John J. Llanaghur, C. M.
Easter 1988

To - Villa Siena
    from the Daughters

D0467438

From the Daughters of Charity
    at O'Connor Hospital

DICTIONARY
OF
AMERICAN
CATHOLIC
BIOGRAPHY

Books by John J. Delaney

Author:

DICTIONARY OF AMERICAN CATHOLIC BIOGRAPHY

DICTIONARY OF SAINTS

POCKET DICTIONARY OF SAINTS

Coauthor:

DICTIONARY OF CATHOLIC BIOGRAPHY with James Edward Tobin

A GUIDE TO CATHOLIC READING with Jack F. Bernard

Editor:

SAINTS ARE NOW

WHY CATHOLIC?

SAINTS FOR ALL SEASONS

A WOMAN CLOTHED WITH THE SUN

CATHOLIC VIEWPOINT SERIES

CATHOLIC PERSPECTIVE SERIES

Anthologist:

THE BEST IN MODERN CATHOLIC READING. Two volumes

Translator:

THE PRACTICE OF THE PRESENCE OF GOD by Brother Lawrence of the
Resurrection

DICTIONARY
OF
AMERICAN
CATHOLIC
BIOGRAPHY

JOHN J. DELANEY

DOUBLEDAY & COMPANY, INC.
GARDEN CITY, NEW YORK
1984

Library of Congress Cataloging in Publication Data
Delaney, John J.
Dictionary of American Catholic biography.
1. Catholics—United States—Biography. I. Title.
BX4670.D45 1984   282'.092'2 [B]   83–25524
ISBN 0-385-17878-6

Dedicated

As always to Ann with love and thanks
for more than a half century
of her love and devotion

With loving remembrance to my mother
and my brother Willie

With gratitude to those
whose friendship has been so precious
to me over the years

ACKNOWLEDGMENTS

My thanks to the following for the information they so kindly sent me at my request: Sister Anselma Mary, S.P., Sister Marie Beck, R.S.H.M., Frank Bruce, Jr., Sister Elizabeth Clifford, O.L.V.M., Sister Marie Coleman, M.M., the Rev. James T. Connelly, C.S.C., John Deedy, John Farina, Fr. Felician Foy, O.F.M., Fr. Paul Grebel, T.O.R., James Langford, Sister Candida Lund, O.P., Kathi Shewring, Jim Doyle, Fr. William Maher, and Daniel Morris. Also to the staff of the Hillside branch of the Queens Borough Public Library for their aid and assistance, particularly Marilyn Lubin and Laurette Newman. And to the staffs of the various research branches of the New York Public Library, especially to Jessie Lee Johnson and Ralph Kirshner of the Donnell Library for their unfailing courtesy and invaluable assistance in the course of my research. And to Pat Kossmann, editor extraordinaire, for her unflagging interest and support from the inception of the idea for this book.

INTRODUCTION

The theme of this volume is well summarized in statements by two famous authors both of whom arrived at a conclusion to which the author of this book heartily subscribes:

The history of the world is but the history of great men.
—Thomas Carlyle

and

There is properly no history; only biography.
—Ralph Waldo Emerson

though I would cavil at Carlyle's remark that history is but the history of *great* men and substitute as the basis of this book the thesis that history is "only biography"— not only of great men but rather of all notable men and women who contributed to the events that constitute history. For history is not merely the recounting of trends and events and of great military and political leaders that it was for so many centuries but for me includes not only great men and women but also those lesser figures who in some manner helped to shape the history of his or her times.

Particularly is this true, it seems to me, of the story of the Catholic Church in the territory that now comprises the United States. Men and women from all walks of life helped evolve the American Catholicism of today. It was not only the cardinals, archbishops, and bishops who molded the Church in this country but the authors and editors, physicians and teachers, statesmen and politicians, priests, nuns, and brothers, industrialists, financiers and labor leaders, actors, entertainers, and athletes —that whole company of Catholics who contributed in some meaningful measure to their Church and their nation.

These men and women and what they accomplished and contributed played a significant role in the development of their Church and their country and saw that Church through the three great constants in the history of Catholicism in the United States: anti-Catholic bigotry, incredible expansion (fueled by waves of immigration), and the constant striving for upward mobility. Each of these factors was of immense importance in the life of the Church. Let us examine them for a moment for they are still very much in evidence in today's American Church.

Much as we Americans pride ourselves on our tolerance there has been a decided strain of bigotry in American history from the days of the original colonies to the present. One form of that bigotry has been the anti-Catholicism which at times was rampant. Many of the colonies had discriminatory laws against Catholics and all too often forbade the presence of Catholic priests in their territory under pain of death. The reasons for this attitude are too varied and complex to allow us any lengthy discussion here beyond noting that except for Maryland all the original colonies were settled by men and women very much influenced by English Protestantism that was rabidly anti-Catholic. Unfortunately they carried their anti-Catholicism with them to the new land and it persisted in the new nation that was forged in the crucible of the Revolution. It was expressed in the most active and often terrifying nativist No-Popery and Know-Nothing movements of the 1830s–50s, the American Protective Association of the 1880s–90s and well into the twentieth century, the twentieth-century Ku Klux Klan which became as anti-Catholic as it was anti-black (its founding purpose); and culminated in our times in the disgraceful explosion of bitter anti-Catholic bigotry in the 1928 presidential campaign when for the first time a major political party, the Democrats, ran a Catholic candidate for president. Nor should be overlooked the need for a presidential candidate as recently as 1960 to defend his religious beliefs before an audience of Protestant ministers in Houston—a meeting which thankfully did much to defuse the anti-Catholic bigotry of the campaign. In the course of these waves of anti-Catholicism, churches and convents were burned, priests and nuns were assaulted, riots of major proportions broke out in major cities and scores of Catholics were killed. (When the Pope's representative, Archbishop Bedini, visited the United States in 1853 he barely escaped being lynched in Cincinnati.)

The second constant was awe-inspiring in its magnitude—the continuous and tremendous expansion of the American Catholic Church from a small despised minority of 30,000 in a population of some 4,000,000 in 1790 to some 52,000,000 Catholics in a population of some 233,000,000 as this Introduction was being written. Together with this increase in the Catholic populace was an enormous expansion of Catholic facilities to meet the needs of this growing population—hierarchy, clergy, religious, churches, schools, hospitals, orphanages, homes for the elderly, facilities to help the needy, and services for the poor and indigent. When John Carroll was consecrated bishop in 1790, he was the only bishop in the United States and had only some 30 priests; today there are some 370 bishops, archbishops, and cardinals, almost 58,000 priests, 121,000 sisters and 7,600 brothers.

The greater part of this increase was due to the successive waves of Catholic immigrants to the United States in the nineteenth and twentieth centuries—the Irish and the Germans in the nineteenth century, the Italians and eastern Europeans in the early twentieth century—over a million in each decade between 1880 and 1890 and over 2,000,000 in the years 1901–10; the almost 3,000,000 Catholics mainly from Ireland and Germany between 1830 and 1880. The influx of Catholic immigrants has been called the most spectacular development in American religious life in the last half of the nineteenth century and this phenomenon of Catholic immigration is with us again today with Hispanic and Asiatic immigration. The overwhelming majority of these immigrants were poor and concomitant with the expansion of Church facilities was a commitment on the part of the Church to aid them. The result was enormously important: the alliance of the Church with the poor and the needy. Indeed, one of the reasons for the anti-Catholicism of the nineteenth century was the opposition of many Americans to the stream of foreigners, mostly poor, pouring into the country, a stream that was the lifeblood of the country. A further

consequence of the commitment of the Church to the impoverished and the oppressed was its support of the labor movement since the labor of many of the new
immigrants was callously exploited; consequently many of the labor leaders were
Catholics seeking to improve the miserable working conditions under which so many
men and women labored.

And the third constant I would mention was and is the ongoing movement among
newly arrived Catholics and their offspring to improve their status in life. It was
partly to meet this urge, though also obviously to safeguard the faith in the hostile
educational environment of the nineteenth century, that Catholic schools and colleges and universities were established on a massive scale; Catholic leaders have
constantly stressed the importance of education for their people. That these institutions continue to serve into our own times is attested by the fact that, despite the
plethora of closings in recent years, there are in the United States some 9,500 Catholic elementary and high schools with a student population of over 3,000,000 and 238
Catholic colleges and universities with some 544,000 students enrolled—still a very
active and flourishing educational community. Another consequence of this striving
for upward mobility was the appearance in the second half of the twentieth century
of a sizable body of highly educated Catholics. It must be remembered that during
the nineteenth and the first half of the twentieth century often the only educated
person in many Catholic communities was the priest and on the larger scene the
bishop. Consequently, most Catholic leaders of many previous eras in the United
States were priests and bishops. But each generation produced a greater number of
highly educated laity than had its predecessor so that by the 1980s there were substantial numbers of Catholic laypersons in positions of national importance in all
fields of human endeavor, including a President of the United States, with a conse-
quent diminishment of religious in secular affairs; and, it should be added an increased number of the laity participating in ecclesiastical matters—a role that most
certainly will increase in the future.

The above is not meant to be a quick course in American Catholicism but merely
sketches three factors that have dominated the Church in the United States. Along
with them must be listed the missionary activities of the priests of the explorer and
colonial periods; the efforts of Archbishop John Carroll to organize the Church in
the United States; the trustee controversy that wracked the Church in the early
nineteenth century; the incredible heroism and dedication of the pioneer priests and
nuns who endured unbelievable hardships to keep and spread the faith on the frontiers; the agonies of the Civil War to Catholic communities, as it was to all Americans; the struggle between the conservatives and the liberals in the late nineteenth
century; the disputes over public aid for Catholic educational institutions and students; the often heated differences between the Americanist and German-speaking
and other languages bishops (the efforts of many Catholics in the nineteenth century
to teach in German in their schools has its counterpart today in the efforts of some
Hispanics to teach in Spanish in their schools); the problems caused by the so-called
"phantom heresy" of Americanism and the apostolic letter of Pope Leo XIII, *Testem
benevolentiae,* condemning it in 1899; and Vatican Council II and the efforts to

implement the decrees of that Council in the United States since 1965. All this and much more that makes up the history of the Catholic Church in the United States is to be found in the lives and activities of the men and women described in the pages that follow.

For to understand these trends one must know of the men and women who created those trends and movements and lived them. And so to the purpose of this book.

It is meant to provide in straightforward fashion factual information about the lives and activities of those Catholic men and women in the United States from the times of the explorers to the present time. It aims to provide the general reader, and hopefully the scholar, brief, concise presentations of essential information about those people included. For the scholar and the expert I would point out that the material, with some few exceptions, is from secondary sources so there is nothing newly discovered or of a startling nature to be found in these pages. However, the idea of collecting these biographies into a single volume in this form with information from sources, which though secondary are reliable, to provide an overall view of the Church in the United States through the lives of those who made that Church is I believe unique, since the information found in this one volume could formerly be found only by searching through hundreds of reference volumes and biographies. Essentially the purpose of the book is to provide in a single volume an up-to-date, easy-to-use compendium of factual information about the people included herein. I have made every effort to screen out errors and discrepancies and the often amazing contradictions in some of the reputable sources I have used. No doubt some errors have crept into the work but I have made every effort to be accurate.

The plan of the book is to give the date and place of birth, educational background, important positions held, activities and place and date of death of the individuals listed. Where the subject worked in the area of literature, art, music, theater, and films, examples of their work are included, such as titles of books, outstanding sculptures, films, and plays, etc. I have made every effort to include everyone who made a significant contribution to the Church and/or nation. I trust the reader will find in these pages practically any Catholic who has played an important role in the development and history of the Church in the United States as well as those Catholics who have made a contribution to the nation in whatever their profession. Undoubtedly, I have failed to include some figure the reader feels should be included. In some cases the omission was deliberate to keep the volume to a sizable length; in other cases some figures were inadvertently missed, for which I apologize. Any worthy suggestions for inclusion in future editions will be welcomed.

For those who might question the inclusion of certain figures I would point out that though I might deplore the actions of some of these persons they were Catholics and were of such importance that their inclusion is justified. Also although I have referred to it several times throughout this Introduction I would emphasize here that this volume is not meant to consist only of ecclesiastical figures or of those men and women who devoted themselves to ecclesiastical work. It is rather meant to encompass all Catholics who have made a notable contribution to their Church and/or to their nation and as such contains biographies of men and women in all walks of life and in all occupations. It should also be noted that no living Catholics are included.

And finally, it is the fervent hope of this author that the impressive collection of Catholics assembled here and their deeds and accomplishments will bring alive to all Catholics in the United States the American Catholic heritage. The Catholic Church has a long and glorious tradition over the past two thousand years and in every country on the face of the earth. The activities of its members in the United States over almost the past five centuries have an honorable place in that tradition. Every American Catholic can be proud of what the men and women of Catholic persuasion have wrought in their time on this planet. May it be an example for us Catholics today and for the American Catholics of future generations.

J.J.D.

DICTIONARY
OF
AMERICAN
CATHOLIC
BIOGRAPHY

A

ABBOTT, ANTHONY. *See* Oursler, Fulton.

ABELL, ROBERT (1792–1873), missionary. Son of Robert Abell, the only Catholic delegate to the Kentucky state constitutional convention of 1799, he was born in Nelson County, Kentucky, on Nov. 25. He studied at St. Rose and St. Thomas seminaries at Bardstown and was ordained in 1818. He engaged in missionary activities in Kentucky, opened several schools in his missionary territory, and was responsible for convincing the Sisters of Charity of Nazareth to found Mt. Carmel Convent and School. He was then sent to Louisville where he built a church in 1824 and ten years later was sent to Lebanon, Kentucky, where he built St. Augustine Church. He was named vice president of St. Joseph College in Bardstown in 1840 and four years later was sent to New Haven where he built St. Catherine's Church. He retired in 1860 because of sciatica and spent the next decade helping pastors in different parts of Kentucky. He was named chaplain of St. Joseph's infirmary in Louisville in 1872 and died there on June 28.

ACCOLTI, MICHAEL (1807–78), missionary. Born of a noble family in Conversano, Italy, on Jan. 29, he entered the Pontifical Academy of Noble Ecclesiastics in Rome in 1830 and two years later joined the Jesuits and entered the Jesuit Sant' Andrea novitiate in Rome. He was ordained in 1842 and the following year was sent to North America with a group of Jesuits headed by Pierre De Smet. He worked as a missionary in Oregon and in 1849 was sent to San Francisco with John Nobilis, the first Jesuits in California since the Society of Jesus had been expelled by Spanish authorities in 1768. He was called back to Oregon in a few months and in 1853 he went to Rome where he was successful in having Jesuit missionary activities in Oregon and California assigned to the Jesuit province of Turin, Italy. He was named superior of the Jesuits in Oregon and served in that capacity until 1855 when he returned to San Francisco where, with Jesuit Anthony Marasci, he founded St. Ignatius College which in time developed into the University of San Francisco. For the next five years he served at San Francisco and at Santa Clara College and died in San Francisco on Nov. 7.

ADRIAN, WILLIAM LAWRENCE (1883–1972), bishop. Born in Sigourney, Iowa, on Apr. 16, he was educated at St. Ambrose College, Davenport, Iowa, (B.A. 1906) and the North American College, Rome (S.T.L. 1911), and was ordained in 1911. He continued his studies at the University of Iowa in the summers of 1914 and 1915, taught at St. Ambrose from 1911 to 1934, and was vice president of the college and principal of the high school there in 1935. After serving as pastor of St. Bridget's Church, Victor, Iowa, in 1935–36, he was consecrated bishop of Nashville, Tennessee, in 1936; he was made an Assistant at the Pontifical Throne in 1961.

He retired in 1969 and died in Nashville on Feb. 13.

AGNEW, WILLIAM HENRY (1881–1931), educator. Born in Westphalia, Kansas, on Oct. 12, he joined the Jesuits in 1900 and studied at St. Louis University (B.A. 1905, M.A. 1907, M.S. 1911). He was ordained in 1915, was head of the science department at Loyola in Chicago for four years, taught theology at St. Louis in 1919–20, and was president of Loyola in 1921–27. He was rector of Sacred Heart Church in Chicago in 1927–28, served as editor of *Queen's Work,* and in 1928 became president of Creighton University, Omaha, Nebraska. He died in Rochester, Minnesota, on Feb. 13.

AGRICOLA. *See* Crèvecoeur, Hector St. John.

AHERN, MICHAEL JOSEPH (1877–1951), educator. Born in New York City on May 25, he studied at St. Francis Xavier College there (B.A. 1896) and joined the Jesuits in 1896. He continued his education at Woodstock, Maryland (M.A. 1902), and became an instructor of chemistry at Boston College in 1902 and of geology at Woodstock in 1906. He resumed his studies at the University of Innsbruck, Austria, in 1907–11 (S.T.D. 1911) and was head of the chemistry department at Canisius College, Buffalo, New York, in 1915–19. He was president of Canisius in 1919–23, was head of the chemistry department at Holy Cross in 1923–25, and was appointed head of the chemistry department at Weston College, Massachusetts, in 1926. He was director of and commentator on the "Catholic Truth Period" radio program in 1929–50 and died in Boston on June 5.

ALDERS, JOSEPH H. (1891–1965), bishop. Born in Cincinnati, Ohio, on Mar. 18, he was educated at Mt. St. Mary of the West Seminary, Cincinnati, from which he graduated in 1916, and Appolinaris University, Rome (J.C.D. 1928). He was ordained in Cincinnati in 1916 and engaged in pastoral work until the United States entered World War I when he became a chaplain in the A.E.F. On his return from the Army, he became secretary to Archbishop Moeller of Cincinnati, was assistant chancellor of the archdiocese in 1919–25, and became chancellor in 1925. He was named titular bishop of Lunda and auxiliary of Cincinnati in 1929 and was appointed first bishop of the newly created diocese of Lansing, Michigan, in 1937; he remained in that position until his death in Lansing on Dec. 1.

ALBERS, WILLIAM (1880–1954), merchant, philanthropist. Born on May 23 in Cincinnati, Ohio, he went to work in his father's grocery store after he graduated from high school. He then joined Schneider Brothers Company and after its amalgamation with the Kroger Grocery and Baking Company became assistant secretary in 1910, vice president and general manager five years later, and was named president of the firm in 1928. His merchandising methods and management led to the phenomenal growth of Kroger from 158 grocery stores to some 5,600 in 1929 when he resigned. He began Albers Super Markets, Inc. which soon had 67 supermarkets in Ohio and Kentucky and then founded and headed the Super Markets Institute in Chicago which pioneered in supermarket promotional techniques that became widely used in supermarket operations all over the country. During World War II he was a member of the National Food Advisory Council and War Food Council. He was active in Catholic circles, was director of the Catholic Youth Organization and the National Council of Catholic Men, and served as a trustee of Catholic University, as a member of the lay advisory board of Xavier University in Cincinnati and was active in several cultural groups in Cincinnati. He was invested as a Knight of St. Gregory in 1934, received several honorary degrees, and was awarded the 1954 citation of the National Conference of Christians and Jews. He died in Cincinnati on June 6.

ALEMANY, JOSEPH SADOC (1814–88), archbishop. Born in Vich, Catalonia, Spain, on July 13, he joined the Dominicans there in 1829 and when Spanish religious houses were closed by the Spanish Government in 1835 he went to Italy to complete his studies for the priesthood; he was ordained at Viterbo in 1837. After a period of pastoral work in Rome, he was sent to the United States in 1840 and worked as a missionary in Ohio, Kentucky, and Tennessee. He served for a time as rector of the diocesan seminary in Nashville, Tennessee, became an American citizen in 1845, and was elected provincial of the American Dominicans in 1849. While attending a general Dominican chapter in Rome in 1850, he was named bishop of Monterey, California, which then had jurisdiction over Upper and Lower California and parts of what are now Nevada and Utah. Lower California was Mexican territory and his jurisdiction over it was bitterly protested by the Mexican Government which refused to turn over to him Lower California's share of the Pious Fund; he later successfully negotiated his claim to his diocese's share of the Fund. He was named first archbishop of San Francisco when that see was established in 1853 at which time Lower California was removed from his jurisdiction. He attended Vatican Council I in 1869–70 and was chairman of a bishops' committee reporting on a uniform catechism for the United States at the Third Plenary Council of Baltimore in 1884. He resigned as archbishop later that year, after having secured Patrick William Riordan as coadjutor, and retired to Spain with the title titular archbishop of Pelusium. He devoted the rest of his life until his death in Valencia on April 14 to pastoral activities and to efforts to have the Order of Preachers restored in Spain. Though buried in Vich, his remains were removed to San Francisco in 1965 and interred in Holy Cross Cemetery.

ALERDING, HERMAN JOSEPH (1845–1924), bishop. Born in Ibbenbüren, Westphalia, Germany, on Apr. 13, he was taken to the United States when an infant by his parents who settled in Kentucky. He studied for the priesthood at St. Gabriel Seminary, Vincennes, Indiana, St. Thomas, Bardstown, Kentucky, and St. Meinrad, Indiana, where he was ordained in 1868. He engaged in pastoral work in Terre Haute and Cambridge City, Indiana, until 1874 when he became procurator of St. Joseph Seminary and pastor of St. Joseph Church in Indianapolis. He was named bishop of Fort Wayne, Indiana, in 1900 and remained in that position until his death there on Dec. 6. He wrote histories of the dioceses of Vincennes and Fort Wayne, organized the parochial school system of his diocese, encouraged secondary education, and saw the population of his see double in the twenty-four years of his bishopric.

ALLEN, EDWARD PATRICK (1853–1926), bishop. Born in Lowell, Massachusetts, on Mar. 17, he studied at Lowell Commercial College and Mt. St. Mary College, Emmitsburg, Maryland, where he was ordained in 1881. He taught at Mt. St. Mary's in 1881–82, was assistant at the Boston cathedral in 1882 and at Framingham, Massachusetts, in 1883, and returned to teach at Mt. St. Mary's in 1884; he served as president from 1884–97. He was named fifth bishop of Mobile, Alabama, in 1897 and served in that capacity the next twenty-nine years until his death in Mobile on Oct. 21. During his bishopric particular attention was paid to ministering to blacks and the rural area inhabitants of the see as its Catholic population almost tripled.

ALLEN, FRANCES MARGARET (1784–1819), nurse. Daughter of Ethan Allen of American Revolution Fort Ticonderoga fame, who died when she was five, and his second wife, Frances Montressor Buchanan Allen, Fanny Allen was born in Sunderland, Vermont, on Nov. 13. She went to Montreal to study under the Sisters of Notre Dame in 1807, was converted to Catholicism the following year, and despite the opposition of her mother and her stepfather, Dr. Jabez Penniman, joined the nursing Sisters of the Hôtel-Dieu of St. Joseph in 1809 and was professed in 1810—the first woman born in New England to enter the religious life. She specialized in pharmacy, was instrumental in bringing many of those she nursed during the War of 1812 into the Catholic Church, and died in Montreal on Dec. 10.

ALLEN, FRED (1894–1956), entertainer. Son of Henry Sullivan, a bookbinder, and Cecily Herlihy Allen, John Florence Sullivan was born in Cambridge, Massachusetts, on May 31, and began his career in entertainment as a juggler at a Christmas party for the em-

ployees of the Boston Public Library where he was then employed. He entered vaudeville as a comedian using juggling as a foil under the names Paul Huckle and Freddy St. James and after a tour of Australia and New Zealand in 1916, became a star under the name of Fred Allen on his return to the United States. He received top billing in an appearance at the Palace Theater in New York City, the dream of all vaudevillians, and appeared in *The Passing Show of 1922* and *The Greenwich Village Follies.* He married Portland Hoffa in 1927, appeared in *The Little Show* (1929) and *Three's a Crowd* (1930) and with the demise of vaudeville he turned to film and radio. He began an hour-long radio show, "Town Hall Tonight," with Portland in 1934 that lasted until 1940 when he launched "Texaco Star Theatre" (1940–49) which each week presented to the listening audience the denizens of "Allen's Alley"—Mrs. Pansy Nussbaum, Senator Beauregard Claghorn, loudmouth Ajax Cassidy, and others. It was one of the most popular radio programs of the time and made Allen and "Allen's Alley" household names throughout the United States. He also wrote two autobiographical books *Treadmill to Oblivion* (1954) and *Much Ado About Me* (1956) and died in New York City on Mar. 17.

ALLEN, GEORGE (1808–76), educator, author. Of Protestant parents, he was born in Milton, Vermont, on Dec. 17, studied French in Canada under a Catholic priest, graduated from the University of Vermont in 1827, and taught languages at Georgia, Vermont, for two years. He was admitted to the bar in 1831, worked as a lawyer for a while, became interested in religion, and in 1834 was ordained an Episcopal minister. He was rector of St. Albans, Vermont, in 1834–37 when he became professor of classics at Delaware College, Newark, Delaware, and in 1845 was named professor of Latin and Greek at the University of Pennsylvania. He became a Catholic in 1847 and died at Worcester, Massachusetts, on May 28. He wrote several books among them *The Life of Phillidor* (1863) and *The Remains of W. S. Graham* (1849).

ALLEN, GRACIE (1905–64), entertainer. Daughter of Edward Allen, an entertainer, and Margaret Darragh Allen, she was born in San Francisco on July 26. She made her stage debut with her father when she was three, was educated at Star of the Sea Convent, and left school when fourteen to join her father and three sisters on the stage. After several years as a member of the Larry Reilly Company, she left the stage to enroll in a secretarial school and while in school met George Burns in 1922 and joined him in a new act, Burns and Allen. They were married in Cleveland in 1926, signed a five-year contract with the Keith Theater chain soon after and in the late twenties were one of the most popular vaudeville acts in the United States. In 1930 she appeared as a guest on Eddie Cantor's radio show and soon the team of Burns and Allen was offered a contract by the Columbia Broadcasting System; by the end of the thirties their radio program was named one of the top three in the United States with an audience in the millions each week. They appeared in several motion pictures, among them *The Big Broadcast* (1932) and *College Holiday* (1936), and in 1950 they appeared on television, again with great success. When Gracie tired of the zany character she had created, that of a scatterbrained woman, she retired in 1958, after almost four decades as one of America's favorite female performers. She died in Los Angeles on Aug. 27.

ALLOUEZ, CLAUDE JEAN (1622–89), missionary. Born in Saint Didier-en-Forez, Haute Loire, France, on June 6, he graduated from Le Puy when seventeen, joined the Jesuits at Toulouse in 1639 and after studying at Billom and Rodez was ordained in 1655. He was sent as a missionary to Canada in 1658 and worked in the St. Lawrence Valley area until 1665 when he was named vicar-general to Bishop Laval of Quebec. He spent the next four years preaching to some twenty different Indian tribes in the Great Lakes region, reputedly baptizing twenty thousand Indians, especially among the Illinois for whom he prepared an Illinois-French prayer book. Portions of his journal were published in the *Jesuit Relations* and he wrote an account of his third trip to the Illinois. His missionary activities were centered in De Pere, Wisconsin, where a monument to him was erected. He died near Niles, Michigan, on the night of Aug. 27–28.

ALTER, KARL J. (1885–1977), archbishop. Born in Toledo, Ohio, on Aug. 18, he was educated at St. John's College there and St. Mary's Seminary, Cleveland, and was ordained in 1910. He engaged in pastoral work in the Toledo diocese, was diocesan director of Catholic Charities in 1914–29 and of the National Catholic School of Social Service in 1929–31, and was appointed third bishop of Toledo in 1931. He occupied that post until 1950 when he was named archbishop of Cincinnati, Ohio, a position he held for nineteen years until his retirement in 1969. He died in Cincinnati on Aug. 23.

ALTHAM, JOHN (1589–1640), missionary. Sometimes called Gravenor or Grosvenor, he was born in Warwickshire, England, joined the Jesuits in 1623 and worked in Devonshire and

London. In 1633, he, Jesuit Andrew White and a Jesuit lay brother, Thomas Gervase, accompanied Leonard Calvert on the *Ark* and the *Dove* in the latter's colonizing expedition to Maryland. They arrived in Maryland in 1634 and though he was plagued by ill health, he worked the rest of his life as a missionary among the Indian tribes of Maryland and Virginia, converting several Indian chiefs to Christianity. He died at St. Mary's, Maryland, on Nov. 5.

ALTHOFF, HENRY (1873–1947), bishop. Born in Aviston, Illinois, on Aug. 28, he received his B.A. from St. Joseph's College, Teutopolis, Illinois, in 1898, his M.A. from St. Francis Solanus College, Quincy, Illinois, in 1899 and continued his studies at the University of Innsbruck, Austria, where he was ordained in 1902. He served as a curate in Damiansville, Illinois, in 1902–03 and in East St. Louis, Illinois, in 1903–04 and was pastor in Okawville and Nashville, Illinois, from 1905 until December 1913 when he was appointed second bishop of Belleville, Illinois. He died on July 3 and was buried in the crypt beneath St. Peter's Cathedral in Belleville.

AMADEUS OF THE HEART OF JESUS, MOTHER MARY (1846–1920), foundress. Sarah Theresa Dunne was born in Akron, Ohio, on July 2, was taught by the Ursulines in Cleveland, and in 1862 she received the Ursuline habit in Toledo, Ohio, taking the name Amadeus of the Heart of Jesus. When the superior of the Toledo Ursulines died in 1874, she was chosen to succeed her though the youngest member of the community. In 1879 she was one of the Ursulines who responded to a plea from Bishop Brondell, first bishop of Helena, Montana, to go to Montana to minister to the Indians and to establish missions; she was appointed by Bishop Gilmour of Toledo superior of any Ursuline foundations she might establish in Montana. She established a mission and a chapel in the Yellowstone Valley, ministered to the Indians and established missions for them, and became known for her austerities and sanctity. At a meeting in Rome ordered by Pope Leo XIII in 1900 to unite the Ursulines all over the world she was confirmed superior of the Montana missions and made provincial. Soon after her return to the United States she was injured in a train collision that left her bedridden for the next nine months and made her a cripple the rest of her life. Despite her affliction, she made several visits to Rome in the next few years and on her return from one of these visits was accompanied by the superior general and was formally installed as first provincial of the "North of the United States" with headquarters in Middletown, New York, where she opened the first general novitiate of the canonically united Ursulines. She sent her first missionary sisters to Alaska in 1905 and in 1910 at the third chapter general of the united Ursulines she was appointed provincial of Alaska. Later that year she went to Alaska and established St. Ursula's-by-the-Sea mission at St. Michael on Norton Sound, a convent at Valdez and St. Mary's Mission, Akulurak, and ministered to the Eskimos, Indians, settlers, and Army personnel. She returned to the United States in 1912, established an Ursuline novitiate for Alaska in Seattle, Washington, and made several trips back to Alaska in the next few years. She died in Seattle and was buried at St. Ignatius Mission in Montana. In her thirty-nine years of missionary work in Montana and Alaska she endured incredible hardships and is often referred to as "Teresa of the Artic" and Great Chief White Woman by the Indians.

AMAT, THADDEUS (1810–78), bishop. Born in Barcelona, Spain, on Dec. 31, perhaps in 1811, he was educated at the Lazarist House of Studies in Barcelona and the motherhouse of the Lazarists in Paris and joined the Lazarists (Vincentians) in Barcelona in 1832. He took his vows in Barcelona two years later, was ordained in Paris in 1838, and was sent to the United States later the same year. He spent the next three years, 1838–41, teaching at St. Vincent de Paul Seminary in New Orleans and in 1841 was appointed master of novices at St. Vincent Seminary, Cape Girardeau, Missouri. During the next twelve years he taught at and served as president of St. Louis Seminary in St. Louis, was president of St. Mary's Preparatory Seminary and pastor of St. Mary's Church, Perrysville, Missouri, pastor of St. Vincent's Church, St. Louis, and was administrator of the diocesan seminary in St. Louis while serving as pastor of Holy Trinity Church there. In 1848 he was named superior of St. Charles Borromeo Seminary in Philadelphia and in 1853 he was named bishop of Monterey, California; he was consecrated in Rome on Mar. 12, 1854, and occupied his see in 1855. He was permitted to change the name of his see to Monterey-Los Angeles in 1859 and took up residence in Los Angeles. During his bishopric he secured diocesan rights to mission properties and his diocese's share of the Pious Fund of California from the Mexican Government and was particularly concerned with the welfare of the Indians in his see. He held synods in 1862, 1869, and 1876, and attended the Second Plenary Council of Baltimore in 1866 and Vatican Council I in 1869–70. Because of ill health caused by a spinal injury, he requested a coadjutor in 1873 and died in Los Angeles on May 12.

AMMEN, DANIEL (1820–98), admiral. Of Swiss-German ancestry, he was born in Brown County, Ohio, on May 15 and was a boyhood friend of Ulysses S. Grant whom he saved from drowning and with whom he developed a close friendship. He was appointed a midshipman in the Navy in 1836 at West Point (the Naval Academy at Annapolis was not founded until 1845), and went on his first sea duty in 1837. During his more than forty years of naval service, he rose to the rank of rear admiral. He was with a squadron sent to China and Japan in 1845–47, a surveying expedition up the Paraguayan River in 1853–54, and on a cruise in the Pacific in 1857–60. During the Civil War he participated in attacks on Confederate forts and the blockade of Southern ports. He was chief of the Bureau of Yards and Docks in 1869–71, of the Bureau of Navigation in 1871–78, and was secretary of the Isthmian Canal Company in 1872–76 and an active proponent of building an Atlantic-Pacific canal through Nicaragua, writing several pamphlets on the subject. He retired in 1878 and died on his estate, "Ammendale," near Washington, D.C., on July 11.

ANDERSON, HENRY JAMES (1799–1875), scientist. Born in New York City on Feb. 6, of a well-to-do family, he studied at Columbia College there, graduated in 1818, and received his medical degree from the College of Physicians in 1823. He became known for his knowledge of mathematics and astronomy and in 1825 was appointed professor of mathematics and astronomy at Columbia—a chair he held for twenty-five years. He went to Europe in 1843 to seek aid for his sick wife, remained there after her death, and in 1848 joined a United States Govern-

21

ment expedition to the Holy Lands for which he wrote two reports, *Geological Reconnaissance of Part of the Holy Land* (1848, 1849); during this period he became a Catholic in 1849. He was active in Catholic affairs, organizing and for a time serving as president of the Catholic Union and of the St. Vincent de Paul Society in New York City and helped build the New York Catholic Protectory. He was named professor emeritus of mathematics and astronomy by Columbia in 1866, went to Australia in 1874 to study the planet Venus in transit, and the following year he joined an expedition exploring the Himalayas and died on the expedition in Lahore, northern Hindustan, on Oct. 19.

ANDERSON, MARY ANTOINETTE (1859–1940), actress. Born in Sacramento, California, on July 28, she attended the Academy of the Presentation in Louisville, Kentucky, and after seeing Edwin Booth's performance in *Richelieu,* she decided to become an actress. She made her first professional appearance in 1875 at Louisville's Macauley Theater as Juliet in *Romeo and Juliet* and two years later debuted in New York as Pauline in *The Lady of Lyons* at the Fifth Avenue Theatre. She soon became one of the most notable actresses of the American stage appearing in Shakespearean roles, Gilbert's *Pygmalion and Galatea, Guy Mannering, The Hunchback,* and *The Winter's Tale* where she played a dual role as Hermione and Perdita—to name a few of her outstanding successes. In 1889, at the height of her fame, she married Antonio de Navarro and went to England with him; she never appeared on the stage again except for several benefit performances during World War I. She published two volumes of memoirs, *A Few Memories* (1896) and *A Few More*

Memories (1936) and died in London on May 29.

ANDREIS, FELIX DE (1778–1820), missionary. Born on Dec. 12 in Demonte, Piedmont, Italy, he was early attracted to the religious life and joined the Congregation of the Missions (the Lazarists or Vincentians) at Mondovi in 1797; he was ordained in 1801. After finishing his theological studies at the Lazarist Alberoni College, he taught there while conducting retreats for the clergy and seminarians. In 1806, he was transferred to Monte Citorio in Rome as professor of theology and continued giving his retreats and missions. In 1815 he met the apostolic administrator of the diocese of Louisiana, Bishop Louis DuBourg, who persuaded him to return to Louisiana with him; though he wanted to go with Bishop DuBourg he was unable to secure his superior's permission until the following year and then went to the United States. He taught at St. Thomas Seminary, Bardstown, Kentucky, for a year and early in 1818 arrived in St. Louis where Bishop DuBourg appointed him vicar-general and rector of the cathedral. He established two schools but never attained his desire to preach to the Indians. He died in St. Louis on Oct. 20.

ANGLIN, MARGARET MARY (1876–1958), actress. Daughter of the Hon. T. W. Anglin, speaker of the Canadian House of Commons, she was born in Ottawa, Canada, on Apr. 3, and was educated at Loretto Abbey, Toronto, and the Convent of the Sacred Heart, Montreal. She studied acting at the Empire School of Dramatic Acting in New York City and graduated in 1894, then married Howard Hull, brother of actor Henry Hull, in September of the same year. She made her acting debut later in 1894 in *Shenandoah,* was a leading lady with James O'Neill in 1896–97, with E. H. Sothern in 1897–98, with Richard Mansfield in 1898–99, and in 1906–07 played with Henry Miller. Among her greatest successes were in Henry Arthur Jones's *Mrs. Dane's Defence* which opened in New York in 1900 and William Vaughan Moody's *The Great Divide* which opened in 1906 with Henry Miller. She toured the United States and Australia in 1909–10, was in Shakespearean repertory as actress manager in 1913, and played in *Lady Windemere's Fan* in 1914. She played in Greek classics at the Greek Theatre, Berkeley, California, in 1915 and produced *Electra* at the Metropolitan Opera House in New York in 1927, the year she was the recipient of the Laetare Medal. Her last stage appearance was in a road company of *Watch on the Rhine.* She died in New York City on Jan. 7.

ANNABRING, JOSEPH (1900–59), bishop. Born in Szaparyliget, Hungary, on Mar. 19, he was brought to the United States when a child and raised in Turtle Neck, Wisconsin. He was educated at St. Francis Seminary, Milwaukee, and at St. Paul (Minnesota) Seminary and the Seminary of Philosophy, Montreal, and was ordained in 1927. He was a curate at Christ the King Cathedral in Superior, Wisconsin, became its rector in 1936, was superintendent of Catholic schools in the diocese in 1944–45 and was made a domestic prelate in 1946. He was appointed bishop of Superior in 1954 and held that position until his death there on Aug. 27.

ANZA, JUAN BAUTISTA DE (b. 1735), explorer. Born in Fonteras, Sonora, Mexico, he early joined the military, became a lieutenant and in 1760 was made captain of the Presidio of Tubac. He set out from the Presidio in 1774 to confirm the theory that there was an overland route that could be used to supply Spanish settlements in California. He led his troops across the Colorado Desert to Monterey, California, and back; he was made a lieutenant-colonel on his return for proving the feasibility of the overland route for supply purposes. He set out on a second trip the following year, this time with settlers as well as soldiers, and arrived at Monterey on Mar. 10, 1776; he then continued his explorations to the present site of San Francisco. He was appointed governor of New Mexico in 1777 and established colonies on the Colorado River in 1780 but they were destroyed the following year by Yuma Indian raids. He was relieved of his governorship in 1788 and then disappeared from the pages of history.

ARBEZ, EDWARD PHILIP (1881–1967), biblical scholar, orientalist. Born in Paris on May 16, he studied at l'Argentière preparatory seminary, the Alix seminary, and Issy, France. He came to the United States in 1901 and joined the Sulpicians, continued his studies at Catholic University, and was ordained at Issy in 1904, when he was formally received as a Sulpician. He was sent to St. Patrick's Seminary, Menlo Park, California, where he taught apologetics, church history, Sacred Scripture, and Hebrew, and remained there until 1928 except for 1917–18 when he was at Catholic University teaching Semitic languages. He returned to Catholic University to teach Sacred Scripture and Old Testament courses until 1938 when he began teaching Semitic languages again; in 1943 he was appointed head of the department of Semitic Languages. He long chafed at the restrictions placed on Catholic biblical scholarship and welcomed its magna carta in

Pope Pius XII's encyclical *Divino afflante Spiritu.* He was a leader in the resultant burst of Catholic biblical scholarship, cofounded the Catholic Biblical Association of America in 1936 and was chairman of its editorial board until 1951; he was one of the leaders in biblical translation which led to the publication of the *New American Bible.* He also worked for the Near Eastern section of the Department of State and was a consultant for the Federal Bureau of Investigation in 1951–61. He died in Washington, D.C., on Dec. 27.

ARGUELLO, LUIS ANTONIO (1784–1830), colonial governor. Born in San Francisco of a distinguished California family (his father, José Dario Arguello was governor of Lower California in 1815–22), he became commandante of California in 1806 and capitain in 1818. In 1821 he led an expedition to explore the Columbia River and the north country. He was governor of California (the area encompassed by California at that time comprised the territory north to Oregon and east to the Rockies) in 1822–25—the first native Californian to hold that office. He died in California.

ARMSTRONG, ROBERT JOHN (1884–1957), bishop. Born in San Francisco on Nov. 17, he was educated at Gonzaga University, Spokane, Washington (M.A. 1912), and the Grand Seminary in Montreal and was ordained in 1910. He was a curate at Our Lady of Lourdes Church in Spokane for the next four years, pastor of St. Paul's Church in Yakima, Washington, in 1914–29, and was appointed bishop of Sacramento, California, in 1929. He founded the diocesan paper, the *Sacramento Register* in 1930 and headed the see until his death in Sacramento on Jan. 14 after a long illness.

ARNOLD, WILLIAM R. (1881–1965), chaplain, general, bishop. Born in Wooster, Ohio, on June 10, he was educated at St. Joseph's College, Rensselaer, Indiana, and St. Bernard's Seminary, Rochester, New York, and was ordained in 1908. He engaged in pastoral work in Peru, Indiana, until 1913 when he joined the Army Chaplain Corps. He served in various Army posts in the United States and the Philippines and in 1937 was made a colonel and appointed chief of chaplains of the United States by President Franklin Roosevelt—the first Catholic to hold that position. He served two four-year terms as chief and rose to the rank of major general in 1944—the first chief of chaplains to hold this rank. He was made a papal chamberlain in 1938, a domestic prelate in 1941, and was consecrated titular bishop of Phocaea and appointed military delegate of the Armed Forces of the United States in 1945. He died in New York City on Jan. 7.

ASHTON, JOHN (1742–c. 1814). Born in Ireland, he joined the Jesuits in 1759, served as a missionary in Yorkshire, England, and then went to the United States. Stationed at a Jesuit house between Baltimore and Washington, D.C., he ministered to the Catholics of Baltimore in 1776–84 and headed the first congregation of Catholics in that city, some forty in number, most of them Acadian refugees. He was elected procurator to manage the estates of the clergy of Maryland and Pennsylvania in 1784 and was placed in charge of building Georgetown College in 1788. He died in Maryland in 1814 or 1815.

ASHURST, HENRY FOUNTAIN (1874–1962), U. S. Senator. Born near Winnemucca, Nevada, on Sept. 13, he spent his early life as a cowboy in Arizona. He then studied at the University of Michigan and was admitted to the Arizona bar in 1897, the year he married Elizabeth McEvoy, and was admitted to practice before the United States Supreme Court in 1908. He became a member of the Arizona Territorial House of Representatives, serving as speaker in 1899, and in 1902 was elected to the Arizona Territorial Senate. He served as district attorney of Coconimo County, Arizona, in 1905–08, and in 1912 was elected one of Arizona's first two senators to the United States Senate. He served five terms in the Senate but was defeated in the Democratic primary for renomination in 1940 and then retired to private life, after serving on the Board of Immigration Appeals in the Department of Justice from 1941 to 1943. He was noted for his oratorical prowess, served as chairman of the Senate Judiciary Committee for many years, and was a supporter of President Wilson's Versailles Treaty and President Franklin Roosevelt's New Deal program. He died in Georgetown, Washington, D.C., on May 31.

AUROROFF, CONSTANTINE (d. 1960). Born in Moscow, he studied at Petrograd and St. Vladimir Seminary, joined a seminarians' strike and participated in an anticzarist demonstration in 1906 to protest the rule of Czar Nicholas II and his government. He migrated to the United States where he was ordained a Russian Orthodox priest in 1914; two years later he left the Russian Orthodox Church to become a Catholic priest of the Byzantine rite. He engaged in parish work in Michigan, Ohio, and Pennsylvania, taught Russian at Pennsylvania State College, and in 1955 was sent to Danbury, Connecticut, where he became pastor of St. Nicholas Church. He taught a Russian language course at Danbury State College in 1958 and died two years later on June 23 in Danbury.

AYALA, JUAN MANUEL DE (fl. c. 1775), explorer. Under instructions from the viceroy of New Spain, Antonio Maria Bucareli, to explore San Francisco Bay, Ayala sailed from San Blas in Mar. 1775 and reached Monterey, California, on June 27, 1775. About July 24, he left for San Francisco Bay and spent most of August and September exploring the Bay. On his return to San Blas, he reported to the viceroy that it was the best port north of Cape Horn and well adapted to settlement.

AYETA, FRANCISCO DE (c. 1700s), missionary. His place and date of birth are unknown but he worked as a Franciscan missionary in New Mexico and Yucatán for many years. He served his order as visitor of the province of New Mexico and the area south of Yucatán, as procurator in Madrid, and as commissary of the Inquisition in New Spain. He was an ardent defender of the Franciscans in New Spain, writing three books in defense of their activities there. He visited the missions in the most remote areas of his territory and in 1678 warned Spanish authorities of hostility and unrest among the Pueblo Indians and the defenselessness of the Spanish colonies in New Mexico, a warning that became a reality in 1680 when the Pueblos attacked and drove the Spaniards out of New Mexico and controlled the area for the next fourteen years. He ministered to some two thousand refugees from the Indians' fury at El Paso, providing them with food and clothing. Where and when he died are unknown.

AYLLÓN, LUCAS VÁSQUES DE (c. 1475–1526), explorer. Probably born in Toledo, Spain, though when is not known for certain, he went to Hispaniola (Santo Domingo) in 1502 and became a member of the Superior Council. In quest of a northwest passage from

25

Europe to Asia, an expedition he dispatched discovered the coast of North Carolina in 1521. In 1524 he set out from Hispaniola and explored the James River in Virginia and the Chesapeake Bay—the first European to do so. Charles V of Spain gave him a grant of the land he had discovered and in 1526 he founded San Miguel de Guanda either in South Carolina or on the Cape Fear River (near the site of Jamestown which the English were to settle eighty years later) with five hundred colonists. The colony was unsuccessful; when Ayllón died of fever in the colony on Oct. 18, the one hundred fifty colonists who had survived the fever and hardships of the settlement returned to Hispaniola. Black slaves were used in San Miguel, the first recorded instance of black slavery in United States territory.

AZARIAS, BROTHER *See* Mullany, Patrick Francis.

B

BABCOCK, ALLEN JAMES (1898–1969), bishop. Born in Bad Axe, Michigan, on June 17, he was educated at Assumption College, Sandwich, Ontario, and the University of the Propaganda in Rome where he received his S.T.B. in 1922 and his S.T.L. in 1924. He was ordained in Rome in 1925, served as curate in several Michigan parishes, was vice-rector of the North American College in Rome in 1936–40, and was made a papal chamberlain in 1938. He was rector of the student chapel at the University of Michigan in 1940–42, of the Blessed Sacrament Cathedral in Detroit in 1942–54, was named a domestic prelate in 1946, and in 1947 was made titular bishop of Irenopolis and auxiliary of Detroit. He was appointed bishop of Grand Rapids, Michigan, in 1954 and remained in that position until his death there on June 27.

BACON, DAVID WILLIAM (1813–74), bishop. Born in Brooklyn, New York, on Sept. 15, he was educated at the Sulpician College, Montreal, and Mt. St. Mary's Seminary, Emmitsburg, Maryland, and was ordained in 1838. He engaged in pastoral work in New York and New Jersey, was founding pastor of the Assumption of our Lady parish in Brooklyn in 1841–55 and was appointed first bishop of Portland, Maine, in 1855. Noted for his oratory, he built the Cathedral of the Immaculate Conception, invited the Sisters of Mercy into his diocese, fought the anti-Catholic Know-Nothing movement and doubled the number of Catholics in his diocese during his nineteen-year bishopric. He attended Vatican Council I and was on his way to Rome again in the summer of 1874 when he fell ill at Brest, France, and was brought back to New York where he died on Nov. 5.

BADIN, STEPHEN THEODORE (1768–1853), missionary. Born in Orléans, France, on July 17, he was educated at Montagu College, Paris, joined the Sulpicians and studied at the Sulpician seminary but was forced to leave France when the Revolutionary government closed the seminary. He went to the United States in 1792 with Benedict Flaget, studied at St. Mary's Seminary, Baltimore, and was ordained in 1793—the first priest to be ordained in the new United States. Later that year he settled at White Sulphur, Kentucky, and covered thousands of miles on horseback ministering to the Catholics in his 120-mile parish; for twelve years he was the only priest there. He fell out with Flaget, now bishop of Bardstown, Kentucky, because of a disagreement over real estate and returned to France in 1812. He became pastor of a parish forty miles from Orléans in 1819 and remained there until 1828 when he returned to the United States. After two years in Michigan and Kentucky, he became a priest of the Cincinnati diocese and ministered to the Potawatomi Indians in Indiana. He opened the first orphanage in Indiana, gave property to Fr. Sorin, one of the founders of Notre Dame, on which Notre Dame University was later built, and was appointed vicar-general in 1837. He was a pastor in Illinois in 1846–48, spent the next two years in Kentucky and then returned to Cincinnati. At the time of his death in Cincinnati on Apr. 19, he had spent sixty years in missionary activities in Kentucky, Tennessee, Ohio, Indiana, Illinois, and Michigan, covering an estimated one hundred thousand miles in his mission travels.

BAILLOQUET, PIERRE (1612–92), bishop. Born in Saintes, France, he joined the Jesuits at Bordeaux in 1631, was ordained, and in 1647 was sent to Canada as a missionary. He spent the rest of his life ministering to the Indians from Acadia in the east to the Illinois country in the west. He died in the Ottawa missions on June 7.

BAKER, FRANCIS ASBURY (1820–65), missionary. Born in Baltimore on Mar. 30, the son of a prominent Baltimore physician, he graduated from Princeton in 1839, left the Methodism of his parents, and joined the Episcopal Church and was ordained a deacon in 1845. He became known for his preaching prowess while an assistant at St. Paul's Church and then rector (1851–53) of St. Luke's Episcopal Church in Baltimore, but in 1853 resigned his ministry and became a Catholic—a step which caused a sensation in Baltimore. He joined the Redemptorists, was ordained Sept. 21, 1856, and the following month with Frs. Isaac Hecker, Augustine Hewit, George Deshon, and Clarence Walworth, all converts, began preaching missions all over the United States. In 1858 Hecker received permission from Pope Pius IX for the five to leave the Redemptorists and found the Society of Missionary Priests of St. Paul the Apostle (the Paulists), dedicated to converting Americans to Catholicism (Walworth withdrew on the eve of the new community's birth). Baker preached missions in parishes all over the country and his impassioned eloquence made him a highly popular missionary. He died in New York City on Apr. 14 of pneumonia brought on by typhoid.

BAKER, JOSEPHINE (1903–75), entertainer. Born in a slum section of St. Louis, Missouri, on June 3, she was early interested in the theater, became a dancer, and when fifteen joined a touring vaudeville troupe. She appeared in the chorus of *Shuffle Along* in New York in 1923 and in the floor show of the Plantation Club and in 1925 went to Paris to appear in *La Revue Nègre* and introduce "le jazz hot" to France. She left to appear in the *Folies Bergère,* opened her own nightclub, Chez Josephine, in 1926 and became the toast of Paris, the epitome of black talent. She was to be a top entertainer the next fifty years. She went into the movies with *Zou-Zou* in 1934 and light opera in *La Créole,* also in 1934, and then appeared in several other motion pictures. She became a French citizen in 1937, was a Red Cross worker at the outbreak of World War II, and was involved with the French underground when the Germans occupied Paris. She entertained troops in North Africa and the Middle East and after the war returned to Paris to star in the *Folies Bergère* and made several world tours. She married French orchestra leader Jo Bouillon in 1947 (her first marriage to French industrialist Jean Lyon had been annulled in 1940) and in the 1950s began adopting babies of various nationalities and races, a dozen in all, and raised them on her estate, Les Milandes, in the Dordogne Valley. She retired from show business in 1956 but returned to the stage in 1959. She died in Paris on Apr. 12.

BAKER, NELSON HENRY (1841–1936). Born in Buffalo, New York, on

Feb. 16, he was educated at Canisius College there and at Our Lady of Angels Seminary at Niagara University and was ordained in 1876. He spent five years as assistant pastor in Lackawanna, New York, was a curate at Corning, New York, and in 1882 was placed in charge of Our Lady of Victory Homes of Charity in Lackawanna. Between 1892 and 1915, he built an industrial school, a maternity hospital, and an infants' home and in 1926 he finished work on Our Lady of Victory Shrine. He was appointed vicar-general of the Buffalo diocese in 1902 and was made a monsignor in 1905. Under his leadership some twenty-five thousand boys were sheltered, educated, and given work and he was responsible for the rehabilitation of thousands of underprivileged men and women. He died in Lackawanna on July 29.

BALBUENA, BERNARD DE (1568–1627), poet. Born in Valdepeñas, he was brought to Mexico by his parents when a boy, was educated there and then returned to Spain for his ordination. He spent twelve years in pastoral work in Jamaica and in 1620 was appointed bishop of Puerto Rico and spent the rest of his life in Puerto Rico until his death there. He was the author of a history of Mexico in the sixteenth century and several books of poetry, chief of which was *El Bernardo o la victoria de Roncesvalles,* a long epic poem on Bernardo del Carpio and the Spanish resistance to Charlemagne's invasion. His poem, *La Grandeza Mexicana,* is considered the beginning of Spanish-American poetry.

BALDWIN, CHARLES SEARS (1867–1935), educator. Born in New York City on Mar. 21, he was educated at Columbia (B.A. 1888, M.A. 1889, Ph.D. 1894) and taught there in 1891–95. He taught English at Yale in 1895–1911 and then returned to New York

where he taught at Columbia and Barnard for the rest of his life. He was greatly interested in the Middle Ages and among the texts, essays, poems, and scholarly works he authored were *A College Manual of Rhetoric* (1902), *College Composition* (1917), *Ancient Rhetoric and Poetic* (1924), *Medieval Rhetoric and Poetic* (1928), *Three Medieval Centuries of Literature in England 1100–1400* (1932), and the posthumous *Renaissance Literary Theory and Practice* (1939). He became a Catholic the year before his death in New York City on Oct. 23.

BALTES, PETER JOSEPH (1820–86), bishop. Born in Ensheim, Bavaria, he was brought, when six, to the United States by his parents who settled in Oswego, New York. He was educated at Holy Cross College, Worcester, Massachusetts, St. Mary's of the Lake Seminary, Chicago, and the Grand Seminary in Montreal where he was ordained. He engaged in parish work in Chicago, became vicar-general to Bishop Henry Juncker of Alton, Illinois, and accompanied him to the Second Plenary Council of Baltimore in 1866 as his theologian. In 1869 he was appointed bishop of Alton succeeding Juncker who had died in 1868; he was noted for his insistence on clerical discipline and on order and uniformity in liturgical ceremonies. He died in Alton on Feb. 15.

BALTIMORE, LORD. *See* Calvert, Cecilius; Calvert, Charles; Calvert, George.

BANDAS, RANDOLPH G. (1896–1969), theologian. Born in Silver Lake, Minnesota, on Apr. 18, he was educated at St. Thomas College (B.A. 1917) and studied for the priesthood at St. Paul (Minnesota) Seminary and was ordained there in 1921. He continued his studies at Angelico University in Rome, receiving his Ph.D. in 1923, and at the University of Louvain, receiving his S.T.D. et M. in 1925. He taught at St. Paul's in 1924–45, was rector in 1945, nonresident professor at Lateran University in Rome in 1958, and a member of the Roman Pontifical Academy in 1960. He became a leader in the catechetical movement and spent most of his life teaching dogmatic theology and catechetics; he taught one of the first formal courses in catechetics. He was first director of the Confraternity of Christian Doctrine for the St. Paul archdiocese and held that position for almost thirty years, was chairman of the National Seminary Committee of the Confraternity of Christian Doctrine in 1945, was a consultant to the Congregation of Seminaries and Universities in Rome, was made a domestic prelate in 1955, and was a *peritus* at Vatican Council II. He was named pastor of St. Agnes Church in St. Paul in 1959 and held that position until his death in St. Paul on July 26. He wrote widely on religious education, had a column in *The Wanderer* for years, and among his books were the pioneer text, *Catechetical Methods* (1929), *Contemporary Philosophy and Thomistic Principles* (1932), *Practical Problems in Religion* (1934), *Catechetics in the New Testament* (1935), *Religion, Teaching and Practice* (1935), the six-volume *Modern Questions* (1941), the eight-volume *Biblical Questions,* and a series of high school texts on the bible and catechetics.

BANNON, JOHN B. (1829–1913), chaplain. Born in Roosky, County Roscommon, Ireland, on Dec. 28, he was ordained at Maynooth, Ireland, in 1853 and came to the United States. He served at St. Louis Cathedral and Immaculate Conception Church in St. Louis and in 1888 was made pastor of St. John's Church there, finishing the construction of a new church in 1860. At the outbreak of the Civil War he decided in favor of the Confederacy, joined the Confederate forces under General Sterling Price in 1862, served as a chaplain in numerous battles including Corinth and Vicksburg, and received his chaplain's commission in 1863. Later that year he was appointed Confederate commissioner to Ireland and labored in his native land to explain the Confederate position by writing letters to newspapers, magazine articles, and widely distributed circulars. He accompanied Bishop Patrick Lynch of Charleston, South Carolina, to Rome in 1864 in an unsuccessful attempt to secure papal recognition of the Confederate States. He then returned to Ireland, joined the Jesuits in 1865, and served at St. Ignatius University College Church and St. Francis Xavier Church in Dublin until his death in Dublin on July 14.

BAPST, JOHN (1815–87), missionary. Son of a well-to-do farmer, he was born at La Roche, Fribourg, Switzerland, on Dec. 17. He began his education when twelve at St. Michael's College in Fribourg, joined the Jesuits in 1835, and was ordained in 1846. He came to New York in 1848 as one of a group of exiled Jesuits and was sent to minister to the Abnaki Indians at Old Town, Maine; he was transferred to Eastport two years later and then to Ellsworth. He traveled all over Maine, founded several temperance societies, and became known for his conversions to Catholicism. He was a victim of the Know-Nothing movement in 1854 when he was dragged from his home in Ellsworth, where he was trying to found a Catholic school, because of his objections to Protestant religious exercises Catholic children in public schools were required by law to attend, and was tarred and feathered by the adherents of Know-Nothingism, barely escaping with his life. After his recovery he continued his missionary journeys throughout the state and spent three years in Bangor where he was honored by the Protestant residents of that town and built the first Catholic church there in 1856. He was rector of the Jesuit scholasticate in Boston in 1860–63 and then was first president of the newly established Boston College in 1864–69. He was superior of all Jesuit houses in Canada and New York in 1869–73, then became superior of a Jesuit residence in Providence, Rhode Island. He died at Mount Hope, Maryland on Nov. 2; the last years of his life were marred by a failing mind attributed to his ordeal at Ellsworth.

BARAGA, FREDERIC (1797–1868), bishop, missionary. Of a wealthy Austrian family of Slovenian extraction, he was born at Malavas, Carniola (now a province of Yugoslavia), on June 29, was baptized Irenaeus Frederic, early dropping his first name, and studied law at the University of Vienna. On graduation in 1821, he opted for the clerical life, broke off his engagement to his fiancée and renounced his inheritance, and later in the same year entered the seminary at Laibach (Ljubljana, Yugoslavia). He was ordained in 1823, served as a parish priest in Smartno and Metlika, and then volunteered his services as a missionary in the United States. He arrived there in 1831 and spent the rest of his life in missionary work among the Indians. He worked among the German Catholics in Cincinnati for a few months early in 1831 and in May was sent to his first Indian mission, Arbre Croche (Harbor Springs, Michigan). He worked among the Ottawas there until 1833 when he was sent to found a new Indian mission at Grand River (Grand Rapids), Michigan; in 1835 he was sent to minister to the Chippewas at La Pointe, Michigan; and in 1843 he went to L'Anse Indian mission on Keweenaw

Bay in Michigan. He spent a decade ministering to the Indians and white Catholics drawn to Upper Michigan by the discovery of iron and copper in northern Michigan, often the only Catholic priest in the whole huge area. When the northern peninsula of Michigan was erected into a vicariate apostolic in 1853 he was named its first bishop with his see at Sault Ste. Marie. The vicariate was raised to a diocese in 1857 and he secured permission from the Holy See in 1865 to transfer its seat to Marquette. He spent the last fifteen years of his life administering his far-flung see traveling incessantly throughout it. He had a voluminous correspondence, composed the first Chippewa grammar and dictionary, *Grammar and Dictionary of the Otchipee* [Chippewa] *Language* (1851–53), and wrote a Chippewa prayer book and several catechetical works in Chippewa as well as a Slovenian prayer book, a book on Indian customs, a book on Our Lady in Slovenian, and a life of Jesus in Ottawa prayer book. He was passionately devoted to the spiritual, material, and intellectual needs of his people and gave tirelessly of his considerable energy to them. He made thousands of converts to Catholicism and was a popular figure not only among the Indians but among all with whom he came in contact; he is remembered in Michigan by the county named after him. He suffered a stroke while attending the Second Plenary Council of Baltimore in 1866, returned to Marquette, and died there on Jan. 19.

BARBER, ABIGAIL (1811–80), *See* Barber, Virgil Horace.

BARBER, CHLOE (1747–1825), *See* Barber, Daniel.

BARBER, DANIEL (1756–1834). Born in Simsbury, Connecticut, on Oct. 2, he was raised a Congregationalist and served in the Continental Army during the American Revolution. When he was twenty-seven he joined the Episcopal Church and when thirty was ordained in Schenectady, New York. He married Chloe Case and in about 1787, with their four children, they moved to Claremont, New Hampshire. After thirty years, he began a study of Catholicism and visited Bishop Cheverus in Boston to discuss Catholicism with him. When Fanny Allen, daughter of Revolutionary-famed Ethan Allen, whom he had baptized in 1807, became a Catholic nun and his son Virgil and his wife were converted in 1817, his study intensified. The following year a visit to his home by a New York Dominican priest, Fr. Charles French, led to his wife, Chloe, and their four children, his sister Mrs. Noah Tyler and her daughter becoming Catholics. Daniel resigned his ministry late the next year, visited friends in Maryland and Washington and while on the trip became a Catholic. Chloe died Feb. 8, 1825, in her seventy-ninth year and Daniel spent the rest of his life with his son Virgil in Maryland and Pennsylvania. He died at the Jesuit house in St. Inigoes, Maryland, on Mar. 24. He wrote *History of Our Times* (1827) and *Catholic Worship and Piety Explained* (1821).

BARBER, JERUSHA (1789–1860). Jerusha Booth was born in New Town, Connecticut, on July 20, married Virgil Horace Barber, and the couple had five children. She joined the Catholic Church with him and their children in 1817 and the following year he joined the Jesuits and she joined the Visitandine nuns, taking her three elder daughters, Mary, Abigail, and Susan, into the convent with her; the youngest, Josephine, was left in the care of the mother of Fr. Benedict J. Fenwick, the Jesuit priest who had received them into the Church. She and Virgil took their

vows together as a Visitandine nun and a Jesuit in the Visitandine convent in Georgetown in 1820. She took the name Mary Augustine. She served her order in convents in Georgetown, Kaskaskia, Illinois, St. Louis, and Mobile, Alabama, where she died on Jan. 1.

BARBER, JOSEPHINE (1816–88). *See* Barber, Virgil Horace.

BARBER, MARY (1810–44). *See* Barber, Virgil Horace.

BARBER, SAMUEL JOSEPH (1814–64). *See* Barber, Virgil Horace.

BARBER, SUSAN (1813–37). *See* Barber, Virgil Horace.

BARBER, VIRGIL HORACE (1782–1847). Son of Daniel Barber, he was born in Simsbury, Connecticut, on May 9, was educated at Dartmouth, and became an Episcopal priest. He was pastor at St. John's Episcopal Church in Waterbury, Connecticut, in 1807–14 and then resigned to become principal of an Episcopal academy in Fairfield, New York. In 1817, he and his wife Jerusha and their five children became Catholics. He opened a school in New York but after seven months he and Jerusha decided to enter the religious life and received ecclesiastical permission to do so. Virgil and his son Samuel went to Georgetown and joined the Jesuits. Jerusha entered the Visitandine convent in Georgetown, taking her three elder daughters, Mary, Abigail, and Susan, and leaving the youngest daughter in the care of the mother of Fr. Benedict J. Fenwick who had received the family into the Catholic Church. He took his vows as a Jesuit and Jerusha made her profession as a Visitandine nun together in the chapel of the Visitandine convent in Georgetown in 1820. After a year in Rome, Virgil returned to Georgetown and was ordained a Catholic priest in Boston in 1822. He was sent to Claremont, New Hampshire, and during the two years he was there (1823–24), built the first Catholic church in the area. He then was sent to Maine where he worked among the Indians for a time after which he returned to Georgetown where he remained until his death on Mar. 25. All five children also embraced the religious life. Mary (1810–44) was born in Waterbury, Connecticut, on Jan. 31 and joined the Ursulines at Mt. Benedict Convent near Charlestown, Massachusetts, in 1826, taking the name Mary Benedicta, and died in the Ursuline convent in Quebec on May 9. Abigail (1811–80) was born in Waterbury on Feb. 5, became an Ursuline nun taking the name St. Francis Xavier and died in the Ursuline convent in Quebec on Mar. 2. Susan (1813–37) also joined the Ursulines, taking the name Mary St. Joseph, and died in the Ursuline convent in Three Rivers, Canada, on Jan. 24. Josephine (1816–88) was born in Fairfield, New York, on Aug. 9 and joined the Visitandines. She died in St. Louis on July 17. Samuel (1814–64) was born in Waterbury on Mar. 19, joined the Jesuits after graduating from Georgetown in 1831, was sent to Rome after his novitiate and was ordained there. He returned to Georgetown in 1840 and died at St. Thomas Manor, Maryland, on Feb. 23.

BARBELIN, FELIX JOSEPH (1808–69). Born in Luneville, Lorraine, France, on May 30, he was educated in his youth by a granduncle, studied at a French seminary, emigrated to the United States, and joined the Jesuits in 1831 at Whitemarsh, Maryland. He taught French for a time at Georgetown, was an assistant pastor of Holy Trinity Church in Georgetown in 1836 and in 1838 was transferred to Old St. Joseph's Church in Philadelphia of which he became pastor in 1844. He established a free school for boys and girls and sodalities for men and women, founded St. Joseph's Hospital, and gathered the first black congregation in Philadelphia and established a school for black children; the Italian congregation he organized at St. Joseph's developed into the first Italian parish in the city. In 1852 he was named first president of St. Joseph's College which he had helped to establish. He died in Philadelphia on June 8, greatly beloved by all the citizens of Philadelphia and was often called the "apostle of Philadelphia."

BARRETT, FRANK A. (1892–1962), U.S. senator. Born in Omaha, Nebraska, on Nov. 10, he was educated at Creighton University there (B.A. 1913, LL.B. 1916), married Alice C. Donoghue in 1919, and moved to Wyoming. He was admitted to the Wyoming bar, spent three years in the U.S. Army in World War I, and on his return began practicing law in Lusk, Wyoming. He was attorney for Niobrara County in 1923–33, became the owner and operator of a sheep and cattle ranch in 1924, served in the state senate in 1933–35 and in the House of Representatives in 1943–51, and was governor of Wyoming in 1951–53. He was elected United States senator from Wyoming in 1952, was defeated for reelection in 1958, married Augusta K. Hogan in 1959 (his first wife had died in 1956), and was general counsel for the United States Agriculture Department in 1959–60. He died in Cheyenne, Wyoming, on May 30.

BARRETT, JAMES FRANCIS (1888–1934), author. Born in Bridgeport, Connecticut, on Sept. 1, he was educated at St. Thomas Seminary, Hartford, Connecticut; St. John's Seminary, Brighton, Massachusetts; and St. Mary's Seminary, Baltimore; and was ordained in

1914. He was a curate at Immaculate Conception Church in Hartford and served as principal of its parish school. He was named pastor of St. Patrick's Church, Farmington, Connecticut, in 1939 and remained in that position until his death on May 29. He was the author of the widely used text, *Elements of Psychology for Nurses* and four novels written in a popular vein, the best known of which were *The Loyalist* and *Winter of Discontent*.

BARRON, EDWARD (1801–54), bishop, missionary. Youngest son of wealthy parents he was born in Ballyneale, County Waterford, Ireland, on June 28. He studied law at Trinity College, Dublin, was admitted to the Irish bar but in 1825 decided to become a priest. He studied for the priesthood at the Propaganda, Rome, where he received his doctorate in divinity, and was ordained in Rome in 1829. He taught at St. John's College, Waterford, for a time and then accepted the invitation of Bishop Kenrick to be rector of the diocesan seminary of Philadelphia, St. Charles Borromeo. After a time he left to engage in parish work, became pastor of St. Mary's Church, and was appointed vicar-general of the see. In 1841 he went to Liberia to work with the Catholics there and in 1842 was consecrated titular bishop of Constantia and prefect apostolic of Upper Guinea which was soon extended to Sierra Leone and most of the western coast of Africa. He recruited Sacred Heart of Jesus priests to aid him and despite great difficulties continued working in Africa until 1845 when a fever he contracted forced him to resign his vicariate and return to the United States. He worked as a missionary priest and in Philadelphia, St. Louis, and Florida, and died in Savannah, Georgia, on Sept. 12, of yellow fever contracted while aiding the stricken during an epidemic.

BARRY, MOTHER GERALD (1881–1961), educator. One of eighteen children of well-to-do farmer Michael Barry and Catherine Dixon Barry, she was born in Inagh, County Clare, Ireland, on Mar. 11 and was christened Catherine Bridget. She emigrated to the United States in her youth, spent several years in business, and in 1913 joined the Most Holy Rosary Congregation of the Dominican sisters of Adrian, Michigan. She took her vows the following year, taught and was principal of several schools in 1914–21, and was novice mistress in 1921–33. She was elected prioress general in 1933 and served in that position until her death in Adrian on Nov. 20. During the years she was prioress general the congregation rapidly expanded; the members of the community increased from 930 to 2,480; two senior colleges, a teachers college, and four girls high schools were built and some seventy parochial schools were opened. A sisters house of studies was opened in Washington and in pursuance of her policy of upgrading the education of her nuns some two hundred nuns were sent to college to get their bachelor and higher degrees. She was first executive chairperson of the Sisters Committee for the National Congress of Religious in the United States at Notre Dame in 1952, and in 1956 she presided at the Chicago meeting of superiors which led to the formation of the Conference of Major Superiors of Women's Religious Institutes.

BARRY, JOHN (1745–1803), naval officer. Born at Tacumshane, County Wexford, Ireland, he took to sea as a youth of ten and when fifteen came to Philadelphia which he made his home for the rest of his life. He commanded several ships in the West Indies trade and in 1775 volunteered for the Continental Navy and was commissioned an officer—the first naval commission of the Continental Congress of the new nation. He was put in charge of its first vessel, the *Lexington*, and participated in the battles of Trenton and Princeton as special aide to General John Cadwalader when his vessel was blockaded in the Delaware River by the British. He returned to the Navy, led several raids on British supply ships in the Delaware River, and in 1778 was put in command of the *Raleigh*. When it was destroyed in an engagement with two British frigates, he escaped with his crew. He was assigned various other vessels, captured several British ships, was wounded while commanding the *Alliance* in an engagement with the *Atlanta* and the *Trespasser* in 1781 and despite his wound captured them both. He was active throughout the rest of the American Revolution and participated in the last naval engagement of the war with the British frigate *Sybille* in 1783. He returned to merchant shipping after the war but when the United States Navy was permanently established in 1794 he was the first of six captains appointed by President Washington—the ranking officer of the Navy. He supervised the construction of the frigate *United States* and commanded her on several cruises. During the undeclared war between France and the United States in 1798–1801, he commanded a fleet in the West Indies to protect American shipping and to harass the French. In 1801 his sea service came to an end when the Navy was put on a peacetime basis. The last years of his life were marred by ill health which caused him to decline to lead American ships against the Barbary pirates. He died soon after in Philadelphia on Sept. 13. He is often called the "father of the American Navy."

BARRY, JOHN (1799–1859), bishop. Born in Oylegate parish, County Wexford, Ireland, in July, he came to the United States at the invitation of Bishop John England of Charleston, South Carolina, under whom he studied, and was ordained in 1825. He was assistant at the cathedral and secretary to Bishop England until 1828 when he was appointed pastor of St. Mary's Church in Charleston; he was transferred to St. Peter's Church in Columbia, South Carolina, in 1829 and the following year to Holy Trinity Church in Augusta, Georgia. He served as chaplain to the Irish Volunteers of Charleston in the Seminole War in 1836. He was honored by city officials for his heroic efforts to aid the stricken people of Augusta in the yellow fever epidemic of 1839, having turned his rectory into a hospital. He was vicar-general of the diocese under Bishops England and Reynolds, attended the fourth Provincial Council of Baltimore as England's theologian, and was named vicar-general of Savannah, Georgia, when the diocese was erected in 1850. When its first bishop, Francis Gartland, died of yellow fever in 1854, Barry was appointed administrator of the see and attended the eighth Provincial Council of Baltimore in 1855; two years later he was appointed second bishop of Savannah. In ill health at the time of his consecration he went to Europe to recover his health and died at the hospital of the Brothers of St. John of God in Paris on Nov. 21.

BARRY, PATRICK (1816–90), horticulturist. Born near Belfast, Ireland, in May, he taught for a time and then in 1836 emigrated to the United States. He became a nurseryman in Flushing, New York, and set up a horticultural business with George Ellwanger in Rochester, New York, in 1849. The firm soon became a leading importer and developer of plants, fruits, and shade trees. In time its nurseries became the largest in the country. Barry wrote widely on horticultural subjects, authored the very successful *A Treatise on the Fruit Gar-*

den (1851), and was editor of *The Gene-see Farmer* from 1844 to 1852 and of *The Horticulturist* from 1852 to 1854. He died in Rochester on June 23.

BARRY, PATRICK FRANK (1868–1940), bishop. Born in Ennis, West Clare, Ireland, on Nov. 15, he was educated at Mungret Apostolic College, Royal University of Ireland, and St. Patrick's Seminary in Carlow where he was ordained in 1895. He went to the United States later that year, was a curate at Jacksonville, Florida, until 1913 and then became a pastor in South Jacksonville. He was vicar-general of the diocese of St. Augustine, Florida, in 1917–22, was administrator of the see in 1921–22 after Bishop Curley had been translated to Baltimore, and in 1922 he was appointed fifth bishop of St. Augustine, a position he held the rest of his life. With his brother Msgr. William Barry and his sister, Mother Gerald Barry, prioress general of the Adrian Dominicans, he founded the liberal arts Barry College for women in Miami shortly before his death on Aug. 13 in Jacksonville, Florida.

BARRY, PHILIP (1896–1949), playwright. Born in Rochester, New York, on June 18, he received his B.A. from Yale in 1919 and served in the American embassy in London for a few months in 1918–19. On his return he did postgraduate work in play writing at Harvard under George P. Baker in the 47 Workshop and was awarded first prize for his first play, *You and I,* in 1922; it was professionally produced the following year in New York. In the years to come he became one of America's best known playwrights noted for his sophisticated comedies of manners and mild social satire. Among his plays were *White Wings* (1926), *Paris Bound* (1927), *Holiday* (1928), *The Animal Kingdom* (1938), *The Philadelphia Story*

(1939) and *Second Threshold* (1951) which was unfinished at his death and completed by Robert Sherwood. His two plays with Catholic themes, *John* (1927), about John the Baptist, and *The Joyous Season* (1934) were not particularly successful. He died on Jupiter Island in Hobe Sound, Florida, on Dec. 3.

BARRYMORE, ETHEL (1879–1959), actress. Daughter of the famous actor, Maurice Barrymore, and the famous actress, Georgiana Drew, she was born in Philadelphia on Aug. 15, and was educated there by the Sisters of Notre Dame de Namur. Though originally she had ambitions to become a concert pianist, she decided instead to become an actress, and made her debut in London in an engagement with Henry Irving. She returned to New York and was a smash hit as the star of *Captain Jinks of the Horse Marines* in 1901 and soon became one of the leading actresses on the American stage, known for her warmth and dignity. She starred in such hits as *Cousin Kate* (1903), *Sunday* (1904), *A Doll's House* (1905), and Somerset Maugham's *Lady Frederick* (1908). She married Russell Griswold Colt, son of the chairman of the United States Rubber Company, in 1909 and the couple had three children, Samuel Pomeroy, Ethel Barrymore, and John Drew. They were divorced in 1923 but she considered it "merely legal" since she was a Catholic; she never remarried. In 1955 she published her autobiography, *Memories* (dedicated to the Sisters of Notre Dame de Namur who had educated her), and in 1956 she hosted the "Ethel Barrymore Theater." She had begun appearing in motion pictures in 1914 and during her lifetime made a score of films and though she never cared for motion pictures, she won the Academy Award for best supporting role in *None But the Lonely Heart* in 1942. She announced her retirement in 1936 but soon returned to Broadway with *The Ghost of Yankee Doodle* in 1937. Her last great stage triumph was in *The Corn Is Green* (1940–42) though she appeared in several Broadway plays after that. She died in Hollywood on June 18 after a half century enthralling audiences as one of America's leading actresses. In 1928 the Ethel Barrymore Theater, named in her honor, opened in New York City.

BARRYMORE, GEORGIANA EMMA (1856–93), actress. Daughter of John and Louisa Lane Drew, of the famous English theatrical family, she was born on July 11, grew up and was educated in Philadelphia. Encouraged by her mother, a famous actress, she began her theatrical career in 1872 at the Philadelphia Arch Street Theatre with a small role in *Ladies' Battle*. She followed her brother John in joining Augustus Daly and his theatrical group and made her debut with the company as Mary Standish in *Pique*. She appeared in numerous Daly productions, among them *The Serious Family, Weak Women, As You Like It*, a revival of *The School for Scandal*, and *The Princess Royal*. Maurice Barrymore was in *The Princess Royal* and the two were married at the end of 1876; they had three children, Lionel, John, and Ethel, all of whom became stars. She worked for a time in Palmer's stock company and at various times appeared in productions with Maurice, Edwin Booth, Lawrence Barrett, and John McCullough until her husband went to California to appear with Madame Modjeska. She joined him there with their three children and in 1884 through the influence of Madame Modjeska she and the children became Catholics. Her last appearances on the stage were in Bisson's *Settled out of Court* and Lestoq's *The Sportsman* in Boston in the fall of 1892. Serious illness cut short her career and she went to Santa Barbara with Ethel in 1893 and died there on July 2.

BARTHOLOME, PETER (1893–1982), bishop. Born in Bellechester, Minnesota, on Apr. 2, he received his B.A. from Campion College in 1914, studied for the priesthood at St. Paul (Minnesota) Seminary in 1914–17, and was ordained in 1917. He served as a curate in Rochester, Minnesota, in 1917–19, was professor of Latin, Greek, and philosophy at St. Mary's College, Winona, Minnesota, in 1919–28, and studied canon law at Apollinare University in Rome in 1928–30. He was chaplain to a group of Franciscan nuns in Rochester in 1929–33, pastor in Caledonia and Rochester in 1933–42, and in 1941 was appointed titular bishop of Lete and coadjutor of St. Cloud, Minnesota. He succeeded to the see in 1953, was named Assistant at the Pontifical Throne the following year, resigned as bishop of St. Cloud in 1968, and was appointed titular bishop of Tanaramusa and died near Ward Springs, Minnesota, on June 17.

BARTON, GEORGE (1866–1940), journalist. Born in Philadelphia on Jan. 22, he began his journalism career as a bit newspaper reporter on the Philadelphia *Inquirer* when he was nineteen. He then became an editorial writer for the Philadelphia *Bulletin*, married Sophia McCauley in 1893, left the *Bulletin* to return to the *Inquirer* as an editorial writer and remained in that position until his death in Philadelphia on Mar. 16. In addition to his news reporting and editorial writing, he wrote some two hundred detective stories, a series of juvenile sports books, and through his interest in history *Little Journeys Around Old Philadelphia* (1926) and *Walks and Talks About Old Philadelphia* (1928), *Columbus the Catholic* (1902), *Angels of* *the Battlefield* (1897), describing the work of nuns on the battlefields of the Civil War, and *Barry Wynn* (1912).

BARZYNSKI, VINCENT (1838–99). Born in Sulislawice, Sandomir, Poland, on Sept. 20, he was baptized Michael but called Vincent after he recovered from an illness during which he had been placed under the protection of St. Vincent Ferrer. He was educated privately because of poor health, entered the Lublin seminary in 1856 and was ordained in 1861, but spent the next six months at home because of illness. He was appointed vicar of Horodlo in 1862 and was then transferred to Tomaszów where he became a member of the Polish underground in the unsuccessful revolt against Russia in 1863. He was forced to flee when his work in the underground was discovered, escaped to Austria, and in 1865 went to Paris. The following year he went to Rome where he joined the newly founded Congregation of the Resurrection and in 1866 emigrated to the United States. He worked among Polish Catholics in the diocese of Galveston, Texas, and then went to Chicago where he was appointed pastor of St. Stanislaus Kostka Church in 1874. He became the leader of the Polish immigrants who came to the Chicago area in great numbers, administered the largest Polish parish school in the United States, helped organize Polish parishes, and founded a Polish orphanage and home for the aged and St. Stanislaus Kostka High School. He established the first Polish-American Catholic paper, *Gazeta Katolica,* and the first Polish daily in the United States, *Dziennik Chicagoski,* and the Polish Roman Catholic Union. He arranged for Polish-American textbooks and Sunday school papers to be published, served as superior of the Chicago Resurrectionists and was first provincial of the congregation's American province in 1898–99, and was active in helping found the Franciscan Sisters of Bl. Kunegunda, a Polish-American sisterhood, and in opposing the radical socialist influences of the times. He was the dynamic force and leader in keeping Poles strong in their faith in their strange new American environment. He died in Chicago on May 2.

BAUMGARTNER, APOLLINARIS (1899–1970), bishop. Born in College Point, New York City, he joined the Capuchins and was ordained at Marathon, Michigan, in 1926. He served as editor of *Seraphic Chronicle and Mission Almanac,* was pastor of St. John Baptist Church in New York City and superior of its community, and was vicar of Sacred Heart Monastery in Yonkers, New York. He was named titular bishop of Joppe and vicar apostolic of Guam in 1945 and died at Agana, Guam, on Dec. 18.

BAYLEY, JAMES ROOSEVELT (1814–77), archbishop. Of a prominent family (one grandfather was the famous surgeon Dr. Richard Bayley; his maternal grandfather was James Roosevelt, a wealthy merchant; and his aunt was St. Elizabeth Seton, first American saint), he was educated at Amherst College, contemplated a naval career but instead studied for the Episcopal priesthood in Hartford, Connecticut. He graduated and was ordained in 1840 and was named rector of St. James Church in Harlem. He resigned his rectorship in 1841 and went to Rome where he became a Catholic the following year. He took his theological studies at St. Sulpice Seminary in Paris and was ordained a Catholic priest in New York in 1844. He became a professor and vice president of St. John's College (Fordham), was acting president in 1846, and then became pastor of a parish at the Quarantine Station on Staten Island. He was made Bishop Hughes's secretary and chancellor of the New York diocese in 1846 and in 1853 was named first bishop of the newly established diocese of Newark, New Jersey. He brought religious communities into the diocese, more than doubled the number of its priests and churches, founded Seton Hall College and Immaculate Conception Seminary, and was an active supporter of the temperance movement. He attended Vatican Council I in 1869–70 and in 1872 was appointed archbishop of Baltimore. Though frequently ill he was active in Indian missions, establishing a missionary affairs association in Washington, D.C., in 1874, helped found the American College in Rome, labored to repair the ravages of the Civil War in his see, and convened the eighth Provincial Synod of Baltimore in 1875, which legislated on the clergy, on clerical dress, mixed marriages, and various other matters, among them church music. He was appointed apostolic delegate in 1875 to bestow the cardinal's hat on Archbishop McCloskey of New York, and he paid off the debt on his own cathedral and consecrated it in 1876. His ill health caused him to ask for a coadjutor (Bishop James Gibbons of Richmond was appointed in 1877) and he went abroad in a vain quest to recover his health. He soon returned to the United States and died in Newark two months later on Oct. 3. His interest in history caused him to publish *A Brief Sketch of the Early History of the Catholic Church on the Island of New York* in 1853 and *Memoirs of Simon Gabriel Bruté, First Bishop of Vincennes* in 1855.

BAYMA, JOSEPH (1816–62), mathematician. Born in Piedmont, Italy, on Nov. 9, he joined the Jesuits in 1832 and became known for his knowledge of mathematics and physics. He was rector of the seminary at Bertinro but went to England when religious were forced by the government to leave Italy. He studied philosophy at Stonyhurst and taught it there for seven years and in 1868 emigrated to California. He became rector of St. Ignatius College in San Francisco, left after three years to teach mathematics at Santa Clara and remained there until his death on Feb. 7. He wrote articles for leading Catholic journals, textbooks on algebra, geometry, trigonometry, and calculus, the widely used *Molecular Mechanics* (1866), a treatment of the constitution of matter, a privately published three-volume work of philosophy, *Realis Philosophia,* and a spiritual book, *The Love of Religious Perfection* (1863).

BAZIN, JOHN STEPHEN (1796–1848), bishop. Born at Duerne, near Lyons, France, on Oct. 15, he was educated in Lyons and was ordained there in 1822. He became a seminary professor but in 1833 volunteered for the American missions. He engaged in pastoral and missionary work in the Mobile, Alabama, area for seventeen years, also serving on the staff of Spring Hill College, organizing Sunday schools for the young, in whom he was particularly interested, and the Catholic Orphan Asylum. He was vicar-general of the diocese and pastor of the cathedral in 1836–47, made a successful trip to France in 1846 bringing back French Jesuits for Spring Hill College, of which he was president in 1832–36, 1839, 1842–44 and 1846, and also Brothers of the Christian Schools for his Boys' Orphan Asylum, and built a new cathedral from his own funds. In 1847 he was named third bishop of Vincennes, Indiana (the see was transferred to Indianapolis in 1898). He died six months after his consecration at Vincennes on Apr. 23; in that short period he was able to restore order in the see and improve bishop-clergy relations that had deteriorated under his predecessor.

BEAUMONT, JOHN COLT (1821–82), naval officer. Son of Andrew Beaumont, a Congressman, and Julia Colt Beaumont, he was born in Wilkes-Barre, Pennsylvania, on Aug. 27, and was appointed a midshipman in 1838. He cruised around the world in the *Constellation* in 1840 and served on the *Ohio* at the fall of Vera Cruz in the Mexican War. During the next decade he served at the Naval Observatory in Washington, D.C., in 1848 and 1852–54, cruised the Mediterranean on the *Independence* in 1849–52, and was a lieutenant on the *Hartford* in the East Indies when the Civil War broke out. During the war he participated in attacks on Confederate installations along the Atlantic coast and Virginia rivers. He was given command of the new monitor *Miantonomoh* on a goodwill cruise to Russia in 1866 and toured European ports with the monitor, which was called the showboat of the American fleet. He rose to the rank of rear admiral and was commandant of the Portsmouth Navy Yard when he retired on Feb. 3, 1882. He died a few months later at Durham, New Hampshire, on Aug. 2.

BEAUREGARD, PIERRE GUSTAVE TOUTANT (1818–93), general. Of French ancestry, he was born in St. Bernard parish near New Orleans on May 28, received an appointment to the United States Military Academy at West Point and graduated second in his class in 1838. He served in the artillery and engineers corps, participated in the siege of Vera Cruz, Mexico, where he was wounded twice, and several other cities during the Mexican War of 1846–48, and was brevetted major. He was appointed a regular captain of engineers in 1853, supervised coastal construction along the Gulf of Mexico coast, and was chief engineer in draining the site of New Orleans in 1858–61. In 1861 he was appointed superintendent of West Point but was allowed to serve only five days because of his secessionist sympathies. He resigned from the United States Army on Feb. 20, 1861, and joined the Confederacy. He was appointed a brigadier-general in the Confederate Army and placed in command of Charleston, South Carolina, where he launched the Civil War with an attack on Union forces at Fort Sumter. He drew up the preliminary plans of the Confederate forces at the Battle of Bull Run in 1861 and took command at Shiloh when the Confederate commander, General A. S. Johnston, was killed but was then forced to take a three-months leave of absence because of ill health. On his return he was made a general, defended Charleston against a Union siege for a year and a half, was with Lee in 1864, and with General J. E. Johnston when Confederate forces tried to stop General Sherman on his march through Georgia from Atlanta to Savannah. Their efforts were futile and they surrendered on Apr. 25, 1865. After the war he became president of the New Orleans, Jackson and Mississippi Railroad and adjutant general of Louisiana and manager of the Louisiana lottery. He refused an offer to head the Romanian army in 1866 and one from the Khedive of Egypt in 1869, and in 1888 he was named commissioner of public works of New Orleans. He wrote *Principles and Maxims of the Art of War* (1863), *Report of the Defence of Charleston* (1864), and *A Commentary on the Campaign and Battle of Manassas* (1891) and died in New Oreleans on Feb. 20.

BEAVEN, THOMAS DANIEL (1851–1920), bishop. Born in Springfield, Massachusetts, on Mar. 1, he was educated at Holy Cross College, Worcester, Massachusetts, and the Grand Seminary in Montreal. He was ordained in Montreal in 1875, was assistant at Spencer, Massachusetts, for three years and pastor the next ten and then was pastor at the Church of the Holy Rosary in Holyoke, Massachusetts, from 1888 until 1892 when he was named second bishop of Springfield, Massachusetts. An able administrator he put the diocese on a sound financial basis, expanded its parochial school system and established orphanages, asylums, hospitals, and other charitable institutions in the diocese. He died in Springfield on Oct. 5.

BECKER, THOMAS ANDREW (1832–99), bishop. Of German Protestant parents, he was born in Pittsburgh on Dec. 20, studied at Allegheny Institute and Western University there and the University of Virginia, and became a Catholic in 1853. He studied for the priesthood at the Propaganda, Rome (S.T.D.) and was ordained in Rome in 1859. He served at St. Peter's Cathedral, Richmond, Virginia, for a time and in 1860 was made a pastor at Martinsburg, West Virginia. He was arrested when he refused to offer certain public prayers in his mission church ordered by public officials which violated his secessionist sympathies. On his release he became a professor at Mt. St. Mary's College in Emmitsburg, Maryland. He became secretary to Archbishop Martin Spalding of Baltimore and helped organize the agenda for the Second Plenary Council of Baltimore in 1866. He then served at St. Peter's Church in Richmond until 1868 when he was named first bishop of the newly established diocese of Wilmington, Delaware. He helped then Archbishop Gibbons prepare for the Third Plenary Council of Baltimore in 1884 and in 1886 was appointed bishop of Savannah, Georgia, a position he held until his death in Washington, Georgia, on July 29. Noted for his linguistic abilities, he produced the chapter on clerical education adopted by the Third Plenary Council of Baltimore, wrote for numerous periodicals (his articles on the role of a true university in the *American Catholic Quarterly Review* in which he advocated the establishment of a national Catholic university attracted widespread attention), supported labor unions, and was active in the temperance movement.

BECKMAN, FRANCIS JOSEPH (1875–1948), archbishop. Born in Cincinnati, Ohio, on Oct. 25, he was educated at Mt. St. Mary of the West Seminary in Cincinnati where he was ordained in 1902. He continued his studies at Louvain and the Gregorian, Rome, where he received his S.T.B. in 1905, S.T.L. in 1907 and S.T.D. in 1908, and taught theology at Mt. St. Mary's the next four years. He was president of its theological seminary in 1912–24 and served as censor librorum for the Cincinnati archdiocese. He was one of the founders of the Catholic Students Mission Crusade in 1918 and later was chairman and director of the Crusade, which was to attain a membership of more than half a million, until 1929. He was made a domestic prelate in 1920 and in 1923 was appointed bishop of Lincoln, Nebraska. He served as apostolic administrator of Omaha, Nebraska, in 1926–28, was appointed an Assistant at the Pontifical Throne in 1928, and was named archbishop of Dubuque, Idaho, in 1930. He founded the Dubuque Symphony Orchestra in 1938, the Columbian Museum, and the National Antiquarian Society. He resigned in 1946 and was appointed titular archbishop of Phulla and died in Chicago on Oct. 17.

BEDFORD, GUNNING S. (1806–70), physician. Of a distinguished family (he was named after his uncle Gunning who was an aide-de-camp to Washington, one of the framers of the Constitution, and a United States judge), he was born in Baltimore and graduated from Mt. St. Mary's College, Emmitsburg, Maryland, in 1825. He received his medical degree from Rutgers Medical College in New Jersey in 1829, spent three years studying abroad, and in 1832 became professor of obstetrics at Charlestown (South Carolina) Medical College. He then taught at Albany Medical College, went to New York in 1836 and there founded the successful University Medical College in 1840 and was professor of obstetrics there; connected with it was the first free obstetrical clinic for the poor. By the time he was forced to retire in 1862 because of ill health he was widely regarded as one of the most distinguished and influential teachers of obstetrics in the United States. He was the author of *Diseases of Women and Children* (1855) and *Practice of Obstetrics* (1861), which were widely used as textbooks in the United States and Europe, and died in New York City on Sept. 5.

BEDINI, GAETANO (1806–64), cardinal, diplomat. Born at Sinigaglia, Italy, on May 15, he was ordained there, was secretary to Cardinal Altieri, papal nuncio to Vienna in 1838, was apostolic internuncio to Brazil in 1846, substitute secretary of state of the Vatican in 1848, commissioner extraordinary of Bologna in 1849–52, and was named titular archbishop of Thebes and apostolic nuncio to Brazil in 1852. He was assigned by Pope Pius IX to visit the United States on his way to Brazil to report on the state of ecclesiastical matters there and to explore the feasibility of establishing an apostolic nunciature in Washington. His visit, June 30, 1853–Feb. 4, 1854, touched off a wave of violent anti-Catholic demonstrations following his meeting with President Franklin Pierce in Washington which was represented by anti-Catholic groups as an attempt to

establish diplomatic relations between the United States and the Vatican. Provoked by Nativists and Know-Nothing adherents who were then at the height of their power, hostile demonstrations were launched in Pittsburgh and Louisville while rioting headed by German revolutionary refugees led to bloodshed and eighteen deaths in Cincinnati. In New York City Italian revolutionaries, led by the ex-priest Alessandro Gavazzi, denounced him and only a warning from a member of a group of conspirators saved Bedini from assassination. When leaving the United States, it was necessary to secrete him aboard the steamer taking him away. He returned to Rome without ever going to Brazil. His report gave a detailed description of the Catholic Church in the United States and stressed the need for, but inopportuneness at that time of, establishing an apostolic nunciature in Washington (an apostolic delegation was not erected until 1893). He was named secretary of the Congregation of Propaganda Fide in 1856, archbishop of Viterbo and Toscanella in 1861, and was created a cardinal later the same year. He died in Viterbo on Sept. 6.

BEGIN, FLOYD L. (1902–77), bishop. Born in Cleveland, Ohio, on Feb. 5, he was educated at St. John's Cathedral College there in 1920–22, the Propaganda in Rome, where he received his Ph.D. and S.T.D. in 1922–28, and received his J.C.D. from Appolinaris University in Rome in 1930. He was ordained in Rome in 1930, was secretary of the Cleveland diocese in 1930–38 after being administrator of St. Anthony's Church in Canton, Ohio, in 1930, and was named *officialis* of the see in 1938. He was national secretary of the Eucharistic Congress, was chaplain of the Rosemary Home for Crippled Children in Euclid, Ohio, was made a papal chamberlain in 1934 and a domestic prelate in 1936, served as vicar-general for religious, and in 1947 was consecrated titular bishop of Sala and auxiliary of Cleveland. He was appointed first bishop of the newly established diocese of Oakland, California, in 1962 and remained in that position until his death there on Apr. 26.

BEHN, HERNAND (1880–1933), executive. Born on St. Thomas, Virgin Islands, on Feb. 19, he was educated in Corsica and Paris. In 1906, he and his brother Sosthenes founded the banking firm of Behn & Company, of which he was president, in Puerto Rico. They branched out to New York City where he organized the International Telephone and Telegraph Company with subsidiaries in forty-two companies. He installed a telephone system in the Vatican in 1930 and developed its radio station, modernized the telephone system in Spain, and was honored three times by the papacy and by France and Spain. He died in St. Jean de Luz, France, on Oct. 7.

BELCOURT, GEORGE ANTHONY (1803–74), missionary. Born in Bay du Febure, Quebec, on Apr. 22, he was educated at the Petit Seminaire Nicolet and ordained in 1827. After parish work in the Montreal District, he was assigned to missionary work among the Chippewa Indians of western Canada in 1831 and established his headquarters at Baie St. Paul, some thirty-five miles west of present-day Winnipeg, and spent the next sixteen years there. In 1848 his support of half-breeds against officials of the Hudson's Bay Company caused such enmity by the officials that he was forced to resign and returned to Quebec. He was given a new assignment and established himself at Pembina on the Red River in North Dakota in 1849. The following year he moved to St. Joseph (Walhalla, North Dakota), encour-

aged the Indians to adopt a more sedentary way of life in place of their nomadic life-style, and built the first sawmill and grist mill in that part of the northwest. He returned to Quebec in 1858 and was later named pastor at Rustico, Prince Edward Island, a position he held until his death at Shediac, New Brunswick. He was the author of *Principes de la langue des Sauvages appelés Saulteux* (1839) and an eye-witness account of a buffalo hunt in North Dakota, an important historical document describing the annual Chippewa event.

BELFORD, JOHN LOUIS (1861–1951), educator. Born in Brooklyn, New York, he was educated at St. Francis Xavier College, New York City, St. Charles College, Maryland, in 1881–83 and St. Mary's Seminary, Baltimore (B.A. 1884, M.A. 1885), and was ordained in 1888. He was a curate at St. Augustine's parish, Brooklyn, in 1888–93, and was first superintendent of schools of the diocese of Brooklyn from 1893 until 1895 when he was sent to Oyster Bay, Long Island, to found St. Dominic parish there. He served until 1900 when he was named pastor of SS. Peter and Paul parish in Williamsburg, Brooklyn; he established Epiphany parish there and in 1905 was transferred to the Church of the Nativity in Brooklyn where he built a new church and parish. He was made a papal chamberlain in 1923 and a domestic prelate in 1926. An outstanding preacher he was also vocal in civic affairs; he bitterly opposed Mayor John Mitchel and Governor Charles Whitman in a controversy over Catholic charitable institutions, opposed Tammany Hall for its graft, and denounced Prohibition and the Ku Klux Klan. He wrote a prayer book for children which sold three million copies, was a member of the executive committee of the Catholic Book Club, and died in Brooklyn on Dec. 12.

BELL, ALDEN J. (1904–82), bishop. Born in Peterborough, Ontario, Canada, on July 11, he was educated at St. Peter's Junior Seminary and St. Patrick's Seminary, Menlo Park, California, and was ordained in Los Angeles in 1932. He received his master of science in social work from Catholic University in 1939, was named assistant director of the Catholic Welfare Bureau in Los Angeles in the same year, served as chaplain in the United States Air Force in the Pacific in 1942–46 during World War II, and was made a papal chamberlain in 1950 and a domestic prelate in 1954. He was named director of Catholic Charities in Los Angeles in 1952, was administrator of St. Vibiana Cathedral there in 1953–62, and was appointed titular bishop of Rhodopolis and auxiliary of Los Angeles in 1956. He was chancellor of the Los Angeles archdiocese in 1956–62 and was appointed bishop of Sacramento, California, in 1962; he retired in 1979 and died in Sacramento on Aug. 28.

BENNETT, JOHN GEORGE (1891–1957), bishop. Born in Dunnington, Indiana, on Jan. 20, he was educated at St. Joseph's College, Collegeville, Indiana, and St. Meinrad's Seminary, Indiana, and was ordained in 1914. He was a curate at St. Patrick's Church, Fort Wayne, Indiana, until 1927 when he was named pastor of St. Joseph's Church in Garret, Indiana, and served as *defensor vinculi* of the Fort Wayne diocesan curia in 1929–44. He was appointed first bishop of the newly established diocese of Lafayette in Indiana in 1944 and remained in that position until his death in Lafayette on Nov. 20.

BENSON, WILLIAM SHEPHERD (1855–1932), admiral. Born on his father's cotton plantation in Bibb County, Georgia, on Sept. 25, he graduated from the United States Naval Academy in 1877 and married Mary Augusta Wyse in 1879. He served on various warships and made a cruise around the world in the *Dolphin* in 1888–89, taught at the Naval Academy in 1890–93 and 1896–98 and was commandant of midshipmen there in 1907–08, and was made a captain in 1909. He was in command of the battleship *Utah* in 1910–13, was commandant of the Philadelphia Naval Yard in 1913–15, and was made both chief of naval operations when that position was established in 1915 and a rear admiral, and in 1916 was made an admiral. He was naval adviser to the American peace commissioners in Paris in 1919 and retired later the same year. He was appointed chairman of the United States Shipping Board by President Wilson in 1920 and served as one of its commissioners until 1928. A convert to Catholicism in early manhood, he was first president of the National Council of Catholic Men in 1921–25 and was active in Catholic affairs, receiving the Laetare Medal in 1917. He was the author of *The Merchant Marine* (1923) and revised Admiral Luce's *Textbook of Seamanship* (1898) and died in Washington, D.C., on May 20.

BENTLEY, ELIZABETH TERRILL (1908–63). Of an old New England family, she was born in New Milford, Connecticut, was educated at Vassar (B.A. 1930) and taught at the Foxcroft School in Virginia in 1930–32. She entered Columbia in the fall of 1932, studied at the University of Florence on a fellowship in 1933–34, and received her M.A. from Columbia in 1935. While in Italy her opposition to fascism marked the beginning of her interest in communism. She joined the Communist Party in New York in 1935, served as a Communist spy during World War II, using the pseudonym Elizabeth Sherman, but became disillusioned with communism and in 1945 became an undercover agent for the Federal Bureau of Investigation. She named more than thirty people before the House of Representatives Committee on Un-American Activities in 1948 that she alleged had supplied her with secret military and political information during the war. Later that year she was converted to Catholicism by Fulton J. Sheen. She lectured on communism all over the country and wrote of her experiences in *Out of Bondage* (1951). She returned to teaching at Mundelein College, Chicago, in 1949–50, at the College of the Sacred Heart, Grand Cocteau, Louisiana, in 1953–58, and for the last five years of her life at the Long Lane School for Girls in Middletown, Connecticut. She died in New Haven, Connecticut, on Dec. 3.

BENZIGER, AUGUST (1867–1955), painter. Son of Adelrich and Marie Koch Benziger of the Catholic publishing family, he was born in Einsiedeln, Switzerland, on Jan. 2, was educated at Downside College, England, and studied art at the Royal Academy, Vienna, and the Académie Julian, Paris. He specialized in portrait painting and soon became known for his technique and idealization of his subject. In time he painted many of the great of his day, among them Presidents William McKinley and Theodore Roosevelt, Popes Leo XIII, Benedict XV, and Pius XI, Cardinals James Gibbons, William O'Connell, and John Farley, and J. P. Morgan and Charles Schwab. He died in New York City on Apr. 13.

BENZIGER, CHARLES (1799–1873). *See* Benziger, Louis.

BENZIGER, J. N. ADELRICH (d. 1878). *See* Benziger, Louis.

BENZIGER, JOSEPH CHARLES (1762–1841). *See* Benziger, Louis.

BENZIGER, LOUIS (d. 1896), publisher. Grandson of Joseph Charles Benziger who was born and died in Einsiedeln, Switzerland (1762–1841), and who had founded the Benziger firm by selling religious articles in Einsiedeln in 1793 and later becoming a bookseller, Louis was the son of Joseph Charles's son Nicholas (1808–64). He and his cousin J. N. Adelrich Benziger, son of Joseph Charles' other son Charles (1799–1873) were placed in charge of a sales branch of the firm in New York City in 1853 by Charles and Nicholas who had succeeded Joseph Charles in 1833 as heads of the business and had begun publishing books in 1835. Louis and J. N. Adelrich headed the company when it began publishing books in the United States in 1860 and in time the American firm of Benziger and Brothers became independent of the Swiss firm and opened book stores in Cincinnati in 1860 and Chicago in 1887 as well as New York City; later it opened stores in San Francisco in 1929 and in Boston in 1937, and became Benziger & Company. It became a major publisher of Catholic books in the United States and in 1867 the title "Printers to the Holy Apostolic See" and in 1888 the title "The Pontifical Institute of Christian Art" were conferred on the firm by the Holy See.

BENZIGER, NICHOLAS (1808–64). *See* Benziger, Louis.

BERGAN, GERALD THOMAS (1892–1972), bishop. Born in Peoria, Illinois, on Jan. 6, he was educated at Spalding Institute there, St. Viator's College in Kankakee, Illinois, and the American College, Rome, and was ordained in Rome in 1915. He served as chancellor of the diocese of Peoria and rector of St. Mary's Cathedral there in 1917–34 and was appointed bishop of Des Moines, Iowa, in 1934. He served in this position until 1948 when he was named archbishop of Omaha, Nebraska. He retired in 1969 and was appointed titular archbishop of Tacarata and died in Omaha on July 12.

BETZ, EVA (1897–1968), author. Daughter of Dr. Michael Forestal and Caroline Cantwell Kelly Forestal, she was born in Fall River, Massachusetts, on Mar. 11, worked as an elementary school teacher in Rhode Island and Massachusetts, married Joseph P. Betz, and engaged in sales promotion work for St. Anthony Guild Press, Paterson, New Jersey. She began free-lance writing and during her career wrote scores of books for young readers, among them *Young Eagles* (1947), *Desperate Drums* (1951), *Knight of Molokai* (1956), *Fanny Allen* (1962), *Story of the Rosary* (1964), and *Lives of the Saints for Boys and Girls* (1965), many written under the pseudonym Caroline Peters. She died in Passaic, New Jersey, on Apr. 7.

BIENVILLE, JEAN BAPTISTE LE MOYNE DE (1680–1767), governor. Eighth son of Charles le Moyne, sieur de Longueil, and brother of Pierre, sieur de l'Iberville, he was born in Longueil on Feb. 24, was orphaned in his boyhood and was raised by his brother Charles. He became a midshipman in the Royal Navy and accompanied his brother Pierre on an expedition to the Hudson Bay region in 1697; the following year he accompanied Pierre on a colonizing expedition to the area around the mouth of the Mississippi River. Pierre left Jean second in command under the Sieur de Sauvole at a settlement Pierre had founded at Biloxi in 1699; when Sauvole died in 1701, Jean assumed command of the settle-

ment and moved it to Mobile Bay in 1702, and became governor of the colony on the death of Pierre in 1706. By heroic effort he kept the colony alive despite famine, Indian attacks and neglect of the colony by France; in 1710 he founded Mobile, Alabama. When wealthy financier Antoine Crozat received an exclusive grant to the Louisiana country from the French crown in 1712, he appointed La Mothe Cadillac (who later founded Detroit) governor and Bienville lieutenant-governor. Bienville led an expedition against the Natchez Indians in 1716 and in 1717 when Cadillac was recalled a new governor was appointed. However, when Crozat was unsuccessful in his quest for gold and precious metals he returned his charter to the king in 1717; a new concession to exploit the colony was at once granted to the Royal Company of the Indies, founded by John Law who appointed Bienville governor. In 1718 he selected a new site for his seat of government and moved it to that site which he named New Orleans. The colony began to expand rapidly and to raise the crops of sugar, cotton, tobacco and rice that grew so well there, and Bienville imported slaves from Guiana; in 1724 he promulgated the *Code Noir* regulating slave life and treatment. For the times it provided a most humane treatment for the slaves and remained in effect until Louisiana became a part of the United States in 1812. When France and Spain went to war in 1719, Bienville sent troops against the Spaniards in upper Louisiana and twice destroyed the Spanish settlement at Pensacola, Florida. His unsuccessful campaign against the Natchez Indians in 1723 led to his dismissal in 1723 and his recall to France in 1725. Unable to defend his administration successfully he was relieved of the governorship. When Louisiana went into a decline, King Louis again appointed him governor and he returned to Louisiana in 1733. An expedition against the Chickasaw Indians in 1736 was a failure but in 1739–40 another expedition was more successful but still indecisive. Exhausted and in ill health from his strenuous efforts on behalf of his colony, he returned to France in 1743 and spent the rest of his life in Paris where he died on Mar. 7.

BINZ, LEO (1900–79), archbishop. Born in Stockton, Illinois, on Oct. 31, he was educated at Loras College, Dubuque, Iowa, St. Mary's Seminary, Baltimore, the Sulpician Seminary, Washington, D.C., and the North American College, the Propaganda (S.T.D. 1924), and the Gregorian (Ph.D. 1926) in Rome. He was ordained in Rome in 1924, taught at the North American College in 1924–26, was a curate at Sterling, Illinois, and pastor at Cherry Valley, Rockford, and Belvidere, Illinois. He became chancellor of the Rockford diocese and was secretary to the apostolic delegate in 1936–42 and was made a domestic prelate in 1939. He was named titular bishop of Pinara and coadjutor and administrator of the diocese of Winona, Minnesota, in 1942. In 1946 he was named titular archbishop of Silyum and coadjutor of Dubuque and succeeded to the see in 1954 after having been made an Assistant at the Pontifical Throne earlier in the year. He was appointed archbishop of St. Paul, Minnesota, in 1961, was a member of the Commission on Bishops and Government of Dioceses at Vatican Council II, and retired in 1975. He took up residence in Maywood, Illinois, and died there on Oct. 9.

BISHOP, WILLIAM HOWARD (1885–1953), founder. Son of Dr. Francis Besant Bishop and Ellen Knowles Bishop, he was born in Washington, D.C., on Dec. 19, attended Harvard in 1907–08 and then decided to study for the priesthood at St. Mary's Seminary, Baltimore. He was ordained in 1915, continued his education at Catholic University, and in 1917 was named pastor of St. Louis parish in Clarksville, Maryland. He founded the Archdiocesan League of the Little Flower to aid needy rural pastors and the first Rural Life Conference of Baltimore in 1925 and was president of the National Rural Life Conference in 1928–33. Concerned with the lack of priests in so many areas he published a plan for a Catholic Home Mission Society to operate in areas where Catholics were few in number and founded the Glenmary Missioners (Home Missioners of America) in 1939. He started a theological seminary at Glendale, Ohio, in 1941 and then founded the Glenmary Lay Brothers Society and the Glenmary Home Mission Sisters in 1952. He died in Glendale on June 11.

BISKUP, GEORGE J. (1911–79), bishop. Born in Cedar Rapids, Iowa, on Aug. 23, he received his B.A. from Loras College, Dubuque, Iowa, in 1933, continued his studies at the Gregorian in Rome in 1933–37, and was ordained in Rome in 1937. He served as a curate at the Dubuque cathedral in 1951–52, was vicar-general of the archdiocese in 1952–65, and in 1957 was appointed titular bishop of Hermeria and auxiliary of Dubuque. He was chaplain of the Presentation Sisters convent in 1952–58 and pastor of the Church of the Nativity in 1958–65 and was appointed bishop of Des Moines, Iowa, in 1965. He was named titular archbishop of Tamalluma and coadjutor of Indianapolis, Indiana, in 1967 and succeeded to the see in 1970. He retired because of ill health in 1979 and died in Indianapolis on Oct. 17.

BLAKELY, PAUL LENDRUM (1880–1943), editor. Son of Laurie John

Blakely, who had been an officer in the Confederate Army, and Lily Hudson Lendrum Blakely, he was born in Covington, Kentucky, on Feb. 29. He joined the Jesuits at the Jesuit novitiate at Florissant, Missouri, in 1897, received his B.A. from Xavier College in 1898 and his M.A. from St. Louis University in 1906, and taught at the University of Detroit in 1906–9, and was ordained in 1912. Two years later he became an associate editor on the Jesuit weekly *America* and in time became its chief editorial writer. From then until his death he wrote some three thousand unsigned comments and more than one thousand signed articles in the magazine on politics, constitutional law, education, and social matters, and several devotional books. He wrote under his own name and at times under the pseudonyms John Wiltbye and Cricket Wainscott. He received his Ph.D. from Fordham in 1918, opposed the creation of a federal department of education proposed in 1920, fought for labor's right to organize and against the abuses of capitalism, and was a fierce supporter of states rights and the rights of parents. He died in New York on Feb. 26.

BLANC, ANTHONY (1792–1860), archbishop. Born at Sury, near Lyons, France, on Oct. 11, he was ordained at Lyons in 1816 by Bishop DuBourg of New Orleans who persuaded him to come to the United States. He arrived in New Orleans the following year, worked as a missionary in Indianapolis in 1820, and spent the next forty years in Louisiana. He was a parish priest in Pointe Coupee and in 1820–30 at Baton Rouge and was made vicar-general by Bishop De Neckere in 1831 but refused the bishop's request to become his coadjutor. When De Neckere died of yellow fever in 1833 Blanc became administrator of the see and in 1835 was named its bishop; during the next twenty-five years he was the leader of southern Catholicism in the South. In 1842 the lay trustees of the cathedral refused his right to name the rector of the cathedral and he put the cathedral under interdict; litigation and controversy followed before he was vindicated by the Louisiana Supreme Court in 1844. He brought many religious communities into the diocese; increased the number of priests, schools, colleges, and convents; established some forty-eight new parishes and founded a diocesan seminary in 1838. He became the first archbishop of New Orleans when the diocese was made an archdiocese in 1850, attended the First Plenary Council of Baltimore in 1852, and was in Rome when Pope Pius IX proclaimed the dogma of the Immaculate Conception in 1854. He died in New Orleans on June 20.

BLANCHET, AUGUSTIN MAGLOIRE (1797–1887), bishop. Son of a Canadian farmer and brother of François Norbert Blanchet, he was born on his father's farm near St. Pierre, Rivière du Sud, Quebec, on Aug. 22. He studied for the priesthood with his brother at the Sulpician seminary in Quebec and was ordained in 1821. After a year's pastoral work, he spent the next four years in missionary activities on the Isle de la Madeleine and Cape Breton Island and then engaged in pastoral work again in parishes in the Montreal vicariate. In 1846 he was appointed first bishop of the newly created diocese of Walla Walla, Washington. He located his see at The Dalles, founded schools and colleges, built hospitals, churches, and missions, began schools for Indians, and brought religious from Canada and Europe into his diocese. When the see of Walla Walla was suppressed in 1850 and translated to Nesqually he located his headquarters in Fort Vancouver, Washington, where he built a log cathedral. He attended the First Plenary Council of Baltimore in 1852, was unable to attend Vatican Council I in Rome in 1869–70 because of his infirmities, and worn out by his decades of arduous missionary work resigned in 1879 and was named titular bishop of Ibora. Often called the "apostle of Washington" and "apostle of the Indians," he died at Fort Vancouver on Feb. 25.

BLANCHET, FRANÇOIS NORBERT (1795–1883), archbishop, missionary. Son of Pierre Blanchet, a Canadian farmer, and brother of Augustin Magloire Blanchet, he was born on his father's farm near St. Pierre, Quebec, on Sept. 3. He was educated with his brother at the Sulpician seminary in Quebec, was ordained in 1819, spent a year at the cathedral in Quebec, and then spent the next seven years ministering to the Micmac Indians and the Acadian settlers of New Brunswick. He was made pastor of St. Joseph de Soulages Church in Montreal in 1827, distinguished himself aiding the victims of the cholera epidemic of 1832, and in 1837 he was appointed vicar-general to Archbishop Signay of Quebec with jurisdiction over the Oregon mission. He traveled the five thousand miles to Vancouver on foot and horseback and by canoe in six and a half months with an assistant, Fr. Modeste Demers, the first priests to visit the area that stretched from the Rockies to the Pacific and from California to Alaska—a mission covering some 375,000 square miles which the two priests covered alone the next four years. In 1843 the Oregon mission was constituted into an apostolic vicariate (the letter from Rome creating the vicariate took eight months to reach him in August 1844) and Fr. Blanchet was named its first vicar apostolic and made titular bishop of Philadelphia (changed in 1845 to Adrasus to avoid confusion with the American Philadelphia) in 1844. He visited Europe after his consecration in Montreal in 1845 to recruit priests, brothers, and sisters for his vicariate and when it was erected into a province in 1846 he was made the first archbishop of Oregon City (the name was changed to Portland in Oregon in 1927)—the first archbishop of the Northwest; at the same time his brother Augustin was named bishop of Walla Walla, Washington, and Fr. Demers was named bishop of Vancouver Island. Methodist ministers in the area bitterly resented the archbishop's success with the Indians and when Marcus Whitman and his party were murdered in 1847 by Indians, they accused Catholics of inciting the Indians to murder Whitman and his companions—a charge that was utterly without foundation and completely disproved. Blanchet called the first provincial council of Oregon in 1848, attended the First Plenary Council of Baltimore in 1852, and went to South America in 1855 and to Canada in 1859 in quest of funds and religious for his province. He strongly opposed Secretary of the Interior Delano when Delano assigned only four of thirty-eight Indian reservations to Catholic missionaries despite the fact more than two thirds of the Indians wanted Catholic missionaries; the dispute led to the formation of the Catholic Indian Commission in Washington, D.C., by the American bishops to assume general supervision over Catholic missions to the Indians. He moved the see to Portland, Oregon, in 1862, attended the Second Plenary Council of Baltimore in 1866, and was at Vatican Council I in 1869–70 and strongly supported the declaration of papal infallibility. He built a cathedral and St. Michael's College in 1871, a hospital under the Sisters of Providence in 1875, and in 1875 had Bishop John Seghers named his coadjutor. He resigned in 1880, after more than four and a half decades of the most strenuous missionary activities, and was named titular archbishop of Amide. He died in Portland on June 18. He was the author of several books, among them *Historical Sketches of the Catholic Church in Oregon* and is often called the "apostle of Oregon."

BLANCHETTE, ROMEO ROY (1913–82), bishop. Born in St. George, Illinois, on Jan. 6, he graduated from Quigley Seminary, Chicago, in 1931 and continued his studies at St. Mary's Seminary, Mundelein, Illinois, (B.A. 1934, S.T.B. 1935, M.A. 1936, S.T.L. 1937) and the Gregorian, Rome (J.C.B. 1938, J.C.L. 1939). He was ordained in 1937, served as a notary on the Chicago archdiocesan marriage court in 1939–49, and was made chancellor of the Joliet, Illinois, diocese in 1949. He was made a domestic prelate in 1950, was vicar-general in 1950–65 and made a protonotary apostolic in 1959, and was named titular bishop of Maxita and auxiliary bishop of Joliet in 1965. He was appointed bishop of Joliet the following year, established a diocesan newspaper and a diocesan office of communications, and resigned in 1979 when he learned he was incurably ill of Lou Gehrig's disease (amyotrophic lateral sclerosis). He attracted national attention the last years of his life by the cheerfulness and fortitude with which he bore the illness that had left him completely paralyzed. He died in Joliet on Jan. 10.

BLANDINA, SISTER. *See* Segale, Blandina.

BLENK, JAMES HUBERT (1856–1917), archbishop. Born of Protestant parents in Neustadt, Bavaria, on July 28, he was brought to the United States when a baby and became a Catholic when twelve. He was educated in New Orleans and New York and taught for a time at the Marists' Jefferson College in Convent, Louisiana, where he joined the Marists. He continued his studies in France and in Ireland and was ordained in 1885. He taught at Jefferson for a time and was named its president in 1891, engaged in parish work in Louisiana, visited various houses of his order in France, England, and Ireland, and in 1899 was appointed bishop of Puerto Rico—the first American to hold that position (Puerto Rico had been ceded to the United States by the Treaty of Paris in 1898 that ended the Spanish-American War). He sued the American Government to regain possession of Church property in Puerto Rico but the matter was not finally resolved until 1908. After seven years there he was appointed archbishop of New Orleans in 1906. He completely rebuilt the Catholic educational system of the see, brought religious orders into the archdiocese, and gave shelter to refugee priests and nuns from Mexico. He died in New Orleans on Apr. 20.

BLENKINSOP, CATHERINE (1816–87), superior. Daughter of Peter Blenkinsop, publisher, she was born in Dublin on Apr. 18, was brought to Baltimore by her parents in 1826, and in 1831 she joined the Sisters of Charity at Emmitsburg, Maryland, taking the name Euphemia. She taught at St. Joseph's School in New York City, St. Peter's School and St. Mary's Asylum in Baltimore, and during the Civil War headed the Sisters of Charity in the Confederate States. She was named superior of the Sisters of Charity in the United States in 1866 and remained in that position until her death in Emmitsburg on Mar. 18.

BLENKINSOP, PETER (19th century), publisher. Born in Dublin, he emigrated to the United States with his family and settled in Baltimore in 1826. There he founded a publishing house and printing press the following year and published the five-volume *A History of the United States* by Charles Constantine Pise (1827–29). In 1830 he began publishing the first Catholic monthly in the United States, *Metropolitan,* which lasted only until December of the same year.

BLENKINSOP, PETER (1818–96), educator. Son of publisher Peter Blenkinsop and brother of William A. Blenkinsop, he was born in Dublin on Apr. 19, was brought to Baltimore by his parents in 1826, studied at St. Mary's College there, and joined the Jesuits in 1834. He taught at Georgetown for a time, was ordained in 1846, taught at Holy Cross College in Worcester, Massachusetts, and was its president in 1854–57. He served as pastor of St. Joseph's churches in Philadelphia and in Maryland and returned to teach at Holy Cross in 1873, also taking charge of the mission at Leicester, Massachusetts. He was at Georgetown in 1880–82 and then was assigned to the Church of the Gesu in Philadelphia where he remained until his death on Nov. 5.

BLENKINSOP, WILLIAM A. (1819–92). Son of Peter Blenkinsop, the publisher, he was born in Dublin and was brought to Baltimore by his parents in 1826. He was educated at St. Mary's College, Baltimore (M.A. 1839) and taught there in 1839–44. He was ordained in 1843, became a priest of the Natchez, Mississippi, diocese and engaged in missionary activities in Mississippi the next seven years. He then became pastor of Chicopee, then part of the Boston see, and built the Church of the Holy Name of Jesus there in 1859. He refused the vicar-generalship of Natchez, was named pastor of SS. Peter and Paul Church in Boston in 1864, and was known for his concern for the poor

and his ecumenical spirit. He spent the last twenty-eight years of his life in Boston and died there on Jan. 8.

BLIEMEL, EMMERAN (1832–64), chaplain. A Benedictine priest who had been born in Bavaria, he was pastor of Assumption parish in Nashville, Tennessee, at the outbreak of the Civil War. When his church was turned into a hospital by Union troops when they captured the city in 1864, he joined the 10th Tennessee Regiment ("the Bloody 10th") as chaplain. He was killed during the battle of Jonesboro outside Atlanta, Georgia, in August while giving absolution to a dying officer—the first Catholic chaplain to die while serving in battle and the only chaplain to die during the Civil War. In 1983 the Sons of Confederate Veterans posthumously awarded him the Confederate Medal of Honor.

BOHACHEVSKY, CONSTANTINE (1886–1961), archbishop. Born in Manaiw, Ukraine, on June 17, he studied at Lwow, Poland, and Innsbruck, Austria (where he received his doctorate), and was ordained in 1909. He returned to Lwow to teach theology while also doing parish work in the city, was spiritual director of the Lwow seminary in 1915, and was consultant to its consistory in 1916. He was named titular bishop of Amissus and apostolic exarch of Ukrainian Catholics in the United States in 1924 with his see at Philadelphia and with jurisdiction over 144 churches, 102 priests, and more than a quarter of a million faithful. During his thirty-seven-year episcopacy, he revived spiritual life among his followers, developed a parochial school system, battled trusteeship, founded a diocesan press, established new churches in accordance with the Byzantine rite, insisted on strict discipline, and established St. Josaphat's Seminary in Washington,

D.C., and opened a cultural museum and library. He has made an Assistant at the Pontifical Throne in 1952, was appointed titular archbishop of Beroe in 1954, and when the Ukrainian Catholic Archeparchy of Philadelphia was established in 1958, he was appointed its first metropolitan. He died in Philadelphia on Jan. 6.

BOLAND, FRANCIS JOSEPH (1896–1960), educator. Born in Everett, Massachusetts, on Jan. 29, he was educated at Notre Dame (B.A. 1918), joined the Congregation of Holy Cross, and was ordained in 1923. He received his Ph.D. from Catholic University in 1924, began teaching economics at St. Edward's College, Austin, Texas, the same year and later become vice president. He returned to Notre Dame, became prefect of discipline, professor of politics and head of the department, and then dean of the college of arts and letters. He served as a Navy chaplain in World War II with the rank of lieutenant commander, was president of Stonehill College, North Easton, Massachusetts, in 1949–55, became chaplain at a veterans' hospital in New York City, and died there on Dec. 31. He was the author of *The Pope and Christian Citizenship* (1941) and coauthored *Catholic Principles of Politics* (1940) with Msgr. John A. Ryan.

BOLAND, THOMAS A. (1896–1979), archbishop. Born in Orange, New Jersey, on Feb. 17, he was educated at Seton Hall University, South Orange, New Jersey (B.A., M.A.), and the North American College, Rome (S.T.D.), and was ordained in Rome in 1922. He was a curate at St. Catherine's Church, Hillside, New Jersey, for a time, taught Scripture and classical languages at Seton Hall until 1926, and for the next twelve years was professor of moral theology and canon law at Im-

maculate Conception Seminary, Darlington, New Jersey. He was chancellor of Newark in 1938–40, was appointed titular bishop of Hirina and auxiliary of Newark, and was rector of Immaculate Conception in 1940–47. He was appointed bishop of Paterson, New Jersey, in 1947, and in 1952 he was appointed archbishop of Newark, New Jersey. His tenure as archbishop was clouded in 1969 when a group of twenty priests accused the archdiocese of racism and bigotry toward blacks, a charge he answered by pointing out the forty housing projects he had sponsored for the poor. He later organized an interfaith coalition of clergymen that sponsored an equal employment program in Newark. He was chairman of the Bishops' Study Commission in Rome in 1962–65, was made an Assistant at the Pontifical Throne in 1965, and retired in 1974. He died in Orange, where he had been hospitalized at St. Mary's Hospital for the previous eight months because of severe arthritis, on Mar. 16.

BOLTON, MOTHER MARGARET (1873–1943), educator. Born in Richfield Springs, New York, on Feb. 12, she graduated from New York State Normal School in 1892 and continued her education at Columbia in 1899–1906. She taught grade school at Patchogue, New York, in 1892, in New York City public schools in 1896–1906, and at the Training School for Teachers in 1906–13, and joined the Congregation of Our Lady of the Retreat in the Cenacle (R.C.) in New York City. She studied theology at the Cenacle in 1914–22 and though she was a member of an enclosed community was granted permission by Pope Pius XI, at the request of several American bishops, to teach her methods of teaching. She was associate professor of religious training at Fordham in 1922–33 and also taught at Boston College, Loyola in Chicago, Providence, and St. John's. She wrote several texts for children's religious instruction which were widely used, among them *Spiritual Way* (1930), a four-book series of religion instruction books for grammar school grades, the six-booklet *Little Child's First Communion* (1935), *Foundation Material for Doctrinal Catholic Action* (1938), and *A Way to Achievement* and died in New York City on Feb. 27.

BONA, STANISLAUS VINCENT (1888–1967), bishop. Born in Chicago on Oct. 1, he was educated at St. Stanislaus College in Chicago (B.A. 1905) and the American College in Rome (Ph.D., D.D., and J.C.L.) and was ordained in 1912. He served in various capacities in Chicago: as curate at St. Barbara's Church in 1912–16; as resident chaplain at the House of Correction in 1916–18; as professor of languages at Quigley Preparatory Seminary in 1918–22; and while pastor of St. Casimir's Church in 1922–31 was made a monsignor in 1931. He was appointed bishop of Grand Island, Illinois, in 1931, and in 1944 was named titular bishop of Mela and coadjutor of Green Bay, Wisconsin, and succeeded to the see the following year. He remained in that position until his death in Green Bay on Dec. 1.

BONACUM, THOMAS (1847–1911), bishop. Born near Thurles, Tipperary, Ireland, on Jan. 29, he was brought to Missouri when a child, was educated at St. Vincent's, Cape Girardeau, Missouri, and Würzburg, Germany, and was ordained in St. Louis in 1870. He was pastor of Holy Name Church in St. Louis, attended the Third Plenary Council of Baltimore in 1884 as Bishop Kenrick's theologian, and though the Council recommended him for bishop of the newly established diocese of Belleville, Illinois, he was not appointed; instead he was named first

bishop of the newly created diocese of Lincoln, Nebraska, in 1887. He held that position until his death in Lincoln on Feb. 4.

BONAPARTE, CHARLES JOSEPH (1851–1921), Secretary of the Navy, U.S. Attorney General. Grandson of Napoleon's brother Jerome and son of Jerome and Susan Bonaparte, he was born in Baltimore on June 9, was educated by private tutors and at Harvard, and graduated from Harvard Law School in 1874. He married Ellen Channing Day in 1875, entered politics as an independent Republican and became identified with reform causes. In 1902 President Theodore Roosevelt named him legal adviser to the Board of Indian Commissioners to investigate conditions in the Indian Territory; he was the recipient of the Laetare Medal in 1903 and was appointed Secretary of the Navy by Roosevelt in 1905. He supported Roosevelt's Navy expansion program and the following year was appointed U.S. Attorney General, a position he held until the end of Roosevelt's term as president in 1909. He was active in reforming the civil service, brought more than fifty suits against trusts and was largely responsible for the dissolution of the American Tobacco Company. He often acted as intermediary for Roosevelt between the Church and the government, though a firm believer in the separation of Church and state, and helped settle the dispute over Church lands in Puerto Rico when that island was ceded to the United States at the end of the Spanish-American War. He returned to private law practice in Baltimore in 1909, supported Roosevelt and the Progressive Party in 1912 but urged party unity in the election of 1916. He was one of the founders of the National Municipal League and later served as its president. He died on his estate, Bella Vista, near Baltimore on June 28.

BONVIN, LUDWIG (1850–1939), composer, conductor. Born in Siders, Switzerland, on Feb. 17, he studied law and medicine but decided to pursue a religious life and joined the Jesuits in Holland in 1874. He was ordained in Liverpool in 1885, studied music, especially early Church music, and in 1887–1907 directed the chorus and orchestra of Canisius College, Buffalo, New York. He also wrote liturgical music, Masses, vespers, hymns, among them *Symphony in G-minor, Morn on the Northern Coast* and *Johanna d'Arc vor dem Scheiterhaufen,* and died in Buffalo on Feb. 18.

BORGESS, CASPAR HENRY (1826–90), bishop. Born in Adrup, Oldenburg, Germany, on Aug. 1, he was brought to the United States by his parents when twelve, was educated at St. Mary's Seminary in Cincinnati, and was ordained in Cincinnati in 1845. After eleven years as pastor of Holy Cross Church in Columbus, Ohio, and a year at Immaculate Conception Church in Cincinnati, he was made rector of St. Peter's Cathedral in Cincinnati in 1859 and chancellor of the diocese in 1860. He was named titular bishop of Calydon and coadjutor and administrator of the diocese of Detroit in 1870 and succeeded to the see the following year as its second bishop. He improved the administration of the diocese, encouraged Catholic education (his invitation to the Jesuits in 1877 led to the foundation of the University of Detroit), and worked to reduce the friction between the different immigrant groups in the diocese. He resigned in 1887 because of ill health and was appointed titular bishop of Phacusites and died in Kalamazoo, Michigan, on May 3.

BOUCHARD, CLAUDE FLORENT (b. 1751). Born in Craon, France, he was ordained for the diocese of Angers in 1777 and served as a chaplain in the French fleet. He was with Admiral de la Sainneville's French fleet aiding the American revolutionists, and when the fleet sailed from Boston in 1788, he deserted and remained in Boston setting himself up as pastor of Boston and calling himself the Abbé de la Poterie. He offered the first public Mass in Boston on Nov. 2, 1788, and after a month in Boston wrote Bishop John Carroll who granted his approval for his ministry in Boston. But his flamboyant life-style and the debts he incurred, his troubles with the French consul and a letter from the archbishop of Paris saying he had been suspended caused Carroll to send Fr. William O'Brien, pastor of St. Peter's Church in New York, to Boston to depose him. Poterie stayed on in Boston until 1790 meanwhile publishing a violent denunciation of Carroll in a pamphlet in 1789, *The Resurrection of Laurent Ricci; or a True and Exact History of the Jesuits,* in which he assailed Carroll as "the new Laurent Ricci in America" and Carroll as "the Friar-Monk-Inquisitor"; he then left for Canada and disappeared from the American scene.

BOUCHARD, JAMES (c. 1823–89), missionary. Son of a Frenchwoman named Bouchard who was captured by the Delaware Indians and married an Indian brave named Kistalua, Watamika was born in Muskagola near Leavenworth, Kansas. When his father was killed in a battle with the Sioux in 1834, he was brought to Marietta College in Ohio by a Protestant minister, assumed his mother's name, and studied to become a Protestant minister. He was converted to Catholicism in St. Louis in 1846 or 1847, joined the Jesuits at

Florissant, Missouri, in 1848, and was ordained in St. Louis in 1855—the first American Indian to be ordained in the United States. He worked as a missionary in the Midwest for several years and then went to San Francisco in 1861 where he became known for his preaching and his missionary work in the mining towns of California. He died in San Francisco on Dec. 27.

BOUQUILLON, THOMAS JOSEPH (1840–1902), theologian. Born in Warneton near Ypres, Belgium, on May 16, he was educated at St. Louis College in Menin, at the preparatory seminary at Roulers, the Bruges major seminary, and the Gregorian in Rome. He was ordained in 1865, continued his studies at the Gregorian, and received his doctorate two years later. He taught moral theology at the Bruges seminary in 1867–77, at Catholic University of Lille, France, in 1877–85, and then retired for the next four years to the Benedictine monastery at Maredsous, Belgium. In 1889 he accepted the chair of moral theology at Catholic University in Washington, D.C., and held that position until his death in Brussels on Nov. 5. He was one of the outstanding moral theologians of his times and a leader in restoring Thomism and moral theology to Catholic education in the United States. He wrote numerous articles and theological treatises among them the two-volume *De Virtutate Religionis* (1880), *Theologia Moralis Fundamentalis* (1903), his outstanding work, *De virtutibus theologicis* (1890), and *Education: To Whom Does It Belong?* (1891), a pamphlet that caused great controversy. He was for a time editor of *Revue des sciences ecclesiastiques,* translated several French and Latin works into English, and helped select some thirty thousand theological works for the Catholic University library.

BOURGADE, PETER (1845–1908), archbishop. Born in Clermont or Puy-de-Dome, France, on Oct. 17, he studied at Billon, came to the United States, and was ordained in 1869 at Santa Fe, New Mexico. He worked as a missionary in Arizona, New Mexico, and Texas until 1885 (except 1872–74 when he was in France recuperating from ill health) when he was appointed titular bishop of Thaumacum and vicar apostolic of Arizona. He was appointed first bishop of Tucson, Arizona, in 1897 when that diocese was established and twenty months later in 1899 was named archbishop of Santa Fe; he remained in that position until his death in Santa Fe on May 17.

BOUSCARIN, TIMOTHY LINCOLN (1884–1971), educator. Born in Cincinnati, Ohio, on Aug. 17, he received his B.A. from Xavier University there in 1902 and from Yale in 1906 and his M.A. from St. Louis University in 1919; he also studied at the University of Cincinnati (LL.B. 1909) and the Gregorian (S.T.D. 1928). He was assistant district attorney for the eastern district of Oklahoma in 1911–13, joined the Jesuits in 1916, and was ordained in 1925. He taught at St. John's College, Toledo, in 1921, became assistant dean of the University of Detroit Law School in 1929, professor at Loyola University, Chicago, in 1930, was professor of canon law at St. Mary of the Lake Seminary in Chicago in 1931–38, and taught canon law at the Gregorian in Rome in 1938–40 and at West Baden College in Indiana in 1941–47. He was procurator general of the Jesuits from 1947 to 1962, during which time he was also consultor of the Congregations for the Propagation of the Faith, and for the Religious, and for the Council. He was professor emeritus of canon law at West Baden in 1962–64 and taught at the Bellarmine

School of Theology, North Aurora, Illinois, in 1964–67. He wrote several books, among them the three volumes and supplements of *Canon Law Digest* and *Canon Law: A Text and Commentary* (1946). He retired to Xavier High School in Cincinnati in 1967 and died in Cincinnati on Feb. 10.

BOWES, EDWARD J. (1874–1946), theatrical executive, entertainer. Born in San Francisco on June 14, his father was killed in a dock accident in 1880 and he had little schooling, leaving school when he was thirteen to work in a real estate office. He made a fortune in real estate in San Francisco, lost it all in the earthquake of 1906 but recouped his fortune when the city was rebuilt. He married actress Margaret Illington in 1909, became her manager and moved to New York and became active in the theater. He served in Army intelligence during World War I and became a major in the reserves, a title he used throughout his theatrical career. He became a partner in building the Capitol Theatre in New York City in 1918, an executive in Goldwyn Pictures Corporation (which became Metro-Goldwyn-Mayer) in 1922, and opened the Capitol Theatre, of which he was vice president and managing director, and other theaters throughout the country. He became popular as an entertainer with the weekly broadcast of "Roxy's Gang" from the Capitol and in 1934 began his "Major Bowes and His Original Amateur Hour" which became one of the most popular radio programs of its time, syndicated in 1934 by the National Broadcasting Company and after 1936 by the Columbia Broadcasting System. A convert to Catholicism, he was known for his philanthropy in the latter part of his life. He retired from radio in 1945 because of heart trouble and died in Rumson, New Jersey, on June 13, leaving the bulk of his estate to charity.

BOYCE, JOHN (1810–64), author. Son of a hotel owner and magistrate, he was born in Donegal, Ireland, was educated at Navan and Maynooth, and was ordained in 1837. He engaged in pastoral work in Ireland until 1845 when he emigrated to the United States as a missionary. He worked first in Eastport, Maine, and from 1847 in Worcester, Massachusetts, where he remained the rest of his life. Early interested in writing, he wrote serials for the Baltimore *Metropolitan* magazine, editorials for the Boston *Pilot,* and a series of popularly written novels under the pseudonym Paul Peppergrass, among them *Shandy Maguire, or Tricks upon Travellers* (1848), *The Spaewife, or the Queen's Secret* (1853) and *Mary Lee, or the Yankee's Ireland* (1859). An eloquent speaker much in demand for his lectures, he died in Worcester on Jan. 2.

BOYLAN, JOHN JOSEPH (1889–1953), bishop. Born in New York City on Oct. 7, he was educated at Mt. St. Mary's College, Emmitsburg, Maryland (M.A.), St. Bernard's Seminary, Rochester, New York, Catholic University, and the Athenaeum, Rome (Ph.D.), and was ordained in 1915. He engaged in parish work in Council Bluffs, Iowa, and from 1918 to 1923, he taught at Dowling College in Des Moines, Iowa, serving as its president in 1927–42. He was made vicar-general of the Des Moines diocese in 1934, served in that post until 1942 and was then appointed bishop of Rockford, Illinois, where he served until his death near Narragansett, Rhode Island, on July 19.

BOYLAN, WILLIAM A. (1869–1940), educator. He was born in New York City on Jan. 6, was educated at St.

Francis Xavier College there, became a teacher in the New York public school system, became a principal in 1901, was district superintendent in 1913–27, and superintendent of schools in 1927. He served in that position until 1930 when he was appointed president of the newly established Brooklyn College and was its president until 1938. He died in New York City on July 8.

BOYLE, HUGH CHARLES (1873–1950), bishop. Born in Cambria City, Pennsylvania, on Oct. 8, he was educated at St. Vincent's College and Seminary, Latrobe, Pennsylvania, and was ordained in 1898. He engaged in parish work, was superintendent of Catholic schools in Pittsburgh in 1909–16, and in 1921 was appointed bishop of Pittsburgh, a position he held until his death on Dec. 22 in Pittsburgh.

BOYTON, NEIL (1884–1956), author. Son of Captain Paul who worked with the Barnum and Bailey Circus and invented and built the Shoot the Chutes in Coney Island, he was born in New York City on Nov. 30, traveled all over the country with his father and was educated at Holy Cross (B.A. 1908). He joined the Jesuits in 1909, taught at St. Joseph's High School in Philadelphia in 1914–16 and at St. Mary's High School in Bombay, India, in 1916–17 but was forced to return to the United States when he contracted tropical fever. He taught at Georgetown Prep, Garrett Park, Maryland, in 1917–18 and then made his theological studies at Woodstock College, Maryland, was ordained in 1921, and received his M.A. from Woodstock in 1922. He again taught at Georgetown Prep in 1923–28, then at Regis High School in 1928–31 and Loyola in 1931–45, both in New York City, and in 1945 was made assistant pastor of St. Ignatius Loyola Church in New York. He wrote more than a score

of books among them *In God's Country* (1923), *Mississippi's Black Robe* (1927), *Blessed Friend of Youth* (1929), *A Yankee Xavier* (1937), and *White Horsemen* (1947). He died in New York City on Feb. 1.

BRADEN, SPRUILLE (1894–1978), diplomat. Born in Elkhorn, Montana, on Mar. 13, son of William Braden, founder of the Braden Copper Company, he was educated at Sheffield Scientific School, Yale (Ph.D. in mining engineering in 1914) and during the next five years worked with various mining companies in South America. He married Marie Humeres Solar, daughter of a prominent Chilean physician in 1915, served as adviser to several South American countries negotiating loans after World War I, helped negotiate a contract for Westinghouse Electric to electrify Chilean state railroads, and acquired control of the Monmouth Rug Company in Englishtown, New Jersey, and developed it into a major firm in its field. He organized the Rehabilitation Corporation in 1932 and entered the diplomatic field in 1933 as a delegate to the Inter-American Conference of American States in Montevideo, Uruguay. He was chairman in 1935–38 of the American delegation to the Chaco Peace Conference and in 1938 was appointed United States minister to Colombia and in 1941 ambassador to Cuba and ambassador to Argentina in 1945. There his strong stand for a democratic government and freedom of the press, his unmasking of Nazi activities in Argentina, a fire that cost the lives of five hundred Chilean miners in a Chilean mine owned by the Braden Copper Company (though neither he nor his father were any longer connected with the firm), and his denunciation of fascism caused much controversy in Argentina. Later in 1945 President Truman appointed him Assistant Secretary of State in charge of Latin American Affairs. He served until 1947 and then spent the later years of his life as a consultant to American companies dealing in South American countries. He died in Hollywood on Jan. 10.

BRADLEY, BERNARD JAMES (1867–1936), educator. Born in East Braintree, Massachusetts, on Feb. 19, he was educated at Mt. St. Mary's College, Emmitsburg, Maryland, and was ordained in 1892. He was a parish priest in Brooklyn for a time and then returned to Mt. St. Mary's where he taught classics and philosophy in 1892–97. He became treasurer and then vice president of St. Mary's and in 1911 was appointed president. During his years as president he built up the college, doubling its enrollment, and put into effect numerous educational reforms. He was made a monsignor in 1914 and died in Washington, D.C., on Sept. 21.

BRADLEY, DENIS MARY (1846–1903), bishop. Born at Castle Island, County Kerry, Ireland, on Feb. 25, his mother took him to the United States after his father died, when he was eight, and settled in Manchester, New Hampshire. He was educated at Holy Cross College and Georgetown, then studied for the priesthood at St. Joseph's Seminary, Troy, New York, and was ordained in 1871. He became a priest of the Portland, Maine, diocese, was named rector of the cathedral and then chancellor of the diocese, and was appointed pastor of St. Joseph's Church in Manchester, Vermont. He made St. Joseph's his cathedral when he was named first bishop of the newly established diocese of Manchester in 1884. He built numerous churches and schools, fought nativism, was a leader in the temperance movement, provided spiritual care for the Catholics scattered throughout the rural areas of his see, held a diocesan synod in 1886, and saw the Catholic population of the diocese double by the time of his death in Manchester on Dec. 13.

BRADY, JOHN J. (1884–1950), chaplain, admiral. Born in New York City on Jan. 8, he studied for the priesthood at St. Joseph's Seminary, Dunwoodie, New York, and was ordained there in 1908. He was an assistant at St. John the Evangelist Church, White Plains, New York, and then at St. Veronica's Church, New York City, while also teaching at Cathedral College while at St. Veronica's. In 1914, he became a naval chaplain, was with the Navy at Vera Cruz, Mexico, in 1914 when the Navy took the city, and during World War I was with the Fifth Marine Division which was involved in some of the bloodiest fighting of the war. He was awarded the Navy Cross, the Croix de Guerre, and the Distinguished Service Cross for his ministrations to the wounded at Château Thierry and Belleau Wood. After the war he served as battle force chaplain aboard the battleship *California*. He retired in 1934 with the rank of captain and in 1936 was named a rear admiral—the first Catholic chaplain to attain flag rank. After his retirement from the Navy, he was named pastor of St. Catherine of Genoa Church in New York City. He served as Military Vicar Delegate for Cardinal Spellman during World War II and was then named pastor of Holy Spirit Church in the Bronx, New York. Ill the last several years of his life, he died in Holy Spirit rectory on Aug. 16.

BRADY, MATTHEW FRANCIS (1893–1959), bishop. Born in Waterbury, Connecticut, on Jan. 15, he was educated at St. Thomas Seminary, Bloomfield, Connecticut, the American College at Louvain and St. Bernard's Seminary, Rochester, New York, and was ordained in Hartford, Connecticut, in 1916. He was assistant pastor at Sacred Heart Church, New Haven, Connecticut, in 1916–18, was a chaplain in World War I, and resumed his pastoral work at Sacred Heart after the war. He was a professor of English at St. Thomas Seminary in 1922–32, a pastor in Hamden, Connecticut, at St. Rita's Church in 1933–38, and in 1938 he was appointed bishop of Burlington, Vermont, and in 1945 was transferred to Manchester, New Hampshire. During his bishopric he founded many new parishes, churches, and schools and established Catholic Charities in the Manchester diocese in 1946. He served as chairman of the education department of the National Catholic Welfare Conference in 1950–56, was named chairman of the United States Bishops' Committee for the Confraternity of Christian Doctrine in 1956, a post he held until his death, and was president of the National Catholic Educational Association in 1957–58. He died in Burlington on Sept. 20.

BRADY, MRS. NICHOLAS F. *See* Macaulay, Genevieve Garvan Brady.

BRADY, NICHOLAS FREDERIC (1878–1930), financier, philanthropist. Born in Albany, New York, on Oct. 25, he was educated at Yale and on his graduation entered his father's public utilities business. He became a Catholic in 1906, married Genevieve Garvan the same year, and inherited a fortune on the death of his father. A skilled financier and manager, he soon increased his inheritance in the public utilities field and various other industries, becoming director of some one hundred corporations during his career. He became known for his charities and philanthropies, helping build the Jesuit novitiate at Wernersville, Pennsylvania, among many of his Catholic charitable works.

In the field of labor he became known for his advocacy of security benefits for his employees. He was awarded the papal *Ordine Supremo del Christe,* which is usually reserved for heads of state, in 1929—the first American citizen to receive the award—and died the following Mar. 27 in Philadelphia.

BRADY, WILLIAM O. (1899–1961), archbishop. Born in Fall River, Massachusetts, on Feb. 1, he was educated at St. Charles College, Cantonsville, Maryland, St. Mary's Seminary, Baltimore (B.A. 1917, M.A. 1918), the Sulpician seminary and Catholic University in Washington, D.C., and was ordained in 1923. He was assigned to the St. Paul, Minnesota, archdiocese, continued his studies at the Collegio Angelico, Rome, in 1924–26, and on his return to St. Paul taught at St. Paul Seminary, St. Catherine College, and St. Paul Diocesan Teachers College. He was rector of St. Paul Seminary in 1933–39 and in 1939 was named bishop of Sioux Falls, Iowa, where he founded a diocesan newspaper. He was appointed titular archbishop of Selymbria and coadjutor of St. Paul in 1956 and succeeded to the see later the same year. He served as treasurer of the National Catholic Welfare Conference for four years and died in Rome on Oct. 1.

BRANN, HENRY ATHANASIUS (1837–1921), educator. Born in Parkstown, West Meath, Ireland, on Aug. 15, he was brought to the United States by his parents when he was twelve. He was educated at St. Francis Xavier College, New York City, St. Mary's College, Wilmington, Delaware, St. Sulpice, Issy, France, and the American College, Rome, in 1862, the first man of that college to be ordained. He taught theology and was vice president of Seton Hall College, South Orange, New Jersey, the next four years, served as pastor in

Jersey City and Fort Lee, New Jersey, and became director of the diocesan seminary in Wheeling, West Virginia, in 1868. He came to New York City in 1870, was founding pastor of St. Elizabeth parish in 1870–89 and then was pastor of St. Agnes parish from 1890 until his death, and was made a domestic prelate in 1910. He wrote articles on purgatory and immortality, the papacy, education, and against the Faribault Plan in defense of Archbishop Corrigan in the school controversy of 1897, *Age of Unreason* (1880), a reply to Robert Ingersoll's theories, a biography of Archbishop Hughes (1892), and *History of the American College* (1912). He died in New York City on Dec. 28.

BRAUER, THEODOR (1880–1942), social theorist, economist. Born in Cleve, Germany, on Jan. 18, he worked for a grain firm for a time and then became interested in unions and the Catholic social movement. He became assistant director of the Catholic People's Union in 1907, staff assistant of the German Federation of Christian Trade Unions in Cologne in 1908, and was editor of its *Central Organ* in 1914–19 and then of its monthly *Deutsche Arbeit.* He became a professor of economics at the Baden Institute of Social Research and professor of labor economics and social legislation at the University of Cologne in 1928 while also directing, after 1930, the labor school of the Christian Trade Unions in Königswinter. He was dismissed from his positions and imprisoned by the Nazis in 1933 and after his release was invited to teach economics at St. Paul College by Archbishop John G. Murray of St. Paul in 1937. He became chairman of the economics department in 1939 and remained in that position until his death in St. Paul on May 19. He was a prolific writer on the Catholic social movement and was one of its outstanding publicists.

BREEN, JOSEPH IGNATIUS (1890–1965). Born in Philadelphia on Oct. 14, he was educated at St. Joseph's College there, worked as a reporter for several Philadelphia and New York papers, and then served in the United States consular service for four years. He was Overseas Commissioner of the National Catholic Welfare Council's Department of Immigration in Rome for two years, worked in public relations for a while, and then on labor disputes for the Peabody Coal Company. In 1930 he moved to Hollywood to help implement the production code for motion pictures that had been drafted by Martin Quigley and Fr. Daniel Lord and in 1934 he became director of the Production Code Administration of the Motion Picture Association of America. In this position he had tremendous authority over the contents of motion pictures by stringently enforcing the Code which stated that nothing in a film should lower the moral standards of audiences, that wrongdoing must not be portrayed sympathetically, and that the law must not be ridiculed. He received a special Oscar from the Motion Picture Academy in 1953, retired in 1954 and devoted himself to Church affairs, and died in Hollywood on Dec. 7.

BREIG, JOSEPH ANTHONY (1905–82), editor. Born in Vandergrift, Pennsylvania, on Feb. 28, he was educated at St. Vincent's College, Latrobe, Pennsylvania, in 1918-20 and Notre Dame, where he edited the university magazine, *The Scholastic,* in 1923–27. After graduating he served as an electrician and steelworker for a time, was editor of the Vandergrift *News* in 1924–34, and in 1930 married Mary Agnes Hoffman. He was a rewrite man and feature writer on the Pittsburgh *Sunday Telegraph* in 1940–45, and in 1945 joined the Cleveland diocesan paper, *The Catholic Universe Bulletin* as assistant managing editor; he worked on the *Universe Bulletin* until his retirement in 1975. Soon after joining the paper he began a column which in time was syndicated by twenty-eight Catholic papers in the United States and Canada. He wrote nine books among them *God in Our House* (1949), *The Devil You Say* (1952), *Under My Hat* (1954), and *The Story of Pope John* (1959). He received the St. Francis de Sales Award of the Catholic Press Association in 1966 and died in Orlando, Florida, on Feb. 6 while visiting his son.

BRENNAN, ANDREW JAMES (1877–1956), bishop. Born in Towanda, Pennsylvania, on Dec. 14, he was educated at Holy Cross College, Worcester, Massachusetts (B.A. 1900), St. Bernard's Seminary, Rochester, New York, and the North American College in Rome (D.D. 1905), and was ordained in 1904. He taught at St. Thomas College, Scranton, Pennsylvania, in 1905–8, served as chancellor of the Scranton diocese in 1908–23 and as rector of St. Peter's Cathedral there in 1914–24, and in 1923 was appointed titular bishop of Thapsus and auxiliary of Scranton. He was rector of St. Mary of Mt. Carmel Church from 1924 until 1926 when he was named bishop of Richmond, Virginia. He founded the diocesan paper, the *Catholic Virginian,* in 1931 and two years later held a diocesan synod. He retired in 1945 and was made titular bishop of Telmissus and died on May 23 at Norfolk, Virginia.

BRENNAN, FRANCIS (1895–1968), cardinal. Born in Shenandoah, Pennsylvania, on May 7, he was educated at St. Charles Borromeo Seminary, Overbrook, Pennsylvania, and the Pontifical Roman Seminary in Rome where he was ordained in 1920. He continued his studies at the Apollinaire (J.U.D. 1924) and on his return to the United States served as assistant pastor at St. Charles Borromeo Church and St. Carthage Church while teaching Latin at West Philadelphia High School for Boys. He was professor of theology and canon law at St. Charles Borromeo Seminary from 1928 to 1949 when he was assigned to the Roman Rota as auditor— the first American to serve on the Rota. He was dean of the Rota in 1959–67, served on several preparatory commissions for Vatican Council II, was consecrated titular bishop of Tubane in Mauretania in 1967, and was made a cardinal the following day by Pope Paul VI. In 1968 he was appointed the first American to be prefect of the Congregation for the Discipline of the Sacraments. During his twenty-eight years in Rome he also served on the Congregations of the Propagation of the Faith and of Sacred Rites and was president of the Vatican Court of Appeals. He died in Philadelphia on July 2.

BRENNAN, THOMAS FRANCIS (1853–1916), bishop. A native of Tipperary, Ireland, where he was born on Oct. 6 or 10, he was educated at Innsbruck, Austria, and was ordained at Brixon, Tyrol, in 1880 for the diocese of Erie, Pennsylvania. He engaged in pastoral work there, was made a papal chamberlain in 1888, and was consecrated first bishop of the newly established diocese of Dallas, Texas, in 1891 but resigned the following year; while bishop of Dallas, he founded the *Texas Catholic,* the first Catholic newspaper in Texas. He was transferred to St. John's, Newfoundland, as titular bishop of Utila and coadjutor of the diocese in 1893, was called to Rome in 1904 and made titular bishop of Caesarea in 1905, and died in Grotta Ferrato, Italy, on Mar. 21.

BRENT, MARGARET (c. 1601–c. 71). One of thirteen children of Richard,

Lord of Admingstone and Larkstore, Gloucester, England, and his wife, Elizabeth Reed, she was born in England and emigrated to Maryland in 1638 with her brothers Giles and Foulke and sister Mary. She had letters from Lord Baltimore ordering Governor Leonard Calvert to grant them extensive holdings to which she added other holdings, the first woman landowner in her own right in Maryland. She was active in the affairs of the colony, raised a troop of volunteers to defend the Calvert property during Claiborne's rebellion, and later became executor of the governor and attorney for proprietary interests in the colony. She was turned down by the Maryland assembly in 1648 when she asked for the right to sit in and vote in that body. Her brother Giles made over his property in Maryland to her in 1642 and when he moved to Virginia in 1646 appointed her his attorney. She went to Virginia herself in 1650 and died there.

BREWSTER, ANNE *See* Edes, Ella B.

BRONDEL, JOHN BAPTIST (1842–1903), bishop. Son of a successful Bruges, Belgium, chair manufacturer, he was born in Bruges on Feb. 23, was educated at the local College of St. Louis in 1851–61 and the American College at Louvain, and was ordained at Mechlin, Belgium, in 1864. A protegé of Bishop Blanchet of Nesqually, Washington Territory, he went as a missionary to the United States in 1866 and to the Washington Territory the following year, and spent the following decade and a half in missionary activities there and north into Alaska. He was particularly successful with the Indians in his territory and was highly regarded by them. In 1879 he was appointed third bishop of Vancouver Island (now Victoria), British Columbia, was made administrator of the vicariate of Montana in 1883, and was named first bishop of

the newly established diocese of Helena, Montana, the following year. His influence with the Blackfeet, Crow, Flathead, and Nez Percé Indians caused the federal government to consult with him frequently about Indian affairs because the Indians trusted him in their dealings with the American Government and regarded him as a father. He increased the number of priests in his diocese from thirteen to fifty-three, greatly expanded the number of churches, schools, hospitals, and charitable institutions in the see, and died in Helena on Nov. 3.

BROOKS, PETER ANTHONY (1893–1948), educator. Born in Watertown, Wisconsin, he began his college education at Chicago, had it interrupted when he served in the artillery during World War I, and completed it at Marquette (B.A. 1921). He joined the Jesuits, was ordained in St. Louis in 1931, taught at Loyola in Chicago, was provincial of the Missouri province of the Society of Jesus in 1937–43, and was named president of Marquette in 1944. He died in Milwaukee, Wisconsin, on May 16.

BROSSART, FERDINAND (1849–1930), bishop. Born in Buechelberg, Bavaria, on Oct. 14, he was educated at St. Nicholas College and the American College at Louvain, Brussels, went to the United States, and was ordained in Covington, Kentucky, in 1892. He was appointed fourth bishop of Covington in 1915, resigned in 1923, and died in Melbourne, Kentucky, on Aug. 6.

BROUILLET, JOHN BAPTIST (1813–84), missionary. Born near Montreal on Dec. 11, he was educated at St. Hyacinth College, Quebec, and was ordained in 1837. He was appointed vicar-general of Nesqually, Washington Territory, accompanied Bishop Augustin Blanchet to Walla Walla, Washington, in

1847, and worked among the Indians as a missionary, establishing the mission of Umatilla. When Marcus Whitman, a Presbyterian minister, and his party were murdered on Nov. 27, 1847 by the Indians near Fort Walla Walla, he managed to warn Whitman's associate, Henry H. Spalding, in time to save his life. Spalding accused Brouillet and other Catholics of inciting the attack and the matter erupted into a national controversy; Brouillet was completely vindicated and the charges proved utterly without foundation. When Bishop Augustin Blanchet of Walla Walla and his brother Bishop François Blanchet of Oregon City objected to President Grant's Indian peace policy of 1870 discriminating against Catholic missionaries, Brouillet went to Washington in 1872 as their representative and became an adviser to Charles Ewing, commissioner of Catholic Indian affairs. Soon after his arrival the Grant policy was revised in accord with his recommendations. When the Bureau of Catholic Indian Missions was officially established in 1879, General Ewing was appointed its commissioner and Fr. Brouillet its director. He died in Washington, D.C., on Feb. 5.

BROUN, HEYWOOD CAMPBELL (1888–1939), journalist. Born in Brooklyn, New York, on Dec. 7, he studied at Harvard in 1906–10 but did not graduate and began his journalistic career by becoming a sports reporter on the New York *Morning Telegraph* in 1910. He left to go with the New York *Tribune* as a sports and feature writer in 1912, was a war correspondent in France during World War I in 1917–19, and on his return became literary and drama critic of the *Tribune* with a daily book review column. He joined the New York *World* in 1921 and began his syndicated column "It Seems to Me" and was soon widely read. Often controversial, he championed the underdog, supported unions, and was critical of social injustices. His bitter columns on the Sacco-Vanzetti case in which he denounced their arrest, conviction, and execution in 1927 caused him to be dismissed by the *World* in 1928 when he refused to stop writing about the case. He joined the Scripps-Howard papers, including the *World-Telegram* in New York City which had absorbed the *World* in 1931, and continued his column, becoming one of the most syndicated columnists in the country. He was unsuccessful in a campaign for Congress in 1930 as a Socialist, organized the American Newspaper Guild in 1933, serving as its president from 1933 until his death, and was converted to Catholicism by Msgr. Fulton J. Sheen in 1939. He left the *World-Telegram* in 1939 because of political differences with the policies of the paper, joined the staff of the New York *Post* and remained on that paper until his death in New York City on Dec. 18. He wrote several books, among them *The A. E. F.* (1918), the autobiographical novel *The Boy Grew Older* (1922), *Anthony Comstock* (1927) with Margaret Leech, *Christians Only* (1931), and several collections of his columns notably *It Seems to Me* (1935) and *Collected Edition,* edited by H. H. Broun in 1941.

BROWN, BENEDICT (1876–1965), prior. Born in Belmond, Iowa, on Jan. 11, he was educated at St. Meinrad College and Seminary at St. Meinrad, Indiana, and was ordained a Benedictine priest in 1905. He served as vice-rector of St. Meinrad's College in 1905–19, was prior of St. Meinrad's Abbey in 1930–38, taught at Marmion Military Academy in 1938–41, and was prior of Marmion Abbey, Aurora, Illinois, in 1947–59. He was also editor of *The Grail* from 1919–59 and died in Aurora on Mar. 11.

BROWN, LEO CYRIL (1900–78), labor arbitrator. Born in Stanberry, Iowa, on Apr. 28, he worked for the Union Pacific Railroad in his youth, served in the Army during World War I, and then began studying at Creighton University, Omaha, Nebraska. He joined the Jesuits at Florissant, Missouri, in 1921 continued his education at St. Louis University (B.A. 1925, M.A. 1926), taught at high schools in St. Louis and Prairie du Chien, Wisconsin, and was ordained in 1934. He received his S.T.L. from St. Mary's College in Kansas in 1935, his M.A. in 1939 and a Ph.D. in economics from Harvard in 1940, taught at Regis College, Denver, in 1940–41, and then went to St. Louis University in 1942. He founded its labor school and was its director in 1942–46 and its Institute of Social Order of which he was director from 1947–62 and served as president of the Catholic Economic Association in 1949. He became recognized as an outstanding mediator in labor disputes, was president of the National Academy of Arbitrators in 1960–61, and was appointed to the Labor Management Panel of the Atomic Energy Commission in 1953, becoming chairman in 1968, and held that position until his death in St. Louis on May 3. He served on several minimum wage commissions, acted frequently as arbitrator in railroad and airline disputes and was named special mediator for the Secretary of Labor to help settle labor-management disputes all over the country. In 1962 he joined the staff of the *New Catholic Encyclopedia* as editor of its social sciences section. He wrote numerous magazine articles and several books, among them *Union Policies in the Leather Industries* (1947), and was a coauthor of *Social Orientations* (1954).

BROWNE, CHARLES FARRAR (1834–67), author, humorist. Born in Waterford, Maine, on Apr. 26, he began working at the age of fourteen as an apprentice printer for the *Skowhegan Clarion*. He left to take a similar position on Boston's *The Carpet-Bag* where his first humorous piece was published in 1852. He worked as a journeyman printer in several Eastern cities, went to Toledo where he wrote columns for *The Commercial*, and then in 1858 he became a reporter on the Cleveland *Plain Dealer*. His satiric accounts of sporting events, séances, and politics under the pseudonym Artemus Ward began to attract national attention and he went to New York to write for *Vanity Fair*, which published many of his articles, and in 1859 he became its editor. He became widely known for his rustic humor and extravagant narratives punctuated with deliberate misspellings. Collections of his writings were published in 1865 and 1867. He also began lecturing with a travesty called "Babes in the Woods" in New York; its instant success caused him to give up journalism for the stage and he soon became famous as a humorist. He began making appearances all over the country. At the height of his success he was stricken with consumption but after two years seemed to have recovered and in 1866 he went to England. His appearances in London's music halls and his letters in *Punch* were received with tremendous enthusiasm and he was extravagantly praised for his distinctively American type of humor. His engagement at Egyptian Hall in London was abruptly terminated when he was taken ill, and he died soon after in Southampton on Mar. 6.

BROWNSON, HENRY FRANCIS (1835–1913), author, soldier, scholar. Son of Orestes Brownson, the celebrated author, and Sarah Healy Brownson, he was born in Canton, Massachusetts, on Aug. 6. He became a Catholic in his youth (his father was converted to Catholicism in 1844), was educated at

Holy Cross College and Georgetown, graduated at sixteen, and then spent the next two years with the Jesuits at Issy, France. He continued his studies at Munich another two years and on his return to the United States studied law and was admitted to the New York bar. He served with the Union Army during the Civil War, attaining the rank of captain, and was wounded in the head and right hand at the battle of Chancellorsville; the latter wound left his hand crippled for life. He was captured by the Confederates but released after several weeks' imprisonment. After the war he remained in the Army; by the time he resigned in 1871 he had become a major. He married Josephine Van Dyke in 1868, founded a law partnership with his brother-in-law Philip Van Dyke in Detroit which became very successful, and was known for his scholarship. He was a regular contributor to *Brownson's Quarterly Review,* wrote a three-volume life of his father, *Life of O. A. Brownson,* also wrote *Faith and Science* and *Equality and Democracy,* and edited a twenty-volume collection of his father's writings. He was the originator of the idea of the first Catholic Congress held in Baltimore in 1892, was the recipient of the Laetare Medal in 1892, and died in Detroit, Michigan, on Dec. 19.

BROWNSON, ORESTES AUGUSTUS (1803–76), philosopher, author. Born in Stockbridge, Vermont, on Sept. 16, his father's death left the family in such straitened conditions that his mother was forced to allow Orestes and his twin Daphne Augusta to be raised on a farm by neighbors. Largely self-taught, he joined the Presbyterian Church in 1822 but left in 1824 to become a Universalist. He was ordained a Universalist minister in 1826 and edited *Gospel Advocate* but three years later joined the Owenites under Robert Dale Owen in Owen's utopian colony. He be-

came a corresponding editor for the cult's *Free Enquirer,* helped organize the short-lived Workingmen's Party, for which he established a journal, but finally became convinced working men's conditions could not be improved by pitting worker against capital through a political organization. He left the Workingmen's Party and in 1831 began preaching as an unaffiliated minister, founding and editing his own paper, *The Philanthropist.* He then joined the Unitarians and served in churches in Walpole, New Hampshire, in 1832–34 and in Canton, Massachusetts, in 1834–36. He organized his own church, the Society for Christian Union and Progress, in 1836 in which year he published *New Views of Christianity, Society and the Church,* denouncing Catholicism and Protestantism and celebrating his "Church of the Future." He joined the Transcendental Group the same year and became so interested in Brook Farm that he sent his son there. He founded his own publication, the *Boston Quarterly Review,* in 1838 and wrote most of the articles it published. His political, literary, philosophical, and political pieces began to attract national attention as he attacked democracy, inheritance of wealth, industrialism, and labor for wages. In the July 1840 issue his strong condemnation of the injustices of industrialism and his advocacy of the abolition of penal codes, private ownership, and all forms of Christianity created a sensation. His radicalism caused consternation in the Democratic Party of which he was a member and Martin Van Buren ascribed his defeat in his bid for reelection as President in 1840 to Brownson's support because the Whigs had used Brownson's writings as proof of the socialistic leanings of the Democratic Party. When the *Boston Quarterly Review* was merged with the *U.S. Democratic Review* of New York in 1842, Brownson continued writing for the latter. A series of articles titled "Origin and Constitution of Government" caused an estrangement with the editor and led Brownson to resign. He resumed publication of his own publication in 1844 with the name changed to *Brownson's Quarterly Review* and in that year he caused a sensation by becoming a Catholic. As a leader of liberalism, his conversion was a bombshell to the Protestant community; it was a step that cost him dearly since he lost large numbers of his followers and readers in New England and almost all his Southern following. In the following years he became one of the most influential Catholic laymen of the nineteenth century, receiving a letter of approbation from the Catholic bishops assembled for the Provincial Council of Baltimore in 1849 and another from Pope Pius IX for his activities on behalf of the Catholic Church in the United States. He used his *Review* for an uncompromising championship of Catholicism and for vigorous attacks on the Church's enemies. In 1853 he was invited to join the faculty of the new Catholic University in Dublin by John Henry Newman who later withdrew the invitation because of Brownson's stand on Americanism. In 1855 he moved to New York where he had a falling out with Bishop John Hughes and in 1857 he moved to Elizabeth, New Jersey. He supported the Union cause in the Civil War, attacking secession and urging the abolition of slavery, suspended his *Review* in 1865 because of ecclesiastical disapprobation of his ontologism but revived it in 1872–75, and died in Detroit on Apr. 17 where he had moved in 1875. Brownson was a prolific writer and his son Henry F. Brownson collected his works in twenty volumes which were published in 1882–87. Brownson was one of the great intellects of the nineteenth century and in the thirty years from 1840 to 1870 made notable contributions in many fields of American life and thought. A valiant champion of his faith but possessed of a curious tactlessness that alienated many, he attained a scholarly eminence rivaled by few men of his time which was especially impressive in view of his almost complete lack of formal education.

BRUCE, FRANK M. (1886–1953), publisher. Son of publisher William George Bruce, he was born in Milwaukee, Wisconsin, on Dec. 25 and was educated at Marquette University (B.A. 1905, M.A. 1910) and the University of Wisconsin (B.A. 1906). He joined his father's firm in 1906, married Alma Mueller in 1910, became secretary-treasurer of the Bruce Publishing Company, and served as secretary of the National School Association. He died in Milwaukee on Feb. 22.

BRUCE, WILLIAM CONRAD (1882–1974), publisher. Son of publisher William George Bruce, he was born in Milwaukee, Wisconsin, on Jan. 17, was educated at Marquette University (B.A. 1901, M.A. 1910), and became an editor in his father's firm, Bruce Publishing Company, in 1902. When his father retired in 1927, he became president. During his presidency the firm purchased the *Catholic School Journal* in 1929, established a book club, the Catholic Literary Foundation, in 1943, which soon developed into the largest Catholic book club in the country, and by the 1950s the firm was a major publisher of Catholic textbooks and trade books in the United States. He was founder and first president of the Serra International and served as president of the National Association of Publishers and Church Goods Dealers. He retired in 1969 when the firm was sold to Crowell Collier & Macmillan and died in Wauwatosa, Wisconsin, on Feb. 23.

BRUCE, WILLIAM GEORGE (1856–1949), publisher. Son of a Great Lakes sailor, he was born in Milwaukee, Wisconsin, on Mar. 17, became a cigar maker when twelve, worked as an accountant for the Milwaukee *Sentinel* and later turned to publishing, though he had only completed the sixth grade of elementary school. He married Monica Moehring in 1881, founded the *American School Journal* in 1891, incorporated his firm as the Bruce Publishing Company, and founded *Industrial Arts and Vocational Education Magazine* in 1914 and *Hospital Progress* in 1920. He retired from the firm in 1927 and turned over its management to his two sons William C. and Frank M. who had joined the firm in 1902 and 1906. Active in civic affairs all his life he served on the Milwaukee Board of Education in 1883–85, became president of the Milwaukee Harbor Commission in 1913, and was a member of that body for thirty-nine years from 1911, and was an early enthusiastic supporter of the St. Lawrence Seaway. He was president of the American State Bank in 1933, was the recipient of the Laetare Medal in 1947, and died in Milwaukee on Aug. 13.

BRUMIDI, CONSTANTINO (1805–80), painter. Son of a Greek father and a Roman mother, he was born in Rome on June 20 and was early attracted to painting, became a pupil at the Academy of Fine Arts and when thirteen was admitted to the Accademia di San Lucia. He painted in several Roman palaces including that of Princess Torionia and worked in the Vatican for three years during the reign of Pope Gregory XVI. He was commissioned, with three other Roman painters, to restore the Raphael frescoes in the Loggia of the Vatican during the pontificate of Pope Pius IX and painted a portrait of that pope. He became a captain of the papal guards and in 1848, when Rossi was assassinated and the Pope fled to Gaeta, he refused to fire on the people for which he was arrested and imprisoned for fourteen months. Pius released him when restored to power and told him to leave Italy. He went to New York and became an American citizen in 1852. He painted portraits for a time and then attracted attention with his "Crucifixion," and altarpiece for St. Stephen's Church. After painting an allegory of the Trinity in the cathedral in Mexico City, he began painting in the Capitol, Washington, D.C., and attracted such favorable attention that he became a government painter and worked in Washington for more than thirty years. His best known works are the allegorical and historical frescoes in the rotunda of the Capitol and his frescoes of Saints Peter and Paul in the Catholic cathedral in Philadelphia. He fell from his scaffold while frescoing the Capitol rotunda in 1879 and never recovered from the shock. He died in Washington, D.C., on Feb. 19.

BRUNINI, JOHN B. (1868–1954), lawyer. Born in Vicksburg, Mississippi, on Dec. 25, he studied law at the University of Virginia and when admitted to the Mississippi bar in 1891, founded the law firm of Brunini and Hirsch. He became a leader of the Mississippi bar, served as a legal adviser for the bishops of Natchez for four decades and carried the Botto case to the Supreme Court where he was successful in establishing the principle that a nun could inherit property and caused a state law prohibiting bequests to religious institutions to be repealed. He was Vicksburg city attorney in 1898–99, engaged in state Democratic Party politics, and served as chairman of the Mississippi Highway Commission and director of the Delta Council. He was active in Catholic affairs and was named a Knight of St.

Gregory in 1928—the first Mississippian to be so honored. He died in Vicksburg on Nov. 8.

BRUNNER, FRANCIS DE SALES (1795–1859), missionary. Born in Mümliswil, Switzerland, on Jan. 10, he was christened Nicolaus Joseph and joined the Benedictines at Maria Stein in 1812, taking the name Francis de Sales. He was ordained in 1819 but after a decade teaching and engaging in missionary work he left the Benedictines in 1829 to join the Trappists at Oehlemberg, Alsace. When the Trappist monastery there was suppressed by the government in 1830 he volunteered his services as a missionary abroad and was ordered to China. As he was about to leave the order was rescinded and instead he founded a school for poor boys at Löwenberg Castle. In 1833 he made a pilgrimage to Rome with his mother Maria Anna and they joined the Archconfraternity of the Most Precious Blood; on his return his mother founded the Sisters of the Most Precious Blood dedicated to perpetual adoration and the education of poor orphans. In 1835 Fr. Brenner joined the Congregation of the Most Precious Blood at Albano, Italy. On his return home he continued his school and preparing boys for the priesthood. In 1843, irked by governmental interference in his school, he and eight other priests accepted an invitation from Archbishop John Purcell of Cincinnati to come to his see. Their arrival on New Year's day the following year marked the foundation of the Congregation of the Precious Blood in the United States. They established themselves near Norwalk, Ohio, built churches and convents and brought the Sisters of the Most Precious Blood to teach in the schools they founded. Brunner made several trips to Europe to secure support for his missions and died on his last trip at Schellenberg convent in Lichtenstein on Dec. 29.

BRUTÉ DE REMUR, SIMON WILLIAM GABRIEL (1779–1829), bishop, missionary. Son of the overseer of the royal possessions in Brittany, he was born in Rennes, France, on Mar. 20; his father died when he was a child. He studied at Rennes until the Revolution when he became a printer and compositor in a plant owned by his mother, who placed him there to avoid his conscription into a children's regiment that took part in the Reign of Terror. He began studying medicine in Paris in 1796 but instead of practicing when he received his medical degree in 1803, he entered St. Sulpice Seminary in Paris, and was ordained a Sulpician priest in 1808. He taught theology at the seminary for two years and then went to the United States with Bishop-elect Flaget of Kentucky. He taught philosophy at St. Mary's Seminary, Baltimore, for two years, engaged in pastoral work in the Chesapeake Bay area for a time, and then taught at Mt. St. Mary's College, Emmitsburg, Maryland. There he became Mother Elizabeth Seton's spiritual director and began their lifelong friendship. He was named president of St. Mary's College, Baltimore, in 1815, returned to Mt. St. Mary's (which was removed from Sulpician control in 1826) in 1818, and remained there until 1834 when he was named first bishop of the newly created see of Vincennes, Indiana. He visited France in quest of priests and funds for his diocese and died in Vincennes on June 26. His unpublished diary and letters are valuable sources of information about the Kentucky frontier and conditions there and of the prominent people he knew in the United States and France.

BRYANT, JOHN DELAVAU (1811–77), physician, author. Son of an Episcopalian minister, he was born in Philadelphia, was educated at the University of Pennsylvania (B.A. 1839, M.A. 1842) and then spent a year studying at the Episcopal General Seminary in New York City. After touring Europe he became a Catholic in 1842, studied medicine at the University of Pennsylvania and received his medical degree in 1848, became prominent in Philadelphia medical circles, and worked in Portsmouth and Norfolk, Virginia, during the yellow fever epidemic there in 1855. His account of his experiences emphasizing the role of neighboring swamps in the epidemic helped to pinpoint the mosquito's role in yellow fever for future researchers. He married Mary Harriet Riston in 1857, edited the *Catholic Herald* for two years, had a controversial novel, *Pauline Seward,* which was very successful, published in 1852, wrote an exposition of the recently promulgated dogma of the Immaculate Conception in 1855, and published an epic poem, "The Redemption," in 1859. He died in Philadelphia.

BUDDY, CHARLES F. (1887–1966), bishop. Born in St. Joseph, Missouri, on Oct. 4, he was educated at St. Benedict's College, Atchison, Kansas, St. Mary's College, Kansas, and the North American College, Rome (Ph.D. 1911, S.T.L. 1913). He was ordained in Rome in 1914, was chancellor of the St. Joseph, Missouri, diocese in 1917–19, director of the Society for the Propagation of the Faith in 1922–36, and vicar forane in 1926–36. He was appointed first bishop of the newly established diocese of San Diego, California, in 1936, a position he held for thirty years until his death in Banning, California, on Mar. 6. During his bishopric he founded the diocesan newspaper, the *Southern Cross,* and the University of San Diego which was

chartered in 1949, encouraged lay participation in Church activities, launched a widespread building program of churches, schools, convents, and charitable institutions, and was appointed an Assistant at the Pontifical Throne in 1964.

BUDENZ, LOUIS F. (1891–1972), journalist, author. Born in Indianapolis, Indiana, on July 17, he was educated at Xavier University, Cincinnati, Ohio, St. Mary's College, Kansas, and the Indianapolis Law School. He was admitted to the Indiana bar in 1912, was associate editor of the union paper, *The Carpenter,* in 1912–13, assistant director of the Central Catholic Verein in 1913–14, edited *Labor Age* in 1921–31, and in 1935 joined the Communist Party. He became one of the leading figures in the Communist Party in the United States, was a member of its national committee in 1939–45, was labor editor of the Communist *Daily Worker* in 1935–37, editor of the *Midwest Daily Record* in 1939–40, and was president and managing editor of the *Daily Worker* in 1940–45. He left the Communist Party in 1945, returned to the Catholic Church, and taught at several Catholic colleges, among them Notre Dame and Fordham. He was a columnist for the National Catholic Welfare Conference (NCWC) News Service in 1946–63 and wrote several books on Communism among them *This Is My Story* (1947), his autobiography, in which he tells of his experiences in the Communist Party. He died in Newport, Rhode Island, on May 2.

BURKE, AEDANUS B. (1743–1802), statesman. Born in Galway, Ireland, he emigrated to the United States, studied law in Stafford County, Virginia, joined the Second South Carolina Regiment during the Revolution, and resigned his commission as lieutenant in 1778. The next month he was appointed one of the associate justices of the state court but when Charleston, South Carolina, fell to the British in 1780 and the courts were suspended he took to the field as a captain of militia. He was a representative in the state legislature in 1781–82 and 1784–89 and was the leader of those favoring leniency for the Loyalists, publishing *An Address to the Freemen of South Carolina* in 1783 appealing for amnesty for them. He opposed ratification of the federal constitution at the South Carolina convention called to ratify it because of the clause permitting reelection of the President, was elected to the first Congress and there opposed the excise tax and the establishment of the United States Bank and urged the assumption of state debts by the national government. When he left Congress, he was appointed to a commission to revise South Carolina laws, was elected chancellor of the Court of Equity in 1799, and died on Mar. 30 in Charleston. Though a forceful proponent of slavery, he was an ardent democrat and had a distrust of any forms of nobility, which he vented in *Considerations on the Order of the Cincinnati* (1783) which was widely circulated in the United States and England and was translated into French and German.

BURKE, JAMES A. (1910–83), congressman. Born in Boston on Mar. 30, he was educated at Suffolk University there, married Aileen McDonald and served in World War II, receiving four Battle Stars. After the war he was a member of the Massachusetts General Court for ten years, served in the Massachusetts House of Representatives for seven years and was elected to the United States House of Representatives in 1958. He served in the House for the next twenty years, was an expert on Social Security and chairman of the sub-committee on Social Security and died on Oct. 13.

BURKE, JOHN (1859–1937), U.S. Treasurer, jurist. Born in Sigourney, Iowa, on Feb. 25, he was educated at the University of Iowa where he received his LL.B., was admitted to the Iowa bar in 1886, and began practicing law in Des Moines. He moved to the Dakota Territory in 1888, was elected county judge in 1889, to the North Dakota House of Representatives in 1890 and Senate in 1892, and married Mary E. Kane in 1891. He was elected governor of North Dakota in 1906—North Dakota's first Catholic governor—and served in 1907–13. During his term in office he enacted a series of liberal measures including the first primary law, a corrupt practices law, and a measure to control public utilities. He served as Treasurer of the United States in 1913–21 and then resumed his law practice. He received 386½ votes for the Democratic vice presidential nomination at the Democratic Convention in 1920, was elected associate justice of the North Dakota Supreme Court in 1924 and served as chief justice in 1929–31 and from 1935 until he died in Rochester, Minnesota, on May 14. He was North Dakota's first representative in Statuary Hall in the Capitol in Washington, D.C., when his statue was enshrined there in 1963.

BURKE, JOHN JOSEPH (1875–1936), editor. Born in New York City on June 6, he was educated at St. Francis Xavier College there and Catholic University, joined the Paulists and was ordained in 1899. He joined the *Catholic World* in 1903 as assistant editor and was its editor from 1904 to 1922. He was also director of the Catholic Publication Society (which later became the Paulist Press), helped found the Catholic Press Association in 1911, and in

1917 founded and was director of the Catholic War Council to coordinate Catholic activities in World War I, and received the Distinguished Service Medal in 1919 for his efforts. After the war he continued the Council as the National Catholic Welfare Council in 1919 with the hierarchy's support (it later became the National Catholic Welfare Conference) to coordinate Catholic activities in the United States and was general secretary of the administrative board until his death. He founded the Chaplains' Aid Society in 1917 and was chairman of the Protestant, Catholic and Jewish Committee of Six in 1917–22 to advise the Secretary of War on religious matters. He helped apply the bishops' Program of Social Reconstruction drawn up in 1919 to alleviate conditions during the depression of the 1930s, was instrumental in helping restore some degree of religious freedom in Mexico in 1928 through his efforts with the State Department and Mexican President Callas, was made a monsignor in 1936, and died in Washington, D.C., on Oct. 30.

BURKE, JOSEPH ALOYSIUS (1886–1962), bishop. Born in Buffalo, New York, on Aug. 27, he was educated at St. Canisius College there and the University of Innsbruck in Austria and was ordained in 1912. He engaged in pastoral work in Buffalo, was a chaplain in the Army during World War I, and in 1943 was named titular bishop of Vita and auxiliary of Buffalo. He was appointed bishop of that see in 1952 and served in that position until he died suddenly in Rome on Oct. 16 while he was attending Vatican Council II.

BURKE, JOSEPH HENRY (1876–1940), educator. Born in Richwood, Wisconsin, on Apr. 10, he was educated at St. Viator College in 1898–99, Notre Dame (B.A. 1904), Holy Cross in 1905–

8, and Catholic University (Ph.D. 1909), and was ordained a priest of the Congregation of Holy Cross in 1909. He joined the faculty at Notre Dame the same year, was prefect of discipline in 1910–16 and dean of studies in 1919–25, and was appointed president of St. Edward's University in Austin, Texas, in 1925. He left in 1931, was on the faculty of St. Thomas Military Academy, St. Paul, Minnesota, and then returned to Notre Dame. He was appointed rector of Dillon Hall there in 1933 and then became pastor in Watertown, Wisconsin, in 1937, and died there on Dec. 30.

BURKE, MAURICE FRANCIS (1845–1923), bishop. Born in Ireland on May 5, he emigrated to the United States, studied at St. Mary-of-the-Lake Seminary, Chicago, Notre Dame, and North American College, Rome, and was ordained in 1875. He engaged in parish work in Chicago in 1875–78, was a pastor in Joliet, Illinois, the next nine years, and in 1887 was appointed first bishop of the newly established diocese of Cheyenne, Wyoming. He was transferred to St. Joseph, Missouri (now Kansas City-St. Joseph), in 1893, was forced to retire in 1921 because of ill health, and died in St. Joseph on Mar. 17.

BURKE, THOMAS (c. 1747–80), governor. Born in County Galway, Ireland, he was probably educated in a Dublin university and emigrated to the United States after a family quarrel. He settled in Norfolk, Virginia, began practicing medicine but abandoned it for the law and in 1771 moved to North Carolina where he received his law license the following year. He was active in protests against the Stamp Act, served in several provincial congresses, helped enact a state constitution (which he helped to write) in 1776, and was elected to the

Continental Congress the same year and there continued his efforts for independence from England, and was severely critical of the Articles of Confederation. He represented North Carolina in the Continental Congress until 1781 when he was elected governor of North Carolina. He was active in raising men and supplies for the struggle against England, was captured by the British but escaped and resumed his duties as governor. He declined to run for the governorship again in 1782 and died the following year at his estate, Tyaquin, near Hillsboro, North Carolina, on Dec. 2.

BURKE, THOMAS MARTIN ALOYSIUS (1840–1915), bishop. Born in Ireland on Jan. 10, he emigrated to the United States and settled in Utica. He studied at St. Michael's College, Toronto, St. Mary's College, Baltimore, and St. Charles College, Ellicott City, Maryland, and was ordained in 1864. He engaged in parish work in Albany, New York, in 1864–94, was appointed vicar-general of the Albany diocese, and in 1894 was consecrated fourth bishop of that see. He built schools and asylums, consecrated Immaculate Conception Cathedral in 1902 and helped settle a strike in Albany the same year, and died in Albany on Jan. 20.

BURNETT, PETER HARDEMAN (1807–95), governor. Son of a carpenter and farmer, George Burnet (he added a second *t* to his father's name), he was born in Nashville, Tennessee, on Nov. 15, and when a child was brought to Missouri by his father. He returned to Tennessee when nineteen, married Harriet W. Rogers, worked as a clerk and became a store owner. He was unsuccessful in this and other businesses, returned to Missouri, studied law, and was admitted to the bar in 1839. When his wife became ill and his debts overwhelming he received permission from his creditors to move to Oregon and in 1843 he and his family moved there. He was a member of the legislative committee in 1844, a judge of the Oregon Supreme Court in 1845, helped set up the territorial government, and was elected to the state legislature in 1848. He became a Catholic in Oregon City in 1846 and two years later he moved to California, leading the first wagon train to the California gold fields. He soon repaid his Missouri debts, was a leader in the movement for statehood for California, was appointed a Superior Court judge in 1849 and was one of the framers of the state constitution. On Nov. 13, 1849, he was elected governor of California—the first citizen of the United States to hold that position. After California was admitted to the Union in 1850, he resigned the governorship in 1851 and resumed his private law practice. He served as chief justice of the California Supreme Court in 1857–58 and founded and was president of the Pacific Bank from 1863 to 1880 when he retired. He died in San Francisco on May 16. During his lifetime he wrote several books, among them *The Path Which Led a Protestant Lawyer to the Catholic Church* (1860), the story of his conversion, *The American Theory of Government* (1861), on the American system with reference to the controversy that led to the Civil War, and *Recollections and Opinions of an Old Pioneer* (1880), a valuable source on Pacific coast history.

BURNS, JAMES ALOYSIUS (1867–1940), educator. Born in Michigan City, Indiana, on Feb. 13, he was educated at Notre Dame (M.A.), joined the Congregation of Holy Cross in 1888, and taught at Sacred Heart College, Watertown, Wisconsin, in 1888–90. He then returned to Notre Dame, was ordained in 1893, and taught chemistry at Notre Dame until 1900 when he was named president of Holy Cross College, Washington, D.C. He received his Ph.D. from Catholic University in 1906, was one of the founders and first vice presidents of the National Educational Association in 1904, and was president of Notre Dame in 1919–22, reorganized the university, raised enrollment, and was named president emeritus in 1922. He returned to Holy Cross in 1926 as president and the following year became provincial of the Indiana province of his Congregation. He was elected first Assistant-General of the Congregation in 1938 and died in South Bend, Indiana, on Sept. 9. He was the author of several books on Catholic education, among them *Principles, Origin and Establishment of the Catholic School System in the United States* (1908), *Growth and Development of the Catholic School System* (1912), and *Catholic Education* (1917).

BURTON, KATHERINE KURZ (1887–1969), author. Daughter of John and Louise Kurz, she was born in Lakewood, Ohio, in Mar., received her B.A. from Western Reserve University, taught for a year at Wheaton College in 1910, and in 1910 married Harry Paynes Burton, an editor. She was associate editor of *McCall's* magazine in 1928–30, of *Redbook* in 1930–33, became a Catholic in 1930, and wrote a woman's page, "Woman to Woman," for *Sign* for twenty years beginning in 1934. During her lifetime she wrote some twenty-five books, mostly popularly written biographies of Catholic figures, among them *Sorrow Built a Bridge* (1937), the story of Rose Hawthorne, *Celestial Homespun* (1943), a life of Isaac Hecker, *In No Strange Land* (1942), *The Great Mantle* (1950), and her autobiography *The Next Thing* (1949). She died in Harrison, New York, on Sept. 23.

BURTSELL, RICHARD LALOR (1840–1912). Born in New York City on Apr. 14, he was educated at the Sulpician seminary, Montreal, and the Propaganda, Rome (Ph.D. in philosophy, 1858; in theology, 1862), and was ordained in 1862. In 1868 he became the founding pastor of Epiphany parish in New York City after having been a curate at St. Ann's Church in 1862–68. He was a firm and vocal supporter of Fr. Edward McGlynn when he was suspended from his priestly duties in 1886 by Archbishop Corrigan for refusing to stop speaking at rallies in support of Henry George's mayoralty campaign and for his support of George's single tax (on land) theory. In 1889 Burtsell was ordered to leave Epiphany and go to a small rural parish in Roundout, New York. His two appeals to Rome for reinstatement were denied and in 1890 he was appointed pastor of St. Anne's Church, Kingston, New York. He was made a papal chamberlain in 1905 and a domestic prelate in 1911 and died in Kingston on Feb. 5. He contributed articles to the *Catholic Encyclopedia* and scholarly journals, was considered an outstanding canonist, and participated actively in civic affairs. He was also responsible for the establishment of St. Benedict the Moor parish, the first Catholic parish in New York City for blacks.

BUSCH, JOSEPH FRANCIS (1866–1953), bishop. Born in Red Wing, Minnesota, on Apr. 18, he was educated at St. Canisius College, Buffalo, New York, Sacred Heart at Prairie du Chien, Wisconsin, the University of Innsbruck, Austria, and Catholic University, and was ordained in Austria in 1889. He became a curate at the cathedral in St. Paul, Minnesota, was secretary to Archbishop Ireland in 1890–92, served as pastor in several parishes in St. Paul, and in 1902 founded the Diocesan Missionary Band of St. Paul of which he was director until 1910 when he was appointed bishop of Lead, South Dakota (transferred to Rapid City in 1930). He was translated to St. Cloud, Minnesota, as its fourth bishop in 1915, was active in the cause of social justice and social action, founded the St. Cloud *Register* (later the St. Cloud *Visitor),* convened three diocesan synods, and died on May 31 in St. Cloud.

BUSSARD, PAUL (1904–83), editor. Born in Essex, Iowa, on Nov. 22, he was educated at St. Thomas College in 1919–22 and St. Paul Seminary in 1922–28, St. Paul, Minnesota, and was ordained in St. Paul in 1928. He continued his education at Catholic University in 1932–37 (Ph.D. 1937) and in Germany in 1934 and became associate editor of *Worship* in 1931. He and Fr. Louis Gale founded the *Catholic Digest* in 1936 and he edited it until his retirement in 1965. He was president of the Catholic Press Association in 1948–50 and died in St. Paul on Feb. 22. He was the author of several books among them *If I Be Lifted Up* (1929), *Living Source* (1936), and *The Sacrifice* (1939).

BUTLER, MOTHER MARIE JO-SEPH (1860–1940), mother superior, educator. Joanna Butler was born in Ballynunnery, Kilkenny, Ireland, of a well-to-do ancient Irish family on July 22. She was educated at the parish school and by the Sisters of Mercy in nearby New Ross, was early attracted to the religious life, and in 1876 entered the Béziers, France, convent of the Congregation of the Sacred Heart of Mary, taking the name Marie Joseph six months later when she was veiled. She made her first profession at Oporto, Portugal, where she was teaching in 1880, was sent to the congregation's school at Braga, Portugal, the following

year, and was appointed superior of the convent and school there in 1883. After a decade there she was sent to the United States in 1893 to take charge of the Congregation's school at Sag Harbor, New York, and to extend the work of the Sacred Heart nuns in the United States. In 1908 she opened Marymount School at Tarrytown, New York, established a novitiate there in 1910, and opened Marymount College in 1918. Over the next two decades she established Marymount schools in Los Angeles, Paris, Rome, and Santa Barbara, California. In 1926 she was elected mother general of her Congregation— the first American to head a congregation with a European motherhouse. She became an American citizen in 1927, expanded the Congregation's schools to England and Brazil, and opened a new novitiate in Ireland. She was a leader in educating of women to participate in world affairs and to become leaders in Catholic activities. She established clinic schools to train Maryknoll students for social work among the poor, helped develop the retreat movement in the United States, and died in Tarrytown on Apr. 23.

BUTLER, PAUL MULHOLLAND (1905–61). Born in South Bend, Indiana, on June 15, he was educated at Notre Dame (LL.B. 1927), was admitted to the Indiana bar in 1927, and early entered politics. He was active in the Indiana Democratic Party, served on various state committees, was chairman of the Democratic National Committee in 1956–60, and often a storm center of the Party for his open criticism of the civil rights stand of Southern Democrats. He died in Washington, D.C., on Dec. 30.

BUTLER, PIERCE (1866–1939), associate justice of the U.S. Supreme Court. Born in a log farmhouse near Northfield, Minnesota, on Mar. 17, he was educated at Carleton College there, a Congregationalist institution (B.S. 1887), read law, and was admitted to the bar in St. Paul in 1888. He began a law practice with Stan Donnelly, became county attorney in 1891, and was elected in 1893 and 1895 to the state senate but was defeated in 1906. He joined the law firm of Butler, Mitchell and Doherty in 1907 and the firm became widely known for his cases involving railroad rates; he was also counsel in several important cases involving the application of the Sherman Anti-Trust Act. In 1922 he was nominated for the United States Supreme Court by President Warren G. Harding and despite the opposition of Senators George W. Norris and Robert A. La Follette, his nomination was confirmed. During his sixteen years on the Supreme Court, his opinions reflected his opposition to the increased centralization of power in the federal government. He wrote more than 300 majority opinions and 140 dissents and became the leader of the conservative bloc on the Court, regularly voting to uphold government restrictions on individuals and striking down government regulation of business. When the New Deal came into power in 1933, he produced numerous dissenting opinions to the regulations it passed, some seventy-three in his last three years on the Court, and he was one of the chief targets of President Roosevelt's proposed reform of the Supreme Court in 1936–37. He died in Washington, D.C., on Nov. 16.

BUTTIMER, CHARLES HENRY (1909–82), superior general. Born of Irish parents in Brighton, Massachusetts, Thomas Joseph Buttimer entered the Christian Brothers novitiate when fifteen and received his habit, taking the name Charles Henry, two years later. He began teaching at St. Mary's School in Yonkers, New York, and in 1933–49 was at De La Salle College, Washington, D.C., where he was teacher, dean, and then superior. In 1956 he founded the Long Island-New England province of the Christian Brothers and in 1966 he was named superior general of the Christian Brothers—the first non-Frenchman named to that post since the Christian Brothers were founded in 1690. He was appointed one of the participants in the 1974 World Synod of Bishops by Pope Paul VI. When his term as superior general ended in 1976 he returned to the United States and lived at the Christian Brothers residence at Narragansett, Rhode Island. He died in South Kingston, Rhode Island, of a stroke on Dec. 15.

BYRNE, ANDREW (1802–62), bishop. Born in Navan, County Meath, Ireland, on Dec. 3 or 5, he was studying for the priesthood at the diocesan seminary there in 1820 when he heard Bishop John England of Charleston, South Carolina, plead for priests for his newly created diocese and accompanied the bishop back to the United States. He was ordained in Charleston in 1827, worked as a missionary in North and South Carolina, became vicar-general of the diocese, and was Bishop England's theologian at the second Provincial Council of Baltimore in 1833. In 1836, because of a disagreement with England, he moved to New York and engaged in pastoral work there. In 1844 he was consecrated first bishop of the newly established diocese of Little Rock, Arkansas. He visited Ireland several times in quest of priests for his new diocese, actively promoted immigration to the Southwest, brought the Sisters of Mercy into his see, and developed missions for the Indians. He attended the sixth Provincial Council of Baltimore in 1846 and the first Provincial Council of New Orleans in 1856 and died in Helena, Arkansas, on June 10.

BYRNE, CHRISTOPHER EDWARD
(1867–1950), bishop. Born in Byrnesville, Missouri, on Apr. 21, he was educated at St. Mary's College, Kansas, (B.A. 1886, M.A. 1896) and St. Mary's Seminary, Baltimore, and was ordained in St. Louis in 1891. He was a curate at St. Bridget's Church, St. Louis, in 1891–97, pastor at Sacred Heart Church, Columbia in 1897–99, of St. Joseph's Church, Edina, Missouri, in 1899–1910 and of Holy Name Church, St. Louis from 1911 to 1918 when he was appointed bishop of Galveston, Texas. He was bishop for thirty-two years, called a diocesan synod in 1930, invited the Congregation of St. Basil into the diocese (the Basilians founded St. Thomas University in 1947), was made an Assistant at the Pontifical Throne in 1941, and died on Apr. 1

BYRNE, EDWIN V. (1891–1963), archbishop. Born in Philadelphia on Aug. 9, he was educated at St. Charles Borromeo Seminary there and was ordained in 1915. He served as a curate at Our Lady of Lourdes Church, Philadelphia, in 1915–17, was a chaplain in the Navy in World War I, and in 1920 became secretary to Bishop James McCloskey of Jaro, Philippine Islands, and vicar-general of the diocese. He was appointed first bishop of the newly established diocese of Ponce, Puerto Rico, in 1925 and four years later was named bishop of San Juan, Puerto Rico. He was named as Assistant at the Papal Throne in 1940, and in 1943 he became archbishop of Santa Fe, New Mexico, a position he occupied until his death there twenty years later on July 25. During his episcopate the military and atomic installations in his see brought in a great influx of Catholic families. To provide for them he increased the number of schools and parishes in the diocese, expanded the facilities and enrollment of the diocesan seminary when he

moved it to Santa Fe and saw the establishment of St. Michael's College in Santa Fe and St. Joseph on the Rio Grande College in Albuquerque, New Mexico.

BYRNE, PATRICK JAMES (1888–1950), missionary. Born in Washington, D.C., on Oct. 26, he was educated at St. Charles College, Catonsville, Maryland, and St. Mary's Seminary, Baltimore, and was ordained in 1915. A week after his ordination he joined the Maryknoll Fathers, the first priest to join that Society. He worked in various positions and then was sent to Korea where he founded a Maryknoll mission in North Korea. He was named prefect apostolic of Pyongyang in 1927, was elected vicar-general of the Society in 1929, and opened the first Maryknoll mission in Japan in 1935 which was soon designated prefecture apostolic of Kyoto. He resigned this post in 1940, remained in Japan during World War II, and in 1947 was named apostolic visitor, later delegate, to Korea. He was consecrated titular bishop of Gazera in 1949, was arrested by the Communists when they invaded South Korea the following year, and died at Ha Chang Ri, Korea, on Nov. 25 while on an infamous "death march" to the Manchurian border with seven hundred other prisoners.

BYRNE, RICHARD (1832–64), general. Born in County Cavan, Ireland, he emigrated to the United States in 1844 and enlisted in the 2nd Cavalry of the United States Army in 1849. He participated in the Indian campaigns in Florida and Oregon, was made a lieutenant in the Union Army at the outbreak of the Civil War, and in 1862 was appointed colonel and commander of the 28th Massachusetts Volunteers, an Irish regiment attached to Meagher's Irish Brigade which served in the Army of the Potomac. The regiment was almost wiped out in fierce fighting at Fredericksburg, Chancellorsville, and Gettysburg and he spent the winter and spring of 1863–64 recruiting replacements. On his return in 1864 he was placed in command of the Irish Brigade and was wounded leading a charge at Cold Harbor, Virginia. He died of his wounds a week later on June 10 in Washington, D.C., before his commission of brigadier general, which had been approved, was signed by President Lincoln.

BYRNE, THOMAS SEBASTIAN (1841–1923), bishop. Born in Hamilton, Ohio, on July 29, he was educated at St. Thomas College, Bardstown, Kentucky, Mt. St. Mary of the West Seminary, Cincinnati, Ohio, and North American College, Rome, and was ordained in Cincinnati in 1869. He taught at Mt. St. Mary of the West until 1875, spent the next twelve years in parish work in Cincinnati and in 1887 was named rector of Mt. St. Mary of the West. He was appointed bishop of Nashville, Tennessee, in 1894 and held that position until his death in Cincinnati on Sept. 4. During his twenty-nine-year episcopate he convoked the first diocesan synod in 1905, decreed all Catholic children in the diocese must attend Catholic schools, brought several religious orders into the see, and approved the establishment of St. Agnes College (changed to Siena College in 1939) in 1922 by the Dominican Sisters of St. Catharine, Kentucky.

BYRNE, WILLIAM (1780–1833), missionary, educator. Born in County Wicklow, Ireland, of a large family he sacrificed his ambition to be a priest to support his family upon the death of his father. When he was twenty-five, he emigrated to the United States, went to Georgetown to become a Jesuit but left, convinced his age and lack of education made becoming a Jesuit impossible and went to Mt. St. Mary's College, Em-

mitsburg, Maryland. He continued his studies at St. Mary's Seminary, Baltimore, was accepted by Bishop Flaget of Bardstown, Kentucky, as a student for the priesthood in his diocese and entered St. Thomas's Seminary in Bardstown and was ordained there in 1819. He was assigned to St. Charles's and St. Mary's missions and to visit Louisville, and in 1821 he opened St. Mary's College near Bardstown with fifty students. Twice it was destroyed by fire but in each case he rebuilt it; after heading it for twelve years he turned it over to the Jesuits who he felt could administer the school better than he could. He was planning a new school in Nashville, Tennessee, when he died of cholera contracted while ministering to a poor black woman on June 5, in Washington, D.C.

BYRNE, WILLIAM (1833–1912), educator. Born in Kilmessan, Meath, Ireland, on Sept. 8, he emigrated to the United States in 1853. He was educated at St. Mary's College, Wilmington, Delaware, and Mt. St. Mary's College, Emmitsburg, Maryland (M.A. 1861), taught at Mt. St. Mary's, was ordained in 1864 for the Boston diocese, and was named chancellor of that see in 1866. He was appointed rector of St. Mary's Church, Charlestown, Massachusetts, in 1874, became active in penal reform and the temperance movement, founding the Boston Temperance Missions and editing the *Young Crusader,* and in 1881 was elected president of Mt. St. Mary's. He solved the college's financial difficulties and returned to Boston and became rector of St. Joseph's Church there in 1884 though he continued his interest in Mt. St. Mary's as a member of its council; its library was named after him. He wrote several religious pamphlets and *A History of the Catholic Church in the New England States* (1899) and died in Boston on Jan. 9.

C

CABOT, JOHN (c. 1450–98), explorer. Giovanni Cabot was born in Genoa, Italy (an honor also claimed by Cabo, Spain), though exactly when is not known. He went to Venice in 1461, became a Venetian citizen in 1476, and made numerous commercial voyages to the East as far as Arabia. There he heard of a fabulously rich country to the east and decided the riches of the Far East could be reached by sailing to the west. Sometime in the 1480s he settled in England, residing chiefly in the port of Bristol, and in 1496, secured a patent from King Henry VII to seek new lands and islands. He set sail from Bristol under the English flag and reached the North American mainland on June 24, 1497, probably at Cape Breton Island or at Newfoundland, according to an entry in the ship's log made by his son Sebastian that some authorities challenge as a later falsification, thus establishing the basis for the English claim to North America. He undertook a second expedition in 1498 with five ships and some three hundred men and sailed along the North American coast probably as far south as Cape Hatteras. He died shortly after his return to England, probably at Bristol, in 1498.

CABRINI, ST. FRANCES XAVIER (1850–1911), saint, foundress. The youngest of thirteen children of Augustine Cabrini, a well-to-do farmer, and Stella Oldini Cabrini, she was born in Sant' Angelo, Lodigiano, Lombardy, Italy, on July 15 and was christened Maria Francesca. Early attracted to missionary work, her family decided she should be a teacher but when she was orphaned at eighteen she decided to become religious. She applied for admission to the Daughters of the Sacred Heart and the Canossan Sisters but was refused by both groups because of her delicate health. In 1874 Bishop Serrati of Lodi asked her to take over a badly managed orphanage in Codogno named House of Providence which had been founded by Antonia Tondini. So fiercely did Antonia resist the new head of the orphanage that Bishop Domenico Galmini in whose diocese the orphanage was located ordered it closed six years later. He then invited Frances to found a new congregation and in 1880 Frances, with seven followers, moved into an abandoned Franciscan friary at Codogno and the Institute of the Missionary Sisters of the Sacred Heart, dedicated to spreading devotion to the Sacred Heart and to the education of girls, was established. The bishop gave formal approval the same year (and the Holy See in 1887) and the institute soon spread to Grumello, Milan, and Rome. While in Rome establishing two houses she met Bishop John Baptist Scalabrini, founder of the Institute of Charles Borromeo (the Scalabrinians), who urged her to send missionaries to the United States to aid Italian immigrants there. Her heart was set on going to China but when Pope Leo XIII told her she was needed in the West and when, in 1889, Archbishop Michael Corrigan of New York City invited her to go there and work with Italian immigrants, she accepted. But when she arrived in New York with five sisters the offer was withdrawn and the Archbishop suggested she return to Italy. Instead she remained and during the next twenty-seven years she traveled all over the United States and despite overwhelming difficulties opened hospitals (the first was Columbus Hospital in New York City in 1892), schools, orphanages, and convents; she also opened foundations in Italy, South America, and Central America. In 1907 she wished to retire as superior but instead a decree was issued making her superior general for life; in 1909 she became an American citizen. By the time of her death in Chicago on Dec. 22, there were in existence some sixty-seven schools, convents, orphanages, hospitals, and other foundations she had established. She was canonized by Pope Pius XII in 1946—the first American citizen to be named a saint; in 1950 Pope Pius named her patroness of immigrants. Her feast day is celebrated on Nov. 13.

CADILLAC, ANTOINE DE LA LOTHE, SIEUR (c. 1656–1730), governor. Son of a parliamentary councillor, he was born in Gascony, France, entered the Army when sixteen and in 1683 went to America to seek his fortune and served in the garrison at Port Royal (Annapolis Royal, Nova Scotia). He was given a grant of land in Maine, which included Mt. Hope and Desert Island, and lived there for a time after he married Marie Thérèse Guyon, daughter of a wealthy merchant, in 1687. He returned to France in 1689 in financial difficulties and while he was there the British sacked and burned his establishment at Port Royal in 1691. King Louis XIV took him under his protection and later in 1691 sent him back to America as an aide of the staff of Comte Louis de Buade Frontenac, the governor of New France, whose favorite he soon became. He rose rapidly on the governor's staff and in 1694 was made commandant of the post at Michillimackinac (Mackinac, Michigan). He ruled with great skill and helped keep the Indians in check, preventing an alliance of the Western Indians with the Iroquois or the English but marred his rule by carrying on an illegal traffic with the Indians selling them brandy at great profit despite the vigorous objections of the Jesuits. He returned to Quebec in 1697 when the posts in the West were abandoned, wrote an account of his experiences at Michillimackinac, and in 1699 returned to France to explain Frontenac's views to the Court. At the same time he pushed his own plan for establishing a post on the Detroit River which he felt would provide the French with a better strategic position against the English than Michillimackinac. Louis granted him permission to build a fortified post at the head of Lake Erie on the Detroit River and in 1701 he built Fort Pontchartrain there which was to develop into the city of Detroit. He also obtained a monopoly on all trade at the post, a step that helped lead to his downfall when the merchants of Montreal protested he was taking away their trade; further the new governor of New France, Philippe de Rigaud, marquis of Vaudreuil, objected to the authority he had arrogated to himself and the Jesuits renewed their complaints about abuses in his trade with the Indians. He was arrested and tried in Quebec in 1704, was acquitted of all charges against him and returned to Detroit, was recalled to France in 1711 and was named governor of Louisiana. The colony was granted to a company founded by Antoine Crozat and he entered into a partnership with Crozat in 1712. He reached Louisiana in 1713 and devoted himself to mining and trading with the

Spaniards. He was again recalled to France in 1716 because of the frequent fierce internal quarrels as he sought to enrich himself and Crozat became disillusioned with him. He was tried and probably imprisoned in the Bastille briefly but was released early in 1717 and restored to royal favor. He retired to Castle Sarazin, his estate in Gascony, and in 1722 was granted a decree restoring his property in Detroit. He was named governor of Castle Sarazin, Tarn-Garonne, France, and died there on Oct. 18. A shrewd, talented man, his greed and caustic temperament time and again embroiled him in difficulties.

CAHENSLY, PETER (1838–1923). Born in Limburg on der Lahn, Nassau, Germany, on Oct. 28, he joined his father's wholesale grocery business and traveled all over Europe on its business. He was an active member of the St. Vincent de Paul Society, became interested in working to alleviate the problems of emigrants and established social action programs to aid them. He became affiliated with the St. Raphael Society to help German emigrants when it was founded in 1871, was its first secretary and in 1899 became its president. The Society was established in the United States in 1883 and in 1890 members of the boards of directors from seven European nations of the St. Raphael Society, meeting in Lucerne, petitioned the Vatican to order separate churches and priests for each nationality in the United States, parochial schools where students would be taught in their native tongues, and representation of national groups in the American hierarchy. The movement became known as Cahenslyism and was fiercely opposed and bitterly denounced by the Americanists of the Church in the United States. Their opposition was successful for the Holy See never acted on the memorandum. Cahensly served in the Prussian House

of Delegates in 1885–1915 and the Reichstag in 1898–1903 and died on Dec. 25.

CALDWELL, MARY GWENDO- LINE (1863–1909), philanthropist. Born in Louisville, Kentucky, she moved to New York City in 1874 after the death of her father who bequeathed her and her sisters a fortune. She studied at Sacred Heart Academy there and became interested in Catholic higher education after meeting John Lancaster Spalding, later bishop of Peoria, Illinois, and then a parish priest in New York City. At the Third Plenary Council of Baltimore in 1884, she donated $300,000 to found the Catholic University of America and is considered its founder. She married the Marquis Jean des Monstiers-Merinoille in Paris in 1896, and was the recipient of the Laetare Medal in 1899 but reportedly renounced her Catholicism in 1904. She died on an ocean liner anchored outside New York Harbor on Oct. 10.

CALLAHAN, PATRICK HENRY (1865–1940), executive. Born in Cleveland, Ohio, on Oct. 15, he was educated at Spencerian Business College there, was briefly a member of the Chicago White Sox baseball team, and worked for the Glidden Varnish Company in Cleveland and Chicago in 1888–92. He married Julia Cahill in 1891, became sales manager of the Louisville (Kentucky) Varnish Company the following year and spent the rest of his life with that company, the last thirty years as president. At the suggestion of Msgr. John A. Ryan he put into effect the Ryan-Callahan plan which gave his employees a share of the company's profits and a voice in management. He was active in Catholic circles, heading the Knights of Columbus Committee on Religious Prejudice in 1914–16, founding the Catholic Laymen's League of

Georgia in 1916, heading the Knights of Columbus Committee on World War Activities in 1917–18, helping found the Catholic Association for International Peace in 1926–27, and was made a Knight of St. Gregory by Pope Pius XI in 1922. He was also active in the Prohibition movement, serving as general secretary of the Association of Catholics Favoring Prohibition and as chairman of the Central Prohibition Committee, and served on several state and national boards of President Franklin Roosevelt's New Deal which he actively supported. He died in Louisville on Feb. 4.

CALLAN, CHARLES JEROME (1877–1962), biblical scholar, author, editor. Born in Royalton, New York, on Dec. 5, he was educated at Canisius College, Buffalo, New York, joined the Dominicans in 1899 and studied for the priesthood at St. Rose Priory, Kentucky, St. Joseph Priory, Ohio, and the Dominican House of Studies, Washington, D.C. He was ordained in 1905 in Somerset, Ohio, with John McHugh whom he had met in the Dominican novitiate and with whom he was to have a lifelong friendship and scholarly collaboration, taught at the Dominican House of Studies in 1909–15, and then went to the newly opened Maryknoll Seminary with Fr. McHugh as professor of biblical exegesis. He was spiritual director of the Maryknoll Sisters Convent in 1917–26 and was pastor of Holy Rosary Church, Hawthorne, New York, in 1929–56. He became coeditor of *Homiletic and Pastoral Review*, with Fr. McHugh, in 1916, was the author or coauthor with Fr. McHugh of some forty books among them *The Catholic Missal*, *The Epistles of St. Paul* (2 volumes, 1922, 1931), *Four Gospels* (1918), *Blessed Be God* (1925), *What is Faith?* (1926), and *The Man of God* (1926). With Fr. McHugh he compiled the

four-volume *A Parochial Course of Doctrinal Instructions* . . . for the priests of the New York archdiocese and both were editors of the Spencer translation of the *New Testament from the Original Greek*. He was appointed consultant to the Pontifical Biblical Commission in 1940, the first native-born American to serve on that committee, and died in Milford, Connecticut, on Feb. 26.

CALVERT, CECILIUS (1606–75), colonial proprietor. The eldest son and heir of George Calvert, first Lord Baltimore, he was born in London and was educated at Oxford, entering Trinity College when he was thirteen. He graduated in 1621 and in 1629 married Anne Arundell of Wardour, also a Catholic. When his father died in 1632, Cecilius became second Lord Baltimore and inherited the charter of Maryland which had been granted but not issued to his father at the time of his death, despite great opposition. The following year he equipped and provisioned two vessels, the *Ark* and the *Dove*, and dispatched his brothers, Leonard as governor and George, with twenty gentlemen and some three hundred laborers to colonize his grant, instructing the new governor to grant complete religious freedom to all Christians in his colony—the only colony to offer freedom of religion to all Christian believers. Although desirous of doing so he was never able to visit his colony as he was kept too occupied in England resisting his enemies who were trying to have the royal grant revoked, gain the plantation for Virginia, and destroy its religion. One of the consequences of his inability to visit the colony was what amounted to self-government for his colony. The charter gave him sole right to make laws for the colony with the advice and consent of the freemen. Since he had issued no code of laws, the freemen met and passed a set of ordinances in 1634–35.

He promptly rejected the laws as infringing on his rights as proprietor and in 1637–38 sent the assembly of freemen his own set of laws which the assembly refused to accept. Another set was then sent him by the assembly which he at first refused to accept but eventually he authorized their acceptance by the governor with the stipulation that future laws passed by the assembly could be approved by the governor and put into effect until submitted for approval or disapproval by the proprietor—thus conceding the right to initiate laws to the colonists. Though the proprietor retained the right of absolute veto, he seldom used this authority, thus in effect granting the colonists the right of self-rule. Control of the government in the colony was temporarily taken from Calvert by Ingle's Rebellion in 1645–47 which caused Governor Leonard Calvert to seek refuge in Virginia until 1647 when he was able to return with sufficient armed force to recapture the government. Again in 1650 a group of Virginia Puritans who had previously been given refuge in Maryland seized control of the colony which was restored to the Calverts in 1658. Throughout this entire period Cecilius spent much of his time warding off attempts to take control of the colony from him. He died in London on Nov. 30.

CALVERT, CHARLES (1637–1715), governor, proprietor. Son of Cecilius Calvert, second Lord Baltimore, and Anne Arundell Calvert, he was born in London on Aug. 27 and married Jane Lowe, widow of Henry Sewall of Matapaney-on-the-Patuxent, Maryland. He was named governor of Maryland by his father in 1661, went to Maryland and served as governor until 1675 when, on the death of his father, he became third Lord Baltimore and proprietor as well as governor of the colony. He resisted the efforts of Protestants in England and in Virginia to make the Church of England the established religion of Maryland and maintained religious freedom there. Meanwhile English Protestants were agitating to establish Protestantism as the religion of the colony and in 1684 Charles returned to England to protect the interests of his colony and to defend his charter. The Protestant Revolution in England in 1688 placed William and Mary on the throne and in 1692 they seized the charter of Maryland for the crown after Protestant settlers in the colony had revolted in 1689. At the same time Calvert's Irish estates were seized when he was accused of being a Catholic outlaw and guilty of treason; King William changed the wording of the charge so the taint of treason was removed. He petitioned the crown in 1711 to restore his proprietorship of Maryland but his request was turned down because of his Catholicism. He died in Epsom, Surrey, England on Feb. 21.

CALVERT, GEORGE (c. 1580–1632), statesman. Son of Leonard Calvert and Alice Crosland Calvert, he was born in Kipling, Yorkshire, England, was instructed by an Anglican clergyman in his youth (though his parents were Catholic they were forced to conform to the Church of England because of anti-Catholic laws), and graduated from Trinity College, Oxford, in 1597. He married Anne Mynne in 1605, met Robert Cecil, principal secretary of state of England, while living in Europe and on his return became Cecil's private secretary in 1606. He was soon appointed a clerk of the crown of assize and peace for the province of Connaught and County Clare in Ireland by King James I and in 1609 was elected to Parliament. He defended the King's policies in Parliament, became clerk of the Privy Council in 1613, served on two commissions appointed by James to investigate the discontent in Ireland and became a favorite of the King whose arguments against the Dutch theologian Vorstius he translated into Latin. He was knighted by the King in 1617, was named one of the principal secretaries of state in 1619 and in that position favored the marriage of the Prince of Wales to the daughter of Philip III of Spain for strategic reasons despite strong opposition in Parliament. He was made a commissioner for the office of treasurer in 1620 and served in Parliament again in 1621 and 1624. He was granted a 2,300-acre estate in Longford, Ireland, in 1621 and was obliged to surrender it when he announced he was a Catholic in 1624 or 1625 since a condition of the grant was that all settlers must be Protestants; he also resigned as secretary when he converted. The grant was returned without condition, the King continued him on in the Privy Council and in 1625 raised him to the peerage as Baron Baltimore of County Longford, Ireland. When King James died in 1625, his successor, Charles I, offered to dispense with the religious supremacy oath if George would remain on the Privy Council but he declined. A member of the Virginia Company in 1609–20, he purchased a plantation in Newfoundland which he named Avalon and a small colony was established at Ferryland; in 1623 he received a patent which gave him quasiroyal authority in the province of Avalon and in 1627 he made a visit to Ferryland and returned in 1628. A Protestant minister named Stourton complained to the Court that Baltimore was allowing Mass to be said in the province but his complaint was ignored. When French ships attacked the fisheries off the coast of Newfoundland, Baltimore's interests were adversely affected and in 1629 he sent his son Leonard to defend them. In 1629 he petitioned for a grant of land in a milder climate and was offered an area in Virginia which he visited and was badly treated by the inhabitants because of his religion. The grant was opposed by the Virginia Company so vigorously that the King withdrew the offer and instead granted him land north and east of the Potomac which was to become Maryland. Before the charter was issued, he died in London on Apr. 15 and it was inherited by his son Cecilius who was to develop the colony.

CALVERT, LEONARD (1606–47). Second son of George Calvert, first lord of Baltimore, and his wife Anne Mynne Calvert, and brother of Cecilius, second Lord Baltimore, he accompanied his father to Newfoundland in 1628 and the following year was sent to Newfoundland to defend his father's colony, Avalon, from attacks by the French. In 1633 his brother Cecilius, now second Lord Baltimore on the death of their father in 1632, sent him as governor to Maryland with two vessels, the *Ark* and the *Dove,* and some three-hundred settlers and twenty gentlemen and his brother George to establish a colony in Maryland. They arrived in 1634 and four months after their departure from England founded St. Mary's on the site of an Indian village. Difficulties began at once from Virginian interference in the new colony. William Claiborne of Virginia had established a fort and a settlement on Kent Island in Chesapeake Bay and refused to acknowledge the authority of the new colony. When he resorted to armed force to defend his settlement Lord Baltimore ordered his arrest in 1634. Claiborne went to England in 1637 to defend his conduct but the King decided in favor of Lord Baltimore; Leonard then established a settlement on Kent Island. In 1643 he returned to England and on his return to Maryland found the disturbances besetting England were having an effect on the colony. A vessel commanded by a Captain

Ingle and commissioned by Parliament appeared at St. Mary's, was captured by the colonists and forced to take an oath against Parliament. Ingle escaped and the following year he and Claiborne, now treasurer of Virginia, returned and aided by dissident Protestants in the colony drove Leonard and many of the Catholic colonists into Virginia and forced Jesuit missionaries in Maryland to return to England. The colony's conquerors then tried to force an oath of allegiance to Protestantism on the Catholics they had captured but all refused to take it. Anarchy reigned until 1646 when Leonard returned with a force of Marylanders and Virginians and captured St. Mary's and the following year Kent Island. He restored the right of self-government and Maryland became a haven for victims of religious persecution, the first colony to put tolerance into actual practice. Leonard died in Maryland on June 9.

CAMPBELL, JAMES (1812–93), U.S. postmaster general. Son of a prosperous Irish immigrant merchant, he was born in Southwark, a suburb of Philadelphia, on Sept. 1. He studied law and was admitted to the Pennsylvania bar in 1833 and became involved in politics. He served as city commissioner and was a member of the board of education of his native city, helped found Girls High School of Philadelphia, was a judge of the courts of common pleas and of oyer and terminer in 1840–50 and was defeated in a bid for election to the state Supreme Court, a victim of the anti-Catholic Know Nothing movement, in 1851. He was appointed attorney general of Pennsylvania in 1852 and the following year was appointed Postmaster General of the United States by President Franklin Pierce, whom he had supported in the 1852 presidential election, and served until 1857. When he was defeated in a bid for the United States Senate in 1861 he retired from politics and resumed his law practice. He was president of the board of trustees of Jefferson Medical College for twenty-five years, vice president of St. Joseph's Orphan Asylum for forty-five years and in 1869 was appointed to the Philadelphia County Board of City Trusts which supervised some forty-two institutions in the city, a position he held until his death in Philadelphia on Jan. 27.

CAMPBELL, JAMES MARSHALL (1895–1971), educator. Born in Warsaw, New York, on Sept. 30, he was educated at Hamilton College, Clinton, New York (B.A. 1917), and Princeton, which he left to serve in the 345th Machine Gun Company during World War I in 1918–19. After the war he resumed his studies at Catholic University (M.A. 1920, Ph.D. in Greek 1933) and at Sulpician Seminary, Washington, D.C., in 1922–26, and was ordained for the Baltimore archdiocese in 1926. He began teaching the classics and Greek at Catholic University and taught there the rest of his life, serving as dean of its College of Arts and Sciences in 1934–38, successfully raising its academic standards during those years. He also served as director of Catholic University's Pacific branch, Dominican College, San Rafael, during summer sessions in 1932–70, and was made a monsignor. He was an outstanding Greek and patristic scholar, wrote widely in various scholarly publications, was the author of *The Greek Fathers* (1929), and coauthored with R. J. Deferrari *A Concordance of Prudentius* (1932), and was associate editor of Catholic University's *Patristic Studies.* He died in Washington, D.C. on Mar. 25.

CAMPBELL, THOMAS JOSEPH (1848–1925), educator, author. Born in New York City on Apr. 29, he was educated at St. Francis Xavier College there

(M.A. 1867), joined the Jesuits at Sault-au-Recollect, Canada, and taught at St. John's College (Fordham) for three years. He then continued his studies at Woodstock College, Maryland, returned to St. Francis Xavier to teach in 1876, and then finished his education at Louvain, Belgium, where he was ordained in 1881. He was president of Fordham in 1885–88, provincial of the New York-Maryland Province of the Jesuits in 1885–93, and served as vice-rector of St. Francis Xavier in 1893. He spent the next two years giving retreats and was again president of Fordham in 1896–1900. He joined the staffs of the *Messenger of the Sacred Heart* and the Apostleship of Prayer in 1900, was editor of the Jesuit magazine *America* in 1910–14, and served at St. Francis Xavier Church in 1916 and at St. Joseph's Church, Philadelphia, in 1917. He then returned to Fordham to teach history until 1925 when he retired; he died at Monroe, New York, on Dec. 14. He wrote several books among them the three-volume *Pioneer Priests of North America* (1908–19), the two-volume *Laymen of North America* (1915), and *The Jesuits, 1534–1921* (1921).

CANCER DE BARBASTRO, LUIS (1500–49), missionary. Born in Aragon, Spain, he joined the Dominicans and after his ordination went to Guatemala as a missionary and worked among the Indians of Vera Paz. He became an ardent follower of Bartolomé de Las Casas in the latter's efforts to improve the lot of the Indians and in 1546 vigorously defended Las Casas before a convocation in Mexico City. He returned to Spain and obtained a commission from Emperor Charles V to head a mission to convert the Indians of Florida and in 1549 sailed from Vera Cruz, Mexico, with two other Dominicans, Fr. Diego de Tolosa and Br. Fuentes, and an Indian woman they had met in Havana,

Magdalen, who served as their interpreter. They landed on the shores of Tampa Bay and soon after were betrayed by Magdalen and killed by the Calusa Indians near the site of present-day Tampa, Florida—the first missionary martyrs of the eastern United States. He wrote a catechism in verse in Zapotecan but it has since been lost.

CANEVIN, JOHN FRANCIS REGIS (1852–1927), bishop. Born in Westmoreland County, Pennsylvania, on June 5, he was educated at St. Vincent's Seminary, Latrobe, Pennsylvania, and was ordained in 1879. He was a curate at St. Paul's Cathedral in Pittsburgh in 1881–96, was chancellor of that see in 1888–93, and then served in several parishes until 1903 when he was appointed titular bishop of Sabrata and coadjutor of Pittsburgh. He succeeded to the see in 1904, expanded diocesan facilities to meet the needs caused by a threefold growth in the population of the diocese, actively supported the lay retreat movement, founded the diocesan Sisters of the Holy Ghost and introduced the Confraternity of Christian Doctrine into the see. He resigned in 1920 and was made titular archbishop of Pelusium the following year and died in Pittsburgh on Mar. 22.

CANTWELL, JOHN JOSEPH (1874–1947), archbishop. Born in Limerick, Ireland, on Dec. 1, he was educated at Sacred Heart College there and St. Patrick's College in Thurles and was ordained in 1899. He emigrated to the United States later the same year, served as a curate at St. Joseph's Church, Berkeley, California, in 1899–1904, founded the Newman Club at the University of California, was secretary to Archbishop Patrick Riordan in 1905–14, and was appointed vicar-general of the archdiocese in 1914. Three years later he was named bishop of

Monterey–Los Angeles, was transferred to Los Angeles–San Diego in 1922 when the dioceses of Monterey-Fresno and Los Angeles–San Diego were formed. He was made archbishop of Los Angeles when that see was made an archdiocese and San Diego was established as a separate diocese in 1936. During his episcopate he greatly expanded the educational and charitable facilities of the see, increased the number of parishes, priests, and religious to accommodate the tremendous increase of Catholics in the archdiocese from 177,000 to 600,000, and founded the Los Angeles minor seminary, Our Lady Queen of Angels, in 1926 and its major seminary, St. John's, in 1939. He held synods in 1927 and 1942, worked to better the conditions of aliens, aided exiled Mexican bishops, and helped form cultural guilds and clubs. He was appointed an Assistant at the Pontifical Throne in 1929 and died in Los Angeles on Oct. 30.

CAREY, HENRY CHARLES (1793–1879), economist. Son of Matthew Carey, the publisher, he was born in Philadelphia on Dec. 15, entered his father's publishing business when he was twelve, became a partner in 1817 and later was head of Carey, Lea and Carey which became a leading American publisher. Though never formally educated, he read omnivorously, became knowledgeable in economics, and when he was forty-two decided to devote himself to economics. Early a free trade advocate, he later embraced protectionism, argued in favor of higher wages for higher profits, and decried the Malthusian theory of population and the Ricardian theory of rent. His conversion to protectionism came in 1844 and he became an intense nationalist and anti-British. He exerted great influence on businessmen and young economists in the United States and headed a group that constituted an American school of political economy. He wrote several pamphlets and books which were widely translated and had international influence, among them the three-volume *Principles of Political Economy* (1837, 1838, 1840), *Harmony of Interests: Manufacturing and Commercial* (1851), *Slave Trade, Domestic and Foreign* (1853), and the three-volume *The Principles of Social Science* (1858–59). He died in Philadelphia on Oct. 13.

CAREY, MATTHEW (1760–1839), publisher, author. Son of a well-to-do baker, he was born in Dublin on Jan. 28 and was crippled for life in a fall in France. He decided not to enter the bakery business and when fifteen became a printer's apprentice. In 1779 a pamphlet he published demanding the repeal of the penal code against Catholics caused such a stir he was forced to flee his native land and went to Paris, France. There he met Lafayette, worked in Benjamin Franklin's printing office, and then returned to Ireland. He ran the *Freeman's Journal* in Dublin and founded the *Volunteers Journal,* dedicated to opposing England's subjugation of Ireland. An article violently attacking the English Parliament and the prime minister in 1784 led to his arrest and imprisonment in Newgate Prison. When freed upon the dissolution of the Parliament he left Ireland in disguise and went to the United States where he settled in Philadelphia. With the loan of four hundred dollars donated by Lafayette he founded the *Pennsylvania Herald* in 1785 and built up its circulation by publishing the debates of the Pennsylvania House of Assembly. He actively supported the new constitution and the debate between his paper and Eleazar Oswald's *Independent Gazeteer* on this and other issues, particularly immigration which Oswald opposed, became so bitter he and Oswald fought a duel (despite his opposition to dueling which he had condemned in the first article he had published in the *Hibernian Journal* in 1777) and Carey was seriously wounded. In 1786 he and five of his friends founded the *Columbian Magazine* but disagreements caused him to leave and he founded the *American Museum* in 1787 and built it into the leading magazine of the period. He married Bridget Flahanen in 1791 and the couple had nine children, one of whom was the economist Henry Charles Carey. When the *American Museum,* despite its editorial success, proved a financial failure he left it in 1792 and began an active career as a bookseller and printer. He became the leading publisher of books in the United States. His publication of many books and their wide distribution encouraged authors and stimulated the growth of American letters; he had published the first edition of the Douay version of the bible in 1790. When an epidemic of yellow fever struck Philadelphia in 1793, he was a member of a committee appointed to aid the stricken and wrote a treatise on the disease. In the same year he helped found the Hibernian Society and in 1796 was one of the founders of the Sunday School Society. Active in politics he at first opposed the rechartering of the United States Bank in 1810, but reversed himself when the matter came before Congress. In 1814 he published *The Olive Branch,* his most famous pamphlet, in which he attempted to unite the Federalists and the Republicans in support of the War of 1812 against England. He never gave up his bitter opposition to England's role in Ireland and in 1818 wrote *Vindiciae Hibernicae,* a defense of Irish and Catholic policies and a refutation of the massacres of 1641. He was involved in the schism led by Father William Hogan at St. Mary's parish in Philadelphia in 1819–22 and wrote several pamphlets supporting Hogan's schism but did so anonymously. He was strongly in favor of high tariffs (he founded the Philadelphia Society for the Promotion of National Industry in 1820 but soon left the organization because he felt it was not aggressive enough) and wrote several pamphlets, among them *Essays on Political Economy* (1822), that greatly influenced the debate on the question of tariffs. He also wrote *Essays on Banking* (1816), *An Appeal to the Wealthy of the Land* (1836), and his *Autobiography* which was published in the *New England Magazine* in 1833–34. He died in Philadelphia on Sept. 16.

CAREY, THOMAS (1904–72), theatrical producer. Born in Chicago on June 14, he was educated at Providence College, was professed a Dominican friar in 1926 and was ordained in 1932, and received his Ph.D. from Catholic University in 1935. He served as assistant professor of psychology at Catholic University the next five years, founded the Blackfriars Guild to encourage Catholic drama with fellow Dominican Urban Nagle in Washington, D.C., in 1932, and in 1937 founded the Blackfriars Institute of Dramatic Arts at Catholic University (which developed into its department of speech and drama), and became first secretary of the National Catholic Theater Conference. He was assistant national director of the Holy Name Society in 1940–52, founded (with Fr. Nagle) the Blackfriars Guild Theater in 1941 in New York City to present Catholic dramas and ten years later took over complete direction of the Theater; in twenty-one years he produced forty-three of the seventy-five plays the Guild produced. The Theater closed six weeks before his death in New York City on May 8 when the building housing the theater was torn down.

CARLIN, JAMES JOSEPH (1872–1930), educator. Born in Peabody, Massachusetts, on Apr. 14, he was educated at Boston College and joined the Jesuits in 1892. He taught theology and canon law at Woodstock College, Maryland, in 1904–19, then philosophy at Holy Cross College, and served as assistant to the Maryland provincial. He was appointed president of Holy Cross in 1918 and served in that post until 1925 when he became president of the Ateneo de Manila in the Philippine Islands. He was named superior of the Jesuit mission in the Philippines in 1927 and died in Los Angeles on Oct. 1.

CARMODY, MARTIN HENRY (1872–1950), Supreme Knight. Born in Grand Rapids, Michigan, on Jan. 23, he was educated at Valparaiso Normal College, Indiana, and the University of Michigan (Ph.D. 1899). He was admitted to the Michigan bar in 1901, set up a law practice in Grand Rapids, and became active in Catholic affairs. He was director of the Boys' Activities department of the Knights of Columbus in 1939, oversaw the expenditure of disaster relief funds and headed boys' conferences, camp and guidance projects, and scholarship grants for the Knights. He worked in the Knights of Columbus forty-million-dollar World War I Armed Forces Welfare Program and was a member of President Herbert Hoover's Commission on Social Welfare, Unemployment Relief and Education. He was elected Deputy Supreme Knight in 1909 and Supreme Knight of the Knights of Columbus in 1927, was made a Knight of St. Gregory by Pope Pius XI in 1929, and was honored by several universities and foreign governments. He died in Grand Rapids on Dec. 9.

CARR, THOMAS MATTHEW (1755–1820), founder. Born in Dublin he was baptized Matthew but took the name Thomas when professed in the Augustinians in Dublin in 1772. He studied at the Augustinian House of Studies at Toulouse and was ordained there in 1778. He returned to Dublin, was prior in 1795, and the following year in response to a plea for priests by Bishop John Carroll he went to the United States and settled in Philadelphia. He founded St. Augustine's parish there, engaged in missionary work, was named vicar-general of Pennsylvania east of the Susquehanna River by Carroll in 1799, and helped settle the trustees' schism at Holy Trinity Church in Philadelphia. In 1796 he was appointed superior of the American Augustinian mission with the title vicar-general—thus becoming the founder of the Augustinians in the United States. He opened St. Augustine's Academy in 1811, published the *Spiritual Mirror* in 1812, and died in Philadelphia on Sept. 29.

CARRELL, GEORGE ALOYSIUS (1803–68), bishop. Born in Philadelphia on June 13, he was educated at Mt. St. Mary's College, Emmitsburg, Maryland, and Georgetown, and was ordained in 1827. He engaged in pastoral work in his native city, joined the Jesuits in 1835, and became pastor of St. Francis Xavier Church in Cincinnati. He was appointed first bishop of the newly established diocese of Covington, Kentucky, in 1853 and during the decade and a half he was bishop of Covington saw the number of Catholics in the see triple. He died in Covington on Sept. 25.

CARROLL, CHARLES (1703–83). Son of Charles Carroll, who had emigrated to Maryland to escape the persecution of Catholics in England, he became attorney general and a wealthy landowner (the source of the great wealth of Charles Carroll of Carrollton) under the third Lord Baltimore. He held several positions in the Maryland government and fought anti-Catholic laws. He and Elizabeth Brooke Carroll were the parents of Charles Carroll of Carrollton and he was known as "of Annapolis" to distinguish him from his son and from his father, who was known as "the attorney general."

CARROLL, CHARLES (1737–1832), statesman. Son of Charles Carroll of Annapolis and Elizabeth Brooke Carroll, he was born in Annapolis, Maryland, on Sept. 19, began his schooling when ten at the Jesuit Bohemian Manor Academy, Maryland, where his cousin John, who was to become the first American bishop, was his classmate. In 1748 they were both sent to the Jesuit college at St. Omer, France; after six years there he spent a year at the Jesuit college in Rheims and then continued his studies at Collège Louis le Grand in Paris. He went to Bourges in 1753 to study law, spent a year there and then returned to Paris where he remained until 1757 when he went to London and studied law at the Temple. He returned to the United States in 1765 and was given a ten thousand-acre estate, Carrollton Manor, in Frederick County, Maryland, by his father; from then on he attached the name of his estate to his name to distinguish him from his father. In 1768 he married his cousin Mary Darnall. When trouble developed between the colonies and England he enthusiastically sided with the colonies. In 1770 he became involved in a dispute with the jurist Daniel Dulaney (Dulaney defended taxes levied by the royal Governor Eden for officeholders' fees and stipends for established clergy), arguing in a series of four articles in the *Maryland Gazette* in 1773 under the pen name "First Citizen," which made him well known, that taxes should not be levied without the consent of the people's representatives. He was elected to the Maryland provincial convention in 1774 though Catholics had been disenfranchised in Maryland since it became a royal colony. He was elected a member of the Provincial Committee of Correspondence later the same year, was a member of the 1775 committee that formed the Maryland Association of the Freeman which adopted a charter and pledged armed resistance to England. He was elected a deputy to the state convention in 1775 and strongly opposed its instructions to the Maryland delegation to the Continental Congress to oppose independence for the colonies and advocated independence. In 1776, he, Benjamin Franklin, and Samuel Chase were appointed a committee of three to go to Canada to try and secure Canada's alliance in the quest for independence for the American colonies; his cousin John, now a priest, accompanied the mission but it failed. His journal is one of the principal sources of information about the mission. On June 28, 1776, largely through his efforts, Maryland instructed its delegates to the Continental Congress to vote for independence. He was elected to the Continental Congress in July and was the first to sign the Declaration of Independence adding his usual "of Carrollton" to his signature so there could be no doubt which Carroll was signing. At that time he was one of the wealthiest men in the colonies and was risking his all in supporting and fighting for independence. On July 19, he was appointed to the Board of War which had charge of the military and with several others foiled the Conway Cabal to displace Washington as commander of the Continental Army. It was mainly through his efforts and example that American Catholics overwhelmingly supported the Revolution. He helped draw up Maryland's constitution as one of a committee of seven appointed by the Maryland colonial convention to do so and resigned from the Continental Congress in 1778 to become a senator in the Maryland Senate; he again resigned from the Continental Congress when reelected in 1780. He served in the Maryland Senate in 1787–89, serving twice as its president, became a leader of the Federalist Party, and was elected Maryland's first senator to the United States Senate in 1789. He supported Alexander Hamilton's economic policies and favored a strong central government. He resigned his Senate seat in 1792 when Congress passed a law forbidding a person to serve simultaneously in the United States Senate and in a state legislature preferring to continue in the Maryland Senate where he served until 1800. He was a member of the committee that settled a boundary dispute between Maryland and Virginia in 1799, opposed Jefferson's election in 1800 and the war with England in 1812, but practically retired from public affairs the last three decades of his life except for his comments on public matters. He died at Doughoregan Manor near Baltimore on Nov. 14, the last surviving signer of the Declaration of Independence. In 1901 his statue was placed in Statuary Hall in the Capitol in Washington, D.C., as Maryland's representative in this assemblage of distinguished Americans.

CARROLL, COLEMAN F. (1905–77), archbishop. Born in Pittsburgh, he was educated at Duquesne University there and St. Vincent's Seminary, Latrobe, Pennsylvania, and was ordained in 1930. He engaged in parish work in 1930–41, received his J.C.D. from Catholic University in 1944, was named pastor of Sacred Heart Church in Pittsburgh in 1951, and was made a domestic prelate the following year. He was appointed titular bishop of Pitanae and auxiliary of Pittsburgh in 1953 and became first bishop of the newly created diocese of Miami in 1958; he was made

Miami's first archbishop in 1968 when it was elevated to an archdiocese. He died of complications from a vascular disease on July 28 in Miami Beach.

CARROLL, DANIEL (1730–96), statesman. Son of Daniel Carroll, an immigrant from Ireland, and well-to-do and educated Eleanor Darnall, and brother of Archbishop John Carroll, he was born in Upper Marlboro, Maryland, on July 22. He was educated abroad in Flanders and on his return to the United States married Elizabeth Carroll and lived the life of a country gentleman, becoming wealthy through his plantation, merchant business, and tobacco farming. He actively supported the colonists against England and early favored independence for the colonies despite strong opposition in Maryland. He was a member of the Maryland Senate and Council in 1777–80 and of the Maryland delegation to the Continental Congress in 1780–84, and was a delegate from Maryland to the Constitutional Convention in 1787–88, one of the two Catholics in that body (the other was Thomas Fitz-Simons of Pennsylvania). He helped have the Constitution adopted in Maryland, served in the House of Representatives in the new Congress in 1789–91, and was a firm believer in a strong central government that should have control of western lands, in religious toleration in all states, and that powers not delegated to the federal government were reserved to the people. He was one of the three members of the commission appointed by Congress to select a new site for the seat of the federal government and favored the present site of Washington, D.C. (he owned one of the four farms that were purchased to make up the District of Columbia), and laid the cornerstone for the new Capitol in 1791. He died in Rock Creek, Maryland, on May 7.

CARROLL, HOWARD JOSEPH (1902–60), bishop. Born in Pittsburgh on Aug. 5, he was educated at Duquesne University there and St. Vincent's College, Latrobe, Pennsylvania, and received his S.T.D. in 1928 from the University of Fribourg, Switzerland, where he had been ordained in 1927. He was a curate at Sacred Heart Church in Pittsburgh in 1928–38 and served as assistant general secretary of the National Catholic Welfare Conference (NCWC) in 1938–44. During World War II he served on the board of directors of the United Service Organizations (USO) and as chairman of its overseas committee and was secretary of the board of trustees of National Catholic Community Services. He was appointed general secretary of the NCWC in 1944, serving until 1957, and was made a papal chamberlain in 1942 and a domestic prelate in 1945. He was appointed first bishop of the newly established diocese of Altoona, Pennsylvania, in 1957 and undertook a widespread building program that included Blessed Sacrament Cathedral in Altoona which he consecrated in 1958. He died in Washington, D.C., on Mar. 21.

CARROLL, JOHN (1735–1815), archbishop. Third son of Daniel Carroll, an Irish immigrant merchant, and Eleanor Darnall, he was born in Upper Marlboro, Maryland, on Jan. 8. He was sent when he was twelve to be educated at the Jesuit Bohemia Manor School, Maryland, where his cousin Charles Carroll was a classmate and in 1748 was sent, with Charles, to study at the Jesuit college in St. Omer, France. His father died in 1750 and three years later he joined the Jesuits. He made his theological and philosophy studies at Liège, Belgium, and was ordained in 1769. He taught at St. Omer and Liège, traveled throughout Europe in 1771–73 as tutor of the son of Lord Stourton and when the Jesuits were suppressed in 1773 he became family chaplain to Lord Arundell at Wardour Castle, England. He returned to Maryland in 1774 and settled on his mother's estate at Rock Creek near Georgetown where he built a small private chapel (Catholic churches were forbidden by law) and spent the next two years in study and serving the Catholics in Maryland and nearby Virginia. He ardently supported the American Revolution and in 1776 he accompanied his cousin Charles, Benjamin Franklin, and Samuel Chase on a fruitless mission from the Continental Congress to Quebec to secure an alliance with Canada in the colonists' war with England or at least the promise of Canadian neutrality. In 1783 he and five priests met, drafted a set of regulations governing the activities of Catholics in the United States and petitioned the Holy See to appoint a superior for the United States and recommended Carroll for that position; the following year Pope Pius VI appointed Carroll superior of the missions in the United States with some of the powers of a bishop including that of confirmation. In the same year he answered an attack on the Church by a Protestant minister, Charles Henry Wharton, an ex-Jesuit, that impugned the loyalty of American Catholics with "An Address to the Roman Catholics of the United States of America," arguing for religious toleration, the first work on Catholicism by an American Catholic published in the United States. In 1786 he moved to Baltimore at Old St. Peter's Church and became a popular figure in the community, active in municipal affairs. He was president of the Female Humane Charity School of Baltimore, one of the three trustees of St. John's College in Annapolis, helped found Georgetown in 1791, and was cofounder of the Maryland Historical Society. He urged Congress to protect religious freedom in the new nation. It is in no small measure due to his efforts that the provision prohibiting any religious test for candidates for any public office in the United States was included in Article 6, Section 3 of the Constitution and that the freedom of religion clause was included in the First Amendment. In 1788, a gathering of twenty-five priests petitioned the Holy See to appoint a bishop for the United States (twenty-four of them voted for Carroll) and the following year Pope Pius VI appointed him the first American bishop in the United States and the first see was established in Baltimore. He held the first national synod in Baltimore in 1791, invited the Sulpicians to Baltimore (they began what was to become St. Mary's College and Seminary), interceded with Washington for a more humane treatment of Indians in 1792, and in 1798 won the famous Fromm Case, which resulted from the trustee controversy plaguing the Church, in which his sole episcopal jurisdiction over all Catholic churches in the United States was affirmed. He conferred episcopal orders for the first time in the United States on his coadjutor, Leonard Neale, in 1800 and in 1806 laid the cornerstone of the cathedral in Baltimore. He was named archbishop in 1808 (when Baltimore was made an archdiocese) with New York, Philadelphia, Boston, and Bardstown, Kentucky, as suffragan sees and in 1810 held the first Provincial Council that drew up a list of regulations for the clergy and laity of the United States. The decrees of this council and the first synod of Baltimore in 1791 provided the first codification of canon law in the United States. Carroll had a genius for organization and under his leadership were propounded the principles and rules that became the cornerstone of the Catholic Church in the United States and led to its future incredible expansion. He was deeply committed to providing religious education for his fellow religionists and was also known as a patron of public education as well. He encouraged religious orders in Europe to establish foundations in the United States and encouraged new foundations, notably the Sisters of Charity of St. Joseph, founded in no small measure because of his encouragement of its founder, St. Elizabeth Ann Seton. Throughout his episcopate he was faced with the problems posed by itinerant priests from Europe, who disputed his jurisdiction, and trustee disputes particularly those in Norfolk, Virginia, Charleston, South Carolina, and Augusta, Georgia, where Irish priests sided with the trustees against him. He was devoted to religious freedom and tolerance, was a friend of the American leaders of his time—Benjamin Franklin, George Washington, and Thomas Jefferson among them—and set an example for future prelates in the Church in the United States in Church relations with the state. The American Catholic Church as we know it today has its roots in its greatest churchman, John Carroll. He died in Baltimore on Dec. 3.

CARROLL, JOHN PATRICK (1864–1925), bishop. Born in Dubuque, Iowa, on Feb. 22, he was educated at St. Joseph's College (later Loras) there and the Grand Seminary, Montreal, and was ordained in 1889. He became a professor of philosophy at St. Joseph's, was appointed its president in 1894, and was made a domestic prelate in 1902. He was famed for his oratory, and in 1904 he was appointed second bishop of Helena, Montana. During his bishopric, he built schools and a new cathedral, which he consecrated in 1924, began construction of Mount St. Charles College (later changed to Carroll College in his honor), and was national chaplain of the Ancient Order of Hibernians in 1910 and 1912. He died in Fribourg, Switzerland, on Nov. 4.

CARSON, CHRISTOPHER (KIT)
(1809–68), frontiersman. Born in Madison County, Kentucky, on Dec. 24, he was taken to the Missouri frontier by his parents when he was a child of two. After the death of his father in 1818 he was apprenticed to a saddler in 1825, an outfitting post on the Santa Fe Trail. He ran away in 1826 with a caravan bound for Santa Fe and continued into Taos, New Mexico, which he made his home and headquarters. In the next few years he worked as a teamster, cook, guide, and hunter for exploring parties and made a reputation with his skill as a guide, scout, and hunter. He was a guide for J. C. Frémont's western expeditions in 1842 (to the Rocky Mountains), in 1843–44 (to Oregon and California), and in 1845 (to California). Frémont's reports of his courage and prowess as a guide and a hunter made him a legend on the western frontier. He carried dispatches to Washington, D.C., from Los Angeles when the latter city was captured in 1846 by American settlers who had revolted against Mexican rule; on the way he met the troops of General Stephen Kearny who commanded him to guide his forces to California. When Kearny's troops were surrounded by Mexican forces in California, Carson and two others made a daring escape through enemy lines at night and brought aid from San Diego. He carried dispatches to the East in 1847 and 1848 and then decided to retire to a sheep ranch but continued as an Indian fighter when Indian forays and depredations continued. In 1853 he was appointed U.S. Indian agent for the Utes and Apaches with headquarters at Taos and filled the position with great success. During the Civil War he commanded the 1st New Mexican Volunteers of the Union Army and led them in campaigns in the Southwest against the Apache, Navaho, and Comanche Indians in New Mexico and Texas. He

was brevetted a brigadier general in 1865 and was commander of Fort Garland, Colorado, in 1866–67. His autobiography, *Kit Carson's Own Story of His Life,* which he dictated to Lt. Col. De Witt C. Peters as he was illiterate until late in life, was published in 1858. At the time of his death at Fort Lyon, near Boggsville, Colorado, on May 23, he had become a legendary figure—Kit Carson, guide, hunter, Indian fighter extraordinaire.

CARTIER, JACQUES (1491–1557), explorer. Little is known of his childhood and youth beyond that he was born in St. Malo, Brittany, probably on Dec. 31. He may have crossed the Atlantic before 1519 (in which year he held the title of master pilot of the King of Spain and married Marie Katherine des Granches, daughter of the high constable of St. Malo) and in 1527 he may have voyaged to Brazil for the Portuguese. In 1534 he was commissioned by Philippe de Chabot, Admiral of France, at the express command of King Francis I, to explore the possibility of a northern route to China and set out with two small ships. In his four-month voyage he sailed along the coast of Newfoundland to Cape Anguille, discovered the Magdalen Islands and Prince Edward Island, continued along the coast of New Brunswick, explored Chaleur Bay, sailed around the Gaspé and landed at Gaspé where he claimed possession of the land for France. The following year the king sent him on a second expedition. He set out with three vessels, explored the St. Lawrence River as far as the present site of Montreal, spent the winter near present-day Quebec, and then returned to France in 1536, bringing several Indians back with him. He made a third voyage to Canada in 1541–42 under the aegis of Sieur de Roberval to head a colonizing plan and wintered at the entrance to

Cap Rouge River. When the Sieur did not appear in the spring with the colonizing party, Cartier sailed for France. On the way he met Roberval and his party but refused to return to Canada with him and continued on his way back to France. In 1543 he led his fourth expedition to rescue Roberval's party but no record of this, his last expedition, has survived. He retired to his manor of Limoilou near St. Malo which the king had given him and remained there until his death on Sept. 1. A description of his third voyage, *Brief récit et succincte narration* was published in 1545. Cartier's primary goal in his expeditions was to discover a Northwest Passage. He failed in this quest but made important geographical discoveries and most important of all his explorations laid the foundations for France's claims in the New World—claims that were to lead to the struggle between France and England which had such an impact on the future development of Canada and the United States.

CASE, ANNA (1893–1984), singer. Born in Clinton, New Jersey, on Oct. 29, she studied under Madame Renard in New York City and made her debut at the Metropolitan Opera as a page in Wagner's *Lohengrin* in 1919, the only American singer without European training to be accepted by the Metropolitan up to that time. Among the operas she appeared in were Bizet's *Carmen,* Verdi's *Aida,* Smetana's *Bartered Bride,* and Mozart's *Magic Flute;* she also traveled extensively in the United States and abroad giving concerts. In 1931 she became a Catholic, married Clarence H. Mackay, chairman of the board of Postal Telegraph Cable Company, the same year and announced her retirement from opera and the concert stage. She died in New York City after a long illness on Jan. 7.

CASEY, LAWRENCE B. (1905–77), bishop. Born in Rochester, New York, on Sept. 6, he was educated at St. Andrew's Seminary (1919–24) and St. Bernard's Seminary (1924–30) there and was ordained in 1930. He served as vice-chancellor of the Rochester diocese in 1932–46, was pastor of Holy Cross Church in 1946–52 and of Sacred Heart Cathedral in 1952–56, was vicar-general of the diocese in 1953–56, and was appointed titular bishop of Cea and auxiliary of Rochester in 1953. He was named bishop of Paterson, New Jersey, in 1966 and died there on June 15. His statements on the Church's position in the Karen Quinlan case were widely publicized.

CASEY, SOLANUS (1870–1957). One of sixteen children of an Irish immigrant couple, Bernard Francis Casey was born in Oak Park, Wisconsin, on Nov. 25. He was raised on a farm, left school when sixteen to help his family and subsequently worked as a lumberjack, a streetcar motorman, and a prison guard. He entered Milwaukee's archdiocesan seminary to study for the priesthood but was forced to leave because of difficulties with the courses which were taught in Latin and German. Sometime later while working as a streetcar motorman in Superior, Wisconsin, he again felt he had a religious vocation, wrote to several religious orders, and was accepted by the Capuchins, entering the Capuchin novitiate in Detroit in 1896. Again he had difficulty in his studies there and also in Milwaukee where he was sent the following year when he found the teaching in the novitiate was in Latin and German, but he persisted and in 1904 he was ordained a simple priest without faculties to preach or to hear confessions. Assigned to Sacred Heart parish in Yonkers, New York, he served as doorkeeper and sacristan and became known for his ministry to the sick. After fourteen years at Sacred Heart, he spent the next three years at Our Lady of Angels parish in Harlem in New York City and in 1924 was sent to St. Bonaventure Friary in Detroit where he served as doorkeeper for three decades. He became widely known in Detroit for his charity and his ministry to the needy and the sick and had miracles attributed to him. He was sent to St. Felix Friary, Huntington, Indiana, and became known there for his compassion and aid to the sick and destitute, returned to Detroit in 1956 and died there on July 31. Always serving in menial positions, his charity and concern for those who sought his aid became legendary and in 1982 the introduction of his cause for beatification was approved by Pope John Paul II.

CASSERLY, EUGENE (1822–83), U.S. senator. Son of Patrick S. Casserly, he was born in Mullingar, Westmeath, Ireland, on Nov. 13 and was brought to the United States, studied at Georgetown and on graduating studied law and was admitted to the bar in 1844. He was editor of *Freeman's Journal* for a time, was corporation counsel in New York City in 1846–47, moved to California in 1850 and became involved in politics. He was publisher of the *Public Balance,* the *True Balance,* and the *Standard,* was elected U.S. senator from California in 1869 but four years later resigned his seat and returned to private law practice in San Francisco where he died on June 14.

CASSIDY, JAMES EDWIN (1869–1951), bishop. Born in Woonsocket, Rhode Island, on Aug. 1, he was educated at St. Charles College, Ellicott City, Maryland, St. Mary's Seminary and Johns Hopkins, Baltimore, and was ordained in 1898. He taught at New York's archdiocesan seminary, St. Joseph's, Yonkers, New York, in 1896–99, engaged in pastoral work in Fall River, Massachusetts, becoming pastor of St. Patrick's Church there, and became vicar-general of the Fall River diocese in 1909. He was appointed titular bishop of Ibora and auxiliary of Fall River in 1930 and became apostolic administrator of the see later the same year. He was appointed coadjutor in 1934 and two weeks later, on the death of Bishop Daniel F. Feehan, succeeded to the see. He remained as bishop of Fall River until his death there on May 17.

CASSIDY, WILLIAM (1815–73), journalist. Born in Albany, New York, on Aug. 12, he was educated at Albany Academy and Union College from which he graduated in 1833. He studied law and in 1843 was appointed state librarian. He became editor of the Albany *Argus* and then of the *Atlas* when the two were merged, was a member of the New York state constitutional convention in 1871, and was appointed to the commission to revise the New York State constitution the following year. He died in Albany on Jan. 23.

CASTAÑEDA, CARLOS EDUARDO (1896–1956), educator. Born in Camargo, Mexico, on Nov. 11, he was educated at the University of Mexico (M.A., Ph.D.), William and Mary College, and the University of Texas. He taught Spanish at William and Mary in 1923–26 and history at the University of Texas in the summers of 1923–26 and then at the University of Mexico, and in 1946 became a professor of history at the University of Texas; he remained in that position until his death in Austin, Texas, on Apr. 5. He was an authority on Texan history and was the author of the monumental seven-volume *Our Catholic Heritage in Texas, 1519–1950*

(1936–58), *The Mexican Side of the Texan Revolution* (1928), *Early Texas Album* (1930), and *The Finding of Texas* (1939). He was president of the American Catholic Historical Association in 1939–40, served as librarian at the University of Texas, was regional director of the Fair Employment Practices Committee in the Southwest during World War II, and was honored by the papacy, Spain, and several universities.

CATALÁ MAGIN *See* Magin, Catalá.

CATALDO, JOSEPH MARY (1837–1928), missionary. Born in Terracina, Italy, on Mar. 17, he joined the Jesuits in 1852 and was ordained in Liège, Belgium, ten years later. He emigrated to the United States two days after his ordination and continued his studies at Santa Clara College in California while also teaching there. In 1865–77 he worked as a missionary among the Indians of the Northwest, was appointed superior of the Rocky Mountain mission in 1877, and sent missionaries to the Indians in Montana, Wyoming, Washington, Oregon, and Alaska. In 1883, he founded Gonzaga College, Spokane, Washington, and in 1892 approved the founding of Immaculate Conception College, Seattle, Washington. He was replaced as superior in 1893 and spent the rest of his life ministering to the Indians of Montana, Oregon, Alaska, and Idaho where he labored among the Nez Percé Indians at St. Joseph's mission at Slickpoo (Culdesac) for many years. He was proficient in eight Indian languages and wrote a grammar, a prayer book, and a life of Christ in the Nez Percé language. He died at Pendleton, Oregon, on Apr. 9.

CAVANAGH, JAMES (1831–1901), general. Born in Tipperary, Ireland, he emigrated to the United States when he was sixteen and became a carpenter in New York City. He enlisted as a private in the 69th Regiment of the militia and was captain of Company C when the Civil War broke out and the regiment was mobilized. After the Battle of Bull Run the regiment was reorganized as the 69th Volunteers of the Irish Brigade with Cavanagh as major. He was wounded at Fredericksburg and was dismissed from the Army because of a disability resulting from the wound. After the war, when the state militia was reorganized as the National Guard, he rejoined the regiment, was made its lieutenant colonel, and in 1867 was elected its colonel. He was brevetted brigadier general in 1893—the first officer of the New York state militia to receive that rank. He retired from the military in 1894 and resumed the position of special customs inspector in New York which he had occupied for several years previously. He died in New York City on Jan. 7.

CAVANAGH, JOHN B. (1908–83), editor. Born in Boness, Scotland, on Sept. 8, he emigrated to the United States, was educated at Catholic University (B.A. 1931, M.A. 1933) and at St. Thomas Seminary, Denver, Colorado, and was ordained in Denver in 1936. He became an associate editor on the *National Catholic Register* in 1936, circulation manager in 1940, and managing director in 1943–60; during his tenure the *Register* group had thirty-two separate diocesan editions. He was made a papal chamberlain in 1949 and a domestic prelate in 1959, became editor and business manager of the *Register* in 1960, retired from the *Register* in 1966, and was pastor of St. Joseph's Church, Fort Collins, Colorado, in 1967–81. He died in Denver of a heart ailment on June 5.

CAVANAUGH, JOHN JOSEPH (1899–1979), educator. Born in Owosso, Michigan, he was educated at Notre

Dame where he was secretary to the president in 1917–19 after he graduated and then went to work for the Studebaker Corporation in South Bend, Indiana, in 1923. He rose to assistant advertising manager in 1926 and then resigned to study for the priesthood. He joined the Congregation of Holy Cross in 1926, resumed his studies at Notre Dame and received his M.A. in 1927. He continued his studies at Catholic University (Ph.L. 1931), was ordained in 1931, and then spent a year at the Gregorian in Rome. He returned to Notre Dame, was prefect of religion there in 1933–38, and in 1940 was named assistant provincial of his Congregation and vice president of Notre Dame. He became president in 1946 and during his six-year term devoted himself to raising academic standards at Notre Dame and reshaping the university curriculum and administration to meet the changing times and the requirements of a quadrupled student body. In 1952–58 he was director of the Notre Dame University Foundation, which initiated a distinguished professors' program, and headed fund-raising campaigns. After this he served in the campus religious ministry at Holy Cross, Worcester, Massachusetts, then returned to Notre Dame where he lived on the campus and died there on Dec. 28.

CHABRAT, GUY IGNATIUS (1787–1868), bishop. Born in Chambres, Cantal, France, on Dec. 28, he studied at St. Fleur Seminary, went to the United States in 1809, and continued his studies at St. Thomas Seminary, Bardstown, Kentucky. He joined the Sulpicians and was ordained by Bishop Flaget in 1811, the first priest to be ordained west of the Alleghenies. He worked as a missionary in Kentucky, was appointed superior of the Congregation of the Sisters of Loretto in 1824, a post he held until 1846, and in 1834

was appointed titular bishop of Bolina and coadjutor of Bardstown. He administered the see in 1835–39 but never succeeded to it (Bishop Flaget did not die until 1850), was stricken with blindness in 1847, resigned and returned to France, and died there on Nov. 21 at Mauriac.

CHAMPLAIN, SAMUEL DE (c. 1567–1635), explorer. Son of Antoine Champlain, a mariner, and Marguerite Le Roy, he was born in Brouage, Saintonge (Charente Inférieur). He was educated by the parish priest, accompanied his father on several voyages in his youth, and when twenty became a soldier under Maréchal d'Aumont in an expedition against the Huguenots. He gave up the military to pursue a seafaring life, went to Spain in 1598 and was given command of the *St. Julien*, a vessel in the annual flotilla sent by Spain to the West Indies. He was gone for thirty-two months and explored the Gulf of Mexico, keeping a journal of his explorations which was published as *Bref Discours* and which suggested the possibility of connecting the Atlantic and Pacific oceans with a canal across the isthmus of Panama. On his return to France in 1601 or 1602 he was appointed royal geographer to King Henry IV. In 1603 he accompanied a fur-trading expedition, sponsored by Aymer de Chastes, to New France, explored the St. Lawrence River to Sault St. Louis, selected Quebec as a site for a future settlement and returned to France the same year, describing his experiences in *Des Sauvages.* The following year he went to Acadia as geographer and historian of a party under Pierre du Guast, Sieur de Monts, who had been granted the trading patent held by de Chastes, and explored the area between the island of Sainte Croix and Port Royal (Annapolis, Nova Scotia). During the next three years he explored the New England coast as far south as Martha's Vineyard and made the first detailed charts of the coast. When de Monts's charter was revoked the colony was abandoned in 1608. Champlain persuaded King Henry IV to permit him to found a colony on the St. Lawrence and he returned with a group of colonists and erected a fort on the site that became Quebec—the first permanent French colony in America. The following year he accompanied a Huron war party in an attack on the Iroquois; in the ensuing battle near Crown Point, New York, the Iroquois were defeated and became the implacable foes of the French—an event that was to have great consequences in the future for France in the struggle that developed between France and England for North America. On this trip Champlain also discovered the lake in northern New York that bears his name. On his return to France in 1610, he entered into a marriage contract with twelve-year-old Hélène Boulle who came to Quebec in 1616 and lived there until 1620; they later separated and she entered a French convent. In 1611 he continued his exploration of the St. Lawrence River and founded a settlement at La Place Royale which in time developed into Montreal; he named the island opposite Ste. Hélène for his wife. He returned to France in 1612 and received the fur trade monopoly of New France. On his return to the New World he set out for the western lakes but only reached Allumette Island in the Ottawa River. In 1615, with Étienne Brulé, he accompanied a party of Hurons to Georgian Bay, a northeastern extension of Lake Huron, and returned southeastward by Lake Ontario, penetrating as far south as Oneida Lake. While attacking an Iroquois stronghold, probably on Nichols Cove, Madison County, New York, with a party of Hurons, they were repulsed and he was severely wounded and spent the winter with the Hurons.

This was the last of his explorations (though later he sent Jean Nicolet on a westward expedition in 1634 that became the basis for French claims to territory as far west as Wisconsin). During the next few years he sought colonists for settlements in the new country and finally persuaded Richelieu to form the Company of One Hundred Associates which sent more settlers in 1627. He was forced to surrender Quebec to an English fleet in 1629 and was taken prisoner. When the colony was restored to France by the treaty of Saint-Germain-en-Laye in 1632, Champlain returned to Quebec as governor the following year and spent the rest of his life there. He died in Quebec on Dec. 25. Champlain is known as the founder of New France and his explorations and settlements provided France with her claims to the New World.

CHANCHE, JOHN MARY JOSEPH (1795–1852), bishop. Born in Baltimore on Oct. 5, he was educated at St. Mary's College and joined the Sulpicians there and was ordained in 1819. He taught at St. Mary's, was appointed its president in 1835, and five years later was named first bishop of the newly created diocese of Natchez-Jackson, Mississippi. He built a cathedral which he dedicated in 1842, worked to build up his diocese, and was active in missionary work among the blacks of his see. He attended the first Plenary Council of Baltimore in 1852 and died later that year in Frederick, Maryland, on July 22.

CHANDLER, JOSEPH RIPLEY (1792–1880), journalist. Born in Kingston, Massachusetts, on Aug. 25, he was educated at the University of Pennsylvania, taught for a time, and in 1815 opened a school for young ladies in Philadelphia. He became an editorial writer for the *Gazette of the United States* in 1822 and four years later with two friends purchased the magazine. He was its editor until 1847 when he was forced to relinquish his post because of ill health; he was also editor of *Graham's American Monthly Magazine of Literature, Art and Fashion* in 1843–49. A Mason from his youth he became Grand Master of the Masons in Philadelphia in 1849 and in that year became a Catholic. He served as a member of the Philadelphia common council in 1832–48, was a delegate to the state constitutional convention in 1837, and was president of the first board of trustees of Girard College in Philadelphia in 1848. He was elected to the House of Representatives in 1849 and served three terms and was an active defender of the rights of Catholics. His brilliant speech in the House of Representatives in 1855, "The Temporal Power of the Pope," attacking the move to deny the full rights of citizenship to Catholics and his oration the same year celebrating the landing "of the Pilgrims in Maryland" were later published in book form. He was United States minister to the Kingdom of the Two Sicilies in 1858–61 and on his return to the United States became involved in philanthropic enterprises, among them the reform of prison conditions, writing several essays advancing his theories. He was the author of the widely used *A Grammar of the English Language* (1821, rev. 1848) and a novel *The Beverly Family* (1875) and died in Philadelphia on July 10.

CHAPELLE, PLACIDE LOUIS (1842–1905), archbishop. Born in Runes, Lozèr, France, on Aug. 28, he was educated at Mende, France, and Enghien, Belgium, emigrated to the United States when he was seventeen, and studied for the priesthood at St. Mary's Seminary, Baltimore, where he received his S.T.D. He was ordained in 1865, served as assistant at St. Joseph's Church and then as pastor of St. John's Church, Baltimore, and from 1869 of St. Joseph's Church. He was Archbishop Spalding's theologian at Vatican I in 1870 and in 1882 was assigned to St. Matthew's Church in Washington as pastor. In 1891 he was named titular bishop of Arabissus and coadjutor to Bishop J. B. Salpointe of Sante Fe, was promoted to the titular archiepiscopate of Sebaste in 1893, and succeeded to the Santa Fe see as its third archbishop in 1894; three years later he was transferred to New Orleans. He was appointed apostolic delegate to Cuba and Puerto Rico and envoy extraordinary to the Philippines in 1898. While in Paris during the signing of the Treaty of Paris ending the Spanish-American War in 1898 he was instrumental in having a clause inserted in the treaty confirming the rights of the Catholic Church to its properties as recognized by the Spanish Government in those territories ceded to the United States by Spain. He was appointed apostolic delegate to the Philippines in 1899, went there in 1900, secured the release of priests and religious held by the rebel leader Emilio Aguinaldo, reorganized the Church in the Philippines, and helped insure a peaceful transition from Spanish to American rule. In appreciation of his work he was named an Assistant at the Pontifical Throne and Count of the Holy Roman Empire. After a visit to Cuba he returned to New Orleans and was planning a visitation of the parishes in Louisiana when he was stricken with yellow fever in the epidemic then wracking the city and died there on Aug. 9.

CHARLEVOIX, PIERRE FRANÇOIS XAVIER DE (1682–1761), explorer, historian. Born in St. Quentin, France, on Oct. 24, he joined the Jesuits in 1698, studied at Collège de Louis le Grand in 1700–4, and went to Quebec in 1705. He spent four years teaching grammar at the Jesuit college there but was recalled in 1709 to teach at Louis le Grand. In 1720 he returned to Canada to explore the West, to visit Jesuit missions, and to seek a new route to the western sea. From Quebec he proceeded by canoe up the St. Lawrence River and through the Great Lakes, continued along the eastern shore of Lake Michigan, reached the Illinois River and then descended the Mississippi to its mouth which he reached in 1722; he attempted to go from there to Santo Domingo but was forced to abandon the expedition when his ship was wrecked in the Gulf of Mexico. He returned to the Mississippi via the coast of Florida, later reached Santo Domingo, and then returned to France. After a trip to Italy, he spent twenty-two years (1733–55) as an editor of the monthly journal of history and science, *Mémoires de Trévoux.* He died at La Flèche on Feb. 1. He wrote several historical works among them a three-volume history of Japan (1736), a life of Mère Marie of the Incarnation (1724), a two-volume history of Santo Domingo (1730), and the multivolume *Histoire et description générale de la Nouvelle France* (1744); an appendix contains a detailed account of his expedition, an invaluable historical record and the only complete description of the interior of America in the first third of the eighteenth century.

CHARTRAND, JOSEPH (1870–1933), bishop. Born in St. Louis on May 11, he was educated at the University of St. Louis and at St. Meinrad Seminary in Indiana and was ordained in Minneapolis in 1892. He engaged in pastoral work in that diocese, was named vicar-general in 1910, and later that year was appointed titular bishop of Flavia and coadjutor of Indianapolis, Indiana. He succeeded to the see in 1918, was transferred to Cincinnati in 1925, but requested and was granted permission to remain in Indianapolis where he died on Dec. 8. During his episcopate numerous schools were built, charitable and religious institutions were founded, and an extensive program of parish building was undertaken.

CHATARD, FRANCIS SILAS (1834–1918), bishop. Son of a physician, he was born in Baltimore on Dec. 13, was educated at Mt. St. Mary's College, Emmitsburg, Maryland, graduated in 1853, and then studied medicine at the University of Maryland. He received his medical degree in 1856 and began to practice but decided the religious life was what he wanted and studied for the priesthood at the Urban College in Rome. He was ordained in Rome in 1862, received his doctorate in divinity in 1863 and in the same year was appointed vice-rector of the American College; he became prorector in 1868 and rector in 1871. He was made a papal chamberlain in 1875 and three years later was appointed bishop of Vincennes, Indiana. He held synods in 1878, 1881, 1886, and 1891, built schools and charitable institutions, established forty-seven new parishes and missions, and moved the see to Indianapolis in 1898, at which time the name of the diocese was changed from Vincennes to Indianapolis, and built the new SS. Peter and Paul Cathedral. He died in Indianapolis on Sept. 7.

CHAVEZ, DENNIS (1888–1962), U.S. senator. Son of David Chavez, a poor farmer-laborer, and Paz Sanchez Chavez, Dionisio was born in Los Chavez, New Mexico, and was brought to Albuquerque by his parents when he was a child. He left school, where his name had been changed to Dennis, in the eighth grade to become a grocery delivery boy and married Imelda Espinosa in 1911. He was assistant engineer in the Albuquerque engineering department in 1905–15 and in 1916 was Spanish interpreter during the reelection campaign of Senator Andribus A. Jones who appointed him a clerk in the U.S. Senate in 1918–19. He passed a special examination to be admitted to Georgetown, studied law, and received his LL.B. in 1920 when he was thirty-two and began practicing law in Albuquerque. He became active in Democratic politics, served in the New Mexico House of Representatives in 1923–24, and was elected to the U.S. House of Representatives in 1930 and reelected in 1932, serving as chairman of the Indian Affairs Committee. He was defeated in a bid for the U.S. Senate by Bronson F. Cutting in 1934 but when Cutting was killed in a plane crash the following year Chavez was appointed to fill his unexpired term. He was elected senator in 1936 and reelected in 1940, 1946, 1952, and 1958. In the Senate he supported New Deal measures and labor-backed legislation, was active in developing the resources of the West and in Latin American affairs, was an advocate of the Good Neighbor policy to Latin America, fought for a permanent Fair Employment Practices Commission, and was a champion of the Indians and Puerto Ricans. He died in Washington, D.C., on Nov. 18, and in 1966 his statue was placed in the Capitol in Washington, D.C., to represent New Mexico.

CHEVERUS, JEAN LOUIS LEFEBVRE DE (1768–1836), cardinal. Born in Mayenne, France, on Jan. 28, he was educated at Collège Louis le Grand and St. Magloire Seminary in Paris and was ordained in 1790. He served as assistant to his uncle in Mayenne and succeeded him as pastor. When he refused to take the oath demanded by the leaders of the French Revolution, he barely escaped with his life to London in 1792. When he received a letter in 1796 from his friend Fr. Francis Matignon, a pastor in Bos-

ton, telling of the desperate need for priests there, he went to the United States and offered his services to Bishop John Carroll who assigned him to New England. He traveled all over New England working as a missionary among the Indians, ministering to Catholics in remote areas, nursing the sick during yellow fever epidemics, built a church in Boston, and became an American citizen. His reputation for learning, tolerance, holiness, and charity made him one of the most popular clergymen in New England even among Protestants who often invited him to preach in their pulpits. He was appointed first bishop of Boston in 1808 and remained in that position until 1823 when ill health caused him to request to be allowed to return to France. He was transferred to Montauban in France, was made archbishop of Bordeaux in 1826, and in 1836 he was made a cardinal. He died in Bordeaux on July 19.

CHRISTIE, ALEXANDER (1848–1925), bishop. Born in Highgate, Vermont, he was educated at St. John's College, Collegeville, Minnesota, and at Montreal. He was ordained in 1877, served as a pastor in Waseca and Minneapolis, Minnesota, and in 1898 was appointed bishop of Vancouver Island. The following year he was named fourth archbishop of Oregon City (changed to the archdiocese of Portland in Oregon in 1928). He built an orphanage for girls at Marylhurst in 1908 and the Lee Anderson Industrial School in 1924 and increased the number of schools, churches, and parishes in his see; among the other institutions founded during his episcopate of a quarter century was Columbia College in 1901 which became the University of Portland. An active proponent of Catholic education and the parochial school system, he fought the 1922 Oregon law that required all children ages eight to sixteen to attend public schools under penalty of fine and/or imprisonment. He was vindicated when the U.S. Supreme Court on June 1, 1925, declared the law unconstitutional by a unanimous decision in the landmark Oregon School Case—two months after he had died in Portland on Apr. 6.

CICOGNANI, AMLETO GIOVANNI (1883–1973), cardinal. Born in Brisighella, Italy, on Feb. 24, he was educated at the Faenza seminary, was ordained in 1905, and continued his studies at the Papal University of the Roman Seminary (D.D. 1907, Ph.D. 1908, J.C.D. 1910). He was with the Congregation of the Sacraments in 1910–14, the Consistorial Congregation in 1914–28, and in 1929 was appointed secretary of the Commission for Codification of Oriental Law. He was named titular archbishop of Laodicea in Phrygia and apostolic delegate to the United States in 1933, serving in that position the next fifteen years and traveling extensively to all parts of the country. He was recalled to Rome in 1958 and made a cardinal by Pope John XXIII, was made secretary of the Oriental Congregation in 1961, and later that year was appointed secretary of state. He resigned in 1969 because of the infirmities of old age and died in Rome on Dec. 17.

CLARK, ELEANOR GRACE (1895–1952), educator. Born in Neenah, Wisconsin, on July 6, she was educated at Oberlin College (B.A. 1918, M.A. 1919) and Bryn Mawr (Ph.D. 1928) and did postgraduate work at London, Oxford, and Edinburgh universities. She was head of the English department at St. Helen's Hall, Portland, Oregon, for two years, taught the following year at Friends School, Morristown, New Jersey and then joined the faculty of Bryn Mawr where she taught from 1923 until 1930 when she moved to Hunter College in New York City where she taught until her death in New York on Apr. 24. She became a Catholic in 1925 and was the author of several works on the Tudor-Stuart period of English history among them *Pembroke Plays* (1928), *Elizabethan Fustian* (1938), *Raleigh and Marlowe,* and *The Bitter Box* (1946).

CLARKE, MOTHER MARY FRANCES (1803–87), foundress. Born in Dublin on Mar. 2, she and four companions formed a congregation to give religious education to children and opened a school in Dublin in 1832. The next year they emigrated to the United States as missionary teachers. Later that year they began teaching at St. Michael's parish in Philadelphia at the invitation of Fr. T. J. Donoghue who organized them into a community with Mother Mary Frances as superior, thus founding the Sisters of Charity of the Blessed Virgin Mary. The congregation was transferred to Dubuque, Iowa, in 1843 and she founded Clarke College there. She received final pontifical approval for the congregation from Pope Leo XIII in 1885 and during the fifty-four years she was superior she founded schools all over the United States; by the end of the century the congregation had more than a thousand members. She died in Dubuque on Dec. 4.

CLEARY, WILLIAM D. (1882–1949), general. Born in Ireland on July 1, he was educated at St. Flannan's College and was ordained in Paris in 1908. He emigrated to the United States, engaged in pastoral work in Brooklyn and New York, and became a chaplain in the Army in 1918. He organized the chaplains' school, which trained more than seven thousand chaplains, in 1942, was appointed deputy chief of Army chaplains and a brigadier general, and died in Washington, D.C., on Aug. 6.

CLEMENS, ALPHONSE HENRY (1905–73), sociologist. Born in St. Louis on Aug. 19, he was educated at St. Louis University (B.A. 1926, M.A. 1936, Ph.D. 1940). He married Bess Wulfers in 1936, was head of the sociology department of Fontbonne College, St. Louis, in 1936–46, and instituted the first undergraduate degree in family life studies. He was on the editorial staff of the *Catholic Herald* in 1936–45, edited *Holy Family* magazine in 1936–38, and served on the War Labor Board, Office of Price Administration, and the National Labor Relations Board in St. Louis during World War II. He joined the faculty of Catholic University in 1952 and remained there until his retirement in 1970. He was president of the American Catholic Sociological Society in 1946–47, became director of the Marriage Counseling Center at Catholic University in 1952, and was considered a leading pioneer in the family apostolate. He wrote numerous magazine articles and several books, among them *The Cana Movement in the United States* (1953), *Marriage and the Family* (1957), and *Design for Successful Marriage* (1964). He died in Washington, D.C., on Sept. 9.

CLIFFORD, CORNELIUS CYPRIAN (1859–1938), educator. Born in New York City on Aug. 24, he was educated at the College of the City of New York and Fordham (B.A. 1879) and joined the Jesuits in 1879. He continued his studies at Woodstock College, Maryland, the University of Innsbruck, Austria, and Louvain, Belgium, and was ordained in England in 1898; he left the Jesuits the following year with the permission of the Society. He taught at Georgetown, Wimbledon, and Roehampton in England and St. Beuno's in Wales and then returned to the United States where he served as editor of the Providence *Visitor* in 1900–3. He taught

at Seton Hall College, South Orange, New Jersey, in 1907–9 and from 1909 until his death in Whippany, New Jersey, on Dec. 4 was rector of St. Mary's Church there. He lectured at Columbia to postgraduate students and Ph.D. candidates for twenty-six years, wrote studies of the breviary and the missal, and was the author of *Introibo* (1903) and *The Burden of Time* (1904).

CLORIVIÈRE, JOSEPH PICOT DE (1768–1826), priest. Born in Nantes, France, on Nov. 4, he was educated at the College of Rennes and the Royal Military School in Paris, served in the Regiment d'Angoulême, the King's Guards, and resigned his commission in 1791 when the French Revolution broke out. He joined the counterrevolutionists, the Chouans, in 1799 and was implicated in a plot to assassinate Napoleon in 1800 but escaped from France dressed as a French soldier and using the name Guitry. He went to the United States in 1803, settled in Savannah, Georgia, using the name Picot de Clorivière, and in 1806 began studying for the priesthood at St. Mary's Seminary, Baltimore. He was ordained in 1812 and was named an assistant to Fr. Simon Gallagher, Irish pastor of St. Mary's Church in Charleston, South Carolina. When Gallagher was suspended by Archbishop Neale, Clorivière was named pastor whereupon the trustees of the parish, in defiance of the archbishop, drove Clorivière out as the Irish parishioners did not want a French priest as pastor. When Gallagher returned to St. Mary's he was supported by the trustees as pastor and one of the most bitter trustee disputes in American Church history ensued. The church was put under interdict and the dispute was not finally resolved until Archbishop Neale's successor, Archbishop Maréchal, sent Fr. Benedict Fenwick to Charleston and appointed Clorivière chaplain at the Visitation Convent in Georgetown, Washington, D.C., in 1817. He spent the rest of his life in that position, donating the proceeds of the sale of his estate in Bretagne to the Sisters and building their chapel. He died there on Sept. 29 and is buried in the crypt of the chapel with Archbishop Neale.

COAKLEY, THOMAS FRANCIS (1880–1961), educator. Born in Pittsburgh on Feb. 20, he was educated at Holy Ghost College (later Duquesne University) (B.A. 1903) and then continued his education at the North American College (S.T.D. 1908) and the Propaganda, Rome. He was ordained in Rome in 1908 and on his return to Pittsburgh he became an assistant at St. Paul's Cathedral. He was named secretary to Bishop Canevin in 1908, served as a chaplain in the Army during World War I and in Germany after. He was pastor of St. Patrick's parish in 1920–23 and then was founding pastor of Sacred Heart Church where he remained until his death on Mar. 5. He wrote widely on education and was one of the founders and first directors of De Paul Institute, a school for deaf and speech-defective children.

COCKRAN, WILLIAM BOURKE (1854–1923), U.S. congressman. Born in Sligo, Ireland, on Feb. 28, he studied there and in France and in 1871 he emigrated to the United States. He became principal of a public school in Tuckahoe, New York, studied law and was admitted to the New York bar in 1876, and moved to New York City. He became involved in politics and at first was opposed to Tammany Hall but joined that organization in 1883. He attracted national attention with his oratory at the Democratic National Convention opposing Grover Cleveland's candidacy for the presidency. He was a member of the House of Representatives in 1887–89 and 1891–95, broke with Tammany Hall in 1896 when, as a gold standard supporter, he backed William McKinley for the presidency against William Jennings Bryan but returned to the Democratic Party in 1900 because of his opposition to imperialism. He was the recipient of the Laetare Medal in 1901, served in the House of Representatives again in 1904–9, and was Grand Sachem of Tammany Hall for three years. He again left the Democratic Party to support Theodore Roosevelt on the "Bull Moose" ticket in 1912 but returned to the Democratic Party once again and was reelected to the House in 1920 and again in 1922. As a congressman, he supported organized labor, opposed restrictions on immigration, and was against prohibition. He was one of the greatest orators of his time, helped found the Perpetual Adoration Society in New York City, was an adviser to New York's archbishops, and died in Washington, D.C., on Mar. 1.

CODY, JOHN PATRICK (1907–82), cardinal. Of Irish immigrant parents, he was born in St. Louis on Dec. 24, entered the St. Louis Preparatory Seminary when twelve, and continued his studies for the priesthood at the North American College and the Appollinaris in Rome (Ph.D. 1928, S.T.D. 1932, J.C.D. 1938), and was ordained in Rome in 1931. He became assistant to the rector of the North American College the following year and in 1933 joined the staff of the Vatican Secretariat of State. He returned to the United States in 1938, became secretary to Archbishop Glennon of St. Louis and chaplain of St. Mary's Home for Girls, and was named chancellor of the archdiocese in 1940. He was named titular bishop of Apollonia and auxiliary of St. Louis in 1947, coadjutor bishop of St. Joseph, Missouri, in 1954, and was named administrator of that see the following year on the resignation of Bishop Le Blond. He was transferred to the newly established diocese of Kansas City-St. Joseph in 1956 as coadjutor and succeeded to the see later the same year on the death of Archbishop O'Hara. In 1961 he was named coadjutor archbishop of New Orleans and became its apostolic administrator in 1962 and its archbishop in 1964. He became involved in a controversy with members of the see as he continued the efforts of his predecessor, Archbishop Rummel, to desegregate Catholic schools of the archdiocese and continued his efforts for interracial justice. In 1965 he was transferred to Chicago where he was recognized as an able administrator but became involved in controversy with some members of the clergy for his traditionally authoritative rule. He was made a cardinal in 1967 and served on several congregations of the Vatican Curia, among them the Sacred Congregation for the Evangelization of People and the Sacred Congregation for the Clergy. He was again involved in controversy in 1968 when he announced a plan for busing black students from overcrowded inner city schools to less crowded suburban schools in white neighborhoods and supported a city plan for desegregating public schools by busing. In 1975 his closing of several inner city schools with high minority enrollment because of growing budget deficits caused a furor and denunciations from interracial groups. He was later praised by the black Catholic clergy of Chicago for his efforts on behalf of inner city Catholic schools that were 75 percent non-Catholic but predominantly minority-attended and for his program of pairing poor, inner city parishes with wealthier parishes by which the latter shared their resources with the poorer parishes. The last years of his life were clouded by the allegations of a Chicago newspaper that he had misused archdiocesan funds for personal purposes; the matter was under investigation by a federal grand jury when he died in Chicago on Apr. 25. Two months after his death, the grand jury refused to hand down an indictment and the investigation was dropped.

COFFEY, JAMES VINCENT (1846–1919), jurist. Born in New York City on Dec. 14, he went to California, studied law and was admitted to the bar in 1869, and practiced law the next six years. He served in the state assembly in 1875–78 and in 1882 was appointed a judge of the San Francisco superior court; he was chief of its probate department the next thirty-seven years. He became a leading authority on probate and his rulings were published in the six-volume *Reports of Decisions in Probate,* popularly referred to as *Coffey's Probate Reports.* He died in San Francisco on Jan. 15.

COLEMAN, JOHN ALOYSIUS (1901–77), stockbroker, philanthropist. Son of a policeman, he was born in New York City on Dec. 24, studied at Trinity High School there, and left to help out his family. He began his career as a page boy at the New York Stock Exchange when he was sixteen, became a stockbroker when he was twenty-one, a member of the New York Curb Exchange in 1923–24 and the youngest member of the New York Stock Exchange in 1924, and formed the Wall Street house of Adler, Coleman in 1928 with Paul Adler. He was a governor of the Exchange for twenty-one years and chairman of its board of governors in 1943–47, married Ann Meehan in 1930, and was a founding member of the Cardinal's Committee of the Laity. He was closely associated with the New York archdiocese's Catholic Charities for half a century and its chairman from

1934 on, and was active in numerous Catholic enterprises. He received many awards, was made a papal chamberlain to Pope Pius XII in 1957, and was presented with the Johannes XXIII Peace and Humanitarian Medal by the Wall Street Synagogue in 1966 in which year Cardinal Spellman named a high school in Kingston, New York, in his honor. He died of heart failure in New York City on Feb. 23.

COLLINS, JOSEPH BURNS (1897–1975), educator, author. Born in Waseca, Minnesota, on Sept. 7, he was educated at St. Mary's College, Winona, Minnesota, St. Paul (Minnesota) Seminary and the Urban College, Rome (S.T.D. 1924), and was ordained in Rome in 1924. On his return to the United States he taught at St. Mary's and the College of St. Teresa in Winona in 1925–30, earned his Ph.D. at Johns Hopkins University in 1934, and after a year teaching at Notre Dame College of Maryland in 1932–33 taught at the Sulpician Seminary, Washington, D.C., in 1933–37, and joined the Sulpicians in 1935. He began teaching moral theology and catechetics at Catholic University in 1938 and continued teaching there until his retirement in 1968. He was director of the National Center for the Confraternity of Christian Doctrine in 1942–67 and continued as a consultant until his death in Washington, D.C., on Jan. 23. He edited *Our Parish Confraternity* in 1942–66 and began *The Living Light* in 1964, wrote widely for magazines and edited or authored more than two dozen books among them *Teaching Religion* (1953) and *Confraternity Teacher's Guide* (1961).

COLLINS, THOMAS PATRICK (1915–73), bishop. Born in San Francisco on Jan. 13, he joined the Maryknoll Fathers, was educated at Maryknoll Seminary, Ossining, New York, and was ordained in 1942. He served as a missionary in Bolivia the next thirty-one years, was named vicar apostolic of Pando, Bolivia, and titular bishop of Sufetula in 1961 and served until 1969 when he retired. He died at Maryknoll on Dec. 7.

COLTON, CHARLES HENRY (1848–1915), bishop. Born in New York City on Oct. 15, he was educated at St. Francis Xavier College there and at St. Joseph's Seminary, Troy, New York, and was ordained in Troy in 1876. He engaged in parish work in New York City until 1897 when he was named chancellor of the archdiocese. He was appointed bishop of Rochester, New York, in 1903, built a new cathedral there, and died there on May 9.

COLUM, MARY MAGUIRE (1887–1957), critic. Mary Maguire was born in Ireland, was educated at Pensionnat Sacré Coeur in Vaals, Netherlands, the Sorbonne, Paris, and the Dominican College and the National University of Ireland in Dublin. She wrote for the *Irish Review, United Irishman,* and *Irish Statesman* and her writing and book reviews attracted the attention of such literary lights as W. B. Yeats, A. E., and James Joyce and she became a member of their Irish literary group. In 1912 he married Padraic Colum and emigrated with him to the United States in 1914. She wrote for numerous literary magazines among them *Scribner's, Saturday Review,* and *The Nation* and did book reviews for the New York *Times;* in 1933–40 she wrote the "Life and Literature" column each month for the *Forum.* She held Guggenheim scholarships in 1930 and 1938, was the recipient of the John Ryder Randall medal from Georgetown in 1938, was elected to the National Institute of Arts and Letters in 1953, and lectured on literature at Columbia in 1952–56. She wrote

From These Roots, a creative interpretation of modern literature, in 1937 and her autobiography, *Life and the Dream,* in 1947 and died in New York City on Oct. 22.

COLUMBA, BROTHER *See* Reilly, Philip James.

CONATY, THOMAS JAMES (1847–1915), bishop. Born in Kilmallough, Cavan, Ireland, on Aug. 1, he was brought to the United States by his parents when he was three years old. He was educated at Holy Cross College, Worcester, Massachusetts, and the Sulpician Seminary, Montreal, and was ordained in Montreal in 1872. He served as an assistant at St. John's Church, Worcester, and was pastor of Sacred Heart Church there in 1880–97 and was a leader in the temperance movement, serving as president of the Catholic Total Abstinence Union in 1887–89. He was founder and president of the Catholic Summer Schools of America, founded *Catholic Home and School Magazine* in 1892 and was its editor until 1897 when he was appointed second rector of the Catholic University. While rector of Catholic University he called several meetings to establish a conference of seminary presidents and professors in 1898 and 1899, and in 1899 the first meeting of the Association of Catholic Colleges and Universities in Chicago in 1899 was held; five years later he was one of the founders of the National Catholic Education Association. He was appointed bishop of Monterey-Los Angeles, California, in 1903 and greatly increased the number of priests, churches, schools, and charitable institutions in the diocese, and was active in the movement to preserve old Catholic landmarks and missions in California. He died in Coronado, California, on Sept. 18.

CONCANEN, RICHARD LUKE (1747–1810), bishop. Born in Kilbegnet, Roscommon, Ireland, on Dec. 27, he was educated at Louvain, Belgium, and San Clemente and the Minerva, Rome, joined the Dominicans in 1764, and was ordained in Rome in 1770. He spent the next forty years at San Sisto e San Clemente in Rome serving as its prior in 1781–83, was librarian of the Minerva and acted as agent for the Irish bishops and Bishop John Carroll of the United States. He was offered two Irish sees but declined and in 1808 was appointed first bishop of the newly established diocese of New York. After his consecration he left for Leghorn to embark for New York but after waiting four months for a ship he returned to Rome. When he went to Naples in 1810 to take a ship to New York, he was detained by the French as a British subject. Before his release could be effected with the French authorities who controlled the city, he died in Naples on June 19.

CONDON, WILLIAM JOSEPH (1895–1967), bishop. Born in Colton, Washington, on Apr. 7, he was educated at Gonzaga College, Spokane (B.A. 1919) and then studied for the priesthood at St. Patrick's Seminary, Menlo Park, California. He was ordained in Spokane in 1917, served as a curate at Our Lady of Lourdes Cathedral there in 1917–18, was pastor of St. Joseph's Church, Waterville, Washington, in 1919–23, of Our Lady of Lourdes Cathedral, Spokane, in 1923–29 and of St. Augustine's Church, Spokane, in 1929–39, and was Bishop Charles White's secretary in 1928–32. He was chancellor of the Spokane diocese in 1927–39, vicar-general in 1933–39, and was appointed third bishop of Great Falls, Montana, in 1939. He greatly increased the number of priests and religious and schools, churches, and charitable institutions in the diocese to meet the tremendous increase in its Catholic population, was made an Assistant at the Pontifical Throne in 1964, and died in Great Falls on Aug. 17.

CONNELL, FRANCIS J. (1888–1967), theologian. Born in Boston on Jan. 31, he was educated at Boston College, joined the Redemptorists in 1907 and studied for the priesthood at Mt. St. Alphonsus Seminary, Esopus, New York. He was ordained in 1913, engaged in parish and missionary work in Brooklyn, New York, taught at Mt. St. Alphonsus in 1915–21 and 1924–40, and received his doctorate in sacred theology from the Angelicum in Rome in 1923. He was president of the seminary department of the National Education Association in 1936–38, first president of the Catholic Theological Society in 1946–47, and was rector of Holy Redeemer College, Washington, D.C., in 1945–50. He taught moral theology at Catholic University in 1940–58, serving as dean of the School of Sacred Theology in 1949–57 and of religious communities at Catholic University in 1958–67, was named a consultor for the Sacred Congregation of Seminaries and Universities in 1956, and was peritus for the American bishops at Vatican Council II in 1962–65. He lectured widely, appeared on radio and television, wrote for religious journals, and was the author of several books, among them *De Sacramentis Ecclesiae* (1935), *Morals in Politics and Professions* (1946), *Outlines of Moral Theology* (1953), and *Fr. Connell Answers Moral Questions* (1959), and translated several devotional works. He was also associate editor of *American Ecclesiastical Review* and *Liguorian* magazine and at the time of his death in Washington, D.C., on May 12 was one of the best known American moral theologians.

CONNELLY, CORNELIA PEACOCK (1809–79), foundress. The youngest of six children by her mother's second marriage to Ralph Peacock, an Englishman, Cornelia Peacock was born in Philadelphia on Jan. 15. Her father died when she was nine, leaving the family practically penniless and her mother died when she was fourteen. In 1831 she married Pierce Connelly, an Episcopal priest, in Natchez, Mississippi, and the couple had five children. Pierce renounced his Episcopal orders in 1835 when Cornelia became a Catholic in New Orleans and he too became a Catholic the following year. In 1844 they received permission from Pope Gregory XVI to separate so that Pierce could become a Catholic priest, provided Cornelia at the same time became a nun. She entered the Sacred Heart Convent in Rome and took her final vows in 1847; Pierce had been ordained in 1845. Cornelia was ordered to help found a new teaching religious order by Pope Gregory and at the invitation of Cardinal Wiseman, who was to become her great friend, she went to England in 1846 to do so; the new order became known as the Society of the Holy Child Jesus with its first house in Derby. In 1849, having failed in an attempt to gain control of the Society and after having taken their children away from Cornelia, Pierce left the Church and sued Cornelia in England for the return of his conjugal rights in a case that was the sensation of the day. He won his case in the Court of Arches but when it came before the Privy Council, he dropped the case, returned to Italy in 1853 as an Episcopal priest in Florence, and died there in 1883. Meanwhile, the Society of the Holy Child Jesus, devoted to the education of girls and women, despite many obstacles, flourished and spread, opening its first American province at Towanda, Pennsylvania, in 1862; its constitutions were given formal approbation by Pope Leo XIII in 1887. Cornelia died in St. Leonard's, England, where the Society had moved soon after its founding, on Apr. 18.

CONNELLY, PIERCE *See* Connelly, Cornelia Peacock.

CONNOLLY, CORNELIUS JOSEPH (1883–1954), anthropologist, educator. Born in Stellarton, Nova Scotia, on Mar. 6, he was educated at St. Francis Xavier College, Antigonish, Nova Scotia (B.A. 1903), and the Grand Seminary, Montreal, and was ordained in 1907. He continued his studies at the University of Munich (Ph.D. 1911), taking up botany, zoology, and anthropology and then taught biology at St. Francis Xavier in 1911–24, doing biological research at Harvard in 1922–24. He began teaching at Catholic University in 1924, was made professor of physical anthropology in 1934, and was made chairman of the department of anthropology in 1949. He published *External Morphology of the Primate Brain,* and died in Washington, D.C., on Apr. 5.

CONNOLLY, FRANCIS XAVIER (1905–65), educator. Born in New York City on June 24, he was educated at Fordham (B.A. 1930, M.A. 1933, Ph.D. 1937) and began teaching at Fordham in 1931. He became a full professor of literature in 1951 and was chairman of the English department for thirteen years. Except for 1943–46 when he served in the Navy, his entire teaching career was spent at Fordham and he also served as adjunct professor of English at Hunter College, New York City, in 1958–59. He was one of the founders of the Catholic Poetry Society, served on the editorial board of the Catholic Book Club, and was the author of several books, among them the novel *Give*

Beauty Back (1950), the widely used textbook, *A Rhetoric Casebook* (1953), *The Art of Rhetoric* (1967), and *Poetry: Its Power and Wisdom* (1960); he also edited four books of poetry with John G. Brunini and compiled *A Newman Reader* (1964). He died in New York City on Nov. 17.

CONNOLLY, JAMES BRENDAN (1868–1957), author. Son of immigrants from the Aran Islands, he was born in South Boston on Oct. 28. He worked for a time with the U.S. Engineer Corps on the southeast Atlantic Coast, took an engineering course at Harvard but left to compete in the first modern Olympics in Athens in 1896; he won the hop, skip, and jump event. He worked on two Boston newspapers, fought in Cuba in 1898 during the Spanish-American War with the 9th Massachusetts Infantry, worked on cattle boats crossing the Atlantic and won second place in the track and field events in the 1900 Olympics in Paris. He began writing short stories about his experiences and had a collection, *Out of Gloucester,* published in 1902, the beginning of his career as one of America's great chroniclers of the sea, ships, and sailing. He then began free-lance writing for such magazines as *Scribner's* and *Harper's* and was correspondent for *Collier's* in the military confrontation with Mexico in 1914 and its naval correspondent during World War I. During his lifetime he had more than a score of books published, among them *Deep Sea Toll* (1905), *Head Winds* (1916), *The U-Boat Hunters* (1918), *Gloucestermen* (1930), and *Sea Borne* (1944), his autobiography. He died in Boston on Jan. 20.

CONNOLLY, JOHN (c. 1750–1825), bishop. Born in Slane, County Meath, Ireland, he joined the Dominicans in his youth, was sent to Liège, Louvain, and Rome to study for the priesthood and was ordained in 1774. He was stationed at San Clemente's, Rome, in 1774–1814, taught theology there, and was librarian at the Casanova Library for several years, was prior of San Clemente's in 1782–92, and was Roman agent for several Irish bishops. He was highly esteemed and through his influence was able to save his convent, church, and library and the Irish, Scots, and English colleges from plundering when the French invaded Rome. He was appointed second bishop of New York and was consecrated in Rome in 1814 but did not reach his see until the following year. His see, consisting of all of New York and New Jersey, had four priests when he arrived. During his episcopate he built several churches and an orphanage, brought the Sisters of Charity into the diocese, and was a strong advocate of a diocese in each state at a time when many dioceses embraced several states. He died in New York City on Feb. 6.

CONNOLLY, MYLES (1897–1964), author, producer. Born in Boston on Oct. 7, he was educated at Boston College (B.A. 1918) and served in the Navy during World War I. After the war he decided to pursue a career in journalism, became an associate editor on the Boston *Post,* was appointed editor of *Columbia* in 1924 and served on the first board of directors of the Catholic Book Club. He went to Hollywood in 1928, began to write scenarios for motion pictures, and during his film career was responsible for the production and writing of some forty motion pictures. He also wrote several books, among them the enormously popular *Mr. Blue* (1928), *The Bump on Brannigan's Head* (1950), *The Noonday Devil* (1951), *The Reason for Ann* (1953), and *Three Who Ventured* (1958). He died in Santa Monica, California, on July 15.

CONNOLLY, TERENCE L. (1888–1961), educator, author. Born on Sept. 26 in North Attleboro, Massachusetts, he joined the Jesuits in 1908, was educated at Woodstock College, Maryland (B.A. 1922, M.A. 1924), and Georgetown, and was ordained at Georgetown in 1922. He taught English at Fordham for several years, was dean of English at Georgetown in 1924, and was professor of English and head of the English graduate program at Boston College in 1926–45; he then served as librarian at Boston College from 1945 until his death in Newton, Massachusetts, on Mar. 21. He was a leading authority on the writings of Francis Thompson, edited the definitive edition of his poetry, *Complete Poems,* and *The Man Has Wings, New Poems and Plays* (1957), and was curator of the Francis Thompson Collection at Boston College. He also edited a collection of poetry by Coventry Patmore.

CONNOR, JOSEPH PIERRE (1896–1952), composer. Born in Kingston, New York, on Nov. 16, he began studying music under his mother, continued at the Wyoming (Pennsylvania) Conservatory of Music and under Ergildo Martinelli, and received his B.A., M.A., and Mus.D. from St. Bonaventure University, Olean, New York. He was ordained and served as pastor of St. John's Church, Teaneck, New Jersey, and of St. Joseph of the Palisades Church, West New York, New Jersey, also serving as chaplain of the New Jersey State Police and the New Jersey State Guard. He was also a well-known pianist and composer of church music and many popular and semi-classical songs under the pseudonyms Pierre Norman and Johnny Openshaw. Among his church musical compositions were a Gregorian Mass in honor of Our Lady of Victory, *The Lord's*

Prayer, Our Father, Ave Maria, and *The Prayer of St. Francis.* Among his popular songs were "The Far Green Hills of Home," "When I Take My Sugar to Tea," "You Brought a New Kind of Love to Me," and "Miracle of the Bells." He also wrote the musical score for several films among them *Big Pond, Young Man from Manhattan, The Perfect Fool,* and *Footlight Parade.* He died in Holy Name Hospital, Teaneck, New Jersey, on Mar. 31.

CONROY, JOHN JOSEPH (1819–95), bishop. Born in Clonaslee, Leix, Ireland, he was educated at the Sulpician College, Montreal, Mt. St. Mary's College, Emmitsburg, Maryland, and St. Joseph's Seminary, Troy, New York, and was ordained in 1842. He served as vice president and then president of St. John's College (Fordham) in 1842–44, engaged in pastoral work in the New York archdiocese until 1864 when he was appointed administrator of the see, attended the first Plenary Council of Baltimore in 1852, and in 1865 was appointed second bishop of Albany, New York. He attended the second Plenary Council of Baltimore in 1866 and Vatican Council I in 1869–70 and resigned his see in 1877 because of ill health. He was appointed titular bishop of Curium the next year and died in New York City on Nov. 20.

CONROY, JOSEPH HENRY (1858–1939), bishop. Born in Watertown, New York, on Nov. 8, he was educated at Montreal College and the Grand Seminary, Montreal and St. Joseph's Seminary, Troy, New York, and was ordained in Troy in 1881. He served as a curate and pastor in upper New York, was named rector of St. Mary's Church, Ogdensburg, New York, in 1883, and became vicar-general of that see in 1901. He was made a domestic prelate in 1905, was appointed titular bishop of

Arindela and auxiliary of Ogdensburg in 1912, and succeeded to that see in 1921. He founded Wadham Hall, the minor diocesan seminary in 1924, and died in Ogdensburg on Mar. 20.

CONSIDINE, JOHN J. (1897–1982), missionary, author. Born in New Bedford, Massachusetts, on Oct. 9, he joined the Maryknoll Fathers in 1917, was educated at Maryknoll College and Seminary and Catholic University (J.C.B. and S.T.L.), and was ordained in 1923. He went to Rome the following year as procurator general (until 1934), founded Fides News Service in 1927, serving as its director until 1934, and was secretary for a papal mission to Ethiopia in 1929. He served as head of Maryknoll Publications, was vicar-general of Maryknoll in 1943–46, and was consultor for the Congregation of the Propagation of the Faith from 1963. He organized and was director of the Latin American Bureau of the U.S. Catholic Conference in 1960–69, founded the Papal Volunteers of Latin America, and was appointed adviser to the Peace Corps by President John F. Kennedy. He wrote several books, among them *When the Sorghum Was High* (1940), *March into Tomorrow* (1942), *World Christianity* (1945), and *Call for Forty Thousand* (1946). He retired to St. Teresa's Residence at Maryknoll in 1976 and died there on May 4.

CONSIDINE, ROBERT BERNARD (1906–75), journalist. Born in Washington, D.C., on Nov. 4, he worked in the U.S. Treasury Department in 1923–27 and while working in the State Department in 1927–30 studied journalism and creative writing at Washington University. He then decided to follow a career in journalism, began as a sportswriter for the Washington *Post* in 1930–33 and the Washington *Herald* in 1933–37 and then transferred to the International

CONWAY, BERTRAND LOUIS

News Service in New York City. He was a syndicated feature writer and sports columnist for the *Daily Mirror* in 1938 and spent almost four decades writing for Hearst publications, serving as war correspondent in England in 1943. He wrote a dozen books among them *The Babe Ruth Story* (1948), *The Maryknoll Story* (1949), *Dempsey* (1960), and *The Irish* (1962) and was coauthor of the enormously successful *Thirty Seconds over Tokyo* (1943). He died in New York City on Sept. 25.

CONWAY, BERTRAND LOUIS (1872–1959), author. Born on May 5 in New York City, he was educated at St. Charles College, Ellicott City, Maryland, St. Paul's College, Washington, D.C., St. Mary's Seminary (B.A., M.A.), Baltimore, and Catholic University (S.T.B. and S.T.L.). He was ordained a Paulist priest in 1896, worked as a missionary for years, and became famous for his convert-making. In 1917 he formed the Catholic Unity League to distribute Catholic books to non-Catholics, was named treasurer of the Paulists in 1931, and was the author of numerous pamphlets and several books, best known of which was *The Question Box* (1903) which sold millions of copies. He died in New York City on Dec. 4.

CONWAY, JOHN DONALD (1905–67), author. Born in Pleasantsille, Iowa, on May 16, he was educated at St. Ambrose College, Davenport, Iowa, (B.A. 1926), the Louvain, Belgium, in 1926–30, and was ordained at Louvain in 1930. He was professor of English at St. Ambrose in 1930–31 and then continued his studies at the Gregorian, Rome, receiving his J.C.L. in 1932. He was chancellor of the Davenport diocese in 1932–42, director of the Propagation of the Faith of that diocese in 1933–49, and was made a papal chamberlain in 1937. He was a chaplain in the Army during World War II attaining the rank of major. After the war he became chaplain of Mercy Hospital in 1946 and officialis of the diocesan marriage tribunal and in 1952 became chaplain of the Catholic Student Center at the University of Iowa. He was president of the Canon Law Society of America in 1958–59, was made a domestic prelate in 1959, and was appointed pastor of St. Mary's Church in Davenport in 1962, remaining in that position until his death in Davenport on Feb. 5. He wrote several books, among them *What They Ask About Marriage* (1955), *What They Ask About the Church* (1958), and *Facts of the Faith* (1959) based on his "Question Box" column that was published in more than fifty diocesan papers.

CONWAY, KATHERINE ELEANOR (1853–1927), editor. Born in Rochester, New York, on Sept. 6, she was educated at Sacred Heart academies in Rochester and New York City and at St. Mary's Academy, Buffalo, New York. She began her journalism career on the Rochester *Daily Union* and a small church magazine, was assistant editor on the *Catholic Union Times* in Buffalo, and in 1883 began working on the Boston *Pilot* as associate editor; she was managing editor there from 1905 to 1908 when she became managing editor of *The Republic* in Boston. She was adjunct professor at St. Mary's College at Notre Dame, Indiana in 1911–15, was the author of *The Golden Years of the Good Shepherd in Boston* (1892), *In the Footprints of the Good Shepherd* (1907), *Fifty Years with Christ, the Good Shepherd* (1925), and *The Color of Life* (1926), and was the recipient of the Laetare Medal in 1907. She died in Boston on Jan. 2.

CONWELL, HENRY (1745–1842), bishop. Born in Moneymore, Derry, Ireland, he studied for the priesthood at the Irish College in Paris, was ordained, and became parish priest at Dungannon. He was vicar-general of the archdiocese of Armagh, Ireland, for twenty-one years and in 1819 when he was seventy-four he was appointed second bishop of Philadelphia after the see had been refused by Fr. Ambrose Maréchal and Fr. Louis de Barth (who had been administering the diocese since 1814), because they did not want to become involved in a diocese wracked by the trustee problem that was causing such dissension in Philadelphia. He arrived in Philadelphia late in 1820 and in an effort to end the trustee problem revoked the priestly faculties of Fr. William Hogan, a step which precipitated a schism headed by Hogan (Hoganism). Hogan left Philadelphia in 1824 but the trustees still resisted Conwell and in 1826 Conwell yielded to the trustees the right to veto his appointments and determine salaries in the diocese, a surrender of his episcopal rights which led to his being called to Rome. He was censured for his actions and forbidden to return to Philadelphia but returned anyway and was suspended. He was later permitted to stay in the city but was not permitted to interfere in the administration of the diocese. Francis Patrick Kenrock was appointed its administrator and coadjutor in 1830. Bishop Conwell spent his last years totally blind and in seclusion and died in Philadelphia on Apr. 22.

COOKE, TERENCE (1921–83), cardinal. Son of Irish immigrants Michael Cooke, a private chauffeur and construction worker, and Margaret Gannon Cooke, he was born in New York City on Mar. 1, and raised by his aunt after his mother died when he was nine. He was educated at Cathedral College, New York City, and St. Joseph's Seminary, Dunwoodie, Yonkers, New York, and was ordained in 1945. He was assis-

tant pastor at St. Athanasius Church in the Bronx in 1946–47 and chaplain at St. Agatha Home, Nanuet, New York, and then continued his studies at Catholic University (Ph.D.) in 1947 and the University of Chicago. He returned to New York City in 1949, was assistant director of the Catholic Youth Organization there in 1949–54, at the same time teaching at Fordham and assisting at St. Jude Church, was procurator of St. Joseph's Seminary in 1954–57, and was secretary to Cardinal Francis Spellman in 1957–58. He was made vice-chancellor of the New York archdiocese in 1958 and supervisor of all archdiocesan construction, was made a domestic prelate and was chancellor in 1961–65, and was named vicar-general and titular bishop of Summa and auxiliary bishop of New York in 1965 and episcopal vicar in 1966, when the see was divided into six vicariates and he was given charge of 175 parishes in Manhattan and the Bronx. He was appointed archbishop of New York in 1968, succeeding Cardinal Spellman who had died in 1967, and automatically became Military Vicar of the Armed Forces of the United States; he was made a cardinal in 1969. Moderate in his approach to social and ecclesiastical problems he was an unrelenting and vigorous foe of abortion (he was chairman of the National Conference of Catholic Bishops' Committee for Pro-Life Activities for ten years), condemned terrorism, denounced racism as a "sickness," and was known for his efficiency and dedication. He coped with the problems unleashed by Vatican Council II by adopting the spirit of the Council in his government of the archdiocese and recast the archdiocese according to the principles of the Council, broadening the decision-making process of the see and decentralizing much of its authority. He was particularly concerned with the welfare of Hispanics who comprised a third of the Catholics in the archdiocese and expanded Cardinal Spellman's program to train priests in Spanish. He inaugurated an inner city scholarship program to help poor minority students attend Catholic schools and put into effect an interparish program wherein more affluent parishes aided poorer parishes, fought for improved welfare benefits, and resolutely continued all Catholic schools in Harlem. At the time of his death he was widely venerated for his spirituality, his rapport with men and women of all faiths, and as an inspired and greatly admired pastor. He died of leukemia, which he had suffered from the last twenty years of his life, in New York City on Oct. 6.

COOPER, JOHN MONTGOMERY (1881–1949), anthropologist. Born in Rockville, Maryland, on Oct. 28, he was educated at St. Charles's College, Catonsville, Maryland, and the North American College, Rome, where he received doctorates in philosophy and theology. He was ordained in 1905, served at St. Matthew's Cathedral, Washington, D.C., and in 1909 began teaching part-time at Catholic University. He served with the National Catholic War Council during World War I, organized the religion department at Catholic University when he began teaching full-time there in 1920, and in 1924 was appointed head of the newly established anthropology department—the first such department in a Catholic college in the United States. He was secretary of the American Anthropological Association in 1931–37 and president in 1940, was made a domestic prelate in 1941, and was a founder of the Catholic Anthropological Conference and editor of its magazine, *Primitive Man* (later *Anthropological Quarterly*). He founded and edited the Anthropological Series of Catholic University, was one of the principal collaborators on the *Hand-*

book of South American Indians (1950), and was noted for the monographs he wrote based on his field research among North American Indians. He died in Washington, D.C., on May 22.

COPLEY, THOMAS (c. 1595–1652), missionary. Eldest son of William Copley of Galton, England, who had been exiled during the reign of Queen Elizabeth I with his family because they were Catholics, he was born in Madrid, became a Jesuit, went to Maryland in 1637 and worked there as a missionary. He was seized in 1645, with Fr. Andrew White, by a group of insurgents and sent back to England in chains. He was finally released when the two priests successfully defended themselves against charges of treason as Catholic priests in England by pointing out they had been forcibly returned to England. In 1648 he returned to Maryland where he died. He is also known under the alias Philip Fisher which he often used.

COPPINGER, JOHN JOSEPH (1834–1909), general. Born in Queenstown, Cork, Ireland, on Oct. 11, he joined the papal army and fought against the Italian unionists and then in 1861 emigrated to the United States. He joined the Army, served in the Civil War as commanding captain of the 14th Infantry and colonel of the 15th New York Cavalry in 1865, served in the Indian Wars in 1866–68, was raised to the rank of colonel in 1891, and four years later was named brigadier general. He was made major general of volunteers at Camp Wheeler, Alabama, during the Spanish-American War, retired from service in 1898, and died in Washington, D.C., on Nov. 4.

CORBETT, TIMOTHY (1861–1939), bishop. Born in Mendota, Minnesota, on July 10, he was educated at Meximieux College, France, and Sulpician seminaries in Montreal and Brighton, Massachusetts, and was ordained in 1886. He served as a curate in the St. Paul, Minnesota, diocese in 1886–89, was pastor of the Holy Rosary Cathedral in Duluth, Minnesota, in 1889–1910, and was appointed first bishop of the newly established diocese of Crookston, Minnesota, in 1910. During his episcopate, he built some fifty churches and twelve schools to meet the needs of the immigrants that flooded into the see, was a strong advocate of Catholic education, and was known for the success of his religious education programs. He resigned the see in 1938 and was appointed titular bishop of Vita and died on July 20 in Crookston.

CORCORAN, FRANCIS VINCENT

(1879–1939), educator. Born in Pittsburgh on May 6, he was educated at St. Mary's Seminary, Perryville, Missouri, in 1892–1901, Collegio Angelicum, Rome (S.T.D. 1903) and the Academy of St. Thomas, Rome (Ph.D.). He joined the Congregation of the Missions (Vincentians) in 1894, was professed in 1897, and was ordained in Paris in 1902. He was professor of philosophy at Kenrick Seminary, St. Louis in 1903–7, of dogma in 1903–30, and was professor of philosophy at Webster College, Webster Groves, Missouri, in 1917–30. He was chairman of the administrative board of St. Louis University in 1927–30, president of De Paul University in Chicago in 1930–35, and rector at Los Angeles from 1936 until his death there on Jan. 28. He founded Kappa Gamma Pi, national honor society for women graduates of Catholic colleges, and was associate editor of *Western Watchman* in 1917–25.

CORCORAN, JAMES ANDREW

(1820–89), theologian, editor. Born in Charleston, South Carolina, on Mar. 30, he was sent to the Propaganda in Rome to study for the priesthood when only fourteen and was ordained there in 1842—the first native South Carolinian to be ordained. He continued his studies at the Propaganda in Rome, became an authority on Semitic languages, especially Syriac, and received his doctorate in theology. He returned to the United States in 1843, taught at the Charleston seminary while engaging in pastoral work, and became editor of the *United States Catholic Miscellany,* the first Catholic literary periodical published in the United States, serving in that capacity in 1848–61. He declined the rectorship of the American College in Rome in 1859, supported the Confederacy during the Civil War, and was pastor of a Wilmington, North Carolina, church in 1861–68. He served as secretary of the Baltimore Provincial Councils in 1855 and 1858 and was principal secretary of the second Plenary Council of Baltimore in 1866. He was theologian for the American hierarchy at Vatican Council I, opposed the definition of the dogma of papal infallibility as inopportune, and prepared the so-called Spalding Formula merely implying papal infallibility, but it was rejected by the Council in favor of a specific statement. After the Council he became professor at the new Philadelphia seminary, St. Charles Borromeo, and remained in that position until his death in Philadelphia on July 16. He was a founding editor of the *American Catholic Quarterly Review* in 1876 and was secretary for the committee of American bishops in Rome in 1883 to prepare for the third Plenary Council of Baltimore. He was made a domestic prelate in 1884 and assisted as secretary at the third Plenary Council of Baltimore in the same year. At the time of his death he had been held in the highest regard for four decades as an expert on theological and canonical subjects.

CORCORAN, MICHAEL (1827–63), general. Son of an Army pensioner, he was born at Carrowkeel, Sligo, Ireland, on Sept. 21, and when nineteen joined the Royal Irish Constabulary. After three years in that organization he resigned and emigrated to the United States in 1849. He settled in New York, enlisted in the 69th Regiment of the New York state militia and rose in rank until he was elected colonel in 1859. He was arrested and ordered court-martialed in 1860 when he defied an order and refused to allow the 69th to march in a military parade honoring the Prince of Wales (later King Edward VII of England). The matter became a sensational cause célèbre but the Civil War broke out before the trial took place and he led his regiment into battle. He was wounded and taken prisoner at the first Battle of Bull Run in 1861 and was imprisoned for thirteen months before being freed in an exchange of prisoners in 1862. He was commissioned a brigadier general, raised a brigade called the Irish Legion (also the Corcoran Legion), and participated in several skirmishes in Virginia. On Dec. 22, he was thrown from his horse while encamped at Fairfax Court House in Virginia and died later that day from his injuries.

CORONADO, FRANCISCO VASQUEZ DE (c. 1510–54), explorer. Born at Salamanca, Spain, he went to Mexico in 1535 with its first viceroy, Antonio de Mendoza, who appointed him governor of Nueva Galicia in 1538. When reports of the fabulous wealth of the Seven Cities of Cibola reached him the viceroy dispatched a two-pronged expedition, one by sea headed by Hernando de Alarçon and the other by land headed by Coronado as captain general, to seek Cibola and colonize the area. Coronado set out from Compostela on the Pacific Coast in 1540 with a force of two hundred Spaniards and a thousand Indians, crossed modern-day Sonora and southeast Arizona and reached Cibola, the Zuñi country of New Mexico. Expeditions he sent out reached the Hopi villages of northern Arizona; another under der Lopez de Cardenas discovered the Grand Canyon; and a third under Hernando de Alvarado went eastward to the pueblos of the Rio Grande and the Pecos. On this expedition Alvarado met an Indian called the Turk who told him of the fabulously wealthy kingdom of Gran Quivira to the east. After wintering on the Rio Grande near present-day Santa Fe, Coronado set out in April 1541, to find Quivira under the guidance of the Turk; he probably passed through the Texas Panhandle to Palo Duro Canyon, went north through Oklahoma into Kansas and finally reached Quivira in northern Kansas only to find it a collection of poor Indian villages. Coronado returned to the Rio Grande, wintered there in 1541–42, and then returned to Nueva Galicia, leaving behind only two Franciscans and one soldier and no settlers in the whole vast territory. The disappointed viceroy dismissed him as governor in 1544 when numerous acts of cruelty led to charges of crimes and negligence against him. He was found guilty of the charges, returned to Mexico City, and spent the rest of his life in obscurity there with his wife and eight children; he died there sometime before Nov. 12. Despite his difficulties, Coronado's expedition was enormously important. Though he did not find the wealth he so avidly sought his report of his expeditions was of great geographic and ethnological value and in time opened up the Southwest for colonization.

CORRIGAN, MICHAEL AUGUSTINE (1839–1902), archbishop. Of Irish-born parents, he was born in Newark, New Jersey, on Aug. 13 and was educated at St. Mary's College, Wilmington, Delaware, and Mt. St. Mary's College, Emmitsburg, Maryland. In 1859, he entered the American College in Rome—one of the twelve members of its first class. He was ordained in Rome in 1863, received his doctorate in divinity from the Propaganda the following year, and then returned to the United States where he taught dogmatic theology and Scripture at Seton Hall College, South Orange, New Jersey, and in 1868 became its president. In the same year he was named vicar-general of the Newark, New Jersey, diocese, which he administered in 1869–70 and 1872–73, and in 1873 was appointed bishop of Newark. He was an able administrator, built several protectories when unsuccessful in an attempt to have Catholic chaplains minister to Catholics in state reform schools, encouraged educational and charitable institutions, and was active in aiding Italian immigrants in the diocese. In 1880 he was named titular archbishop of Petra and coadjutor of the archdiocese of New York and in 1885 succeeded to the see as its third archbishop. He convoked a synod in 1886 to put into effect the decrees of the third Plenary Council of Baltimore which he had attended in 1884, built a new theological seminary at Dunwoodie that opened in 1896, and finished the towers of St. Patrick's Cathedral. He vigorously opposed the Socialist candidate for mayor of New York, Henry George, and his single tax theory in the 1886 mayoralty election and clashed with Fr. Edward McGlynn, pastor of St. Stephen's Church, a social reformer and active supporter of George, and McGlynn's economic and political views which the archbishop believed distorted Catholic teaching. When McGlynn refused the archbishop's order not to appear at a rally for George, he was suspended and early in 1887 removed from his pastorate when he would not obey a summons to go to Rome and was then

excommunicated. McGlynn finally did go to Rome when Archbishop Satolli, the apostolic delegate to the United States, lifted the censure in 1892. The archbishop transferred McGlynn to the pastorate of St. Mary's Church in Newburgh, New York, and he remained there until his death; ironically Archbishop Corrigan presided at his funeral Mass. Noted for his conservative views, Corrigan sharply disagreed with Archbishop Ireland, archbishop of St. Paul, over the Church's attitude toward public school education—a disagreement that was exacerbated when Ireland supported Sylvester Malone for a vacancy on the Board of Regents of New York's State University against Corrigan's choice of Bishop McQuaid of Rochester. Corrigan also opposed the appointment of Bishop Keane as rector of the new Catholic University in Washington, D.C., and frequently differed with Cardinal Gibbons's treatment of various issues. He vigorously supported parochial schools, labored to accommodate the large number of Italian immigrants settling in New York, and was a great builder and an excellent administrator of the New York see. He died in New York City on May 5.

CORRIGAN, PATRICK (1835–94), priest. Born in Longford, Ireland, on Jan. 1, he was brought to the United States when he was thirteen, was educated at All Hallows College, Dublin, St. Mary's College, Wilmington, Delaware, and St. Mary's Seminary, Baltimore, and was ordained in 1860. He engaged in pastoral work in the diocese of Newark, New Jersey, and became pastor of Our Lady of Grace Church, Hoboken, New Jersey. He was a friend of Archbishop Ireland and an enthusiastic Americanist, opposed Cahenslyism, and in 1883, his pamphlet, *Episcopal Nominations*, advocating that priests be allowed to participate in the nominations

117

of bishops, caused a furor. He early advocated an apostolic delegate to the United States, supported a New Jersey bill to make parochial schools part of the public school system, and was subjected to an ecclesiastical trial and forced to apologize to Bishop Winand M. Wigger for his attacks on the bishop and the bishop's connection with the sixth German Conference in 1892. He tried to rent his parochial school to the public school system and when Bishop Wigger refused permission he closed it. He died in Hoboken on Jan. 9.

CORRIGAN, WILLIAM RAYMOND (1889–1943), historian. Born in Omaha, Nebraska, on Jan. 28, he was educated at Creighton University there in 1902–6, joined the Jesuits in 1908 and continued his studies at St. Stanislaus Seminary in 1908–12 and St. Louis University (B.A., M.A.). He spent four years in missionary work and in teaching at St. John's College in Belize, British Honduras, in 1915–19, finished his theological studies at Colegio Maximo, Sarria, Spain, and was ordained in Manresa, Spain, in 1922. He completed his graduate studies in history at Bonn and Munich universities (Ph.D. 1927), taught at Marquette University, Milwaukee, Wisconsin, in 1919–20, at the University of Detroit in 1927–31 when he was also chaplain of Marygrove College in Detroit and at the Jesuit theologate at St. Mary's College, Kansas, from 1931 until 1932. Then he became head of the history department at St. Louis University, a position he held until his death there on Jan. 19. He edited the *Historical Bulletin* from 1932, was associate editor of *Mid-America* from 1935 and assistant editor of *Catholic Historical Review* from 1937, and wrote *The Church and the Nineteenth Century* (1938) and articles for history magazines.

CORY, HERBERT ELLSWORTH (1883–1947), critic. Born of Congregationalist parents in Providence, Rhode Island, on Oct. 8, he was educated at Brown (B.A. 1906) and Harvard (Ph.D. 1910), taught at Harvard in 1908–9 and English at the University of California in 1909–18; he edited the University's *Chronicle* in 1912–14. During World War I, he served on the War Labor Policies Board in Washington, D.C., in 1918, did research at Johns Hopkins in 1918–22, and in 1923 became professor of liberal arts and head of the department at the University of Washington where he remained until his death on Feb. 1. He became a Catholic in 1933, wrote of the experience in *The Emancipation of a Freethinker,* and was the recipient of the De Smet Medal in 1940. He wrote several other books, among them *The Critics of Edmund Spenser* (1911), *Edmund Spenser, a Critical Study* (1917), *Progress* (1941), and *The Significance of Beauty in Nature and Art* (1947).

COSGROVE, HENRY (1834–1906), bishop. Born in Williamsport, Pennsylvania, on Dec. 19, he was taken to Davenport, Iowa, by his parents in 1845, was educated at St. Mary's Seminary, The Barrens, Missouri, Mt. St. Bernard's Seminary, Table Mound, near Dubuque, Iowa, and the St. Louis diocesan seminary, Carondolet, Missouri. He was ordained in 1857, engaged in parish work at St. Marguerite's Church, Dubuque, Iowa, and became its pastor in 1861, and was named vicar-general of the newly created diocese of Davenport in 1881 and rector of the cathedral. He was appointed second bishop of Davenport in 1884. He built Sacred Heart Cathedral, St. Ambrose College, and St. Vincent's diocesan orphanage, increased the number of priests, parishes and schools in the diocese, and was active in projects to settle Catholic immigrants in the Midwest. In ill health the last two years of his life, he died in Davenport on Dec. 22.

COTTER, JOSEPH B. (1844–1909), bishop. Born in Liverpool, England, on Nov. 19, he emigrated to the United States and was educated at St. Vincent's College, Beatty, Pennsylvania, and St. John's College, Collegeville, Minnesota, and was ordained in 1871. He served as pastor of St. Thomas Church, Winona, Minnesota, and in 1889 was appointed first bishop of the newly established diocese of Winona. During his episcopate, he expanded the facilities of the diocese doubling the number of priests and greatly increasing the number of churches and schools. He died in Winona on June 28.

COTTON, FRANCIS R. (1895–1960), bishop. Born in Bardstown, Kentucky, on Sept. 19, he was educated at St. Meinrad's Seminary, Indiana, St. Mary's Seminary, Baltimore, and Sulpician College, Washington, D.C. He was ordained in 1920, did postgraduate work at the Apollinaris, Rome, and then engaged in pastoral work at the procathedral in Bardstown, and St. Cecilia's Church, Louisville, Kentucky. He became assistant chancellor and then chancellor of the Louisville diocese and in 1937 was appointed bishop of the newly created diocese of Owensboro, Kentucky. He died there on Sept. 25.

COUDERT, FRÉDÉRIC RENÉ (1832–1903), lawyer. Born in New York City on Mar. 1, he studied at Columbia, graduated in 1850, and was admitted to the New York bar in 1853. He began practicing law in New York, gained a reputation as an international lawyer and was for many years counsel for the French, Italian, and Spanish governments in the United States. He was a delegate to the Antwerp conference in 1877 to revise the system of averages for losses at sea, representing the New York City Chamber of Commerce, and in 1880 was a participant in an international conference at Berne, Switzerland, to discuss codification of the law of nations. He was one of the counsel for the United States at the international Bering Sea fur-seal arbitration in Paris in 1893–95 that settled the fur dispute between the United States and Great Britain and was a member of President Cleveland's Venezuela Boundary Commission in 1899 which settled the boundary dispute between Venezuela and British Guiana. In 1892–98 he was government receiver for the Union Pacific Railroad. Though active in political reform movements, he refused appointment as minister to Russia and to the U.S. Supreme Court and several other political appointments but did serve as an unsalaried member of the New York City Board of Education in 1883–84 and was a trustee of many educational institutions. He was also active in Catholic affairs, serving as president of the United States Catholic Historical Association, lectured under the auspices of the Catholic Union in 1873, and aided in the management of the St. Vincent de Paul Orphan Asylum for many years. He died in Washington, D.C., on Dec. 20. He was the author of *International Law, the Rights of Ships* (1895), and *Addresses; Historical, Political, Sociological* (1905).

COUDERT, FRÉDÉRIC RENÉ, JR. (1871–1955), lawyer. Son of Frédéric René Coudert, the famed international lawyer, and Elizabeth McCredy Coudert, he was born in New York City on Feb. 11, was educated at Columbia (B.A. 1890, M.A. 1891), received his law degree from Columbia Law School in 1894 and was admitted to the New York bar. He joined the family law firm and was admitted to practice before the U.S. Supreme Court in 1896 where he argued many cases of international scope, among them the landmark Insular cases on the status of Puerto Rico after the Spanish-American War. He was counsel for the British Government during World War I in the Appam Prize case and was attorney for Russia against the Lehigh Railroad in the Black Tom disaster. He strongly favored arbitration as the means of settling disputes among nations and international organizations, such as the Hague Tribunal and the League of Nations, and supported the Atlantic Charter. He was president of the American Society of International Law in 1942–46 and was the author of *Certainty and Justice* (1913) and *A Half Century of International Problems* (1954). For five decades he was a leading figure on the international scene and greatly influenced the direction of internationalism and American foreign policy during that time. He died in New York City on Apr. 1.

COUGHLIN, CHARLES EDWARD (1891–1979). Son of a Great Lakes seaman, Indiana-born Thomas Coughlin, and Amelia Mahaney Coughlin, a Canadian, he was born in Hamilton, Ontario, on Oct. 25, was educated at St. Michael's College, University of Toronto, and was ordained in 1916. After teaching for several years at Assumption College, Sandwich, Ontario, he became a curate at St. Agnes Church, Detroit, and in 1923 was incardinated into the Detroit diocese. He was a curate at St. Augustine's Church, Kalamazoo, Michigan, and St. Leo's Church, Detroit, was pastor at North Branch, Michigan, and in 1926 he was sent to found a parish at Royal Oak, Michigan; he built the Shrine of the Little Flower and remained as pastor there until his retirement in 1966. After the Ku Klux Klan burned a cross in the churchyard

of his church he requested and was granted time on Detroit's radio station WJR to explain Catholicism. Broadcast from the Shrine of the Little Flower the first broadcast caused little reaction. But in time his talks attracted more and more attention; when he turned from strictly religious subjects to social and political issues in 1930 his audience grew by leaps and bounds until eventually it was estimated forty million listeners tuned in each Sunday afternoon to listen to him. At first he attacked Communism but soon broadened his attacks to include the "money changers" and in time he became anti-Semitic and pro-Nazi. He supported Franklin D. Roosevelt in the presidential election of 1932 but broke with him after Roosevelt was elected President, eventually becoming a rabid anti-New Dealer. He became isolationist and anti-union, organized the National Union for Social Justice in 1934, and in 1936 founded *Social Justice,* a magazine to promote the principles of the Union, which included abolition of private banking, nationalization of certain resources, and a central government bank to control prices. In 1936 he formed the Union Party to oppose Roosevelt in the presidential election and ran William Lemke, a North Dakota congressman, for president, vowing to go off the air if Lemke did not receive nine million votes. When Lemke received only one million votes he did go off the air, but returned seven weeks later. He renewed his anti-Semitic attacks, violently opposed the entrance of the United States into World War II, and became the center of isolationist and pro-Nazi groups after Pearl Harbor. His attacks became so violent on what he called the British-Jewish-Roosevelt conspiracy that Church authorities pressured him into going off the air and the government barred *Social Justice* from the mails for violating the Espionage Act, forcing the magazine out of business in 1942. He retired as pastor of the Shrine of the Little Flower (he had built a new Shrine from a million dollars in contributions) in 1966 and lived the last years of his life in seclusion, though he did write several tracts denouncing Communism and Vatican Council II. He died at his home in Birmingham, Michigan, on Oct. 27.

COUGHLIN, MARY SAMUELS (1868–1959), mother general. Born in Faribault, Minnesota, on Apr. 7, she graduated from Bethlehem Academy in 1885, joined the Congregation of the Most Holy Rosary and received the Dominican habit in 1886. She taught in parish schools for several years, was elected the Congregation's bursar general in 1901, prioress of St. Clara Convent, Sinsinawa, Wisconsin, in 1904 and mother general in 1910. During her generalship she established sixty-three foundations, saw some 1,450 sisters make their profession, transferred Santa Clara College from Sinsinawa to River Forest, Illinois, in 1922 as Rosary College, established Edgewood College of the Sacred Heart in Madison, Wisconsin, in 1927, and opened a European house of studies in Fribourg, Switzerland, in 1917 and Pius XII Institute, a graduate school of fine arts, at Villa Schifanoia, Florence, Italy, in 1948. She encouraged graduate study for her nuns, sending them to American and European universities, opened the Congregation to black applicants and opened five schools for blacks, and was the first president of the American Dominican Mothers General Conference in 1935–37. She died at the Congregation's motherhouse, St. Clara Convent, at Sinsinawa, Wisconsin, on October 17.

CRABITES, PIERRE (1877–1943), jurist. Born in New Orleans on Feb. 17, he was educated at Immaculate Conception College there (B.A. 1895), Tulane (LL.B. 1898), and the University of Paris. He was admitted to the Louisiana bar in 1900, practiced law for a time in New Orleans, and then went to Egypt to learn Arabic. He was selected by President Taft in 1911 to be American judge at the Mixed Tribunals in Cairo and remained there the next twenty-five years. During trips home from Egypt he was a special lecturer at Louisiana State University law school. When World War II broke out, he was sent on special diplomatic service to Cairo and in 1942 he was appointed special aide to the American minister in Iraq. He died in Iraq on Oct. 9. He was the author of several books on Egypt and Sudan including *Ismail, the Maligned Khedive* (1933), *Gordon, the Sudan and Slavery* (1933), and *The Spoliation of Egypt* (1940). He also wrote a biography of Eduard Beneš of Czechoslovakia, on the Spanish Civil War, and on Pope Clement VII and King Henry VIII.

CRAIGIE, PEARL MARY TERESA (1867–1906), author. Eldest daughter of John Morgan Richards, a Boston executive, and Laura Hortense Arnold Richards, Pearl Richards was born on Nov. 3 in Boston and was taken to England as an infant. She was educated at University College, England, and in 1887 married Reginald Walpole Craigie, an Englishman; the marriage was shortlived and she soon obtained a legal separation and custody of their only child. She began writing and soon became known for her moralistic novels and as a dramatist, writing under the pseudonym John Oliver Hobbes. She published more than a dozen books and half a dozen plays. Among the former were *The Sinner's Comedy* (1892), *A Study in Temptation* (1893), *The School for Saints* (1897), and *Robert Orange* (1900); among her plays were the one-act *Journey's End in Lovers' Meeting* (1894), written for Ellen Terry, *The*

Ambassador (produced in 1898), and *The Wisdom of the Wise* (1900). She was converted to Catholicism in 1892 and many of her later works reflected her new religious beliefs. She died on Nov. 3.

CRAWFORD, FRANCIS MARION (1854–1909), author. Son of Thomas Crawford, distinguished American sculptor, and Louise Ward, sister of Julia Ward Howe, he was born in Bagni di Lucca, Italy, on Aug. 2 and was educated at St. Paul's School, Concord, New Hampshire, Cambridge, the Technische Hochschule, Karlsruhe, and Heidelberg in Germany, and studied Sanskrit at the University of Rome. He went to India in 1879, edited the *Indian Herald* in Allahabad in 1879–80 and became a Catholic there in 1880. He returned to Rome because of illness and in 1881 went to Boston where he wrote his first novel, *Mr. Isaacs* (1882) in six weeks. He returned to Italy, married Elizabeth Berdan in 1884 and they settled in Sorrento where he spent the rest of his life. He wrote biography, history, travel books, a study of the novel, *The Novel: What It Is* (1893), and cosmopolitan and colorful novels though sometimes critized for inaccurate details. His first novel had brought him immediate fame and he eventually published some forty novels. Among his books were *Dr. Claudius* (1883), *Marzio's Crucifix* (1887), *Saracinesca* (1887), *A Cigarette Maker's Romance* (1890), which was made into a drama, *Constantinople* (1895), *Via Crucis* (1898), *The Life of Pope Leo XIII* (1904), and *The Diva's Ruby* (1908). He also wrote *Francesca da Rimini* in which Sarah Bernhardt starred in Paris. He died at Sorrento, Italy, on Apr. 9.

CREIGHTON, EDWARD (1820–74), executive, philanthropist. The fifth child of Irish immigrants who came to the United States in 1805, he was born near Barnesville, Belmont County, Ohio, on Aug. 31. He had only a rudimentary education and when he was eighteen went into business as a wagoner when his father gave him a team of horses and a wagon. He became interested in building telegraph lines when he contracted to deliver telegraph poles from Dayton, Ohio, to Evansville, Indiana, and started erecting lines himself with one between Dayton and Cincinnati, Ohio. In 1856 the line he built to St. Joseph, Missouri, gave him a reputation in the field and when it was decided to erect a transcontinental line he was chosen to survey the route and in 1861, he built the section between Julesburg, Colorado, and Salt Lake City. When the line was finished he was made general superintendent of the Pacific Telegraph, a position he resigned in 1867 to return to the lucrative trucking business. He married Mary Lucretia Wareham (his brother John married her sister Sarah Emily Wareham), was one of those who stocked the Western plains with cattle, and was one of the founders of the First National Bank of Omaha and was its president until stricken with a stroke that caused his death in Omaha on Nov. 5. He had accumulated a large fortune during his lifetime and had contributed generously to many charities but he died before realizing his dream of founding a free Catholic college. However, his wife Mary (d. Jan. 23, 1876) left a large bequest toward the founding of Creighton University, the first free Catholic college in the United States.

CREIGHTON, JOHN A. (1831–1907), philanthropist. The youngest of nine children of Irish immigrant parents and brother of Edward Creighton, he was born in Licking County, Ohio, on Oct. 15. He studied at St. Joseph's College, Somerset, Ohio, intending to become an engineer but abandoned his plan when his mother died in 1854. He became associated with his brother in building transcontinental telegraph lines and in his freighting business. He opened a miners' supply store in Virginia City, Montana, during the gold rush there and served on the Vigilance Committee that helped free Montana of the desperadoes and bandits plaguing the area and offered to fight against the Indians in 1867, though his services were not needed. In 1868, he married Sarah Emily Wareham (her sister Mary Lucretia Wareham married his brother Edward) and the couple settled in Omaha, Nebraska. He built a large fortune from investments in western mines and Omaha real estate and he and his wife contributed generously to Creighton University; on Sarah's death in 1888 he built Creighton Memorial St. Joseph's Hospital as a memorial to her. He was a benefactor of many worthy causes, among them a monastery for the Poor Clares in Omaha and the Creighton Home for Girls (built after his death), and he left large bequests in his will to Creighton University. He was made a Knight of St. Gregory and a Count of the Papal Court by Pope Leo XIII in 1895 and received the Laetare Medal in 1900. He died in Omaha on Feb. 7.

CRESPI, JUAN (1721–82), explorer. Born in Mallorca, Spain, he joined the Franciscans and in 1749 was sent to San Fernando College, Mexico, with Francisco Palou and Junípero Serra. He was placed in charge of Mission Purisima Concepción in Lower California in 1767 and two years later joined the expedition of Gaspar de Portolá to occupy San Diego and Monterey in California; the expedition explored the coast to Portolá, discovering San Francisco Bay on the way on Nov. 1. In 1770 he founded Mission San Carlos Borromeo at Carmel and made it his headquarters until his death there twelve years later.

In 1774 he acompanied Juan Perez's expedition to the North Pacific and Alaska as its chaplain and left a diary of the exploration which is an invaluable historical record of these explorations.

CRÉTIN, JOSEPH (1799–1857), bishop. Born at Montluel, Ain, France, on Dec. 10, he was educated at l'Argentière, Aix, and St. Sulpice Seminary, Paris, and was ordained in 1823. He became curate in 1823 and then pastor in 1831 at Ferney and built a new church and a school for boys. In 1838 he responded to the visit and appeal of Bishop Loras, first bishop of Dubuque, Iowa, for priests for his diocese and accompanied the bishop back to the United States. On his arrival at Dubuque, he was appointed vicar-general of the diocese. He engaged in missionary work in Iowa and Wisconsin among the Winnebago Indians, went to Europe in 1847 seeking priests, and in 1850 he was appointed first bishop of the newly established diocese of St. Paul, Minnesota. He was consecrated in Belley, France, the next year, returned to the United States with seven priests for his new see, built a new cathedral (his first one was a log cabin) and a hospital in 1853, established a cemetery, and brought the Sisters of St. Joseph and the Brothers of the Holy Family into the see in 1851 and 1855. A leader in the temperance movement, he founded the Catholic Temperance Society of St. Paul in 1852 and promoted Catholic colonization by encouraging Catholic immigrants from Europe to settle on the plains of Minnesota. In 1855 he began the building of St. Paul's present cathedral but died in St. Paul on Feb. 22 before it was finished.

CRÈVECOEUR, HECTOR ST. JOHN (1735–1813), agriculturist. Christened Michel-Guillaume Jean de Crèvecoeur, he was born near Caen,

France, on Jan. 31 and when sixteen went to England. He emigrated to Canada, served with Montcalm, and then traveled through the Great Lakes and Ohio Valley regions as a surveyor. In 1759 he went to New York and spent the next decade traveling widely especially in New York and Pennsylvania. He married Mehetable Tippett of Yonkers in 1769, settled down on his farm, Pine Hill, in Orange County, New York, and introduced several European crops to America, notably alfalfa. In 1780 he left for France on business but on the way was arrested in New York by the British who accused him of being a spy. After being imprisoned for several months, he was freed and finally reached his native land where he introduced the potato to the farmers of Normandy. His glowing description of the New World caused several hundred of his countrymen to emigrate to Pennsylvania where they established a colony which flourished at first but eventually was destroyed by Indian marauders. On his return to his farm in 1783 he found his house had been burned in an Indian raid, his wife was dead, and his children had disappeared; he later found them in the care of a friendly merchant. He became French consul to the United States in New York after the Revolution, worked to improve relations between France and the United States, and helped found New York's first Catholic church, St. Peter's, in 1785 and served as a trustee. He left the United States in 1790 and returned to France where he died at Sarcelles on Nov. 12. Crèvecoeur wrote for American newspapers under the name Agricola and a collection of his letters was published as *Letters from an American Farmer* (1784), an invaluable description of American rural life of that period; they were written under the pseudonym J. Hector St. John which he said was his real name, claiming Crèvecoeur

was an addition to the family name. A collection of his letters discovered in 1922 was published as *Sketches of Eighteenth-Century America.*

CRIMMINS, JOHN DANIEL (1844–1917), contractor. Born in New York City on May 8, he was educated at St. Francis Xavier College there and then joined his father's contracting firm. It soon became one of the largest such firms in the city and constructed most of New York City's railroad lines, built skyscrapers, hospitals, and churches, and constructed the first underground telephone and telegraph lines. Crimmins pioneered in the use of steam drills in excavation work. He participated in Democratic politics and Irish-American groups, served as commissioner of parks, and was known for his philanthropies to Catholic organizations and his contributions to St. Patrick's Cathedral. He died in New York City on Nov. 9.

CRIMONT, JOSEPH RAPHAEL (1858–1945), bishop. Born in Ferrières, near Amiens, France, on Feb. 2, he was educated at College de la Providence, Amiens, in 1869–75, and joined the Jesuits in 1875. He continued his studies at St. Acheul, Amiens, in 1875–80 and St. Helier on the Isle of Jersey in 1884–86, and went to the United States in 1886. He was ordained in 1888 after further studies at Woodstock College, Maryland, where he received his S.T.D. He worked among the Crow Indians as superior of St. Xavier's mission in Big Horn County, Montana, from 1890 until 1894 when he was appointed superior of the Holy Cross mission on the Yukon, Alaska, and was stationed there until 1901. He served as president of Gonzaga College, Spokane, Washington, from 1901 until 1904 when he was appointed prefect apostolic of Catholic missions in Alaska. He was named titular bishop of Ammaedera and vicar apostolic of Alaska in 1917 and spent the rest of his life in Alaska until his death on May 20 in Juneau, Alaska.

CROSBY, HARRY LILLIS "BING" (1903–77), entertainer. Born in Tacoma, Washington, on May 2, he early earned the sobriquet "Bing" for his interest in a comic strip called "The Bingville Bugle." When the family moved to Spokane, he attended Gonzaga High School and entered Gonzaga University in 1921 and in the same year began his career when he joined a local band called the Musicaladers. He left the university in 1925 and with a friend, Al Rinker, went to Los Angeles. The two worked on the vaudeville circuit and in 1927 were hired by Paul Whiteman as a singing act; when they were unsuccessful in New York City, Whiteman dropped them. With Harris Barris they formed the Rhythm Boys and became an instant success with such numbers as "Mississippi Mud" and "From Monday On." In 1930 they appeared in the motion picture *The King of Jazz,* then returned to Whiteman's band. When Whiteman fired Crosby for his lackadaisical attitude they went back to Los Angeles and again were a success in nightclubs. Bing married Dixie Lee in 1930 and when the Rhythm Boys disbanded he played in several Mack Sennett shorts; in 1932 his record, crooning "I Surrender Dear" on CBS in New York, made him a nationwide hit. He had a sensational twenty-week run at the Paramount Theater in New York and in 1932 appeared in the picture *The Big Broadcast of 1932* and appeared in several other pictures over the next few years. In 1934 he signed with Decca Records and became one of the bestselling singers of all time with such hits as "When the Blue of the Night Meets the Gold of the Day," "Don't Fence Me In," "Sweet Leilani," and "White Christmas," the bestselling record of all time. He made some seventy motion pictures among them *Anything Goes* and *Pennies from Heaven* (1936) and *Sing You Sinners* (1938). In 1936 he became the star of NBC's Kraft Music Hall which was a nationwide hit. In 1940 Crosby, Bob Hope, and Dorothy Lamour appeared together for the first time in the movie *The Road to Singapore;* its immediate success led to a whole series of *Road* pictures, among them *The Road to Zanzibar* (1941), *The Road to Morocco* (1942), and *The Road to Bali* (1952). Among other pictures he appeared in were *Holiday Inn* (1942) in which he sang "White Christmas," *Going My Way* (1944) in which his portrayal of Fr. O'Malley won him an Academy Award, and its sequel, *The Bells of St. Mary's* (1945), *Blue Skies* (1946), *Here Comes the Groom* (1951), *The Country Girl* (1954), and *Stagecoach* (1966). In 1952 he made his television debut on a telethon with Bob Hope and in the years to come his television specials were enormously popular. His autobiographical *Call Me Lucky* was published in the *Saturday Evening Post* in 1953 and in book form the following year. Crosby was one of the greatest and most beloved entertainers of all time—highly successful on the stage, in nightclubs, in motion pictures, and on radio and television. He died of a heart attack while playing golf on La Moraleja golf course near Madrid, Spain, on Oct. 14.

CROWLEY, PATRICK EDWARD (1864–1953), railroader. Born in Chattaraugus, New York, on Aug. 25, he left school when thirteen and became a messenger for the Erie Railroad in 1878. He moved to the New York Central Railroad in 1889 and rose from dispatcher to vice president in 1915. During World War I he was federal manager when the governor took over control of the railroads and in 1924 he was named president of the New York Central. He also served as president of the Rutland Railroad and as a director of Emigrant Industrial Savings Bank, Western Union, and the Railroad Credit Corporation. He resigned as president of the New York Central in 1932, became a member of the railroad advisory board and held that position until he retired in 1940. He died in Mount Vernon, New York, on Oct. 1.

CROWLEY, PATRICK FRANCIS (1911–74), cofounder. Born in Chicago on Sept. 23, he was educated at Notre Dame (B.A. 1933) and Loyola University, Chicago, (J.D. 1937), and married Patricia Caron in 1937. He and Patricia founded the Christian Family Movement in the United States in 1943 in Chicago to promote the Christian family way of life; it became a national movement in 1949. They were awarded the Laetare Medal in 1966 and he became president of the International Confraternity of Christian Family Movements. He died in Chicago on Nov. 24.

CRUZ, JUAN DE LA (d. c. 1544). *See* Padilla, Juan de.

CUDAHY, EDWARD ALOYSIUS (1860–1941), executive. Born in Milwaukee, Wisconsin, on Feb. 1, he entered the meat supply business in 1875 and spent his entire career in that industry. With his brother Michael and Philip Armour, he established the Armour-Cudahy Packing Company in 1887 and in 1890 he became vice president of the Cudahy Packing Company when Michael bought out Armour's share of the business and renamed the firm. He became president on Michael's death in 1910 and became chairman of the board when his son Edward became president in 1925. He was well known for his philanthropies, among them the library he donated in honor of his wife at Loyola University, Chicago. He died in Chicago on Oct. 18.

CUDAHY, MICHAEL (1841–1910), executive. Born in Callan, Kilkenny, Ireland, on Dec. 7, he was brought to the United States in 1849 by his parents and entered the meat packing business in 1856. In 1870 he introduced the refrigeration process which revolutionized the industry and five years later he became a partner in Armour & Company of Chicago. In 1887 he and his brother Edward and Philip Armour bought out Thomas J. Lipton's slaughterhouse in Omaha, Nebraska, and founded the Armour-Cudahy Packing Company. He bought out Armour's interest in the firm in 1890 and renamed it the Cudahy Packing Company, serving as its president with Michael as vice president, and held this position until his death in Chicago on Nov. 27.

CUDDIHY, ROBERT JOSEPH (1862–1952), publisher. Born in New York City on Dec. 31, he began working for the working for the publishing firm established by the Rev. I. K. Funk and A. W. Wagnalls in 1878 and in 1890 was named publisher of the newly launched *Literary Digest*. He acquired the controlling interest in Funk and Wagnalls in 1914 and remained at its head until he retired in 1948. He developed the ideas for the Schall-Herzog *Encyclopedia of Religious Knowledge, The Jewish Encyclopedia,* Funk and Wagnalls's *Standard Dictionary of the English Language,* and the enormously successful *Standard Encyclopedia* which sold more than twenty-five million copies. Though a Catholic, he made available in the United States many of the works of the great Protestant theologians. He sold off the *Literary Digest* in 1937 the year after its poll of the 1936 presidential election had predicted the election of Alfred M. Landon over Franklin D. Roosevelt, who overwhelmed his opponent (Landon captured the electoral votes of only two states), though its poll had been consistently accurate in previous presidential elections since 1920. Cuddihy was widely known for his charitable and philanthropic work, was honored by several foreign governments and the Vatican for it, and died in New York City on Dec. 22.

CULLEN, BERNARD A. (1903–60). Born in New York City on Aug. 3, he was educated at Cathedral College there and St. Joseph's Seminary, Yonkers, New York, and was ordained in 1930. He engaged in pastoral work in the New York archdiocese, became interested in the plight of the American Indians and became director of the Marquette League for American Indian missions. He was made a papal chamberlain in 1954 and died in Miami, Florida, on Sept. 3.

CUMMINGS, JEREMIAH WILLIAMS (1814–66). Born in Washington, D.C., on Apr. 15, he was brought to New York City when a boy by his mother after the death of his father. He decided to become a priest, studied briefly at the seminary in Nyack, New York, and was then sent to the Propaganda in Rome by Bishop Dubois. He received his doctorate in divinity and was ordained in Rome in 1847, was assigned to old St. Patrick's Cathedral on his return to New York, and became known for his musical and linguistic abilitites and his oratorical prowess. Bishop John Hughes appointed him to found St. Stephen's parish in New York in 1848 and he finished building its church in 1854; he developed the parish into one of the outstanding parishes in the diocese, known for its liturgical ceremonies and music and his sermons. A

friend of Orestes Brownson whom he persuaded to move to New York from Boston, he wrote numerous articles for *Brownson's Review* and supported many of Brownson's often unpopular positions. With a group of other priests and laymen, he opposed the European domination of teaching in American Catholic colleges and seminaries and was highly critical of the effectiveness of Catholic higher education and seminary training; his article on "Vocations to the Priesthood" in *Brownson's Review* in 1860 evoked the ire of Archbishop Hughes who responded with one of his best known articles, "Reflections on the Catholic Press." Cummings favored a more ecumenical approach to non-Catholics in contrast to the hostility toward non-Catholics then prevalent in Catholic circles and supported the concept of ecumenism. He was the author of *Italian Legends* (1854), *Songs for Catholic Schools* (1862), and *Spiritual Progress* and was pastor of St. Stephen's until his death in New York City on Jan. 4.

CUMMINS, PATRICK (1880–1968), scholar. Born in Burlington Junction, Missouri, on Apr. 19, he joined the Benedictines at Conception Abbey, Missouri, in 1889, changing his name from John Thomas Benedict to Patrick and was professed in 1900. He studied at St. Anselm's, Rome (S.T.D. 1905) and Maximilian University, Munich, Germany, and on his return to the United States taught and was master of novices at Conception Abbey. He was appointed rector of St. Anselm's in 1921 but returned to Conception Abbey in 1925 when his proposals to revise St. Anselm's curriculum was rejected by the Congress of Abbots. He was a leader in the liturgical movement and the revival of interest in the bible among Catholics and was president of the Catholic Biblical Association in 1947–

48. In 1941 he proposed the Catholic Biblical Association put aside its intended new translation of the Old Testament from the Vulgate and instead undertake a translation from the original languages; the project was begun in 1943 and the result was The New American Bible. He died at Conception Abbey on Feb. 14.

CUNNINGHAM, DAVID F. (1900–79), bishop. Born in Walkerville, Montana, on Dec. 3, he was educated at St. Michael's College, Toronto, Canada, St. Bernard's Seminary, Rochester, New York, and Catholic University and was ordained in 1926. He served as assistant pastor at St. Ambrose Church, Endicott, New York, until 1929 when he resumed his studies at Catholic University and received his licentiate in canon law in 1930. He served as secretary to bishops Daniel Curley in 1930–33, John Duffy in 1933–37, and Walter A. Foley in 1937–50, was made a domestic prelate in 1941, was made pastor of St. John the Baptist Church in Syracuse and vicar-general of the diocese in 1946, and in 1950 was named titular bishop of Lampsacus and auxiliary of Syracuse. He attended Vatican Council in 1962–65, was appointed coadjutor of Syracuse in 1967, and succeeded to the see three years later. He retired in 1976 and died in Syracuse on Feb. 22.

CUNNINGHAM, JOHN FRANCIS (1842–1919), bishop. Born in Kerry, Ireland, he emigrated to the United States and was educated at St. Benedict's College, Atchison, Kansas, and St. Francis Seminary, Milwaukee, Wisconsin, and was ordained in Leavenworth, Kansas in 1865. He served in the Leavenworth diocese, became vicar-general and in 1898 was appointed third bishop of Concordia, Kansas. He built numerous charitable institutions and schools during his episcopate and died on June 23 in Concordia.

CURLEY, DANIEL (1869–1932), bishop. Born in New York City on June 16, he was educated at St. Francis Xavier College there, St. Joseph's Seminary, Troy, New York, and the North American College, Rome, and was ordained in Rome in 1894. He was assigned to pastoral work in New York City, was secretary to Archbishop Corrigan in 1901–2, and served as pastor of Our Lady of Solace parish from 1902 until 1923 when he was appointed bishop of Syracuse, New York, a position he held until his death there on Aug. 3.

CURLEY, JAMES (1796–1889), astronomer. Born in Athleague, Roscommon, Ireland, on Oct. 26, he had a meager education in his youth though he was extremely proficient in mathematics. He emigrated to the United States in 1817, settled in Philadelphia, worked as a bookkeeper for a time, and then taught mathematics in Frederick, Maryland. He entered the seminary in Washington, D.C., in 1826 to study for the priesthood and when it closed the following year he joined the Jesuits. He taught at Frederick for a time, was sent to teach and study theology at Georgetown in 1831, became an American citizen in 1832, and was ordained in 1833. He spent the rest of his life at Georgetown, serving as chaplain at the Visitation Convent there for fifty years and teaching at Georgetown for forty-eight years. He planned and superintended the building and was first director of the Georgetown Astronomical Observatory which was opened in 1844 and was soon recognized as a first-class observatory. He determined the longitude of Washington, D.C., which differed from that of the Naval Observatory's calculations, and had his observations determined to be correct when the transatlantic cable was laid in 1858. He authored *Annals of the Astronomical Observatory of Georgetown College, D.C.* (1852), and died at Georgetown on July 24.

CURLEY, JAMES MICHAEL (1874–1958), governor. Son of a hod carrier, he was born in Boston on Nov. 20, entered politics as soon as he graduated from high school and was elected to the city council when he was twenty-five. He served in the Massachusetts legislature in 1902–3, was alderman in 1904–9 and councilman in 1910–11, and became a power in the Democratic Party in Boston. He served in the United States House of Representatives in 1911–15 and was mayor of Boston in 1914–18, 1922–26, and 1930–34, and was governor of Massachusetts in 1935–37. He again served in Congress in 1943–46 and was reelected mayor in 1946; while still mayor he was convicted in 1947 of mail order fraud in connection with war contracts and sentenced to federal prison. After serving five months of his sentence he had the balance commuted by President Harry Truman and he returned to finish his term as mayor. He was defeated in 1949 in a bid for reelection as mayor. Curley was one of that group of powerful political figures that dominated politics in many of the large cities of the United States in the first half of the twentieth century and had a great influence on national politics. His autobiography *I'd Do It Again* was published in 1957 and the highly successful novel *The Last Hurrah* by Edwin O'Connor (later made into a motion picture starring Spencer Tracy) was reputedly based to a large extent on his colorful life and career. He died in Boston on Nov. 13.

CURLEY, MICHAEL JOSEPH (1879–1947), archbishop. Born in Athlone, Westmeath, Ireland, on Oct. 12, he was educated at Mungret College, Limerick, the Royal University, Dublin (B.A.), and the Propaganda, Rome (S.T.L.), and was ordained in 1904. He emigrated to the United States in 1904 and became pastor at De Land, Florida, and an American citizen. He served there until 1914 when he was named bishop of St. Augustine, Florida. He greatly increased the number of churches in the diocese and led the fight against a state law forbidding white women to teach black children; the law was eventually declared unconstitutional. He was appointed archbishop of Baltimore to succeed Cardinal Gibbons in 1921. He was an avid supporter of Catholic education, building some sixty-six schools during his episcopate, sponsored St. Mary's Seminary, helped complete St. Charles College, Catonsville, Maryland, and was chancellor of Catholic University. In 1939 he was appointed first archbishop of Washington, D.C., while remaining as archbishop of Baltimore (the archdiocese of Washington, D.C., was not separated from the archdiocese of Baltimore until 1947), and died in Baltimore on May 16.

CURRAN, EDWARD LODGE (1898–1974), priest. Born in Brooklyn, New York, on Mar. 23, he was educated at St. John's University (B.A. 1918), Catholic University (S.T.B.), and was ordained in 1922. He continued his education at Columbia (M.A. 1925) and Fordham (Ph.D. 1928), studied law at Brooklyn Law School (LL.B. 1932), and was admitted to the New York City bar in 1932 and the New York State bar the following year. He taught literature at Cathedral College, Brooklyn, in 1922–32 and was dean there in 1927–32. He was an implacable foe of Communism and in 1932 he founded the International Catholic Truth Society and was its president. He served as pastor of St.

CURRAN, JOHN JOSEPH

Stephen's Church in Brooklyn in 1941–62 and of St. Sebastian's Church in Woodside, Queens, New York, from 1962 until his death in Woodside on Feb. 14. He was the author of several books and pamphlets, among them *Great Moments in Catholic History* (1938), *Facts about Communism* (1937), and *Pope of Peace.*

CURRAN, JOHN JOSEPH (1859–1936), priest. Born in Hawley, Pennsylvania, on June 20, he started working in the Pennsylvania coal mines when a child of seven, decided on a priestly vocation and studied for the priesthood at Wyoming Seminary, Kingston, and St. Vincent Seminary, Latrobe, Pennsylvania, and the Grand Seminary, Montreal. He was ordained in Scranton, Pennsylvania, in 1887 and spent the rest of his life ministering to the coal miners of Pennsylvania as curate of St. Rose's Church, Carbondale, as founding pastor of Holy Savior Church, Wilkes-Barre in 1895 and as pastor of St. Mary's Church, Wilkes-Barre, from 1919 until his death. He became famed for his support of the coal miners in their struggle for better working conditions and of John Mitchell, president of the United Mine Workers, and achieved national recognition for his role in the bitter anthracite strike of 1902; President Theodore Roosevelt thanked him for his aid in settling the strike. He was instrumental in settling other strikes, was made a papal chamberlain in 1930, and died in Wilkes-Barre on Nov. 7.

CURRIER, CHARLES WARREN (1857–1918), bishop. Born in St. Thomas, West Indies, on Mar. 22, he was educated at the Redemptorist preparatory college in Roermond, Holland, was professed a Redemptorist in 1875, finished his studies at Wittem, and was ordained in 1880. He served as a missionary in Surinam, South America, for thirteen months, came to the United States in 1882 because of ill health and engaged in missionary activities in Maryland, Boston, and New York City. Ill health caused him to ask for a dispensation from his Redemptorist vows which was granted and in 1892 he joined the Baltimore archdiocese, serving there for the next twenty-one years, as pastor of St. Mary's Church in Washington, D.C., from 1913. He was an editorial writer for the *Catholic Mirror* in 1893–94, wrote for magazines, and was the author of several books, among them *Carmel in America* (1890), *History of Religious Orders* (1894), *Dimitrios and Irene* (1894), and *Lands of the Southern Cross* (1911). He was a director of the Spanish-American Athenaeum in Washington and an authority on Hispanic matters, and served as official U.S. government representative at numerous Spanish-American conferences. In 1913 he was appointed first bishop of the newly established diocese of Matanzas in Cuba but was soon forced to resign because of ill health. He was named titular bishop of Etalomia and died in Baltimore on Sept. 23.

CURTIS, ALFRED ALLEN (1831–1908), bishop. Born in Rehoboth, Somerset County, Maryland, on July 4, he was raised an Episcopalian, became an Episcopal priest in 1859, and served as minister at Chestertown, Maryland. While on a visit to England in 1872, he was converted to Catholicism by Cardinal Newman; on his return to the United States he studied for the Catholic priesthood at St. Mary's Seminary, Baltimore, where he was ordained in 1874. He engaged in pastoral activities in the Baltimore diocese, was secretary to Archbishop James Roosevelt Bayley and Cardinal Gibbons, and was chancellor of the archdiocese in 1874–86, and was appointed second bishop of Wilmington, Delaware, in 1886. He inherited a heavy diocesan debt which he paid off in the next decade, brought Benedictine and Ursuline sisters into the diocese, built the Visitation monastery, and established a mission for blacks under the Josephites. He resigned the see in 1896 because of ill health and was appointed titular bishop of Echinus. He administered the Wilmington see in 1896–97 and was vicar-general of Washington, D.C., in 1897–98 and died in Baltimore on July 11.

CUSACK, THOMAS FRANCIS (1862–1918), bishop. Born in New York City on Feb. 22, he was educated at St. Francis Xavier College there, graduated in 1880, and then studied for the priesthood at St. Joseph's Seminary, Troy, New York, and was ordained there in 1885. He engaged in pastoral work and was director of the New York archdiocesan missionaries from 1897 to 1904 when he was named titular bishop of Themiscyra and auxiliary of New York and rector of St. Stephen's parish. In 1915, he was appointed fifth bishop of Albany, New York, and devoted himself to convert work and missions for Catholics, establishing diocesan offices for the Propagation of the Faith and Catholic Charities. He died in Albany on July 12.

CUSHING, RICHARD (1895–1970), cardinal. Born in Boston on Aug. 24, he was educated at Boston College and St. John's Seminary, Brighton, Massachusetts (D.D., LL.D.), and was ordained in 1921. He spent a year in pastoral work and then was appointed to the Boston archdiocesan office of the Society for the Propagation of the Faith; he was appointed its director in 1928 and developed it into the most outstanding Propagation of the Faith office in the United States. In 1939 he was named titular bishop of Mela and auxiliary of Boston and on the death of Cardinal O'Connell in 1944 was appointed archbishop of Boston; he was made a cardinal in 1958. During his episcopate eighty churches were built in the archdiocese, some sixty new religious orders were brought into the see, the number of schools was increased, three colleges were chartered and Pope John XXIII Seminary for mature men seeking to enter the priesthood was established at Weston, Massachusetts. He built the first chapel at an airport, established the first diocesan center for radio and television, and founded the Missionary Society of St. James the Apostle in 1958, which allowed diocesan priests to spend several years in missionary work in South America. He established six new hospitals, founded homes for the aged and handicapped children, and was known for his devotion to the aged and the handicapped. He was active in the social and ecumenical movements of the times, attended Vatican Council II, and was a friend of the Kennedy family, delivering the invocation at John Kennedy's inauguration as President of the United States in 1961 and presiding at his funeral rites in 1963. Suffering from cancer the last two decades of his life and from asthma, he resigned in 1970 and died two months later in Boston on Nov. 2. At the time of his death Cardinal Cushing was one of the best known and most beloved priests in the United States and had a reputation for charitable benefactions unsurpassed by anyone in the United States and indeed throughout the world.

D

DABLON, CLAUDE (c. 1618–97), missionary. Born in Dieppe, France, in Feb., he joined the Jesuits when he was twenty-one and was sent to Canada in 1655. He was sent to minister to the Iroquois Indians near present-day Syracuse, New York, and built St. Mary's chapel for the French settlers where Mass was said for the first time in New York. He accompanied Fr. Gabriel Druillettes on an exploration of Hudson Bay in 1661 in an attempt to discover a Northwest Passage and to establish missions among the Cree Indians along the way. In 1668, with Fr. Claude Jean Allouez and Fr. Jacques Marquette, he crossed the Great Lakes, explored the area around Lake Superior, and discovered copper mines in the region. In 1669 he was placed in charge of the western missions, spent the winter of 1669–70 with the Winnebago Indians and dispatched Marquette on his trip down the Mississippi River. He founded Sault Ste. Marie, Michigan, in 1668, and in 1670 was appointed superior general of all Canadian missions, a position he held until 1680 and to which he was reappointed in 1686, serving this time until 1693. As superior he was director of the great expansion of missionary and exploring activities of the Jesuits. He died in Quebec on May 3. His contributions to the Jesuit *Relations* are an important part of that invaluable collection and it was he who was responsible for preserving and publishing Marquette's letters and charts.

DABROWSKI, JOSEPH (1842–1903), priest. Born in Zoltance, Poland, on Jan. 27, he was educated at Lublin gymnasium and the University of Warsaw and fought against Russia in the Polish revolt of 1863. When the revolt was unsuccessful, he fled to Germany in 1864, continued his studies at Lucerne and Berne, Switzerland, went to Rome to study for the priesthood and was ordained in 1869 when he emigrated to the United States. He worked with Polish immigrants, brought the Felician sisters to the United States in 1874, and served as pastor at Polonia, Wisconsin, from 1870 to 1882, when ill health forced him to retire. He went to Detroit and despite his poor health began building SS. Cyril and Methodius Seminary there in 1884; it opened in 1887, devoted to the training of bilingual Polish-American priests, and he served as its rector for nineteen years until his death in Detroit on Feb. 15.

DAEGER, ANTHONY THOMAS (1872–1932), bishop. Born in North Vernon, Indiana, he was educated at St. Francis Seminary, Cincinnati, Ohio, joined the Friars Minor taking the name Albert, continued studying for the priesthood and was ordained in 1896. He engaged in pastoral work in Ohio, Missouri, and Nebraska and in 1902 became a missionary to the Indians at Pena Blanca, New Mexico. He worked with the Indians there until 1919 when he was appointed bishop of Santa Fe,

New Mexico. During his episcopate he began a short-lived seminary at Las Vegas to help alleviate the shortage of priests in his diocese and encouraged religious orders to open foundations in the see. He died in Santa Fe on Dec. 2.

DAHOOD, MITCHELL (1922–82), biblical scholar. Born in Anaconda, Montana, on Feb. 2, he joined the Jesuits in 1941, was educated at Boston College (B.A. 1947, M.A. 1948) and Johns Hopkins University (Ph.D. 1951), where he studied under the famous biblical scholar William F. Albright, and was ordained in 1954. He became a professor of Ugaritic languages and literature at the Pontifical Institute of Biblical Studies, Rome, in 1956, held the chair of Northwest Semitic Languages on the faculty of Near Eastern Studies of the Institute for more than twenty-five years, was dean of the faculty in 1975–78, and was elected president of the Catholic Biblical Association of America in 1980. He became a world-famous authority on the correlation between the Hebrew text of the Old Testament and Ugaritic and, toward the end of his life, Eblaite. He wrote hundreds of articles on the subject and several books, among them *Ugaritic Hebrew Philology* (1965) and a three-volume translation and commentary on the Psalms in the Anchor Bible series (I, 1966; II, 1968; III, 1970). He also directed the scholarly monograph series *Analecta Orientalia* and *Studia Pohl* from 1972 until his death in Rome on Mar. 8. During the last years of his life, he worked on the texts and language of the tablets discovered at Tel el-Mardikh (ancient Ebla), Syria.

DALEY, JOSEPH T. (1915–83), bishop. Born in Connerton, Pennsylvania, on Dec. 1, he was educated at St. Charles Borromeo Seminary, Overbrook, Philadelphia, and was ordained

in 1941. He was named titular bishop of Barca and auxiliary of Harrisburg, Pennsylvania, in 1963, was made coadjutor in 1967 and succeeded to the see in 1971. He remained as bishop of Harrisburg until his death there on Sept. 2.

DALEY, RICHARD (1902–76), mayor. Born in Chicago on May 15, he took a commercial course at De La Salle Institute there and on graduation took a job in the stockyards. He began studying law at night at De Paul University in 1923, received his LL.B. in 1933 and was admitted to the Illinois bar later that year. He married Eleanor Guilfoyle in 1936, was involved in local Democratic politics (from the time he was twelve), was a precinct captain when twenty-one, and in 1936 formed a law firm with Peter V. Fazio. He was state representative in 1936–38, state senator in 1939–46, and deputy controller of Cook County in 1946–49. He was appointed state revenue collector in 1948, was elected Cook County clerk in 1950 and chairman of the Cook County Democratic Central Committee in 1953, and began building his own political machine. He was elected mayor of Chicago in 1955 and reelected at each mayoralty campaign for the rest of his life. He began to play an important role in state affairs and in 1960 he played a decisive role in the nomination of John F. Kennedy as Democratic candidate for the presidency; Kennedy credited him with his victory since the Illinois vote which Daley delivered to him at the national convention was crucial to his securing the nomination. When Kennedy was elected president, Daley became a power in national politics. In 1968 he was severely criticized for police actions against demonstrators during the national Democratic convention in Chicago. Daley's administrations were marked on the one hand by his complete control of the city through his political machine, characterized by persistent charges of corruption in the city government, and on the other hand by the fact he revitalized the city, was a top-flight administrator, and was credited with conducting the most effectively run city in the country. A master politician he was the last of the big city "bosses" of the twentieth century. He died in Chicago on Dec. 20, after having suffered a stroke in 1974.

DALY, AUGUSTIN (1838–99), theatrical manager, dramatist. Born in Plymouth, North Carolina, on July 20, he was brought to New York City when a youngster by his parents. He became interested in the theater, directed amateur theatrical productions, and in 1859 became drama critic of the New York *Sunday Courier;* by 1867 he was writing dramatic criticism for five New York newspapers. In 1867 he made his debut as a manager with *Under the Gaslight* and two years later he opened his first theater, the Fifth Avenue, in New York. In 1879 he established the famous Daly's Theater on Broadway with a company headed by John Drew and Ada Rehan and produced outstanding productions of Shakespearan comedies and adaptations of plays from the French and German (he is credited with more than eighty plays). He opened a theater in London (later known as Daly's) in 1893 and annually took his company there. He became America's most famous theatrical manager and his troupe became internationally renowned. He was hailed for his inspired direction though he was often denounced by members of his company for his high-handed practices and dictatorial manner. He was the recipient of the Laetare Medal in 1894 and died in Paris on June 7.

DALY, EDWARD CELESTIN (1894–1964), bishop. Born in Cambridge, Mas-

sachusetts, on Oct. 24, he was educated at Boston College in 1912–14, joined the Dominicans in 1914, continued his studies at the Dominican House of Studies, Washington, D.C., and was ordained in 1921. After studying canon law at Catholic University in 1921–24 and teaching at the House of Studies, he served as secretary and archivist to the apostolic delegation in Washington in 1923–48. He was appointed bishop of Des Moines, Iowa, in 1948 and held that position until he was killed in a plane crash near Rome on Nov. 23 after leaving the third session of Vatican Council II. He had been named an Assistant at the Pontifical Throne in 1958.

DALY, JAMES J. (1872–1953), editor. Born in Chicago on Feb. 1, he was educated at St. Ignatius College there (B.A. 1890) and St. Louis University (M.A.), joined the Jesuits in 1890, and was ordained in St. Louis in 1905. He joined the staff of *America,* the Jesuit journal of opinion, and was literary editor in 1909–11, taught at various Jesuit colleges and schools, was assistant editor of *Queen's Work* in 1920–24, was literary editor of *Thought* in 1924–39, and became professor of English at the University of Detroit in 1931. He wrote several books, among them *Life of St. John Berchmans* (1921), two collections of essays, *A Cheerful Ascetic* (1931) and *The Road to Peace* (1936), a collection of poetry, *Boscobel* (1934), and *Nicholas Frederic Brady* (1935). He died in Detroit on Aug. 17.

DALY, JOHN JOSEPH (1905–64), journalist. Born in Naugatuck, Connecticut, on Aug. 3, he was educated at Catholic University (B.A. 1927), was city editor of the Naugatuck *Daily News* in 1927–36, state and city editor of the Waterbury *Republican* in 1936–46, and became editor and general manager of the *Catholic Virginian* in 1946, holding that position until his death in Richmond, Virginia, on Nov. 5. He was active in the Catholic Press Association and served two terms as president in 1958–61.

DALY, MARCUS (1841–1900), copper magnate. Born in Ireland on Dec. 5, he emigrated to the United States when he was fifteen and after a period in New York City went to California where he worked as a pick and shovel miner. He began working for J. G. Fair and J. W. Mackay, dubbed the "silver kings," and in 1876 was sent by his company to investigate the silver mines at Butte, Montana. About this time he persuaded George Hearst and several other capitalists to help him acquire the Anaconda silver mine and several neighboring mines; when its silver lode was exhausted he bought out the shareholders and then exploited the fabulously wealthy copper ore under the worked-out silver veins, organized the Anaconda Copper Mining Company and the Amalgamated Copper Company, and built a smelter at Anaconda and connected it by rail with Butte. He made millions on his copper operations and expanded his interests into coal mines, timber, banks, power plants, and railroads to supply the mines. In the last decade of the nineteenth century, he engaged in a power struggle with William A. Clark for control of the mines and political machinery of Montana—the war of the copper kings. He was a member of the Montana constitutional convention in 1884, contributed half a million dollars to the presidential campaign of William Jennings Bryan in 1896, and became involved in farming and cattle raising; his ranch in the Bitter Root Valley became famous; he also established the influential Anaconda *Standard.* He died in Anaconda, Montana, on Nov. 12.

DALY, THOMAS AUGUSTINE (1864–1941), journalist, author. Born in Philadelphia on May 28, he was educated at Villanova College near there in 1880–87 and Fordham in 1887–89 but left Fordham in his sophomore year. He was a reporter on the Philadelphia *Record* in 1891–98, was general manager of the Catholic *Standard and Times,* the Philadelphia diocesan newspaper, in 1898–1915, was a columnist on the Philadelphia *Evening Ledger* in 1915–18, associate editor of the Philadelphia *Record* in 1919–29, and was a columnist on the Philadelphia *Evening Bulletin* from 1929 until his death in Philadelphia on Oct. 4. He married Naunie Barrett in 1896, wrote several books, all with a light touch and mostly autobiographical, including a series of humorous books in Italian dialect, among them *Canzoni* (1906), *Carmina* (1909), *Madrigali* (1912), and *McAroni Ballads* (1919); his *Songs of Wedlock* was published in 1916 and *Selected Poems* in 1936, and he coauthored *The House of Dooner* with Christopher Morley (1928).

DAMIANO, CELESTINE J. (1911–67), archbishop. Born in Dunkirk, New York, on Nov. 1, he was educated at St. Michael's College, Toronto, Canada, and the Propaganda, Rome, and was ordained in Rome in 1935. He served as a curate at St. Joseph's Church, Niagara Falls, and St. Lucy's Church, Buffalo, New York, and was pastor of Our Lady of Loreto Church in Falconer, New York. In 1947–52 he was with the Propagation of the Faith in Rome. He was appointed titular bishop of Nicopolis in Epiro and apostolic delegate to South Africa in 1953 and was appointed bishop of Camden, New Jersey, with the personal title of archbishop, in 1960. He was a member of the Preparatory Commission for Vatican Council II, which he attended, and died in Camden on Oct. 2.

DAMIEN THE LEPER *See* Veuster, Ven. Joseph de.

DANEHY, THOMAS JOSEPH (1914–59), bishop. Born in Fort Wayne, Indiana, on May 19, he was educated at Sacred Heart Seminary, Detroit, St. Joseph College, Rensselaer, Indiana, and St. Gregory's Seminary, Cincinnati, joined the Maryknoll Fathers in 1934, and was ordained in Rome in 1939. He taught at Clarks Summit, Pennsylvania, and was then assigned to the Gold Coast in Africa but in 1942 was among the first Maryknoll priests sent as missionaries to Bolivia where he spent the rest of his life working among the Aymara Indians at the headwaters of the Amazon River. He was made apostolic administrator of the vicariate of Pando in 1948 and five years later was made titular bishop of Bita; he was often called "the jungle priest." He died in Lima, Peru, on Oct. 9.

DAVID, JOHN BAPTIST MARY (1761–1841), bishop. Born in Couëron, Brittany, France, on June 4, he was educated at the Oratorian college in Nantes and the seminary there, joined the Sulpicians in 1783, and was ordained two years later. He lectured at the minor seminary at Angers until 1791 when the French Revolution closed the seminaries in France and went to the United States with Frs. Benedict Flaget, Stephen Badin, and Guy Chabrat in 1792. He worked as a missionary and was pastor of St. Mary's Church, Bryanton, Maryland, until 1803 when he began teaching philosophy at Georgetown. After a year he transferred to St. Mary's Seminary, Baltimore, serving as temporary president in 1810–11, and became an adviser to Mother Seton's Sisters of Charity. In 1811, he accompanied

Flaget, now bishop of the newly created diocese of Bardstown, Kentucky, and became famous for his missionary activities. He founded St. Thomas Seminary at Bardstown and was its superior and founded St. Joseph's College, helped found St. Mary's College, and in 1912 founded the Sisters of Charity of Nazareth, serving as their ecclesiastical superior the rest of his life. In 1817 he was appointed titular bishop of Mauricastro and coadjutor of Bardstown, though not consecrated until 1819 when the cathedral at Bardstown was completed. He succeeded to the see in 1832, resigned the following year after attending the second Provincial Council of Baltimore, and died in Nazareth, Kentucky, on July 12. He wrote several devotional works that were popular for a generation, among them *True Piety* (1814), *Compilation of Church Music* (1815), and *Catechism of the Diocese of Bardstown* (1825), a catechism for children, and translated works of St. Robert Bellarmine and St. Alphonsus Liguori.

DAVIS, JAMES J. (1852–1926), bishop. Born in Tinvawn, Killarney, Ireland, probably on Nov. 7, he was educated at the Carmelite college, Donemagin, and St. Patrick's College, Carlow, and was ordained in 1878. Later in the same year he emigrated to the United States, settled in Dubuque, Iowa, and engaged in pastoral and missionary activities. He was named chancellor of the diocese of Davenport, Iowa, and in 1904 was appointed titular bishop of Milopotamus and coadjutor of Davenport; he succeeded to the see as its third bishop in 1906. He retained that position until his death in Davenport on Dec. 2.

DAY, DOROTHY (1897–1980), social activist. Daughter of John I. Day, a journalist who specialized in racing news, and Grace Satterlee, she was born in Bath Beach, Brooklyn, New York, on Nov. 8 and was taken to Oakland, California, by her parents when she was six; they moved to Chicago when the San Francisco earthquake destroyed all their possessions. She attended the University of Illinois for two years, moved to New York in 1915 when her father took a job on the New York *Morning Telegraph* and got a job with the Socialist newspaper, *The Call.* She left after eight months to work on the Communist paper, the *Masses,* until 1917 when it was suppressed by the government. During this period she was associated with the Communist movement and a friend of many of the radical journalists of the times among them Mike Gold, Floyd Dell, and Max Eastman. She was arrested during a woman's suffrage demonstration in Washington, D.C., in Nov. 1917, was an ardent pacifist during World War I, and became a close friend and companion of Eugene O'Neill. She studied nursing for a year, married in 1919 and went to Europe in 1920 and then returned to Chicago where she worked for the Communist cause. Her novel, *The Eleventh Virgin,* was published in 1924 when she returned to New York. There she lived with Forster Batterman and in 1926 bore him a child. She had her daughter, Tamar Therese, baptized a Catholic, decided to become a Catholic herself and did so in 1927, and left Batterman upon becoming a Catholic. In 1932 she met Peter Maurin, a meeting destined to change her life. In 1933 they began publishing *The Catholic Worker,* devoted to making known the papal encyclicals on social justice, and she devoted herself to helping the needy and the down-and-outers. She established her first house of hospitality in New York City in 1935 and they soon began to spread; by the time of World War II there were forty houses of hospitality and six communal farms. During World War II, she pro-

claimed her pacifism anew; in the 1950s the Catholic Workers refused to pay federal taxes or participate in air raid drills. She was arrested in 1973 during a demonstration by farm workers led by Cesar Chavez, suffered a heart attack in 1975, and died in New York City five years later, on Nov. 29. She had spent forty-five years in the Catholic Worker movement, espousing voluntary poverty, poverty marches, participating in breadlines and soup kitchens for the destitute, and fighting for Christian principles. She wrote her autobiography, *The Long Loneliness,* in 1952 and was awarded the Laetare Medal in 1972.

DE FALCO, LAWRENCE MICHAEL (1915–79), bishop. Born in McKeesport, Pennsylvania, on Aug. 25, he was educated at St. Vincent's College, Pennsylvania, St. John's Seminary, Arkansas, and the Gregorian, Rome (J.C.L. 1955), and was ordained in Little Rock, Arkansas, in 1942. He served as a curate in Fort Worth and Dallas, Texas, in 1942–53, was pastor of Our Lady of Perpetual Help Church, Dallas, in 1956–62, also serving as secretary of the diocesan court in 1956–59, was pastor of St. Patrick's co-Cathedral in 1962–63, and was vice officialis of the diocese in 1958–62. He was appointed bishop of Amarillo, Texas, in 1963, retired in 1969, and died less than a month later in Amarillo on Sept. 22.

DE GRASSE, FRANÇOIS PAUL. *See* Grasse, François Joseph Paul, Comte de.

DELANY, JOHN BERNARD (1864–1906), bishop. Born in Lowell, Massachusetts, on Aug. 9, he was educated at Holy Cross College, Worcester, Massachusetts, Boston College, and St. Sulpice Seminary, Paris, and was ordained in 1891. He engaged in parish work in

Manchester and Portsmouth, New Hampshire, and in 1898 was named chancellor of Manchester. He served as secretary to Bishop Denis M. Bradley of that see and in 1904 was appointed its second bishop. He founded the diocesan magazine, *Guidon,* and edited it until 1904. He died in Manchester on June 11.

DELANY, SELDEN PEABODY (1874–1935), author. Born in Fond du Lac, Wisconsin, on June 24, he was educated at Harvard (B.A. 1896) and Western Theological Seminary, Chicago, and became an Episcopal priest in 1899. He served in churches in Massachusetts and Wisconsin, was dean of the Episcopal All Saints Cathedral in Milwaukee in 1907–15, and was curate at the Church of St. Mary the Virgin in New York City in 1915–29 and rector in 1929–30, and edited the *American Church Weekly* in 1930. One of the leaders of the High Church movement in the United States, he became a Catholic in 1930; his conversion led to hundreds of Episcopalians following him into the Catholic Church. He studied for the Catholic priesthood at Beda College, Rome, and was ordained a Catholic priest in Rome in 1934. On his return to the United States he became a chaplain at Thevenet Hall, Highland Mills, New York, where he remained until his death on July 5. He was the author of *Why Rome?* (1930), *Rome from Within* (1935), and *Married Saints* (1935).

DEMPSEY, BERNARD WILLIAM (1903–60), educator, economist. Born in Milwaukee, Wisconsin, on Jan. 21, he was educated at Marquette University there, joined the Jesuits in 1922 and continued his studies at St. Louis University (B.A. 1928, M.A. 1929, S.T.L. 1936), and was ordained in 1935. He did postgraduate work at Harvard (Ph.D. in economics, 1940), taught eco-

nomics at St. Louis in 1940–52, becoming regent of the School of Commerce and Finance in 1942, and taught economics at Nirmala College, New Delhi, India, in 1952–53. He returned to St. Louis in 1953 and became director of the economics department at Marquette in 1954 and held that position until his death in Milwaukee on July 23. He was one of the founders of the Catholic Economic Association and served as its president and wrote widely on the economic implications of the papal encyclicals and profit sharing. Among his books were *Interest and Usury* (1948), *Reorganization of the Social Order* (1936), and *The Frontier Wage* (1960).

DEMPSEY, JOHN JOSEPH (1879–1958), congressman, governor. Born in White Haven, Pennsylvania, on June 22, he left school when he was thirteen and worked at various jobs, among them water boy for work crews on the Lehigh Railroad, and then began working as telegraph operator for the Brooklyn Union Elevated Company; in time he became vice president of the Brooklyn Rapid Transit Company, formed by the merger of Brooklyn Union Elevated Company and Kings County Elevated Company. He resigned in 1919, entered the oil business, moved to Santa Fe, New Mexico, and was president of Continental Oil and Asphalt Company from 1919 to 1920 when he resigned to become an independent oil operator. He became president of the U.S. Asphalt Corporation in 1928, entered politics, was director of the National Recovery Administration (NRA) for New Mexico in 1933, and then became director of the Federal Housing Administration. He was elected to the House of Representatives in 1934 and served in that body until 1941. He was a member of the U.S. Maritime Commission for six months in 1941, was under secretary of the Interior Department in 1941–42, and was elected governor of New Mexico in 1942, serving in 1943–47. He was an unsuccessful candidate for the Democratic nomination for the U.S. Senate in 1946, was elected to Congress again in 1950 and served from 1951 to 1958 when he died in Washington, D.C., on Mar. 11.

DEMPSEY, MARY JOSEPH, SISTER (1856–1939), hospital administrator. Born in Salamanca, New York, on May 14, she was brought to Rochester, Minnesota, by her parents when she was a child and joined the Third Order Regular of the Congregation of Our Lady of Lourdes in 1878. She taught in parochial schools until 1889 when she was assigned to the new St. Mary's Hospital in Rochester. She was appointed its superintendent in 1892 and greatly expanded its facilities with the aid of Drs. William W., Charles H., and William J. Mayo who later established the Mayo Clinic; she was Dr. William J.'s first surgical assistant. She founded St. Mary's School of Nursing in 1906, helped organize the Catholic Hospital Association, serving as its first vice president, and died in Rochester on Mar. 29, internationally renowned in the field of medicine.

DEMPSEY, TIMOTHY (1867–1936), priest. Born in Cadamstown, Offaly, Ireland, on Oct. 21, he studied for the priesthood at St. Mary's Seminary, Mullingar, and St. Patrick's Foreign Mission College, Carlow, and was ordained for the American priesthood in 1871. He served as a curate at Indian Creek, Moberly, and St. Louis, Missouri, and was appointed pastor of St. Patrick's Church, St. Louis, in 1898. Early interested in social work, he aided paroled convicts, founded inexpensive hotels for workingmen and women, established a free lunchroom for destitute people during the Depression, provided a burial area for the indigent, and opened a nursery. He died in St. Louis on Apr. 6.

DENNING, JOSEPH M. (1866–1927), priest. Born in Cincinnati, Ohio, on Apr. 19, he was educated at Xavier College (B.A. 1887, M.A. 1890) and St. Mary of the West Seminary there and was ordained in 1891. He engaged in pastoral work in Cincinnati, Oxford, Hillsboro, and Marion, Ohio, until 1922 when he was named consul general at Tangiers, Morocco, by President Warren G. Harding—the first Catholic priest to hold a position in the U.S. consular service. He returned to Cincinnati in 1924 and died there on July 26.

DE ROALDÈS, ARTHUR WASHINGTON (1849–1918), physician. Born in Opelousas, Louisiana, on Jan. 25, he was educated at the University of France (B.A. 1865, B.S. 1866) and studied medicine at the University of Louisiana where he received his medical degree in 1870. He served in the Franco-Prussian War as a surgeon, was decorated for bravery, and returned to New Orleans in 1872. He directed the Charitable Hospital of Louisiana in New Orleans in 1880–83, founded the Eye, Ear, Nose, and Throat Hospital of New Orleans in 1889, and served as emeritus professor of eye, ear, nose, and throat diseases at Tulane University. He participated in many international medical congresses and received numerous awards and honors from foreign governments and the papacy for his gratuitous medical services. Interested in blindness for many years, he lost his own sight several years before his death in New Orleans on June 12.

DERRY, GEORGE HERMANN (1878–1949), educator. Born in Portland, Maine, on May 27, he was educated at Holy Cross College, Worcester,

Massachusetts, Stonyhurst College, England, Johns Hopkins University, and the Catholic Institute, Paris, where he received his S.T.D. He taught at St. Francis Xavier College, New York City, in 1904–6, at Holy Cross in 1906–8, was principal of Jordan High School, Lewiston, Maine, in 1908-9, of Milford, Massachusetts, High School in 1911–14, married Agnes L. Mann in 1913, and taught at English High School in Boston in 1914–17. He was assistant professor of political science at the University of Kansas in 1917–19, head of the economics department at Bryn Mawr in 1919–20 and of Union College, Schenectady, New York, in 1920–25, and was head of the sociology department at Marquette in 1925–27. In 1927 he became president of Marygrove College, Detroit, a position he retained until he became president of St. Joseph's College, Portland, Maine; he also served as international director of social education for the Knights of Columbus. He died in Gloucester, Massachusetts, on Jan. 18.

DESHON, GEORGE (1823–1903), missionary. Of a distinguished Huguenot family tracing its family to the seventeenth century in America, he was born in New London, Connecticut, on Jan. 30. He was appointed to West Point in 1839, where he was a roommate of Ulysses S. Grant and graduated second in the class of 1843. He taught mathematics and ethics there and rose to the rank of captain but resigned in 1850; in the same year, influenced by General William S. Rosecrans, he became a Catholic. Later in the year he joined the Redemptorists in Baltimore, was ordained in 1855, and worked with Frs. Isaac Hecker, Clarence Walworth, Francis Baker, and Augustine Hewit up and down the East Coast. They secured release from their Redemptorist vows from Pope Pius IX in 1858 and he

helped found the Missionary Society of St. Paul the Apostle (the Paulists) in New York City. He served as novice master for several years, was active on the missions, and was in charge of the financial affairs of the community. He helped plan and build St. Paul's Church in New York City in 1859, was elected third superior general of the Paulists in 1879, and served in that position until his death. He founded a Paulist house in Chicago in 1903, published in 1860 *Guide for Catholic Young Women,* which went into twenty-five printings, and a collection of his sermons in 1901, and died in New York City on Dec. 30.

DE SMET, PIERRE JEAN (1801–73), missionary. Born at Termonde (Deudermonde), Belgium, on Jan. 30, he emigrated to the United States in 1821, after meeting the missionary Charles Nerinckx. He joined the Jesuits at Whitemarsh, Maryland, in 1821 and was sent to Florissant, near St. Louis, Missouri, thus becoming one of the founders of the Jesuit Missouri province; he was ordained there in 1827. He returned to Belgium because of ill health and left the Jesuits but after four years recovered his health, returned to the United States, and was readmitted to the Jesuits. In 1838 he went on his first missionary tour among the Indians, founding St. Joseph's Mission at Council Bluffs, Iowa, among the Potawatomi. In 1840, he was sent to the Northwest and began his ministry to the Rocky Mountains Indians, establishing missions in Montana and Iowa. In 1843 he went to Europe to recruit missionaries and to solicit funds and returned by way of Cape Horn to Astoria, Oregon, at the mouth of the Columbia River, bringing with him six Sisters of Notre Dame de Namur. In 1846 he journeyed to the Yellowstone Valley where he negotiated a peace truce between the Blackfeet Indians and other Indian tribes with whom they had warred and established a mission among them. On his return he was recalled to St. Louis and was made provincial secretary and treasurer, ending his active missionary work. By now he was recognized by the federal government for his great influence with the Indians whose cause he pleaded in Washington and Europe and in his prolific writings. In 1851 he was requested by Washington to attend a conference of Indian tribes, restless over the influx of white settlers into California and Oregon, at Fort Laramie and succeeded in pacifying them. In 1858 he was chaplain on General Harney's expedition against the Mormons (the "Mormon War") and acted as a pacificator in the matter; he is reported to have advised Brigham Young where to settle with his Mormons. He then accompanied Harney to the Oregon and Washington territories where he again succeeded in quieting the Indians. At the outbreak of the Civil War he warned of unrest among the Sioux and when they went on the warpath in 1862 he was asked to accompany an armed force against them; when he learned of the punitive nature of the expedition he refused to accompany it. Again in 1867 the government appealed to him to help placate the Indians and he traveled to the Upper Missouri to listen to the Indians' complaints but was forced to return to St. Louis because of illness before the Peace Commission came to a decision. The following year he was again asked to join the Peace Commission and traveling alone went to Sitting Bull's war camp of some five thousand warriors. His advice was taken by the Sioux and a peace treaty was signed by the Sioux on July 2. He made one more visit to the Sioux in 1870 before his death in St. Louis on May 23. More than any white man Fr. De Smet was trusted by the Indian tribes west of the Missouri and he worked ceaselessly on their behalf.

Aside from his constant intercessions for them with the United States Government, he made several trips to Europe visiting practically every European country seeking aid for the Indians. He wrote profusely and vividly of his trips among and experiences with the Indians and his books are valuable sources of the history of the West, notably his *Letters and Sketches* (1843), *Oregon Missions and Travels* (1847), *Western Missions and Missionaries* (1859), and *New Indian Sketches* (1863).

DESMOND, DANIEL FRANCIS (1884–1945), bishop. Born in Haverhill, Massachusetts, on Apr. 4, he was educated at Holy Cross College, Worcester, Massachusetts (B.A. 1906) and Duquesne University, studied for the priesthood at St. John's Seminary, Brighton, Massachusetts, and was ordained in 1911. He served as a curate at Beachmont in 1911–12, Medford in 1913–16, and as pastor in Somerville in 1917–32, all in Massachusetts, except for 1918–19 when he was a chaplain in the Army during World War I. In 1932 he was appointed bishop of Alexandria, Virginia, and held that position until his death there on Sept. 11.

DE SOTO, HERNANDO (c. 1500–42), explorer. Of an impoverished noble family, he was born at Barcarrota, Spain, and was educated at the University of Salamanaca through the generosity of Pedrarias Dávila. He became a soldier, was made a captain of cavalry by Dávila, now governor of Darien, when he accompanied Dávila to Central America about 1519. He took part in the conquest of Honduras and Nicaragua in 1523 by the expedition led by Francisco Fernández de Córdoba and was second in command of an expedition headed by Francisco Pizarro that set out in 1532 from Panama to conquer Peru; after his discovery of the capital of the Incas he was ambassador to Atahualpa, lord of the Incas. He became friendly with Atahualpa who was imprisoned by Pizarro, played a prominent role in the capture and sack of Cuzco and the surrounding area, and returned to Spain furious with Pizarro for his murder of Atahualpa. He settled in Seville with the fortune in gold that was his share of the booty taken from the Incas, married Inés de Bobadilla, daughter of Governor Dávila, in 1537 and lived the life of a noble. He sold his estate later the same year to return to his life of explorer and conqueror in the New World and was appointed governor of Cuba with the right of conquest of Florida, and was made a marquis by Emperor Charles V in 1537. On Apr. 6, 1538, he set out from Spain with a flotilla of vessels and almost a thousand fighting men to conquer Florida which he felt had treasure equal to that of Peru. The expedition was delayed in Cuba while he established his rule, naming Gonzalo de Guzmán, lieutenant governor of Santiago, and his wife Inés de Bobadilla director of affairs of state and in rebuilding Havana, which had been sacked and burned by the French. He left Havana in May 1539, landed on the Florida coast, probably near Ucita on Charlotte Bay, and spent the next three years in a search for the gold, silver, and jewels he never found that led the party halfway across the continent. After spending the winter of 1539–40 near Tallahassee the expedition went north through Georgia and the Carolinas, into Tennessee and then south into Alabama where he was wounded in a fierce battle with the Indians. Throughout the trip he was constantly deceived by the Indians who fed him stories of wealthy cities, which never materialized, farther along the way; for his part he treated the Indians with the greatest contempt and cruelty. So obsessed was he with finding treasure that he did not reveal to his men in late 1540 that Spanish ships were off the coast for fear they would desert. In 1541 they set out westward, crossed the Mississippi, the first white men to do so, and journeyed up the Arkansas River to Oklahoma. When no treasure turned up and after wintering in 1541–42 on the Cayas River, they returned to the Mississippi which they reached on Apr. 16. De Soto was stricken with fever and died probably on May 21. He was buried secretly in the river so the Indians who feared him would not know he had died. The remainder of the party turned west, crossed the Red River to northern Texas and then returned to the Mississippi and followed it south to the sea; a small remnant of the shattered expedition finally reached Vera Cruz in 1543. De Soto's expedition, though it ended disastrously, was one of the most important Spanish explorations of the sixteenth century; it was the first extensive exploration of the Southeast, discovered the Mississippi, and provided the first description of the southern Indian tribes and the whole southeastern portion of what was to become the United States.

D'ESTAING, CHARLES HECTOR *See* Estaing, Pierre Baptiste Charles Henri Hector, Comte d'.

DEVER, ANDREW W. (1903–58), governor. Born in Boston on Jan. 15, he was educated at Boston University (LL.B. 1926), was admitted to the Massachusetts bar the same year when he also ran for state senator and was defeated. He was elected to the Massachusetts General Court in 1928 and served for three consecutive terms until 1934 when he was elected attorney general of Massachusetts serving until 1941. He was unsuccessful in a bid for the governorship in 1941, served as a commander in the Navy during World War II, and was defeated in the election for lieutenant governor in the 1946 election. He was elected governor of Massachusetts in 1948 and reelected in 1950 but was defeated in a bid for a third term. As governor he supported minimum wage, unemployment compensation, mental care, and highway construction legislation and was committed to aid for mentally retarded children. After his defeat he continued active in Democratic Party politics and was the keynoter at the 1952 National Democratic Convention. He died in Boston on Apr. 11.

DEVEREUX, JOHN C. (1774–1848), merchant, mayor. Son of a farmer, he was born near Enniscorthy, Wexford, Ireland, on Aug. 5 and emigrated to the United States in 1797. He gave dancing lessons in Connecticut for a time and in 1802 settled in Utica, New York, where he prospered and became wealthy as a store owner. He was elected first mayor of Utica in 1840, founded the Utica Savings Bank with his brother Nicholas and the two of them brought the Sisters of Charity to Utica to run an orphanage and contributed generously toward its founding. He died in Utica on Dec. 11.

DEVEREUX, NICHOLAS (1791–1855), real estate developer, philanthropist. Son of Thomas Devereux and Catherine Cornish Devereux and youngest brother of John C., he was born on his father's farm near Enniscorthy, Wexford, Ireland, on Dec. 29. He emigrated to the United States in 1806 and soon became involved in real estate which made him wealthy. He purchased 400,000 acres of land in Allegany and Cattaraugus counties in New York, started a settlement for Irish immigrants, and with his brother John founded the Utica Savings Bank. On a visit to Rome in 1854 he returned with six Franciscans to whom he made a generous donation to found a monastery at Allegany; in time it developed into St.

Bonaventure University. He proposed building a seminary in Rome for the education of American priests and though he did not live to see his idea come to fruition, a donation from his widow helped the North American College to come into existence. He taught Sunday school at Utica, printed and circulated an edition of the New Testament in 1828, and was a generous contributor to Catholic institutions. He died in Utica on Dec. 29.

DEYMANN, CLEMENTINE (1844–96). Born in Klein-Stavenburg, Hanover, Germany, on June 24, he came to the United States with his parents in 1863, studied at the Teutopolis in Illinois, and joined the Franciscans in 1867, changing his name from John Henry to Clementine. He was ordained in St. Louis in 1872 and taught at the Teutopolis until 1879 when he became chaplain of the state prison at Joliet, Illinois, and spiritual director of the School Sisters of St. Francis. He was appointed pastor of the German parish in Joliet in 1880 and two years later of the German parish in Chillicothe, Missouri, and was elected definitor of the Franciscan Sacred Heart Province in 1885 and 1891. He was named superior of the boys orphanage at Watsonville, California, in 1886 and was appointed provincial visitor for the California area, helping to obtain Franciscan parishes in Los Angeles, San Francisco, Oakland, and Sacramento. In 1896 he was appointed first commissary provincial of the newly erected Franciscan commissariat of the Pacific coast; he died later the same year on Dec. 4 in Phoenix, Arizona. He was the author of several manuals for the Franciscans and their third order and devotional works and also translated several devotional works.

DICKINSON, CLARE JOSEPH, MOTHER (1755–1830), foundress.

Frances Dickinson was born in Middlesex, England, on July 12, was early attracted to the religious life and when sixteen entered the Carmelite monastery in Antwerp, Holland, and took her vows in 1773 with the names Clare Joseph. In 1790 at the request of Fr. Charles Neale, a Maryland Jesuit who was the Antwerp Carmelites' confessor, and several friends, Mother Bernardine Matthews as prioress and Sister Clare Joseph as subprioress and two other sisters were sent to America and established a foundation near Port Tobacco, Maryland—the first Carmelite foundation in the United States. When Mother Bernardine died in 1800, Bishop Carroll appointed Mother Clare prioress; when canonical elections were held she was elected by the nuns and held the office for thirty years. She introduced devotion to the Sacred Heart in the Carmel dedicating its chapel to the Sacred Heart. Ill the last years of her life she died at the Port Tobacco Carmel on May 27.

DIETZ, PETER ERNEST (1878–1947), labor priest. Of German immigrant parents, he was born in New York City on July 10, was educated at the Society of Divine Word Seminary in Moedling, Germany, St. Francis Xavier College, New York City, the University of Connecticut and Washington (D.C.) University, and was ordained in 1904. He was pastor of Sacred Heart Chapel, Oberlin, Ohio, in 1904–21 and early became interested in the application of the principles of Pope Leo XIII's encyclical, *Rerum novarum,* to social problems in the United States, particularly in the field of labor. He was a firm supporter of the labor union movement and a friend of such labor leaders as Philip Murray, Matthew Woll, and John Mitchell and was active in labor unions, attending the national conventions of the American Federation of Labor

where he fought socialistic influences. He edited the *Bulletin* and *Newsletter* of the Social Service Commission of the American Federation of Catholic Societies, the English section of the German Catholic Central Verein's *Central Blatt* and *Social Justice* and organized the Verein's first social institute. He was forced to discontinue his public activities in the labor movement when a group of Catholic members of the Chamber of Commerce protested his activities to Archbishop McNicholas of Cincinnati and he was forced to close his American Academy for Christian Democracy there. He spent the rest of his life as pastor of St. Monica's parish in Milwaukee, Wisconsin, and died there on Oct. 11.

DILLON, WILLIAM THOMAS (1892–1964), educator. Born in Brooklyn, New York, on July 4, he was educated at St. John's College and Seminary there (B.A. 1913, M.A. 1917) and was ordained in 1917. He served as assistant at St. Francis of Assisi Church in Brooklyn until 1920 when he was appointed head of the philosophy department at St. Joseph's College for Women in Brooklyn. He studied law at Brooklyn Law School (LL.B. 1924) and was admitted to the New York bar in 1925 when he also received his J.D. He was dean of St. Joseph's in 1927–45, served as president of the Catholic Philosophical Association, which he had helped found, in 1937, and was made a domestic prelate in 1938. He was president of St. Joseph's from 1945 until 1955 when he became pastor of St. Teresa's Church in Brooklyn. He died in Brooklyn on Oct. 12.

DOHENY, EDWARD LAURENCE (1856–1935), oil magnate, philanthropist. Born near Fond du Lac, Michigan, on Aug. 10, he worked in the surveying service of the federal government in

1872–76, unsuccessfully prospected for gold in Arizona and Mexico in 1876–88, and then taught school in New Mexico. He studied law and was admitted to the bar but in 1891 went to California in another futile quest for gold. He moved to Los Angeles in 1892 and began drilling for oil with his partner, Charles A. Canfield; this time he was more successful and they gained control of some eighty-one wells in the Los Angeles area. He went to Mexico, leased 250,000 acres of land near Tampico for oil prospecting and struck oil. When an oil glut left him with no market for oil, he began to produce asphalt from his oil fields and secured lucrative contracts to pave the streets of many Mexican cities. When the growth of the automobile industry brought renewed and increased demand for oil, he founded the Mexican Petroleum Company of California. He was accused of aiding the revolution that overthrew President Diaz of Mexico in 1910 but denied any complicity in the revolt. In 1922 he received a contract to build a naval fuel station at Pearl Harbor and drilling rights to 32,000 acres of naval reserve land at Elk Hills, California. When it was learned he had sent Secretary of the Interior Albert B. Fall one hundred thousand dollars in cash in 1921 (he claimed it was a loan), he and Fall were indicted by the government for bribery in 1925 after a Senate investigation. He was acquitted of conspiracy in 1926 and of giving a bribe in 1930 but all the leases he had received from Fall were canceled. He gave much of his wealth to institutions and Catholic charities and built a library at the University of Southern California, Los Angeles, in memory of his only son Edward who had been murdered in 1929. He died in Beverly Hills, California, on Sept. 8 after having been bedridden for three months.

DOHERTY, EDWARD (1890–1975), journalist, author. Son of a Chicago police lieutenant, he was born in Chicago on Oct. 30, studied for the priesthood at the Servite Monastery, Granville, Wisconsin, for two years and then left and went to business school. He began his journalism career as a copy boy and later as a reporter for the *City Press* and after three years there left to become a reporter on the Chicago *Examiner* and then on the *Record-Herald*, the *Tribune*, the *Herald*, and finally on the *American*. He married Marie Ryan (d. 1918) in 1914, worked for a time on the Tampico *Tribune*, Mexico's only English-language newspaper, returned to Chicago, and was sent to Hollywood in charge of the Chicago *Tribune*'s news bureau there. He then went to New York City, where he joined *Liberty* magazine and wrote articles, fiction, and serials, writing some one thousand articles during the fifteen years he was with *Liberty*. He married Mildred Frisby outside the Church in 1919; though she wanted to become a Catholic and be married in the Church, she was killed in a fall in California before she could realize her wish. He married Catherine de Kolyshkine (Baroness Catherine de Hueck) in 1943 and worked with her at Madonna House, in Combermere, Ontario. He studied for the priesthood and was ordained a priest of the Melchite rite, an Eastern Catholic rite which permits the ordination of married men, in 1969, when he was seventy-nine, and died in Renfrew, Ontario, on Mar. 4. Doherty was one of the best-known journalists of his time and was the author of numerous newspaper and magazine articles and of twenty-two books, among them *Gall and Honey* (1941), *Splendor of Sorrow* (1943), *My Russian Wife* (1946), *Tumbleweed* (1948), *Fabi-*

ola (1951), *My Hay Ain't In* (1952), and *Lambs in Wolfskins* (1953).

DOMENEC, MICHAEL (1816–78), bishop. Born in Ruez, near Tarragona, Spain, on Dec. 27, he began studying at Madrid but was forced to flee with his father to Paris when he was fifteen when the Carlist movement failed. He joined the Vincentians in Paris in 1832, studied for the priesthood at the Vincentian seminary there, emigrated to the United States in 1838, and finished his theological studies at St. Mary's Seminary, The Barrens, Missouri. He was ordained there in 1839, worked as a missionary in Missouri while teaching at St. Mary's, and in 1845 was sent with a group of Vincentians to teach and take charge of St. Vincent's Seminary, Germantown, Pennsylvania; he was also pastor at Nicetown and in 1851 became founding pastor of St. Vincent de Paul Church in Germantown. He was appointed second bishop of Pittsburgh in 1860 and had a difficult episcopate because of the divisions caused by the Civil War and the depressions that followed. He was an ardent supporter of the North during the war, and at the behest of the federal government went to Spain on behalf of the Union. The diocese of Pittsburgh was divided at his request in 1876, and he chose and became bishop of the lesser of the two sees, Allegheny City, which was thus created. He resigned a year later because of ill health and retired to Tarragona, where he died on Jan. 7.

DONAHOE, PATRICK (1811–1901), publisher. Born in Munnery, Cavan, Ireland, on Mar. 17, he was brought to Boston by his parents in 1821. When he was fourteen he became a printer's apprentice on the *Columbia Sentinel* and later on the *Transcript*. He began to work on the *Jesuit* (later the *Literary and Catholic Sentinel* and in 1836 *The*

Pilot) when Bishop Fenwick bought it, in 1832, and entered into a partnership with Henry L. Devereux, its printer, to take it over from the bishop; he became sole owner in 1838. The paper soon became one of the most influential Catholic newspapers in the country. He also began selling religious articles, becoming the largest religious-articles dealer in New England, and established a book publishing house and founded a bank. In 1872 the great Boston fire destroyed his printing plant; after it was rebuilt it was again destroyed by fire the following year. These disasters, failure of his insurance company, and injudicious loans plunged him into bankruptcy and caused his bank to fail in 1876. He sold the paper to Archbishop Williams and John Boyle O'Reilly so he could pay back some of the depositors of the bank, and he then started publishing *Donahoe's Magazine* and began a travel agency. He bought *The Pilot* back from the archdiocese in 1890 and devoted the rest of his life to its management. He was the recipient of the Laetare Medal in 1893, and died in Boston on Mar. 18.

DONAHUE, JOSEPH P. (1870–1959), bishop. Born in New York City on Nov. 6, he was educated at the College of the City of New York and Manhattan College. He studied for the priesthood at St. Joseph's Seminary, Troy, New York, and was ordained in 1895. After serving as a curate at Mamaroneck, New York, and as pastor of Ascension Church, in New York City, he was appointed to the diocesan board of consultors, made a monsignor, and became vicar-general of the archdiocese. He was named titular bishop of Emmaus and auxiliary bishop of New York in 1945, served as chairman of the archdiocesan school board, worked with Catholic Charities, the orphan asylum, and the Eucharistic League, and died in New York City on Apr. 26.

DONAHUE, PATRICK JAMES
(1849–1922), bishop. Born in Malvern, Worcestershire, England, on Apr. 15, he was educated at the University of London, graduating in 1869, and at Columbia (George Washington) University, Washington, D.C., after emigrating to the United States in 1873. He was admitted to the bar, practiced law in Washington in 1876–82, and then studied for the priesthood at St. Mary's Seminary, Baltimore, where he was ordained in 1885. He was named chancellor of the Baltimore archdiocese the next year and rector of the Baltimore Cathedral in 1891 and was appointed third bishop of Wheeling, West Virginia, in 1894. He died in Wheeling on Oct. 4 after a twenty-eight year episcopate during which all the activities of the diocese were greatly expanded.

DONGAN, THOMAS (1634–1715), governor. Son of John Dongan, baronet and member of the Irish Parliament, he was born in Castletown, Kildare, Ireland. When he was fourteen, the family, Stuart partisans, went into exile in France on the death of King Charles I, in 1649. Thomas served in an Irish regiment in England and in France and rose to the rank of colonel in 1674. He returned to England in 1678 and in the same year secured an appointment to serve in the Army in Flanders and later that year was appointed lieutenant governor of Tangiers by King Charles II. Four years later, the lord proprietor of New York, James, Duke of York, appointed him governor of that colony, then bankrupt and in a state of rebellion. He was the first Catholic governor of that colony. He convened New York's first representative assembly in 1683, which passed "A Charter of Liberties" establishing representative government under the Duke of York. He made the Assembly the equal of the British Parliament, established courts, and enumerated principles that later became the cornerstone of the American constitution: religious liberty, no taxation without representation and only by the people's representatives, and the right of suffrage, with election by a majority of votes. After the American Revolution, it was to become the framework of England's colonial policy in Canada and Australia. The first Mass on Manhattan Island was said in 1683 in a chapel he opened on a site where later the customs building was built, and he established a Latin school under the direction of his chaplains, Jesuit Frs. Thomas Harvey, Henry Harrison, and Charles Gage; he granted them a tract of land called King's Farm, but James later vetoed the grant, and in 1705 it became the property of Trinity Church. He also planned a Jesuit mission at Saratoga, an Irish settlement in central New York, and an expedition to explore the Mississippi and take possession of its valley for the English—all of which were vetoed by James. He settled boundary disputes with Connecticut, Pennsylvania, and Canada, and in 1684 negotiated treaties with the Iroquois which were to have long-term consequences: years later, the Iroquois remained loyal to the British during the Revolution. He established a post office in New York in 1685 and granted charters to New York and Albany in 1686, which remained in effect for over a century and established the forms of other city governments in New York. He early recognized and took steps to curb the growing powers of the French to the north and in 1687–88 raised a force to protect Albany. When the Duke of York became King James II, in 1685, the Board of Trade and Plantations vetoed the "charter" passed in 1683, a veto James approved, and New York became a royal colony. The New York Assembly was dissolved in 1687 by the King, who appointed Sir Edmund Andros governor of the consolidated provinces of New York, the Jerseys, and New England in 1688. Dongan was offered the command of a regiment but refused the offer and retired to his estate on Staten Island. He was forced to flee a religious persecution in 1689, returned to England in 1691, and became second Earl of Limerick in 1698, on the death of his heirless brother William, governor of Munster. He died in London on Dec. 14. Dongan was one of the most capable of the colonial governors and ruled with great ability and understanding, displaying a tolerance of religious differences seldom found in the rulers of those times.

DONNELLY, FRANCIS PATRICK (1869–1959), educator. Born at Pittston, Pennsylvania, on Dec. 10, he was educated at Villanova (Pennsylvania) College and St. John's College (Fordham), joined the Jesuits in 1888, continued his education at Jesuit Teachers College, Frederick, Maryland, and Woodstock College, Maryland (B.A. 1894, M.A. 1895, Ph.D. 1922), and was ordained in 1903. He taught classics and rhetoric for fifty years, at Boston College in 1895–98 and 1920–22, Holy Cross College in 1898–1900 and 1916–20, at Jesuit Teachers College, Poughkeepsie, New York, in 1906–15 and 1922–29, and at Fordham from 1929, also serving as rector of St. Aloysius Church, in Washington, D.C., in 1915–16. He was editor of *Messenger of the Sacred Heart* in 1905–8 and wrote some twenty devotional works, among them *The Heart of Revelation* (1913), *Grains of Incense* (1934), and *Heart of the Mass* (1940), as well as texts on education, writing, criticism, and analyses of Latin writers, among them *Model English I* (1902) and *II* (1919), *Art Principles in Literature* (1923), *Literary Art and Modern Education* (1927), and *Principles of Jesuit Education* (1934); he also

translated Cicero's *Milo* (1936) and edited Newman's *Second Spring*. He died in Poughkeepsie on Apr. 18.

DONNELLY, GEORGE JOSEPH (1889–1950), bishop. Born in St. Louis on Apr. 23, he studied at Kenrick Seminary in his native city and was ordained in 1921. He served as chaplain of the convent of the Sacred Heart and Mullanphy Orphan Asylum and became chancellor of the St. Louis archdiocese. He was made a papal chamberlain in 1934, was named titular bishop of Coela and auxiliary of St. Louis in 1940, and was appointed bishop of Leavenworth (changed to Kansas City, Kansas, in 1947) in 1946. He provided the first buildings for Donnelly College in Kansas City in 1949, and died in Kansas City the following year on Dec. 13.

DONOVAN, WILLIAM J. "WILD BILL" (1883–1959), soldier, lawyer. Born in Buffalo, New York, on Jan. 1, he was educated at Columbia University (B.A. 1905, LL.B. 1907) and was admitted to the New York bar in 1907. He began practicing in Buffalo, married Ruth Ramsey in 1914, and at the outbreak of World War I joined the Army as captain of Troop I, 1st Cavalry, of the New York National Guard. He advanced in rank to colonel of the "Fighting 69th," became a household name for his gallantry in action, was wounded three times, and was awarded the Medal of Honor for an assault he led near Landres and St. Georges, in France, in 1918. After the war he was unsuccessful as Republican candidate for lieutenant governor in 1922, was U.S. district attorney for western New York in 1922–24 and assistant U.S. Attorney General in 1924–29 and was defeated for the governorship in 1932. He was recalled to active duty at the outbreak of World War II as a major general, was head of the Office of Strategic Services (OSS) in

1942–45 and was United States ambassador to Thailand in 1953–54. He was honored by England, France, Poland, Belgium, Italy, Norway, Siam, and the papacy and several universities; he died in Berryville, Virginia, where he had a farm, on Feb. 8.

DOOLEY, THOMAS ANTHONY (1927–1961), doctor, humanitarian. Born in St. Louis on Jan. 17, he began his premedical studies at Notre Dame but when the United States entered World War II he left to become a medical corpsman in the Navy. On his return from the war, in 1946, he continued his studies at Notre Dame and at St. Louis University and received his medical degree from St. Louis in 1953. He was commissioned a medical officer in the Navy and was sent to Japan and assisted North Vietnamese refugees who had fled to South Vietnam at a refugee camp he established at Haiphong. His efforts in treating some six hundred thousand refugees caused the South Vietnamese Government to honor him, and he was also awarded the Navy's Merit of Honor–the youngest medical officer ever to receive it; he was twenty-eight at the time. His best-selling *Deliver Us from Evil* (1956) described the collapse of Vietnam from Communist pressure and infiltration, and his experiences with the refugees; the proceeds from the book he donated to the founding of a hospital in northern Laos and to starting a nursing home. He resigned from the Navy in 1956, and in 1958 wrote of his experiences in *The Edge of Night*. With Dr. Peter Commanduras, he founded the Medical International Corporation (MEDICO) to provide health services in undeveloped areas throughout the world; by 1960 they were working in ten countries. He spent much time in Laos giving medical aid to the natives. In 1959 he fell down an embankment there, injuring his chest; a tumor developed, which was diagnosed as malignant, and he underwent surgery later in the year. Despite his affliction he continued his work, raised almost $2 million for MEDICO with his lectures and books, and oversaw the establishment of seven hospitals in four Asian countries. He also wrote *The Night They Burned the Mountain* (1960) and *Dr. Tom Dooley, My Story* (1962). He died in New York City on Jan. 18.

DORNIN, BERNARD (1761–1836), publisher. Born in Ireland, he was forced to flee his native land in 1803 because of his political activities; he emigrated to the United States. He began a publishing and bookselling concern in New York, the first publisher in the city to devote himself to publishing Catholic books; he printed a New Testament in Brooklyn in 1805 and Pastorini's *History of the Church* in 1807. He moved to Baltimore in 1809 and to Philadelphia in 1817, became the leading publisher of Catholic books in the United States, but in the 1830s sold his business and moved to Ohio to live near his daughter. He died there in 1836.

DORSEY, ANNA HANSON (1815–96), novelist. The daughter of the Rev. William McKenney, a chaplain in the U.S. Navy, she was born in Georgetown, D.C., and married Lorenzo Dorsey in 1837; three years later, influenced by the Catholic revival in England, they became Catholics. She began writing novels that gave a sympathetic and understanding view of Catholic life and became one of the leading religious authors of her time. Among the more than thirty books she wrote over half a century were *The Student of Blenheim Forest* (1847), her first novel, *Flowers of Love and Memory, The Palms, The Flemings, Warp and Woof, Guy, the Leper, Nora Brady's Vow, The Mad Penitent of Todi,* and *Beth's Promise.*

She was the recipient of the Laetare Medal in 1899, twice received the benediction of Pope Leo XIII, and died in Washington, D.C., on Dec. 26.

DOUGHERTY, DANIEL (1826–92), lawyer. Born in Philadelphia on Oct. 15, he was educated there and was admitted to the bar in 1849. He became known for his oratorical prowess and became one of the nation's leading lawyers. He lectured extensively, warmly supported the Union during the Civil War, worked for President Lincoln's reelection in 1864, but after his reelection supported the Democratic Party. He made speeches nominating General Winfield Scott Hancock for the Democratic presidential nomination at the national Democratic convention in 1880 and Grover Cleveland in 1888, delivered an address at the first Catholic Congress in Baltimore in 1889, and was known as the "silver-tongued orator." He was the recipient of the Laetare Medal in 1891; he died in Philadelphia on Sept. 5.

DOUGHERTY, DENNIS J. (1865–1951), cardinal. Of Irish immigrant parents, he was born in Ashland, Pennsylvania, on Aug. 16 and worked in the coal mines when a boy. He entered Ste. Marie College, Montreal, when he was sixteen, transferred to St. Charles Borromeo Seminary in Philadelphia two years later, continued his studies at the North American College, Rome, where he received his D.D., and was ordained in Rome in 1890. He taught at St. Charles Borromeo until 1903, when he was appointed bishop of Nueva Segovia, in the Philippines, the first American bishop of that see. He was faced with a schism headed by Padre Gregorio Alipay (who had apostatized and started his own church with his native followers when his petition for a native bishop had been refused by the Holy

See) and was successful in a court action to force Alipay to return all the church properties he claimed to the Catholic Church. He was transferred to Jaro, in the Philippines, in 1908 and was appointed bishop of Buffalo, New York, in 1915. He revitalized its parochial-school system, established fifteen new parishes, and paid off the debt on the cathedral in the three years he was bishop of Buffalo. He was named archbishop of Philadelphia in 1918, and in 1921 became the fifth American to become a cardinal. He was an active supporter of the temperance movement, vigorously opposed Communism, and constantly sought to raise the moral tone of motion pictures. He greatly expanded the facilities of his see during his episcopate, creating 112 new parishes and building 145 schools, including 53 high schools, 4 colleges and a seminary, 12 hospitals and 11 homes for the aged. He died in Philadelphia on May 31.

DOUGHERTY, JOSEPH PATRICK (1905–70), bishop. Born in Kansas City, Kansas, on Jan. 11, he was educated at the University of Portland, Oregon, and St. Patrick's Seminary, Menlo Park, California, and was ordained at Seattle, Washington, in 1930. He taught at St. Edward's Seminary, Kenmore, Washington, in 1931–34, received his M.A. from the University of Washington in 1934, and was vice-chancellor of the Seattle diocese in 1934–42. He was appointed chancellor in 1942, was director of the diocesan Society for the Propagation of the Faith, and in 1951 was appointed first bishop of the newly created diocese of Yakima, Washington. During his episcopate he greatly increased the facilities of the diocese to accommodate its rapidly growing Catholic population, sponsored an apostolate to the many Spanish-speaking migrant workers in the diocese, and made the Catholic mission on the Yakima Indian reservation a parish. He resigned in 1969, was named an auxiliary bishop of Los Angeles later the same year, and died a year later on July 10 in Washington, D.C.

DOUTRELEAU, STEPHEN (b. 1693), missionary. Born in France on Oct. 11, he joined the Jesuits when he was twenty-two and was ordained. He went to Louisiana in 1727, was at Vincennes, Indiana, the following year, and in 1730 set out again for New Orleans. Unaware that the Natchez Indians were on the warpath, his party was attacked on the way while he was saying Mass at the mouth of the Yazoo River; a companion was killed, and he was wounded, but the party managed to escape and proceeded to New Orleans. He became chaplain of French troops in Louisiana and in New Orleans and of a hospital in New Orleans for a time, returned to his mission with the Illinois Indians, and in 1747 returned to France. When and where he died are unknown.

DOWLING, AUSTIN (1868–1930), archbishop. Born in New York City on Apr. 6, he graduated from Manhattan College in 1887, studied for the priesthood at St. John's Seminary, Brighton, Massachusetts, and Catholic University, and was ordained in 1891. He was a curate in Providence for a short time, taught at St. John's in 1894–96, edited the diocesan newspaper, the Providence *Visitor,* for two years, and then engaged in pastoral work in Providence and Warren, Rhode Island, in 1898–1905. He was named rector of SS. Peter and Paul Cathedral in Providence in 1905, became bishop of Des Moines, Iowa, in 1912 (the see having been erected in 1911), and founded Des Moines Catholic College (now Dowling College) in 1918 and built up the parochial-school system. He was appointed second archbishop of St. Paul, Minnesota, in 1919, helped organize the National Catholic Welfare Conference, and was treasurer of its first administrative board, worked to improve the diocesan educational system, and built the archdiocesan preparatory seminary, Nazareth Hall, in 1923, the St. Paul Diocesan Institute, a teachers college for sisters, in 1927, and several high schools. He also served as episcopal chairman of the education department of the National Catholic Welfare Conference, and died in St. Paul on Nov. 29.

DOWLING, EDDIE (1894–1976), actor. The fourteenth of seventeen children of French-Canadian Charles Goucher and Irish-born Bridget Dowling, he was born in Woonsocket, Rhode Island, on Dec. 9 and was christened Joseph Nelson. He was attracted to the entertainment world at a very young age, served as a cabin boy on several ocean liners, was a member of the boys choir of St. Paul's Cathedral, in London, and then returned to the United States to pursue an acting career. He made his stage debut with the New England Stock Company, appeared in his first role on Broadway in 1919 in *The Velvet Lady* and the *Ziegfeld Follies,* and following a stint in Hollywood, appeared in several musical comedies. He produced *Richard II* in 1937, appeared in several dramas, including *Here Come the Clowns* in 1938 and in 1945 *The Glass Menagerie,* and in 1932 was active in the presidential campaign on behalf of his friend Franklin D. Roosevelt, serving as chairman of the Democratic Stage, Screen and Radio Committee. He was first president of the USO Camp Shows during World War II, retired from the theater in the early 1960s, and died in a nursing home in Smithfield, Rhode Island, on Feb. 18. During his career he won a Pulitzer prize as producer of *The Time of Your Life* in 1940 and four New York Drama Critics Circle awards.

DOYLE, MARY PETER (1898–1971), educator. Born in Rockford, Illinois, on Oct. 29, she was educated at St. Clara's College (now Rosary College, River Forest), Sinsinawa, Wisconsin (B.A. 1920), the Theodore Irvine Studio and Francis Robinson Duff Studio for the Theatre, New York City, in 1920–22, and the University of Wisconsin (M.A. 1923). She taught at Hall School, Rockford, in 1920–22, joined the Dominican Sisters of the Congregation of the Most Holy Rosary at Sinsinawa in 1924, and taught at Trinity High School in 1924–27 and at Rosary College, River Forest, Illinois, in 1927–40. She was chairperson of the speech department in 1929–43 and received her Ph.D. from Columbia in 1935. She was active in the Catholic theater movement and director of the Midwest Region of the Catholic Theatre Conference and in speech groups, was dean of Rosary College in 1942–43, and was president in 1943–49. She was vicaress-general of her Congregation at Sinsinawa in 1949–67, returned to Rosary in 1968 to teach part-time in the English department, and died in Dubuque, Iowa, on June 17.

DOYLE, MICHAEL FRANCIS (1877–1960), jurist. Born in Philadelphia on July 12, he was educated at the University of Pennsylvania, where he received his law degree in 1897, did postgraduate work there in 1897–99, and was admitted to the Philadelphia bar in 1897. He became an authority in the field of international law, and at the outbreak of World War I represented the State Department in Europe, taking care of Americans stranded in Europe by the outbreak of the war. He also acted as counselor in the American legation in Switzerland and the American embassy in Austria, assisted in the organization of United States relief to Belgium in 1915 and to Ireland during the troubles in 1915–16; when Sir Roger

Casement was accused of treason by the government in 1916, he defended him (Casement was found guilty and hanged). When the United States entered World War I, he served as special assistant chief of ordnance for the War Department in the Philadelphia area in 1917–18, helped avert several strikes, and was counsel for the Atlantic Shipbuilders' Council, representing shipyard employees on the Atlantic coast. He defended the Irish patriot Eamon de Valera, who was sentenced to death (though the sentence was later commuted to a life sentence), and several other Irish revolutionaries in the uprising of 1922, and was an adviser to the Irish Free State Commission drafting the Irish Free State constitution in 1922. He was counsel for Haiti and Santo Domingo to the State Department in 1922 and was chairman of the American committee at the League of Nations in Geneva in 1929–39. He was a United States delegate to the Inter-American Conference for Peace, in Buenos Aires in 1936, was appointed a member of the permanent court of arbitration at The Hague by President Franklin Roosevelt in 1938, and was reappointed by President Truman, serving until 1951, and was special counsel to the President of the Philippine Republic from 1945. He had helped found the National Conference of Catholic Charities in 1910 and the Catholic Near East Welfare Association, serving for many years as the latter's counsel. After the United States and the U.S.S.R. resumed diplomatic relations, in 1933, he secured permission from the Soviet Union for American missionaries to minister to American citizens in Moscow. He also was president of the American electoral college in 1937, 1941, 1945, and 1949. Honored by many European, Asian and Latin-American countries, including France, Bulgaria, the Dominican Republic, the

Philippines, Spain, and the Vatican (six times) and by many colleges and universities, he was named a papal chamberlain in 1959; he died in Philadelphia on Mar. 25.

DREW, GEORGIANA EMMA *See* Barrymore, Georgiana Emma Drew.

DREXEL, FRANCIS ANTHONY (1824–85), banker. Son of Francis Martin Drexel, an Austrian immigrant who founded the well-known banking firm of Drexel & Company, and Catherine Hookey, he was born in Philadelphia on June 20 and entered his father's business in his youth. When his father died, in 1863, he became senior member of the firm, and by the time of his death, in Philadelphia on Feb. 15, he was widely regarded as one of the foremost financiers in the country and was widely known for his philanthropic works. By his first wife, he had two daughters, Elizabeth (d. 1890) and Katharine (who founded the Sisters of the Blessed Sacrament for Indian and Colored People and spent much of the fortune she inherited from her father in that congregation's enterprises). On his death he bequeathed a large portion of his estate to charitable and religious enterprises.

DREXEL, KATHARINE (1858–1955), founder. Daughter of wealthy banker Francis Drexel and Hannah Jane Langstroth, who died when she was an infant, she was born in Philadelphia on Nov. 26. She was educated at home by governesses, traveled widely, and in 1885, on the death of her father, she inherited a fortune, which she decided to devote to religious work. She helped reestablish and support many schools on Indian reservations, and in 1889 she joined the Sisters of Mercy. But desirous of doing missionary work among blacks and Indians, she left and in 1891 founded the Sisters of the Blessed Sacra-

ment for Indians and Colored People and served as its superior until 1937. Ill since 1934, when she had suffered a stroke, she was elected vicar-general, and though she participated in the affairs of her congregation, she was obliged to curtail her activities. She was confined to a wheelchair the last years of her life until she was completely bedridden. During the years she was superior she established some sixty-three schools, among them Xavier University, launched in New Orleans in 1925 and dedicated in 1932, the first Catholic university in the United States for blacks, developed teachers and catechists for her schools and Indian centers, and by the time of her death, in Cornwall Heights, Pennsylvania, on Mar. 3, the congregation had forty-nine houses and hundreds of sisters.

DROSSAERTS, ARTHUR JEROME (1862–1940), archbishop. Born in Breda, the Netherlands, on Sept. 11, he was educated at the Haaren seminary, where he received his D.D. and was ordained in 1889. He emigrated to the United States in 1890, engaged in parish work in the New Orleans diocese, and in 1918 was appointed bishop of San Antonio, Texas. He founded St. John's Seminary, in San Antonio, in 1920, aided refugees from the religious persecution in Mexico, held diocesan synods in 1921 and 1930, and when the see was made an archdiocese, in 1926, became San Antonio's first archbishop. He was named an Assistant at the Pontifical Throne in 1934, and died in San Antonio on Sept. 8.

DRUM, HUGH ALOYSIUS (1879–1951), general. Son of an army officer, he was born in Fort Brady, Michigan, on Sept. 19. He was studying at Boston College when he was commissioned a second lieutenant by President McKinley in 1898; he did not receive his B.A.

until 1921. He served in the Philippines in 1899–1901, and was cited for bravery, and again in 1908–10; he married Mary Reaume in 1903 and served in the Mexican border skirmish in 1912–14. He was assistant chief of staff and aide-de-camp to General Funston in 1914–17, served General Pershing in the same capacity, and accompanied Pershing to France when America entered World War I. He was brigadier general and chief of staff of the American First Army in 1918–19, and after the war was commander of General Services schools in 1920–21, of coastal air defenses of the II Corps area in 1922, and was assistant chief of staff in 1923–26; while in this latter post he became embroiled in the controversy over a separate air force, insisting that aviation belonged under army control. He was commander of the 1st Infantry Brigade in 1927, inspector general of the U.S. Army in 1930, and commander of the V Corps area in 1931–33. After serving as deputy chief of staff in 1933, he was commander of the Hawaiian Department in 1935–37 and in 1937 was appointed commander of the VI Corps Area and the Second Army; he was assigned command of the II Corps Area and First Army Headquarters in 1938. He expected to be appointed army chief of staff in 1939, but George Marshall was appointed instead and he was promoted to lieutenant general and put in charge of the initial training of the First Army when it was activated in 1940. He then became head of the Eastern Defense Command. He was the recipient of the Laetare Medal in 1940, retired with the rank of lieutenant general in 1943, served as commander of the New York State Guard until 1948, and was named president of the Empire State Building Corporation in New York City in 1944; he died there on Oct. 3.

DRUMGOOLE, JOHN CHRISTOPHER (1816–88). Born in Granard, Longford, Ireland, on Aug. 15, he was brought to New York in 1824 and in his youth supported his widowed mother by working as a shoemaker, as sexton of St. Mary's Church, and in a small bookstore he founded. Desirous of becoming a priest since his boyhood, he studied at St. Francis Xavier and St. John's colleges, and when forty-nine entered Our Lady of the Angels Seminary, Niagara, New York. He was ordained there in 1869, became an assistant at St. Mary's, and was then put in charge of St. Vincent's Home for Homeless Boys begun by the St. Vincent de Paul Society. He founded St. Joseph's Union to raise funds to support the home, built the larger Mission of the Immaculate Virgin in New York in 1881, and then purchased land on Staten Island to build Mount Loretto with vocational schools and other buildings capable of housing two thousand boys annually. He became world famous for his work with homeless children, and helped secure passage of a New York State law mandating that homeless children be placed in a home or institution of their own religion. He died in New York City on Mar. 28.

DRUMM, THOMAS W. (1871–1933), bishop. Born in Fore, Westmeath, Ireland, on July 12, he emigrated to the United States in 1888, studied at St. Joseph's, Dubuque, Iowa, the Grand Seminary, Montreal, and Catholic University, and was ordained in Montreal in 1901. He engaged in pastoral work in Iowa and in 1919 was appointed second bishop of Des Moines, a position he held until his death there on Oct. 24.

DUBOIS, JOHN (1764–1842), bishop. Born in Paris on Aug. 24, he was educated at Collège Louis le Grand (where he was a classmate of Robespierre) and St. Magloire Seminary there, and was ordained in 1787. He was assistant at St. Sulpice and chaplain to the Sisters of Charity in Paris until forced to flee in 1791 by the French Revolution. He emigrated to the United States, settled in Norfolk, Virginia, where he resided for a time at the residence of James Madison, and was taught English by Patrick Henry. He engaged in missionary work in Norfolk and Richmond, became an American citizen, was named pastor of Frederick, Maryland, in 1794 and built its first Catholic Church, and worked as a missionary in western Maryland and Virginia. He joined the Sulpicians in 1808, opened a boys school at Emmitsburg, Maryland, and when financial difficulties beset the school broadened its scope at first and then in its place founded Mt. St. Mary's College. He was consecrated third bishop of New York in 1826, sought priests and financial aid for his diocese (all of New York and half of New Jersey) in visits to France and Rome in 1829, and was unsuccessful in attempts to found a seminary. Throughout his bishopric, he was beset by the trustee problem, which was finally settled by his successor, but despite his difficulties tripled the number of priests and churches in the diocese during his tenure. Ill health caused him to request a coadjutor, and John Hughes was appointed his coadjutor in 1837; he took over the administration of the see in 1839, when Bishop Dubois went into retirement. Bishop Dubois died in New York City on Dec. 20.

DUBOURG, LOUIS WILLIAM VALENTINE (1766–1833), archbishop. Born at Cap François, Santo Domingo, on Feb. 14, he was taken to France when an infant, studied at the Collège Guyenne and St. Sulpice, Paris, and was ordained in 1788. He was superior at the Issy seminary when the French Revolution broke out and he was forced to leave France. He emigrated to the United States in 1794, joined the Sulpicians in Baltimore in 1795, was president of Georgetown College in 1796–99, and then went to Havana, Cuba, to open the Sulpician college there. When the project failed, he returned to the United States, where he founded and was first superior of St. Mary's College in 1803 in Baltimore. He was superior of the Sisters of Charity in 1809–10, and in 1812 was appointed apostolic administrator of Louisiana and the Floridas. He supported the Americans in the War of 1812 and congratulated General Andrew Jackson on the steps of the cathedral for his victory over the British in 1815; later the same year he went to Rome to be consecrated bishop of New Orleans. On his return, in 1818, he settled in St. Louis (then in Upper Louisiana), founded a seminary and a college at The Barrens, near St. Louis, and the St. Louis Latin Academy, which in time developed into St. Louis University. He moved to New Orleans in 1820. His tenure was troubled by the machinations of a French Capuchin, Anthony de Sedella, who refused to accept the purchase of Louisiana in 1803 by the United States and by the dissension caused by the candidates for DuBourg's coadjutor. Bishop Rosati was appointed coadjutor in 1824, and Dubourg's resignation was accepted in 1826. Though intending to retire, Dubourg instead was appointed bishop of Montauban, France, in 1826, and in 1833 he was made archbishop of Besançon, France, where he was a strong supporter for the Society for the Propagation of the Faith, which was founded by his vicar-general, Abbé Inglesi, and Pauline Marie Jaricot. He died in Besançon on Dec. 12.

DUBUIS, CLAUDE MARY (1817–95), bishop. Born in Coutouvre, Loire,

France, on Mar. 10, he was educated at the seminary at l'Argentière, the seminary of St. Jodard, France, and the Grand Seminary, Lyon, France; he joined the Congregation of the Holy Cross and was ordained in Lyon in 1844. He was sent to the United States and worked as a missionary in the Galveston, Texas, diocese from 1844 until 1862, when he was appointed second bishop of Galveston. In 1866 he founded the Sisters of Charity of the Incarnate Word, in San Antonio, Texas, attended Vatican Council I, in 1869–70, and in 1881 resigned the administration of the diocese but kept the title of bishop of Galveston until 1892, when he was appointed titular bishop of Arca. He retired to Vernaison, France, and died there on May 22.

DUCHESNE, BL. ROSE PHILIPPINE (1769–1852), founder. Daughter of Pierre François Duchesne, a noted lawyer active in political affairs, she was born in Grenoble, France, on Aug. 29. She was educated at the Convent of the Visitation Sainte Marie d'en Haut, was attracted to the religious life, and despite her father's opposition joined the Visitation nuns in 1788. She was forced to leave the convent by the antireligious decrees of the French Revolution and returned home in 1792. She spent the next decade in charitable work in Grenoble, and after the Concordat of 1801 restored religious peace, she was successful in her attempt to reestablish the convent. She and the few followers who had returned joined the newly founded Society of the Sacred Heart in 1804, with Sainte Marie d'en Haut its second convent. She was transferred to Paris in 1815 and founded the first Sacred Heart convent there, and in 1818 with four companions she was sent to the United States. The group settled at St. Charles, near St. Louis, and established the first house of the Society in the United States. They moved to nearby Florissant the following year, and despite great hardships she had established six houses along the Mississippi by 1828. In 1840, when seventy-one, she resigned as superior and founded and taught at a school for the Potawatomi Indians at Sugar Creek, Kansas. Ill health caused her to return to St. Charles after a year, and she died there on Oct. 18. She was known for her holiness and sanctity and was beatified in 1940, with her feast day Nov. 17.

DU COUDRAY, PHILIPPE CHARLES JEAN BAPTISTE (1738–77), soldier. Born in Reims, France, on Sept. 8, he entered the military at an early age, became an army engineer, and soon achieved an outstanding reputation for his military knowledge and abilities. He was adjutant-general of artillery in 1776, when he volunteered to go to America to aid the colonists in their revolt against England. Promised the rank of major general in charge of artillery by Benjamin Franklin and Silas Deane, then American agents in France, he encountered great opposition from other officers in the Continental Army because of the high rank; instead he was made inspector general in 1777 in charge of fortifications along the Delaware River. He was drowned on Sept. 11 when his horse bolted while he was crossing the Schuylkill River at Philadelphia.

DUCRUE, FRANCIS BENNON (1721–79), missionary. Born in Munich, Bavaria, of French parents on June 10, he joined the Jesuits in 1738 and was sent to California as a missionary ten years later. He was superior of the California missions in 1767, when the Jesuits were expelled from Mexico and all Spanish possessions by King Charles III. He returned to Europe and died in Munich on Mar. 30. He wrote an account of his journey from California back to Mexico and then to Europe in 1767 and an account of the Jesuits's expulsion from Mexico with emphasis on California, which are valuable historical accounts.

DUFF, EDWARD ALOYSIUS (1883–1953), chaplain. Born in Philadelphia on May 31, he was educated at St. Charles College, Ellicott City, Maryland, St. Charles Borromeo Seminary, Philadelphia, and St. Mary's Seminary, Baltimore, and was ordained for the Charleston, South Carolina, diocese in 1911. He served as an assistant at the Charleston cathedral and as chaplain at the Charleston Navy Yard, and in 1913 he became an assistant at St. Mary's Church, Greenville, South Carolina. He joined the Navy as a chaplain in 1915, served in London, Paris, and Venice and on several warships, was on Admiral William S. Sims's staff during World War I, was promoted to captain in 1925, and was appointed chief of navy chaplains in 1936—the first Catholic chaplain to hold that post. The following year, he was assigned to the *California* as chaplain of the Pacific fleet and held that position until his retirement, in 1938. He died in Philadelphia on Feb. 11.

DUFFY, FRANCIS PATRICK (1871–1932), chaplain. Born in Cobourg, Ontario, Canada, on May 2, he was educated at St. Michael's College, Toronto, St. Francis Xavier College, New York City, and St. Joseph's Seminary, Troy, New York, and was ordained in Cobourg in 1896. He continued his studies at Catholic University until 1898, when he became an instructor in philosophy at the new St. Joseph's Seminary, Yonkers, New York, and remained there until 1912; he was also an editor of the *New York Review* in 1905–8. He was founding pastor of Our Sav-

ior's parish, Bronx, New York City, in 1912, and in 1914 he became chaplain of the 69th Regiment of the New York National Guard. During World War I he became famous as the chaplain of the now-called "Fighting 69th" and was decorated by the American, Canadian, and French governments. After the war he served as president of the Catholic Summer School, Cliff Haven, New York, and in 1920 he was appointed pastor of Holy Cross Church, New York City, a position he held until his death, in New York on June 23. He helped prepare Al Smith's reply to an article in the *Atlantic Monthly* by Charles Marshall casting aspersions on Smith's loyalties as a Catholic to the American ideal and on Catholics in general as Americans during the 1928 presidential campaign, and wrote his autobiography, *Father Duffy's Story* (1919). Several books and a motion picture told of his wartime experiences, and a statue of him was erected in Times Square, New York City—the first statue of a Catholic priest erected on public property in the state of New York.

DUFFY, FRANCIS RYAN (1888–1979), U.S. senator. Born in Fond du Lac, Wisconsin, on June 23, he was educated at the University of Wisconsin (B.A. 1910, LL.B. 1912) and was admitted to the Wisconsin bar in 1912. He practiced law in Fond du Lac, served as a major in the Motor Transport Corps in 1917–19, married Louise Haydon in 1918, and resumed his law practice after the war. He was national vice-commander of the American Legion in 1923–24, served in the U.S. Senate in 1933–39 but was unsuccessful in a bid for reelection in 1938; he was judge of the U.S. District Court for the Eastern District of Wisconsin in 1939–49. He was appointed to the U.S. Court of Appeals, 7th Circuit, in 1949 and was chief judge in 1954–59 and senior U.S. Circuit Judge from 1966 to 1978. He died on Aug. 16 and was buried at Fond du Lac.

DUFFY, JAMES ALBERT (1873–1968), bishop. Born in St. Paul, Minnesota, on Sept. 13, he was educated at St. Thomas College and St. Paul Seminary and was ordained in 1899. He served as a curate at Immaculate Conception Church, Minneapolis, in 1899–1902 and was pastor of St. Ann's Church, Le Sueur, Minnesota, but resigned because of ill health. He later became pastor of the cathedral at Cheyenne, Wyoming, and chancellor of that diocese. He was consecrated first bishop of the newly established diocese of Kearney, Nebraska (transferred to Grand Island in 1917), resigned his see in 1931, and was appointed titular bishop of Silando; he died in Grand Island on Feb. 12.

DUFFY, JOHN ALOYSIUS (1884–1944), bishop. Born in Jersey City, New Jersey, on Oct. 29, he was educated at Seton Hall College, South Orange, New Jersey, and the North American College, Rome (S.T.D. 1908), and was ordained in Rome in 1908. He taught at Seton Hall and Immaculate Conception Seminary, Darlington, New Jersey, until 1915, when he was appointed chancellor of the diocese of Newark, New Jersey. He served as vicar-general in 1924–33 and as pastor of St. Joseph's Church, Jersey City, and was appointed bishop of Syracuse, New York, in 1933; he was transferred to Buffalo in 1937 and held that post until his death, on Sept. 27.

DUGGAN, JAMES (1825–99), bishop. Born in Maynooth, Kildare, Ireland, on May 22, he studied there, emigrated to the United States in 1842, and continued his studies at St. Vincent's Seminary, Cape Girardeau, Missouri, and St. Louis, and was ordained in 1847. He

was superior of the St. Louis seminary at Carondelet in 1847–50, engaged in parish work in the St. Louis diocese, and was administrator of the Chicago diocese in 1853. He was appointed vicar-general in 1854 and titular bishop of Antigone and coadjutor of St. Louis in 1857, and was again sent to Chicago to administer the vacant see in 1858. He was appointed fourth bishop of Chicago the following year, and during his episcopate he expanded the diocese's parochial-school system, attended the second Plenary Council of Baltimore in 1866, became mentally ill in 1869, and was placed in a St. Louis asylum (he was retired in 1870), where he remained until his death on Mar. 27.

DU LHUT, DANIEL GREYSOLON. *See* Duluth, Daniel Greysolon.

DULUTH, DANIEL GREYSOLON (1636–1700), explorer. Born of noble parents at St. Germain-en-Laye, near Paris, he joined the French Army in his youth, was made a lieutenant in 1657, and in 1664 was made a gendarme of the King's Guard. He took part in the campaign in Flanders and in 1674 went to Canada, where his uncle had settled in Montreal. He was recalled to service in France later the same year, participated in the battle of Seneffe in which the French under Louis II de Condé defeated the Dutch, and then returned to Canada. In 1678 he and his brother La Tourette with six soldiers set out on an expedition to the West to pacify the Indians and end the war between the Chippewas and the Sioux. He succeeded in restoring peace and then explored Lake Superior and the sources of the St. Lawrence and the Mississippi rivers, built forts at Kaministikwia (Fort William) and Fort La Tourette, on Lake Nipigon, and claimed the Sioux country for France. His explorations were interrupted in 1680 by his negotiations with the Issati Sioux for the release of Michael Aco and Fr. Louis Hennepin, who had been captured when dispatched by La Salle from his expedition to explore the upper Mississippi Valley. When he returned to Mackinac he was charged with illegal trading and was obliged to go to France, where he cleared himself and received a royal commission. He was off on a new expedition in 1683 and became very influential with the Indians, who admired him, and kept them allied with the French. He was recalled from this trip in 1684 to lead an expedition, with Nicolas Perrot, against the Iroquois and brought the Western Indians into an alliance with the French campaign against the Iroquois. He returned to Kaministikwia to lead an expedition in quest of the Western Sea but was again called on to fight the Iroquois. In 1686 he founded a post at Detroit, and in 1690 was made a captain and put in command of Fort Frontenac but was forced to retire because of lameness in 1695; he spent his last years in Montreal, where he died on Feb. 25. Du Lhut (as he spelled his name) was one of the greatest of seventeenth-century French explorers and was mainly responsible for keeping the Lake Superior and upper Mississippi country for the French. He wrote of his 1676–78 journey, but the account has been lost; a plan he drew up for a string of forts has survived. Duluth, Minnesota, was named in his honor.

DUMETZ, FRANCISCO (d. 1811), missionary. A native of Mallorca, Spain, though when he was born is not known; he joined the Franciscans there and was one of a group of Franciscans sent to the order's missionary college in Mexico City. Later the same year he was sent to California, and the following year reached Monterey and was assigned to the San Diego mission. He was sent to San Carlos mission in 1792,

served there for fifteen years, was then sent to San Buenaventura mission, and in 1797 founded San Fernando mission. He ministered to the Indians there, spent 1803–4 at San Gabriel and then returned to San Fernando; he later returned to San Gabriel and spent the rest of his life and died there on Jan. 14 after four decades of missionary work in California.

DUNN, JAMES PHILIP (1884–1936), composer. Born in New York City on Jan. 10, he was educated at the College of the City of New York, studied music at Columbia under Edward MacDowell, and became an organist in New York and New Jersey churches. He was an associate editor of *Singing,* wrote *The Galleon,* an opera, three symphonic poems *(Annabelle Lee, Lovesight,* and *We),* songs, an overture on black themes, and works for violin and piano. He died in Jersey City, New Jersey, on July 24.

DUNN, JOSEPH (1874–1951), scholar. Born in New Haven, Connecticut, on Aug. 26, he was educated at Yale (B.A. 1895, Ph.D. 1898), taught Latin at Catholic University in 1898–91, was named a fellow in Gaelic in 1901, and studied Gaelic at Harvard, Freiburg im Breisgau, and Rennes until 1904, when he was appointed to the Ancient Order of Hibernians Chair of Celtic at Catholic University. He lectured on Celtic at Yale and the College of the City of New York in 1928–29 and 1931–32, translated lives of SS. Patrick and Alexis and the Irish epic *Tain Bo Cuailnge* (1914), and contributed to the Catholic Encyclopedia. He died in New Haven on Apr. 9.

DUNNE, EDWARD JOSEPH (1848–1910), bishop. Born in Gortnahoe, Tipperary, Ireland, on Apr. 23, he was brought to the United States when he was a boy and was educated at Old St. Mary-of-the-Lake, Chicago, and St. Mary's Seminary, Baltimore. He was ordained for the Chicago diocese in 1871, engaged in pastoral work in Chicago, and was pastor of All Saints Church, Chicago, when he was named second bishop of Dallas, Texas, in 1893. During his bishopric the cathedral, an industrial school for blacks, and colleges and sanitoriums were built in the diocese. He died on Aug. 5 while on a visit to Green Bay, Wisconsin.

DUNNE, EDMUND MICHAEL (1864–1929), bishop. Born in Chicago on Feb. 2, he was educated at St. Ignatius College there, Niagara University, New York, Séminaire de Fioriffe, at Louvain, Belgium, and the Gregorian, Rome. He was ordained in Louvain in 1887, engaged in pastoral work in several Chicago parishes, and was made chancellor of that archdiocese in 1905. He was appointed second bishop of Peoria, Illinois, in 1909 and continued the building program begun by his predecessor, initiating the building of twenty-one churches and thirteen schools. He resigned in 1908 after suffering a paralytic stroke in 1905, and died in Peoria on Oct. 7.

DUNNE, M. FREDERIC (1874–1949), abbot. Born in Ironton, Ohio, on Apr. 25, he joined the Trappists at Gethsemani, Kentucky, when he was twenty and was ordained in 1901—the first American Trappist. He served as vice-president of Gethsemani College and was prior of the monastery for more than thirty years, until 1935, when he was elected fifth abbot of Gethsemani. During his abbacy he modernized the monastery, established foundations in Georgia and Utah, and increased the community to almost two hundred monks. He died in Knoxville, Tennessee, on Aug. 4.

DUNNE, PETER FINLEY (1867–1936), humorist, journalist. Son of Peter Dunne and Ellen Finley Dunne, he was born in Chicago on July 10 and after his graduation from high school, in 1884, worked on the staffs of several Chicago newspapers. He began as an errand boy on the Chicago *Telegram,* became a reporter, and in 1888, when twenty-one, became city editor of the Chicago *Times.* In 1892 he began writing sketches in Irish dialect about Martin Dooley, an imaginary saloonkeeper, for the Chicago *Post.* The dialogues between "Mr. Dooley" and his constant companion, "Hinnissey," made Dunne known for his acidly humorous comments on politics and the social foibles of the times, but their gibes at the Spanish-American War won him a nationwide fame. He was managing editor of the Chicago *Journal* from 1899 to 1900, when he moved to New York, where he worked for *McClure's Magazine,* briefly edited the New York *Morning Telegraph,* was an editor of *American Magazine* in 1907–13, and was an editor of *Collier's* from 1915 until William Collier died. He wrote nondialect columns, "In the Interpreter's House" and "From the Bleachers," which were known for their wit and good common sense but never attained the popularity of the "Dooley" sketches. He wrote little after 1920, but eight volumes of his humorous observations were collected and published in book form beginning with *Mr. Dooley in Peace and in War,* in 1898, and concluding with *Mr. Dooley on Making a Will,* in 1919. He died in New York City on Apr. 24.

DUNNE, PETER MASTEN (1889–1957), historian. Born in San Jose, California, on Apr. 16, he was educated at Santa Clara College, California, and joined the Jesuits at Los Gatos, California, in 1906. He continued his studies at Gonzaga University, Spokane, Washington (B.A. 1912, M.A. 1914), taught in high schools in San Francisco and Santa Clara, and from 1919 studied theology at Hastings, England, where he was ordained, in 1921. He returned to the United States, served on the staff of *America* magazine in 1924–25, taught at Santa Clara College and the Los Gatos seminary in 1926–30 and then at the University of San Francisco. He received his doctorate from the University of California in 1934, became chairman of the history department of the University of San Francisco the same year, had his first book, *Mother Mary of St. Bernard,* published in 1929, and subsequently wrote numerous historical articles and books, among them *Pioneer Black Robes on the West Coast* (1940), *Pioneer Jesuits in Northern Mexico* (1944), *Blackrobes in Lower California* (1952), and a textbook, *Latin America* (1947), with Fr. John Francis Bannon. He died in San Francisco on Jan. 15.

DUPONCEAU, PETER STEPHEN (1760–1844), jurist, linguist. Born at St. Martin, Île de Ré, France, on June 3, Pierre Étienne du Ponceau was destined for the military but was forced to abandon this career because of poor eyesight. He entered the Benedictine college at St. Jean Angely in 1773, and in 1777 accompanied Baron Steuben to the United States as his secretary. He was given the rank of captain in the Continental Army but was forced to resign his commission in 1781 because of ill health, and settled in Philadelphia. He studied law there, became a citizen of Pennsylvania in 1781, and was under secretary to Robert Livingston, the American secretary of foreign affairs, in 1781–83, was admitted to the Pennsylvania bar in 1785, and became a leading authority on international law and practice. He was a member of the American Philosophical Society in 1791 and was its president from 1827 until his death, in Philadelphia on Apr. 1. He early displayed a marked proclivity for languages and wrote numerous papers on linguistic subjects for various volumes published by the Philosophical Society; his contributions to philology brought him international recognition, and his treatise on the grammatical system of several Indian tribes won the French Institute's Volney Prize in 1835.

DURANTE, JIMMY (1893–1980), entertainer. Born on the Lower East Side of New York's Manhattan on Feb. 10, he was a newsboy in his youth, left school in the seventh grade, worked at various jobs, and when seventeen began working at Diamond Tony's Saloon, in Coney Island—the beginning of his professional career. He formed a jazz band and played at the Club Alamo, in Harlem, where he met Jeanne Olson (whom he married in 1921) and Eddie Jackson. He opened the Club Durante in 1923, then met Lou Clayton, and he and Clayton and Jackson worked out a comedy routine; the new team became a tremendous success in nightclubs and then in vaudeville, playing to packed houses all over the country. They appeared in Florenz Ziegfeld's *Show Girl* in 1929 and Cole Porter's *The New Yorkers* in 1930, and after the latter closed, the team broke up. Durante appeared and was a great success in the movie *Get-Rich-Quick Wallingford,* in 1932, which was followed by a succession of second-rate films. He appeared in New York in *Strike Me Pink* (1933) and in *Jumbo* (1935), and among the other Broadway shows he was in were *Red, Hot and Blue* and *Stars in Your Eyes.* He made a comeback in films in *Music for Millions* (1944), *Two Girls and a Sailor* (1945), and *Two Sisters from Boston* (1946), which were hits, and began to appear on radio and then on television, where he captured the nation with his clowning, large nose (which earned him the nickname "Schnozzola"), honky-tonk piano playing, and gravelly voiced singing, especially of "I'm Jimmy That Well Dressed Man" and "Ink-a Dink-a Doo" and his "Goodnight Mrs. Calabash, wherever you are" sign-off. He died in Santa Monica, California, on Jan. 29.

DURBIN, ELISHA JOHN (1800–87), missionary. Born near Boonesboro, Madison County, Kentucky, on Feb. 1, he was sent to St. Thomas Preparatory Seminary, in Nelson County, in 1816, studied under David Flaget and Joseph Rosati there, and then continued his studies at St. Joseph's Seminary, Bardstown, where one of his instructors was Francis Kenrick, later archbishop of Baltimore. He was ordained at Bardstown in 1822 and two years later was assigned to an area of some eleven thousand square miles in western and southwestern Kentucky. From his headquarters in Morganfield, Kentucky, he spent the next sixty years traveling some half million miles on foot and on horseback throughout his vast missionary domain and also in Indiana, Illinois, and Tennessee, ministering to the Catholics of that far-flung area. In 1844 the infirmities of old age caused him to request relief from the incessant traveling and he was assigned to a small mission in Princeton, Kentucky. When he suffered a stroke, the following year, he was made chaplain of an academy at Shelbyville, Kentucky, and he died there on Mar. 22. He is often called "the apostle of Western Kentucky" and the "patriarch priest of Kentucky."

DURIER, ANTHONY (1833–1904), bishop. Born at St. Bonnet-des-Quarts, France, on Jan. 30 (some authorities say in Rouen on Aug. 8, 1832), he was educated at the Rouen seminary, emigrated to the United States, and continued his studies at Mt. St. Mary of the West Seminary, Cincinnati, and was ordained

in 1856. He engaged in parish work in New Orleans for twenty-seven years (1857–84), when he was appointed bishop of Natchitoches, Louisiana (transferred to Alexandria in 1910); he remained in that position until his death there on Feb. 28.

DURKIN, MARTIN PATRICK (1897–1955), union official. Born in Chicago on Mar. 18, he left evening high school to become a steamfitter's assistant when he was seventeen. He served in the Army during World War I, became business representative of the Chicago pipefitters union in 1921, and was head of the Illinois state labor department in 1933–41; in that position he bettered unemployment benefits and conciliation services. In 1941 he left the department to become secretary-treasurer of the United Association of Journeymen and Apprentices of the Plumbing and Pipe Fitting Industry and was elected president of the 225,000-member union in 1943. He was appointed Secretary of Labor in President Eisenhower's Cabinet, though he was a Democrat, in January 1953, but resigned in Sept. when changes in the proposed Taft-Hartley Act were not introduced despite his support for the changes. He returned to his position as president of the plumbers's union, serving in that post until he died, in Washington, D.C., on Nov. 13.

DUTTON, IRA BARNES (1843–1931), missionary. Born in Stowe, Vermont, on Apr. 27, he left Vermont and settled in Wisconsin, served in the Civil War as a Union lieutenant, and after the war worked ten years in the War Department's claims department. He became a convert to Catholicism in 1883, joined the Trappists in Gethsemani, Kentucky, as a lay brother with the name Joseph, and in 1886 went to Molokai, in the Hawaiian Islands, to work with Fr. Damian among the lepers of that leper colony. When Damian died, in 1888, Br. Joseph became administrative assistant of the colony. He founded Baldwin Home, for leper men and boys, and was honored by the Hawaiian Government for his work with the lepers. He died in Honolulu on Mar. 26.

DWENGER, JOSEPH GREGORY (1837–93), bishop. Born of German parents at Strattotown, near Minster, Ohio, on Sept. 7, he was orphaned as a boy when his father died when he was three and his mother when he was twelve. He was educated by the Fathers of the Precious Blood, joined the Congregation of the Precious Blood in 1854, studied for the priesthood at St. Mary of the West Seminary, Cincinnati, Ohio, and was ordained in 1859. He was professor at the Community's seminary until 1862, when he was assigned to pastoral work; in 1867–72 he was engaged in preaching missions. He was theologian for Bishop John Purcell of Cincinnati at the second Plenary Council of Baltimore, in 1866, was appointed second bishop of Fort Wayne, Indiana, in 1872, and in 1889 donated land for his congregation's St. Joseph's College, near Rensselaer, Indiana. A fervent supporter of the parochial-school system, he built his into a model school system. He was often referred to as "the orphan's friend" for his interest in orphans and built an orphanage for boys at Lafayette in 1875 and one for girls at Fort Wayne in 1886. He led the first official American pilgrimage to Lourdes in 1874 and with Bishops Moore and Gilmour was chosen to bring the decrees of the third Plenary Council of Baltimore, in 1884, to Rome. He died at Fort Wayne on Jan. 22. The plan he instituted for his school system was adopted by the fourth Provincial Council of Cincinnati, in 1882, which in turn was practically adopted as the basis for parochial-school systems at the third Plenary Council of Baltimore.

DWIGHT, THOMAS (1843–1911), anatomist. Born in Boston on Oct. 13, he was converted to Catholicism with his mother in 1856. He was educated at Harvard, received his medical degree in 1867, and continued his studies abroad at Munich. On his return to the United States he was appointed instructor in comparative anatomy at Harvard in 1872 and served as editor of the *Boston Medical and Sociological Journal.* In 1883 he succeeded Oliver Wendell Holmes as Parkman professor of anatomy at Harvard. He reconstituted Harvard's medical school and arranged the osteology section of the Warren Peabody Museum of Anatomy, was president of the Association of American Anatomists in 1893–95, and practiced surgery at Boston City Hospital and Carney Hospital, in Boston, until 1900, when he devoted himself to teaching and research. He published several treatises on bone structures, among them *Variation of the Bones of the Head and Foot* (1907) and *Thoughts of a Catholic Anatomist* (1911), attempted to reconcile the theory of evolution and the teaching of the Church, and was president of the Catholic Union of Boston in 1873–78 and of the St. Vincent de Paul Society. He died in Nahant, Massachusetts, on Sept. 8.

DWORSCHAK, LEO F. (1900–76), bishop. Born on a farm near Independence, Wisconsin, on Apr. 6, he was educated at St. John's University, Collegeville, Minnesota (B.A. 1922), and Catholic University (S.T.B. 1925), and was ordained in 1926. He served as a curate at St. Anthony's Church, Fargo, North Dakota, in 1929–39, was made chancellor of the Fargo diocese in 1935 while serving as secretary to the bishop

DWYER, ROBERT JOSEPH

of Fargo in 1929–39, and in 1940 became vicar-general; he was made a domestic prelate in 1941. He was appointed titular bishop of Tium and coadjutor of Rapid City, South Dakota, in 1946, was auxiliary bishop of Fargo in 1947–60, and succeeded to that see in 1970; he held that position until his death in Fargo on Nov. 5.

DWYER, ROBERT JOSEPH (1908–76), bishop. Born in Salt Lake City, Utah, on Aug. 1, he was educated at St. Mary's Manor, Pennsylvania, and St. Patrick's Seminary, Menlo Park, California, where he received his M.A., and was ordained in Salt Lake City in 1932. He served as a curate in the cathedral there in 1932–34 and as chaplain at St. Mary of the Waratch Convent there in 1934–38, continued his studies at Catholic University in 1938–41 (Ph.D.) and was diocesan superintendent of schools in Salt Lake City in 1941–52. He had *The Gentile Comes to Utah* published in 1941, was editor of the diocesan newspaper, *Intermountain Catholic,* for ten years, and in 1952 he was appointed bishop of Reno, Nevada—the first native of Utah to become a bishop. He held that position until 1960, when he was named archbishop of Portland in Oregon. He retired in 1974 because of ill health and moved to Piedmont, California; during his retirement he served as publisher/editor of the *National Catholic Register* and chairman of the board of *Twin Circle.* He died in Oakland, California, on Mar. 24.

E

EARLS, MICHAEL (1875–1937), educator. The eldest of ten children, he was born at Southbridge, Massachusetts, Oct. 2. He worked in mills to pay for his education at Holy Cross College, Worcester, Massachusetts (B.A. 1896), and Georgetown (M.A. 1897), and spent the next year traveling through Europe as a tutor. He began to study for the priesthood at the Grand Seminary, Montreal, joined the Jesuits in 1899 at the Jesuit novitiate in Frederick, Maryland, and while taking his philosophy and theology at Woodstock (Maryland) College, he taught at Boston College. He was ordained at Woodstock in 1912, was professor of rhetoric at Holy Cross in 1916–26, being father minister of the Jesuit community there in 1926–29, and taught English in 1929–31. He was superior of Manresa Institute, South Norwalk, Connecticut, the next two years, served as parish priest at St. Mary's Church, in Boston, in 1933–35, and then, after a short stay at Keyser Island, Connecticut, to write, he was recalled to Holy Cross and was faculty director of the Alumni Association in 1935. He died in New York City on Jan. 31. He published novels, essays, short stories, and poetry, among them *Under College Towers* (essays, 1926), *From Bersabee to Dan* (poetry, 1924), *The Hosting of the King* (poetry, 1935), and *Manuscripts and Memories* (essays, 1936).

ECCLESTON, SAMUEL (1801–51), archbishop. Born near Chestertown, Maryland, on June 27, he came under the influence of Catholicism when his mother married a Catholic after the death of his father, a Presbyterian. He was educated at St. Mary's College, Baltimore, where he became a Catholic, studied for the priesthood at St. Mary's Seminary, Baltimore, and was ordained there in 1825. He joined the Sulpicians and continued his education at Issy, France, and on his return to the United States, in 1827, he was made vice president of St. Mary's College and two years later became president. He continued in this position until 1834, when he was appointed titular bishop of Thermia and coadjutor of Baltimore. He succeeded to the see as its fifth archbishop a month later and at the same time became administrator of the diocese of Richmond, Virginia, an administration that lasted until Bishop Whelan was appointed bishop of Richmond, in 1841. He was active in expanding the educational facilities of his see, brought several orders of brothers into the archdiocese, including the Christian Brothers in 1841, held five provincial councils in Baltimore, helped build the cathedral with his personal contributions, and saw the opening of St. Charles's College, in Baltimore, in 1848. He died at Georgetown, D.C., on Apr. 22.

EDES, ELLA B. (1832–1916). Of an old New England family, she was born on Dec. 7, became a Catholic in 1852, and about 1866 she settled in Rome and became secretary of Cardinal Alessandro Barnabo, prefect of the Congregation of the Propagation of the Faith. After 1870, she became Roman correspondent, particularly of ecclesiastical affairs, for several newspapers, among them the London *Tablet,* New York *Herald,* New York *World* (under the pseudonym Anne Brewster), Brooklyn *Eagle,* and the New York *Catholic News.* She acted as agent for Archbishop Corrigan of New York and conservative members of the American hierarchy, and was often at odds with the progressive group headed by Archbishop Ireland of St. Paul. She retired because of ill health in 1908 and moved to northern Italy, where she died, near Pinerolo on Feb. 27.

EGAN, MAURICE FRANCIS (1852–1924), diplomat, author. Born in Philadelphia on May 24, he was educated at La Salle College there (B.A. 1873, M.A. 1875), began writing for Philadelphia newspapers, and taught while continuing his studies at Georgetown in 1875–78. His first novel, *That Girl of Mine,* was published in 1879, as was his first volume of poems, *Preludes.* He married Katharine Mullin in 1880, worked on *Magee's Illustrated Weekly* in 1877–79 and on *Freeman's Journal* as editor in 1881, becoming part owner in 1888; he became professor of English literature at Notre Dame in 1888. He was professor of English literature at Catholic University in 1895–1907 and became an adviser to Presidents McKinley and Roosevelt, helping to settle the "friar's land" dispute in the Philippines. President Roosevelt appointed him minister to Denmark in 1907, and he negotiated the purchase of the Danish West Indies (now the American Virgin Islands) by the United States in 1917; he remained as minister until 1918, when illness caused him to resign. He had turned down posts as ambassador to Austria-Hungary in 1913 and later to Japan. He was awarded the Laetare Medal in 1910, and was the author of more than thirty books, among them *Everybody's*

Saint Francis (1912), *Ten Years Near the German Frontier* (1919), *Confessions of a Book Lover* (1922), and *Recollections of a Happy Life* (1924). He died in Brooklyn on Jan. 15.

EGAN, MICHAEL (1761–1814), bishop. Born in Galway or Limerick, Ireland, he joined the Franciscans when he was eighteen, was educated at St. Anthony's College, Louvain, Belgium, and Immaculate Conception College, Prague, where he was ordained, and in 1787–90 he was guardian of St. Isidore's College. He then served as guardian of Franciscan friaries in Ennis, Roscrea, and Castlelyons, all in Ireland, and in 1802 he went to the United States. He served at St. Mary's Church, Lancaster, Pennsylvania, was named pastor of St. Mary's Church, Philadelphia, in 1803, and was appointed first bishop of the newly erected diocese of Philadelphia in 1808; he was not consecrated until 1810, in Baltimore, because of the delay in arrival of the papal bulls of his appointment, which were held up because of the Napoleonic Wars. His brief episcopate was marked by the bitter dispute with the trustees of St. Mary's, which he had selected as his cathedral, who claimed the right to appoint and remove pastors. The trustee struggle was to continue for years, exacerbated by the activities of two Irish priests, the Dominican William Harold and his uncle James, not only in Philadelphia but in other cities as well, bringing disruption to the Church in the United States and retarding its progress. Bishop Egan died in Philadelphia on July 22.

EGAN, PATRICK (1841–1919), diplomat. Born in Ballymahon, Longford, Ireland, on Aug. 13, he began working for a milling company when he was fourteen and rose in the company until, in 1872, he became one of its managing directors. He reorganized the company and made it the largest joint stock company in Ireland. He became a leader in the land movement to improve the condition of the Irish peasants, helped found the Amnesty Association, to secure the release of Irish prisoners, and helped Charles Parnell in his successful campaign in Meath in 1874. He was named to the executive council and became chairman of the Irish Land League when it was founded, in 1879, and the following year was accused of treason by the British Government and tried with Parnell and eleven others. They were acquitted, but when the British suspended the writ of habeas corpus to imprison them, Egan fled to Paris and took the treasury of the National Land League to Paris to prevent its confiscation. He resigned as treasurer in 1882, returned to Ireland, and was again threatened with arrest. He emigrated to the United States in 1883, settled in Lincoln, Nebraska, became active in the grain and milling business and the Republican Party, and helped organize the Irish National League of America, in Philadelphia in 1883, serving as its president in 1884–86. He supported James G. Blaine for the presidency in 1884 and at the Republican National Convention in 1888, but later swung a large Irish vote to Benjamin Harrison, who was elected President of the United States. Blaine became Secretary of State and appointed Egan minister to Chile (he had received his citizenship papers in 1888). He was faced with the outbreak of a revolution in that country in 1890, and when the revolutionists were victorious, negotiated a settlement with them—despite intense anti-American feeling (the United States had supported the existing government)—of the deaths of two American sailors who had been killed when a mob attacked a group of twelve American sailors in Valparaíso. In 1888–89 he disproved the sensational charges of the London *Times* stating he and Parnell were involved in the Phoenix Park murders by proving that the charges were based on forgeries. During his term as minister to Chile, he worked to improve diplomatic relations and commercial arrangements between the two countries. He resumed his business career in New York in 1893, continued his activities on behalf of the Irish Home Rule movement, and died in New York City on Sept. 30.

EGLOFFSTEIN, FREDERICK W. VON (1824–85), printer. Born at Aldorf, near Nuremberg, Bavaria, on May 18, he served in the Prussian Army in his youth and then emigrated to the United States. He established a printing business with Samuel Sartain, an engraver, and introduced half-tone engraving using glass screens with an opaque varnish with photography to produce engravings. He left his business to join the Union Army at the outbreak of the Civil War, was commissioned a colonel, and was wounded in a skirmish in North Carolina in 1862; at the end of the war he retired with the brevet rank of brigadier general. He resumed work on his new engraving process, founded the Heliographic Engineering and Printing Company, in New York City, but when unsuccessful in convincing the federal government to adopt his system for printing currency, abandoned the project. He became a member of the United States engineering department, engaged in submarine research at Rock Island, Illinois, and participated in the blasting operations at Hell Gate, in New York's East River. He died in New York City.

EIS, FREDERICK (1843–1926), bishop. Born in Arbach, Germany, on Jan. 20, he was brought to the United States by his parents in 1855. He was educated at St. Francis Seminary, Milwaukee, Wisconsin, and Joliette Seminary, Quebec, and was ordained in 1870. He engaged in parish work in Sault Sainte Marie and Marquette, Michigan, until 1899, when he was named administrator of the diocese of Marquette. He was appointed bishop of that see later in 1899 and held that position until he resigned, in 1922, and was made an Assistant at the Pontifical Throne and titular bishop of Bita. He died in Marquette on May 5.

ELDER, BENEDICT (1882–1961), editor. Born in Taylorsville, Kentucky, on June 19, he was educated at Gethsemani College, studied law at Western Reserve, Cleveland, Ohio, where he received his law degree, and was admitted to the Kentucky bar. He practiced law at Louisville, was managing editor of the Louisville diocesan paper, *The Record,* in 1919–46, and was active in the Catholic Press Association, serving as its president in 1930–32 and as its general counsel in the thirties. He died in Louisville on Jan. 12.

ELDER, GEORGE (1793–1838), educator. Born in Hardin's Creek, Marion County, Kentucky, on Aug. 11, he entered Mt. St. Mary's College, Emmitsburg, Maryland, when he was sixteen, studied for the priesthood at St. Mary's Seminary, Baltimore, and was ordained at Bardstown, Kentucky, in 1819. He became an assistant at the Bardstown cathedral, founded a college for lay students at the Bardstown (St. Joseph's) seminary, and in 1820–23 erected a separate building for the college, which in time became one of the outstanding educational institutions in the West. In 1827 he was appointed pastor of St. Pius parish in Scott County, Kentucky, but three years later he returned to St. Joseph's as president and held that post until his death, at Bardstown on Sept.

28. He was also an editor and contributor to the Louisville diocesan paper, *The Catholic Advocate,* founded in 1836, and wrote the satirical column "Letters to Brother Jonathan," on contemporary education and controversy.

ELDER, WILLIAM HENRY (1819–1904), bishop. Born in Baltimore on Mar. 22, he was educated at Mt. St. Mary's College, Emmitsburg, Maryland, and the Propaganda, Rome, where he received his doctor of divinity degree and was ordained in 1846. On his return to the United States, he became a professor of dogmatic theology at Mt. St. Mary's and served there until 1857, when he was appointed third bishop of Natchez, Mississippi. During the Civil War he was arrested for refusing the order of the commander of Union forces occupying Natchez to have prayers for the President of the United States said during Mass in the Catholic churches in his diocese; his conviction by the military was reversed in Washington. He was hailed for his heroic efforts to aid those stricken by the yellow fever epidemic of 1878, and in the midst of the epidemic was notified that he had been appointed coadjutor to Archbishop Alemany of San Francisco. His appeal for a postponement was granted, but in 1880 he was appointed titular bishop of Avara and coadjutor of Cincinnati, Ohio. He succeeded to the see as its second archbishop in 1883, and despite the financial difficulties he inherited he presided over the fourth provincial council, in 1882, and convened the fifth, in 1889, held two diocesan synods, in 1886 and 1898, founded thirty-two new parishes and missions and expanded the facilities of the see, reopened Mount St. Mary of the West Seminary in 1887, enlarged St. Joseph's Orphan Asylum, and founded St. Gregory's Preparatory Seminary in 1890. He died in Cincinnati on Oct. 31.

ELLARD, GERALD (1894–1963), liturgist. Born in Commonwealth, Wisconsin, on Oct. 8, he joined the Jesuits in 1912, was educated at Gonzaga University, Spokane, Washington (B.A. 1918), the University of St. Louis (M.A. 1925), and the University of Munich (Ph.D. 1931), and was ordained in 1926. He taught at St. Louis in 1931–32 and St. Mary's College, Kansas, from 1932 until his death, in Cambridge, Massachusetts, on Apr. 1. He was an outstanding liturgist, lectured widely on the liturgy, pioneered in liturgical reforms, was one of the founders of the National Liturgical Conference, and wrote numerous books on liturgical matters, among them *Christian Life and Worship* (1933), *Life and Worship* (1933), *Men at Work at Worship* (1940), *The Dialogue Mass* (1942), *The Mass of the Future* (1948), *Evening Mass* (1954), and *The Mass in Transition* (1956), a revision of *The Mass of the Future.*

ELLIOTT, WALTER (1842–1928), missionary. Son of Irish immigrants, he was born, four months after his father's death, in Detroit on Jan. 6. He was educated at Notre Dame, served with the 5th Ohio Volunteers during the Civil War, and was taken prisoner by the Confederates. On his return to Detroit, he studied law and was admitted to the bar. When he heard Fr. Isaac Hecker preach, in 1868, he decided to become a Paulist priest and went to New York to join the Paulists. He was ordained in 1872, was assigned to parish work for a time, and then began a half century of giving and directing missions all over the United States and training priests for mission work. He soon became one of the most effective and most popular missionaries of his day, was especially interested in converting non-Catholics to Catholicism, trained diocesan priests in mission work, and in 1902, with Fr. Alexander Doyles, founded on the campus of Catholic University the Apostolic Mission House to train them. He became its first rector and, except for 1909–12, when he was general consultor of the Paulist community in New York City, held that position the rest of his life. He organized the Catholic Missionary Union with its monthly organ, *The Missionary,* and was a leader of the Catholic Total Abstinence Union. He wrote several books, among them *Missions to Non-Catholics* (1893), *The Life of Christ* (1902), *The Spiritual Life* (1914), and a collection of his sermons, *Mission Sermons* (1926). But what attracted most attention in his life was his biography of Fr. Isaac Hecker, founder of the Paulists. A devoted friend and confidant of Hecker for many years, he began work on the biography immediately on the death of Hecker, in 1888. It first appeared as articles in the *Catholic World* and appeared in book form in 1891; six years later, it was published in France with an introduction by Abbé Felix Klein. Its publication in France caused a furore in European religious circles, particularly in France; it was denounced by the conservatives and acclaimed by the progressives as a vindication of their policies in its depiction of the Paulists's religious activities. The furore erupted into a major controversy over Americanism and led to Pope Leo XIII's apostolic letter *Testem benevolentiae,* in 1898, denouncing the so-called phantom heresy of Americanism. The book was withdrawn from circulation and, though "without prejudice," deeply affected Elliott. He died in Washington, D.C., on Apr. 18.

ELWELL, CLARENCE EDWARD (1904–73), bishop. Born in Cleveland, Ohio, on Feb. 4, he was educated at John Carroll University there (B.A. 1923), St. Mary's Seminary, Cleveland, the University of Innsbruck, Austria, where he was ordained in 1929, Western

Reserve University (M.A. 1934), and Harvard (Ph.D. 1938). He was assistant pastor at St. Cecilia's Church, in Cleveland, in 1929–33, taught education at St. John's College, Cleveland, in 1933, and was diocesan director of Cleveland's Catholic high schools and academies in 1938–46 and superintendent of the diocese's schools in 1946–66. He was named a domestic prelate in 1949 and a protonotary apostolic in 1960, auxiliary bishop of Cleveland in 1962, and was appointed bishop of Columbus in 1968, a position he occupied until his death there, on Feb. 16.

EMMET, THOMAS ADDIS (1825–1919), gynecologist, historian. Grandnephew of the Irish patriot Robert Emmet and son of Dr. John Patten Emmet, professor of science at the University of Virginia, he was born near Charlottesville, Virginia, on May 29. He studied at the University of Virginia but left in 1846 to study medicine at Jefferson Medical College, Philadelphia, graduating in 1850. He became resident physician at Emigrant's Refuge Hospital, Blackwell's Island, New York City, the following year and left in 1855 to join the staff of Women's Hospital in New York (where he served the next forty-five years) and was appointed surgeon in chief in 1861. He became world famous for his obstetrical knowledge, operative skills, and cures of women's diseases, and developed new methods of treating childbirth injuries and the Emmet operation for the repairs of tears in the womb. He became a Catholic in 1897, was told he was dying of cancer when he was seventy but did not retire until he was seventy-five, and lived to his nineties. An advocate of Irish home rule, he wrote the two-volume *Ireland under English Rule* (1903), attacking England's treatment of Ireland, and headed the Irish National Federation in 1891–1901. He early began collecting manuscripts of American historical importance, became an authority on American manuscripts, and in time built one of the finest collections of American manuscripts, particularly of the Revolutionary period, which contained a complete series of letters by the signers of the Declaration of Independence; it is now in the New York Public Library. He was honored papally and was awarded the Laetare Medal in 1898, and died in New York City on Mar. 1. His *Principles and Practice of Gynecology* (1879) and *Diseases of Women* became standard textbooks on the subjects.

ENGELHARDT, ZEPHYRIN (1851–1934), historian. Born in Bilshausen, Hannover, Germany, on Nov. 13, he was christened Charles Anthony and was brought to the United States by his parents when he was an infant. He was educated at St. Francis Seminary, Cincinnati, Ohio, joined the Franciscans, taking the name Zephyrin, in 1873 and was ordained in St. Louis in 1878. He taught at St. Joseph's College, Cleveland, until 1880 and was then assigned to the Menominee Indian mission at Keshena, Wisconsin, and in 1895 to the Franciscan monastery at Superior, Wisconsin. He published a catechism, *Kateshim,* in Menominee in 1884, and founded the Indian monthly *Anishina Enamiad* in the Ottawa language in 1896, edited *Messenger of St. Francis* and *Pilgrim of Palestine,* and was named vice-commissary of the Holy Land in 1887. After a brief term in that position in New York City, he spent the next thirteen years at Indian missions in California, Michigan, and New Mexico. He was then sent to Santa Barbara, California, and except for a short time at an orphanage near Watsonville, he spent the rest of his life at Santa Barbara; he died there on Apr. 27. He was the outstanding authority on the missions of the Southwest and wrote prolifically on the subject: the four-volume *Missions and Missionaries of California* (1909–15), *The Franciscans in California* (1897), *The Franciscans in Arizona* (1899), and a life of Kateri Tekakwitha were among his books.

ENGLAND, JOHN (1786–1842), bishop. One of ten children, he was born in Cork, Ireland, on Sept. 23, studied law at Cork, but after two years there entered St. Patrick's College, Carlow, and was ordained in 1808. He was appointed lecturer at the cathedral and soon began to draw large crowds with his eloquent preaching, attended inmates in the city jail, and helped secure better conditions for prisoners being transported to Australia. He was president of the newly established diocesan St. Mary's College in 1812–17, was a staunch supporter of Irish rights, and was one of the leaders in the fight for Catholic emancipation that led to the Catholic Emancipation Act of 1829, enacted by the British Parliament. He so vociferously opposed allowing the government a voice in the selection of Irish and English Catholic bishops that he was transferred to the small village of Bandon in 1817. Three years later he was appointed bishop of Charleston, South Carolina, an impoverished diocese that consisted of the Carolinas and Georgia. He soon became involved in the trustee controversy that was wracking the Church in the United States and in 1822 incurred the wrath of Bishop Conwell of Philadelphia by interfering in the Hogan schism in that city by offering to accept Hogan into his diocese; the bishops of New York and Baltimore also objected to his interference in what they felt were matters outside his province. He abolished pew rent and the trustee system in a constitution he provided for his diocese, but his solution of the trustee system—establishing a dioc-

esan board of clerical and lay advisers to help govern his see—was strongly opposed by his fellow bishops. He persuaded the South Carolina legislature to grant him a charter for his diocesan corporation (a move opposed by ecclesiastical trustees), was the first Catholic priest to address Congress, in 1826 (the month before he received his final citizenship papers), convinced Bishop James Whitfield of Baltimore to convene the first Provincial Council of Baltimore, in 1829, and held conventions of clergy and laity and a clergy synod in 1831. He encouraged classical learning, established the Philosophical and Classical Seminary, in Charleston, in 1832 and was an active member of the Philosophical Society of Charleston. He ordered a book society to be established in each congregation in 1822 and in the same year founded the *United States Catholic Miscellany,* the first fully Catholic newspaper in the United States, and in 1823 was put in charge of Florida with the powers of vicar-general. He opened St. John the Baptist Seminary in 1825 to provide priests for his diocese, founded the Sisters of Our Lady of Mercy in Charleston in 1827, and brought the Ursulines into the diocese in 1833. He was especially devoted to the needs of the blacks of the diocese, opened a school for free blacks in 1835 (though he was soon forced to close it), and rendered heroic services ministering to the victims of the cholera and smallpox epidemics that regularly beset Charleston. He visited the chief cities of the United States and went to Europe in quest of priests, funds, books, and vestments for his diocese. He actively participated in civic matters, helped to organize the Anti-Duelling Society, strenuously opposed the doctrine of nullification, and though personally opposed to slavery did not believe it could be abolished in his adopted country. He was sent to Haiti in 1833 as apostolic delegate, the first United States bishop to be chosen for such a mission, and drafted a concordat that was turned down by Pope Gregory XVI because of the concessions he had made; though the mission proved unsuccessful, Gregory made him an Assistant at the Pontifical Throne. He edited a catechism and prepared a new edition of the Missal and contributed many columns to the *United States Catholic Miscellany;* he was a prolific writer, and his successor, Bishop Ignatius Reynolds, collected his writings in five volumes in 1849. He vigorously promoted the concept of a native American clergy, constantly quarreled with French priests, especially the Sulpicians, for what he believed were their monarchical tendencies as opposed to his own concept of democracy, and made repeated visitations of the parishes and missions of his far-flung see. He fought for the cause of Irish freedom all his life but turned down the offer of an Irish see to remain in his own debt-ridden diocese. He was noted for his fearless defense of his faith, his learning, his apostolic zeal, and his personal poverty; his death, in Charleston on Apr. 11, was mourned by people of all faiths. England was one of the most dynamic prelates in the history of the American Church, a champion of democracy, and a fervent patriot who anticipated many of the later developments in the Church.

ESPELAGE, BERNARD THEODORE (1892–1971), bishop. Born in Cincinnati, Ohio, he joined the Franciscans in 1910, was educated at Franciscan seminaries and Catholic University (J.C.L. 1926), and was ordained in Oldenburg, Indiana, in 1918. He served as assistant pastor in Roswell, New Mexico, in 1918–19, was chancellor of the archdiocese in 1919–34, and was pastor of St. Francis Cathedral there in 1934–39 and of Holy Family Church, in Oldenburg, in 1939–40. He was appointed

first bishop of the newly created diocese of Gallup, New Mexico, in 1940; at the time of his resignation, in 1969, he had established eighteen new parishes and missions and built Sacred Heart Cathedral. He died in Gallup on Feb. 19.

ESTAING, PIERRE BAPTISTE CHARLES HENRI HECTOR, COMTE D', MARQUIS DE SAILLANS (1729–94), admiral. Born at the Château de Ruval, Auvergne, France, on Nov. 24, he entered the Army in his youth and, as a nobleman, was commissioned a colonel. He was made a brigadier general in 1757 and was sent to the East Indies during the Seven Years' War and was wounded and taken prisoner at the siege of Madras in 1758. On his release he was given command of two vessels of the Franch East Indies fleet and led a naval force that destroyed British establishments in Sumatra and the Persian Gulf. On his way back to France, in 1760, he was captured by the British and imprisoned in Plymouth. On his release, he became a lieutenant general of the Navy in 1763, was governor of the Antilles in 1763–66 and inspector of the Navy at Brest for five years. He was made a vice admiral in 1777 and the following year was dispatched with a fleet of seventeen ships to aid the American colonists in their struggle for freedom. He was unsuccessful in his first attempt to engage Admiral Howe's fleet off the coast of Newport, Rhode Island, but when a confrontation between the two fleets did take place, a violent storm scattered the ships of both fleets. He then sailed to the West Indies, captured St. Vincent and Grenada, and fought a drawn battle with Admiral John Byron's fleet in 1779. In cooperation with American forces under General Benjamin Lincoln he launched an unsuccessful attempt to capture Savannah, Georgia, in 1779 and was wounded. He returned to France in 1780 and fell into disfavor with the court, but in 1783 he was reinstated and placed in command of a Franco-Spanish fleet before Cádiz, but the peace was signed before any action took place. He at first favored the French revolutionary ideas, was elected to the Assembly of Notables in 1789 and, although commandant of the National Guard at Versailles during its storming by a Parisian mob in 1789, took no action against the mob. He became an admiral in 1792. When he spoke up for Marie Antoinette at her trial, in 1793, he was charged with being a royalist and was guillotined in Paris on Apr. 28.

EUPHEMIA, MOTHER *See* Blenkinsop, Catherine.

EUSTACE, BARTHOLOMEW JOSEPH (1887–1956), bishop. Born in New York City on Oct. 9, he graduated from St. Francis Xavier College there in 1910 and then studied for the priesthood at St. Joseph's Seminary, Yonkers, New York, and the North American College, Rome, where he received his S.T.D. and was ordained in 1914. He was a curate at Blessed Sacrament Church in New Rochelle, New York, for a time and then taught at St. Joseph's in 1916–37. He served as chaplain at the Pelham Bay Training Station in World War I, and in 1937 was appointed first bishop of the newly created diocese of Camden, New Jersey. He inherited a substantial debt and a shortage of priests, and during his almost two decades as bishop he established thirty-two parishes and built nineteen elementary schools, six high schools, and two hospitals, and added 115 priests to the see; he was the author of *Baptism Ritual* (1935) and *Rites for Small Churches* (1935). He died in Camden on Dec. 11.

EWING, CHARLES (1835–83), general. Fifth child of Thomas Ewing and

Maria Boyle Ewing, he was born in Lancaster, Ohio, on Mar. 6, was educated at the Dominican college near Lancaster, Gonzaga College, Spokane, Washington, and the University of Virginia. He began practicing law in St. Louis in 1860, and at the start of the Civil War was commissioned a captain in the 13th Infantry of the Union Army. He was with General William Tecumseh Sherman, his brother-in-law, during the latter's Arkansas and Missouri campaigns and was wounded three times at Vicksburg. He was made a lieutenant colonel in 1862, inspector general of the XV Army Corps the following year, and was with Sherman on his march through Georgia. He was commissioned brigadier general in 1865, was cited for his bravery at Vicksburg and at Atlanta, and stayed in the Army after the war as brevet colonel; he resigned in 1867 to resume his law practice in Washington, D.C. He was appointed to handle Catholic Indian affairs by Archbishop James Roosevelt Bayley of Baltimore and was named commissioner of the Bureau of Catholic Indian Missions in 1874 when it was officially established, worked to restore to the Catholic Indian missions the schools they had run the previous two decades, and was made a Knight of St. Gregory by Pope Pius IX in 1877. He died in Washington, D.C. on June 20.

EWING, HUGH BOYLE (1826–1905), jurist, general, diplomat. Son of Thomas Ewing, he was born at Lancaster, Ohio, on Oct. 31, was educated by private tutors and at West Point (though he did not graduate), went to California in 1849 during the gold rush, and returned to Lancaster in 1852 to study law. He was admitted to the bar, practiced in St. Louis in 1854–56 and in Leavenworth, Kansas, in 1856–58 with the firm of Ewing, Sherman (his foster brother) & McCook. He returned to Lancaster, and at the outbreak of the Civil War joined the Union Army. He was brigade inspector of Ohio Volunteers in 1861, fought under Generals McClellan and Rosecrans in their West Virginia campaign, was commissioned colonel in command of the 30th Ohio Volunteers and was promoted to brigadier general in 1862 after the battle of Antietam. He fought at Vicksburg in 1863, was placed in command of the 4th Division, XV Army Corps, participated in the Chattanooga campaigns and the capture of Missionary Ridge, and was placed in command of the district of Kentucky; he was brevetted major general at the close of the war in 1865. He served as United States minister to The Hague in 1866–70, and on his return to the United States practiced law until 1874, when he retired to his estate at Lancaster; he died there on June 30. He wrote a number of magazine articles and the books *A Castle in the Air* (1888) and *The Black List; a Tale of Early California* (1893).

EWING, J. FRANKLIN (1905–68), anthropologist. Born in New York City on Oct. 14, he was educated at Woodstock College (Maryland) (B.A. 1928, M.A. 1929) after joining the Jesuits, taught physics at Ateneo de Manila, Philippines, in 1929–32 and was ordained at Woodstock in 1935. He continued his studies at Woodstock (S.T.L. 1936) and the University of Vienna in 1937–38, received his Ph. D. from Harvard in 1947, and began teaching anthropology at Fordham in 1949. He became director of the Institute of Mission Studies in 1953, wrote *The Ancient Way* (1964), and died at Peekskill, New York, on May 20.

EWING, PHILEMON BEECHER (1820–96). Eldest son of Thomas Ewing and Maria Boyle Ewing, he was born in Lancaster, Ohio, on Nov. 3, was edu-

cated at Miami University, Oxford, Ohio, graduating in 1838, and then studied law. He was admitted to the bar in 1841, formed the law firm of T. Ewing & Son with his father and became a well-known figure in state and federal courts. He married Mary Rebecca Gillespie, sister of Mother Mary of St. Angela of the Sisters of the Holy Cross of Notre Dame, in 1848, supported his father's political activities, and was himself active in politics as a Whig and then as a Republican. He was appointed judge of the Court of Common Pleas in 1862, vigorously opposed Republican reconstruction policies, and was nominated to Ohio's supreme court in 1873. During the 1860s and 1870s he engaged in the banking business and helped develop the Hocking Valley coal fields, in Ohio. He was a delegate to the Catholic congresses of 1889 and 1893, and died at Lancaster on Apr. 15.

EWING, THOMAS (1789–1871), statesman. Son of George Ewing, an officer in the Continental Army during the American Revolution, and Rachel Harris Ewing, he was born in West Liberty, Virginia (Liberty, West Virginia) on Dec. 28. He was given his early education by his sister Sarah, worked in Kanawha salt mines to earn money for his education, and then entered Ohio University, where he received his B.A. in 1815, the first degree granted by a western college. He studied law, was admited to the Ohio bar in 1816, and began his law practice. He was a successful practitioner in local and national courts, decided to enter politics, served as prosecuting attorney for Fairfield County for several years, and in 1830 was elected United States Senator from Ohio. He favored a protective tariff, advocated rechartering the United States Bank, supported Whig policies, presented a memorial to abolish slavery, and helped bring about a reorganization of the Post Office Department. He was defeated for reelection in 1836, resumed his law practice, was appointed Secretary of the Treasury in 1841 by President William Henry Harrison but resigned later in the same year with the entire Cabinet when President Tyler vetoed a bill to recharter the Bank of the United States which Ewing favored. He returned to private law practice, was appointed Secretary of the newly established Department of the Interior in 1849, and organized the department; he urged the building of a transcontinental railroad. He resigned in 1850, when he was appointed senator from Ohio to fill an unexpired term, but was defeated in a bid for reelection in 1851 and resumed his law practice, becoming renowned for his brilliance in cases before the United States Supreme Court. He was a member of the Peace Conference seeking to avert the Civil War in 1860,

strongly favored the Union position during the war, and afterward vigorously opposed the reconstruction policies of Congress and supported President Andrew Johnson and his policies. Johnson appointed him Secretary of War in 1868, but the Senate never acted on his appointment. He had married Maria Willis Boyle, an Irish Catholic, in 1820 and had permitted her to raise their six children as Catholics. Though the Ewings had this large family, they adopted nine-year-old William Tecumseh Sherman when his father died, in 1829. In 1869, while arguing a case before the United States Supreme Court, he collapsed and was baptized in the courtroom; he was received into the Catholic Church by his old friend Archbishop John Purcell of Cincinnati in 1871 and died soon after in Lancaster, on Oct. 26.

F

FARIMAN, VIRGIL B. *See* Klarmann, Andrew F.

FARIBAULT, JEAN BAPTISTE (1775–1860), trader. Son of Barthélemy Faribault, a Parisian lawyer who had migrated to Canada, he was born at Berthier, Quebec, on Oct. 29, worked in a mercantile establishment for a time, and in 1796 joined the Northwest Fur Company. In 1798 he was sent to Michilimackinac (Mackinac) Island, in northwestern Lake Huron, and spent the next decade there trading with the Potawatomi and Sioux Indians. In 1805 he married Pélagie Hanse, half-breed daughter of Major Hanse (or Aisne) of Mackinac, and the couple settled in Prairie du Chien, Wisconsin, in 1809, and he began trading with the Indians on his own. Though it was claimed he favored the Americans in the War of 1812, he was in the British militia that attacked Prairie du Chien in 1814. After the war he became an American citizen, in 1815, and resumed his trading at Prairie de Chien. He moved to Pike Island, in the Minnesota River, near Fort Snelling, in 1819, to St. Peter (Mendota), Minnesota, in 1826, and spent the last years of his life in Faribault, Minnesota (which was named after his eldest son, Alexander), and died there on Aug. 20. He was known for his considerateness of the Indians and for his strong Catholic faith, which he endeavored to impart to them; he gave a house to be used as a chapel to Fr. Lucien Galtier, first resident missionary in Minnesota, where a county was named in Faribault's honor.

FARLEY, JAMES ALOYSIUS (1888–1976), Postmaster General. Born in Grassy Point, New York, on May 30, he graduated from Packard Commercial School in New York City in 1906 and began his career as a bookkeeper in New York in the same year. He early became interested in politics, was town clerk in Grassy Point in 1912–19, port warden of the Port of New York in 1918–19, a member of the New York State Athletic Commission in 1922–23, and its chairman in 1925–33. He served in the New York State Assembly in 1923, became sales manager of the Universal Gypsum Company in 1926, and then established his own firm, James A. Farley & Company, dealing in building materials. In 1929 his firm merged with five others as General Builders Supply Corporation, and he served as its president until 1933. He was secretary of the New York State Democratic Committee in 1928–30 and chairman in 1930–44, and he was chairman of the Democratic National Committee in 1932–40. He was an early supporter of Franklin D. Roosevelt for the presidency and played a major role in the nomination and election of Roosevelt as President in 1932; Roosevelt appointed Farley Postmaster General in 1933. He masterminded the 1936 presidential election campaign that led to Roosevelt's landslide victory in which he captured the electoral votes of forty-six of the forty-eight states, but broke with the President when Roosevelt decided to seek an unprecedented third term, in 1940. Never enamored of the New Deal and many of the New Dealers, he opposed Roosevelt at the National Democratic Convention in 1940 and sought the nomination himself but was easily defeated by Roosevelt. He refused Roosevelt's request that he run the campaign and resigned as national chairman of the Democratic National Committee and as Postmaster General. After the 1940 reelection of Roosevelt, he ceased to be important on the national scene, though he continued active in New York State politics. He was appointed chairman of the board of the Coca-Cola Export Corporation in 1940 and was reelected president of General Builders Supply Corporation in 1949. He was the recipient of many awards and honorary degrees, wrote two books, *Behind the Ballots* (1938) and *Jim Farley's Story* (1948), and died in New York City on June 9.

FARLEY, JOHN MURPHY (1842–1918), cardinal. John Farrelly was born in Newton Hamilton, Armagh, Ireland, on Apr. 20, was early attracted to the priesthood, studied at St. Macartan's College, Monaghan, and in 1864 emigrated to New York, where he continued his studies at Fordham. The following year, he entered St. Joseph's Seminary, Troy, New York, went to the North American College, Rome, in 1866, and was ordained a priest of the New York archdiocese in 1870. He was a curate at St. Peter's parish, on Staten Island, until 1872, when he became Cardinal John McCloskey's secretary, changing his name to Farley, and in 1884 became a papal chamberlain. He was vicar-general of the archdiocese in 1891–92, when he was also pastor of St. Gabriel's Church, was made a domestic prelate in 1892, and in 1895 was consecrated titular bishop of Zeugma and auxiliary of New York. He was appointed fourth archbishop of New York in 1902 and was created a cardinal in 1911. During his episcopate he doubled the number of parochial schools in the archdiocese, opened Cathedral College minor seminary in 1903, supported Catholic University, was a patron of the Catholic Encyclopedia, and backed the concept of college education for women. He held diocesan synods every three years, was active in aiding immigrants, and received the founders of Maryknoll into the archdiocese in 1911. He wrote a history of St. Patrick's Cathedral in 1908, and in 1918, a biography of Cardinal McCloskey, whom he greatly admired; he died of pneumonia in New York City on Sept. 17.

FARMER, FERDINAND. *See* Steinmeyer, Ferdinand.

FARRELL, WALTER (1902–51), theologian. Born in Chicago on July 21, he was educated at Quigley Preparatory Seminary there, joined the Dominicans in Somerset, Ohio, in 1920, and after further study at St. Rose Priory, Kentucky, and the Dominican House of Studies, Washington, D.C., he was ordained in 1927. He continued his studies at the University of Fribourg, Switzerland (S.T.D. 1930), and on his return to the United States taught dogmatic theology at Somerset. In 1933 he began teaching at the Dominican House of Studies, Washington, D.C., was appointed regent of studies of the Dominicans' eastern province, St. Joseph's, in 1939, and the following year received his S.T.M. in Rome; later the same year he became president of the pontifical faculty of theology at the Washington house of studies. After serving as a chaplain in the Navy in 1942–45, he went to the Dominican House of Studies in River Forest, Illinois, as retreat master. He did much to renew interest in the teachings of St. Thomas Aquinas, writing the immensely popular four-volume *Companion to the Summa* (1938–42) and helping found *The Thomist* in 1939; his unfinished life of Christ, *Only Son,* was posthumously published in 1953. He died in River Forest on Nov. 23.

FARRELLY, JOHN PATRICK (1856–1921), bishop. Born in Memphis, Tennessee, on Mar. 15, he was educated at Georgetown, Nôtre Dame de la Paix, Namur, Belgium, and the Propaganda, Rome. He was ordained in 1880, engaged in parish work in the Nashville diocese, and in 1904 was named spiritual director of the North American College, Rome. He was appointed fourth bishop of Cleveland, Ohio, in 1909, and the following year the diocese was divided to create the diocese of Toledo. During his episcopate he greatly increased the number of churches, schools, and hospitals in the see and organized the charitable activities of the diocese under the Catholic Charities Corporation. He died in Cleveland on Feb. 12.

FARROW, JOHN VILLIERS (1906–63), motion-picture director and producer, author. Born in Sydney, Australia, on Feb. 10, he was educated privately there, in England, and in Europe; raised an Anglican, he later returned to Catholicism. He spent his youth as a soldier of fortune, traded in the South Sea islands with his own schooner, participated in two South American revolutions, and was a member of several scientific expeditions. He then went to Hollywood and became a director, with his first successful picture, *My Bill,* released in 1937; but he left for service in the British and Canadian navies during World War II. He was medically discharged in 1942 for typhus and returned to Hollywood, where he became a top-flight producer and director. Among the more than forty films he directed were *Wake Island* (1942), for which he received the New York Film Critics Award as best director of the year, *Five Came Back, Two Years Before the Mast, Back from Eternity, Botany Bay,* and *Hondo.* He also wrote screenplays (he received the Academy Award for best screenplay for *Around the World in 80 Days)* and books, among them an English-Tahitian dictionary (1932), *Damien the Leper* (1937), *Pageant of the Popes* (1942), and *The Story of Thomas More* (1954). He married screen star Maureen O'Sullivan in 1936 and the couple had seven children, one of whom, Mia Farrow, also became a screen star. He received numerous awards, among them a knighthood of the Grand Cross of the Order of the Holy Sepulchre, from Pope Pius XI, and honorary commander of the Order of the British Empire, from Queen Elizabeth II. He died in Beverly Hills, California, on Jan. 28.

FAY, SIGOURNEY WEBSTER (1857–1919). Born in Philadelphia on June 16, he was educated at the University of Pittsburgh and the Episcopal Divinity School in Philadelphia, and was ordained an Episcopal priest in 1903. He taught theology at the Episcopal Nashotah House seminary, Fond du Lac, Wisconsin, and then became associated with a group of Anglican clergymen called Companions of the Holy Saviour. When the Episcopal Convention of 1907 permitted clergymen of other denominations to preach in Episcopal churches, he became a Catholic; he was ordained a Catholic priest in 1910. He served as headmaster of the Newman School for Boys, Hackensack, New Jersey, for several years, and in 1917 joined the Red Cross. While in Italy, he learned of a clause to be inserted in the peace conference ending World

War I that excluded the Holy See from the conference. He devoted himself to having the clause eliminated but died in New York City on Jan. 10 while preparing to go to London to pursue his efforts with English leaders.

FEBIGER, JOHN CARSON (1821–98), admiral. Born in Pittsburgh on Feb. 14, he entered the Navy as a midshipman in 1838 and served in South American, African, and East Indian waters. When the Civil War broke out, he was with the East Indian squadron, which returned to the United States at once. He was made a commander in 1862 and put in command of the *Kanawha,* of the West Gulf blockading squadron, and in 1864 was put in command of the side-wheeler *Mattabesett.* In May 1864 he fought a four-hour battle with the confederate ram *Albemarle* in Albemarle Sound, North Carolina, causing the ram to withdraw. After the war, he commanded the *Ashuelot,* of the Asiatic squadron, in 1866–68, was made a captain in 1868, served as inspector of naval reserve lands in 1869–72, and was made a commodore in 1874, serving on the board of examiners until 1876, when he was made commandant of the Washington Navy Yard, serving in that post until 1880. He became a rear admiral in 1882 and retired later in that year. He took up residence in Easton, Maryland, and died in Londonderry, near Easton, on Oct. 9.

FEEHAN, DANIEL FRANCIS (1855–1934), bishop. Born in Athol, Massachusetts, on Sept. 24, he was educated at St. Mary's College, Montreal, graduating in 1876, and St. Joseph's Seminary, Troy, New York; he was ordained in Troy in 1879. He served as pastor in Fitchburg and West Brighton, in the Springfield, Massachusetts, diocese, and in 1889 was made pastor of St. Bernard's Church, Fitchburg. He

served in that position until 1907, when he was appointed second bishop of Fall River. He greatly expanded the facilities of the diocese, establishing thirty-six new parishes, orphanages, day nurseries, and welfare agencies; he died in Fall River on July 19.

FEEHAN, PATRICK AUGUSTINE (1829–1902), bishop. Born in Kilenaule, Tipperary, Ireland, on Aug. 29, he was educated at Castle Knock College and then went to Maynooth, where he was appointed to the Dunboyne Establishment, a higher course of ecclesiastical studies for those students who have distinguished themselves in the ordinary courses. In 1850 he accompanied his family to the United States, continued his studies at the Carondelet theological seminary, St. Louis, and was ordained in St. Louis in 1852. He taught Sacred Scripture at Carondelet Seminary and in 1854 became its president, was named pastor of St. Michael's Church in 1858 and was transferred to Immaculate Conception Church as its pastor soon after. His concern for the poor and his ministrations to wounded soldiers during the Civil war gained him a widespread reputation. In 1864 he was named bishop of Nashville, Tennessee, an appointment he declined at first because of illness, but accepted in 1865 after the death of his mother. During his fifteen years as bishop, he built up the war-ravaged diocese, attended Vatican Council I, in 1869–70, and during the cholera epidemics in Nashville in 1873, 1878, and 1879 won the esteem of his fellow citizens for his heroic labors among those stricken. He was one of the founders of the Catholic Knights of America, a fraternal insurance company, in 1877, and was its spiritual director, and in 1880 was appointed first archbishop of Chicago when that see was made an archdiocese. He defended the Ancient Order of Hibernians at the third Plenary Council of Baltimore, in 1884, when several bishops attacked secret societies, convened the first archdiocesan synod, in 1887, labored to integrate the vast number of immigrants pouring into his see into the American way of life, and began the *New World,* the archdiocesan newspaper. During his tenure as archbishop, he more than doubled the number of priests in the see, encouraged Catholic education, built up the parochial-school system (increasing the number of Catholic schools from 88 to 166), was noted for his charitable works, and was a leader in the Catholic social movement. The last days of his life were clouded by his excommunication of Fr. Jeremiah Crowley, pastor of St. Mary's Church, the leader of a group of Irish-born clergymen who vehemently objected to his appointment of Peter J. Muldoon, a native-born priest, as his auxiliary bishop in 1901 when illness rendered the archbishop incapacitated. He died of an apoplectic stroke in Chicago on July 12.

FEENEY, DANIEL J. (1894–1969), bishop. Born in Portland, Maine, on Sept. 12, he was educated at Holy Cross College, Worcester, Massachusetts, and the Grand Seminary, Montreal, and was ordained in 1921. He engaged in pastoral work until 1946, when he was named titular bishop of Sita and auxiliary of Portland. He was appointed ordinary of the see in 1948, coadjutor in 1952, and succeeded to it in 1955; he held that position until his death, in Portland on Sept. 15.

FEENEY, LEONARD (1897–1978), author, lecturer. Born in Lynn, Massachusetts, on Feb. 15, he joined the Jesuits when he was seventeen, in 1914. He took his novitiate at St. Andrew-on-Hudson, Poughkeepsie, New York, taught at Canisius High, Buffalo, and Holy Cross College, and studied for the priesthood at Woodstock (Maryland) College and Weston (Massachusetts) College and was ordained at Weston in 1928. Early attracted to writing, he had his first book, *In Towns and Little Towns,* a book of poetry, published in 1927; in the years to come he produced a steady stream of short stories, biographies, essays, and poetry. He continued his studies at St. Beuno College, North Wales, Wadham College and Campion Hall, Oxford, and took summer courses at the Sorbonne, Paris. On his return to the United States he taught at Boston College until 1936, when he became literary editor of the Jesuit weekly *America;* he remained in that position until 1940. He was president of the Catholic Poetry Society, broadcast on the "Catholic Hour," taught at Weston, and lectured widely. He became permanent chaplain of St. Benedict Center, at Harvard, in 1943, and in 1949 Feeney and Catherine Goddard Clarke, who had founded the Center in 1940, formed a religious community of men and women in Cambridge, Massachusetts, to follow a monastic life according to the Benedictine spirit. He came under ecclesiastical disapproval for his narrow and rigorous interpretation of St. Cyprian's adage "Outside the Church there is no salvation" as the teaching of the Church. A letter from the Supreme Congregation of the Holy Office to Archbishop Richard Cushing of Boston, his archbishop, in 1949 disapproved of his position and he was dismissed from the Jesuits later in 1949 and excommunicated by Rome in 1953. The community moved to a farm in 1958 at Still River, Massachusetts, in the diocese of Worcester, and in 1972 Bishop Bernard Flanagan of Worcester, Cardinal Humberto Medeiros of Boston, and Cardinal John Wright of the Congregation for the Clergy succeeded in having all ecclesiastical censures against Fr. Feeney removed, and eventually most of the members of his group were reconciled with the Church. He died in Still River, on Jan. 30. Among his books were *Fish on Friday* (1934), *Boundaries* (1936), *You'd Better Come Quietly* (1939), *The Leonard Feeney Omnibus* (1943), and *Your Second Childhood* (1945).

FEENEY, THOMAS JOHN (1894–1955), bishop. Born in Boston on Sept. 4, he was educated at Boston College, joined the Jesuits in 1915, and continued his education at Woodstock (Maryland) College and Weston (Massachusetts) College. He taught at Canisius High School, Buffalo, New York, in 1920–21, was a missionary to the Philippines in 1921–24, and was ordained at Weston in 1927. He taught at the Jesuit juniorate in Massachusetts in 1928–30, served as associate editor of *Jesuit Missions* in 1931 (when his *Padre of the Press* was published) to 1939, and was then appointed superior of the Jesuit missions in Jamaica, British West Indies. He served in this post until 1945, when he became procurator of the New England Province of the Jesuits. In 1947–51, he was superior of the Marshall Islands missions and was named titular bishop of Agno and vicar apostolic of the Caroline-Marshall Islands in 1951. He died in Magnolia, Massachusettes, on Sept. 9. He wrote numerous articles and stories and *Letters from Likiep* (1952).

FENLON, JOHN FRANCIS (1875–1943), educator. Born in Chicago on June 23, he was educated at St. Mary's Seminary, Baltimore, and Johns Hopkins University and was ordained in Chicago in 1896. He served as a curate at the Chicago cathedral in 1896–98, joined the Sulpicians in 1900, and continued his studies at the Minerva, Rome, where he received his doctorate in theology in 1900. After further stud-

ies in oriental languages at the Sapienza, Rome, he returned to the United States in 1901 and taught Sacred Scripture at St. Joseph's Seminary, Yonkers, New York, in 1901–4 and at St. Mary's Seminary, Baltimore, in 1904–19. He was superior of the Sulpician House of Studies, St. Austin's College, Washington, D.C., in 1904–11 and of Divinity College, Catholic University, in 1911–24, acted as secretary of the annual bishops' meeting, and helped establish the National Catholic Welfare Conference. He became president of Catholic University's Theological College in 1924 and was president of St. Mary's Seminary and provincial superior of the Sulpicians in the United States from 1925 until his death, in Holland, Michigan, on July 31. He wrote for many Catholic periodicals and articles for the Catholic Encyclopedia, opened the new St. Mary's Seminary of Theology at Roland Park, Baltimore, in 1929 and began St. Edward's Seminary, Seattle, Washington, in 1932.

FENWICK, BENEDICT JOSEPH (1782–1846), bishop. Descendant of one of the original Catholic settlers of Lord Baltimore's Maryland, he was born near Leonardstown, Maryland, on Sept 3. He attended Georgetown with his brother Enoch in 1793 and in 1805 entered the Sulpician seminary in Boston to study for the priesthood. He joined the Jesuits when the Society of Jesus was restored, in 1806, continued his studies at St. Mary's Seminary, Baltimore, and was ordained in 1808. He was sent to New York with Anthony Kohlmann as copastor of St. Peter's Church and administered the diocese of New York in 1815–17. He returned to Georgetown in 1817 as president and the following year was sent to Charleston, South Carolina, acting as vicar-general, and was appointed to the post officially in 1820. He ended several schisms in Charleston and in 1822 returned to Georgetown as procurator of the Jesuits in the United States and minister of Georgetown; he was president of the College again in 1822–25. He was appointed second bishop of Boston (the diocese then included all of New England) in 1825. During his episcopate he fought anti-Catholicism (which caused a mob to burn down the Carmelite convent in Charlestown, Massachusetts, in 1834), founded *The Jesuit, or Catholic Sentinel* (it eventually became the Boston *Pilot),* attended the first Provincial Council of Baltimore, in 1829, held the first diocesan synod, in 1842, was a strong supporter of Catholic education, and founded Holy Cross College, at Worcester, Massachusetts, in 1843—the first Catholic college in New England. He died in Boston on Aug. 11 after a long illness. At the beginning of his episcopate, there were only nine thousand Catholics, three priests, and eight churches and the cathedral in the diocese; at his death there were some fifty churches with attendant priests, and the number of Catholics was estimated at fifty-three thousand, and Boston had become one of the leading dioceses in the United States.

FENWICK, EDWARD DOMINIC (1768–1832), bishop. Born in St. Mary's County, Maryland, on Aug. 19, he was orphaned when six and was privately educated in his youth on the Fenwick manor. He then studied at Holy Cross College, Bornhem, Belgium, and Liège, and joined the Dominicans. He was professed in 1790, was ordained at Ghent in 1793, taught at Holy Cross for a year, and then was imprisoned by the invading French when he was left in charge of the College when the English Dominicans in Bornhem fled to England to escape the invaders. On his release, he went to England, where he taught at Carshalton College, near London. On

his return to the United States, in 1804, he settled in Kentucky and established the motherhouse of the Dominicans in the United States near Springfield, Kentucky, in 1806. He founded the College of St. Thomas Aquinas and St. Rose's Church and Priory in 1807 and at his request was relieved as superior to serve as a missionary in Kentucky and Ohio. In 1821 he was appointed first bishop of the newly created diocese of Cincinnati, Ohio, and made Administrator Apostolic of Michigan and the eastern part of the old Northwest Territory. He toured Europe the following year, seeking priests and funds for his diocese, completed the new St. Peter in Chains Cathedral in 1826 to replace the log cabin that had served as his cathedral, and was appointed American provincial of the Dominicans for life in 1828. He was a staunch supporter of Catholic education, brought the Sisters of Charity into the see, and founded the Athenaeum, St. Francis Xavier College, in Cincinnati, in 1829. In 1831 he founded the *Catholic Telegraph-Register,* the diocesan paper, using printing presses he had brought back from Europe which had been given to him as a gift to print the paper. He died of cholera contracted during an epidemic in Wooster, Ohio, on Sept. 26.

FERMI, ENRICO (1901–54), nuclear physicist. Born in Rome on Sept. 29, he early displayed a genius for mathematics and physics, studied at the Scuola Normale Superiore, the University of Pisa (Ph.D. 1922), Ruprecht Karls University, Heidelberg, Germany, and with Paul Ehrenfest at Leiden, and in 1926 became lecturer on mathematical physics and mechanics at the University of Florence. In 1927 he was appointed professor of theoretical physics at the University of Rome and developed a statistical model of the atom the same year. He was the first physicist appointed to the Accademia Italia in 1929, and in the late twenties began research in nuclear chemistry, producing artificially radioactive isotopes of numerous elements, discovering that slow neutrons are more effective than faster neutrons in 1934; he received a Nobel Prize for his discoveries in 1938. He also proposed the theory that proton and neutron are differing states of the same particle, the nucleon. He left Italy in 1938 to escape the restrictions of fascism, was professor of physics at Columbia in 1939–42, and began researching nuclear fission. In 1942 he transferred to the University of Chicago and guided the construction of the first atomic pile. He became a citizen of the United States in 1944, and that fall he went to Los Alamos, New Mexico, at the request of J. Robert Oppenheimer, and engaged in the research that led to the detonation of the first atomic bomb, on July 16, 1945. He returned to Chicago at the end of 1945 as professor of physics; he died there of cancer on Nov. 28. He was the recipient of numerous awards, among them the Congressional Medal of Merit in 1946, the Award of Merit from the President of the United States in 1954, and the first Enrico Fermi Award from the Atomic Energy Commission in 1954. *The Collected Papers of Enrico Fermi* were published in two volumes in 1962 and 1965; other documents and unpublished manuscripts are in the library of the University of Chicago.

FERRON, MARIE ROSE (1902–36). The tenth of fifteen children of a Canadian couple, she was born at St. Germain de Grantham, Quebec, on May 24. The family emigrated to the United States and settled in Woonsocket, Rhode Island, in 1925. There she reportedly experienced the stigmata and endured great suffering before her death, on May 11. The claims made by her followers have never been accepted or approved by the Church.

FIDELIS OF THE CROSS. *See* Stone, James Kent.

FINK, FRANCIS A. (BILL) (1912–71), editor. Born in Fort Wayne, Indiana, on Oct. 12, he was educated at Notre Dame (B.A. 1930) and married Helen E. Hartman in 1931. He became associated with *Our Sunday Visitor* in 1930 and served on that paper for forty years in various positions, eventually becoming its managing editor. He was also publisher of *Family Digest* and business manager of *The Priest,* was active in the Catholic Press Association, and was its president in 1950–53. He died in Fort Wayne on Dec. 4.

FINK, MICHAEL LOUIS MARY (1834–1904), bishop. Born in Triftersburg, Bavaria, on July (or perhaps June) 2, he came to St. Vincent Archabbey, Westmoreland County, Pennsylvania, with Archabbot Wimmer's first group, about 1850, took his vows as a Benedictine in 1854, and was ordained in 1857. He engaged in pastoral work in New York, New Jersey, Kentucky, and Kansas until 1868, when he was appointed prior of St. Benedict Priory, Atchison, Kansas. In 1871 he was appointed titular bishop of Encarpia and coadjutor of the vicariate of Kansas and the Indian Territory; he succeeded as vicar in 1874 and three years later was appointed first bishop of the newly erected diocese of Leavenworth, Kansas. He encouraged Catholic immigration to his see, helped raise money in eastern states for the farmers whose crops were destroyed by grasshoppers in 1874, and when Leavenworth was suppressed, in 1891, was transferred to Kansas City. He returned to Leavenworth when the diocese was restored, in 1897, and died in Kansas City, Kansas, on Mar. 17.

FINN, FRANCIS JAMES (1859–1928), author. Born in St. Louis in Oct., he was educated at St. Mary's College, Kansas, joined the Jesuits, and studied at the Jesuit novitiate in Florissant, Missouri, and Woodstock (Maryland) College (also teaching during his studies there at St. Mary's, St. Xavier College, Cincinnati, and Marquette), and was ordained in 1893. Four years later he began teaching English at St. Xavier's and during his tenure there became the pioneer writer of books for Catholic boys. He wrote some twenty-seven enormously popular books for boys, among them *Tom Playfair* (1891), *Claude Lightfoot* (1893), *Lucky Boy* (1917), *His Luckiest Year* (1918), *On the Run* (1922), and *Sunshine and Freckles* (1925). He died in Cincinnati, Ohio, on Nov. 2.

FINN, WILLIAM JOSEPH (1881–1961), musician. Born in Boston on Sept. 7, he was educated at St. Charles College, Ellicott City, Maryland, the New England Conservatory of Music, St. Paul's College, and Catholic University; he joined the Paulists in 1900. He was ordained in 1906, studied music in Europe, and organized the Paulist Choristers, which he headed the next thirty-six years, at St. Mary's Church, Chicago, in 1904. He was transferred to New York City in 1908 and over the years built the Paulist Choristers into a world-famous group. He was a chaplain in 1917–18 during World War I and after the war made frequent tours of the United States and Canada and often conducted such musical organizations as the Los Angeles Symphony Orchestra and the Hollywood Bowl Chorus. He was forced to retire because of ill health in 1940 and died in Bronxville, New York, on Mar. 20. He wrote music

textbooks, among them *A Manual of Church Music* (1905), *Fr. Finn's Christmas Carol Book* (1917), *Compline Hymn* (1935), *Principles of Choral Technique* (1935), *The Art of the Choral Conductor* (1939), and his autobiography, *Sharps and Flats in Five Decades.*

FINNEGAN, GEORGE JOSEPH (1885–1932), bishop. Born in Potsdam, New York, on Feb. 22, he was educated at Notre Dame, the Gregorian, Rome, and Laval University, Quebec. He joined the Congregation of Holy Cross in 1902 and was ordained in Rome in 1915. He engaged in missionary work, was a chaplain in the Army, and in 1920–24 was rector of Holy Cross Seminary. He served as vice president of Notre Dame in 1924–26, was elected provincial of his congregation in 1926, and the following year was appointed bishop of Helena, Montana; he held that position until his death, in Helena on Aug. 14.

FINOTTI, JOSEPH MARY (1817–79), author. Born in Ferrara, Italy, on Sept. 21, he joined the Jesuits in Rome in 1833, studied in several Jesuit institutions in Italy and emigrated to the United States in 1845. He continued his education at Georgetown College, was ordained at Georgetown, D.C., in 1847, and was appointed pastor of St. Mary's Church, in Alexandria, Virginia, with additional missionary duties in Maryland and Virginia. He left the Jesuits in 1852 and went to Boston, where he was appointed a pastor in Brookline and later in Arlington, Massachusetts. He was literary editor of the Boston *Pilot* for many years and left Boston in 1876 to go West to seek relief from his rheumatism, taught at St. Mary's Seminary, Omaha, Nebraska, and then became pastor at Central City, Colorado, in 1877 and held that position until his death there on Jan. 10. He wrote numerous books, among them *Month of Mary* (1853), *Life of Blessed Paul of the Cross* (1860), *Diary of a Soldier* (1861), *The Spirit of St. Francis de Sales* (1866), and *Peter Claver* (1868). But his most ambitious literary effort was his unfinished Bibliographia Catholica Americana, a catalogue of 295 Catholic books published in the United States before 1821; the first volume, of books published to 1820 inclusive, was published in 1872, but the second volume, of books published from 1821 to 1875, was unfinished at the time of his death.

FIRST CITIZEN *See* Carroll, Charles (1737–1832).

FISHER, PHILIP. *See* Copley, Thomas.

FITTON, JAMES (1805–81), missionary. Born in Boston on Apr. 10, he was educated at Virgil Barber's academy, at Claremont, New Hampshire, and by Bishop Benedict Fenwick, who ordained him in 1827. He spent the next quarter of a century traveling the length and breadth of New England ministering to the Catholics there, serving as pastor of the first Catholic church in Hartford, Connecticut, in 1830–36, and of Christ Church, Worcester, Massachusetts, in 1836–43; he built Our Lady of the Isle Church, in Newport, Rhode Island. He suffered constant harassment and insults as he went about his work from "Know-Nothing" adherents during this most virulently anti-Catholic period in American history. While pastor at Worcester, he purchased a plot of land and erected a building for the education of young men, Mt. St. James Seminary. He donated it to Bishop Fenwick in 1842; it became the site of Holy Cross College. After serving in Newport in 1844–55, he was named pastor of Most Holy Redeemer Church in East Boston, in 1855 and spent the rest of his life

there; he died in Boston on Sept. 15. He served as editor of the Hartford *Catholic Press* and wrote several books, among them *Youth's Companion* (1833), *Sketches of the Establishment of the Church in New England* (1872), and *St. Joseph's Manual* (1877).

FITZGERALD, EDWARD (1833–1907), bishop. Born in Limerick, Ireland, on Oct. 28, he was brought to the United States in 1849 and entered the Lazarist seminary at The Barrens, Missouri, the following year. He continued his studies at Mt. St. Mary of the West Seminary, Cincinnati, Ohio, and Mt. St. Mary's Seminary, Emmitsburg, Maryland, and was ordained in Emmitsburg in 1857. He became pastor of St. Patrick's Church, Columbus, Ohio, in 1857 and resolved a trustee dispute that had the parish under an interdict. In 1866 he was preconized second bishop of Little Rock, Arkansas. He attended Vatican Council I in 1869–70 and was one of the two bishops (the other was Bishop Aloisio of Caiazzo, Italy) who voted against the doctrine of papal infallibility, though he submitted immediately when the doctrine was approved by the Council in 1870. He also attended the third Plenary Council of Baltimore, in 1884, where he advocated prudence in legislating compulsory attendance of Catholic children at parochial schools, though he was a firm supporter of Catholic education in his diocese. During his episcopate he brought Benedictine monks and Holy Ghost Fathers into the see, encouraged the immigration of Catholics to his diocese, and in 1894 dedicated the first Catholic church for blacks in Arkansas, at Pine Bluff. At the beginning of his bishopric there were four churches, five priests, and sixteen hundred Catholics in the diocese; by the time of his death there were forty-one churches and thirty-three missions, sixty priests and twenty

FITZGERALD, EDWARD ALOYSIUS

thousand Catholics. He resigned and retired to Hot Springs in 1906 because of ill health and died there on Feb. 21.

FITZGERALD, EDWARD ALOYSIUS (1893–1972), bishop. Born in Cresco, Iowa, on Feb. 13, he was educated at Loras College, Dubuque, Iowa (B.A. 1913), and the Grand Seminary, Montreal (J.C.B. 1916); he was ordained in Dubuque in 1916. He taught at Loras in 1916–20, was dean of studies there in 1920–41, was cofounder of Delta Epsilon Sigma in 1939, and served as pastor of Sacred Heart Church, Osage, Iowa, in 1941–46 and of St. Joseph's Church, Elkader, and was diocesan dean in 1946. He was named titular bishop of Cantanus and auxiliary of the archdiocese of Dubuque in 1946 and was vicar-general from 1946 to 1949, when he was appointed bishop of Winona, Minnesota. He retired in 1969 and was made titular bishop of Zerta, and died in Winona on Mar. 30.

FITZGERALD, JOHN (c. 1739–99), patriot. Nothing is known of his early life beyond that he had been well educated. He settled in Alexandria Virginia, about 1769, engaged in the import-export business, acquired real estate in Alexandria, and married Jane Digges in 1779. A friend of George Washington, he was a firm supporter of the colonists in their quarrel with England, and when the Revolution broke out he became captain of the 3rd Virginia Infantry, in 1776, and major of the 9th Virginia Infantry the following year. He became secretary and aide-de-camp to Washington in November 1776 and after being wounded at the battle of Monmouth, in 1778, he resigned from the Army. He resumed his business career in Alexandria and became active in politics. He was alderman in 1779, mayor of Alexandria in 1792–94, and collector of the port of Alexandria in 1793–99. He was also active in education affairs, serving as collector for the Georgetown College Building Fund, was director of the Library Company of Alexandria in 1794 and of the Alexandria Bank in 1798, and helped raise funds to build St. Mary's, Alexandria's first Catholic church, in 1795. He died in Alexandria on Dec. 2.

FITZGERALD, JOHN FRANCIS (1863–1950), mayor. Born in Boston on Feb. 11, he was educated at the Boston Latin School and attended Harvard Medical School for a year but was obliged to drop out to help support the family (there was eleven children). He worked in the Boston customs house, began an insurance business, and in 1889 married Mary Josephine Hannon. He entered politics, was elected to the Boston city council in 1892, was a state senator in 1893–94, and served in the U.S. House of Representatives in 1895–1901. In Congress he defended civil-rights legislation for southern blacks, helped persuade President Cleveland to veto literacy tests for immigrants in 1891, and attacked the meat industry for the quality of the meat it shipped to the Army during the Spanish-American War. On his retirement from Congress he purchased the weekly *The Republic* and became the most powerful political boss in Boston. He was mayor of Boston in 1906–7 and again in 1910–14. As mayor he helped and supported organized labor and expanded aid to the urban poor but was accused of tolerating vice, bypassing civil-service regulations to build up his political machine through patronage and contract awards, and had his administration assailed as the most corrupt in Boston history by the Good Government Association. He supported Woodrow Wilson for the presidency in 1912, was defeated in a bid for the U.S. Senate in 1916, and in

1918 was denied a seat in the House, though apparently the winner by 238 votes, when a congressional committee declared fraud had been involved and awarded the election to his opponent, Peter Tague. He was defeated in a bid for the governorship in 1922, lost the gubernatorial nomination in the Democratic primary in 1930, and then devoted himself to private business, serving as a member of the Boston port authority. He died in Boston on Oct. 2. His daughter Rose married Joseph P. Kennedy, financier and ambassador to Great Britain, and three of his grandsons were President John F. Kennedy and Senators Robert and Ted Kennedy.

FITZGERALD, JOHN M. (1888–1952), engineer. Born in New York City, he received his degree in engineering from Manhattan College in 1907 and then joined the city board of water supply, remaining with that body until his death, in New York City on Apr. 1, except for two years in the Army during World War I. He worked on the Shandaken tunnel of the Catskill water supply system for New York City, was engineer in charge of the Delaware aqueduct of the Kensico system, and was named chief engineer of the board in 1948.

FITZGERALD, WALTER JAMES (1883–1947), bishop. Born in Peola, Washington, on Nov. 17, he joined the Jesuits in 1902 and was educated at Los Gatos (California) Normal School, Gonzaga University, Spokane, Washington (B.A. 1910, M.A. 1912), and Immaculate Conception College, Montreal. He taught at Seattle College in 1906–9, Gonzaga in 1912–15, was ordained in 1918, and taught at Gonzaga again in 1919–20. He was president of Gonzaga in 1921–27, of Manresa Hall Seminary, Point Townsend, Washington, in 1927–29, and of Seattle College

in 1929–30. He was vice-provincial of the Oregon province of the Jesuits in 1931 and was elected provincial in 1932, serving in that position until 1938, when he was appointed titular bishop of Tymbrias and coadjutor vicar apostolic of Alaska and succeeded to the vicariate in 1945. He died on July 19 and was buried in St. Michael's Cemetery, Spokane, Washington.

FITZGIBBON, MARY IRENE (1823–96). Catherine Fitzgibbon was born in Kensington, England, on May 11 and was brought to Brooklyn, New York City, when her parents emigrated to the United States when she was nine. In 1850 she joined the Sisters of Charity at Mount St. Vincent, New York, taking the name Mary Irene, and then taught at St. Peter's Academy, in New York. She became interested in abandoned children when many were left at St. Peter's Convent, of which she became superior in 1858, so in 1869 she founded the Foundling Home for abandoned children (later the New York Foundling Hospital). In 1870 the city gave her a square block to build a larger home; she raised funds to build the Foundling Hospital, which opened in 1873, and cared for tens of thousands of children during her twenty-seven years as superior of the hospital. Also interested in rehabilitating unwed mothers, she founded St. Ann's Maternity Hospital for homeless mothers in 1880; she founded the Hospital of St. John for children and Nazareth Hospital for convalescent children the following year, and in 1884 Seton Hospital, at Spuyten Duyvil, New York, for tubercular men. She died in New York City on Aug. 14.

FITZMAURICE, EDMOND JOHN (1880–1962) archbishop. Born in Tarbert, Kerry, Ireland, on June 24, he was educated at St. Brendan's, Killarney, College of St. Trond, Belgium, and the

North American College, Rome. He was ordained in 1904, emigrated to the United States the same year, was a curate at Annunciation Church, Philadelphia, in 1904–6, taught theology at St. Charles Borromeo Seminary, Philadelphia, in 1906–14, and became an American citizen in 1910. He was chancellor of the archdiocese of Philadelphia in 1914–20 and was rector of St. Charles Borromeo from 1920 until 1925, when he was appointed fourth bishop of Wilmington, Delaware. He resigned in 1960 because of ill health and was named titular archbishop of Tomi. During his episcopate, the Catholic population of the diocese grew from thirty-four thousand to eighty-five thousand, and to meet this growth he founded eighteen new parishes, saw thirty-one elementary and high schools begun, founded Catholic Charities, the Society for the Propagation of the Faith, and the Confraternity of Christian Doctrine in the diocese, and brought nine new religious communities into the see. He died in Wilmington on July 25.

FITZMAURICE, JOHN EDMUND (1829–1920), bishop. Born in Newtorn Sandes, Kerry, Ireland, on Jan. 8, he emigrated to the United States, studied for the priesthood, and was ordained in Philadelphia in 1862. He engaged in parish work until 1866, when he was named rector of St. Charles Borromeo Seminary, Philadelphia, and in 1897 was appointed titular bishop of Amisus and coadjutor of Erie, Pennsylvania; he succeeded to the see two years later. During his two decades as bishop he established thirty-two parishes and four parochial schools to accommodate the increased population of his see (65,000 to 115,000). He died in Erie on June 18.

FITZPATRICK, JOHN BERNARD (1812–66), bishop. The son of Irish immigrant parents, he was born in Boston on Nov. 1, was educated at Collège de Montréal and St. Sulpice Seminary, Paris, and was ordained in Paris in 1840. He served for a time as assistant at the Boston cathedral, was then pastor of the church in East Cambridge, and in 1844 was named titular bishop of Callipolis and coadjutor of Boston; in that year, he received Orestes Brownson into the Church. He succeeded to the see as Boston's third bishop, in 1846, and attended the sixth Provincial Council of Baltimore, in 1846, and the first Plenary Council of Baltimore, in 1852. During his episcopacy he vigorously fought the anti-Catholicism of the times that destroyed Catholic churches in Bath and Manchester, New Hampshire, in 1854, worked to aid the Irish immigrants who poured into his see, was a staunch supporter of Catholic schools and colleges, and was well known for his interest in literature. In 1861 he received an honorary doctorate in divinity from Harvard, the first Catholic to be so honored by that institution. In declining health his last days, he died in Boston on Feb. 13.

FITZPATRICK, JOHN CLEMENT (1876–1940), archivist, historian. Born in Washington, D.C., on Aug. 10, he was educated at St. Mary's College, Pennsylvania (M.A. 1918), and in 1894 joined the staff of the *U.S. Government Advertiser.* He became a member of the manuscripts division of the Library of Congress and was assistant chief in 1902–27. He wrote brochures on manuscript collecting and cataloguing and edited Martin Van Buren's *Autobiography* (1920), the *Complete Diaries of George Washington* (1925), and four volumes of the journals of the Continental Congress (1904–37). He was appointed acting chief of the manuscript division of the Library of Congress in 1927 but when passed over for the position of chief the following year, he resigned. He became editor of the thirty-nine-volume George Washington Bicentennial Commission edition of the collected works of our first President (1931–44), was president of the American Catholic Historical Association in 1928–29, and died in Washington, D.C., on Feb. 10. Among the books he wrote were *Notes on the Care, Cataloguing and Arranging of Manuscripts.* (1913), *Handbook of Manuscripts in the Library of Congress* (1918), *Washington's Expenses as Commander in Chief* (1917), and *The Spirit of the Revolution* (1924).

FITZPATRICK, THOMAS PATRICK (1844–1919), executive. Born in Grafton, Massachusetts, on Dec. 17, he began working in a Boston store when he was eighteen, became a traveling salesman three years later, and in 1871 joined Brown, Durell & Co., a large wholesale dry-goods firm; in time he became its president and treasurer. He became known for his philanthropies, helped establish the Working Girls' Home, in Boston, and contributed generously to Boston College and Catholic University. He was active in Irish affairs and cultural matters, the Catholic Union, and Young Men's Catholic Association, and received the Laetare Medal in 1905 for his philanthropic endeavors. He died in Boston on Jan. 15.

FITZSIMMONS, JAMES EDWARD "SUNNY JIM" (1874–1966), racehorse trainer. Born on July 23 on a farm that later became part of the Sheepshead Bay race track in Brooklyn, New York, he began his career in horse racing as an errand boy at the Brannon Brothers Stable in 1885. He was a jockey in 1889–94 but increasing weight forced him to retire and he turned to training horses, at first running a public stable and also racing his own horses. In 1924 he became trainer for the horses of William Woodward's Belair Stud Farm and the following year he took on the horses of Mrs. Henry Carnegie Phipps's Wheatley Stables; her son Ogden and grandson Ogden became his patrons in time and it was for them that he trained his most famous horses. He became one of the most famous of all horse trainers and saddled some 2,275 winning horses. He won racing's Triple Crown (Kentucky Derby, the Preakness, and the Belmont Stakes) with Gallant Fox in 1930 and with Omaha (a son of Gallant Fox) in 1935. He had three winners of the Kentucky Derby (with Johnstown in 1939 in addition to the above), five of the Belmont Stakes, six of the Dwyer, eight of the Lawrence Realization, and eight of the Saratoga Cup. He officially ended his racing career when he resigned his position with the Phipps family in 1963. Nicknamed "Sunny Jim" for his kindly disposition and known for his aid and advice to newcomers to the field of horse racing, he was affectionately dubbed "the grand old man of thoroughbred racing" in his later years. He died in Miami, Florida, on March 11.

FITZSIMON, LAURENCE JULIUS (1895–1958), bishop. Born in San Antonio, Texas, on Jan. 31, he was educated at St. Anthony's College there, the North American College, Rome, and St. Meinrad's Seminary, Indiana. He served in the Navy in World War I, was ordained in 1921, and taught at St. John's Seminary, San Antonio, in 1925. He was pastor at Runge and then at Seguin, in 1925–41, was made chancellor of the San Antonio archdiocese in 1941, and later the same year was appointed bishop of Amarillo, Texas, a position he held until his death there on July 2. During his episcopate he opened a children's home in Panhandle in 1953, built twenty new churches and missions, and was instrumental in greatly expanding the facilities of the Catholic Archives of Texas, in Austin, an outstanding collection of material on the Church in the Southwest.

FITZ SIMONS, THOMAS (1741–1811), merchant. Born in Ireland, he emigrated to the United States sometime before 1758 (exactly when is not known), married Catherine Meade in Philadelphia in 1763, and set up a merchandising business with her brother George as partner that lasted until 1784. He was active in the events leading up to the American Revolution, serving on the city and county committees of correspondence in 1774 and on the Provincial Committee and the Council of Safety, was a deputy to the Carpenter's Hall conference that led to the Continental Congress, and was elected one of the Pennsylvania Provincial Delegates in 1774—the first Catholic in public office in Pennsylvania—and served in the Continental Congress later that year. When war broke out with England, his company donated £5,000 for the support of the Continental Army, and he organized a militia company in 1775. He participated in the battles of Trenton and Princeton and then joined with other Philadelphia merchants supplying the Continental Army and his vessels became privateers. He was a member of the Congress under the Articles of Confederation in 1782, was a delegate to the Constitutional Convention that framed the Constitution in 1787 (he and Daniel Carroll of Maryland were the only Catholic members), was a signatory of the Constitution, and was elected a member of the first Congress, serving on the House Ways and Means Committee. He was reelected twice but defeated in a bid for a fourth term in 1784; his defeat was described by Madison in a letter to Jefferson. He was an ardent Federalist, supported a protective tariff, and was opposed to universal suffrage. He was also active in Philadelphia business and civic affairs, was founder and a trustee of the Bank of North America, founder and President of the Insurance Company of North America, president of the Delaware Insurance Company and the Philadelphia Chamber of Commerce, a member of the board of trustees of the University of Pennsylvania, and one of the founders of Georgetown College. Financial reverses in 1805 virtually bankrupted him and he never fully recovered financially. He died in Philadelphia on Aug. 26.

FLAGET, BENEDICT JOSEPH (1763–1851), bishop. Born at Contournat, Auvergne, France, on Nov. 7, after the death of his father, he was orphaned when his mother died when he was two; he was raised by an aunt and uncle in Billom. He entered the Sulpician seminary at Clermont when he was seventeen, joined the Sulpicians in 1783, continued his studies at the seminary at Issy, and was ordained in 1787. He taught theology at Nantes for two years, until it was closed by the French Revolution, returned to Billom, and the following year went to the United States with John Baptist David and Stephen Badin. He was sent as a missionary to the Indians around Fort Vincennes, Indiana, of which he was also pastor, and arrived there late in 1792. After two years he was recalled to teach at Georgetown; in 1798 he was sent to Havana and failed in an attempt to establish a Sulpician college while he was stationed there; he returned three years later with twenty-three students for St. Mary's College, Baltimore, where he taught from 1801 to 1808, when he was appointed first bishop of the newly created diocese of Bardstown, Kentucky. He declined the appointment but on a visit to Paris in 1809 was told by his superior he should be in Bardstown and had been commanded to accept by the Pope. He returned to the

United States, was consecrated in Baltimore in 1810, and arrived at Bardstown in the middle of 1811, more than three years after his appointment. He spent the next thirty-nine years traveling through and administering his far-flung see, which included the whole area from the Allegheny Mountains to the Mississippi River. He soon acquired great influence in the young American Church and was usually consulted in the selection of bishops for American sees. He sent missionaries to the Indians, consecrated his new cathedral in Bardstown in 1819, consecrated his old friend, Fr. J. B. M. David, his coadjutor there a week later, worked among the Indians in 1819–21, held the first synod of Bardstown, in 1823, and attended the first Provincial Council of Baltimore, in 1829. He resigned as bishop in 1832 in favor of Bishop David but so strong was the reaction of the priests and people of the diocese against his resignation that Rome recalled David's appointment to the see. He was a strong advocate of education and founded St. Thomas Seminary in 1812, colleges, asylums, and churches during his episcopate. In 1834 Bishop Chabrat became his coadjutor, and the following year he went to Europe and spent four years visiting some forty-six dioceses seeking priests and aid for his diocese. On his return, in 1839, he transferred the seat of the diocese to Louisville, Kentucky. He consecrated his third coadjutor, Martin John Spalding, in 1848 (Bishop David had died in 1841 and Bishop Chabrat had gone blind in 1847 and returned to France), and died in Louisville on Feb. 11, beloved by all for his holiness and sterling character.

FLANAGAN, EDWARD JOSEPH (1886–1948), sociologist. Born in Roscommon, Ireland, on July 13, he studied at Sligo and Summer Hill College, and on his graduation, in 1904, emigrated to the United States, where he continued his education at Mt. St. Mary's College, Emmitsburg, Maryland (B.A. 1906), and St. Joseph's Seminary, Dunwoodie, New York. He was forced to leave St. Joseph's after a year because of ill health and went to Omaha to live with his brother, Fr. Patrick Flanagan, to recover his health. On his recovery, Bishop Richard Scannell of Omaha sent him to continue his studies at the Gregorian, Rome. He was again forced to leave because of ill health, but in 1908 he went to the University of Innsbruck, Austria, and was ordained there in 1912. He served as a curate at O'Neill, Nebraska, and then, in 1913, became assistant to the pastor of St. Patrick's Church, in Omaha. He established the Workingmen's Hotel, a home for destitute workers, in Omaha in 1913, and four years later began an orphanage in an old house in downtown Omaha with two juvenile delinquents who had been paroled in his custody by the courts and three homeless orphans and ninety dollars he had borrowed from a friend. From this humble beginning developed Boys Town, which became the most famous home for homeless, delinquent, and destitute boys in the world. It became a model for similar institutions in many other countries as it grew and flourished. The story of Boys Town became a best-selling book by Fulton and Will Oursler and a motion picture with Spencer Tracy starring in the role of Fr. Flanagan. Boys Town became an incorporated village eleven miles from Omaha in 1939 capable of caring for more than a thousand boys from six to eighteen and with its own government. In 1947 General Douglas MacArthur invited Fr. Flanagan to Japan and Korea to advise the governments of those countries on youth problems. Fr. Flanagan died in Berlin on May 15 while making a survey of youth conditions in Austria and Germany at the request of the War Department and establishing an organization to rehabilitate war orphans in Germany.

FLASCH, KILIAN CASPER (1831–91), bishop. Born in Retastadt, Bavaria, on July 16 (or 9), he was brought to the United States by his parents when he was ten. They settled near Milwaukee, and Kilian was educated at Notre Dame and St. Francis Seminary, Milwaukee; he was ordained in 1859. He engaged in pastoral work, taught at St. Francis, was named its rector in 1877, and two years later was appointed second bishop of La Crosse, Wisconsin. During his decade as bishop he greatly increased the number of churches and schools in the see, and he died in La Crosse on Aug. 3.

FLETCHER, ALBERT L. (1896-1979), bishop. Born in Little Rock, Arkansas, on Oct. 28, he was educated at Little Rock College and St. John's Seminary, in Little Rock, and was ordained in 1920. He taught at Little Rock College in 1920–23, was its president in 1923–25, and taught theology at St. John's in 1925–29. He was chancellor of the Little Rock diocese in 1926–33, was made a papal chamberlain in 1929, was vicar-general in 1933–46, and was made a domestic prelate in 1934. He was named auxiliary bishop of the see in 1939 and was appointed its bishop in 1946. He retired in 1972 and died in Little Rock on Dec. 6.

FLICK, LAWRENCE FRANCIS (1856–1938), physician. Born in Carrolltown, Pennsylvania, on Aug. 10, he was educated at St. Vincent's College, Latrobe, Pennsylvania, and studied medicine at Jefferson Memorial College, Philadelphia, where he received his medical degree in 1879. He began to practice medicine in Philadelphia, contracted tuberculosis, and moved to Cali-

fornia in 1881 in quest of a cure; he developed a method to control the disease and returned to Philadelphia in 1883. He specialized in the study of tuberculosis and, convinced it was contagious, advocated isolation of tubercular patients in special hospitals—a theory that evoked great controversy among his fellow doctors. He founded the Pennsylvania Society for the Prevention of Tuberculosis in 1892, the Free Hospital for Poor Consumptives in 1892, and a sanitorium at White Haven, Pennsylvania, which he headed until 1935, and was president and medical director of the Henry Phipps Institute for the Study, Prevention and Treatment of Tuberculosis from 1903 to 1910, when it became affiliated with the University of Pennsylvania. Also interested in history, he founded the American Catholic Historical Society of Philadelphia in 1884, serving as its president in 1893–96 and 1913–14, and was a founder and first president of the American Historical Association in 1919. He helped found the Philadelphia Institute for the Study and Prevention of Nervous and Mental Diseases in 1929, and was its president until 1935; he died in Philadelphia on July 7. He was the author of several books, among them *Consumption, a Curable and Preventable Disease* (1903), *The Development of our Knowledge of Tuberculosis* (1925), and *Tuberculosis, a Book of Practical Knowledge to Guide the General Practioner of Medicine* (1937).

FLOERSH, JOHN ALEXANDER (1886–1968), archbishop. Born in Nashville, Tennessee, on Oct. 5, he was educated at the Propaganda, Rome (Ph.D. 1907, D.D. 1911), and was ordained in Rome in 1911. He served in several parishes for a year and then was secretary to the apostolic delegate in Washington, D.C., in 1912–22. He was consecrated titular bishop of Lycopolis and coadjutor of Louisville, Kentucky, in 1923; he succeeded to the see in 1924 and became the first archbishop of the see when it was elevated to an archdiocese in 1937. He resigned in 1967 and was made titular archbishop of Sistroniana; he died in Louisville on June 11. During his episcopate he established Catholic Charities in the see and a school board, opened several high schools, and announced the establishment of Bellarmine College, in 1949.

FLOYD, JOHN (1783–1837), governor, physician. Born at Floyd Station, Kentucky, on Apr. 24, two weeks after his father was killed by Indians, he was educated at Dickinson College, Carlisle, Pennsylvania, but illness prevented his graduation. He married Letitia Preston in 1804, studied medicine at the University of Pennsylvania, and practiced at Lexington, Virginia, and then Christiansburg, where he became known for his medical skills. He served as a surgeon in the War of 1812 until 1814, when he was elected to Virginia's General Assembly; in 1817 he was elected to Congress and served there the next twelve years. He supported Andrew Jackson's policies in Florida and opposed the censure of the President, was one of four Virginia representatives who voted for the Missouri Compromise, and is credited with introducing to Congress the bill for the occupation and territorial organization of Oregon. He returned to medical practice in 1829–30, and in 1830 was elected governor of Virginia by the state legislature; he was reelected in 1831 to a three-year term. He favored developing transportation facilities for the state, was at first sympathetic to abolition but then came out in favor of slavery and state sovereignty. The conversion of Floyd and his family in 1832 to Catholicism caused a sensation. He retired from the governor's office in 1834 and suffered a stroke soon after; he died on Aug. 16.

FLOYD, JOHN BUCHANAN (1806–63), cabinet officer, governor. Son of John Floyd, congressman and governor of Virginia, and Letitia Preston Floyd, he was born in Smithfield, Virginia, on June 1 and was educated at Columbia College, South Carolina, graduating in 1829. He married Sally Buchanan Preston in 1830, practiced law in Virginia with indifferent success, and then went to Arkansas, where he became a cotton planter. Ill health caused him to return to Virginia in 1837, and he became active in politics. He was elected to the Virginia General Assembly in 1847 and 1848 and was governor of the state in 1849–52. He returned to his law practice in 1852, was reelected to the General Assembly in 1855, and became leader of the Democratic Party in Virginia. He was appointed Secretary of War by President Buchanan in 1857, was accused of misuse of his office for issuing acceptances to army contractors which were substituted for Indian trust bonds in the Department of the Interior, but was cleared of any wrongdoing. He was also accused of transferring arms and equipment from northern to southern arsenals to arm the South for the conflict that seemed certain to burst on the nation, but historians now largely discount this charge, though his inefficient administration of the War Department during his term did not help the Union cause when war did come. A firm supporter of states' rights (though opposed to secession), he opposed the strengthening of Fort Sumter, in Charleston Harbor, and resigned in 1860 when President Buchanan refused to support his order countermanding the removal of Major Robert Anderson from Fort Moultrie to Fort Sumter. He then became an ardent secessionist, and at the outbreak of the Civil War, in 1861, he raised a brigade of volunteers for the Confederacy. He was removed from his command by Confederate President Davis for withdrawing his forces from Fort Donelson, which led to its capture by Union forces in 1862; two months later he was made a major general by the Virginia General Assembly. Soon after, his health broke, and he died near Abingdon, Virginia, on Aug. 26.

FLYNN, JOHN ALOYSIUS (1900–65), educator. Born in Philadelphia on Sept. 20, he was educated at St. Joseph's College there (B.A. 1918) and Princeton and studied for the priesthood at St. Vincent's Seminary, Germantown, Pennsylvania. He was ordained in the Congregation of the Mission (Vincentians) in 1928, received his doctorate in sacred theology from the Angelicum, Rome, in 1928, and then taught at St. Vincent's Seminary in 1928–33 and 1936–38, St. Bernard's Seminary, Rochester, New York, in 1933–35, and Niagara University in 1935–36. He became professor of psychology at St. John's University, New York, in 1938, was dean of the teachers college there in 1942–47, and in 1947 was named twelfth president of St. John's. He began building an entire new campus in Jamaica, Queens County, New York, and during the fourteen years of his presidency St. John's became the largest Catholic university in the United States. He died in New York City on July 21.

FLYNN, JOHN THOMAS (1882–1964), journalist, commentator. Son of John Flynn, a lawyer, and Margaret O'Donnell Flynn, he was born in Bladensburg, Maryland, on Oct. 25 and was educated at Georgetown (LL.B. 1902). Despite his law degree, he decided not to practice law, married Alice Bell in 1910, was a press officer for the German embassy in the United States

before World War I, and during the war was a reporter for the New Haven *Register,* later becoming its city editor. He joined the New York *Globe* in 1920, was managing editor from 1920 to 1923, when it folded, and then did free-lance writing. He was a columnist for *The New Republic* in 1931–40 and began a career as a political commentator. At first liberal, he became critical of the New Deal and one of President Franklin Roosevelt's severest critics; he decided the President was part of a conspiracy that led to intervention in World War II and that Roosevelt had provoked the Japanese into the attack on Pearl Harbor. He opposed the entry of the United States into World War II and became an ardent anti-Communist but denounced American aid to the French in Vietnam. An early supporter of Senator Joseph McCarthy, he broke with him in 1956 over the Senator's support of the British and the French during the Suez crisis of 1956. He wrote hundreds of magazine articles and fourteen books, among them *God's Gold* (1932), *Country Squire in the White House* (1940), *The Roosevelt Myth* (1948), and *While You Slept* (1951). He died in Amityville, New York, on Apr. 13.

FOERY, WILLIAM ANDREW (1890–1978), bishop. Born in Rochester, New York, on July 6, he was educated at St. Bernard's Seminary there (S.T.L., Ph.D., and D.D.); he was ordained in 1916. He served as a curate at Our Lady of Mt. Carmel Church in 1916–22 and as pastor in 1922–32 and was pastor of Most Holy Rosary Church in 1932–37, both in Rochester. He was appointed bishop of Syracuse in 1937 and held that position until 1970, when he retired and was made titular bishop of Miseno-Cape. During his episcopate he doubled the number of priests and religious in the diocese and launched a campaign to develop the see's high schools. It was at his request that the Jesuits founded LeMoyne College, in Syracuse, in 1946 and the Franciscans began Maria Regina College in 1960. He was made an Assistant at the Pontifical Throne in 1961. He died in Syracuse on May 10.

FOIK, PAUL JOSEPH (1880–1941), librarian, historian. Born in Stratford, Ontario, on Aug. 14, he came to the United States in 1900, joined the Congregation of Holy Cross the following year, and studied at Notre Dame. He was ordained in 1911, continued his studies at Catholic University (Ph.D.), was head librarian at Notre Dame in 1912–24, became head librarian at St. Edward's University, Austin, Texas, and taught there and was dean of the college of arts and sciences. He was cofounder of the Catholic Library Association, serving as its vice president in 1930–34, founded the Texas Catholic Historical Society, was archivist of the Catholic Archives of America, and collected some seventy thousand documents and manuscripts of historical importance. He served as associate editor of *Mid-America,* was chairman of the editorial board of the *Catholic Periodical Index,* contributed articles to major historical journals, wrote *Pioneer Catholic Journalism in the U. S.* (1930), and edited the first four volumes of *Our Catholic Heritage in Texas, 1519–1950.* He died in Austin on Mar. 1.

FOLEY, JOHN SAMUEL (1833–1918), bishop. Brother of Bishop Thomas Foley, administrator of the Chicago diocese in 1870–79, he was born in Baltimore on Nov. 5, was educated at St. Mary's Seminary there and the Apollinaris, Rome, and was ordained in Rome in 1856. He served as a curate and then was pastor in Baltimore archdiocesan churches and in 1888 was appointed fourth bishop of Detroit.

During the thirty years of his term as bishop of Detroit, he provided services for the thousands of immigrants drawn to Detroit by the new automobile industry, opened many national churches (Italian, Slovak, Lithuanian, Hungarian, Romanian), encouraged the growth of religious orders in the see, and increased the number of priests from less than 100 to 318 in 246 churches and missions to serve the increase in the Catholic population from one hundred thousand to just under four hundred thousand. He ended a schism among Polish groups in the diocese and established a special seminary for students of Polish descent; he died in Detroit on Jan. 5.

FOLEY, THEODORE (1913–74), superior general. Born in Springfield, Massachusetts, on Mar. 3, he was educated at Holy Cross Preparatory Seminary, Dunkirk, New York, joined the Passionists in 1933, and was ordained in Baltimore in 1940. He taught philosophy while continuing his education at Catholic University (D.S.T. 1944), at St. Michael's Seminary at Union City, New Jersey, in 1944–45 and was director of the Passionist seminarians in 1953–56. He was elected rector of St. Paul's Monastery, Pittsburgh, in 1956, consultor to the Passionist superior general in Rome in 1958, and six years later was elected superior general. He was reelected in 1970; he died in Rome on Oct. 9.

FOLEY, THOMAS PATRICK ROGER (1822–79), bishop. Brother of John Samuel Foley, bishop of Detroit in 1888–1918, he was born in Baltimore on Mar. 6, was educated at St. Mary's College and Seminary there, and was ordained in Baltimore in 1846. He engaged in missionary work in Maryland for a time, was assistant pastor at St. Patrick's Church, Washington, D.C., and then was appointed rector of the Baltimore cathedral. In 1851 he became chancellor of the Baltimore archdiocese, was secretary of the first Plenary Council of Baltimore, in 1852, and notary of the second, in 1862, and in 1870 was appointed titular bishop of Pergamus and coadjutor and administrator of Chicago, the bishop of which, James Duggan, had been judged to be mentally ill. During his administration of the see, which lasted until his death, he greatly expanded the facilities of the see, brought numerous religious orders into the diocese to care for the wave of immigrants coming to Chicago, and rebuilt many of the institutions of the diocese, including the cathedral, which had been destroyed in the Great Fire of 1871. He never succeeded to the see, as Bishop Duggan lived until 1899; he died in Chicago on Feb. 19.

FORD, FRANCIS XAVIER (1892–1952), martyr, bishop. Son of Austin B. Ford, publisher of the *Irish World* and *Freeman's Journal,* he was born in Brooklyn, New York, on Jan. 11, was educated at Cathedral College, New York City, and entered the Maryknoll seminary in 1912—its first student. He was ordained in 1917, and the following year was sent as one of Maryknoll's first four missionaries to China. He worked in Yeongkong, southern China, opened the first Maryknoll seminary for Chinese students in 1921, and in 1925 was named perfect apostolic of a new mission in northern Kwangtung (Meihsien), with Kaying as its headquarters. In 1935 he was appointed titular bishop of Etenne and vicar apostolic of Kaying. He was chairman of the Chinese Catholic Welfare Conference for southern China, was active in aiding the victims of that war-ravaged country during World War II, and returned to the United States for a visit after the war. On his return he found the Communists had overrun Kaying. He was arrested in 1950, and for the next fourteen months the Communists tortured and vilified him at a series of public trials during a two hundred-mile trip to Canton. He is reported to have died in prison in Canton on Feb. 21 as a result of the tortures to which he had been subjected, though his death was not revealed by Communist officials until Aug. 16.

FORD, JEREMIAH DENIS MATHIAS (1873–1958), scholar. Born in Cambridge, Massachusetts, on July 2, he studied for a time at Cork when his parents returned to Ireland, but on his return to the United States entered Harvard, graduated in 1894, and received his doctorate in Romance philology in 1897. He had begun teaching at Harvard in 1895 and spent the next forty-five years teaching there. He married Winifred Fearns in 1902, was appointed Smith professor of French and Spanish in 1909, was chairman of the Romance Languages and Literature Department in 1911–43, and in the course of the years became internationally famous as an authority on Spanish and Portuguese literature. He wrote widely on linguistics and belles lettres; among his books were *Old Spanish Sibilants* (1900), *Old Spanish Reading* (1911), and *Main Currents of Spanish Literature* (1919), and he translated several Spanish works as well as collaborating on bibliographies of Cervantes. He was editor of *Speculum* in 1927–36, held office in many scholarly societies, among them the presidency of the Dante Society in 1922–40, of the American Academy of Arts and Sciences in 1931–33, and the American Catholic Historical Association in 1935. He received honors from many universities in the United States and Europe and was the recipient of the Laetare Medal in 1937, retired in 1943, was elected to the French Academy in

1945, and died in Cambridge on Nov. 14.

FORD, JOHN (1895–1973), motion-picture director. Born Sean O'Feeney in Cape Elizabeth, Maine, on Feb. 1, he was taken to Portland by his parents when a child. He was unsuccessful in an attempt to get an appointment to the U.S. Naval Academy and studied for a short time at the University of Maine. He then joined his brother Francis in Hollywood in 1914 and began his film career as a prop man at Universal, changing his name to John Ford. He became an assistant director later the same year, directed several short films, and signed a contract in 1919 with Fox to direct; the following year, he married Mary McBryde Smith. His first important film was *Cameo Kirby,* which introduced John Gilbert, soon to be one of Hollywood's brightest stars, and in the next half century Ford became Hollywood's most famous director; many of his films are classics. His first well-known movie was *The Informer,* which he filmed in an incredible three weeks and which won him the 1935 Academy Award for best director. He made some 130 pictures and won Academy Awards also for *Stagecoach* (1939), *The Long Voyage Home* and *The Grapes of Wrath* (both 1940), *The Quiet Man* (1952), and the documentary *The Battle of Midway* (1942), which he had filmed while heading a photographic unit established in 1941 for the U.S. Navy; he left the Navy with the rank of admiral of the U.S. Naval Reserve. Among his other well-known films are *Young Mr. Lincoln* (1939), *Drums Along the Mohawk* (1939), *They Were Expendable* (1945), *The Fugitive* (1947; based on Graham Greene's *The Power and the Glory), Fort Apache* (1948), *She Wore a Yellow Ribbon* (1949), *The Searchers* (1956), and *The Man Who Shot Liberty Valance* (1962). He received the American Film Institute's first Life Achievement Award and the Presidential Medal of Freedom in 1973, and is generally considered to be one of the greatest artists the cinema has produced. He died in Palm Springs, California, on Aug. 3

FOREST, JOHN. *See* Loviner, John Forest.

FOREST, JOHN ANTHONY (1838–1911), bishop. Born in St. Martin-la-Sauveté, St. Germain, Loire, France, on Dec. 25, he was educated in France for the priesthood but had only reached his diaconate when he emigrated to the United States, in 1863. He was ordained in New Orleans in the same year, engaged in missionary work at St. Mary's settlement, Lavaca County, Texas, became pastor of Sacred Heart Church, in Hallettsville, and in 1895 was consecrated third bishop of San Antonio. During his episcopate, the Catholic population of the diocese increased from sixty-six thousand to almost one hundred thousand and many of the missions became parishes as the missionary period of the diocese came to an end. He died in San Antonio on Mar. 11.

FOSTER, JOHN GRAY (1823–74), general. Born in Whitefield, New Hampshire, on May 27, he was educated at Hancock Academy and the U.S. Military Academy at West Point and graduated in 1846. He participated in the Mexican War with the Engineer Corps and was wounded at Molina del Rey in 1847. In 1852–54 he worked on a coastal survey and then taught engineering at West Point in 1855–57. He was strengthening the fortifications at Fort Moultrie, in Charleston (South Carolina) Harbor when the Civil War broke out; he transferred his troops to Fort Sumter and was brevetted major for his gallantry in defense of Sumter during the Confederate attack on it.

Later in 1861 he was commissioned brigadier general of volunteers and served in the North Carolina campaign that year. He became a Catholic late in 1861 and commanded the Department of North Carolina and Virginia with the rank of major general in 1862–63. In July 1863 he was sent to the relief of General Ambrose Burnside, under siege at Knoxville, Tennessee, and succeeded him as commander of the Department of Ohio later that year, but was soon forced to relinquish this command because of injuries he sustained in a fall from his horse. After his recovery he was with Sherman in 1864 on the latter's march to the sea and was brevetted brigadier general in the regular Army for his gallantry in action in the capture of Savannah. He was brevetted major general in the U.S. Army in 1865, commanded the Department of Florida in 1865–66, and in 1867 was commissioned lieutenant general, Corps of Engineers. He supervised several river and harbor improvement projects, conducted several experiments in submarine operations, wrote *Submarine Blasting in Boston Harbor,* and died in Nashua, New Hampshire, on Apr. 2.

FOURNIER, MOTHER ST. JOHN (1814–75), foundress. Born in Arbois, France, on Nov. 13, she was christened Julie; she entered the Order of the Immaculate Conception of Mary in 1820; she took her vows in 1832 but left to join the Sisters of St. Joseph of Lyons when she learned they were planning an American foundation. She received the habit in 1836, taking the name St. John, learned to teach the deaf, and went to teach in St. Louis. She was sent to Philadelphia with three other sisters at the request of Bishop Kenrick in 1837 to work at St. John's Orphanage, and the Sisters of St. Joseph of Philadelphia were founded. The following year she opened St. Patrick's School in Pottsville

and in 1849 took over St. Joseph's Hospital (the first Catholic hospital in Philadelphia) but was forced to give it up a decade later for lack of funds. She established the motherhouse of her community at Mt. St. Joseph, Chestnut Hill, Philadelphia, in 1858, and during the Civil War her sisters serves as nurses on the battlefields. While she was superior, she established thirty-eight schools and two orphanages; she died in Philadelphia on Oct. 15.

FOWLER, GENE (1891–1960), journalist, author, scenario writer. Son of Charles Francis and Dora Grace Devlan, Eugene Parrott Devlan was born in Denver, Colorado, on Mar. 8. His father deserted his family two months after he was born, and he was adopted by his stepfather, Frank Fowler, who had married Fowler's mother after she divorced Devlan, in 1894. Gene attended the University of Colorado but left after a year, became a night signal clerk for the American District Telegraph Company, and in 1912 began his newspaper career as a reporter on the Denver *Republican.* He then worked for the *Rocky Mountain News,* became assistant sports editor on the Denver *Post,* and in 1918 went to New York to report on sports for the New York *American.* He became sports editor of the *Daily Mirror* in 1924, returned to the *American* as managing editor in 1925, and joined *The Morning Telegraph* as managing editor in 1928. He was fired when his publisher discovered he had increased its payroll, and he began free-lance writing. He went to Hollywood in 1931 as one of the highest-paid scenario writers in the industry and was enormously successful; he later established his own film-producing company. He became a Catholic in 1950. In addition to his film scenarios he wrote several novels and biographies which were extremely successful, among them *The Great Mouthpiece* (1931), on the criminal lawyer William J. Fallon; *Timberline* (1933); *Father Goose* (1934), a life of Mack Sennett; *Good Night, Sweet Prince* (1943), on John Barrymore; *Beau James* (1949), on Mayor James J. Walker of New York; and *Schnozzola* (1951), about comedian Jimmy Durante. He also wrote the autobiographical *A Solo in Tom Toms* (1946) on his early life. He died in West Los Angeles, California, on July 2.

FOX, JOSEPH JOHN (1855–1915), bishop. Born in Green Bay, Wisconsin, on Aug. 2, he was educated at St. Francis Seminary, Milwaukee, and Louvain, Belgium, and was ordained in Mechlin, Belgium, in 1879. He engaged in pastoral work in Wisconsin, became secretary to Bishop Francis Krautbauer of Green Bay, and was vicar-general of that diocese in 1894–1904. He was made a domestic prelate in 1898 and was appointed bishop of Green Bay in 1904. He resigned because of ill health in 1914 and was appointed titular bishop of Ionopolis; he died three months later in Green Bay on Mar. 14.

FULCHER, GEORGE A. (1922–84), bishop. Born in Columbus, Ohio, on Jan. 30, he was educated at St. Charles Borromeo Seminary there, Mt. St. Mary's Seminary of the West, Norwood, Ohio, and the North American College and the Angelicum, Rome. He was ordained in 1948, was editor of the Columbus diocesan paper, *Catholic Times,* and in 1976 was consecrated titular bishop of Morobisdo and auxiliary of Columbus. He was appointed bishop of Lafayette in Indiana in 1983 and was killed the following year in an automobile accident near Rockville, Indiana, on Jan. 25.

FUREY, FRANCIS J. (1905–79), archbishop. Born in Summit Hill, Pennsylvania, on Feb. 22, he was educated at St. Charles Borromeo Seminary, Philadelphia and the Pontificio Seminario Romano Maggiore (Ph.D. 1926, S.T.D. 1930), Rome, and was ordained in Rome in 1930. He served as secretary to Cardinal Dennis Dougherty in 1930–36, was president of Immaculata College, Pennsylvania, in 1936–46, and rector of St. Charles Borromeo Seminary in 1946–58; he was made a domestic prelate in 1947. He was appointed titular bishop of Temnus and auxiliary of Philadelphia in 1960, and two years later was appointed to the Administrative Tribunal of Vatican Council II. He was named coadjutor bishop and apostolic administrator of San Diego, California, in 1963 and succeeded to the see in 1966. He was transferred to San Antonio, Texas, as archbishop of that see in 1969 and remained in that position until his death, in San Antonio on Apr. 23 of cancer. During his episcopate he was a leading supporter of social causes among Hispano-Americans and was particularly concerned with the Mexican-Americans in the archdiocese, who constituted an overwhelming majority of the Catholics in his see; he also served as chairman of the Campaign for Human Development.

G

GABRIELS, HENRY (1838–1921), bishop. Born in Wannegem, Belgium, on Oct. 6, he was educated at Audenarde, St.-Nicolas, Ghent, and Louvain, and was ordained in 1861. After his ordination he emigrated to the United States and began teaching at St. Joseph's Seminary, Troy, New York, in 1864. He taught there for twenty-eight years, serving as president from 1871 until 1892, when he was consecrated second bishop of Ogdensburg, New York. He wrote a book on rubrics and translated C. H. Vosen's *Rudiments of Hebrew Grammar,* and died in Ogdensburg on Apr. 23.

GABRO, JAROSLAV (1919–80), bishop. Born in Chicago on July 31, he was educated at St. Procopius College, Lisle, Illinois, St. Charles College, Baltimore, St. Basil's College, Stamford, Connecticut, and Catholic University, and was ordained in Philadelphia in 1945. He served in Ukrainian Catholic parishes in Pennsylvania, Missouri, Michigan, and New York and was pastor of Assumption Church, Perth Amboy, New Jersey, in 1949–61. He was dean of the New Jersey deanery in 1958–61, was made a papal chamberlain in 1958, and was consecrated bishop of St. Nicholas diocese for Ukrainian Catholics in midwestern and western United States in 1961. He made his headquarters in Chicago, was a strong critic of religious repression in Russia, and died in Chicago on Mar. 28.

GALBERRY, THOMAS (1833–78), bishop. Born in Naas, Kildare, Ireland, on May 28, he was brought to the United States by his parents when he was three, was educated at Villanova College, Philadelphia, and graduated in 1851. He joined the Augustinians the following year, was ordained in 1856, and taught at Villanova. He served as pastor in Havertown, Pennsylvania, Troy, New York, and Lawrence, Massachusetts, in 1858–72 and became superior of Augustinian missions in the United States. He was president of Villanova in 1872–75, was elected provincial of the newly established St. Joseph province of the Augustinians in 1874— the first Augustinian provincial in the United States—and the following year was appointed fourth bishop of Hartford, Connecticut. He founded the diocesan newspaper, the *Connecticut Catholic* (renamed the *Catholic Transcript* in 1898) in 1876; he died in New York City on Oct. 10 while he was on the way to Villanova.

GALES, LOUIS (1896–1978), magazine founder. Born on May 24 in Racine, Wisconsin, he was educated at St. Francis Seminary, Milwaukee, Catholic University, and St. Paul (Minnesota) Seminary. He intended to be a Paulist priest but instead was ordained for the St. Paul archdiocese in St. Paul in 1926. He served as an assistant pastor in the St. Paul archdiocese for the next twelve years, and in 1932 founded the Catechetical Guild; in 1936, with Fr. Paul Bussard, he founded the *Catholic Digest,* which in the next several years became the most widely circulated Catholic magazine in the United States. He retired from the *Digest* in 1964 when it became part of the College of St. Paul, was pastor of St. Mary's Church, in St. Paul, and then was chaplain for many years at the Ancker Hospital, in St. Paul, and to the Little Sisters of the Poor. He died in St. Paul on Apr. 7.

GALITZIN, ELIZABETH (1797–1843). Daughter of Prince Alexis Andreyevich and Countess Protasof, she was born in St. Petersburg (Leningrad), Russia, on Feb. 22 and followed the example of her mother in leaving the Russian Orthodox Church to become a Catholic. She joined the Society of the Sacred Heart in Metz, Lorraine, in 1828, made her final profession in Paris in 1832, and became secretary to St. Madeleine Sophie Barat, founder of the Society, in 1834. She was elected assistant general in 1839, and the following year went to the United States to visit the Society's foundations there, founding convents in New York City and McSherrystown, Pennsylvania, and gave approval to the founding of a mission to the Potawatomi Indians at Sugar Creek, Kansas. She returned to France in 1842, realized that the changes she had imposed on the American foundations were too drastic, and returned to the United States in 1843 to restore the rule B1. Philippine Duchesne had applied. She visited convents in the United States and Canada and was at St. Michael, Louisiana, when stricken with yellow fever while ministering to the victims of the fever; she died there on Dec. 8.

GALLAGHER, HUGH PATRICK (1815–82), missionary, editor. Born in Donegal, Ireland, on May 12, he emi-grated to the United States in 1832, studied for the priesthood at St. Charles Borromeo Seminary, Philadelphia, and was ordained in 1840. He engaged in parish work at St. Peter's Church, in Butler, in western Pennsylvania, championed the Irish immigrants working in the coal mines there, was editor of the Pittsburgh *Catholic* for a time, promoted the temperance movement, and in 1844 was appointed rector of the Theological College of Pittsburgh. He was transferred to Loretto later in 1844 and while a theologian at the first Plenary Council of Baltimore, in 1852, met Archbishop Joseph Alemany, who persuaded him to work with him in the newly established archdiocese of San Francisco. He worked as a missionary in northern California, founded the *Catholic Standard* in 1853, the first Catholic weekly on the West Coast, and then went to Europe to seek aid for the Church in California. He brought back priests, seminarians, Sisters of Mercy, and Presentation Sisters. He built the first Catholic church in Nevada at Genoa in 1861 and other churches and schools, was involved in civic affairs (his plan to improve Golden Gate Park was adopted in 1869), and labored to assist immigrants to California. He died in San Francisco on Mar. 10.

GALLAGHER, MICHAEL JAMES (1866–1937), bishop. Born in Auburn, Michigan, on Nov. 18, he was educated at Assumption College, Sandwich, Ontario, Canada, Mungret College, Limerick, Ireland, and the University of Innsbruch, Austria, where he was ordained in 1893. He engaged in pastoral work in Michigan, was made pastor of St. Andrew's Cathedral, Grand Rapids, Michigan, became the bishop's secretary in 1896, and was chancellor of the Grand Rapids diocese in 1900–12. He served as vicar-general in 1912–16, was consecrated titular bishop of Tipaca and coadjutor of Grand Rapids in 1915, and succeeded to the see the following year. He was transferred to Detroit in 1918, and during his nineteen-year episcopate there he devoted himself to meeting the needs of his rapidly growing diocese. He began some 105 parishes (33 for national groups), doubled the number of priests, from 318 to more than 800, founded Sacred Heart Seminary in 1919, and established colleages, hospitals, and retreat houses. He died in Detroit on Jan. 20.

GALLAGHER, NICHOLAS ALOYSIUS (1846–1918), bishop. Born in Temperanceville, Ohio, on Feb. 14, he was educated at Mt. St. Mary of the West Seminary, Cincinnati, and was ordained in Columbus, in 1868. He engaged in parish work in Columbus, served as president of St. Aloysius Seminary there in 1871–76, became pastor of St. Patrick's Church, and acted as administrator of the diocese in 1878–80 on the death of Bishop Rosecrans. He was vicar-general in 1880–82, and in 1882, at Galveston, Texas, he was consecrated titular bishop of Canopus and named administrator of the diocese of Galveston. He succeeded to the see in 1892 and remained in that position until his death, in Galveston on Jan. 21.

GALLAGHER, SIMON FELIX (1756–1825). Born in Ireland, he graduated from the University of Paris and became a priest in Dublin. In 1793 he requested an assignment from Bishop John Carroll, bearing a letter of recommendation from Bishop John Troy of Dublin, and was assigned a pastorate in Charleston, South Carolina, and also taught at the College of Charleston. He soon became involved in a dispute with the trustees of his parish, and in 1800 he was suspended for intemperance and the trustees refused to accept the replacement Bishop Carroll sent. Gal-

lagher was soon reinstated, and in 1812 Carroll sent Fr. Joseph Picot de Clorivière as his assistant to minister to French parishioners. When Clorivière went to Europe in 1814, Gallagher secured the services of Fr. Robert Browne, pastor at Augusta, Georgia, to aid him; when Clorivière returned, Gallagher and Browne refused to allow him to resume his duties, and the trustees upheld them, declaring that the trustees decided who the priests of the parish would be. When Carroll died, his successor, Archbishop Leonard Neale, confirmed Clorivière's right to return, suspended Gallagher and Browne, placed the church under interdict, and ordered Clorivière to open another church. He sent Fr. Benedict Fenwick to settle the matter, but the dispute was not finally resolved until 1820, when Charleston was made a diocese and Bishop John England reinstated Gallagher but with no duties. Gallagher was granted his request to move to St. Augustine, Florida, in 1822; he went to Havana the following year, then to New Orleans, and by 1825 was in Natchez, Mississippi, as pastor of St. Mary's Church. He died in Natchez on Dec. 13.

GALLEN, HUGH (1924–82), governor. Born in Portland, Oregon, on July 30, he was brought to Medford, Massachusetts, when he was six. He moved to Littleton, New Hampshire, in his youth, worked in the Civilian Conservation Corps (CCC) during the depression of the 1930s and at various other jobs, among them carpenter, laborer, truck driver, and car salesman, eventually acquiring the General Motors francise for Littleton. He served on several civic and business boards and councils, entered politics, and became chairman of the Democratic state committee and supported Senator Edmund Muskie for the presidency in 1972. In 1973, he was elected the first Democrat in four decades to the New Hampshire state legislature, from Littleton, and was elected governor of New Hampshire in 1978; he was reelected in 1980 but defeated in a bid for a third term in 1982. During his second term he was faced with a budget deficit and vetoed a state budget in 1981, the first New Hampshire governor to do so, defeated a proposal to build a nuclear plant in Seabrook, and by the end of his second term was in such deep personal financial difficulties he was forced to close his automobile agency. Stricken late in his second term by a blood infection, he died at Brigham and Woman's Hospital, in Boston, on Dec. 29.

GALLITZEN, DEMETRIUS AUGUSTINE (1770–1840), missionary. Son of Prince Dmitri Alekseyevich Gallitzen, descended from one of the wealthiest and most illustrious Russian families, and Countess Amalie, daughter of the celebrated Prussian Field Marshal von Schmettau, he was born at The Hague (where his father was Russian ambassador) on Dec. 22. He was baptized in the Greek Orthodox Church, was educated as was befitting a Russian prince, with outstanding tutors, and was subjected to rigid discipline. His mother, who had been baptized a Catholic but had allowed her faith to lapse, returned to Catholicism in 1786, and when Dmitri was seventeen he joined her in her religion. He served as aide-de-camp to Austrian General von Lillien for a time, but in 1792 his parents sent him on a two-year trip to America and the West Indies. He used the pseudonym Schmet, or Smith, in the United States to avoid any problems he might encounter as a prince in the democratic country, and was known for many years as Augustine Smith. On his arrival in the United States, despite the disapproval of his family and friends, he decided to become a priest and entered St. Mary's Seminary, in Baltimore. He was ordained in 1795, the first priest to receive all orders from tonsure to ordination in the new nation, and engaged in missionary activities at first in Baltimore and then among the frontiersmen and Indians of southern Pennsylvania and northern Virginia. In 1796, while attending a sick woman at a settlement some one hundred fifty miles from Conewago, where he was stationed, he conceived the idea of establishing a Catholic settlement there. He purchased land adjoining a four hundred-acre tract that had been donated to Bishop John Carroll by Captain Michael McGuire in 1788 in the Alleghenies in present-day Cambria County, Pennsylvania, received permission from Bishop Carroll to proceed with his project, and was given ecclesiastical jurisdiction over a hundred-mile radius. He began by building a church in 1799 and soon attracted settlers. He named the settlement Loretto. In time he built a whole town, with sawmills, grist mills, tanneries, and other industries, sold tracts of land to new settlers at little or no cost, and by 1827 found himself in deep debt when the Russian Government disinherited him for becoming a Catholic priest; his inheritance was turned over to his sister's husband. A public appeal for funds was launched in 1827 and endorsed by Bishop Carroll, and the proceeds from the appeal allowed him to repay all his debts by the end of his life. He was often calumniated by his enemies and opponents of the Church and frequently engaged in controversy in defense of the Church, but in time he became widely known for his untiring efforts on behalf of his flock, for his sanctity, and for his humility. He accepted the post of vicar-general of Western Pennsylvania in 1827 but firmly resisted all efforts to have him appointed bishop of Cincinnati and of Detroit. He died at Loretto on May 6 after more than forty years of missionary service that had transformed Loretto and the surrounding area from a wilderness to a flourishing community.

GALVIN, WILLIAM LELAND (1886–1960), jurist, executive. Born in Baltimore on Dec. 27, he was educated at Calvert Hall, received his law degree from the Maryland School of Law, and became a partner in the law firm of Galvin & McCort. He was treasurer of his father's Horstmeier Lumber Company, became director in several bank and trust companies, including the U.S. Fidelity and Trust Company and the Commonwealth Bank of Baltimore, and in 1924 became legal adviser to the archdiocese of Baltimore. He served on several state agencies, including the Maryland Board of State Aid and the Maryland State Department of Public Welfare, was active in hospital, school, and orphanage work, serving on some dozen advisory boards, and was one of the founding directors of Maryland Hospital Services, Inc. (Blue Cross). He became treasurer of Catholic University in 1938, serving in that position the rest of his life, was made a Knight Commander of St. Gregory in 1939 and a Knight of the Holy Sepulchre in 1953; he died in Baltimore on Apr. 12.

GANNON, JOHN MARK (1877–1968), bishop. Born in Erie, Pennsylvania, on June 12, he was educated at St. Bonaventure University, New York (B.A. 1899), Catholic University (S.T.B. 1900) and Apollinare University, Rome (D.D., D.C.L., 1903), and was ordained in 1901. He served as pastor at McKean, Oil City, Cambridge Springs, and Meadville, Pennsylvania, until 1917, when he was appointed titular bishop of Nilopolis and auxiliary bishop of Erie, Pennsylvania. He was diocesan superintendent of schools in 1912–20, pastor of St. Andrew's Church, and administra-

tor of the diocese from June until August 1920, when he became Erie's bishop. He founded Cathedral College (which in time became Gannon College) in Erie in 1933, was episcopal chairman of the Catholic Press Association, and was made an Assistant at the Pontifical Throne in 1944 and given the personal title of archbishop in 1953. During his forty-six-year bishopric, he greatly expanded the facilities of the see, established twenty-four new parishes, tripled the number of priests in the diocese, opened St. Mary's minor seminary and Cathedral Preparatory School for Boys, and provided larger facilities for hospitals and homes in the diocese. He resigned in 1966 and was made titular bishop of Tacarata; he died in Erie on Sept. 5.

GANNON, ROBERT I. (1893–1978), author, educator. Born in St. George, Staten Island, New York City, on Apr. 20, he was educated at Georgetown (B.A. 1913), Woodstock College (Maryland) (M.A. 1919), the Gregorian, Rome (S.T.D. 1927), and Christ's College, Cambridge (M.A. 1930). He joined the Jesuits, taught at Fordham in 1919–23, and was ordained in 1926. He was at St. Peter's College, Jersey City, New Jersey, in 1930–36, serving for a time as dean, and at the Hudson College of Commerce and Finance, which he organized, in 1932–35. He served as president of Fordham in 1936–49, saw its student body drop from eight thousand to three thousand during World War II, but built it back after the war to more than thirteen thousand, and was president of the Association of Universities and Colleges of the State of New York in 1946–49. He was director of Manresa Retreat House, on Staten Island, in 1949–52 and then became pastor of St. Ignatius Church and rector of Loyola School and Regis High School, in New York City. He held these positions until

1958, when he became superior of the Jesuit Mission House, where he remained until 1967, when he became retreat master of St. Ignatius Retreat House, in Manhasset, Long Island, New York. He died in New York City on Mar. 12. He received numerous honorary awards from colleges and universities, was a much-sought-after after-dinner speaker, and was a friend and confidant of Cardinal Spellman of New York, whose biography, *The Cardinal Spellman Story* (1962), he wrote. He was also the author of *Techniques of the One-Act Play* (1925), *After Black Coffee* (1947), *The Poor Old Liberal Arts* (1962), and *Up to Now: the Story of Fordham* (1967).

GANSS, HENRY GEORGE (1855–1912), composer. Born in Darmstadt, Germany, on Feb. 22, he was brought to the United States as a child and was educated at St. Vincent's College and Seminary, Latrobe, Pennsylvania. He was ordained in 1878, held pastorates at Milton, Carlisle, and Lancaster, and was chaplain at the government's Indian school in Carlisle. Cardinal Gibbons appointed him financial agent of Catholic Indian Missions, and in 1904 he founded the Marquette League in New York to support Indian missions. Interested in history, he wrote articles for Catholic magazines and the Catholic Encyclopedia, and was very much involved in musical activities. He organized bands and musical groups, wrote piano pieces, hymns (best known was "Long Live the Pope"), and five masses. He died in Lancaster on Dec. 25.

GARAKONTHIE, DANIEL (c. 1600–76), Iroquois chieftain. After visiting Montreal in 1645 as a member of an Indian peace delegation and remaining as a hostage to the Indians' pledge of peace, he returned to Onandaga, headquarters of the Iroquois Confederacy, and was a close ally of the French. In 1661, after two years of warfare between the French and the Onandagas and Cayugas, the Indians sued for peace at his instigation, and Fr. Simon Lemoyne was sent to Onandaga to decide how sincere the Indians were about peace. He and Garakonthie became close friends, and the Indian accompanied Lemoyne back to Canada with nine French captives. Over the next few years he sought to effect peaceful relations between the French and the Iroquois and urged the French to send missionaries to the Indian tribes. He was baptized by Bishop François Laval in Quebec in 1670, taking the name Daniel, learned to read and write so he could read the bible, and died at Onandaga, New York. His name is also spelled Garaconthié and Garacontié.

GARCÍA DIEGO Y MORENO, FRANCISCO (1785–1845), bishop. Born in Lagos de Morenó, Jalisco, Mexico, on Sept. 17, he was educated at St. Joseph's Conciliar Seminary, at Guadalajara, joined the Franciscans at Guadalupe in 1801, continued his studies at Our Lady of Guadalupe College, Zacatecas, and was ordained in 1808 in Monterrey. He engaged in missionary work, taught at Our Lady of Guadalupe College, served as master of novices in 1816–19 and prefect in 1822–25, and in 1832 was made superior of the college. He went to California with ten Mexican Franciscans from Zacatecas to take charge of the missions there when the Mexican Government decided to expel all Spanish friars from California, in 1832. He made his headquarters at Santa Clara in 1833 and restored many of the missions but saw his work undone when the Mexican Government passed a decree converting the mission churches to parishes under secular control. He returned to Mexico to fight the decree and secured suspension of the secularization until a diocesan organization could be obtained from Rome. In 1840, Pope Gregory XVI separated the Californias from the diocese of Sonora, created the diocese of California, and appointed Fr. Diego bishop of Upper and Lower California, with his see at San Diego—the first bishop of California. He moved the seat of the diocese to Santa Barbara in 1842, was placed in charge of the Pious Fund, but later in the same year Mexican President Santa Anna confiscated the Fund and the diocese lost its source of income. Fr. Diego struggled to overcome the poverty of the see, opened the first seminary on the Pacific coast at Santa Inés mission in 1844, and died at Santa Barbara on Apr. 30.

GARDINER, HAROLD CHARLES (1904–69), critic, author. Born in Washington, D.C., on Feb. 6, he joined the Jesuits at St. Andrew-on-Hudson, Poughkeepsie, New York, in 1922, studied at Woodstock (Maryland) College (B.A. 1928, M.A. 1929, S.T.L. 1935) in 1926–29 and 1932–36, and taught Latin, Greek, and English literature at Canisius College, Buffalo, New York, in 1929–31 between his Woodstock studies. He was ordained in 1935, continued his theological studies at Tronchiennes (Drongen), Belgium, and received his Ph.D. in English literature from Cambridge in 1941. He joined the staff of *America* as literary editor in 1940 and during the next two decades became the most influential critic in the American Catholic press, helping to formulate new understanding among Catholics of the relationship between morality and literature and promoting literary excellence among Catholic authors. He was chairman of the editorial board of the Catholic Book Club in 1948–62, and in 1962 he left *America* to become literary editor of the New Catholic Encyclopedia in Washington, D.C. On the completion of the Encyclopedia, in 1967, he became editor of Corpus Books and remained in that position until his death, in Denver, Colorado, on Sept. 3. He edited and wrote numerous books, among them *Norms for the Novel* (1953), the four-volume *Great Books* (1947–53), *Catholic Viewpoint on Censorship* (1958), *In All Conscience* (1959), and a modern version of *The Imitation of Christ* by Thomas à Kempis (1955).

GARESCHÉ, EDWARD (1876–1960), founder. Born in St. Louis on Dec. 27, he was educated at St. Louis University (B.A. 1896, M.A. 1898) and studied law at Washington University, where he received his law degree in 1898. From 1898 to 1900, when he joined the Jesuits, he practiced law, studied for the priesthood at the Jesuit novitiate at Florissant, Missouri, and taught at St. Mary's College, Kansas; he then taught philosophy and theology at St. Louis University, in 1908–12. He was ordained in 1912 and after a year on the staff of *America,* he was assigned to promote the Sodality of Our Lady and founded *The Queen's Work* in 1914, serving as editor until 1922, when its circulation was 160,000. He founded the Knights of the Blessed Sacrament in 1918, taught at Marquette, and edited *Hospital Progress* for the Catholic Hospital Association in 1925–28. In 1928 he founded the International Guild of Catholic Nurses, which was to reach a membership of more than 300,000, and in 1929 he became director of the Catholic Medical Mission Board, serving in that post until his death. In 1935 he founded the Daughters of Mary, Health of the Sick, and became superior general. He wrote some sixty books and booklets on a wide variety of subjects, among them volumes of inspirational reading; collections from his articles in *The Queen's Work* such as "Your Soul's Salvation," "The Things Immortal," and "Paths to Goodness"; poetry, as *The Four Gates* (1913), *War Mother* (1918), and *The Torrent and Other Poems* (1929); textbooks, as *Ethics and the Art of Conduct for Nurses* (1929); prayers, as *Moments with God* (1931); art criticism, as *Great Christian Artists* (1924); and as *Mary, the Most Beloved Woman* (1919). He died in Framingham, Massachusetts, on Oct. 2.

GARESCHÉ, JULIUS PETER (1821–62), soldier. Born near Havana, Cuba, on Apr. 26, he studied at Georgetown, where he became a Catholic, for four years, until 1837, when he was appointed to the U.S. Military Academy at West Point. He graduated in 1841, served on the frontier and on garrison duty the next five years, participated in the Mexican-American War, and in 1855 was appointed assistant adjutant general. He was active in Catholic circles, wrote for *Freeman's Journal* and *Brownson's Quarterly Review* and was made a Knight of St. Sylvester in 1851. He became chief of staff to General William S. Rosecrans, commander of the Army of the Cumberland, early in the Civil War, was made lieutenant colonel in 1862, and was killed at the battle of Stone River, Tennessee, on Dec. 31.

GARIN, ANDRÉ (1822–95), missionary. Born in Côte-Saint-André, Isère, France, on May 7, he was educated at the minor seminary there, joined the Oblates of Mary Immaculate in 1842, and was sent to Canada, where he was ordained in 1845. He spent the next twelve years ministering to the Indians of eastern Canada from the Saguenay River to Hudson Bay and Labrador, served as superior at Plattsburg and Buffalo, New York, and then spent twenty-seven years at Lowell, Massachusetts, where he built several churches and schools. He died in Lowell on Feb. 16.

GARRAGHAN, GILBERT JOSEPH (1871–1942), historian. Born in Chicago on Aug. 14, he was educated at St. Ignatius College (now Loyola) there (B.A. 1889), joined the Jesuits in 1890, and was ordained in 1904. He taught at Xavier College, Cincinnati, Ohio, Creighton College, Omaha, Nebraska, and St. Louis University (Ph.D. 1919). He was assistant provincial of the Missouri province of the Jesuits in 1911–12 and 1927–28 and professor of history at the graduate school of St. Louis University in 1925–32; he became research professor of history at Loyola University of Chicago in 1935. He was editor of *Mid-America* in 1929–33, spent 1933–35 collecting documents from archives in Belgium, England, France, and Italy, and became one of the outstanding Catholic historians of his time, an authority on American frontier history. He wrote books on the Church in Kansas City (1919) and Chicago (1921), *Chapters in Frontier History* (1934), biographies of La Salle and Marquette (whose letters he edited), the monumental three-volume *Jesuits of the Middle United States* (1938), covering the years 1823–1923, and the scholarly *Guide to Historical Method* (1946). He died in Chicago on June 6.

GARRIGA, MARIANO SIMON (1886–1965), bishop. Born in Point Isabel, Texas, he was educated at St. Mary's College, Kansas City, Kansas, and St. Francis Seminary, Milwaukee, Wisconsin; he was ordained in 1911. He was made a papal chamberlain in 1934 and a domestic prelate the following year; in 1936 he was consecrated titular bishop of Siene and coadjutor of Corpus Christi, Texas, the first native Texan to be consecrated. He succeeded to the see in 1949, greatly expanded its facilities, and died in Corpus Christi on Feb. 21.

GARRIGAN, PHILIP JOSEPH (1840–1919), bishop. Born in White-gate, Cavan, Ireland, on Sept. 8, he was brought to the United States by his parents in 1844; they settled in Lowell, Massachusetts. He was educated at St. Charles College, Ellicott City, Maryland, graduating in 1862, and studied for the priesthood at St. Joseph's Seminary, Troy, New York; he was ordained there in 1870. He was a curate at St. John's Church, Worcester, Massachusetts, for a short time and then became rector of St. Joseph's Church in 1872. He was appointed pastor in Fitchburg, in 1875 and served there until 1888, when he was appointed first vice-rector of Catholic University. He helped found Trinity College, in Washington, D.C., and was appointed first bishop of the newly created diocese of Sioux Falls, Iowa, in 1902. During his administration he doubled the number of schools in the diocese so that three of every four Catholic children in the see were enrolled in Catholic schools. He died in Sioux Falls on Oct. 14.

GARTLAND, FRANCIS XAVIER (?1805–54), bishop. Born in Dublin on Jan. 19 (perhaps in 1808), he emigrated to the United States, studied at Mt. St. Mary's College and Seminary, Emmitsburg, Maryland, and was ordained in Philadelphia in 1832. He was engaged in pastoral work in the Philadelphia diocese in 1832–50, was vicar-general in 1845–50, and was consecrated first bishop of the newly established diocese of Savannah, Georgia, in 1850. He remained in that position until his death there of yellow fever on Sept. 20.

GARVAN, FRANCIS PATRICK (1875–1937), lawyer, executive. Born in East Hartford, Connecticut, on June 13, he was educated at Yale and Catholic universities and studied law at New York University Law School, where he received his law degree in 1899. He became assistant district attorney in New York County the same year, married Mabel Bradley in 1910, and returned to private law practice. In 1917–19 he was director of the bureau of investigation of the alien property custodian, became alien property custodian in 1919, and a U.S. assistant attorney general. As custodian he controlled German chemical patents confiscated by the U.S. Government during the war, and as attorney general he participated in the anti-Communist campaign of Attorney General A. Mitchel Palmer and helped organize the Federal Bureau of Investigation. In 1919 he was founding president of the Chemical Foundation, a nonprofit corporation formed to develop German patents seized by the United States, a step that greatly helped the post-World War I growth of the United States chemical industry. He was dean of the Fordham University Law School in 1919–23 and was the author of several books, among them *Birth Control of New American Industries* (1934) and *Scientific Method of Thought in Our National Problems* (1936), was honored by several universities, and died in New York City on Nov. 7.

GARVEY, EUGENE AUGUSTINE (1845–1920), bishop. Born in Carbondale, Pennsylvania, on Oct. 5, he was educated at St. Charles College, Ellicott City, Maryland, and St. Charles Borromeo Seminary, Philadelphia, and was ordained in Scranton, in 1869. He served as pastor in several Pennsylvania towns and from 1871 to 1899 at Williamsport; he was consecrated bishop of Altoona in 1910, a position he held until his death there on Oct. 22.

GARVIN, JOHN E. (1865–1918), author. Born in San Antonio, Texas, on Feb. 24, he joined the Marianist Brothers, received his B.A. from the University of Dayton, Ohio, in 1898 and a licentiate in physics and mathematics from Stanislaus College, Paris, France, and became principal of St. Martin's Academy, in Baltimore. He became known for his conferences to religious and his addresses on educational subjects, wrote *The Centenary of the Society of Mary* (1917), translated Henry Rousseau's *Life of Guillaume Joseph Chaminade* into English, and died in Washington, D.C., on Oct. 7.

GASSON, THOMAS IGNATIUS (1859–1930), educator. Born in Sevenoaks, Kent, England, on Sept. 23, he was educated at St. Stephen's, London, and Woodstock College, Maryland, after joining the Jesuits, and was ordained in 1891. He taught at Boston College, was its president in 1907–14, and purchased its present Chestnut Hill site. He became dean of the graduate school at Georgetown, left in 1924 to become dean of studies at Loyola, Montreal, and held that position until his death there on Feb. 27.

GASTON, WILLIAM JOSEPH (1778–1844), jurist. Son of Dr. Alexander Gaston, an Irish Presbyterian surgeon and ardent patriot who had been murdered during the American Revolution by Tories, he was born in New Bern, North Carolina, on Sept. 19. He was the first student to enroll at Georgetown, in 1791, left after two years because of ill health, and then went to the College of New Jersey (Princeton), graduating in 1796. He studied law, was admitted to the bar, practiced at New Bern, and two years later, when only twenty-two, was elected to the North Carolina Senate, despite a clause in the state constitution barring Catholics from public office; from 1800 to 1832, he served four terms in the North Carolina Senate and seven terms in the North Carolina House of Commons. He

served in the United States House of Representatives in 1813–17, obtaining a charter from Congress for Georgetown in 1815, and became one of the leaders of the Federalist Party. In Congress he supported the Bank of the United States and denounced the Administration's war policies in the War of 1812. At the end of his second term he resumed his law practice and in 1833 was elected chief justice of the North Carolina Supreme Court, a position he held the rest of his life. At the state constitutional convention of 1835 he was mainly responsible for changing the clause in the North Carolina constitution that practically disenfranchised Catholics, but was unsuccessful in his opposition to an amendment depriving free blacks of the vote. He died in Raleigh, North Carolina, on Jan. 23 while presiding over a session of the North Carolina Supreme Court.

GAYARRÉ, CHARLES ÉTIENNE ARTHUR (1805–95), historian. Grandson of Étienne Boré, Louisiana's first successful sugar planter, he was born in New Orleans on Jan. 9 and received his early education at a school for the sons of rich planters near his native city. He then studied at the College of Orleans, France, from which he graduated in 1825, went to Philadelphia the following year to study law in the office of William Rawle, and was admitted to the Pennsylvania bar in 1828 and that of his native state the following year. He was elected to the Louisiana state legislature in 1830, was appointed assistant attorney general in 1838 and presiding judge of the city court of New Orleans the following year, and was elected to the United States Senate in 1835 but was unable to fulfill his duties because of ill health. He spent eight years in France in an effort to recover his health and spent much of the time researching documents on Louisiana in archive collections; the result was his two-volume *Histoire de la Louisiane* (1846–47), the first of his books and invaluable for its information based on original documents. In time he developed this into his monumental four-volume *History of Louisiana* (1848, 1852, 1854, 1866), in which he incorporated his earlier *Poetry and Romance of the History of Louisiana* (1844). He was elected to the state legislature in 1844, was secretary of state of Louisiana in 1846–53, and developed the state library and historical holdings. He was one of those who founded the Know-Nothing Party in Louisiana but in 1855 was excluded from the party because he was a Catholic. An early supporter of the Confederacy, he later advocated freeing and arming the slaves in 1863 when he realized the Confederacy was doomed. He lost his fortune during the Civil War, was reporter of the Louisiana Supreme Court decisions in 1873–76, was a leader in literary circles in Louisiana, and served as president of the Louisiana Historical Society in 1860–88. Often called "the historian of Louisiana," he died in New Orleans on Feb. 11. He also wrote *The School for Politics* (1854), *Fernando de Lemos* (1872), and *Aubert Dubayet, or the Two Sister Republics* (1882).

GERARD, MOTHER *See* Phelan, Mother Mary Gerard.

GERCKE, DANIEL JAMES (1874–1964), archbishop. Born in Philadelphia on Oct. 9, he was educated at St. Joseph's College (B.A. 1891) and St. Charles Borromeo Seminary there, and was ordained in 1901. He served as curate at St. Joseph's Church, Girardville, Pennsylvania, in 1901, at Holy Trinity later the same year, St. Mary's Church in 1903, and St. Gregory's in 1905–7, all in Philadelphia. He went as a mission-

ary to the Philippine Islands and served at Vigan in 1903–5, and after he served at St. Gregory's was vicar-general of Nueva Caceres in 1910–19; he was made a domestic prelate in 1915. He returned to Philadelphia in 1919 and served as rector of the cathedral until 1923, when he was appointed third bishop of Tucson, Arizona. During his episcopate, the number of Catholics in the diocese more than quadrupled and he completed the diocesan seminary Regina Cleri and increased the facilities of the see to meet the demands of the increased Catholic populace. He was made an Assistant at the Pontifical Throne in 1951, retired because of ill health and advanced age in 1960, and was made titular bishop of Cotadeum; he died in Tucson on Mar. 19.

GERKEN, RUDOLPH ALOYSIUS (1887–1943), archbishop. Born in Dyersville, Iowa, on Mar. 7, he was educated at Pio Nono College, Milwaukee, Wisconsin, St. Joseph's College, Rensselaer, Indiana, and the University of Dallas, Texas, and then taught in Texas public schools from 1910 to 1912, when he became an instructor at the University of Dallas. He decided to become a priest, studied at Kenrick Seminary, St. Louis, in 1913–17, and was ordained in 1917. He was pastor of Sacred Heart Church in Abilene, Texas, in 1917–19 and of St. Rita's Church, in Ranger, in 1919–27 and dedicated the first church of St. Thérèse, the Little Flower, in the United States, in Pioneer in 1923. He was appointed first bishop of the newly created diocese of Amarillo in 1927, founded Prince Memorial College there in 1928, and in 1933 was transferred to the archdiocese of Santa Fe, New Mexico, as its archbishop. He remained in that position until his death, on Mar. 2 in Santa Fe of a heart ailment.

GEROW, RICHARD OLIVER (1885–1976), bishop. Born in Mobile, Alabama, on May 3, he was educated at Mt. St. Mary's College, Emmitsburg, Maryland (B.A. 1904, M.A. 1906) and the North American College, Rome (S.T.D. 1909), and was ordained in Rome in 1909. He was assistant at the Mobile cathedral and prochancellor in 1909, became chancellor, and in 1920 was named rector of the cathedral. He was appointed bishop of Natchez-Jackson, Mississippi (changed to diocese of Jackson in 1977), in 1924, was a staunch advocate of civil rights, doubled the number of priests and parishes in the diocese, completed the chancery offices in Jackson in 1948, and established three new hospitals and a lay retreat house during the twenty-three years he was bishop of the see. He was made an Assistant at the Papal Throne in 1949, resigned his see in 1967, and died in Natchez on Dec. 20.

GIBAULT, PIERRE (1735–1802), missionary. Born in Montreal on Apr. 7, in his youth, he traveled to the Mississippi Valley with a fur brigade, then studied for the priesthood at the Quebec seminary and was ordained in 1760. He was sent to the Illinois country by Bishop Briand as a missionary with the title vicar-general and settled at Kaskaskia. He was the only Catholic priest in what is now Illinois and Indiana and acquired great influence with the French settlers and the Indians. Despite Bishop Briand's order forbidding clergy or laity to aid the American revolutionists, he persuaded the inhabitants of Kaskaskia not to resist George Rogers Clark and his forces when they approached the settlement in 1778 and joined the American cause; he likewise persuaded the settlers and Indians of Cahokia and Vincennes to accept American rule—actions that ensured the success of Clark's campaign and made Gibault responsible in no

small measure for winning the old Northwest for the United States. He left Kaskaskia to live at Ste. Geneviève in 1782 and then left Ste. Geneviève for New Madrid, Missouri, then in Spanish territory, in 1789, when Bishop John Carroll assumed episcopal jurisdiction over the area encompassing Kaskaskia. He applied to Spanish civil authorities and the bishop of Louisiana for priestly faculties and was appointed pastor of New Madrid in 1792; he died there on Aug. 15.

GIBBONS, EDMUND F. (1868–1964), bishop. The youngest son of a stonecutter, he was born in White Plains, New York, on Sept. 16, studied at Niagara University for a time, and then continued his studies at Our Lady of Angels Seminary, Niagara, New York, and the North American College, Rome, (S.T.D. 1893); he was ordained in Rome in 1893. He was secretary to Bishop Stephen Ryan of Buffalo in 1893–96, was assistant at St. Mary's Church, Niagara Falls, in 1896–98, and was inactive the next two years because of illness. He was superintendent of Buffalo's Catholic schools in 1900–16 and was appointed pastor of Silver Springs in 1902 and of St. Vincent's Church, Attica, in 1904–15. He became pastor of St. Teresa's Church, Buffalo, in 1916 and was appointed bishop of Albany in 1919. He was a staunch supporter of the Catholic press and founded the diocesan weekly *The Evangelist* in 1926; a firm believer in Catholic education, he greatly increased the number of schools in the see, founded the diocesan minor seminary, Mater Christi, in 1954, and established the College of St. Rose in Albany and Siena College for women in Loudonville; he also opened two retreat houses. With Bishop Cantrell of Los Angeles he was cofounder of the National Legion of Decency and was first episcopal chairman of the National Organization for Decent Literature. He retired to Mater Christi Seminary because of ill health in 1954 and was named titular bishop of Verbe; he died in Albany on June 19.

GIBBONS, FLOYD PHILLIPS
(1887–1939), journalist. Raphael Floyd Phillips Gibbons was born in Washington, D.C., on July 16 and studied at Georgetown University's preparatory school but was expelled in his fourth year for a boyish prank. He began his newspaper career on a newspaper in Lucca, North Dakota, became a reporter on the Minneapolis *Daily News* in 1907, the Milwaukee *Free Press* in 1909, the Minneapolis *Tribune* in 1910, and two years later the Chicago *Tribune.* He was with General John J. Pershing's forces in Mexico seeking Pancho Villa in 1916 for the *Tribune,* was on the S.S. *Laconia* in 1917 when it was torpedoed by U-boats, becoming famous for his reporting of that incident, and was with Pershing when he landed in France in 1917. He was wounded doing front-line dispatches during World War I and lost his left eye, which he covered with a black patch that became his trademark, and in 1919–27 he directed the *Tribune*'s foreign news service for Europe and North Africa and edited the European edition of the *Tribune.* The stories he filed were avidly read all over the country, among them his reports on the Irish revolution in 1919, the French-Riff hostilities in 1925, the Polish revolution in 1935, and the Spanish Civil War in 1936; perhaps his most spectacular reportorial exploit was his reporting on the 1921 famine in Russia and an interview with Stalin. He later became a well-known radio commentator, dubbed "the fastest talker on the air," lectured extensively, and wrote several books on his experiences, the Depression of the 1930s, and the New Deal; among his books were *How the*

Laconia Sank (1917), *And They Thought We Wouldn't Fight* (1918), *The Red Knight of Germany* (1927), and *The Red Napoleon* (1929). He died in Stroudsburg, Pennsylvania, on Sept. 24.

GIBBONS, JAMES (1834–1921), cardinal.
Son of Irish immigrants Thomas and Bridget Gibbons, he was born in Baltimore on July 23 and was taken to Ireland when he was three, when his family returned to Ireland for his father's health. His father died in 1847, and his mother returned to the United States with her five children and settled in New Orleans in 1853. He was educated at St. Charles College, Ellicott City, Maryland, in 1855–57 and St. Mary's Seminary, Baltimore, and was graduated and ordained for the Baltimore archdiocese in 1861. He served as assistant at St. Patrick's Church, Baltimore, for a short time and then became pastor of St. Bridget's Church, Canton, Maryland, also serving as chaplain to Union soldiers at Forts McHenry and Marshall during the Civil War. He became secretary to Archbishop Martin Spalding of Baltimore in 1865 and assistant chancellor of the archdiocese the following year, and helped in the preparations for the second Plenary Council of Baltimore, in 1866. When the vicariate apostolic of North Carolina was established, in 1868, he was named titular bishop of Adramyttum and its vicar. He attended Vatican Council I, as its youngest bishop, in 1869–70, was named administrator of the vacant diocese of Richmond, Virginia, in 1872, and was appointed its bishop the next year, while still administering the vicariate of North Carolina. In 1876, he published *The Faith of Our Fathers,* an enormously popular work (it was probably the best-selling Catholic book in the history of the Church in the United States), which made him well known all over the country. He was named coad-

jutor of Baltimore in 1877 and succeeded to the see on Oct. 19, on the death of Archbishop James Roosevelt Bayley; he was forty-three years old and was to head the premier see in the United States for forty-four years, among them some of the most momentous in American Catholic history. He presided over and was apostolic delegate to the third Plenary Council of Baltimore, in 1884, and at the conclusion of the Council was recognized as the leader of the American Church. He was made a cardinal in 1886, and the following year, being a firm believer in the American way of life, took the occasion of his taking possession of his titular church in Rome, Santa Maria in Trastevere, to reiterate his faith in the American system of government in a speech that was widely heralded. During the controversies of the 1880s between differing nationalities and over national churches, he was a moderating influence though constantly stressing the obligations of American citizenship and the oneness of the Catholic faith. In the controversies of the 1890s over Catholic education he staunchly defended Catholic education and the right of Catholics to have their own schools while agreeing in general with Archbishop Ireland and his Faribault plan. He was a defender of organized labor, and in 1887 his memorial to Pope Leo XIII persuaded the Holy See not to condemn the Knights of Labor, as had been done by the hierarchy of Canada in 1883. He was also instrumental in preventing the books of Henry George from being placed on the Index in 1887, insisting such an act would cause more harm than good though he thoroughly opposed George's single tax and economic theories and deplored the support accorded George and his theories by Msgr. McGlynn in New York City. He became a leader in the cause of social justice (many scholars believe his championship of social justice paved the way for Pope Leo XIII's *Rerum novarum* in 1891), pleaded for black missions, and although initially cool to the idea of a Catholic University of America, as proposed by Archbishop Ireland and Bishop John Spalding, became its firm supporter, serving as chancellor when it opened, helping save it from financial disaster in 1904, and defending it throughout his lifetime. In 1903 he was the first American to vote in a papal election, in the conclave that elected Pope Pius X. He was the leader in defending the American Church from charges of "Americanism" (the so-called phantom heresy), was a friend of six American presidents, who often consulted him on church-state matters, especially the problems brought on in church-state relations in the Philippines after the United States acquired those islands as a result of the Spanish-American War, and performed many of the functions of an apostolic delegate before the establishment of the Apostolic Delegation (to which he objected), in Washington, D.C., in 1893; to most Americans he was the symbol of the Catholic Church in the United States. Through much of his regime he exercised *de facto* primacy among his fellow bishops, and Baltimore, though never so designated officially by Rome, was in effect the primatial American see. Though not a crusading leader—indeed he was a conciliationist—he was a prudent and for the most part progressive influence on the American Church. At the time of his death, in Baltimore on Mar. 24, he was one of the most influential and most admired churchmen in the country, the epitome of the ideal churchman. Besides *Faith of Our Fathers,* he also wrote *Our Christian Heritage* (1889), *The Ambassador of Christ* (1896), *Discoveries and Sermons* (1908), and *A Retrospect of Fifty Years* (1916).

GIBSON, HUGH SIMONS (1883–1954), diplomat. Born in Los Angeles on Aug. 16, he was educated by private tutors in his youth and graduated from École Libre des Sciences Politiques, Paris, in 1907. He entered the United States diplomatic service the following year and served as secretary of the legations at Tegucigalpa, Honduras, in 1908, London in 1909–10, Havana in 1911–13, and Brussels in 1914–16. He aided Herbert Hoover's relief work during and after World War I, was the first minister to the newly created Poland in 1919–24, married Ynes Reyntiens in Brussels in 1922, and was U.S. minister to Switzerland in 1924–27, where he unofficially attended sessions of the League of Nations in Geneva and was chairman of the U.S. delegation to the Preparation Commission for the disarmament conference in 1926–27. He became ambassador to Belgium in 1927, participated in disarmament conferences in London in 1930 and in Brussels in 1932–33, and was ambassador to Brazil in 1933–37, during which time he was also a member of the mediatory group seeking to negotiate a peace in the Chaco War, between Bolivia and Paraguay (1932–35). He was again ambassador to Belgium and also to Luxembourg in 1937–38; he retired from diplomatic service in 1938, when he also became a Catholic. He served as European director of the Commissions for Polish Relief and for Belgian relief in 1940–41 and was director of the Intergovernmental Committee on Movement of Migrants from Europe in 1952. He died in Geneva on Dec. 12. He authored several books, among them *Rio* (1937), *Belgium* (1939), *The Road to Foreign Policy* (1944), *Problems of Lasting Peace*, with Herbert Hoover (1942), and *The Basis of Lasting Peace* (1945).

GILFILLAN, FRANCIS (1872–1933), bishop. Born in Aghavas, Carrigallen, Leitrim, Ireland, on Feb. 16, he was educated at St. Patrick's Seminary, Carlow, and emigrated to the United States. He continued his studies at Catholic University, was ordained in 1895, and engaged in pastoral work in the St. Louis archdiocese until 1922, when he was appointed titular bishop of Spiga and coadjutor of St. Joseph, Missouri (diocese of Kansas City-St. Joseph since 1956). He succeeded to the see in 1923 and remained in that position until his death, in St. Joseph on Jan. 13.

GILLESPIE, MOTHER MARY OF ST. ANGELA (1824–87), educator. Born in Brownsville, Washington County, Pennsylvania, on Feb. 21, she was baptized Eliza Maria, and studied under the Dominican sisters at Somerset, Ohio, and at the Visitation Convent at Georgetown, D.C. The niece of Senator Thomas Ewing of Ohio, she became one of the leading social lights in Washington, noted for her beauty and intelligence. She organized a Catholic school, taught in a secular Maryland school, opened a Sunday school for blacks, and helped raise money for the relief of the Irish in the famine sweeping Ireland. In 1853 she decided to enter the religious life and join the Sisters of Mercy, but while visiting her brother at Notre Dame met Fr. Edward Sorin, who persuaded her to join the Holy Cross Sisters. She joined in 1853, taking the name Mary of St. Angela, made her novitiate at the convent of the Sisters of Bon Secours, in Caen, France, and made her profession later that year. On her return to the United States, in 1855, she was made directress of St. Mary's Academy (serving until 1870), at Bertrand, Michigan, and transferred it to its present location, near Notre Dame, in South Bend, Indiana. During the Civil War she organized her nuns into a nursing corps and established eight military hospitals and two hospital ships to care for sick and wounded soldiers and sailors. After the war she returned to St. Mary's, compiled two sets of readers for Catholic schools, Metropolitan and Excelsior readers, and in 1869, when the Holy Cross Sisters in the United States decided to separate from the mother community in France to form an independent community, she was elected superior, thus being the foundress of the Sisters of the Holy Cross in the United States. While she was superior, the congregation founded thirty-five schools and other institutions all over the country; she helped to found *Ave Maria* in 1865 and contributed numerous articles to it. She was made mistress of novices at St. Mary's when she relinquished her superiority, and in 1886 was again named head of St. Mary's and occupied that position until her death, at St. Mary's convent on Mar. 4.

GILLESPIE, NEAL HENRY (1831–74), educator. Brother of Mother Mary of St. Angela, foundress of the Holy Cross Sisters in the United States, he was born in Washington County, Pennsylvania, on Jan. 19. He was educated at Notre Dame, receiving the first degree conferred by that institution in 1849, and in 1851 joined the Congregation of Holy Cross and entered its novitiate at Notre Dame. He continued his studies in Rome and was ordained there in 1856. On his return to the United States, he served as vice president and director of studies of Notre Dame from 1856 to 1859, when he was appointed president of St. Mary of the Lake College, Chicago. He was at the motherhouse of the congregation in Le Mans, France, in 1863–66, became editor of *Ave Maria* on his return, in 1866, and held that position until his death at St. Mary's College, Notre Dame, on Nov. 12.

GILLIS, JAMES MARTIN (1876–1957), missionary, preacher. Born in Boston on Nov. 12, he was educated at St. Charles College, Baltimore, and St. John's Seminary, Boston, and joined the Paulists in 1898. He continued his studies at Catholic University (S.T.L. 1903), was ordained in 1901, was novice master and professor at St. Paul's College, Washington, D.C. in 1907–10, and spent the next twelve years in missionary work. He became editor of the *Catholic World* in 1922, and soon his editorials in the *Catholic World,* his widely syndicated newspaper column, "Sursum Corda," begun in 1928, his radio programs on "The Catholic Hour" in 1930–41, and his books made him one of the most influential Catholic priests of his time. He was an eloquent and highly effective preacher, frequently controversial and always outspoken, and drew large, enthusiastic crowds wherever he preached. He resigned as editor of the *Catholic World* in 1948 because of the illness that plagued the last years of his life; he died in New York City on Mar. 14. Among his books were *False Prophets* (1925), *The Catholic Church and the Home* (1928), *Christianity and Civilization* (1932), *This Our Day* (two volumes, 1933, 1949), *So Near Is God* (1953), and *This Mysterious Human Nature* (1956).

GILMORE, JOSEPH M. (1893–1962), bishop. Born in New York City on Mar. 22, he was taken to Montana by his parents when he was four. He was educated at Columbia College, Dubuque, Iowa (B.A. 1911), and the Propaganda, Rome (S.T.D. 1915), and was ordained in Rome in 1915. He taught at Carroll College, Helena, Montana, in 1915–19, was pastor of St. Teresa's Church, Whitehall, in 1920–25, and of St. Helena's Church, Butte, in 1925–27;

he served as chancellor of the Helena diocese in 1927–36. He was consecrated fifth bishop of that diocese in 1936, and during his episcopate he established Catholic Charities, the Serra Club, and the Christian Family Movement in the diocese, completed the renovation of the cathedral in 1959, and began new churches and schools and a rebuilding program. He was named an Assistant at the Pontifical Throne in 1958 and died in San Francisco on Apr. 2.

GILMORE, PATRICK SARSFIELD (1829–92), musician. Born in Ballygar, Galway, Ireland, on Dec. 25, he emigrated to the United States in 1848, settled in Boston, and organized several bands there and in Salem. In 1858 he founded Gilmore's Band, which in time became the best-known military concert band in the United States. He and the members of his band enlisted in the 24th Massachusetts Volunteers at the outbreak of the Civil War and served under General Burnside in South Carolina. In 1869 he organized the National Peace Jubilee, and in 1872 the International Peace Jubilee, in Boston, two of the largest musical festivals up to that time, with some thirty thousand singers and two thousand instrumentalists participating and with hundreds of thousands of spectators in attendance. He became bandmaster of New York's 22nd Regiment in New York City in 1873 and played at Gilmore's Garden (later Madison Square Garden). He toured all over the United States and Europe with Gilmore's Band and was touring in 1892, celebrating the four-hundredth anniversary of Columbus's discovery of America, when he was stricken and died in St. Louis on Sept. 24. He was often called "the father of military bands" and was responsible for elevating the brass band to a distinguished musical status, bringing it into concert halls all over the world. He also wrote many popular songs and marches.

GILMOUR, RICHARD (1824–91), bishop. Born in Glasgow, Scotland, on Sept. 28, he was brought to the United States when thirteen by his parents. He became a Catholic in 1842, studied for the priesthood at St. Michael's Seminary, Pittsburgh, and Mt. St. Mary's College, Emmitsburg, Maryland, and was ordained in Cincinnati, Ohio, in 1852. He engaged in pastoral and missionary work in Ohio, served in Cincinnati, built churches in Portsmouth and Ironton, taught at Mt. St. Mary of the West, in Cincinnati, in 1868 and then became pastor of St. Joseph's Church, Dayton. He was appointed second bishop of Cleveland, in 1872, fought anti-Catholicism in his see, was an active supporter of Catholic education, and was responsible for a successful appeal to the United States Supreme Court that a tax imposed on school property in Cleveland in 1875 was unconstitutional *(Gilmour v. Pelton,* 1883). He was unsuccessful, though, in the struggle he and other bishops waged to secure public funds for private schools. He held diocesan synods in 1872 and 1882, firmly supported the concept of independence of the American hierarchy, and was a firm supporter of the Catholic press, founding the diocesan paper, *The Catholic Universe,* in 1871. In 1878 he established the diocesan archives when he started a collection of historical data on every Catholic parish and institution in the diocese. He was involved in disputes with several religious communities over his demand that their properties be held by the bishop and with several of his priests over his strict discipline. He was active at the third Plenary Council of Baltimore, in 1884, and was one of the bishops designated to bring its conciliar acts to Rome. During his episcopate he established seventy-three new churches and fifty-two new schools, built four hospitals, and brought new religious orders into the see (the Jesuits opened St. Ignatius College—later John Carroll University—in Cleveland in 1886). He was an ardent supporter of the concept of a native clergy, though he provided immigrants with churches and priests of their own while urging them to become American Catholics. He strongly opposed the Germanizing influence on the Church in the United States in a memorial he and Bishop John Moore of St. Augustine, Florida, presented while they were in Rome in 1885 and strongly supported Cardinal Gibbons in the latter's defense of the Knights of Labor and American labor unions. He was the author of two extremely popular textbook series, Bible History (1869) and Catholic National Readers (1874–89), popularly known as the Gilmour Readers. He died in St. Augustine on Apr. 13.

GIROUARD, PAUL JOSEPH (1898–1964), bishop. Born in Hamilton, Rhode Island, on Dec. 27, he was educated at La Salette Seminary, Hartford, Connecticut, the La Salette novitiate, Bloomfield, Connecticut, and the Gregorian, Rome, and was ordained a La Salette priest in Rome in 1927. He was sent as a missionary to Madagascar (Malagasy Republic) the following year and was appointed prefect apostolic of Morondava in 1955 and then first bishop of the newly erected diocese of Morondava, remaining in that position until his death there in Feb.

GLASS, JOSEPH SARSFIELD (1874–1926), bishop. Born in Bushnell, Illinois, on Mar. 13, he graduated from St. Vincent's College, Los Angeles, in 1869, joined the Vincentians in 1891, and studied for the priesthood at St.

Mary's Seminary, The Barrens, Missouri, and the Minerva, Rome. He was ordained in Los Angeles in 1897, taught theology at St. Mary's for a time, and was president of St. Vincent's College in 1901–11. He was also pastor of St. Vincent's Church, in Los Angeles, from 1901 to 1915, when he was consecrated second bishop of Salt Lake City, Utah. During World War I he was one of the four bishop directors of the National Catholic War Council, was a founder of the National Catholic Welfare Conference, and was an enthusiastic supporter of the liturgical revival. He died in Los Angeles on Jan. 26.

GLEASON, ROBERT W. (1917–82), educator, author. Born in White Plains, New York, on May 19, he was educated at Fordham (B.A. 1939, M.A. 1947, Ph.D. 1948), joined the Jesuits, and continued his studies at Woodstock (Maryland) College (S.T.L. 1952) and was ordained at Woodstock in 1952. He went to Rome for further studies at the Gregorian (S.T.D. 1953), was assistant professor of theology at Fordham in 1955–58, and was appointed chairman of the department of theology and religion in 1958 and held that position until his death, in the Bronx, New York City, on Nov. 11. He wrote some fifteen books, among them World to Come (1958), Christ and the Christian (1959), Counseling the Catholic (1960), and To Live in Christ (1961).

GLEASON, FRANCIS DOYLE (1895–1983), bishop. Born in Carrollton, Missouri, on Jan. 17, he joined the Jesuits in 1912 and was educated at Mt. St. Michael's, Spokane, Washington, and Oña, Spain, where he was ordained in 1926. He served as rector of Bellarmine College, Tacoma, Washington, for a time, was pastor of St. Stanislaus Church, Lewiston, Iowa, and then was rector of the Jesuit novitiate at Sheridan, Oregon, and St. Mary mission, Omak, Washington. He was consecrated titular bishop of Cotenna and vicar apostolic of Alaska in 1948, and in 1962 was appointed first bishop of the newly established diocese of Fairbanks, Alaska. He retired in 1968 and was made titular bishop of Cuicul, in Numidia, and later that year was made an Assistant at the Pontifical Throne. He died in Fairbanks on Apr. 30.

GLENNON, JOHN JOSEPH (1862–1946), cardinal. Son of a naturalized American citizen, he was born in Kinnegad, Meath, Ireland, on June 14 and was educated at St. Finian College, Mullingar, and All Hallows College, Dublin. He emigrated to the United States in 1883 and was ordained the following year in Kansas City, Missouri. He served as a curate at St. Patrick's Church there for a time and then continued his education at Bonn, Germany. On his return to the United States, in 1888, he was stationed at the cathedral in Kansas City and in 1892 became vicar-general of Kansas City. He was administrator of the see from 1894 to 1896, when he was appointed titular bishop of Pinara and coadjutor of the diocese. He was transferred to St. Louis as coadjutor in 1903 and succeeded to the see later in that year as archbishop. During his forty-two-year episcopate he established forty-three new parishes, increased the number of priests from 442 to 928, expanded the secondary school, college, and charitable institutions of the archdiocese, built Kenrick Seminary in 1913–15 and St. Louis Preparatory Seminary in 1930–31, helped integrate immigrants to St. Louis into the American way of life, and constructed St. Louis Cathedral, which was dedicated in 1926. He encouraged colonization projects in the see and the National Catholic Rural Life Movement and was one of the founders of the National Catholic War Council (which developed into the National Catholic Welfare Conference). He was made an Assistant at the Pontifical Throne in 1921 and was created a cardinal in 1946, when he was eighty-four; he died in Dublin three weeks later, on the way home from the consistory in Rome that had made him a cardinal.

GLORIEUX, ALPHONSE JOSEPH (1844–1917), bishop. Born in Dottignies, Belgium, on Feb. 1, he was educated there, at Courtrai College, the American College, Rome, and Louvain, and was ordained in 1867. He was a missionary in Oregon for a time and president of St. Michael's College, Portland, Oregon, from 1871 to 1885, when he was consecrated titular bishop of Apollonia and second vicar apostolic of Idaho. He was appointed first bishop of the newly established diocese of Boise, Idaho, in 1893 and held that position until his death, in Portland on Aug. 25.

GLOVER, GOODY (d. 1688). Also known as Goodwife Ann, she was an Irish Catholic woman living in Boston. She rebuked the daughter of John Goodwin for accusing her daughter, a laundress, of stealing some of the Goodwin family linen. When the girl "became bewitched" and three other members of the family exhibited such signs as barking like dogs and purring like cats, Cotton Mather and several ministers prayed over them and decided they were possessed by a witch. The magistrates decided the witch must be Goody Glover, citing such evidence as "she was a wild Irish woman" and could say the Lord's prayer in Latin but not in English, convicted her of being a witch, and had her executed.

GLYNN, MARTIN HENRY (1871–1924), governor. Born in Kinderhook, New York, on Sept. 27, he was educated at St. John's College (Fordham), graduating in 1894, joined the staff of the Albany *Times-Union,* and became its managing editor in 1895. He studied law, was admitted to the bar in 1897, and entered politics the following year and was elected to Congress and served in that body in 1899–1901. He was defeated in a bid for reelection in 1900 but was elected New York State Comptroller in 1906 and lieutenant governor in 1912. During the impeachment proceedings against Governor William Sulzer, in 1913, he was acting governor, and when Sulzer was convicted and removed from office, in 1913, he completed Sulzer's term. He was defeated in the race for governor in 1914, was temporary chairman of the 1916 Democratic National Convention (it was from his keynote address that the phrase "he kept us out of war," which became the Democratic slogan in the election of 1916 that reelected Woodrow Wilson President, was coined) and served on the Federal Industrial Commission in 1919–20. During the Irish rebellion of 1921, he acted as liaison between Prime Minister Lloyd George of Great Britain and Eamon de Valera in their effort to settle the Irish question. He died in Albany on Dec. 14.

GMEINER, JOHN (1847–1913). Born in Bavaria, he was brought to the United States by his parents, who settled in Milwaukee, Wisconsin, in 1849. He was educated at Milwaukee's St. Francis de Sales Seminary, was ordained in 1870, and served for a time at St. Boniface Church, Germantown, Wisconsin. He then taught at St. Francis de Sales preparatory school and served at the cathedral at Milwaukee and at Cassville, Platteville, Oshkosh, and Waukesha in 1873–83; he edited *Columbia* in 1873–76. He was appointed professor at St. Francis de Sales Seminary in 1883, taught at St. Thomas

Seminary in St. Paul, until 1889, and then served in parishes in Mendota and in St. Paul and Buffalo, in Minnesota; in 1902 he was sent to a German parish in Springfield, Minnesota. He became an authority on German immigrants and immigration, opposed Cahenslyism and the concept of perpetuating the German language and customs among German immigrants on American soil, and was a staunch supporter of Americanism. He wrote articles for magazines and was the author of several books, among them *The Spirits of Darkness and their Manifestation on Earth* (1886), *The Church and the Various Nationalities in the United States—Are German Catholics Unfairly Treated?* (1887), *The Church and Foreignism* (1891), and *Modern Cosmology* (1891).

GOESBRIAND, LOUIS DE (1816–99), bishop. Son of Henri, Marquis de Goesbriand and Émilie de Bergean, he was born in St. Urban, Finistère, France, on Aug. 4, was educated at the Quimper seminary and St. Sulpice, Paris, and was ordained in 1840. He came to the United States, engaged in pastoral work in the Louisville, Kentucky, diocese, served at St. Francis de Sales parish, Toledo, Ohio, and was vicar-general of Cleveland in 1847–53. He was consecrated first bishop of the newly established diocese of Burlington, Vermont, which had five priests, ten churches, and twenty thousand Catholics when he was consecrated, in 1853. He went to Europe in 1855 seeking funds and priests in France and Ireland for his see, held the first diocesan synod the same year, built a cathedral, which he dedicated in 1867, and attended Vatican Council I, in 1869–70. He wrote several books, among them *Catholic Memories of Vermont and New Hampshire* (1886) and *Christ on the Altar* (1890), and retired to a nursing home in Burlington because of advanced age and failing health in 1892; he died there on Nov. 3. During his episcopate the Catholic population almost tripled (two thirds of which was of French-Canadian birth or origin), the number of priests increased to fifty-two and the churches to seventy-eight, and he established twenty-four new schools and brought seven congregations of nuns into the see.

GORMAN, DANIEL MARY (1861–1927), bishop. Born in Wyoming, Iowa, on Apr. 12, he was educated at St. Joseph's College, Dubuque, Iowa, and St. Francis Seminary, Milwaukee, Wisconsin, and was ordained in 1893. He began teaching at St. Joseph's (later Dubuque University) in 1894 and was its president from 1904 until 1918, when he was consecrated second bishop of Boise, Idaho; he remained in that position until his death, at Lewiston, Idaho, on June 9.

GORMAN, RALPH (1897–1972), editor. Born in Binghamton, New York, on Oct. 4, he was educated at the Passionist preparatory college in Baltimore, was professed a Passionist in 1917, and studied in Passionist monasteries in 1917–24. He was ordained in 1924, continued his studies at Catholic University (S.T.L. 1925) and École Biblique et Archéologique, Jerusalem, in 1925–27. He joined *Sign* magazine in 1935 as associate editor and was managing editor in 1942–66, during which time *Sign* was one of the leading Catholic magazines in the United States. He retired in 1966, suffered a stroke in 1972, and died in Scranton, Pennsylvania, on Oct. 17. He wrote two books: *The Last Hours of Jesus* and *The Trial of Christ— Reappraised.*

GORMAN, THOMAS KIELY (1892–1980), bishop. Born in Pasadena, California, on Aug. 30, he was educated at St. Patrick's Seminary, Menlo Park, California, and St. Mary's Seminary, Baltimore (S.T.B. 1917), was ordained in 1917, and continued his education at Catholic University (J.C.B. 1917, J.C.L. 1918) and Louvain (Doctor of Sacred History 1925). He served as assistant pastor at St. Clare's Church, Oxnard, California, and at St. Bibiana's Cathedral, Los Angeles, in 1918–22 and was editor of the Los Angeles diocesan newspaper, *The Tidings,* in 1926–31. He was consecrated first bishop of the newly established diocese of Reno, Nevada, in 1931, was made an Assistant at the Pontifical Throne in 1942, was assistant chairman of the National Catholic Welfare Conference (NCWC) press department in 1942–51 and chairman in 1951–57, was appointed titular bishop of Rhasus and coadjutor of the diocese of Dallas, Texas, in 1952, and succeeded to the see in 1954. He resigned in 1969 and was appointed titular bishop of Pinlel; he died in Dallas on Aug. 16.

GOUPIL, ST. RENÉ (1607–42), martyr. Born in Anjou, France, he joined the Jesuits and studied for a time at the Jesuit novitiate in Paris but was forced to leave because of deafness. He studied medicine at Orléans Hospital and became a successful surgeon, but, desirous still of participating in Jesuit missionary work, went to Quebec in 1640 and worked as a *donné* (lay assistant) at the Sillery mission, near Quebec, and at Quebec's Hôtel-Dieu (hospital). In 1642 he joined Fr. Isaac Jogues, who was leaving on a missionary trip to the Hurons; they were captured by the Iroquois, the Hurons' deadly enemies, and for three months they were subjected to the most terrible tortures and mutilations. On Sept. 29, at the Iroquois village of Osserneon, near Albany, New York, René was tomahawked to death in Fr. Jogues's presence, the first of the North American Martyrs. Jogues escaped but was later martyred by the Mohawks. The North American Martyrs were canonized by Pope Pius XI in 1930, with Oct. 19 their feast day. A shrine at Auriesville, New York (the site of Osserneon), was opened in 1884 to commemorate the martyrdom of St. René Goupil and also St. Isaac Jogues and St. Jean de Lalande, who were martyred there in 1646; it is also the birthplace of St. Kateri Tekakwitha.

GRACE, JOSEPH PETER (1872–1950), executive. Born in Great Neck, New York, on June 29, he was educated at Columbia (B.A. 1894) and New York Law School (LL.B. 1895) and went into the shipping business. By 1909, when he became its president, he had developed William R. Grace & Co. into a world-famous shipping company. He became chairman of the board of trustees in 1929, when he established Pan American-Grace Airways (Pan Am), was widely known for his philanthropies, and served on the boards of many charitable institutions. He died in Great Neck on July 15.

GRACE, THOMAS (1841–1921), bishop. Born in County Wexford, Ireland, on Aug. 2, he was educated at St. Peter's there and All Hallows, Dublin, and was ordained in 1876. He emigrated to the United States the same year, engaged in parish and missionary work in Nevada, and was rector of the Marysville, California, cathedral for eight years. He was pastor of the Sacramento cathedral in 1881–96, was administrator of that diocese in 1895–96, and was preconized bishop of the diocese of Sacramento, California, in 1896; he held this position until his death there on Dec. 27.

GRACE, THOMAS LANGDON (1814–97), bishop. Born in Charleston, South Carolina, on Nov. 16, he was ed-

ucated at the Cincinnati, Ohio, seminary and St. Rose's Priory, Bardstown, Kentucky, and joined the Dominicans there in 1831. He went to Rome in 1839 for further studies at the Minerva and was ordained there in the same year. He returned to the United States in 1844, engaged in pastoral work in Kentucky and then for thirteen years in Memphis, Tennessee, and was appointed second bishop of St. Paul, Minnesota, in 1859. During his episcopate he was a firm adherent of Catholic education and greatly expanded the educational facilities of the diocese, brought in many new religious orders, encouraged immigration, and worked to aid new immigrants (he founded the Minnesota Irish Emigration Society in 1864) and was known for his charitable works. He resigned in 1884 and was appointed titular bishop of Menith; five years later he was named titular archbishop of Siunia. He died in St. Paul on Feb. 22.

GRACE, WILLIAM RUSSELL (1832–1904), merchant, philanthropist. Born in Queenstown (Cobh), Ireland, on May 10, he ran away to sea for two years when a boy, worked in a Liverpool ship chandlers firm, and in 1850 went to Peru and joined a ship chandlers firm there. He became a partner in the firm of Bryce & Company, ship chandlers, at Callao; in time it evolved into Grace Brothers & Co. and W. R. Grace & Co., in New York, in 1856. He married Lillius Gilchrist, daughter of a Maine shipbuilder, in 1859, became ill soon after, and was forced to resign. After his recovery, he settled in New York City, and when Peru began building railroads, Grace concerns supplied practically everything needed for the system. He became a confidential adviser to the Peruvian Government, armed and equipped the Peruvian Army in 1875–79, and helped purchase its Navy. He supplied Peru with munitions for its war with Chile in 1875, and when Peru was defeated, he and several colleagues underwrote the national debt in return for extensive concessions: silver mines, guano deposits, railroads. He expanded the business to other South American countries, dealing in Peruvian textiles, Brazilian rubber, and Chilean nitrates; he enlarged his interests, founding the New York and Pacific Steamship Company, operating the first regular steamer service to the west coast of South America. He contributed generously to Irish famine relief in 1878–79, was elected mayor of New York City in 1880—its first Catholic mayor—opposed Tammany Hall with a reform administration, and was reelected in 1884; he refused a third term. In 1897 he established Grace Institute, for the practical education of women in dressmaking, stenography, typing, bookkeeping, and the domestic sciences with tuition free, and was noted for his charity to workers' families and the poor. He died in New York City on Mar. 21.

GRANAHAN, KATHRYN O'HAY (c. 1896–1979), U.S. Treasurer. Kathryn Elizabeth O'Hay was born in Easton, Pennsylvania (she would never say when), was educated at Mt. St. Joseph College, Chestnut Hill, Pennsylvania, and began her public career as a supervisor of public assistance. She married William T. Granahan in 1943, a five-term congressman, and worked closely with him. When he died, in 1956, she ran for Congress the same year and was elected—the first woman to represent a Philadelphia congressional district. She was reelected in 1958 and served on several committees and investigated the use of the mails to distribute pornographic materials as chairlady of the Postal Operations subcommittee. She was named U.S. Treasurer in 1963 and served in that post until she died, in Norristown, Pennsylvania, on July 10.

GRANJON, HENRY REGIS (?1863–1922), bishop. Born in St. Étienne, Loire, France, on June 15 (or perhaps on Apr. 15, 1859), he was educated at St. Chamond College and St. Sulpice, in Paris, and the Apollinaris and the Minerva, in Rome. He was ordained in Lyons, France, in 1887, emigrated to the United States, and engaged in missionary work in Arizona. He was the first national director of the Society for the Propagation of the Faith, establishing its headquarters in St. Mary's Seminary, Baltimore, from 1897 until 1900, when he was appointed second bishop of Tucson, Arizona, which position he held until his death, in Brignais, France, on Nov. 9.

GRASSE, FRANÇOIS JOSEPH PAUL, COMTE DE (1722–88), admiral. Born near Toulon, France, of an old and noble family, he entered the naval service of the Knights of Malta in 1734, when he was eleven, and served during the Turkish and Moorish wars. He joined the French Navy in 1739, was captured by the British in 1747 and held in England for two years, and on his release served under La Galissonnière during the Seven Years' War and under d'Ache in the East Indies. He was made a captain in 1762, and in 1778, when the French became allied with the American colonists in their war for freedom, he was wounded while commanding the *Robuste* in the naval engagement off the island of Ushant, off the coast of Brittany, between the fleets of Count d'Orvilliers and Admiral Keppel. On his recovery he was made rear admiral, served under Count d'Estaing in the West Indies, and on his return to France was promoted to lieutenant général des armées navals (admiral). He sailed from Brest in 1781 with a large fleet destined for the West Indies, defeated a British fleet under Admiral Samuel Hood, and captured Tobago. He came north to Virginia at the request of Washington and Rochambeau and blockaded the York and James rivers, thus bottling up Cornwallis at Yorktown. When a fleet from Newport under Admiral de Barras sailed from Newport, Rhode Island, to rendezvous with him, an English fleet under Admirals Thomas Graves and Hood tried to prevent the two French fleets from uniting and to reinforce Cornwallis. He defeated the British force and thus played a crucial role in the great victory at Yorktown; the British surrendered there on Oct. 19, 1781, and though the war continued until 1783, Cornwallis's defeat was really the end. De Grasse then sailed to Martinique, and in April 1782 engaged the fleet of Admiral Rodney. The battle was indecisive, but four days later the two fleets fought again and the British were victorious and took De Grasse captive. He was held in England until the Revolution ended, when he returned to France. While in London, he published an account of the battle with Rodney blaming his captains for the defeat, and on his return to France he demanded a court-martial of his subordinates. The trial was held in 1784 and resulted in their exoneration. When he demanded a second trial, the King refused an audience with him and he retired from public life in disfavor. He died four years later, in Paris, on Jan. 11.

GRASSO, ELLA (1919–81), governor. Of Italian immigrant parents, Ella Rosa Tambussi was born in Windsor Locks, Connecticut, on May 19 and was educated at Chaffee School, Windsor, and Mount Holyoke College, South Hadley, Massachusetts (B.A. 1940, M.A. 1942). After graduation she became interested in politics, worked for the Federal Manpower Commission in Connecticut during World War II, married Thomas A. Grasso in 1942, engaged in political activities for the Democratic Party, and

was elected to the House of Representatives of the Connecticut General Assembly in 1952 and again in 1954. She was elected secretary of state of Connecticut in 1958 and was repeatedly reelected serving twelve years in this position. At the National Democratic Convention in Chicago in 1968 she supported a defeated resolution opposing the war in Vietnam and in 1970 was elected to the federal House of Representatives; she was reelected in 1972. She helped pass the Emergency Employment Act of 1971 and educational and fair-labor-practices bills and opposed abortion legislation. She was elected governor of Connecticut in 1974 —the first woman to be elected the governor of a state in her own right—and was reelected in 1979 but resigned in 1980 because of illness. She died of cancer in Hartford, Connecticut, on Feb. 5. During her administrations she was obliged to curtail state programs due to economies she put into effect because of the recession.

GRAVENOR, JOHN. *See* Altham, John.

GRAVIER, JACQUES (1651–1708), missionary. Born in Moulins, France, he studied under the Jesuits there and in 1670 joined the Society of Jesus. He studied theology at Louis-le-Grand College, Paris, and in 1685, after his ordination, was sent to Canada to work as a missionary. Two years later he was sent to Michilimackinac and in 1689 replaced Fr. Claude Allouez in the Illinois mission at the head of Peoria Lake (now Rockford, Illinois), which had been begun by Fr. Jacques Marquette. He was made superior of the Michilimackinac (Mackinac, Michigan) mission with the title vicar-general in 1696, and four years later he returned to the Illinois mission. In 1706 he restored the mission founded by Fr. Allouez on the St. Jo-

seph River near the present site of Notre Dame and was wounded in an attack
by the Peoria Indians; an arrowhead
embedded in his arm could not be removed by a surgeon in Paris, and he
died of the wound two years later, on
Feb. 12, near present-day Mobile, Alabama. He had traveled all over the Middle West and South to the Louisiana
Territory, ministering and preaching to
the Indians; he was the author of the
manuscript (now at Harvard) Dictionary of the Peoria Language, the principal literary monument of the now ex-
tinct Illinois Indians.

GREEN, JOSEPH MICHAEL (1917–
82), bishop. Born in St. Joseph, Michigan, on Oct. 13, he studied for a year at
Maher's Business College and then decided to become a priest. He studied at
St. Joseph's Seminary, Grand Rapids,
St. Gregory's Seminary, Cincinnati
(B.A. 1943), and St. Mary's Seminary,
Norwood, Ohio, and was ordained in
1946. He continued his studies at the
Lateran, Rome (J.C.D. 1954), was secretary to Bishop Joseph Albers of Lansing, Michigan, in 1955–57, vice-chancellor of that see in 1957–62, and vicar-
general in 1962. He was named titular
bishop of Trispia and auxiliary of Lansing in 1962, was appointed bishop of
Reno, Nevada, in 1967, resigned in
1974, and died in Pontiac, Michigan, on
Aug. 30.

**GREEN, WILLIAM JOSEPH
"BILLY," JR.** (1910–63), political
leader, congressman. Son of William Joseph Green, a saloonkeeper, and Annie
Theresa Duffy Green, he was born in
Philadelphia on Mar. 5. He studied at
St. Joseph's College there in 1930–31
but left to enter politics. He operated an
insurance business, was a Pennsylvania
insurance examiner and then U.S. chief
marshal; in 1937 he married Mary E.
Kelly. He served in the Army Quarter-

master Corps during World War II, was
elected to Congress while in the Army
but was defeated in a bid for reelection
in 1946; he was reelected in 1948 and in
each congressional election from then
on until his death. By the 1950s he had
built and headed a powerful political
machine in Philadelphia that exerted influence in national politics; he helped
nominate Adlai Stevenson for the presidency at the 1956 National Democratic
Party Convention and became a friend
of John F. Kennedy, whom he vigorously supported. He was indicted in
1956 on charges of conspiracy to de-
fraud the government by taking a bribe,
but was acquitted. He suffered a bladder
attack in Dec. 1963 and died soon after,
on Dec. 21.

GREENE, EDWARD LEE (1843–
1915), botanist. Born in Hopkinton,
Rhode Island, on Aug. 20, he was taken
to Ohio and then Wisconsin by his parents when he was a child. He began
studying at Albion College, Albion,
Michigan, under the Swedish botanist
Knure Kumlein, but when the Civil
War broke out he joined the 63rd Regiment, of Wisconsin, and served as a private throughout the war. On his return
he resumed his education at Albion, received his bachelor's degree, and was
ordained an Episcopal priest. He was
rector of a parish in Berkeley, California, when he resigned and became a
Catholic, in 1885. He soon made a
name for himself as a botanist, was a
professor of botany at the University of
California in 1885–95, taught at Catholic University in 1896–1904, and was an
associate of botany at the Smithsonian
Institution from 1904 until 1913, when
he became head of the Graduate School
of Sciences at Notre Dame, where he
established the Edward Lee Greene Library with an outstanding collection of
books on botany. He held this position
until his death, in Washington, D.C. on

Nov. 10. He wrote *Landmarks of Botanical History* (he was working on the second volume when he died), *Manual of Botany for San Francisco Bay,* and the five-volume *Pittonia and West American Oaks,* and contributed articles to more than forty scientific journals, many of them foreign, for he was fluent in thirty languages. He established that Cesalpino, rather than Linnaeus, was the founder of scientific biology, classified and named some five thousand plants he had discovered, and while at the Smithsonian found methods of exterminating plants that were injurious to grazing cattle. At the time of his death he was considered the most learned and accurate of the systematic botanists and the father of the neo-American school of botanical nomenclature.

GRIFFIN, JAMES ALOYSIUS (1883–1948), bishop. Born in Chicago on Feb. 27, he was educated at St. Ignatius College (now Loyola) there, the Propaganda, Rome (Ph.D. 1906, D.D. 1910), and the North American College, Rome, and was ordained there in 1910. He was a curate at St. James Church, Chicago, in 1910–15 and St. Brendan's Church, Chicago, in 1915–17, was pastor of Assumption Church, in Coal City, Illinois, in 1917–21 and of St. Mary's Church, Joliet, 1921–24, when he was appointed fourth bishop of Springfield. He was active in civic affairs, was national chaplain of the Ancient Order of Hibernians, conducted several successful building campaigns, and built Immaculate Conception Cathedral, dedicating it in 1928. He died in Springfield on Aug. 5.

GRIFFIN, JOHN HOWARD (1920–80), author. Born in Dallas, Texas, on June 16, he was educated at Lycée Descartes and École de Médecin, Lyons, the University of Poitiers, Conserva-toire de Fontainebleau, and the Abbey of Solesmes, all in France, and studied music privately. He served in the U.S. Air Force in 1941–45 and lost his sight from diabetes and wounds suffered in the South Pacific. He became a Catholic in 1952, recovered his sight in 1957, and became involved in the civil rights movement. His *Black Like Me,* based on his experiences in the South after he had dyed his skin black, caused a sensation when it was published, in 1961. Among his other books were *The Devil Rides Outside* (1952) and *Nuni* (1956), written while he was blind, *Land of the High Sky* (1959), *A Hidden Wholeness: The Visual World of Thomas Merton* (1970), and *The Hermitage Journals,* published posthumously in 1981. He died in Fort Worth, Texas, on Sept. 9.

GRIFFIN, MARTIN IGNATIUS JOSEPH (1842–1911), journalist. Born in Philadelphia on Oct. 23 of Irish immigrant parents, he was educated in public and parochial schools and began his journalism career in Philadelphia. In 1867 he became part owner and editor of the *Sunday School Journal* and the *Guardian Angel* and was an assistant editor of the Philadelphia *Catholic Standard* from 1870 to 1873. He was appointed secretary of the Irish Catholic Benevolent Union in 1872 and founded its *Journal* in 1873, serving as editor until 1894, and was one of the founders of the Catholic Total Abstinence Union of America. He helped found the American Catholic Historical Society of Philadelphia, in 1884, and became its librarian, and was owner and editor of *American Catholic Historical Researches* in 1881–1911. Known for his objective historical research, he constantly stressed the need for authenticity in American Catholic writing. He wrote several biographies, parish histories, and historical works, among them *History of Commodore John Barry* (1903) and the three-volume *Catholics and the American Revolution* (1907–11). He died in Philadelphia on Nov. 10.

GRIFFIN, ROBERT STANISLAUS (1857–1933), admiral. Born in Fredericksburg, Virginia, on Sept. 27, he graduated from the U.S. Naval Academy in 1878 and served under George W. Melville, the arctic explorer and engineer. He began to specialize in engineering in 1899, was an engineer of the North Atlantic Fleet in 1901–5 and in 1908 was assigned to the Bureau of Steam Engineering, where he spent the rest of his career; he became its chief and a rear admiral in 1913, serving during the period when coal was replaced by oil in ships and the electric drive was developed. He was the first editor of the *Journal of the Society of Naval Engineers* and was president of the Society in 1908, 1912, and 1913. During World War I he was in charge of naval construction and the repair program of the Navy. He retired in 1921, wrote *History of the Bureau of Engineering, Navy Department, during the World War,* and died in Washington, D.C., on Feb. 21.

GRIFFIN, WILLIAM ALOYSIUS (1885–1950), bishop. Born in Newark, New Jersey, on Nov. 20, he was educated at Seton Hall College, South Orange, and Immaculate Conception Seminary, Darlington, and was ordained in 1910. He taught at Seton Hall until 1915, when he was assigned to parish work as rector of St. Michael's Church, Jersey City, and was first director of the Society for the Propagation of the Faith in the diocese of Newark. He was made a papal chamberlain in 1929, was named national treasurer of the Society for the Propagation of the Faith in 1935, and then became rector of Immaculate Conception Seminary. He was appointed titular bishop of Sanavus and auxiliary of Newark in 1938, and two

years later became bishop of Trenton. During his bishopric he established thirty-five new parishes, eight regional catechetical centers, and fourteen parochial centers. He died in Trenton on Jan. 1.

GRIFFITHS, JAMES HENRY AMBROSE (1903–64), bishop. Born in Brooklyn, New York, on July 16, he was educated at St. John's College there (B.A. 1923, M.A. 1929) and the Almo Collegio Crapranica, the Gregorian (J.C.B. 1925, S.T.D. 1927), and the Pontifical School of Archives (Dipl. 1926), all in Rome, and was ordained in Rome in 1927. He was a curate at St. Joseph's Church, Babylon, New York, in 1927–28, Our Lady of Mercy Church in 1928–29 and St. Augustine's Church in 1929–31, in Brooklyn, taught at Dominican Normal School, Amityville, New York, in 1927–29, and was vice-chancellor of the Brooklyn diocese in 1935–43. He was made a papal chamberlain in 1938, was one of the founders of the Canon Law Society of America and its president in 1941–42, served as chancellor of the Military Ordinariate in 1943–55, and was appointed titular bishop of Gaza and auxiliary of New York in 1949. He left the Military Ordinariate in 1955 to become pastor of St. Monica's Church, New York City, and occupied that position until his death there on Feb. 24. In 1959 he was appointed official observer of the Holy See at the United Nations and also represented the Vatican at technical and refugees conferences there.

GRIMES, JOHN (1852–1922), bishop. Born in Brooklawn, Limerick, Ireland, on Dec. 18, he was educated at the Jesuit college there, St. Hyacinthe College, and the Grand Seminary, Montreal, and was ordained in Albany in 1882. He engaged in pastoral work in Syracuse and became pastor of St.

Mary's Church there and was made a domestic prelate in 1904. He was consecrated titular bishop of Hemeria and coadjutor of Syracuse in 1909, succeeded to the see in 1912, and remained in that position until his death, in Syracuse on July 26.

GRIMMELSMAN, HENRY JOSEPH (1890–1972), bishop. Born in Cincinnati, Ohio, on Dec. 22, he was educated at St. Joseph's College, Rensselaer, Indiana, the University of Innsbruck, Austria, and Mt. St. Mary's Seminary of the West, Cincinnati, and was ordained in 1915. He was professor of Sacred Scripture and vice-rector of Mt. St. Mary's until 1932, when he was appointed rector of the Pontifical College Josephinium, Columbus, Ohio. He was made a domestic prelate in 1933 and was consecrated first bishop of the newly erected diocese of Evansville, Indiana, in 1944. He greatly increased the number of priests, churches, and schools in the diocese, expanded hospital facilities, and erected a new chancery building in 1957 and Sarto Retreat House in 1961. He retired and was named titular bishop of Tabla in 1965. He died on June 26 in Evansville. He was the author of exegetical works on Exodus (1927) and Ruth (1931).

GRONBERGER, SVEN MAGNUS (1866–1916), anthropologist. Born in Söderköping, Sweden, on Aug. 19, he emigrated to the United States and secured a higher education while working in a drugstore in New York City. He was converted to Catholicism by the Dominican Sisters of St. Catherine's Hospital while ill there when he was about thirty. He secured a position on the library staff of the Smithsonian Institution, in Washington, D.C., and wrote several scientific monographs, among them *The Frogs of the District of Columbia, The Palearctic Birds of Greenland,* and *The Origin of the Goths.* He died in Washington, D.C., on Apr. 24.

GROSS, WILLIAM HICKLEY (1837–98), bishop. Born in Baltimore, Maryland, on June 12, he was educated at St. Charles College there, worked in his father's hardware store for a time, and joined the Redemptorists in 1857. He studied for the priesthood at the Redemptorist seminary in Annapolis, Maryland, and was ordained in 1863, served as chaplain in a nearby prison for war prisoners, preached missions in 1863–71, and became first rector of the Redemptorist mission church in Roxbury, Massachusetts, in 1871. Two years later he was appointed bishop of Savannah, Georgia. He built a new cathedral, established a college/seminary in Macon, Georgia, and was active at the third Plenary Council of Baltimore, in 1884, particularly concerned with the black apostolate, in which he was deeply involved. He was a supporter of Cardinal Gibbons and the progressive group of the American hierarchy, and in 1885 he was transferred to Oregon City (changed to the diocese of Portland, in Oregon, in 1928) as its archbishop—the first native American prelate in the Far West. His see included Oregon, Washington, Idaho, Montana, Alaska, and British Columbia, and during his thirteen-year tenure he was particularly concerned with Indian missions, brought new religious orders into the see, founded the Sisters of St. Mary of Oregon, and ministered to the orphans of the area. He died in Baltimore on Nov. 14.

GROSVENOR, JOHN. *See* Altham, John.

GRUDEN, JOHN CAPISTRAN (1884–1962), theologian. Son of a farmer, he was born in Idria, West Slovenia, on Oct. 21, was attracted to the religious life, and emigrated to the United States in 1901. He studied for the priesthood at the St. Paul (Minnesota) Seminary, was ordained in 1907, served as assistant at St. Agnes Church, St. Paul, and then did postgraduate work at Catholic University (S.T.L. 1910). He taught at St. Paul Seminary for twenty-seven years, becoming an authority on the spiritual and mystical life of the Church and the social contexts of the sacraments, and in 1937 became pastor of St. Agnes, remaining in that position until he retired, in 1955. He was a pioneer in the liturgical revival and wrote *The Mystical Christ* (1937), which had a widespread impact; he died in Orlando, Florida, on Oct. 28.

GRUENTHANER, MICHAEL (1887–1962), biblical scholar. Son of German immigrant parents, he was born in Buffalo, New York, on Oct. 1, joined the Jesuits in 1905, studied at St. Louis University (M.S.C. 1913), taught natural sciences at Marquette in 1913–16 and at the University of Detroit in 1916–17, and was ordained in 1920. He continued his studies at the Pontifical Biblical Institute, Rome, and in 1926 received his doctorate in Sacred Scripture—the first American to receive this degree from the Pontifical Biblical Institute. He taught scripture at St. Mary's Seminary, Mundelein, Illinois, in 1925–26, 1928, at Weston (Massachusetts) College in 1928–31, and at St. Marys (Kansas) College from 1931, and was chancellor of the Graduate School of Sacred Theology for laywomen at St. Mary's College, South Bend, Indiana, in 1946–55. He was one of the pioneers in the Catholic biblical movement in the United States and one of the founders of the Catholic Biblical Association of America, was editor of the *Catholic Biblical Quarterly* in 1941–51, contributing many articles to it, and was an authority on the Book

of Daniel. He died at St. Mary's (South Bend) on Sept. 14.

GRUENTHER, ALFRED MAXIMILIAN (1899–1983), general. Son of Christian M. Gruenther, a newspaper editor, and Mary Shea Gruenther, he was born in Platte Center, Nebraska, on May 23. In his youth he thought of becoming a priest or a doctor, but when he was fifteen he decided on a military career, entered West Point, and graduated fourth in his class in 1918. He was assigned to Fort Knox in 1920, where he took up bridge and directed tournaments; in time he became an internationally known bridge-tournament director and refereed many notable bridge matches. He married Grace E. Crum in 1922, taught mathematics at West Point, advanced in rank to captain only in 1935 because of slow promotions in the peacetime Army, and in 1937 attended the Command and General Staff School and in 1939 the Army War College. When the United States entered World War II, he was made deputy chief of staff of the Third Army, under Brigadier General Dwight D. Eisenhower, went to London with Eisenhower, and was chief American planner of the Allied invasion of North Africa. He also served as chief of staff under General Mark Clark, planned the invasion of Italy, and then became deputy commanding general of U.S. forces in Austria, advancing to brigadier general in 1942 and major general in 1943. After the war he was deputy commander of the National War College in 1946–47, then army chief of staff for plans and operations and in 1951, at fifty-three, became the youngest four-star general in army history when he became chief of staff at North Atlantic Treaty Organization (NATO) headquarters. He was then appointed commander of Supreme Headquarters Allied Powers, Europe (SHAPE) at Marly-le-Roi, near Paris, and in 1953–56 was Supreme Commander of NATO—one of the most powerful generals in the world. He retired from the Army in 1956 and served as president of the American Red Cross in 1957–64, modernizing and streamlining its operation. After he left the Red Cross he was chairman of the English-Speaking Union of the United States in 1966–68 and was director of half a dozen major organizations and corporations, including Pan Am, New York Life Insurance Company, Federated Department Stores, Inc., and the American Heritage Foundation. He was the recipient of the Laetare Medal in 1956, received honorary degrees from some thirty-eight universities, and was awarded the Distinguished Service Medal with two oak-leaf clusters from the United States and was honored by a score of other nations. He died in Walter Reed Hospital, in Washington, D.C., on May 30.

GUÉRIN, MOTHER THEODORE (1798–1856), foundress. Born in Étables, Brittany, France, on Oct. 2, she was christened Anne Thérèse, was educated at a private school, and took care of her invalid mother until 1823, when she joined the Congregation of the Sisters of Providence at Ruillé-sur-Loire. She was superior of a school at Rennes in 1825–33 and in Soulaines until 1840, when she and five companions went to the United States in response to an appeal from Bishop de la Hailandière to found a house in Vincennes, Indiana. She at once opened an academy for girls —the first in Indiana—and founded the motherhouse of the Sisters of St. Mary-of-the-Woods, Indiana, and ten schools during her superiorship. She died at St. Mary-of-the-Woods on May 14; the cause for her beatification has been presented to Rome.

GUERTIN, GEORGE ALBERT (1869–1931), bishop. Born in Nashua, New Hampshire, on Feb. 7, he was educated at St. Charles College, Sherbrooke, Quebec, and at St. Hyacinthe College, Quebec, and St. John's Seminary, Brighton, Massachusetts, and was ordained in Manchester, New Hampshire, in 1892. He served in several New Hampshire parishes until 1900, when he was named pastor of St. Anthony's Church, Manchester. He was consecrated bishop of Manchester in 1907, and during his episcopate inaugurated a widespread school expansion program and was obliged to contend with friction from the French-Canadian populace and clergy over some of his policies, which they opposed as being inimical to their national interests, and to a lesser extent from the Poles of the diocese. He died in Morristown, New Jersey, on Aug. 6.

GUILDAY, PETER (1884–1947), historian. Born in Chester, Pennsylvania, on Mar. 25, he was educated at St. Charles Borromeo Seminary, Philadelphia, and Louvain, Belgium, and was ordained in Louvain in 1909. He spent five years researching Church history in archives in France, Belgium, Spain, and Italy, continued his studies at the universities of Bonn and London while an assistant at St. Mary's Church, London, and in 1914 received his doctorate in historical sciences from Louvain. He began teaching history at Catholic University the same year and continued there until his death. He founded the *Catholic Historical Review* in 1915 and served as its editor until 1941, when ill health caused his retirement, and was secretary of the National Catholic War Council during World War I. He founded the American Catholic Historical Association in 1919 and served as its president;

he became the leading American Catholic Church historian of his times. He helped revive interest in American Catholic history with programs leading to master's and doctor's degrees at Catholic University and during his three decades at Catholic University assembled an important collection of transcripts and photostats of Catholic history documents of the United States of the eighteenth to twentieth centuries which he gathered from American and European sources. He was given honorary degrees by eight universities, was made a domestic prelate in 1935, and was honored by the Belgian Government in 1962 for his work in the restoration of Louvain's library, which had been destroyed in World War I. Among his many books were the two-volume *Life and Times of John Carroll* (1922), *Life of John Gilmary Shea* (1926), *An Introduction to Church History* (1925), the two-volume *Life and Times of John England* (1927), *History of the Councils of Baltimore, 1791–1884* (1932), and *Catholic Philosophy of History* (1936); he was also editor of *National Pastorals of the American Hierarchy, 1792–1919* (1923). He died in Washington, D.C., on July 31 after a long illness.

GUILFOYLE, MERLIN JOSEPH (1908–81), bishop. Born in San Francisco on July 15, he was educated at St. Joseph's minor seminary in Mountain View and St. Patrick's Seminary, Menlo Park, California, in 1927–33; he was ordained in San Francisco in 1933. He continued his studies at Catholic University (J.C.D. 1937), was made a domestic prelate in 1949, and was appointed titular bishop of Bulla and auxiliary of San Francisco in 1950. He was pastor of Mission Dolores in 1950–69, was cofounder of the St. Thomas More Society, a lawyers guild, wrote a book on San Francisco and another on California, and had a column in the San Francisco *Monitor* for twenty years. He was appointed bishop of Stockton in 1969, retired in 1979, and died in Stockton on Nov. 20.

GUILFOYLE, RICHARD THOMAS (1892–1957), bishop. Born in Adrian (De Lancey), Pennsylvania, on Dec. 22, he was educated at St. Bonaventure College, Buffalo, New York, and was ordained in Buffalo in 1917. He served as a curate at St. Stephen's Church, Oil City, Pennsylvania, in 1917–21, was named secretary to Bishop John Gannon of Erie, Pennsylvania, in 1921 and was pastor of St. Peter's Cathedral there; he was chancellor of the Erie diocese in 1923–36 and was made a papal chamberlain in 1924. He was appointed bishop of Altoona, Pennsylvania, in 1936; he remained in that position until his death, on June 10.

GUINEY, LOUISE IMOGEN (1861–1920), poet. Daughter of General Patrick Guiney and Janet Margaret Doyle Guiney, she was born in Roxbury, Boston, Massachusetts, on Jan. 7 and was educated at Notre Dame Academy there, at the Academy of the Sacred Heart, Providence, Rhode Island, and by private tutors. She early evinced an interest in writing, had her first poems published in the Boston *Pilot*, obtained a Post Office appointment in Auburndale, in Boston, in 1894–97 despite strong religious opposition to an Irish-Catholic postmistress, worked in the public library in Boston, and wrote for newspapers and magazines including *Scribner's* and *Atlantic Monthly*. She left the United States and settled in England in 1901, after her mother's death, and lived the rest of her life in Oxford. She had numerous books of poetry published, among them *Songs at the Start* (1884), *The White Sail* (1887), and *A Roadside Harp* (1893); essays, *A Little English Gallery* (1894) and *Patrins*

(1897); short stories, *Lovers' St. Ruth* (1896); biographies, *Hurrell Froude* (1904), *Robert Emmet* (1904), and *Blessed Edmund Campion* (1908); she edited collections of the works of Matthew Arnold, James Clarence Mangan, and Henry Vaughan. The first volume of *Recusant Poets,* 1535–1735, a study of such poets in England, was published posthumously in 1938. She was dubbed "the laureate of the lost" for her research on neglected authors and was largely responsible for the revival of interest in such authors as Henry Vaughan and William Hazlitt. She died in Chipping Campden, England, on Nov. 2. Many of her letters and first editions of her works are housed in a collection at Albertus Magnus College, in New Haven, Connecticut.

GUINEY, PATRICK ROBERT (1835–77), general. Born in Parkstown, Tipperary, Ireland, on Jan. 19, perhaps in 1836, he was taken to the United States by his parents, who settled in Portland, Maine, when he was six. He studied at Holy Cross College (but only for a year and never graduated), studied law under Judge Walton in Lewiston, Maine, and was admitted to the Maine bar in 1856. He married Janet Margaret Doyle in 1859 and moved to Boston to set up his law practice; the couple had two children, one of whom was Louise Imogen Guiney, the poet. At the outbreak of the Civil War, he joined the 9th Massachusetts Regiment as a private, and by the end of the war had risen to the rank of brigadier general. He took part in thirty battles, was decorated for bravery, and was seriously wounded and partially blinded at the battle of the Wilderness. On his return from the war, despite the illness he suffered the rest of his life because of his war injuries, he ran unsuccessfully for Congress, was an assistant district attorney for Suffolk County in 1865–69, was one of the

founders of the Catholic Union of Boston, and was active in civic organizations in Boston, where he died on Mar. 21.

GUMMERMANN, JOHN (1876–1960), educator. Born in Kirmsees, Bavaria, on July 27, he became a Capuchin in 1895, taking the name Basil, and was ordained in 1902. He served in parishes in Wisconsin, Minnesota, Michigan, and Brooklyn and Yonkers, in New York, taught at St. Lawrence Seminary, Mt. Calvary, Wisconsin, and for the last twenty-four years of his life was professor of theology at St. Anthony's Friary, Marathon, Wisconsin; he was also director and later commissary provincial of the Third Order of St. Francis. He died in Wausau, Wisconsin, on Feb. 13.

GUNN, JOHN EDWARD (1863–1924), bishop. Born in Fivemiletown, Tyrone, Ireland, he was educated at St. Mary's, Ireland, the Marist college in Paignton, England, the Catholic University of Ireland, Dublin, and the Gregorian, Rome. He was professed in the Society of Mary in 1884, was ordained in Rome in 1890, and was sent to the United States. He taught at the Marist House of Studies, Washington, D.C., in 1892–98 and served as pastor in Savannah, Georgia, from 1898 to 1911, when he was preconized bishop of Natchez-Jackson, Mississippi. He was known for his oratory and administrative abilities; he established nine new parishes in the diocese and died in New Orleans on Feb. 19.

GURIAN, WALDEMAR (1902–54), author. Born in St. Petersburg (Leningrad), Russia, on Feb. 13, he was brought to Germany by his mother when he was a child and was baptized a Catholic when she was converted to Catholicism from Judaism. He was educated at the Dominican Collegium Albertinum and the universities of Bonn, Munich, Breslau, and Cologne, where he received his Ph.D. in 1923 and decided on journalism as a career. He was an editor of the *Kölnische Volkszeitung* in Cologne in 1923–24, went to Switzerland as a refugee from the Nazi regime in Germany, and edited *Die Deutsche Briefe* in 1934–37, when he went to the United States. He became an associate professor of political science at Notre Dame in 1937, founded and was editor of *Review of Politics* in 1929, and wrote a series of books on *Bolshevism* (1932), *The Future of Bolshevism* (1936), *Hitler and the Christians* (1937), *The Rise and Decline of Marxism* (1938), and on Maurras, French Catholicism, and French socialism. He died in South Bend, Indiana, on May 26.

H

HAAS, FRANCIS JOSEPH (1889–1953), bishop. Born in Racine, Wisconsin, on Mar. 18, he was educated at St. Francis Seminary, Milwaukee, and was ordained in Racine in 1913. He was a curate at Holy Rosary Church, Milwaukee, in 1913–15, taught literature at St. Francis in 1915–19, and then continued his studies at John Hopkins University and Catholic University (Ph.D. 1922). He was a professor of sociology and dean of the college department at St. Francis, then professor of sociology at Marquette University, Milwaukee, and edited *Salesianum* in 1922–31 and lectured at the Milwaukee School of Social Research in 1925–31. He was president of the Catholic Association for International Peace in 1929–31, and from 1931 to 1935 he was director of the National School of Social Service and taught economics at Catholic University. He was appointed a member of the Labor Advisory Board of the NRA and the National Labor Board in 1933, was labor representative on the General Code Authority, and was federal mediator in the Minneapolis truck drivers' strike in 1934. He was dean of St. Francis college department in 1935–37, served on the Labor Policies Board of the Works Progress Administration (WPA) in 1935–39, and was on the federal Department of Labor's Conciliation Board from 1935 until his death. He was chairman of the board set up to mediate the cigar makers' strike in Tampa, Florida, in 1935, was a member of the Wisconsin Labor Relations Board in 1937–39, was made a domestic prelate in 1937, was appointed to the National Resources Planning Board in 1940, and the following year went to Puerto Rico as chairman of a board to study wage problems there. In 1937 he was named dean of the newly established School of Social Science at Catholic University, serving until 1943, and became chairman of the Council Against Intolerance and the American Association for Labor Legislation. He served on many committees and councils, founded the Catholic Council on Industrial Problems, and was again professor of sociology and dean of the college department of St. Francis in 1943. In that year he was consecrated bishop of Grand Rapids, Michigan, and remained in that position until his death, in Grand Rapids on Aug. 29. During his career he wrote many pamphlets for the governmental agencies in which he served and *Shop Collective Bargaining* (1922) and *Man and Society* (1930).

HAFEY, WILLIAM JOSEPH (1888–1954), bishop. Born in Springfield, Massachusetts, on Mar. 14, he was educated at Holy Cross College, Worcester (B.A. 1909), studied law at Georgetown Law School in 1909–10 and theology at Mt. St. Mary's College, Emmitsburg, Maryland (M.A. 1914), and was ordained in Baltimore in 1914. He served as a curate at St. Joseph's Church, Baltimore, in 1914–20, was chancellor of the archdiocese of Baltimore in 1920–25, and was appointed first bishop of the newly created diocese of Raleigh, North Carolina, in 1925. He was transferred to

Scranton, Pennsylvania, as coadjutor and apostolic administrator in 1937 and succeeded to the see in 1938. He held the see's first diocesan synod, in 1949, directed a successful fund-raising campaign, and saw King's College founded by the Holy Ghost Fathers in 1946 at his request. He died in Scranton on May 12.

HAGERTY, JAMES EDWARD (1869–1946), sociologist. Born in Rolling Prairie, Indiana, on Aug. 1, he was educated at Indiana University (B.A. 1892), did graduate work in sociology and economics at the Universities of Chicago (1896–97), Wisconsin (1897–98), Berlin and Halle, Germany (1898–99), and Pennsylvania (Ph.D. 1900). In 1901 he became assistant professor at Ohio State University, where he introduced the first marketing course at an American university, in 1905, was then professor of the economics and sociology department, and in 1922 was named chairman of the new sociology department. He was dean of the university's College of Commerce and Journalism, which he organized, in 1916–27, and director of its School of Social Administration in 1927–32. He was a recognized authority on industrial relations and penology, was federal Food Administrator for Ohio in 1918 during World War I, and was president of the Catholic Conference on Industrial Problems in 1928–37. He wrote on crime, finances, and social problems; among his books were *Mercantile Credit* (1913) and *Twentieth Century Crime—18th Century Methods of Control* (1934). He died in Columbus, Ohio, on Nov. 10.

HAGSPIEL, BRUNO M. (1885–1961), editor. Born in Schoenwiese, West Prussia, on Mar. 14, he was educated in West Prussia, Upper Silesia, and Austria, joined the Society of the Divine Word in Silesia in 1897, and was or-

dained in Vienna in 1910. He went to the United States the same year and taught at St. Mary's Seminary, Lisle, Illinois, and became a citizen in 1919. He founded the *Little Missionary* in 1914 and edited it for ten years, and *Our Missions* in 1921 and edited it for six years, wrote the five-volume *Along the Mission Trails* (1925), and became rector of St. Mary's in 1925. He was elected provincial superior of the Society of the Divine Word in the United States in 1928, was mission procurator in 1934, and served as rector of St. Francis Seminary, Duxbury, Massachusetts, in 1942–48. The last ten years of his life were spent as retreat master at the Divine Word Seminary, Girard, Pennsylvania; he died in nearby Erie on Feb. 14.

HAGUE, FRANK (1876–1956), politician, mayor. Born in Jersey City, New Jersey, on Jan. 17, he left elementary school in the sixth grade to become a machinist, but soon became active in politics. He became a constable in the Hudson County sheriff's office when he was twenty-one, then a member of Jersey City's street and water board; he was elected to the Jersey City Board of Commissioners in 1913 and in the next four years built up a political machine in Jersey City that in time made him the most powerful political figure in New Jersey and a power in national affairs. He was elected mayor in 1917 and reelected each election until his resignation, in 1947. He was elected to the Democratic National Committee in 1922, went to the Democratic National Convention in 1932 as a supporter of Alfred E. Smith for the presidency but soon switched to Franklin D. Roosevelt and supported Roosevelt during his presidential years. He was defeated in the courts in his attempts to prevent the Congress of Industrial Organizations (CIO) from organizing workers in Jersey City, supported Charles Edison for governor in 1940, but after Edison was elected they became bitter enemies and Hague defeated Edison's attempt to have a new state constitution ratified. His nephew, Frank Hague Eggers, succeeded him as mayor when he resigned, but when Eggers was defeated, in 1949, Hague attempted a comeback; that was unsuccessful, and he was deposed from control of the New Jersey Democratic Party; in 1952 he was ousted from the Democratic National Committee by the state Democratic organization. Hague was one of the last of the powerful political bosses who controlled many of the major American cities in the first half of the twentieth century and became notorious for his boast: in Jersey City "I am the law." He died in New York City on Jan. 1.

HAID, LEO MICHAEL (1849–1924), bishop. Son of German immigrants, he was born near Latrobe, Pennsylvania, on July 15, was educated at the scholasticate of St. Vincent's Abbey, Beatty, Pennsylvania, and joined the Benedictines in 1869. He was ordained in Beatty in 1872 and taught at St. Vincent's until 1885, when he was elected first abbot of the recently founded Maryhelp (Belmont) Abbey, Garibaldi, North Carolina (later changed to Belmont). In 1887 he was appointed vicar apostolic of North Carolina and was consecrated titular bishop of Messene the following year—the first abbot-bishop in the United States. He was president of the American Cassinese Congregation in 1890–1902, was appointed abbot ordinary when Belmont Abbey was made an abbot nullius by Pope Pius X, in 1910, and founded institutes and priories at Bristow, Virginia (1893), Savannah, Georgia (1902), and Richmond, Virginia (1911). He helped develop St. Mary's College (changed to Belmont Abbey College in 1913), and was named

an Assistant to the Pontifical Throne in 1914; he died at the abbey on July 24.

HAILANDIÈRE, CÉLESTIN RENÉ LAURENT GUYNEMER DE LA (1798–1882), bishop. Born at Friandin, Brittany, France, on May 2, he was educated at the seminary in Rennes and was ordained in Paris in 1825. He volunteered for the American missions and was sent to the United States in 1836, worked in the Vincennes, Indiana, diocese under Bishop Bruté and became vicar-general. He was in France begging for financial aid for the diocese when he was named titular bishop of Axierne and coadjutor of Vincennes, in 1839; he succeeded to the see at once as its second bishop when Bishop Bruté died, before Hailandière was consecrated. He brought the Eudists to the diocese to establish a theological seminary at Vincennes and Fr. Sorin and the Holy Cross Fathers to establish a college and a novitiate. In 1842 he gave them a tract of land, and the following year the first building of Notre Dame was erected. He also brought to his diocese the Sisters of Providence, under Mother Theodore Guérin, who founded St. Mary-of-the-Woods, and the Sisters Marianites of Holy Cross, who founded Notre Dame du Lac mission in 1843. He resigned in 1847 because of disagreement with his clergy and returned to France, where he died in Friandin on May 1.

HALDEMAN, SAMUEL STEHMAN (1812–80), scientist, philologist. Born in Locust Grove, Pennsylvania, on Aug. 12, he was educated at a classical school at Harrisburg and at Dickinson College, Carlisle, Pennsylvania, and then managed his father's sawmill, studying natural history in his spare time. He married Mary Hough in 1835 and the next year began experimenting with the use of anthracite in his brother's ore-smelting plants. He worked on a geological survey of New Jersey in 1836, lectured on zoology at the Franklin Institute, Philadelphia, in 1842–43, became a Catholic in 1846, and was a professor of natural history at the University of Pennsylvania in 1851–55 and of geology at Pennsylvania Agricultural College, and in 1853–58 was professor of natural sciences at Delaware College, Newark, Delaware. In 1868 he became the first professor of philology at the University of Pennsylvania and held this position until his death, at Chickies, Pennsylvania, on Sept. 10. He wrote *Freshwater Mollusca of the United States* (1842), books on insect sounds and on orthography, etymology, Indian languages, and variations within European vernaculars. He was deeply interested in language and spelling reform, became an expert on American Indian dialects, and intensively studied vocal sounds, writing on variations within European vernaculars. Among his books in this field were *Elements of Latin Pronunciation* (1851), *Analytic Orthography* (1860), *Outlines of Etymology* (1877), and *Word-Building* (1881).

HALLINAN, PAUL JOHN (1911–68), archbishop. Born in Painesville, Ohio, on Apr. 8, he was educated at Notre Dame (B.A. 1932) and St. Mary's Seminary, Cleveland, Ohio, in 1932–37; he was ordained in 1937. He was a curate at St. Aloysius Church, Cleveland, in 1937–42, served as a U.S. Army chaplain in the Far East in 1942–45, receiving a Purple Heart in 1944, and on his return was a curate at the cathedral in Cleveland, 1945–47. He was archdiocesan director of Newman Clubs in 1947–48, served as Catholic chaplain at Western Reserve University for eleven years, and was national chaplain of the Newman Clubs in 1952–54. He was appointed bishop of Charleston, South Carolina, in 1958 and became first arch-

bishop of Atlanta, Georgia, when that see was made an archdiocese, in 1962. He was a vigorous leader in efforts to end racial segregation and to promote integration and was in the forefront of the ecumenical movement and in implementing the liturgical changes of Vatican Council II. He died in Atlanta on Mar. 27.

HAMILTON, GEORGE ERNEST (1855–1946), educator. Born in Charles County, Maryland, on Mar. 5, he was educated at Georgetown (B.A. 1872, LL.B. 1874, M.A. 1882) and was admitted to the District of Columbia bar in 1874. He joined the law firm of Richard T. Merrick and Judge Martin F. Morris and in time became a partner. He represented the Baltimore and Ohio Railroad and other railroads, became professor of law at Georgetown in 1885 and was dean in 1900–3, and served as presidential trustee of the Corcoran Gallery. He died in Washington, D.C., on May 24.

HANNA, EDWARD JOSEPH (1860–1944), archbishop. Born in Rochester, New York, on July 21, he was educated at the Rochester Free Academy in 1875–79, the Propaganda in 1879, and the North American College, Rome, in 1879–85; he was ordained in Rome in 1885. He taught theology at the Propaganda in 1886–87, classics at St. Andrew's preparatory seminary in 1887–93, and theology at St. Bernard's Seminary, Rochester, New York, in 1893–1912 while continuing his studies at Cambridge in 1900–1 and the University of Munich in 1906. He was appointed titular bishop of Titiopolis and auxiliary of San Francisco in 1912, became third archbishop of that see in 1915, and was chairman of the administrative board of the National Catholic Welfare Conference in 1919–35. He received the American Hebrew Medal for his efforts to better relations between

Christians and Jews in 1932, was appointed chairman of the National Mediation Board to settle the longshoremen's strike in San Francisco in 1934, and during his tenure as archbishop established forty-four new parishes, forty-two elementary schools and high schools, and St. Joseph's College, in Mountain View, California. He resigned his see in 1935 and was appointed titular archbishop of Gortyna and went to Rome, where he died on July 10.

HANNAN, JEROME DANIEL (1896–1965), bishop. Born in Pittsburgh, Pennsylvania, on Nov. 29, he was educated at Duquesne University (B.A. 1916) and St. Vincent's Seminary, Beatty, Pennsylvania (D.D. 1920); he was ordained in 1921; he received his J.C.D. from Catholic University in 1934. He served at Holy Trinity Church, McKeesport, in 1921 and Holy Rosary Church, Pittsburgh, in 1921–23 and was appointed chaplain of Mt. Marcy Academy, Pittsburgh, in 1923. He was secretary to Bishop Hugh C. Boyle of Pittsburgh in 1923–31, assistant chancellor of that diocese in 1934–40, taught canon law at Catholic University in 1940–51, serving as vice-rector in 1951–54, and was appointed fifth bishop of Scranton, Pennsylvania, in 1954. He built a new building to centralize diocesan offices and St. Pius X diocesan seminary in Dalton, and was the author of several textbooks and canon-law books, among them *Religion Hour* (1925), *The Canon Law of Wills* (1934), and *Chancery Cases* (1941). He died in Rome on Dec. 15.

HANNEGAN, ROBERT EMMET (1903–49), Postmaster General. Born in St. Louis on June 30, he was educated at St. Louis University, graduating in 1925 with a law degree, was admitted to the bar, and became active in politics. He became a member of the Democratic City Committee in 1933, played a leading role in the reelection of Harry S Truman as United States senator in 1940, and was named collector of internal revenue for the eastern district of Missouri in 1942 and commissioner of internal revenue in 1943. He was elected chairman of the Democratic National Committee in 1944, helped secure Truman's nomination for Vice President at the 1944 Democratic Convention, and helped him win the Democratic nomination for the presidency in 1948 and then the presidency in the election that fall. Probably Truman's closest political adviser, he served as Postmaster General of the United States in 1945–47 but was forced to resign because of ill health. He was a joint owner of the St. Louis Cardinals baseball team in the 1940s; he died in St. Louis on Oct. 6.

HARAHAN, WILLIAM JOHNSON (1867–1937), railroad executive. Born in Nashville, Tennessee, on Dec. 22, he graduated from St. John's College, New Orleans, in 1885 and began his railroad career working on the Louisville and Nashville Railroad. He then worked on the Chesapeake and Ohio Railroad, became engineer in charge of structures on the Baltimore and Southwestern in 1890, and left to become roadmaster of the Pontiac division of the Illinois Central in 1892 and in time became general manager and vice president. He was assistant to the president of the Erie Railroad in 1907–10, became vice president in 1911, was president of the Sea Board Air Line in 1912–20, of the Chesapeake and Ohio in 1920–29, and also of the Hocking Valley Railroad in 1920–29. Ill health caused his retirement in 1929, but he resumed the presidency of the Chesapeake and Ohio in 1935 and was also president of the Nickel Plate and Père Marquette Railroad in 1935–37. He was active in Catholic affairs, was a trustee of the National Council of Catholic Men, and was honorary vice president of the Catholic Conference on Family Life. He died in Clifton Forge, Virginia, on Dec. 4.

HARDEE, WILLIAM JOSEPH (1817–73), general. Born on the Hardee estate in Camden County, Georgia, he graduated from the U.S. Military Academy in 1838 and served in the 2nd Dragoons in the war against the Florida Indians. In 1840, he was sent to St. Maur military school, in France, to study cavalry operations and was attached to the French cavalry. On his return to the United States he was assigned a post in Fort Jessup, Louisiana, and in 1844 was promoted to captain of dragoons. He served in the Mexican War with great distinction and was made major of the 2nd Cavalry in 1855 when he published *United States Rifle and Light Infantry Tactics,* which became an army textbook known as "Hardee's Tactics." He was made lieutenant colonel and appointed commandant of West Point in 1836, and when the Civil War broke out he opted for the Confederacy and was made a colonel in the Confederate Army. He organized the Arkansas brigade that became known as Hardee's Brigade, became a lieutenant general in 1862, and was put in charge of the military department of South Carolina, Georgia, and Florida in 1864. He was forced to evacuate Savannah and then Charleston by Sherman's army and had joined his army to the Army of Tennessee when the war ended. After the war he settled on his farm in Alabama; he died in Wytheville, Virginia, on Nov. 6.

HARDEY, MARY ALOYSIA (1809–86), superior. Of an old Maryland Catholic family, she was born at Piscataway, Maryland, on Dec. 8, was taught by Sacred Heart nuns in Grand Coteau, Louisiana, when her family moved to that state, in 1822, and in 1825 joined the Society of the Sacred Heart, taking the name Aloysia. She was professed in 1833, was appointed assistant superior of St. Michael's Convent in 1835 and superior the next year, and in 1841 she came to New York City with Mother Galitzen, at the invitation of Bishop John Dubois, to open the first Sacred Heart school there; in time it was to become Manhattanville College. She went to Rome in 1842 and then to Paris, where she was instructed by Mother Barat, foundress of the society, and in 1844 she became superior vicar of Sacred Heart houses in the eastern United States and Canada, and from 1847 to 1872 worked from the new center called Manhattanville. She spent these years traveling all over the United States and Canada, opening some thirty convents and twenty-five schools. She was appointed assistant general in 1871, necessitating her moving to the motherhouse, in Paris, made return visits to the United States as visitrex, was a member of the general council of the society, and died in Paris on June 17.

HARKINS, MATTHEW (1845–1921), bishop. Born in Boston on Nov. 17, he was educated at Holy Cross College, Worcester, Massachusetts, the University of Douai, France, and St. Sulpice, Paris, and was ordained in 1869. He engaged in parish work in Arlington and Boston, and in 1887 was appointed second bishop of Providence, Rhode Island. He was particularly concerned with providing for the spiritual needs of large French-Canadian and Italian groups in his diocese, providing national churches for them, devoted much time to works of charity, building a hospital, an asylum for infants, and a home for working girls, brought many religious orders into the see, and invited the Dominicans to found a college in the diocese in 1915, which opened in 1919 as Providence College. He died in Providence on May 25.

HARLAND, HENRY (1861–1905), novelist. Son of Thomas Harland, a Connecticut lawyer; he was born in St. Petersburg (Leningrad), Russia, on Mar. 1 and was educated at the College of the City of New York and at Harvard, where he studied for a year. He began to work in the Surrogate's Court of New York and in the next few years wrote a trilogy on Jewish life, *As It Was Written* (1885), *Mrs. Peixada* (1886), and *The Yoke of the Thorah* (1886), and seven other novels under the pen name Sidney Luska. In 1887 he went to Paris and then to London, where he and his wife wrote a drama, *The Light Sovereign* (1889); he wrote short stories for various magazines and edited with Aubrey Beardsley the quarterly *Yellow Book* in 1894–97, when his ill health caused publication to cease. He became a convert to Catholicism in 1897 and then published his most popular novels, all on themes of Catholic interest: *The Cardinal's Snuff Box* (1898), *The Lady Paramount* (1902), and *My Friend Prospero* (1904). He died in San Remo, Italy, on Dec. 20 and was buried in Norwich, Connecticut.

HARNEY, JOHN MILTON (1789–1825). Son of a Revolutionary War officer and brother of General William Harney, he was born in Delaware on Mar. 9, studied medicine, and settled in Kentucky. He spent some time traveling in Europe, accepted an appointment in the Navy, and lived in South America for several years. On his return to the United States he edited a newspaper, became a Catholic, and after the death of his wife joined the Dominicans and served as a missionary in Kentucky. He had a number of poems of merit published in several periodicals and may well be called the first American Catholic poet of any consequence. He died at Somerset, Kentucky, on Jan. 15.

HARNEY, WILLIAM SELBY (1800–89), general. Son of a merchant who had been an officer in the American Revolution, he was born near Haysboro, Tennessee, on Aug. 27. He studied at an academy there, was appointed to the U.S. Army as a second lieutenant in 1818, served in the Black Hawk and Florida Seminole Indian wars, was made a lieutenant colonel of the Dragoons in 1836, and served in the Mexican-American War under General Winfield Scott. After the war, he was stationed in the Platte country during the Sioux uprisings of 1855 and defeated them in the battle of Sand Hill, on the Platte River. During this time he met and became a friend of Fr. Pierre De Smet, who helped him restore peace. In 1858 he became a brigadier general commanding the Oregon Territory, and his seizure of San Juan Island, near Vancouver, Canada, precipitated a boundary dispute with Great Britain (he was an ardent expansionist) and led to his recall; he was placed in command of the Department of the West, headquartered in St. Louis, in 1861. When the Civil War broke out he was suspected of southern sympathies but was captured by Confederate forces while on the way to Washington, D.C.; he was released shortly after. On his retirement, in 1863, he was brevetted major general. He spent some time on his estate at Pass Christian, Mississippi, and St. Louis, and died in Orlando, Florida, on May 9.

HART, CHARLES ALOYSIUS (1893–1959), educator, philosopher. Born in Ottawa, Illinois, on Sept. 6, he was educated at St. Viator's College, Bourbonnais, Illinois (B.A. 1917, M.A. 1919) and St. Paul's (Minnesota) Seminary; he was ordained in Peoria, Illinois, in 1919. He continued his studies at Catholic University (S.T.A. 1920, J.C.B. 1920, Ph.D. 1930), became an instructor in philosophy there in 1921, and was on the faculty the rest of his life, also teaching at Notre Dame College, Baltimore, in 1933–54. He was active in the neo-scholastic movement and the revival of Thomism, contributed numerous papers to the American Catholic Philosophical Association, of which he was national secretary in 1930–59, and was made a domestic prelate in 1957. He wrote several books, among them *The Thomistic Concept of Mental Faculty* (1930), *Metaphysics for the Many* (1957), and *Thomistic Metaphysics* (1959); he died in Washington, D.C., on Jan. 29.

HART, LUKE EDWARD (1880–1964), Supreme Knight. Born in Maloy, Iowa, on July 31, he was educated at Drake University and the University of St. Louis, where he received his LL.B. in 1905, the year he married Catherine O'Connor. He began practicing law in St. Louis, was admitted to practice in federal courts and before the United States Supreme Court in 1913, and became active in the Knights of Columbus. An influential figure in the Knights since 1918, when he was elected to the board of directors, he became supreme director in 1918–22 and was supreme advocate from 1922 until 1953, when he became Supreme Knight, a position he held until his death, in New Haven, Connecticut, on Feb. 19. During his tenure, the Knights passed the one-million membership mark, sponsored a nationwide Catholic advertising program, contributed more than a million dollars toward the construction of the National Shrine of the Immaculate Conception, in Washington, D.C., and financed the microfilming of some forty thousand priceless documents in the Vatican Library and built a library at St. Louis University to house the films. He was a

member of the organization committee of the National Catholic War Council in 1917 and a member of the executive committee that formed the United Service Organizations (USO), was president and general manager of the Hamilton-Brown Shoe Company in 1934–38, and was elected president of the National Fraternal Congress in 1951. He was honored by Popes Pius XI and XII and by the French Government for a statue of Lafayette at Metz presented by a Knights of Columbus committee of which he was chairman.

HART, PHILIP ALOYSIUS (1912–76), United States senator. Son of a bank president, he was born in Bryn Mawr, Pennsylvania, on Dec. 10, was educated at Georgetown (B.A., 1934), studied law at the University of Michigan Law School (J.C.D., 1937), was admitted to the Michigan bar in 1938 and began practicing law with a Detroit law firm. He served as a second lieutenant in World War II in 1941–46 and was wounded and decorated. In 1943 he married Jane Cameron Briggs, daughter of industrialist Walter D. Briggs (who later became an anti–Vietnam War activist), and he returned to practice in Detroit in 1946. He became Michigan's corporations securities commissioner in 1949, was appointed federal director of the Michigan Office of Price Stabilization in 1951, and was named United States District Attorney for the Eastern District of Michigan in 1952. He became legal adviser to Governor G. Mennen Williams in 1953, was elected lieutenant governor of Michigan in 1954, and was reelected in 1956. Hart was elected to the United States Senate in 1958 and reelected in 1964 and 1970. In the Senate he supported antitrust, equal opportunity, civil rights, and consumer protection legislation and opposed the Vietnam War. He served as Michigan chairman of the American

Christian Palestine Committee to further Israel's development in 1951–58 and was often called "the conscience of the Senate." He died in Washington, D.C., on Dec. 26.

HARTLEY, JAMES JOSEPH (1858–1944), bishop. Born in Columbus, Ohio, on June 5, he was educated at Mt. St. Mary's Seminary of the West, Cincinnati, Ohio, and Holy Angels Seminary in Niagara, New York, and was ordained in Columbus, Ohio, in 1882. He was a curate at St. Peter's Church and organized the Holy Name parish, both in Steubenville, Ohio, and in 1903 was appointed fourth bishop of Columbus. He was one of the founders of the Catholic Press Association in 1911 and served as its honorary president until his death, helped found St. Charles's Seminary in 1923, was named an Assistant at the Pontifical Throne in 1929, and died of a heart attack in Columbus on Jan. 12.

HARTMAN, LOUIS FRANCIS (1901–70), biblical scholar. Born in New York City on Jan. 17, he was educated at St. Mary's College (North East, Pennsylvania), St. Mary's (Ilchester, Maryland), Mt. St. Alphonsus (Esopus, New York), and St. Mary's (Annapolis, Maryland). He was professed a Redemptorist in 1922. After his ordination in 1927, he studied Greek, Hebrew, and Syrian at Catholic University and continued his studies at the Pontifical Biblical Institute, Rome (S.S.L. 1931). He taught Old Testament at Esopus for two years and pursued further biblical studies at the Biblical Institute Faculty of the Ancient Near East, where he received his licentiate in Oriental Languages in 1936. Then he returned again to Esopus, where he taught Old and New Testament the next twelve years. He became general secretary of the Catholic Biblical Association in 1948

and moved to Washington, D.C., where he worked on the Confraternity translation of the bible (which became The New American Bible). He taught at Catholic University from 1950 until his death in Washington, D.C. on Apr. 22, became editor of Scripture, the ancient Near East, Judaism, and Islam for the New Catholic Encyclopedia in 1962 and contributed some sixty articles to it; he also edited the Encyclopedic Dictionary of the Bible (1963).

HARTY, JEREMIAH JAMES (1853–1927), archbishop. Of Irish immigrant parents, he was born in St. Louis on Nov. 7, studied at the University of St. Louis, entered St. Vincent's Seminary, Cape Girardeau, Missouri, in 1873, and was ordained in 1878. He engaged in parish work in St. Louis, founded St. Leo parish, and was temporary administrator of the see from 1902 to 1903, when he was appointed first American archbishop of Manila, Philippine Islands. He was faced with grave problems, among them his lack of knowledge of the language, misunderstandings with government officials, claims of the American Government to hospitals that had been operated by the Church and the Spanish authorities, the Aglipayan schism, antifriar sentiment among the populace, financial difficulties, and the seizure of Church properties by schismatics. He convoked the first provincial council of the Philippine Islands in 1907, reorganized seminaries, initiated law suits to recover Church property, rebuilt churches and schools, and fought the Alipayanism schism. He was forced to return to the United States in 1916 because of ill health, and he was named archbishop-bishop of Omaha, Nebraska. During his episcopate, he established thirteen parishes and nine parochial schools, organized Catholic Charities, the Society for the Propagation of the Faith and other societies in the diocese, and aided Fr. Flanagan of Boys Town. He was forced to leave the diocese in 1925 because of ill health and died in Los Angeles on Oct. 29.

HASSARD, JOHN ROSEGREENE (1836–88), journalist, author. Born in New York City on Sept. 4, he was raised an Episcopalian but became a Catholic in 1851, when he was fifteen. He studied at and graduated from St. John's College (Fordham) in 1855 and then entered the diocesan seminary to study for the priesthood but was forced to leave because of ill health. He was Archbishop John Hughes's secretary until Hughes's death in 1864, was literary editor of the New York *Tribune,* and in 1865 became the first editor of *Catholic World.* He joined the *Chicago Republican* as assistant editor at the behest of Charles A. Dana, and when that publication collapsed, Hassard returned to the *Tribune* in 1866 as music and literary editor; his music criticism was highly regarded, and he was one of the early and very active promoters of the Wagnerian school of music composition. He was also New York correspondent for the London *Daily News.* He married Isabella Hargeous in 1872, and the two traveled extensively in Europe. He was the author of several books, among them *The Wreath of Beauty* (1864), a biography of Archbishop Hughes (1866), *A Life of Pope Pius IX* (1877), and the *New York Tribune's History of the United States* (1887) and *History of the United States* (1878), used widely as a text in Catholic schools. He died in New York City on Apr. 18.

HAUGHERY, MARGARET GAFFNEY (c. 1813–82). Margaret Gaffney was born in Cavan, Ireland, was brought to Baltimore by her parents when she was a child in 1818, and was orphaned four years later. She was raised by a Welsh family who befriended her, married Charles Haughery in 1835, and they moved to New Orleans. When her husband and child died the following year, she began working in the orphan asylum in New Orleans and decided to devote her life to charitable enterprises, financing her activities from her dairy and bakery—the first steam bakery in the South, it soon became famous. An astute businesswoman, though she never learned to read or write, she amassed a large fortune and gave most of it to charity. She helped found the Female Orphan Society of the Sisters of Charity in 1840, clearing it of debt, ministered to the victims of the yellow fever epidemics that swept New Orleans in the 1850s and to the Confederate prisoners during the Civil War. She was extremely popular with the people of New Orleans, who erected a statue in her honor in 1894, one of the first public monuments to a woman in the United States. She died in New Orleans on Feb. 9, mourned by the entire city. She was often called "the orphan's friend" and "the mother of orphans," and on her death she bequeathed her estate to the orphan asylum she had helped to found.

HAVEY, FRANCIS PATRICK (1864–1945), educator. Born in County Meath, Ireland, on Mar. 4, he was brought as an infant to the United States by his mother; they settled in New Haven, Connecticut. He was educated at St. Charles College (Ellicott City, Maryland), St. Bonaventure College (Allegany, New York), St. John's Seminary (Boston), and received his D.D. from the Catholic Institute (Paris). He was ordained in 1889 and served as curate at the cathedral in Hartford, Connecticut, from 1889 until 1896, when he joined the Sulpicians. He resumed his studies at Issy-sur-Seine, France, for the next two years, and on his return to the

United States he became professor of Church history at Dunwoodie Seminary, New York, and taught there in 1898–1904. He was superior of the House of Philosophy at St. John's Seminary, Brighton, Boston, in 1905–11, after having been a professor of moral theology there in 1904–6, was rector in 1906–11, and was superior of St. Austin's College, Washington, D.C., in 1911–14. He was vice president of St. Charles College, Catonsville, Maryland, in 1912–13 and became professor of Church history and ascetic theology at St. Mary's Seminary, Baltimore, in 1914. He was superior of the Sulpician Seminary in 1919–25 and then continued teaching there as professor of moral theology. He was the author of several books, among them *Meditations on the Passion and Eastertide* (1928), *The Way of the Cross in the Seminary* (1935), and the three-volume *Holy Hour Meditations for Seminarians and Priests* (1951). He died in Baltimore on Mar. 13.

HAWKS, EDWARD (1878–1955), author. Born in Crickhowell, Glamorganshire, Wales, on Feb. 17, he was educated at private schools and at the University of London. When he was twenty-one, he went to Canada to prepare for the Anglican ministry. He studied at Bishop's College, Lennoxville, Canada, and then worked as a missionary in mining camps in northern Canada. He entered the Episcopal Seminary at Nashotah, Wisconsin, received his orders, and then taught Latin and Greek there. He became a member of the Anglican Companions of the Holy Saviour, but when the Episcopal Church permitted non-Episcopalians to preach in its pulpits in 1907, he resigned as teacher at Nashotah and the following year became a Catholic—as did William McGarvey, who had founded the Companions, and most of his congregation. In 1911 Hawks was ordained a priest of the Philadelphia archdiocese, served as a parish curate, and during World War I was a chaplain in the Canadian Army. He returned to Philadelphia in 1919, established St. Joan of Arc parish, and remained there until his death on Jan. 22. He wrote a popular column for the *Catholic Standard and Times,* the diocesan paper, for twenty-four years and wrote several books, among them *Pedigree of Protestantism* (1936), *Difficulties of Fr. Callaghan* (1939), and *How It Looks Now* (1939). He was made a domestic prelate in 1936, was in Spain in 1936–38 to report on the Spanish Civil War, and was decorated by Spain for his support of the Nationalist government.

HAWTHORNE, JULIAN (1846–1934), author. Son of Nathaniel Hawthorne, the famous American author, he was born in Boston on June 22, was educated at Lowell Scientific School of Harvard, and later studied civil engineering in Dresden, Germany. He worked in the New York City Docks Department as a hydrographic engineer in 1870–72 under General George McClellan and spent the next decade in Europe and England, where he served on the staff of the *Spectator* and devoted himself to writing. On his return to the United States, he continued his writing and was a book reviewer for New York and Philadelphia newspapers. In 1913 he was convicted of fraudulent use of the mails for publicity he wrote for a Canadian gold-mining company and spent a year in the Atlanta federal penitentiary; he wrote of his experiences there in *The Subterranean Brotherhood.* After his release from prison, he edited the book section of the Pasadena (California) *Star* and died in San Francisco on July 14.

HAWTHORNE, ROSE *See* Lathrop, Rose Hawthorne.

HAYDEN, JEROME E. (1902–77), psychiatrist. Born in Pittsburgh, Pennsylvania, on Dec. 2, he studied at the University of Pittsburgh and received his medical degree in 1927. He taught on the medical school faculty for a time and then went to Louvain, where he received his doctorate of philosophy in 1937. He practiced medicine in Pittsburgh on his return and in 1943 joined the Benedictines at St. Anselm's Monastery, Washington, D.C. He was ordained in 1947, continued his studies at Catholic University, the University of Montreal, and McGill University, Toronto. In 1949 he became a member of the department of psychiatry and psychology at Catholic University; he also became president of St. Gertrude's School for retarded girls in Washington the same year. In 1957, at the request of Cardinal Richard Cushing of Boston, he founded Marsalin Institute in Holliston, Massachusetts, dedicated to promoting mental health through the prevention, early detection, and treatment of emotional illness and to harmonizing Catholic doctrine with psychiatry; he devoted the rest of his life to the institute. He wrote numerous articles for learned journals, lectured widely on mental health and the priesthood, and died in Boston on July 18.

HAYDEN, MOTHER MARY BRIDGET (1814–90), educator. Margaret Hayden was born in Kilkenny, Ireland, on Aug. 26, was taken by her parents to Perrysville, Missouri, when she was six, and was educated by the Sisters of Loretto at the Foot of the Cross at Bethlehem and St. Vincent's Academy at Cape Girardeau. In 1830, when her father died, she left school to help out at home, joined the Sisters of Loretto in 1841, and received the habit later that year, taking the name Margaret Bridget. In 1847, with Mother Concordia Henning as superior and with two other Sisters of Loretto, she was sent to take charge of a new government school for Indians at Osage Mission (later St. Paul), Kansas, and succeeded Mother Concordia as superior in 1859. She left in 1863 to become superior of St. Vincent's Academy, Cape Girardeau, but returned in 1867 to find mainly white children at the mission school since the Osages had been moved to Indian Territory (now Oklahoma) by an 1865 treaty. She expanded the school into St. Ann's Academy and in time developed it into one of the outstanding institutions of learning in the Southwest. She died at Osage Mission on Jan. 23.

HAYES, CARLTON JOSEPH HUNTLEY (1882–1964), historian. The son of Dr. Philetus A. Hayes and Permelia Mary Hayes, Baptists, he was born on a farm near Afton, New York, on May 16, was educated at Columbia (B.A. 1904, M.A. 1905, Ph.D. 1909), and became a Catholic in 1904. He began teaching history at Columbia in 1907 and taught there, with the exception of several years during World Wars I and II, until 1950, when he was named professor emeritus on his retirement. He was a lecturer in 1907–10, assistant professor in 1910–15, associate professor in 1915–19, professor in 1919–34, and Seth Lowe Professor from 1935 until his retirement. He served in the United States Army Military Intelligence Division of the General Staff in World War I and was United States ambassador to Spain in 1942–45 during World War II. An opponent of totalitarianism in Germany, Italy, and Russia, he was criticized as being too friendly with the Franco regime in Spain, but everyone agreed he played an important role in keeping Franco neutral during the war and not interfering with the Anglo-American military invasion of North Africa. He was a specialist in the history of the North Atlantic community and an authority on nationalism, and wrote some twenty-seven books, among them *British Social Politics* (1913), the two-volume *Political and Social History of Modern Europe* (1916), which was a standard text in many colleges and universities for years, *Essays on Nationalism* (1926), *Historical Evolution of Modern Nationalism* (1931), *A Political and Cultural History of Modern Europe* (two volumes, 1932–36), *Modern Europe to 1870* (1953), *Christianity and Western Civilization* (1954), *Contemporary Europe Since 1870* (1958), and *Wartime Mission in Spain* (1945), based on his experiences as ambassador to Spain; his *Modern History* (1923)—a high school text written with Dr. Parker T. Moon was criticized for its Catholic orientation and for being too international in outlook. He was president of the American Catholic Historical Association in 1930 and of the American Historical Association in 1945, and was cofounder of the National Conference of Christians and Jews, serving as its Catholic cochairman in 1926–46. He received numerous honorary awards and degrees, among them the Laetare Medal in 1946, and died at his Jericho farm near his native Afton on Sept. 3.

HAYES, JAMES T. G. (1898–1980), bishop. Born in New York City on Feb. 11, he was educated at Woodstock College in Maryland (M.A. 1923) and at Tronchiennes, Belgium. In 1921 he was ordained as a Jesuit priest. He taught at Regis High School, New York City, in 1914–18, was professor of Greek, Latin, English, and mathematics at Boston College in 1918, was dean of discipline at Fordham in 1923–25, and was sent to the Philippines as a missionary in 1926. He was superior of the Jesuit Mindanao Mission in 1927–30 and of all Jesuits in the Philippines in 1930–33, and was appointed first Catholic bishop of Cagayan in 1933 and in 1951 its first archbishop. He retired in 1970 and died in Cagayan de Oro, Philippine Islands, on Mar. 28.

HAYES, PATRICK JOSEPH (1867–1938), cardinal. A son of Irish immigrants, he was born in New York City on Nov. 20 and was orphaned when six. He was educated at Manhattan College (B.A. 1888, M.A. 1894) and at St. Joseph's Seminary, Troy, New York, and was ordained in 1892. He continued his studies at Catholic University (S.T.L. 1894), was a curate at St. Gabriel's Church, New York City, in 1894, and was secretary to Bishop John M. Farley in 1895–1903. When Farley became archbishop of New York in 1902, he appointed Hayes as chancellor of the archdiocese in 1903 and delegated him to found Cathedral College, a preparatory seminary. He was its first president in 1903–14, was made a domestic prelate in 1907, and was appointed titular bishop of Tagaste and auxiliary of New York to Cardinal Farley in 1914. He was pastor of St. Stephen's Church, New York City, in 1915–17, was named first ordinary of the United States Armed Forces in 1917, a position he retained all his life, and after the death of Cardinal Farley in 1918, he was appointed fifth archbishop of New York in 1919. He was one of the founders of the National Catholic Welfare Conference in 1924, established Catholic Charities in the New York archdiocese (he was often called "the Cardinal of charities"), and was made a cardinal by Pope Pius XII in 1924. During his episcopacy, he founded some sixty new parishes in the archdiocese, was a supporter of the temperance movement, was president of the Catholic Near East Welfare Association, and was the personal representative of Pope Pius XI at the National Eucharistic Congress in Cleveland in 1935.

Ill from 1932, he died in New York City the night of Sept. 3–4.

HAYES, RALPH LEO (1884–1970), bishop. Born in Pittsburgh on Sept. 21, he was educated at Duquesne University there and the North American College, Rome (D.D. 1910), and was ordained in Rome in 1910. On his return to the United States, he served as superintendent of schools, censor librorum and secretary of the Confraternity of Christian Doctrine of the Pittsburgh diocese, and was pastor at St. Catherine of Siena Church in Pittsburgh. He was appointed fourth bishop of Helena, Montana, in 1933 and served in that position until 1935, when he was named rector of the North American College in Rome and titular bishop of Hierapolis. He was transferred to Davenport, Iowa, as its bishop in 1944, and during his episcopate he greatly increased the enrollment in diocesan schools, built new elementary and high schools to accommodate the increase, added substantially to the number of priests and religious in the see, and was made an Assistant at the Pontifical Throne in 1958. He retired in 1966 and was named titular bishop of Naraggia. He died in Davenport on July 4.

HEALY, GEORGE PETER ALEXANDER (1813–94), painter. The son of a sea captain, he was born in Boston on July 15, was early attracted to art as a career, and though he had no formal art training he began drawing at sixteen and painting at eighteen, when he set up a studio in Boston. He went to Paris to study in 1834, and in the decade and a half that he spent there and in London, he achieved a reputation as an outstanding portrait painter. He returned to the United States in 1855 and took up residence in Chicago. He went back to Europe ten years later, lived in Paris and Rome, and returned to Chicago in 1892,

dying there on June 14. He executed some seven hundred portraits, many of outstanding figures of his times, among them a series of the U.S. Presidents (Corcoran Gallery), Abraham Lincoln (Newberry Library, Chicago), Daniel Webster and Henry Wadsworth Longfellow (Boston Museum of Fine Arts), Chief Justice Taney (Capitol, Washington, D.C.), Louis Philippe, François Guizot, and a self-portrait (Uffizi, Florence), and Mrs. John C. Cruger and a self-portrait (Metropolitan Museum, New York). He also painted historical scenes such as *Webster Replying to Hayne* (Faneuil Hall, Boston), *Franklin Urging the Claims of the American Colonists Before Louis XVI,* for which he received a gold medal at the Paris Universal Exposition in 1855, and *The Peacemakers* (White House). He wrote his autobiography, *Reminiscences of a Portrait Painter* (1894), and was an honorary member of the National Academy of Design.

HEALY, JAMES AUGUSTINE (1830–1900), bishop. The son of Michael Morris Healy, an Irish immigrant plantation owner, and Elizabeth Smith, a black slave, he was born in Macon, Georgia, on Apr. 6 and was sent to the North by his father in 1837 to be educated and to get out of the slavery states of the South. He studied at Holy Cross College, Worcester, Massachusetts, and graduated in its first class in 1849; then he studied for the priesthood at Grand Seminary, Montreal, and St. Sulpice, Paris. He was ordained in Paris in 1854 and on his return to the United States became secretary to Bishop John Fitzpatrick of Boston. He was appointed chancellor of the Boston diocese in 1855 and vicar-general in 1857, became founding pastor of St. James Church, Boston, in 1866, and in 1875 was appointed second bishop of Portland, Maine. During his twenty-five-year episcopate, he was a strong supporter of Catholic education, labored to help the French-Canadians in the see, and increased the number of parishes (sixty), missions (sixty-eight), schools (eighteen), convents, hospitals, and orphanages in the diocese. He was made an Assistant at the Pontifical Throne in 1900 and died soon after in Portland on Aug. 5.

HEALY, PATRICK JOSEPH (1871–1937), Church historian. Born in Waterford, Ireland, on July 26, he was educated at Mt. Melleray College, Cappoquin, Ireland, emigrated to the United States, and studied for the priesthood at St. Joseph's Seminary, Dunwoodie, Yonkers, New York. In 1897 he was ordained. He engaged in postgraduate studies in Church history at Catholic University (CB.Th. 1898, L.Th. 1899, S.T.D. 1903) and at Bonn and Heidelberg universities, Germany; then he returned to New York, where he was an assistant at Holy Innocents' parish for a short time. He then returned to Catholic University, was named Patrick Quinn Professor of Church history in 1910, and served as dean of the faculty of theology several times. He edited the *Catholic University Bulletin* in 1911–14, wrote articles for various historical magazines, and was the author of *The Valerian Persecution* (1905). He died in Washington, D.C., on May 18.

HECKER, ISAAC THOMAS (1819–88), founder. Born in New York City on Dec. 18, he began working in the family bakery business when he was eleven, became a Transcendentalist, and was a member of the Brook Farm community in 1842–43. Then he became a member of the Fruitlands community and was a friend of Thoreau, Emerson, Bronson Alcott, and Orestes Brownson. Hecker became a Catholic in 1844, joined the Redemptorists the following year, and

studied for the priesthood at the Redemptorist St. Trond College in Belgium. He was ordained in London in 1849, spent a year there as a parish priest, and then returned to the United States in 1851 to become a member of a Redemptorist mission band with four other American converted Redemptorists: Augustine Francis Hewit, Clarence A. Walworth, George Deshon, and Francis Asbury Baker. They gave missions all over the United States that were spectacularly successful, and though many of them were with immigrants over the next six years, Hecker became convinced of the need of a special ministry to native American non-Catholics. He decided to try to establish an American English-speaking Redemptorist house to work among native Americans, and in 1857, with the encouragement of Archbishop John Hughes of New York, he went to Rome to seek permission of his Redemptorist superiors to establish such a foundation; three days after his arrival, through a misunderstanding, he was expelled from the Redemptorists by the general for having made the trip without the necessary permission. He appealed to Pope Pius IX, and the Pope dispensed him from his Redemptorist vows and gave him and his four mission-band companions permission to found a new congregation devoted to converting non-Catholic Americans to Catholicism. On his return to the United States in 1858, with three of his four Redemptorist companions—Baker, Hewit, and Deshon—founded the Congregation of the Missionary Priests of St. Paul the Apostle (the Paulists); Walworth, the other member of the group, had withdrawn in a dispute over the form of the vows, among other matters. Hecker was elected superior and spent the next thirty years building up the congregation and founding communications media to disseminate the aims of the Paulists. He founded *The Catholic World* in 1865 and edited it until his death. The next year he established the Catholic Publication Society (which in time was to become the Paulist Press) to distribute inexpensive Catholic books and pamphlets on a national scale. *The Young Catholic,* a magazine for juveniles, was founded by Hecker in 1870 and became the leading exponent of the apostolate of the printed word in the United States. He attended Vatican Council I in 1869–70 as Archbishop Martin Spalding's theologian, and the following year he suffered the first of a series of nervous breakdowns that plagued him the rest of his life, leaving him practically an invalid the last five years of his life; he died in New York City on Dec. 22. He was the author of three books: *Questions of the Soul* (1855), *Aspirations of Nature* (1857), and *The Church and the Age* (1887). Ironically, a French translation of Fr. Walter Elliott's *The Life of Father Hecker* with a preface by Abbé Felix Klein, published in Paris in 1898, ten years after Hecker's death, provoked an uproar and caused the controversy which led to the condemnation of the Americanism heresy (often called the phantom heresy) by Pope Leo XIII in *Testem benevolentiae* in 1899, though neither Fr. Hecker nor indeed any American priest was ever accused of holding the ideas condemned in that encyclical.

HEELAND, EDMOND (1868–1948), bishop. Born in Elton, Limerick, Ireland, on Feb. 5, he was educated at All Hallows College, Dublin, and was ordained in Dublin in 1890. He went to the United States the same year, was curate at St. Raphael's Cathedral, Dubuque, Iowa, in 1890–93 and pastor in 1893–97, became an American citizen in 1895, and served as pastor of Sacred Heart Church, Fort Dodge, Iowa, in

1897. He was named titular bishop of Gerasa and auxiliary of Sioux City, Iowa, in 1919, was rector of the cathedral in 1919–20, and was appointed bishop of Sioux City in 1920. During his episcopate he held three synods, incorporated the various agencies of the diocese, and helped establish the College of Our Lady of Grace in Sioux City, when he donated a seventy-acre tract of land to the Sisters of the Third Order of St. Francis of the Holy Family. He died in Sioux City on Sept. 20.

HEENEY, CORNELIUS (1754–1848), merchant, philanthropist. Born in Dublin, he learned merchandising there and in 1784 emigrated to the United States. He went to work for a fur dealer in New York, and when he retired, he and John Jacob Astor, a fellow employee, became partners in the business; after a few years Heeney left to go on his own and in time became wealthy. When Heeney was elected to the New York State Assembly in 1818, he was one of the first Catholics to hold public office in New York; he was also reelected for four more terms. He retired from business in 1837 to a farm he purchased in Columbia Heights, Brooklyn, and died there on May 3. He was noted for his charitable works and willed that his sizable fortune be put into an estate and incorporated as the Brooklyn Benevolent Society and be devoted to aiding the poor and orphans. Among his more notable philanthropies were his contributions to St. Peter's Church, which he helped to reorganize in 1785 (he served as trustee and treasurer), his encouragement of Mother Elizabeth Seton to establish the Sisters of Charity, and his aid in securing the site of St. Patrick's Cathedral in New York City.

HEFFRON, PATRICK RICHARD (1860–1927), bishop. Born in New York City on June 1, he took business courses at St. John's, Collegeville, Minnesota, and in 1878 entered the Grand Seminary, Montreal, to study for the priesthood. He continued his studies at the Sapienza and the Apollinaris, Rome, and was ordained at Montreal in 1884. He was named pastor of the St. Paul, Minnesota cathedral in 1889, served as rector of the St. Paul Seminary from 1897 until 1910, when he was named second bishop of Winona, Minnesota. In 1913 he founded St. Mary's College in Winona and the diocesan paper, *The Winona Courier.* He died in Winona on May 23.

HEISS, MICHAEL (1818–90), archbishop. Born in Pfahldorf, Bavaria, on Apr. 12, he was educated at the Georgianum, Munich, and intended to study law, but he changed his mind and studied for the priesthood at the Eichstätt Seminary. He was ordained in 1840. He engaged in pastoral work in and about Raitenbuch until 1842, when he emigrated to the United States at the invitation of Bishop John Purcell of Cincinnati and was affiliated with the diocese of Louisville, Kentucky. In 1844 he became secretary to Bishop John Henni of the newly established diocese of Milwaukee, Wisconsin, later was pastor of St. Mary's Church there, and served as the first rector of St. Francis Seminary (the Salesianum) in 1856–68. He was a highly regarded theologian (he wrote *De Matrimonio* and *The Four Gospels)* and played an active role in preparing the agenda for the second Plenary Council of Baltimore in 1866. He was appointed first bishop of the newly created diocese of La Crosse, Wisconsin in 1868, attended Vatican Council I in Rome in 1869–70, and strongly favored the definition of papal infallibility and was appointed titular archbishop of Hadrianople and coadjutor of the archdiocese of Milwaukee in 1880 at the request of Bishop Henni; he succeeded to the see

the following year. His accession aroused new nationalistic conflicts in the American church, sparked by John Shea's article in the *American Catholic Quarterly* in 1883 decrying the lack of American-born bishops in the western United States. The matter was further exacerbated in 1886, when Archbishop Heiss sent Fr. Peter Abbelen to Rome to present the case for the Germans in the United States (a move vigorously protested by Bishops John Ireland and Keane), and in an 1887 interview for the Milwaukee *Sentinel* Heiss stressed the necessity of continued use of the German language by German immigrants and the need for more German bishops—all further infuriating the Americanists led by Bishop Ireland. Heiss was a strong supporter of Catholic schools but opposed the establishment of the Catholic University. He died in La Crosse on Mar. 26.

HEITFELD, HENRY (1859–1938), United States senator. Born in St. Louis on Jan. 12, he was brought by his parents to Seneca, Kansas, when he was eleven, and in 1882 he went to Washington. He moved to Idaho the following year and engaged in farming and stock raising at Lewiston, married Anna M. Jacobs in 1884, and became involved in politics as a Populist. He was elected to the Idaho Senate in 1894, was reelected in 1896, and in 1897 was elected to the United States Senate as a Populist. In the Senate he supported measures for national irrigation projects, for the exclusion of Chinese immigrants, and for the construction of a canal across Central America, favoring the Nicaraguan route. He retired from the Senate in 1903, remained active in state politics, and received the Democratic nomination for governor in 1904 but was defeated in the election. He was mayor of Lewiston in 1905–9, register of the United States Land Office at Lewiston in 1914–22, and on the board of county commissioners in 1930–36, serving two terms as chairman. He retired to Spokane, Washington, in 1938 and died there on Oct. 21.

HENDERSON, ISAAC AUSTIN (1850–1909), author. Born in Brooklyn, New York, he was educated at private schools and Williams College, where he received his B.A., M.A., and a doctorate in civil law. He joined the staff of the *Saturday Evening Post,* of which his father was a partner; in 1872 he became assistant publisher in 1875 and two years later was named publisher. He sold the interest he held in the *Post* in 1881 and went to Europe, lived in London and in Rome, and began writing novels and dramas. Among his books were the novels *The Prelate* (1886) and *Agatha Page* (1888), dramatized as *Agatha* (produced at the Boston Museum in 1892) and also dramatized as *The Silent Battle* (produced in London in 1892); a second drama, *The Mummy and the Humming Bird,* was produced in 1902. He became a Catholic in 1896, devoted much of his time to helping poor boys in the Trastevere section of Rome, was made a papal chamberlain by Pope Pius X in 1903, and died in Rome in March.

HENDRICK, THOMAS AUGUSTINE (1849–1909), bishop. Born in Penn Yan, New York, on Oct. 29, he was educated at St. John's College (Fordham), Seton Hall College (South Orange, New Jersey), and St. Joseph's Seminary (Troy, New York), and was ordained in 1873. He engaged in parish work in the diocese of Rochester, New York, for the next thirty years, serving as president of the Rochester Society for the Prevention of Cruelty to Children and as a member of the New York State Board of Regents in 1900–4. A friend of Theodore Roosevelt, he was appointed the first American bishop of Cebu, Phil-

ippine Islands, in 1903, after the United States had taken possession of the Islands following the Spanish-American War. He spent his episcopate restoring order to his diocese and rebuilding the many churches that had been destroyed in battles between American troops and the native *insurrectos* during the war. He reopened some fifty elementary schools, appointed pastors to vacant parishes, brought priests from abroad into the see, and joined his fellow prelates in fighting the Aglipayan schism and securing the return of Church property seized by the Aglipayans. He died in Cebu on Nov. 29.

HENDRICKSEN, THOMAS FRANCIS (1827–86), bishop. Born in Kilkenny, Ireland, on May 5, he was educated at St. Kieran's there, at Maynooth and All Hallows, Dublin, and was ordained at All Hallows by Bishop Bernard O'Reilly of Hartford, Connecticut, who persuaded him to emigrate to his American diocese. On his arrival in the United States, Hendricksen served as pastor in Waterbury, Connecticut, and in 1872 was consecrated first bishop of the newly erected diocese of Providence, Rhode Island. He began building a new cathedral (completed in 1886), established the diocesan paper, the *Weekly Visitor* (now the *Providence Visitor),* in 1875, brought Jesuits, Ursulines, and Little Sisters of the Poor into the see, and grappled with the nationalistic problems created by the great influx of French Canadians into the diocese. He died in Providence on June 11.

HENNACY, AMON (1893–1970). Born in Negley, Ohio, on July 24, he became a Socialist when he was seventeen and left college in his junior year. He served two years in prison for refusing to register for the draft during World War I, met Selma Nelms, and they had two children and settled in

Waukesha, Wisconsin. The family moved to Milwaukee in 1931, after he was fired from his dairy job for organizing a strike. There he met Peter Maurin and Dorothy Day and became associated with the Catholic Worker movement. He joined the Workers in 1950, became a Catholic in 1952, engaged in radical antiwar activities, and wrote numerous autobiographical articles for the *Catholic Worker.* He left the paper in 1961, moved to Salt Lake City, Utah, and announced he had left the Church. He died in Salt Lake City on Jan. 14 in the midst of a fast while picketing, and though he was annointed just before his death, it is not known if he was reconciled to the Church.

HENNEPIN, LOUIS (1640–1701?), explorer. Born in Ath, Hainault, Belgium, little is known of his childhood and youth until he joined the Recollects (a branch of the Franciscans) when he probably took the name Louis (he had been baptized Johannes). He studied for the priesthood at the Recollect monastery at Béthune, Artois (Pas-de-Calais), France, and was ordained. He spent some time visiting churches and Recollect convents as he begged and preached in Italy and Germany, and he spent a year as a preacher in the Recollect convent at Halles, Hainaut. While serving as a mendicant in Calais, he became intrigued with seafarers' tales of journeys to far lands, but instead of going as a missionary to these far lands he went to Holland, where he preached and ministered to the wounded soldiers of the war raging between the French and the Spaniards, who then controlled the Netherlands. In 1675 he was ordered to Canada as a missionary and on the way met Robert de la Salle on the ship. He spent the next four years as chaplain at the hospital in Quebec and was then sent, at the request of La Salle, to be chaplain at

Fort Frontenac (Kingston, Ontario), a La Salle seigniory on Lake Ontario, and spent the next two and a half years there. In 1678 he set out as chaplain of La Salle's expedition to the Illinois country and spent the winter at Fort Niagara on the Niagara River near Lake Erie. In 1679 the expedition set out on the *Griffon,* the first ship on the Great Lakes; La Salle crossed to the Mississippi by way of Illinois and in 1680 sent Louis Hennepin with the expedition led by Michael Aco which first explored the upper Mississippi. They ascended the river to Minnesota, where two months after their departure, on Apr. 12, 1681, they were captured by a party of Issati Sioux Indians. While a captive, Hennepin first saw and named the Falls of St. Anthony, where Minneapolis was later founded. Five months later they were freed through the intercession of Daniel Duluth, who was also on an exploring expedition. Hennepin joined Duluth on his expedition, returned to Quebec, and in 1682 returned to Europe, where he spent the next year at his order's monastery at St. Germain-en-Laye writing *Description de la Louisiane* (1683), telling of his travels and describing the customs and life of the Indians he had encountered. Though he falsely claimed he was the leader of the expedition that explored the upper Mississippi, his work is one of the most important descriptions of seventeenth-century American exploration, describing for the first time such places as the upper Mississippi and Niagara Falls. A disagreement with his superiors caused him to leave France about 1690, and he established himself at Utrecht, the Netherlands, where he published *Nouveau Voyage* in 1696 and *Nouvelle Découverte d'un très grand Pays . . .* in 1697 (published in England together as *New Discovery of a Vast Country in America* in 1698), in which he claimed to have explored the Mississippi to its upper reaches and down to the Gulf of Mexico and back—obviously impossible, since there just would not have been enough time for him to have made the trip in the two months that elapsed from the time he set out and his capture by the Sioux in Minnesota. He was refused permission to return to Canada and fell out of favor with King Louis XIV, who ordered the governor of Canada to arrest him and return him to France if he put in an appearance in Canada. As a result he dedicated his books to King William III of England, who gave him a grant of money. He is known to have been in Rome in 1701, but he then disappears from the historical record; probably he died in Rome soon thereafter. His writings are all sources of valuable information about the country and its inhabitants, despite the fact that they are marred by his penchant for exaggeration and his unscrupulous use of other writers' material.

HENNESSY, JOHN (1825–1900), archbishop. Born in Bulgaden, Limerick, Ireland, on Aug. 20, he was educated at All Hallows College, Dublin, and emigrated to the United States when he was twenty-two. He completed his studies for the priesthood at the seminary in Carondelet, Missouri, was ordained in St. Louis in 1850, and spent the next few years in pastoral work. He returned to Carondelet in 1854 to teach, was president of the seminary in 1857, acted as the representative in Rome of Archbishop Peter Kenrick of St. Louis in 1858–59, and on his return became pastor of St. Joseph, Missouri. He was appointed third bishop of Dubuque, Iowa, in 1866, and during his three and a half decades as bishop and archbishop (he became Dubuque's first archbishop when the see was elevated to an archdiocese in 1893), he founded St. Joseph's College and Seminary in 1873, brought new priests, especially from Ireland and Germany, into the diocese, was a fervent supporter of the Catholic parochial school system, and brought in numerous teaching sisters to staff his schools. He attended the third Plenary Council of Baltimore in 1884 and there favored the establishment of a Catholic university in the United States, founded the Sisters of the Holy Ghost in 1890, and established 118 new parishes to care for the spiritual needs of the flood of Catholic immigrants brought to Iowa by the railroads that were being built. He died in Dubuque on Mar. 4.

HENNESSY, JOHN JOSEPH (1847–1920), bishop. Born near Cloyne, Cork, Ireland, on July 19, he was brought to the United States by his parents when he was a child and was educated at the Christian Brothers College in St. Louis, St. Francis Seminary in Milwaukee, Wisconsin, and St. Vincent's in Missouri. He was ordained when he was twenty-two by special permission because of his youth, engaged in missionary work in Missouri, and was procurator of the St. Louis Protectory in 1878–86. He edited *Youth's Magazine* in 1880–86, was rector of St. Joseph's parish, and in 1888 was appointed second bishop of Wichita, Kansas, to succeed its first bishop-elect, James O'Reilly, who had died before he was consecrated. He was apostolic administrator of the diocese of Concordia, Kansas, in 1891–98 and served as bishop of Wichita until his death there on July 13.

HENNI, JOHN MARTIN (1805–81), archbishop. Born in Misanenga, Grisons, Switzerland, on June 13, he studied at St. Gall, Lucerne, and the Propaganda, Rome, and emigrated to the United States in 1828 to complete his studies for the priesthood at the seminary in Bardstown, Kentucky. He was ordained in Cincinnati, Ohio, in 1892, taught at the Athenaeum in Cincinnati (now known as St. Xavier University), for a time, and then took a census of the Germans in the area and ministered to them so successfully that he was called "the apostle of the Germans." He was named vicar-general of the Cincinnati diocese in 1834, was second pastor of the first German parish, Holy Trinity, erected in Cincinnati in 1834, and in 1837 founded the first German Catholic newspaper published in the United States, *Der Wahrheitsfreund.* He edited the paper for the next six years. He inaugurated a system of bilingual schools in Cincinnati, wrote a catechism in German, organized English classes for German adults, and planned a bilingual seminary to train a native clergy. He was appointed first bishop of the newly established diocese of Milwaukee, Wisconsin, in 1893, brought numerous religious orders into the see, and was a firm believer in the need for a strong Catholic press, establishing *Der Seebote* in 1852 and *Die Columbia* in 1872 and encouraging other newspapers. He was a leader in the struggle against anti-Catholic groups, was a firm adherent of the American principles of equality and tolerance, was a fervent believer in agriculture as the basic industry for the nation, though he was opposed to settlement by colonization as too prone to lead to speculation and favored homesteading and government land sale. He promoted education at all levels, building the German parochial schools in his see to a level of excellence commended by the second Provincial Council of Cincinnati in 1858. He encouraged the founding of Marquette and St. Francis de Sales Seminary in 1856, when he also dedicated St. John the Evangelist Cathedral. He convened synods in 1847 and 1853 and developed Milwaukee into the leading "German diocese" in the country; his selection of Bavarian-born Michael Heiss as his coadjutor in 1880 set off a storm of protests from the Americanists led by Archbishop John Ireland. He attended Vatican Council I in 1869–70, where he opposed the inclusion of papal infallibility on the conciliar agenda but voted for its definition. In 1875 he became an archbishop when Milwaukee was elevated to an archdiocese. He died in Milwaukee on Sept. 7.

HENRICHS, LEO (1867–1908). Born in Östrich, Germany, on Aug. 15, he was baptized Joseph and raised in Cologne, emigrated to the United States, joined the Franciscans at Paterson, New Jersey, in 1886, and took the name Leo. He engaged in pastoral work in Franciscan churches the next sixteen years after his 1891 ordination in Newark, New Jersey, and in 1907 he was appointed pastor of St. Elizabeth Church in Denver, Colorado. On Feb. 23, while distributing communion in his church, he was shot to death by Joseph Alia, an anarchist.

HENRY, HUGH THOMAS (1862–1946), author. Born in Philadelphia on Nov. 27, he was educated at La Salle College, the University of Pennsylvania, and St. Charles Borromeo Seminary, all in Philadelphia, and was ordained in 1889. He taught English and Latin at St. Charles Borromeo in 1889–94 and church music and literature in 1889–1917. He directed the choir and was also the principal of Philadelphia Catholic High School in 1902–19. He was twice president of the American Catholic Historical Society of Philadelphia and its corresponding secretary in 1910–13, became professor of homiletics at Catholic University in 1919, serving until 1937, and died in Jessup, Pennsylvania, on Mar. 12. He was an authority on church music and hymnals, wrote poetry, edited *Church Music* in 1905–12, wrote an annual section of the *Records of the American*

Catholic Historical Society, and was the author of *Eucharistica* (1912), *Hints to Preachers* (1924), *The Lord's Prayer* (1935), *Christmas Customs and Symbols* (1925), and *Preaching* (1941).

HERBERMANN, CHARLES GEORGE (1840–1916), editor, writer, educator. Born in Saerbeck, Westphalia, Germany, on Dec. 8, he was brought to the United States by his parents in 1851. They settled in New York City, and he was educated at St. Francis Xavier College there and taught at that college in 1858–69. He received his M.A. from St. John's College (Fordham) in 1860 and his Ph.D. from St. Francis Xavier in 1865, and began to teach Latin and literature at the College of the City of New York in 1869, a teaching career at the City College that was to last until his retirement in 1915. He was appointed librarian of the college in 1873, helped found the Catholic Club of New York, and with John Gilmary Shea founded the United States Catholic Historical Society. He reorganized the society after Shea's death and was its president in 1898–1916, was editor of nine volumes of its *Historical Records and Studies,* and wrote articles for its publications. He was editor in chief of The Catholic Encyclopedia in 1905–16, was honored by several universities and the papacy, received the Laetare Medal in 1913, and was made professor emeritus at City College in 1915. He was the author of *Business Life in Ancient Rome* (1880) and *The Sulpicians in the United States* (1916) and published *Letters of Charles Carroll of Carrollton.* He died in New York City on Aug. 24.

HERZFELD, KARL F. (1892–1978), physicist. Born in Vienna on Feb. 24, he was educated at the Universities of Göttingen, Zürich, and Vienna (Ph.D. 1914), and served in the Austrian Army during World War I (1914–18) as a second lieutenant. He was on the faculty of the University of Zürich in 1920–26, emigrated to the United States, was a professor of physics at Johns Hopkins in 1926–36, and married Regina Flannery in 1938. He was professor of physics at Catholic University from 1936 until 1968, when he was made professor emeritus, serving as head of the physics department in 1936–61. He did research on the electronic structure of molecules, ultrasonics, thermodynamics, and the kinetic theory of gases, and was honored with the United States Navy's Meritorious Public Service Award in 1964 (he had done research for the Navy as a civilian in 1941–44), and was also honored by numerous colleges and universities. He died in Washington, D.C. on June 3.

HESLIN, THOMAS (1847–1911), bishop. Born in Longford County, Ireland, on Apr. 17 (or Dec. 21), he emigrated to the United States after he had completed his classical studies at the invitation of Archbishop John Odin of New Orleans. He studied for the priesthood at St. Vincent de Paul Seminary, New Orleans, was ordained in 1869 at Mobile, Alabama, and engaged in parish work in the New Orleans archdiocese. He was serving as pastor of St. Michael's Church there when he was appointed fifth bishop of Natchez-Jackson, Mississippi (changed to the diocese of Jackson in 1977) in 1889, and he remained in that position until his death in Natchez on Feb. 22.

HESS, BEDE FREDERICK (1885–1953), minister-general. Born in Rome, New York, on Nov. 16, he was educated at St. Francis College, Trenton, New Jersey, and joined the Order of Friars Minor Conventual in 1900. He was professed the next year, continued his studies at the University of Innsbruck, Austria (S.T.D. 1908), and was ordained there in 1908. He taught Latin at St. Francis College and scholastic philosophy at St. Anthony-on-Hudson, Rensselaer, New York, in 1909–14. He was director of the Immaculate Conception Province Mission Band in 1918–32, while also serving as pastor of St. Catherine of Siena Church, Seaside Park, New Jersey, and of Sacred Heart Church, Bay Head, New Jersey, in 1918–32. He edited the Franciscan magazine, *The Minorite* (later *The Companion),* in 1924–32, was provincial director of the Minorite Tertiary Province of the Immaculate Conception Province in 1925–32, was chairman of the National Executive Board of the Third Order of St. Francis in the United States in 1925–32, and was minister-provincial of the Immaculate Conception province in 1932–36. He was elected minister-general of the Friars Minor Conventuals in 1936—the first native-born American to be accorded this honor—and was reelected in 1948. During his generalate, the study and liturgy of the Order were reorganized and the activities of the Order were expanded, particularly in the field of mission work. He helped preserve Assisi when the Nazis occupied Italy during World War II. He wrote several treatises on the Third Order and on the constitutions of his Order, and died in Assisi on Aug. 8.

HESS, VICTOR FRANCIS (1883–1964), physicist. Born in Schloss Waldstein, Styria, Austria, on June 24, he studied at the Universities of Vienna, Innsbruck, and Graz (Ph.D. 1906). He lectured at the Veterinary Academy, Vienna, in 1908–20 and served in the Austrian Army in World War I as chief of the X-ray department of Reserve Hospital No. 15 in Vienna. He lectured in physics at the University of Vienna in 1910–20, becoming first assistant to the director of the Vienna Radium Institute and associate professor in 1911. He was assistant professor at the University of Vienna in 1919 and associate professor at the University of Graz in 1920. He was chief physicist at the New York Radium Corporation in New York City and Orange, New Jersey, in 1921–23, consultant physicist of the U.S. Bureau of Mines in 1922 and professor of experimental physics at the University of Graz in 1923–31 and at the University of Innsbruck in 1931–37. He was head of the physics department at the University of Graz in 1937–38. In 1938 he fled from Austria two months before the *Anschluss* and came to the United States to head the physics department at Fordham University, where he taught until he retired and was named professor emeritus in 1956; he had become a United States citizen in 1944. He received numerous awards for his work in physics: the Lieben Prize of the Academy of Science, Vienna, 1919; the Ernst Abbe Prize, Carl Zeiss Stiftung, Jena, 1932, and others. In 1936 he shared with Carl D. Anderson the Nobel Prize for physics for his work with cosmic rays; he had discovered them in balloon ascents in 1911–12, when his instruments revealed that the radiation which ionizes the atmosphere is of cosmic origin. He was the author of numerous scientific works, among them *Atmospheric Electricity* (1928), *Ionization Balance of the Atmosphere* (1933), and *Cosmic Radiation and Its Biological Effects* (1949) with Jakob Eugster. He died in Mount Vernon, New York, on Dec. 17.

HESSION, MARTIN J. (1892–1936), educator. Born in Waltham, Massachusetts, on Jan. 28, he joined the Christian Brothers, taking the name Cornelius Malachy, in 1905 and taught in schools in New York and New Jersey until 1922. He was director of studies at Pocantico Hills, New York, from 1922 until 1927, when he became president of Manhattan College. During his presidency he broadened the curriculum and increased the faculty and the number of students attending the college. He was minister-provincial of the New York province of the Christian Brothers in 1932–35 and died in New York City on Apr. 29.

HESTORN, EDWARD (1907–73), archbishop. Born in Ravenna, Ohio, on Sept. 9, he was educated at Notre Dame in 1921–28 and at the Gregorian, Rome (Ph.D. 1931), and was ordained in Rome in 1934. He was professor of philosophy at Moreau Seminary at Notre Dame in 1936–38, received his S.T.D. in 1937 and his J.C.D. in 1941 from Catholic University. He served as assistant procurator-general of the Congregation of Holy Cross and assistant superior of Holy Cross International College, Rome, in 1938–40. In 1940, when World War II broke out, he returned to the United States, was assistant secretary to the apostolic delegate in Washington, D.C. in 1942–47, was elected acting procurator-general in 1947 and procurator-general of the Congregation of Holy Cross in 1950 and was superior of Holy Cross International College, Rome, in 1947–62. He served on the Congregations of Sacraments and of Religious, and was a member of the Preparatory Commission on Religious Experiences for Vatican Council II. He was English-language Press Officer at Vatican Council II, was secretary of the Sacred Congregation for Religious and Secular Institutes in 1969, and was appointed president of the Pontifical Commission on Social Communications in 1971. He received the title of titular archbishop of Numidia in 1972. He died in Denver, Colorado, on May 2. He was the author of *The Priest of the Fathers* (1945) and *The Holy See at Work,* and he translated the two-volume *Circular Letters of Father Moreau* (1943–45) and *Basil Moreau* (1955).

HEUSER, HERMAN JOSEPH (1852–1933), editor, author. Born in Potsdam, Germany, on Oct. 28, he was educated at Berlin and Breslau, emigrated to the United States in 1870, and continued his studies for the priesthood at St. Charles Borromeo Seminary, Overbrook, Philadelphia. He was ordained in 1876 and began teaching at St. Charles and spent the rest of his life there. He served for a time as assistant editor of the *American Catholic Quarterly Review,* founded the *American Ecclesiastical Review* in 1899, was its editor in 1899–1914 and 1919–27, and built it into one of the most influential clerical journals in the United States. He was the founder and director of the Dolphin Press, published *The Dolphin* in 1900–8, wrote the constitutions of the Sisters of Mercy of Mercion, Pennsylvania, and of Mother Drexel's Sisters of the Blessed Sacrament. He was appointed apostolic delegate for all Catholic publications in the United States in 1907 during the Modernism controversy. He authored some fifteen books, among them *Canon Sheile of Doneraile* (1917), *Autobiography of an Old Breviary* (1925), *From Tarsus to Rome* (1927), and *House of Martha in Bethany* (1927). He died at St. Charles Borromeo Seminary on Aug. 22.

HEWIT, AUGUSTINE FRANCIS (1820–97). Descended from a distinguished New England family and the son of the Rev. Nathaniel Hewitt, a prominent Congregational minister, and Rebecca Hillhouse Hewitt, daughter of United States Senator James Hillhouse, Hewit (he dropped the second *t* from the family name) was born in Fairfield, Connecticut, on Nov. 27. He was educated at Phillips Academy, Andover, and Amherst College, Amherst, Massachusetts, and graduated from Amherst in 1839. Beginning in 1840, he studied theology at the Congregational seminary at East Windsor, Connecticut, and was licensed to preach in 1842, but soon thereafter he became an Episcopalian and an ardent follower of the Oxford movement. He was ordained a deacon in 1843, but in 1846, impressed by the conversion of John Henry Newman to Catholicism in England the previous year, he became a Catholic. He decided to become a priest, studied privately under Dr. Patrick N. Lynch and Dr. James A. Corcoran, and was ordained by Bishop Ignatius Reynolds of Charleston, South Carolina, the following year. Hewit taught at Bishop England's college for a time, worked on an edition of England's works, joined the Congregation of the Most Holy Redeemer (the Redemptorists) in 1849, and worked on missions with Frs. Isaac Thomas Hecker, Clarence Walworth, Francis A. Baker, and George Deshon. When Fr. Hecker was dispensed from his Redemptorist vows in 1858, they joined together and founded the Institute of St. Paul the Apostle (the Paulists) in New York later that year. Hewit drafted the community's first constitutions, helped establish (in 1865) and became managing editor (in 1866) of the *Catholic World,* wrote profusely, and became one of the foremost Catholic apologists in the United States. He was unanimously chosen in 1889 to succeed Fr. Hecker as superior after Hecker died in 1888 and held this position for the rest of his life. He was a firm supporter of the Catholic University, established the Paulist St. Thomas College at the university in 1889 and a Paulist foundation at San Francisco in 1894, and was the author of several books, among them *Life and Sermons of Francis Asbury Baker* and *Problems of the Age;* he also edited *Highways of Life.* He died in New York City on July 3.

HICKEY, JOSEPH ALOYSIUS (1883–1955), prior-general. Born in Chicago on May 30, he was orphaned when a child and raised by Fr. Maurice Dorney, pastor of St. Gabriel's Church, Chicago. He was educated at Villanova College (University), Philadelphia (B.A. 1903), joined the Augustinians there, and was professed at Villanova in 1903 and sent to Rome to continue his studies at the Augustinian International College of St. Augustine and the Apollinaris, where he received his doctorate in canon law in 1908. He was ordained in Rome in 1906, and on his return to the United States he was stationed in Chicago for a short period. Then, in 1910, he was sent to Villanova, where he served as rector of postulants, regent of studies, provincial secretary, prior of Corr Hall Seminary, and in 1924–25 as president of the college. He was elected fourth assistant-general of the Augustinians in 1925 and held that position 1925–47, while also serving as rector of the International College and teaching law at Catholic University. He was named consultor of the Sacred Congregation of Sacraments in 1928. He was elected prior-general of the Augustinians in 1947—the first American to hold that position—and during his term in that office, 1947–53, he reorganized the order. He returned to the United States in 1953 and died at Villanova on July 9.

HICKEY, PATRICK (1846–89), editor, publisher. The son of a Shakespeare scholar who was an inspector of schools, he was born in Dublin on Feb. 14, was educated at St. Vincent's College, Castlenock, in 1857–61, Holy Cross College, Clontarf, for a year, and entered St. Patrick's College, Maynooth, in 1863. He tutored for a time, and then in 1866 he emigrated to the United States. He worked on *Scientific American* for a time, was a reporter on the New York *World* for six years, married Agnes Kavanagh in 1871, and in 1872 resigned from the *World* and

founded the *Catholic Review,* a weekly
publication. In 1877 he founded the *Illustrated Catholic American* and in 1887
a supplement to it, *The Catholic American,* a weekly, serving as editor and
publisher of all three publications until
his death in Brooklyn, New York, on
Feb. 21. He was twice honored by the
Vatican, by Fordham, and by Notre
Dame with its Laetare Medal in 1888.

HICKEY,   THOMAS   FRANCIS
(1861–1940), archbishop. Born in Rochester, New York, on Feb. 4, he was educated at St. Andrew's Seminary there,
St. John's (Fordham) College, in New
York City, and St. Joseph's Seminary, in
Troy, New York. He was ordained in
Rochester in 1884. He served as a curate at St. Francis de Sales Church, Geneva, and at Moravia, New York, and
was appointed chaplain of the state industrial school in 1895. He was named
rector of the Rochester cathedral in
1898 and vicar-general of that diocese in
1900, and was consecrated titular
bishop of Berenice and coadjutor of
Rochester in 1905. He succeeded to the
see in 1909, was appointed Assistant at
the Pontifical Throne in 1925, and was
Rochester's bishop until 1928, when he
resigned and was appointed titular archbishop of Viminacium. He died in
Rochester on Dec. 10.

HICKEY, WILLIAM AUGUSTINE
(1869–1933), bishop. Born in Worcester,
Massachusetts, on May 13, he was educated at Holy Cross College there, at St.
Sulpice in Paris, and at St. John's Seminary, Brighton, Boston. He was ordained in Boston in 1893 and engaged
in parish work in the Boston archdiocese through 1903. He was pastor at St.
Aloysius Church, Gilbertville, Massachusetts, in 1903–17 and at St. John's
Church, Clinton, Massachusetts, 1917–
19. In 1919 he was consecrated as titular bishop of Claudiopolis and coadjutor

of Providence, Rhode Island. He was at
once named administrator of the see because of incumbent Bishop Lowney's ill
health and succeeded to the see in 1921.
During his episcopate he conducted one
million-dollar drive to build new high
schools and another to clear Providence
College's debt, and inaugurated an annual charity drive. He had to deal with
a group of dissident French Canadian
clergy and lay people who were sparked
by the French-language newspaper, *La
Sentinelle,* in Woonsocket and who objected to the parish assessments he levied. When they brought the matter to
the civil courts, he excommunicated
them, only lifting the excommunica-
tions in 1929. He translated Émile Le
Camus's *The Life of Christ* in 1906 (3
volumes). He died in Providence on
Oct. 4.

HICKEY, WILLIAM MACE (1906–
83), executive. Born in Boston on July
2, he was educated at Harvard Engineering School (B.S. in Electrical Engineering 1927), began working in engineering with Stone & Webster, Inc., in
Boston and married Lucy Murphy in
1929. He went to Washington, D.C., in
1934 to work as an examiner in the
Public Utility Division of the Securities
and Exchange Commission, became
president of the United Corporation in
1943, and served in that capacity until
1976, when he became chairman of the
board; the company became Baldwin-
United Corporation in 1978, and he was
named chairman of the executive committee. He served as chairman of the
board of several power companies,
among them International Power Company and Canadian International Power
Company, and was director of several
domestic and foreign companies, among
them the Bolivian Power Company and
Financiadora Venezolana de Creditos.
He was also president of the Spanish Institute, was honored by the Spanish and

Venezuelan governments, and died in New Rochelle, New York, on May 14.

HILDEBRAND, DIETRICH ADOLPH VON (1889–1977), philosopher. The son of Adolf von Hildebrand, a well-known sculptor, he was born in Florence, Italy, on Oct. 12 and studied philosophy at the University of Munich and the University of Göttingen, where he received his Ph.D. in 1912. He became a Catholic in 1914, was an assistant surgeon in 1914–18 at the Poliklinik of Munich during World War I, and in 1918 he became a *Privatdozent* at the University of Munich and an associate professor in 1924. He was forced to flee from Germany in 1933 because of his opposition to Nazism; he went to Florence and then to Vienna, where he founded and was editor of the Catholic review *Der Christliche Ständestaat,* in which he continued his bitter attacks on Nazism. In 1935 he became a professor at the University of Vienna. When the Nazis invaded Austria in 1938, he was again forced to flee, to Switzerland. He became a professor at the Catholic University of Toulouse in 1939 and also lectured at the Grand Seminaire; when France fell in 1940, he had to flee a third time and came to the United States later that year via Portugal and Brazil. He joined the faculty of Fordham in 1942 as professor of philosophy and in the following years introduced the method and insight of the German phenomenologists to Americans through his teaching and writings. He was out of sympathy with the changes in the Church inaugurated by Vatican Council II and increasingly drew apart from the mainstream of Catholic intellectual life in his later years. He retired in 1960 and died in New Rochelle, New York, on Jan. 26. He wrote some one hundred articles on philosophy and morality and more than thirty books, among them *In Defense of Purity*

(1933), *Marriage* (1942), *Liturgy and Personality* (1943), *Transformation in Christ* (1948), *Fundamental Moral Attitudes* (1950), *The Trojan Horse in the House of God* (1967), *Celibacy and the Crisis of Faith* (1971), and his major work *Christian Ethics* (1953).

HILGARD, EUGENE WALDEMAR (1833–1916), agriculturist. Born in Zweibrücken, Bavaria, on Jan. 5, he was brought to the United States when he was three by his parents, who settled in Belleville, Illinois. He was educated at the University of Heidelberg, Germany (Ph.D. 1853), and at Zürich and Freiberg. He became assistant state geologist of Mississippi in 1855, serving in that position until 1873, joined the Smithsonian Institution in Washington, D.C. as a chemist in charge of its laboratories in 1858, married Alexandrina Bello in 1860, and became a Catholic. When the Civil War broke out, he served in the Confederate forces. After the war he taught at the universities of Mississippi in 1866–73 and Michigan in 1873–75 and was a professor of agriculture at the University of California, 1875–1904, when he was named professor emeritus. He was director of the Agricultural Experiment Station at Berkeley, California, in 1888–1904. He became the nation's outstanding authority on soil chemistry and reclamation of alkaline soil, introduced scientific methods of cotton cultivation, helped end mid-America's "desert region" with his *Soils of the Arid and Humid Regions* (1906), and opened the way to studies of the Gulf Coast plains with his geological work. He was honored by several institutions, including Columbia in New York, the Academy of Sciences in Munich, and Paris, and with the gold medal at the Paris Exposition in 1900. He died in Berkeley, California, on Jan. 8.

HILLINGER, RAYMOND PETER (1904–71), bishop. Born in Chicago on May 2, he was educated at St. Mary of the Lake Seminary, Mundelein, Illinois, and was ordained in 1932. He served as a curate at St. Aloysius Church, Chicago, 1932–35, was a member of the Chicago Archdiocesan Mission Band in 1935–50, and was rector of the Angel Guardian Orphanage in 1950–53. In 1953 he was appointed bishop of Rockford, Illinois, and was transferred to Chicago in 1956 as auxiliary and titular bishop of Derbe, because of ailing health. He died in Chicago on Nov. 13.

HOBAN, EDWARD F. (1878–1966), archbishop. Born in Chicago on June 27, he was educated at St. Ignatius College (Loyola University) there, St. Mary's Seminary, Baltimore (B.A. 1900, M.A. 1901) and the Gregorian University, Rome (Ph.D. 1905). He was ordained in 1903, was named chancellor of the Chicago archdiocese in 1905, and became titular bishop of Colonia and auxiliary of Chicago in 1921. He was appointed bishop of Rockford, Illinois, in 1928, established the diocesan newspaper, *The Observer,* organized Catholic Charities in the diocese, expanded the see's facilities, and was made an Assistant to the Pontifical Throne in 1937. He was named coadjutor bishop of Cleveland in 1942, succeeded to the see as its sixth bishop in 1945, and was given the personal title of archbishop by Pope Pius XII in 1951. During his episcopate in Cleveland, he increased the number of parishes there, rebuilt and consecrated the cathedral in 1948, expanded the diocesan facilities, and opened Borromeo Seminary. He died in Cleveland on Sept. 22.

HOBAN, JAMES (c. 1762–1831), architect. Born in Callon, Kilkenny, Ireland, he was educated at the Dublin Society Schools and in Paris, and worked as an architect on several Dublin buildings. He had emigrated to the United States by 1789 and began his American career in Charleston, South Carolina, where he designed the South Carolina state capitol in 1791 (it was burned in 1865). He moved to Washington, D.C., the following year and won the competition for the design of the President's Mansion, now known as the White House. He built the White House in 1792–99 and rebuilt it after the British burned it down in 1814 during the War of 1812. He was one of the supervising architects working on the Capitol executing the designs of Dr. William Thornton and worked on various public buildings in the service of the federal government for forty years. Many of the noble structures of early Washington were due to the collaboration of Hoban and Thornton. He died in Washington on Dec. 8.

HOBAN, MICHAEL JOHN (1853–1926), bishop. Born in Waterloo, New Jersey, on June 6, he was educated at St. Francis Xavier College (New York City), Holy Cross College (Worcester, Massachusetts), St. John's College (Fordham), St. Charles Borromeo Seminary (Overbrook, Philadelphia), and the North American College (Rome), where he was ordained in 1880. He engaged in parish work in the dioceses of Scranton and Pittston, Pennsylvania, was pastor at Troy, Pennsylvania, and in 1887 founded St. Leo's parish in Ashley. He remained in that position until 1896, when he was consecrated as titular bishop of Halius and coadjutor bishop of Scranton. He succeeded to the see three years later, doubled the number of priests and churches in the diocese, improved its parochial school system, and founded an infant asylum, a home for the aged, and St. Michael's Industrial School for neglected boys. He died in Scranton on Nov. 13.

HOBBES, JOHN OLIVER *See* Craigie, Pearl Mary Teresa.

HOCHWALT, FREDERICK G. (1909–66), educator. Born in Dayton, Ohio, on Feb. 5, he was educated at the University of Dayton (B.A. 1931) and St. Gregory's and Mt. St. Mary's of the West seminaries, in Cincinnati, Ohio, and was ordained in 1935. He spent the next two years as an assistant pastor and teaching high schools in Cincinnati, then continued his education in 1937–43 at Catholic University (M.A. 1939, Ph.D. 1943), and in 1940–43 served again in Cincinnati parishes. He was appointed director of the Department of Education of the National Catholic Welfare Conference (NCWC) in 1944, remaining in that position until 1966, and was secretary of the National Catholic Education Association (NCEA) in 1944–68. In these positions he encouraged cooperation between public and parochial school educators, supported high professional standards for Catholic education and the development of distinctly Catholic curriculums by parochial schools, and was unsuccessful in his efforts to include non–public school children in some of the benefits of the 1965 Federal Education Act. He served at several UNESCO meetings and on United States educational missions to Japan in 1946 and 1950 as an adviser, was made a papal chamberlain in 1944 and a domestic prelate in 1947, and was honored by a dozen Catholic colleges and universities. He died on the S.S. *Coronia* en route to Venice on Sept. 5.

HOEHN, MATTHEW (1898–1959), librarian. Born in Newark, New Jersey, on Feb. 4, he was educated at St. Anselm's College, Manchester, New Hampshire (B.A. 1921), joined the Benedictines in 1918, was professed in 1919, and was ordained in 1926. He taught at St. Anselm's and St. Bene-

dict's Preparatory School in Newark, studied library science at Columbia (B.L.S. 1936), and became librarian at St. Benedict's. He gathered biographical information on 620 Catholic authors and published it in *Catholic Authors: Contemporary Biographical Sketches, 1930–47* (1948) and added 374 new biographies in a second volume published in 1952. He was prior of St. Mary's Abbey, Newark, in 1946–56 and died in Newark on May 12.

HOGAN, ALOYSIUS JOSEPH (1891–1943), educator. Born in Philadelphia on Aug. 5, he was educated at St. Joseph's College there (B.A.), joined the Jesuits in 1908, continued his studies at Woodstock College, Maryland (M.A.), the Gregorian, Rome (S.T.D.), and Cambridge (Ph.D.), and was ordained. He taught classics at Boston College in 1915–20 and was dean of studies at the Jesuit House of Classical Studies at St. Andrew-on-the-Hudson, Poughkeepsie, New York, in 1928–30 and at St. Isaac Jogues Novitiate, Wernersville, Pennsylvania, in 1930. He was president of Fordham in 1930–36, reorganized its graduate school and general faculty and encouraged the Fordham University Press; during his presidency Fordham became a major power in intercollegiate athletics. He was dean of graduate studies at Georgetown from 1936 until his death in Washington, D.C., on Dec. 17.

HOGAN, JOHN BAPTIST (1829–1901), educator. Born near Ennis, Clare, Ireland, on June 24, he went to France in 1844, studied at the preparatory seminaries at Bordeaux and St. Sulpice, Issy, and joined the Sulpicians in 1851. He was ordained the following year, taught at St. Sulpice in 1853–84 and went to the United States as first president of the newly erected St. John's Seminary, Brighton, Boston, in 1884–

89. He was named president of the graduate theological seminary at Catholic University in 1889, returned to St. John's five years later, and spent the rest of his career as its president. He resigned because of ill health and returned to France, dying in Paris on Sept. 29. Usually called Abbé Hogan, he was the author of *Clerical Studies* (1898) and *Daily Thoughts* (1899).

HOGAN, JOHN JOSEPH (1829–1913), bishop. Born in Bruff, Limerick, Ireland, he received his education in classical studies in Ireland, emigrated to the United States in 1848, studied for the priesthood at the diocesan seminary at St. Louis, and was ordained there in 1852. He engaged in pastoral and missionary work in St. Louis and in northwestern Missouri for the next sixteen years, and in 1865 was indicted when he refused to take a test oath that the Missouri constitution required; the case eventually went to the United States Supreme Court, which declared unconstitutional the section of the Missouri constitution requiring the oath. In 1868 he was appointed bishop of the newly established diocese of St. Joseph, Missouri, rebuilt churches, schools, and charitable institutions, and was instrumental in bringing the Benedictines to found Conception Abbey. When the diocese of Kansas City, Missouri, was created in 1880, he was transferred there as its first bishop, also continuing as administrator of St. Joseph until 1893. He remained in that position until his death in Kansas City on Feb. 21. During his episcopate he increased the number of priests, religious communities, and churches in the diocese and built the cathedral of the Immaculate Conception. He was the author of several books, among them *On the Mission in Missouri* (1892).

HOGAN, WILLIAM (1788–1848), schismatic. He was born in Ireland, but little is known of his early life beyond that he was ordained in Ireland and worked as a priest in the diocese of Limerick. He is reported to have been suspended for five years prior to his emigration to the United States and to have declared his intention to become a Protestant clergyman. He settled in the New York diocese in Albany, but in 1820 he moved to Philadelphia without the permission of New York's Bishop John Connolly and attached himself to St. Mary's Cathedral there. He became a favorite of the lay trustees who were feuding with Philadelphia's Bishop Henry Conwell and soon was a leader in the trustee movement that so disrupted the early American Catholic Church. When Conwell suspended him, Hogan attacked the bishop publicly. A series of court actions followed his proposal that an American Catholic Church be founded in which congregations would choose their pastors—a philosophy that became known as Hoganism. The Pennsylvania Supreme Court ruled in favor of the bishop, but the trustees declared that they, not the diocese or the bishop, owned the property, and closed the cathedral. Meanwhile, Hogan's notoriety and loose moral life (he supposedly was married twice) forced him to resign, and he became involved in anti-Catholic activities, writing pamphlets with such titles as *Popery As It Was* and *Nunneries and Auricular Confessions*. He was named United States consul at Nuevitas, Cuba, in 1843 and died in Nashua, New Hampshire, on Jan. 3, without having been reconciled with the Church.

HOGUET, JOSEPH PETER (1882–1946), physician. Born in Long Branch, New Jersey, on Aug. 16, he graduated from Harvard in 1904 and studied medicine at Columbia, where he received his medical degree. He married Helen Gourd in 1912, was a surgeon in the United States Army during World War I, and at the end of the war resumed his practice in New York City. He taught at Cornell Medical College and became head surgeon at French Hospital in New York City but was forced to relinquish that position when he lost his hand in an automobile accident in 1930. He became president of the Medical Guild Foundation in 1940, supplied medical and ambulance equipment during World War II, and was decorated for his activities by the French Government. Well known for his philanthropies, he died in New York City on June 17.

HOLLAND, JOHN PHILIP (1840–1914), inventor. Born in Liscanor, Clare, Ireland, on Feb. 29, he was educated at Ennistymon and Limerick, taught in Ireland 1858–72, and emigrated to the United States in 1873. He settled in Paterson, New Jersey, married Margaret Foley, and taught in a Catholic parochial school. While in Ireland he had developed plans for a submarine which he hoped would end the domination of the seas by the British Navy and help secure Irish independence, but he was forced to abandon his experiments for lack of money. In the United States, with funds he received from the Fenians, he built a fourteen-foot underwater craft operated by a steam engine and one crewman, and tested it in the Passaic River in 1878; the test ended when the craft sank (it was recovered in 1927 and placed in the Paterson Museum). Three years later, again with Fenian support, he built the *Fenian Ram,* a nineteen-ton, thirty-one-foot submarine manned by a crew of three. He tested it successfully in New York Harbor, submerging it to sixty feet, and incorporated into its structure the major principles of the modern submarine. Rebuffed in initial attempts to interest the United States Navy in 1875, when he offered the Navy his plans, he secured the support of Lieutenant (later Rear Admiral) W. W. Kimball and attracted public attention to his inventions, but it was not until 1895 that the sum of $150,000 was made available to him so that he could proceed with construction of the *Plunger.* His construction plans were vetoed by Admiral George W. Melville and the craft was a failure. With his own funds he built the fifty-three-foot, seventy-five-ton *Holland* and launched it in 1898—the first submarine with two power plants, a gasoline engine for surface operation, and an electric motor for submarine operation. The Navy then ordered six of the craft in 1900, and Great Britain, France, and Japan soon placed orders. In 1904 he was successful in building the first respirator for use in escaping from submarines under water. He died in Newark, New Jersey, on Aug. 12.

HOLLAND, ROBERT EMMET (1892–1946), editor. Born in Olympia, Washington, on Feb. 21, he joined the Jesuits in 1908, studied at St. Andrew-on-the-Hudson, Poughkeepsie, New York, and was ordained in 1923. He taught English and classical literature at Jesuit high schools in Boston and Philadelphia, served as a missionary in the Philippines in 1926, and was principal of Canisius High School, Buffalo, New York, in 1928–32. He then became director of the Fordham University Press and became known for the distinctive design of the press's books. He died in New York City on Aug. 2. He was the author of several books for youngsters, a biography of St. John Francis Regis, and the *Song of Tekakwitha,* a poem on that Indian saint.

HOMAN, HELEN WALKER (1893–1961), author. The grandniece of James G. Blaine, unsuccessful candidate for the presidency in a sensational election in 1884, when he lost New York by a scant 1,000 votes because of a remark about the Democrats as the party of "rum, Romanism, and rebellion" by one of his supporters in New York. Helen Walker Blaine was born in Helena, Montana, on Oct. 17. She was educated at Notre Dame of Maryland (Baltimore) and Pensionat Cyrano (Lausanne, Switzerland), and studied law at the New York University Law School (LL.B. 1919). She then embarked on a journalism career, was editor of the Pelham *Sun* in 1919–20, managing editor of the *Forum* in 1920–22, editor of *The New Republic* in 1924, and assistant editor of *Commonweal* in 1924–27. She married Dominique A. Homan in 1927 and in 1938 became director of the School of Journalism at Notre Dame College, Staten Island, New York. She was admitted to the New York bar in 1940 and during World War II was correspondent for the National Catholic Welfare Conference News Service. After the war she devoted herself to teaching and began writing books; among them were *By Post to the Apostles* (1933), *Letters to the Martyrs* (1951), *Star of Jacob* (1953), *Knights of Christ* (1957), and several books for young readers. She died in New York City on Apr. 7.

HORSTMANN, IGNATIUS FREDERICK (1840–1908), bishop. Born in Philadelphia on Dec. 16, he was educated at St. Joseph's College and St. Charles Borromeo Seminary there and the North American College, Rome, where he was ordained in 1865, receiving his doctorate in divinity the following year. On his return to the United States, he taught at St. Charles Borromeo until 1877, when he was named rector of St. Mary's Church, Philadel- phia, and in 1885 he became chancellor of the archdiocese of Philadelphia. He was consecrated bishop of Cleveland in 1892, brought the first Hungarian priest into that diocese that year for the many Hungarians who had settled in Cleveland, and appointed Bishop Koudelka auxiliary bishop to minister to Slavics— the first auxiliary bishop of special jurisdiction in the United States. He founded St. John's College, Toledo, in 1898 and established the Cleveland Apostolate, the first diocesan missionary band in the country. He died of a heart attack in Canton, Ohio, on May 13 while making a visitation there.

HOWARD, EDWARD DANIEL (1877–1983), archbishop. Born in Cresco, Iowa, on Nov. 5, he was educated at Columbia College, Dubuque, Iowa (B.A. 1899), St. Mary's College, Kansas, and St. Thomas Seminary, St. Paul, Minnesota, and was ordained in 1906. He was a professor at Columbia College in 1906–21 and served as its president from 1921 until 1924, when he was appointed titular bishop of Isauria and auxiliary of Davenport, Iowa. He was appointed bishop of Oregon City in 1926, and in 1928, when the see was moved to Portland, Oregon, and became an archdiocese, he became its archbishop. During his forty-year episcopate, 1926–66, he established twenty-three new parishes, centralized the school system and built new schools, increased the number of priests in the diocese from 174 to 430 to care for the increase in the Catholic population from 61,000 to 186,000, promoted the liturgical movement, and established Catholic Charities in the see. He was made an Assistant at the Pontifical Throne in 1938, retired in 1966, and was made titular archbishop of Albule. He died in Beaverton, Oregon, on Jan. 2. At the time of his death, he was the oldest living prelate in the world.

HOWARD, FRANCIS WILLIAM (1867–1944), bishop. Born in Columbus, Ohio, on June 21, he was educated at Niagara University and Mt. St. Mary's Seminary of the West, Cincinnati, Ohio, and was ordained in Columbus in 1891. He served as a curate at the Columbus cathedral, was pastor of Holy Trinity parish, Jackson, Ohio, in 1891–95, and continued his studies the next three years at Columbia and for another year in Rome. On his return he was chaplain at St. Francis and St. Anthony hospitals, Columbus, and then was pastor of Holy Rosary Church there in 1905–23. He was made first general secretary of the National Catholic Education Association in 1904 and served in that position until 1928; he was president of the association in 1929–35 and was named a domestic prelate in 1920. He was appointed bishop of Covington, Kentucky, in 1923, established the Bishop's School for talented boys, was made an Assistant at the Pontifical Throne in 1928, and died in Covington on Jan. 18.

HOWARD, TIMOTHY HOWARD (1837–1916), jurist, author. Born in Ann Arbor, Michigan, on Jan. 27, he was educated at the University of Michigan, served with the 12th Michigan Infantry during the Civil War, and after the war continued his studies at Notre Dame (B.A. 1864, M.A. 1866). He taught at Notre Dame until 1879, when he began practicing law and entered politics. He served as clerk of St. Joseph's County Circuit Court, Indiana, was elected to the city council of South Bend, Indiana, was attorney for the city and the county for a time, was elected to the state senate in 1886, and was associate justice of the Indiana Supreme Court in 1893–99; he was the recipient of the Laetare Medal in 1898. He served on several state commissions and was a member of the commission established to codify Indiana state law in 1903–05,

became professor of law at Notre Dame in 1906, and died in South Bend, Indiana, on July 9. He was the author of several books, among them *Excelsior* (1868), *History of Notre Dame,* (1895), *The Laws of Indiana* (1900), *The Indiana Supreme Court* (1900), and *Musings and Memories* (1905).

HOWLETT, WILLIAM JOSEPH (1847–1936), missionary. He was born of Irish immigrant parents, in Monroe County, New York, on Mar. 6, was brought to Michigan by his parents when he was six, and was educated at St. Thomas Seminary, Bardstown, Kentucky, in 1868–69, the Sulpician Seminary at Issy-sur-Seine, France, the Grand Seminary, Paris, and the University of Würzburg, Bavaria. He was ordained in Paris in 1876 and on his return to the United States served as a missionary and pastor in the Denver diocese for the next thirty-six years, 1897–1913. He then was chaplain at the Sisters of Loretto motherhouse, Loretto, Kentucky, for twenty-three years, 1913–36. He was the author of several works, among them biographies of Bishop Joseph Macheboeuf of Denver and *The Life of Rev. Charles Nerinckx* (1916), and several historical works—most notably a *Historical Tribute to St. Thomas Seminary at Poplar Neck* (1906). He died at Loretto on Jan. 17.

HOYNES, WILLIAM (1846–1933), jurist. Born near Callan, Kilkenny, Ireland, on Nov. 8, he was brought to the United States by his parents when he was a child and served with Wisconsin infantry and cavalry units during the Civil War. After the war he studied at Notre Dame, was graduated, and then studied law at the University of Michigan, receiving his law degree in 1872. He became a newspaperman, was editor of daily papers in New Brunswick, New Jersey, and Peoria, Illinois, until 1882, and then practiced law in Chicago. He taught law at Notre Dame, became dean of its law school, and held that position until he retired in 1918. He died in South Bend, Indiana, on Mar. 28.

HROBAK, PHILIP (1904–64), editor. Born in Cleveland, Ohio, on May 1, he was educated at St. Procopius College, Lisle, Illinois (B.A. 1926) and then did postgraduate work at New York University in 1927–29. He taught chemistry at St. Procopius High School in 1924–27, was a laboratory instructor at New York University in 1927–29, and taught languages and science at Slovak Benedictine High School in 1929–38. In 1938 he became editor of the weekly Slovak newspaper, *Jednota,* and held that position until his death. He was president of the Slovak League of America and wrote a Slovak dictionary and grammar and numerous articles on Slovak affairs. He died in Harrisburg, Pennsylvania, on Jan. 10.

HUBBARD, BERNARD ROSECRANS (1888–1962), explorer. The son of an Episcopal priest, he was born in San Francisco on Nov. 24 and became a Catholic in his youth. He was educated at St. Ignatius College, San Francisco, and the University of Santa Clara, Santa Clara, California, and joined the Jesuits in 1908. He continued his studies at Los Gatos (B.A. 1913), Gonzaga University, Spokane, Washington (M.A. 1921), and the University of Innsbruck in 1921–25, while also teaching at various Jesuit institutions in the United States and Europe. He was ordained in 1925, began teaching at the University of Santa Clara in 1925, was appointed head of the geology department in 1926, and in that year made the first of thirty-two trips he was to make to Alaska. He became famed for his explorations in Alaska and the Far North, was considered the foremost authority on Alaska,

and earned the name "glacier priest" for his ascents of previously unclimbed mountain peaks, his work in Alaska and among the Eskimos, his geological studies, and his exploits. Among the latter were the first winter ascent of Mt. Katmai in 1932, his crossing of the hazardous Bering Strait with eight companions in a canoe to prove how ancient peoples might have come to North America, crossing crevasse-ridden ice packs, exploring the inside of a volcano during a gas explosion, and living with the Eskimos for eighteen months on King Island off Seward Peninsula in 1937–38. During World War II, he ministered to the members of the American Armed Forces in Alaska in 1943–44 and served as an adviser to the military on terrain, weather, clothing, and food. He was a popular lecturer, wrote several books— among them *Mush, You Malemute* (1932) and *Cradle of Storms* (1935)— and made several motion pictures, among them *Aniachak, Adventures of Father Hubbard,* and *Alaska's Silver Millions.* He died at Santa Clara on May 28.

HUBBELL, JOHN LORENZ (1853–1930), trader, sheriff. Born in Pajarito, New Mexico, on Nov. 27, he became a trader to the Navajo Indians and settled in Ganado, Arizona, in 1876. He built up the handicrafts of the Navajos and Hopis to worldwide fame, became wealthy through his trading, and was the Indians' friend and defender. He was twice sheriff of Apache County during its most lawless period, served two terms in the territorial legislature, and died in Ganado on Nov. 12.

HUBER, RAPHAEL M. (1886–1963), historian. Born in Louisville, Kentucky, on Nov. 2, he joined the Friars Minor Conventual in 1897, studied at St. Francis College, Trenton, New Jersey, and at the University of Innsbruck. He was ordained in Innsbruck in 1906. He continued his studies at Innsbruck, receiving his doctorate in theology in 1909, and then taught at St. Francis and was master of clerics there until 1912. He spent the next sixteen years in pastoral work in Trenton, Indianapolis, Syracuse, and Northville, New York, and was rector of St. Bonaventure College, New York, in 1923–27. He was an English-speaking confessor at St. Peter's in Rome in 1927–37 and taught Church history at Catholic University in 1937–53 and then at St. Anthony-on-Hudson, New York, until his death there on Sept. 22. He was the author of several books on Franciscan themes, among them *The Portiuncula Indulgence* (1938), *Documented History of the Franciscan Order* (1944), and *St. Anthony of Padua* (1948).

HUCKLE, PAUL *See* Allen, Fred.

HUDSON, DANIEL ELDRED (1849–1934), editor. Born in Nahany, Massachusetts, on Dec. 18, he worked in a bookstore and for a publisher in Boston, studied at Holy Cross College, Worcester, Massachusetts, and in 1871 joined the Congregation of Holy Cross at Notre Dame. He was professed in 1872 and ordained in 1875, when he became editor of the magazine *Ave Maria,* a position he held until forced to retire because of illness in 1929. He died at Notre Dame on Jan. 12.

HUGHES, JOHN J. (1856–1919), superior general. Born in New York City on Dec. 6, he was educated at St. Charles College, Ellicott City, Maryland, and at St. Francis Xavier College, New York City (B.A. 1878), joined the Paulists in 1879, and was ordained in 1884. He was a missionary in Indiana but was obliged to give up his missionary work because of a weak voice and became a parish priest. He served as assistant superior of the Paulists under Frs. Deshon and Searle, also serving as pastor of St. Paul's Church, New York City, and was elected superior general of the Paulists in 1909. He was reelected in 1914 and died in New York City on May 6.

HUGHES, JOHN JOSEPH (1797–1864), archbishop. The son of an Irish farmer, he was born at Annaloghan, Tyrone, Ireland, on June 24 and followed his father to the United States in 1817, settling at Chambersburg, Pennsylvania. Though he had studied horticulture in Ireland and worked as a gardener and as a laborer in quarries, his real desire was to become a priest. In 1819 he went to Mt. St. Mary's College, Emmitsburg, Maryland, at first as a gardener and the following year as a student. He was ordained in 1826, engaged in pastoral work in Philadelphia and Bedford, Pennsylvania, was a theologian at the first Provincial Council of Baltimore in 1829 and later the same year he founded St. John's Orphan Asylum and became secretary of auxiliary Bishop Francis Kenrick in 1830. He became pastor of St. Mary's Church in Philadelphia, which for years had been a center of a trusteeship controversy. The controversy was ended when Bishop Kenrick closed the church and its cemetery until the trustees acceded to the demands of the ordinary in 1832. Hughes built St. John the Evangelist Church and was its pastor later the same year. Under Bishop Kenrick, Hughes founded the *Catholic Herald* with Fr. Michael Hurley in 1833. His spirited defense of Catholicism in a debate with a well-known Presbyterian clergyman, the Rev. John A. Breckenridge, in 1836 attracted widespread attention, and the following year Hughes was appointed titular bishop of Basileopolis and coadjutor of New York, where he was consecrated in 1838. He was named administrator of the see in 1839 and went to Europe that year, seeking financial aid to alleviate the huge diocesan debt he had inherited. On his return he became embroiled in a bitter dispute with the Public School Society over the treatment of Catholic children in the public schools of New York but was unsuccessful in his attempts to secure public support for Catholic schools from the state legislature. He then established an independent Catholic school system which became one of the outstanding Catholic school systems in the country. He became bishop of New York when Bishop John Dubois died in 1842 and was at once confronted with a dispute with the trustees of St. Peter's Church. He resolved the dispute when the trustees filed for bankruptcy and he bought the church and named his own committee to manage it. He eventually ended the trustee problem in New York by obtaining ecclesiastical control of Church property. A resolute and ardent defender of Catholicism, he fought anti-Catholicism all his life, especially the Native Americans and Know-Nothings, and denounced the plan of the anti-Catholic Native American political party to hold a rally in New York City after anti-Catholic riots and demonstrations in Philadelphia in 1844; he convinced the mayor of New York to forbid the rally to avert the rioting and bloodshed he was sure would ensue. His remark to Mayor Robert Morris and his successor James Harper that "if a single Catholic church is burned in New York, the city will become a Moscow"—an allusion to the fires with which the Russians greeted Napoleon in Moscow in 1812—no doubt helped convince them. Prominent in public as well as Church affairs, he was asked by President Polk to accept a diplomatic mission to Mexico in 1845, but he declined. He addressed Congress in 1847 and accepted a mission from the federal government

in 1861 to go to France to present the Union side of the Civil War to Napoleon III and to dissuade him from recognizing the Confederacy—which Napoleon never did. A strong supporter of Pope Pius IX, he raised a large sum of money for the beleaguered pontiff in 1860. During the Draft Riots in New York City, July 13–16, 1863, though seriously ill, he addressed the rioters from the balcony of his residence, an action which played no small role in ending the riots. Though not an abolitionist, he actively supported the federal government throughout the Civil War because of his fervent belief in the American political system and country as an asylum for the oppressed of other countries. He was deeply concerned about the welfare of immigrants (he founded the Irish Emigrant Society in 1841) and worked unceasingly to better their conditions; he believed immigrants and Americans should be formed into a common citizenry and opposed national churches as divisive. He became archbishop when the diocese of New York was elevated to an archdiocese in 1850, and during his episcopacy the archdiocese rapidly expanded. The number of priests grew from 40 to 150, churches from 50 to 85, and the number of Catholics in the see doubled to 400,000, even though 4 dioceses (Albany, Brooklyn, Buffalo, and Newark) were formed from the original area of the New York see during his term as ordinary. He opened St. John's College and Seminary (Fordham) in 1841 and established St. Joseph's Seminary, Troy, in 1862, transferring the seminary students from St. John's there at that time, and strongly supported Catholic educational and charitable institutions; he was a leading proponent of the establishment of the North American College (which opened in 1859) in Rome. He attracted numerous religious orders to New York (he welcomed the newly established Paulist Fathers to the see in 1858), laid the cornerstone of St. Patrick's Cathedral (derisively dubbed "Hughes's folly" because it was located so far out in the country) in 1856, and died in New York City on Jan. 3.

HUNKELER, EDWARD JOSEPH (1894–1970), archbishop. Born in Medicine Lodge, Kansas, on Jan. 1, he studied at the Pontifical College Josephinum, Worthington, Ohio, from 1907 to 1919, when he was ordained there. He was pastor of Sts. Philip and James Church (Wynot, Nebraska) in 1919–27, of Blessed Sacrament Church (Omaha, Nebraska) in 1927–36, and of St. Cecilia's Cathedral (Omaha) in 1936–45. He was made a domestic prelate in 1937, became vicar-general of the archdiocese, and in 1945 was appointed bishop of Grand Island, Nebraska. The see was transferred to Kansas City, Kansas, in 1951, and when it was made an archdiocese in 1952, he became its first archbishop. He retired in 1969 and died on Oct. 1 in Crookston, Minnesota.

HUNT, DUANE GARRISON (1884–1960), bishop. Born in Reynolds, Nebraska, on Sept. 19, he was educated at Cornell College in Mount Vernon, Iowa (B.A. 1907), and was a high school teacher in Iowa, 1907–11. He studied law at the University of Iowa in 1911–12 and at the University of Chicago in 1912–13, and taught public speaking at the University of Iowa in 1913–16. He became a Catholic in 1913, taught at the University of Utah through 1916. Then he decided to become a priest and studied for the priesthood at St. Patrick's Seminary, Menlo Park, California. He was ordained in 1920, served as rector of the cathedral in Salt Lake City, Utah, became chancellor and then vicar-general of that diocese, and was made a papal chamberlain in 1924 and a domestic prelate in 1930. He edited the diocesan

paper, *The Intermountain Catholic* in 1930–32, was administrator of the see briefly in 1937, and later the same year was appointed its bishop. An outstanding preacher, he had a popular radio program on Catholic topics for several years beginning in 1927, wrote *The People, the Clergy, and the Church* (1936), and was made an Assistant at the Pontifical Throne in 1946. He died in Salt Lake City on Mar. 31.

HUNTINGTON, JEDEDIAH VINCENT (1815–62), novelist, editor. Born in New York City on Jan. 20, he was educated at Yale and at New York University, from which he graduated in 1835. He then studied medicine at the University of Pennsylvania and received his medical degree in 1838, though he never practiced medicine. He taught psychology at St. Paul's Episcopal School near Flushing, New York, for three years, became an Episcopal priest in 1841, and rector of the Episcopal church in Middlebury, Vermont. He resigned in 1846 and spent the next three years in England and Rome. In 1849 he and his wife became Catholics in Rome. On his return to the United States, he edited *Metropolitan Magazine* in Baltimore and then *The Leader* in St. Louis, but each soon failed. He had *Poems and Translations from the Greek* published in 1843, and in the years thereafter he wrote several popularly written and widely read novels, among them *Lady Alice* (1849) and the partly autobiographical *Alban, or the History of a Young Puritan* (1851) and its sequel, *The Forest* (1852), *America Discovered: a Poem* (1852), *Blonde and Brunette* (1859), and *Rosemary* (1860). He spent the last few years of his life in southern France, where he died of tuberculosis at Pau on Mar. 10.

HUNTON, GEORGE K. (1888–1967), interracial leader. Born in Claremont,

New Hampshire, on May 24, he was educated at Holy Cross College, Worcester, Massachusetts, and studied law at Fordham (LL.B. 1910). He worked in the offices of the Legal Aid Society in Harlem, the Lower East Side, and Brooklyn in New York City, 1912–15, served as a flights record sergeant in World War I, and then engaged in private law practice. He was executive secretary of the Cardinal Gibbons Institute, an agricultural school for blacks in Ridge, Maryland, 1931–34, and there met Fr. John LaFarge. Hunton decided to devote himself full time to the fight for racial justice, and he and Fr. LaFarge founded the Catholic Interracial Council of New York in 1943. Hunton became its executive secretary and editor of its journal *Interracial Justice;* he held these positions until his retirement in 1962. He was made a national director of the National Association for the Advancement of Colored People (NAACP) in 1955 and published his autobiography, *All of Which I Saw, Part of Which I Was,* in 1967. Though blind the last two years of his life, he remained active in the movement for interracial justice until his death in Brooklyn, New York, on Nov. 11.

HURLEY, EDWARD NASH (1864–1933), executive. Born in Galesburg, Illinois, on July 31, he worked briefly as a railroad man in his youth; he and his brother invented a piston air drill, and to market it in 1896 they founded the Standard and Pneumatic Tool Company, which became extremely successful in its field. He retired in 1902 but six years later became president of the First National Bank of Wheaton, Illinois, and founded the Hurley Machine Company, which he developed into one of the leading producers of electrical labor-saving devices for the home. He was appointed trade commissioner to Latin America by President Woodrow Wilson in 1913, was chairman of the Federal Trade Commission in 1915–17, became chairman of the United States Shipping Board and president of the Emergency Fleet Corporation in 1917; during World War I he directed the building of the enormous merchant fleet required for the war. It was the largest merchant fleet ever assembled up to that time and consisted of some 14,000,000 tons of shipping. He retired from public service to private business in 1919 and devoted himself to civic affairs and writing. He was honored by the American, French, and Italian governments and was the recipient of the Laetare Medal in 1926. He helped organize the Chicago World's Fair in 1933 and was the author of *The New Merchant Marine* (1920) and *The Bridge to France* (1927), on the merchant marine and his role in building it, and of *The Awakening of Business* (1917). He died in Chicago on Nov. 14.

HURLEY, JOSEPH PATRICK (1894–1967), archbishop. Born in Cleveland, Ohio, on Jan. 21, he was educated at John Carroll University there in 1912–15, at St. Bernard's Seminary in Rochester, New York, in 1915–16, and at St. Mary's Seminary, Cleveland, in 1916–19 (B.A., M.A.). He was ordained in Cleveland in 1919, served as curate at St. Columba's Church of Youngstown, Ohio, in 1919–23, at St. Philomena's Church of East Cleveland in 1923, and at Immaculate Conception Church, Cleveland, in 1923–27. He was secretary of the apostolic delegation to India in 1928–31 and to Japan in 1931–34, serving as *chargé d'affaires* in 1933–34. He was attaché to the papal secretariat of state in 1934–40—the first American to become an official member of the secretariat—was made a domestic prelate in 1934, and in 1940 was appointed bishop of St. Augustine, Florida. He vigorously opposed isolationism in the United States prior to America's entrance into World War II and castigated the Nazis, demanding American intervention in the war against Germany. When the Communists gained control of Yugoslavia in 1945 and relations between the Church and Tito's regime reached the breaking point, Pope Pius XII sent him to Yugoslavia as his papal nuncio—the first American to attain this rank. He served as nuncio until 1949 and helped secure the release of Archbishop Stepinac from prison in 1951 after the archbishop had been sentenced to a sixteen-year prison term in 1946 by the Communist government of Hungary. He was given the personal title of archbishop by Pope Pius XII in 1950. While attending the first Synod of Bishops in Rome, in September 1967, he was taken ill, returned to Florida, and died the following month in Orlando on Oct. 30.

HURLEY, MICHAEL (c. 1780–1837), superior. Of Irish immigrant parents, he was probably born in Ireland and about 1797 became the first American to join the Augustinians. He went to Italy to study for the priesthood, was ordained in 1803, and returned to the United States to be an assistant at St. Augustine's Church in Philadelphia. He was at St. Peter's Church in New York City in 1805–7, where he met and became a close friend and spiritual adviser to Mrs. Elizabeth Bayley Seton. He returned to Philadelphia, became pastor of St. Augustine's in 1820, and six years later became superior of the Augustinians in the United States in 1826. He performed heroically in the cholera epidemic of 1832, for which he was praised by city officials. He died there on May 15.

HUSSLEIN, JOSEPH CASPAR (1873–1952), sociologist. Born in Milwaukee, Wisconsin, on June 10, he studied at Marquette there, joined the Jesuits when he graduated in 1891, and continued his studies at St. Louis University (M.A. 1906) and Fordham (Ph.D. 1919). He was ordained in 1905. He became interested in socioeconomic matters, was associate editor of the Jesuit magazine, *America,* 1911–27, taught sociology at St. Ignatius College (Cleveland), Fordham, and St. Louis. In 1929 he became head of the sociology department at St. Louis and founded its School of Social Service in 1936, directing it for the next decade. He wrote numerous books, among them *The Church and Social Problems* (1912), *The World Problem—Capital, Labor, and the Church* (1918), *The Reign of Christ* (1928), *The Mass of the Apostles* (1929), *The Christian Social Manifesto* (1931), and edited a two-volume collection of encyclicals of Popes Leo XIII and Pius XI on social problems, *Social Wellsprings* (1940, 1942); he also was general editor of the *Science and Culture* series and the *Religion and Culture* series. He died in St. Louis on Oct. 19.

HYLAN, JOHN FRANCIS "RED" (1888–1936), mayor. Born in Hunter, New York, on Apr. 20, he worked as a railroad worker for a time and then settled in Brooklyn, New York, where he became an engineer on New York's transit system. He studied law at New York Law School, graduating in 1897, practiced law and entered politics as a Democratic Party worker. He was city magistrate in 1906–14 and judge of King's County Court in 1914–18. In 1917 he was elected mayor of New York City, following a bitter campaign in which he was supported by Tammany Hall and charged with being the candidate of the anti-American element of New York's Irish and German populace who opposed England in World War I, then raging in Europe. He was reelected in 1921 but failed to win a third term when he was defeated in the Democratic Party primary in 1925 by James J. Walker. His terms in office were filled with controversies: he proposed municipal ownership of the subways and staunchly supported a five-cent fare; he launched an investigation of alleged pro-English bias in textbooks, an investigation that was widely criticized; his appearance at a pro-German meeting sparked an American Legion attack on him; and his handling of patronage was widely criticized. He was appointed a justice of the Children's Court in 1925 by his successor, James J. Walker, who had defeated him for the mayoralty nomination earlier that year. He died in Forest Hills, New York City, on Jan. 12.

HYLAND, FRANCIS E. (1901–68), bishop. Born in Philadelphia on Oct. 9, he studied for the priesthood at St. Charles Borromeo Seminary, Overbrook, Philadelphia (B.A. 1926) and at Catholic University (J.C.D. 1928) and was ordained in Philadelphia in 1927. He was made a private chamberlain in 1933, was secretary to the apostolic delegation in 1938, and was made a domestic prelate the same year. He was rector of Resurrection Church, Chester, Pennsylvania, in 1929–41 and of Our Lady of Lourdes Church, Philadelphia, 1941–49, after which he was named titular

bishop of Gomphi and auxiliary of the Savannah–Atlanta, Georgia, diocese; he was appointed first bishop of Atlanta when it was established as a separate diocese in 1956. He resigned in 1961, was appointed titular bishop of Bisica and an Assistant at the Pontifical Throne. He retired to St. Charles Borromeo Seminary and died in Philadelphia on Jan. 31.

HYLE, MICHAEL WILLIAM (1901–67), bishop. Born in Baltimore on Oct. 13, he studied for the priesthood at St. Mary's Seminary there (B.A. 1922) and the Urban College, Rome (S.T.L. 1926) and was ordained in 1927. He engaged in parish work in Washington, D.C., 1927–43, was pastor in Libertyville, Maryland, 1943–46, at Bradshaw, Maryland, 1946–57, and at St. Mary's Church, Baltimore, 1957–58. He was appointed titular bishop of Christopolis and coadjutor of Wilmington, Delaware, in 1958 and succeeded to the see in 1960. He established a diocesan newspaper and a Catholic information center in Wilmington, founded new parishes, and struggled with the problems of urban decay in his see. He died in Wilmington on Dec. 26, of a heart attack.

I

IBERVILLE, PIERRE LE MOYNE D' (1661–1706), explorer, soldier, founder of Louisiana. Son of Charles Le Moyne, Sieur de Longueuil in Canada and a native of Dieppe, France, and Catherine Thierry, Iberville was born in Villa Marie (Montreal) on July 20 and entered the French Navy in 1675, when he was fourteen. He spent the next decade in the Navy, returned to Canada in 1685, when his father died, and in 1688 joined an expedition under Chevalier de Troyes to drive the English from the James Bay extension of Hudson Bay; they attacked three English trading posts and captured a fortune in furs. He led attacks on British trading posts in 1686, 1689, 1694, and 1697, and on the last expedition he sank three British warships, though he had but one, and when his ship, the *Pelican,* was wrecked in a storm he led an assault on the strongest British post, Fort Nelson, and captured it. In 1690 he accompanied his brother Jacques in an attack on Schenectady, New York, which destroyed the settlement, but he was unsuccessful in a 1692 attempt to capture Fort Pemaquid on the coast of Maine; in 1696 he attacked it again and this time succeeded in capturing it. He advocated an attack on New York but never put his plan into effect; his series of battles to drive the English from North America ended with the signing of the treaty of Ryswick between England and France in 1697. He went to France in 1697 and was chosen by the minister of marine to lead an expedition to rediscover the mouth of the Mississippi River and to colonize Louisiana. He set out from Brest with his younger brother Bienville and four ships on Oct. 24, 1698. He was joined by the warship *François* at Santo Domingo, reached the Gulf of Mexico early in 1699, founded Old Biloxi (now Ocean Springs, Mississippi), and on Mar. 2 was the first to definitely ascertain the mouth of the Mississippi from the Gulf of Mexico. He built a fort on the northeast side of the Bay of Biloxi and went back to France in May. He returned to Louisiana in December, sailed up the Mississippi to present-day Natchez, and again returned to France in May 1700. He returned to Louisiana in December, sent his brother Bienville to found Fort Louis of Mobile, and left Louisiana for the last time in 1702. In 1706, with France and England again at war, he captured the West Indies islands of Nevis and St. Christopher from the English and was planning to launch an attack on Boston and New York and other English settlements on the Atlantic coast when he was stricken with yellow fever and died aboard his ship in Havana Harbor on July 9. He was the first great Canadian, a military genius whose dream of giving France a continent was not appreciated by those in power in the French Government; had he been given greater support, the future of North America might have unfolded in a much different manner than it did.

IRELAND, JOHN (1838–1918), archbishop. Born in Burnchurch, Kilkenny,

273

Ireland, and baptized on Sept. 11, he was brought to the United States in 1848 by his parents, who lived first in Burlington, Vermont, then in Chicago, and finally settled in St. Paul, Minnesota, in 1852. The bishop there, Joseph Crétin, sent him to study for the priesthood at the Meximieux preparatory seminary and the Marist seminary near Toulouse, France, and he was ordained at St. Paul in 1861. He served as chaplain with the 5th Minnesota Regiment during the Civil War but was forced to resign because of ill health in 1863. He served at the St. Paul cathedral and became its rector in 1867. He soon became known for his oratory, his leadership in the temperance movement, and his opposition to corrupt politicians. He was appointed titular bishop of Maronea and coadjutor of St. Paul in 1875, and became its bishop in 1884 when Bishop Thomas Grace retired. He soon became involved in civic affairs in his see and nationally, came to be recognized as the leader of the liberal faction of the American hierarchy and a spokesman for the Americanists, and was constantly involved in controversy. His "The Catholic Church and Civil Society" address at the third Plenary Council of Baltimore in 1884 on the patriotism of Catholics attracted nationwide attention; it was a theme he fervently proclaimed throughout his life. He encouraged emigration to the West through his St. Paul Catholic Colonization Association which made it easy for immigrants to purchase land, brought more than four thousand families from the slums of eastern cities to western Minnesota and Nebraska, and was responsible for the founding of numerous towns and villages throughout the West. In 1888 he became the first archbishop of St. Paul when that see was elevated to an archdiocese. With Bishop John Joseph Keane of Richmond, Virginia, he headed the fight for a national Catholic University,

which was established in 1887, vigorously opposed the establishment of national churches, fought to have English used exclusively in Catholic schools, and was the leader in 1891 in the successful fight to defeat Peter Paul Cahensly's memorial to Pope Leo XIII requesting that bishops in the United States be appointed on the basis of the proportion of each national group in the United States. He had joined with Cardinal Gibbons in 1887 in persuading Pope Leo not to condemn the Knights of Labor, as the Canadian bishops had done earlier, and he was a constant supporter of labor though opposed to the use of violence in strikes and labor disputes. He came out strongly in favor of racial equality in 1891 and supported public schools, though he believed Catholic schools were necessary because of anti-Catholic bias in public schools. His Faribault plan, which he put into effect in Faribault and Stillwater, Minnesota, in 1891, caused tremendous controversy. The plan called for turning over parochial schools to local school boards which paid for their upkeep and teachers' salaries (usually the teachers were nuns), with religious education being given in the same schools by the same teachers after regular school hours. It raised such opposition, even among Catholics, that though the decision from Rome in *Tolerari potest* in 1892 permitted such an arrangement under specific circumstances, the plan was abandoned in 1892. Ironically one of the most bitter opponents of the Faribault plan was Archbishop Michael Corrigan of New York, where a similar plan had been in effect in Poughkeepsie, New York, from 1873 until 1890, when the public school superintendent discontinued it. Ireland then devoted himself to expanding the parochial school system of his see. He established St. Thomas Seminary (now College) in 1885, St. Paul Seminary in 1894, and helped establish St. Catherine College in 1905. In 1892 he went to France and incurred the wrath of conservative Catholics there as he urged support for Pope Leo's *railliement* in support of the new republic and lauded the position of the Church in the United States, emphasizing the doctrine of separation of Church and state which was so prominent a feature of the American system of government. In 1894 he became involved in a bitter dispute with Archbishop Corrigan of New York and Bishop Bernard McQuaid of Rochester, New York, when he supported Fr. Sylvester Malone against Bishop McQuaid in an election for a seat on the board of regents of the state of New York; he was denounced by Bishop McQuaid from his pulpit in the Rochester cathedral for interfering in matters outside his ecclesiastical jurisdiction. Ireland led opposition to anti-Catholic political parties and politicians, opposed William Jennings Bryan's candidacy for the presidency and his bimetallism as well as the brewing Spanish-American War, though he supported the United States when war actually broke out in 1898. The following year Pope Leo's encyclical, *Testem, benevolentiae,* was issued warning against ideas said to be abroad in the United States (called by many the "phantom Americanism" heresy), and though it named no names, it was widely believed to be aimed at the liberals in the American hierarchy headed by Ireland; all denied that the reprobated attitudes condemned in the encyclical existed. He laid the cornerstone of St. Paul's Cathedral in 1907, urged American preparedness when war broke out in Europe in 1914, and actively supported the Allies. He died in St. Paul on Sept. 25. Throughout his life Ireland encouraged scholarship and wrote numerous essays for learned magazines. His essays, collected in *The Church and Modern Society* (1896), delineated the problems encountered by the Church in a democratic and pluralistic society. A fervent believer in the American system, he spoke out forthrightly on national and ecclesiastical problems, and despite frequent criticism by those who thought he was too American on the one hand and by those who thought he was too Catholic on the other hand, he was recognized by all as one of the outstanding religious figures of his times.

IRELAND, MOTHER SERAPHINE (1842–1930), educator. Sister of Archbishop John Ireland, Ellen was born in Kilkenny, Ireland, in July and was brought to the United States by her parents, who in time settled in Minnesota. She studied at St. Joseph's Academy, St. Paul, and in 1858 joined the Sisters of St. Joseph, taking the name Seraphine. She taught in the elementary and secondary schools of her order and in 1882 became provincial superior of the St. Joseph province of the Sisters of St. Joseph. She developed the College of St. Catherine in St. Paul, founded for women, into a leading women's college, and on her retirement in 1921 she had increased the number of sisters in her province from 116 to 913 and the number of schools from 8 to 60, and had established 5 hospitals and two orphanages. She died in St. Paul on June 20.

IRENE, SISTER. *See* Fitzgibbon, Mary Irene.

IRETON, PETER LEO (1882–1958), bishop. Born in Baltimore on Sept. 21, he was educated at St. Charles College (Ellicott City, Maryland), St. Mary's Seminary (Baltimore), and the Apostolic Mission House (Washington, D.C.), and was ordained in 1906. He engaged in pastoral work in parishes in Washington and Baltimore, was made a domestic prelate in 1929, and became rector of St. Anne's Church and director of the Holy Name Society in Baltimore. He was appointed titular bishop of Cime and coadjutor and apostolic administrator of Richmond, Virginia, in 1935 and succeeded to the see ten years later in 1945, when its ordinary, Bishop Andrew J. Brennan, who had been paralyzed in 1934, resigned. During his episcopate, Bishop Ireton brought new religious orders into the see, opened new hospitals, maternity homes, and information centers, founded the Richmond Diocesan Missionary Fathers, requested the establishment of Marymount Junior College in Arlington by the Sacred Heart of Mary nuns, and began to integrate Catholic schools in the diocese. He was made an Assistant at the Pontifical Throne in 1956 and died in Washington, D.C. on Apr. 27.

ISSENMAN, CLARENCE G. (1907–82), bishop. Born in Hamilton, Ohio, on May 30, he was educated at St. Gregory's Seminary, Cincinnati, Ohio (B.A.), the University of Fribourg, Switzerland (S.T.D.), and the Angelicum, Rome (Ph.D.). He was ordained in 1932. He became secretary of Archbishop John McNicholas of Cincinnati and associate editor of the *Catholic Telegraph Register* in 1938, was pastor of St. Susanna Church in Mason, Ohio, in 1941–42 and professor of moral theology at Mt. St. Mary's Seminary of the West, Cincinnati, in 1942. In 1945 he was named chancellor of the Cincinnati archdiocese and was also made a domestic prelate. He was pastor of the St. Louis Church, Cincinnati, in 1945–56, was made a prothonotary in 1949, and was consecrated titular bishop of Phytea and auxiliary of Cincinnati in 1954. He was pastor of St. Peter in Chains Cathedral, Cincinnati, in 1956–58, and in 1957 was appointed bishop of Columbus, Ohio; in 1964 he was appointed coadjutor and administrator of the Cleveland diocese and succeeded to the see in 1967. He was active in the Catholic press, served as episcopal chairman of the National Catholic Welfare Conference, was honorary chairman of the Catholic Press Association in 1965–67, and stressed the need for professionalism in Catholic journalism and led the successful battle against censorship of the National Catholic Welfare Conference News Service. He completed a twenty-million-dollar building program and retired in 1974. He died in Cleveland on July 27.

ITURBI, JOSÉ (1895–1980), pianist, conductor. Born in Valencia, Spain, on Nov. 28, he was destined for a musical career from birth. His parents entered him in the Escuela de Musica de Maria Jordan when he was five; by the time he was seven, he was performing in public. He entered the Conservatorio de Musica in Valencia in 1903 and studied privately with Joaquín Malats and then at the Conservatoire de Musique in Paris, graduating with first honors when he was seventeen. He married Marie Giner in 1916, was appointed head of the piano department of the Geneva Conservatory in 1919, and after two years of further study began giving concerts. He toured the European capitals beginning in 1923 and made his American debut in 1928 with the Philadelphia Orchestra under Leopold Stokowski, all to great acclaim. In 1933 he made his debut in Mexico City as a conductor, directed in New York, Philadelphia, Detroit, Rochester, and Hollywood during the next few years, and in 1936 was appointed conductor of the Rochester Philharmonic Orchestra, a post he held for several seasons. In 1941 he played Liszt's Piano Concerto in E-flat while conducting the Philadelphia Orchestra at Carnegie Hall in New York City—a feat which drew wild applause from the audience and praise from the critics. He took out American citizenship papers the same year. Flamboyant in style, he was frequently engaged in controversy, as when he stated women could not attain the musicianly standards of men in a 1937 newspaper interview, or when he refused to continue the broadcast of a concert in 1937 when Jan Peerce and Lucy Monroe sang popular songs, or when he refused in 1941 to appear on the same program with Benny Goodman. He appeared in several motion pictures, among them *Thousands Cheer* (1943) and *Anchors Aweigh* (1945), continued his concert tours until he was eighty-four, and died in Hollywood on June 28.

IVES, LEVI SILLIMAN (1797–1867). Born in Meriden, Connecticut, on Sept. 16, he left school to enlist in the Army during the War of 1812, served for a year, and then studied for the Presbyterian ministry at Hamilton College, Clinton, New York. He became an Episcopalian in 1819 and was ordained a priest in the Episcopal Church in 1823, served congregations in New York and Pennsylvania, and in 1831 was consecrated the first Episcopal bishop of North Carolina. He was active in educating and promoting the welfare of blacks in his diocese, though he defended the institution of slavery. He was impressed by the Oxford movement, and founded a religious community, the Brotherhood of the Holy Cross, in 1845 at Valle Crucis, North Carolina. He was arraigned before an Episcopal Church convention for his support of the Oxford movement and for following Catholic practices. Although the charges were dismissed in 1848, the Brotherhood was dissolved. He went to Rome in 1852 and became a Catholic; his wife, daughter of Bishop John Henry Hobart of the Episcopal diocese of New York, also became a Catholic shortly after. On his return to the United States, he became an instructor in English at St. Joseph's Seminary and at St. John's College (Fordham) and devoted himself to charitable activities. He founded the Catholic Male Protectory in New York City in 1863 and became its first president. He died in New York City on Oct. 13.

J

JAMES, DANIEL R. "CHAPPY", JR.
(1920–78), general. Youngest of seventeen children, he was born in Pensacola, Florida, on Feb. 11, intended to become a mortician at Tuskegee Institute, Tuskegee, Alabama, but decided to major in physical education and received his B.S. in that subject. He learned to fly there and in 1943 joined the Army Air Corps as a second lieutenant. He trained pilots for the all-black 99th Pursuit Squadron, was sent to the Philippines as flight leader of the 12th Fighter Bomber Squadron in 1949, and during the Korean "police action" flew 101 combat missions. He was placed in command of the 437th and 60th Fighter Interceptor Squadrons at Otis Air Force Base, Massachusetts, after the Korean conflict, was made a major while there and was a staff officer at Air Force headquarters in Washington, D.C., in 1957–60. He was in England in 1960–64 and then commanded operations of the 4453rd Combat Crew Training Wing at Davis-Monthan Air Force Base in Arizona. He flew seventy-eight combat missions over North Vietnam as wing vice commander in 1967 and in 1969 was made commander of Wheelus Air Force Base in Libya. He was at the Pentagon in 1970–73 as Deputy Assistant Secretary of Defense for Public Affairs and while there was raised from one-star to three-star general. In 1974 he was made vice commander of the Military Airlift Command at Scott Air Force Base in Illinois and was made a four-star general—the first black man to attain that rank. The following year he was made commander-in-chief of the North American Air Defense Command (NORAD) in charge of all United States and Canadian strategic air defense forces, headquartered at an underground center in Colorado Springs, Colorado. He retired in 1978, suffered a heart attack soon after, and died in Colorado Springs on Feb. 25. Throughout his career he championed racial equality in the Armed Forces and encouraged minorities to follow in his footsteps.

JANSSEN, JOHN (1835–1913), bishop. Born in Keppeln, Prussia, on Mar. 3, he studied at the Münster seminary and went to the United States in 1858 at the request of Bishop Henry Juncker of Alton (now diocese of Springfield), Illinois. He finished his theological studies, was ordained later the same year, and engaged in missionary work in Illinois. He was secretary to Bishop Juncker and was vicar of the diocese in 1870–86, except for 1877–79, when he was pastor of St. Boniface Church, Quincy, Illinois. He was administrator of the see from 1886 to 1888, when he was consecrated first bishop of the newly established diocese of Belleville, Illinois. During his quarter-of-a-century episcopate, he greatly increased the number of priests, churches, schools, and hospitals in the diocese. He died in Belleville on July 2.

JANSSENS, FRANCIS AUGUST ANTHONY JOSEPH (1843–97), archbishop. Born in Tillburg, North Brabant, Holland, on Oct. 17, he was educated at Bois-le-Duc Seminary and the American College, Louvain, Belgium, and was ordained in Ghent in 1867. He emigrated to the United States in 1868, became pastor of the cathedral at Richmond, Virginia, in 1870 and vicar of that diocese in 1872, and was made administrator of the see when Bishop James Gibbons was transferred to Baltimore as coadjutor in 1877. He was appointed bishop of Natchez-Jackson (changed to the diocese of Jackson), Mississippi, in 1881. He built up the diocese and became known for his interest in developing a black Catholic clergy and for his work among the Choctaw Indians. In 1888 he completed St. Mary's Cathedral and later the same year was appointed archbishop of New Orleans. He opened new parochial schools, welcomed Mother Cabrini to his see, established the corporate structures of the parishes of the archdiocese, actively promoted native vocations, labored to help blacks and immigrant Italians, and founded a seminary at Ponchatoula, Louisiana. He died at sea on June 9 while on his way to New York on the steamer *Creole,* the first step of a trip to Europe, where he hoped to raise funds to help liquidate the heavy diocesan debt he had inherited and had substantially reduced during his episcopate.

JEANMARD, JULES BENJAMIN (1879–1957), bishop. Born in Breaux Bridge, Louisiana, on Aug. 15, he was educated at St. Joseph's Seminary, Gessen, Louisiana, Holy Cross College, Worcester, Mass., St. Louis Seminary, New Orleans, and Kenrick Seminary, St. Louis. He was ordained in 1903, was a curate at New Orleans' St. Louis Cathedral in 1903–6, was secretary to Archbishop James Blenk in 1906–14, and served as chancellor of the New Orleans archdiocese in 1914–17. He was administrator of the see in 1917–18, was administrator of the new diocese of La-

fayette, Louisiana, for six months in 1918, and was appointed its first bishop the same year—the first Louisianan to become a bishop. He was made an Assistant at the Pontifical Throne in 1943, resigned in 1956 because of ill health, and was named titular bishop of Bareta. He died at Lake Charles, Louisiana, on Feb. 23.

JERITZA, MARIA (1887–1982), opera singer. Daughter of a concierge, Marie Jedlitzka was born at Brünn, Austria (Brno, Czechoslovakia), on Oct. 6 and changed her name to Maria Jeritza in her early twenties. Though her family was poor, she studied dramatics and singing in her youth and made her debut as a member of the Olmütz Opera Company in 1910 in the role of Elsa in Wagner's *Lohengrin.* She won a position at the Vienna Volksoper five months later in the role of Elisabeth in Wagner's *Tannhäuser.* Appearances in Offenbach's *La Belle Hélène* in Munich and as Strauss's first Ariadne in Stuttgart evoked favorable reaction and when Emperor Franz Josef was impressed with her Rosalinda in *Die Fledermaus* she was invited to join the Vienna Opera. Her debut in 1912 in the title role of *Aphrodite* launched her on a career that made her one of the great stars of opera and earned her the adulation of opera fans all over the world. She joined the Metropolitan Opera in 1921 and sang some twenty roles for the Metropolitan before she left in 1932. She then sang all over the United States and Europe and made several motion pictures. During her career her most famous roles were Tosca, Santuzza, Sieglinde, Elsa, Elisabeth, Octavian, Turandot, and Minnie and she sang with all the great male singers, notably Alfred Piccaver and Beniamino Gigli. She was married three times, to Austrian businessman Baron Leopold Popper de Podharagn, whom she divorced in 1934, Hollywood film executive Winfield Sheehan (d. 1945) in 1935, and New Jersey businessman Irving P. Seery (d. 1966) in 1948. She was noted for her flamboyant life-style, was active into her eighties, and died on July 10 at St. Mary's Hospital, Orange, New Jersey, after a long illness.

JOGUES, ST. ISAAC (1607–46), missionary, martyr. Born of well-to-do parents in Orléans, France, on Jan. 10, he joined the Jesuits in 1624, studied at the Jesuit school in Orléans, and was ordained in 1636. He taught literature for a time at Rouen and then at his request was sent as a missionary to Canada; he was immediately sent to work among the Hurons on Georgian Bay. He worked among them for the next six years with great success, traveling in 1641 as far as Sault Ste. Marie, which he named, in his missionary work. In 1642 he and his party were captured by a band of Iroquois Mohawk Indians, traditional enemies of the Hurons, near Three Rivers, Quebec, and taken to their village of Ossernenon (now Auriesville) on the Mohawk River, New York. For the next thirteen months he was subjected to incredible tortures (among them being forced to watch the torture and murder of René Goupil, one of the group) but when about to be put to death was smuggled aboard a Dutch ship and taken to New Amsterdam—the first Catholic priest to set foot on Manhattan island. He then returned to France, where he was given a hero's welcome at the court. Early in 1644 he returned to Canada, again at his request, and resumed his missionary activities. In 1646 he was sent to negotiate a peace with the Mohawks at Ossernenon, was well received by the Indians, and was successful in his mission; on this trip he discovered Lake George, which he named Lac du St. Sacrement. At his request he was sent back to the Iroquois later in the year, but this time he received a different reception. The Indians blamed him for a pestilence that had struck the tribe and for a blight that had decimated their crops. He was taken captive, with his companion Jean Lalande, near Lake George, tortured, and brought to Ossernenon, where on Oct. 18 he was tomahawked to death. He was canonized in 1930 by Pope Pius XI as one of the Martyrs of North America; their feast day is Oct. 19.

JOHANNES, FRANCIS (1874–1937), bishop. Born in Mittelstren, Bavaria, on Feb. 17, he was brought to the United States in 1882, studied at St. Benedict's College, Atchison, Kansas, and St. Francis Seminary, Milwaukee, Wisconsin, and was ordained in 1897. He engaged in pastoral work in St. Joseph, Missouri, in 1897–1928, serving as pastor from 1918 until 1928, when he was appointed titular bishop of Thasus and coadjutor of Leavenworth (changed to Kansas City in 1947), Kansas, and succeeded to the see in 1929. He served in that position until his death in Denver, Colorado, on Mar. 13.

JOHNSTON, RICHARD MALCOLM (1822–98), author, educator. Son of a Baptist minister, he was born near Powelton, Georgia, on Mar. 8, was educated at Mercer University, Macon, Georgia, and after graduation taught for a year. He then studied law, was admitted to the bar in 1843, and practiced until 1857, when he began teaching literature at the University of Georgia. He continued there until the outbreak of the Civil War closed the university and he opened a small school for boys on a farm near Sparta, Georgia. After the war, he founded the Penn Lucy School near Baltimore and in 1875 became a Catholic, following his wife and children. He began to write at the urging of Sidney Lanier, the poet, and when the attendance at his school, which was mostly Baptist, declined after his conversion to Catholicism, he devoted himself entirely to writing and lecturing. His stories of Georgia life, *Dukesborough Tales* (1871), *Old Mark Langston* (1884), *The Widow Guthrie* (1890), and *The Primes* (1891) became immediately popular when published in *Southern Magazine* and *The Century*. He also wrote *Essays* (1881), a biography of Alexander H. Stephens (with W. H. Browne), and a text on English literature. He died in Baltimore on Sept. 23.

JOLIET or JOLLIET, LOUIS (1645–1700), explorer. Son of a wagon maker, he was born near Quebec before Sept. 21, studied at the Jesuit school there, received minor orders in 1662 but abandoned the religious life to become a trader among the Indians. He went to France in 1667 to study hydrography and then spent the next four years trapping and traveling all over the Great Lakes area. In 1672 he was sent by Governor Frontenac to seek the *grande rivière* (the Mississippi) beyond the Great Lakes. He and his party, which included Fr. Jacques Marquette, wintered at the Straits of Mackinac and the following spring set out on the epic-making trip through the heartland of America—down the Wisconsin River to the Mississippi (sighted June 17, 1673), which they followed south down its west bank until they passed the mouth of the Arkansas River. Then, convinced it emptied into the Gulf of Mexico, they ascended its east bank. He arrived back in Quebec in August 1674 and, though his maps and full reports were lost when his canoe overturned in the Lachine Rapids, his condensed reports led to plans to colonize the Mississippi Valley, though his request to establish a colony among the Illinois was refused. He married Claire-Françoise Bissot, was granted the island of Anticosti in the Gulf of St. Lawrence in 1680, where he erected a fort (captured in 1690 by the English, who took his wife into captivity while he was on an exploring expedition to Labrador and the Hudson Bay area), and was appointed royal hydrographer in 1697 and granted the seigniory of Joliette, south of Quebec. He died there after May 4 and before Oct. 18.

JONES, WILLIAM AMBROSE (1865–1921), bishop. Born in Cambridge, New York, on July 21, he was educated at Villanova, Philadelphia, joined the Augustinians in 1886, and made his profession the next year. He was ordained in Philadelphia in 1890, engaged in parish work in Philadelphia and Atlantic City, New Jersey, for several years, and was master of novices at the Augustinian scholasticate at Villanova from 1895 until 1899, when he was sent to Cuba as pastor of old San Agustín Church there. He opened St. Augustine College, Havana, in 1901 and was its president until 1907, when he was consecrated first American bishop of San Juan, Puerto Rico, a position he held until his death in Philadelphia on Feb. 17.

JORDAN, EDWARD BENEDICT (1884–1951), educator. Born in Dunmore, Pennsylvania, on Dec. 17, he was educated at St. Thomas College, Scranton, Pennsylvania (B.S. 1903), Mt. St. Mary's College, Emmitsburg, Maryland (B.A. 1905), and the Propaganda, Rome (S.T.D. 1909), and was ordained in Rome in 1909. He taught biology and education at Mt. St. Mary's in 1910–21 and was vice president in 1918–20, taught education at Catholic University in 1921–30 and was secretary of the College of Arts and Sciences there in 1930–37. He was secretary of the Catholic Sisters College in Washington, D.C., in 1921–36 and became dean in

1936, the year he was made a domestic prelate. He lectured on psychology at Trinity College, Washington, D.C., in 1931–37, became vice-rector of Catholic University and national director of the International Federation of Catholic College Alumnae in 1934, and was director of ecclesiastical studies in 1950. He translated Frans de Hovre's *Philosophy and Education* (1931) and *Catholicism in Education* (1934) and died in Washington on July 19.

JORDAN, ELIZABETH (1865–1947), author, journalist. Born in Milwaukee, Wisconsin, on May 9, she was educated at Notre Dame Convent there, graduated in 1884, and determined to become a nun. She was dissuaded by her father, who steered her into a career in journalism. She attended business school, did some reporting for the St. Paul *Globe* and the Chicago *Tribune,* and then went to New York City, where she joined the staff of the New York *World* in 1890. She worked on the *World* until 1900, writing a daily column, "True Stories of the News," and serving as assistant editor of its Sunday edition in 1897–1900, when she became editor of *Harper's Bazaar.* When William Randolph Hearst bought *Harper's Bazaar,* she stayed on as literary editor to Harper and Brothers, book publishers, until 1918. She was story editor for Goldwyn Pictures briefly in 1918, and in 1922 became dramatic critic for *America,* a position she held until her retirement in 1945. She early began writing novels and during her career wrote some thirty-nine books, among them *Tales of Destiny* (1902), *Many Kingdoms* (1908), *Wings of Youth* (1917), *The Lady of Petlands* (1923), *Life of the Party* (1935), and the autobiographical *Three Rousing Cheers* (1938); she also wrote a comedy, *The Lady from Oklahoma,* which ran only thirteen performances when produced

in New York in 1913. She died in New York City on Feb. 24.

JUERGENS, SYLVESTER PETER (1899–1969), superior general. Born in Dubuque, Iowa, on Mar. 27, he was educated at Chaminade College, Clayton, Missouri, joined the Society of Mary (the Marianists) at Ferguson, Missouri, in 1910, and continued his education at the University of Dayton, Ohio (B.A. 1918). He taught at his Society's schools in Texas, Illinois, and Missouri in 1912–22 and then resumed his studies at the University of Fribourg, Switzerland (S.T.L., S.T.D.) in 1922–27. He was ordained in Fribourg in 1927, was professor of philosophy at Maryhurst Normal, Kirkwood, Missouri, in 1927–31, served as president of Chaminade College in Clayton in 1931–36, was provincial of the St. Louis province of the Marianists in 1936–46, and was elected superior general of the Society of Mary in 1946 —the first American to be named to that position—and served until 1956. He was the author of several books, among them *Newman on the Psychology of Faith in the Individual* (1928), with P. A. Resch, and *Martha, Martha!* (1930). He died in St. Louis on Nov. 21.

JUGE, GABRIEL (1879–1959), superior general. Born in St. Julien, Chapteuil, France, he joined the Brothers of the Sacred Heart, taking the name Albertinus, in 1893, taught at Paradis, and when anticlerical legislation closed many of the French Catholic schools, he emigrated to the United States in 1903. He taught at the Metuchen, New Jersey, novitiate of his order from 1903 to 1922, except in 1906–8, when he taught in the South. He became provincial of the Brothers of the Sacred Heart in the United States in 1922, assistant to the superior general in 1931, and superior of his order in 1937–52. He spent the next four years as novice master in Écully, France, and then returned to the United States, where he died in Metuchen on Dec. 7.

JUNCKER, HENRY DAMIAN (1809–68), bishop. Born in Fénétrange, Lorraine, on Aug. 22, he began studying for the priesthood at the Pont-à-Mousson Seminary and then emigrated to the United States, where he finished his studies at St. Francis Xavier Seminary, Cincinnati, Ohio. He was ordained in Cincinnati in 1836 and worked as a missionary and pastor in Ohio until 1857, when he was consecrated first bishop of the newly established diocese of Alton (transferred to Springfield in 1923), Illinois. Later that year he went to Europe, where he was successful in securing priests and funds for his diocese, among them Franciscans of the Holy Cross Province whom he helped found St. Joseph Seminary and College in 1862; also founded by the Franciscans at his urging was the liberal arts Quincy College which in time became the minor seminary of the see. During his episcopate, he enlarged the cathedral and encouraged the building of churches and schools to accommodate the needs of the Irish and German immigrants who were flocking into Illinois. He attended the second Plenary Council of Baltimore in 1866 and the Centenary of the Holy Apostles in Rome in 1867, and died the following year in Alton on Oct. 2.

JUNGER, AEGIDIUS (1833–95), bishop. Born in Burtscheid, Germany, on Apr. 6, he studied at the American College, Louvain, and was ordained in 1862. He served as an assistant to Fr. Brouillet at Walla Walla, Washington, for the next two years and was then recalled to Vancouver by Bishop Blanchet of Nesqually and served as his secretary in 1864–79. He was appointed second bishop of Nesqually (changed to the diocese of Seattle in 1907) in 1879 when Bishop Blanchet resigned. He was a strong advocate of Catholic education, built sixty new churches and sixteen schools, brought numerous religious orders into the see, built a new cathedral at Vancouver, British Columbia, in 1884, and saw Gonzaga College (University) opened in Spokane, Washington, in 1886. He died in Vancouver on Dec. 26.

K

KAIN, JOHN JOSEPH (1841–1903), archbishop. Born in Martinsburg, West Virginia, on May 31, he was educated at St. Charles College, Baltimore, and was ordained in Baltimore in 1866. He was pastor at Harper's Ferry, West Virginia, until 1875, when he was consecrated second bishop of Wheeling, West Virginia. He was procurator of the third Plenary Council of Baltimore in 1884 and was appointed titular bishop of Oxyrynchia and coadjutor of St. Louis in 1893. He was administrator of the archdiocese of St. Louis in 1893–95 and was appointed archbishop of the see in 1895. He held archdiocesan synods at which he reorganized the archdiocese, reactivated Kenrick Seminary, and began building a new cathedral. He left St. Louis after the arrival of John Joseph Glennon as coadjutor in 1903 and died in Baltimore six months later on Oct. 13.

KATERI TEKAKWITHA, BL. *See* Tekakwitha, Bl. Kateri.

KATZENBERGER, WILLIAM E. (1876–1963), educator. Born in Baltimore on Nov. 13, he was educated at St. Vincent's Seminary and the University of Pennsylvania, joined the Vincentians in 1895, and was ordained in 1903. He taught at St. John's College, Brooklyn, New York, in 1906–12 and then at Niagara University, except for the years 1927–29 at St. Vincent's, from 1912–59, serving as president of Niagara in 1918–27. He went to Conception Church in Baltimore in 1959, where he spent the rest of his life. He died on July 27.

KATZER, FREDERICK XAVIER (1844–1903), archbishop. Born in Ebensee, Upper Austria, on Feb. 7, he studied at the seminary in Freinberg, near Linz, and then with a group of volunteers for the American missions, emigrated to the United States in 1864. He continued his studies for the priesthood at St. Francis Seminary, Milwaukee, Wisconsin, and was ordained there in 1866. He taught at St. Francis until 1875, when he became secretary to newly appointed Bishop Krautbauer of Green Bay, Wisconsin, was named vicar-general of the diocese in 1878 and administrator of the see when Bishop Krautbauer died in 1885, and was consecrated bishop of Green Bay the following year. The Wisconsin legislature passed the Bennett law in 1889, making teaching in all schools compulsory in English, and he and other Wisconsin Catholic bishops joined Lutheran church authorities in fighting the legislation on behalf of the numerous German language schools in Wisconsin, and forced its repeal in 1890. He was appointed third archbishop of Milwaukee in 1891, despite the opposition of the Americanists led by Archbishop John Ireland, who felt he was too German-oriented to be appointed archbishop of an American archdiocese and had recommended Bishop John L. Spalding of Peoria, Illinois, for the see. Katzer supported the establishment of parochial schools in every diocese at the third Plenary Council of Baltimore in 1884 and opposed Ireland's Faribault plan. He brought the Sisters of the Divine Savior to the United States in 1895, opposed the presidential candidacy of William Jennings Bryan in 1896, and died at Fond du Lac, Wisconsin, on July 20.

KAVANAGH, EDWARD (1795–1844), statesman, diplomat. Son of a prosperous Irish immigrant merchant and shipbuilder, he was born in Newcastle, Maine, on Apr. 27. He studied at Georgetown in 1810–11 and St. Mary's College, Baltimore, in 1811–12, and for the priesthood under Fr. Francis Matignon in Boston, but when his father's business was ruined by the War of 1812, he abandoned his plans for the priesthood to devote himself to his father's business. He went to Europe in 1815 to press claims of the business against the French and the British governments and on his return to the United States studied law and was admitted to the bar. He became interested in politics, was elected to the Maine legislature in 1826 and the state Senate in 1828, and was secretary of the Senate in 1830. He served in Congress in 1831–35, was named American chargé d'affaires at Lisbon, Portugal, in 1835, and negotiated the first trade treaty between the United States and Portugal. He resigned in 1841 and returned to Maine, where he was again elected to the Senate and was made its presiding officer in 1843. He was one of the four commissioners sent to Washington to present Maine's claims in the northeast boundary controversy with England (he had earlier prepared a report on the matter to Maine's governor in 1831) which was eventually settled by the Webster-Ashburton Treaty in 1842 which defined the boundary between Maine and Canada. When Governor Fairfield of Maine resigned in 1843 to enter the United States Senate, Kavanagh, as president of the Maine Senate, succeeded to the office—the first Catholic governor of any New England state. He was forced to resign because of ill health nine months later and died the following month in Newcastle on Jan. 21.

KEANE, JAMES JOHN (1857–1929), archbishop. Born in Joliet, Illinois, on Aug. 26, he was educated at St. John's Seminary, Collegeville, Minnesota, St. Francis Xavier College, New York City, and the Grand Seminary, Montreal, and was ordained in St. Paul, Minnesota, in 1882. He engaged in pastoral work in St. Paul for a time, then became an instructor at St. Thomas College, where he was appointed rector in 1888. He served as pastor for a time and in 1902 was appointed third bishop of Cheyenne, Wyoming, serving in that position until 1911, when he was appointed archbishop of Dubuque, Iowa—the first American-born ordinary of that see. During his episcopate he encouraged educational and charitable foundations in the archdiocese, worked to develop the archdiocesan college, Dubuque College (later Columbia College), founded the see's paper, *The Witness,* in 1921, and died in Dubuque on Aug. 2.

KEANE, JOHN JOSEPH (1839–1918), archbishop. Born in Ballyshannon, Donegal, Ireland, on Sept. 12, he was brought to Canada by his parents when they emigrated there in 1846. They moved to Baltimore in 1848 and John studied at St. Charles College, Ellicott City, Maryland, and St. Mary's Seminary, Baltimore, and was ordained in Baltimore in 1866. He served as a curate in Washington, D.C., parishes until 1878, when he was appointed fifth bishop of Richmond, Virginia. He ardently supported the establishment of a Catholic University of America at the third Plenary Council of Baltimore in

1884 and, with Archbishop John Ireland, representing the committee established by the council to found the university, secured the approval of the Holy See. Despite the opposition of the conservative members of the American hierarchy, he was appointed first rector of the university in 1888 and was named titular bishop of Vasso the following year. He gained a national reputation as a university administrator, became one of the leaders of the liberal faction of the American hierarchy, helped prevent the condemnation of the Knights of Labor, convinced the Roman authorities to reject the Abbelen memorial, and strongly opposed Cahenslyism. He was removed as rector in 1896 by papal order, reportedly because of his liberalism. He was appointed titular archbishop of Damascus in 1897 and went to Rome as a consultor of the Congregation of Propaganda and of the Congregation of Studies. He returned to the United States in 1899, worked to secure endowments for Catholic University for a year, and was appointed archbishop of Dubuque, Iowa, in 1900. He was active in encouraging religious education, opened new parishes, formed a mission band for the archdiocese, vigorously promoted the temperance movement and held synods in 1902, 1905, and 1908. He resigned in 1911 because of ill health and was appointed titular archbishop of Cios and served as vicar-general under Archbishop James John Keane, his successor. He died in Dubuque on June 22. He was the author of several books, among them *Onward and Upward* (1902), a collection of his sermons, and *Emmanuel* (1915).

KEANE, PATRICK JOSEPH (1872–1928), bishop. Born in Kerry, Ireland, on Jan. 6, he was educated at St. Patrick's College, Carlow, emigrated to the United States, and finished his studies for the priesthood at Catholic University. He was ordained in 1895 and engaged in pastoral work in San Francisco until 1920, when he was appointed titular bishop of Samaria and auxiliary of Sacramento, California. He succeeded to the see in 1922, labored to provide the diocese with a modern parochial school system, and died in Sacramento on Sept. 1.

KEARNEY, JAMES E. (1884–1976), bishop. Born in Salt Lake City, Utah, on Oct. 28, he graduated from Teachers' College of New York, taught for a time, and then studied for the priesthood at St. Joseph's Seminary, Dunwoodie, Yonkers, New York, and Catholic University, where he received his S.T.L. He was ordained in 1908, served as a curate at St. Cecilia's Church and taught at Cathedral College, New York City, and became pastor of St. Francis Xavier Church, Bronx, New York. He served as superintendent of Catholic schools in the Bronx and in 1932 was appointed fourth bishop of Salt Lake City. He held this position until 1937, when he was transferred to Rochester, New York, as its fifth bishop. He founded St. John Fisher College there in 1947, retired in 1966, and died in Rochester on Jan. 12.

KEATING, EDWARD (1875–1965), editor. Born in Kansas City, Kansas, on July 9, he was brought to Colorado by his widowed mother in 1880 and, when fourteen, joined *The Republican* in Denver as copyholder in the proofreading room. He worked on various Denver newspapers as proofreader, reporter and editor from 1889 until 1911, serving as managing editor of the Denver *Rocky Mountain News* in 1906–11, was owner of the Pueblo *Daily News* in 1912–14, and in 1919 became first managing editor of *Labor,* the paper of the railroad workers, a position he held until his retirement thirty-four years later. Also interested in politics, he was Denver city auditor in 1889–1901, was president of the Colorado State Board of Land Commissioners in 1911–13, and served in Congress in 1913–19, voting against the entrance of the United States into World War I. He retired as manager-editor of *Labor* in 1953 and was made manager-editor emeritus. He wrote *Labor* (1953), a history, and *Gentleman from Colorado* (1964). He died in Washington, D.C., on Mar. 18.

KEELY, PATRICK CHARLES (1816 or 1820–96), architect. Son of an architect, he was born in Kilkenny, Ireland, on Aug. 9, 1816, or Thurles, Ireland, on Aug. 9, 1820, and was probably trained by his father. He emigrated to the United States in 1841 and soon became a leading church architect in neo- or Victorian Gothic style, designing sixteen Catholic cathedrals and some seven hundred other churches. Among his works are the Cathedral of the Holy Cross in Boston, Cathedral of the Holy Name in Chicago, Cathedral of SS. Peter and Paul, Providence, Rhode Island, St. Peter's Cathedral, Erie, Pennsylvania, and St. Francis Xavier Church in New York City. His name is also spelled Keily and Kiely. He was awarded the Laetare Medal in 1884 and died in Brooklyn, New York, on Aug. 11.

KEILEY, ANTHONY M. (1833–1905), jurist. Born in Paterson, New Jersey, on Sept. 12, he was educated at Randolph-Macon College, Boydton, Virginia, and was admitted to the bar. He served in the Confederate Army during the Civil War and was captured, writing of his experiences in *In Vinculis* (1866), served in the Virginia House of Delegates in 1864–71, and was mayor of Richmond, Virginia, in 1871–76. After serving as Richmond city attorney in 1875–85 and as chairman of the state Democratic committee, he was ap-

pointed U.S. minister to Italy by President Cleveland in 1885. The Italian Government refused to accept him because of his public criticism of its seizure of Rome; the government of Austria-Hungary also refused to accept him when he was appointed minister to that country because his wife was a member of a prominent Richmond Jewish family. In 1886 he was appointed a judge of the International Court of the First Instance at Cairo and in 1894 he was appointed U.S. representative on the Higher Court of Appeals at Alexandria, Egypt. He resigned in 1902 and died in Paris on Jan. 27. He had also served as president of the National Irish Catholic Benevolent Union for twelve years.

KEILEY, BENJAMIN JOSEPH (1847–1925), bishop. Born in Petersburg, Virginia, on Oct. 13, he was educated at St. Charles College, Ellicott City, Maryland, and the North American College, Rome, and was ordained in 1873. After serving as pastor in Delaware and Atlanta and Savannah, Georgia, he was named vicar-general of Savannah in 1887. He was consecrated bishop of that diocese in 1900, founded the Catholic Layman's Association of Georgia, and resigned in 1922 because of blindness. He was appointed titular bishop of Scillium and died in Atlanta on June 17.

KEILY, PATRICK CHARLES. *See* Keely, Patrick Charles.

KELLER, JAMES G. (1900–77). Born in Oakland, California, on June 27, he entered St. Patrick's Seminary, Menlo Park, California, to study for the priesthood but left after three years. He returned in 1918 only to leave in 1921, when he joined the Maryknoll Fathers. He finished his studies for the priesthood at Maryknoll Seminary, Ossining,

New York, and Catholic University (S.T.B. 1924, M.A. 1925), and was ordained in Oakland in 1925. He was assigned to the Maryknoll house in San Francisco and engaged in publicity and fund-raising for Maryknoll missioners in China and Maryknoll centers throughout the United States. In 1930 he was put in charge of a Maryknoll promotion center in New York City and in 1945 he founded The Christophers, dedicated to the belief that each individual can help change the world and improve it; its monthly *News Notes,* begun in 1946, in time was distributed to more than a million people. He produced documentary films spreading the Christopher message, wrote a widely syndicated newspaper column, "Three Minutes a Day," in 1950–68, produced a television program, "Christopher Close-up," in 1953–68, and was the author of more than twenty-five bestselling books, among them *You Can Change the World* (1948), from which a movie was made in 1950, *Three Minutes a Day* (1949), *Careers That Change Your World* (1951), and his autobiography, *To Light a Candle* (1963). He also inaugurated the annual Christopher Awards to writers, directors, and producers for books, motion pictures, and television productions of outstanding artistic merit that affirmed the highest value of the human spirit. He retired because of illness in 1969 and died in New York City on Feb. 7.

KELLEY, FRANCIS ALPHONSUS (1888–1931), chaplain. Born in Cohoes, New York, on Apr. 19, he was educated at St. Michael's College, Toronto, Canada, and St. Bernard's Seminary, Rochester, New York, and after his ordination, served as pastor in Albany, Troy, and Cairo, all in New York. He was chaplain of the 27th Division during World War I and was decorated by the American and British governments. In 1919 he became the first national chaplain of the American Legion. He died in Catskill, New York, on Oct. 15.

KELLEY, FRANCIS CLEMENT (1870–1948), bishop. Born in Vernon River, Prince Edward Island, Canada, on Nov. 24, he was educated at St. Dunstan's College, Charlottetown, Canada, and Nicolet Seminary at Laval University, Quebec, and was ordained for the diocese of Detroit in 1893. He was pastor in Lampeer, Michigan, in 1893–1907 and served as a chaplain with the 32nd Michigan Regiment in the Spanish-American War. In 1905 he founded the Catholic Church Extension Society of the United States to serve the needs of home missions and served as its president for the next nineteen years. He founded *Extension* magazine in 1906 and was its editor; in time he built its circulation to over three million subscribers. The Society built seven thousand churches and over the years provided regular support for needy priests and seminarians and missionary assistance of every kind. He represented the Mexican bishops at the World War I peace conference in Paris and while there began negotiations unofficially with Italian Premier Vittorio Orlando to settle the "Roman Question." Two years later he was Vatican envoy to England to settle problems concerning German and Austrian missions and during the Carranza revolution in Mexico he represented the Mexican bishops and established St. Philip Neri Seminary in Castroville, Texas, for priests and seminarians exiled from Mexico. He was made a domestic prelate and then a prothonotary apostolic in 1915 and in 1924 was appointed bishop of Oklahoma (changed to the diocese of Oklahoma City and Tulsa in 1930). He opened some sixty churches in the diocese, continued his mission work, fought the Ku Klux Klan, and died in

Oklahoma City on Feb. 1. He was honored by Italy and Austria and by numerous universities and colleges and wrote numerous books, among them *The Last Battle of the Gods* (1907), *Charred Wood* (a novel published under the pen name of Myles Murdach in 1917), *The Forgotten God* (1932), *Problem Island* (1937), *The Bishop Jots It Down* (1939), and *Pack Rats* (1942).

KELLY, DENNIS FRANCIS (1868–1938), merchant. Born in Chicago, he went to work when a boy for Mandel Brothers, a department store in Chicago, in 1879, was manager in 1901–23, and joined The Fair in 1923, becoming its president in 1925. He was first president of Catholic Charities of the archdiocese of Chicago in 1918 and served as president of the National Retail Dry Goods Association in 1931. He died in Bergen, Norway, on July 22.

KELLY, EDWARD DENIS (1860–1926), bishop. Born in Hartford, Michigan, on Dec. 30, he was educated at Mt. St. Mary of the West Seminary, Cincinnati, Ohio, St. Charles College, Ellicott City, Maryland, and St. Joseph Seminary, Troy, New York, and was ordained in Sandwich, Ontario, Canada, in 1886. He engaged in pastoral work in the Detroit diocese in 1886–1911 and in 1910 was appointed titular bishop of Cestrus and auxiliary of Detroit and consecrated the following year. He was translated to Grand Rapids, Michigan, as its third bishop in 1919 and remained in that position until his death there on Mar. 26.

KELLY, EDWARD JOSEPH (1890–1956), bishop. Born in The Dalles, Oregon, on Feb. 26, he was educated at St. Mary's College there, Columbia University, Oregon, St. Patrick's Seminary, Menlo Park, California, and North American College, Rome. He was ordained in 1917, worked as a missionary in the Baker City, Oregon, diocese in 1917–19, and became secretary to Bishop Joseph McGrath of Baker City in 1919, who made him chancellor of the see. He was named bishop of Boise, Idaho, in 1928 and served in that position until his death in Boise on Apr. 21.

KELLY, EUGENE (1808–94), banker. Born in County Tyrone, Ireland, on Nov. 25, he emigrated to New York in 1834 and engaged in the dry-goods business there with the Donnelly Company. He moved to Maysville, Kentucky, and then to St. Louis, establishing dry-goods concerns, and in 1850 went to California during the gold rush days. He engaged in merchandising, founding Murphy, Grant & Company, and banking, founding Donohoe, Kelly & Company, amassed a fortune, and returned to New York in 1856. He married Margaret Anna Hughes, niece of Archbishop John Hughes, in 1857 and concentrated his business interests in New York City. He contributed generously to charitable and educational institutions, notably Catholic University (he was a member of its original board of trustees), and supported Irish home rule, serving as president of the National Federation for Irish Home Rule. He helped rehabilitate a number of Southern railroads after the Civil War and died in New York City on Dec. 19. The Lady Chapel in St. Patrick's Cathedral in New York City was built through a memorial gift donated by his family after his death.

KELLY, FRANCIS MARTIN (1886–1950), bishop. Born in Houston, Minnesota, on Nov. 15, he was educated at St. Thomas Academy, St. Paul, Minnesota, Catholic University (Ph.B. 1909), and the Propaganda, Rome (S.T.D. 1913), and was ordained in Rome in 1913. He was secretary to Bishop Patrick Heffron of Winona, Minnesota, in 1914, taught philosophy at St. Mary's College, serving as vice-rector in 1918–26, and College of St. Teresa, both in Winona, in 1915–26, and was chancellor of the diocese of Winona in 1919–22. He was consecrated titular bishop of Mylasa and auxiliary of Winona in 1926, becoming its bishop in 1928. He resigned and was appointed titular bishop of Nasal in 1949 and died in Rochester, Minnesota, on June 24.

KELLY, GERALD ANDREW (1902–64), theologian. Born in Denver, Colorado, on Sept. 30, he joined the Jesuits at Florissant, Missouri, in 1920, studied at the University of St. Louis (B.A., M.A., S.T.L.), and was ordained in 1933. He continued his studies at the Gregorian, Rome, and taught moral theology at St. Mary's College, Kansas, for twenty-six years, giving summer courses to nuns and lay people at several colleges, and was managing editor of *Review of Religious* in 1942–59. He became recognized as a leading theologian in the field of medico-moral problems and was chairman of the committee that drew up the ethics code of the Catholic Hospital Association. He contributed to scholarly magazines (particularly worthy of note was the series he did in *Theological Studies* summarizing current developments in theology between 1946 and 1952) and wrote several books, among them *Modern Youth and Chastity* (1941), *Guidance for Religious* (1956), *Medico-Moral Problems* (1957), and, with John C. Ford, the two-volume *Contemporary Moral Theology* (1958, 1963). He died in Kansas City, Missouri, on Aug. 2.

KELLY, GRACE (1929–82), princess, actress. Daughter of John B. Kelly, onetime bricklayer who became wealthy through the construction business, and Margaret Majer Kelly, she was born in Philadelphia on Nov. 12. She studied at the Stevens School in Philadelphia and, early attracted to the entertainment world, at the American Academy of Dramatic Arts in New York City. She engaged in modeling, appeared in television dramas, and made her stage debut in *The Father* in New York City with Raymond Massey in 1949. She made her first screen appearance as a bit player in *Fourteen Hours* in 1951 and the following year played her first major role in *High Noon*, with Gary Cooper. She returned to New York for a short-lived play and then returned to Hollywood, where in the next few years she appeared in several pictures, among them *Mogambo, Dial M for Murder, Rear Window, The Country Girl*, with Bing Crosby, for which she won an Oscar, *The Bridges of Toko-Ri, To Catch a Thief,* and *High Society*. She met Prince Rainier of Monaco at the Cannes Film Festival in 1954 and, after a storybook romance that captivated the world, they were married in Monaco in 1956. She ruled as his consort until Sept. 14, when she died in Monaco of a second stroke the day after being stricken while driving her car, causing it to crash.

KELLY, HUGH (1858–1908), merchant, financier. Of Irish immigrant parents, he was born in Chicago on Sept. 24, was brought to New York City by his parents when he was a child, and graduated from the College of the City of New York in 1871. He began his business career with Gomez & Monjo, a West Indian trading firm, left to found, with Manuel Rionda, a company engaged in the West Indian trade in 1883, the year he married Mary E. McCabe, and the following year founded the house of Hugh Kelly (incorporated as Hugh Kelly & Co. in 1903) to engage in the cane sugar business. He became an expert in the field, built sugar factories in Santo Domingo, Cuba, and Puerto Rico and served as school commissioner in New York in 1895–98. He was president of the Maritime Exchange in 1896–98, New York State Commerce Commissioner in 1898–1900, and a director and trustee of numerous business, religious, social, and cultural organizations. When the Oriental Bank failed in the depression of 1908, he became its president, restored it to financial solvency, and then resigned, refusing to take any compensation for his services. He died in New York City on Oct. 30.

KELLY, JOHN BERNARD (1888–1957). Born in New York City on Jan. 12, he was educated at Cathedral College and City College there and St. Joseph's Seminary, Dunwoodie, New York, and was ordained in 1913. He engaged in parish work at Our Lady of Good Counsel Church in New York City, became spiritual director of the Catholic Big Brothers and the Catholic Writers Guild of America (for twenty-two years), and organized the Golden Book Awards. He wrote a biography of Cardinal Patrick Hayes and two volumes of verse, *The Son of Man and other Essays and Poems* (1927) and *The Romance of Truth* (1935), and died in New York City on June 27.

KELLY, PATRICK (1779–1829), bishop. Born in Kilkenny, Ireland, on Apr. 16, he studied at Maudlin Street College there and St. Patrick's, Lisbon, Portugal, and was ordained in 1802. He taught at St. Patrick's, Maudlin Street College, and St. John's in Ireland and served as president of St. John's from 1816 until 1820, when he was consecrated first bishop of the newly created diocese of Richmond, Virginia. The creation of the diocese had been vigorously opposed by Archbishop Ambrose Maréchal of Baltimore, from whose see it had been carved, as unwarranted; the new bishop also encountered such difficulties with various groups in the new see that in 1822 he asked to be relieved of his duties in Richmond and the diocese reverted to the administration of the archdiocese of Baltimore. He was transferred to the diocese of Waterford and Lismore, Ireland, and he died in Waterford on Oct. 8.

KELLY, WILLIAM (1811–88), scientist. Born of a well-to-do landowner in Pittsburgh on Aug. 21, he was educated in that city's public schools. Though interested in metallurgy from his youth, he entered the dry-goods business in his native city and became a junior partner in McShane & Kelly. He married Mildred A. Gracy, daughter of a wealthy tobacco merchant in Eddyville, Kentucky, and settled there and bought iron-ore land. With his brother he founded the Suwanee Iron Works & Union Forge, with his father-in-law as a partner, and began producing sugar kettles for the farmers in the area. Seeking an alternative fuel to charcoal, he discovered the carbon in molten iron can be burned by air blast, making the molten iron even hotter. Between 1851 and 1856 he built seven converters to develop his process, only to learn in 1856 that Henry Bessemer had developed that same process in England and had been granted a United States patent. He was able to convince the American patent authorities he had developed the process prior to Bessemer's and was issued a patent as original inventor (his patent was renewed in 1871 when Bessemer's was refused). He was bankrupted by the panic of 1857 and sold the patent to his father for one thousand dollars. When his father refused to return the patent, thinking he was too incompetent in business (his wife and father-in-law thought he was mentally unbalanced when he originally told them of his discovery, so obsessed had he been with it), he went to Daniel J. Morrell of the Cambria Iron Works in

Johnstown, Pennsylvania, whose encouragement and aid led him to build an eighth converter of the tilting type which made soft steel cheaply and became an essential process in steelmaking during the "steel age" that was just beginning. Kelly left Johnstown after five years, founded an axe manufacturing business in Louisville, Kentucky, retired when he was seventy, and died in Louisville on Feb. 11.

KENEDY, ARTHUR (1878–1951), publisher. Son of Patrick John Kenedy, the publisher, and Elizabeth Weiser Kenedy, he was born in Brooklyn, New York, on Apr. 30. He graduated from De La Salle Institute and then studied at Georgetown but was forced to leave after two years to run the family business because of his father's illness. He married Anna Mercedes Reid (d. 1918) in 1912 and was president of P. J. Kenedy & Sons from 1906 to 1927, when he became chairman of the board. While on his honeymoon in Europe he arranged with the English publisher Burns, Oates & Washbourne to market their publications in the United States; among them were the autobiography of St. Thérèse of Lisieux, the works of Archbishop Goodier, and John Stoddard's *Rebuilding a Lost Faith.* He secured the rights to the Official Catholic Directory in 1911, helped bring out the Catholic Encyclopedia, and in 1908 was among those who organized the National Association of Catholic Publishers and Dealers in Church Goods. He died in New York City on Feb. 3.

KENEDY, JOHN (1794–1866), publisher. Born in County Kilkenny, Ireland, on Apr. 13, he became a schoolmaster, emigrated to the United States, and settled in Boston. He moved to Baltimore, married Ellen Timon, and began a small bookstore in 1832. He entered the publishing field with an abridgment of Alfonso Rodríquez's *The Practice of Christian Perfection* in 1834. When his wife died in 1836 he moved to New York, married Bridget Smith in 1842, and his firm, P. J. Kenedy & Son (named after their son Patrick John), became a leading publisher of Catholic prayer books, bibles, catechisms, and devotional books. He began buying up copyrights from publishers in financial difficulties, notably *Faith of Our Fathers* by Cardinal James Gibbons and *The Manual of Prayers,* which were enormously successful, and a line of bibles from John J. Murphy of Baltimore. He died in New York City on June 25.

KENEDY, LOUIS (1882–1956), publisher. Son of Patrick John Kenedy, the publisher, and Elizabeth Weiser Kenedy, he was born in Brooklyn, New York City, on Oct. 13 and educated at Georgetown. He entered his father's firm in 1901 and was president from 1927 to 1952, when he became chairman of the board. He was editor of The Official Catholic Directory, which the firm had acquired in 1911, served as president of the National Council of Catholic Men and the National Association of Catholic Publishers and Dealers in Church Goods, and was one of the founders of the Statisticians of American Religious Bodies. He died in New Rochelle, New York, on Nov. 17.

KENEDY, PATRICK JOHN (1843–1906), publisher. Son of John Kenedy, he was born in New York City on Sept. 4, worked in his father's bookstore after school, and became a partner in the firm, John Kenedy & Son, in 1865. He became owner on his father's death in 1866 and served as president of the firm, which he incorporated as P. J. Kenedy & Sons, until his death. He married Elizabeth Teresa Weiser in 1873, expanded the firm's prayer book line and devotional books, added religious goods, and continued his father's practice of purchasing other publishers' stock and plates—from Excelsior Catholic Publishing House in 1877, Baltimore Publishing Company in 1894, Henry McGrath of Philadelphia in 1898 —and built his list to some five hundred titles. Pope Leo XIII conferred on him the honorary title of printer to the Holy See, and he died in New York City on Jan. 4.

KENNA, JOHN EDWARD (1848–93), United States senator. Born in Kanawha County, Virginia (now West Virginia), on Apr. 10, he had no formal education in his youth and in 1864 joined the Confederate forces under General Joseph O. Shelley. When Shelley surrendered to Union forces at Shreveport, Louisiana, in 1865, Kenna returned to West Virginia, studied at St. Vincent's College, Wheeling, West Virginia, and was admitted to the bar in 1870. He became prosecuting attorney for Kanawha County in 1872, justice pro tempore on the Circuit Court of Appeals in 1875, and was elected to the United States House of Representatives in 1876. After three terms in the House he was elected to the United States Senate in 1882 and served in that body until his death in Washington, D.C., on Jan. 11. He was chairman of the Democratic Congressional Committee in 1886 and 1888, supported President Cleveland's demand for tariff reform in 1887 and for federal regulation of railroads, and sought federal aid to improve navigation on the Kanawha River. In 1901 his statue was placed in the Capitol in Washington to represent West Virginia.

KENNALLY, VINCENT IGNATIUS (1895–1977), bishop. Born in Boston on June 11, he was educated at Boston College in 1914–15, joined the Jesuits in 1915, taught at the Atteneo de Manila in 1922–25, and continued his studies at Woodstock College, Maryland (B.A., M.A. 1922). He was ordained in 1928, taught philosophy at Boston College in 1929–30, was assistant editor of *Jesuit Missions* in 1930–31, and was superior at Cagayan de Oro, Philippine Islands, in 1933–39. He was rector and master of novices at Novaliches in 1940–45, apostolic administrator of the vicariate of the Caroline and Marshall Islands in 1946–51, vice-provincial of the Jesuit vice-province of the Philippine Islands in 1952–56, and was named titular bishop of Sassura and vicar apostolic of the Caroline and Marshall Islands in 1956. He retired in 1971 and died on Truk, the Caroline Islands, on Apr. 12.

KENNEDY, JOHN FITZGERALD (1917–63), President of the United States. Son of wealthy financier Joseph P. Kennedy, who served as ambassador to Great Britain in 1937–40, and Rose Fitzgerald, daughter of John Francis "Honey Fitz" Fitzgerald, who was a powerful political figure in Massachusetts and two-time mayor of Boston, he was born at Brookline, Massachusetts, on May 29. He studied at fashionable Choate Preparatory School, briefly at Princeton, and then at Harvard, where he graduated cum laude in 1940; his bachelor thesis, *While England Slept,* based on his observations while he was secretary to his father in London, attracted special attention and became a bestseller. He enrolled for graduate studies at Stanford, but when World War II threatened to draw in the United States, he enlisted in the Navy in 1941. He served as a PT boat commander in the Pacific during the war and was injured in action off the Solomon Islands when his boat was sunk by a Japanese destroyer; the back injuries he sustained in that engagement were to plague him the rest of his life. He managed to save his crew by his heroic actions, but his injuries and the malaria he contracted caused him to be invalided home. After the war he entered politics and in 1946 was elected to the United States House of Representatives; he was reelected the next two terms. In 1952 he was elected to the United States Senate, and re-elected in 1958. He married Jacqueline Bouvier in 1953. After suffering a reoccurrence of his back injuries, he underwent several operations in 1955, and in 1956 published *Profiles in Courage,* which was awarded the Pulitzer Prize and focused national attention on him. He surprised the National Democratic Convention in 1956 by the strength of his bid for the vice presidency and in 1960, after a resounding victory in the West Virginia primary where he had been given slight chance of winning, he was nominated as the presidential candidate of the Democratic Party. He was elected thirty-fifth President of the United States by a narrow popular margin in a bitter campaign notable for its anti-Catholicism (the decisive events of the campaign were his meeting in Houston, Texas, with a group of Protestant ministers, where he counteracted much of the opposition due to his religion, and his television debates with Richard M. Nixon). He was the first Catholic President and, at forty-three, the youngest man ever to be elected President. His term in office was characterized by high ideals, which caused it to be referred to as Camelot, though at the time of his death his legislative program was largely unenacted and stalled in Congress; the major items of his domestic program, known as the New Frontier, were enacted after his death during the presidency of Lyndon B. Johnson. They called for an accelerated space program, expanded civil rights for blacks, federal aid to education, medical care for the aged through social security, and aid to depressed areas throughout the nation. In foreign affairs, two crises in Cuba drew worldwide attention and concern.

The first was the abortive Bay of Pigs raid in 1961 in which he authorized and supported a group of American-trained Cuban exiles' attempt to invade Cuba and unseat its Communist dictator, Fidel Castro; the attempt resulted in the complete defeat of the invading forces. The second crisis was the Cuban missile crisis of 1962 in which a threatened nuclear war between the United States and Russia was averted, after Kennedy imposed a naval blockade of Cuba to prevent Soviet vessels from delivering further missiles to Cuba, when Russia dismantled the missile bases and withdrew the ballistic missiles capable of attacking the United States it had installed in Cuba. Despite this confrontation between the two nations, the United States and Russia signed a treaty in 1963 banning the testing of nuclear weapons underseas and in space. In the same year Kennedy expanded American aid to anti-Communist forces in Vietnam, a move that was to have enormous consequences in the years to come. Kennedy's Alliance for Progress programs and his Peace Corps (American volunteers working in poor countries) were very well received. On Nov. 22, 1963, while on a visit to Dallas, Texas, President Kennedy was assassinated by Lee Harvey Oswald, acting, according to a presidential commission report, alone and not as part of a political conspiracy, as had been suggested by some investigators.

KENNEDY, JOSEPH PATRICK (1888–1969), financier, diplomat. Son of Patrick Joseph Kennedy, a Boston saloon-keeper politician, and Mary Hickey Kennedy, he was born in Boston on Sept. 6 and was educated at the prestigious Boston Latin School and Harvard (B.A. 1912). After he graduated he was a state bank examiner in 1912–14, married Rose Fitzgerald, daughter of John F. "Honey Fitz" Fitzgerald, who was twice mayor of Boston, in 1914, and in 1914 he became president of the Columbia Trust Company. He was assistant general manager of the Fore River, Massachusetts, plant of Bethlehem Shipbuilding Corporation during World War I, 1917–19, and after the war he became manager of the stock division of the investment banking firm of Hayden, Stone and Company. When Stone retired in 1922, Kennedy struck out on his own as a stock market operator. During the next decade and a half he acquired a fortune in the stock market. In 1926 he moved to New York City, where he continued dealing in stocks, making huge profits. Anticipating the 1929 stock market crash, he liquidated his holdings before the crash and turned to the real estate and movies field. He had earlier bought a New England theater chain and now became president and chairman of the board of Film Booking Offices of America, 1926–29, chairman of the board of directors of Keith-Albee-Orpheum Corporation, 1928–29, and president and chairman of the board of directors of Pathé Exchange, Inc., 1929–30. He was an early supporter of Franklin D. Roosevelt for the presidency (he published *I'm for Roosevelt* in 1936), made a fortune in the liquor business when Prohibition was repealed in 1933, was chairman of the Securities and Exchange Commission in 1934–35, and was chairman of the United States Maritime Commission in Mar.–Dec. 1937. In December of that year he was appointed first Irish-American United States Ambassador to Great Britain. He supported England's Prime Minister Neville Chamberlain in his negotiations with Hitler, believed England would fall to the Nazis if war broke out, and advocated a policy of isolationism for the United States. A press interview he gave stating these views caused a break with President Roosevelt and he resigned as ambassador in November 1940. He returned to his successful business operations, notably in real estate, in New York City. He was appointed a member of the Commission on the Organization of Executive Branches of the U.S. Government in 1947 and was reappointed in 1953. He suffered a stroke in 1961 which left him paralyzed the last years of his life, and he died at Hyannisport, Massachusetts, on Nov. 18. Of his four sons, Joseph was killed in World War II, John became President of the United States, and Robert and Edward (Ted) became United States senators.

KENNEDY, ROBERT FRANCIS (1925–68), United States Attorney General, senator. Son of Joseph P. Kennedy and Rose Fitzgerald Kennedy and brother of President John F. Kennedy and senator Edward Kennedy, he was born in Brookline, Massachusetts, on Nov. 20. He entered Harvard, interrupted his studies to serve in the Navy during World War II in 1944–46, returned to complete his studies, receiving his B.A. in 1948, and then studied law at the University of Virginia (LL.B. 1951). He married Ethel Skakel in 1950, was an attorney in the Justice Department in 1951–52, and managed his brother John's campaign for the United States Senate in 1952. He served on the Senate Permanent Committee on Investigation in 1953–55 and became known for his investigation of the Teamsters Union as chief counsel for the Senate Select Committee on Improper Activities in Labor and Management in 1957–59. He managed John's successful presidential campaign in 1960, was named United States Attorney General in 1961, and was John's confidant and adviser in governmental matters. When John was assassinated in 1963, Robert resigned as Attorney General in 1964 and ran for and was elected United States senator from New York. He opposed the government's Vietnam policies and in 1968 began a campaign for the Democratic nomination for President. He was shot by an Arab fanatic, Sirhan Bishara Sirhan, in a Los Angeles hotel shortly after midnight on the night of June 4, after just having won the California primary. He died in Los Angeles the next day, June 6.

KENNEDY, THOMAS (1887–1963), labor leader. Born in the mining town of Lansford, Pennsylvania, on Nov. 2, he began working in coal mines when he was twelve, became active in the labor movement when he joined the local union of the United Mine Workers of America (UMW) in 1903, and was president of District 7, UMW, Hazelton, in 1910–25. He married Helen Melley in 1912 and was unanimously elected secretary-treasurer of the UMW by the executive board in 1925, serving in that position until 1948. He was elected lieutenant governor of Pennsylvania in 1934, serving for four years while retaining his union post, and was defeated for the Democratic nomination for governor in 1938, though he remained active in Democratic Party politics. He was appointed a member of the National Defense Mediation Board in 1941 and of the National Labor Board in 1942, during World War II, but soon resigned from each, was vice president of the UMW in 1948–60 and was president from 1960 until his death. He became chairman of the board of trustees of the Health and Welfare Fund for Anthracite Miners in 1946 and was chairman of Labor's Non-Partisan League. He died in Hazelton, Pennsylvania, on Jan. 19.

KENNY, WILLIAM JOHN (1853–1913), bishop. Born in Delhi, New York, on Jan. 12 (or Oct. 9 or 14), he was educated at St. Bonaventure College, New York, and was ordained in St. Augustine, Florida, in 1879. He was

pastor of several parishes in Florida, vicar-general of the diocese of St. Augustine in 1889–91, administrator of the diocese in 1901–2, and was consecrated its third bishop in 1902. He held that position until his death in Baltimore on Oct. 23.

KENRICK, FRANCIS PATRICK (1797–1863), archbishop. Brother of Archbishop Peter Richard Kenrick of St. Louis, he was born in Dublin on Dec. 3, received a classical education in Ireland, and, when eighteen, was sent to the Propaganda in Rome to study for the priesthood. He was ordained in 1821 and went to the United States in response to a plea from Bishop Benedict Flaget of Bardstown, Kentucky, for priests. He taught at St. Joseph's Seminary in Bardstown for nine years, becoming known for his eloquent preaching and convert-making. Bishop Flaget appointed him his secretary and took him to the Provincial Council of Baltimore in 1829 as his theologian. In 1830 he was appointed titular bishop of Arata and coadjutor of Philadelphia with full jurisdiction. In 1831 he abolished the lay trustees system, which had plagued Bishop Conwell, by summarily closing and putting under interdict St. Mary's Church, where the trustees had been most recalcitrant, until they capitulated. He opened what was in time to become St. Charles Borromeo Seminary in 1832 and was highly praised for his work in the cholera epidemic of 1832. He convoked the first diocesan synod in 1832, holding two more in 1842 and 1847, was a founder of the *Catholic Herald* in 1833, and in 1842 succeeded to the see. He helped end the Nativists' anti-Catholic riots in 1844, during which St. Michael and St. Augustine churches were burned, began a new cathedral, actively encouraged Catholic education, and built new schools and increased the number of churches in the diocese from twenty-two to ninety-four and the number of priests from thirty-five to one hundred one. He was appointed archbishop of Baltimore in 1851, presided over the first Plenary Council of Baltimore the following year as apostolic delegate, and in 1853 established the Forty Hours' Devotion in the United States. He attended the promulgation of the doctrine of the Immaculate Conception in Rome in 1854, after having collected the opinions of the American bishops on its promulgation. With Archbishop John Hughes of New York, he was a leading proponent for founding the American College in Rome (it opened in 1859 on property donated by Pope Pius IX), promoted the temperance movement, and encouraged each parish in Baltimore to establish a parochial school. He was considered the foremost Catholic moral theologian of his time in the United States, wrote four volumes of *Theologica Dogmatica* (1834–40), three volumes of *Theologica Moralis* (1860–61), and a commentary on Job and provided a new revision of the Douai Bible (1849–50). He died in Baltimore on July 8.

KENRICK, PETER RICHARD (1806–96), archbishop. Brother of Archbishop Francis Patrick Kenrick, archbishop of Baltimore, he was born in Dublin on Aug. 17, worked for a time as a clerk in his father's office after his father's death, and then studied for the priesthood at St. Patrick's College, Maynooth, where he was ordained in 1832. He was attracted to the Lazarists but when his mother died, he joined his brother, then coadjutor bishop of Philadelphia, there in 1833, became president of St. Charles Borromeo Seminary, editor of the diocesan paper, the *Catholic Herald,* rector of the cathedral, and then vicar-general of the diocese. In 1837–38 he was pastor of St. Paul's Church in Pittsburgh. While in Rome in 1840, he was approached by Bishop Joseph Rosati to become his coadjutor, and he was consecrated titular bishop of Adrasus and coadjutor of St. Louis in 1841. He succeeded to the see when Bishop Rosati died in Rome in 1843, founded the *Catholic Cabinet,* and became a real estate investor in his efforts to pay off the heavy diocesan debt he had inherited. He was appointed first archbishop of St. Louis in 1847, when the see was elevated to an archdiocese, fought the "Drake constitution," passed in 1865 by a rump convention after the defeat of the Confederates, which required all clergymen to take a loyalty oath. He ordered all clergymen in his jurisdiction to refuse to take the oath and eventually succeeded in having the act declared unconstitutional by the United States Supreme Court in 1866. He attended Vatican Council I in 1869 and opposed the doctrine of papal infallibility as inopportune at the eighteenth congregation, did not attend the public session at which it was approved on July 18, 1870, but submitted when it was promulgated. The original area of his archdiocese of Missouri, Arkansas, and half of Illinois had sixteen dioceses carved out of it during his episcopate, but despite this loss of territory, his see greatly increased the number of priests, religious, churches, and institutions in it. He resigned in 1895 and was named titular archbishop of Marcianopolis and died in St. Louis on Mar. 4.

KEOGH, JAMES (1834–70), editor, theologian. Born in Enniscorthy, Wexford, Ireland, on Feb. 4, he was brought to the United States by his parents, who settled in Pittsburgh in 1841. He studied for the priesthood at the Propaganda, Rome, receiving his doctorates in philosophy in 1851 and in theology in 1855, and was ordained in 1856. He served as pastor in Latrobe, Pennsylvania, and in 1857 was appointed professor of dogmatic theology at St. Michael's Seminary, Glenwood, Pennsylvania. He became president of the seminary in 1862 and was editor of the diocesan newspaper, the Pittsburgh *Catholic,* serving until 1865, when he resigned both posts because of disagreement over his management of the seminary and the editorial policies of the paper. He then lectured at St. Charles Borromeo Seminary, Overbrook, Philadelphia, became first editor of the newly founded Philadelphia *Catholic Standard* in 1866, and was one of the secretaries of the second Plenary Council of Baltimore in 1866. Ill health caused his retirement in 1868 and he died in Pittsburgh on July 10.

KEOGH, JOHN (1877–1960), Newman Club chaplain. Born in Philadelphia on Nov. 29, he was educated at Temple University and St. Charles Borromeo Seminary there and was ordained in 1909. He served as curate at St. Mary's Church, Phoenixville, Pennsylvania, in 1909, assistant chaplain at Philadelphia General Hospital in 1909–11, and assistant rector at Sacred Heart Church from 1911 to 1913, when he was appointed first full-time Catholic chaplain at the University of Pennsylvania, where the first Newman Club had been founded in 1893, serving in that post until 1938. In 1917 he became first national chaplain of the Federation of College Catholic Clubs (National Newman Club Federation) and remained national chaplain until 1935. He became the leader in the successful struggle to establish Newman programs in secular colleges and universities, earning the title "father of the Newman apostolate" for his efforts, and served for years as president of the Catholic Total Abstinence Union. He was appointed pastor of St. Gabriel's parish in Philadelphia in 1938 but remained active in the Newman apostolate the rest

of his life; he was one of the founders of the John Henry Newman Honorary Society, serving as its chaplain from 1945. He was made a domestic prelate in 1959, when he also received the Cardinal Newman Award—the first priest to be so honored—and died in Philadelphia on Oct. 14.

KEOGH, FRANCIS PATRICK (1890–1961), archbishop. Born in New Britain, Connecticut, on Dec. 30, he was educated at St. Thomas Seminary, Bloomfield, Connecticut, St. Sulpice, Issy, France, and St. Bernard's Seminary, Rochester, New York, and was ordained in 1916. He served as a curate at St. Rose Church, Meriden, Connecticut, and was director of the Hartford diocese's Society for the Propagation of the Faith and Catholic Mission Aid Society. He became chaplain of the House of the Good Shepherd in Hartford and was named assistant chancellor of the diocese in 1919, serving in that position until he was named bishop of Providence, Rhode Island, in 1934. During his episcopate, he expanded the educational and charitable facilities of the see, paid off the debt he had inherited, founded a minor seminary and Salve Regina College for the education of women in Newport, contributed to the expansion of Providence College, and labored to reconcile the French- and the English-speaking members of the diocese. He was appointed archbishop of Baltimore in 1947, was elected episcopal chairman of the education department of the National Catholic Welfare Conference (NCWC) in 1949, of the legal department in 1953, and of the social action department in 1954, and served as chairman of the administrative board of the NCWC in 1950–52 and 1955–58 and on several mission society committees. He built Mary Our Queen Cathedral, dedicated in 1959, and several charitable institutions. He died in Washington, D.C., on Dec. 8 after several years of declining health.

KERBY, WILLIAM JOSEPH (1870–1936), educator. Born in Lawler, Iowa, on Feb. 20, he was educated at St. Joseph's College (Loras College), Dubuque, Iowa, and St. Francis Seminary, Milwaukee, Wisconsin, and was ordained in 1892. He continued his studies at Catholic University, receiving his licentiate in 1894, and then taught at St. Joseph's in 1895–96. He studied sociology at the universities of Bonn and Berlin, received his doctorate in social and political science from Louvain in 1897, and began teaching at Catholic University as head of its sociology department; he also served as dean of the faculty of philosophy to 1919. He was one of the founders of the National Conference of Catholic Charities in 1910, was its secretary in 1910–20 and secretary of the District of Columbia Board of Charities in 1920–26, and founded the *Catholic Charities Review* in 1916. He edited the *Saint Vincent de Paul Quarterly* in 1911–17 and the *Ecclesiastical Review* from 1927, wrote *The Social Mission of Charity* and *Problems of the Better Hope* and several other books. He died in Washington, D.C., on July 27. He firmly believed social reform was the only way socialism could be curbed, was deeply involved all through his life with aiding the needy and underprivileged, and may well be called the founder of scientific Catholic social work.

KERENS, RICHARD C. (1842–1916), executive, diplomat. Born in Kilberry, Meath, Ireland, on Nov. 12, he was brought as an infant to the United States by his family, who settled in Iowa. He was involved in transportation for the Union Army during the Civil War and after the war became a contractor for Southern Overland Mail at Fort Smith, Arkansas. He married Frances Jane Jones in 1867, moved to San Diego, California, in 1874, became involved in railroading, and in 1876 moved to St. Louis. In the next four years he became a railroad magnate, helping to establish half a dozen railroads, among them the West Virginia Central & Pittsburgh, the Cotton Belt and Northern, and the San Pedro, Los Angeles & Salt Lake. He also became involved in lumber and mining interests in West Virginia and became a wealthy man. He was U.S. representative on the U.S. Inter-Continental Railway Commission, which prepared a survey of fifteen Latin American nations, and served as ambassador extraordinary and plenipotentiary to Austria-Hungary in 1909–13. He contributed generously to the building of churches, received numerous honors, among them the Laetare Medal in 1904, and died in Merion, Pennsylvania, on Sept. 4.

KERNAN, FRANCIS (1816–92), U.S. senator. Born in Steuben County, New York, on Jan. 14, he graduated from Georgetown in 1836, studied law at Watkins and Utica, New York, was admitted to the bar in 1840, and became one of the best-known lawyers in the state. He entered politics, was alderman and school commissioner in Utica, official reporter of New York's Court of Appeals in 1848–57, a state assemblyman in 1860–62, and a member of the United States House of Representatives in 1863–65. When defeated for reelection in 1864, he returned to his law practice, was a delegate to the New York Constitutional Convention in 1867, and was unsuccessful in a bid for the governorship of New York in 1872, but in 1874 he was elected first Democratic United States senator from New York in twenty-four years by the state legislature; he was defeated for reelection in 1880. He nominated Samuel J. Tilden for the presidency at the Democratic Convention in St. Louis in 1876, actively supported Grover Cleveland for the presidency at the Democratic Convention in Chicago in 1884 and died in Utica on Sept. 7.

KETCHAM, WILLIAM HENRY (1868–1921), missionary. Born in Summer, Iowa, on June 1, he was converted to Catholicism in 1885 while studying at St. Charles College, Grand Cocteau, Louisiana. He studied for the priesthood at Mt. St. Mary of the West Seminary, Cincinnati, Ohio, was ordained at Guthrie, Oklahoma, in 1892, and became a missionary to the Creek and Cherokee Indians. He extended his work to the Choctaws in 1897, built schools and mission centers for the Indians, and in 1901 was named director of the Bureau of Catholic Indian Missions in Washington, D.C., serving in this position until 1921. He established the *Indian Sentinel* in 1902, fought for and regained for Indian parents the right to have their children attend schools of their own choice and to receive religious instruction, and established new mission schools and expanded missionary efforts among the Indians. In 1912 he was appointed a member of the U.S. Board of Commissioners of Indian Affairs by President Taft, was made a domestic prelate in 1919, and died of an apoplectic stroke in Tucker, Mississippi, on Nov. 14, while visiting the Choctaws in Mississippi.

KEVENHOERSTER, JOHN BERNARD (1869–1949), bishop. Born in Alten-Essen, Prussia, on Nov. 1, he was brought to the United States by his parents in 1881, studied at St. John's College and Seminary, Collegeville, Minnesota, and the University of Minnesota, joined the Benedictines in 1892, took his vows the following year, and was ordained at St. John's Abbey, Collegeville, in 1896. He taught at St. John's for a time in 1907, was pastor of St. Anselm's Church, Bronx, New York City, from 1907 until 1929, and was made vicar forane of Bahamas Missions in 1929. He was made a domestic prelate and prelate apostolic in 1932 and was consecrated titular bishop of Camuliana and first prefect apostolic of the Bahamas in 1933. He became vicar apostolic of the Bahamas in 1941, when the prefecture was raised to a vicariate apostolic, established nineteen churches and missions and fourteen schools in his vicariate, was made an Assistant at the Pontifical Throne in 1946, and died in Nassau, Bahamas, on Dec. 9.

KEYES, ERASMUS DARWIN (1810–95), soldier. Son of a prominent physician, he was born in Brimfield, Massachusetts, on May 29. He studied at West Point, graduated in 1832, rose to the rank of captain in 1837, and served as aide-de-camp to General Winfield Scott in several Indian campaigns in 1837–41. He taught at West Point in 1844–48, was on the West Coast in 1851–60, serving in campaigns against the Indians in Washington and on the Spokane Expedition in 1858, was made a major in 1858, and was General Scott's military secretary in 1860–61. He served in the Union Army during the Civil War, rising to the rank of major general of volunteers in command of the IV Army Corps in the Army of the Potomac, and in 1862 was brevetted brigadier general, United States Army. He was involved in a dispute with General Dix over participation in expeditions against White House and West Point, Virginia, was refused his request for an official investigation of the matter, and in 1864 resigned from the Army and went to California. He became president of the Maxwell Gold Mining Company in 1867–69, vice president of the Humboldt Savings and Loan Society in 1868–70, and was active in the banking business. He became a Catholic in 1866 and died in Nice, France, on Oct. 14. Among his published works is *Fifty Years' Observation of Men and Events* (1884).

KEYES, MICHAEL JOSEPH (1876–1959), bishop. Born in Dingle, Kerry, Ireland, on Feb. 28, he studied under the Christian Brothers there in 1892–93 and emigrated to the United States in 1896. He joined the Marists in 1901, was professed in 1905, studied at the Marist seminary in Washington, D.C., and was ordained there in 1907. He taught at Catholic University while receiving his S.T.L. and J.C.L. there from 1911 until 1922, and became an American citizen in 1921, when he was consecrated bishop of Savannah, Georgia. He resigned in 1935 and was appointed titular bishop of Aeropolis, was made an Assistant at the Pontifical Throne, and died in Washington, D.C., on July 31.

KIELY, PATRICK CHARLES. *See* Keely, Patrick Charles.

KIERAN, JAMES MICHAEL (1863–1936), educator. Born in New York City on Aug. 23, he was educated at the College of the City of New York and St. Francis Xavier College there and taught in New York's public schools in 1883–1900, becoming a principal in 1900. He began teaching philosophy and education at Hunter College in New York City in 1904, founded the New York Academy of Public Education in 1912, was dean of Hunter in 1927–28, and was president from 1928 until his retirement in 1933. During his presidency at Hunter, he developed Hunter's Bronx campus, made major contributions to women's education, and initiated Newman Clubs in non-Catholic colleges. He died in New York City on Apr. 25.

KIERAN, JOHN FRANCIS (1892–1981), journalist. Son of James M. Kieran, who was president of Hunter College in New York City in 1928–33, he was born in the Bronx, New York City, on Aug. 2, and was educated at the College of the City of New York and Fordham (B.S. 1912). Through a family friend he got a position in the sports department of the New York *Times* in 1915 and became the *Times* reporter for golf. He served in France during World War I and on his return was assigned to cover baseball. In 1922, he moved to the New York *Herald-Tribune* when promised a byline—*Times* sports writers wrote anonymously then—but he returned to the *Times* in 1926 to write a column, "Sports of the Times," with his byline—the first on the *Times.* In 1938 he became a panelist on the "Information Please" program on the NBC radio network; the program became enormously successful and ran for ten years. He again left the *Times* in 1943 to write a general-interest column for the New York *Sun,* and in 1947 he became editor of the Information Please Almanac, an offshoot of the radio program. He was renowned for his encyclopedic knowledge, was a leading ornithologist, and was the author of several ornithological books, among them *Nature Notes* (1941), *Introduction to Birds* (1946), and the highly praised *Natural History of New York City* (1959). He died in Rockport, Massachusetts, on Dec. 10.

KILEY, MOSES ELIAS (1876–1953), archbishop. Born in Margaree, Inverness, Nova Scotia, on Nov. 13, he was educated at St. Laurent College, Montreal, St. Mary's Seminary, Baltimore, and the North American College and the Propaganda, Rome (S.T.D. 1911), and was ordained in Rome in 1911. He was a curate at St. Agnes Church, Chicago, in 1911–16, was first diocesan director of Catholic Charities in Chicago in 1916–26, was made a domestic prelate in 1924, and was spiritual director of the North American College in Rome in 1926–34. He was named a consultor on the Vatican's Russian Commission in 1929, was appointed fifth bishop of Trenton, New Jersey, in 1934 and served there until 1940, when he was appointed archbishop of Milwaukee, Wisconsin. He served in that position until his death in Milwaukee on Apr. 15.

KILGALLEN, DOROTHY MAE (1913–65), journalist, TV and radio personality. The daughter of James Lawrence Kilgallen, a newspaperman, and Mary Jane (Mae) Ahern Kilgallen, she was born in Chicago on July 3, was brought to New York City by her parents in 1923, and was educated at the College of New Rochelle. She began working at the *Evening Journal* in New York City during the summer in 1931, had a byline when she was twenty, and became known for her coverage of murder trials and social events. She received widespread publicity for a round-the-world race on commercial airlines in 1936 and became a newspaper celebrity for her coverage of the coronation of King George VI of England in 1937. She took over the syndicated column "The Voice of Broadway" in the *Journal-American* in 1938, married Richard Kollmar, an actor, in 1940, and in 1945 they began their "Breakfast with Dorothy and Dick" radio show, which became widely popular. She became a panelist on the television program "What's My Line?" in 1950 and, with its exposure, became one of the best-known journalists in the United States. Her "The Voice of Broadway" column was carried by 146 newspapers and "What's My Line?" had some ten million viewers. She died accidentally in New York City on Nov. 8 of a combination of barbiturates and alcohol which proved deadly.

KILMER, ALINE MURRAY (1888–1941), poet. Born in Norfolk, Virginia, on Aug. 1, Aline Murray was educated at the Rutgers Preparatory School and the Vail-Deane School, Elizabeth, New Jersey, from which she graduated in 1907. She married Joyce Kilmer in 1908, became a Catholic with him in 1913, and after his death in 1918 lectured on literary topics and became recognized as a poet in her own right. She published four books of poetry, *Candles That Burn* (1919), *Vigils* (1921), *The Poor King's Daughter* (1925), and *Selected Poems* (1929); a book of essays, *Hunting a Hairshirt* (1923); and two children's books. She died in Stillwater, New Jersey, on Oct. 1.

KILMER, JOYCE (1886–1918), poet. Alfred Joyce Kilmer was born in New Brunswick, New Jersey, on Dec. 6, attended Rutgers College there for two years, and then transferred to Columbia, from which he graduated in 1908. He taught Latin at a New Jersey high school for a year and then moved to New York City, where he worked on the staff of the Standard Dictionary. He married Aline Murray, a poet, in 1908, began contributing poems to magazines, and was literary editor of the Episcopalian *Churchman*. He became a Catholic in 1913 and joined the staff of the New York *Times Magazine* and *Book Review* the same year. He published collections of essays, *The Circus* (1916) and *Literature in the Making* (1917), and poems, *Trees* (1915), *Main Street* (1917), and *Joyce Kilmer's Anthology of Catholic Poets* (1917). His poem, "Trees," first published in *Poetry* magazine in 1913, was immensely popular, as were the lectures he gave. He enlisted in the 165th New York Infantry ("the Fighting 69th"), when the United States entered

World War I, and was killed in the battle along the Ourcq River in France on July 30.

KINDEKENS, PETER (d. 1873). Born in Denderwindeke, Belgium, at an unknown date, he offered his services to Bishop Peter Lefevere of Detroit and, after his ordination in 1842, became vicar-general of Detroit, also serving as pastor of St. Ann's Cathedral and director of St. Thomas Seminary in Detroit. He designed a new cathedral for Detroit, was Bishop Lefevere's representative in a dispute with the Redemptorists of the see in Rome in 1856, and while there began inquiries about the establishment of the American College in Rome. Unable to secure the needed support, he developed an alternative plan to establish an American college at Louvain, had the idea accepted and in 1857 was sent to Louvain by Bishops Lefevere and Martin Spalding of Louisville, Kentucky, to establish the American College of Louvain and became its first rector. He returned to the United States in 1860, resumed his post as vicar-general of Detroit and died there on Mar. 23.

KINO, EUSEBIO FRANCISCO (c. 1645–1711), missionary. Born in Segno in the Tirol, Italy, and baptized on Aug. 10 (the day he was probably born), Eusebio Chino or Chini (Kino as he became known was the French and Spanish version of his name; the German version was Kühn) studied at Trent and Innsbruck and joined the Jesuits in 1665, after promising St. Francis Xavier he would do so if he recovered from a near-fatal illness that beset him in 1663. He continued his studies at Innsbruck and Ingolstadt, was a professor of mathematics at the latter for a time, and after his ordination was sent in 1680 to Mexico (though he wanted to be sent to China) as a missionary. He reached there in 1681, published *Exposición astronomica del Comete,* his observations at Cádiz of the comet of 1680–81, and in 1682 was appointed royal cartographer for the Atondo, a colonizing expedition to Lower California; it crossed the Rio Grande and discovered the overland route to California, establishing that Lower California was a peninsula, not an island as had been thought. The project was abandoned in 1685 and two years later he was sent to work among the Pimas in Primería Alta (now southern Arizona and northern Sonora) and established a mission at Nuestra Señora de los Dolores. An indefatigable explorer, he made some forty journeys from Señora de los Dolores, acquired enormous influence among the Indians of the area, and was so successful in his missionary work that he was called "the apostle of the Pimas." He traveled all over southwestern North America and his reports and maps provided the first information of this vast hitherto-unknown country. He introduced cattle ranching into the Southwest, bringing into the region cattle, horses, and sheep, and pioneered in the planting of wheat, European cereals and fruit. He was stricken while saying Mass at Santa Magdalena, Sonora, Mexico, and died there on Mar. 15. His hundreds of letters, maps, which won him acclaim as a master cartographer, and his autobiography, *Favores celestiales* (undiscovered until 1907 and published in 1919 in two volumes as *Kino's Historical Memoir of Primería Alta,* edited by the noted historian H. E. Bolton), are invaluable sources of information about seventeenth-century southwest United States. His statue was enshrined in the Capitol in Washington, D.C., in 1965 by Arizona as a person worthy of national commemoration.

KIRLIN, JOSEPH (1868–1926), author. Born in Philadelphia on Mar. 20, he was educated at La Salle College there (B.A. 1886), studied for the priesthood at St. Charles Borromeo Seminary, Overbrook, Philadelphia, and Catholic University, and was ordained in 1892. After receiving his bachelor's degree in sacred theology the following year, he became an assistant at St. Patrick's Church, Philadelphia, lectured widely on the Eucharistic movement, was founding pastor of the Most Precious Blood parish, Philadelphia, in 1907, and was named a papal chamberlain in 1920. He wrote several books, among them a history of the Church in Philadelphia, *Catholicity in Philadelphia* (1909), *One Hour with Him* (1923), *Our Trust in Him* (1925), *With Him in Mind* (1926), and the posthumously published *Christ the Builder* (1929), and *His Priestly Virtue and Zeal,* on the Curé of Ars. He died in Philadelphia on Nov. 26.

KITE, ELIZABETH SARAH (1864–1954), historian, archivist. Daughter of a Quaker preacher, she was born in Philadelphia on Dec. 4, studied in Germany, Switzerland, France, and England, taught science at Southwest Institute, San Diego, California, in 1893–95 and at Coffin School, Nantucket, Massachusetts, in 1898–1903, and became a Catholic in 1906. She carried out studies for the Psychological Laboratory, Vineland, New Jersey, on mental deficiency and degeneration in 1909–18 and wrote *The Kallinak Family* and *A Social Survey of the People of the Pine 5,* and engaged in social work at Camp Dix, New Jersey, during World War I. She became interested in history, was made archivist for the American Catholic Historical Society of Philadelphia in 1932, and wrote numerous magazine articles on the French role in the American Revolution. Among her books were the two-volume *Beaumarchais and the War of American Indepen-*

dence (1918), *L'Enfant and Washington* (1929), *Correspondence of George Washington and the Comte de Grasse* (1931), *Lafayette and His Companions on the Victoire* (1934), and *Catholic Part in the Making of America* (1936). She died in Philadelphia on Jan. 5.

KLARMANN, ANDREW F. (1866–1931), author. Born in Oberhaid, Bavaria, Germany, he worked as a hod carrier in his youth and in 1881 emigrated to the United States with his brother Charles. He began studying for the priesthood at St. Vincent's Seminary, Latrobe, Pennsylvania, but was delayed in his studies when the seminary was destroyed by fire and he then contracted malaria. He continued his studies, was ordained a priest for the Brooklyn, New York, diocese in 1892, and served for nine years as curate of All Saints Church there. He was named pastor, in 1901, of St. Elizabeth Church and became founding pastor, in 1909, of St. Thomas the Apostle, both in Queens, New York City. While at St. Elizabeth's he began writing under the pseudonym of Virgil B. Fairman and produced a series of novels and plays, among them his first novel, *The Princess of Gar-sar* (1907), *Nizra* (1908), *Fool of God* (1912), *Lark's Creek* (1927), *King's Banner* (1930), essays in rhyme, *Lost Ring* (1923), and *Felix Aeternus,* plays, and *Vision* (1912), an operetta. He also wrote *The Crux of Pastoral Medicine,* which was his thesis for his master's degree. He died in New York City on Mar. 24.

KLUBERTANZ, GEORGE P. (1912–72), philosopher. Born in Columbus, Ohio, on June 29, he joined the Jesuits in 1931 and was ordained in 1944. He received his Ph.D. from the Pontifical Mediaeval Institute, Toronto, Canada, under Étienne Gilson, whose friendship he retained throughout his life. On his return to the United States in 1949, he taught at St. Louis University, serving as dean of its College of Philosophy and Letters in 1952–70, resigned this position in 1970, and became acting dean of the School of Divinity of the university in 1971. He died on July 5 while on a sabbatical at Gonzaga University, Spokane, Washington, and Regis College, Denver, Colorado. He wrote several books, among them *Introduction to the Philosophy of Being* (1952), *The Philosophy of Human Nature* (1953), and *Habits and Virtues* (1965).

KOHLMANN, ANTHONY (1771–1836). Born in Kaiserberg, Alsace, on July 13, he was forced to flee to Switzerland in his youth because of the French Revolution, studied at the College of Fribourg, was ordained there, and in 1796 joined the Fathers of the Sacred Heart. He served in the military as a chaplain in Austria and Italy for two years and then became director of the seminary at Dillingen, Bavaria. He taught at Berlin, headed a college founded by the Fathers of the Faith of Jesus in Amsterdam, and in 1800 joined the newly recognized Jesuits in Russia and entered the Jesuit novitiate in Dunebourg. He volunteered to go to the United States in 1804, taught at Georgetown, and ministered to several German parishes in Pennsylvania and Maryland and in 1808 was sent to New York, which had been created a diocese but did not yet have its bishop, as vicar-general to administer the diocese until its newly appointed bishop arrived from Italy. He put into effect needed reforms, founded several schools, and became involved in a landmark case while rector at St. Peter's Church. He was instrumental in having stolen goods returned to their owner, a James Keating. When Keating demanded the name of the thief, Fr. Kohlmann refused on the grounds he had received the informa-

tion in confession and was bound not to reveal any information so acquired because he was bound by the seal of the confessional. Keating took the matter to court. In a decision of the Court of General Sessions handed down by De Witt Clinton, later governor of the state, Fr. Kohlmann was upheld. The principle involved, the confidentiality of information given duly accredited priests and ministers, was enacted into a state law on Dec. 10, 1828. The book he wrote about the trial, *The Catholic Question in America* (1813), caused great controversy, which led him to write a reply to several Unitarian ministers, *Unitarianism, Theologically and Philosophically Considered* (1821). He returned to Georgetown as master of novices in 1815, became president of Gonzaga College, the Jesuit scholasticate in Washington, D.C., and, when it was discontinued as a seminary in 1824, was appointed to the chair of theology at the Gregorian, Rome. He held that position and served as consultor to several Congregations until 1829, when he was assigned as confessor at the Jesuit Church of the Gésu in Rome. He died of pneumonia in Rome on Apr. 11.

KOŚCIUSZKO, TADEUSZ ANDRZEJ BONAWENTURA (1746–1817), general. Born near Novoguidok, Lithuania (now Poland), on Feb. 12, he studied at the Jesuit college in Breeze and two military academies and the Royal School of engineering at Mézières, France. On his return to Poland in 1774, he attained the rank of captain in the Polish Army. At the outbreak of the American Revolution he went to America and offered his services to the Continental Army; he was commissioned an officer of engineers in 1776 and served throughout the war with great distinction, attaining the rank of brigadier general. He took part in the Saratoga campaign, fortified West Point in 1778, and in 1780 fought under General Nathanael Greene in the Carolina campaign. At the end of the war he received a vote of thanks for his services from Congress, a pension, and the rank of brigadier general and then returned to Poland, where he lived in retirement. He rejoined the Polish Army as major general in 1789, fought under Prince Poniatowski against the Russians, and defeated a force of eighteen thousand men with only four thousand men at Dubienka. When King Stanislaus surrendered and Poland was partitioned by Russia and Prussia a second time in 1793, he resigned his commission and retired to Leipzig. The following year he issued a call from Kraków for a national uprising against the Prussians and Russians and led the revolt. He defeated a force of six thousand Russian soldiers with four thousand peasants armed with scythes and farming tools at Raciawice, and formed a provisional government. He was defeated by a Prussian force and a Russian pincer movement at the battle of Maciejowice, where he was wounded and captured by the Russians. After two years imprisonment he was freed by Emperor Paul on parole in 1796 and again retired. He visited the United States in 1797 and was given a hero's welcome and showered with honors by the grateful young nation. On his return to Europe he settled on his estate at Bienville, near Paris, refused Napoleon's request in 1806 to join in his invasion of Poland, as he felt he could not do so in view of his parole to Russia, and in 1816 he moved to Switzerland. He died at Solothurn, Switzerland, on Oct. 15 from injuries suffered in a fall from a horse. Kościuszko is one of the great heroes of Poland in that unhappy nation's quest for freedom and is justly revered in the United States for his aid to the colonists fighting for their freedom in the Revolution.

KOUDELKA, JOSEPH MARIA (1852–1921), bishop. Born in Chlistovo, Czechoslovakia, on Dec. 8, he studied at Klattau, Bohemia, and in 1868 emigrated to the United States with his parents and settled in Manitowoc, Wisconsin. He finished his studies for the priesthood at St. Francis Seminary, Milwaukee, Wisconsin, was ordained in 1875, and then engaged in pastoral work at St. Procopius parish in Cleveland, Ohio, until 1882. He became deeply involved in aiding Bohemian immigrants to the United States, edited the Bohemian weekly *Hlas (Voice)* in 1882–83, and prepared a series of textbooks for Bohemian Catholic schools. He was rector of St. Michael's Church in Cleveland from 1883 until 1907, when he was appointed titular bishop of Germanicopolis and auxiliary of Cleveland with special jurisdiction over the Slavs in that diocese—the first auxiliary bishop of special jurisdiction appointed in the United States. He was transferred to Milwaukee as an auxiliary in 1911 and was appointed second bishop of Superior, Wisconsin, in 1913. He increased the number of churches, missions, and schools in the see and increased the priests from eighty-six to ninety-eight during his administration and died in Superior on June 24.

KRAUTBAUER, FRANCIS XAVIER (1824–85), bishop. Born in Bruck, Bavaria, on Jan. 12, he studied at Ratisbon seminary and Munich and was ordained in Ratisbon in 1850. He emigrated to the United States, engaged in pastoral work in Buffalo and Rochester, New York, and in 1859 was made spiritual director of the American Sisters of Notre Dame. He was consecrated second bishop of Green Bay, Wisconsin, in 1875 and remained in that position until he died there suddenly on Dec. 17.

KREISLER, FRITZ (1875–1962), violinist, composer. Son of a prominent physician, he was born in Vienna on Feb. 2, studied violin under his father, and was admitted to the Vienna Conservatory when he was seven. He won its Gold Medal when he was ten, studied under Lambert Joseph Massart and Léo Delibes at the Paris Conservatoire, graduated in 1887, and won that year's Premier Grand Prix de Rome for his violin playing when he was twelve. He began the first of many American tours in 1888 and on his return to Vienna, after two years at the Piaristen Gymnasium, gave up music to study medicine at the University of Vienna in 1892. He returned to music two years later and made his debut with the Vienna Philharmonic in 1898 and the following year made his Berlin debut. He married Harriet Lies Woerz, an American divorcée, in 1902, and served as a captain in the Austrian Army briefly in World War I; he was released after being wounded in September 1914 and wrote of his wartime experiences in *Four Weeks in the Trenches; the War Story of a Violinist* (1915). He returned to the concert stage, was greeted with some hostility during an American tour as an enemy alien in 1917 (the United States had entered World War I in April and one of the nations against whom war had been declared was Austria-Hungary), and many of his engagements were canceled. After the war he played all over the world, universally acclaimed as the greatest violinist of his time. When Hitler came to power in Germany, Kreisler, who had built a home in Berlin, was harassed by the government when, in 1933, he refused to play in Germany until artists of all nationalities were allowed to perform there. The sale and broadcast of his music were banned in Germany and he left and went to France and became a French citizen in 1938. He moved to the United States in 1939, made it his permanent home, and became an American citizen in 1943. He and his wife were received back into the Catholic Church by Bishop Fulton J. Sheen and they renewed their marriage vows in a Catholic ceremony. He retired from music in 1950. In addition to his incomparable skill on the violin, Kreisler composed concertos, chamber music, operettas, and violin solos, among them the light violin pieces *Caprice viennois, Liebesfreud, Liebesleid, Schön Rosmarin,* and *Tambourin Chinois* and the operettas *Apple Blossoms* (1919), *Sissy* (1932), and *Rhapsody* (1944). He died in New York City on Jan. 29.

KUCERA LOUIS BENEDICT (1888–1957), bishop. Of Bohemian parents, he was born in Wheatland, Minnesota, on Aug. 24, was educated at St. Thomas College and the diocesan seminary, St. Paul, Minnesota, and the Catholic University, and was ordained in St. Paul in 1915. He engaged in parish work as a curate in Tama, Iowa, was a professor of Latin and prefect of discipline at Loras College, Dubuque, Iowa, in 1916–25, and was pastor of Holy Trinity Church, Protivin, Iowa, from 1925 to 1930, when he was appointed bishop of Lincoln, Nebraska. He remained in that position until his death in Lincoln on May 9.

KUNDIG, MARTIN (1805–79). Born in Switzerland on Nov. 15, he studied at Einsiedeln and Lucerne, Switzerland, and Rome and in 1828 he and John Henni (future first bishop of Milwaukee, Wisconsin) emigrated to the United States at the invitation of Fr. Frederic Résé, vicar-general of Cincinnati, Ohio. He continued his studies at Bardstown, Kentucky, was ordained in 1829 for the diocese of Cincinnati, and engaged in pastoral work in southern Ohio. He founded several parishes, became known for his work in the cholera epidemic of 1834, and was involved in civil matters. He served as superintendent of the Wayne County poorhouse, was appointed a regent for the University of Wisconsin, helped immigrants in their land purchases and in becoming citizens, was a leader in the temperance movement, and worked to improve the harbor facilities of Milwaukee. He became pastor of St. Mark's Church, Kenosha, Wisconsin, and opened the first public school in Wisconsin there in 1845, served as vicar-general of Milwaukee for thirty years, and was rector of the cathedral there in 1859–79; he is credited with building twenty-two churches in southeastern Wisconsin. He died in Milwaukee on Mar. 6.

L

LACKAYE, WILTON (1862–1932), actor. Born in Loudon County, Virginia, on Sept. 30, he studied in Ottawa for two years and at Georgetown and then studied for the priesthood for a time but decided it was not for him. He studied law briefly and then became involved in the theater, making his first success with the Lawrence Barrett Dramatic Club in Washington, D.C. He was with a stock company in Dayton, Ohio, later joined the Carrie Swan Company, appeared in New York in 1883 as Leo in *She,* was with Fanny Davenport's company in 1886–87 and in August 1887 joined Augustin Daly's company. He played many roles and made a tremendous hit as Svengali in *Trilby* in 1894. Among the other roles that made him a leading actor in the American theater were in *Dr. Belgraft* in 1896–97, as Sir Lucius O. Trigger in *The Rivals* in 1898, and in *The Royal Secret* in 1897–98. He married Alice Evans in 1895, was one of the founders of Actors' Equity Association and the Catholic Actors' Guild in 1914 and died in Long Island City, New York, on Aug. 22.

LA FARGE, CHRISTOPHER GRANT (1862–1938), architect. Son of John La Farge, the famous painter, and brother of John La Farge, the Jesuit, he was born in Newport, Rhode Island, on Jan. 5, studied at the Massachusetts Institute of Technology for two years in 1880–81 and then worked for a year in the office of Henry Hobson Richardson, architect. In 1883 he engaged in architectural work in his father's office in New York City and in 1886 he and his classmate, George Lewis Heins, formed an architectural firm. He became known for his architectural designs when the firm created the original designs for the Cathedral of St. John the Divine in New York City, though the trustees discarded the original plan after the death of Heins in 1907 and only the apse is La Farge's. After the death of Heins he became a member of La Farge and Morris in 1910–15, of La Farge, Warren and Clark in 1926–31 and of La Farge and Son in 1931–38. Among the buildings he designed are the interior of St. Paul the Apostle Church in New York City, the Catholic chapel at West Point, the Packard Library, Salt Lake City, buildings at Trinity College, Hartford, Connecticut, St. Matthew's Church, Washington, D.C., the Houghton Memorial Chapel at Wellesley College, Massachusetts, and the U.S. Naval Hospital, Brooklyn, New York; he also designed many of the subway stations for New York City's first subway system. He served as director and vice president of the American Institute of Architects and died in Saunderstown, Rhode Island, on Oct. 11.

LA FARGE, JOHN (1835–1910), painter. Born in New York City on Mar. 31, he was educated at St. John's College (Fordham) and Mt. St. Mary's College, Emmitsburg, Maryland, graduating in 1853. He planned to study law but in 1856 went to Paris, studied for a time in Thomas Couture's studio and met many of the pre-Raphaelites in England and decided on an art career. On his return to the United States, he studied art under William Morris Hunt, a Couture disciple, in Newport, Rhode Island, and began his career as a painter of landscapes and figure compositions. He married Margaret Mason, granddaughter of Commodore Matthew Perry and great-granddaughter of Benjamin Franklin, and the couple had nine children, among whom were Christopher Grant, Bancel, and John. He was on the committee that established the Metropolitan Museum of Art in 1870 and in 1876 he was commissioned to decorate Trinity Church in Boston and for the rest of his life he devoted himself mainly to mural painting and the manufacture and design of stained glass; he revived the art of stained-glass portraiture. His murals in Trinity Church and the Church of the Ascension and St. Paul's Church in New York City became famous and are unsurpassed in the United States. Among his finest works are windows in churches in Buffalo, New York, and in Worcester, Massachusetts, the "Peacock Window" in the Worcester Art Museum and the "Battle Window" at Harvard, many of which were equal in beauty to those of the great medieval masters. He was also known for his water colors and drawings, particularly those he did based on his visit to the South Seas in 1886 with his close friend, Henry Brooks Adams. Many of his easel paintings are to be found in leading American museums. He was also a pioneer in the study of Japanese art, which had great influence on his style. A man of the widest culture and erudition, his lectures on art are greatly admired for their style and balanced judgment, many of which were collected and published in book form, among them *Considerations on Painting* (1895), *An Artist's Letters from Japan* (1897), *The Higher Life in Art* (1908), *Reminiscences of the South Seas* (1912),

and *The Gospel Story in Art* (1913). He died in Providence, Rhode Island, on Nov. 14.

LA FARGE, JOHN (1880–1963), journalist, author, social worker. Of a distinguished American family and son of the noted artist John La Farge, he was born in Newport, Rhode Island, on Feb. 13. He was educated at Harvard (B.A. 1901), decided to become a priest (Theodore Roosevelt persuaded his father to give his consent), and continued his studies at the University of Innsbruck, where he received his licentiate in theology and was ordained in 1905. He joined the Jesuits later the same year, entered the Jesuit novitiate at St. Andrew's-on-Hudson, Poughkeepsie, New York, later the same year, taught at Canisius College, Buffalo, New York, Loyola College, Baltimore, and in 1908 entered Woodstock College, Maryland, where he received his M.A. in theology in 1910. He served as a chaplain in the prisons and hospitals on Blackwell's Island, New York City, and after nine months there was assigned in 1911 to Leonardstown, Maryland, and spent the next fourteen years there ministering to the Catholics in the rural areas of St. Charles County. He worked to improve the conditions of the blacks there, was instrumental in opening eight schools, including the Cardinal Gibbons Institute, a trade school for black boys and girls, in 1924, and two years later he became as assistant editor on the Jesuit magazine *America;* he remained on its staff for thirty-seven years until his death, serving as executive editor in 1944–48. He founded the Catholic Layman's Union of New York in 1928 and became a leader in the movement for social and interracial justice. In 1934 he founded the Catholic Interracial Council (by 1958 forty councils had been established all over the country) and became the leading American Catholic spokesman on the race question. In 1938 he was asked by Pope Pius XI to prepare a draft of an encyclical on the issue of racism. With Frs. Gustave Gundlach and Gustave Desbuquois, he drew up the draft but its transmittal to the Pope was held up and not submitted to Pius until January 1939, when he was desperately ill; when the Pope died on Feb. 10, 1939, the encyclical was never promulgated. Fr. La Farge wrote hundreds of articles for *America* and other journals and was the author of ten books, among them *The Race Question and the Negro* (1943), *No Postponement* (1950), *The Catholic Viewpoint on Race Relations* (1956), *An American Amen* (1958), *Reflections on Growing Old* (1973), and his autobiography, *The Manner Is Ordinary* (1954). He died in New York City on Nov. 24. During his lifetime Fr. La Farge was an uncompromising foe of Communism and a leader in the fields of liturgy and ecumenism, but above all he is known for his role as chief Catholic spokesman of his times for the cause of human rights for blacks.

LAFAYETTE, MARQUIS DE, MARIE JOSEPH PAUL YVES ROCH GILBERT DU MOTIER (1757–1834), general. Born in the Château de Chavaniac, Auvergne, France, on Sept. 7, he was brought to Paris in 1768 and studied at the Collège du Plessis. When his mother and grandfather died in 1770 (his father had been killed at the battle of Minden in 1759 when he was two), he inherited his grandfather's fortune. He joined the King's Musketeers in 1771, became a lieutenant in 1773, and married Marie Adrienne Françoise de Noailles in 1774, when he was seventeen. He became a captain soon after his marriage, determined to go to America in 1775 to help the Americans in their struggle against the English and in 1776 left active service in the French Army and went to America

the following year. The Continental Congress voted him the rank of major general and he met General Washington in Philadelphia on Aug. 1; the two became close friends. He played an active role in the Revolution, was slightly wounded at the battle of Brandywine, was put in charge of a division of Virginia light troops and shared the hardships of Valley Forge during the winter of 1777–78. He participated in the battle of Monmouth with distinction, acted as liaison in the failed attack on Newport by the French fleet under d'Estaing and American land forces, and in 1778 returned to France, where he sought increased French aid for the Americans. He returned to America in 1780, acted as an intermediary between Washington and the Comte de Rochambeau, commander of the French army in the colonies, helped prevent the capture of Richmond, Virginia, by British forces under General Phillips, and then was pursued by a superior force under General George Cornwallis but escaped. He took part in the attack on Cornwallis at Yorktown that led to Cornwallis's surrender in 1781 and returned to France in December. He was given a tremendous reception when he visited the United States in 1784 and on his return to France engaged in plans to establish a charter of freedom for his native land. He continued aiding the United States, helped adjust the frontier between the United States and Spanish possessions in America, and helped secure a most favored nation position for American exports to France. He was a member of the Assembly of Notables in 1787, urged the convocation of the States General, was a member of that body in 1789 and sponsored a declaration of rights. He served on the Constitutional Assembly, where he was among the leaders promoting liberal measures, and was elected vice president of the National Assembly and put in command of the National Guard the day after the fall of the Bastille, July 14, 1789. He tried to act as mediator between the various factions, becoming one of the most popular figures in France, but when he ordered his troops to fire into a crowd gathered on the Champs de Mars in 1791 to petition for dethronement of the king, his popularity rapidly declined. He retired to private life early in 1791 but was recalled to head a French army against Austria in 1792. He supported the monarchy and opposed the Jacobins, was branded a traitor in 1792 and forced to flee to Liège. He was captured and imprisoned by the Austrians in Austria in 1792–97 but was released by Napoleon when the Treaty of Campo Formio was signed in 1797, though he and his family lived in exile until 1799, when he returned and lived at La Grange forty miles from Paris. He lived in retirement during the reign of Napoleon, acknowledging his rule but opposing some of his measures, was a liberal member of the Chamber of Deputies in 1818–24, and was leader of the liberal opposition in 1825–30. He visited the United States in 1824–25 and received an unparalleled and enthusiastic reception, returned to France late in 1825 and played a prominent role as a leader of the moderates in the Revolution of July 1830. He died in Paris on May 20. Lafayette was a lifelong friend and admirer of the United States, constantly held up the United States as an example to his countrymen and as a promise for all mankind, and became the symbol of the bond of friendship between the United States and France. He spent some $200,000 of his own funds (a huge fortune in those days) to help the colonists and refused any compensation for his services, though Congress in 1794 voted him $24,424 for his salary during the American Revolution and in 1803 Congress voted him a grant of 11,520 acres of land in Louisiana; the Cham-

brun family, his direct descendants, are honorary American citizens.

LA GORCE, JOHN OLIVER (1879–1959), geographer. Born in Scranton, Pennsylvania, on Sept. 22, he was educated at Georgetown and after his graduation became a telegrapher. He wrote for newspapers and magazines from 1903 until 1905, when he joined the staff of the National Geographic Society as a secretary and remained with that organization in various capacities until his retirement in 1957. He held advertising and editorial positions, became a life trustee in 1927, and was president of the Society and editor-in-chief of its *National Geographic* in 1954–57. He traveled widely, was a friend of scientists, wrote numerous articles and edited *Book of Fishes* and was the author of several books, among them *The Warfare on Our Eastern Coast, Devil Fishing in the Gulf Stream, Puerto Rico, the Gateway of Riches,* and *Jamaica, Isle of Many Rivers.* La Gorce Mountains in Antarctica, La Gorce Arch in Utah, and a mountain and glacier in Alaska are named after him, and in 1933 he was appointed postmaster of Little America, Antarctica. He was honored by several colleges and died in Washington, D.C., on Dec. 23.

LALANDE, ST. JEAN DE (d. 1646), martyr. Born in Dieppe, France, he went to Quebec in 1644 and offered his services to the Jesuit missionaries of Canada as a *donné* (lay brother) and accompanied Fr. Isaac Jogues on a trip to the Mohawks in 1646. When Jogues was blamed by the Indians for a pestilence that had swept the tribe and a drought that had decimated their crops, they were both taken captive near Lake George in New York and brought to the Indian village of Ossernenon (now Auriesville, near Albany, New York). They were subjected to terrible tortures and on Oct. 19 Lalande was tomahawked and beheaded, the day after Fr. Jogues had been tortured to death. He was canonized in 1930 by Pope Pius XI as one of the North American Martyrs. Their feast day is celebrated on Oct. 19.

LALEMENT, ST. GABRIEL (1610–49), martyr. Born in Paris on Oct. 10, he joined the Jesuits in 1630, taught at Moulins and studied at Bourges, and was ordained in 1638. He taught at La Flèche and Moulins until 1646, when he was sent to Canada at his request. He spent the next two years in Quebec and then was sent to the Huron missions as assistant to Fr. (St.) Jean de Brébeuf at St. Ignace. Two months after his arrival a war party of Iroquois Indians, mortal enemies of the Hurons, attacked St. Ignace and captured the two priests after massacring all the other inhabitants. They were subjected to terrible tortures and after being forced to watch Fr. de Brébeuf's torture and murder, Lalement was put to death the following morning on Mar. 17. He was canonized in 1930 by Pope Pius XI as one of the North American Martyrs. Their feast day is celebrated on Oct. 19.

LALOR, TERESA (c. 1769–1846), foundress. Born in Ballyragget, Kilkenny, Ireland, she was early attracted to the religious life and was about to enter a convent in Ireland when she decided to emigrate to the United States with her sister, the wife of an American merchant, in 1794. She began a community in Philadelphia with two companions under the direction of Fr. Leonard Neale of that city and taught in a school for girls. When the yellow fever epidemic of 1797–98 closed her school, Fr. Neale, now president of Georgetown, invited her to Georgetown. She opened a school in 1799 (it became Georgetown Academy) and when the Poor Clare nuns returned to France in 1804, Fr. Neale bought their property and turned it over to Teresa; in 1813, Neale, now archbishop of Baltimore, allowed her to take simple vows. In 1816 Archbishop Neale received permission from Pope Pius VII to raise the community to the rank of monastery and later the same year the sisters, now thirty-five in number, took their solemn vows with Teresa as superior—the beginning of the Order of the Visitation in the United States; she and Archbishop Neale are considered the cofounders. She retired as superior in 1819 and died in Baltimore on Sept. 9 after having expanded the Order to Mobile, Alabama, St. Louis, Baltimore, and Brooklyn, New York.

LAMB, HUGH LOUIS (1890–1959), bishop. Born in Modena, Pennsylvania, on Oct. 6, he was educated at St. Charles Borromeo Seminary, Overbrook, Philadelphia, the North American College and the Propaganda, Rome, and was ordained in 1915. He engaged in parish work in Philadelphia, taught at St. Charles Borromeo from 1918 to 1921, when he became secretary to Cardinal Dennis Dougherty of Philadelphia, and was named assistant superintendent of Catholic schools in Philadelphia in 1923. He became chancellor of the see in 1926, was made a monsignor the following year, and was appointed titular bishop of Helos and auxiliary of Philadelphia in 1935 and vicar-general the following year. In 1951 he was named first bishop of the newly created diocese of Greenburg, Pennsylvania, and when Cardinal Dougherty died on May 31, four days after Bishop Lamb's consecration, the bishop was named administrator of the archdiocese of Philadelphia and served in that position until the following January, when he was installed in his own diocese. He launched a fund-raising campaign to build a chancery, a hospital, and a high school and built eight new elementary schools before his sudden death on Dec. 8 at Jeanette, Pennsylvania.

LAMBERT, LOUIS ALOYSIUS (1835–1910), editor. Born in Charleroi, Pennsylvania, on Apr. 13, he was educated at St. Vincent's Seminary, Latrobe, Pennsylvania, and the St. Louis Seminary at Carondelet, Missouri, and was ordained for the diocese of Alton, Illinois, in 1859. He engaged in pastoral work in Alton, Cairo, and Shawneetown, Illinois, served as chaplain of the 18th Illinois Infantry in the early years of the Civil War, and was pastor at Cairo in 1863–68. He taught for a time at the Paulist novitiate in New York City and in 1869 was incardinated into the diocese of Rochester, New York, and was named pastor at Waterloo, New York. He founded the Buffalo *Catholic Times* in 1877 (later merged with the Rochester *Catholic Times*), serving as editor until 1880, and engaged in controversy with Robert Ingersoll, the popular agnostic, which attracted widespread attention. In 1892 he founded the Philadelphia *Catholic Times,* serving as its editor for two years. He became involved in a controversy with Bishop McQuaid of Rochester, who denounced him to Rome for recalcitrance in 1890, and he was ordered to stay in his own diocese of Rochester. He was transferred to Scottsville, New York, as pastor of Ascension parish and remained in that position until his death. He edited the New York *Freeman's Journal* from 1895 to 1910, published *Notes on Ingersoll* (1883), refuting Ingersoll's philosophy, *Tactics of Infidels* (1887), and *Christian Science Before the Bar of Reason* (1908), and translated Paul Merz's *Thesaurus Biblicus,* the first Catholic concordance of the bible published in the United States. He died in Newfoundland, New Jersey, on Sept. 25.

LAMBERVILLE, JACQUES DE (1641–1710), missionary. Born in Rouen, France, he joined the Jesuits in 1661, was sent to Canada in 1675, and spent the rest of his life as a missionary to the Iroquois Indians. He and his brother Jean became extremely influential among the Indians and helped pacify them after they had been mistreated and aroused by Governors de la Barre and Denonville. Among his Indian converts was Kateri Tekakwitha, whom he instructed and baptized in 1675 and who was beatified in 1980. He returned to Quebec in 1709 and died there the following year.

LAMBERVILLE, JEAN DE (1633–1714), missionary. Born in Rouen, France, he joined the Jesuits in 1656 and was sent to Canada in 1669. He engaged in missionary work among the Onondaga and Iroquois Indians for four years and with his brother Jacques had great influence with them, especially the Iroquois, constantly striving to maintain peace between the French and the Iroquois. He saved Governor de la Barre's punitive expedition against the northern Indians from disaster in 1683 (he constantly urged a policy of moderation and compromise) and when Governor de Denonville in 1685–86 attempted to avenge de la Barre's capitulation he worked to restore peace. He returned to France because of ill health and died in Paris before he was able to return to his mission, as he so ardently desired.

LAMBING, ANDREW ARNOLD (1842–1918), author, historian. Born in Manorville, Pennsylvania, on Feb. 1, he studied for the priesthood at St. Michael Seminary, Glenwood, Pennsylvania, and was ordained in 1869. He was at St. Francis College, Loretto, Pennsylvania, for a time, at Pittsburgh in 1873–85 and Williamsburg in 1885–1918, served as censor of the diocese and president of the diocesan school board, founded the Ohio Valley Catholic Historical Society in 1884, and wrote widely for religious magazines. He wrote many popular books and works of history and was an authority on early Pennsylvania history. Among the former were *The Orphan's Friend* (1875), *Come Holy Ghost* (1901), and *Fountain of Living Water* (1907); among the latter were *A History of the Catholic Church in the Dioceses of Pittsburgh and Allegheny* (1880) and *Foundation Stones of a Great Diocese* (1912). He served as editor of *Historical Researches in Western Pennsylvania, Principally Catholic,* was made a domestic prelate in 1915, and died in Williamsburg, Pennsylvania, on Dec. 24.

LAMY, JOHN BAPTIST (1814–88), archbishop. Born in Lempdes, Puy de Dôme, France, on Oct. 11, he studied at the seminary of Montferrand and was ordained in 1838. He went to the United States in response to an appeal for priests from Bishop John Purcell of Cincinnati, Ohio, the following year and served as a missionary in Ohio and Kentucky. In 1850 he was appointed titular bishop of Agathon and vicar apostolic of New Mexico (comprising Arizona, Colorado, and New Mexico and parts of Utah and Nevada) when that region was ceded to the United States as a result of the Mexican war. He became first bishop of Santa Fe, New Mexico, when that diocese was created in 1853. His journeys under the utmost difficulties to the farthest reaches of his vicariate and diocese became legendary and in time he was considered the exemplar of a Catholic missionary on the frontier. He established the first school for teaching English in Santa Fe in 1852, brought priests and religious into his diocese, founded St. Michael College in Santa Fe in 1859, built and repaired Catholic churches and charitable institutions and

the unfinished Cathedral of San Francisco de Assis, dedicated in 1886, and transformed a decaying diocese into a flourishing see. In large measure his tireless labors were responsible for the renewed hold of the Catholic faith on the white settlers and Indians of the Southwest. He traveled to Europe in 1853 seeking priests and financial aid for his see and in 1875 became the first archbishop of Santa Fe when it was made a metropolitan see. He resigned in 1885 and was appointed titular archbishop of Cyzicus and died in Santa Fe on Feb. 13. His life was portrayed in one of Willa Cather's finest novels, *Death Comes for the Archbishop* (1927).

LANE, JOSEPH (1801–81), legislator, governor. Born in Asheville, North Carolina, on Dec. 14, he emigrated to Indiana when a youth and married Mary Hart there in 1820. He entered politics, was elected to the Indiana legislature in 1822, and served in its assembly and senate for seven terms. He fought in the Mexican-American War, attained the rank of brigadier general, and when he was discharged from the Army was appointed territorial governor of Oregon in 1848 by President Polk. He organized the territory, suppressed Indian uprisings caused by the flood of miners into southern Oregon's gold mines, and captured the Cayuse Indians accused of the murder of the Whitman Party in 1847. He was territorial delegate to the United States Congress in 1851–58, was elected to the United States Senate when Oregon became a state in 1859 and, a Southern sympathizer, ran for vice president on the presidential ticket of the southern Democrats, who had nominated John C. Breckinridge as their presidential candidate, in 1860. When Lincoln was elected, he retired to his farm, became a Catholic with several members of his family in 1867 and died in Roseburg, Oregon, on Apr. 19.

LANE, LORAS THOMAS (1910–68), bishop. Born in Cascade, Iowa, on Oct. 19, he was educated at Notre Dame (Ph.B. 1932), Loras College, Dubuque, Iowa (B.A. 1933), the Gregorian, Rome (S.T.L. 1937), the University of Iowa (M.A.), and Catholic University, where he received his J.C.D. He was ordained in Rome in 1937, was a curate at Nativity Church, Dubuque, in 1937–40, taught Spanish and economics at Loras in 1940–44 and was its president in 1951–56. He was named titular bishop of Benscenna and auxiliary of Dubuque in 1951 and was appointed bishop of Rockford, Illinois, in 1956. During his episcopate he launched an extensive building program of schools and churches, established new parishes, held a synod in 1958, saw Dubuque College for Women established in 1963 at St. Charles, and was elected chairman of the Committee on Priestly Formation of the National Council of Catholic Bishops in 1966. He died in Chicago on July 22.

LANE, RAYMOND A. (1894–1974), bishop. Born in Lawrence, Massachusetts, on Jan. 2, he was educated at St. John's College, Danvers, Massachusetts, and Maryknoll Preparatory Seminary, Scranton, Pennsylvania, where he was the seminary's first student in 1913. He was ordained in 1920, served as procurator for Maryknoll and in 1923 was sent to China as a missionary. In 1925 he was sent to Manchuria, was superior of the Maryknoll Mission there in 1925–29, was rector of the Maryknoll Seminary in New York in 1929–32, and was appointed prefect apostolic of Fushun, Manchuria, in 1932. He was named titular bishop of Hypaepa and vicar apostolic of Fushun in 1940. He was imprisoned by the Japanese during World War II, was superior general of Maryknoll in 1946–56, and died on July 31 in San Francisco.

LANZA, MARIO (1921–59), singer. Born Alfredo Arnold Cocozza in South Philadelphia on Jan. 31, he early evinced great promise as a singer and had as his great ambition to be an opera singer. He took music and singing lessons and in 1942 met Serge Koussevitzky, who was in charge of the Berkshire Music Center at Tanglewood, Lenox, Massachusetts, and who offered him a Tanglewood scholarship. At this time he changed his name, using his mother's maiden name. His singing in *The Merry Wives of Windsor* at the festival attracted attention and he was signed for a tour by Columbia Concerts but had his career interrupted when he was inducted into the Army in 1943. He sang in several army groups and shows, was discharged in 1945 and married Betty Hicks the same year, when he also sang at the Hollywood Bowl. In 1947 he was heard by Louis B. Mayer, the movie tycoon, who signed him to a seven-year movie contract. His movie debut in *That Midnight Kiss* (1949) was a tremendous success and he appeared in a succession of films, among them *The Toast of New Orleans* (1950), *The Great Caruso* (1951), *Because You're Mine* (1952), *The Seven Hills of Rome* (1958), and *For the First Time* (1959). Forced to battle overweight all his life, he was on a diet at the Villa Giulia Clinic in Rome, Italy, when he died of a blood clot in the heart on Oct. 7.

LA RICHARDIE, ARMAND DE (1686–1758), missionary. Born in Périgueux, France, on June 7, he joined the Jesuits in 1703 in Bordeaux and was ordained. He was sent as a missionary to Canada in 1725, spent two years as an assistant at Lorette and learning the Huron language, and in 1728 was sent to the Petun-Huron Indians to reestablish a mission in the area around present-day Detroit. He spent the next twenty-three years in missionary work until 1751, founding the first Catholic mission in Ohio among the Hurons near Sandusky, except for a time in 1746–47 when he was recovering from a paralysis in Quebec, when he was forced to return to Quebec with a reoccurrence of the same illness. He remained in Quebec until his death there on Oct. 4.

LARKIN, JOHN (1801–58), educator. Of Irish parents, he was born in Newcastle-on-Tyne, England, on Feb. 2, studied at Ushaw College, Ushaw, England, and traveled throughout the East. On his return he joined the Sulpicians in Paris, studied at St. Sulpice Seminary, Paris, and was sent to St. Mary's Seminary, Baltimore, where he completed his studies for the priesthood and was ordained in 1827. He taught at the Sulpician college in Montreal until 1840, when he returned to the United States and joined the Jesuits in 1841. He taught at Mt. St. Mary's, Kentucky, founded St. Ignatius Literary Institution in Louisville, Kentucky, in 1841, became famed for his oratorical prowess, and in 1846 went to teach at St. John's College (Fordham) in New York City, serving as vice president for a year. The following year he founded and became first president of St. Francis Xavier College in New York City and was seeking funds for the college, which had been destroyed by fire, when he was appointed bishop of Toronto in 1850. He declined and in 1851 became president of St. John's College. He went to England in 1854 to preach missions, returned to New York in 1856 and served as a parish priest at St. Francis Xavier Church until his death in New York City on Dec. 11.

LARRAZOLA, OCTAVIANO AMBROSIO (1859–1930), governor. Born in Allende, Chihuahua, Mexico, on Dec. 7, he went to Tucson in 1870 as the protégé of Bishop J. B. Salpointe and accompanied Salpointe to Santa Fe when he became its archbishop in 1875. He studied at St. Michael's College there, taught school at Tucson for a year, and then was a high school principal in San Elizario, Texas, in 1879–84. He was a court clerk in El Paso district in 1884–88, studied law and was admitted to the bar in 1888, and served as district attorney for Western Texas in 1890–94. By now he was well known as a champion of the natives, who constituted half of the population of the territory and had a provision written into the state charter prohibiting discrimination against Spanish-speaking voters. He was defeated in elections for Congress in 1900, 1906, and 1908 but was governor of New Mexico in 1919–21. He was defeated in a bid to be elected justice of the state supreme court in 1924, and in 1928 he was appointed United States senator to fill the unexpired term of Andrieus A. Jones. He died in Albuquerque, New Mexico, on Apr. 7.

LA SALLE, RENÉ ROBERT CAVELIER SIEUR DE (1643–87), explorer. Born in Rouen, France, and baptized on Nov. 22, he studied at the Jesuit college there and joined the Jesuits in Paris when fifteen but left the Society in 1665. The following year he went to Canada, where the Sulpicians granted him land on the western end of the island of Montreal and he engaged in the fur trade. During the next two years he learned eight Indian dialects and in 1669 he explored the Ohio River and went as far as Lake Michigan and discovered the Illinois River. He was appointed commander of Fort Frontenac on Lake Ontario by Governor Frontenac in 1673 and the following year returned to France to make plans for further expeditions and was made esquire. He was commissioned by the crown to build forts and to explore the Mississippi Valley in 1677, and in 1679, with a group that included Henri de Tonty, Michael Aco, and Fr. Louis Hennepin, he built a blockhouse at the mouth of the Niagara River and sailed across Lakes Erie, Huron, Michigan, and to Green Bay in the *Griffon*, a forty-five-ton gunboat they had built—the first sailing vessel on the Great Lakes. He proceeded overland to the Illinois River, building Fort Miami on the site of present-day St. Joseph, Michigan, and the Fort Crèvecoeur on the Illinois near present-day Peoria, Illinois. He dispatched a party under Fr. Hennepin and Aco to explore the Upper Mississippi while he returned overland to Frontenac for supplies. On his return he found Tonty had been forced to abandon Fort Crèvecoeur because of attacks by Iroquois Indians which had caused his men to mutiny and drive him into the wilderness. He organized a federation of the Illinois, Miami, and several smaller Indian tribes to fight the Iroquois, captured the mutineers and brought them back to Montreal in chains, and then set out to find Tonty. They were reunited at Mackinac Island on Feb. 6, 1681, and with Fr. Zenobe Membré and a small party he set out early in 1682 on his epic-making expedition to descend the Mississippi River (which he named Colbert) to its mouth. On Apr. 9, they reached the Gulf of Mexico. He named the entire region he had traversed Louisiana and took possession of it for France. Tonty returned to the Illinois and began to reconstruct the fort and La Salle joined him and Fort Saint Louis was built in 1682–83. In 1682 the new governor, Antoine Lefebre, Sieur de la Barre, deprived La Salle of his authority and he returned to France. He reported his discoveries to the king, who made him viceroy of North America and authorized him to govern and colonize the area between Lake Michigan and the Gulf of Mexico.

In 1684 he set out from France with four vessels for the mouth of the Mississippi but was unable to find it from the Gulf of Mexico. He landed on what is now the Texas shore and made two futile attempts to reach the Mississippi overland; his men grew restless, mutinied when he made a third attempt and during this attempt shot and killed him on Mar. 19 on the bank of the Brazos River in Texas.

LASANCE, FRANCIS XAVIER (1860–1946), author. Born in Cincinnati, Ohio, on Jan. 24, he was educated at Xavier College there and at St. Meinrad's Abbey, Indiana, and was ordained in his native city in 1883. He served as a curate and pastor in Kenton, Reading, Dayton, Lebanon, and Monroe, all in Ohio, from 1883 until 1890, when ill health forced him to retire. After an unsuccessful trip to Europe to recoup his health, he was appointed chaplain to the Sisters of Notre Dame de Namur in Cincinnati and spent the greater part of the rest of his life there writing some thirty devotional books on the Mass for religious and children and compiled a variety of popular missals and prayer books. His best-known book is the missal *My Prayer Book* (1913); some of his other books are *Visits to Jesus in the Tabernacle* (1898), *Mass Devotions* (1901), *Young Man's Guide* (1910), *Reflections for Religious* (1920), *Rejoice in the Lord* (1920), *Our Lady Book* (1924), *Let Us Pray* (1925), *Sweet Sacrament We Adore Thee* (1930), and *New Missal for Everyday* (1932). He died in Cincinnati on Jan. 11.

LATHROP, GEORGE PARSONS (1851–98), author. Born near Honolulu, Hawaiian Islands, on Aug. 25, he was educated in New York City and Dresden, Germany, and on his return to New York decided to devote himself to a literary career. He married Rose Hawthorne, daughter of Nathaniel Hawthorne, while on a visit to London in 1871, lived in New York for a time, and moved to Boston in 1875, when he became associate editor of the *Atlantic Monthly.* He left the *Atlantic* two years later for newspaper work in Boston and New York and produced a prodigious number of articles for newspapers and periodicals. He founded the American Copyright League in 1883, which in time secured international protection for copyrights, and was one of the founders of the Catholic School of America in 1892. He and his wife became Catholics in 1891 while living in New York. In addition to his magazine and magazine output, he also published books of poetry, fiction, and history; among his books were *Rose and Roof-Tree* (1875), *Dreams and Days* (1892), *Afterglow* (1871), and, co-authored with his wife, *A Story of Courage* (1894), a history of Visitation Convent in Washington, D.C. He edited the works of Nathaniel Hawthorne in 1883 and adapted *The Scarlet Letter* for Walter Damrosch's opera, which was produced in 1896. He died in New York City on Apr. 19. After his death his wife became a Dominican sister as Mother Mary Alphonsa and founded a religious order.

LATHROP, ROSE HAWTHORNE (1851–1926), foundress. Daughter of Nathaniel Hawthorne, Rose Hawthorne was born in Lenox, Massachusetts, on May 20. She was raised in England (her father was then in the consular service there) and Italy and returned to the United States in 1860. In 1871 she married George Lathrop in London, had a book of poems, *Along the Shore,* published in 1888, and in 1891 she and her husband became Catholics. Two years later she left him when he became an alcoholic, but they were reunited in 1894. She began ministering to victims of cancer on New York's Lower East Side, left George for good later in 1894 but was reunited with him on his death bed in 1898. She joined the Dominicans the following year, taking the name Mother Mary Alphonsa, and devoted herself to caring for penniless sufferers of incurable cancer. She founded St. Rose's Free Home for Incurable Cancer in the slums of New York City in 1901, established Rosary Hill Home in Hawthorne, New York, for the same purpose, where the patients were cared for by a community she founded in 1900, the Servants of Relief for Incurable Cancer (the incorporated name of the Dominican Congregation of St. Rose of Lima). Widely honored for her medical and charitable works, she also wrote stories and sketches and *Memories of Hawthorne* (1897) and co-authored with her husband *A Story of Courage* (1894), a history of the Visitation Convent in Washington, D.C. She died in Hawthorne on July 9.

LAVANOUX, MAURICE (1894–1974), architect. Born in New York City on June 10, he was educated at Mt. St. Louis Institute, Montreal in 1906–11, Columbia University Extension in 1912–17, and Atelier Hirons, New York City, in 1915–17. He served in World War I as an interpreter for the American Army in France in 1917–18 and as a lieutenant in the French Army in 1919, continued his studies at Atelier Laloux, Paris, in 1919–20, and spent the next fifteen years in architecture at Gustave E. Steinback, New York, and Maginnis and Walsh, Boston, as draftsman and researcher. He was one of the founders of the Liturgical Arts Society in 1928 and served as its secretary, launched *Liturgical Arts Quarterly* in 1932 and was its editor until 1972, when it was discontinued for lack of funds. He lectured and wrote widely on church art and architecture all over the United States and

Canada, was consulted on many ecclesiastical structures, and became the leader in the movement to improve the quality of ecclesiastical art and architecture in the United States. After his retirement from *Liturgical Arts Quarterly,* he became editor of *Stained Glass* magazine and worked closely with the Contemporary Christian Art Gallery in New York City. He was made a Knight Commander of St. Gregory in 1967, received an honorary citation of membership from the American Institute of Architects in 1968 and honorary degrees from several colleges and universities. He died in New York City on Oct. 21.

LAVELLE, MICHAEL JOSEPH (1856–1939), educator. Born in New York City on May 30, he was educated at Manhattan College (B.A. 1873, M.A. 1875), St. Joseph's Seminary, Troy, New York, and was ordained in 1879. He served as a curate at St. Patrick's Cathedral in New York City in 1879–86 and was its pastor for more than fifty years, from 1887 until his death in New York City on Oct. 17. He was named vicar-general in 1902 and was made a domestic prelate in 1902 and a prothonotary apostolic in 1929. He founded the Catholic Institute for the Blind (now Lavelle School of the Blind) and Cathedral High School, the first free Catholic high school in New York, was one of the founders of the Catholic Summer School of America at Plattsburg, New York, and was its president in 1896–1903 and chairman of its board of trustees in 1924–39. He was active in numerous welfare and cultural activities.

LAVIALLE, PETER JOSEPH (1820–67), bishop. Born in Lavialle, Auvergne, France, on July 15, he made his preparatory studies for the priesthood in France and in 1841 emigrated to Louisville, Kentucky, to join a relative, Bishop Guy Chabrat, coadjutor of that diocese. He finished his studies for the priesthood at St. Thomas Seminary, Bardstown, Kentucky, was ordained in 1841, and served as an assistant at the cathedral and secretary of Bishop Flaget, ordinary of Louisville. He taught at St. Thomas from 1849 until Bishop Martin Spalding named him president of St. Mary's College in 1856 and he served in that position until he was appointed bishop of Louisville in 1865. He brought the Dominicans into the see and founded the Sisters of the Third Order Regular of St. Francis, attended the second Plenary Council of Baltimore in 1866, returned from the Council in ill health, retired to Nazareth, Kentucky, and died there the following year on May 11.

LAWLER, JOHN JEREMIAH (1862–1948), bishop. Born in Rochester, Minnesota, on Aug. 4, he was educated at St. Francis Seminary, Milwaukee, Wisconsin, and Louvain, Belgium, and was ordained in 1885. After further study at Louvain where he was vice-rector of the American College in 1885–87, he became professor of Sacred Scriptures at St. Thomas College, St. Paul, Minnesota, was pastor of St. Luke's Church and then of the cathedral in St. Paul, and in 1910 was appointed titular bishop of Greater Hermopolis and auxiliary of St. Paul. He became bishop of Lead, South Dakota, in 1916 (transferred to Rapid City in 1930) and remained in that position until his death there on Mar. 11.

LAWRENCE, DAVID LEO (1889–1966), governor. Son of a teamster, he was born in Pittsburgh on June 18 and early became involved in politics in his native state. He soon became a major political force and in 1920 was chairman of the Allegheny County Democratic organization. He was Collector of

Internal Revenue for Western Pennsylvania in 1933–34, secretary of the Commonwealth of Pennsylvania in 1935–38, and was accused several times of negotiating illegal contracts and forcing state employees to make campaign contributions but was acquitted each time. He was elected mayor of Pittsburgh for four consecutive terms in 1945, 1949, 1953, and 1957 and saw Pittsburgh cited as one of the eight best governed cities in the nation by *Fortune* magazine in 1958. He was a firm supporter of President Franklin D. Roosevelt, was credited with engineering the nominations of Harry Truman for vice president in 1940, and in 1960 helped nominate John F. Kennedy for the Democratic nomination for President though he at first opposed him. The only four-time mayor of Pittsburgh, he was responsible for the rejuvenation of that city, which became a showcase of urban renewal, and served as president of the United States Conference of Mayors in 1950–52. He was elected governor of Pennsylvania in 1958—the first Catholic to hold that office—and when his term expired in 1963, he resumed the leadership of Pennsylvania's Democratic Party, a role he filled until his death in Pittsburgh on Nov. 21.

LEBLOND, CHARLES HUBERT (1883–1958), bishop. Born at Celina, Ohio, on Nov. 21, he was educated at John Carroll University and St. Mary's Seminary, Cleveland, Ohio, and was ordained in 1906. He served as curate at St. John's Cathedral, Cleveland, in 1909–11, was director of St. Anthony's Home for Boys in 1911, and was diocesan director of Catholic Charities and Homes in 1911–13. He was appointed bishop of St. Joseph, Missouri (redesignated diocese of Kansas City–St. Joseph in 1956), in 1933, resigned and was appointed titular bishop of Orcistus in 1956 and died in St. Joseph on Dec. 30.

LE BUFFE, FRANCIS PETER (1885–1954), author. Born in Charleston, South Carolina, on Aug. 21, he was educated at Gonzaga College, Washington, D.C., joined the Jesuits in 1901 and studied at St. Andrew-on-Hudson, Poughkeepsie, New York, and Woodstock College, Maryland (M.A. 1915), and was ordained at Woodstock in 1915. He was ill the next three years, was regent of the School of Law at Fordham in 1920–22 and received his Ph.D. from Fordham in 1922 and was dean of Fordham's School of Social Service from 1923 to 1926, when he joined the editorial staff of *America,* also serving as managing editor of *Thought.* After 1939 he wrote articles, pamphlets, and books, among them the enormously popular *My Changeless Friend.* He served as director of the Catholic Press Association in 1936–38, was president of the Catholic Anthropological Conference in 1939, and founded the Eastern Jesuit Philosophical Association in 1926 and the Jesuit Anthropological Association in 1936. He died in New York City on May 27. Among his other books were *Jurisprudence with Cases to Illustrate Principles,* with J. V. Hayes (1924), the five-pamphlet *Let Us Pray* and the three-pamphlet *As It Is Written* series.

LEDVINA, EMMANUEL BOLESLAUS (1868–1952), bishop. Born in Evansville, Indiana, on Oct. 28, he was educated at St. Meinrad College and Seminary, Indiana, and was ordained in Indianapolis in 1893. He served as a curate in Evansville and Indianapolis, Indiana, was pastor of St. Joseph's Church, Princeton, Indiana, in 1895–97, and was first general secretary and vice president of the Catholic Church Extension Society in 1907–21. He was made a domestic prelate in 1918 and was consecrated bishop of Corpus Christi, Texas, in 1921. Faced with far-reaching mission needs in his diocese, he appealed to the Extension Society, which donated more than half a million dollars to the diocese, which helped put it on a self-sustaining basis. He was made an Assistant at the Pontifical Throne in 1931, resigned his see in 1949, and died in Corpus Christi on Mar. 15.

LEE, THOMAS SIM (1745–1819), governor. Born in Prince George's County, Maryland, on Oct. 29, he inherited a large fortune and in 1771 married Mary Digges, a Catholic. He opposed the British at the outbreak of the Revolution and became a major in the Prince George's County militia. He was appointed to the Provincial Council in 1777 and in 1779 was elected governor of Maryland over Samuel Chase. Ineligible for reelection, he served in Congress under the Articles of Confederation, declined to serve in the Constitutional Convention in 1787, and was reelected governor in 1792. He supported the federal government during the Whiskey Rebellion, reorganized the state militia, and retired from politics in 1794. According to family tradition he became a Catholic, established St. Mary's Church, Petersville, Maryland, as a thanksgiving for the recovery of his wife from a serious illness, and died in Frederick County, Maryland, on Nov. 9.

LEFEVERE, PETER PAUL (1804–69), bishop. Born in Roulers near Ghent, Belgium, on Apr. 29, he studied under the Lazarists in Paris and became a Lazarist in 1828. He emigrated to the United States the same year, continued his studies for the priesthood at St. Mary's Seminary, Perrysville, Missouri, and was ordained there in 1831. He engaged in pastoral work at St. Paul's parish, Salt River, Missouri, and missionary work in its mission stations in Missouri, Illinois, and Wisconsin from 1832 to 1841, when he was appointed titular bishop of Zela and coadjutor and administrator of the diocese of Detroit. Though he never succeeded to the see (Bishop Frederic Résé, bishop of Detroit, did not die until 1871, two years after Bishop Lefevere), he built up its Catholic educational facilities, brought religious orders into the diocese, issued a set of diocesan statutes in 1843, and held a synod in 1859. He was unsuccessful in an effort to secure public funds for his schools in 1852–53, built SS. Peter and Paul Cathedral, which opened in 1845, and secured for the bishops of Detroit ownership of Church property. At the time of his death, he had increased the number of priests from 18 to 88 and the churches from 25 to 160 in the lower peninsula of Michigan. With Bishop Martin Spalding of Louisville, he was mainly responsible for the founding of the American College at Louvain, Belgium, in 1857. He died in Detroit on Mar. 4.

LEIBOLD, PAUL FRANCIS (1914–72), bishop. Born in Dayton, Ohio, on Dec. 22, he was educated at the University of Dayton (B.A. 1936), St. Gregory Seminary and Mt. St. Mary of the West Seminary, Cincinnati, and was ordained in 1940. He was assistant chancellor of the Cincinnati archdiocese in 1942–48, chancellor in 1948–58, and was made a papal chamberlain in 1948 and a domestic prelate in 1950. He was named titular bishop of Trebanna and auxiliary of Cincinnati in 1958 and served as vicar-general in 1958–66 and was consecrated bishop of Evansville, Indiana, in 1966. He was appointed archbishop of Cincinnati in 1969 and remained in that position until his death in Cincinnati on June 1.

LEIPZIG, FRANCIS PETER (1895–1981), bishop. Born in Chilton, Wisconsin, on June 29, he was educated at St. Francis Seminary, Milwaukee, Wisconsin, Mt. St. Angel Seminary, Oregon, and St. Patrick's Seminary, Menlo Park, California, and was ordained in 1920. He served as a curate at McMinnville, Corvallis, and Sheridan, Oregon, and the cathedral at Portland, Oregon, served as diocesan consultant and rural dean, and was pastor of St. Mary's Church and was teaching at its high school in Eugene, Oregon, when he was appointed bishop of Baker, Oregon, in 1950. He retired in 1971 and died in Beaverton, Oregon, on Jan. 17.

LEMCKE (or LEMKE), HENRY (1796–1882), missionary. Born in Rhena, Mecklenburg, Germany, on July 27, he attended the Lutheran cathedral school at Schwerin, Germany, and the University of Rostock, Mecklenburg-Schwerin, and became a Lutheran minister in 1820. He was converted to Catholicism in 1824 and was ordained a Catholic priest at Ratisbon in 1826. He emigrated to the United States in 1834, was at Holy Trinity Church, Philadelphia, for a time and was then sent to Loretto, Pennsylvania, as assistant to Prince Demetrius Gallitzen. He bought some land in 1836 and founded Carrolltown on it, succeeded Prince Gallitzen on his death as pastor of Loretto in 1846, and helped bring the first Benedictines to the United States; they settled at Latrobe, Pennsylvania, and founded the priory of St. Vincent (later archabbey) under Fr. Boniface Wimmer, and in 1852 Fr. Lemcke joined them. He went to Kansas in 1855 and helped found St. Benedict's Abbey at Atchison, was pastor at several churches in Elizabeth, New Jersey, from 1861—when his biography of Prince Gallitzen was published—until 1877, when he returned to Car-

rolltown. He spent the rest of his life there until his death there on Nov. 29.

L'ENFANT, PIERRE CHARLES (1754–1825), engineer, architect. Son of a painter of the royal court, he was born in Paris on Aug. 2, was educated as an artist by his father and as an engineer and joined Lafayette in 1777 as a volunteer to help the colonists in their revolt against England. He served in the Continental Army throughout the American Revolution, was wounded at the siege of Savannah in 1779 and captured at Charleston, and was brevetted major in Washington's army in 1783. After the war he remodeled New York's City Hall for the first Congress in 1789, arranged Federal Hall in Philadelphia, and when the District of Columbia was selected as the site of the federal government, he drew up the plans for the city of Washington in 1791. He was dismissed by Washington the following year for failing to get along with the commissioners of the District and the President as well; he had also antagonized the Congress and was opposed by Jefferson. He refused an appropriation for his plan for the capital and spent the next years designing private and public buildings and fruitlessly petitioning Congress for further compensations for his plans for the capital. Among the projects in which he was engaged was a commission, later in 1792, from a society headed by Alexander Hamilton and Robert Morris to lay out a manufacturing town around the falls at Passaic, New Jersey; again difficulties with the directors caused him to leave. He declined an appointment as professor of engineering at West Point in 1812 and instead worked on plans for fortifications near Washington during the War of 1812 but left government service when he again quarreled with his superiors. He spent the rest of his life at the estate of a friend, William Dudley Digges, near Blandensburg,

Maryland, and died there on June 14, in poverty and forgotten. Ironically, in 1889 his plans were exhumed from the archives and in 1901 the capital was developed along the lines he had laid down; and finally in 1909 the nation honored him with a state funeral and burial in Arlington Cemetery.

LENIHAN, MATTHIAS CLEMENT (1854–1943), bishop. Brother of Thomas Matthias Lenihan, he was born in Dubuque, Iowa, on Oct. 6, was educated at St. Joseph's College there, St. John's College, Prairie du Chien, Wisconsin, in 1870–72, Columbia College, Dubuque, in 1873–76 and the Grand Seminary, Montreal, and was ordained in Montreal in 1879. He was pastor at Vail and Denison, Iowa, in 1880–87, was vicar forane and missionary director at Marshalltown, Iowa, in 1887–1904, and was appointed first bishop of the newly created diocese of Great Falls, Montana, in 1904. He was a vigorous supporter of the temperance movement, established a parochial school system in the diocese, dedicated St. Ann's Cathedral in 1907 and increased the number of priests from fourteen to fifty-one, parishes from eleven to forty-five, schools from two to fifteen during his episcopate, and resigned and was made titular bishop of Preslavo in 1930. He died in Dubuque on Aug. 19.

LENIHAN, THOMAS MATTHIAS (1843–1901), bishop. Brother of Matthias Clement Lenihan, bishop of Great Falls, Montana, in 1904–30, he was born in Mallon, Cork, Ireland, on May 21, was educated at St. Thomas College, Bardstown, Kentucky, St. Vincent's Seminary, Cape Girardeau, Missouri, and St. Francis Seminary, Milwaukee, Wisconsin, and was ordained in 1868. He engaged in pastoral work until 1897, when he was consecrated second bishop of Cheyenne, Wyoming, a position he

held until his death in Dubuque, Iowa, four years later on Dec. 15.

LERAY, FRANCIS XAVIER (1825–87), archbishop. Born in Château Giron, Brittany, France, on Apr. 20, he studied at Rennes and in 1843 emigrated to the United States. He continued his studies at St. Mary's Seminary, Baltimore, and Spring Hill College, Alabama, and then went to Natchez, Mississippi, with Bishop John Chanche, the new see's first bishop, and was ordained there in 1852. He engaged in missionary work in Mississippi, became a pastor in Vicksburg, where he brought Sisters of Mercy from Baltimore to establish a school, and was a chaplain in the Confederate Army during the Civil War. He was consecrated bishop of Natchitoches, Louisiana, in Rennes, France, in 1877 and was appointed titular bishop of Janopolis and coadjutor and apostolic administrator of New Orleans in 1879, at the same time continuing as administrator of Natchitoches until 1883, when he was appointed archbishop of New Orleans. He abolished the cathedral's board of trustees, which had frequently quarreled with previous bishops, reduced the immense archdiocesan debt he had inherited from his predecessor, and died in Château Giron on Sept. 23 while visiting France in a vain effort to recover his health.

LEVADOUX, MICHAEL (1746–1815), missionary. Born at Clermont-Ferrand, Auvergne, France, on Apr. 1, he entered the Sulpician seminary at Clermont in 1769, studied at the Sulpician novitiate for a year and then at St. Sulpice in Paris, and was ordained a Sulpician priest in Paris in 1774. He was director of the Limoges seminary from 1774 to 1791, when he accompanied Fr. Francis Nagot and a group of other Sulpicians to found a school at Baltimore, where Bishop John Carroll had decided to establish St. Mary's Seminary—the first American seminary under Sulpician auspices. Fr. Lavadoux was treasurer for a year until 1792, when he was sent west as Bishop Carroll's vicar-general in the Middle West and engaged in missionary work in the area around Cahokia, Kaskaskia, and Prairie de Rocher in Illinois. He became parish priest of St. Ann's Church, Detroit, in 1796 and ministered to the Indians and settlers of the area until 1801, when he was recalled to Baltimore. He returned to France in 1803, was appointed superior of St. Fleur Seminary in Auvergne and remained there until Napoleon dispersed the Sulpicians in France in 1811. When they were reinstated in 1814, he was named head of the seminary of Le Puy-en-Velay and remained in that position until his death there on Jan. 13.

LEVEN, STEPHEN A. (1905–83), bishop. Born in Blackwell, Oklahoma, on Apr. 30, he was educated at St. Gregory's College, Oklahoma, St. Benedict's College, Kansas, and the American College and the Institut Supérieur de Philosophie, Louvain, Belgium (Ph.D. 1938). He was ordained in 1928, was a curate at the Oklahoma City cathedral and secretary to Bishop Francis C. Kelley for two years, was pastor at Bristow and Drumright, Oklahoma, in 1932–35, and was vice-rector of the American College at Louvain in 1935–38. He was pastor at Tonkawa in 1938–48 and Enid in 1948–56, both in Oklahoma, was made a papal chamberlain in 1949 and a domestic prelate in 1955, and was named titular bishop of Bure and auxiliary bishop of San Antonio, Texas, in 1955. He was appointed bishop of San Angelo, Texas, in 1969 and remained in that position until he retired in 1979. He died in San Angelo on June 28.

LEWIS, FRANK J. (1867–1960), executive. Born in Chicago on Apr. 9, he became a roofer and president of his own roofing materials and coal-tar products company, which became a leading producer of roofing, paving materials, and coal-tar chemicals. He retired in 1927 and established the Lewis Foundation and became famous for his philanthropies. He gave millions of dollars to charitable causes, founded the Lewis Memorial Maternity Hospital in Chicago in 1931, and donated Lewis Towers, a skyscraper office building in Chicago, to Loyola University in 1945. Three years later he established the Stritch School of Medicine in Chicago and the Illinois Club for Catholic women, and in 1955 he donated a Chicago office building to De Paul University. He donated generously to the Catholic Church Extension Society, to St. Ambrose College, Lockport, Illinois, was papally honored three times, and was made a papal count. He died in Chicago on Dec. 21.

LILLIS, THOMAS FRANCIS (1862–1938), bishop. Born in Lexington, Missouri, on Mar. 3, he was educated at Niagara University, New York, where he received his B.A. and at St. Benedict's College, Kansas, and was ordained in Kansas City, Missouri, in 1885. He served as a curate at Shackleford, Missouri, in 1885–87, was pastor at Westport, Missouri, in 1887–88 and of St. Patrick's Church, Kansas City, Missouri, in 1888–1904 and was consecrated bishop of Leavenworth, Kansas, in 1904. He was appointed titular bishop of Cibyra and coadjutor of Kansas City, Missouri (Kansas City–St. Joseph since 1956), in 1910 and succeeded to the see in 1913. He was appointed Assistant at the Pontifical Throne in 1935 and died in Kansas City on Dec. 29.

LILLY, JOSEPH (1893–1952), biblical scholar. Born in Cape Girardeau, Missouri, on July 1, he joined the Congregation of the Mission (the Vincentians) and was ordained in 1918. He taught Sacred Scripture at Catholic University in 1942–46 and was a charter member of the Catholic Biblical Association of America, serving as its general secretary in 1942–48. He wrote profusely on biblical matters, was a member of the committee to revise the 1941 edition of the Confraternity of Christian Doctrine New Testament and with James Kleist translated the New Testament from the original Greek. The Kleist-Lilly New Testament was published posthumously in 1954. He died in St. Louis on Mar. 21.

LILY OF THE MOHAWKS. *See* Tekakwitha, Bl. Kateri.

LINTON, MOSES LEWIS (1808–72), physician. Born in Nelson County, Kentucky, he graduated from Transylvania University, Lexington, Kentucky, and then continued his medical studies in Edinburgh and Paris. He returned to the United States in 1840, practiced medicine in Springfield, Kentucky, and in 1842 became a member of the medical faculty of St. Louis University, at first as professor of obstetrics and then of the principles and practice of medicine. He established the *St. Louis Medical and Surgical Journal* in 1843, serving as its editor, opposed homeopathy, emphasizing nature's role in the curing of diseases, theorized on microbes before Pasteur's discoveries, and wrote *Outlines of Pathology* (1851), *Medical Science and Common Sense* (1859), and *Medicine for the Millions* (1860). He died in St. Louis on June 1.

LOMBARDI, VINCENT THOMAS (1913–70), football coach. Born in Brooklyn, New York City, on June 11, he was educated at Fordham (B.S. 1937), played football there and was one of the famous "Seven Blocks of Granite" of Fordham's football team. He continued studying law at Fordham's School of Law at night in 1937–39, took his first coaching job at St. Cecilia High School in Englewood, New Jersey, in 1939 and over the next few years his teams won six New Jersey championships and in one stretch won thirty-six games in a row. He married Marie Planitz in 1940, returned to Fordham as freshman football coach in 1947, became assistant coach at West Point in 1949, and in 1954 went to the New York Giants as offensive coach. In 1959 he became head coach and general manager of the Green Bay Packers, whose record the previous year was one victory, ten losses, and one tie. In his second year as coach in 1960 the Packers won the Western Conference championship and in 1961, 1962, 1965, 1966, and 1967 were National Football League champions, winning Super Bowl games in 1962, 1963, and 1968; he then retired as coach but remained another year as general manager. While coach of the Packers he had changed them from the doormat of the National Football League to the team with the best winning record. He became manager of the Washington Redskins in 1969, coached them only that year and died the next year on Sept. 3 of cancer in Washington, D.C. He had a .738 winning percentage as professional coach with a 96-34-6 record. With W. C. Heinz he authored *Run to Daylight!* (1963).

LOMBARDO, GUY (1902–77), orchestra leader. Son of an Italian immigrant tailor, Gaetano Albert Lombardo was born in London, Ontario, Canada, on June 19. Early interested in music, he formed a band and began playing overnight stands and at local roadhouses. He began to play in dance halls (regularly at the Winter Garden dance hall in London in the twenties) and vaudeville and in 1924 went to the United States, where he evolved the distinctive Lombardo style of music. When he appeared on a Cleveland radio station, he attracted the attention of Jules Stein, head of Music Corporation of America (MCA), and became a client of MCA. He was booked into the Granada Cafe in Chicago in 1927 as "Guy Lombardo and his Royal Canadians" and when they appeared on a Chicago radio station they were an immediate hit. He toured the nation with his band and made his first New York appearance in New York City at the Roosevelt Hotel in 1929. His band became one of the nation's most outstanding, appearing on national radio networks and in hotels and nightclubs from New York to California. It reputedly recorded three hundred hit songs, and it appeared in several films. His band was among the highest paid in the world. Despite the waning interest in big bands, Lombardo's group continued to be popular, and his playing of "Auld Lang Syne" with "the sweetest music this side of heaven" from New York's Waldorf-Astoria Hotel on New Year's Eve at the stroke of twelve, begun in 1929, continued for half a century and became a national institution. The musicals he produced at Jones Beach, New York, were tremendously successful. He died in Houston, Texas, on Nov. 5.

LONGSTREET, JAMES (1821–1904), general. Born in Edgefield District, South Carolina, on Jan. 8, he was brought to Georgia by his parents when he was ten and then to Alabama by his mother after his father's death in 1833. He was appointed to the United States Military Academy at West Point in 1838, graduated in 1842, served in Indian campaigns and the Mexican War, and was made a major in 1858. He resigned his commission at the outbreak of the Civil War in 1861 and joined the Confederate Army as a brigadier general. He took part in the first battle of Bull Run and the Peninsula campaign, fought in the second battle of Bull Run, at Antietam, and at Fredericksburg, and was made a lieutenant general in 1862. He held a semi-independent command south of the James River in 1862–63 and commanded the right wing of Lee's army at Gettysburg in 1863; many military experts believe his delay in taking the offensive cost Lee the battle. He fought at Chickamauga in the Chattanooga campaign, unsuccessfully besieged Knoxville in 1863, and returned to Virginia in 1864 and distinguished himself in the Battle of the Wilderness that year in which he was severely wounded. He was in the last defense of Richmond and surrendered with Lee to Grant. After the war he engaged in the cotton brokerage and insurance business in New Orleans. A personal friend of General Grant, he joined the Republican Party and was ostracized by his embittered colleagues. He was appointed surveyor of customs in New Orleans by now President Grant and later supervisor of internal revenue and postmaster. He moved to Georgia in 1875, became a Catholic in 1877, was U.S. minister to Turkey in 1880–81 and was U.S. railroad commissioner in 1897–1904. He died in Gainesville, Georgia, on Jan. 2. He was long unpopular in the South for his harsh criticism of Lee and for becoming a Republican. Military scholars and historians are sharply divided over his military ability, though it is generally agreed he was an excellent tactician but a poor strategist. He wrote several books on the Civil War, most important of which was *From Manassas to Appomattox* (1896) and the four-volume *Battles and Leaders of the Civil War* (1887–88).

LOOTENS, LOUIS (1827–98), bishop. Born in Bruges, Belgium, on Mar. 17, he was educated at the seminary there and at St. Nicholas Seminary in Paris. He was ordained in Paris in 1851. He emigrated to Canada the following year in response to a plea from Bishop Modeste Demers of Vancouver for missionaries and he served on Vancouver Island for nine years. He then went to California, where he continued his missionary work until 1868, when he was appointed titular bishop of Castabala and first vicar apostolic of Idaho. He established himself in Granite City, Idaho, attended Vatican Council I in 1869–70 and saw the first church built in Boise in 1870. He resigned in 1876 and died in Victoria, Vancouver Island, British Columbia, on Jan. 13.

LORAS, JEAN MATHIAS PIERRE (1792–1858), bishop. Son of Jean Mathias, who was guillotined for his participation in the Girondist revolt against Jacobin Paris in 1793, he was born in Lyons, France, on Aug. 30. He was a fellow student of St. Jean Vianney, the curé of Ars, as a boy in Écully, studied at the St. Irenaeus Seminary, Lyons, and was ordained in Lyons in 1815. He taught at the minor seminary in Meximieux, became superior in 1817, was named superior of L'Argentière seminary in 1824 and resigned in 1827 to work in the home missions of Lyons. In 1828 he volunteered for the American missions in response to a plea from Bishop Michael Porter of Mobile, Alabama, for priests for his diocese. He taught at Spring Hill College, Alabama, served as vicar-general of the Mobile diocese in 1830–37 and was president of Spring Hill College in 1833–37. He was appointed first bishop of the newly established diocese of Dubuque, Iowa, in 1837, spent the next eighteen months in Europe seeking priests for his diocese, and arrived in Mobile in 1839. He encouraged German and Irish immigrants to settle in his sparsely settled diocese, refused an archbishopric in France, brought the Sisters of Charity of the Blessed Virgin Mary to Dubuque, where at his request they located their mother house in 1843, founded Mt. St. Bernard Seminary in 1850, and with Bishop John Hughes of New York succeeded in their efforts to have Catholic chaplains in the Army during the Mexican War. He died in Dubuque on Feb. 19, having increased the number of priests in the diocese from one with three churches to forty-eight with sixty churches and the number of faithful from a tiny flock to fifty-four thousand during his episcopate.

LORD, DANIEL ALOYSIUS (1888–1955), author, editor, playright, producer. Born in Chicago on Apr. 23, he was educated at St. Ignatius College (Loyola University) there (B.A.) and St. Louis University (M.A.) and joined the Jesuits in 1909. He studied at the Jesuit novitiate at Florrisant, Missouri, for four years, was assigned to the editorial staff of *Queen's Work* in 1913 (an association that was to continue until his death), taught English at St. Louis University in 1917–20, and was ordained in 1923. He became editor of *Queen's Work* in 1925, serving in that capacity until 1948, and also in 1925 organized the Sodality of Our Lady and the Knights and Handmaids of the Blessed Sacrament, both of which developed into nationwide groups, directed the Institute of Social Order of the Society of Jesus in 1943–47, and organized and directed Summer Schools of Catholic Action (establishing the first school in 1931) all over the United States. He wrote some three hundred pamphlets and sixty-six booklets which sold more than twenty million copies on religious, social, and economic topics, religious songs, fifty plays, twelve musicals, and six pageants, including the pageant for Detroit's centennial celebration in 1951 and *Joy to the World* for the Marian Year celebration in Toronto in 1954. He helped develop the Motion Picture Production Code for the motion picture industry in 1929, with Martin Quigley, helped organize the Legion of Decency and wrote forty-eight children's and thirty adult books, among them *Armchair Philosophy* (1918), *Our Nuns* (1921), *Religion and Leadership* (1933), *Our Lady in the Modern World* (1940), *Notes for the Guidance of Parents* (1944), *His Passion Forever* (1950), and his autobiography, *Played by Ear* (1956). He died of throat cancer in St. Louis on Jan. 15.

LORD, ROBERT HOQARD (1885–1954), educator, author. Born in Plano, Illinois, on July 20, he was educated at Northwestern University, Harvard (B.A. 1906, M.A. 1907, Ph.D. 1910), and the Universities of Vienna, Berlin, and Moscow in 1908–10. He taught history at Harvard in 1910–26, was a member of the American delegation to the Paris Peace Conference in 1918–19 as an authority on German and Polish affairs, became a Catholic in 1920, and was president of the American Catholic Historical Association in 1922. He decided to become a priest, entered St. John's Seminary, Brighton, Boston, in 1926, and was ordained in Boston in 1929. He served as a curate at St. Cecilia Church, Boston, in 1929–30, taught Church history at St. John's in 1930–44, and was vice-rector of the seminary in 1933–44. He was appointed pastor of St. Paul's Church, Wellesley, Massachusetts, in 1944, and was made a domestic prelate in 1950. He was the author of several books, among them *The Second Partition of Poland* (1915), *The Origins of the War of 1870* (1924), and with C. H. Haskins *Some Problems of the Peace Conference* (1920) and with

E. T. Harrington the three-volume *History of the Archdiocese of Boston* (1945). He died in Boston on May 22.

LOUGHLIN, JAMES F. (1851–1911). Born in Auburn, New York, on May 8, he studied at the Propaganda, Rome (S.T.D.), and was ordained in 1874. He served as a curate in the Philadelphia archdiocese, taught theology at St. Charles Borromeo Seminary, Overbrook, Philadelphia, and in 1886 became founding pastor of Our Lady of the Rosary parish in Philadelphia. He was named chancellor of the archdiocese in 1892, was made a domestic prelate in 1899, and became rector of the Nativity of the Blessed Virgin parish in Philadelphia. He conducted Catholic reading clubs, was one of the founders of the Catholic Summer School of America, serving as its second president, helped form the National Union of Catholic Young Men's Societies, serving as its president, and was active in his opposition to the Faribault Plan of Archbishop John Ireland for Catholic schools. He died in Barbados, West Indies, on Mar. 17.

LOUGHLIN, JOHN (1817–91), bishop. Born in Drumboneffe, Down, Ireland, on Dec. 20, he was brought to the United States when he was six by his parents, who settled in Albany, New York. He was educated at the college of Chambly near Montreal and Mt. St. Mary's Seminary, Emmitsburg, Maryland, and was ordained for the New York diocese in 1840. He engaged in pastoral work in Utica and New York City, was vicar-general of the New York diocese in 1850–53, and was appointed first bishop of Brooklyn when that diocese was established in 1853. There were 12 churches and 15,000 Catholics in the diocese, which included all of Long Island, but by the time of his death thirty-eight years later there were

125 churches, 93 schools, 2 colleges, a diocesan seminary, and numerous charitable institutions and some 400,000 Catholics in the diocese. He invited the Vincentian Fathers to found St. John's College in Brooklyn in 1870, attended the second and third Plenary Councils of Baltimore in 1866 and 1884 and Vatican Council I in 1869–70, when he was made an Assistant at the Pontifical Throne, and died in Brooklyn on Dec. 29.

LOUISE, SISTER *See* Schrieck, Sister Louise Van Der.

LOVINER, JOHN FOREST (1896–1970), publisher. Born in Columbus, Ohio, on June 13, he was educated at St. Joseph's Seraphic Seminary, Callicoon, New York, and joined the Franciscans in 1916, taking the name of the English martyr Bl. John Forest. He continued his studies at St. Stephen's Monastery, Croghan, New York, and St. Bonaventure College and Seminary, Allegany, New York (M.A.), and was ordained in 1923. The following year he began St. Anthony's Guild to solicit funds for seminarians and missionaries and a few years later expanded its activities to include the printing and publishing of books and began publication of *The Anthonian,* a quarterly, in 1927. In a short time St. Anthony's Guild became one of the leading publishers of catechetical literature in the United States; among its outstanding publications were the *St. Anthony's Treasury,* The National Catholic Almanac, and The New American Bible. Fr. John Forest, as he was called, died at Lafayette, New Jersey, on Sept. 12 after having been associated with St. Anthony's Guild for almost forty-seven years.

LOWE, ENOCH LOUIS (1820–92), governor. Born in Frederick, Maryland, on Aug. 10, he was educated by the Jesuits at Clongowes College, Dublin, Ireland, and Stonyhurst, England. He returned to the United States in 1839, studied law and was admitted to the bar in 1842, and married Esther Windsor Polk in 1844. Though barely of legal age for the position, he was elected governor of Maryland in 1851, served until 1854, and then resumed his law practice in Baltimore. He was strongly pro-Southern and tried to bring Maryland to the Confederate side at the outbreak of the Civil War and, when unsuccessful, went into exile in Georgia. He refused to take the oath required of Southern supporters in Maryland after the war and moved to New York in 1866 and practiced law until his death there on Aug. 23.

LUCAS, FIELDING, JR. (1781–1854), publisher, bookseller. Born in Fredericksburg, Virginia, on Sept. 3, he was early interested in the publishing business, became Baltimore's leading publisher, and after the death of Matthew Carey in 1839 was the leading publisher of Catholic books in the United States. He published books on dogma and apologetics, textbooks, devotional books, and, in 1833–57, Metropolitan Catholic Almanac, a continuation of the U.S. Catholic Almanac, which he had acquired in 1833. Though a major publisher of Catholic books, he did not become a Catholic until his last illness. He died in Baltimore on Mar. 12.

LUCAS, HENRY S. (1889–1961), historian. Born in Jamestown, Michigan, on Mar. 6, he was educated at Olivet College (B.A. 1913), the University of Michigan (Ph.D. 1921), and the universities of Leiden, in 1919–20, and Ghent, in 1925–26, under the noted historians Johan Huizinga and Henri Pirenne and specialized in the medieval and renaissance periods. He joined the faculty of the University of Washington, Seattle, in 1921 and taught there until 1959. He was converted to Catholicism in 1947 and was president of the American Catholic Historical Association in 1949. He wrote numerous scholarly articles, and among the books he authored were *The Low Countries in the Hundred Years' War, 1326–1347* (1929), *The Renaissance and the Reformation* (1934), and *Netherlanders in America* (1955). He died in Seattle, Washington, on Dec. 29.

LUCEY, ROBERT EMMET (1891–1977), archbishop. Born in Los Angeles on Mar. 16, he was educated at St. Vincent's College there, St. Patrick's Seminary, Menlo Park, California, and the North American College, Rome (S.T.N.). He was ordained in 1916 and was serving as pastor of St. Anthony's Church, Long Beach, California, when he was appointed bishop of Amarillo, Texas, in 1934; he was transferred to San Antonio, Texas, in 1941 as its second archbishop. He was known for his outspoken support of labor and the Congress of Industrial Organizations (CIO) and his efforts in social welfare and race relations issues. He supported the Allies at the outbreak of World War II and was a charter member of the Committee to Defend America by aiding the Allies. He retired in 1969 and died in San Antonio on Aug. 1.

LUDDEN, PATRICK ANTHONY (1836–1912), bishop. Born in Breaffy, Mayo, Ireland, on Feb. 4, he was educated at St. Jarlath's College, Tuam, and the Grand Seminary, Montreal, and was ordained in Montreal in 1864. He engaged in pastoral work in Albany, New York, was rector of the Immaculate Conception Cathedral there and was vicar-general of the Albany diocese in 1872–78. He was rector of St. Peter's Church, Troy, New York, from 1879 until 1886 when he was appointed first

bishop of the newly established diocese of Syracuse, New York. He built a new cathedral which he consecrated in 1910 and died in Syracuse on Aug. 6.

LUERS, JOHN HENRY (1819–71), bishop. Born in Luetten near Münster, Westphalia, Germany, on Sept. 29, he was brought to the United States in 1831, was educated at St. Francis Xavier Seminary, Cincinnati, Ohio, and was ordained in Cincinnati in 1846. He engaged in pastoral work in Cincinnati until 1857, when he was appointed first bishop of the newly created diocese of Fort Wayne, Indiana. He attended the second Plenary Council of Baltimore in 1866, increased the number of schools in his diocese from three to forty, and died in Cleveland on June 29 of apoplexy after ordaining a class of seminarians there.

LUSKA, SIDNEY. *See* Harland, Henry.

LYNCH, DOMINICK (1754–1825), merchant, philanthropist. Born in Galway, Ireland, he went to Bruges, Flanders, after his marriage to Jane Lynch, a cousin, in 1780, to manage his father's business there and made a fortune in trade. In 1783 he entered a partnership in a commercial enterprise with Don Thomas Stoughton, a merchant dealing in Spanish trading; the partnership was dissolved in 1795 amid great acrimony and with lawsuits. He moved to New York City in 1785, invested in real estate and the China trade, and bought land in upstate New York for a town he named Lynchville, which developed into the city of Rome. He became known for his philanthropy to Catholic causes and institutions and, with Stoughton, advanced the purchase money in 1786 for the property bought from the trustees of Trinity Church on which New York's first Catholic church, St. Peter's, was built and served as one of its trustees. He handled subscriptions for the building of Georgetown and donated his estate in Westchester County, now Clason Point, Bronx, to the Christian Brothers after his wife's death and in time it became the Academy of the Sacred Heart. In 1789 he was one of the four Catholic laymen who signed "An Address from the Roman Catholics of America to George Washington, Esq., President of the United States" congratulating him on his inauguration as president. He died in the Bronx on June 5.

LYNCH, JOSEPH PATRICK (1872–1954), bishop. Born in St. Joseph, Michigan, on Nov. 16, he was educated at St. Charles College, Ellicott City, Maryland, St. Mary's Seminary, Baltimore, and Kenrick Seminary, St. Louis, and was ordained in 1900. He served as a curate at the cathedral in Dallas, Texas, in 1900–2, was pastor of St. Stephen's Church, Weatherford, Texas, in 1902–3, built St. Rita's Church, Handley, in 1909 and St. Edward's Church, Dallas, in 1911 and was named vicar-general of the diocese of Dallas in 1910. He was administrator of the see in 1910 and was appointed its third bishop in 1911. He convened diocesan synods in 1912 and 1934, increased the number of priests in the diocese from 83 to 185 and the parishes from 52 to 83, and expanded the educational facilities of the see. He was made an Assistant at the Pontifical Throne in 1936 and died in Dallas on Aug. 19.

LYNCH, PATRICK NEISEN (1817–82), bishop. Born in Clones, Monaghan, Ireland, on Mar. 19, he was brought to South Carolina in 1819 when he was a child. He was educated at St. John the Baptist Seminary, Charleston, South Carolina, and the Propaganda, Rome, where he received his doctorate in divinity, and was ordained in Rome in 1840. On his return to the United States, he was named an assistant at the Charleston cathedral, was editor of the *United States Catholic Miscellany*, taught at St. John's, was pastor of St. Mary's Church in 1845–47, and then was rector of St. John's until its closing in 1851. He was made vicar-general of the see in 1850. He was appointed coeditor of the collected writings of John England in 1845 and in 1850 was named to supervise the building of St. John and St. Finbar Cathedral and was treasurer of a project to aid fever victims in 1852–53. He was administrator of the diocese from 1854 until 1858, when he was appointed Charleston's third bishop. In 1864 he went to Rome as special commissioner of the Confederate States of America to present the Confederate side of the Civil War to Pope Pius IX and to counteract Union propaganda in Europe, but by then the Confederacy was doomed. The cathedral, the bishop's residence, the diocesan library, and most of the city's schools were destroyed by a disastrous fire that swept the city in 1861 and by the bombardment of the city by Union forces and then by the occupation of the city by General Sherman's army in the closing days of the Civil War. Bishop Lynch spent most of the remaining days of his episcopate raising funds to pay off the huge debt he incurred rebuilding the cathedral and the many institutions of the diocese that had been destroyed; by the time of his death he had managed to erase the debt. He attended Vatican Council I in 1869–70 and favored promulgation of the dogma of papal infallibility, helped heal the wounds between North and South during his visits to Northern cities to raise funds, and died in Charleston on Feb. 26.

LYNSKEY, ELIZABETH MARY (1896–1954), educator. Born in Minneapolis, Minnesota, on Sept. 28, she was educated at the University of Minnesota (B.A. 1919, M.A. 1920). She taught social science at the high school in Spooner, Minnesota, in 1919–20, history at West High School, Minneapolis, in 1921, and was head of the social science department at the Itasca Junior High School, Coleraine, Minnesota, in 1922–26. She joined the political science department of Hunter College, New York City, in 1927 and in time became professor emeritus. She received her Ph.D. in 1929 from the Brookings Graduate School of Economics and Government, Washington, D.C., was one of the founders of the Catholic Association for International Peace, serving as its vice president, and was liaison for the C.A.I.P. to the United Nations. She was sent to Australia by the War Department as an expert on the study of social studies, was contributing editor to *Commonweal* in 1938–44 and in 1948, and wrote and lectured on international and church-state relations; she was the author of *The Government of the Catholic Church* (1952). She died in Minneapolis on Nov. 30.

LYONS, CHARLES WILLIAM (1868–1939), educator. Born in Boston on Jan. 31, he joined the Jesuits in 1890, was educated at Woodstock College, Maryland, and was ordained in 1904. He taught at St. Francis Xavier, New York City, in 1905–7, Boston College in 1907–8, and was president of Gonzaga College, Washington, D.C., in 1908–9, St. Joseph's College, Philadelphia, in 1909–14, Boston College in 1914–18, and Georgetown University in 1924–28. He spent the rest of his life in mission and retreat work and died in Dorchester, Massachusetts, on Jan. 31.

M

MACAULAY, GENEVIEVE GARVAN BRADY (1884–1938), philanthropist. Genevieve Garvan was born in Hartford, Connecticut, on Apr. 11 and was educated at Manhattanville College of the Sacred Heart, Purchase, New York, and Sacred Heart Convents in Dresden, Germany, and Paris. She married Nicholas F. Brady, the financier, in 1906 and with him became involved in many charitable and philanthropic activities. She founded the Carroll Club in New York City for girls, was chairman of the national board of the Girl Scouts in 1928 and later of the World Committee of Girl Scouts, and supported a variety of philanthropic and charitable works, among them summer camps, welfare relief, the Curie radium fund, the Jesuit novitiate at Wernersville, Pennsylvania, the retreat home and rest center at Manhasset, New York, and funds for additions to Georgetown University's library. Her husband died in 1930, leaving her a fortune, and in 1937 she married William J. Babington Macaulay, Irish Free State minister to the Vatican, and she moved to Rome. She was honored papally four times for her charities and by the French and Belgian governments for war service and was the recipient of the Laetare Medal in 1934. She died in Rome on Nov. 24 and the bulk of her estate was distributed among Catholic charities.

MACAULAY, WILLIAM J. BABINGTON (1893–1964), diplomat. Born in Limerick, Ireland, he studied at the Sorbonne, served in the British Navy in World War I, and then entered the British civil service. He joined the diplomatic corps of the Irish Free State on its establishment in 1922, served as first secretary of the Irish legation in Washington in 1925–30, became Irish consul general in New York in 1930, and was appointed minister to the Holy See in 1934, a position he held until his retirement in 1941. He married Mrs. Nicholas F. Brady, the well-known philanthropist, in 1937, became an American citizen in 1944, and moved to Florence, Italy, in 1961 and died there on Jan. 1.

MACDONNELL, JAMES FRANCIS CARLIN (1881–1945), poet. Son of a coachman, he was born in Bay Shore, New York, on Apr. 7. His father died when he was a boy. He entered a grammar school in Norwalk, Connecticut, but never graduated, worked in a shoe store, made two short trips to Ireland, educated himself, and became a salesman in Macy's department store in New York City. His first work, *My Ireland,* was published in 1917 at his own expense, and in 1919 *Cairn of Stones* was published. His poetry was praised by Christopher Morley and Thomas Augustus Daly but, except for a few poems in magazines, he never published again. He devoted himself to a study of the bible for fifteen years from 1924 and died in New York City on Mar. 11.

MACELWANE, JAMES BERNARD (1883–1956), geophysicist, seismologist. Born near Port Clinton, Ohio, on Sept. 28, he joined the Jesuits in 1903, studied at John Carroll University, Cleveland, Ohio, and St. Louis University (B.A. 1910, M.A. 1911, M.S. 1912), was ordained in 1918 and received his Ph.D. from the University of California in 1923. He taught mathematics at St. John's College, Toledo, Ohio, in 1907–8, physics at St. Louis University in 1912–13, and was assistant professor of physics there in 1913–15 and 1918–19. He was assistant professor of geology at the University of California in 1923–25, also serving as the director of the seismographic stations he helped organize in California. He was professor of geophysics and director of the department at St. Louis University from 1925, was dean of the graduate school in 1927–33 and chairman of the Council of Regents in 1929–33 and in 1944 was named dean of the Institute of Geophysical Technology. He was an authority on seismology and the discoverer of a method of tracking hurricanes at sea, was president of the Seismological Society of America in 1928–29 and chairman of the seismological section of the American Geophysical Union in 1938–41; he was named to the National Science Foundation by President Franklin Roosevelt in 1944. The author of numerous articles for scientific magazines, he also wrote several books, among them *When the Earth Quakes* (1946), *Introduction to Theoretical Seismology, Part I, Geodynamics* (1930), *Seismometry, Part II* (1932), and coauthored *Internal Constitution of the Earth* (1939) and *Compendium of Meteorology* (1951). He died in St. Louis on Feb. 15.

MACGEBEUF, JOSEPH PROJECTUS (1812–89), bishop. Born in Riom, Puy de Dôme, France, on Aug. 11, he studied there and at Montferrand and was ordained in Clermont-Ferrand in 1836. He went to the United States in 1839 in response to a plea for priests from Bishop John Purcell of Cincinnati,

Ohio, engaged in missionary work in northwest Ohio for eleven years, and then spent a decade under Bishop John Lamy of Santa Fe as a missionary in New Mexico and Arizona. He was vicar-general for Bishop Lamy until 1860, when he and Fr. John B. Raverdy were sent to Denver, Colorado, where he labored until 1868, when he was appointed titular bishop of Epiphania and vicar apostolic of Colorado and Utah. In 1887 the vicariate of Colorado was made a separate diocese with the episcopal see at Denver and he was appointed its first bishop (Utah had been transferred to the jurisdiction of the archbishop of San Francisco in 1870). During his episcopate he increased the number of priests in his diocese from 3 to 64, and at his death in Denver on July 10, there were 112 churches and chapels, 10 schools, and 9 hospitals in the diocese.

MACGINLEY, JOHN BERNARD (1871–1969), bishop. Born in Tirconaill, Ireland, on Aug. 19, he was educated at St. Eunan's Seminary and Blackrobe College, Ireland, was ordained in 1895 and received his D.D. from the North American College, Rome, the following year. He emigrated to the United States in 1896, was a curate at Our Lady of the Rosary Church, Philadelphia, until 1898, when he became a professor of Latin and moral theology at St. Charles Borromeo Seminary, Overbrook, Philadelphia, and became a naturalized American citizen in 1903. He was rector of the seminary at Vigan, Philippine Islands, in 1903–5 and a curate at St. Charles Church in Philadelphia from 1905 until 1910, when he was appointed bishop of Nueva Caceres in the Philippines. He was appointed first bishop of the Monterey-Fresno, California, diocese in 1924 and remained in that position until 1932, when he resigned because of ill health. During his episcopate he devoted much of his time and energy to education, rebuilding schools and building new ones, established catechetical centers, and founded a diocesan newspaper. He was appointed titular bishop of Croe later in 1932 and retired to Killybegs, Donegal, Ireland, where he died on Oct. 18.

MACK, CONNIE (1862–1956), baseball manager. Cornelius McGillicuddy was born in East Brookfield, Massachusetts, on Dec. 23, worked in a shoe factory in his youth, became a member of the local baseball team as a catcher, played on minor league teams at Meriden in 1884 and Hartford, Connecticut, in 1885 and the following year became a member of the Washington Senators. In 1890 he joined the Brotherhood of Professional Baseball Players battling the owners and left Washington to play with Buffalo of the Players' League. When the league collapsed that fall he joined the Pittsburgh Pirates in 1891, serving as manager from 1894 until 1896, when he was dismissed. He managed Milwaukee of the Western League with great success the next four years and when the league was renamed the American League in 1901 he moved to Philadelphia and became part owner. He managed the Philadelphia Athletics the next forty years and became one of the most famous managers in baseball, as his Athletics won nine American League championships and five World Series. In 1922 he acquired half ownership of the club when Benjamin F. Shibe died, and he rebuilt the team into a powerhouse. He had practically dismantled it in 1914, when he sold most of his stars to meet expenses, but its 1929 team was one of the all-time greats of baseball. In 1933 he repeated his 1914 tactic to great criticism, and in 1937 he acquired full control of the Athletics. Despite the poor showing of his teams in these later years, he was selected as one of the original thirteen personalities to be honored

in the baseball Hall of Fame at Cooperstown, New York, in 1937. His sons took over control of the club in 1940, though he retained the meaningless title of president. The Athletics' stadium, Shibe Park, was renamed Connie Mack Park in 1953. The sons sold the franchise in 1954 to a Chicago businessman, Arnold M. Johnson, who moved it to Kansas City. "The grand old man of baseball," as he was called, died fifteen months later in Georgetown, Philadelphia, on Feb. 8.

MACKAY, CLARENCE HUNGERFORD (1874–1938), executive, philanthropist. Son of John William Mackay, he was born in San Francisco on Apr. 17, was educated at Vaugirard College, Paris, and Beaumont College, Windsor, England, and graduated in 1892. He entered his father's business in 1894 in New York City, became a director of the Commercial Cable Company and Postal Telegraph Cable Company in 1896, vice president the following year, and in 1902, on his father's death, became president. He married Katherine Duer in 1898, completed the laying of the transatlantic cable in 1904, became president of the Mackay Radio and Telegraph Company and in 1928 chairman of the board of a new company which merged his father's holdings into the International Telephone and Telegraph Corporation. He served on the board of directors of many banks, railroads, and trust companies and was chairman of the board of American Exchange National Bank, Canadian Pacific Railroad, and Pacific Postal Telegraph Cable Company. The Postal Telegraph–Commercial Cable empire he had inherited from his father was shattered by the depression that shook the United States after the stock market crash in 1929; the Postal Telegraph and Cable Corporation went into receivership in 1935, though he remained as its head until his death. The Associated Companies in 1938 and the Mackay land lines merged with Western Union in 1943; however, overseas International Telephone and Telegraph continued to handle Mackay interests. Mackay was famous as a host—his receptions for the Prince of Wales in 1924 and Charles Lindbergh in 1927 were legendary—and as a philanthropist. He established the John W. Mackay School of Mines at the University of Nevada and a chair in electrical engineering at the University of California and during World War I established the Mackay-Roosevelt hospital unit. He was twice honored by the Vatican, was chairman of the board of St. Vincent's Hospital in New York City and of the New York Philharmonic Society, was a director of the Metropolitan Opera (he married the noted opera soprano Anna Case in 1931, the year after his first wife died) and a trustee of the Metropolitan Museum of Art. In 1926 he was awarded the Medal of the National Institute of Social Sciences. He was treasurer of Lincoln Farm Association, which acquired the Lincoln farm in Kentucky and preserved the log cabin in which President Lincoln was born. He died in New York City on Nov. 12.

MACMANUS, SEUMAS (1869–1960), author. Born in Donegal, Ireland, he spent his boyhood herding cattle and sheep and working on farms. When he was sixteen he was appointed a pupil-teacher at Iniskillon Model School in neighboring County Fermanagh and spent the next fifteen years teaching there and at Kinawley National School, and writing stories and poems for Irish newpapers. He then became a master at Glen Cuach School but in 1899 emigrated to the United States and began writing for such magazines as *Harper's, Century,* and *McClure's.* He married Anna Johnson (the Irish poet Ethna

Carberry) in 1901; she died the following year and he married Catalina Violante Páez in 1911. He wrote poems and plays about the fairies and ancient folk tales of his native Ireland and among the twenty-five books and more than a dozen plays he wrote were *The Bend of the Road* (1898), *Donegal Fairy Stories* (1900), *Irish Nights* (1905), *Top o' the Mornin'* (1920), *The Story of the Irish Race* (1921), *Dark Patrick* (1939), *The Rocky Road to Dublin* (1938), and *Heavy Hangs the Golden Grain;* among his plays were *The Woman of Seven Sorrows, Father Peter's Miracle,* and *The Hard-Hearted Man.* He died in New York City on Oct. 23.

MACNEVEN, WILLIAM JAMES (1763–1841), physician. Born in Ballynahown, Galway, Ireland, on Mar. 21, he was educated abroad since penal laws prevented Catholics from receiving an education in Ireland. He studied at Prague and medicine at Vienna, where he received his doctor in physic degree in 1784 and then returned to Dublin to practice. He was arrested in 1798 for involvement in revolutionary activities and sent to jail in Scotland. He was freed and exiled in 1802, went to Paris, where he was unsuccessful in an attempt to get Napoleon to send French troops to Ireland, and emigrated to the United States in 1805. He received his M.D. from Columbia College the same year and three years later he was appointed professor of midwifery at the recently established College of Physicians and Surgeons—one of its seven professors. Two years later he was made professor of chemistry and in 1816 he was appointed to the chair of materia medica. In 1825 he helped found the Irish Emigrant Assistance Association of New York to encourage Irish immigrants to move from seaboard cities to rural areas of the country where work was more readily available. In 1826 he resigned his chair at the College of Physicians and Surgeons because of a dispute with the New York Board of Regents and accepted the materia medica chair at Rutgers Medical School. He wrote several textbooks, among them *Exposition of the Atomic Theory* (1820), political tracts and literary pieces and for many years was coeditor of the *New York Medical and Philosophical Journal.* He died in New York City on July 12.

MACNUTT, FRANCIS AUGUSTUS (1863–1927), diplomat, author. Born in Richmond, Indiana, on Feb. 15, he was educated at Phillips Academy, Exeter, New Hampshire, and Harvard Law School, spent some time traveling abroad, and in 1883 became a Catholic. He studied for the priesthood at the Pontifical Academy of Noble Ecclesiastics in Rome in 1887–89, decided he did not have a vocation for the priesthood, and entered the diplomatic service. He was first secretary of the United States legation in Constantinople (Istanbul) in 1892–93, married Margaret van Cortlandt Ogden in 1898, and took up residence in Rome. Pope Leo XIII, who had made him an honorary papal chamberlain in 1895, assigned him active duty at the papal court—the first American to be so honored—and in 1904 Pope Pius X named him one of the four ranking chamberlains. He retired to private life the following year at Schloss Ratzotz near Bressanone, Italy, where he devoted himself to writing. He wrote seven books, among them *Fernando Cortes and the Conquest of Mexico, 1485–1547* (1909), *Bartholomew de las Casas* (1909), and his posthumously published memoirs, *A Papal Chamberlain* (1936). He died in Bressanone on Dec. 30.

MADDEN, JOHN THOMAS (1882–1948), economist. Born in Worcester, Massachusetts, on Oct. 26, he was edu-cated at New York University (B.S.C. 1911), became a certified public accountant in New York City in 1911, began teaching at New York University School of Commerce the same year and became its dean in 1925. He wrote widely on economic matters—inflation, currency stabilization, and international finance —was a governor of the New York Stock Exchange, president of the American Association of Collegiate Schools of Business in 1928–29, of the Alexander Institute in 1929–35, and of the International Accountants Society from 1929 until his death in New York City on July 2. Among the several books he wrote were *Principles of Accounting* (1918), *Accounting Practice and Auditing* (1919), and with Marcus Nadler *Foreign Securities* (1929) and *International Money Market* (1934), and with Nadler and Harry Sauvain *America's Experience as a Creditor Nation* (1936).

MADELEVA, MARY (1887–1964), poet, educator. Mary Evaline Wolff was born of a pioneering family of German descent in Cumberland, Wisconsin, on May 24. She was educated at the University of Wisconsin and St. Mary's College, Notre Dame, and joined the Congregation of the Sacred Heart in 1908. When she received her B.A. from St. Mary's in 1909 she began teaching there while studying for her M.A. at Notre Dame, which she received in 1918. She was head of St. Mary's English department in 1914–19 and taught at her order's schools in Ogden, Utah, in 1919–22 and Woodland, California, in 1922–25. She continued studies for a doctorate in English at the University of California and in 1925 was the first woman to receive that degree at the university. She had early begun writing poetry and had her first collection, *Knight's Errant and other Poems,* published in 1923. She served as president of St. Mary-of-the-Wasatch College in

Salt Lake City in 1931–33, after having taught English there in 1926–31, studied at Oxford, England, and traveled in Europe and the Holy Land in 1933–34, was named president of St. Mary's College, Notre Dame, Indiana, in 1934, continuing in that position until 1961, and was president of the Catholic Poetry Society of America in 1942–48. Considered one of the leading Catholic poets of her time, she had published some seventy books of poetry and essays, among them *Pearl: a Study in Spiritual Dryness* (1925), *Chaucer's Nuns and Other Essays* (1925), *Penelope and Other Poems* (1927), *A Question of Lovers and Other Poems* (1935), *Collected Poems* (1947), *The Four Last Things: Collected Poems* (1959), *My First Seventy Years* (1959), and *Conversations with Cassandra* (1961). Sister Madeleva greatly influenced higher education for Catholic women, established the first graduate school in sacred doctrine for women, was one of the pioneers in the Sister Formation Movement, and under her presidency St. Mary's grew from a small school with 250 students to a modern college with 1,000 students. She received numerous awards for her poetry and seven honorary degrees and died in Boston on July 25.

MAES, CAMILLUS PAUL (1846–1915), bishop. Born in Courtrai, Belgium, on Mar. 13, he was educated at St. Amandus College there, seminaries at Roulers and Bruges and the American College, Louvain, Belgium, and was ordained in Mechlin, Belgium, in 1865 for the diocese of Detroit. He went to the United States, served as pastor of St. Peter's Church, Mount Clemens, in 1869–71, St. Mary's Church, Monroe, in 1871–73, and St. John the Baptist Church in Monroe in 1873–80, all in Michigan, and was chancellor of the Detroit diocese in 1880–85. He was

consecrated third bishop of Covington, Kentucky, in 1885, built a new cathedral, wiped out a large debt he had inherited, established thirty parishes, and extended the mission work of the diocese to eastern Kentucky, brought the Sisters of Divine Providence into his see in 1889, and founded two diocesan papers, *New Cathedral Chimes* and *Christian Year* in 1912. He opposed Archbishop John Ireland's Faribault school plan but was a vigorous supporter of Catholic University (he was secretary of its board of trustees), which Ireland also espoused. He founded the Priests' Eucharistic League in 1893, and was its president in 1893–1915, and the following year its magazine, *Emmanuel,* which he edited until 1903, and was chairman of the board of bishops for the American College, Louvain, Belgium, in 1897–1919. He died in Covington on May 11.

MAGIN CATALÁ (1761–1830), missionary. Born at Montblanch, Catalonia, Spain, probably on Jan. 29, he joined the Franciscans in Barcelona in 1777 and was ordained probably in 1785. He was granted permission to go to America as a missionary, sailed from Cádiz in 1786 and was stationed at the San Fernando missionary college in Mexico City. He served as chaplain on a ship sailing between Mexico and Nootka (Vancouver) Sound in 1793 and the following year was sent to the Santa Clara mission in California. He spent the next thirty-six years, beset by arthritis that often crippled him so badly he could hardly walk, ministering to the Indians of the mission and the surrounding areas. He died at Santa Clara on Nov. 22. He was widely known for his holiness and austere way of life and was reputed to have performed miracles and to have the gift of prophecy. The process for his beatification was instituted by Archbishop José Alemany of San Francisco in 1884.

MAGINNIS, CHARLES DONAGH (1867–1955), architect. Born in Londonderry, Ulster, Ireland, on Jan. 7, he studied at Cusack Academy and architecture in Dublin, emigrated to the United States in 1884 and joined the firm of Edmund Wheelwright in Boston as a designer. He founded his own firm, Maginnis and Walsh, in 1898 and became famous for the seminaries, hospitals, churches, schools, and monuments he designed all over the country. Among his outstanding works are the Shrine of the Immaculate Conception and the chapel of Trinity College in Washington, D.C., the Cathedral of Mary Our Queen in Baltimore, the bronze doors of St. Patrick's Cathedral in New York City, Maryknoll Seminary, Ossining, New York, the Notre Dame chapel, for which the firm was awarded the Architects' Gold Medal for Ecclesiastical Architecture in 1927, and buildings at Holy Cross College and Boston College. He was awarded the Laetare Medal in 1924, received the gold medal of the American Institute of Architecture three times, served as the Institute's president in 1937–38, was first president of the Liturgical Arts Society, received numerous degrees, and was made a Knight of Malta in 1945. He died in Brookline, Massachusetts, on Feb. 15.

MAGNIEN, ALPHONSE (1837–1902), educator. Born in Bleymard, Mende, France, on June 9, he studied at the minor seminary at Chirac and the diocesan seminary at Orléans and was ordained in 1862. He taught at La Chapelle St. Mesmin Seminary the next two years, joined the Sulpicians, and taught at Nantes in 1864–65 and Rodez in 1866–69. He emigrated to the United States in 1869 and became professor of philosophy and Scriptures at St. Mary's Seminary, Baltimore, was appointed superior of the seminary in 1878 and held that position until ill health caused him to resign in 1902. He died in Baltimore two months later on Dec. 2. During his quarter of a century as superior of one of the nation's outstanding seminaries, which he had helped build to that preeminent position, he had a profound effect on several generations of seminarians. Abbé Magnien was also often consulted by members of the hierarchy and was a confidant and adviser of Cardinal James Gibbons, who appointed him his director of the Society for the Propagation of the Faith in 1896. He helped found St. Austin's College at Catholic University and was a theologian at the third Plenary Council of Baltimore in 1884.

MAGNIEN, FRANCIS JOSEPH (1887–1947), bishop. Born in Wilmington, Illinois, on Mar. 18, he was educated at Loyola University, Chicago, St. Mary's College, Kansas, and the North American College, Rome, and was ordained in 1913. He engaged in parish work in the Chicago archdiocese and was pastor of St. Mary's Church, Evanston, Illinois, from 1927 to 1940, when he was appointed seventh bishop of Marquette, Michigan. He founded new parishes in the rural areas of the diocese, established catechetical schools and a program of lay retreats, and began the diocesan newspaper, the *Northern Michigan*. He died in Marquette on June 13.

MAGUIRE, JOHN WILLIAM ROCHFORT (1883–1940), educator, labor arbitrator. Born in County Roscommon, Ireland, on Aug. 11, he studied at All Hallows School, England, emigrated to Canada and then the United States, and began to work for the *Spokane Review* as a reporter. He continued his studies at Western Theological Seminary, Chicago, to become an Episcopal priest but left and became a Catholic. He continued his studies at St. Viator College, Bourbonnais, Illinois, joined the Clerics of St. Viator who ran the college and then went to Catholic University for further study. He was ordained in Washington, D.C., in 1914 and after receiving his M.A. from Catholic University the following year, he taught economics and sociology at St. Viator's for the next two decades, except for a time when he served as a chaplain in World War I. He became active in the labor movement, was a strong supporter of labor and of the social goals outlined in the Bishops' Program of Reconstruction issued in 1918, and served as arbitrator in numerous labor-management disputes, notably in the 1934 Kohler Company strike and the Warner Construction Company dispute in 1939. He died in Miami, Florida, on Feb. 11.

MAHONEY, BERNARD JOSEPH (1875–1939), bishop. Born in Albany, New York, on July 24, he was educated at Mt. St. Mary's College, Emmitsburg, Maryland (B.A. 1899, M.A. 1901) and the North American College, Rome, and was ordained in 1904. He was a curate at St. Peter's Church, Troy, New York, in 1904–9, was spiritual director of the North American College, Rome, in 1909–22, and was consecrated bishop of Sioux Falls, South Dakota, in 1922. He held that position until he died in Rochester, Minnesota, on Mar. 20.

MALLORY, STEPHEN RUSSELL (1813–73), United States senator. Son of an American engineer, he was born on the island of Trinidad, West Indies, was educated at the Jesuit college at Springhill, Mobile, Alabama, studied law and was admitted to the bar in Florida about 1839. He served in the Semi-

nole War of 1835–42, was a probate judge in Florida for a time, and was appointed collector of customs in Key West in 1854. He was elected to the United States Senate in 1851 and re-elected in 1857 and was chairman of the Senate committee on naval affairs. He resigned his seat in the Senate at the outbreak of the Civil War in 1861 and became a member of the cabinet of the Confederate States of America when President Jefferson Davis appointed him secretary of the navy. He hoped to break the Union blockade of the Confederate states with ironclads but was unsuccessful in efforts to secure any from England and France, though he did get a few ironclads built, notably the *Virginia* (the old *Merrimack)* and the *Mississippi,* which eventually had to be destroyed to keep them out of Union hands. He was arrested at the end of the war, after fleeing with Davis, at his home in La Grange, Georgia, and was imprisoned in Fort Lafayette on the Narrows in New York Harbor. He was released on parole in 1866 after ten months' imprisonment and returned to Florida, where he practiced law at Pensacola until his death there on Nov. 9.

MALONE, SYLVESTER (1821–99), social reformer. Born in Trim, Meath, Ireland, on May 8, he studied in his youth in a Protestant academy and in 1838 began studying for the priesthood at St. Joseph's Seminary, Dunwoodie, Yonkers, New York. He was ordained for the New York diocese in 1844, became pastor of SS. Peter and Paul Church in the Williamsburg section of Brooklyn the same year, where he remained until his death. He built up the parish and a church and was theologian for Bishop John Loughlin at the second Plenary Council of Baltimore in 1866. He soon attracted attention by his liberal views and outspoken statements on ecclesiastical and civic matters. He favored abolition, supported the Irish Land League, spoke up for the rights of blacks, and was a supporter of the public school system. In 1894 he was elected to the New York State Board of Regents over Bishop Bernard McQuaid, who publicly rebuked Archbishop John Ireland of the archdiocese of St. Paul, Minnesota, for his support of Malone. His election enraged Archbishop Corrigan of New York, who had supported McQuaid, and Malone further annoyed the archbishop when he wrote to Pope Leo XIII decrying the suspension of Msgr. Edward McGlynn imposed by Corrigan. Malone died in Williamsburg on Dec. 29.

MALONEY, MARTIN (1848–1929), executive, philanthropist. Born in Ballingarry, near Thyrles, Ireland, on Nov. 14, he was brought to the United States by his parents in 1854. He worked in mines in Pennsylvania and then opened a plumbing shop in Scranton. He invented a gasoline burner for streetlamps that made him wealthy, became president of the Pennsylvania Heat, Light and Power Company, organized the United Gas Improvement Company, and became associated with other utility organizations. He was known for his philanthropies, among them his gift that helped repair St. John Lateran in Rome, the Mahoney Memorial Home for the Aged in Scranton, the chemical laboratory at Catholic University, and a medical clinic at the University of Pennsylvania he donated. Pope Leo XIII made him a papal marquis and Pope Pius X made him a papal chamberlain. He died in Philadelphia on May 8.

MALONEY, THOMAS J. (1859–1933), executive. Born in Covington, Kentucky, on July 12, he worked in the tobacco fields in his youth, became superintendent of manufacture for P. Lorillard & Co. and was made a vice president when it merged with the American Tobacco Company in 1900. He was elected president in 1911 and served in that capacity until he retired in 1924. He donated a quarter of a million dollars to the Georgetown University cancer research laboratory, a million dollars to the Newark, New Jersey, diocese, was honored with two papal decorations, and died in Teaneck, New Jersey, on Jan. 18.

MALY, EUGENE H. (1920–80), biblical scholar. Born in Cincinnati, Ohio, on Sept. 6, he was educated at the Athenaeum there (B.A. 1940) and Mt. St. Mary of the West Seminary, also in Cincinnati, and was ordained in 1943. He became professor of Sacred Scriptures at St. Mary's and then of theology, continued his studies at the Angelicum (S.T.D. 1948) and the Pontifical Biblical Institute (S.S.D. 1959), both in Rome, and became a leading American scriptural authority. He was chairman of the editorial board of *The Bible Today* and president of the Catholic Biblical Association, wrote *World of David and Solomon* (1966) and *Prophets of Salvation* (1967) and contributed to the Jerome Biblical Commentary. He died in Cincinnati on July 30.

MANION, CLARENCE (1896–1979), educator. Born in Henderson, Kentucky, on July 7, he was educated at St. Mary's College, Kentucky (B.A. 1915) and Catholic University (M.A. 1916, Ph.D. 1917). He served in the Transportation Corps of the United States Army as a second lieutenant during World War I in 1917–19 and after the war studied law at Notre Dame (J.D. 1922). He taught history and politics at Notre Dame in 1919–22, practiced law in Evansville in 1922–25, and began teaching law at Notre Dame in 1925; he was dean of the law college in 1941–52. He was director of the Indiana National

Emergency Council in 1935–40, married Virginia O'Brien in 1936, and was a member of the Indiana State Board of Education in 1947–61. He became a leading conservative, founded the Natural Law Institute at Notre Dame in 1947 and in 1954 the Manion Forum on radio and television, and wrote several books, among them *Sources of the Federal Constitution* (1917), *American History* (1926), *Lesson in Liberty* (1939), *Catholics in Our Country's Story* (1929), *Let's Face It* (1956), and *Conservative American* (1964). He died in South Bend, Indiana, on July 28.

MANODUE, PATRICK (1831–95), bishop. Born in Desart, Kilkenny, Ireland, on Mar. 15, he studied at Callan and then joined his oldest brother, who was trying to provide for the family of seven orphaned children, and they went to the United States in 1848 and settled in Connecticut. He decided to become a priest, studied at St. Mary of the Lake Seminary, Chicago, for three years and then went to California, where he worked as a miner to make money to finish his studies for the priesthood; he continued his studies at St. Sulpice Seminary in Paris and was ordained in Paris in 1861. He returned to California the following year, worked as a missionary among the Indians there and in Nevada, and became founding pastor of St. Mary's-in-the-Mountains Church, Virginia City, Nevada. He traveled all over Nevada, converting many of the Indians to Catholicism, and in 1870 was named vicar-general of the diocese of Grass Valley, California. He was named titular bishop of Cerramos and coadjutor of Grass Valley in 1881 and succeeded to the see in 1884. When the boundary of the diocese was enlarged and its episcopal see moved to Sacramento, California, in 1886 he became first bishop of Sacramento. He was active in public affairs, became most influential among the miners and was instrumental in settling several disputes between them and the mine owners, built the Cathedral of the Blessed Sacrament in Sacramento, and died there on Feb. 27.

MANUCY, DOMINIC (1823–85), bishop. Born in Mobile, Alabama, on Dec. 20, he was educated at Spring Hill College, Alabama, was ordained for the Mobile diocese in 1850, and engaged in pastoral work in Montgomery and Mobile the next twenty-four years. He was named titular bishop of Dulma and vicar apostolic of Brownsville, Texas, in 1874 and was transferred to Mobile in 1883 as its third bishop, though still administering Brownsville. He resigned as bishop of Mobile the following year, attended the third Plenary Council of Baltimore in 1884, remained as administrator of Mobile until 1885, and was then appointed vicar apostolic of Brownsville and titular bishop of Maronea. He died in Mobile on Dec. 4.

MARDAGA, THOMAS J. (1913–84), bishop. Born in Baltimore, Maryland, on May 14, he was educated at St. Charles College, Catonsville, Maryland (B.A. 1936), and St. Mary's Seminary, Baltimore (S.T.L. 1940), and was ordained in 1940. He served as archdiocesan director of the Catholic Youth Organization and of the Confraternity of Christian Doctrine, was rector of the basilica of the Assumption in Baltimore, and in 1966 was named titular bishop of Mutugenna and auxiliary of Baltimore. He was appointed bishop of Wilmington, Delaware, in 1968, served on the Administrative Committee and on the Committee of Doctrine of the National Conference of Catholic Bishops, and died of cancer in Wilmington on May 28.

MARÉCHAL, AMBROSE (1764–1828), archbishop. Born in Ingres near

343

Orléans, France, on Aug. 28, he studied law but decided he wanted to be a priest. He studied at the diocesan seminary at Orléans, joined the Sulpicians in 1787, and was ordained in Paris in 1792. He was forced to flee to the United States the same year to escape the clerical persecution of the French Revolution and with three fellow Sulpicians settled in Baltimore. He engaged in missionary work in eastern Maryland the next seven years and in 1799 began teaching theology at St. Mary's College, Baltimore, and in 1801 at Georgetown. He was recalled to France to teach in 1803 and was asked to become his coadjutor by Bishop Richard Corcoran, newly appointed first bishop of the newly established diocese of New York, in 1808, but nothing came of it when Corcoran died in Naples, Italy, before taking possession of the see. He taught at the diocesan seminaries of St. Flour, Lyons, Aix, and Marseilles until 1811, when the Sulpicians were again expelled from France, and he returned to the United States in 1812 to teach at St. Mary's Seminary, Baltimore; he was temporary president in 1815. He refused an appointment as bishop of Philadelphia in 1816, but the next year he was appointed titular bishop of Stauropolis and coadjutor bishop of Baltimore and succeeded to the see as archbishop later the same year. He abolished trusteeism in the see, dedicated the cathedral at Baltimore in 1821, and was involved in a dispute with the Jesuits over a plantation which was resolved in his favor when he visited Rome in 1821. He was also involved in a dispute with a group of recalcitrant Irishmen in Virginia and South Carolina over his selection of bishops for the dioceses of Richmond and Charleston, which were carved out of the Baltimore see. The Irishmen resented the French priests Maréchal sent to minister to them and asserted they had the right to choose their own bishops. The matter was settled when Rome emphatically denied them such a right but appointed two Irishmen, Patrick Kelly and John England, as bishops, though Maréchal would have preferred French prelates. He fell ill after a journey to Canada in 1826 and never fully regained his health. He died in Baltimore on Jan. 20 before his new coadjutor, and successor, James Whitfield, had been consecrated.

MARGARET BOLTON, MOTHER
See Bolton, Mother Margaret.

MARGIL, VEN. ANTONIO DE JESÚS (1657–1726), missionary. Born in Valencia, Spain, on Aug. 18, he joined the Franciscans there in 1673 and was ordained in 1682. He volunteered for the American missions and was sent to Vera Cruz, Mexico, with twenty-two other friars, in 1683 and was stationed at the Santa Cruz missionary college. He traveled all over Mexico and Central America ministering to the Indians, was appointed first guardian of the newly established missionary college of Our Lady of Guadalupe, Zacatecas, in 1708, and in 1716 headed a team of five religious that founded three missions in Texas. When they were destroyed by the French, he spent a year near the present city of San Antonio, Texas, and then reestablished the missions. He was in Louisiana for a time and founded the mission of San Miguel de Linare in what is now Sabine County and built the first church in Louisiana. He then made his famous walk, barefooted, from Louisiana to Guatemala on which he is reported to have converted sixty thousand Indians to Catholicism. He was obliged to return to the college of Our Lady of Guadalupe when reelected guardian in 1722, but on the completion of his term he returned to missionary work among the Indians in Mexico. He died in Mexico City on Aug. 6. He is called "the apostle of Guatemala," and his reputation for sanctity and the miracles he is reported to have performed caused Pope Gregory XVI to declare in 1836 that his virtues were heroic.

MARIE (or MARY) JOSEPH, MOTHER *See* Butler, Mother Marie Joseph.

MARIQUE, PIERRE JOSEPH (1872–1957), educator. Born in Seilles, Belgium, on Jan. 24, he graduated from the College of St. Servais, Liège, served in the Belgian Army, and then taught for several years. In 1903 he emigrated to the United States and continued his studies at New York University, where he received his Ph.B. in 1910 and Ph.D. in 1912. He taught at Seton Hall College, South Orange, New Jersey, French at the College of the City of New York in 1914–18 and at Columbia, and in 1918 became professor of education at Fordham and later became head of the education department at the College of Mt. St. Vincent, New York City. He wrote several books, notably the two-volume *History of Christian Education* (1924–32) and *Philosophy of Education.* He died in New York City on Apr. 10.

MARLING, JOSEPH MARY (1904–79), bishop. Born in Centralia, West Virginia, on Aug. 21, he was educated at St. Joseph's College, Rensselaer, Indiana, (B.A. 1923) and studied for the priesthood at St. Charles Seminary, Carthagena, Ohio, in 1923–29 and was ordained a priest of the Precious Blood in 1929. He continued his studies at Catholic University (S.T.L. 1932, Ph.D. 1934), taught at St. Charles Seminary in 1934–37 and Catholic University's School of Education in 1937–38 and was elected provincial of the Society of the Precious Blood in 1938. He was named auxiliary bishop of Kansas City

in 1947 and was appointed first bishop of the newly created diocese of Jefferson City, Missouri, in 1956 serving in that position until 1969 when he retired. He died in Kansas City, Missouri, on Oct. 2.

MARQUETTE, JACQUES (1637–75), missionary, explorer. Of a distinguished French family, he was born in Laon, France, on June 1, joined the Jesuits when he was seventeen, took his novitiate at Nancy and spent the next years studying at the University of Pont-à-Mousson in 1656–59 and 1664–65 and teaching at Charleville in 1661–63 and Langres in 1663–64. He was ordained in Toul in 1666 and was sent to Canada later in that year to work as a missionary among the Indians. He was assigned to Three Rivers, ministered to the Indians there and studied Indian languages and became proficient in six dialects. He was recalled to Quebec in the spring of 1668 and assigned to his first western mission to the Ottawa Indians at Sault Ste. Marie, where he built a house and a chapel. After eighteen months there he was sent in 1669 to Holy Ghost Mission at La Pointe on Chequamegon Bay near present-day Ashland, Wisconsin, on Lake Superior, where he ministered to the Hurons and met a group of Illinois from the south who told him of a mighty river that flowed southward. They asked him to come to their land and instruct them and he was about to embark on the trip to the Illinois country when a threatened attack by the Dakota Sioux caused him to withdraw with his Ottawas and Hurons to the straits of Mackinac, where he built Saint Ignace Mission in 1671. He received permission from his superiors to seek the river and was appointed by Governor Frontenac to accompany Louis Joliet and five other Frenchmen on an expedition to find it. The expedition set out on May 17, 1673. It skirted the northern shore of Lake Michigan, entered Green Bay, followed the Fox and Wisconsin rivers to the Mississippi, which they reached on June 17 and named River of the Conception. They followed the river down to the Arkansas, ascertained it flowed not westward into the Gulf of California, as had been believed, but south to the Gulf of Mexico—the first white men to establish the existence of a water highway from the St. Lawrence River to the Gulf of Mexico. They then returned to Canada for fear of the Spaniards, whom they believed were inhabiting the lower reaches of the Mississippi. Marquette remained at St. Francis Xavier Mission at the head of Green Bay to recover his health, which had been severely affected by the journey, while Joliet returned to Quebec with news of their momentous explorations and discoveries. In 1674 Marquette set out for the Illinois Indian country to found a mission among the Illinois, spent the winter near present-day Chicago, and reached the Illinois in the spring of 1675. Falling ill again, he left three weeks later to return to Saint Ignace but died on the way back near present-day Ludington, Michigan, at the mouth of Père Marquette River on May 18. Two years later Indians brought his body back to Saint Ignace Mission at Mackinac; his bones were unearthed in 1877 and are now at Marquette University. The explorations of Joliet and Marquette were of tremendous importance in opening a huge new territory to colonization and in establishing France's claims to the lands west of the Mississippi. Marquette made maps of the region through which the party traveled, and his journal of the expedition, written at Mackinac, describing the country, its flora and fauna and its Indian inhabitants, is an invaluable document of American history. His statue representing the state of Wisconsin was enshrined in the Capitol in Washington, D.C., in 1895.

MARTIN, AUGUSTE MARIE (1803–75), bishop. Born in St. Malo, France, on Feb. 1, he studied under Abbé Jean Marie de Lamennais and was ordained in Rennes in 1828. He engaged in pastoral work there, taught at Collège Royale in 1828–39, and was serving as chaplain there when he met Bishop Célestine de la Haylandière of Vincennes, Indiana, who persuaded him to come to Vincennes. He was vicar-general of the diocese for six years when ill health caused him to go to Louisiana in 1845. He settled in New Orleans and was vicar-general of the archdiocese from 1849 until 1853 when he was appointed first bishop of the newly formed diocese of Natchitoches, Louisiana (transferred to Alexandria in 1910). He made several trips to Europe seeking priests for his diocese, attended the second Plenary Council of Baltimore in 1866 and Vatican Council I and at the Council was a strong supporter of the dogma of papal infallibility. He died in Natchitoches on Sept. 29.

MARTIN, CLARENCE EUGENE (1880–1955), lawyer. Born in Martinsburg, West Virginia, on Mar. 13, he was educated at West Virginia University, Morgantown, West Virginia (LL.B. 1899), and Catholic University (LL.M. 1901). He was admitted to the bar in West Virginia in 1901, established the law firm of Martin and Seibert in Martinsburg in 1904, when he married Agnes G. McKenna, and was city attorney in 1904–6. He became one of the leading lawyers in the state, was a member of the West Virginia Judicial Council in 1933–41, 1952–53, and was chairman of the Martinsburg Housing Department in 1938–41. He resigned these positions to accept an appointment by Governor

Holt as United States senator to fill an unexpired term, but the appointment was defeated in the state legislature. He was president of the American Catholic Historical Association in 1927 and of the American Bar Association in 1932–33 and helped found the Thomas More Society of America at the American Bar Association meeting in Boston in 1936. He received several honorary degrees and was made a Knight Commander of the Order of St. Gregory the Great by Pope Pius XI in 1929. He died in Martinsburg on Apr. 24.

MARTINELLI, SEBASTIANO (1848–1918), cardinal. Born in Santa Anna near Lucca, Italy, on Aug. 20, he joined the Augustinians when he was fifteen and was ordained. He taught theology for a time, was elected prior general of his order in 1889 and again in 1895, and was named archbishop of Ephesus in 1896. He was sent to the United States the same year as second apostolic delegate succeeding Cardinal Satolli, was made a cardinal in 1901, returned to Rome in 1902, became prefect of the Congregation of Rites in 1904, and served on the canon law commission in 1906–17. He died in Rome on July 4.

MARTY, MARTIN (1834–96), bishop. Son of a shoemaker, he was born in Schwyz, Switzerland, on Jan. 12, was educated at the Jesuit college at Hofmatt, St. Michael's College, Fribourg, and the Benedictine college at Einsiedeln. He joined the Benedictines in 1855, was ordained in 1856, and taught at Einsiedeln in Switzerland in 1856–60 and emigrated to the United States in 1860. He became prior of St. Meinrad's Priory, Indiana, in 1865, founded St. Meinrad's College there the following year, and became abbot (it had been made an abbey in 1870) in 1871. He was appointed titular bishop of Tiberias and vicar apostolic of Da-kota in 1879 when the vicariate was established and became first bishop of Sioux Falls, South Dakota, when that diocese was erected in 1889. He was deeply concerned with the welfare of the Indians in his vicariate and see (the Sioux were placed under his abbey in 1876), encouraged Catholic immigration to the West, convened synods in 1892 and 1893, and served on the United States Board of Indian Missions in 1893. He was transferred to St. Cloud, Minnesota, in 1895, continuing to administer Sioux Falls until 1896, and died in St. Cloud on Sept. 19. He was the author of a history of the Benedictines and a biography of Bishop John Henni of Milwaukee.

MARX, ADOLPH (1915–65), bishop. Born in Cologne, Germany, on Feb. 18, he was educated in Germany, came to the United States in 1934, continued his studies at St. Mary's Seminary, La Porte, Texas, and was ordained in Corpus Christi in 1940. After further studies at Catholic University (J.C.D. 1943), he was secretary to Bishop Emmanuel Ledvina of Corpus Christi in 1943–44, a curate at Refugio, Texas, in 1944–45 and at Corpus Christi in 1945–48, and became an American citizen in 1947. He was pastor of Holy Cross Church, Corpus Christi, in 1948–50, was made chancellor of the diocese in 1948 and a domestic prelate in 1950, and was named titular bishop of Citrus and auxiliary of Corpus Christi in 1956. He was appointed first bishop of the newly established diocese of Brownsville, Texas, in 1965 and died of a heart attack four months later while visiting his parents in Cologne on Nov. 1.

MARY FRANCES, MOTHER. *See* Clarke, Mother Mary Frances.

MARY JOSEPH, MOTHER *See* Rogers, Mother Mary Joseph.

MARY OF ST. ANGELA, MOTHER
See Gillespie, Mother Angela.

MASSE, BENJAMIN LOUIS (1905–78), editor, author. Born in Green Bay, Wisconsin, on June 17, he was educated at St. Norbert College, joined the Jesuits in 1925, and continued his studies at St. Louis University (B.A. 1930, M.A. 1932), L'Immaculée Conception in Montreal, Marquette, and Fordham and was ordained in 1938. He taught at St. Louis University in 1940–41 (after receiving his S.T.L. in 1939) and joined the editorial staff of *America* as an associate in 1941. During his thirty years with *America* he wrote more than five hundred signed articles and over five thousand unsigned comments and editorials on the social and labor issues of the times. He was executive editor of the *Catholic Mind* in 1942–55 and on its fiftieth anniversary edited *The Catholic Mind: 1903–53,* and was the author of *Justice for All* (1964). He was for a time professor of ethics at Xavier Labor School in New York City and spent the last seven years of his life in pastoral work at Holy Family Church, New Rochelle, New York. He died in New Rochelle, New York, on Sept. 28.

MATHIS, MICHAEL AMBROSE (1885–1960), liturgist. Son of a German immigrant carpenter, he was born in South Bend, Indiana, on Oct. 6, joined the Congregation of Holy Cross in 1901, studied at Holy Cross Seminary at Notre Dame (B. Litt. 1901) and was ordained in 1914. He taught Scripture at Holy Cross College in Washington, D.C., in 1915–24, where he studied architecture for a year, and studied Scripture at Catholic University (S.T.B. 1914, S.T.L. 1917, S.T.D. 1920). He was appointed procurator for the Holy Cross missions in 1915, founded the Holy Cross Foreign Mission Society and *The Bengalese,* its mission magazine, in

1919, serving as its editor until 1933, and was president of the Catholic Anthropological Conference in 1920. He founded the Holy Cross Foreign Mission Seminary in Washington, D.C., in 1924 and served as superior for seven years. In 1925, with Mother Anna Dengel, he founded the Society of Catholic Medical Mission Sisters—the first community of women to combine the religious life with the practice of medicine. He was a professor at Notre Dame in 1939–41 and founded the first graduate school of liturgy there in 1947, and in 1954 he organized an annual seminar for architects and artists at Notre Dame; he then became chaplain at St. Joseph's Hospital in South Bend, Indiana. He was one of the leaders of the liturgical movement in the United States and was active in the Liturgical Conference, serving on its board of directors in 1948–56. He died at Notre Dame on Mar. 10.

MATIGNON, FRANCIS ANTHONY (1753–1818), missionary. Born in Paris on Nov. 10, he joined the Sulpicians, studied at St. Sulpice Seminary in Paris, and was ordained in 1778. He received his doctorate in theology from the Sorbonne in 1785, taught theology at the College of Navarre, and was forced to flee to England when the French Revolution closed the college and he refused to take the oath supporting the civil constitution of the clergy. He emigrated to Baltimore in 1792, was assigned to parish and missionary work in Boston and New England by Bishop John Carroll, built Holy Trinity Church in Boston from funds he raised from Protestants and which was designed by Charles Bulfinch, healed the divisions between the French and the Irish in the area, and became an American citizen in 1795. He distinguished himself by his heroic work during the epidemic of 1798, created a favorable climate for

Catholicism in Boston among previously hostile Protestants, and refused Bishop Carroll's efforts to have him named first bishop of Boston, preferring to spend the rest of his life serving as pastor and aide to John de Cheverus, who was named Boston's first bishop in 1808. He died in Boston on Sept. 19.

MATRE, ANTHONY (1866–1934), executive. Born in Cincinnati, Ohio, on Dec. 16, he studied organ and choir directing at Pio Nono Normal School, became editor of *Teacher and Organist,* and was one of the founders of the American Federation of Catholic Societies (the forerunner of the National Catholic Welfare Conference), serving as secretary in 1901–17. He was also one of the founders and was president of the Marquette National Fire Insurance Company of Chicago and was president of the Great Western Fire Insurance Company and was active in numerous Catholic societies. He was one of the first Americans to be made a Knight of the Order of St. Gregory and was professor of English at St. Mary's Mission House, Techny, Illinois, for several years before his death at Elmhurst, Illinois, on Jan. 16.

MATTHEWS, FRANCIS PATRICK (1887–1952), executive, Secretary of the Navy. Born in Albion, Nebraska, on Mar. 15, he was educated at Creighton University, Omaha, Nebraska (B.A. 1910, LL.B. 1913) and was admitted to the Nebraska bar in 1913. He married Claire Hughes in 1914, represented insurance companies and banks and became president of the Securities Investment Corporation and the First Federal Savings and Loan Association of Omaha; most of his business assets were wiped out during the depression of the thirties, though he recovered in the forties. He was an enthusiastic supporter of President Franklin Roosevelt and his

New Deal in 1932 and was general counsel for the Reconstruction Finance Corporation (RFC) in Nebraska and Wyoming in 1933–38. During World War II he was head of the executive committee of National Catholic Community Service in 1942, was vice president of the United States Organization (USO) and the National War Fund and supervised relief services for the War Fund and War Prisoner's Aid in the liberated areas of Europe. He fiercely opposed Communism, was named to the President's Committee on Human rights in 1946, the report of which became the basis of President Truman's civil rights program, and worked for Truman's election as President in 1948. He was appointed Secretary of the Navy by President Truman in 1949, worked with Secretary of Defense Louis A. Johnson for the unification of the armed forces, and successfully squelched "the revolt of the admirals" opposing the diminished role of the Navy by firing Admiral Louis E. Denfeld, chief of naval operations. He resigned in 1951 during the Korean War when the White House disavowed the military steps he proposed to end the war. He was then appointed ambassador to Ireland and held that position until his death in Omaha on Oct. 18.

MATTHEWS, MOTHER MARY BERNARDINE (1732–1800), prioress. Ann Matthews was born in Charles County, Maryland, joined the English-speaking Discalced Carmelites in Hoogstraeten, Belgium, in 1754 and was professed the next year, taking the name Bernardina Teresa Xavier of St. Joseph. She became mistress of novices, served as mother prioress for twenty-eight years, and after all religious orders in the Netherlands were suppressed in 1782, she established a foundation near Port Tobacco, Maryland, in 1790—the first Carmelite monastery in the United

States—and became its first prioress. She died in Port Tobacco on June 12.

MATTHEWS, WILLIAM (1770–1854), missionary, educator. Of an old colonial family, he was born in Port Tobacco, Maryland, on Dec. 16, studied at Liège, Belgium, taught for a short time at Georgetown, and entered St. Mary's Seminary, Baltimore, in 1797. He was ordained in 1800—the first native-born American to be ordained in the United States—and engaged in missionary work in southern Maryland. He became second pastor of St. Patrick's Church, Washington, D.C., in 1804, a position he held the rest of his life, and was appointed president of Georgetown in 1809. He was cofounder of the first public library in Washington, serving as president in 1821–34, and donated the land next to St. Patrick's on which Gonzaga College was built. He established St. Vincent's Female Orphan Asylum and St. Joseph's Home for Boys with his donations and was named vicar-general of the diocese of Philadelphia in 1828 to aid the enfeebled and almost blind Bishop Henry Conwell. He later declined appointment as bishop of Philadelphia to remain in Washington and died there on Apr. 30.

MATZ, NICHOLAS CHRYSOSTOM (1850–1917), bishop. Born in Munster, Lorraine, France, on Apr. 6, he was educated at Finstigen, France, and Mt. St. Mary of the West Seminary, Cincinnati, Ohio, and was ordained in 1874. He engaged in pastoral and missionary work in Colorado and Utah, was named titular bishop of Telmissus and coadjutor of Denver, Colorado, in 1887 and succeeded to that see in 1889 as its second bishop. During his twenty-eight-year episcopate he had to contend with growing anti-Catholic feeling, conflicts between German and Irish Catholics in the diocese, and financial problems, but he erected Our Lady of the Immaculate Conception Cathedral, held the first diocesan synod in 1910, brought the Theatines into the diocese, and expanded diocesan facilities, especially for education, in which he was deeply interested. He died in Denver on Aug. 9.

MAURIN, ARISTIDE PETER (1877–1949), philosopher. Born on a farm near Oultet, Languedoc, France, on May 9, he worked on the family farm in his youth, studied at the Christian Brothers St. Privat's School near Paris, became a novice in 1893, and took his first vows as a Christian Brother two years later, taking the name Adorator Charles. He taught at the Order's schools in and around Paris, served in the French Army in 1898–99, and became interested in the Sillon movement headed by Marc Sangnier. He took his three-year vows in 1899, but when anticlerical Émile Coombs was elected Premier of France in 1902 and proceeded to close the religious schools, Maurin left the Christian Brothers on New Year's Day, 1903, and joined the Sillon movement. In 1909 he emigrated to western Canada, where he worked a farm with a partner, but he left it to work in the wheat fields and then as a ditch digger on the Canadian Pacific Railroad when his partner was killed in a hunting accident. He emigrated to the United States in 1911, worked as a laborer in different parts of the country, and in 1925 came to New York City. He met Dorothy Day in 1932. The following year they began the Catholic Worker movement with the publication of *The Catholic Worker,* devoted to promoting and promulgating the social program of the Catholic Church. One of his urgent pleas was for the members to practice the works of mercy and to establish Houses of Hospitality, and the first House was opened in an empty barbershop under Dorothy Day's apartment in

New York City. Branches of the Catholic Worker movement began opening all over the country and in 1936 the New York group began the first farming commune, near Easton, Pennsylvania. In the same year a collection of Maurin's columns in *The Catholic Worker, Easy Essays,* was published in book form. During the last eleven years of his life Peter constantly traveled throughout the country, preaching his Green Revolution—to fight Marxist teachings with Christian doctrines—visiting the various houses and communes and lecturing and preaching on street corners. In ill health the latter years of his life, he spent his last five years at Maryfarm, a Catholic Worker farm at Newburgh, New York, and died there on May 15.

MAYNARD, THEODORE (1890–1956), author. The son of English Protestant missionaries, he was born in Madras, India, on Nov. 3. He came to the United States and worked there in 1909–10, then returned to England, where he studied for the Protestant ministry but instead became a Catholic in 1913. After spending seven months in a Dominican novitiate in 1915, he decided he did not have a vocation for the priesthood and left. He became a freelance journalist, worked for the British Government in World War I, and in 1918 married Sara Casey of South Africa, an author in her own right. The couple had seven children. He returned to the United States in 1920, resumed his education and received his B.A. from Fordham, his M.A. from Georgetown, and his Ph.D. from Catholic University, while teaching at San Rafael Dominican College, California, in 1921–25, St. John's College, Brooklyn, and Manhattanville College of the Sacred Heart, New York, in 1925–27, Fordham in 1927–29, Georgetown in 1929–34, and Mt. St. Mary's College, Emmitsburg, Maryland, in 1934–36. He lectured widely but was forced to give up teaching and lecturing because of ill health in 1936, and he then devoted himself to writing. He produced many books of poetry and history and biographies and textbooks. Among them are: *De Soto and the Conquistadores* (1930); *The Story of American Catholicism* (1941); biographies of Francis Xavier (1936), St. Vincent de Paul (1939), Simon Bruté *(The Reed and the Rock,* 1942), Orestes Brownson (1943), Frances Cabrini (1945), and Thomas More (1947); *Saints for Our Times* (1952); poetry, *Exile, and Other Poems* (1928) and *Man and Beast* (1936); criticism, *Our Best Poets, English and American* (1922); his autobiography, *The World I Saw* (1938); two anthologies, *The Book of Modern Catholic Verse* (1926) and *The Book of Modern Catholic Prose* (1927); and the posthumously published *Catholics in American History* (1957). He became president of the Catholic Poetry of America Society in 1948. He married Kathleen Sheen in 1946 (his first wife, Sara, had died in 1945) and died in Port Washington, New York, where he spent the last years of his life, on Oct. 18.

MAZZUCHELLI, SAMUEL CHARLES (1806–64), missionary. Son of a prominent banker, he was born in Milan, Italy, on Nov. 4 and was educated by the Somaschi Fathers in Lugano and at Faenza, where he joined the Dominicans in 1823 and made his profession in 1824. He continued his studies at St. Sabina and the Minerva, Rome, and was sent to the United States in 1828, continued his studies at St. Rose's Priory, Kentucky, and was ordained in Cincinnati, Ohio, in 1830. He was assigned to missionary work on Mackinac Island, Michigan, the next three years, the only permanent priest in the upper Great Lakes region, and in 1833 established in Green Bay, Wisconsin, the first Catholic school in Wisconsin (for Menominee Indian children). He later moved his headquarters to Galen, as the center of his missionary activities, which were to take him all over the midwestern United States, ministering to the Indian tribes and building churches, schools, convents, and public buildings in dozens of places. He excelled in music, painting, and architecture and designed all his churches and many public buildings, including the first statehouse of Iowa at Iowa City. He made an unsuccessful attempt to convert Joseph Smith, the Mormon leader, to Catholicism in 1843, attended the fifth Provincial Council of Baltimore the following year as theologian for Bishop Jean Loras of Dubuque, Iowa (when Bishop Loras took possession of his see in 1839 Fr. Mazzuchelli was the only priest in his far-flung diocese), and in the same year while recuperating from a severe illness in Italy, he wrote his *Memoirs,* which did not appear in English until 1910. He was made missionary apostolic to establish the Dominicans along the upper Mississippi in 1844, opened a college for boys, Sinsinawa Mound College, Sinsinawa, Wisconsin, in 1846 and served as its first president in 1845–48 and was founder and first president of the Dominican Congregation of the Most Holy Rosary at Sinsinawa in 1847. He served for a time as chaplain of Wisconsin's first territorial legislature and was pastor of Benton, Wisconsin, from 1849 until he died there on Feb. 23, while ministering to the stricken during an epidemic.

McANDREWS, JAMES WILLIAM (1862–1922), general. Born in Hawley, Pennsylvania, on June 29, he graduated from West Point in 1888 and fought in the Sioux Indian campaign in 1890–91 and in Cuba and the Philippines during the Spanish-American War. He served in the Philippines in 1899–1902 and in

Alaska in 1905–6, was a member of the General Staff Corps in 1916–17, and during World War I he was in command of the 18th Infantry Regiment of the 1st Division in France; he helped organize the war college at Langres and was chief of staff to General John Pershing. He became commandant of the General Staff College in Washington, D.C., after the war, became a major general in 1921, was honored by the French, British, Italian, and Belgian governments and died in Washington, D.C., on Apr. 30.

McAULIFFE, MAURICE FRANCIS (1875–1944), bishop. Born in Hartford, Connecticut, on June 17, he was educated at Mt. St. Mary's College, Emmitsburg, Maryland, St. Sulpice Seminary, Paris, and St. Willibald's Seminary, Eichstätt, Germany. He was ordained in 1900, taught at St. Thomas Preparatory Seminary, Hartford, Connecticut, and was its vice president in 1906–22 and president in 1922–34, was made a domestic prelate in 1924, and was named titular bishop of Dercos and auxiliary of Hartford in 1925. He was appointed bishop of that diocese in 1934 and during his episcopacy invited the Jesuits to found a boys' preparatory school at Fairfield in 1942 (which led to Fairfield University), renovated St. Joseph's Cathedral, established the Diocesan Labor Institute and interracial centers and died in Hartford on Dec. 15.

McAVOY, THOMAS TIMOTHY (1903–69), historian. Born in Tipton, Indiana, on Sept. 12, he was educated at Notre Dame (B.A. 1925) and joined the Congregation of Holy Cross in 1925. He continued his studies at the College of the Holy Cross, Washington, D.C., was ordained in 1929 and received his M.A. from Notre Dame in 1930 and his Ph.D. from Columbia in 1940. He began teaching history at Notre Dame in

1933 and spent his entire career there, serving as head of the history department in 1939–60 and as archivist. He became one of the leading historians of Catholic history in the United States and built the manuscript collection at Notre Dame into one of the finest in American Catholic history in the country. He was for many years managing editor of *Review of Politics,* lectured widely and wrote numerous articles for magazines, and was the author of several books, among them *The Great Crisis in American Catholic History, 1895–1900* (1957) and *A History of the Catholic Church in the United States* (1969). He died at Notre Dame on July 7.

McBRIDE, LLOYD (1916–83), labor leader. Born in Farmington, Missouri, on Mar. 16, he went to work at a steel fabricating plant in St. Louis after graduating from junior high school when fourteen. He joined Local 1295 of the Steel Organizing Committee (later United Steelworkers of America) in 1936 and after organizing a sitdown strike at the plant in 1937, he was elected president of the local the following year, when he was twenty-two. He was made president of the St. Louis Industrial Council in 1940, became president of the Council for Missouri of the Congress of Industrial Organizations (CIO) in 1942. He served in the Navy during World War II and in the decade after the war became increasingly influential in the labor movement and was elected fourth president of the United Steelworkers of America after a bitter election. During his presidency the Steelworkers membership declined to 750,000 from a previous high of 1.4 million in 1979 as the steel industry experienced its worst slump since the depression of the 1930s. Despite opposition from some locals, he supported the no-strike agreement of his predecessors and at first opposed negotiated contract con-

cessions to the industry. He died in Pittsburgh, Pennsylvania, on Nov. 6 of a heart ailment.

McCABE, FRANCIS XAVIER (1872–1948), educator. Born in New Orleans on Feb. 6, he was educated at St. Mary's Seminary, Perrysville, Missouri (B.A. 1889, M.A. 1890), and was ordained a Vincentian priest in 1896. He was a professor of chemistry at St. Vincent's College, Los Angeles, in 1896–1906, serving as vice president in 1902–6, engaged in home mission work the next four years, and was president of De Paul University, Chicago, in 1910–20. During his tenure as president he established a law school and introduced coeducation. He was rector of St. Vincent's Church, Kansas City, Missouri, in 1920–23 and again in 1927–28, was director of missions for the western province of his order for two years, and was rector of St. Stephen's Church, New Orleans, in 1925–26. He served as rector of St. Thomas Seminary in 1926–27, was appointed director of the Vincentian Auxiliary in 1928, and died in New Orleans on July 3.

McCAFFREY, JOHN HENRY (1806–81), educator. Born in Emmitsburg, Maryland, on Sept. 6, he was educated at Mt. St. Mary's College and Seminary there, was ordained a deacon in 1831 but was not ordained a priest until 1838. He taught at Mt. St. Mary's, serving as vice president in 1834–37, and after further study at St. Mary's Seminary, Baltimore, he was ordained in 1838. He returned to Mt. St. Mary's and was elected president, serving until 1872, when ill health caused him to resign. During his thirty-four-year tenure at Mt. St. Mary's he built it into one of the leading seminaries in the country, though its existence was threatened during the Civil War, when most of the students left (only seven men graduated in

1863 and two in 1864) and it was in grave financial difficulties. A catechism he prepared in 1856 became the basis of the famous Baltimore Catechism, which was adopted as the standard catechism for use in the United States at the second Plenary Council of Baltimore in 1866. He died in Emmitsburg on Sept. 26.

McCARRAN, PATRICK ANTHONY (1876–1954), United States senator. Born of Irish immigrant parents near Reno, Nevada, on Aug. 8, he studied at the University of Nevada but never graduated because he was forced to leave in his senior year to help his father, who had been crippled. He studied law, married Martha Harriet Weeks in 1903, engaged in farming and sheep raising, and was admitted to the Nevada bar in 1905. He began his long political career by being elected to the Nevada legislature in 1902, was district attorney for Nye County in 1907–9, engaged in private law practice in Reno in 1909–13, and was elected associate justice of the Nevada Supreme Court in 1913, serving as chief justice in 1917–18. He was president of the Nevada Bar Association in 1920–21, vice president of the American Bar Association in 1922–23, and chairman of the Nevada State Board of Bar Examiners in 1931–32. A major figure in Nevada politics for a quarter of a century, he entered the national scene when he was elected to the United States Senate in 1932, after unsuccessful bids in 1916 and 1926, and became one of its most influential members; he spent the rest of his life in that body, being reelected in 1938, 1944, and 1950. Though a Democrat, he often clashed with President Roosevelt and President Truman in his roles as a member of the committee on foreign cooperation and the Senate judiciary committee and as chairman of the Internal Security subcommittee. He was often the center of violent controversies, vigorously opposed the plan of President Roosevelt to pack the Supreme Court in 1937, and often opposed other New Deal measures. He sponsored the 1938 bill creating the Civil Aeronautics Authority and favored the creation of an independent air force in the armed forces. He opposed lend-lease to England in 1941, attacked the abandonment of the Nationalist Chinese Government and the refusal of NATO nations to admit Spain into the North Atlantic Treaty Organization, fiercely opposed Communism and Communist influence in government, and secured congressional override of President Truman's veto of the Internal Security Act of 1950. He was the sponsor in the Senate of the McCarran-Walter Immigration and Nationality Act of 1952, which was passed over President Truman's veto. He died in Hawthorne, Nevada, on Sept. 28 and in 1960 his statue was placed in National Statuary Hall in the Capitol, Washington, D.C., to represent the state of Nevada.

McCARTHY, DENIS ALOYSIUS (1870–1931), poet. Born in Carrick-on-Suir, Tipperary, Ireland, on July 25, he was educated by the Christian Brothers there and when he was fifteen he went to the United States. He joined the staff of the *Sacred Heart Review* in Boston in 1895, serving as associate editor in 1900–17, married Ruphine Morris in 1901, wrote for newspapers and magazines, and edited the *North American Teacher*. He lectured on the Chautaqua circuit, worked for the Knights of Columbus during World War I, and as his poetry output developed became associated with several educational and literary groups in the Boston area. Among his books of verse are *A Round of Rimes* (1909), *Voices from Erin* (1910), *Songs of Sunrise* (1918), *Ould Father Toomey and Other Poems* (1926), and *The Harp* *of Life* (1929). He died in Arlington, Massachusetts, on Aug. 18.

McCARTHY, JOSEPH EDWARD (1877–1955), bishop. Born in Waterbury, Connecticut, he was educated at Holy Cross College, Worcester, Massachusetts, and St. Sulpice Seminary, Paris, and was ordained in 1903. He became vice president of St. Thomas Preparatory School, Hartford, Connecticut, and in 1932 was appointed bishop of Portland, Maine. During his episcopate, he refunded the diocesan debt, saw St. Francis College in Biddeford—the only college in the diocese for men—open in 1943 and, ill the last few years of his life, died in Portland on Sept. 8.

McCARTHY, JOSEPH RAYMOND (1909–57), United States senator. Of a farming family, he was born in Grand Chute, Wisconsin, on Nov. 14, received his LL.B. from Marquette in 1935, and was admitted to the bar the same year. He began practicing law in Waupaca and Shawano, Wisconsin, was elected district attorney of Shawano County in 1936, was a judge of the Wisconsin Circuit Court in 1940–42, and served in the United States Marines in the Pacific in 1942–45 during World War II, achieving the rank of captain before his discharge. He was defeated in 1944 in a bid for the United States Senate but two years later defeated Robert M. LaFollette, Jr., for the Republican nomination and went on to win the election. He attracted national attention with a speech in 1950 in Wheeling, West Virginia, in which he charged the State Department had been infiltrated with Communists, who were shaping American foreign policy. From then on he was an unrelenting opponent of Communism and continually attacked those he classified as Communists and subversives. He became chairman of the Senate Committee on Government Operations and of its investigative arm, the Permanent Subcommittee on Investigations, when he was reelected in 1952 and the Republicans gained control of Congress in 1953. The methods he employed in his investigations aroused great controversy and found their way into Webster's Third New International Dictionary as the term "McCarthyism," defined as "a political attitude of the mid-twentieth century closely allied to know-nothingism and characterized chiefly by opposition to elements held to be subversive and by the use of tactics involving personal attacks on individuals by means of widely publicized indiscriminate allegations, especially on the basis of unsubstantiated charges." His investigations in 1954 were a sensation when he accused Secretary of the Army Robert T. Stevens and his aides of concealing evidence of espionage activities he claimed to have uncovered at Fort Monmouth, New Jersey. In turn the Army accused McCarthy and his chief counsel, Roy Cohn, of attempting to secure preferential treatment for G. David Schine, a former committee aide for McCarthy's committee, now a private in the Army. McCarthy was cleared of the charges in a widely publicized hearing, but by that time he had alienated many of the Republican leaders, including President Eisenhower. In December 1954 the Senate censured him for his contempt of a Senate elections subcommittee investigating the conduct and financial affairs of McCarthy's 1952 election, for abusing several senators, and for his insulting remarks about the Senate during the Senate censure proceedings. His influence declined after this censure and went into further eclipse when the Democrats gained control of the Congress in the 1954 election. He married Jean Kerr in 1953, spent his last years in relative obscurity, and died of hepatitis in Bethesda, Maryland, on May 2.

McCARTHY, JUSTIN JOSEPH (1900–59), bishop. Born in Sayre, Pennsylvania, on Nov. 26, he was educated at Seton Hall University, South Orange, New Jersey (B.A. 1923), and the Propaganda, Rome (M.A. 1925, S.T.L. 1927), and was ordained in Rome in 1927. He taught Scripture and homiletics at Immaculate Conception Seminary, Darlington, New Jersey, in 1927–41 and ascetical theology, and was spiritual director from 1941. He was made a papal chamberlain in 1941, domestic prelate in 1949, and was pastor in South Orange in 1953. He was named titular bishop of Doberus and auxiliary bishop of Newark, New Jersey, in 1954 and in 1957 was appointed second bishop of Camden, New Jersey. During his episcopate he expanded the educational facilities of the see, established new parishes, and developed a Puerto Rican apostolate. He died suddenly in Elizabeth, New Jersey, on Dec. 26.

McCARTY, WILLIAM TIBERTUS (1889–1972), bishop. Born in Crossingville, Pennsylvania, on Aug. 11, he was educated at Redemptorist seminaries in North East, Pennsylvania, Ilchester, Maryland, and Esopus, New York, was professed a Redemptorist in 1910, and was ordained in Esopus in 1915. He taught at St. Mary's College, North East, in 1916–17, Mt. St. Alphonsus, Esopus, in 1918–26, served as prefect of studies there in 1921–30, and was rector in 1933–39. He was provincial of the Baltimore province of the Redemptorists in 1939–43, was named titular bishop of Anaea and Military Delegate to the Armed Forces in 1943, and served in that capacity until 1947, when he was appointed coadjutor bishop of Rapid City, Iowa. He succeeded to the see the following year and remained in that position until 1969, when he retired and was appointed titular bishop of Rotdon. He died in Rapid City on Sept. 14.

McCAULEY, VINCENT J. (1906–82), bishop. Born in Council Bluffs, Iowa, on Mar. 8, he joined the Congregation of Holy Cross in 1924, made his first profession of vows in 1926, received his B.A. from Notre Dame in 1930, and made his theological studies at Holy Cross Foreign Mission Seminary, Washington, D.C. He was ordained in 1934, did graduate studies in English at Boston College in 1934–36, was a missionary in India in 1936–44, and was rector of Holy Cross Foreign Mission Seminary in 1944–52. He worked in the Holy Cross Foreign Mission Society until 1958, when he headed the first band of Holy Cross priests to Uganda, East Africa, and founded Fort Portal mission. He was consecrated first bishop of Fort Portal when it was created a diocese in 1961, retired as bishop of Fort Portal in 1972 in favor of a native priest he had trained, and was executive secretary of the Association of Member Episcopal Conferences of Eastern Africa (AMECEA) from 1973 until 1979, when he resigned to devote himself to raising funds for AMECEA's projected Institute for Higher Theological Studies at Eldoret, Kenya. He returned to the United States in September 1982 for treatment of cancer and died while undergoing surgery at St. Mary's Hospital, Rochester, Minnesota, on Nov. 1.

McCLELLAN, WILLIAM (1874–1951), biblical scholar. Born in West Chester, Pennsylvania, on Mar. 25, he was educated at Peirce College, Philadelphia, in 1891–92 and the University of Pennsylvania (B.A. 1899), studied for the priesthood at General Theological Seminary of the Episcopal Church in New York City (B.D. 1902) and was ordained in 1902. He served at St. Elizabeth Church in Philadelphia until 1908, when his objections to the "open pulpit" movement in Anglicanism (by which ministers of other denominations were allowed to preach in Episcopal churches) caused him and a group of other Episcopal clergymen to become Catholics. He joined the Jesuits in 1909, studied at Woodstock College, Maryland (M.A. 1914, S.T.D. 1919), was ordained in 1918 and was appointed professor of Old Testament at Woodstock. He wrote on biblical themes for various magazines, including a treatise on the old Latin psalter in the *Catholic Biblical Quarterly,* and was an expert on herpetology, on which he also wrote. He died in Woodstock on May 8.

McCLOSKEY, JOHN (1810–85), cardinal. Son of Irish immigrant parents, he was born in Brooklyn, New York, on Mar. 10 and entered Mt. St. Mary's College and Seminary, Emmitsburg, Maryland, in 1822. After twelve years' study there he was ordained in New York City in 1834—the first native New Yorker to be ordained a secular priest. He was named professor of philosophy at the new seminary at Nyack, New York, in 1834 and when it was destroyed by fire in its first year went to Europe and spent the next three years traveling and studying at the Gregorian in Rome. On his return to the United States in 1837 he was appointed pastor of St. Joseph's Church, Sixth Avenue, in New York City and when the trustees refused to accept him as pastor, demanding the right to select their own pastor, he won them over in time so that they accepted him. In 1841 he was appointed first president of St. John's College (Fordham), while retaining his pastorate at St. Joseph's, and in 1844 he was appointed titular bishop of Axiere and coadjutor of New York with the right of succession. He was responsible for the conversion to Catholicism of

James Roosevelt Bayley in 1842 and Isaac Hecker in 1844 and when the diocese of Albany was erected in 1847 he was appointed its first bishop. During the seventeen years he was bishop there he greatly expanded the facilities of the diocese, establishing some 88 new churches and 13 schools, increasing the number of priests from 34 to 84, building four new orphanages and the new Immaculate Conception Cathedral, bringing new religious communities into the see and establishing St. Joseph's Provincial Seminary in Troy. He was appointed second archbishop of New York in 1864 and was preconized cardinal in 1875—the first American so honored—by Pope Pius IX, formally receiving his red hat from Pope Leo XIII in 1878. During his more than two decades as ordinary of New York he became one of the leading Catholic prelates in the United States. During his episcopate he held two diocesan synods and the fourth Provincial Council of New York in 1883, increased the number of priests in the archdiocese by 250, churches and chapels by 144, schools from 53 to 97 and the number of students in them from 16,000 to 37,000. He established new hospitals, homes and asylums, rebuilt St. Patrick's Cathedral on Mott Street when it was destroyed by fire in 1866, and then built a new St. Patrick's Cathedral on Fifth Avenue, which was dedicated in 1879, and encouraged Silliman Ives to found the New York Catholic Protectory. He attended Vatican Council I in 1869–70, where he opposed the definition of the dogma of papal infallibility as inopportune at that time but voted for it at the final session. In 1884 he was instrumental in having the State Department intervene with the Italian Government to prevent the expropriation of the North American College in Rome on the grounds that it was owned by American citizens. He died at Mt. St. Vincent-on-

Hudson, New York City, where he had spent the last year of his life in retirement, on Oct. 10.

McCLOSKEY, WILLIAM GEORGE (1823–1909), bishop. Born in Brooklyn, New York, on Nov. 10, he studied law in New York for a time but opted for the religious life and studied for the priesthood at Mt. St. Mary's College and Seminary, Emmitsburg, Maryland, and was ordained in New York in 1852. He served as a parish priest in New York City for ten months and then returned to St. Mary's to teach Scripture, theology, and Latin. He was director of the seminary from 1857 until 1859, when he was named first rector of the North American College in Rome, the unanimous choice of the American bishops. In the years to come he greatly expanded the college and its facilities despite the difficulties caused by the American Civil War. He was appointed fourth bishop of Louisville, Kentucky, in 1868 and established Preston Park Seminary the following year. He attended the second Plenary Council of Baltimore in 1866, Vatican Council I in Rome in 1869–70, and the third Plenary Council of Baltimore in 1884. During his episcopate he brought many religious orders into the see, increased the number of churches from 64 to 165 and the number of priests from 80 to 200, established a diocesan newspaper, *The Record,* in 1879 and was a strong supporter of the parochial school system in his diocese. He was often embroiled in disputes with the clergy and religious orders in the diocese, suppressed St. Mary's College, and caused the School Sisters of Notre Dame and the Sisters of St. Francis of Mt. Olivet to leave the diocese, as well as many priests, including his secretary and chancellor, John L. Spalding, who became first bishop of Peoria, Illinois, in 1876. He died in Louisville on Sept. 17 at Preston Park Seminary.

McCORMACK, JOHN FRANCIS (1884–1945), tenor. Born in Athlone, Ireland, on June 14, he was educated by the Marist Brothers, who taught him to read music, at the local school and at the Immaculate Conception of Summerhill College at Sligo. He was accepted by the choir of Dublin's Marlborough Street Cathedral, where he was given vocal tutoring by Vincent O'Brien in 1903 and in the same year won first prize in the *Feis Ceoil,* the national Irish festival. He studied under Vincenzo Sabatini in Milan in 1905–6, made his operatic debut as Fritz in Mascagni's *L'Amico Fritz* in Savona, Italy, in 1906 and was signed for the Royal Opera House, appearing at Covent Garden in London in 1907. He made his American operatic debut with Oscar Hammerstein's Manhattan Opera House in 1909 as Alfredo in *La Traviata* and sang with the Chicago-Philadelphia Opera House Company, the Metropolitan, the Boston Grand Opera Company, the Chicago Grand Opera Company, and the Monte Carlo Opera Company. He became enormously popular through the hundreds of Victrola records he made and by his concerts, singing Irish folk songs and simple ballads. He settled in New York City at the outbreak of World War I in 1914, for which he was severely criticized in England and Canada, became an American citizen in 1919, and was known for his Catholic charities, for which he was honored by Pope Benedict XV in 1921 and by Pope Pius XI in 1928. He was the recipient of the Laetare Medal in 1933. He lived in Ireland the last years of his life, caught a chill at a concert which developed into pneumonia, and he died at Booterstown just outside of Dublin on Sept. 16.

McCORMACK, JOHN W. (1891–1981), congressman. Son of bricklayer Joseph H. McCormack and Ellen O'Brien McCormack, he was born in South Boston, Massachusetts, on Dec. 21. He left school to work as a newsboy when he was thirteen when his father died and later as an office boy in a law office, where he began reading law. He passed the bar examinations when he was twenty-one, began practicing law, and entered politics. He served in the Army in World War I, was elected to the Massachusetts House of Representatives in 1920 and served in the state Senate from 1923 to 1926, and was elected to the United States House of Representatives in 1928, after having been defeated in a bid for the Democratic nomination in 1926; he was re-elected in each subsequent election until he died. He was appointed to the House Ways and Means Committee, became Democratic leader of the House in 1940, and supported President Roosevelt's New Deal legislation. He was appointed chairman of the House Committee Investigating Un-American Activities in 1934, was first chairman of the House Scientific and Astronauts Committee, and in 1958 sponsored legislation creating the National Aeronautics and Space Administration (NASA). He was elected Speaker of the House in 1961—the first Catholic to hold that position—and earned a reputation as a compromiser; in the 1944, 1952, and 1956 Democratic National Conventions he employed this gift to bridge the gap between Northern liberals and Southern conservatives. Journalists reported strained relations between him and President Truman which he denied. He was honored by the papacy and more than a dozen colleges and died in Dedham, Massachusetts, on Nov. 22. McCormack served in the House of Representatives for forty-three years and during those years he was a champion of civil rights, supported aid to the needy, opposed Communism, was on good terms with various religious denominations (he was affectionately called "the Archbishop" and "Rabbi John"), and was one of the colorful political figures of his times.

McCORMICK, ANNE ELIZABETH O'HARE (1882–1954), journalist. Born of American parents in Wakefield, Yorkshire, England, on May 16, Anne O'Hare was educated in private schools in the United States and England, St. Mary of the Springs College, Columbus, Ohio, where she received her B.A., and the University of Dayton, where she received her LL.D. She began her newspaper career as associate editor on the Cleveland, Ohio, diocesan paper, the *Catholic Universe Bulletin*, wrote free-lance poetry and articles for the New York *Times Magazine, Atlantic Monthly*, and other magazines and married Francis J. McCormick, a Dayton engineer and importer, and frequently accompanied him on his trips abroad. She wrote several articles from abroad for the New York *Times* in 1920, was made a regular *Times* correspondent in 1922, and after 1925 wrote exclusively for the *Times*, except for a series in *Ladies' Home Journal* in 1933–34. Eventually she was given a thrice-weekly column, "Abroad." She covered the hectic years of the rise of Mussolini (she was one of the first correspondents to assess correctly his impact), Hitler, and Stalin, events in Asia, the United Nations, and the Korean War and interviewed practically every important world figure. In 1936 she became the first woman to be appointed to the editorial board of the *Times*, a position she held the rest of her life, and the following year she received the Pulitzer Prize for reporting—the first woman to receive this award. She was named Woman of the Year in 1939, was awarded Theta Phi Alpha's Siena

McCORMICK, JOHN P.

Medal as the outstanding Catholic woman in the United States in 1940 and the Laetare Medal in 1944, was a delegate to the United Nations Educational, Scientific and Cultural Organizations (UNESCO) conferences in 1946 and 1948 and was elected to the National Institute of Arts and Letters in 1947. She received honorary degrees from sixteen colleges, was the author of *The Hammer and the Scythe* (1928), and died in New York City on May 29. Two collections of her columns, *The World at Home* (1956) and *Vatican Journal, 1921–54* (1957), were published posthumously.

McCORMICK, JOHN P. (1904–81). Born in Baltimore on Aug. 1, he was educated at Catholic University (B.A. 1926, M.A. 1927, S.T.B. 1931, Ph.D. 1935) and was ordained in Washington, D.C., in 1931. He joined the Sulpicians the following year, was assistant to the president of Divinity College at Catholic University in 1932–34, taught at St. Charles College, Maryland, in 1934–43, and was president of St. Edward's Seminary, Kenmore, Washington, in 1943–49. He was rector of the Theological College at Catholic University in 1949–68, was a peritus at Vatican Council II, and was a leader in the post-conciliar seminary reform in the United States. He died in Catonsville, Maryland, on Oct. 13.

McCORT, JOHN JOSEPH (1860–1936), bishop. Born in Philadelphia on Feb. 16, he was educated at La Salle College and St. Charles Borromeo Seminary there and was ordained in Philadelphia in 1883. He then taught church history and mathematics at St. Charles until 1889, when he was named pastor of Our Mother of Saviour Church. He became a domestic prelate and vicar-general of the Philadelphia archdiocese in 1910 and two years later was consecrated titular bishop of Azotus and auxiliary of Philadelphia. He was appointed coadjutor bishop of Altoona, Pennsylvania, in 1920, succeeded to the see later the same year, and was made an Assistant at the Pontifical Throne in 1933. He died in Altoona on Apr. 21.

McDERMOTT, ARTHUR VINCENT (1888–1949), general. Born in Brooklyn, New York, on Aug. 27, he was educated at Columbia in 1906–8 and New York Law School (LL.B. 1912), was admitted to the bar in 1913, and engaged in law practice in New York City as a member of the firm of Burke and Burke. He joined the National Guard, served in the Mexican campaign and with the 106th Infantry in World War I, and was wounded and was Judge Advocate General of the New York National Guard in 1919–40. He married Genevieve Markey in 1919, became involved in politics, and was deputy city controller in New York City in 1938–40. He was recalled to military service in 1940, was director of the Selective Service System for New York in 1940–47, and was made a brigadier general in 1947. He died in New York City on Dec. 18.

McDERMOTT, TERENCE STEPHEN (1887–1963). Born in Eagle Grove, Iowa, on Mar. 14, he joined the Dominicans and studied at St. Joseph's Novitiate, Somerset, Ohio, Catholic University (S.T.L.), Dominican House of Studies, Washington, D.C., and Providence College, Rhode Island (LL.D. and S.T.D.), and was ordained in 1913. He taught at the Dominican House of Studies in 1914–17, was an Army chaplain during World War I in 1917–19, and was pastor of Holy Name Church, Kansas City, Missouri, in 1919–26 and pastor and prior of St. Catherine's Church and Convent in New York City in 1926–29. He was prior of the Dominican House of Studies in Washington,

D.C., in 1929–30, was provincial of the Dominican province of St. Joseph for six terms in 1930–55, and was vicar-general of his order in 1954–55. He died in New York City on Apr. 5.

McDEVITT, PHILIP RICHARD (1858–1935), bishop. Born in Philadelphia on July 12, he graduated from La Salle College there, studied for the priesthood at St. Charles Borromeo Seminary, Overbrook, Philadelphia, and was ordained in Philadelphia in 1885. He was superintendent of Catholic schools in the Philadelphia archdiocese in 1899–1916 and was president of the American Catholic Historical Society in 1910, when he was made a domestic prelate. He was appointed bishop of Harrisburg, Pennsylvania, in 1916, became episcopal chairman of the press department of the National Catholic Welfare Conference (NCWC) in 1918 and died in Harrisburg on Nov. 11.

McDONALD, BROTHER BARNABAS EDWARD (1865–1929). Born in Ogdensburg, New York, on July 25, he joined the Christian Brothers in 1885 and while vocational recruiter in 1890–1901 became interested in the plight of orphan boys. He founded St. Philip's Home for urban working boys in 1902, introduced the "cottage system" at Lincoln Agricultural School, which he established at Lincolndale, New York, in 1909, and helped found the National Conference of Catholic Charities the same year. He was director of Catholic Charities in Toronto in 1919–22 and introduced the Boy Scouts there, was executive secretary of the Boys Life Bureau of the Knights of Columbus and founded the Columbian Squires, and established a program for directors of boys' activities at Notre Dame. He received numerous awards for his work with boys and died in Santa Fe, New Mexico, on Apr. 22.

McDONNELL, CHARLES EDWARD (1854–1921), bishop. Born in New York City on Feb. 1, he studied at St. Francis Xavier College there and the North American College, Rome, and was ordained in Rome in 1878. After receiving his doctorate in divinity, he engaged in pastoral work in New York, became secretary to Cardinal John McCloskey in 1884 and his successor Archbishop Michael Corrigan in 1885, and was chancellor of the archdiocese in 1885–87. Made a papal chamberlain in 1890, he was appointed second bishop of Brooklyn, New York, in 1892. He held two diocesan synods, in 1894 and 1898, brought many religious orders into the see, established new parishes, built two hospitals and several charitable institutions, and increased the number of national churches in the diocese to accommodate the immigrants settling in the see. He led three diocesan pilgrimages to Rome in 1900, 1902, and 1904 and died in Brooklyn on Aug. 8.

McDONNELL, THOMAS JOHN (1894–1961), bishop. Born in New York City on Aug. 18, he was educated at Cathedral College, Fordham (M.A. 1921) and St. Joseph's Seminary, Dunwoodie, Yonkers, New York, and was ordained in New York City in 1919. He engaged in pastoral work in New York City as a curate at St. Patrick's Church, Staten Island, in 1919–23 and at the Church of the Annunciation in New York City in 1923–36, was appointed secretary to Auxiliary Bishop John Dunn in 1923, was director of New York's Society for the Propagation of the Faith in 1923–36, and was editor of *Good Work* magazine in 1923–36. He was appointed national director of the Society for the Propagation of the Faith in 1936 and held this position until 1950. He was appointed titular bishop of Sela and auxiliary of New York in 1947 and was named coadjutor of Wheeling, West Virginia, in 1951 but never succeeded to the see, as he died there on Feb. 25 the year before its ordinary, Bishop John J. Swint.

McENTEGART, BRYAN JOSEPH
(1893–1968), bishop. Born in New York City on Jan. 5, he was educated at Manhattan College (B.A. 1913) and Catholic University (M.A. 1918) and was ordained in 1917. His interest in social welfare work led him to continue his studies at the New York School of Social Work, and he graduated in 1920. He was director of the children's division of New York Catholic Charities in 1920–41, director of the Child Welfare League of America in 1931–37, and president of the New York State Conference of Social Work in 1940 and of the National Conference of Catholic Charities in 1941. He was national secretary of the Catholic Near East Welfare Association in 1941–43 and executive director of Catholic Relief Services in 1943. He was appointed fifth bishop of Ogdensburg, New York, in 1943, where he served until 1953, when he was named titular bishop of Aradi and director of Catholic University, a position he held until 1957, when he was appointed fourth bishop of Brooklyn, New York. In 1966 he was given the personal title of archbishop by Pope Paul VI. He retired in 1968 and was made titular archbishop of Gabii and died two months later in Brooklyn on Sept. 30.

McFADDEN, JAMES AUGUSTINE
(1880–1952), bishop. Born in Cleveland, Ohio, on Dec. 24, he was educated at St. Ignatius College and St. Mary's Seminary there and was ordained in Cleveland in 1905. He was a curate at St. Agnes Church, Cleveland, in 1905–14, the founding pastor of St. Agnes Church, Elyria, Ohio, in 1914–17, and was rector of St. Mary's Seminary in 1917, serving in that position until 1923.

He was made chancellor of the Cleveland diocese and a domestic prelate in 1927 and was named titular bishop of Bida and auxiliary of Cleveland in 1932. He was appointed first bishop of the newly established diocese of Youngstown, Ohio, in 1943 and remained in that position until he died in Youngstown on Nov. 16.

McFARLAND, FRANCIS PATRICK
(1819–74), bishop. Son of Irish immigrants, he was born in Franklin, Pennsylvania, on Apr. 16, studied at Mt. St. Mary's College, Emmitsburg, Maryland, graduated in 1844, and after teaching there for a time was ordained in New York in 1845. He taught at St. John's College (Fordham) for a year, served as pastor of St. John's Church, Watertown, New York, until 1851, when he was transferred to Utica, New York, and in 1857 he was appointed vicar apostolic of Florida but declined the appointment. He was appointed third bishop of Hartford, Connecticut, later the same year, attended Vatican Council I in 1869–70, and, in ill health, asked to be allowed to resign. Instead, to relieve his burden, his see was divided into two dioceses, Providence and Hartford, in 1872. He moved from Providence, where he had been living, to Hartford, built St. Aloysius for orphans and dependent children, and a convent and chapel for the Sisters of Mercy which he dedicated in 1873 and which became the procathedral for the diocese. He died in Hartford on Oct. 2.

McFAUL, JAMES AUGUSTINE
(1850–1917), bishop. Born near Larne, Antrim, Ireland, on June 6, he was brought to the United States when an infant by his parents, who settled in New York City at first and then moved to Bound Brook, New Jersey. He was educated at St. Vincent's Seminary, Beatty, Pennsylvania, St. Francis Xavier

College, New York City, and Seton Hall College, South Orange, New Jersey, and was ordained in 1877. When the diocese of Trenton, New Jersey, was established in 1881, he was appointed an assistant at St. Mary's Church there, became pastor of St. Mary Star of the Sea Church, Long Branch, New Jersey, and in 1890 was appointed rector of the cathedral in Trenton. He became the bishop's secretary and chancellor of the see and in 1892 was named vicar-general. He acted as administrator of the diocese when Bishop Michael O'Farrell died in 1894 and later the same year was appointed second bishop of Trenton. He devoted much of his activity to social welfare work, was particularly concerned with aiding immigrants, increased the number of churches, schools, and other institutions in the diocese and put the see on a sound financial basis. In 1901 he was one of the prime movers in the founding of the American Federation of Catholic Societies which represented some two million Catholics. He died in Trenton on June 16.

McGARRY, WILLIAM JAMES (1894–1941), educator. Born in Hamilton, Massachusetts, on Mar. 14, he joined the Jesuits in 1911, and studied at Woodstock College, Maryland (B.A. 1917, M.A. 1918, S.T.D. 1926) and Fordham (Ph.D. 1922). He taught mathematics and philosophy at Fordham in 1918–22, was ordained in 1925, and continued his studies at Rome and Jerusalem and received his licentiate in Sacred Scripture from the Pontifical Biblical Commission in Rome in 1930. He taught Scripture at Weston School of Theology, Massachusetts, in 1930–37, serving as dean of philosophy in 1930–33, and was president of Boston College in 1937–39. Ill health caused him to resign in 1939 and he went to New York, where he served as associate editor of *Thought* and was first editor of *Theolog-*

ical Studies. He wrote several books, among them *The Biblical Commission* (1931), *Anthropology and the Knowledge of God* (1932), *Paul and the Crucified* (1939), and *Unto the End* (1941). He died in New York City on Sept. 23.

McGARVEY, WILLIAM (1861–1924), author. Born in Philadelphia on Aug. 14, he was educated at General Theological Seminary, New York City, and the Nashotah Seminary, Wisconsin, and was ordained a priest of the Episcopal Church in 1886. He served as a curate at the Church of the Evangelists and then as rector of St. Elizabeth's Church, Philadelphia, was master of the Anglican Companions of the Holy Saviour and chaplain general of the Anglican Sisters of Mary until 1908, when he became a Catholic. He studied for the Catholic priesthood at St. Charles Borromeo Seminary, Overbrook, Philadelphia, and Catholic University and was ordained in 1910. He served as curate at Holy Child and then St. James Church in Philadelphia until 1919, when he was appointed rector of the Church of the Holy Infancy, Bethlehem, Pennsylvania, and remained in that position until he died in San Diego, California, on Feb. 27. He wrote several books before his conversion to Catholicism and for Catholic periodicals afterward.

McGAVICK, ALEXANDER J. (1863–1948), bishop. Born in Fox Lake, Illinois, on Aug. 22, he was educated at St. Viator's College, Kankakee, Illinois (M.A. 1887), and was ordained in 1887. He was assigned as a curate at All Saints Church, Chicago, was named pastor of St. John's Church in 1897, and was consecrated titular bishop of Narcopolis and auxiliary of Chicago in 1899 and made pastor of Holy Angels Church in 1900. Despite ill health, which hampered him the rest of his life, he was active in social programs, founded welfare and youth groups, and was one of those who helped revitalize the National Catholic Welfare Conference. He was appointed bishop of La Crosse, Wisconsin, in 1921 and during his episcopate he built thirty-eight diocesan buildings, established high school programs in fourteen schools, and continued his activity in social work. He died in La Crosse on Aug. 25.

McGEE, THOMAS D'ARCY (1825–68), editor. Born in Carlingford, Louth, Ireland, on Apr. 13, he received his early education from a hedge schoolmaster in Wessex and emigrated to the United States in 1842, when he was seventeen. He became an editor on the staff of the Boston diocesan paper, *The Pilot,* and his articles and speeches on England's domination of Ireland attracted widespread attention. He became associate editor in 1844, returned to Ireland the following year, and took a position on the London editorial staff of *Freeman's Journal* in Dublin but left for a position on the *Nation* because of his stand in favor of the revolutionary Young Ireland Party. He was a leader in the Irish revolt of 1848, serving as secretary of the Irish Confederation, and was arrested and imprisoned by the British for his activities. He escaped to the United States disguised as a priest and started the *Nation* in New York, but when Archbishop John Hughes objected to his revolutionary ideas and his inflammatory articles against England and priests in Irish politics and placed an episcopal ban on the *Nation,* it collapsed in 1849. He changed the name of the paper to *The American Celt* and published it in Boston, then in Buffalo, and then back in New York in 1850–57. While editing these papers, he fought Know-Nothingism, organized night schools for adult immigrants, and in 1856 was the moving spirit in the Buffalo Convention to organize Irish-Catholic settlements in rural areas of the United States and Canada. In 1857 he moved to Montreal and published *The New Era* there, entered Canadian politics, served in the Legislative Assembly in 1858–67, became a prominent figure in Canadian politics, played a major role in confederating the British colonies in Canada into the Dominion of Canada, and completely changed his position and supported England's role in Ireland. He was elected to the first Dominion Parliament in 1867 and was minister of agriculture and immigration in 1864–68. His new stand about England and Ireland, his denunciation of Fenian raids in Canada and his attacks on revolutionary activities in Ireland and support of those activities by Irishmen all over the world caused great bitterness and much hatred toward him by his fellow countrymen. He was assassinated by a Fenian, Patrick James Whelan, an Irish immigrant, at Ottawa, Canada, on Apr. 7. He was the author of several books, among them *Irish Writers of the Seventeenth Century* (1846), *History of the Attempt to Establish the Protestant Reformation in Ireland* (1853), *History of the Irish Settlers in North America* (1851), and the three-volume *History of Ireland* (1862–69) and a collection of poetry, *Poems* (1869).

McGILL, JOHN (1809–72), bishop. Born in Philadelphia on Nov. 4, he graduated from St. Joseph's College there in 1828, read law, and was admitted to the bar. Instead of pursuing a career in law, he decided to become a priest, studied at St. Thomas Seminary, Kentucky, and St. Mary's Seminary, Baltimore, and was ordained in Bardstown, Kentucky, in 1835. He engaged in pastoral work in Kentucky, became editor of the *Catholic Advocate,* and was named vicar-general of the diocese of

Bardstown by Bishop Martin J. S. Spalding. He was appointed third bishop of Richmond, Virginia, in 1850, convened Richmond's first diocesan synod in 1855, fought the anti-Catholicism of the Know-Nothing movement and supported the Confederacy in the Civil War. After the war, he rebuilt the diocese, attended Vatican Council I, where he preached, in 1869–70, and was the author of several books, among them *The True Church* (1862) and *Our Faith, Our Victory* (1865). He died in Richmond on Jan. 14.

McGINLEY, PHYLLIS (1905–78), poet. Born in Ontario, Oregon, on Mar. 21, she and her family moved to Colorado and then Utah when she was very young and she was educated at Sacred Heart Academy, Ogden, Utah, and the universities of Utah and California. She taught school in Utah for a year, went to New York and worked as a free-lance writer and advertising copy editor, and became assistant editor of *Town and Country* magazine. She had her first book of poems, *On the Contrary,* published in 1934 and became noted for the skill, wit, and lucidity of her light, sprightly poems and for her children's books. She married Charles Hayden in 1937. She was elected to the National Academy of Arts and Letters in 1955, was awarded the Pulitzer Prize in 1961 for *Times Three: Selected Verse from Three Decades* (1960), and received the Laetare Medal in 1964. Among her books are: *A Pocketful of Wry* (1940), *The Horse Who Lived Upstairs* (1944), *All Around the Town* (1948), *A Short Walk from the Station* (1951), *Make Believe Twins* (1953), *Love Letters of Phyllis McGinley* (1954), *Province of the Heart* (1959), and *Saint-Watching* (1969). She died in New York City on Feb. 22.

McGINNIS, WILLIAM F. (1867–1932), editor. Born in Brooklyn, New York, on Dec. 28, he was educated at St. John's College, Brooklyn, and the North American College, Rome, and was ordained in 1891. He engaged in pastoral work on Long Island, was pastor in Westbury there in 1904–9 and of St. Thomas Aquinas Church, Brooklyn, from 1919 until his death. He founded the Metropolitan Truth Society in 1899, which became the International Truth Society when incorporated in 1910 to defend Catholicism against misrepresentation and to expound the teachings of Catholicism through the written and the spoken word, and served as its president and was editor of its journal, *Truth.* He was made a monsignor in 1926 and died in Brooklyn on May 16.

McGIVNEY, MICHAEL JOSEPH (1852–90), founder. Born in Westbury, Connecticut, on Aug. 12, he was educated at St. Hyacinth, Canada, Niagara University, New York, and St. Mary's College, Baltimore, and was ordained in 1877. He served at St. Mary's Church, New Haven, Connecticut, and in 1882, helped by parishioners, he founded the Knights of Columbus, a fraternal benefit society of Catholic men, serving as its corresponding secretary and national chaplain the rest of his life. In the next two decades the Knights spread to every state and territory of the United States, Canada, Mexico, and the Philippines and became one of leading Catholic organizations in the country, noted for its charitable, fraternal, patriotic, social and educational activities, with more than a million members. Fr. McGivney died in Thomaston, Connecticut, on Aug. 14.

McGLOIN, FRANK (1846–1921), jurist. Born in Gort, Galway, Ireland, on

Feb. 22, he was brought to New Orleans as an infant by his parents, studied at St. Mary's College, Perry County, Missouri, and fought on the side of the Confederacy in 1862–65 during the Civil War. He was admitted to the Louisiana bar in 1866, became editor of the *Hibernian* in 1868, resisted the Radical government during the Reconstruction era, was a member of the state constitutional convention in 1879, and became senior justice of the Louisiana Court of Appeals in 1880, serving two terms. With Edward Douglass White, later chief justice of the United States Supreme Court, he fought the lottery movement in Louisiana in the 1880s. He was the author of several books, among them *The Conquest of Europe, The Light of Faith* (1905), and a novel, *The Story of Norodom,* and was made a Knight Commander of the Order of St. Gregory in 1910. He died near Baton Rouge, Louisiana, on Aug. 30.

McGLYNN, EDWARD (1837–1900). Born in New York City on Sept. 27, he was educated at the Urban College of the Propaganda, Rome, where he received his doctorate in divinity and was ordained in Rome in 1860. He engaged in pastoral work in New York City as assistant at St. Joseph's Church and in 1866 was named pastor of St. Stephen's Church, the largest and most influential parish in the city. He became involved in social reform activities, was a founder of the Anti-Poverty Society, favored state education for children rather than parochial schools, and was an ardent supporter of the single tax on land theory of Henry George. When George ran for mayor in 1886, McGlynn worked for him during his political campaign. His activities in the campaign brought him into conflict with Archbishop Michael Corrigan, who vigorously opposed George and believed McGlynn's economic beliefs violated Church teaching.

McGlynn refused the archbishop's order not to speak at a political rally for George, whereupon the Archbishop suspended him from his priestly duties for two weeks and again later in the year; early in 1887 McGlynn was removed as pastor of St. Stephen's. When Cardinal Simeoni, prefect of the Congregation of the Propagation, ordered McGlynn to Rome to repudiate his land tax theories, the pastor refused and then refused the summons of Pope Leo XIII. He was excommunicated. He continued his activities on behalf of the single tax theory as president of the Anti-Poverty Society and in 1892 was reinstated by Archbishop Satolli, Pope Leo's personal delegate (ablegate) to the United States, who declared McGlynn's single tax views did not violate Catholic teaching after Satolli and four professors at Catholic University had examined him. He was received by the Pope in 1893 and the following year was transferred to Newburgh, New York, by Archbishop Corrigan as pastor of St. Mary's Church there. He never did retract his views on the single tax theory, though the Holy Office stated George's land tax theory deserved to be condemned in 1889 and transmitted the condemnation to Corrigan in 1893, mandating it be kept secret —this at the request of Cardinal Gibbons, who feared its publication would lead to further exacerbation of the McGlynn matter. McGlynn remained as pastor of St. Mary's until his death in Newburgh on Jan. 7; Archbishop Corrigan presided at his funeral Mass.

McGOLRICK, JAMES (1841–1918), bishop. Born in Borrisokane, Tipperary, Ireland, on May 1, he was educated at All Hallows College, Dublin, was ordained there in 1867, and emigrated to the United States the same year. He was an assistant at the cathedral in St. Paul, Minnesota, in 1867 and was pastor of Immaculate Conception Church, St.

Paul, from 1868 to 1889, when he was appointed first bishop of the newly created diocese of Duluth, Minnesota, a position he occupied until his death in Duluth on Jan. 23. During the twenty-eight years of his episcopate he greatly increased the number of priests, religious, and laity in the diocese, was faced with a schism in 1906 when the parishioners of St. Mary's parish in Duluth affiliated with the Polish National Catholic Church, was particularly interested in the welfare and education of the see's large Indian population, and built many new churches, schools, hospitals, and charitable institutions.

McGOVERN, PATRICK ALOYSIUS ALPHONSUS (1872–1951), bishop. Born in Omaha, Nebraska, on Oct. 14, he was educated at Creighton University, Omaha (B.A. 1891), and Mt. St. Mary of the West Seminary, Cincinnati, Ohio, and was ordained in Omaha in 1895. He was pastor of his native parish's St. Philomena Cathedral in Omaha in 1898–1907 and of St. Peter's Church, Omaha, the next five years. In 1912 he was appointed bishop of Cheyenne, Wyoming. He held a diocesan synod in 1913, was made an Assistant at the Pontifical Throne in 1937, and died in Cheyenne on Nov. 8.

McGOVERN, THOMAS (1832–98), bishop. Born in Swanlinbar, Cavan, Ireland, he emigrated to the United States, studied at St. Mary's Seminary, Baltimore, and St. Charles Borromeo Seminary, Overbrook, Philadelphia, and was ordained in Philadelphia in 1861. He engaged in pastoral work in Philadelphia until 1887, when he was appointed second bishop of Harrisburg, Pennsylvania, a position he held until his death there on July 25.

McGOWAN, RAYMOND AUGUSTINE (1892–1962), social activist. Born in Brookfield, Missouri, on July 23, he was educated at St. Benedict's College, Atchison, Kansas, St. Bernard's Seminary, Rochester, New York, the North American College, Rome, and Catholic University and was ordained in Washington, D.C., in 1915. He engaged in pastoral work in Missouri in 1916–19, serving as a chaplain in the Army in 1918 during World War I, and in 1919 was assigned to the National Catholic War Council (later National Catholic Welfare Conference, NCWC). He was one of the founders of the Catholic Association for International Peace in 1927, serving as its executive secretary, and was appointed director of NCWC's Social Action Department in 1945, succeeding Msgr. John A. Ryan. He worked to apply Catholic social principles to the American economic scene, founded the Catholic Conference on Industrial Problems, serving as its secretary in 1923–47, and became deeply involved in the labor movement in the United States, stressing the need for mutual cooperation between labor and management to solve industrial problems. He was assigned to NCWC's Latin American Bureau in 1933, traveled widely throughout Latin America, and was appointed by President Roosevelt to study changes needed in Puerto Rico's organic law. He was made a domestic prelate in 1952, retired as director of NCWC's Social Action Department in 1954, and died in Kansas City, Missouri, on Nov. 13. He wrote numerous articles on the papal encyclicals, labor management relations, and Latin America and the pamphlets *Europe and the United States* (1931) and *Towards Social Justice* (1933).

McGRANERY, JAMES P. (1895–1962), United States Attorney General. Born in Philadelphia on July 8, he was an observation pilot in the U.S. Air Forces of the A.E.F. in World War I, studied law at Temple University, Philadelphia (LL.B. 1928), was admitted to the Pennsylvania bar in 1928, and established a successful law practice. He entered politics, headed Al Smith's presidential campaign in Philadelphia in 1928, was appointed chairman of the Philadelphia Registration Commission in 1935 and served until he was elected to the House of Representatives in 1936, after an unsuccessful bid in 1934. He was reelected the next three terms, consistently supported the policies of President Roosevelt, and was known for his anti-Communism. He resigned from Congress in 1943 to become assistant to the United States Attorney General and served in that position until 1946, when he was appointed judge of the United States District Court of Eastern Pennsylvania. In that post he presided at the much publicized trial of atom spy Harry Gold in 1950. He resigned his judgeship in 1952 when appointed United States Attorney General by President Truman; he retired from public life the following year and resumed his law practice in Washington, D.C., and Philadelphia. Honored by several universities and Pope Pius XII, he died in Palm Beach, Florida, on Dec. 23.

McGRATH, JAMES HOWARD (1903–66), United States Attorney General, governor. Born in Woonsocket, Rhode Island, on Nov. 28, he was educated at Providence College (Ph.B. 1926) and Boston University (LL.B. 1929) and was admitted to the Rhode Island bar in 1929, when he married Estelle A. Cadorette. He was city solicitor of Central Falls, Rhode Island, in 1930–34 and was U.S. district attorney for Rhode Island from 1935 to 1940, when he was elected governor of that state; he was reelected in 1942 and 1944. He resigned in 1945 when appointed United States Solicitor General. In 1946 he was elected United States senator and while in the Senate favored the Administration's foreign policy, supported liberal measures, broader social security coverage, and sponsored the National Insurance Bill and opposed racial discrimination and the Taft-Hartley Act. He was chairman of the National Democratic Committee in 1947–49 and resigned as senator in 1949 when appointed Attorney General of the United States by President Truman. He served until 1952, when he returned to private practice, was campaign manager for Estes Kefauver's successful bid for the Democratic nomination for the vice presidency in 1956, served as director of several banks and corporations, was made a Knight of the Equestrian Order of the Sepulchre of Jerusalem, and died in Providence, Rhode Island, on Sept. 2.

McGRATH, JOSEPH FRANCIS (1872–1950), bishop. Born in Kilmacow, Kilkenny, Ireland, on Mar. 1, he was educated at the Grand Seminary, Montreal, and was ordained there in 1895. He engaged in pastoral work in the Boston archdiocese, spent two years as a missionary among the Indians of northern Michigan, and then became curate at the cathedral in Seattle, Washington. He was rector of St. Patrick's Church, Tacoma, Washington, from 1907 to 1918, when he was appointed bishop of Baker, Oregon, a position he held until his death there on Apr. 12.

McGRAW, JAMES J. (1874–1928), banker. Born in Leavenworth, Kansas, on Aug. 21, he moved to Oklahoma and settled in Tulsa, became president of a lumber company, and was a Republican national committeeman in 1916–20. During World War I he was in charge of the expenditures of the Knights of Columbus in France, for which he was decorated by Belgium and France, became president of the Exchange National Bank in 1921, and held that position until his death in Hot Springs, Arkansas, on Mar. 3.

McGROARTY, JOHN STEVEN (1862–1944), poet. Born in Boston Township, Pennsylvania, on Aug. 20, he was educated at the Harry Hillman Academy, Wilkes Barre, Pennsylvania, married Ida Lubrecht in 1890, served as treasurer of Luzerne, Pennsylvania, in 1890–93, studied law, and was admitted to the bar in 1894. After practicing law for two years, he went to Butte, Montana, as a lawyer on the staff of Marcus Daly, the copper magnate, went to Mexico on a mining venture after Daly's death in 1900, and then moved to California the following year. He joined the staff of the Los Angeles *Times,* began writing poetry and wrote a drama, *The Mission Play,* about Fr. Junípero Serra that was performed some 3,200 times in San Gabriel. He became interested in the old California missions, served in Congress in 1935–39 and wrote plays, histories, and poetry, among them *Wander Songs* (1908), *The King's Highway* (1909), *California, Its History and Romance* (1912), the three-volume *Los Angeles* (1921), and the four-volume *California of the South* (1933). He was honored by Pope Pius XI for his work on the missions, was named poet laureate of California by the state legislature in 1933, and died in Tujunga, Los Angeles, on Aug. 7.

McGROARTY, SISTER JULIA (1827–1901), educator, superior. Born in Inver, Donegal, Ireland, on Feb. 13, Susan McGroarty was brought to Cincinnati, Ohio, by her parents in 1831 and was professed a Sister of Notre Dame de Namur, taking the name Julia, in 1848. She taught at Notre Dame Academy, Roxbury, Massachusetts, in 1848–60 and at a school for blacks in Philadelphia in 1877–82. She was named superior of the Sisters of Notre Dame de Namur east of the Rocky Mountains in 1886, and in 1892 was also named superior of the California province. She inaugurated new educational methods in the Notre Dame de Namur schools and founded fifteen houses, including Trinity College for Women in Washington, D.C., in 1897 and a provincial house and novitiate in Cincinnati, Ohio. She died in Peabody, Massachusetts, on Nov. 12.

McGUCKEN, JOSEPH THOMAS (1902–83), archbishop. Born in Los Angeles, California, on Mar. 13, he was educated at the University of California Los Angeles (UCLA), St. Patrick's Seminary, Menlo Park, California, and the North American College, Rome (D.D. 1928). He was ordained in Rome in 1928, served as secretary to Archbishop John J. Cantwell of Los Angeles in 1929–38, was made a papal chamberlain in 1937 and a domestic prelate in 1939, and was named titular bishop of Sanavo and auxiliary of Los Angeles in 1941. He was vicar-general of that diocese in 1948–55, was appointed coadjutor of the diocese of Sacramento, California, in 1955 and succeeded to the see in 1957. He was appointed archbishop of San Francisco in 1962, was chairman of the Press Department of the National Catholic Welfare Conference (NCWC) and was appointed an Assistant at the Pontifical Throne in 1966. He retired as archbishop of San Francisco in 1977 and died there on Oct. 26.

McGUINNESS, EUGENE JOSEPH (1889–1957), bishop. Born in Hallertown, Pennsylvania, on Sept. 6, he was educated at St. Charles Borromeo Seminary and Villanova, Philadelphia, and the University of Santo Tomás, Manila, Philippine Islands, and was ordained in Philadelphia in 1915. He served as curate at St. Agatha's and St. John's churches and the cathedral in

Philadelphia, was assistant director of the diocesan Society for the Propagation of the Faith in 1917–19 and field secretary in 1919–20, second vice president in 1920–24, and first vice president of the Extension Society in 1924. He was also an associate editor of *Extension Magazine.* He was executive secretary of the American Board of Catholic Missions in 1923–27, was made a domestic prelate in 1929, and was consecrated bishop of Raleigh, North Carolina, in 1937. He was named coadjutor bishop of Oklahoma City–Tulsa, Oklahoma, in 1944, succeeded to the see in 1948, and remained as bishop until his death in Oklahoma City on Dec. 27.

McGUIRE, CHARLES BONAVEN-TURE (1768–1833), missionary. Born in Dungannon, Tyrone, Ireland, on Dec. 16, he studied at Louvain and was ordained a Franciscan priest. He left France during the Revolution, traveled throughout Europe on Franciscan matters, and in 1817 emigrated to the United States. He served as a missionary in western Pennsylvania in 1817–20, was pastor of St. Patrick's Church, Pittsburgh, in 1820–33 and laid the cornerstone of St. Paul's Church, then one of the largest churches in the United States, in Pittsburgh in 1829. He died in Pittsburgh on July 17.

McGUIRE, CONSTANTINE EDWARD (1890–1965), economist. Born in Boston on Apr. 4, he was educated at Boston Latin School and Harvard (Ph.D. 1915) and became assistant secretary general of the Inter-American High Commission to coordinate the financial policies of Latin American countries. He joined the Institute of Economics (later the Brookings Institute) in 1922 and resigned in 1929 to work as consulting economist to several Latin American countries. He lectured at universities in Europe and the United

States, was treasurer of the American Historical Association in 1930–36 and president of the American Catholic Historical Association in 1933. He helped found the School of Foreign Service at Georgetown, was a consulting editor for the Encyclopaedia Britannica, and was the author of *Germany's Capacity to Pay* (1923), with Harold G. Moulton, and *Italy's International Economic Position* (1926), and died in New York City on Oct. 22.

McGURKIN, EDWARD A. (1905–83), bishop. Born in Hartford, Connecticut, on June 22, he was educated at Maryknoll (New York) Seminary and was ordained a Maryknoll priest in 1930. He was English editor of Fides News Service in 1930–32, secretary to Cardinal Fumasoni-Biondi, prefect of the Sacred Congregation for the Propagation of the Faith in 1932–34, and was procurator general of Maryknoll and rector of the Maryknoll Seminary in Rome in 1934–38. He went to Manchuria in 1938 as a missionary, was interred by the Japanese during World War II, and was superior of Manchuria in 1946–54. He was named superior of Maswa, Tanzania, in 1954 and was appointed first bishop of the newly established diocese of Maswa (renamed the diocese of Shinyanga in 1957) in 1956 and resigned as bishop of Shinyanga in 1975. He died at Memorial Hospital, Tarrytown, New York, on Aug. 28.

McHUGH, SISTER ANTONIA (1873–1944). Born in Omaha, Nebraska, on May 17, she joined the Sisters of St. Joseph of Carondelet in St. Paul, Minnesota, studied at the University of Chicago, Columbia, and the University of Minnesota and became professor of history at the College of St. Catherine in St. Paul in 1911. She was dean in 1914–28 and president in 1928–37, also serving as superior of the sisters in 1931–37. She promoted advanced education for her sisters at American and European universities, added lay professors to the faculty of St. Catherine's and had a chapter of Phi Beta Kappa established there—the only Catholic women's college in the United States to have a Phi Beta Kappa chapter at that time —and expanded the physical and educational facilities of the college during her presidency. She died in St. Paul, Minnesota, on Oct. 11.

McHUGH, JOHN AMBROSE (1880–1950), theologian. Born in Louisville, Kentucky, on Nov. 2, he joined the Dominicans at St. Rose Priory, Springfield, Kentucky, in 1897 and was professed in 1898. He was ordained at St. Joseph's Priory, Somerset, Ohio, in 1905, finished his theological studies at St. Maria sopra Minerva, Rome (S.T.L. 1907) and the University of Fribourg, Switzerland, and taught at the Dominican House of Studies in Washington, D.C., from 1908 to 1915, when he became a professor of theology and philosophy at the Maryknoll Seminary, Ossining, New York. He became coeditor of *Homiletic and Pastoral Review,* with Fr. C. P. Callan, in 1916 and over the years the two coauthored some thirty books on the liturgy, Scripture, theology, homiletics, and devotion, among them the four-volume *A Parochial Course of Doctrinal Instructions . . . ,* the two-volume *Moral Theology* (1929), *Blessed Be God* (1925), *Catholic Missal,* and *Man of God* (1927). He was president of the Catholic Biblical Association of America in 1938 and died at Ossining on Apr. 9.

McINERNEY, MICHAEL J. (1877–1963), architect. Born in Lock Haven, Pennsylvania, he studied at Duquesne and Pittsburgh universities and then for the priesthood at Belmont Abbey, North Carolina, where he was ordained a Benedictine priest in 1905. He became known for his architectural work over the next six decades and designed some four hundred churches, schools, convents, rectories, and hospitals, notably St. Benedict's Church in Baltimore and St. Benedict's in Richmond. He died in Belmont Abbey on Mar. 3.

McINTYRE, JAMES FRANCIS (1886–1979), cardinal. Born in New York City on June 25, he began working as a messenger for the Wall Street securities firm of H. J. Horton & Company and rose in rank to become office manager. After ten years in business, on the death of his father, he decided to become a priest and studied at Cathedral College, New York City, and St. Joseph's Seminary, Dunwoodie, Yonkers, New York, and was ordained in New York's St. Patrick's Cathedral in 1921. He was a curate at St. Gabriel's Church in 1921–22, assistant chancellor in 1923–34 and chancellor in 1934–41 of the New York archdiocese, was made a domestic prelate in 1937 and was put in charge of the finances of the archdiocese. He was known for his financial acumen for keeping the see's finances in good order during the great depression of the thirties, was named titular bishop of Cyrene and auxiliary of New York in 1940, and in 1946 was named titular archbishop of Paltus and coadjutor of New York with the right of succession. Two years later he was appointed archbishop of Los Angeles. His episcopate witnessed the phenomenal growth of the Catholics in that archdiocese from 625,000 to 1,600,000 and to meet this increase he greatly expanded the facilities of the see; the number of parishes grew from 211 to 313, schools from 159 to 366, and other facilities and services were increased in similar manner. In 1953 Pope Pius XII made him a cardinal—the first from a see west of St. Louis. Considered an ultraconservative, he was frequently involved in controversy both within and without the Church. In 1952 and again in 1958 he successfully fought attempts to levy property taxes on Church-sponsored schools in California; he fought for federal aid for parochial schools when federal aid was first extended to public schools; and he opposed a measure of the California legislature liberalizing abortion. He was often criticized for not taking a more active role in the struggle for civil rights, especially during the attempt to nullify California's housing laws, but his supporters cited numerous instances where he had supported civil rights. He was opposed to many of the new policies instituted in the Church after Vatican Council II, was often embroiled in disputes with religious orders in the archdiocese, notably the Jesuits and the Immaculate Heart of Mary nuns (with whom he clashed over their ideas to modernize the order), and frequently barred clerics from speaking in his see. He resigned in 1970, was ill the last years of his life and confined to St. Vincent's Hospital in Los Angeles, where he died on July 16.

McKAY, CLAUDE (1890–1948), author. Born in Sunny Vale, West Indies, on Sept. 15, he studied there and wrote poetry in his youth, came to the United States in 1912, studied for a short time at Tuskegee Normal and Industrial Institute in Alabama and then transferred to Kansas State College, where he remained until 1914. He then went to New York City, worked as a porter and waiter, and wrote for *Pearsons Magazine* at the invitation of its editor Frank Harris. In 1918–22 he was an associate editor on the staffs of the *Liberator* and the *Dreadnought*, both revolutionary in tone, and then went to London, where his book of poems, *Spring in New Hampshire and Other Poems* (1920), was published. He became a spokesman

for the American Workers Party, left soon after for Russia, whose government appalled him, and spent the next twelve years in Europe. On his return to New York, he met Ellan Tarry, a writer and a convert to Catholicism, who helped him through illness in 1941–42. In 1944 he went to Chicago, became a Catholic, and worked for the Catholic Youth Organization and Friendship House there and died in Chicago on May 22. Among the leading black writings of the post World War I era, much of his earlier work was marked by extreme realism, and he was often exploited as the champion of causes never fully defined. He wrote poetry, such as *Harlem Shadows* (1922), and novels, among them *Home in Harlem* (1927), *Banjo* (1929), *Banana Bottom* (1933), and the autobiographical *A Long Way from Home* (1937).

McKEE, JOSEPH V. (1889–1956), mayor. Born in New York City on Aug. 18, he was educated at Fordham (B.A., M.A., LL.B, and LL.D.), taught Greek at Fordham for a term, married Cornelia E. Kraft in 1918, and served seven terms in the New York State legislature in 1918–24. He was appointed a judge in the New York City courts to fill an unexpired term in 1924–25, and then was elected for the full term but resigned in 1926 and was president of the New York City Board of Aldermen in 1926–33. He was acting mayor of the city in Sept.–Nov. 1932 when Mayor James J. Walker resigned as a result of the Seabury investigation. He resigned as president of the Board of Aldermen in 1933 to take up private law practice and was named president of the Title Guarantee and Trust Company in 1933. He died in New York City on Jan. 28.

McKENNA, BERNARD A. (1875–1960). Born in Philadelphia on July 8, he graduated from La Salle College there (B.A. 1895) and St. Charles Seminary and was ordained in 1903. He continued his studies at Catholic University (S.T.B. 1904, S.T.L. 1905) and the North American College, Rome (D.D. 1918) and served in several parishes in the Philadelphia archdiocese. In 1915 he was appointed first director of the National Shrine of the Immaculate Conception in Washington, D.C., helped raise funds, with Bishop Thomas Shahan, rector of Catholic University and founder of the Shrine, whose secretary he was, and supervised its construction. He taught theology at Catholic University in 1919–33, holding the chair of the Immaculate Conception there from 1925, was appointed a domestic prelate in 1929, and in 1933 became pastor of Holy Angels Church in Philadelphia, a position he held until his death in Philadelphia on July 20. He was president of the American Catholic Historical Society of Philadelphia in 1941–43 and was the author of several books, among them *The Immaculate Conception* (1929) and *Memoirs of the First Director of the National Shrine of the Immaculate Conception* (1959).

McKENNA, CHARLES HYACINTH (1834–1917), missionary. Born in Fillalea, Derry, Ireland, on May 8, he emigrated to the United States in 1859, entered Sinsinawa Mound College, Wisconsin, to study for the priesthood, and joined the Dominicans at St. Joseph's Priory, Somerset, Ohio, in 1863. He was ordained in Cincinnati, Ohio, in 1863, was novice master at St. Rose Priory, Springfield, Kentucky, in 1868–70, and was then sent to New York's St. Vincent Ferrer Church where, except for 1878–81 when he was pastor in Louisville, Kentucky, he remained until his retirement. He became known for his missionary preaching and was made a preacher general by the Dominicans in 1881 and was director general of the

Holy Name Society and Rosary Confraternity; it was mainly through his efforts that the Holy Name Society became so popular in the United States and he is often called "the apostle of the Holy Name Society." He wrote several devotional works, among them *How to Make the Mission* (1873) and *The Angelic Guide* (1899). He retired to the Dominican House of Studies in Washington, D.C., in 1914 and died in Jacksonville, Florida, on Feb. 21.

McKENNA, JOSEPH (1843–1926), Associate Justice of the United States Supreme Court. Born in Philadelphia on Aug. 10, he studied for the priesthood at St. Joseph's College there, decided he did not have a vocation for the priesthood, and continued his studies at Bernicia Collegiate Institute in California, where he graduated in 1865. He was admitted to the California bar the same year, practiced law and entered politics, and married Amanda Frances Borneman in 1869. He served in the state legislature in 1875–76, where he supported legislation regulating railroads in the state and requiring compulsory school attendance and opposed the use of public funds for private schools. He was defeated in three attempts to be elected to Congress in 1876, 1878, and 1880, in large measure because of his Catholicism, but he was successful in 1884 and was reelected for three subsequent terms. In Congress he supported railroads, high tariffs, anti-Chinese legislation, free silver and veterans' pensions, and voted against the establishment of the Interstate Commerce Commission in 1887. He resigned from Congress in 1897 when he was appointed United States Attorney General by President McKinley. He served only eight months when McKinley nominated him for Associate Justice of the Supreme Court. Despite vigorous opposition in the Senate, his nomination was confirmed and he served on the Court for twenty-seven years. He resigned from the Court in 1925 and died the following year in Washington, D.C., on Nov. 21.

McKEOUGH, MICHAEL J. (1892–1960), educator. Born in Green Bay, Wisconsin, on Sept. 18, he joined the Premonstratension Order (the Norbertines) in 1912, was educated at St. Norbert College, West De Pere, Wisconsin (B.A. 1914), was professed in 1914, and was ordained at St. Norbert's in 1917. He was a chaplain in World War I in 1918–19, continued his studies at Catholic University after the war (M.A. 1920, Ph.D. 1926) and was a founder and director of Camp Tivoli for boys in Cecil, Wisconsin, in 1925–30. He was professor of philosophy at St. Norbert's in 1928–32, headmaster at Archmere prep school for boys at Claymont, Delaware, in 1932–36 and principal of Southeast Catholic High School in Philadelphia in 1936–45, and taught education at Catholic University in 1945–51. He edited *Catholic Educational Review* in 1947–49, became head of the department of education at St. Norbert's in 1951 and dean in 1952, and died in Green Bay on June 5.

McKINNON, WILLIAM DANIEL (1858–1902). Born in Melrose, Prince Edward Island, Canada, on Aug. 1, he emigrated to California when he was seventeen, graduated from Santa Clara College, studied for the priesthood at Mission San José, California, and St. Mary's Seminary, Baltimore, and was ordained in 1887. He lectured widely, combating the American Protective Association's anti-Catholicism, served as chaplain for the 1st California Volunteers in the Spanish-American War in 1898 and during the American siege of Manila helped convince the Spanish commander of the helplessness of his situation and to surrender. He worked in the Philippines when the Americans took over, helped reestablish schools, directed relief work, and ministered to the victims of typhus and smallpox plagues that racked the islands, and died of an attack of amoebic dysentery in Manila on Sept. 25. A statue to his memory was erected in Golden Gate Park, San Francisco, with funds raised by civilian and military personnel.

McLAUGHLIN, CHARLES BORROMEO (1913–78), bishop. Born in New York City on Sept. 26, he was educated for the priesthood at St. Joseph's Seminary, Dunwoodie, Yonkers, New York, and St. John's Seminary, Little Rock, Arkansas, and was ordained in 1941. He was named titular bishop of Risinium and auxiliary of Raleigh, North Carolina, in 1964 and was appointed first bishop of the newly formed diocese of St. Petersburg, Florida, in 1968 and occupied that position until he died there on Dec. 14.

McLAUGHLIN, THOMAS HENRY (1881–1947), bishop. Born in New York City on July 15, he was educated at St. Francis Xavier College there (B.A. 1900) and the University of Innsbruck, Austria, and was ordained in 1904. He was a chaplain in Austria while studying for his S.T.D. at Innsbruck, which he received in 1908, and on his return to the United States the same year he became professor of theology at Seton Hall College, South Orange, New Jersey. He served as dean of Seton Hall in 1914–21, was president of the college in 1922–33, and was made a domestic prelate in 1923. He was named rector of Immaculate Conception Seminary, Darlington, New Jersey, and vicar-general of the diocese of Newark, New Jersey, in 1933. He was made a prothonotary the following year and in 1935 was named titular bishop of Nisa and auxiliary of Newark. He was appointed first bishop of the newly established diocese of Paterson, New Jersey, in 1937 and remained in that position until his death in Paterson on Mar. 17.

McLOUGHLIN, JOHN (1784–1857), pioneer, trader. Born in La Rivière du Loup, Quebec, Canada, on Oct. 19, he was raised at the home of his maternal grandmother when his father died when he was a boy. He studied in Canada and medicine in Scotland and became a doctor but soon gave up his practice to become a trader with the Northwest Fur Company. When it merged with the Hudson's Bay Company in 1821, he remained in charge of Fort William on Lake Superior, the company's chief place of business, and in 1824 was sent to Fort George (Astoria) near the mouth of the Columbia River as chief factor with supervision of the Columbia District. The following year he moved the company's headquarters to Fort Vancouver (Vancouver, Washington) on the northern side of the Columbia River; in the twenty-two years he was in charge of the company in the Columbia River area—then hotly contested by the British and the Americans—he used his power and authority to keep the Indians in check, treating them with fairness, and to expand trade. Though known as a stern businessman, he was noted for his justice and personal generosity and during his career, which was marked by the absence of Indian wars, he was on good terms with the missionaries of all denominations and was equally so with American settlers. He became a Catholic in 1842, aided the first of the Oregon homemaking immigrants, when they arrived in 1843, with food, clothing, and seed. Since most of these settlers were Americans, the Hudson's Bay Company, an English corporation, forced his resignation in 1846. He then settled in Oregon City, which he had founded and

developed, and in 1849 applied for American citizenship. A suit by Methodist ministers, whom he had once aided, deprived him of all his land on the grounds he was a British subject when he filed his land claim and hence, according to the Donation Land Law of 1850, the claim was invalid. He died heartbroken and a pauper in Oregon City on Sept. 3. Five years after his death the Oregon legislature restored his lands to his heirs. He was known as "the father of Oregon," and his statue was placed in the Capitol in Washington, D.C., to represent Oregon in 1953. His letters and reports to the governor and committee of the Hudson's Bay Company were published in three volumes in 1941–45.

McMAHON, BRIEN (1903–53), United States senator. James O'Brien McMahon was born in Norwalk, Connecticut, on Oct. 6 and was educated at Fordham (B.A. 1924) and studied law at Yale (LL.B. 1927), was admitted to the Connecticut bar in 1927, and began practicing law in Norwalk. He became a judge on the Norwalk City Court in 1933, resigned to become a special assistant to United States Attorney General Homer S. Cummings in 1933–35, and was Assistant Attorney General in charge of the Criminal Division of the Department of Justice in 1935–39 and specialized in tax and criminal cases. He left government service in 1939 to resume his private law practice, married Rosemary Turner in 1940, and was elected to the United States Senate in 1944 and again in 1950. Though only a freshman in the Senate in 1945, he sponsored that fall a bill to establish the special Committee on Atomic Energy and later became its chairman. He opposed granting the military control of atomic energy and played a major role in the passage of the Atomic Energy Act of 1946, which established the

Atomic Energy Commission, headed by civilians, which was given control of atomic energy. The law also established the Joint Committee on Atomic Energy, of which he was elected chairman in 1946, serving until 1948, and again became chairman in 1949. Deeply concerned about the threat of Communism to the free world, he advocated American reliance on atomic weapons for defense, fought successfully for the accelerated production of atomic bombs and the building up of a large stockpile, and was a leader in the fight to develop the hydrogen bomb. He also favored expanded use of atomic energy for civilian use. He was numbered among the liberal bloc in the Senate, supported President Truman's legislative program, proposed international arms reduction, and favored establishment of a fund for worldwide economic development to be administered by the United Nations. He also served on the Foreign Relations and Interstate Commerce Committees of the Senate and was a strong supporter of civil rights measures. He was proposed as Democratic candidate for the vice presidency by Connecticut Democrats in 1952, was forced to withdraw as a candidate because of serious illness when the Democratic National Convention convened, and died four days later in Washington, D.C., on July 28.

McMAHON, JOHN JOSEPH (1875–1932), bishop. Born in Hinsdale, New York, on Sept. 27, he was educated at St. Bonaventure College, Olean, New York, and the Propaganda, Rome, and was ordained in Rome in 1900. He engaged in pastoral activities in the Buffalo, New York, diocese, worked among the Italian immigrants, was assistant superintendent of schools in the Buffalo diocese in 1904, became chancellor of the see and then vicar-general, and was diocesan visitor to communities of nuns

in the diocese. He was appointed bishop of Trenton, New Jersey, in 1928, was especially known for his interest in the youth of the see during his five-year episcopate, and died in Buffalo on Dec. 31.

McMAHON, JOSEPH HENRY (1862–1939). Born in New York City on Nov. 18, he was educated at Manhattan College (B.A. 1880, M.A. 1881) and was ordained in 1886. He served as a curate at St. Patrick's Cathedral in 1886–1901, headed the Cathedral Free Circulating Library from its founding in 1887 until it was merged with the New York Public Library in 1904 and developed it into the largest Catholic circulating library in the United States. He organized the Cathedral Library Association in 1889 to raise funds to support it and was one of the founders of the Catholic Summer School of America in 1892. He was founding pastor of Our Lady of Lourdes parish in New York City in 1901, was made a domestic prelate in 1921, and died in New York City on Jan. 6.

McMAHON, LAWRENCE STEPHEN (1835–93), bishop. Born in St. Johns, New Brunswick, Canada, on Dec. 26, he was raised in Cambridge, Massachusetts, was educated at St. Mary's College, Baltimore, Holy Cross College, Worcester, Massachusetts, and in Montreal, France, and Italy and was ordained in Rome in 1860. He became an assistant at the Boston cathedral, served as chaplain of the 28th Massachusetts Regiment during the Civil War, was pastor in Bridgewater and New Bedford, Massachusetts, and was named first vicar-general of the diocese of Providence, Rhode Island, in 1872. He was appointed bishop of Hartford, Connecticut, in 1879, finished building St. Joseph's Cathedral and dedicated it in 1892, and greatly expanded the number of parishes, chapels, schools, and convents in his see. He died suddenly at Lakeville, Connecticut, on Aug. 21.

McMAHON, MARTIN THOMAS (1838–1903), soldier, jurist. Born in Laprairie, Canada, on Mar. 21, he was taken when an infant to the United States by his parents, who eventually settled in New York City. He was educated at St. John's College (Fordham), graduating in 1855, and then went to Buffalo to study law. He became a special agent of the post office and was sent to California, where he was admitted to the bar in Sacramento in 1861. At the outbreak of the Civil War, he raised the first cavalry company on the West Coast but resigned his captaincy when he learned the regiment was not to be sent east. He went to Washington, became an aide-de-camp to General George B. McClellan, and served in the Army of the Potomac throughout the war. He was awarded the Medal of Honor for his bravery at the battle of White Oak Swamp and was brevetted major general of volunteers by the end of the war. He resigned from the Army in 1866, was corporation counsel for New York City in 1866–67, and was minister to Paraguay in 1868–69. On his return he resumed his law practice in New York. He was city receiver of taxes in 1872–85, served as United States marshal for southern New York in 1883–89, was elected to the state Assembly in 1891 and the Senate in 1892 and was elected judge of the Court of General Sessions in 1896, a position he held until his death in New York City on Apr. 21.

McMAHON, THOMAS JOHN (1909–56). Born in Tuxedo Park, New York, on Apr. 5, he was educated at Cathedral College, New York City, graduating in 1926, St. Joseph's Seminary, Dunwoodie, Yonkers, New York, in 1928–30, and the Propaganda, Rome

(S.T.B. 1932), and was ordained in Rome in 1933. He continued his studies at the Gregorian (S.T.D. 1935), was administrator of Sacred Heart Church, Newburgh, New York, in 1936 and taught Church history at St. Joseph's Seminary in 1936–43. He became national secretary of the Catholic Near East Welfare Association in 1943 and was made a papal chamberlain in 1945 and a domestic prelate in 1948. He wrote articles for history periodicals, was editor of the United States Catholic Historical Society publications, and in 1949 was appointed president of the Pontifical Mission for Palestine, spending much of his time the next five years in the Near East. He resigned in 1954 because of ill health and became founding pastor of the Church of Our Saviour in New York City and was one of the organizers of the Fordham Conference on Eastern Rites. He died in New York City on Dec. 6.

McMASTER, JAMES ALPHONSUS (1820–86), editor. Son of a prominent Presbyterian minister, he was born in Duanesburg, New York, on Apr. 1, studied at Union College but left in 1839 before graduating, studied at Columbia and for the Episcopal priesthood at Union Theological Seminary, New York City, in 1840–44 but was converted to Catholicism in 1845 and decided he wanted to become a Catholic priest. He joined the Redemptorists and was sent to study at St. Trond, Belgium, with Isaac Hecker and Clarence Walworth, but soon decided he did not have a vocation for the priesthood and returned to the United States in 1846. He became a journalist as a writer for the New York *Tribune* and then the New York *Freeman's Journal and Catholic Register,* owned by Bishop John Hughes, and in 1848 bought the paper and was its editor until his death. Under his editorship it became the first Catholic magazine of national influence and circulation. He began quarreling almost immediately with Bishop Hughes over the Irish question, vigorously differed with Orestes Brownson on philosophical matters, and became a rabid abolitionist. His editorial attacks on the President and the policies of the federal government led to his arrest at the outbreak of the Civil War in 1861 and the suppression of *Freeman's Journal* when the United States postmaster declared it treasonable and seditious and barred it from the mail. He was imprisoned briefly at Fort Lafayette in 1861 but was allowed to resume publication in April 1862. Uncompromising in the positions he took and fiercely independent of any hierarchical interference, he was a strong supporter of Catholic education and, after the events of 1870 in Italy, of the papacy. His paper, at one time one of the most influential in the country, had little impact and small circulation by the time death ended his stormy career in Brooklyn, New York, on Dec. 29.

McMULLEN, JOHN (1832–83), bishop. Born in Ballynahinch, Down, Ireland, on Jan. 8, he studied for the priesthood at St. Mary of the Lake Seminary, Chicago, and the Propaganda, Rome, and was ordained in 1858. He engaged in pastoral work in the Chicago diocese in 1858–61, was pastor of St. Mary's Church in 1861–66, founded the short-lived *Catholic Monthly Magazine* in 1865, and continued his pastoral activities in 1861–81. He was named vicar-general of the Chicago diocese in 1877, was its administrator in 1879–80, and was consecrated first bishop of the newly established diocese of Davenport, Iowa, in 1881. He was a vigorous promoter of Catholic education, founded St. Ambrose College in Davenport in 1882, and died in Davenport on July 4.

McNAMARA, MARTIN DEWEY (1896–1966), bishop. Born in Chicago on May 12, he was educated at Cathedral College, St. Mary's Seminary, Baltimore, and Catholic University and was ordained in 1922. He taught at Quigley Preparatory Seminary, Chicago, in 1925–37, was named pastor of St. Francis Xavier Church, Wilmette, Illinois, in 1937 and was made a domestic prelate in 1946. He was consecrated first bishop of the newly established diocese of Joliet, Illinois, in 1949, greatly expanded the facilities of the see, especially educational institutions, dedicated St. Raymond Nonnatus Cathedral in 1955 and died in Rochester, Minnesota, on May 23.

McNEIRNY, FRANCIS (1828–94), bishop. Born in New York City on Apr. 25, he was educated at Montreal College and the Grand Seminary, Montreal, and was ordained in New York in 1854. He engaged in pastoral work in the New York archdiocese, was appointed chancellor of the see in 1857 and was secretary to Archbishop John Hughes in 1859, and was named titular bishop of Rhesina and coadjutor of Albany, New York, in 1871. He became administrator of the see in 1874 and succeeded to the see in 1877 as its third bishop. He brought several religious orders into the diocese, reorganized the chancery office, conducted regular clerical conferences and synods, and enlarged the Albany cathedral. He died in Albany on Jan. 2.

McNICHOLAS, JOHN TIMOTHY (1877–1950), archbishop. Born in Kiltimagh, Mayo, Ireland, on Dec. 15, Timothy was brought to the United States by his parents in 1881 when he was four years old. He was educated at St. Joseph's College, Philadelphia, St. Rose Priory, Springfield, Kentucky, St.

Joseph's House of Studies, Somerset, Ohio, and the Minerva, Rome (S.T.L. 1904, S.T.M. 1907). He joined the Dominicans in 1894, taking the name John, and was ordained in Somerset in 1901. He taught at the Dominican House of Studies at Somerset and was also master of novices, and the next year he was named regent of studies and a professor at the newly opened Dominican House of Studies, Immaculate Conception College at Catholic University. He became national director of the Holy Name Society (which was to achieve a membership of a million and a half men) and editor of the *Holy Name Journal* in 1909, continuing in these positions while also serving as pastor of St. Catherine of Siena Church in New York City in 1913–16. He became assistant to the master general of the Dominicans in Rome in 1917 and taught at the Angelicum. The following year he was appointed bishop of Duluth, Minnesota. He brought new religious orders into the diocese, established a mission band, devoted much attention to clerical training, and was made an Assistant at the Pontifical Throne in 1923. He was translated to Indianapolis, Indiana, in 1925 but never took possession of the see, since he was appointed archbishop of Cincinnati, Ohio, later that year. During his quarter-century episcopate at Cincinnati, he sponsored convert programs and an apostolate to blacks, built up the educational facilities of the archdiocese, and encouraged post graduate study for his priests, championed the rights of labor, founded the Athenaeum of Ohio in Cincinnati, and opened the Institutum Divi Thomae in 1935. He fought for social and racial justice, firmly believed in the principle of separation of church and state, and was an uncompromising foe of Communism. He was episcopal chairman of the education department of the National Catholic Welfare Conference (NCWC)

in 1930–35 and 1942–45, was president of the National Catholic Educational Association in 1946–50, was chairman of the episcopal committee on motion pictures, which founded the Legion of Decency, in 1933–43, and was chairman of the administrative board of the NCWC for five terms, 1945–50. He died in Cincinnati on Apr. 22.

McNICHOLAS, JOSEPH A. (1923–83), bishop. Born in St. Louis on Jan. 13, he was educated at Cardinal Glennon College and Kenrick Seminary and St. Louis University and was ordained for the St. Louis archdiocese in 1949. He was assistant pastor of the St. Louis cathedral from 1949 to 1955, when he became assistant pastor of Most Holy Name of Jesus parish in St. Louis, and in 1966 he became chaplain of St. Joseph's Home for Boys in St. Louis. He was named titular bishop of Scala and auxiliary bishop of St. Louis in 1969 and was named pastor of the old cathedral, the Basilica of St. Louis, the same year and in 1975 was appointed sixth bishop of Springfield, Illinois. He died of a coronary thrombosis at St. John's Hospital, Springfield, on Apr. 17.

McNICHOLS, JOHN PATRICK (1875–1932), educator. Born in St. Louis on Feb. 24, he was educated at St. Louis University and St. Stanislaus Seminary, Missouri, joined the Jesuits in 1891, and was ordained in 1906. He taught at Xavier College, Cincinnati, Ohio, and Champion College, Prairie du Chien, Wisconsin, was dean at Marquette in 1919–21, and was president of the University of Detroit from 1921 until his death at Ann Arbor, Michigan, on Apr. 26. During his presidency of the University of Detroit, he inaugurated an expansion program and established a department of aeronautical engineering and a graduate school; he was also the author of several textbooks on rhetoric.

McNULTY, JAMES A. (1900–72), bishop. Born in New York City on Jan. 16, he was educated at Seton Hall College, South Orange, New Jersey (M.A. 1923), Immaculate Conception Seminary, Darlington, New Jersey, and the Louvain, Belgium, and was ordained at Louvain in 1925. He served as assistant pastor in Jersey City and Newark, was diocesan director of the Confraternity of Christian Doctrine, taught at the Teachers Institute for Religious, and in 1947 was named titular bishop of Methone and auxiliary of Newark, New Jersey. He helped increase the number of parishes and high schools in the archdiocese and founded the archdiocesan newspaper, *The Advocate,* and in 1953 he was appointed bishop of Paterson, New Jersey. He was transferred to Buffalo, New York, in 1963 and was praised for his commitment to social justice but was severely criticized for his retrenchment policy, which led to the closing of several schools and the curtailment of many diocesan agencies, all of which was forced upon him by the huge debt he had inherited. He died in Buffalo on Sept. 4.

McQUAID, BERNARD JOHN (1823–1909), bishop. Son of Irish immigrants, he was born in New York City on Dec. 15, was raised by the Sisters of Charity at St. Patrick's Orphanage there when he was orphaned in 1832, when he was nine, and was educated at Chambly College near Montreal and St. John's Seminary, Fordham. He was ordained in New York in 1848, was assistant to the pastor at Madison, New Jersey, and in 1853, when the diocese of Newark, New Jersey, was established, was appointed rector of the cathedral there. He helped found Seton Hall College, South Orange, New Jersey, in 1856

and was its president in 1856–68, served as chaplain to the New Jersey Brigade during the Civil War, and was captured by the Confederates. He was named vicar-general of Newark in 1866 and attended the second Plenary Council of Baltimore later that year as a theologian. He was appointed first bishop of Rochester, New York, when that diocese was established in 1868. A firm believer in Catholic education, he built an outstanding parochial school system in the diocese, establishing some forty elementary schools, founded sixty-nine new parishes, built many charitable institutions, was instrumental in having a law passed that provided for paid chaplains in state penal and welfare institutions, brought new religious orders into the diocese, and expanded every activity of the see. He founded St. Andrew's Preparatory Seminary in 1870 and opened St. Bernard's Seminary, which became a model seminary for the whole country, in 1893, fought unsuccessfully for funds for public schools from the state, and opposed the attendance of Catholic children at public schools. He attended Vatican Council I in 1869–70 and opposed the definition of papal infallibility as inopportune at that time but accepted the dogma when it was passed by the Council and proclaimed by Pope Pius IX. He and his friend Archbishop Michael Corrigan of New York were leaders of the conservative faction of the American hierarchy and opposed the liberal Americanizers headed by Archbishop John Ireland of St. Paul, with whom he clashed repeatedly, and John Keane, rector of Catholic University and later bishop of Dubuque, Iowa, and Denis O'Connell, rector of the North American College in Rome. He supported Archbishop Corrigan in the McGlynn affair, strongly opposed the Faribault Plan advanced by Archbishop Ireland in 1891, and denounced Ireland to Rome when the archbishop of St. Paul supported Benjamin Harrison, a Republican, for the presidency in 1892, on the grounds that the Republican Party was supported by the anti-Catholic American Protective Association and hence Ireland was disloyal to the Church when he supported the Republican Party. Always insensitive to any infringement of his jurisdiction, he was critical of Cardinal Gibbons for his favorable attitude toward the Americanists and for the jurisdiction Gibbons exercised as head of the unofficial primatial see of the United States. He opposed the appointment of an apostolic delegate to the United States and in 1894 denounced Ireland from his cathedral pulpit for Ireland's support of Sylvester Malone, a Brooklyn priest and supporter of Fr. McGlynn, for a seat on the board of regents of New York's state university against McQuaid, an action he felt was an unwarranted intrusion of an outsider in New York affairs. He died in Rochester on Jan. 18.

McSHANE, DANIEL L. (1888–1927), missionary. Born in Columbus, Indiana, on Sept. 13, he was educated at St. Joseph's, joined the Catholic Foreign Missionary Society of America (Maryknoll), was one of the Society's first six novices, continued his studies at St. Mary's Seminary, Baltimore, and in 1914 was the first Maryknoll candidate to be ordained a priest at St. Patrick's Cathedral in New York City. He taught at the Maryknoll Vénard minor seminary, Scranton, Pennsylvania, for a time, headed the Maryknoll house in San Francisco, and was sent to China as a missionary in 1919. He worked in the Kwangtung province, opened an orphanage at Loting, and died, on June 4, of smallpox he caught from a child who had been left at the orphanage.

McSHERRY, JAMES (1819–69), author. Born at Liberty Town, Maryland, on July 29, he graduated from Mt. St. Mary's College, Emmitsburg, Maryland, in 1838, studied law, and was admitted to the bar in 1840. He set up practice in Gettysburg, Pennsylvania, but returned to Maryland and married Eliza Spurrier in 1841 (their oldest of five children, James, became chief justice of the Maryland Court of Appeals) and practiced law at Frederick City until his death there on July 13. He wrote several books, among them *History of Maryland* (1849) and *Père Jean, or the Jesuit Missionary* (1849).

McSHERRY, JAMES (1842–1907), jurist. Son of James McSherry and Eliza Spurrier McSherry, he was born in Frederick, Maryland, on Dec. 30, and was a student at Mt. St. Mary's College, Emmitsburg, Maryland. His studies were interrupted when he was arrested and imprisoned at Fort McHenry, Baltimore, in 1861 because of his outspoken support of the Confederacy. After his release, he studied law at his father's office, was admitted to the bar in 1864, and married Louise McAleer in 1866. He was appointed to the Maryland Circuit Court of Appeals in 1887 and was elected to the full term later that year. He was appointed chief justice of the Maryland Court of Appeals in 1896 and occupied that position until his death in Frederick on Oct. 23.

McSHERRY, RICHARD (1817–85), physician. Son of a physician, he was born in Martinsburg, Virginia (now West Virginia), on Nov. 21, was educated at Georgetown and the University of Maryland, studied medicine at the University of Pennsylvania, and received his M.D. in 1841 after having served as assistant surgeon in the Army in 1838–40 during the Seminole War. He was assistant surgeon in the Navy from 1843 until 1856, when he went into private practice in Baltimore. He was one of the founders and first president of the Baltimore Academy of Medicine, wrote for medical journals and several books, and died in Baltimore on Oct. 7.

McSORLEY, JOSEPH (1874–1963), superior, author. Born in Brooklyn, New York, on Dec. 9, he was educated at St. John's College there (B.A. 1891, M.A. 1893), joined the Paulists in 1896 and continued his studies at Catholic University, where he became the first Paulist to receive his doctorate in sacred theology in 1897. He was ordained later that year in New York City, served as a curate at St. Paul's Church in New York in 1897–99 and was master of novices at St. Thomas College, Washington, D.C., in 1902–7. He then returned to New York City, where he became known for his retreats at St. Paul's, was chaplain in the United States Army in World War I in 1918–19, was pastor of St. Paul's in 1919–24, and served as superior general of the Paulists in 1924–29. While superior, he began radio station WLWL, the first Catholic radio station in the United States. He spent the next three years in mission work at St. Peter's Church in Toronto and then returned to New York, where he remained until his death there on July 3. He was a contributing editor to the *Catholic World* from 1932 and the author of numerous books, among them *A Primer of Prayer* (1934), *An Outline History of the Church by Centuries* (1943), and *Father Hecker and His Friends* (1952).

McVINNEY, RUSSELL J. (1898–1971), bishop. Born in Warren, Rhode Island, on Nov. 25, he was educated at St. Charles College, Ellicott City, Mary-land, St. Bernard's Seminary, Rochester, New York, and the American College, Louvain, and was ordained in Louvain in 1924. He was a curate at St. Patrick's Church, Harrisville, in 1924–29 and assistant pastor at Pawtucket, in 1929–35, both in Rhode Island, and at the same time taught at St. Raphael's Academy. He left St. Edward's in 1935 to study journalism for a year at Notre Dame. On his return he was assigned to SS. Peter and Paul Cathedral in Providence and was associate editor on the diocesan paper, the *Providence Visitor*. He became rector of Our Lady of Providence Seminary, Warwick, Rhode Island, in 1941 and served in that position until he was appointed bishop of Providence, Rhode Island, in 1948, the first native Rhode Islander to hold that position. He expanded the educational and charitable facilities of the diocese, enlarged the diocesan seminary at Warwick, and founded the Sisters of Our Lady of Providence in 1955 and the Brothers of Our Lady of Providence in 1959. He died at his summer home at Watch Hill, Rhode Island, on Aug. 10.

MEADE, GEORGE (1741–1808), merchant. Grandfather of General George Meade of Civil War fame, he was born in Philadelphia on Feb. 27, was educated on Barbados, where his father had lived for a time, and captained a vessel trading between Barbados and Philadelphia in his youth. He and his brother established the firm of Garrett and George Meade in Philadelphia and engaged in importing and shipping and built up an extensive and profitable business; it became George Meade & Company with his brother-in-law, Thomas FitzSimons, his partner when Garrett retired. He was a fervent patriot, contributed large sums to the cause of the patriots, and served on various committees and the Public Defence Association during the Revolution. He served on the Philadelphia Common Council in 1789–99 and chaired the board of management of Philadelphia prisons, was one of the original members of the Friendly Sons of St. Patrick in 1771, and an incorporator of the Hibernian Society in 1792. He helped in the building and founding of St. Mary's Church in Philadelphia. His investments in undeveloped land in various sections of the country in 1795 were adversely affected by the financial crisis of 1796 and eventually, in 1801, he was obliged to go into bankruptcy. He died in Philadelphia on Nov. 9.

MEADE, RICHARD WORSAM (1807–70), naval officer. Grandson of George Meade and brother of General George Gordon Meade, he was born in Cádiz, Spain, where his father was naval agent for the United States, returned to the United States with his mother when he was ten, and was educated at St. Mary's College, Baltimore. He was appointed a midshipman from Pennsylvania in 1826, served on cruises in the Pacific in 1827–30, the West Indies in 1833–35, and during the Mexican War on the *Scorpion* and the *Potomac.* He was commander of the *Massachusetts* on a Pacific cruise in 1853–55 and was made a commander in 1855, served on the receiving ship *North Carolina* in New York during the early days of the Civil War, and in 1862 was made captain of the *San Jacinto,* which grounded in the Bahama Islands in 1865. Though his heroic efforts saved all on board and the ship's supplies, he was suspended for three years by a court-martial, retired on disability resulting from injuries sustained in the shipwreck, and suffered a stroke and died in Brooklyn, New York, on Apr. 16.

MEADE, RICHARD WORSAM III (1837–97), admiral. Son of Captain Richard Worsam Meade, he was born in New York City on Oct. 9 and was appointed to the United States Naval Academy when he was thirteen and graduated in 1856. He was with the Pacific squadron when the Civil War broke out but was invalided home with fever in 1861 and became ordnance instructor in Boston on the receiving ship *Ohio.* He was in command of the *Louisville* with the Mississippi squadron in 1862, returned to New York the same year with a reoccurrence of his illness, and was in charge of the naval battalion during the draft riots in New York City in July 1863. He was put in command of the *Marblehead* on the Charleston blockade in 1863–64 and for gallantry in action against batteries at Storm Inlet, North Carolina, in 1863 was commended; he then commanded the *Chocura* in the Gulf of Mexico until the end of the war. He taught at the Naval Academy in 1865–68, was promoted to commander in 1868, commanded the *Narragansett* on a 60,000-mile cruise in the Pacific in 1871–73, made the first American treaty with Samoa for a coaling station in Tutuila in 1872, and was then assigned to ordnance duty in Brooklyn. He commanded the *Vandalia,* North Atlantic squadron, in 1879–82, was commander of the *Dolphin* in 1885–86, and was president of the Navy Board of Inventory, which revised the Navy's accounting system, in 1886–87. He was commandant of the Washington Navy Yard in 1887–90 with the rank of captain and was appointed commander of the North Atlantic squadron. He was made a rear admiral in 1894. He resigned in 1895, retired to Germantown, Pennsylvania, and died of appendicitis in Washington, D.C., on May 4. He wrote *Manual of the Boat Exercise at the U.S. Naval Academy* (1868) and *A Treatise on Naval Architecture* (1868) and articles on naval subjects. He translated several French naval treatises.

MEAGHER, THOMAS FRANCIS (1823–67), general, patriot. Son of a wealthy merchant who served for a time in Parliament, he was born in Waterford, Ireland, on Aug. 23. He studied at the Jesuit college of Clongowes Wood in Kildare in 1833–39 and the English college at Stonyhurst in 1839–43 and became known for his oratorical prowess. He was an early supporter of Daniel O'Connell but broke with him over his moderate policies, demanding more radical and revolutionary action. He joined the Young Ireland party in 1845, was one of the founders of the Irish Confederacy and a member of its so-called "War Directory," and in 1848 went to Paris seeking aid for it. On his return he was arrested for a fiery speech he delivered in Dublin and charged with sedition. He was found guilty of treason at a trial in Clonmel in October 1848 and sentenced to be hanged, but the sentence was commuted in 1849 and he was banished to the penal colony of Tasmania. He married the daughter of a farmer there in 1851 and the following year escaped and went to New York City, where he received a hearty welcome from his countrymen there. He lectured, studied law, and was admitted to the bar in 1855. He became editor of the *Irish News* the following year and the leader of the Irish in New York. He married Elizabeth Townsend in 1855 (his first wife had died the previous year) and was on an exploring trip to Central America in 1857, which he described in an article in *Harper's Magazine* on his return. At the outbreak of the Civil War, he joined the Union Army with the 69th New York Volunteers and then organized the Irish Brigade in New York City in 1861–62. He was its brigadier general. He resigned as its commander in 1863 when it was almost annihilated in battles at Second Bull Run, Antietam, Chancellorsville, and Fredericksburg, where he was wounded, and was not allowed to recruit new members. He was recommissioned in 1864 and put in command of the military district of Etowah, Tennessee. Later he was assigned to General William T. Sherman's forces in Savannah, where he was mustered out of service. In 1865 he was appointed Territorial Secretary of Montana by President Johnson. His strong support of President Johnson's Reconstruction policies caused great hostility toward him in the Territory and two years later he drowned under mysterious circumstances when he fell from a steamer at Fort Benton, Missouri, on July 1 while on a tour of the Territory.

MEANY, GEORGE (1894–1980), labor leader. Son of a plumber, he was born in New York City on Aug. 16, became a plumber's apprentice in 1910 and a journeyman in 1915, when he was admitted to the union and became involved in union affairs. He was business manager of Plumbers Local Union No. 463 in New York in 1922–34, was elected president of the New York State Federation of Labor in 1934, and was unanimously elected secretary-treasurer of the American Federation of Labor (AFL) in 1939. He was appointed to the National Defense Mediation Board by President Franklin Roosevelt in 1941, was a strong supporter of the reunion of the AFL and the Congress of Industrial Organizations (CIO), strongly opposed the Taft-Hartley Act, defeated John L. Lewis's bid for a place on the executive council of the AFL (which led to Lewis's withdrawal of the United Mine Workers of America from the AFL at the AFL Convention in 1947), and made several trips to trade union conventions in Europe, where he denounced Communism. In 1952, on the death of William Green, Meany was elected president of the AFL by its executive council. and the selection was unanimously affirmed at the AFL convention in St. Louis the following year by the membership. He continued efforts to heal the breach between the AFL and CIO, and in 1955, when the two labor organizations were reunited, he was elected president of the merged AFL-CIO and served in that position until 1979. Throughout his career, Meany labored for better wages and working conditions for his union people, the elimination of Communism and racketeering from locals, and the rights of labor. He died in Washington, D.C., on Jan. 1.

MEDEIROS, HUMBERTO SOUSA (1915–83), cardinal. Born in Arrifes, São Miguel Island, in the Azores on Oct. 6, he emigrated to the United States in 1931 with his parents, who settled in Fall River, Massachusetts. He began working in a textile mill, sweeping floors while attending high school, studied for the priesthood at Catholic University, earning his master's degree and licentiate in sacred theology, became an American citizen in 1940, and was ordained in 1946. He served as assistant pastor at Fall River, New Bedford, and Somerset, Massachusetts, and continued his studies at North American College, Rome. He became assistant chancellor of the diocese of Fall River in 1952, when he also received his doctorate in theology from Catholic University, and then became chancellor and vicar for the religious in the diocese. He was named pastor of St. Michael's Church, Fall River, in 1960 and six years later was appointed bishop of Brownsville, Texas. He became a champion of immigrant workers there, often traveling with them, vigorously supported labor unions, helped sponsor housing projects for the poor, and established eighteen new parishes. He also served as chairman of the American bishops' committee on Latin America

and the committee on farm labor. He was appointed archbishop of Boston in 1970 to succeed retiring Cardinal Richard Cushing—the first person of non-Irish heritage to be archbishop of that see. He was an unrelenting foe of abortion, initiated parish reforms in the archdiocese, and continued his support of labor unions. He was made a cardinal in 1973 and died in Boston ten years later on Sept. 17 after undergoing emergency heart surgery.

MEEHAN, THOMAS FRANCIS (1854–1942), editor, historian. Born in Brooklyn, New York, on Sept. 19, he was educated at St. Francis Xavier College, New York City (B.A. 1873, M.A. 1874), decided to pursue a journalism career, and was appointed managing editor of *The Irish American* by its owner, his father, in 1874 and served in that position until 1904. He was also New York correspondent for the Baltimore *Sun* in 1888–94 and for the Philadelphia *Ledger* in 1896–1902, was on the staff of the New York *Herald* in 1894–96, and was assistant managing editor of The Catholic Encyclopedia in 1906–9, contributing more than a hundred articles to it. He joined the editorial staff of *America* in 1909, when that magazine was founded, and served on it until his death. He contributed articles to numerous magazines, was president of the United States Catholic Historical Society and became editor of its *Records and Studies* in 1916, after having collaborated with Charles J. Herbermann, president and editor of the Society since 1905, and was also editor and helped prepare the five-volume *Catholic Builders of the Nation* (1925). He died in New York City on July 7.

MEERSCHAERT, THEOPHILE (1847–1924), bishop. Born in Roussignies, Belgium, on Aug. 24, he studied at Renaix, Audenarde, and the American College, Louvain, and was ordained in Mechlin (Malines), Belgium, in 1871. He emigrated to the United States the following year, engaged in missionary work in Mississippi, was named rector of St. Mary's Cathedral in Natchez in 1880, and became vicar-general of the diocese. He was its administrator in 1888, was appointed titular bishop of Sidyma and first vicar apostolic of the Oklahoma and Indian Territories in 1891, and ministered to the Indians and white settlers of that area. When Oklahoma City was established as a diocese in 1905, he was appointed its first bishop. He increased the number of priests, religious, and churches in the diocese, was made an Assistant at the Pontifical Throne in 1916, and died in Oklahoma City on Feb. 21.

MEHEGAN, MOTHER MARY XAVIER (1825–1915), foundress. Born in Skibbereen, Cork, Ireland, on Feb. 15, Catherine Josephine Mehegan went to the United States in 1844 with her sister Margaret and joined the New York Sisters of Charity in 1847, taking the name Mary Xavier. With two other sisters she opened St. Vincent's Hospital in New York City. In 1858 she and Sister Mary Catherine Nevin were invited by Bishop James Bayley of Newark, New Jersey, to train five novices and the following year the community was formally inaugurated in Newark, the founding of the New Jersey Sisters of Charity. During the Civil War the sisters worked in Trenton and Newark hospitals, and after the war the congregation expanded into New York, Connecticut, and Massachusetts, with its mother house in Madison, New Jersey. In 1899 Mother Xavier founded the College of St. Elizabeth at Convent Station, New Jersey, the state's first college for women. She died at Convent Station on June 24 after having been superior for fifty-seven years.

MELCHER, JOSEPH (1807–73), bishop. Born in Vienna on Mar. 19, he studied at the Modena, Italy, seminary, was ordained there in 1930, and the following year was a chaplain at the ducal court. He emigrated to the United States, engaged in pastoral work in Little Rock, Arkansas, became vicar-general of the St. Louis archdiocese, and in 1855 declined an appointment as bishop of Quincy, Illinois. He was appointed first bishop of the newly established diocese of Green Bay, Wisconsin, in 1868 and held that position until his death there on Dec. 20.

MEMBRE, ZENOBIUS (1645–87), missionary. Born in Bapaume, Pas-de-Calais, France, he joined the Franciscan Recollet Fathers of St. Joseph Province and after his ordination was sent on the Canadian mission in 1675. He accompanied La Salle to the Illinois country in 1675 and worked among the Illinois Indians, with little success, and in 1682 accompanied La Salle on his epic-making trip down the Mississippi River to the Gulf of Mexico. He then returned to Europe, was made superior of the Franciscan monastery at Bapaume, and in 1684 again accompanied La Salle, on his ill-fated expedition to the Gulf of Mexico. He was killed during an Indian massacre two years later at Fort St. Louis, which the expedition had built on the Texas shore.

MÉNARD, RENÉ (1604–61?), missionary. Born in Paris, he joined the Jesuits and after his ordination was sent on the Canadian mission in 1640. He worked among the Hurons and Iroquois in 1641–50 and in 1659 set out for the West. He established a post at Keweenaw Bay in Upper Wisconsin in 1661, visited groups of Catholic Hurons in the Chippewa and Black rivers region, and then crossed the Wisconsin River and ascended it on the way to the land of the Dakotas. He was never heard from again and is believed to have been murdered by a band of Sioux Indians near the site of present-day Merrill, Wisconsin, after he became separated from his guides at a portage.

MENGARINI, GREGORIO (1811–86), missionary. Born in Rome on July 21, he joined the Jesuits in 1828, taught grammar at Rome, Modena, and Reggio, studied at the Roman College, and was ordained in 1840. Impressed by an appeal from Bishop Rosati of St. Louis for priests to work as missionaries in 1839, he went to the United States, spent a short time at Georgetown, and in 1841 accompanied Fr. De Smet to minister to the Flathead Indians in Montana. When the mission to the Flatheads was closed in 1849, he went to Oregon and the following year to California, where he helped to establish Santa Clara mission, which in time was to grow into the University of Santa Clara. He spent the rest of his life at Santa Clara, serving as treasurer and vice president for thirty years until ill health and failing sight caused his retirement. He died at Santa Clara on Sept. 23. He was the author of several linguistic studies, among them *Salish or Flathead Grammar* and *A Dictionary of the Kalispel or Flathead Indian Language* (two volumes, 1877–79).

MERCER, MABEL (1900–84), singer. Born in Burton-on-Trent, Staffordshire, England, on Feb. 3, of a black American, who died before she was born, and a white English vaudevillian and actress whose family was in show business, she joined her family's act as a dancer when she was fourteen. After World War I she became a member of a quartet in Paris and when the quartet broke up she began singing on her own and built a reputation for her unique style, characterized by her phrasing and ability to inter-

pret and convey to her audiences the emotional sense of a lyric. She came to the United States in 1928 and soon developed a devoted following, including many singing stars of popular music whose own styles were influenced by hers, among them Frank Sinatra, Billie Holiday, Nat "King" Cole, and Bobby Short. She performed at night spots, cafes, and on the concert stage, retired in 1979 but returned to the stage briefly to appear at several benefit concerts in 1982. She was awarded the Medal of Freedom by President Reagan in 1983 and died the following year of heart disease in the Berkshire Medical Center, Pittsfield, Massachusetts, on April 20.

MERRICK, MARY VIRGINIA (1866–1955), social worker. Of an old Maryland family, she was born in Washington, D.C., on Nov. 2, was crippled in her youth and spent her entire life in a wheelchair or in bed. She was educated privately, was early interested in helping the poor, and in 1886 founded the Christ Child Society to provide for the heads of families of poor children at Christmas. It expanded its activities by establishing summer camps, a boys' club, a settlement house, and a convalescent home. In time the Society spread to other cities and by the time of her death there were thirty-seven chapters with some twelve thousand workers. She served as president of the Society until her death, was awarded the Laetare Medal in 1915 and other honors, and died in Washington, D.C., on Jan. 10. She was the author of *The Altar of God* (1920) and translated *Life of Christ for Children* and *Acts of the Apostles* from the French.

MERTON, THOMAS (1915–68), monk, author. Son of Owen Merton, a New Zealand artist, and American Ruth Jenkins, he was born in Prades, France, on Jan. 31 and spent his youth traveling in Europe and England. He was educated at a French lycée in Montauban, France, an English private school, Ripley Court, and Cambridge. His mother died when he was six and his father when he was sixteen. He came to the United States in 1932 to live with his mother's parents, attended Columbia, where he edited the yearbook, *The Columbian,* in 1937, received his B.A. in 1938 and his M.A. in 1939, and was a candidate for the Rensselaer Poetry Prize in 1939. He taught at Columbia briefly, joined a group of young Communists, and served in a Catholic settlement house in Harlem. In 1938 he became a Catholic. He taught at St. Bonaventure University, Olean, New York, in the summer of 1941, decided to become a priest, and in December joined the Trappists at Gethsemani, Kentucky, taking the name of Louis. He made his solemn vows in 1949 and was ordained in 1949. A writer from the days of his childhood, he wrote his autobiography, *The Seven-Storey Mountain,* describing his spiritual pilgrimage leading to Catholicism and the Trappists, and it became an immediate bestseller on publication in 1948. Over the next decades he was to write scores of books of poetry, on spirituality and contemplation, on the Trappists, on the problems of the world and religious, and on Far Eastern religions. Through his often controversial writings, which caused his superiors to pronounce a ban on his writing twice, he became a leader in the struggle for civil rights and racial justice, in the ecumenical movement, the antiwar movement, and the renewal of monastic life. He served as novice master at Gethsemani for ten years, resigned as novice master in 1965 to live as a hermit on the monastery's grounds, and in 1968 went to the Far East to attend a number of religious conferences and to address a meeting of Asian Christian contemplatives at Bangkok,

Thailand. He died there on Dec. 10 when a faulty electric fan he was moving fell on him and electrocuted him. Among his best-known books are: *Thirty Poems* (1944), *The Waters of Siloe* (1949), *Seeds of Contemplation* (1949), *The Ascent to Truth* (1951), *The Sign of Jonas* (1952), *No Man Is an Island* (1955), *Conjectures of a Guilty Bystander* (1966), and *Mystics and Zen Masters* (1967). He also wrote novels but destroyed all of them except *My Argument with the Gestapo,* published posthumously in 1969. His reflections on his fateful last journey, *The Asian Journal of Thomas Merton,* was also published posthumously, in 1973.

MESSMER, SEBASTIAN GEBHARD (1847–1930), archbishop. Born in Goldach, Switzerland, on Aug. 29, he was educated at St. George Seminary, St. Gall, Switzerland, the University of Innsbruck, Austria, and later in 1888 at the Apollinaris, Rome (D.C.L.). He was ordained in Innsbruck in 1871 and went to the United States later that year, where he taught theology at Seton Hall College, South Orange, New Jersey, until 1889. He was a secretary for the third Plenary Council of Baltimore in 1884, helped draft its decrees and, with Denis O'Connell (appointed rector of the North American College in Rome the next year), edited them for publication. He went to Catholic University in 1889 and taught canon law until 1891, when he was appointed bishop of Green Bay, Wisconsin. While bishop there he built schools, asylums, and hospitals, supported the Germans in their controversies with the Irish, vigorously opposed the Bennett Law of 1893, which required that English be used in all schools, opposed socialism, and supported efforts to settle Catholic immigrants in rural areas. He supported Peter Cahensly's petition to Rome for better representation of foreign nationalities in the American hierarchy and opposed Archbishop John Ireland's Faribault Plan for Catholic schools. He was translated to Milwaukee, where he was made an archbishop in 1903 and was appointed an Assistant at the Pontifical Throne in 1906. During his twenty-six-year episcopate in Milwaukee he became most influential among the German-speaking Catholics of the Midwest and used that influence for the support of the United States war effort in World War I. He greatly expanded the number of schools, hospitals, and charitable institutions in the archdiocese, was a staunch supporter of Catholic education, and was responsible for the appointment of a Catholic chaplain at the University of Wisconsin in 1904. He edited and wrote several canonical treatises and wrote articles for scholarly journals. He died in Goldach on Aug. 4.

MEŠTROVIĆ, IVAN (1883–1962), sculptor. Born in Vrpolje, Slavonia, Austria (now in Yugoslavia), on Aug. 15, he was a shepherd when a boy and then was apprenticed to a marble cutter. He studied carving under his father, went to Split in 1898 and studied under Pavle Bilinić, and in 1900–4 studied at the Vienna Academy of Fine Arts under Edmund von Hellmer. He went to Paris in 1907, where he was befriended by Auguste Rodin, and won international recognition for his talent as a sculptor at the Serbian Pavilion at the International Exhibition in Rome in 1911 when he was awarded first prize. He became noted for his bold modern sculptures, many in wood, and was a leader in the nationalistic art revival. He was rector at the Academy of Fine Arts in Zagreb, Croatia, in 1923–41, was imprisoned for four and a half months in 1941 during World War II for his pro-Allied leanings but was freed through Vatican intervention and went to Switzerland. He refused to live under Tito's dictatorship in

Yugoslavia after the war, lived in Rome for a time, and then came to the United States in 1947. He had a one-man exhibit at the Metropolitan Museum of Art, the first living sculptor to be so honored, and headed the department of plastic art at the University of Syracuse in 1947–55. He became an American citizen in 1954 and the following year went to Notre Dame, where he remained until his death in South Bend, Indiana, on Jan. 16. He received the gold Award of Merit for sculpture from the American Academy of Arts and Letters in 1953, was elected to that body in 1960, and was honored by numerous universities and colleges. Among his outstanding pieces are his statue of the Serbian hero Marko Kraljević, sculptures commemorating the battle of Kosovo, a war memorial in Canada, his Pietà at Notre Dame, his Mary, Queen of the Universe at the Shrine of the Immaculate Conception, Washington, D.C., St. Francis of Assisi, My Mother at Prayer, sculptures of Pope Pius XII, Cardinal Stepinac, and President Herbert Hoover and two equestrian statues of North American Indians in Grant Park, Chicago.

MEYER, ALBERT GREGORY (1903–65), cardinal. Son of a German-American grocery store owner, he was born in Milwaukee, Wisconsin, on Mar. 9 and was early attracted to the religious life. He was educated at St. Francis Seminary, Milwaukee, and the North American College and the Urban College of the Propaganda in Rome, and was ordained in Rome in 1926. He received his S.T.D. from the North American College in 1927, continued his education at the Pontifical Biblical Institute (S.S.L. in 1929), and then served as a curate at St. Joseph's parish, Waukesha, Wisconsin, for a year. He joined the faculty of St. Francis Seminary in 1931, was named its rector in

1937, became a monsignor in 1938, and was named sixth bishop of Superior, Wisconsin, in 1946. He inaugurated a construction and renovation program, established a diocesan edition of the Milwaukee *Herald-Citizen,* held a diocesan synod and established the diocesan Council of Catholic Women in 1950. He was appointed archbishop of Milwaukee, Wisconsin, in 1953 and again inaugurated in his new see an extensive expansion program, establishing new parishes, building new schools and churches, and enlarging existing institutions of higher learning. He encouraged the growth of lay organizations, instituted new administrative procedures, and was elected to the administrative board of the National Catholic Welfare Conference (NCWC) in 1956, where he was chairman of its education department. He was chairman of the National Catholic Education Association in 1956–57 and from 1953 was a member of the American Board of Catholic Missions. He was translated to Chicago in 1958 and made a cardinal by Pope John XXIII the following year. He vigorously supported efforts to obtain social justice for blacks, ended segregation in all Catholic institutions in Chicago in 1961, and was a leader in the ecumenical and liturgical movements. He embarked on a tremendous expansion program of church facilities in the archdiocese, creating thirty new parishes, constructing seventy-three churches and sixty-nine new elementary schools, while building additions to eighty-two schools, fifteen new high schools, forty-one convents, thirty-seven rectories, six hospitals, and four homes for the aged. He reorganized archdiocesan finances, established an archdiocesan Parish Welfare Fund, and emphasized and encouraged spiritual activities and bible study. He was chairman of the Bishops' Commission on the Liturgical Apostolate in 1960–61 and of the Bishops' Committee for Migrant Workers, and after he was made a cardinal in 1959 he was appointed to the Congregations of the Propagation of the Faith, of Seminaries and Universities, and of the fabrics of St. Peter's, was named to the Pontifical Commission for Biblical Studies in 1962, and the following year was appointed to the papal commission for the revision of canon law. In 1964 he was made a member of the Supreme Congregation of the Holy Office. At Vatican Council II he was recognized as the intellectual leader of the American hierarchy, was one of the twelve presidents of the Council, and was a leader of the progressive group. He became internationally known for his interventions and especially for his leadership in the unsuccessful attempt to force the president of the Council to permit discussion on the freedom of religion declaration at the third session in 1964. When Cardinal Tisserant announced the preliminary vote on religious freedom would be postponed until the fourth session, he and Cardinals Ritter of St. Louis and Léger of Montreal presented a petition signed by one thousand bishops to Pope Paul VI to proceed with the vote at the current session, but the Pope refused to overrule Tisserant's decision. A believer in collegiality, he felt the Church must become involved in the world's problems and in efforts to help solve them. He was appointed a member of the Congregation of the Holy Office in 1964. Exhausted from his efforts at the third session of the Council, he entered Mercy Hospital in Chicago early in 1965 and, after brain surgery, died there on Apr. 9.

MICHAUD, JOHN STEPHEN (1843–1908), bishop. Born in Burlington, Vermont, on Nov. 24, he was educated in Montreal, Holy Cross College, Worcester, Massachusetts, and St. Joseph's Seminary, Troy, New York, and was ordained in 1873. He engaged in pastoral work in Vermont until 1892, when he was appointed titular bishop of Modra and coadjutor of Burlington. He succeeded to the see as its second bishop in 1899 and held that position until his death in New York City on Dec. 22. He helped found Vermont's first Catholic hospital, Fanny Allen Hospital, in Winooski Park, brought the Society of St. Edmund into the diocese in 1899, which founded St. Michael's College in Winooski Park in 1904, the only Catholic college for men in Vermont, and wrote *History of the Catholic Church in the New England States* (1899).

MICHEL, VIRGIL (1890–1938), liturgist. Born in St. Paul, Minnesota, on Jan. 26, George Francis Michel joined the Benedictines in 1909, taking the name Virgil, was educated at St. John's College and Seminary, Collegeville, Minnesota (B.A. 1912, M.A. 1913), and was ordained in 1916. He continued his studies at Catholic University (Ph.D. 1918) and Columbia, taught at St. John's in 1918–24, and pursued further studies at St. Anselm's College, Rome, and Louvain. He became interested in the liturgical movement while in Europe and on his return to St. John's in 1925 founded the liturgical magazine *Orate Fratres* (later *Worship),* and was its editor, and the Liturgical Press. He taught philosophy at St. John's in 1925–30 and was named dean of the college in 1933. He soon became a leader in the liturgical movement and, except for the years 1930–33 that he spent with the Chippewa Indians, he devoted the rest of his life to that apostolate. Among the many activities in which he participated were the Catholic social movement, the revival of Thomism, adult religious education, and the welfare of Indians. While with the Chippewas he reorganized the Indian missions in the Duluth and Crookston dioceses and held an In-

dian Congress in 1932. He organized the first liturgical summer school at St. John's, founded the Institute for Social Studies and was its director in 1935. He died at Collegeville on Nov. 26. He wrote books on the liturgy, the teachings of Thomas Aquinas, and the social teachings of the Church, among them *Christian Social Reconstruction* (1937) and *The Liturgy of the Church* (1937), coedited with Fr. Basil Stegman the ten-volume Christ-life series in religion (1934–35), and translated *Liturgy the Life of the Church* (1926), *Spirit of the Liturgy* (1926), and Martin Grabmann's *Thomas Aquinas* (1928).

MIDDLETON, THOMAS COOKE (1842–1923), historian. The oldest of nine children of Quaker parents, he was born in Philadelphia on Mar. 30; the whole family became Catholic in 1854. Thomas studied at Villanova College (University) in 1854–58, joined the Augustinians, and was sent to study at their novitiate at Tolentino, Italy, where he took his vows in 1859. He continued his studies at St. Agostino, Rome, was ordained in Rome in 1864, and returned to the United States the following year. He began teaching at Villanova and remained there for fifty-eight years, serving as president in 1876–78. He was one of the founders of the American Catholic Historical Society of Philadelphia in 1884, serving as its president in 1884–90, edited its *Records of the American Catholic Historical Society* in 1899–1905, wrote numerous articles on ecclesiastical subjects and personages, and was the author of *Historical Sketch of Villanova* (1893) and *Augustinians in the United States* (1909). He died at Villanova on Nov. 19.

MIÈGE, JEAN BAPTISTE (1815–84), bishop. Born in La Forêt, Haute-Savoie, France, on Sept. 18, he was educated at Conflans College, the diocesan seminary at Moutiers, and the Roman College, Rome. He joined the Jesuits in Milan in 1836 and was ordained in Rome in 1847. He emigrated to the United States the following year, taught at St. Louis University and did missionary work in the St. Louis archdiocese until 1850, when he was appointed titular bishop of Messene and first vicar apostolic of the Indian Territory east of the Rocky Mountains. He established his headquarters at St. Mary's Mission, Kansas, among the Potawatomi Indians, but transferred his headquarters to Leavenworth, Kansas, in 1855 when the Kansas-Nebraska Act of 1854 brought an influx of settlers and violence to the area. He brought Carmelites, Sisters of Charity of Leavenworth, and Benedictines into the vicariate to aid in the missionary work in his huge territory (it extended from the Missouri River to the Rockies and from southern Kansas to Canada). In 1859 the Benedictines established a priory that developed into St. Benedict's College, Atchison, Kansas. In 1857 his vicariate was divided and he was assigned the Kansas Territory, though he continued to administer the Nebraska vicariate as well until 1859. He consecrated his cathedral in Leavenworth in 1868, attended Vatican Council I in 1869–70, toured South America for three years to raise funds for his vicariate in 1871–74, and resigned his vicariate in 1874. He was assigned to the Jesuit house of studies at Woodstock, Maryland, as spiritual director, was sent to Detroit in 1877, founded the University of Detroit and served as its president until 1880, when he returned to Woodstock as spiritual director, where he remained until his death on July 21.

MILES, GEORGE HENRY (1824–71), dramatist. Born in Baltimore, on July 31, he graduated from Mt. St. Mary's College, Emmitsburg, Mary-land, in 1843, studied law and practiced in Baltimore, and began to write. He had a novel, *The Truth of God,* published anonymously in the *United States Catholic Magazine* in 1847 and two years later won a $1,000 prize offered by Edwin Forrest for the best original drama with his *Mohammed, the Arabian Prophet,* which was produced in New York City in 1851. He gave up his law practice to devote himself to writing, had *Hernando de Soto* produced in Philadelphia in 1852, married Adaline Tiers in 1859, and a few months later was appointed professor of English literature at Mt. St. Mary's College; he retired from teaching in 1867 to devote himself full time to writing. Among his other plays were *Mary's Birthday* (1852), *Señor Valiente* (1859), and *The Seven Sisters* (1860); he also wrote poetry, *Christine, A Troubadour's Song and Other Poems* (1866) and *Christmas Poems* (1866), and three novels, and a detailed study of *Hamlet* for *The Southern Review* in 1870. He is considered the first American Catholic dramatist of any significance. He died at his home near Emmitsburg on July 24.

MILES, RICHARD PIUS (1791–1860), bishop. Born in Prince Georges County, Maryland, on May 17, he was educated at St. Rose of Lima Priory, Springfield, Kentucky, joined the Dominicans in 1810, and continued his studies at St. Thomas College, near Springfield. He was ordained in 1816, taught at St. Thomas's, and engaged in missionary work. In 1828 he went to Ohio. He became superior of St. Rose's in 1833, of St. Joseph's Priory, Ohio, three years later, and in 1837 was elected provincial of his province. Later the same year he was appointed first bishop of the newly established diocese of Nashville, Tennessee, and was consecrated in 1838 in Bardstown, Kentucky. He was one of the four bishops delegated to take the decrees of the fourth Provincial Council of Baltimore in 1840 to Rome, toured Europe seeking priests and funds for his diocese, and founded St. Athanasius Seminary in 1839. He built Seven Dolors Cathedral in 1847 and died in Nashville on Feb. 21. His see was one of the poorest in the country when he was appointed its bishop, with a few hundred Catholics, one church, and no priests, but by the time of his death it had fourteen churches, nine schools and an orphanage, and some twelve thousand Catholics served by thirteen priests, and in 1851 the Dominican Sisters established St. Agnes Academy (now Siena College) in Memphis, Tennessee.

MILLAR, MOORHOUSE IGNATIUS XAVIER (1886–1956), educator. Born in Mobile, Alabama, on Mar. 7, he was raised an Anglican but became a Catholic with his mother when he was eleven. He was educated privately in France in 1895–98 and Germany in 1898–1900 and at Loyola High School, Baltimore, in 1901–3. He joined the Jesuits in 1903, continued his studies at the Jesuit novitiate, St. Andrew-on-Hudson, New York, in 1903–8, taught at Holy Cross College, Worcester, Massachusetts, in 1911–12, Canisius College, Buffalo, New York, in 1912–16, and then studied theology at Woodstock College, Maryland, in 1916–20. He was ordained in 1919, taught at Fordham in 1920–21, Georgetown in 1922–23, and constitutional law at Fordham in 1923–37, where he founded and became director of the Department of Political Philosophy and Social Science at the graduate school in 1929, serving until his retirement in 1953. He was associate editor of *Thought,* contributed to numerous magazines, and wrote *Unpopular Essays in the Philosophy of History* (1928) and, with Msgr. John A. Ryan, *The State and the Church* (1922), a con-troversial text on church-state relations which became widely used in Catholic colleges. He died in New York City on Nov. 14.

MING, JOHN JOSEPH (1838–1910), author, educator. Born in Gyswyl, Unterwalden, Switzerland, on Sept. 20, he was educated at the Benedictine college in Engelberg, Switzerland, joined the Jesuits in 1856, studied philosophy at Aachen in 1861–64 and theology at Maria Laach in 1865–69 and was ordained in 1868. He spent a year in Westphalia, lectured on theology at Gorz, Austria (Gorizia, Italy), in 1871 and emigrated to the United States in 1872 when the Jesuits were expelled from Austria. He spent two years in pastoral work and then taught philosophy at Spring Hill, Alabama, Buffalo, Prairie du Chien, Wisconsin, and St. Louis University, where he spent the last twenty years of his life. He was a pioneer in the Catholic sociological field, wrote magazine articles on ethics, the temporal power of the pope, evolution, and socialism and several books, among them *The Data of Modern Ethics Examined* (1894), *The Characteristics and the Religion of Modern Socialism* (1908), and *The Morality of Modern Socialism* (1909). He died in Parma, Ohio, on June 17.

MINTON, SHERMAN (1890–1965), Associate Justice of the United States Supreme Court. Born on a farm near Georgetown, Indiana, on Oct. 20, he was educated at Indiana University Law School (LL.B. 1915) and Yale (LL.M. 1916) and began to practice law in New Albany, Indiana, in 1916. He married Gertrude Gurt, a Catholic, in 1917, was a captain in World War I, and after the war resumed his law practice in New Albany. He was public counselor for Indiana's Public Service Commission in 1933–34 and in 1934 was elected to the United States Senate. In the Senate he was a vigorous supporter of the New Deal of President Franklin Roosevelt, served as the President's liaison with Congress, was an ardent supporter of his "court packing" bill in 1937, and was defeated for reelection to the Senate in 1940. He was appointed to the U.S. Circuit Court of Appeals for the Seventh Circuit in 1941, served on a board to investigate the coal strike of 1948, and the following year was appointed an Associate Justice of the United States Supreme Court by President Harry Truman. Although considered a liberal while on the Circuit Court, he mainly voted with the conservative members of the Court. He retired in 1956 because of ill health, served briefly on the U.S. Court of Claims in 1957, became a Catholic in 1961, and died in New Albany on Apr. 9.

MITCHELL, JAMES PAUL (1900–64), Secretary of Labor. Born in Elizabeth, New Jersey, on Nov. 12, he was unsuccessful in an attempt to enter the Naval Academy in Annapolis in 1916 and became a grocery clerk after graduating from high school. He opened his own store in Rahway, which failed in 1923, the year he married Isabelle Nulton, and worked as a truck driver and then as a door-to-door salesman until 1926, when he joined Western Electric. In time he engaged in personnel work, was Emergency Relief Administrator in Union County, New Jersey, in 1932–36, returned to Western Electric in 1936 as supervisor of training, and in 1938 became director of the industrial relations department of the Works Progress Administration (WPA) in New York City. During World War II, he was director of the industrial personnel department of the War Department in 1942–45, administering a million civilian army employees; he was also a member of the joint Army and Navy

personnel board in 1943–45. After the war he was director of personnel and labor relations for R. H. Macy & Co., in New York City in 1945–47 and of Bloomingdale's in 1947–53, and was a member of the personnel advisory board of the Hoover Commission in 1948. He was named Assistant Secretary of the Army in charge of manpower in 1953 by President Eisenhower and later that year was appointed Secretary of Labor, a position he held until 1960. While Secretary of Labor, he reorganized the department, raising it to new stature among the cabinet departments, was instrumental in settling major labor disputes, notably the steel strikes of 1956 and 1959–60, and was a liberalizing influence in the Republican Party's attitude toward labor. He aided migrant workers, worked to widen employment opportunities for blacks and older and handicapped persons, and constantly applied the principles of Pope Leo's *Rerum novarum* and Pius XI's *Quadragesimo anno* to labor matters (he was the recipient of the *Rerum novarum* Award in 1953). He early realized the implications of automation in industry and what it would do to individuals and is generally considered one of the outstanding secretaries of labor. After he left the Labor Department he became chairman of the Railroad Retirement Board, was unsuccessful in his campaign as Republican candidate for the governorship of New Jersey in 1961, and then retired from public life and devoted himself to business. He became senior vice president of Crown Zellerbach Corporation, a paper manufacturing firm in San Francisco in 1962, and held that position until his death in New York City on Oct. 19 while on a business trip.

MITCHELL, JOHN (1870–1919), labor leader. Son of a miner, he was born in Braidwood, Illinois, on Feb. 4, was orphaned when he was six, and was raised by his devout Presbyterian stepmother. He began working in the coal mines of northern Illinois when he was twelve, joined the Knights of Labor in 1885, but, when a strike in Spring Valley in 1888 failed with disastrous results for the miners, he became convinced of the need of a separate miners' union. He joined the local branch of the United Mine Workers of America when it was founded in 1890, married Katherine O'Rourke, a miner's daughter, in 1891, and in 1894 was discharged after a strike by the national UMWA in 1894. He became a member of the union's state Executive Board in 1897, was elected national vice president, and in 1898 was elected president. His leadership of the anthracite coal miners during the 1902 strike, which led to substantial wage and benefit increases for the miners, elicited national attention and support for the union. He became a Catholic in 1907 and remained as president of the UMWA until 1908, sometimes in bitter conflict with more radical members of his union over his insistence on "the sacredness of contract," when he became head of the trade-agreement department of the National Civic Federation. He resigned in 1911 and was appointed chairman of the New York State Industrial Commission, a position he held until his death in New York City on Sept. 9.

MITTY, JOHN JOSEPH (1884–1961), archbishop. Born in New York City on Jan. 20, he was orphaned as a child and was educated at Manhattan College and St. Joseph's Seminary, Dunwoodie, Yonkers, New York, and was ordained in 1906. He continued his studies at Catholic University (S.T.B. 1907), the Pontifical Seminary, Rome (S.T.D. 1908), and the University of Munich, and then served as a curate at St. Veronica's Church in New York City

in 1909. He taught at St. Joseph's from 1909 until the United States entry into World War I, when he served as an army chaplain in 1917–19. After the war he was pastor of Sacred Heart Church, Highland Falls, New York, and chaplain at the United States Military Academy at West Point in 1919–22 and then was pastor of St. Luke's Church in New York City in 1922–26. He was appointed bishop of Salt Lake City, Utah, in 1926 and in 1932 was named coadjutor archbishop of San Francisco; he succeeded to the see in 1935. During his twenty-six-year episcopate at San Francisco, he presided over an enormous expansion program to accommodate the huge increase of Catholics in the archdiocese from some 400,000 to over 1,000,000. He increased the number of parishes from 171 to 256, built more than 500 buildings, including 120 new churches, 119 new elementary schools, 13 high schools, 28 youth centers and orphanages, retreat houses, and hospitals, while adding more than 500 priests to the see. He initiated postgraduate studies for priests, social service counseling, established a diocesan television program, provided aid for migrant workers, and encouraged the ecumenical movement and supported the United Nations when it was founded in San Francisco in 1945. He died at St. Patrick's Seminary, Menlo Park, California, on Oct. 15.

MODJESKA, HELENA (1840–1909), actress. Daughter of a music teacher, Helena Opid was born in Kraców, Poland, on Oct. 12, was early attracted to the theater, made her amateur stage debut in 1861 in Bochnia, Poland, and began her professional career the following year. She married Gustav Modrzejewski while in her teens and used a variation of his name, Modjeska, as her stage name. She married Count Charles Bozenta Chlapowski in 1868 after Modrzejewski died. She joined the Imperial Theatre in Warsaw and soon became Poland's leading actress. In 1876 her nationalistic views caused difficulties with the regime (Poland was then under Russian rule) and she and her husband moved to the United States. She made her American debut in San Francisco in 1877 in an English version of *Adrienne Lecouvreur* and when she played the title role in New York later that year she became as famous in the United States as she had been in Europe. She visited Poland and London in 1882 and 1884, brought Ibsen's *A Doll's House,* in which she had starred as Nora, to the United States in 1883—Ibsen's first production in the United States—and then appeared in numerous Shakespearean roles, in the title role in J. C. F. von Schiller's *Mary Stuart,* and in Dumas's *La Dame aux Camelias,* and toured with Edwin Booth in 1889–90. She was a close friend of Ethel Barrymore, who attributed her conversion to Catholicism to her. She attempted a tour in 1907, but it was canceled because of her frail health, and she died on Bay Island, East Newport, California, on Apr. 9.

MOELLER, HENRY (1849–1925), archbishop. Born in Cincinnati, Ohio, on Dec. 11, he was educated at St. Francis Xavier Seminary there and the North American College, Rome, and was ordained in Rome in 1876. He taught at Mt. St. Mary's Seminary, Cincinnati, served as secretary to Bishop Francis Chatard of Vincennes, Indiana, and then Archbishop William Elder of Cincinnati, and was named chancellor of the Cincinnati archdiocese in 1886. He was appointed bishop of Columbus, Ohio, in 1900; he paid off a large diocesan debt and in 1903 was made titular bishop of Aeropolis and coadjutor of Cincinnati. He succeeded to the see in 1904, raised the educational standards and facilities in his archdiocese, and was active in the National Catholic Welfare Conference (NCWC). He helped found the American Board of Foreign Missions, of which he was chairman, to raise funds for missionary activities, worked to improve diocesan educational facilities, founded a diocesan bureau of Catholic Charities, established new parishes, built a new diocesan seminary, and saw Cincinnati made the national headquarters for Catholic Charities as well as for the Catholic Students Mission Crusade. In 1922 he went to Rome to defend the NCWC and its activities with Bishop Joseph Schrembs, was made an Assistant at the Pontifical Throne in 1923, and died in Cincinnati on Jan. 5.

MOLLOY, THOMAS E. (1885–1956), bishop. Born in Nashua, New Hampshire, on Sept. 4, he was educated at St. Anselm's College, Manchester, New Hampshire, St. Francis College and St. John's Seminary, Brooklyn, and the North American College, Rome. He was ordained in 1908, was curate at St. John's Chapel, Brooklyn, for a time and was secretary to Auxiliary George Mundelein in 1909–15. He accompanied Mundelein to Chicago when the auxiliary bishop was appointed archbishop of that see in 1915. He returned to Brooklyn the following year, became an assistant at Queen of All Saints parish and spiritual director of Cathedral College, taught philosophy at St. Joseph's College for Women, and was president of the college in 1916–20. He was appointed titular bishop of Lorea and auxiliary of Brooklyn in 1920, and was appointed third bishop of that diocese in 1921. He founded Immaculate Conception Seminary, Huntington, Long Island, in 1930, tripled the number of priests in the diocese, doubled the number of high schools, established ninety new parishes, opened one hundred new schools, expanded the charitable and social services facilities of the see, and saw the opening of Molloy College for women at Rockville Centre, Long Island. He was given the personal title of archbishop in 1951 and died in Brooklyn on Nov. 26.

MONAGHAN, FRANCIS JOSEPH (1890–1942), bishop. Born in Newark, New Jersey, on Oct. 30, he was educated at Seton Hall College (University), South Orange, New Jersey (B.A. 1911, M.A. 1913), and the North American College, Rome (S.T.D. 1915), and was ordained in 1915. He was a curate at St. Paul of the Cross Church, Jersey City, New Jersey, in 1915–26 and assistant at St. Mary's Church, Roselle, New Jersey, for a time in 1926. Then he taught at Immaculate Conception Seminary, South Orange (later moved to Darlington), New Jersey, in 1926–33 and was president of Seton Hall College in 1933–36. He was made a papal chamberlain in 1934, was consecrated titular bishop of Mela and auxiliary of Ogdensburg, New York, in 1936, and succeeded to the see in 1939. He remained in this position until he died of a cerebral hemorrhage from a fall from a train at Watertown, New York, on Nov. 13.

MONAGHAN, JAMES CHARLES (1857–1917), economist. Born in Boston, on Oct. 11, he began working in mills when his father was crippled when he was eight and was educated at Brown University (B.A. 1885, M.A. 1903). He continued his studies in Germany at Mannheim, Heidelberg, Leipzig, Berlin, and Chemnitz in 1885–1900. He was a member of the Providence, Rhode Island, city council in 1884–85 while a student at Brown, and after working for the election of President Cleveland in 1884, he was appointed U.S. consul at Mannheim and served there in 1885–89. He returned to the United States in 1890, married Dorothy T. Ryan in 1892, studied law, and was consul at Chemnitz in 1893–97. He was editor of the Philadelphia *Manufacturer* in 1899–1900, taught the theory and practice of domestic and foreign commerce at the University of Wisconsin in 1900–3, and was chief of the division of consular reports of the Department of Commerce and Labor in 1903–6. He occupied the chair of economics and history at Notre Dame in 1906–8 and was U.S. consul at Kingston, Jamaica, West Indies, in 1914. He was highly regarded as a leading authority on commercial economy, was the recipient of the Laetare Medal in 1918, lectured nationally for the Knights of Columbus, was president of the Columbus Travel Society and secretary of the National Society for Promotion of Industrial Education, and died in Brooklyn, New York, on Nov. 12.

MONAGHAN, JOHN JAMES JOSEPH (1856–1935), bishop. Born in Sumter, South Carolina, on May 23, he was educated at St. Charles College, Ellicott City, Maryland, and St. Mary's Seminary, Baltimore, and was ordained in 1880. He engaged in pastoral work in South Carolina, was chancellor of the Charleston diocese in 1887–88 and assistant to the vicar-general in 1888–97, and was consecrated bishop of Wilmington, Delaware, in 1897. He served in that position until 1925, when he resigned because of illness and was appointed titular bishop of Lydda. During his administration he held the third diocesan synod in 1898, established seven new parishes and seven missions and eight new schools, and died in Wilmington on Jan. 7.

MONAGHAN, JOHN PATRICK (1890–1961), labor educator. Born in Dunamore, Tyrone, Ireland, on Feb. 12, he emigrated to the United States, was educated at St. Francis College, Brooklyn, St. Joseph's Seminary, Dunwoodie, Yonkers, New York, the North American College, Rome, and Fordham and was ordained. After his ordination he taught at Cathedral College, New York, and Fordham's graduate school and became involved in labor matters. He was one of the leading promoters of Catholic principles of social action, helped establish Catholic labor schools in 1935, and was one of the founders and national chaplain of the Association of Catholic Trade Unionists (ACTU) in 1937. He served as director of the Association's labor schools, operated youth centers in New York, pioneered in adult education and made St. Margaret Mary Church on Staten Island, New York, of which he was pastor in 1939–54, known all over the country for its liturgical practices. He was named pastor of St. Michael's Church, New York City, in 1954, was made a domestic prelate in 1957 and remained as pastor of St. Michael's until he died in New York City on July 26.

MONROE, ANDREW FRANCIS (1824–72), nephew of President James Monroe, was born in Charlottesville, Virginia, on Mar. 5. He graduated from the United States Naval Academy and served in the Mexican War and, while on a naval expedition to China in 1853, became a Catholic. He resigned from the Navy and joined the Jesuits the following year, studied for the priesthood, and was ordained in Montreal in 1860. He taught at St. Francis Xavier College, New York City, and died in New York on Aug. 2.

MONTANI, NICOLA ALOYSIUS (1890–1948), composer, conductor, liturgical music educator. Born in Utica, New York, on Nov. 6, he studied music at the Conservatory of St. Cecilia in Rome and with a group of scholars from Solesmes in 1906 on the Isle of Wight. On his return to the United States he was choirmaster of St. John the Evangelist Church in Philadelphia in 1906–23 and St. Paul the Apostle Church in New York City in 1923–25. He gave courses in several schools, established the Palestrina Choir, and with Frs. Leo Manzetti and J. M. Petter founded the Society of St. Gregory of America in 1914, and was editor of *The Catholic Choirmaster,* devoted to promoting the cause of liturgical music, in 1914–48. He was liturgical editor for G. Schirmer & Co. and the Boston Music Co., taught and lectured on music at several colleges throughout the country, and was director of music at Immaculate Conception Seminary, Darlington, New Jersey, in 1932–47. He was head of the music department at Seton Hall College, South Orange, New Jersey, and of the Institute of Sacred Music for the archdiocese of Newark and was a pioneer in promoting liturgical music in Catholic churches in the United States. He wrote masses and motets, was honored in 1926 by Pope Pius XI for his activities in the field of liturgical music, received the first Liturgical Music Award of the Society of St. Gregory in 1947, and died in Philadelphia on Jan. 11. He was the author of *St. Gregory Hymnal* (1920) and the two-volume *The Essentials of Sight Singing* (1931).

MONTAVAN, WILLIAM F. (1874–1959). Born in Scioto County, Ohio, on July 14, he was educated at Notre Dame (B.A. 1892, M.A. 1895), the Institut de Sainte-Croix, Paris, and Catholic University in 1897–1901. He was superintendent of schools in Tabayas Province, Philippine Islands, in 1915, worked as U.S. commercial attaché in Peru in 1915–18, and represented the International Petroleum Company in South America in 1918–25. When he returned to the United States in 1925, he became director of the legal department of the National Catholic Welfare Conference (NCWC) and served in this position until his retirement in 1951. He wrote numerous pamphlets for the NCWC on Mexico, Spain, Haiti, and subjects of topical interest such as sterilization, school laws, and legislative matters affecting the Church. He devoted much time and effort to the religious conflict in Mexico during the Mexican civil war, for which he was made a Knight of St. Gregory in 1928, was correspondent for Catholic newspapers with the Forbes Commission to Haiti in 1930, and was sent to Madrid the following year to represent the Church at the constitutional convention there. He served as an adviser to the U.S. State Department on Latin American affairs, lectured on health, education, and welfare, and was a consultant to the U.S. Catholic Hospital Association. He died in Washington, D.C., on Feb. 15.

MONTGOMERY, GEORGE THOMAS (1847–1907), bishop. Born in Davies County, Missouri, on Dec. 30, he was educated at St. Mary's Seminary, Baltimore, and was ordained in 1879. He went to California, became chancellor of the San Francisco diocese, and in 1894 was consecrated titular bishop of Tumi and coadjutor of the diocese of Monterey–Los Angeles. He succeeded to the see in 1896, was a fervent supporter of the rights of the Church and of Catholic education, fought the anti-Catholicism of the American Protection Association, insisted Catholics live up to their obligations as American citizens, and defended the rights of the Indians, especially the rights of Indian parents to educate their children as they desired. He was appointed titular archbishop of Osimo and coadjutor of San Francisco in 1903 but never succeeded to the see. He died on Jan. 10 in San Francisco before Archbishop Patrick Riordan, the ordinary of the see.

MOODY, JOHN (1868–1958), economist, author. Born in Jersey City, New Jersey, on May 2, he was educated in Bayonne schools but was forced to leave when he was fifteen because of family financial difficulties and began his business career as an errand boy with a wholesale firm. He became an office boy with the brokerage house of Spencer, Trask & Company in 1890 and rose to be an accountant and then a securities analyst. He married Agnes Addison in 1900, when he also published the first edition of *Moody's Manual of Railroads and Corporation Securities* with fifty dollars he had borrowed; he founded *Moody's Magazine* in 1905 and *Moody's Analysis of Investments* in 1909. He opened his own investment service in New York City and soon established offices abroad. He wrote on investments, capital, trusts, and management and among the books he wrote were *The Truth About Trusts* (1904), *The Investor's Primer* (1907), *How to Invest Money Wisely* (1912), *Masters of Capital* (1917), *The Railroad Builders* (1919), and *The Remaking of Europe* (1921). He became a Catholic in 1931 and wrote of his conversion in his autobiographies *The Long Road Home* (1933) and *Fast by the Road* (1942); he also wrote the biography *John Henry Newman* (1945). He was president of the Liturgical Arts Society, was knighted by Pope Pius XI, and died in La Jolla, California, on Feb. 16.

MOON, PARKER THOMAS (1892–1936), historian. Born in New York City on June 5, he was educated at Columbia (B.A. 1913), became a Catholic in 1914, and the following year began his career as a historian and an instructor at Columbia. He became known for his knowledge and understanding of contemporary history and international affairs and was a member of the American Commission at the Paris Peace Conference in 1918–19, serving as secretary of the International Committee on Territorial Problems. After the Conference he resumed teaching at Columbia, earned his Ph.D. in 1921, when he married Edith Conway, and rose in rank in the academic world until he became a professor in 1931. He wrote prolifically, was editor of the *Political Science Quarterly* from 1921 and of *Proceedings of the Academy of Political Science* from 1928, until his death in New York City on June 11. He was president of the American Catholic Historical Association in 1926 and of the Catholic Association for International Peace in 1931–34. Among his books are *A Syllabus of Imperialism and World Politics* (1919), *The Labor Problem and the Social Catholic Movement in France* (1921), *Imperialism and World Politics* (1926), and with Carlton J. Hayes *Modern History* (1923), *Ancient History* (1929), and *World History* (1932).

MOONEY, EDWARD FRANCIS (1882–1958), cardinal. Born in Mount Savage, Maryland, of Irish immigrant parents, on May 9, he was educated at St. Charles College, Ellicott City, Maryland, St. Mary's Seminary, Baltimore (B.A. 1905, M.A. 1906), and the North American College, Rome (Ph.D. 1907, D.D. 1909), and was ordained in 1909. He taught dogmatic theology at St. Mary's Seminary, Cleveland, Ohio, in 1909–16, was headmaster of the Cathedral Latin School, which he founded, in 1916–22, and was pastor of St. Patrick's Church, Youngstown, Ohio, in 1922–23. He was spiritual director of the North American College from 1923 to 1926, when he was named titular bishop of Irenopolis and apostolic delegate to India. While in India he received, into communion with Rome, Mar Ivanios,

Mar Theophilus, and eight Bethany monks, members of the Catholicos party of the Jacobite Church, in 1930, helped solve the dispute between the Indian bishops of native dioceses and the Portuguese missionaries on the east coast, and ended Portuguese ecclesiastical control over some of India's Catholics, a problem that had festered for four centuries. He also helped to establish eleven new missionary territories and transferred three dioceses to native Indian bishops. He was apostolic delegate to Japan in 1931–33 and ended a dilemma facing Japanese Catholics by deciding Catholics could attend Shinto shrines that were mandated by the civil government when he ruled the rites celebrated at these shrines were civil not religious. He was appointed bishop of Rochester, New York, in 1933 and was named to the administrative board and was chairman of the Social Action Department of the National Catholic Welfare Conference (NCWC) in 1933–37. He was elected chairman of the administrative board in 1935 and served in that position in 1935–39 and 1941–45 and in that post was, in effect, spokesman for the Catholic Church in the United States. He was first chairman of the Bishops' War Emergency and Relief Committee, first president of National Catholic Community Service, and cochairman of the Clergy Committee of the United Services Organization (USO). He was appointed first archbishop of Detroit when that see was made an archdiocese in 1937 and was at once faced with strife in the automobile plants of the city caused by efforts to organize the workers; he supported unionization with his statement that Catholics had an obligation to join unions. He soon became nationally recognized as a champion of workingmen's rights and of social justice. He inherited an enormous debt when he became archbishop and reorganized the financial structure of his archdiocese. After World War II, he greatly expanded the services and facilities of the see to meet the tremendous increase in its Catholic population from half a million to a million and a quarter. He established one hundred new parishes, built new schools, catechetical centers and social service centers, hospitals and homes, and opened St. John's Provincial Seminary in 1949. He was made a cardinal by Pope Pius XII in 1946 and died in Rome on Oct. 25 while attending the conclave that elected Pope John XXIII. One of the matters he faced at Detroit was the activities of Fr. Charles E. Coughlin, pastor of the Shrine of the Little Flower, Royal Oak, Michigan, who gained a tremendous following with his radio program. At first devoted to social reform, in time it became anti-Semitic and pro-Nazi and was filled with such invective and hatred that it drew widespread criticism and eventually Fr. Coughlin was pressured into going off the air by ecclesiastical authority.

MOORE, EDWARD ROBERTS (1894–1952), sociologist, author. Born in New York City on Jan. 9, he was educated at Fordham (B.A., M.A., Ph.D.), St. Joseph's Seminary, Dunwoodie, Yonkers, New York, and Catholic University and was ordained in 1919. He became an assistant at St. Peter's Church in New York City in 1919–23, was stationed at St. Gregory's parish in 1923–29, was director of the social action division of Catholic Charities in 1923–41, and returned to St. Peter's in 1929 and became pastor in 1937. He taught at the Fordham School of Social Service in 1924–38, worked with the Catholic Youth Organization, was active in social services, slum clearance, and low-cost housing units and was a member of the New York City Housing Authority in 1934–44. He helped estab-

lish the Legion of Decency nationally in 1935, when he also served on President Roosevelt's Advisory Commission of the National Youth Administration. He was made a papal chamberlain in 1941 and a domestic prelate in 1948. He wrote of his experiences at St. Peter's, New York's oldest Catholic church, where Mother Seton became a Catholic, in *Roman Collar* (1951) and coauthored a novel on Mother Seton's life, *Heart in Pilgrimage* (1948). He died in New York City on June 2.

MOORE, JOHN (1834–1901), bishop. Born in Rossmead, Mayo, Ireland, on July 27, he emigrated to the United States and settled in Charleston, South Carolina, in 1848. He studied for the priesthood at St. John the Baptist Seminary there, Courbrée College, France, and the Propaganda, Rome, and was ordained in Rome in 1860. He served as a curate at the Charleston cathedral during the Civil War, was pastor of St. Patrick's Church in 1865–77 and vicar-general of the diocese in 1871–77, and was consecrated second bishop of St. Augustine, Florida, in 1877. He attended the third Plenary Council of Baltimore in 1884 and was one of the two bishops designated to take its decrees to Rome. He died in St. Augustine on July 30.

MOORHEAD, LOUIS DAVID (1892–1951), physician. Born in Chicago on Nov. 22, he was educated at Loyola (B.A. 1913, M.A. 1916) and Chicago (B.S. 1914, M.S. 1915, M.D. 1917) universities and was senior house surgeon at Cook County Hospital in 1917–19. He taught surgery at the school of medicine at Loyola in 1918–28, was dean in 1918–41, and was head of the department of surgery in 1929–41. He served on the staffs of several hospitals in Chicago, was on the medical board of the archdiocese of Chicago and personal physician to Cardinals Mundelein and

Stritch, and was director of Catholic Charities and on the board of trustees of several hospitals. He was one of the founders of the American Board of Surgery, served the health, police, and fire departments of Chicago, and was twice honored by the papacy. He died in Chicago on Sept. 14.

MORA, FRANCIS (1827–1905), bishop. Born in Vich, Catalonia, Spain, on Nov. 25, he studied at the seminary there and, while still a student, was persuaded by Bishop Thaddeus Amat of Monterey, California, in 1855 to emigrate to California. He was ordained in Santa Barbara in 1856, engaged in missionary work at San Juan Bautista Mission in 1856–60, and was superior of San Luis Obispo Mission in 1861–66. He continued his work in Los Angeles, became pastor of Our Lady of Angels Church and vicar-general of the diocese, and in 1873 was consecrated titular bishop of Mosynopolis by Thaddeus Amat, who was then bishop of Monterey–Los Angeles. He succeeded to the see on the death of Bishop Amat in 1878. He brought religious orders into the diocese and financial order to the see, after paying off the major debts he had inherited, and opened new schools and charitable institutions, resigned in 1896 because of ill health, and was appointed titular bishop of Hieropolis. He then returned to Spain, where he died at Sarriá on Aug. 3.

MORAN, EUGENE FRANCIS (1872–1961), shipping executive. Son of Michael Moran, who founded what was to become the Moran Towing and Transportation Company, and Margaret Haggerty Moran, he was born in Brooklyn, New York, on Mar. 24. He left grade school before graduation to begin working on one of his father's tugs. He worked for the Lancashire Fire Insurance Company to learn about marine insurance from 1887 to 1889 and then joined the family firm. He married Julia Claire Browne in 1897 and on the death of his father in 1906 became president; in 1930 he also became chairman of the board. He built the company's fleet into one of the largest tugboat fleets in the world, operating in New York Harbor and other American cities. He was instrumental in persuading the Army Corps of Engineers to deepen and broaden the channel leading into New York, retired as president of the firm in 1940, was chairman of the Port of New York Authority in 1942–59 and a member of the New York Transit Authority. He wrote *Famous Harbors of the World* (1953) and, with Louis Reed, the juvenile *Tugboat* (1956). He died in Palm Beach, Florida, on Apr. 13.

MORRIS, JOHN BAPTIST (1866–1946), bishop. Born in Hendersonville, Tennessee, on June 29, he was educated at St. Mary's College, Bardstown, Kentucky, and the Urban College, Rome, and was ordained in Rome in 1892. He engaged in pastoral work in the Nashville, Tennessee, diocese, became pastor of St. Charles Cathedral, Nashville, and was Bishop Joseph Rademacher's secretary and chancellor and also vicar-general of the Nashville diocese in 1902–6. He was named titular bishop of Acmonia and coadjutor of Little Rock, Arkansas, in 1906 and succeeded to the see the following year. He founded the short-lived Little Rock College in 1908, St. John's Home Missions Seminary in 1911, and St. Joseph's Orphanage and the diocesan newspaper *The Guardian,* convoked the first diocesan synod in 1909, and was made an Assistant at the Pontifical Throne in 1931. He died in Little Rock on Oct. 22.

MORRIS, MARTIN FERDINAND (1834–1909), jurist. Born in Washington, D.C., on Dec. 3, he graduated from

Georgetown in 1854, joined the Jesuits on graduation but was forced to leave the Society to care for his mother when his father died. He studied law and was admitted to the bar, practiced in Baltimore in 1863–67, and then returned to Washington to form a partnership with Richard T. Merrick. He was one of the founders of Georgetown Law School in 1871. When Merrick died in 1885, he formed a new partnership with George E. Hamilton. When the Court of Appeals of the District of Columbia was established in 1893, President Grover Cleveland appointed him an associate justice on it. He died in Washington on Sept. 12.

MOYLAN, STEPHEN (1737–1811), general. Brother of Francis Moylan, who became bishop of Cork, and son of John Moylan, a well-to-do merchant, he was born in Cork, Ireland, was educated in Paris because of the penal laws then in effect in Ireland against Catholics, traveled in England and Europe, and in 1765 entered the shipping business in Lisbon, Portugal. He emigrated to the United States in 1768 and became a successful merchant in Philadelphia, where he helped found the Friendly Sons of St. Patrick in 1771 and served as its first president. He joined the Continental Army in 1775 as muster-master general and the following year became aide-to-camp and secretary to George Washington; he was appointed first quartermaster general later in the year. He resigned in December 1776 to raise a troop of cavalry, Moylan's Dragoons, and served with great distinction at Valley Forge and the battle of Germantown, in the Hudson River valley, with Wayne in Pennsylvania and General Nathanael Greene in his Carolina campaign and with Lafayette at Yorktown. While serving under Casimir Pulaski in 1777, his quarrel with Pulaski led to a court-martial at which he was acquitted

and was later vindicated. He succeeded to Pulaski's cavalry command in 1778, married Mary Ricketts Van Horn the same year, and was brevetted brigadier general in 1783. After the war he resumed his business career, became register and recorder of Chester County, Pennsylvania, in 1792, when he was again elected president of the Friendly Sons of St. Patrick, and was appointed Pennsylvania commissioner of loans by Washington in 1793. He died in Philadelphia on Apr. 13.

MRAK, IGNATIUS (1818–1901), bishop. Born in Hotoyle, Austria, on Oct. 16, he studied at the Laibach diocesan seminary and was ordained in 1837. He went to Lugano, Italy, as a tutor, spent two years there, and in 1840 he returned to Laibach, where he served as an assistant until 1845, when he emigrated to the United States. He worked as a missionary among the Indians in Michigan, was named vicar-general by Bishop Frederick Baraga of Marquette, Michigan, and was appointed second bishop of that diocese when Baraga died in 1868. He labored to increase the number of priests in the see and to maintain its churches and schools and was forced to resign in 1878 because of ill health and was named titular bishop of Antinoe. When his health improved, he resumed his missionary activities among the Indians of Michigan until 1899, when he retired. He spent the rest of his life as chaplain at St. Mary's Hospital in Marquette and died there on Jan. 2.

MUDD, SAMUEL ALEXANDER (1833–83), doctor. Of an old, distinguished Maryland Catholic family, he was born on Dec. 21 on his father's farm, Oak Hill, near Bryantown, Maryland. He entered St. John's College, Frederick, Maryland, in 1849, went to Georgetown in 1851 and graduated in

1854, and then studied medicine at Baltimore Medical College (University of Maryland), where he graduated in 1856. He returned to his father's farm and began practicing medicine. In 1857 he married Sarah Frances Dyer and they built their own home, Rock Hill Farm, on land his father gave him from his farm. A slave owner and tobacco planter, he was sympathetic to the Confederacy when the Civil War broke out. He met John Wilkes Booth on Nov. 20, 1864, at St. Mary's Church, Bryantown, while Booth was professedly seeking land and had him stay at his home overnight. He again met Booth in Washington, D.C., on Dec. 23, and on Apr. 15, 1865, while Booth was fleeing the authorities after having murdered President Lincoln, Mudd treated him for a broken leg. Later he was arrested for complicity in the murder of the President and though he swore he had not recognized Booth, who, he said, was in disguise, he was tried, convicted, and sentenced to life imprisonment on June 30, 1865. He was imprisoned for three and a half years at Fort Jefferson, Dry Tortugas, in the Gulf of Mexico, where he rendered heroic service during an epidemic of yellow fever in 1867 and was pardoned by President Johnson in 1869. He returned home and resumed his medical practice, contracted pneumonia while visiting patients during the winter of 1882, and died on Jan. 10 and was buried at St. Mary's Church in Bryantown. Mudd's trial and conviction have been the subject of numerous studies and scholars now believe his conviction was a miscarriage of justice.

MUELLER, JOSEPH MAXIMILIAN (1894–1981), bishop. Born in St. Louis on Dec. 1, he studied at the Josephinum Seminary in Worthington, Ohio, and was ordained there in 1919. He was a curate at Carlyle, Mt. Carmel, East St. Louis and Belleville, founded and was first pastor of Blessed Sacrament parish in Belleville in 1926–30 and was rector of St. Peter's Cathedral in Belleville in 1930–47. He was made a domestic prelate in 1939 and in 1947 was appointed titular bishop of Sinda and coadjutor of Sioux City, Iowa, with the right to succession. He succeeded to the see the following year as its third bishop, established a diocesan newspaper, the *Globe,* and developed the concept of free interparochial high schools serving and supported by clusters of parishes. He was made an Assistant at the Pontifical Throne in 1957, retired in 1970, and died at the Marian Health Center in Sioux City on Aug. 9.

MUENCH, ALOISIUS (1889–1962), cardinal. Born in Milwaukee, Wisconsin, on Feb. 18, he was educated at St. Francis Seminary there and the University of Wisconsin (M.A. 1919) and was ordained in 1913. He served as a curate at St. Michael's Church, Milwaukee, in 1913–17 and as a chaplain at the University of Wisconsin in 1917–19 and then continued his studies at the University of Fribourg, where he received his D.Sc. in 1921. He did graduate work at Cambridge, Louvain, Sorbonne, and Oxford in 1921–22 and on his return to the United States in 1922 taught dogma at St. Francis Seminary and served as its rector in 1929–35. He was made a domestic prelate in 1934 and the following year was appointed third bishop of Fargo, North Dakota. He devised the Catholic Church Expansion Fund to aid parishes in financial difficulty because of the depression of the thirties, founded a diocesan paper, *Catholic Action News,* convoked the first diocesan synod in 1941, established the Priests Mutual Aid Fund for disabled and retired priests, and was an active supporter of the Catholic Central Verein. He denounced the Morgenthau plan at the end of World War II which advocated the abolition of German industry and the turning of the country into a rural economy, pleading for justice in the treatment of former enemies in his 1946 pastoral letter, "One World in Charity." He was episcopal chairman of the National Catholic Rural Life Conference in 1939–40 and was appointed apostolic visitator to West Germany by Pope Pius XII in 1946 and military vicar delegate by the National Catholic Welfare Conference (NCWC) for American members of the Armed Forces in Germany; he became adviser to General Lucius Clay on matters concerning the Church and the American army of occupation. He was given the personal title of archbishop as titular archbishop of Selembryia in 1950, was appointed papal nuncio to West Germany in 1951, serving until 1960, and became dean of the diplomatic corps there. He resigned as bishop of Fargo in 1959 when he was appointed a member of the Roman Curia and made a cardinal—the first American to hold office in the Curia. He also served on the advisory staffs of the Sacred Congregations of Religious Rites and of Extra-ordinary Ecclesiastical Affairs. He died in Rome on Feb. 15.

MULDOON, PETER JAMES (1863–1927), bishop. Born in Columbia, California, on Oct. 10, he was educated at St. Mary's College, Kentucky, and St. Mary's Seminary, Baltimore, and was ordained for the Chicago archdiocese in 1886. He engaged in pastoral work in Chicago, was chancellor of the archdiocese and Archbishop Patrick Feehan's secretary in 1888–95 and was named pastor of St. Charles Borromeo Church in Chicago in 1895. He held that position the next thirteen years and was named titular bishop of Tamassus and auxiliary of Chicago in 1901, an appointment of a native-born American so vehemently opposed by some of the Irish-born clergy that Archbishop

Feehan excommunicated one of the most vociferous leaders of the opposition, Fr. Jeremiah Crowley, rector of St. Mary's Church in Oregon, Illinois. He was appointed first bishop of the newly established diocese of Rockford, Illinois, in 1908 and in 1917 was appointed bishop of Monterey–Los Angeles but declined the appointment to remain in Rockford. He became known for his espousal of social reforms, was sympathetic to the labor movement and a defender of unions, and in 1911 was appointed chairman of the Federation of Catholic Societies. He acquired national recognition as chairman of the National Catholic War Council in 1917–18 and when the hierarchy decided to replace the Council with a peacetime organization he pleaded for its approval while in Rome with Bishop Joseph Schrembs of Cleveland after initial approval had been revoked. The National Catholic Welfare Conference (NCWC) was finally approved by the Holy See and Bishop Muldoon became chairman of the NCWC's Social Action Department, was made an Assistant at the Pontifical Throne in 1921, and died in Rockford on Oct. 8.

MULHOLLAND, ST. CLAIR AUGUST (1839–1910), general. Born in Lisburn, Antrim, Ireland, on Apr. 11, he was brought to the United States when a boy by his parents, who settled in Philadelphia. Interested in the military from his boyhood, he was active in the local militia and at the outbreak of the Civil War was commissioned lieutenant of the 116th Pennsylvania Volunteers, which was attached to Meagher's Irish Brigade. He served with distinction throughout the war, became a lieutenant colonel in 1862, was wounded at Fredericksburg in 1862, performed with great skill and valor at Chancellorsville and Gettysburg in 1863, and was wounded again at the battle of the Wilderness in 1864, the year he married Mary Dooner. He was wounded a third time at the Po River in 1864, was brevetted major general of volunteers for his actions around Petersburg, and returned to civilian life after the war. He served as Philadelphia's chief of police in 1868–71, was appointed United States pension agent at Philadelphia by President Cleveland, serving in that position for twelve years, when he was reappointed by Presidents McKinley and Roosevelt and was awarded the Congressional Medal of Honor in 1895 for his bravery and brilliant command of the picket line covering the withdrawal of the Army of the Potomac across the Rappahannock River after the battle of Chancellorsville. He died in Philadelphia on Feb. 17.

MULLANPHY, JOHN (1758–1833), merchant, philanthropist. Born near Enniskillen, Fermanagh, Ireland, he went to France in 1778 and served in the Irish Brigade but returned to Ireland in 1789 when the French Revolution broke out. He married Elizabeth Brown and they emigrated to the United States in 1792. They lived in Philadelphia and Baltimore, and in 1799 he opened a book store in Franklin, Kentucky. He moved to St. Louis in 1804, went into the real estate business, fought in the War of 1812, and was with Andrew Jackson at the battle of New Orleans in 1815. After the war he made a fortune in real estate in St. Louis and speculating in cotton during and after the war, thus becoming Missouri's first millionaire. He spent much of his fortune in his later years on charitable enterprises, helping to establish religious orders in St. Louis, and building churches, convents, orphanages, and hospitals. He died in St. Louis on Aug. 29.

MULLANY, BROTHER AZARIAS OF THE CROSS (1847–93), educator, author. Born near Killenaule, Tipperary, Ireland, on June 29, Patrick Francis Mullany emigrated to the United States in 1857 and was educated in Deerfield, Massachusetts, at the Christian Brothers' Assumption Academy, Utica, New York, and joined the Christian Brothers, being professed in 1862 and taking the name Azarias of the Cross. He taught in Albany, New York City, and Philadelphia schools and in 1866 became professor of mathematics and literature at Rock Hill College, Ellicott City, Maryland, and served as president in 1879–86. He spent the next two years studying in European libraries and on his return to the United States became professor of literature at De La Salle Institute in New York City, a position he occupied until his death in Plattsburgh, New York, on Aug. 20. He organized Catholic reading circles, helped found the Catholic Summer School of America at Plattsburgh, and wrote voluminously on education and literature. Among his outstanding books were *An Essay Contributing to a Philosophy of Literature* (1874), *The Development of Old English Thought* (1879), *Aristotle and the Christian Church* (1888), *Books and Reading* (1889), and *Phases of Thought and Criticism* (1892).

MULLEN, TOBIAS (1818–1900), bishop. Born in Tyrone, Ireland, on Mar. 4, he was studying for the priesthood at Maynooth when he volunteered for the American missions and went to the United States in 1843. He was ordained in Pittsburgh in 1844, engaged in pastoral work in the Pittsburgh diocese, was vicar-general, and edited the *Pittsburgh Catholic* until 1868, when he was consecrated third bishop of Erie, Pennsylvania. He founded and edited the

Lake Shore Visitor, was particularly interested in aiding the immigrants in his see, inaugurated a widespread building program in the diocese, tripled the number of priests, parishes, and parochial schools and built St. Peter's Cathedral, which he consecrated in 1893. He suffered a stroke in 1897, resigned in 1899, and was appointed titular bishop of Germanicopolis. He died in Erie on Apr. 22.

MULLOY, WILLIAM THEODORE (1892–1959), bishop. Born in Ardoch, North Dakota, on Nov. 9, he was educated at St. Boniface College, Wisconsin, and St. Paul Seminary, Wisconsin, and was ordained in 1916. He engaged in pastoral work in the Fargo, North Dakota, diocese, became active in rural life work, and was director of the diocesan Rural Life Conference in 1934–43 and president of the National Catholic Rural Life Conference in 1935–37. He was pastor of St. Mary's Cathedral in Fargo when appointed bishop of Covington, Kentucky, a position he occupied until his death in Covington on Jan. 1.

MULRY, THOMAS MAURICE (1855–1916), executive. Born in New York City on Feb. 13, he studied nights at Cooper Union there after graduating from De La Salle Academy, went with his family to Wisconsin to engage in farming, and in 1872 joined his father's excavating business, Mulry & Sons, in New York City. He married Mary E. Gallagher in 1880, eventually took over Mulry & Sons, and then went into real estate, insurance, and banking, becoming president of the Emigrant Industrial Savings Bank in 1906. He became involved in charitable ventures, especially the Society of St. Vincent de Paul, which he had joined when he was seventeen, and in 1915 he became president of its Superior Council of the United States, which he had helped to found. He had a great influence on the Catholic Charities movement in the United States, worked to improve conditions in charitable institutions and for cooperation between public and private welfare agencies. He was one of the founders of the National Conference of Catholic Charities and one of its vice presidents, helped establish the Fordham School of Social Sciences, was president of the National Conference of Charities and Correction in 1907, was the recipient of the Laetare Medal in 1912, and was one of a committee of three appointed by President Theodore Roosevelt to organize the first White House Conference on Children in 1909. He died in New York City on Mar. 10.

MUNDELEIN, GEORGE WILLIAM (1872–1939), cardinal. Born in New York City on July 2, he was educated at Manhattan College, St. Vincent Seminary, Latrobe, Pennsylvania, and the Propaganda, Rome, and was ordained in Rome in 1895. He became secretary to Bishop Charles McDonnell of Brooklyn, was chancellor of that diocese in 1897–1909, was made a domestic prelate in 1906, and was named titular bishop of Loryma and auxiliary of Brooklyn in 1909. He was appointed archbishop of Chicago in 1915, founded St. Mary of the Lake Seminary in Area, Illinois (the name of the seminary was changed to Mundelein in 1924, as was the name of the town), and Quigley Preparatory Seminary in 1916, and greatly expanded the number of churches, schools, hospitals, orphanages, and other institutions of the archdiocese, and in 1918 he established the Associated Catholic Charities in his see. He was made a cardinal in 1924, was elected president of the American Board of Catholic Missions in 1925, and was an early and vocal opponent of Nazism (it was he who labeled Adolf

Hitler "an Austrian paperhanger"), vigorously supported social reforms and measures to aid the workingman, and was a friend of the needy and a friend and adviser of President Franklin Roosevelt. He died in Chicago on Oct. 2.

MUNDWILER, FINTAN (1835–98), abbot. Born in Dietikon, Switzerland, on July 12, he was educated at Einsiedeln, Switzerland, joined the Benedictines there in 1854, and was ordained in 1859. He was then sent, with Martin Marty, future bishop of Sioux Falls and St. Cloud, to teach at the newly established St. Meinrad's Monastery in Indiana. He also engaged in missionary work in the surrounding area, founded St. Benedict's parish in Terre Haute, Indiana, in 1864, and when St. Meinrad's was made an abbey in 1869 he was made prior; he was elected its second abbot in 1880. He rebuilt the abbey after it was destroyed by fire in 1887, founded a commercial college at Jasper, Indiana, and St. Joseph's Abbey in Louisiana in 1889, and saw New Subiaco in Arkansas made an abbey in 1891. He was the first president of the Swiss-American Congregation of Benedictines, founded in 1881. He died at St. Meinrad's on Feb. 14.

MURPHY, FRANCIS PARNELL (1877–1958), governor. Born on a farm at Winchester, New Hampshire, on Aug. 16, he began his career working for the Child Chamberlain Company, a shoe manufacturer, in Newport, Rhode Island, in 1898, married Mae Herrick in 1902, moved on to J. F. McElwain Company in Nashua, also a shoe manufacturer, and in time rose to a partnership and vice presidency and was a director of the firm. He served on Governor Winant's staff in 1925–26, was a delegate to the New Hampshire Constitutional Convention in 1930, and was elected to the New Hampshire state legislature in 1931, where he served as chairman of the Ways and Means Committee. He was elected to the Governor's Council in 1933 and in 1938 was elected first Catholic governor of New Hampshire, serving two terms in 1937–41. As governor he signed a bill creating the New Hampshire State Police, approved an interstate agreement for flood control, and supported flood control projects in the Merrimack and Connecticut watershed, and introduced the merit system for state employees. He was defeated in a bid for the United States Senate in 1942 and then retired from public life and resumed his role with the McElwain company. He died in Nashua, New Hampshire, on Dec. 19.

MURPHY, FRANK (1890–1949), Associate Justice of the United States Supreme Court, governor. Born in Sand Beach (Harbor Beach), Michigan, on Apr. 13, he was educated at the University of Michigan (B.A. 1912, LL.B. 1914) and was admitted to the Michigan bar in 1916. He was a captain in the Army during World War I, studied for a time while in Europe at Lincoln's Inn, London, and Trinity College, Dublin, and on his return to the United States served as assistant United States attorney for the Eastern District of Michigan in 1919–22. He was defeated in a bid for Congress in 1920, resigned as U.S. attorney in 1922, and resumed his private law practice. He was elected a judge of Detroit's Recorder's Court in 1923 and reelected in 1929. In 1930 he was elected mayor of Detroit when Mayor Charles Bowles was ousted in a recall vote; he was reelected in 1931. He became an ardent New Dealer when Franklin D. Roosevelt was elected President and resigned as mayor in 1933 when he was appointed governor general of the Philippine Islands by Roosevelt; he was named High Commissioner when the Philippines became autonomous in 1935. He resigned his ten-year term in 1936 to run for governor of Michigan at the request of President Roosevelt and was elected. His settlement of the automobile workers sit-down strike in Flint, Michigan, in 1937 made him a national figure and brought him much praise, though his failure to act more forcibly and eject the strikers was later severely criticized when sit-down strikes spread throughout the country. He was defeated in a bid for reelection in 1938 and the following year President Roosevelt appointed him United States Attorney General. He was active in launching antitrust suits against capital and labor, set up a civil rights division in the Department of Justice, and crusaded against crime and corruption, was an ardent defender of civil liberties, freedom of religion and of speech, and of the rights of labor. In 1940 Roosevelt appointed him Associate Justice of the United States Supreme Court and during his tenure on the Court he joined the liberal bloc. Except for a brief period in 1942, when he left the Court to serve as an army officer, he served on it the rest of his life. He died in Detroit on July 19.

MURPHY, FREDERICK E. (1872–1940), journalist. Born in Troy, Wisconsin, on Dec. 5, he graduated from Notre Dame in 1893, joined the staff of the Minneapolis *Tribune* the same year, became interested in farm problems and wrote extensively and in depth on them. Ill health caused him to retire to his own farm in 1918 and he became more involved in the problems of farmers from his own actual experiences as the owner and operator of the four-thousand-acre Femco Cattle Farms. He returned to the *Tribune* as president and editor in 1921 and became a leading spokesman for western farmers, was recognized as a leading authority on American agriculture, was a delegate to the World Wheat Conference in 1933, and was named a permanent American delegate on the International Wheat Advisory Committee. He served as president of several firms, among them Manistique Pulp and Paper Company, Manistique Light and Power Company and Mutual Holding Company, and died in New York City on Feb. 14.

MURPHY, FREDERICK VERNON (1879–1958), architect. Born in Fond du Lac, Wisconsin, on Feb. 16, he studied at Columbian (George Washington) University, Washington, D.C., in 1899–1901 and the École des Beaux Arts, Paris. He became professor of architecture and head of the architecture department at Catholic University from 1910, founded the firm of Murphy and Locraft, and married Marjorie Mary Cannon in 1936. He became an outstanding architect of ecclesiastical buildings, among them St. Charles College Chapel, Catonsville, Maryland, Sacred Heart Church, Washington, D.C., St. Francis de Sales Church, Buffalo, New York, and St. Mary's Church, Mobile, Alabama. He also designed public buildings and among his outstanding work in this field were the John Kernan Memorial Library and the Papal Legation, Washington, D.C. He was consulting architect for the National Shrine of the Immaculate Conception, Washington, D.C., and he was a member of the design committee for the House of Representatives Office Building, the new National Museum, and the Naval Hospital. He died in Chevy Chase, Maryland, on May 4.

MURPHY, HENRY VINCENT (1888–1960), architect. Son of an Irish immigrant farmer, he was born in Horseheads, New York, on Mar. 4 and graduated from Pratt Institute School of Architecture, Brooklyn, New York, in 1909. He began working as a drafts-man with the Public Service Commission in New York and in 1911 took a similar position in the office of Henry McGill in New York. He left in 1919 to become a partner in the firm of Collins, Murphy and Lehman in Brooklyn, which became Murphy and Lehman in 1925, and from 1929 he worked for his own firm, Henry V. Murphy, specializing in designing schools and churches. He married Marie Tracy in 1923 and in time became one of the outstanding ecclesiastical architects in the United States. Among his best-known works are Mary Louis Academy (1947), four buildings of St. John's University (1946), and Archbishop Molloy High School (1950), all in Jamaica, Queens, New York City, Our Lady of Refuge Church (1953), Brooklyn and St. Francis of Assisi Church (1950), Norristown, Pennsylvania. He served on the board of design for the Brooklyn civic center for six years, received numerous architectural awards, and died in Brooklyn, New York, on May 17.

MURPHY, JOHN BENJAMIN (1857–1916), surgeon. Born near Appleton, Wisconsin, on Dec. 21, he studied medicine at Rush Medical College, Chicago, and received his medical degree in 1879. He interned at Cook County Hospital, continued his studies at Vienna for two years, and then returned to Chicago. He became one of the leading surgeons in the United States and revolutionized methods of internal surgery. An eminent teacher and highly regarded for his surgical innovations, he was a pioneer in gall bladder work, developed new techniques in blood vessel surgery and of the intestinal tract, developing a device to link severed ends of the intestines, and of the chest, especially his technique of collapsing a lung in the treatment of pulmonary tuberculosis. He was professor of surgery at

Northwestern in 1901–5 and 1908–16 and at Rush in 1905–8, was consulting surgeon in many Chicago hospitals, and served as president of the American Medical Association in 1910. His notes on his clinical consultations, the five-volume *The Surgical Clinics of John B. Murphy, M.D., at Mercy Hospital, Chicago* (1912–16), received wide circulation. He was honored by the governments of England, France, and Germany, several universities, and Pope Benedict XV and he was the recipient of the Laetare Medal in 1902. He died on Mackinac Island, Michigan, on Aug. 11.

MURPHY, JOHN JOSEPH (1812–80), publisher. Born in County Tyrone, Ireland, on Mar. 12, he was brought to the United States when he was ten by his parents, who settled in Delaware. He went to Philadelphia to learn the printing trade and about 1835 established a book and stationery store in Baltimore. He began publishing books the following year and soon became one of the leading U.S. publishers of Catholic books. Among them was Cardinal Gibbons's *The Faith of Our Fathers* (1876), which sold several million copies. He also was a prominent printer and received a papal gold medal in 1855 for publishing the documents relating to the dogma of the Immaculate Conception and was given the title "Typographer of the Holy See" for his publication of the decrees of the second Plenary Council of Baltimore in 1866. He published *U.S. Catholic Magazine* in 1842–49, *Catholic Youth Magazine* in 1859–61, and the *Metropolitan Catholic Almanac and Laity's Directory.* He also published publications of the Maryland Historical Society for a quarter century. He died in Baltimore on May 27.

MURPHY, ROBERT DANIEL (1894–1978), diplomat. Born in Milwaukee, Wisconsin, on Oct. 28, he worked in his teens to pay for his education at Marquette Academy and Marquette University and in 1917 entered the United States diplomatic service as a consular clerk in the American legation in Bern, Switzerland. On his return to the United States in 1919 he worked in the Treasury Department, took evening law courses at George Washington University (LL.B. 1920, LL.M. 1928), and was admitted to the District of Columbia bar. He served in Germany for a time, was consul at Seville, Spain, in 1925–26 and at Paris in 1930–36, and was made first secretary of the embassy by Ambassador William C. Bullitt and in 1939 counselor. He was chargé d'affaires briefly in 1940, participated, under the nom de plume of Lieutenant Colonel McGowan, in negotiations with the Vichy leaders of France, and in 1942 persuaded Admiral Jean Darlan to sign an armistice arrangement. He was principal planner of Allied landings in North Africa during World War II in 1942 and chief civil affairs officer on General Eisenhower's staff in North Africa and the President's personal representative, with the rank of minister, to North Africa. He participated in the negotiations for Italy's surrender in 1943 and was named United States political adviser for Germany with the rank of ambassador in 1944, continuing as political adviser to the military in 1949. He was named United States ambassador to Belgium in 1949, ambassador to Japan in 1952–53, and Deputy Under Secretary of State for Political Affairs and Assistant Secretary of State for United Nations affairs in 1953. He was Deputy Under Secretary of State in 1954–59, was one of the four diplomats named Career Diplomat in 1956, helped settle the Yugoslav-Italian dispute over Trieste later the same year, and in 1958 helped in the negotiations between France and Tunisia which led to Tuni-

sia's freedom. He was Undersecretary of State for political affairs in 1959–60, was the recipient of the Laetare Medal in 1959, and became honorary chairman of Corning Glass International in 1967. He was the author of *Diplomat Among Warriors* (1964) and died in New York City on Jan. 9.

MURPHY, THOMAS EDWARD (1856–1933), educator. Born in New York City on Jan. 27, he was educated at St. Francis Xavier College there and joined the Jesuits in 1875. He continued his studies at Quebec and Woodstock College, Maryland, and was ordained in 1890. He served as vice president of Georgetown from 1891 to 1893, when he was named president of St. Francis Xavier, was transferred to Holy Cross College, Worcester, Massachusetts, in 1900 and was its president in 1911, and was then appointed rector of St. Ignatius Church, Brooklyn, New York, and remained in that position until his death in Brooklyn on Dec. 14.

MURPHY, WILLIAM FRANCIS (1885–1950), bishop. Born in Kalamazoo, Michigan, on May 11, he was educated at St. Joseph College, Kitchener, Ontario, Canada, Assumption College, Sandwich, Ontario, Canada, and the Propaganda, Rome (S.T.D. 1908), and was ordained in Rome in 1908. He continued his studies at the Apollinaris, Rome (J.C.L. 1909), and then returned to the United States. He was a curate at St. Thomas Church, Ann Arbor, Michigan, in 1910–12, at Holy Cross Church, Marine City, Michigan, in 1912–19, and at SS. Peter and Paul Cathedral, Detroit, Michigan, in 1919–21. He was founding pastor of St. David's Church, Detroit, in 1921–38, was made a domestic prelate in 1934, and was appointed first bishop of the newly established diocese of Saginaw, Michigan, in 1938. During his episco-

MURRAY, ALBERT A.

pate, he established a diocesan paper, the *Catholic Weekly,* in 1942, convoked the first diocesan synod, established a chancery office, the League of Catholic Women and the Clergy Benefit Society in 1939, a diocesan Catholic Charities in 1943, and a Mexican apostolate in 1947 for the Spanish-speaking of the diocese and migrant workers. He died in Saginaw on Feb. 7.

MURRAY, ALBERT A. (1889–1964), editor. Born in Baltimore on Jan. 18, he was educated at the University of Maryland, where he studied law, St. Paul's College, and the Theological College, Catholic University, and was ordained a Paulist priest in 1926. He was business manager of the *Catholic World* in 1926–28 and was a member of the Paulist Fathers Mission Band in 1926–46, preaching all over the country. He founded *Information* magazine in 1946 and was its editor until 1958. He wrote several pamphlets and *Prayer for Daily Needs* (1947) and died in New York City on Feb. 26.

MURRAY, GEORGE DOMINIC (1889–1956), admiral. Born in Boston on July 6, he graduated from the United States Naval Academy in 1911, served at the Anacostia Naval Air Station in 1918, was squadron commander of the first aviation unit in the Philippines in 1923–25, married Corinne Montague Mustin in 1925, and served as naval attaché in London, Paris, Berlin, and The Hague, 1930–33. He was air officer on the U.S.S. *Saratoga* in 1933–35 and executive officer in 1937–38, commanded the U.S.S. *Langley* in 1938–39 and the U.S.S. *Enterprise* in 1941–42, and was task force commander, U.S.S. *Hornet,* flagship, in 1942. He served at Pensacola, Florida, in 1942–43, was commander of the Air Force, Pacific Fleet, in 1944–45, and accepted the surrender of the Japanese on Truk Atoll in 1945.

He was commandant of the 9th Naval District in 1946–47, commander of the 1st Task Force Fleet in 1947–48 and of the Western Sea Frontier and Pacific Reserve Fleet from 1948 to 1951, when he retired and became a director of Pacific Telephone and Telegraph Company. He died in San Francisco on June 18.

MURRAY, JAMES EDWARD (1876–1961), United States senator. Born on a farm near St. Thomas, Ontario, Canada, on May 3, he graduated from St. Jerome's College, Berlin (Kitchener), Ontario, in 1897. He moved to the United States the same year, studied law at New York University (LL.B. 1900), became an American citizen in 1900, received his LL.M. in 1901, and was admitted to the Montana bar that year. He built up a successful law practice in Butte, married Viola Edna Horgan in 1905, and was county attorney for Silver Bow County in 1906–8. He campaigned for the election of Franklin Roosevelt for President in 1932, was chairman of the state advisory board for the Public Works Administration in Montana in 1933–34, was appointed to fill an unexpired term in the United States Senate in 1934, and then was reelected five terms until his retirement in 1961. He was a leader of the liberal group in the Democratic Party and supported most of the domestic policies of President Roosevelt, though he remained silent on the President's plan to reorganize the Supreme Court. He was an isolationist until World War II broke out, when he was on the side of the internationalists, though he opposed the Selective Service Act of 1940. He cosponsored the Employment Act of 1946, was coauthor, with Senator Robert Wagner of New York, of legislation broadening social security, old age, and unemployment benefits and also introduced the first Medicare bill. He was chairman of several Senate committees, opposed the Taft-Hartley Act, and unsuccessfully urged the creation of a Missouri Valley Authority. He died in Butte on Mar. 23.

MURRAY, JOHN COURTNEY (1904–67), theologian. Son of an attorney, he was born in New York City on Sept. 12, was raised in Queens and planned to become a lawyer. He studied at St. Francis Xavier College in New York from 1916 until 1920, when he joined the Jesuits. He continued his studies at Weston College, Massachusetts, in 1924–27, received his M.A. from Boston College in 1927, taught in the Philippines for three years, and was ordained in 1932. He continued his education at Woodstock College, Maryland (S.T.L. 1934), and at the Gregorian, Rome (S.T.D. 1936), and in 1936 joined the faculty at Woodstock as professor of dogmatic theology, remaining on the staff until his death; he was visiting professor of philosophy at Yale in 1951–52. He became widely known as an expert on church-state relations as he sought to reconcile the traditions of the Catholic Church with the demands of America's pluralistic society. Among his other concerns were interracial justice, civil rights, the promotion of civil and religious freedom, peace and ecumenism, but the study of church-state relations was his paramount interest. He became the center of controversy in the fifties when his proposal that the Vatican give its blessing to the relationship between church and state that existed in the United States attracted international attention. In 1954 his Jesuit superiors in Rome demanded he stop writing and lecturing on the subject—which he did —and he was required to clear all his writing with Jesuit headquarters in Rome. He came into his own at Vatican Council II when Cardinal Francis Spell-

man of New York invited him to Rome as his peritus. He became the best-known peritus at the Council and was the architect of the Declaration on Religious Freedom passed by the Council in 1965, which some authorities consider the major contribution of the Council. He received numerous honorary degrees and was named director of the La Farge Institute in 1966. He died of a heart attack in New York City on Aug. 16. Most of Murray's theses were presented in essays in *Theological Studies,* of which he became an editor in 1941, and in his books, among them *We Hold These Truths* (1961), *The Problem of God* (1963), and *Problems of Religious Freedom* (1965).

MURRAY, JOHN GREGORY (1877–1956), archbishop. Born in Waterbury, Connecticut, on Feb. 26, he was educated at Holy Cross College, Worcester, Massachusetts (B.A. 1897), and the North American College, Rome, and Louvain, Belgium, and was ordained at Louvain in 1900. He taught Greek and Latin at St. Thomas Seminary, Hartford, Connecticut, in 1900, was named chancellor of the Hartford diocese in 1903, and was appointed titular bishop of Flavias and auxiliary of Hartford in 1919. He was transferred to Portland, Maine, as its fifth bishop in 1925 and in 1931 was named archbishop of St. Paul, Minnesota. During his episcopate in St. Paul, he established eighty-seven new parishes, doubled the enrollment in Catholic elementary schools, built new high schools, organized an archdiocesan Confraternity of Christian Doctrine and a Catholic labor school in Minneapolis in 1933, built retreat houses, homes for the aged, and the Newman Center and chapel at the University of Minnesota in 1953, and brought new religious orders into the see. He died in St. Paul on Oct. 11.

MURRAY, JOHN O'KANE (1847–85), author, physician. Born in Antrim, Ireland, on Dec. 12, he was brought to the United States by his parents when he was nine. He studied at St. John's College (Fordham) and then medicine at the University of the City of New York and practiced medicine in Brooklyn until 1880, when ill health forced him to retire. He devoted himself to writing and over the next few years wrote popular-interest books on Church history, lives of the saints, Irish poetry, and English history and literature, among them *Popular History of the Catholic Church in the United States* (1876), *Poets and Poetry* (1877), *Little Lives of the Great Saints* (1879), *Catholic Pioneers of America* (1881), and *Lessons in English Literature* (1883). He died in Chicago on July 30.

MURRAY, LAWRENCE O. (1864–1926), financier. Born in Addison Hill, Steuben County, New York, on Feb. 18, he was educated at Niagara and New York universities (LL.B. 1893), was admitted to the bar in 1893, and practiced law in New York City. He was secretary to the assistant of the Treasury in 1893–96, was chief of the organization division of the Treasury Department in 1896–98 and was deputy controller of the currency in 1898–99. He was trust officer with the Trust Company of America in New York City in 1899–1902 and of the Central Trust Company of Chicago in 1902–4, was assistant secretary of the Department of Commerce and Labor in 1904–8, and was controller of the treasury in 1908–13. He was in the accounting section of the Signal Corps during World War I and served with the American Red Cross and was field secretary of the Knights of Columbus. He died in Elmira, New York, on June 10.

MURRAY, PHILIP (1886–1952), labor leader. Born in Blantyre, Scotland, on May 25, of Catholic immigrants from Ireland, he left school after the sixth grade, when he was ten years old, and went to work with his father in the coal mines. He came to the United States with his parents in 1902, went to work in the coal mines of Pennsylvania, and was elected president of a United Mine Workers of America (UMW) local formed in 1904 after a strike called when he was fired for accusing a checkweighman of cheating failed; the union lost the strike but he was launched on the career that was to make him one of the outstanding American labor leaders of the twentieth century. The following year he was elected a member of the UMW's international board and in 1916 he became president of District 5 and in 1920 was appointed vice president of the UMW by John L. Lewis, the beginning of an association that was to last the next two decades. He successfully led membership drives during the New Deal era under the National Industrial Recovery Act and fought for the formation of industrial unions at the American Federation of Labor (AFL) Convention in 1935. When the craft unions rejected the concept, eight industrial unions led by the UMW formed the Committee for Industrial Organization (CIO), with John L. Lewis as president. Murray was appointed chairman of the Steel Workers Organizing Committee (SWOC) in 1936 and in the next two years signed contracts, with Big Steel recognizing the right of SWOC to organize, although Little Steel did not. Murray's recommendation of a strike led to bloody confrontations (ten workers were killed at the Republic Steel plant in South Chicago in 1937) and eventually the steel companies were compelled to sign union contracts by the National Labor Relations Board. Murray worked to settle disputes among unions in the CIO and for the reunion of the CIO and the AFL (vetoed by Lewis in 1937) and in 1940 was elected president of the CIO after Lewis made good his threat to resign if President Roosevelt was reelected in 1940. Lewis and Murray parted company in 1942 when at Lewis's instigation the International Policy Board of the UMW removed Murray from the vice presidency of the UMW on the grounds his activities for SWOC were incompatible with his duties as vice president of the UMW. The break between the two men was completed when the UMW withdrew from the CIO and SWOC became the United Steel Workers of America with Murray as president, a position he held the rest of his life with the presidency of the CIO. He supported the government during World War II and was a member of the Combined War Labor Board. He was a supporter of the movement among blacks to end discrimination in union membership and had the CIO condemn racial discrimination. In 1943 he organized the CIO's Political Action Committee, which became active in the political life of the country, and fought for a guaranteed annual wage and union pensions, vigorously opposed the Taft-Hartley bill, and was active in securing what he considered proper CIO representation on international labor bodies, actions which led to the formation of the World Federation of Trade Unions in 1945. In 1949 he expelled Communist-dominated unions from the CIO, losing almost a third of the CIO's membership in the process. He died in San Francisco on Nov. 9.

MURRAY, THOMAS EDWARD (1860–1929), engineer, inventor. Son of a carpenter, he was born in Albany, New York, on Oct. 21, and was forced to go to work in his youth when his father died. In 1881 he became an operating engineer at the Albany Waterworks pumping plant and in 1887, when he married Catherine Bradley, he joined Anthony N. Brady's Municipal Gas Company in Albany and rose in the ranks until he was overseer of all the company's activities, including its plants in other areas. In 1895 he moved to New York City, where he consolidated the company's properties there into the New York Edison Company in 1900, becoming senior vice president in 1924; after the merger of New York Edison Company and the Brooklyn Edison Company in 1928 he became vice chairman of the board of directors of the merged companies. He was responsible for the building of many of the power stations supplying New York with electricity, designed steam power and hydroelectric plants in various parts of the country, and founded several corporations of his own (among them, Thomas Murray, Inc., and the Murray Radiator Company) to market and develop many of the eleven hundred patents issued to him (only Thomas A. Edison had more). He served as president of the Institute of Electrical Engineers, was the recipient of the Gold Medal of the American Museum of Safety for his safety devices, and was the author of several books, among them, *Electric Power Plants* (1910), *Power Stations* (1922), and *Applied Engineering* (1926). He was active in Catholic affairs, was made a Knight of St. Gregory and a Knight of Malta, and died at his summer home, "Wickapogue," Southampton, New York, on July 21.

MURRAY, THOMAS EDWARD (1891–1961), member of the Atomic Energy Commission. Born in Albany, New York, on June 20, he studied mechanical engineering at the Sheffield

Scientific School at Yale, receiving his degree in mechanical engineering in 1911, worked for two years as an engineer with the New York Edison Company, and then joined his father's firm, the Metropolitan Engineering Company, and became president on his father's death in 1929 and later of Thomas E. Murray, Inc., and the Murray Manufacturing Company. During World War I, he developed several welding techniques in the manufacture of mortar shells, married Marie Brady in 1917, and after the war developed several processes for auto radiators and rear-axle housings. He became famous for his inventions, patenting some two hundred, and as a leader in the business world; he was director of the finance committee of the Chrysler Corporation, was named receiver of the bankrupt Interborough Rapid Transit Company and Manhattan Railway Company in New York City in 1932, and served as trustee of several banks and of the welfare fund of the United Mine Workers. He became known also for his settlements of labor disputes in World War II. He resigned from his various positions when President Truman appointed him to the United States Atomic Energy Commission (AEC) in 1950. As a member of the AEC he at first advocated rapid expansion of AEC facilities to produce nuclear weapons and accelerated research on the hydrogen bomb and pushed for the development of nuclear propulsion systems for warships, submarines, and aircraft. Later he became increasingly concerned over the potential of nuclear weapons to destroy civilization and advocated a ban on multimegaton nuclear devices, though he favored the continued testing and production of tactical nuclear weapons and the development of nuclear power for peaceful purposes. When his term on the AEC expired in 1957 he was not reappointed by President Eisenhower, whereupon he was appointed a consultant to the Joint Congressional Committee on Atomic Energy. He failed in an attempt to secure the nomination of the Democratic Party for the United States Senate in 1958. He urged the resumption of nuclear testing by the United States in 1960 (it had been halted in 1958). He was twice honored by the papacy for his charitable works and with honorary degrees from numerous universities and colleges and received the Laetare Medal in 1952. He died in New York City on May 26.

MUSSIO, JOHN ANTHONY KING (1902–78), bishop. Born in Cincinnati, Ohio, on June 13, he was educated at Xavier University there, Notre Dame, Mt. St. Mary of the West Seminary, Cincinnati, and the Angelicum, Rome, and was ordained in Cincinnati in 1935. He engaged in pastoral work in the Cincinnati archdiocese, became chancellor, and in 1945 was appointed first bishop of the newly established diocese of Steubenville, Ohio. During his thirty-two-year episcopate, he greatly increased the number of priests and institutions in the diocese, established a major and a minor seminary, and saw the College of Steubenville opened by the Third Order Regular of St. Francis and the first issue of the Steubenville *Register* published in 1946. He retired in 1977 and died in Steubenville on Apr. 15.

N

NAGLE, URBAN (1905–65), author, theatrical producer. Edward John Nagle was born in Providence, Rhode Island, on Sept. 10, was educated at Providence College (B.A.), joined the Dominicans, taking the name Urban, in 1924, and was professed the following year. He studied for the priesthood at the Dominican House of Studies, River Forest, Illinois, the Dominican House of Theology, Washington, D.C., and Catholic University (Ph.D. 1934). He was ordained in Washington in 1931 and the following year, with Fr. Thomas Carey, founded the Blackfriars Guild, dedicated to producing dramas in the Catholic tradition; in time there were to be Guild chapters in twenty cities. He taught English and drama at Providence College in 1934–40, directed the Providence chapter of the Guild which was founded in 1935, and was a cofounder of the Catholic Theatre Conference in 1937. He was assigned to New York City in 1940 to work on the *Holy Name Journal,* became its editor and served in that position until 1946. He was producer and moderator of the New York chapter of the Blackfriars in 1940–51, which soon developed into an outstanding theatrical group. He wrote several plays produced by the Blackfriars, among them *Savanorola* (1938), *Lady of Fatima* (1948), and *City of Kings* (1949), and published his autobiography, *Behind the Masque,* in 1951. He was chaplain of St. Mary of the Springs, Columbus, Ohio, the last years of his life and died in Cincinnati, Ohio, on Mar. 11.

NAGOT, FRANCIS CHARLES (1734–1816), educator. Born in Tours, France, on Apr. 19, he was educated at the Jesuit college there, joined the Sulpicians in Paris in 1753, and was ordained in 1860. He taught at the Nantes seminary, received his doctorate in theology from the University of Nantes, and in 1768 was made superior of the Little Company of Saint-Sulpice in Paris. He became superior of the Little Seminary of Saint-Sulpice in 1770 and vice-rector of the Grand Seminary of Saint-Sulpice in 1789. The following year he went to London to discuss the establishment of a seminary for the new diocese of Baltimore in the United States. He was named superior of the group of Sulpicians sent to the United States and in 1791 opened the first seminary in the United States, St. Mary's in Baltimore. He opened a minor seminary at Pigeon Hill, Pennsylvania, in 1806, but it failed in 1809 and the students were sent to Mt. St. Mary's Seminary, Emmitsburg, Maryland. Nagot resigned as superior soon after but remained at St. Mary's until his death there on Apr. 9.

NAJMY, JUSTIN (1898–1968), apostolic exarch. Born in Aleppo, Syria, on Apr. 23, he was educated at the Greek college and the Propaganda, Rome, and was ordained in 1926. He was consecrated titular bishop of Augustopolis in Phrygia and apostolic exarch for Melkites in the United States in 1966, made his headquarters in Boston, and died in Manchester, New Hampshire, on June 11.

NAVAGH, JAMES JOHNSTON (1901–65), bishop. Born in Buffalo, New York, on Apr. 4, he was educated at Canisius College, Buffalo, New York (B.A.), and Niagara (New York) College (M.A.), and was ordained in Buffalo in 1929. He was a curate at Holy Cross Church, Buffalo, in 1929–37, pastor of Our Lady of Carmel Church, Brant, New York, in 1937–40, and of St. Joseph's Church, Fredonia, New York, in 1940–42. He was named first director of the missionary apostolate of the diocese of Buffalo in 1939, titular bishop of Ombi and auxiliary of Raleigh, North Carolina, in 1952, and was appointed bishop of Ogdensburg, New York, in 1957. He served as director of the National Catholic Rural Life Conference and in 1963 he became fourth bishop of Paterson, New Jersey. He was the author of *The Apostolic Parish* (1950) and died of a heart attack in Rome while attending the fourth session of Vatican Council II on Oct. 2.

NEALE, LEONARD (1746–1817), archbishop. Born near Port Tobacco, Maryland, on Oct. 15, he was sent to France when he was twelve and studied at St. Omer, Flanders, Bruges, and Liège. He joined the Jesuits in 1767 and was ordained. When the Jesuits were suppressed by Pope Clement XIV in 1773, he went to England and engaged in pastoral work there until 1779, when he went to British Guiana as a missionary. He was forced to return to the United States in 1783 because of ill health, worked at the Port Tobacco mission, and was appointed pastor of St. Mary's Church, Philadelphia, in 1793. He became Bishop John Carroll's vicar-general and was named president of Georgetown, then an academy, in 1798; he developed the academy into a college

in 1801. He was appointed titular bishop of Gortyna and coadjutor to Bishop Carroll in 1793 but the bulls did not arrive until 1800. He remained as president of Georgetown until 1806 and succeeded to Archbishop Carroll's see of Baltimore as its second archbishop in 1815, when he was almost seventy. In 1816, he and Teresa Lalor, who had been under his spiritual direction since 1797, founded the Visitation Order of nuns in the United States when he received a grant from Pope Pius VII declaring her community part of the Visitation Order. During his brief episcopate he was plagued by schisms in Philadelphia and Charleston, South Carolina. He died in Georgetown on June 18.

NECKERE, LEO RAYMOND DE (1800–33), bishop. Born in Wevelghem, Belgium, on June 6, he was educated at Roulers and the Lazarist seminary at Ghent and went to the United States in 1817 in response to a call for priests from Bishop Louis Dubourg of Louisiana. He continued his studies for the priesthood at St. Thomas Seminary, Kentucky, and St. Mary of the Barrens, Missouri, and was ordained a Lazarist priest in 1822. He taught at St. Mary's for a time, engaged in missionary activities in Missouri and Louisiana, and was named vicar-general of New Orleans in 1827. He was appointed bishop of that diocese in 1829 and during his episcopate visited Europe several times to recover his health and brought back statues and sacred vessels for the churches of the diocese, books for the seminary library, and a printing press. He died on Sept. 4, four years after his consecration, in New Orleans of the plague he had contracted while ministering to its victims.

NEILL, CHARLES PATRICK (1865–1942), educator, labor mediator. Born in Rock Island, Illinois, on Dec. 12, he was brought to Austin, Texas, by his parents in 1871 and was educated at Notre Dame, the University of Texas, Georgetown (B.A. 1891), and the University of Chicago. He began teaching at Notre Dame in 1891, left in 1894 to study for his Ph.D. at Johns Hopkins, which he received in 1897, and was professor of political economy at Catholic University in 1897–1905. He married Esther Waggaman in 1901, served as assistant recorder for the commission handling labor-management disputes in the anthracite coal industry, and was United States Commissioner of Labor from 1905 until 1913, when he was named commissioner of labor statistics in the newly created Department of Labor. In these positions he helped mediate railroad disputes and prepared a report on his investigation of the meatpacking industry that led to the federal inspection law of 1906; he also prepared a report on child labor for Congress and was one of those who drafted the Newlands Act regulating railroad disputes in 1913. He left the Department of Labor in 1913 to specialize in mediating labor disputes, became manager of the bureau of information of Southeastern Railways and was in charge of labor problems in 1915–39. He helped promote industrial safety and supported state workmen's compensation laws and was president of the American Statistical Association in 1916–17. He served on the U.S. Railroad Board of Adjustments in 1919–21, on the U.S. Coal Commission in 1922–23, received the Laetare Medal in 1922, and died in Washington, D.C., on Oct. 3. He is reported to have arbitrated more than three thousand labor disputes during his career.

NERAZ, JOHN CLAUDIUS (1828–94), bishop. Born in Anse, Rhone, France, on Jan. 12, he was educated at St. Jodard Seminary there, the Aix seminary, and the Grand Seminary, Lyons. He emigrated to the United States in 1851, was ordained at Galveston, Texas, and engaged in missionary work in eastern and southern Texas. He was appointed first vicar-general of San Antonio, Texas, in 1870, was administrator of the see in 1880–81, and in 1881 was appointed its second bishop, a position he held until his death in San Antonio on Nov. 15. He was also appointed administrator of the vicariate apostolic of Brownsville, Texas, in 1885, when its bishop, Dominic Manucy, died, and administered it until the appointment of the new vicar apostolic, Bishop Pedro Verdaguer, in 1890.

NERINCKX, CHARLES (1761–1824), missionary. Son of a doctor and the eldest of fourteen children, he was born in Herffelingen, Belgium, on Oct. 2, was educated at Enghien, Gheel, Louvain, and the Mechlin seminary and was ordained in 1781. He was named vicar of the Mechlin cathedral in 1785, became known for his concern for the poor, and in 1784 became pastor of Everberg-Meerbeke. He was ordered arrested by the revolutionary French Directoire but went into hiding for four years, and in 1804 he emigrated to the United States, where he stayed briefly at Georgetown. The following year he was assigned to missionary work in Kentucky by Bishop John Carroll and worked from Bardstown with Stephen T. Badin. He refused the bishopric of New Orleans in 1809 to remain with his people, organized the first Holy Name Society in Kentucky in 1809, was especially interested in the education of children, and in 1812 founded the Congregation of the Sisters of Loretto at the Foot of the Cross devoted to Christian education—the first native American religious community. He made two trips back to Europe to secure missionaries and funds for his mission, was instrumental in bringing back Jesuits from Belgium to work as missionaries in the West, among them Pierre de Smet, and also brought back with him a number of valuable paintings, which were given to the Louisville diocese. A dispute with Bishop Guy Chabrat over the rule of the Sisters of Loretto caused him to decide to leave Kentucky to minister to the Indians in Missouri, and he died at St. Genevieve, Missouri, while on the way.

NEUMANN, JOHN NEPOMUCENE, ST. (1811–60), bishop. The third child of Agnes and Philip Neumann, he was born in Prachatitz, Bohemia, on Mar. 28 and was early attracted to the religious life. He entered the Budweis diocesan seminary in 1831 and two years later the theological school at Charles Ferdinand University, where he finished in 1835. Though not yet ordained in 1836, he volunteered for the New York diocese, went to the United States, and was ordained in New York City the same year. He spent the next four years in missionary work, especially among German-speaking Catholics in upstate New York, and in 1840 joined the newly established branch of the Redemptorists in Pittsburgh; in 1842 he was the first Redemptorist to be professed in the United States. He continued his missionary work in Maryland, Ohio, Pennsylvania, and Virginia and was very popular among the German populace. In 1844 he was named superior of the Redemptorists in Pittsburgh, where three years later he built St. Philomena Church. He became vice-regent and vice-provincial of the American Redemptorists, became an American citizen, built SS. Peter and Paul Church in Baltimore in 1848, and was named rector of St. Alphonsus Church there in 1851. He was appointed fourth bishop of Philadelphia in 1852, reorganized the diocese, inaugurated a widespread program of church and school

building, organized the parochial schools into a diocesan system, and established a preparatory seminary at Glen Riddle, Pennsylvania, in 1859. He was an active proponent of Catholic education (on his consecration as bishop of Philadelphia there were two Catholic schools there; on his death there were a hundred) and wrote, while rector at Pittsburgh in 1845, two catechisms, known as the Redemptorist Catechisms, that were endorsed by the American bishops at the first Plenary Council of Baltimore in 1852 and were widely used in Catholic schools the next thirty-five years. He brought numerous religious orders into his see, helped save the colored Oblate Sisters of Baltimore from dissolution, was the first American bishop to introduce the Forty Hours' Devotion into his see on a diocesan-wide scale in 1853, and founded the Sisters of the Third Order of St. Francis in Philadelphia in 1855. At the time of his death in Philadelphia on Jan. 5, he was renowned and venerated for his holiness, charity, spiritual writing, pastoral work, and preaching. He was canonized in 1977 by Pope Paul VI, the first male citizen of the United States to be so honored; his feast day is celebrated on Jan. 5.

NEVILS, COLEMAN (1878–1955), educator. William Coleman Nevils was born in Philadelphia on May 29 and was educated at St. Joseph's College there (B.A., M.A.), joined the Jesuits in 1896, and taught at high schools in Boston and New York City in 1903–8. He received his Ph.D. from Woodstock College, Maryland, and was ordained there in 1911, was a professor of rhetoric at St. Andrew's-on-Hudson, Poughkeepsie, New York, and of philosophy at Holy Cross College, Worcester, Massachusetts, and went to Georgetown in 1918, serving as dean in 1918–19, as chancellor in 1919–24, and regent of the

School of Foreign Service from 1920 until he was appointed dean of Shadowbrook Jesuit House of Studies in 1924. He returned to Georgetown as president in 1928, reorganized its School of Foreign Service, and was a member of the United States delegation to the international Red Cross conference in Tokyo in 1934. He left Georgetown in 1935, was rector of Loyola School and Regis High School and pastor of St. Ignatius Church in New York City in 1935–42, and was president of Scranton University in 1942–47, when the Maryland province of the Society of Jesus acquired it in 1942. He received several honorary degrees and was honored by several foreign governments, wrote *Miniatures of Georgetown* (1934), *Saving Sense* (1947), and *Moulders of Men* (1953), was named superior of Campion House in New York City in 1947 and spiritual director of the Jesuit community of St. Ignatius in 1953. He died in New York City on Oct. 12.

NEWMAN, THOMAS A. (1903–78), bishop. Born in Waterbury, Connecticut, on Nov. 3, he joined the La Salette Fathers and was educated at the La Salette Seminary, Ipswich, Massachusetts, and the Gregorian, Rome, and was ordained a priest of the Missionaries of Our Lady of La Salette in 1929. He was consecrated first bishop of Prome, Burma, in 1961 and died in Hartford, Connecticut, on Mar. 9, after having spent forty years as a missionary in Burma.

NEWTON, JOHN (1823–95), general. Son of General Thomas Newton, a congressman for twenty-nine years, and his second wife, Margaret Jordan Pool Newton, he was born in Norfolk, Virginia, on Aug. 24. He graduated from West Point, second in his class, in 1842, taught engineering there, engaged in army engineering projects on the Atlantic and Gulf of Mexico coasts, rose to the rank of captain in 1856, and was named chief engineer of the Utah expedition in 1858. At the outset of the Civil War, he was engaged in fortification work on Delaware Bay and became chief engineer of the Department of Pennsylvania and of the Shenandoah, spent 1861–62 working on the defenses of Washington, D.C., and as brigadier general of volunteers in charge of a brigade engaged in its defense and served under General McClellan during the Peninsula Campaign. He participated with great distinction and gallantry in numerous battles, among them Antietam, Fredericksburg, Chancellorsville, and Gettysburg, where he commanded the I Army Corps and was brevetted a colonel of regulars. He participated in the invasion of Georgia and the capture of Atlanta and then commanded the districts of West Florida. He was commissioned lieutenant colonel of engineers in the regular Army after the war in 1865 and was stationed in New York City in 1866, where he was in charge of fortifications and made numerous improvements to New York Harbor, the Hudson River north to Troy, and the harbors of Lake Champlain. Among his most celebrated engineering feats were the destruction of Hallett's Reef and of Flood Rock (or Middle Reef) in Hell Gate Channel in the East River, New York City, in 1876 and in 1885, which removed these dangerous navigational hazards. He was promoted to the rank of brigadier general and chief of engineers in 1884, retired in 1886, and was appointed New York City Commissioner of Public Works the next day. He received the Laetare Medal in 1886, resigned as Commissioner in 1888, and became president of the Panama Railroad Company, a position he held until his death in New York City on May 1.

421

NIEUWLAND, JULIUS ARTHUR (1878–1936), chemist. Born in Hansbeke, Belgium, on Feb. 14, he was brought to the United States when a child and was educated at Notre Dame (B.A. 1899). He joined the Congregation of Holy Cross, was ordained in 1903, and continued his studies at Catholic University (Ph.D. 1904). He taught chemistry and botany at Notre Dame in 1904–18 and was dean of the School of Science in 1920–24, founded *American Midland Naturalist* in 1909 and edited it for five years, and became professor of chemistry in 1918. He was curator of the botanical herbaria at Notre Dame. He engaged in research in the production of synthetic rubber from 1906, attracted the attention of Du Pont du Nemours & Company to his research with a paper he read at the American Chemical Society at Rochester in 1925, and worked with them to produce a new synthetic rubber, neoprene, in 1931. A reference in his doctoral thesis, *Some Reactions of Acetylene,* led to the development of Lewisite, World War I's poison gas, by Dr. W. Lee Lewis in 1917 (the gas was never used by the Allies). He died in Washington, D.C., on June 11.

NILAN, JOHN JOSEPH (1855–1934), bishop. Born in Newburyport, Massachusetts, on Aug. 1, he was educated at St. Raphael's College, Nicolet, Canada, and St. Joseph's Seminary, Dunwoodie, Yonkers, New York, and was ordained in 1878. He engaged in pastoral work in Massachusetts, was pastor of St. Joseph's Church, Amesbury, Massachusetts, in 1892–1910, and was consecrated second bishop of Hartford, Connecticut, in 1910. During his episcopate, he enlarged the diocesan bureau of social service and expanded the charitable facilities of the diocese, organized a Council of Catholic Women, constructed a new St. Thomas Seminary at Bloomfield in 1930, and saw the Dominican Sisters open Albertus Magnus College in New Haven in 1925—the first Catholic college for women in Connecticut. He died in Hartford on Apr. 13.

NIZA, MARCOS DE (c. 1495–1558), missionary, explorer. Little is known of his early life, though he was probably a Savoyard and born in Nice, France. He was a Franciscan priest with a reputation for learning when he set out for New Spain in 1531 as the leader of a group of Franciscans on their way to Peru. He was a member of expeditions there between 1531 and 1535, was in Guatemala in 1535–36, went to Mexico in 1537, and the following year set out with an expedition to explore the lands north of Mexico, discovering the Zuñi country in Arizona and New Mexico; probably duped by Zuñi legends, he identified the Indian pueblos as the fabulously rich Seven Cities of Cíbola. An expedition headed by Coronado was dispatched to exploit the wealth of the area with Fray Marcos as guide in 1540 and when no fabulously rich cities were discovered he was sent back to Mexico in disgrace. He was provincial of the Franciscan Holy Ghost province in Mexico in 1540–43, was sent to Jalapa to recover from paralysis he had acquired on his explorations, and died in Mexico City on Mar. 25.

NOA, THOMAS L. (1892–1977), bishop. Born at Iron Mountain, Michigan, on Dec. 18, he was educated at St. Francis Seminary, Milwaukee, Wisconsin, in 1907–11 and the North American College, Rome (Ph.D.), and was ordained in Rome in 1916. He continued his studies at the Propaganda (S.T.D. 1917), taught at St. Joseph's Seminary, Grand Rapids, Michigan, in 1917–27, and was its rector in 1927–46. He was made a domestic prelate in 1935, was named titular bishop of Salona and co-adjutor of Sioux City, Iowa, in 1946, and was appointed bishop of Marquette, Michigan, in 1946. He retired in 1968 and died in Marquette on Mar. 13.

NOBILI, JOHN (1812–56), missionary. Born in Rome on Apr. 8, he joined the Jesuits in Rome in 1828, taught at Jesuit colleges in Loretto and Fermo, Italy, and was ordained in 1843. He volunteered as a missionary to America and arrived at Fort Vancouver in the Oregon country with Michael Accolti and Peter De Smet, worked among the Indians and settlers in New Caledonia (British Columbia) in 1845–48, evangelized the Babine Indians, established chapels in many of the Hudson's Bay Company trading posts, and worked as far north as southern Alaska. He made his final profession as a Jesuit in 1849, was sent to California with Accolti in the same year, worked in St. Francis parish, San Francisco, and San Jose pueblo fifty miles south. In 1850 he was assigned to administer Santa Clara Mission near San Jose. He established Santa Clara College—the first Catholic college in California—in 1851, received a state charter in 1855, and was first president of Santa Clara. He died there on Mar. 1.

NOGAR, RAYMOND J. (1916–67), philosopher. Born in Monroe, Michigan, on Nov. 19, he received his B.A. from the University of Michigan, began graduate work in sociology but became a Catholic in 1939 and joined the Dominicans the following year. He studied theology at Aquinas Institute, River Forest, Illinois (S.T.L., Ph.D.), and was ordained in 1948. He began teaching at the Aquinas Institute and, except for 1956–57, when he taught at the Angelicum, Rome, taught there the rest of his life. He became a popular lecturer, helped found the Albertus Magnus Lyceum, devoted to the study of the relationship of philosophy and science, and was its executive secretary. He wrote numerous scholarly articles for periodicals and several books, among them *Science in Synthesis* (1952), *The Wisdom of Evolution* (1963), *The Lord of the Absurd* (1967), and the posthumously published *The Problem of Evolution* (1973). He died in River Forest on Nov. 17.

NOLD, WELDELIN J. (1900–81), bishop. Born in Bonham, Texas, on Jan. 18, he was educated at St. Mary's Seminary, La Porte, Texas, and the North American College, Rome (S.T.D.), and was ordained in Rome in 1925. He engaged in pastoral work in Texas, was pastor of Christ the King Church, Dallas, in 1941–47, was made a domestic prelate in 1942 and a protonotary apostolic in 1946, and was appointed titular bishop of Sasima and coadjutor of Galveston, Texas, the following year. He succeeded to the see in 1950 and during his episcopate he increased the number of parishes in the diocese, helped establish four new coeducational high schools, and opened several new retreat houses. He had an apostolic administrator appointed in 1963 because of his failing eyesight but did not resign until 1975. He died in Houston, Texas, on Oct. 1.

NOLL, JOHN FRANCIS (1875–1956), archbishop. Born in Fort Wayne, Indiana, on Jan. 25, he was educated at St. Lawrence College, Mount Calvary, Wisconsin, and Mt. St. Mary of the West Seminary, Cincinnati, and was ordained in 1898. He served as assistant at Elkhart and Logansport for nine months and was pastor at Kendalville in 1899–1902, Besançon in 1902–6, Hartford City in 1906–10, and Huntington in 1910–25, all in Indiana, and was made a domestic prelate in 1921. He founded the weekly newspaper *Our*

Sunday Visitor and was its editor. He built a huge printing plant in Huntington, Indiana, in 1912, and by the time of his death he had built *Our Sunday Visitor* into the largest Catholic newspaper in the United States. In 1923 he built a Training School and Novitiate for the Society of Missionary Catechists in Huntington and in 1925 he was consecrated bishop of Fort Wayne. He built a preparatory seminary, two high schools, and an orphanage and established a diocesan Catholic Charities, a diocesan Council of Catholic Women, and a Catholic Youth Organization. He served as treasurer of the American Board of Catholic Missions for seventeen years, was chairman of the Department of Lay Organizations of the National Catholic Welfare Conference, and was chairman of the National Organization for Decent Literature. He was made an Assistant at the Pontifical Throne in 1941, was given the personal title of archbishop in 1953, and suffered a stroke shortly after. He had Bishop Leo A. Pursley named apostolic administrator and died in Fort Wayne on July 31. He wrote several books, among them the enormously popular *Father Smith Instructs Jackson* (1913) and *The Decline of Nations* (1940), a history of the Fort Wayne diocese, and some fifty pamphlets.

NORMAN, PIERRE *See* Connor, Joseph P.

NORRIS, JAMES JOSEPH (1907–76), relief worker. Born in Roselle Park, New Jersey, on Aug. 10, he was educated at Seton Hall College, South Orange, New Jersey (B.A. 1933) and Fordham's School of Social Science in 1938–41. He married Amanda Tisch in 1941, early decided to devote his life to working to alleviate problems of pov-erty and injustice, worked for the Automatic Electric Company in 1934–37, and was assistant director of National Catholic Community Service in 1941–42 and executive director in 1942–44. He was a commander in the Naval Armed Guard during World War II in 1944–46, European director of Catholic Relief Services (CRS) in 1946–59, and became assistant to the director of CRS in 1959, remaining in that position until his death in Rumson Park, New Jersey, on Nov. 17. He helped establish the International Catholic Migration Commission (ICMC) to aid migrants and refugees, working with Msgr. Giovanni Battista Montini (later Pope Paul VI), and served as its president in 1951–76. He was chairman of the International Migratory Organizations in 1955–57. He was the only layman to address a plenary session of Vatican Council II in 1964 and his talk on poverty led to the establishment of the Pontifical Commission for Justice and Peace by Pope Paul VI in 1967, of which he was a member. He was honored by the papacy, by the governments of several foreign nations, among them Poland, Germany, and Greece, and by several colleges.

NORRIS, KATHLEEN (1880–1966), author. Born in San Francisco on July 16, Kathleen Thompson was privately educated except for a few months at the University of California. Early attracted to writing, she began her career on the San Francisco *Call,* where in 1909 she met and married Charles Gilman Norris, a novelist. She had her first short story published in 1910 and in time became one of the most prolific and popular novelists of her time, writing on romanticized domestic themes. She wrote some eighty novels, among them *Mother* (1911), *Saturday's Child* (1914), *Margaret Yorke* (1930), *Manhattan Love Song* (1934), and *Through a Glass*

Darkly (1957). She also had several collections of short stories published, wrote two autobiographies, *Noon* (1925) and *Family Gathering* (1959), and had more than twenty of her novels made into movies. She died in San Francisco on Jan. 18.

NORTHROP, HENRY PINCKNEY (1842–1916), bishop. Born in Charleston, South Carolina, on May 5, he was educated at Georgetown, Mt. St. Mary's College, Emmitsburg, Maryland, and the North American College, Rome, and was ordained in Rome in 1865. He engaged in pastoral and mission work in North and South Carolina until 1882, when he was consecrated titular bishop of Rosalia and vicar apostolic of North Carolina. He was appointed fourth bishop of Charleston in 1883 and continued as vicar apostolic of North Carolina for another four years. He rebuilt many of the church buildings destroyed in an earthquake in 1886 and dedicated St. John the Baptist Cathedral in 1907. He died in Charleston on June 7.

NORTON, MARY TERESA HOPKINS (1875–1959), congresswoman. Daughter of Irish immigrants Thomas Hopkins, a well-to-do contractor, and Marie Shea Hopkins, Mary Teresa was born in Jersey City, New Jersey, on Mar. 7. She graduated from Jersey City High School in 1892 and spent the next four years managing her father's household. When her father remarried, she attended Packard Business School in New York City and after graduating in 1896 spent the next thirteen years as a stenographer and secretary. She married Robert Francis Norton in 1909. After their child died in infancy, she engaged in child welfare work and in 1916 became president of the Day Nurseries Association of Jersey City. Encouraged

by Mayor Frank Hague she entered politics in 1920 as a member of the Democratic State Committee, serving as chairlady in 1932–35, and was a delegate to Democratic National Conventions from 1924 to 1944. She was elected to Congress in 1924—the first woman to be elected to Congress on the Democratic ticket—and served in Congress until 1951. She supported Al Smith for the Democratic Party nomination for President in 1928 and 1932 and then became an ardent New Dealer and supporter of Franklin Roosevelt. She steered President Roosevelt's Wages and Houses Bill through the House of Representatives in 1938, led the fight in the House for the Fair Labor Standards Act of 1938, and fought unsuccessfully against the Taft-Hartley Act of 1947. She was chairlady of the House Committee on the District of Columbia in 1932–37—the first woman to chair a major congressional committee—and the House Committee on Labor from 1937 to 1947, when she resigned from the Committee, served as adviser to the U.S. Government delegation at the Conference of International Labor Organizations in Paris in 1945, and headed the House Administration Committee in 1949. She received the Siena Medal in 1947 as the outstanding Catholic woman of the year. She retired from Congress in 1951 and was appointed consultant to the United States Secretary of Labor, moved to Greenwich, Connecticut, in 1956, and died there on Aug. 2.

NUSSBAUM, PAUL JOSEPH (1869–1935), bishop. Born in Philadelphia on Sept. 7, he joined the Passionists in 1847 and was ordained in Brazil in 1894. He engaged in missionary work in Brazil and the United States, was second consultor of the eastern province of the Passionists in 1911, and was appointed first bishop of the newly established diocese of Corpus Christi, Texas, in 1913. He resigned seven years later and was named titular bishop of Gerasa and in 1922 was appointed bishop of Marquette, Michigan, a position he held until his death there on June 24.

O

OBRECHT, M. EDMOND (1852–1935), abbot. Born in Stotzheim, Alsace, on Nov. 13, he joined the Trappists at La Grand Trappe, France, when he was twenty-three and was ordained in 1879. He was sent to Rome to serve as secretary to the procurator general of the Trappists, went to the United States in 1892 to collect funds for the Abbey of Tre Fontane, Rome, which had been selected as the generalate of the three observances of the Trappists which had been formed into one order. He returned to Rome four years later, was sent to an abbey in the French Jura, and then was sent to Gethsemani in Kentucky. He prevented the closing of the monastery, was elected its abbot in 1898, and over the next years served as visitor to monasteries in Europe, Asia, Africa, and North America. He also served as apostolic administrator of Marian Hill Mission in South Africa. He died at Gethsemani on Jan. 4.

O'BRIEN, EDWARD CHARLES (1860–1927), executive. Born at Fort Edward, New York, on Apr. 20, the son of a well-to-do farmer, he was educated at the Granville (New York) Military Academy, engaged in the flour commission business in Plattsburg, New York, and then became involved in foreign commerce and maritime shipping. He was disbursing clerk for the House of Representatives in 1889–91, was United States Commissioner of Navigation in 1892–93, and was briefly commissary general of the State of New York in 1895 but resigned to become commis-

sioner of docks in New York City, serving in 1895–98. He retired to private life, organized and was president of the International Express Company and the Pan-American Express Company, and was United States minister plenipotentiary to Paraguay and Uruguay in 1905–8. He helped end the revolution in Paraguay in 1908 (for which he was thanked by both sides), resigned from the diplomatic service in 1909, and spent the rest of his life promoting trade in and with Latin America. He died in Montevideo, Uruguay, on June 21 while working on a plan to build a highway between the capitals of Uruguay and Argentina.

O'BRIEN, EDWARD JOSEPH HARRINGTON (1890–1941), anthologist, author. Born in Boston on Dec. 10, he studied for a time at Boston College and then Harvard but graduated from neither of them. He was assistant editor of *Poetry Journal* in 1912–15 and of *Poet Lore* in 1914–15 and lived abroad after 1922. He married Romer Wilson, an English novelist, and after her death in 1930 he married Ruth Gorgel. He was European story editor for Metro-Goldwyn-Mayer, the motion picture company, in 1937–39 and died at Garrod's Crossing, Buckinghamshire, England, on Feb. 25. He began issuing an annual collection of *The Best Short Stories* in 1915 and it soon became recognized as the outstanding collection in the field, though his selections were often controversial. He continued editing an annual volume the rest of his life.

He also edited, with John Cournos, the first four volumes of *The Best British Short Stories* and published other collections of fiction. He wrote poetry, *White Fountains* and *Distant Music,* and several books of prose, among them *The Forgotten Threshold* and *The Advance of the American Short Story,* and two plays, *The Flowing of the Tide* and *The Bloody Fool.*

O'BRIEN, HENRY JOSEPH (1896–1976), archbishop. Born in New Haven, Connecticut, on July 21, he was educated at St. Thomas Seminary, Hartford, Connecticut, in 1914–17, St. Bernard's Seminary, Rochester, New York, in 1917–19, and Louvain, Belgium, in 1919–23, and was ordained in Louvain in 1923. He was a curate at Windsor Locks in 1923–24 and in Fairheld in 1924–26. He taught at St. Thomas in 1926–40, serving as vice president of the seminary in 1932–34 and as president in 1934–40. He was named titular bishop of Sita and auxiliary of Hartford in 1940 and was appointed bishop of Hartford in 1945; he became Hartford's first archbishop when it was made an archdiocese in 1953. During his fifteen-year tenure as ordinary, he was outspoken in his opposition to abortion and birth control, favored state aid to Catholic educational institutions, and helped fight discrimination in employment, announcing in 1965 that the archdiocese would not do business with concerns that discriminated. He resigned in 1968 because of ill health and was named titular bishop of Utina. He died in Hartford on July 23.

O'BRIEN, JOHN (1897–1963), educator. Born in Chicopee, Massachusetts, on May 22, he was educated at Holy Cross College, Worcester, Massachusetts (B.A. 1918), joined the Jesuits in 1918, and continued his studies at Weston, Massachusetts (M.A. 1924). He taught at Holy Cross in 1924–27, was ordained in 1930, and went to Rome for further studies at the Gregorian (Ph.D. 1933). On his return he taught at Boston College in 1933–48, serving as chairman of the philosophy department the last ten years, and was president of Holy Cross in 1948–54. He taught philosophy at Fairfield (Connecticut) University in 1954–62 and then at Boston College until his death in Newton, Massachusetts, on Nov. 21.

O'BRIEN, JOHN A. (1893–1980), author. Born in Peoria, Illinois, on Jan. 20, he was educated at the Spalding Institute there, at Holy Cross College, Worcester, Massachusetts, and at St. Viator College, Bourbonnais, Illinois (B.A., M.A.). He continued his studies at Catholic University, was ordained in 1920, and received his doctorate in psychology from the University of Illinois in 1920. He served as superintendent of the diocesan schools of Peoria for a time and attracted national attention in the 1920s with his lectures on Catholicism at the University of Illinois, where he taught for twenty-two years. He was a leader in family planning, was unsuccessful in an attempt in 1968 to convince Pope Paul VI to rescind his condemnation of artificial birth control, was a pioneer in the Newman Club chaplaincy, and advocated changes in Church law to permit priests to marry. He wrote some forty books and pamphlets, most popular of which were *The Truths Men Live By* (1946), *The Road to Damascus* (1949), and *The Faith of Millions* (1938), which sold millions of copies and was translated into ten languages. He became professor of theology at Notre Dame in 1940 and was an author-in-residence there the last years of his life. Notre Dame awarded him its Laetare Medal in 1973 and he died there on Apr. 18.

O'BRIEN, MATTHEW ANTHONY (1804–71), missionary. Born in Nenagh, Tipperary, Ireland, in May, he was educated in Ireland, emigrated to the United States in 1826, and settled in Kentucky. He taught at St. Mary's College, Marion County, Kentucky, beginning in 1829, joined the Dominicans at St. Rose Priory, Springfield, Kentucky, was professed in 1837, and was ordained two years later. After completing his studies at St. Rose's, he engaged in pastoral work at St. Joseph's parish near Somerset, Ohio, for five years and then was elected provincial of the Dominicans' St. Joseph province in 1850. During his provincialate he opened St. Joseph's College, Somerset, Ohio, preached throughout the Midwest, and in 1854–57 was prior of St. Rose's; he reopened St. Thomas College there and built the parish church. He spent the rest of his life in missionary activity, except for two years when he was pastor of St. Peter's Church, Ontario, Canada. He died in Springfield, Kentucky, on Jan. 15.

O'BRIEN, MICHAEL JOSEPH (1870–1960), historian. Born in Fermoy, Cork, Ireland, he studied at St. Colman's there, emigrated to the United States, and in 1889 began working in the accounting department of the Western Union Telegraph Company, remaining with that firm until he retired in 1936. He was historiographer of the Irish-American Historical Society and edited several of its *Journals,* was librarian of the Friendly Sons of St. Patrick, and was a founder of the Catholic Writers Guild. He was particularly interested in the Irish contribution to American history and wrote more than twenty books on the Irish in the American Army during the Revolution, Irish schoolmasters of the colonial period, and Irish settlers in New York and New England, among them *Pioneer Irish in New England* (1937), *Hercules Mulligan, Confidential Correspondent of George Washington* (1937), *In Old New York* (1938), and *George Washington's Association with the Irish* (1937). He died in Yonkers, New York, on Nov. 11.

O'BRIEN, MORGAN JOSEPH (1852–1937), jurist. Born in New York City on Apr. 28, he was educated at St. John's College (Fordham), B.A. 1872, St. Francis Xavier College (M.A. 1873), and Columbia Law School (LL.B. 1875) and was admitted to the bar and began practicing law in New York City. He married Rose M. Crimmins in 1880, entered politics, was appointed New York City corporation counsel in 1887, and was elected to the Supreme Court later the same year. He was elevated to the appellate division in 1896 and became its presiding judge in 1905. He resigned the next year and resumed his private law practice, was president of the New York Bar Association, and was a trustee and director of several banks and insurance companies, among them the Provident Loan Society, the Metropolitan Life Insurance Company, and the Bank of Manhattan Trust Company, and of numerous civic bodies. He helped reorganize the Equitable Life Assurance Society after the revelations of the investigators of insurance companies. He was appointed chairman of the Temporary Planning and Survey Committee in 1926, was an ardent champion of municipal reform, and in 1936, as chairman of the Citizen's Charter Campaign Committee, he offered a new charter for the city. He worked with Cardinals Farley and Hayes on charity drives and presided over the second Catholic Congress of the United States in Chicago in 1893. He died in New York City on June 16.

O'BRIEN, PAT (1899–1983), actor. Born in Milwaukee, Wisconsin, on Nov.

11, William Joseph O'Brien took his grandfather's name, Patrick, and was known throughout his career as Pat. He was a student at Marquette Academy, where he met and began a lifetime friendship with Spencer Tracy, and when the United States entered World War I the two joined the Navy. After the war he studied law at Marquette University for a time but decided to pursue an acting career and went to New York City, where he studied acting at Sargent's School for Drama. He launched his career as a chorus boy in the musical *Adrienne* in 1923, played in various Broadway productions and in stock, among them the role of Walter Burns in *The Front Page* in 1926, and met Eloise Taylor in 1927 while the two were playing in a Chicago production of *Broadway;* they were married in 1931. He made his first big hit in films as Hildy Johnson, the newspaper reporter, in *The Front Page* (1931), and in the next two decades appeared in more than a hundred motion pictures and was famed for his portrayals of priests and military men. Best known of his pictures were *Angels with Dirty Faces* (1938), with his friend Jimmy Cagney, as Fr. Connolly, *The Fighting 69th* (1940) as its chaplain, Fr. Duffy, again with Cagney, and *Knute Rockne—All American* (1940), in which he portrayed the legendary Notre Dame football coach and in which an aspiring young actor, Ronald Reagan, later President of the United States, appeared. His last role in motion pictures was a small part in *Ragtime* in 1981, in which Jimmy Cagney starred. He appeared in radio and on television and spent the last years of his life in nightclubs and doing summer stock; his last appearance was with his wife Eloise in *On Golden Pond.* He died in Santa Monica, California, on Oct. 15 of a massive coronary attack. His autobiography, *The Wind at My Back,* was published in 1964. Some of his other pictures were *Here Comes the Navy* (1934), *Ceiling Zero* (1935), *The Iron Major* (1943), *Bombardier* (1943), *Marine Raiders* (1944), *Secret Command* (1944), *Fighting Father Dunne* (1945), and *Okinawa* (1952).

O'BRIEN, WILLIAM DAVID (1878–1962), archbishop. Born in Chicago on Aug. 3, he was educated at De Paul University there (B.A. 1899, M.A. 1902), studied for the priesthood at Kenrick Seminary, St. Louis, and was ordained in 1903. He joined the Catholic Church Extension Society in 1907, became editor of *Extension Magazine,* and in 1925 was appointed president of the Society, serving in that post for thirty-seven years. He became pastor of St. John's Church, Chicago, was made a domestic prelate in 1926, and was appointed titular bishop of Calinda and auxiliary of Chicago in 1934. He was appointed permanent secretary of the American Board of Catholic Missions in 1946 and served in that position until his death. He was made an Assistant at the Pontifical Throne in 1947 and given the personal title of archbishop as titular archbishop of Calinda. He died in St. Pierre, Indiana, on Feb. 19. During the years he was president of the Church Extension Society, it supported needy clergy and seminarians, built thousands of churches, and developed the Extension lay volunteer program to recruit, train, and assign lay missionary workers.

O'BRIEN, WILLIAM VINCENT (c. 1740–1816). Born in Dublin, he joined the Dominicans at San Clemente, Rome, and made his profession there in 1761. He studied at the Dominican house of studies at Bologna, Italy, and was ordained there and then preached in Ireland for seventeen years, earning the title preacher general of the Dominicans. He went to the United States and worked in Philadelphia and New Jersey and in 1787 was appointed pastor of St. Peter's Church in New York City. He healed the differences between various factions among its parishioners and in 1789 was sent to Boston by Bishop John Carroll to depose Fr. Claudius de la Poteris, a French priest who was called "an unworthy priest" by the archbishop of Paris and whose conduct in Boston called for his dismissal. Fr. O'Brien went to Mexico City in 1790 seeking funds for St. Peter's and returned with vestments, paintings, and funds to improve the church. He ministered to the victims of yellow fever epidemics in 1795 and 1798, opened the first free Catholic school in the state at St. Peter's in 1800, and was forced into partial retirement because of illness in 1806 and full retirement in 1808. He died in New York City on May 14.

O'CALLAGHAN, EDMUND BAILEY (1797–1880), historian. Born in Mallow near Cork, Ireland, on Feb. 28, he studied in Ireland and in 1820 went to Paris to study medicine. He emigrated to Canada in 1823, began practicing medicine in Quebec and then Montreal, and became involved in the National Patriotic movement, supporting Louis Papineau, leader of the French opposition to English rule. He became editor of the movement's paper, *The Vindicator,* in 1834, was elected to the Quebec provincial council in 1836, and when he took part in Papineau's unsuccessful rebellion in 1837, he was accused of treason and fled to the United States. He resumed his medical practice in Albany, New York, in 1838, edited and wrote for the industrial journal *Northern Light* in 1842–44, and became interested in New York history. He published his two-volume *History of New Netherlands* in 1846–48, gave up his medical practice to devote himself to historical research, and published some

twenty books, among them the four-volume *Documentary History of New York* (1849–51) and the eleven-volume *Documents Relating to the Colonial History of the State of New York* (1853–61). He was made keeper of the historical manuscripts of New York State in 1848 and held that post the next twenty-two years. In 1870, he became historiographer of New York City and began editing its records; they were never published because of lack of financing when the Tweed Ring scandal broke, though he had edited fifteen volumes which, except for two volumes, had been printed but not bound. He was the first to call attention to the historical value of the *Jesuit Relations* as a treasure trove of historical lore and information and edited and published several volumes of *Jesuit Relations.* Among his other publications were *A List of Editions of the Holy Scriptures . . . Printed in America Previous to 1860* (1861), *The Register of New Netherland, 1626 to 1674* (1865), and *Laws and Ordinances of New Netherland, 1638–1674* (1868). He died in New York City on May 29.

O'CALLAGHAN, JEREMIAH (c. 1780–1861), missionary. Born in Cork, Ireland, he was ordained for the diocese of Cloyne in 1805, but when he quarreled with his bishop over the latter's strict views on usury and criticism of banking, he was refused a post by other bishops until 1830, when Bishop Benedict Fenwick of Boston accepted him. He was sent to Vermont as a missionary and worked from Burlington with Fr. John B. Daly with great success. He was procurator of the clergy at the first Boston diocesan synod in 1842, returned to Massachusetts when Burlington was made a diocese in 1853, and served at Northampton and Holyoke. He wrote numerous polemical pamphlets in reply to anti-Catholic writers and preachers; best known of his pamphlets was *Usury Funds and Banking* (1834), which he wrote while in Burlington. He died in Holyoke on Feb. 23.

O'CALLAGHAN, ROGER (1912–54), Orientalist. Born in New York City on Oct. 12, he joined the Jesuits in 1929, studied in Toronto and Rome and then Near Eastern archaeology, history, and languages under the noted biblical scholar W. F. Albright at Johns Hopkins University, Baltimore, and at the Oriental Institute of the University of Chicago. He taught biblical history, geography, and languages at the Pontifical Biblical Institute in Rome until 1953, when he took part in the excavation under American auspices at Nippur, Iraq. He was killed in an automobile accident near Baghdad on Mar. 5.

O'CALLAHAN, JOSEPH TIMOTHY (1905–64), chaplain. Born in Roxbury, Boston, on May 14, he joined the Jesuits in 1922, was educated at St. Andrew-on-Hudson novitiate, Poughkeepsie, New York, and Weston (Massachusetts) College (M.A. 1929) and then taught at Boston College until 1931, when he returned to Weston. He was ordained in 1934, continued his studies at Georgetown, where he received his Ph.D. and licentiate in theology, taught physics and mathematics at Holy Cross College, Worcester, Massachusetts, and became head of its mathematics department in 1940. He joined the Navy Chaplain Corps the same year and served on the aircraft carrier *Ranger* during the North African invasion during World War II and then was transferred to the carrier *Franklin* in the Pacific. He received nationwide attention and the Congressional Medal of Honor for his heroism ministering to the dead and wounded of the *Franklin,* though wounded himself, when the carrier was severely damaged by Japanese kamikazi pilots near Kobe, Japan. After the war he served as chaplain on the aircraft carrier *Franklin D. Roosevelt,* was discharged from the Navy in 1946, and returned to Holy Cross, where he suffered a stroke in 1949. He wrote of his experiences on the *Franklin* in *I Was a Chaplain on the Franklin* (1956) and died in Worcester on Mar. 18.

O'CONNELL, ANTHONY, SISTER (1814–97), nurse. Born in Limerick, Ireland, on Aug. 15, Mary O'Connell was brought to the United States as a child, studied with the Ursulines at Charlestown, Massachusetts, and joined the Sisters of Charity, taking the name Anthony, in 1835. She went to Cincinnati in 1837 to care for orphans, was active there in hospitals, asylums, and St. John's Hotel for invalids, which she established, and in 1852 was one of the seven founders of the Sisters of Charity of Cincinnati, serving as procuratrix-general for two terms. Her work as a nurse in military hospitals during the Civil War earned her the title "the Florence Nightingale of America." When the Marine Hospital in Cincinnati was presented to the Congregation, it was named the Good Samaritan and she was named its administrator, serving until 1882; she was also administrator of St. Joseph's Infant Home, opened in 1873, the first hospital for unmarried mothers and abandoned infants in the Cincinnati area. She died in Cincinnati on Dec. 8.

O'CONNELL, DANIEL M. (1885–1958), editor. Born in Louisville, Kentucky, on Aug. 27, he was educated at St. Mary's Hospital, Kansas, joined the Jesuits in 1903, and continued his education at St. Louis University, where he received his B.A., M.A., and, in 1910, his Ph.D. He was ordained in St. Louis in 1918, taught at Campion College in 1919–20 and then at Xavier University, Cincinnati, where he was dean in 1924–30, was prefect of studies of the Jesuit

Chicago Province in 1930–34, and became first secretary of the National Jesuit Educational Association in 1934. He served on the staff of the Jesuit journal *America*, founded Spiritual Book Associates in 1934, and later taught at the University of Detroit and West Baden, Indiana. He edited several of Cardinal Newman's works for college use and died in West Baden on July 29.

O'CONNELL, DENIS JOSEPH (1849–1927), bishop. Born in Donoughmore, Cork, Ireland, on Jan. 28, he studied at St. Charles College, Ellicott City, Maryland, and the Propaganda, Rome, and was ordained in 1877. He engaged in pastoral work in Richmond, Virginia, and served as secretary to Bishop George Conroy of Armagh when that prelate was on a papal mission to Canada, and was on the preparatory commission for the third Plenary Council of Baltimore in 1884. He was named rector of the North American College in Rome in 1885, was made a domestic prelate in 1887, and acted as intermediary for the American bishops to the Holy See. He was vicar of Santa Maria Church in the Trastevere section of Rome in 1895–1903, was a strong supporter of Archbishop John Ireland and the Americanist group in the American hierarchy, and strongly supported the United States in the Spanish-American War in 1898. He was named rector of Catholic University in 1903 and was at once faced with near disaster for the university when its broker went into bankruptcy and it lost two thirds of its investment portfolio. He weathered this storm and served as rector until 1907, when he was appointed titular bishop of Sebaste and auxiliary of San Francisco. In 1904 he was elected first president of the Catholic Educational Association, which was formed when the Conference of Seminary Presidents and Professors, the Association of Catholic Colleges and Universities, and the Parish School Conference voted to merge. He was appointed bishop of Richmond, Virginia, in 1912, resigned because of ill health in 1926, and was named titular archbishop of Mariamme. He died in Richmond on Jan. 1.

O'CONNELL, EUGENE (1815–91), bishop. Born in Kingscourt, Cavan, Ireland, on June 18, he was educated at the Navan seminary and St. Patrick's, Maynooth, and was ordained at Maynooth in 1842. He taught at the Navan seminary and All Hallow's College until 1851, when he was persuaded by Bishop José Alemany of California to come to the United States to head the diocesan seminary at Santa Inez, California. The following year he became head of St. Thomas Seminary, San Francisco, and in 1854 he returned to Ireland to teach theology and as dean of All Hallows College. He was consecrated titular bishop of Falviopolis and vicar apostolic of Marysville, the territory west of the Colorado River in the northwestern United States when that vicariate was established in 1861. He became first bishop of Grass Valley (moved to Sacramento in 1886) in 1868, when the vicariate was formed into that diocese, resigned in 1884 because of ill health, and was appointed titular bishop of Joppa. He retired to Los Angeles, where he died on Dec. 4.

O'CONNELL, JOHN PATRICK (1918–60), theologian. Born in Chicago on Jan. 12, he was educated at Quigley Seminary there and St. Mary of the Lake Seminary, Mundelein, Illinois (M.A., S.T.D.), and was ordained in 1943. He served as a parish priest for a time, taught at Barat College, Lake Forest, Illinois, and was named editor of the Catholic Press, Inc., of Chicago, which published bibles, missals, and devotional books, by Cardinal Stritch. He was an active promoter of the liturgical apostolate and served as secretary, treasurer, and on the board of directors of the Liturgical Conference. He was studying the feasibility of a new edition of the Catholic Encyclopedia when he died in Chicago on Feb. 20.

O'CONNELL, WILLIAM HENRY (1859–1944), cardinal. Born in Lowell, Massachusetts, on Dec. 8, he studied for the priesthood at St. Charles College, Ellicott City, Maryland, but left in 1877 to enter Boston College (B.A. 1881). He returned to study for the priesthood at the North American College, Rome, in 1881 but was forced to forego studies for his doctorate because of illness. He was ordained in 1884, engaged in pastoral work at St. Joseph's churches, Medford and Boston, until 1895, when he was appointed rector of the North American College and served in that position until 1901. During his six years as rector of North American College, he put its finances in order, doubled its enrollment, and purchased Santa Caterina for summer sessions. He was made a domestic prelate in 1897. He was consecrated third bishop of Portland, Maine, in 1901, declined an appointment as archbishop of Manila in 1903 (he felt his support of Spain in the Spanish-American War in 1898 would hinder him as its archbishop), and in 1905 he was sent to Japan as special papal envoy. He submitted a report of recommendations for missionary activities for Japan—including the founding of a Catholic university in Tokyo—that was adopted. He was appointed titular bishop of Constantia and coadjutor of Boston in 1906 and succeeded to the see on the death of Archbishop John Williams the following year. He at once began a complete reorganization of the archdiocese and launched an unprecedented expansion of its facilities. During his administration he added 128 parishes to the archdiocese, increased the number of priests from 600 to some 1500 and brought 20 religious communities into the see, doubled the number of Catholic elementary schools and tripled the number of high schools, founded 3 women's colleges, tripled the number of seminarians at St. John's Seminary, built the Crehan Library, enlarged St. John's Seminary, and purchased the *Pilot* and made it the diocesan paper. In civic matters, he preached against graft in politics, was a fervent supporter of the United States in World War I and of self-determination for Ireland, opposed the proposed constitutional amendment on child labor on the grounds it infringed on the rights of parents and of the states, and helped develop the National Catholic Welfare Conference from the National Catholic Welfare Council of World War I. He was made a cardinal in 1911 and in 1922 his vigorous protest over the ten days allowed between the death of a pope and the convening of a conclave to elect his successor, which had caused him to miss the conclaves that elected Pope Benedict XV in 1914 and Pope Pius XI in 1922, caused Pope Pius XI to extend the time to eighteen days. In 1937 Harvard University awarded him a doctorate in letters—the first American Catholic prelate to be so honored. His *Sermons and Addresses* were collected in eleven volumes and his *Recollections of Seventy Years* was published in 1923. He died in Boston on Apr. 22.

O'CONNOR, EDWIN GREENE (1918–68), author. Son of a physician and a former schoolteacher, he was born in Providence, Rhode Island, on July 29. He graduated from Notre Dame in 1939, worked as a radio announcer, and during World War II served with the Coast Guard. After the war he wrote short stories and radio scripts, produced several radio shows, and had his first book, *The Oracle,* published in 1951. His *The Last Hurrah* (1956) was an immediate best-seller, as was *The Edge of Sadness* (1961), for which he received the Pulitzer Prize in 1962. He also wrote *I Was Dancing* (1964) and *All in the Family* (1966). He died in Boston on Mar. 23.

O'CONNOR, FLANNERY (1925–64), author. Born in Savannah, Georgia, on Mar. 25, Mary was brought when twelve by her parents to Milledgeville, Georgia, and spent most of her life there. She was educated at Georgia State College for Women, graduated in 1945, and received her M.A. in creative writing from the University of Iowa in 1947. She moved to New York City in 1947 and, when she fell ill, in 1950 returned to Georgia; her illness was diagnosed as disseminated lupus and after her discharge from Emory Hospital in Atlanta in 1951 she moved with her mother to a farm, "Andalusia," the family owned five miles from Milledgeville and lived there the rest of her life. She had her first story, "The Geranium," published in *Accent* in 1946, and in 1952 her first novel, *Wise Blood,* was published. It was met with critical literary acclaim but was also widely criticized for its horrendous satire, violence, and unusual humor. In 1955, *A Good Man Is Hard to Find,* a collection of ten short stories, was published and was accorded the same reception. By the time her last book, *Everything That Rises Must Converge,* nine short stories, was published posthumously in 1965, she was recognized as one of the outstanding authors of her time, treating in her books the theology of sin (the conflict of wills in the sinner) and freedom. Her only other books were *The Violent Bear It Away* (1960), a novel, and *Mystery and Manners* (1969), essays on writing; all her short stories were collected in *Complete Stories* (1971). She died in

Milledgeville on Aug. 3. She published a relatively small corpus of writing but is considered among the finest writers of the twentieth century. Though her characters are grotesque, the situations bizarre, and violence very much in evidence, her stories are always profoundly moral, stressing the awareness of sin, free will, and the need for redemption.

O'CONNOR, JAMES (1823–90), bishop. Born in Queenstown (Cobh), Ireland, on Sept. 10, he emigrated to the United States when he was fifteen, studied for the priesthood at St. Charles Borromeo Seminary, Overbrook, Philadelphia, and the Propaganda, Rome, and was ordained in Rome in 1848. He served as a missionary under his brother Michael, bishop of Pittsburgh, until 1857, when he was named rector of St. Michael's Seminary, Pittsburgh; he became rector of St. Charles Borromeo in 1862 and was made pastor of St. Dominic's Church, Holmesburg, Pennsylvania, in 1872. He was cofounder of the *American Catholic Quarterly Review* in Philadelphia in 1876 and was appointed vicar apostolic of Nebraska and consecrated titular bishop of Dibona later the same year. The construction of the Union Pacific Railroad and the extension of the Burlington Railroad had brought a flood of settlers into Nebraska and in 1885, after the Dakotas had been established as a separate vicariate in 1880, the vicariate of Nebraska was erected into the diocese of Omaha, consisting of Nebraska and Wyoming, and Bishop O'Connor was named ordinary of the new see. He greatly expanded the facilities of the diocese, especially the number of churches and schools, to accommodate the heavy influx of Catholics among the settlers, built a college in Omaha which was completed in 1879 and is now Creighton University, brought several orders of sisters into the diocese, and, in 1889, acting with Katharine Drexel, formed the Sisters of the Blessed Sacrament, devoted to missionary work among Indians and colored people. He was also active in the movement to bring Catholic immigrants into the area, notably the group of Irish in Greeley County, Nebraska, in the 1880s, organized the Catholic Relief Society of America, brought into the see Franciscans and Jesuits from central Europe to minister to the Poles and Bohemians who had settled in the vicariate and diocese, and founded the Catholic Mutual Relief Society of America in 1889. He died in Omaha on May 27.

O'CONNOR, JAMES FRANCIS THADDEUS (1886–1949), jurist. Born in Grand Forks, North Dakota, on Nov. 10, he was educated at the University of North Dakota (B.A. 1907) and Yale (LL.B. 1909, M.A. 1910), was known at Yale for his oratorical prowess and was captain of the Yale debating team and taught at Yale as an instructor in 1909–12. He was admitted to the North Dakota bar in 1908 and practiced at Grand Forks until 1925, became interested in politics, served in the North Dakota legislature in 1915–19, taught at the University of North Dakota Law College in 1917–20, and was defeated in bids for the governorship in 1920 and the United States Senate in 1922. He moved to California in 1925, resumed his law practice there, and was a law associate of Senator William McAdoo. He was again unsuccessful in a bid for governor and in 1933 was appointed Comptroller of the Currency by President Franklin Roosevelt, a position he held the next five years. He was a member of the Federal Reserve Board in 1933–36 and became a United States District Judge in 1940. He wrote of his experiences as comptroller in *Banks Under Roosevelt* and died in Los Angeles on Sept. 29.

O'CONNOR, JOHN JOSEPH (1855–1927), bishop. Born in Newark, New Jersey, on June 11, he was educated at Seton Hall College, South Orange, New Jersey, the North American College, Rome, and the Louvain, and was ordained in 1877. From 1878 until 1892 he taught philosophy at the diocesan seminary and became its rector and in 1892 was named vicar-general of Newark. He was rector of St. Joseph's Church, Newark, from 1895 until 1901, when he was appointed bishop of Newark. He raised funds to continue work on the new cathedral, moved Immaculate Conception seminary to Darlington in 1926, and died the next year at South Orange on May 20.

O'CONNOR, MICHAEL (1810–72), bishop. Born near Queenstown (Cobh), Ireland, on Sept. 27, he was educated in France and at the Propaganda, Rome, and was ordained in Rome in 1833. He continued his studies and received his doctorate in divinity from the Propaganda the following year, taught Sacred Scripture at the Propaganda, and was vice-rector of the Irish College in Rome. He then returned to Ireland and became a curate at Fermoy, emigrated to the United States about 1839 at the invitation of Bishop Francis Kenrick of Philadelphia, became rector of St. Charles Borromeo Seminary, Overbrook, Philadelphia, and in 1841 was named vicar-general of Western Pennsylvania. He was appointed first bishop of Pittsburgh when that diocese was established in 1843. When the see was divided into two dioceses, Pittsburgh and Erie, in 1853 he elected to become bishop of Erie; the following year, after five months in Erie, he returned to Pittsburgh because of the demand of the people and priests of Pittsburgh. While in Rome attending the proclamation of the dogma of the Immaculate Conception in 1854, he joined the other American bishops there in a request to Pope Pius IX for permission to establish a North American College in Rome. During the time he was bishop of Pittsburgh, he held a synod, finished the cathedral in Pittsburgh in 1854, increased the number of priests in the diocese from sixteen to sixty-four, the churches from forty-three to seventy-eight as the Catholic population grew from twenty-five thousand to fifty thousand, brought many religious orders into the see, and opened a chapel for blacks in Pittsburgh. He was an active proponent of Catholic education and fought for public funds for parochial schools, founded St. Michael's Seminary and two colleges and the diocesan paper, *The Pittsburgh Catholic,* in 1844, and donated land to the Benedictines for St. Vincent Archabbey in Beatty in 1846 and to the Franciscans in 1847 for St. Francis College in Loretto. In 1852 he introduced the Passionists to the United States when he brought them into his diocese. He resigned as bishop of Pittsburgh in 1860 to become a Jesuit, and made his profession in Boston in 1862. He taught at Boston College in 1863, then became *socius* to the Jesuit Maryland province, and spent the rest of his life in missionary work, devoting himself to ministering to blacks. He died in Woodstock, Maryland, on Oct. 18.

O'CONNOR, THOMAS FRANCIS (1899–1950), historian. Born in Syracuse, New York, on Aug. 14, he was educated at Holy Cross College, Worcester, Massachusetts (B.A. 1922) and Syracuse University, New York (M.A. 1927), and taught at Little Rock University, Arkansas, in 1928–30, St. Louis University in 1931–37 and 1948–50, and St. Michael's College, Winooski Park, Vermont, in 1937–39. He was historiographer of the diocese of Syracuse and

then in 1944–48 of New York, was president of the American Catholic Historical Association in 1946–47, and wrote numerous articles for historical journals. He died in St. Louis on Sept. 15.

O'CONNOR, WILLIAM PATRICK (1886–1973), bishop. Born in Madison, Wisconsin, on Oct. 18, he was educated at St. Francis Seminary, Milwaukee, Wisconsin, was ordained in 1912, and continued his studies at Catholic University (Ph.D.). He was a chaplain in World War I and was awarded the Croix de Guerre for his bravery in action, taught philosophy at St. Francis after the war, became pastor of St. Thomas Aquinas Church, Milwaukee, and was president of the American Catholic Philosophical Association in 1939. He was appointed bishop of Superior, Wisconsin, in 1941 and became first bishop of Madison, Wisconsin, when that diocese was established in 1946. During his episcopate, he emphasized Catholic education, more than doubled the enrollment in the Catholic elementary schools and in Confraternity of Christian Doctrine (CCD) programs in the diocese, brought religious orders into the see to establish educational institutions, built homes for the aged, remodeled and enlarged St. Raphael's Cathedral in 1955, and held a synod in 1956. He resigned in 1967 and died in Madison on July 13.

O'CONOR, CHARLES (1804–84), lawyer. Son of Irish immigrant Thomas O'Conor, noted journalist and historian, he was born in New York City on Jan. 22, was apprenticed to a lampblack manufacturer in 1816, became an office boy in a law firm the next year, studied law, and was admitted to the bar in 1824. He was a member of the New York State Constitutional Convention in 1846, was unsuccessful in the election of 1848 for lieutenant governor, and was appointed United States district attorney for the Southern District of New York in 1853. He became one of the best-known attorneys of his time and participated in many of the outstanding cases of the era; most sensational of his cases was the divorce case of Edwin Forrest, the celebrated tragedian, in which he represented the wife of the actor in 1851–52 and secured a decree of absolute divorce with alimony for Mrs. Forrest. He believed slavery was a just institution and was a proponent of states' rights and was senior defense counsel for Jefferson Davis when the President of the Confederate States of America was tried for treason in 1865. He was treasurer of the New York Law Institute, serving as its president in 1869, and was vice president of the New-York Historical Society. He was special counsel for the State of New York in the proceedings that exposed the corruption and fraud of the Tweed Ring in New York City in 1871–75, and was nominated for the Presidency in 1872 by the "Straight-out Democrats," a group which had splintered off from the Democratic Party because of its nomination of Horace Greeley; he took no part in the election. He was counsel for Samuel Tilden in 1877 before the Electoral Commission in the disputed presidential election of 1876, retired in 1881, and died on Nantucket Island on May 12. Many authorities consider him the greatest of all American jurists. He wrote of his encounter with Boss Tweed in *Peculation Triumphant* (1875), and the papers of his principal cases, which were bequeathed to the New York Law Institute, fill one hundred volumes.

O'CONOR, HERBERT ROMULUS (1897–1960), governor, U.S. senator. Born in Baltimore on Nov. 17, he was educated at Loyola College there (B.A. 1917, LL.D. 1924) and the University of Maryland (LL.B. 1920), was admitted to the bar in 1920, when he married Eugenia Byrnes, and began practicing law in Baltimore. He became active in politics, was an assistant state attorney in 1921–22, was state attorney of Baltimore in 1924–30, and was elected attorney general of Maryland in 1934. He served two terms as governor of Maryland in 1939–47 and was U.S. senator from Maryland from 1946 until his retirement in 1953. In the Senate he was chairman of the crime committee and of the internal security subcommittee, in which position he vigorously opposed Communism, stopping the shipment of war materials to the Chinese Communists during the Korean conflict. After he left the Senate in 1953, he became counsel of the American Maritime Institute in Washington, D.C., and held that position until his death in Baltimore on Mar. 4.

O'CONOR, THOMAS (1770–1855), journalist. Father of Charles O'Conor, the noted lawyer, he was born in Dublin on Sept. 1 and emigrated to the United States in 1801. With William Kernan, he established a settlement on a 24,000-acre tract of land in Steuben County, New York, but in time abandoned the project and returned to New York City. In 1803 he married the daughter of Hugh O'Conor, a fellow countryman, and in 1810 he founded and edited the *New York Shamrock or Hibernian Chronicle* until 1817, when it ceased publication; he revived it as the *Globe* in 1819 but it lasted only a year. He also founded and edited the *Military Monitor* in 1819, published several pamphlets on Irish and Catholic questions, wrote a history of the War of 1812, and was a staunch supporter of Irish freedom and of the Church. He was really the first Irish editor and publisher in the United States. He died in New York City on Feb. 9.

O'DANIEL, VICTOR FRANCIS (1868–1960), historian, archivist. Born in Cecilville, Kentucky, on Feb. 15, he was educated at St. Rose Priory, Springfield, Kentucky, joined the Dominicans there in 1886, continued his studies at St. Joseph Priory, Somerset, Ohio, and was ordained in Columbus, Ohio, in 1891. He engaged in further studies at the Dominican House of Studies, Louvain (S.T.L.), in 1893–95 and on his return to the United States taught theology at St. Rose's and St. Joseph's in 1895–1901 and at the Dominican House of Studies at Bernicia, California, in 1901–6 and the Dominican House of Studies, Washington, D.C., in 1906–13. He received his master of sacred theology degree in 1909 and, after two years sabbatical in Europe researching archives, resumed his teaching. He was allowed to give up teaching in 1913 to devote himself entirely to historical research and to the building of his province's archives. He was historian of the Dominican St. Joseph province from 1907 until his death and organized the Dominican archives in Washington, D.C. He and Peter Guilday founded the *Catholic Historical Review* in 1915, and he served as associate editor in 1921–27. He wrote numerous articles for the *Review* and biographies of Bishop Edward D. Fenwick of Cincinnati, Fr. Charles H. McKenna, "apostle of the Holy Name Society," and Bishop Richard Pius Miles, bishop of Nashville, Tennessee, *The Order of the Dominican Province of St. Joseph* (1942), and *The Dominicans in Early Florida* (1930). He died in Washington, D.C., on June 12.

O'DEA, EDWARD JOHN (1856–1932), bishop. Born in Roxbury, Boston, on Nov. 23, he was educated at St. Michael's, Oregon, St. Ignatius, San Francisco, and the Grand Seminary, Montreal, and was ordained in 1882. He engaged in pastoral work in the Oregon City diocese, was secretary of Bishop William Gross of that diocese (made archbishop in 1885) in 1882–92, and became pastor in Portland, Oregon. He was consecrated third bishop of Nesqually, Washington, at Vancouver, Washington, in 1896, held a diocesan synod in 1898 at which he reorganized the diocese, encouraged Catholic education, brought religious orders into the see, and ministered to the Indians and immigrants of the diocese. He transferred the see to Seattle in 1907, dedicated St. James Cathedral the same year, opened the Briscoe Memorial Home and Training School for orphan boys in 1909, was made an Assistant at the Pontifical Throne 1925, and opened St. Edward Seminary in 1931. He died in Seattle on Dec. 25. During his administration he had increased the number of churches from 42 to 90 and the number of diocesan priests from 40 to 113 to minister to the increased Catholic population, which rose from 42,000 to 100,000.

ODIN, JOHN MARY (1801–70), archbishop. Son of a farmer, he was born in Hauteville, Ambierle, Loire, France, on Feb. 25, worked on his father's farm as a boy, and was educated at Roanne and Verrières classical schools, L'Argentière and Alix colleges, and the Sulpician Seminary in Lyons. While still a seminarian he went to the United States in response to a plea from Bishop Louis Dubourg of New Orleans in 1822, was sent to the Lazarist seminary at The Barrens near St. Louis, joined the Lazarists there and was ordained in 1823. He taught at the seminary and became its president and engaged in missionary work in Missouri, Arkansas, and Texas. He accompanied Bishop Joseph Rosati to the second Provincial Council of Baltimore as his theologian in 1833 and was delegated to take its decrees to Rome. He spent the next two years traveling about Europe raising funds for the American missions and on his return opened a school at Cape Girardeau, Missouri, and continued his missionary activities. He was sent to Texas in 1840 as vice-prefect, declined an appointment as coadjutor of Detroit in 1841, and when Texas was made a vicariate apostolic in 1841 he was appointed vicar and consecrated titular bishop of Claudiopolis in 1842. When Texas became an independent republic in 1836 he secured recognition of the Church's possessions under the former (Mexican) government from the new Texas government. He went to Europe in 1845 in a quest of priests for his vicariate and in 1847 was appointed first bishop of the newly established diocese of Galveston, Texas. He was a strong supporter of Catholic education, brought religious orders into the see, opened new churches and schools, and increased the number of priests from twenty-five to forty-six. He was appointed second archbishop of New Orleans in 1861, a few days after the Civil War broke out. He went to Europe in 1863 and returned with fifty priests and seminarians for the see. During the Civil War he acted as contact for the Holy See in the South. He was in Europe again in 1867 to attend the eighteenth centenary of the martyrdom of St. Peter and in 1869–70 for Vatican Council I, fell ill during the Council, and returned to his native Hauteville and died there on May 25. During his administration he held two diocesan synods, strictly enforced clerical discipline, and after the war was faced with the problem of freed Catholic slaves, who as slaves were admitted to the Catholic churches and sacraments but as free men were unwelcome.

O'DONAGHUE, DENIS (1848–1925), bishop. Born in Daviess County, Indiana, on Nov. 30, he was educated at St. Meinrad and St. Thomas colleges, Bardstown, Kentucky, and the Grand Seminary, Montreal, and was ordained in 1874. He engaged in pastoral work in the Indianapolis diocese, was chancellor of the diocese of Vincennes in 1874–1900, and served as rector of St. Patrick's Church in Indianapolis in 1885–1910. He was consecrated titular bishop of Pomario and auxiliary of Indianapolis in 1900 and ten years later was appointed bishop of Louisville, Kentucky. During his episcopate he organized the Catholic Orphans Society and the Clerical Aid Society, had St. Joseph's College reopened under the Xaverian Brothers, and built twenty-one churches and twenty-seven schools and established four new parishes. He resigned in 1924 because of failing health, was named titular bishop of Lebedus, and died in Louisville on Nov. 7.

O'DONNELL, CHARLES LEO (1884–1934), poet, educator. Born in Greenfield, Indiana, on Nov. 15, he was educated at Notre Dame, graduated in 1899, and joined the Congregation of Holy Cross. He continued his studies at Holy Cross College, Washington, D.C., received his doctorate in 1910, and was ordained in the same year. He taught English literature at Notre Dame from 1910 to 1928, except for 1918–19, when he was chaplain of the Rainbow Division of the United States Army during World War I, and in 1919 was elected provincial of his province. He became superior general of the Congregation of Holy Cross in 1925, was named president of Notre Dame in 1928, serving until 1934, and built its law school and its new stadium. He edited *Notre Dame Verse,* wrote articles for national magazines, and was the author of three books of poetry, *The Dead Musician and Other Poems* (1916), *Cloister and Other Poems* (1922), and *A Rime of the Road and Other Poems* (1928). He died in

South Bend, Indiana, on June 4 after a year's illness.

O'DONNELL, KENNETH P. (1924–77), presidential aide. Born in Worcester, Massachusetts, on Mar. 24, he flew a bomber during World War II, studied for a time at Boston College and then at Harvard, where he met Robert Kennedy, and graduated in 1949. He became a public relations consultant, worked on John F. Kennedy's first run for the United States Senate in 1952, was a Massachusetts state representative in 1952–57, was administrative assistant to Robert Kennedy in 1957 when Kennedy was counsel to the Senate Rackets Committee, and the following year joined the Washington staff of John F. Kennedy. With Robert he organized John's presidential campaign in 1960 and was appointments secretary for John while he was President, 1961–63, and was one of his closest confidants. He was in the car behind that of President Kennedy when Kennedy was assassinated in Dallas in 1963 and after the assassination stayed on with the Johnson administration until 1965, when he resigned and returned to private business as head of his own public relations and management firm. He ran unsuccessfully for governor of Massachusetts in 1966 and 1970 and in 1968 was manager of Robert Kennedy's presidential campaign and was present when he was assassinated in Los Angeles in 1968. He was coauthor with David F. Powers of *Johnny, We Hardly Knew Ye* (1972) and died at Beth Israel Hospital in Boston on Sept. 9.

O'DWYER, JOSEPH (1841–98), physician. Born in Cleveland, Ohio, on Oct. 12, he was educated in the public schools of London, Ontario, studied medicine for two years under a Dr. Anderson and then at the College of Physicians and Surgeons in New York City, and graduated in 1865. He became resident physician at the Charity Hospital on Blackwell's (now Roosevelt) Island, New York City, and then engaged in private practice and married Catherine Begg. He joined the staff of the New York Foundling Hospital in 1872, became a specialist in children's diseases, served as president of the American Pediatric Society, and developed a successful method of intubation of the larynx to aid breathing in diphtheria cases where the patient was suffocating because the larynx had become closed. He invented the instruments needed in that operation. Despite the initial unfavorable criticism of the process from the contemporary medical establishment, it was soon widely adopted. He was among the first to recognize the value of diphtheria serum and engaged in research on the treatment of pneumonia in his later years. He died in New York City on Jan. 7.

OERTEL, JOHN JAMES MAXIMILIAN (1811–82), journalist. Born in Ansbach, Bavaria, on Apr. 27, he was educated at the Lutheran University of Erlangen, Germany, and became a Lutheran minister. He came to New York City in 1837, was concerned over Lutheran practices in New York, and went to Missouri in 1839 with ninety-five Prussian immigrants to join the Saxon congregation (now the Missouri Synod of the Lutheran Church), and again became dissatisfied with the way his religion was being practiced there. He returned to New York and became a Catholic in 1840. He taught German at St. John's (Fordham) College, edited the German Catholic weekly *Wahrheitsfreund* in Cincinnati, and in 1846 founded the *Katholische Kirchenzeitung* in Baltimore, which he developed into the leading German-language Catholic newspaper in the United States. He moved the newspaper to New York in

1851, published *Altes und Neues* in 1869, and died in Jamaica, New York, on Aug. 21.

O'FARRELL, MICHAEL JOSEPH (1832–90), bishop. Born in Limerick, Ireland, on Dec. 2, he was educated at All Hallows College, Dublin, and St. Sulpice, Paris, joined the Sulpicians, and was ordained in Limerick in 1855. He was sent to Montreal to teach theology at the Grand Seminary there and then left the Sulpicians and became rector of St. Peter's Church in New York City. He was consecrated first bishop of the newly established diocese of Trenton, New Jersey, in 1881. During his episcopate he attended the third Plenary Council of Baltimore in 1884, expanded the facilities of the see, formed new parishes and missions, built an orphanage and a home for the elderly, and died in Trenton on Apr. 2.

O'FLANAGAN, ROBERT DERMOT (1901–72), bishop. Born in Lahinch, Clare, Ireland, on Mar. 9, he was educated at Belvedere College and Milltown Park, Dublin, and Ignatius-kolleg, Valkenburg, Holland, and was ordained at Valkenburg in 1929. He taught at Clongowes Wood College, Kildare, Ireland, in 1930–32, went to Alaska and was pastor of Holy Name Church, Anchorage, in 1933–51, became an American citizen, was vicar delegate of subvicariate XI in the military ordinariate, and was appointed first bishop of the newly created diocese of Juneau, Alaska, in 1951. He resigned in 1968 because of ill health, was made titular bishop of Trecalae, and died in La Mesa, California, on Dec. 31.

O'GORMAN, JAMES (1804–74), bishop. Born near Nenagh, Tipperary, Ireland, he was educated by the Trappists at Mt. Melleray, Waterford, Ireland, joined the Trappists there in 1838, was professed the following year, and was ordained in 1843. He was sent the same year with a group of other Trappists to the United States and helped found the Trappist monastery at Mt. Melleray, Dubuque, Iowa, in 1847. In 1859 he was appointed vicar apostolic of Nebraska and consecrated titular bishop of Raphanae. During his fifteen-year vicariate he increased the number of priests in his immense vicariate (Nebraska, the Dakotas west of the Missouri River, Wyoming and Montana west of the Rockies) from three to nineteen and the Catholic population from three hundred families to over eleven thousand, helped improve the conditions of the Indians, and brought the Sisters of Mercy into the Nebraska Territory in 1864. He died in Cincinnati, Ohio, on July 4 and was buried in Omaha.

O'GORMAN, THOMAS (1843–1921), bishop. Born in Boston on May 1, he was brought to Chicago in 1848 by his parents, who later moved to St. Paul, Minnesota. He was selected for the priesthood by Bishop Joseph Cretin of St. Paul and studied with John Ireland in St. Paul and then in seminaries at Maximieux and Montbel, France. He was ordained in St. Paul in 1865, was pastor in Rochester and Faribault, Minnesota, and in 1877 joined the Paulists and became a member of the Paulist mission bands. He left the Paulists and returned to Faribault in 1882 and was named first rector of the new St. Paul Seminary and president of St. Thomas College in St. Paul in 1885. He served until 1890, when he was appointed to the chair of Church history at Catholic University; while there he published a *History of the Roman Catholic Church in the United States* (1895). He was appointed second bishop of Sioux Falls, South Dakota, in 1896 and went to Rome in 1902 as a member of the Taft

Commission at the request of President Theodore Roosevelt to help settle the "friar-land claims" in the Philippines. During his episcopate he encouraged education in his see and established Columbus College in Chamberlain, South Dakota, in 1909, founded several hospitals, completed St. Joseph's Cathedral in Sioux Falls in 1919, greatly increased the number of priests, churches, and missions in the diocese and saw the Catholic population double during his administration. He died in Sioux Falls on Sept. 18.

O'HARA, EDWIN VINCENT (1881–1956), archbishop. Born in Lanesboro, Minnesota, on Sept. 6, he was educated at St. Thomas College, St. Paul, Minnesota, St. Paul (Minnesota) Seminary, Catholic University, and L'Institut Catholique, Paris, and was ordained in St. Paul in 1905. He was assistant and later pastor of St. Mary's Cathedral, Portland, Oregon, in 1905–20, superintendent of Catholic schools of the Portland diocese in 1906–20, founded *St. Isidore's Plow* (later *Catholic Rural Life),* and was chairman of the Oregon Industrial Welfare Commission in 1914–18 and of the Portland Housing Commission in 1915–20. He served as a chaplain in the Army during World War I and was pastor in Eugene, Oregon, in 1920–28. In 1923 he convened a meeting of eighty clerics concerned with the problems of rural life in the United States at which the National Catholic Rural Life Conference was founded. He was director of the Rural Life Bureau of the National Catholic Welfare Conference (NCWC) in 1920–30 and was appointed bishop of Great Falls, Montana, in 1930. He was one of the leaders in the catechetical movement in the United States and became chairman of the episcopal committee of the Confraternity of Christian Doctrine in 1935, serving in that position until his death, and was

chairman of the Social Action Department of the NCWC in 1936–42. In 1939 he was appointed bishop of Kansas City, Missouri, was made an Assistant at the Pontifical Throne in 1949, was elected president of the International Rural Life Conference in 1951, and in 1954 was given the personal title of archbishop. He was an enthusiastic supporter of the Confraternity translation of the bible *(The New American Bible),* wrote several books, among them *Pioneer Catholic History of Oregon* (1909) and *The Church and the Country Community* (1927), and died in Milan, Italy, on Sept. 11.

O'HARA, FRANK (1876–1938), educator. Born in Lanesboro, Minnesota, on Mar. 24, he was educated at the University of Minnesota (B.A. 1900), Notre Dame (M.A. 1901), and the University of Berlin (Ph.D. 1904). He was editor of the *Seattle* (Washington) *Catholic Progress* in 1904–5, was professor of economics at Notre Dame in 1905–7, director of Interlaken School, Indiana, in 1907–8, and taught economics at Catholic University from 1909–38, serving as dean of the university's school of philosophy in 1920–24. He founded and was dean of Columbus University, the Knights of Columbus evening school, in Washington, D.C., in 1919, and died in Washington on July 30.

O'HARA, GERALD PATRICK (1895–1963), archbishop. Born in Green Ridge, Scranton, Pennsylvania, on May 4, he was educated at St. Charles Borromeo Seminary, Overbrook, Philadelphia, was ordained in Rome in 1920, and continued his studies at the Pontifical Seminary, Rome (D.D. 1921), and the Apollinaris Seminary, Rome (J.U.D. 1924). He was secretary to Cardinal Dennis Dougherty of Philadelphia from 1926 until 1929, when he was consecrated titular bishop of Heliopolis and auxiliary of Philadelphia. He was appointed bishop of Savannah, Georgia, in 1935 and was president of the American Catholic Historical Society in 1934–36. He served as regent ad interim at the apostolic nunciature in Bucharest, Romania, in 1946–50 and when he protested the Communist government's persecution of the Church in Romania he was expelled from that country. He was given the personal title of archbishop in 1951, was apostolic nuncio to Ireland from 1951 to 1954, when he was named apostolic delegate to Great Britain and occupied that position until his death in London on July 16; he resigned as bishop of Savannah in 1959.

O'HARA, JOHN FRANCIS (1888–1960), cardinal. Son of the American consul to Uruguay, he was born in Ann Arbor, Michigan, on May 1 and was educated at Collegio del Sagrado Corazón College, Montevideo, Uruguay, and Notre Dame (B.A. 1911). He entered the Congregation of Holy Cross novitiate in 1912, continued his studies at Holy Cross College and Catholic University in Washington, D.C., and was ordained in 1916. He taught religion and was prefect of religion at Notre Dame in 1917–35, established and was dean of the College of Commerce in 1920–24 and vice president in 1933–34. He became president of Notre Dame in 1934, serving until 1939, and instituted a building program, enlarged the faculty, and began a program to exchange students with South American universities. He also established a Latin-American news service for some seventy-five newspapers in Central and South America and was active in the National Foreign Trade Council. He was appointed a delegate to the eighth Inter-American Congress at Lima, Peru, by President Franklin Roosevelt, surveyed South American school systems, and at the invitation of President Contreras of Vene-

zuela headed a social services commission in that country in 1939. He was appointed Military Delegate to assist the Military Vicar of U.S. Armed Forces, Cardinal Francis Spellman, and was consecrated titular bishop of Mylasa in 1939. He reorganized the military ordinariate, supervised the five thousand priests who ministered to the American Armed Forces during World War II, and visited camps all over the world. He was appointed bishop of Buffalo, New York, in 1945 and while ordinary of that see established new parishes, renovated the cathedral, and brought religious communities into the diocese. He was transferred to Philadelphia as archbishop of that archdiocese in 1951 and in 1958 was made a cardinal. A vigorous proponent of Catholic education, he built fifty-five new elementary schools and fourteen high schools and developed Philadelphia's parochial school system into one of the finest in the United States; he was particularly interested in education for the retarded. He established thirty new parishes in the archdiocese and died in Philadelphia on Aug. 28.

O'HARA, THEODORE (1820–67), editor. Born in Danville, Kentucky, on Feb. 11, he graduated from St. Joseph's College, Bardstown, Kentucky, in 1839, studied law, and was admitted to the bar in 1842. He was a clerk for a short time in the Treasury Department, Washington, D.C., became a reporter on the Frankfort (Kentucky) *Yeoman,* and served in the Mexican War and was brevetted major. He was involved in filibustering expeditions in 1849–50 and was an editor on the Louisville (Kentucky) *Times* in 1852 and on the Mobile (Alabama) *Register* in 1856–61. He served in the Confederate Army during the Civil War, was staff officer with Generals Johnson and Breckinridge, and after the war became a Georgia merchant. He wrote the poem "The Bivouac of the Dead" in commemoration of the Kentuckians who fell at Buena Vista in the Mexican War; the last four lines of its opening stanza are inscribed over the entrance to the National Cemetery at Arlington, Virginia. He died of malaria in Guerryton, Alabama, on June 6.

O'HARA, WILLIAM (1816–99), bishop. Born in Dungiven, Derry, Ireland, on Apr. 14, he received his early education in Ireland, studied for the priesthood at the Propaganda, Rome, and was ordained in Rome in 1842. He became an assistant at St. Patrick's Church, Philadelphia, taught at St. Charles Borromeo Seminary there and became its rector, and was pastor of St. Patrick's in 1856–68. He was named vicar-general of the Philadelphia archdiocese in 1860 and was consecrated first bishop of the newly created diocese of Scranton, Pennsylvania, in 1868. During his administration he increased the number of priests in the diocese from 25 to 152 and churches from 50 to 121, built St. Patrick's Orphanage and the House of the Good Shepherd, formed the independent Scranton Congregation of the Sisters Servants of the Immaculate Heart of Mary in 1871, and brought new religious orders into the see. He founded St. Thomas College in Scranton in 1888. He died in Scranton on Feb. 3.

O'HERN, CHARLES ALOYSIUS (1881–1925), rector. Born in Lawrence, Kansas, on Dec. 31, he was educated at St. Ignatius College, Chicago, the North American College, the Roman Academy of St. Thomas Aquinas (Ph.D. 1905), and the Propaganda (D.D. 1907) in Rome and was ordained in 1906. He was appointed vice-rector of the North American College in 1907, became rector in 1917, and retained that position until his death. He was made a privy

chamberlain to Pope Pius X in 1911 and to Pope Benedict XV in 1914 and was named a domestic prelate in 1917. He died in Rochester, Minnesota, on May 13.

O'HERN, JOHN FRANCIS (1874–1933), bishop. Born in Olean, New York, on June 4, he was educated at St. Andrew's and St. Bernard's seminaries, Rochester, New York, and the Propaganda, Rome, and was ordained in 1901. He engaged in parish work in Rochester, was named vicar-general of that diocese in 1923, was made a domestic prelate the following year, and was apostolic administrator of the see in 1927–28. He was appointed third bishop of Rochester in 1929 and held that position until his death there on May 22.

OLDENBACH, FREDERICK LOUIS (1857–1933), meteorologist. Son of a furrier, he was born in Rochester, New York, on Oct. 21 and was educated at Canisius College, Buffalo, New York. After his graduation he joined the Jesuits in 1881. He was sent to Europe to study in the Netherlands, returned to the United States in 1885, taught at Canisius in 1885–87, and spent the next four years studying theology at Ditton Hall, England. He was ordained in 1892, began teaching physics and chemistry at St. Ignatius College (now John Carroll University) in Cleveland, Ohio, and then astronomy and meteorology. He founded a meteorological observatory at the college in 1896, personally assembled a large universal meteorograph given the college by the Smithsonian Institution in 1898, and designed and built in 1899 the first ceraunograph to detect and continuously record static observances associated with thunderstorms. He founded a seismological observatory in 1900, was instrumental in the founding of the Jesuit Seismological

Service in 1909, and died in Cleveland on Mar. 15.

O'LEARY, MICHAEL (1875–1949), bishop. Born in Dover, New Hampshire, on Aug. 16, he was educated at Mungret College, Limerick, Ireland, and the Grand Seminary, Montreal, and was ordained in Montreal in 1897. He was a curate at St. Anne's Church, Manchester, in 1898–99 and St. John's Church, Concord, in 1899–1904, was made chancellor of the Manchester diocese in 1904, served as secretary to Bishop John Delany there, and was named vicar-general of the see in 1914. He was consecrated third bishop of Springfield, Massachusetts, in 1921 and held that position until his death there on Oct. 10.

O'MAHONEY, JOSEPH CHRISTOPHER (1884–1962), U.S. senator. Son of Irish immigrant parents, he was born in Chelsea, Massachusetts, on Nov. 5 and was educated at the Cambridge Latin School and Columbia. After graduation in 1908, he went West and worked as a newspaperman, settling in Boulder, Colorado, and married Veronica O'Leary in 1913. He moved to Cheyenne in 1916 to become city editor of the Cheyenne *State Leader* and when his publisher, John B. Kendrick, went to Washington, D.C., in 1917 as United States senator, he accompanied him as his executive secretary. He studied law at Georgetown, receiving his law degree in 1920, returned to Cheyenne to practice law, and engaged in politics. He managed Kendrick's reelection campaign in 1922, served on the Democratic National Committee in 1929–34, and was vice-chairman in 1933. He was Far West campaign manager for Franklin D. Roosevelt in the presidential election of 1932. For several months in 1933 he was first assistant postmaster general until he was appointed U.S. senator to fill Senator Kendrick's unexpired term when Kendrick died in 1933; he was elected to the Senate in 1934 and reelected in 1940 and 1946. He resumed his law practice in 1952 when defeated for the Senate by Governor George Barrett but was again elected in 1954 to take the place of the late Senator Lester C. Smith. Because of ill health (he suffered a stroke in 1959) he did not seek reelection in 1960. He died in the Naval Hospital in Bethesda, Maryland, on Dec. 1. During his quarter of a century in the Senate, he was an ardent New Dealer, though he helped to defeat President Roosevelt's plan to reorganize the Supreme Court in 1937. He worked to encourage new and small businesses and vigorously supported strict enforcement of antitrust laws and efforts to restrict monopolies. He served on the Appropriations, Judiciary and Interior (of which he was chairman in 1949–52) committees and actively promoted the admission of Alaska and Hawaii to statehood.

O'MALLEY, FRANK WARD (1875–1932), author. Born in Pittston, Pennsylvania, on Nov. 30, he studied art at the Art Students' League in Washington, D.C., Notre Dame and the Pennsylvania Academy of Fine Arts in 1894–1902. He went to New York City in 1902 and after several years as a commercial artist turned to humorous writing and began to write for the New York *Morning Telegraph.* He became a reporter for the *Sun* in 1906 and remained in that position until 1920, when he resigned to write for the *Saturday Evening Post.* He became widely known for his humorous, satirical articles on the life of the times. He was the author of several books, including *The War-Whirl in Washington* (1918) and *The Swiss Family O'Malley* (1928), and collaborated on two plays, *The Head of the House* (1909) and *A Certain Party* (1910), with E. W. Townsend. He died in Tours, France, where he had lived for several years, on Oct. 19.

O'MEARA, JOSEPH (1898–1983), educator. Born in Cincinnati, Ohio, on Nov. 8, he was educated at Xavier University there (B.A. 1921) and the University of Cincinnati (LL.B. 1923) and was admitted to the Ohio bar. He practiced law in Cincinnati in 1924–52, married Jean Callow in 1928, and was dean of the Notre Dame Law School from 1952 to 1968, when he retired. He became known for his criticism of the United States Supreme Court decision of 1973 permitting abortion and was a longtime member of the American Civil Liberties Union and director of the Indiana branch until 1974, when he resigned in protest against that organization's stand that nonpublic—including Catholic—hospitals had to provide facilities for abortions. He died in South Bend, Indiana, on June 17.

ONAHAN, WILLIAM JAMES (1836–1919), executive. Born at Leighlin Bridge, Carlow, Ireland, on Nov. 24, he lived for a time in Liverpool, England, emigrated to the United States in 1851, lived in New York, and then moved to Chicago, where his family lived in 1854. He began his business career as an office boy and shipping clerk in a flour commission brokerage firm, became interested in politics, and in 1860 married Margaret Duffy. He served as civilian secretary for the Irish Brigade and recruited for the Union Army in the Civil War. In 1863 he was named a member of the Chicago Board of Education. He became president of the Home Savings Bank, served as city collector, city comptroller, and president of the public library, and was active in Catholic affairs. He aided several religious orders, helped Archbishop John Ireland and Bishop O'Connor in promoting Irish Catholic colonization projects in Minnesota and Nebraska, helped organize the first Catholic Layman's Congress in Baltimore in 1889, and was chairman of the Columbia Congress, which met with the Parliament of Religious in Chicago in 1893. He was Chicago correspondent for the New York *Freeman's Review,* wrote for magazines, and was the author of several books, among them *The Religious Crisis in France, Our Faith and Our Flag,* and *The Influence of the Catholic Layman.* Considered the outstanding Catholic layman of his time in the United States, he was awarded the Laetare Medal in 1890 and was made honorary private chamberlain by Pope Leo XIII in 1895. He died in Chicago on Jan. 12.

OÑATE, JUAN DE (c. 1549–c. 1624), explorer. Son of Cristóbal de Oñata, who became governor of Nueva Galicia in 1538 and one of the richest men in America, and Dona Catalina de Salazar, daughter of Gonzalo de Salazar, royal factor and enemy of Hernán Cortés, he was born somewhere in New Spain (Mexico) and early became active in the service of the king. He married Isabel Tolosa, a descendant of Cortés and Montezuma, and in 1595 received a royal contract to explore and colonize New Mexico. Because of political maneuverings, his expedition was delayed until 1598, when he set out from Zacatecas with four hundred settlers and Indians and cattle. He took possession of New Mexico for the Spanish crown, establishing San Juan de los Caballeros, thirty miles north of present-day Santa Fe, New Mexico—the first permanent Spanish settlement in New Mexico. He organized the area into districts for governmental and missionary purposes, put down with great cruelty the Indian revolt at Acoma in 1599, and in 1601, in search of Quivira, he led an expedition that crossed Oklahoma and reached the plains around present day Wichita, Kansas. In 1605 he led another expedition westward to find a route to the South Sea and descended the Colorado River to the Gulf of California. On his return to the colony he found discontent rife and sought to resign in 1607 but it was not until 1609 that he was relieved by a new governor. He was tried for misconduct in office (though in reality because he had not found treasure on his expeditions) and was convicted in 1614 and perpetually banished from New Mexico, and from Mexico for four years, and fined six thousand ducats. He appealed in 1622 but was not granted the king's pardon though he may have succeeded in doing so in 1624 when he was in Spain on an unsuccessful quest for a position in Mexico or the Philippines. Oñate's explorations, which opened up a whole new territory for Spain, were never appreciated nor was their importance understood by the Spanish authorities. His exploits were celebrated in *Historia de la Nueva México* by Gaspar de Villagrá, one of his lieutenants.

ONDRAK, AMBROSE L. (1892–1961), abbot. Born in Chicago on July 28, he was educated at St. Procopius College, Lisle, Illinois (B.A. 1918), the University of Chicago, and the University of Illinois and was professed a Benedictine in 1913. He was ordained in 1918, taught at St. Procopius Abbey and College in 1918–24, was a curate at St. Michael's Church, Chicago, in 1924–46, and in 1946 became the fourth abbot of St. Procopius Abbey. He became a leader in the movement for Christian unity and established the Apostolate for Christian Unity. When the abbey was granted the privilege of bi-ritualism in 1954, he was made an archimandrite. He was active in aiding Catholics in Czechoslovakia against Communist persecution, was appointed to the Theological Commission preparing for Vatican Council II, and died in Chicago on Dec. 23.

O'NEILL, ARTHUR BARRY (1858–1925), author. Born in St. George, New Brunswick, Canada, on Sept. 1, he was educated at St. Joseph's College, Memramcook, New Brunswick (B.A. 1880), joined the Congregation of Holy Cross in 1877, and was ordained in 1882. He taught at St. Joseph's in 1882–1904, except for two years at Notre Dame in 1890–92 studying for his M.A. (1891) and teaching; he returned to Notre Dame in 1904 and became an associate editor of *Ave Maria* magazine. He contributed articles to Catholic magazines and wrote poetry and books for the clergy, notably *Between Whiles* (1899), *The Cross and the Flag* (1908), *Clerical Colloquies* (1916), *Priestly Practice* (1914), and *Sacerdotal Safeguards* (1918). He died at Notre Dame on Aug. 1.

O'NIELL, CHARLES AUSTIN (1869–1951), jurist. Born in Franklin, Louisiana, on Sept. 7, he was educated at the Christian Brothers college in Memphis, Tennessee, and studied law at Tulane. He was admitted to the bar in 1893, married Bettie Singleton Gordey the next year, was a district judge in St. Mary's Parish in 1908–12, and was named to the state Supreme Court in 1912. He was named its chief justice in 1922 and his decisions on municipal zoning set nationwide precedents. When Governor Huey Long was brought to trial on impeachment charges in 1929 he presided at the trial until the proceedings were dropped and then successfully resisted Long's efforts to have him removed from the bench. He died in New Orleans on Mar. 8.

OPENSHAW, JOHNNY *See* Connor, Joseph P.

O'REGAN, ANTHONY (1809–66), bishop. Born in Lavalleyroe, Mayo, Ireland, he was educated at St. Patrick's College, Maynooth, Kildare, and was ordained in Tuam in 1833. He taught Scripture and theology at St. Jarlath College, Tuam, became president in 1844, and five years later, at the invitation of Bishop Peter Kenrick of St. Louis, he went to the United States to be head of the new theological seminary at Carondelet, Missouri. He was consecrated third bishop of Chicago in 1854, was severely criticized by some of the clergy for his administration of the see from the time of his arrival, dismissed four diocesan priests constituting the faculty of St. Mary of the Lake Seminary, thus closing it, and excommunicated Charles Chiniquy, a Canadian priest admitted to the diocese by his predecessor, for his unorthodox and peculiar behavior. Unable to cope with the situation, he resigned in 1858 and was appointed titular bishop of Dora. He retired to Brompton, London, England, and died there on Nov. 13.

O'REILLY, BERNARD (1803–56), bishop. Born in Columkille, Ireland, he made his classical studies in Ireland and in 1825 emigrated to the United States. He continued his studies at the Grand Seminary at Montreal, Canada, and St. Mary's College, Baltimore, and was ordained in New York City in 1831. He engaged in pastoral work in Brooklyn, then in Rochester, New York, where he became pastor of St. Patrick's Church, and was especially involved with the men building the Erie Canal from 1832 to 1847, when he was appointed vicar-general of the diocese of Buffalo, New York, and director of the diocesan seminary. He was appointed titular bishop of Pompeionopolis and coadjutor of Hartford, Connecticut, in 1850, and succeeded to the see later the same year as its second bishop. He founded St.

Mary's Seminary at Providence, Rhode Island, and brought the Sisters of Mercy into the diocese in 1851 and at the height of the Know-Nothing movement the same year faced down a Know-Nothing mob seeking to demolish their convent. He went to Dublin seeking priests for his diocese, where he established thirty-four new churches, fourteen new schools, and three orphan asylums. He died at sea on the S.S. *Pacific,* on which he had embarked at Liverpool on Jan. 23 while returning from another visit to Ireland seeking Brothers of the Christian Schools for the diocese, when it was lost at sea with all its passengers.

O'REILLY, BERNARD (1820–1907), historian. Born in County Mayo, Ireland, on Sept. 29, he emigrated to Canada in his youth, entered Laval University, Montreal, in 1836, and was ordained in 1843. He engaged in pastoral work in the Quebec diocese, then joined the Jesuits and taught at St. John's College (Fordham). During the Civil War he was chaplain of the Irish Brigade of the Army of the Potomac, left the Jesuits after the war, and joined the editorial staff of the New American Encyclopedia; he also wrote articles for the New York *Sun* while traveling in Europe after finishing his work on the Encyclopedia. He was made a monsignor in 1887 and when he returned to New York City he became chaplain at Mt. St. Vincent Convent there, a position he held until his death in New York on Apr. 26. He wrote several books, among them biographies of Popes Leo XIII (1877) and Pius IX (1877) and of John McHale, archbishop of Tuam (1890).

O'REILLY, CHARLES JOSEPH (1862–1923), bishop. Born in Carlton, New Brunswick, on Jan. 4 (perhaps in 1860), he was educated at St. Joseph's College, Memramcook, New Brunswick, and the Grand Seminary, Montreal, and was ordained in Portland, Oregon, in 1890. He engaged in pastoral work in Oswego and Tegardville in the Oregon City archdiocese, became pastor of the Church of the Immaculate Heart of Mary in Portland in 1894, and was editor of the *Catholic Sentinel.* When the diocese of Baker City, Oregon, was established in 1903 he was appointed its first bishop. He was transferred to the diocese of Lincoln, Nebraska, in 1918 and remained in that position until his death in Lincoln on Feb. 4.

O'REILLY, JAMES (d. 1887), bishop-elect. Appointed first bishop of Wichita, Kansas, when that diocese was erected in 1887, he died on July 26 before the papers of establishment and consecration arrived from Rome.

O'REILLY, JAMES (1855–1934), bishop. Born in Lisgrea, Cavan, Ireland, on Oct. 10, he was educated at All Hallows College, Dublin, and was ordained in 1880. He emigrated to the United States, engaged in pastoral work in parishes in Minnesota, and was pastor of St. Anthony of Padua Church in Minneapolis in 1886–1910. He was consecrated second bishop of Fargo, North Dakota, in 1910 and held that position until his death there on Dec. 19. During his episcopate he established thirty-four new parishes, built fifty-six churches, twenty-four schools, and seven hospitals but was faced with financial difficulties in many of his parishes due to the depression and drought that devastated many areas of the diocese in the later years of his life.

O'REILLY, JOHN BOYLE (1844–90), editor. Born at Douth Castle, Drogheda, Ireland, where his father was headmaster of a school, on June 28, he was educated at the National School, worked as a printer on the Drogheda *Argus* and on the staff of *The Guardian*

in Preston, England, and then joined the 10th Hussars as a trooper. On his return to Ireland in 1863, he became involved in a revolutionary movement and joined the Fenians. He was arrested, convicted of rebellion, and sentenced to twenty years in prison in Western Australia. He escaped on an American whaler in 1869 and arrived in the United States in November, joined the staff of the Boston *Pilot,* and was appointed its editor in 1870. He and Archbishop John Williams became owners of the *Pilot* in 1876 and he remained as editor until his death. He married Mary Murphy in 1872, became one of the outstanding Catholic editors in the United States in the last half of the nineteenth century, and was known for his love of freedom, his championship of blacks, Indians, and Jews as well as the Irish and his support of Catholic education, social reform, and art and literature. He wrote numerous newspaper and magazine articles and published several books, among them four volumes of poetry, *Songs from the Southern Seas* (1873), *Songs, Legends and Ballads* (1878), *Statues in the Block* (1881), and *In Bohemia* (1886), a novel, *Moondyne Joe* (1875), based on his experiences in Australia, and *Ethics of Boxing and Manly Sport* (1888). He died in Hull, Massachusetts, on Aug. 10.

O'REILLY, PATRICK THOMAS (1833–92), bishop. Born in Kilnaleck, Ireland, on Dec. 24, he was brought to the United States as a youth and settled in Boston. He was educated at St. Charles College, Ellicott City, Maryland, and St. Mary's Seminary, Baltimore, and was ordained for the Boston diocese in 1857. He served as assistant at St. John's Church, Worcester, Massachusetts, until 1862, when he went to Boston to reorganize St. Joseph's parish. He returned to Worcester as pastor of St. John's Church in 1864 and in 1870 was appointed first bishop of the newly established diocese of Springfield, Massachusetts. During his twenty-two-year episcopate the Catholic population of the diocese tripled, the number of priests was increased from 43 to 196, the number of parishes from 43 to 96 and schools from 2 to 30; he expanded the charitable facilities of the see and established a group of Sisters of Providence in Holyoke as a diocesan institute in Springfield in 1892. He died in Springfield on May 28.

O'REILLY, BROTHER POTAMIAN (1847–1917), educator, scientist. Born in Baillieborough, Cavan, Ireland, on Sept. 29, Michael Francis O'Reilly was brought to New York City in his youth by his parents, was impressed by the Brothers of the Christian Schools who taught him, and joined the Christian Brothers in 1859, when he entered their novitiate in Montreal; he took the name Potamian and spent the rest of his life teaching. He taught at St. Joseph's College, London, in 1870–93, becoming its president, and earned his doctorate in science at the University of London in 1883—the first Catholic to do so—specializing in electricity and magnetism. He made the first medical use of the X ray in Ireland while teaching at De La Salle Normal School in Waterford, was transferred back to the United States in 1896, and was professor of physics and first dean of engineering at Manhattan College in New York City until his death in New York on Jan. 20. He became known as a historian of electrical science, wrote for numerous electrical and engineering periodicals, and was the author of *Essays on Electrical Experimenters and Experiments* (1893), *Makers of Electricity* (1909), with J. J. Walsh, and the monumental annotated guide to the most complete electrical library then extant, *Catalogue of the Wheeler Gift of Books, Pamphlets and Periodicals in the Library of the American Institute of Electrical Engineers* (1909).

O'REILLY, THOMAS CHARLES (1873–1938), bishop. Born in Cleveland, Ohio, on Feb. 22, he was educated at John Carroll University and the Spencerian Business College there and the North American College, Rome, and was ordained in Rome in 1898. He continued his studies at the Propaganda, Rome (S.T.D. 1899), and, on his return to Cleveland, served as a curate at St. John the Evangelist Cathedral in 1899–1901. He taught at St. Mary's Seminary in Cleveland in 1901–10, was chancellor of the diocese and pastor of the cathedral in 1911–28, and was vicar-general in 1916–21. He was vicar-general of religious from 1922 until 1927, when he was appointed third bishop of Scranton, Pennsylvania. He reorganized the diocesan administration, brought the Oblates of St. Joseph to the United States to his see in 1931, and sponsored Eucharistic gatherings that drew thousands. He died in Miami Beach on Mar. 25.

ORONA (d. 1802), chieftain. A chief of the Penobscot Indians of the Abenaki Confederacy in Maine, many of whom were converted to Catholicism by French Jesuits in the seventeenth century and fought on the side of the French in the wars between the French and the English, he offered the services of his tribe to the American colonists at the outbreak of the Revolution and requested that a priest be sent to his tribe, as they had not had a missionary in forty years. They fought on the American side throughout the Revolution but the Massachusetts government was unable to send them a priest, since Jesuits had been outlawed in the colony and New England for years. After the war the Indians made another appeal to

Bishop John Carroll and in 1785 a Sulpician, Fr. Francis Ciquard, sent from France for the purpose, was sent to the Penobscots and established a mission at Oldtown on an island near Bangor, Maine. Orona died there.

O'RORKE, PATRICK (1837–63), soldier. Born in County Cava, Ireland, on Mar. 25, he was brought to the United States when he was one year old by his parents, who settled in Rochester, New York. He went to work as a marble cutter, was appointed to West Point, and graduated in 1861 with highest honors. At the outbreak of the Civil War, he became colonel of the 140th New York Volunteers, participated in the battle of Chancellorsville, and was killed during the battle of Gettysburg while defending Little Round Top in July.

O'ROURKE, JOHN JOSEPH (1875–1958), biblical scholar. Born in New York City on June 16, he joined the Jesuits in 1895, studied at Stonyhurst and Oxford, England, and the University of St. Louis, and was ordained in 1910. After teaching in the United States the next several years, he went to Rome in 1913 to teach biblical Greek and papyrology and New Testament exegesis at the Biblical Institute, and was rector of the Institute in 1924–30. He expanded the faculty, bringing in professors of Near Eastern languages, such as Egyptian, Iranian, Armenian, and Sanskrit, founded a subsidiary house in Jerusalem, secured faculties for the Biblical Institute to grant doctorates in Sacred Scripture, and arranged for archaeological excavations at Teleilat Ghassul in 1930. After his term as rector ended, he taught Greek and biblical geography at the Institute until 1937, when he returned to New York. He was superior of the Jerusalem house of the Institute in 1947–49 and on his return to New York served as a spiritual direc-

tor until his death in New York on Mar. 27.

ORTYNSKY, STEPHEN SOTER (1866–1916), bishop. Born in Ortynycki, Galicia, Austria, on Jan. 29, he was educated at Kraców, where he received his doctorate in divinity, was professed a monk of the Order of St. Basil the Great in 1889, and was ordained in 1891. He taught at the University of Lawrow, Galicia, became head of the St. Paul Monastery in Michaelovka, Galicia, and was known for his preaching and intense nationalism. He was sent to the United States and appointed titular bishop of Daulia and vicar-general to the Latin rite bishops in 1907 to minister to all Catholics of the Byzantine-Slavonic rite in the United States—the first Ukrainian Catholic bishop in this country. He had great success in keeping Ruthenians and Ukrainians in the Church, founded St. Mary of the Immaculate Conception Church in Philadelphia in 1909, and four years later was granted full ordinary jurisdiction over the clergy and faithful of the Byzantine-Slavic rite in the United States, thus removing them from the jurisdiction of the Latin bishops and establishing the exarchate system for Byzantine-Slavic Catholics in the United States. He established his episcopal see in Philadelphia and designated St. Mary's his cathedral, greatly increased the number of Byzantine-Slavic Catholic churches and priests, encouraged religious education and founded schools, brought Sisters of the Order of St. Basil (Basilians) to Philadelphia, and founded the fraternal order, the Providence Association, and established a diocesan paper, *Ameryka,* for his people. He died in Philadelphia on Mar. 24.

O'RYAN, JOHN (1874–1961), general. Born in New York City on Aug. 21, he was educated at the College of the City of New York, studied law at New York University (LL.B. 1898), and was admitted to the bar in 1898. He practiced law in New York as a member of the firm of Corbin and O'Ryan in 1901–12 and married Janet Holmes in 1902. He had joined the National Guard in 1897 and in 1912, when he had risen to the rank of major general and was commander of the New York State Guard, he joined the regular Army. He graduated from the War College in 1914, commanded the 6th New York Division on the Mexican border in 1916, and was in command of the 27th Division in France and Belgium in 1917–19 during World War I. He resumed his law practice after the war, was chief counsel of the U.S. Senate Committee investigating the U.S. Veterans Bureau in 1923, served on the New York Transit Commission in 1921–26, and was appointed New York City police commissioner in 1934. He was among those favoring preparedness before World War II, was chairman in 1940 of Fighting Funds for Finland to aid Finland in her struggle with Russia, and died in New Salem, New York, on Jan. 29. He was honored by Great Britain, France, Belgium, Italy, and the United States and wrote *The Story of the 27th Division* and *The Modern Army in Action.*

O'SHAUGHNESSY, EDITH COUES (1870–1939), author. Daughter of Elliot and Jeanie McKinney Coues, she was born in Columbia, South Carolina, was educated at Notre Dame Convent, Baltimore, and by private tutors, and in 1901 in Rome she married Nelson O'Shaughnessy (d. 1932), who was later in the American diplomatic service. She wrote of her life as the wife of an American diplomat in *A Diplomat's Wife in Mexico* (1916) and *Diplomatic Days in Mexico* (1917), recounting her experiences in Mexico while her husband was

chargé d'affaires. She accompanied him to his various posts in Berlin, St. Petersburg, Vienna, and Bucharest. Among her other books were *My Lorraine Journal* (1918), *Intimate Pages of Mexican History* (1920), *Viennese Medley* (1924), *Other Ways and Other Flesh* (1929), and *Marie Adelaide, Grand Duchess of Luxembourg* (1932). She died in New York City on Feb. 18.

O'SHAUGHNESSY, NELSON JARVIS (1876–1932), diplomat. Born in New York City on Feb. 12, he was educated at Georgetown and St. John's College, Oxford, England (B.A. 1899), and then studied international law at London's Inner Temple. He married Edith Louise Coues in Rome in 1901, continued his studies in Europe and in 1904 entered the American foreign service. He was appointed secretary of the American legation in Copenhagen in 1904 and served in Germany, Russia, Austria-Hungary, and Romania until 1911, when he was appointed secretary of the American legation in Mexico City. When Ambassador Henry Lane Wilson was recalled to Washington he was in charge of the legation as chargé d'affaires. His good relations with the new Mexican dictator, Victoriano Huerta, caused difficulty with President Woodrow Wilson, who believed Huerta had murdered his predecessor, Francisco Madero. When it was reported to the President that Shaughnessy's friendship with Huerta was affecting his judgment of Mexican events and he failed in attempts to secure a satisfactory settlement of the Tampico incident in 1914 in which American sailors were arrested, U.S. Marines occupied Vera Cruz and he was recalled. He served briefly in the embassy in Vienna later in 1914 and resigned in 1916. He worked for the Western Union Telegraph Company in South America during World War I, represented a group of Yugoslavian bondholders in the 1920s, and died in Vienna on July 25.

O'SHEA, WILLIAM JAMES (1863–1939), educator. Born in New York City on Oct. 10, he was educated at the College of the City of New York (B.S. 1887) and Manhattan College (M.S. 1889) and began teaching in the New York public school system in 1887. He became a principal in 1901, district superintendent in 1906, and associate superintendent in 1918. During World War I he was vice-chairman of Liberty Loan and Relief drives, was named superintendent of schools in 1924, worked to advance pension plans, and retired in 1934 after forty-seven years in the public school system. During his career he wrote sixteen English textbooks and was honored by France and Belgium in 1923 for his relief work. He died in New York City on Jan. 16.

O'SULLIVAN, JEREMIAH (1842–96), bishop. Born in Kanturk, Cork, Ireland, on Feb. 6, he emigrated to the United States in 1863, studied at St. Charles College, Ellicott City, Maryland, and St. Mary's Seminary, Baltimore. He was ordained in Baltimore in 1868 and engaged in pastoral and missionary activities until 1885, when he was consecrated fourth bishop of Mobile, Alabama. He became known for his administrative ability and his oratorical prowess, built towers on the Mobile cathedral, and worked to restore his diocese from the ravages of the Civil War, from which it was still suffering. He died in Mobile on Aug. 10.

O'TOOLE, GEORGE BARRY (1886–1944), educator. Born in Toledo, Ohio, on Dec. 11, he was educated at St. John's University there (B.A. 1906, M.A. 1908) and the Propaganda, Rome (Ph.B., Ph.L., Ph.D., S.T.B., S.T.L., and S.T.D.), and was ordained in Rome

in 1911. He was secretary to Bishop Joseph Schrembs of Toledo in 1912–15, pastor of St. Aloysius Church, Bowling Green, Ohio, in 1915–17, and professor of philosophy at St. Vincent Archabbey, Latrobe, Pennsylvania, in 1917–18 and of theology in 1923–24. He served as a chaplain in the Army during World War I in 1918–19, attaining the rank of captain, and in 1919 returned to teaching at St. Vincent's; he was also professor of animal biology at Seton Hill College, Greenburg, Pennsylvania, in 1919–20 and 1923–24. He visited China in 1920–21 to help the Benedictines launch the Catholic University of Peking and served as its rector from 1925 until 1933, when the Benedictines were forced to leave China and return to the United States. He became head of the philosophy department at Duquesne University, Pittsburgh, in 1934, the year he was made a domestic prelate, and left Duquesne in 1937 to become a professor of philosophy at Catholic University and editor of *The China Monthly* in 1939. He served in these last two positions until his death in Washington, D.C., on Mar. 26. He wrote several books and pamphlets, among them *The Case Against Evolution* (1925).

OURSLER, FULTON (1893–1952), author. Born in Baltimore on Jan. 22, he left high school before graduating, worked at various jobs, as water boy for a construction gang and packer in a department store, and then worked for two years in a law office, intending to become a lawyer. He decided instead to become a writer, worked on the Baltimore *American* in 1910–12 as a reporter and in 1912–18 as music and dramatic critic, married Rose Keller Kargan in 1911, and moved to New York City in 1918 to become editor of *The Music Trades.* He became editor-in-chief of *Metropolitan Magazine* in 1922, married Grace Perkins, an author and an actress, in 1925 (his first wife had died), coauthored the play *The Walking Gentlemen* with her, and began writing short stories, plays, and novels. In 1931 he became editor-in-chief of McFadden publications, which included the weekly *Liberty* and ten monthly magazines with a combined circulation of 16 million, and, as editor-in-chief of *Liberty* in 1931–42, he introduced the now-familiar concept of publishing novels in a condensed version. After a trip to Jerusalem, described in *A Skeptic in the Holy Land* (1936), he became a convert to Catholicism and frequently appeared on the "Catholic Hour" radio program. In 1944 he became senior editor of *Reader's Digest,* a position he held until his death of a heart attack in New York City on May 24. He wrote some thirty books, among them eight mystery sto-

ries written under the pseudonym Anthony Abbot; these latter were very successful and led to his working with the police in solving actual crimes and lecturing on methods of criminal detection to the Federal Bureau of Investigation (the FBI). He also wrote several plays, among them *Behold This Dreamer!* (1927), *The Spider* (1927), *All the King's Men* (1929), and scenarios for motion pictures. But his most popular works were books with a religious theme: the enormously successful *The Greatest Story Ever Told* (1949), from which a movie was made, *Why I Know There Is a God* (1950), *Modern Parables* (1950), *The Greatest Book Ever Written* (1951), *A Child's Life of Jesus* (1951), and the posthumously published *The Greatest Faith Ever Known* (1953).

P

PACE, EDWARD ALOYSIUS (1861–1938), psychologist. Born in Starke, Florida, on July 3, he was educated at St. Charles College, Ellicott City, Maryland (B.A. 1880), and the North American College and the Propaganda, Rome (S.T.B. 1883, S.T.D. 1886), and was ordained in 1885. He was rector of the cathedral at St. Augustine, Florida, in 1886–88, continued his studies at the University of Leipzig (Ph.D. 1891), Louvain, and Paris, where he studied psychology and was a professor of psychology in 1891–94 and of philosophy in 1894–1935 at Catholic University. He was dean of the school of philosophy in 1895–99, 1906–14, and 1934–35 and served as vice-rector of the university in 1925–36. He established the first psychology laboratory at a Catholic college at Catholic University in 1891, was founder and first director of the Institute of Pedagogy (which became the department of education) at Catholic University in 1899, and helped found Trinity College in 1900. He was cofounder, with Thomas Edward Shields, of the *Catholic Educational Review* in 1911 and was its first editor, was made a prothonotary apostolic in 1920, and was the first editor of *Studies in Psychology and Psychiatry* in 1926. He was one of the founders of the American Catholic Philosophical Association in 1926 and was its first president and editor of its *New Scholasticism,* was associate editor and contributor to the Catholic Encyclopedia and was president of the American Council of Education in 1925–26. A pioneer among Catholics in the new science of psychology, he was the first Catholic priest to receive a doctorate in psychology, was a charter member of the American Psychological Association, and wrote hundreds of articles on psychology, philosophy, theology, and education. He died in Washington, D.C., on Apr. 26.

PADILLA, JUAN DE (c. 1500–c. 1544), martyr, missionary. Born in Andalusia, Spain, he became a Friar Minor of the Andalusian province, came to Mexico about 1528, was chaplain of an expedition headed by Nuño de Guzmán to Nueva Galicia and Culiacán in 1529–30 and defended the rights of the Indians. He was a missionary to the Indians in 1531–40 and was founding superior of the convents at Tzapotlán, Tuchpán, and Tulantcinq. He went to Tehuantepec in 1533 to join an expedition to the Orient with Hernán Cortés, but when it did not materialize, he returned to his Indians. He joined Francisco Coronado's expedition to New Mexico in 1540, reaching the Hopi pueblos in 1540 and the Rio Grande pueblos and the Pecos in 1541. The following year he was again with Coronado in his quest for Quivira, in the course of which the expedition reached central Kansas. When Coronado abandoned his search, Padilla, with Fr. Juan de la Cruz and Br. Louis de Ubeda and six others, decided to remain behind to evangelize the Indians, and they established a mission on the Rio Grande in New Mexico. With six companions Fr. Padilla set out to evangelize other Indian tribes and all seven were murdered by Indians at some unknown place in the Southwest at an unknown date, about Nov. 30; some authorities conjecture it may have been in eastern Colorado or western Kansas. Fr. de la Causa and Br. de Ubeda were also murdered at the mission. They were the first Christian missionaries to suffer martyrdom within the present boundaries of the United States.

PALLADINO, LAWRENCE BENEDICT (1837–1927), missionary. Born in Tiglieto, Italy, on Aug. 15, he studied for a time at Genoa's minor seminary, became a Jesuit novice at Querciuoli in Modena in 1855, was forced to continue his studies in Austria and France because of the anticlericalism of the Italian nationalists, and was ordained in Nice, France, in 1863. He emigrated to California in 1864, taught at St. Ignatius College, San Francisco, until 1867, and then spent the next sixty years (forty-four in Montana) ministering to the settlers and Indians of the Pacific Northwest. When the diocese of Helena, Montana, was established in 1884, he served as secretary to its Bishop John B. Broudel and later was vicar-general of the diocese and pastor of St. Francis Xavier Church in Missoula, Montana. In 1894 he published *Indian and White in the Northwest: A History of Catholicity in Montana,* an invaluable source of information about the early history of Montana. He died in Missoula on Aug. 19.

PALLEN, CONDÉ BENOIST (1858–1929), author. Born in St. Louis on Dec. 5, he was educated at Georgetown and the University of St. Louis (Ph.D. 1885), taught at St. Louis for a short time, and then continued his studies in Rome. On his return to St. Louis he was made editor of *Church Progress* and opposed Archbishop John Ireland and his policies in 1895–97. He was managing editor of the Catholic Encyclopedia in 1905–13 and president of its publishing firm, the Encyclopedia Press, in 1913–20, and was president of the Layman's League for Retreats and Social Studies in 1912–13. He lectured widely, was an ardent foe of socialism, and engaged in editorial work for the New International Encyclopedia and Encyclopedia Americana. He wrote several books on philosophy, poetry, and education, among them *Philosophy of Literature* (1897), *What Is Liberalism?* (1899), *Collected Poems* (1915), *Education of Boys* (1916), *The Story of Literature* (1917), and *As Man to Man* (1927). He died in New York City on May 26.

PALMER, GRETTA (1905–53), author. Born in St. Louis on Sept. 13, she was educated at Vassar, worked on the staff of *The New Yorker* and then the New York *World-Telegram* and in 1934 began free-lance writing. She was a war correspondent in World War II, remained in the Far East after the war to write of postwar conditions there, and became a Catholic in 1946. She wrote a syndicated column, "The Top of My Head," for the National Catholic Welfare Conference (NCWC) feature news service and several books, among them *God's Underground* (1949) and *God's Underground in Asia* (1952). She died in New York City on Aug. 15.

PALÓU, FRANCISCO (c. 1722–c. 1789), missionary. Born in Palma on the island of Majorca, Balearic Islands, on Jan. 22, he joined the Friars Minor there in 1739, studied at Lullian University there under Fr. Junípero Serra, whose lifelong companion he became, and was ordained in 1747. He joined Fr. Serra in volunteering for the American missions in 1749 and they were sent to the missionary college of San Fernando in Mexico City and then to Sierra

Gorda and San Sabas (now in Texas). Fr. Serra was recalled to Mexico in 1760 and Fr. Palóu continued working in the Indian missions of the Sierra Gorda, north of Querétaro, until 1767, when he was sent with Fr. Serra as superior and fourteen other Franciscans to Lower California to take over the missions of the Jesuits, who had been expelled from Spain and Spanish territories. He succeeded Fr. Serra as president of the Lower California missions in 1769, when Serra was sent to Upper California with the Portolá expedition, and while in that position engaged in a protracted struggle with Governor Barri in a successful defense of the Indians and the missionaries. In 1773 he went to Upper California and on the way erected a cross marking the boundary between Lower and Upper California, which was to help fix the United States–Mexican boundary after the Mexican War (1846–48). He acted as president at Monterey until Fr. Serra returned the following year, and later that year he accompanied Captain Rivera's expedition that discovered San Francisco Bay. He founded San Francisco de Asís de la Dolores Mission, popularly called Mission Dolores, in San Francisco in 1776, became president of the California missions on the death of Fr. Serra in 1784, and was recalled to San Fernando the following year. He was elected president of the college in 1786 and remained in that post until his death there on Apr. 6. While at Mission San Dolores he wrote the four-volume *Noticias de la Nueva California* (1874), the source history of the early years of California's colonization, and was also author of a life of Fr. Serra (1787), which contains the history of the first nine California missions.

PARDOW, WILLIAM O'BRIEN (1847–1909). Born in New York City on June 13, he was educated at St. Francis Xavier College there, graduated in 1864, and joined the Jesuits that year. He continued his studies in Canada and Woodstock College, Maryland, taught at St. Francis Xavier from 1871 until 1875, when he went to France to finish his studies, and was ordained there in 1877. He returned to the United States when the Jesuits were expelled from France in 1880, served as assistant of the provincial of the Maryland–New York province in 1884–88, was rector of St. Francis Xavier in 1891–93 and provincial in 1893–97 and established the American Jesuits' first foreign mission in Jamaica, British West Indies. He was a popular preacher—known throughout the country for his eloquence—and retreat master, served as pastor of St. Ignatius Church in New York City in 1901–6 and 1907–9, and was master of tertians in 1888–91 and 1903–6. He died in New York City on June 13.

PARDY, JAMES V. (1898–1983), bishop. Born in Brooklyn, New York, on Mar. 9, he joined the Maryknoll Fathers in 1925, received his B.A. from St. Francis College, Brooklyn, New York, in 1927 and his S.T.B. from Catholic University in 1930. After ordination in 1930, he taught at Maryknoll Junior Seminary in Pennsylvania, 1930–32, went to Korea in 1932 as a missionary, and was named superior of Maryknoll missions there in 1939. He served as a chaplain in the United States Army in 1943–45, was interned by the Japanese for ten months during World War II, and was rector of Maryknoll Junior Seminary in Massachusetts in 1945–48. He was director of the Maryknoll formation of candidates program in 1948–51, returned to Korea in 1951, and was again made superior of Maryknoll missions in Korea in 1953. He was vicar-general of Maryknoll in 1956. He was consecrated titular bishop of Irenopolis and first vicar apostolic of Cheong-Ju,

Korea, in 1958 and was appointed first bishop of the newly established diocese of Cheong-Ju in 1962. He resigned his bishopric of Cheong-Ju in 1969 and died at El Camino Real Hospital in Mountain View, California on Feb. 16.

PARISEAU, MOTHER JOSEPH OF THE SACRED HEART (1823–1902), missionary. Esther Pariseau was born at St. Elziar de Laval, Canada, on Apr. 16 and was accepted into the Sisters of Providence in 1843 by Mother Gamelin, foundress of the order, in Montreal, taking the name Joseph of the Sacred Heart. In 1856, at the request of Bishop Augustin Magloire Blanchet of Nesqually, Washington, she and four other Sisters of Providence went to the Washington Territory and she spent the rest of her life working in the Northwest. She began the first Catholic school in the Northwest in 1857 at Fort Vancouver, where the Sisters had settled, and established St. Joseph Hospital in 1858 —the first hospital in the Northwest. During the next four decades she traveled by horseback and later by train from California to Alaska and from the Pacific to the Indian villages of Montana and Idaho and built twenty-nine hospitals, schools, and homes, designed most of them herself, and actually constructed some of them (she was an accomplished carpenter). She died in Seattle on Jan. 19. In 1953 the American Institute of Architects acclaimed Mother Joseph as the Pacific Northwest's first architect; the West Coast Lumbermen's Association named her the first Northwestern artist to work in the medium of wood. Her statue representing the state of Washington was placed in National Statuary Hall in the Capitol, Washington, D.C., in 1981 after Governor Dixy Lee Ray, Washington's first woman governor, signed a bill authorizing it in May 1977.

PARSONS, WILFRID (1887–1958), editor. Born in Philadelphia on Mar. 17, he joined the Jesuits in 1903, taught at Boston College and Holy Cross College, and studied at Woodstock (Maryland) College (M.A. 1908) and at the Jesuits' seminary at Louvain in 1907–09 (Ph.D. 1910). He was ordained at Woodstock in 1918, received his S.T.D. from Woodstock the following year, and continued his studies at the Gregorian, Rome (S.T.M. 1921). On his return to the United States he taught theology at Woodstock in 1922–24 and was editor of the Jesuit weekly *America* in 1925–36, in which post he ardently supported New Deal policies and sharply criticized Fr. Charles E. Coughlin and founded the quarterly *Thought* in 1926. He taught political science at Georgetown in 1936–40, 1948–50, and 1954–58, was dean of Georgetown's Graduate School in 1938–40, librarian and archivist in 1938, and reorganized the library. He was professor of political science at Catholic University's Graduate School in 1940–49 and wrote several books, among them *The Pope and Italy* (1929), *Mexican Martyrdom* (1936), *Early Catholic Americana* (1939), and *The First Freedom* (1948). He died in Washington, D.C., on Oct. 28. His *Early Catholic Americana* listed more than a thousand books and their locations published by Catholics from 1729 to 1830.

PAUL, FATHER. *See* Wattson, Paul James.

PAYERAS, MARIANO (1769–1823), missionary. Born in Inca, island of Majorca, Balearic Islands, on Oct. 10, he joined the Franciscans in Palma in 1784 and was sent to the missionary college of San Fernando in Mexico City in 1793. For the rest of his life he served in California missions, at San Carlos,

459

Monterey, in 1796–98, Soledad in 1798–1803, San Diego in 1803–4, and Purísima Concepción in 1804–23. While at Purísima Concepción he compiled a catalogue in Indian which was used by other friars but never published. He was *presidente* (superior) of the missions in 1815–20 and in 1819 San Fernando College elected him *comisario-prefecto* of the missions; in that position he visited all the missions from San Diego to Sonoma north of San Francisco. Six months before his death he was on an expedition to the Russian settlements in Sonoma County. He died on Apr. 28.

PEEBLES, BERNARD MANN (1906–76), patrologist. Born in Norfolk, Virginia, on Jan. 1, he was educated at Hampden-Sydney College, Virginia, the University of Virginia (B.A. 1926), and Harvard (M.A. 1928, Ph.D. 1940). He was an instructor in Greek at the University of Virginia in 1928–29 and in 1932–34 a fellow in the School of Classical Studies in the American Academy, Rome. While in Rome he became a Catholic. He taught at Fordham in 1934–35 and 1939–41, Harvard in 1937–39, St. John's College, Annapolis, Maryland, in 1941–48, except for 1942–45, when he was with the Army during World War II, and Catholic University in 1948–71, serving as chairman of the Department of Greek and Latin in 1962–70. He retired from full-time teaching in 1971 but remained active in teaching and editorial work. An authority on classical and medieval Latin and patristics and probably the foremost authority on St. Martin of Tours, he was also an editor of *Traditio,* coeditor of the *Fathers of the Church* series, and author of *The Poet Prudentius* (1951), translated St. Augustine's *Enchiridion* (1947) and Sulpicius Severus' *Life of St. Martin, Letters, Writings* (1949), and contributed to scholarly monographs and periodicals. He was murdered by an assailant in Washington, D.C., on Nov. 22.

PEGIS, ANTON CHARLES (1905–78), philosopher. Born in Milwaukee, Wisconsin on Aug. 24, he was educated at Marquette (B.A. 1928, M.A. 1929) there and the University of Toronto (Ph.D. 1931), and was converted from the Greek Orthodox Church to Catholicism in 1930. He taught philosophy at Marquette in 1931–37 and at Fordham's graduate school in 1937–40. In 1944 he became a professor of the history of philosophy at the Pontifical Institute of Mediaeval Studies at the University of Toronto. He was a disciple of Étienne Gilson, became a leader in the revival of Thomism in the United States, and was president of the Pontifical Institute of Mediaeval Studies in 1946–54 and president of the American Catholic Philosophical Association in 1946–47. He was editorial director of the Catholic Textbook Division of Doubleday & Company in New York City in 1954–61 and then returned to the Pontifical Institute of Mediaeval Studies in Toronto. He wrote profusely and lectured widely on the teachings of Thomas Aquinas. He translated and edited *On the Truth of the Catholic Faith* by Aquinas, edited the two-volume *Writings of St. Thomas Aquinas* (1945), *Introduction to St. Thomas* (1948), *The Wisdom of Catholicism* (1949), and wrote *St. Thomas and the Greeks* (1939), *Christian Philosophy and Intellectual Freedom* (1955), *The Middle Ages and Philosophy* (1963), and *St. Thomas and Philosophy* (1964). He died in Toronto on May 13.

PELLICER, ANTHONY DOMINIC (1824–80), bishop. Born in St. Augustine, Florida, on Dec. 7, he was educated at Spring Hill College, Mobile, Alabama, and St. Vincent de Paul Seminary, New Orleans, and was ordained in Mobile in 1850. He engaged in pastoral work in the Mobile diocese, was vicar-general in 1867–74, and was appointed first bishop of the newly established diocese of San Antonio, Texas. He held this position until his death in San Antonio on Apr. 14.

PEÑALVER Y CÁRDENAS, LUIS IGNACIO (1749–1810), archbishop. Born in Havana, Cuba, on Apr. 3, he was educated at St. Ignatius College there until 1768 when King Charles III of Spain closed all Jesuit institutions in his realms. He continued his studies at the University of Havana, received his doctorate in theology in 1771, and was ordained in 1772. He was named vicar-general of Santiago in 1773, helped found a public library and an asylum, and spent most of his personal fortune ministering to the victims of a hurricane that had struck Cuba in 1772. He was named titular bishop of Tricca and ordinary of the diocese of Louisiana and Florida in 1793 and arrived in New Orleans on July 17, 1795. He was dismayed at the lack of spirituality in the lives of its inhabitants, struggled to improve their faith, encouraged Catholic education, and helped the poor. He completed what became the Cathedral of St. Louis in New Orleans, was transferred to Guatemala City, Guatemala, as archbishop in 1801, resigned the see in 1806, and returned to Havana. He died there on July 17.

PENNINGS, BERNARD HENRY (1861–1955), abbot. Born in Gemert, Holland, on June 9, he was educated at the Norbertine Berne Abbey in Heeswick, Holland, and joined the Premonstratensian (Norbertine) Order there in 1879. He was ordained in 1886, was novice master in 1886–93, and volunteered for the American mission, which the Berne Abbey had undertaken at the request of Bishop Sebastian G. Messmer of Green Bay, Wisconsin, in 1893. He worked with Dutch and Belgian immigrants in northern Wisconsin, was especially effective in combating the proselytizing efforts among the Belgian immigrants of Joseph René Vilatte, "archbishop of the Old Catholic Church in America," and in 1898 was named prior of the first permanent foundation of the Premonstratensian Order in North America at West De Pere, Wisconsin; when it was raised to an abbey by Pope Pius XI in 1925 he was named abbot, a position he held until his death at West De Pere on Mar. 17. He became provincial of American Norbertines, and when his community established St. Norbert College in West de Pere, he served as its president.

PEPPERGRASS, PAUL. See Boyce, John.

PERCHÉ, NAPOLEON JOSEPH (1805–83), bishop. Born in Angers, France, on Jan. 10, he taught philosophy when he was eighteen, studied for the priesthood at the Beaupré seminary, and was ordained there in 1829. He engaged in pastoral work in Murr, near Angers, until 1837, when, at the request of Bishop Benedict Flaget of Bardstown, Kentucky, he went to the United States and was appointed pastor of Portland. He went to New Orleans with Bishop Anthony Blanc in 1841 and became almoner of the Ursulines in New Orleans, holding that position for twenty-eight years. He founded *Le Propagateur Catholique* in 1842 to support now Archbishop Blanc in his dispute with wardens of the cathedral, who claimed the authority to select curates, and he edited it until forced to resign because of ill health in 1857. He was appointed titular bishop of Abdera and coadjutor of New Orleans in 1870 and succeeded to the see later the same year as its third archbishop. During his episcopate he reestablished the diocesan seminary (though forced to close it in 1881 because of financial difficulties), brought religious orders into the see, and because of his charity to those ruined by the Civil War ran up a huge diocesan debt. He died in New Orleans on Dec. 27.

PERSICO, IGNATIUS (1823–95), cardinal. Born in Naples, Italy, on Jan. 30, he joined the Capuchins in 1839 and was ordained in 1846. He was sent as a missionary to India in 1846, became a secretary to Bishop Hartmann, the vicar apostolic, and helped establish the Bombay *Catholic Examiner* in 1850 and was its first editor. He went to Rome in 1853 to explain the Goanese schism to Pope Pius IX and then went to London, where he secured English recognition of Catholic rights in India. He was named titular bishop of Gratianopolis and auxiliary to Bishop Hartmann in 1854, visitor of the vicariate in Agra in 1855, and later was made its vicar apostolic. In 1860 he returned to Italy because of ill health. He offered his services to the diocese of Charleston, South Carolina, in 1867, attended the tenth Provincial Council of Baltimore in 1869, and was appointed fourth bishop of Savannah, Georgia, in 1870. He was again forced to resign because of ill health in 1872, was made titular bishop of Bolina, and was apostolic delegate to Canada in 1874 and to Malabar in 1877. He was appointed bishop of Aquino, Italy, in 1879, resigned because of ill health in 1887, and was appointed titular archbishop of Damietta, Egypt, and sent to Ireland as apostolic delegate. He was made a cardinal in 1893 and died in Rome on Dec. 7.

PESCHGES, JOHN HUBERT (1881–1944), bishop. Born in West Newton, Minnesota, on May 11, he was educated at St. John's College, Collegeville, Minnesota, in 1891–99 and the St. Paul (Minnesota) seminary in 1899–1905, and was ordained in Winona, Minnesota, in 1905. He continued his studies at Catholic University in 1905–6, was pastor of St. Mary's Church, Geneva, Minnesota, in 1906, engaged in missionary work in 1907–10, was pastor of Mt. Carmel Church, Easton, Minnesota, in 1910–13, and became vice president of St. Mary's College, Winona, in 1913. He was president of St. Mary's from 1918 until 1933, was made a domestic prelate in 1925, and was named pastor of St. Augustine's Church, Winona, in 1933. He was appointed second bishop of Crookston, Minnesota, in 1938 and during his episcopate he established the Confraternity of Christian Doctrine in the diocese, encouraged organizations for agricultural development and the religious education of rural youngsters, and died in Crookston on Oct. 30.

PETER, SARAH WORTHINGTON KING (1800–97). Daughter of Thomas Worthington, United States senator and sixth governor of Ohio, she was born in Chillicothe, Ohio, on May 10. She married General Edward King, son of Rufus King, in 1816, when she was sixteen. The couple took up residence in Cincinnati in 1831 and she became known for her work with the poor, orphanages, and Sunday schools and her efforts to improve the role of women. She was widowed in 1836 and moved to Cambridge, Massachusetts, married the British consul in Philadelphia, William Peter, in 1844, and founded the Philadelphia School of Design for Women. When Peter died in 1853 she returned to Cincinnati, went to Europe in 1854, and was commissioned to buy works of art for the Ladies' Academy of Art, in which she was greatly interested (and which developed into the Cincinnati Art Museum); while in Rome she became a Catholic in 1855. She continued her charitable and educational work with the Sisters of Charity and the Sisters of Notre Dame and brought the Franciscan Sisters to work in Cincinnati hospitals and the Sisters of Mercy from Ireland and helped support their foundations. She worked as a field nurse with the Franciscan Sisters and in Cincinnati hospitals and war prisons during the Civil War, brought the Little Sisters of the Poor to Cincinnati in 1868 and also the Passionist Fathers, and died in Cincinnati on Feb. 6.

PETERS, CAROLINE *See* Betz, Eva.

PETERSEN, THEODORE C. (1883–1966), scholar. Born of Lutheran parents at Nayudupet, Madras, India, on Feb. 1, he studied for the Lutheran ministry at Lutheran Foreign Missionary Seminary in Hermannsburg, Germany, but just before his ordination became a Catholic in 1907. He went to the United States to work with German Catholics in the Middle West but instead entered the Paulist seminary in Washington, D.C., and was ordained a Paulist priest in 1912. He continued his studies in Semitics at Catholic University (Ph.D. 1913) and theology (S.T.L. 1914), taught philosophy at St. Paul's College in 1919–25 and Scripture in 1932–36, was research assistant to Professor Henry Hyverat, founder of Catholic University's department of Semitic and Egyptian Languages and Literature, in 1929–35, and was an associate professor of Hebrew, Arabic, and Coptic at Catholic University in 1941–48. He became recognized as a leading authority on things Coptic, supervised the establishment of the Institute of Christian Oriental Research at Catholic University, and engaged in private Coptic research from 1952 until his death in Washington, D.C., on Mar. 14.

PETERSON, JOHN BERTRAM (1871–1944), bishop. Born in Salem, Massachusetts, on July 15, he was educated at the Marist college in Van Buren, Maine, St. Anselm College, Manchester, New Hampshire (B.A. 1895), and St. John's Seminary, Brighton, Boston, and was ordained in 1899. He continued his studies in Church history at Catholic University, the University of Paris, and the School of History, Rome, and taught Church history on his return to St. John's in 1901–2 and moral theology the next twenty years. He was one of the founders of the National Catholic Educational Association in 1904 and served as its president for five years. He was rector of St. John's in 1911–26, was made a domestic prelate in 1915, held numerous diocesan positions, and became pastor of St. Catherine of Genoa parish in Somerville, Massachusetts, in 1926. He was named titular bishop of Hippo and auxiliary of Boston in 1927 and was appointed bishop of Manchester, New Hampshire, in 1932. During his episcopate he worked to offset the effects of the depression of the thirties in New Hampshire, was episcopal chairman of the Educational Department of the National Catholic Welfare Council (NCWC), and was made an Assistant at the Pontifical Throne in 1834. He died in Manchester on Mar. 15.

PFLAUM, GEORGE A. (1903–63), publisher. Born in Dayton, Ohio, on June 18, he was educated at the University of Dayton and in 1923 joined his father's publishing firm, George A. Pflaum Publishers, Inc. He became president in 1933, greatly expanded the firm's activities during his thirty-year presidency, and added eight new periodicals to its list, among them *Young Catholic Messenger, Junior Catholic Messenger, Our Little Messenger,* and *Treasure Chest.* He died in Dayton on Nov. 20.

PHELAN, DAVID SAMUEL (1841–1915), editor, author. Born in Sydney, Nova Scotia, on July 16, he was taken to St. Louis in 1853 by his family and studied for the priesthood at Cape Girardeau, Missouri. He was ordained in 1863, served as assistant at the cathedral in St. Louis for a short time, became pastor at Indian Creek and then at Edina, Missouri, and began publication of the *Missouri Watchman* (later the *Western Watchman* of St. Louis) at Edina. He became pastor of Annunciation parish in St. Louis in 1868, served in Pacific, Missouri, and then returned to St. Louis as pastor of Our Lady of Mt. Carmel Church in 1873, serving as pastor until his death in St. Louis on Sept. 21. He was often involved in controversy through the editorial positions of the *Watchman.* While in Edina, he was arrested for refusing to take Missouri's test oath, which he had attacked in the *Watchman,* but was soon released. He was outspoken in his criticism of the hierarchy, denounced Cahenslyism and the condemnation of the Ancient Order of Hibernians by some bishops, opposed the educational decrees of the third Plenary Council of Baltimore, and was a supporter of Archbishop John Ireland and a bitter opponent of the American Protective Association in St. Louis.

PHELAN, MOTHER MARY GERARD (1872–1960), educator. Born in Kilkenny, Ireland, on Jan. 17, Anastasia Phelan was educated by the Religious of the Sacred Heart of Mary (RSHM) in Waterford and Lisburn, Ireland, and joined the congregation at Béziers, France, taking the name Gerard in 1893. She continued her education at Cambridge, served as headmistress at Crosby, England, and in 1907 went to the United States to aid Mother Mary Joseph Butler found Marymount School. Later the same year she and Mother Mary Joseph founded the first Marymount College for women at Tarrytown, New York; she and Mother Mary Joseph worked during the next three decades establishing Sacred Heart foundations all over the United States, Europe, and England. She continued her education studies at Oxford, the Sorbonne, Catholic University, and Fordham and received her M.A. and Ph.D. and served in various positions in her congregation, including the presidency of Marymount and provincial of the North American province, until 1946, when she was elected superior general succeeding Mother Joseph. She was reelected in 1952 and during her term in office the congregation established twenty-eight schools and colleges in eleven countries, including Marymount College in New York. She died in Tarrytown on Mar. 22.

PHELAN, JAMES DUVAL (1861–1930), U.S. senator, banker. Born in San Francisco on Apr. 20, he was educated at St. Ignatius College there (B.A. 1881) and the University of California, where he received his law degree in 1882. He traveled throughout Europe and on his return began practicing in San Francisco. He gave up law for banking and in time became president of the U.S. Bank and Trust Company of San Francisco. He was chairman of the Relief and Reconstruction Committee after the disastrous San Francisco earthquake and fire in 1906, and in 1907 he was elected mayor of San Francisco and was elected for the two succeeding terms. During his administration he secured the adoption of a new city charter, inaugurated a public works program, and attacked corruption in the city government. He went to Europe in 1913 to attract foreign governments to participate in the Panama Pacific International Exposition of 1915 and was elected U.S. senator from California in 1914. While in the Senate he worked on railroad and public land legislation and an Oriental exclusion law. When he was defeated for reelection in 1920 he retired from politics, resumed his business career, and died in San Jose, California, on Aug. 7. He bequeathed much of his estate to Catholic and educational institutions.

PHELAN, RICHARD (1828–1904), bishop. Born in Sralee, Ballyragget, Kilkenny, Ireland, on Jan. 1, he was educated at St. Kieran College, Kilkenny, came to the United States in 1844 in response to a plea for priests from Bishop Michael O'Connor of Pittsburgh, and continued his studies at St. Mary's College, Baltimore. He was ordained in Pittsburgh in 1854, engaged in pastoral work in the diocese, and was named its vicar-general. He was appointed titular bishop of Cibyra and coadjutor of Pittsburgh in 1885 and succeeded to the see in 1889, where he was an able administrator. During his decade and a half as bishop of Pittsburgh he was particularly concerned with aiding the thousands of immigrants who flooded into the diocese to work in the coal mines and the steel mills of western Pennsylvania and formed them into congregations with pastors who spoke their language. He died in Idlewood, Pennsylvania, on Dec. 20.

PHILLIPS, CHARLES JOSEPH MacCONAGTY (1880–1933), author. Born in New Richmond, Wisconsin, on Nov. 20, he was educated at De La Salle College, Toronto, worked on a railroad for a time, and then entered journalism. He was managing editor of the *Northwestern Chronicle* in St. Paul, Minnesota, 1901–3, edited *The New Century* in Washington, D.C., in 1903–6 and *Republican Voice* in New Richmond from 1906 to 1907, when he went to San Francisco as editor of the archdiocesan

paper, *The Monitor,* in 1907–15. He continued his education at St. Mary's College, Oakland, California, where he received his degree in 1914, and at Catholic University, Oxford, and Florence, Italy. He served with the Knights of Columbus and the American Red Cross during World War I and engaged in relief work in France, Germany, and Poland in 1918–22. He spent two years after his return to the United States recovering his health and in 1924 became a professor of literature at Notre Dame, a position he held until his death in South Bend, Indiana, on Dec. 29. In 1925 a series of articles he wrote for the National Catholic Welfare Conference revealed for the first time the persecution of the Catholic Church in Mexico. While at Notre Dame he founded the University Theatre, was associate editor of *Catholic World,* and was cofounder of and edited *Pan, Poetry and Youth,* a poetry magazine for youth, in 1925. He began writing poetry in his youth and wrote poetry, drama, fiction, biography, and on the Polish people. Among his books were *Back Home—An Old-fashioned Poem* (1908) and *High in Her Tower* (1927), poetry, and *The Divine Friend* (1915), a poetic play; *The Shepherd of the Valley* (1918) and *Tarcisius* (1917), plays; *The Doctor's Wooing* (1926), a novel; a biography of Abraham Lincoln and the posthumously published *Paderewski* (1934); and *The New Poland* (1923).

PICOT DE CLORIVIÈRE, JOSEPH. *See* Clorivière, Joseph Picot de.

PICQUET, FRANÇOIS (1708–81), missionary. Born in Bourg, Bresse, France, on Dec. 4, he was educated at the Lyons seminary, the Sorbonne, where he received his doctorate, and St. Sulpice, Paris, and was ordained a Sulpician priest in 1734. At his request he was sent as a missionary to Canada the same year, worked with the Indians around Montreal, and became fluent in the Algonquin and Iroquois languages. He expanded his missionary activities to western New York, founded an Indian mission in 1749 on the site of Ogdensburg, and in 1751 traveled all around Lake Ontario. He convinced the Five Nations, traditional allies of the English, to remain neutral in the war between France and England in 1743–48, presented a report on how to keep Canada in French hands to the minister of the navy in France in 1751, and on his return to Canada in 1754 led his Indians against the English colonists in the resumption of hostilities between France and England the next six years. He was ordered home in 1760 to escape the wrath of the English, who had set a price on his head, engaged in pastoral work until 1772, when he returned to Bresse and became a canon of the cathedral of Bourg. He died in Verjon, Ain, France.

PINTEN, JOSEPH GABRIEL (1867–1945), bishop. Born in Rockland, Michigan, on Oct. 3, he was educated at St. Francis Seminary, Milwaukee, Wisconsin, and the Propaganda, Rome, and was ordained in Rome in 1890. He engaged in pastoral work in Michigan, became chancellor of the Marquette diocese and rector of the cathedral, and was vicar-general of the see from 1916 until 1921, when he was appointed bishop of Superior, Wisconsin. He was transferred to Grand Rapids, Michigan, in 1926, retired in 1940, and was appointed titular bishop of Sela. He died on Nov. 6.

PISE, CHARLES CONSTANTINE (1801–66), editor, author. Born in Annapolis, Maryland, on Nov. 22, he was educated at Georgetown and joined the Jesuits in 1820 as a scholastic. He soon left the Jesuits to become a secular

priest, probably continued his education at Mt. St. Mary's College, Emmitsburg, Maryland, and St. Mary's College, Baltimore, and was ordained in 1825. He taught at Mt. St. Mary's College and served as a curate at the Baltimore cathedral in 1827–32 and then at St. Patrick's Church, Washington, D.C. While at St. Patrick's, on motion of Senator Henry Clay, he was appointed chaplain of the United States Senate in 1832—the first Catholic priest to be so honored. He was stationed in New York City in 1834–49 and was founding pastor of St. Charles Borromeo Church in Brooklyn from 1850 until his death in Brooklyn on May 26. He was known nationally for his preaching prowess, founded *Literary Magazine* in 1841, edited the *Metropolitan Record,* and was coeditor of the *Catholic Expositor,* which was published only from 1842 to 1844, and of the *Weekly Reporter and Catholic Diary.* He also wrote poems and a play, a five-volume *History of the Catholic Church* (1827–30), *Altheia* (1845), and *Christianity and the Church* (1850).

PITAVAL, JOHN BAPTIST (1858–1928), archbishop. Born in St. Genis-Terre-Noire, France, on Feb. 10, he studied at the Lyons seminary, went to the United States, where he finished his studies for the priesthood at St. Charles College, Ellicott City, Maryland, and was ordained in Santa Fe, New Mexico, in 1881. He engaged in missionary work in the Southwest, was consecrated titular bishop of Sora and auxiliary of Santa Fe in 1902, administered the see in 1908, and was appointed its archbishop in 1909. He resigned in 1918 and was appointed titular archbishop of Amida and died in Denver, Colorado, on May 23.

PLAGENS, JOSEPH CASIMIR (1880–1943), bishop. Born in Detroit on

Jan. 29, he was educated at the University of Detroit (B.A. 1899, M.A. 1902) and St. Mary's Seminary, Baltimore (S.T.B. 1903) and was ordained in 1903. He was pastor of St. Michael's Church, Pt. Austin, Michigan, in 1906–11, St. Florian's Church, Detroit, in 1911–19, and Sweetest Heart of Mary Church, Detroit, in 1919–35; he was made a domestic prelate in 1923. He was consecrated titular bishop of Rhodiopolis and auxiliary of Detroit in 1924, retaining his pastorate, and was vicar-general of the see from 1924 until 1935, when he was appointed sixth bishop of Marquette, Michigan. While bishop there he instituted a modernizing and expansion program, reconstructed fire-gutted St. Peter's Cathedral, and organized a Catholic youth program in the diocese. He was transferred to Grand Rapids, Michigan, in 1940 and remained in that position until his death in Grand Rapids on Mar. 31.

PLASSMANN, THOMAS BERNARD (1879–1959), educator. Born in Avenwedde, Westphalia, Germany, on Mar. 19, he came to the United States in 1894 and was educated at St. Francis Solanus College, Quincy, Illinois (M.A. 1898), joined the Franciscans in 1898, and studied for the priesthood at the Franciscan scholasticate in Paterson, New Jersey. He was ordained in 1906 and continued his oriental and biblical studies at Catholic University (Ph.D. 1907), the Apollinaris College, Rome (S.T.D. 1909), and Bonn and Louvain universities. He began teaching Sacred Scripture and dogmatic theology at St. Bonaventure College, Allegany, New York, in 1910 and was its president in 1920–49. During his presidency he instituted a major building program, began Christ the King Seminary for candidates for the diocesan priesthood, expanded the graduate program, and added schools of business administra-

tion and St. Elizabeth Teacher's College for sisters, and increased the student enrollment from three hundred to twenty-two hundred. He was provincial of the New York province of the Franciscans from 1949 to 1952, when he returned to St. Bonaventure and became rector of Christ the King Seminary, a position he held until his death in Olean on Feb. 13. He was founder and for twenty-eight years president of the Franciscan Educational Conference in 1919–47, helped establish the Franciscan Institute and served as president of the Catholic Biblical Association and the Catholic Historical Association. He was a contributor to the Catholic Encyclopedia, was on the editorial board of the Confraternity of Christian Doctrine version of the bible, and wrote several books, among them *The Significance of Beraka* (1913), *The Book Called Holy* (1935), *The Priest's Way to God* (1938), *From Sunday to Sunday* (1948), *The Upper Room* (1953), and *Radiant Crown of Glory* (1954).

PLUMPE, JOSEPH CONRAD (1901–57), editor. Born in Cloverdale, Ohio, on Apr. 12, he was educated at the Pontifical College Josephinum, Worthington, Ohio (B.A. 1922, M.A. 1924), and was ordained in Toledo, Ohio, in 1928. He continued his studies at the universities of Münster (Ph.D. 1932) and Berlin, Germany, taught at the Josephinum in 1932–41, and Latin and Greek at Catholic University in 1941–57. He was founder-editor of the patristic series, *Ancient Christian Writers,* and wrote *Mater Ecclesia* (1943). He died in Worthington on Dec. 8.

PLUNKETT, CHRISTOPHER J. (1867–1939). Born in Dublin on July 1, he was educated at Blackrock College and Royal University of Ireland in 1882–89 and at Langonnet, Chevilly (Paris), and Grignon, France, and was ordained in France as a priest of the Congregation of the Holy Cross in 1893. He emigrated to the United States, taught at Duquesne University, Pittsburgh, in 1894, and then was pastor of Philadelphia's St. Peter Claver Church in 1895–1912. He was founding pastor of St. Mark's Church, New York City's first Catholic parish for blacks, in 1912–31, and for the next two years was a missionary at Arecibo, Philippine Islands, in 1931–33. He was elected provincial of the American congregation of his order in 1933 and died in New York City on Aug. 17.

PONCE DE LEÓN, JUAN (c. 1460–1521), explorer. Of a noble family, he was born in San Servos, León, Spain, served as a page in the household of Pedro Nuñez de Guzmán in his youth, and fought against the Moors in Granada. In 1493, he accompanied Columbus on his second journey to the New World and settled in Hispaniola. He became aide to Governor Nicolás de Ovando and was put in charge of Higüey, the eastern part (now the Dominican Republic) of Hispaniola, by Ovando in 1502. There he heard from the Indians of fabled treasure in the neighboring island of Borinquén (Puerto Rico) and headed an expedition there in 1508. He found gold, was appointed governor of Borinquén in 1509, conquered the natives, established the first European settlement on the island, and amassed a fortune before being replaced by Diego Columbus in 1512. When Carib Indians told him of a fabled spring which restored youth on a rich island called Bimini north of Cuba, he secured a patent from Charles V in 1512 giving him jurisdiction over the island and making him governor, and in 1513 he set out with an expedition of three ships from Puerto Rico to discover the island. He sailed through the Bahamas and landed in Florida about

175 miles south of present-day St. Augustine—the first European presence on the North American mainland in this period, though he thought it was an island. He followed the coastline south and then explored Florida's west coast as far as Cape Romano. Though he found neither treasure nor his "fountain of youth" on this expedition, he secured another grant in 1514, giving him jurisdiction over Bimini and the "island" of Florida. He led an unsuccessful campaign against the Caribs south of Borinquén in 1515 and then, after a period in Spain, returned to Borinquén until 1521, when he set out to colonize Florida. He began building houses for the settlers on the west coast of Florida, probably in the vicinity of Charlotte Harbor or Tampa Bay, but the party was driven off by hostile Indians. He was severely wounded during the attack and died of the wound on a ship on the way to Cuba.

PORRO Y PEINADO, FRANCISCO (1738), bishop. A Spanish Franciscan at the Convent of the Holy Apostles in Rome, he was appointed bishop of New Orleans to succeed its first bishop, Luis Peñalver y Cárdenas, who had been transferred to Guatemala in 1801. Authorities differ on what happened to him, but all agree he never set foot in his see. One chronicle states he was never consecrated; another that he was and died on the eve of his leaving; and one authority believes that in 1803 he was translated to Tarazona, Spain, where he died on Jan. 3. At any rate, the confusion caused by the transfer of Louisiana from Spain to France in 1800 and from France to the United States in 1803 caused the Holy See to put New Orleans under the jurisdiction of Bishop John Carroll of Baltimore, and New Orleans remained without its own bishop until Louis Dubourg was appointed in 1818.

PORTIER, MICHAEL (1795–1859), bishop. Born in Montbrison, Loire, France, on Sept. 7, he was educated at the Lyons seminary and in 1817 emigrated to the United States in response to a plea for priests from Bishop Louis Dubourg of Louisiana. He completed his studies for the priesthood at St. Mary's Seminary, Baltimore, and was ordained in St. Louis in 1818. He engaged in pastoral and educational activities in New Orleans, became its vicar-general, and when Alabama and the Floridas were erected into a vicariate apostolic in 1825, he was appointed vicar apostolic and consecrated titular bishop of Oleans in St. Louis in 1826. He was the only priest in the vicariate and in 1829 he went to France seeking priests and funds. On his return, he found his vicariate had been elevated to the status of a diocese, Mobile, Alabama, and he was its first bishop. He established Spring Hill College at Mobile in 1830, attended the seventh Provincial Council of Baltimore in 1849, and was designated by the Council to take its decrees to Pope Pius IX at Gaeta, managed to bring in ten priests to serve the nine parishes and nine mission stations he had established in the diocese, consecrated the Cathedral of the Immaculate Conception in Mobile in 1850, and brought several religious orders into the see. He died in Mobile on May 14.

POTERIE, ABBÉ DE LA. *See* Bouchard, Claude Florent.

PRENDERGAST, EDMOND FRANCIS (1843–1918), archbishop. Born in Clonmel, Tipperary, Ireland, on May 3, he went to the United States in 1859, studied at St. Charles Borromeo Seminary, Overbrook, Philadelphia, and was ordained in 1865. He engaged in work in the Philadelphia see, became pastor of St. Malachy's Church, was vicar-general of the archdiocese in 1895–97, and was consecrated titular bishop of Scilium and auxiliary of Philadelphia in 1897. He succeeded to the see as its third archbishop in 1911 and during his administration established thirty new parishes, opened West Catholic High School for boys and Hallahan High School for girls, increased the number of charitable institutions in the see, and erected Misericordia Hospital and brought new religious orders into the archdiocese. He died in Philadelphia on Feb. 26.

PRESTON, THOMAS SCOTT (1824–91), author, founder. Born in Hartford, Connecticut, on July 23, he studied at Washington College (Trinity) there and General Theological Seminary, New York City, and was refused ordination by the Episcopal bishop of New York because of his strong High Church stance. He was ordained an Episcopal priest by Bishop De Lancey of Western New York in Holy Innocents Church at West Point, New York, in 1847. He served as a curate at St. Luke in the Fields Church in New York City until 1849, when he and his brother William and St. Luke's pastor, Dr. John Murray Forbes, became Catholics. He studied for the Catholic priesthood at St. Joseph's Seminary, Fordham, was ordained in 1850, was a curate at Old St. Patrick's Cathedral for a short time, and then was appointed pastor of St. Mary's Church, Yonkers, New York, in July 1851. He became secretary to Archbishop John J. Hughes of New York in 1853 and two years later was named chancellor of the archdiocese. He was appointed pastor of St. Ann's Church in 1862 and vicar-general in 1863, and remained at St. Ann's until his death in New York City on Nov. 4. With Mother Veronica Starr he founded the Sisterhood of the Divine Compassion in 1873 and was made a domestic prelate in 1881 and a prothonotary apostolic in 1888. He was the author of fifteen books, among them *Lectures on Reason and Revelation* (1868), *Vicar of Christ* (1878), *Protestantism and the Church* (1882), and *God and Reason* (1884).

PRICE, THOMAS FREDERICK (1860–1919), founder. Son of Alfred Lanier Price, editor of the Wilmington *Daily Journal,* he was born in Wilmington, North Carolina, on Aug. 19 and when sixteen decided he wanted to become a priest. He studied at St. Charles College, Catonsville, Maryland, graduated in 1881, and continued his studies at St. Mary's Seminary, Baltimore. He was ordained in Wilmington in 1886 and served as a curate there and in Asheville and was appointed pastor of St. Paul's Church, New Bern, in 1887. He traveled all over North Carolina doing missionary work and in 1897 founded *Truth,* a magazine of Catholic apologetics. He founded an orphanage in Raleigh in 1898 and *The Orphan Boy* magazine and in 1902 founded Regina Apostolorum, a center for training priests to work for the conversion of the South, which eventually failed. While attending a mission conference in Washington, D.C., in 1904 he met Fr. James Anthony Walsh and in 1911 the two received papal approval to found the Catholic Foreign Mission Society of America (Maryknoll)—the first native American missionary society. In 1918 he led the first group of four Maryknoll priests to China, where they established a mission at Yeungkong in southern China. He died the following year in Hong Kong on Sept. 12 of gangrene from appendicitis.

PUGH, GEORGE ELLIS (1822–76), U.S. senator. Son of Lot Pugh, a successful merchant, and Rachel Anthony Pugh, he was born in Cincinnati, Ohio, on Nov. 28, was educated there at Xavier College and Miami University, Oxford, Ohio (M.A. 1843), and was admitted to the Ohio bar in 1843. He began to practice law in Cincinnati, served in the Mexican War as a captain of the 4th Ohio Infantry, and was commended for bravery and served in the Ohio House of Representatives in 1848–49. He was city solicitor of Cincinnati in 1850, state attorney general in 1852–54, and was Ohio's first native son to serve in the United States Senate in 1855–61. In the Senate he consistently opposed the intervention of Congress in the slavery dispute in the territories but opposed the acceptance of the proslavery Lecompton (Kansas) constitution in 1858 and the demands of the Southern faction of the Democratic Party at the 1860 Democratic Convention that the Northern Democrats accept the extreme pro-Southern viewpoint on slavery. He was defeated in a bid for reelection to the Senate in 1861 and in the election of 1863 for lieutenant governor of Ohio in 1863, and again for Congress in 1864. In 1865 he assisted Charles O'Conor in the defense of Jefferson Davis after the Civil War. Descended from Quaker stock, he became a convert to Catholicism soon after the death of his Catholic wife, Therese Chalfont Pugh, in 1868. Though elected a delegate to Ohio's constitutional convention of 1873, he declined to serve and died in Cincinnati on July 19.

PULASKI, CASIMIR (c. 1748–79), general. The eldest son of Count Joseph Pulaski and Maria Zislinska Pulaski, he was born in Winiary, Podolia, Poland, on Mar. 4 and was destined for the bar. However, in his youth he received military training in the guard of Duke Charles of Courland and in 1768 was one of the leaders in the Confederation of Bar, formed by his father to free Poland from foreign domination by rebelling against Stanislas II. When the revolt was put down his estates were confiscated and he was forced to flee to Prussia and then to Turkey in 1772, where he was unsuccessful in an attempt to persuade Turkey to attack Russia, and in 1775 to Paris. In 1776 he offered his services to Benjamin Franklin in Paris to aid the colonists in their revolt against England. He joined Washington in Boston the following year with the rank of brigadier general and as a cavalry commander. He served with distinction at Brandywine, Germantown, and in the New Jersey campaign, commanding the cavalry during the winter of 1777–78 at Trenton and serving with General Anthony Wayne. He refused to serve under Wayne, resigned his command in 1778, and formed the Pulaski Legion. He was ordered to South Carolina in 1779 in support of General Benjamin Lincoln, was defeated when he attacked General Augustine Prevost advancing north from Savannah, and then joined Lincoln in the attack on Savannah in 1779 in command of the American and French cavalry. He was seriously wounded leading a cavalry charge on enemy lines on Oct. 9, was taken aboard the *Wasp* in Savannah harbor for surgery, and died of his wounds off St. Helena's Island, South Carolina, on Oct. 11. It is not known whether he was buried at sea, at Greenwich, Georgia, or on St. Helena's Island.

PURCELL, JOHN BAPTIST (1800–83), archbishop. Born in Mallow, Cork, Ireland, on Feb. 26, he was unable to secure a college education in Ireland because of the laws then discriminating against Catholics and emigrated to the United States when he was eighteen to secure a higher education. He spent a year as a tutor and then teaching at Asbury College in Baltimore and in 1820 entered Mt. St. Mary Seminary, Em-

mitsburg, Maryland, to study for the priesthood. After three years there, he continued his studies at St. Sulpice Seminary in Paris, where he was ordained in 1826. After another year of studies he returned to the United States, taught at Mt. St. Mary's, and in 1829 became its president. He was appointed bishop of Cincinnati, Ohio, in 1833 and after attending the third Provincial Council of Baltimore, which began on the day of his consecration in Baltimore, he traveled to his see city, which had one church. An ardent champion and defender of the Church, his series of public debates with Alexander Campbell, founder of the Campbellite wing of the Presbyterian Church, who had accused the Catholic Church of being an enemy of culture and Americanism, in 1837 attracted widespread attention and led to a flood of conversions to Catholicism. He launched an expansion of diocesan facilities and services to provide for the needs of his people and the immigrants who were flocking into the area. He built a new cathedral, St. Peter in Chains, which was consecrated in 1846, founded St. Francis Xavier College, opened Mt. St. Mary of the West Seminary in 1851, and was a fervent supporter of the Catholic school system which he built up in the see. He made trips to Europe in 1835, 1838, and 1843 seeking priests and religious for his diocese and held diocesan synods in 1855, 1858, and 1861. He was made an archbishop in 1851 when Cincinnati was made an archdiocese and at the same time was made an Assistant at the Pontifical Throne. In 1853 he quelled a Know-Nothing mob bent on burning the cathedral during the visit of Archbishop Bedini, papal nuncio to Brazil, who had been sent to the United States by Pope Pius IX. He strongly supported the Union during the Civil War and called for the emancipation of slaves in 1862, five months before President Lincoln issued the Emancipation Proclamation. He attended Vatican I in 1869–70, where he questioned the opportuneness of the declaration of papal infallibility, though he accepted it when it was proclaimed. His last years were clouded by the financial disaster that befell the archdiocese in 1878, caused by the collapse of an archdiocesan fund managed by his brother, Fr. Edward Purcell. He retired from active duty as archbishop in 1880 and died at the Ursuline convent at St. Martin's, Brown County, Ohio, on July 4. During his administration the Catholic population of the Cincinnati see increased from 7,000 to 500,000 in Ohio. To meet this tremendous growth, he increased the number of priests from 14 to 480 and the number of churches from 16 to 510 and similarly increased the other facilities of the see.

PUTZER, JOSEPH (1836–1904), theologian. Born in Rodaneck, Tirol, Austria, on Mar. 4, he joined the Congregation of the Most Holy Redeemer (the Redemptorists) in 1856, studied at St. Barbara's Seminary, Mautern, Austria, and was ordained in 1859. He taught at St. Barbara's until 1861, when he became a missionary at Eggenburg and Innsbruck, Austria. After fourteen years in this work he was sent to the United States in 1876, began teaching at St. Alphonsus Seminary, Baltimore, in 1880, and engaged in parish work at St. Michael's Church, Baltimore, until 1884, when he was made superior of St. Mary's Church, Buffalo, New York. He was appointed to the chair of moral theology at St. Mary's House of Studies, Ilchester, Maryland, in 1887, also teaching canon law, and remained in that position, except for 1893–96, when he was superior at St. Mary's Church, until his death there on May 15. He wrote numerous articles for Catholic magazines and *Instructio de Confessariis* and completely revised Konings's *Commentarium in facultates apostolicas*.

Q

QUARTER, WILLIAM (1806–48), bishop. Born in Killurine, Ireland, on Jan. 21, he studied at Maynooth College, County Kildare, Ireland, and in 1822 emigrated to America and finished his studies for the priesthood at Mt. St. Mary's College, Emmitsburg, Maryland, and was ordained for the New York diocese in 1829. He was pastor of St. Peter's Church there the next four years, was named pastor of St. Mary's Church in 1833, and was consecrated first bishop of the newly established diocese of Chicago in 1844. He was active in aiding immigrants, inaugurated the first theological conferences in the United States in 1847, built thirty churches, many with his own funds, held a diocesan synod in 1846, and opened St. Mary of the Lake Seminary in 1846. He died suddenly in Chicago on Apr. 10.

QUIGLEY, JAMES EDWARD (1855–1915), bishop. Born in Oshawa, Ontario, Canada, on Oct. 15, he was brought to the United States when he was a child by his parents and graduated from St. Joseph's College, Buffalo, New York, in 1872. He studied for the priesthood at Our Lady of the Angels Seminary, Niagara Falls, New York, at Innsbruck and the Propaganda, Rome, where he received his doctorate in theology, and was ordained in Rome in 1879. He was rector of St. Vincent's Church, Attica, New York, in 1879–84, St. Joseph's Cathedral, Buffalo, New York, in 1884–86, and St. Bridget's Church, Buffalo, from 1886 to 1897, when he was consecrated bishop of Buffalo. He actively fought socialism and encouraged labor unionism and attracted national attention by mediating the dock strike in Buffalo in 1899. In 1903 he was appointed archbishop of Chicago. During his episcopate he held an archdiocesan synod, founded Cathedral College of the Sacred Heart as a preparatory seminary in 1905, greatly increased the number of priests, religious, and ecclesiastical buildings in the see, continued his outspoken opposition to socialism, and helped establish the Catholic Church Extension Society in Chicago under Fr. Francis Kelly in 1905. He died in Buffalo on July 10.

QUIGLEY, MARTIN JOSEPH (1890–1964), publisher. Born in Cleveland on May 6, he was educated at Niagara University in 1906–8 and the Catholic University of America in 1908–9 and worked as a newspaper reporter in Cleveland, Detroit, and Chicago in 1910–13. He entered the motion picture industry when he founded the trade paper *Exhibitors Herald* in 1915, founded, and was president of, the Quigley Publishing Company in 1916, which in the next several decades acquired or founded several motion picture trade journals, among them *Motography* in 1917, *The Moving Picture World* in 1925, *Motion Picture News (Herald)* in 1931, *Motion Picture Almanac,* and *International Television Almanac.* He acquired great influence in motion picture circles and in 1929, with Fr. Daniel Lord, authored the Motion Pic-

QUIGLEY, THOMAS J.

ture Production Code, a statement of moral principles for the guidance of motion picture producers, which was adopted by all the major film companies in 1930. He received numerous papal honors and industry awards, was the author of *Decency in Motion Pictures* (1937), and died in New York City on May 4.

QUIGLEY, THOMAS J. (1905–60), educator. Born in Pittsburgh on Mar. 4, he was educated at Duquesne University there (B.A. 1927) and St. Vincent Seminary, Latrobe, Pennsylvania, and was ordained in Latrobe in 1931. He served as a curate in the Pittsburgh diocese in 1931–37, was superintendent of diocesan schools in 1939–56, and was president of the National Catholic Music Educators Association and editor of *Musart.* He was named pastor of St. Canice Church in 1956 and died in Pittsburgh on Dec. 26.

QUINLAN, FRANCIS JOSEPH (1852–1936), physician. Son of Irish immigrant parents, he was born in New York City on Dec. 24, graduated from St. Francis Xavier College there in 1872, taught for three years, and then studied medicine at Columbia University's College of Physicians and Surgeons, where he received his M.D. in 1878. He continued his medical studies at Heidelberg, Vienna, and Berlin and after interning at St. Vincent's Hospital in New York City served in the U.S. Army Medical Corps in the Dakota Territory, Montana, and Idaho in 1879–83. He left the Army in 1883 and began private practice specializing in diseases of the ear, nose, and throat. He was professor of otology and laryngology at New York Polyclinic School and Hospital, of diseases of the nose and throat at Fordham, and served on the staffs of several New York hospitals. He married Matilda Venn in 1896 (d. 1931) and Eliza-

beth Maurer in 1932, was active in charitable work and a leader in his field of medicine, and was the recipient of the Laetare Medal in 1906. He was president of the Irish Historical Society in 1908–10 and of the Catholic Club in 1911–12 and was the author of several medical monographs, among them *Throat Complications of Typhoid Fever, Post-Nasal Catarrh,* and *Pampilloma of Larynx.* He died in Amawalk, New York, on July 24.

QUINLAN, JOHN (1826–83), bishop. Born in Cloyne, Cork, Ireland, on Oct. 19, he emigrated to the United States in 1844, studied for the priesthood at Mt. St. Mary's College, Emmitsburg, Maryland, and was ordained in Cincinnati in 1853. He engaged in pastoral and missionary work in the Cincinnati archdiocese and was rector of its Mt. St. Mary of the West Seminary from 1854 until 1859, when he was consecrated second bishop of Mobile, Alabama, in New Orleans. He labored to repair the damages suffered by the diocese during the Civil War, expanded the Catholic activities of the see, brought in clergy from Ireland, and increased the number of priests in the diocese from ten to forty-five and the number of churches and mission stations from eighteen to thirty-six and rebuilt Spring Hill College in Mobile which had been destroyed by fire in 1869. He died in Mobile on Mar. 9.

QUINN, DANIEL (1861–1918), Greek scholar. Son of an Irish immigrant, he was born in Yellow Springs, Ohio, on Sept. 21, studied at Mt. St. Mary College and Seminary, Emmitsburg, Maryland (B.A. 1883, M.A. 1886), and was ordained in 1887. He then studied archaeology at the American School for Classical Studies at Athens and philosophy at the University of Athens and after further study at the University of Munich began teaching Greek at Mt.

St. Mary's. After two years there he was appointed to the chair of Greek at Catholic University but spent 1892–93 in further studies at the University of Berlin and the University of Athens (Ph.D. 1893) before assuming the chair as head of the Greek Department at Catholic University in 1893. He resigned in 1897, traveled in Greece until 1904, and was rector of Leonine College in Athens in 1902–5. On his return to the United States, he served as pastor of St. Paul's Church, Yellow Springs, until 1912, also serving as professor of Greek at Antioch College there in 1906–12, and from 1912 was pastor of St. Vincent de Paul Church, Cincinnati, where he died on Mar. 3. He was highly regarded for his research in Grecian philology and archaeology, wrote many articles on the subject, and was the author of *Helladian Vistas* (1908).

QUINN, DANIEL JOSEPH (1864–1940), educator. Born in New York City on May 12, he studied at the North American College, Rome, for the diocesan priesthood but joined the Jesuits in 1888. He was ordained in 1899, became noted for his oratory, and became a professor at Boston College. He served as president of Fordham in 1906–11, amended the charter of St. John's College in New York to change its corporate name to Fordham in 1907, and died in New York City on Mar. 9.

R

RADEMACHER, JOSEPH (1840–1900), bishop. Born in Westphalia, Michigan, on Dec. 3, he studied at St. Vincent's Seminary, Latrobe, Pennsylvania, and was ordained in Fort Wayne, Indiana, in 1863. He engaged in pastoral work in that diocese the next two decades and in 1883 he was appointed fourth bishop of Nashville, Tennessee. During his administration in Nashville, he built thirteen churches, five schools, and three hospitals and in 1893 was transferred to Fort Wayne. While bishop of Fort Wayne, he increased the number of churches and schools in the diocese and remodeled the cathedral before suffering a mental breakdown in 1898. The see was administered during his illness by the vicar-general, Fr. J. H. Guendling, until he died in Fort Wayne on Jan. 12.

RAFFEINER, JOHN STEPHEN (1785–1861), missionary. Born in Mals, Austrian Tyrol, on Dec. 26, he studied for the priesthood at the Benedictine abbey in Fiechtand in Rome and began studying medicine. After receiving his medical degree in 1813, he practiced in Italy, Austria, and Switzerland but returned to his studies for the priesthood and was ordained in Brixen in 1825. He engaged in pastoral work in the Brixen diocese until 1833, when he volunteered for the American missions and went to the United States. Though intended for the Cincinnati diocese, he remained in New York City and organized its first German congregation at St. Nicholas Church, which was dedicated in 1836.

He traveled all over New York and New Jersey organizing and ministering to German congregations and settling disputes, founded Holy Trinity Church for German immigrants in 1841, and by the time of his death had established some thirty churches. He was appointed vicar-general for New York's German Catholics in 1843 and continued in that position until his death and acted as vicar-general for Bishop John Loughlin of Brooklyn when that diocese was established in 1853. He died in Brooklyn, New York, on July 16.

RAFINISQUE, CONSTANTINE (1783–1840), naturalist. Son of a prosperous French Marseilles merchant, he was born in Galatea, a suburb of Constantinople (Istanbul) on Oct. 22. He was educated by private tutors, became deeply interested in natural history, and in 1802 went to Philadelphia, where he spent the next three years in the Clifford Brothers Counting House. During these years he traveled the Atlantic seaboard states and on his return to Italy resided at Palermo, where he engaged in the export business and devoted himself to studying the natural history of plants and fish. He wrote treatises on the flora of Virginia, Maryland, Pennsylvania, Delaware, and North Carolina, among them the highly regarded *Flora Columbica* on the Potomac region. He became professor of natural science at the University of Naples, edited the journal of Specchio delle Scienze, a learned society, and in 1815 returned to the United States, entering the country dramatically when his ship was wrecked off Fisher's Island in Long Island Sound, and became a permanent resident. He visited the regions of the United States he had not covered on his first travels and from this trip came his monumental *The American Herbalist.* He also taught at Transylvania University in Kentucky from 1818 to 1826, when he became professor of science and medicine at Franklin Institute, Philadelphia, a position he occupied until his death in Philadelphia on Sept. 18. He was a pioneer in his field and as Louis Agassiz, the noted Swiss-American geologist and zoologist, said, "Both in Europe and America, he anticipated all his contemporaries . . ." Some of his theories on evolution considerably predate Darwin. Though he was criticized for vagueness and scientific inaccuracy by some, he did reorganize and improve the systematic study of botany in the United States. The last years of his life were marred by a mental breakdown and were spent alone and in abject poverty. He wrote some forty-three treatises, which were collected and published in a uniform edition in 1884; among them were *Medical Flora or Manual of the Medical Botany of the United States of America* (1828–30), *New Flora and Botany of North America* (1836), and his autobiography, *A Life of Travels and Researches in North America and South Europe* (1836).

✓**RAIMONDI, LUIGI** (1912–75), cardinal. Born in Lussito d'Acqui, Italy, on Oct. 25, he studied for the priesthood at the Acqui diocesan seminary and was ordained in 1936. After further study at the Gregorian and the Pontificia Academia dei Nobili Ecclesiastici, he joined the Vatican diplomatic service. He served in various diplomatic posts for the Holy See the next three decades until 1967, when he was named apostolic delegate to the United States. He traveled all over the country, was papal representative at the funerals of President Eisenhower and Kennedy, and in 1973 was made a cardinal. He left the United States soon after to become Prefect of the Sacred Congregation for Saints' Causes where he took special interest in the causes of Mother Elizabeth Seton and Bishop John Neumann and died of a heart attack at the Vatican on June 24.

RÂLE, SEBASTIAN (1654–1724), missionary. Born in Pontarlier, France, on June 20 (perhaps on Jan. 4, 1657), he joined the Jesuits at Dôle, France, in 1675, studied at Carpentras, taught at Nîmes and completed his theology at Lyons in 1638. The following year he went to Canada as a missionary. He worked among the Abenaki and Huron Indians around Quebec and among the Illinois from 1691 to 1693, when he was recalled and sent to work with the Abenakis on the Kennebec River in present-day Maine, where he spent the last thirty years of his life. He acquired great influence with the Indians and was accused by the English of inciting them to attack the English colonists; during Queen Anne's War (1702–13), his mission at Norridgewock, Maine, was destroyed by the English in 1705. When the Peace of Utrecht was signed in 1713, he rebuilt the village but hostilities broke out in 1721 between the English and the Abenakis (by now completely Catholic), who accused the colonists of encroaching on their territory and raided the English settlements. The English placed a price on Râle's head and in 1721 raided Norridgewock and burned its chapel, but he escaped. In 1724 Fr. Râle was murdered and scalped in a surprise English attack on Norridgewock on Aug. 23. He was the author of two letters included in the *Jesuit Relations* and compiled an Abenaki dictionary, seized during the raid in

1721; it is now in the Harvard Library and was edited by John Pickering in 1833. His name is sometimes spelled Rasle.

RANDALL, JAMES RYDER (1839–1908), journalist. Born in Baltimore on Jan. 1, he studied at Georgetown but did not graduate because of illness and made a trip to Brazil and the West Indies to recover his health. On his return to the United States he worked in a printing shop in Baltimore and then moved to Florida and in 1859 to New Orleans. The following year he began teaching at Poydras College, a Creole school in Pointe-Coupée Parish, Louisiana. He was a firm supporter of the Confederacy but could not join the Confederate military because of his health. He wrote *Maryland, My Maryland* after hearing a classmate had been wounded in 1861, and it was first published in the April 26, 1861, issue of the New Orleans *Sunday Delta*. After the war he became associate editor of the Augusta (Georgia) *Constitutionalist,* was secretary to Senator Joseph E. Brown in Washington, D.C., for a time, and in 1866 married Katherine Hammond. He wrote for various periodicals, including the Baltimore *Catholic Mirror* and the New Orleans *Morning Star,* and died in Atlanta on Jan. 14.

RANDALL, JOHN STEPHEN (1906–81), editor. Born in Newark, New Jersey, on Mar. 30, he was educated at St. Bernard's Seminary, Rochester, New York, and was ordained in 1931. He served as a curate at Sacred Heart Cathedral in Rochester in 1931–36, at Holy Family Church, Auburn, New York, in 1936–37, was chaplain of the Carmelite Sisters in Rochester in 1938, served as diocesan director of the Society for the Propagation of the Faith in 1938–66, and was pastor of Immaculate Conception Church there in 1952–66.

He resigned to devote more time to his position on the diocesan paper. Always interested in the Catholic press, he was managing director of the diocesan paper, *The Catholic Courier Journal,* in 1942–71 and was active in the Catholic Press Association for almost forty years, serving as its president in 1956–58. He resigned as managing editor to become assistant secretary of the Catholic Near East Relief Association in 1971. After many years' effort he established a national advertising sales bureau for Catholic newspapers, Catholic Major Markets, a sales agency representing many Catholic newspapers, and was its secretary-treasurer in 1967–70. He was instrumental in the founding of the Catholic Journalism Scholarship Fund in 1961 and in the later years of his life helped to establish and operate the Catholic Golden Age Club. He died in Rochester on July 15.

RANSDALL, JOSEPH EUGENE (1858–1954), U.S. senator. Born in Alexandria, Louisiana, on Oct. 7, he was educated in private schools there and Union College, Schenectady, New York (B.A. 1882), studied law, and was admitted to the bar in Louisiana in 1883. He married Olive Irena Powell in 1885, practiced law at Lake Providence in 1883–99, was district attorney for Louisiana's eighth judicial district in 1884–97, and was a member of the state constitutional convention in 1898, became interested in cotton planting in 1897, purchased the Olivedell Pecan Grove, and served in the U.S. House of Representatives from 1900 to 1913, when he was elected a U.S. senator. He served until 1931. In Congress he supported the expansion of the merchant marine, advocated the development of waterways, helped pass the Flood Control Act of 1928 and introduced the bill creating the National Institute of Health; he also helped create the National Merchant Marine Association in 1919. Defeated for reelection by Huey Long in 1930, he became executive director of the National Institute of Health when he was seventy-three and died in Lake Providence, Louisiana, on July 27.

RAPPE, LOUIS AMADEUS (1801–77), bishop. Born in Andrehem, France, on Feb. 2, he was educated at Boulogne College, was ordained in Arras in 1829, and went to the United States as a missionary in 1840. He engaged in missionary work at Maumee, Ohio, for a short time, was founding pastor of St. Francis de Sales parish, Toledo, Ohio, in 1840–47, and when the Cleveland diocese was established in 1847 he was appointed its first bishop. He held five diocesan synods, brought new religious orders into the see, was a strong believer in Catholic education, established new parishes, schools, and charitable institutions, a diocesan seminary in 1848, and founded two colleges, St. John's in Cleveland and St. Louis in Louisville, which did not endure very long, and was active in charitable affairs. He resigned in 1870 and engaged in missionary work among the French in Vermont until he died in St. Albans, Vermont, on Sept. 8.

RASKOB, JOHN JACOB (1879–1950), financier, industrialist. Born in Lockport, New York, on Mar. 19, he studied accounting and stenography in a local business college and in 1898 joined the Holly Manufacturing Company. He married Helena S. Green in 1906 (the couple had twelve children) and while working at the Johnson Company in Lorain, Ohio, met Pierre S. du Pont—a meeting that was to have momentous consequences in the business world. He became du Pont's secretary and in time his close confidant and associate. When du Pont and two cousins, Alfred I. and Coleman, took over the family firm, Raskob oversaw the financial arrangements for the expansion of the company and it acquired a practical monopoly in explosives. He established the company's financial division and he and du Pont pioneered many of the modern financial tools of modern corporations. When du Pont became president (he had been treasurer) Raskob replaced him as treasurer in fact and in 1914 by title. He interested the du Ponts in investing in the newly founded General Motors Company in 1914, and he became chairman of the General Motors finance committee, in which post he introduced modern financing methods in the company. In 1919, he established the General Motors Acceptance Corporation, which revolutionized the automobile business by introducing installment sales. When General Motors encountered grave financial difficulties in the recession of 1920, Raskob persuaded Pierre to have the Du Pont Company invest heavily in General Motors. They secured control of the corporation, forced out its president and founder, William C. Durant, and replaced him with Pierre as president and chairman of the board. Pierre brought in Alfred P. Sloane, Jr., to manage General Motors, but Raskob continued to manage its finances and to provide financing for its huge expansion in the 1920s. When Alfred E. Smith ran for the presidency in 1928 Raskob left General Motors and became national chairman of the Democratic Party at Smith's request. After Smith's defeat he continued as chairman, worked with Smith to build and operate the Empire State Building in New York City, and worked for Smith's nomination at the 1932 Democratic Convention. He was replaced as national chairman by James A. Farley when Franklin D. Roosevelt was nominated for the presidency and in 1934 helped found the conservative Liberty League to combat the New Deal but took little interest in it and devoted himself to traveling and Catholic charitable and civic causes. He died on his farm near Centerville, Maryland, on Oct. 15; most of his estate went to the Raskob Foundation for Catholic Charities, which he had established in 1945.

RASLE, SEBASTIAN *See* Râle, Sebastian.

RAUSCH, JAMES S. (1926–81), bishop. Born in Albany, Minnesota, on Sept. 4, he was educated at St. Thomas College, St. Paul, Minnesota, the University of Minnesota, and the Gregorian in Rome and was ordained in 1856. He was associate general secretary of the National Council of Catholic Bishops (NCCB) and the U.S. Catholic Conference in 1970–72 and general secretary in 1972–77, and was named titular bishop of Summa and auxiliary of St. Cloud, Minnesota, in 1973. He was appointed bishop of Phoenix, Arizona, in 1977 and remained in that position until his death there on May 18.

RAVALLI, ANTONIO (1811–84), missionary. Born in Ferrara, Italy, on May 16, he joined the Jesuits in the Italian province of Emilia in 1827, taught in Turin, Piedmont, and other Italian cities, and in 1843, in response to a plea from Fr. Pierre De Smet for missionaries, he went to the United States with him to work in the Oregon Territory. He worked at St. Ignatius Mission among the Kalispel Indians on the Upper Columbia River, Washington, in 1845 and was then transferred to St. Mary's Mission among the Flathead Indians in western Montana. Forced to leave in 1850 because of the hostile Blackfeet Indians, he was put in charge of Sacred Heart Mission among the Coeur d'Alenes (Skitswish) in northern Idaho in 1854. He is credited with keeping peace among the northern tribes when an Indian uprising led by the

Yakima took place in 1856–57. He served at Santa Clara College in 1860–63 and when St. Mary's Mission was reestablished in 1866 he returned and spent the rest of his life there until his death (Stevensville, Montana) on Oct. 2.

RAYMBAUT, CHARLES (1602–43), missionary. Born in France, he joined the Jesuits in Rouen in 1621, became procurator of the Quebec mission, and in 1637 he went to Quebec. He worked among the Nipissing Algonquin Indians in 1640 and with Fr. Jogues visited the Chippewas in 1641–42, traveling as far west as Sault Ste. Marie, probably the first white man to visit this outlet of Lake Superior, and died in Quebec—the first Jesuit to die in Canada.

READY, MICHAEL JOSEPH (1893–1957), bishop. Born in New Haven, Connecticut, on Apr. 9, he was educated at St. Vincent's College, Latrobe, Pennsylvania (B.A. 1913, M.A. 1915), St. Bernard's Seminary, Rochester, New York, and St. Mary's Seminary, Cleveland, Ohio, where he was ordained in 1918. He served as a curate at St. Mary's Church, Painesville, Ohio, in 1918–19, taught Latin at Cathedral Latin School, Cleveland, in 1919–22, was a curate at Holy Name Church, Cleveland, in 1922–27, and was diocesan director of the Society for the Propagation of the Faith in 1927–31. He was general secretary of the National Catholic Welfare Conference (NCWC) in 1936–44, was made a papal chamberlain in 1934 and a domestic prelate in 1937, and was appointed bishop of Columbus, Ohio, in 1944. During his tenure he established eighteen new parishes, fourteen schools, and the Catholic Welfare Bureau. He died in Columbus on May 2.

REED, VICTOR J. (1905–71), bishop. Born in Montpelier, Indiana, on Dec.

23, he graduated from St. Joseph College, Muskogee, Oklahoma, in 1924 and studied for the priesthood at St. John's Seminary, Arkansas, and the North American College, Rome (S.T.L.), and was ordained in Rome in 1929. He served as a curate of St. Joseph Cathedral, Oklahoma City, in 1930–35 and for the next four years studied at the Louvain (Ph.D. 1939). He was made assistant chancellor of the diocese and pastor of St. Francis Xavier Church, Stillwater, Oklahoma, in 1939, was rector of Holy Family co-Cathedral in Tulsa, Oklahoma, in 1947–57, and in 1957 was named titular bishop of Limisa and auxiliary of Oklahoma City–Tulsa. He became fourth bishop of that see the following year, expanded high school facilities in the diocese, established several catechetical facilities, and dedicated the new diocesan seminary, St. Francis de Sales, in Oklahoma City. He died in Oklahoma City on Sept. 8.

REEDY, JOHN LOUIS (1925–83), editor, columnist. Born in Newport, Kentucky, he was educated at Notre Dame (B.A. 1948) and Holy Cross College, Washington, D.C., and was professed in the Congregation of Holy Cross in 1945. He was ordained in 1952, joined the staff of *Ave Maria* magazine, and was its executive editor from 1954 to 1970, when the magazine ceased publication. He was director of Ave Maria Press from 1945 until his death and was president of Spiritual Book Associates. For a time after 1970 he published a newsletter, *A. D. Correspondence.* He wrote a widely read column that was syndicated in some forty Catholic newspapers and was a champion of the press and of professionalism in the Catholic press. He died at Notre Dame, Indiana, on Dec. 2.

REEVE, BENJAMIN (1880–1936), author. Born in Patchogue, New York, on Oct. 15, he graduated from Princeton in 1903, edited the Cape May (New Jersey) *Daily Star* during summer vacations while at Princeton, studied law at New York Law School but decided to pursue writing as a career. He married Margaret A. Wilson and became assistant editor of *Public Opinion* in 1906, was editor of *Our Own Times* in 1906–10, and was a member of the staff of *Survey* in 1907. He wrote some forty novels, many of them detective stories featuring the character Craig Kennedy, who made his appearance in *Cosmopolitan Magazine* in 1910, which were great successes and was considered America's foremost writer of detective fiction for years; he also wrote *The Golden Age of Crime* (1931), a study of racketeering in the period after World War I. He and his wife became converts to Catholicism in 1926. He covered murder trials for newspapers the last fifteen years of his life, was interested in crime prevention and wrote a radio series on the subject. He died in Trenton, New Jersey, on Aug. 9. His character Craig Kennedy was sometimes called the American Sherlock Holmes.

REHRING, GEORGE J. (1890–1976), bishop. Born in Cincinnati, Ohio, on June 10, he was educated at Mt. St. Mary of the West Seminary there and was ordained in 1914. He served as a curate at SS. Peter and Paul Church, Reading, Pennsylvania, in 1914–21, was pastor of Guardian Angel Church in Cincinnati in 1921–23, and was a professor of theology at Mt. St. Mary of the West in 1923–40. He continued his studies at the Collegio Angelico, Rome, in 1926–28 (S.T.D.), was made a domestic prelate in 1932, and was consecrated bishop of Lunda and auxiliary of Cincinnati in 1937. He was also pastor of St. Mary's Church from 1940 until 1950, when he was appointed bishop of Toledo, Ohio. He inaugurated a major building and redevelopment program, was appointed an Assistant at the Pontifical Throne in 1964, retired in 1967, and died in Toledo on Feb. 29.

REID, CHRISTIAN *See* Tiernan, Frances Christine.

REID, RICHARD (1896–1961), editor. Born in Winchester, Massachusetts, on Jan. 21, he was educated at Holy Cross College, Worcester, Massachusetts (B.A. 1918, M.A. 1922), Columbia, and Fordham (LL.B.). He served in the Army in World War I, taught at St. Francis Xavier High School, New York City, in 1918–19, and then became a journalist, serving on the editorial staff of the Augusta, Georgia, *Chronicle* in 1919–20 and was news editor and columnist of the Augusta *Herald* in 1920. He was executive secretary of the Georgia Catholic Laymen's Association in 1920–40 and edited the Catholic newspaper of the Southeast, *The Bulletin,* so successfully it became a major force in combating bigotry in Georgia. He married Katherine O'Leary in 1923, was admitted to the Georgia bar in 1929, and practiced there as a member of the law firm of Mulherin & Reid until 1940. He was president of the Catholic Press Association in 1932–34, general counsel of the National Council of Catholic Men in 1937–40, visiting lecturer at Notre Dame in 1937–40, and served as trustee or adviser of many Catholic organizations. He was appointed editor of the *Catholic News* in New York City in 1940 and in that position, which he held until his death, he strongly defended interracial justice and became a nationally recognized champion of the Catholic Church and of the Catholic role in public life. He was thrice honored by the papacy, received the Laetare Medal in 1936 and in 1946 the Hoey Medal for his work in interracial justice. He was the author of *The Morality of the Newspaper* (1937), a collection of the lectures he had delivered at Notre Dame, and was coauthor, with Edward Moffett, M.M., of *Three Days to Eternity* (1947). He died in New Rochelle, New York, on Jan. 24.

REILLY, JOSEPH JOHN (1881–1951), educator, author. Born in Springfield, Massachusetts, on Jan. 16, he was educated at Holy Cross College, Worcester, Massachusetts (B.A. 1904), Columbia (M.A. 1909), and Yale (Ph.D. 1912). He taught at Fordham in 1904–7 and the College of the City of New York in 1907–10, served as chief examiner for the Massachusetts Civil Service Commission in 1912–21, and was president of the National Association of Civil Service Commissions in 1920–21. He was superintendent of schools in Ware, Massachusetts, in 1921–26, married Anna Walsh in 1922, and became a member of the English Department of Hunter College in New York City in 1926, holding that position until his death in New York on Jan. 23. He also served as librarian in 1928–48 and taught at Fordham's Summer School in 1927–31. He became a leading authority on John Henry Newman and was the author of several critical studies and collections, among them *Lowell as Critic* (1915), *Newman as a Man of Letters* (1925), *Dear Prue's Husband and Other People* (1932), *Of Books and Men* (1942), and *The Fine Gold of Newman,* a collection he edited.

REILLY, PHILIP JAMES (1879–1961), educator. Born in Ireland, he was educated in the National Schools there and emigrated to the United States in 1903. He joined the Brothers Third Order Regular of St. Francis, taking the name Columba in 1903, and was professed in 1904. He continued his studies at St. Francis College, Brooklyn, New York (B.A.), Fordham (M.A.), St. John's University, Brooklyn, and Manhattan College and taught at St. Francis Prep in 1904–19. He was president of St. Francis College in 1925–34 and 1936–52, superior general of the Franciscan Brothers of Brooklyn in 1925–34 and 1937–40, and was president emeritus of St. Francis from 1952 until his death in Brooklyn on Aug. 13.

REILLY, WENDELL (1875–1950), biblical scholar. Born in North Hatley, Quebec, Canada, on Mar. 25, he studied at the Grand Seminary, Montreal, and was ordained in Sherbrooke, Quebec, in 1898. He continued his studies at the Institut Catholique in Paris the next two years and then began teaching at St. Mary's Seminary, Baltimore. He continued his studies (in Oriental languages) at Catholic University in 1901 and at the Sulpician Institute in 1902 and received his S.T.D. from the Institut Catholique. He taught at St. John's Seminary, Brighton, Boston, in 1903–7, studied Scripture at École Biblique in Jerusalem and then at the Pontifical Biblical Commission in Rome, and received his S.S.D.—the first American to receive this degree. On his return to the United States, he taught at St. John's until his retirement in 1947. He helped found the Catholic Biblical Association of America in 1936 and in 1939 the *Catholic Biblical Quarterly,* serving as its editor-in-chief in 1939–47, was an editor of the Confraternity of Christian Doctrine's translation of the New Testament (1941), for which he translated "Epistle to the Ephesians" and was one of the two Americans selected for the Westminster revision of the bible, translating and providing a commentary on John's Gospel. He died in Baltimore on Oct. 7.

REINERT, CARL M. (1913–80), educator. Born in Boulder, Colorado, on July 4, he was educated at St. Louis University (B.A. 1935, M.A., Ph.D. 1935–38) and St. Mary's (Kansas) College (S.T.D. 1945). He joined the Jesuits, was ordained in 1944, served as assistant principal of Campion (Wisconsin) High School in 1945–48 and as principal in 1948–50, and was president of Creighton University, Omaha, Nebraska, in 1950–62. He was appointed president of Catholic University Development Foundation in 1962 and died in Omaha on Aug. 13.

REINHOLD, HANS ANSCAR (1897–1968), liturgist. Born in Hamburg, Germany, on Sept. 6, he was educated at the universities of Innsbruck, Freiburg, Münster, and the Pontifical Institute of Archaeology, Rome, served in the German Army in World War I, and, after studying to be a Benedictine at Maria Laach, decided he did not have a Benedictine calling. He was ordained a diocesan priest in Innsbruck in 1925, served as chaplain at St. John's School, Niendorf, in 1925–28 and as a seamen's chaplain in Bremerhaven in 1925–35, where he inaugurated many liturgical innovations, such as a dialogue Mass with the priest facing the congregation (later put into effect after Vatican Council II). He was threatened with arrest in 1935 by the Nazis because of his criticism of Nazi leaders and policies and fled to England. He went to the United States in 1936, had difficulty securing an ecclesiastical assignment because of his liturgical innovations and his suspected Communist sympathies but was finally accepted in the archdiocese of Seattle, Washington. He founded a seaman's club at Yakima and was pastor at Sunnyside, Washington, from 1944 to 1956, when difficulties with his bishop caused him to leave; he was eventually accepted into the Pittsburgh diocese in

1961 by Bishop John Wright and died there of Parkinson's disease on Jan. 26. Reinhold was a leader in the liturgical movement, serving as one of the first presidents and longtime national director of the North American Liturgical Conference, and many of the reforms he advocated were put into effect after Vatican Council II. He lectured widely and wrote articles for Catholic magazines and was the author of several books on liturgical and social reform, among them *The American Parish and the Roman Liturgy* (1958), *Bringing the Mass to the People* (1960), *Dynamics of Liturgy* (1961), *Liturgy and Art* (1966), and his autobiography; he also edited several collections, among them *Soul Afire* (1945) and *Churches, Their Plan and Furnishings* (1948), with P. F. Anson.

REPPLIER, AGNES (1855–1950), author. Born in Philadelphia on Apr. 1, she was educated at Eden Hall Sacred Heart Academy and at Miss Irwin's school there and was expelled from both for her independence. Encouraged by Fr. Isaac Hecker and Thomas Bailey-Aldrich, she began to contribute short stories and essays to the *Catholic World* and *Atlantic Monthly* and had her first book, *Books and Men*, published in 1888. For the next three decades she turned out a steady stream of books of informal essays, which made her the ranking essayist in the United States and one of the outstanding essayists in the English language. When the essay faded in popularity after World War I, she turned to religious biography. Among her books were *Points of View* (1891), *Essays in Miniature* (1892), *Compromises* (1904), *In Our Convent Days* (1905), on her experiences at Eden Hall, the autobiographical *A Happy Half-Century* (1908) and *Counter Currents* (1916); her biographies were *Mère Marie of the Ursulines* (1931), *Père Marquette* (1929), and *Junípero Serra*

(1933). Her last two books were *In Pursuit of Laughter* (1936), essays, and *Eight Decades* (1937), her autobiography. She was honored by several universities, was awarded the gold medal of the American Academy of Arts and Letters, and received the Laetare Medal in 1911. She died in Philadelphia on Dec. 15.

RESCH, PETER ANTHONY (1895–1965), author. Born in Chicago on Feb. 27, he was educated at Chaminade College, Clayton, Missouri, was professed in the Society of Mary (Marianists) in 1912, and continued his studies at the University of Dayton, Ohio (B.A. 1919), and later at the University of Fribourg, Switzerland (S.T.D. 1926). He taught at Marianist schools in San Antonio, Texas, Iowa, and Canada from 1913 to 1927, when he was ordained. He was professor at Chaminade College in 1927–28 and vice president in 1928–29 and was novice master at Maryhurst Novitiate, Kirkwood, Missouri, in 1929–42. He served as superior of Marianist seminaries at St. Meinrad (Indiana) Seminary in 1942–46, was provincial of the St. Louis province in 1954–56, wrote for Catholic periodicals, and was the author of several pamphlets and books, among them *Key of Heaven* (1927), *Our Blessed Mother* (1939), *Shadows Cast* (1948), *A Life of Mary, Co-Redemptrix* (1954), and translated several books from the French, notably Henri Lebon's two-volume *The Marianist Way* (1951).

RÉSÉ, JOHN FREDERIC (1791–1871), bishop. Born in Weinenburg, Hanover, Germany, on Feb. 6, he was orphaned as a child, became a tailor, and was drafted into the Army in 1813 and fought at Waterloo. He studied for the priesthood at the Propaganda, Rome, was ordained in 1822, and went to Africa as a missionary. Forced to return to Germany because of illness two years later, he went to the United States in 1825, when he recovered and was sent as a missionary to the then Northwest Territory—the first German priest in that area. He went to Germany in 1828 in quest of missionaries and financial aid and was responsible for the formation of the Leopoldine Society of Vienna to provide aid for German churches and schools in the United States in the winter of 1828–29; he was also responsible for the founding of the Ludwig Mission Society in Munich in 1838 to give financial assistance to Catholic missions in America and Asia. He was named vicar-general for Michigan-Wisconsin in 1830, was administrator of the diocese of Cincinnati in 1832, and the following year was appointed first bishop of the newly established diocese of Detroit, Michigan. He founded St. Philip's College at Hamtramck, Michigan, in 1836, suffered a mental breakdown in 1837, and, after Bishop Peter Lefèvre was appointed his coadjutor in 1841, spent the rest of his life in Europe seeking to regain his health. He died in Hildesheim, Germany, on Dec. 30. His name is sometimes spelled Reze.

REVERMANN, THEODORE H. (1877–1941), bishop. Born in Louisville, Kentucky, on Aug. 9, he was educated at St. Meinrad (Indiana) Abbey, Canisius College, Buffalo, New York, the University of Innsbruck, Austria, and the Gregorian, Rome, and was ordained in Innsbruck in 1901. He continued his theological studies at Innsbruck and canon law at Rome, taught at Preston Park Seminary, and was chaplain to Mt. St. Mary's, Louisville, Kentucky, in 1901–4 and pastor of St. Edward's Church, Jeffersontown, Kentucky in 1904–21 and of St. Francis of Assisi Church, Louisville, in 1921–26. He was appointed bishop of Superior, Wisconsin, in 1926. He remained in this position until his death in Superior on July 18.

REY, ANTHONY (1807–47), educator. Born in Lyons, France, on Mar. 19, he was first destined for a business career but entered the Jesuit college at Fribourg, joined the Jesuits in 1827, and was ordained. After teaching for a time at Fribourg and Sion in Valais, he went to the United States in 1840 as professor of theology at Georgetown University. He was transferred to pastoral work at St. Joseph's Church, Philadelphia, in 1843 and was pastor of Trinity Church, Georgetown, D.C. In 1845 he was named vice president of Georgetown University. He was a chaplain in the Army in 1846 during the Mexican War and was killed by a band of Mexican guerrillas on Jan. 19 near Ceraloo, Mexico, where he had gone to conduct services for a congregation of Mexicans and Americans.

REYNOLDS, FRANK (1923–83), TV newsman. Born in East Chicago, Indiana, on Nov. 29, he studied at Wabash College for a year and then dropped out. He served in the Army during World War II in 1943–45 and received a Purple Heart award, married Henrietta Mary Harpster in 1947, worked at WJOB, Hammond, Indiana, in 1947–50, WBKB-TV in 1950, and WBBM-CBS, Chicago, in 1951–63. He was ABC correspondent in Chicago in 1963–65 and in 1965 became ABC network correspondent in Washington, D.C. He was offered the anchor post on ABC's "Evening News" in 1967 and declined but accepted the following year. After eight years covering major stories he returned in 1978 as chief anchorman on ABC's "World News Tonight." He was known for his liberal views, won the George Foster Peabody Award for excellence in broadcast journalism in 1967 and an Emmy Award in 1980 for his work on ABC's "Post-Election Special Edition" and died in Washington, D.C., of acute viral hepatitis after having suffered from multiple myeloma, a form of bone cancer, for some time.

REYNOLDS, IGNATIUS ALOYSIUS (1798–1855), bishop. Born in Bardstown, Kentucky, on Aug. 22, he was educated at St. Thomas Seminary there and St. Mary's Seminary, Baltimore, and was ordained in 1823. He taught at St. Joseph's College, Bardstown, was its president in 1827–30, and then engaged in missionary work. He was the superior of the Sisters of Charity of Nazareth in 1833–34 and vicar-general of the diocese of Louisville from 1841 until 1844, when he was consecrated second bishop of Charleston, South Carolina. He built a new cathedral, edited and published the five-volume *Works* of his predecessor, Bishop John England, in 1849 and petitioned to have Georgia removed from the territory of his see, which was done with the creation of the diocese of Savannah, Georgia, in 1850. He died in Charleston on Mar. 6.

REYNOLDS, QUENTIN JAMES (1902–65), journalist. Son of James J. Reynolds, assistant superintendent of schools in Brooklyn, New York, he was born there on Apr. 11. He was educated at Brown University (Ph.D. 1924) and began his career in journalism as a reporter for the New York *World* in 1926 to pay for his law studies at Brooklyn Law School, where he received his law degree in 1931. When the *World* was merged with the *Telegram* and became the *World-Telegram*, he remained with the new paper but soon was discharged in an economy drive. He obtained a job with the International News Service (INS) and became an INS feature writer in Berlin. On his return to the United States in 1932 he became associate editor of *Collier's Weekly*, for which he wrote some four hundred articles. In 1940 *Collier's* sent him to cover World War II in Europe, and the gripping stories he filed from France and England and later from North Africa and Italy attracted nationwide attention; many of them were later gathered into a book. His radio address to Herr Schicklgruber (Adolf Hitler) won him the esteem of the British, whose courage during the London blitz he had lauded. During the closing phases of World War II he reported on the activities of the United States Navy in the Pacific, and on his return to the United States he engaged in free-lance writing, lecturing, and appearances on radio and television. He was awarded $175,000 in 1954 in a libel suit he brought against Westbrook Pegler, who had called him a coward and an absentee war correspondent in his column in 1949. Among Reynolds's books were *The Wounded Don't Cry* (1941), *London Diary* (1941), *Only the Stars Are Neutral* (1942), *The Battle of Britain* (1953), and his autobiography, *By Quentin Reynolds* (1963). He died at Travis Air Force Base in California on Mar. 17.

REZE, FREDERIC. *See* Résé, Frederic.

RHODE, PAUL PETER (1871–1945), bishop. Born in Neustadt, Germany, on Sept. 18, his father died the year after his birth and he was brought to the United States by his mother in 1879, when he was eight years old. He was educated at St. Mary's College, Kentucky, St. Ignatius College, Chicago, and St. Francis Seminary, Milwaukee, Wisconsin, and was ordained in 1894. He served as a curate at St. Adelbert's Church, Chicago, in 1894–96, was pastor of St. Peter's, St. Paul's, and St. Michael's churches, Chicago, in 1896–1909, and was named titular bishop of Barca and auxiliary of Chicago in 1908

—the first priest of Polish lineage to be raised to the episcopate in the United States. He was vicar-general of the diocese from 1909 until 1915, when he was appointed bishop of Green Bay, Wisconsin, a position he held until his death there on Mar. 3.

RHODES, MARY (c. 1782–1853), educator. Born in Maryland (exactly where and when are unknown), she was educated by the Nuns of the Visitation at their school in Georgetown, D.C., and opened a school in a log cabin near St. Charles Church, Harden's Creek, near Bardstown, Kentucky, while visiting her brother Bennet in 1811. Two companions, Christina Stewart and Anne Havern, joined her and in 1812, under the direction of Fr. Charles Nerinckx and with the approval of Bishop Benedict Flaget of Bardstown, they formed a religious community on Apr. 25, 1812, and took the habit as Friends of Mary at the Foot of the Cross devoted to Christian teaching. Shortly after, her sister Anne Rhodes and Sarah Havern joined them, and Anne was named first superior. When Anne died six months later on Dec. 11, Mary was chosen superior; the four took their final vows in 1813 and Fr. Nerinckx received papal approval for the community and its rule in 1817. The order flourished, opened its first branch house at Calvary, Kentucky, in 1816, soon came to be called the Sisters of Loretto at the Foot of the Cross, and spread throughout the southern and midwestern United States; it received final papal approval in 1907. Mary retired as superior in 1822, was almost totally blind in her last years, and died at the mother house at Loretto, Kentucky, on Feb. 27.

RICE, JOSEPH JOHN (1871–1938), bishop. Born in Leicester, Massachusetts, on Dec. 6, he was educated at Holy Cross College, Worcester, Massachusetts, Laval University, Montreal (S.T.B., J.C.B.), and the Gregorian, Rome (S.T.L., D.D.), and was ordained in 1894. He engaged in missionary work among the Indians of northern Maine for a short time and then taught at St. John's Seminary, Brookline, Boston, and was rector in 1894–1910. He was appointed third bishop of Burlington, Vermont, in 1910. During his episcopate, three high schools were erected, Trinity College for women was opened in Burlington in 1925, and De Goesbriand Memorial Hospital was built in 1923. He died in Burlington on Apr. 1.

RICHARD, GABRIEL (1767–1832), missionary. Born in Saintes, France, on Oct. 15, he was educated at the college there and the Sulpician seminaries at Angers and Issy, joined the Sulpicians in 1790, and was ordained the following year. He taught mathematics at Issy in 1792 until he was forced to flee the anti-clerical policies of the French Revolutionary Government and went to the United States. He engaged in missionary work among the Indians of Illinois and Michigan, became pastor of St. Ann's Church in 1798 in Detroit, where he established an elementary school in 1802, and was made vicar-general of the area in 1804. He traveled extensively throughout the Middle West, fought to protect and aid the Indians, built schools, hospitals, and churches, brought the first printing press to Detroit and published the first Catholic newspaper printed in the United States, *The Michigan Essay or Impartial Observer,* in 1809. He was imprisoned by the British in Canada in 1813 when they occupied Detroit during the War of 1812, cofounded the University of Michigan in 1817 and served as its vice president, became an American citizen in 1823, and was territorial delegate for Michigan to the United States House of Representatives in 1823–25—the first

Catholic priest to serve in that body. He supported bills to give land grants to state universities and was instrumental in having a bill passed that authorized federal road-building in Michigan. He was defeated in a bid for reelection in 1824 and devoted the rest of his life to his pastoral and missionary activities. In 1827 the Congregation of the Propagation authorized the establishment of a diocese in Michigan with its see at Detroit and with Richard its first bishop. Though the nomination was confirmed by Pope Leo XII and the diocese was officially created, it was decided to withhold the order pending a new study. When the size of Richard's debt and the smallness of the Catholic population were revealed, it was decided not to issue the order. Richard died in Detroit on Sept. 13 of cholera he contracted while caring for plague victims.

RICHTER, HENRY JOSEPH (1838–1916), bishop. Born in Neuenkirchen, Oldenburg, Germany, on Apr. 9, he emigrated to the United States in 1854, was educated at St. Joseph's College, Kentucky, Xavier College and Mt. St. Mary of the West Seminary, Cincinnati, Ohio, and the North American College, Rome, and was ordained in Rome in 1865. He taught at Mt. St. Mary's in 1865–70 and became vice president, was then rector at St. Laurent and chaplain at Mt. St. Vincent's, and in 1883 was consecrated first bishop of the newly created diocese of Grand Rapids, Michigan. He greatly increased the number of priests in the diocese from 34 to 133, the number of churches and missions from 66 to 183, and parish schools from 11 to 66. He established Michigan's first diocesan seminary, St. Joseph's Minor Seminary, in 1909 during his episcopate. It was at his suggestion that the Dominican Sisters of Grand Rapids became a separate community in 1894. He died in Grand Rapids on Dec. 26.

RIDDER, CHARLES H. (1888–1964), publisher. Son of Henry Ridder, cofounder of the New York *Catholic News,* and Lena Croker Ridder, he was born in New York City on June 11, studied at Packard Business School there, and then worked in several publishing houses. In 1910 he joined the *Catholic News,* served in various capacities on the paper and became general manager, married Alice A. Lytle in 1916 (d. 1941), and on his father's death in 1936 became president of the *Catholic News,* a position he held until his death in New York City on Oct. 10. He was active in the Catholic Press Association, serving two terms as its president in 1938–40, married Elizabeth Sullivan in 1944, and was president of the United States Catholic Historical Society in 1954–56, after serving as its treasurer in 1943–53. He was honored by Pope Pius XII in 1950 and 1952 and by Pope John XXIII in 1959 and died in Poughkeepsie, New York, on Oct. 10.

RIDDER, HERMAN (1851–1915), publisher. Of the famous German publishing family, he was born in New York City on Mar. 5, began his career as an errand boy, and then became an insurance agent. In 1878 he entered journalism when he founded the *Katholische Volksblatt* and in 1886 the New York *Catholic News,* which attained wide circulation. He was treasurer and manager of the daily *Staats-Zeitung* from 1890 until 1907, when he became its president. He became active in Democratic Party politics, bitterly opposed Tammany Hall, and was treasurer of the National Democratic Committee in 1908. He was a director of the Associated Press in 1900–15 and its treasurer in 1907–8, was president of the American Newspaper Publishers' Association in 1907–11, vice president of the Hudson Fulton Commemorative Celebration in 1907, and was manager of the New

York State Board of Charities. He died on Nov. 1.

RIDDER, VICTOR FRANK (1886–1963), publisher. Son of Herman Ridder, publisher of *Staats-Zeitung* and other newspapers, and Mary Amend Ridder, he was born in New York City on Apr. 4 and was educated at Columbia, graduating in 1910. He began his newspaper career in 1905 and when his father died in 1915, he and his brothers, Joseph and Bernard, took over the management of the *Staats-Zeitung* and eventually built a nationwide chain of nine newspapers and two television and three radio stations. He served as chairman of the board of Northwest Publications and as vice president of Ridder Publications, was active in the Boys Club from 1907 and the Boy Scout movement from 1910, served in various civic posts, and was director of the Marquette League for Catholic Indian Missions. He died in New York City on June 14.

RIGGS, THOMAS LAWRASON (1888–1943), author. Born in New London, Connecticut, on June 28, he was educated at Yale (B.A. 1910), spent a year traveling abroad, and then continued his studies at Harvard (M.A. 1912). He taught English at Yale in 1912–17 and served in the Yale Ambulance Corps in World War I in 1917–18 and in Mobile Hospital No. 3 in Paris the next year. After the war he studied for the priesthood at Catholic University in 1920–21 and St. Thomas Seminary, Hartford, Connecticut, in 1921–22 and was ordained in Hartford in 1922. He was appointed chaplain of the Catholic Club in 1922, the first Catholic chaplain at Yale, and also served as administrator of Our Lady of Pompeii Church in East Haven. He founded the Thomas More Association for Catholic students at Yale in 1937, which built the Thomas More Chapel, and was chaplain of the Thomas More Club, successor of the Catholic Club, in 1938–43, taught religion at Albertus Magnus College in New Haven in 1925–38, and was one of the founders of *Commonweal*, to which he contributed articles. He was the author of *The Book of Kildare and Other Verses* (1911) and *Saving Angel* (1943) and died in New Haven on Apr. 26. After his death Yale established the T. Lawrason chair for Roman Catholic studies in his honor.

RING, THOMAS FRANCIS (c. 1841–98). Born in Boston, he early joined the family paper stock importing business and in 1867 married Elizabeth Crowley. He founded the first central council of the St. Vincent de Paul Society in 1888 and organized the structure later adopted by the Society. He was a member of the Boston Board of Overseers in 1886–95, was first vice president of the Associated Charities when it was founded in 1893 and became an officer in the National Conference of Charities and Corrections—the first Catholic to hold office in that Conference. He spoke at numerous major gatherings, notably the second Laymen's Congress in Chicago in 1893 and the International Congress of Charities, Corrections and Philanthropy, the latter at the invitation of President Rutherford B. Hayes. He died in Boston on Sept. 16. One of the leading Catholic laymen of his times in the United States, he is often called the "American Ozanam."

RIORDAN, PATRICK WILLIAM (1841–1914), archbishop. Of Irish parents who moved to Chicago when he was seven, he was born in Chatham, New Brunswick, Canada, on Aug. 27. He was educated at Notre Dame, graduating in 1858, and St. Mary of the Lake Seminary, Chicago, and was chosen as one of the first twelve students for the North American College, Rome. Ill health caused him to leave Rome and he continued his studies at the College of the Holy Ghost, Paris. He was ordained at Mechlin, Belgium, in 1865, and received his doctorate in theology from the American College, Louvain, the following year. He taught at St. Mary of the Lake until 1868, when he served as pastor at Woodstock and then at Joliet and Chicago, and in 1883 he was named titular archbishop of Cabesa and coadjutor of San Francisco; he succeeded to the see the following year. He attended the third Plenary Council of Baltimore in 1884 and was named president of the bishops' commission for the Indian and black missions. He favored the establishment of national churches and built many in his archdiocese. He built St. Mary's Cathedral in 1891 and opened St. Patrick's Seminary, Menlo Park, California, in 1898, the year he took over the archdiocesan newspaper, *The Monitor*. He was instrumental in having a law passed granting tax exemption to California churches in 1910 and helped settle successfully the Pious Fund dispute with Mexico before the International Permanent Court of Arbitration at The Hague in 1902. (The Mexican government defaulted on its agreement in 1913 and has ignored The Hague tribunal's decision since.) He was forced to rebuild many of the schools, churches, and other ecclesiastical buildings of the see after the devastating San Francisco earthquake of 1906. During his episcopate he established 70 new parishes, added 250 priests to the archdiocese, and built 56 new schools. He died in San Francisco on Dec. 27.

RITTER, JOSEPH E. (1892–1967), cardinal. Born in New Albany, Indiana, on July 20, he was educated at St. Meinrad (Indiana) Seminary and was ordained in Indianapolis, Indiana, in 1917. He served as a curate at SS. Peter and Paul Cathedral, Indianapolis in 1917–20 and was rector in 1920–23 and vice president of the diocesan newspaper. He was named titular bishop of Hippus and auxiliary of Indianapolis in 1933, was appointed its seventh bishop the following year, and in 1944 was made an archbishop when Indianapolis was elevated to an archdiocese. He was appointed archbishop of St. Louis in 1946 and attracted national attention in 1947, when he ordered all churches and schools in the archdiocese of St. Louis integrated and threatened excommunication to those who resisted the implementation of his order. He was made an Assistant at the Pontifical Throne in 1956 and was created a cardinal in 1961. He was an enthusiastic supporter of the aggiornamento of Pope John XXIII and Vatican Council II and anticipated many of the reforms proposed by the Council by his emphasis on greater lay participation in Church affairs, tangible commitments to social justice, especially for blacks, liturgical reform, the ecumenical movement, and aid to deprived nations. He was a firm believer in the Catholic school system, headed the Bishops Committee on the Liturgical Apostolate and was a leader of the progressive faction at Vatican Council II. He died in St. Louis on June 10.

ROBINSON, HENRY MORTON (1898–1961), author. Born in Boston on Sept. 7, he served as a gunner's mate in World War I after graduating from high school in 1917, studied at Columbia (B.A. 1923, M.A. 1924) after the war, began writing, and had his first novel, *Children of Morningside* (1924), published while he was a senior at Columbia. He taught at Columbia in 1924–27, married Gertrude Ludwig in 1926, and was editor of *Contemporary Verse* in 1925–27, while teaching at Columbia. He did free-lance writing in 1927–35 and wrote stories, poems, and articles for national magazines. He was an associate editor of *Reader's Digest* in 1935–42 and a senior editor in 1942–45. After that he was a roving reporter. He married Vivian Wyndham in 1953 (he and his first wife had been divorced) and wrote several novels, among them *The Perfect Round* (1945), *The Great Snow* (1947), the enormously popular and controversial *The Cardinal* (1950), and *Water of Life* (1960); poetry, *Buck Fever* (1929), *Second Wisdom* (1937); a biography, *Stout Cortez* (1931); and *A Skeleton Key to Finnegans Wake* (1944), which he coauthored with Joseph Campbell. He died in New York City on Jan. 13.

ROBINSON, PASCHAL (1870–1948), archbishop, diplomat. Born in Dublin on Apr. 26, Charles Robinson was brought to the United States when he was an infant, studied law but became a newspaperman and was an associate editor of *North American Review* in 1892–96. He entered St. Bonaventure College, Allegany, New York, and joined the Franciscans, taking the name Paschal, in 1896 and was ordained in Rome in 1901. He spent the next decade studying and writing, was appointed associate editor of *Archivum Franciscanum Historicum* in 1907, taught medieval history at Catholic University in 1913–19, and was named a fellow of the Royal Historical Society of England in 1914. He was named to assist the United States educational and economic commission at the Versailles Peace Conference in 1919, was apostolic visitor to the Custody of the Holy Land in 1920–21 and then to the Latin Patriarchate in Jerusalem and the Uniate churches in Palestine, Transjordan, and Cyprus in 1925–28, and served as consultant to several Roman congregations. He was appointed titular bishop of Tyana in 1927, was mediator between ecclesiasti-

cal and English authorities on Malta, and in 1930 was sent to Ireland as first papal nuncio there in three hundred years. He served in that position until his death in Dublin on Aug. 27. He wrote numerous magazine articles and was the author of several books, among them *The Real St. Francis* (1903), *The Writings of St. Francis* (1906), and *The Life of St. Clare* (1910).

ROBINSON, WILLIAM CALLYHAN (1834–1911), jurist. Born in Norwich, Connecticut, on July 26, he was educated at Wesleyan University, Dartmouth, and General Theological Seminary, New York City, married Anna E. Haviland in 1857, engaged in missionary work in Pittston, Pennsylvania, and was ordained in the Episcopal Church in 1859. He was rector of St. Luke's Church in Scranton, Pennsylvania, until 1863, when he became a Catholic. He then studied law and was admitted to the bar in Luzerne County, Pennsylvania, in 1864 and then moved to New Haven, Connecticut, in 1865, where he began a law practice and taught law at Yale in 1869–95. He was a judge of the Common Pleas Court of New Haven, in 1869–71, a member of the state legislature in 1874, judge of the Court of Common Pleas in 1874–76, and chairman of the Connecticut Tax Commission in 1884–86. He married Ultima Marie Smith in 1891 (his first wife had died), was appointed head of the newly established law department at Catholic University in 1896, reorganized the school of social sciences and its curriculum, and was dean of the law school until his death in Washington, D.C., on Nov. 6. He wrote a life of E. B. Kelly in 1855 and several law treatises, among them *Notes on Elementary Law* (1875), *Clavis Rerum* (1883), and the three-volume *The Laws of Patents for Useful Inventions* (1890).

ROBOT, ISIDORE (1837–87), missionary. Born in Tharoiseau, Burgundy, France, on July 18, he joined the Benedictines at the Monastery of Sainte-Marie de la Pierre-qui-Vire, France, when he was twenty and was ordained in 1862. He was a military chaplain in the Franco-Prussian War and in 1871 emigrated to the United States, where he engaged in missionary work in northern Louisiana, concerning himself particularly with the Indians there. In 1875 he went to Indiana Territory to minister to the Choctaws and Pottawatomies, founded St. Mary's Monastery of the Benedictine Congregation Cassinese of the Primitive Observance at Sacred Heart Mission, Oklahoma (now Pottawatomie County), and in 1876 was appointed first prefect apostolic of the Indian Territory, with his headquarters at Sacred Heart Mission. He built a school for Indian boys and one for Indian girls and in 1878, when his monastery was elevated to an abbey, he was named its abbot. He attended the third Plenary Council of Baltimore in 1884 and there pleaded the cause of Indian missions, went to Europe in 1885 seeking recruits and finances for his missions, and resigned his prefecture in 1886. He died the following year in Dallas, Texas, on Feb. 15.

ROCHAMBEAU, JEAN BAPTISTE DONATIEN DE VIMEUR, COMTE DE (1725–1807), marshal. Born in Vendôme, France, on July 1, he was educated at the Jesuit college at Blois and entered the Army when he was sixteen. He distinguished himself in the War of the Austrian Succession, became aide-de-camp to the Duke of Orleans in 1746, served in the Minorca expedition in 1756 and the Seven Years' War in 1756–63, and was made a brigadier general and inspector of cavalry in 1761. He was appointed governor of Villefranche-en-Roussillon in 1776 and when King Louis XVI decided to aid the American colonists in their revolt against England he made Rochambeau a lieutenant general and dispatched him to America in command of six thousand French troops. He arrived in Newport, Rhode Island, in 1780 and remained there for a year because the French fleet was blockaded off Narragansett. He joined Washington's army on the banks of the Hudson River above New York City in 1781 and the two drew up the plan to strike south at Cornwallis instead of attacking General Clinton in New York, which Rochambeau opposed. He was with the American forces at Lord Cornwallis's surrender at Yorktown, which practically ended the war, though it dragged on until peace was signed in 1783. He returned to France in 1783, was made a marshal in 1790, and was placed in charge of the Army of the North, fighting against the Austrians the following year. He resigned after a disagreement with the army commander, Charles Dumouriez, barely escaped the guillotine during the Reign of Terror in France when he fell out of favor with the terrorists and was imprisoned and brought to trial. He had his rank restored by Napoleon, who made him an officer of the Legion of Honor and granted him a pension. He spent the last years of his life writing his *Mémoires,* which were published posthumously in Paris in 1809. He died at Thoré, Loire-et-Cher, France, on May 10.

ROCKNE, KNUTE KENNETH (1888–1931), football coach. Born in Voss, Norway, on Mar. 4, he was brought to the United States when he was five by his parents, who settled in Chicago. He was educated at Notre Dame (B.S. 1914) and played on the team that brought Notre Dame to national attention in the football world with its defeat of Army in 1913. He became assistant football coach and a chemistry teacher at Notre Dame and in 1918 was made head coach. During his tenure as head coach, Notre Dame became a power in national football and he became one of the greatest coaches in the annals of intercollegiate football. During his thirteen years as coach, his teams won 105 out of 122 games and were undefeated and untied in 1919, 1920, 1924, 1929, and 1930, one of the most prestigious records of any football coach. He revolutionized football theory by stressing offense, developing the precision backfield (the famous Notre Dame shift), and perfecting line play. He became a Catholic in 1925 and died in a plane crash near Bazaar, Kansas, on Mar. 31. He wrote *Coaching* (1925), *Four Winners* (1925), *Football* (1927), and his autobiography; several books were written about him and a motion picture, *The Knute Rockne Story* starring Pat O'Brien, and among those who appeared in it was Ronald Reagan, who later became fortieth President of the United States.

ROCKWELL, JOSEPH HORACE (1862–1927), educator. Born in Boston on Nov. 19, he was educated at Boston College, joined the Jesuits at Frederick, Maryland, and continued his studies there and at Woodstock College, Maryland, in 1881–96, except when he taught at St. Francis Xavier College, New York City, in 1887–92, and was ordained in 1895. He taught at St. Francis Xavier in 1896–98 and at Boston College in 1899–1901, was vice president of Boston College in 1901–7, was assistant to the provincial of the Maryland–New York province for four years, and was president of St. Francis Xavier College in 1911–18 and of Brooklyn College in 1913–18, when it was affiliated with St. Francis Xavier. He was president of the Association of College Presidents of New York State, was provincial of the

Maryland–New York province of the Jesuits in 1918–22, and when the New England province was established in 1926 he became its procurator, serving in that position until his death in Boston on Aug. 1.

ROEMER, THEODORE (1889–1953), educator, historian. Born in Appleton, Wisconsin, on Jan. 19, he attended St. Lawrence College preparatory seminary at Mt. Calvary, Wisconsin, joined the Capuchins in 1906, and was professed in 1907. He was ordained in 1913, began teaching at St. Lawrence in 1915, taught at St. Anthony Seminary, Marathon, Wisconsin, in 1919–21, and then engaged in pastoral work in the Milwaukee archdiocese. He went to Catholic University to study American Catholic history (M.A. 1931), continued his studies at Louvain in 1931–32, and engaged in research in Germany and Italy. On his return to the United States, he engaged in further studies at Catholic University (Ph.D. 1933) and then resumed his teaching at St. Lawrence College, where he remained until his death at Mt. Calvary on Jan. 7. He served as associate editor of *Franciscan Studies,* wrote articles for the Catholic Encyclopedia supplement, and wrote several books, among them *Pioneer Capuchin Letters* (1936), which he translated, *Ten Decades of Alms* (1942), and a textbook, *The Catholic Church in the United States* (1950).

ROGERS, MOTHER MARY JOSEPH (1882–1955), foundress. Mary Josephine Rogers was born in Boston on Oct. 27, graduated from Smith College in 1905 and Normal School, Boston, in 1908, and in 1906 while at Smith formed the Catholic Mission Study Club. Through it she met Fr. James A. Walsh, cofounder of Maryknoll in 1911, and volunteered to help the new Society. She was put in charge of the Teresians, lay women helping the Society, serving in that position from 1912 until 1920, when the Teresians became a diocesan religious community of the third order of St. Dominic, the Maryknoll Sisters of St. Dominic, with Mary Joseph as mother general. Twenty-two women made their first vows in 1921 and Mother Joseph made her final profession at Shingishu, Korea, in 1924. During her tenure as mother general of the Maryknoll Sisters from 1921 to 1946, when she resigned, she founded a teaching college for her sisters at Maryknoll and a cloistered branch of her community, and by the time of her death more than eleven hundred Maryknoll Sisters were serving all over the world. She died in New York City on Oct. 5.

ROHLMAN, HENRY P. (1876–1957), archbishop. Born in Appelhulsen, Westphalia, Germany, on Mar. 17, he was educated at St. Lawrence College, Mt. Calvary, Wisconsin, Columbia College, Dubuque, Iowa, and the Grand Seminary, Montreal. He was ordained in Montreal in 1910, served as a curate at St. Mary's Church, Dubuque, did postgraduate work in sociology at Catholic University, and was pastor of St. Mary's Church, Waterloo, Iowa. He was business manager at Loras College, Dubuque, in 1917–24, pastor of Nativity Church, Dubuque, in 1923, and was consecrated fourth bishop of Davenport, Iowa, in 1927. He was appointed titular archbishop of Macra in Rodolphi and coadjutor and apostolic administrator of Dubuque in 1944, succeeding to that see in 1946. He was named Assistant at the Apostolic Throne in 1950, resigned in 1954, and was appointed titular archbishop of Cotrada. He died in Dubuque on Sept. 13.

ROMNEN, HEINRICH A. (1897–1967), educator. Born in Cologne, Germany, on Feb. 21, he served in the German Army in World War I, studied law at Münster and Bonn (J.U.D. 1930) after the war, founded the Institute for Social and Economic Order and headed it in 1929–33 at Monchengladbach, and was with the legal department of Aschinger, Inc., in Berlin in 1933–38. He was persecuted and imprisoned by the Nazis for his activities in the field of Catholic action, left Germany and went to England, and in 1938 emigrated to the United States. He taught at St. Joseph's College, West Hartford, Connecticut, in 1938–46 and became an American citizen in 1944. He was an expert in civil and canon law, was a leader in the revival of interest in natural law, and devoted much time and energy to the struggle for social justice, emphasizing Catholic teaching on social thought. He taught at St. Thomas College, St. Paul, Minnesota, in 1946–53 and the University of Minnesota in 1952–53 and was at Georgetown from 1953 until his death in Arlington, Virginia, on Feb. 19. Among the books he wrote were *The State in Catholic Thought* (1945) and *The Natural Law* (1947).

ROSATI, JOSEPH (1789–1843), bishop. Born in Sora, Italy, on Jan. 12, he studied at the diocesan seminary, joined the Congregation of the Missions (called Vincentians or Lazarists) in 1807, and studied at their seminary in Rome, where he was ordained in 1811. He engaged in missionary work in the Papal States until 1815 and the following year went to the United States at the behest of Bishop Louis Dubourg of Louisiana and the two Floridas. He taught theology at St. Thomas Seminary, Bardstown, Kentucky, and was rector until 1818 when, at Bishop Dubourg's order, he established St. Mary's Seminary at The Barrens near St. Louis. He also engaged in missionary work throughout Missouri and became Bishop Dubourg's vicar-general. He became superior of the Vincentians in the United States in 1820 and two years later was appointed titular bishop of Tenagra and vicar apostolic of the newly established vicariate of Mississippi and Alabama. When he declined the appointment, explaining that the area had too few people and was too poor to support a priest, the appointment was revoked and the vicariate suppressed. In 1824, he was again appointed titular bishop of Tenagra and also coadjutor to Bishop Dubourg, with residence at St. Louis, and when Louisiana was divided into the dioceses of New Orleans and St. Louis he was assigned to the New Orleans see. When he objected, he was appointed bishop of St. Louis in 1827, while at the same time administering the diocese of New Orleans. He built St. Louis Cathedral, which was dedicated in 1834, was apostolic delegate to negotiate an agreement between Haiti and the Holy See in 1842, and was appointed an Assistant at the Apostolic Throne the following year. Taken ill while in Rome, he was unable to return to St. Louis before he died on Sept. 25.

ROSECRANS, SYLVESTER NORTON (1827–78), bishop. Brother of William Starke Rosecrans, the Civil War general, he was born in Homer, Ohio, on Feb. 5, studied at Kenyon College Seminary of the Episcopal diocese of Ohio, and was converted to Catholicism in 1845. He went to New York, continued his studies at St. John's College (Fordham), and on his graduation in 1846 studied for the priesthood at Mt. St. Mary of the West Seminary, Cincinnati, Ohio, and the Propaganda, Rome. He was ordained in 1852, taught at Mt. St. Mary's, became associate editor of the diocesan newspaper, the *Catholic Telegraph,* and in 1859 was named president of Mt. St. Mary's College. He

was consecrated titular bishop of Pompeiopolis and auxiliary of Cincinnati in 1862, and was appointed first bishop of the newly created diocese of Columbus, Ohio, in 1868. He saw the opening of the Academy (now College) of St. Mary of the Springs in 1868, founded St. Aloysius Seminary in Columbus in 1871, dedicated St. Joseph's Cathedral in 1878, and died the next day, Oct. 21, in Columbus.

ROSECRANS, WILLIAM STARKE (1819–98), general. Brother of Sylvester Rosecrans, bishop of Columbus, Ohio (1868–78), he was born in Kingston Township, Delaware County, Ohio, on Sept. 6, and attended West Point, graduating in 1842. He served briefly in the engineer's corps and then returned to West Point to teach engineering in 1843–47. He married Ann Eliza Hegeman in 1843, became a Catholic in 1845, and spent 1843–53 in various posts in New England. He resigned from the Army in 1853 to engage in private business but returned at the outbreak of the Civil War in 1861 and was made a colonel and chief engineer of the department of Ohio and was soon made a brigadier general. He held commands in Virginia, Mississippi, and Tennessee and in 1863 was badly defeated at the battle of Chicamauga by General Bragg. He was relieved there and sent to command the department of Missouri for a short time and then was sent to Cincinnati to await orders. Though receiving the brevet rank of major general in 1865, he was given no new command. In 1867 he resigned from the Army. He was United States minister to Mexico in 1868–69 and in 1869–88 was involved there and in California in railroad and mining enterprises. He was a member of the House of Representatives from California in 1881–85, was register of the U.S. Treasury Department in 1885–93, and in 1889 was commissioned a brigadier general on the retired list of the regular Army by Congress. He was the recipient of the Laetare Medal in 1896 and died on his ranch at Redondo, near Los Angeles, California, on Mar. 11.

ROSS, JOHN ELLIOT (1884–1946), author. Born in Baltimore on Mar. 14, he was educated at Loyola College there (B.A. 1902), George Washington (M.A. 1908) and Catholic universities (S.T.B., Ph.D. 1912), Washington, D.C., and was ordained a Paulist priest in 1912. He continued his studies at the Papal University, Rome (S.T.D. 1913), spent two years at St. Mary's Church, Chicago, served as chaplain at the University of Texas in 1914–23, while also serving as pastor of St. Austin's Church, Austin, Texas, taught at Our Lady of the Lake College, San Antonio, Texas, in 1921–22, and then at St. Paul's College, Catholic University, for a year. He was chaplain at Columbia in 1925–29, taught and was chaplain at the universities of Iowa, in 1929, and Illinois, 1930–31, and then spent much of his time working with the National Council of Christians and Jews. He was the author of several books, among them *Consumers and Wage Earners* (1912), *The Right to Work* (1917), *Christian Ethics* (1918), *How Catholics See Protestants* (1928), and *Truths to Live By* (1929), and collaborated on *The Religions of Democracy* (1941). He died in New York City on Sept. 18.

ROUQUETTE, ADRIEN EMMAN-UEL (1813–87), missionary, author. Born in New Orleans on Feb. 13, he was devoted to the Choctaw Indians in his youth. He was educated at the Collège d'Orléans there, Transylvania University, Lexington, Kentucky, and at Paris, Rennes, and the Collège Royal, Nantes, France. On his return to New Orleans, he became editor of *Le Propagateur Catholique* and studied law, but his in-terest in religion led him to study for the priesthood and he was ordained in 1845. He was assigned to St. Louis Cathedral, became noted for his eloquence, and after fourteen years at the cathedral left to minister to the Indians. He established mission chapels for the Choctaws in the bayous of St. Tammany Parish, became an authority on Choctaw culture and language, and wrote several books, among them *Les Savances, poésies Americains* (1841), *Wild Flowers* (1848), *La Question Américaine* (1855), and *Catherine Tegahwitha, the Saint of Caughnawaga* (1873). He died in New Orleans on July 15.

ROWLEY, MOTHER RITA (1913–63), superior general. Born in County Leitrim, Ireland, on Aug. 7, she received her secondary school diploma from University College, Dublin, in 1931 and later that year came to the United States and joined the Religious of the Sacred Heart of Mary at St. Joseph's novitiate, Tarrytown, New York. She completed her undergraduate studies at Marymount College, Tarrytown (B.A. 1936), continued her studies at the Sorbonne, Paris, and McGill University, Montreal (M.A. 1940), took graduate courses at Fordham, and received her Ph.D. from Laval University, Quebec, in 1948. She was a member of the faculty of Marymount Academy, Tarrytown, in 1936–39, made her final profession in 1938, and was on the faculty of Marymount College, Tarrytown, in 1939–43. She was appointed superior of Marymount Junior College, New York City, in 1943, became an American citizen in 1940, and was appointed superior and dean of Marymount College, New York City, in 1948 and of Marymount College, Tarrytown, in 1953. She was named provincial superior of the Eastern Province of North America of her Institute in 1959 and in 1960 she was elected seventh superior general of the Religious of the Sacred Heart of Mary and held that position until her death in New York City on July 1. She opened schools in Florida, St. Louis, and Chicago, modernized the habit of her nuns, and created two new assistant generals to give representation to all of the six provinces of the Institute.

ROY, PERCY ALBERT (1889–1949), educator. Born in New Orleans on Jan. 8, he was educated at Immaculate Conception College there (B.A. 1907), joined the Jesuits in 1908, taught at Jesuit High School, New Orleans, in 1915–17 and at St. Charles College, Grand Cocteau, Louisiana, in 1917–20, continued his studies at St. Louis University (M.A. 1922), and was ordained in St. Louis in 1922. He received his Ph.D. from Woodstock College, Maryland, in 1925, was principal of Jesuit High School, New Orleans, in 1925–34, regent at Loyola University in 1934–36, and dean of faculties in 1937. He was active in the National Catholic Educational Association, serving as president of its secondary school department in 1935–37, and was president of Loyola from 1939 until 1945, when he became pastor of St. Ann's Church, West Palm Beach, Florida. He died there on July 1.

RUMMEL, JOSEPH FRANCIS (1876–1964), archbishop. Born in Steinmauren, Baden, Germany, on Oct. 14, he was brought to the United States by his parents when he was six and became an American citizen with them in 1888. He was educated at St. Anselm's College, Manchester, New Hampshire, (B.A. 1896), St. Joseph's Seminary, Dunwoodie, New York, in 1896–99, and the North American College, Rome (S.T.L. 1903). He was ordained in Rome in 1902, earned a doctorate in sacred theology from the Pontifical Urban University in 1903, and then served as curate at St. Joseph's Church, New York City, in 1903–7. He was pastor of St. Peter's Church, Kingston, New York, in 1907–15, was vicar forane (dean) of Ulster and Sullivan counties, New York, in 1912–15, pastor of St. Anthony of Padua Church, Bronx, New York, in 1915–24, and was made a papal chamberlain in 1924. He was pastor of St. Joseph of the Holy Family Church, Harlem, New York, in 1924–28 and executive director of the German Relief Committee in 1923–24. He was appointed fourth bishop of Omaha, Nebraska, in 1928, convened a diocesan synod in 1934, continued work on the unfinished cathedral, and established a uniform accounting system for the parishes of the diocese. He was appointed ninth archbishop of New Orleans in 1935, reorganized and modernized the administration of the archdiocese, established forty-eight parishes, convened the seventh diocesan synod in 1949, and encouraged lay groups stressing the need for them. He was an eloquent speaker, was active with the National Catholic Welfare Conference (NCWC), serving on its administrative board and as episcopal chairman of its Legal Department, its lay organizations (the National Council of Catholic Nurses was organized in Chicago under his auspices), and the Catholic Committee for Refugees; his aid to the needy and the homeless brought him honors from France, Italy, Holland, and Haiti. He attracted national attention for his efforts to achieve racial equality with the publication of his pastoral letter "Blessed Are the Peacemakers" in 1935, stating there was no segregation in heaven, his pastoral letter in 1956, "The Morality of Racial Segregation," denouncing segregation as morally wrong and sinful, and his directive in 1962 integrating Catholic schools in the New Orleans archdiocese and threatening disobedience with excommunication.

His stand on integration caused some of the laity to refuse to obey, whereupon he excommunicated three of the leaders of the revolt. Ill health and near blindness the last fifteen years of his life caused him to request a coadjutor, and Archbishop John Cody was appointed in 1961. He retired in 1962, announcing the appointment of Archbishop Cody as apostolic administrator, and died in New Orleans on Nov. 8.

RUSSELL, MOTHER MARY BAPTIST (1829–98), foundress. Sister of Baron Charles Russell of Killowen, Down, Ireland, who became the first Catholic Lord Chief Justice of England in centuries in 1894, Kate Russell was born in Newry, Down, Ireland, on Apr. 18, where she was tutored by a governess and in private schools. In 1848 she entered the convent of the Sisters of Mercy in Kinsale, received the habit the next year, taking the name Mary Baptist, and made her final profession in 1851. In response to a plea from Archbishop Joseph Alemany of San Francisco for nuns, she was sent to California in 1854 as superior of a group of eight nuns and novices. They devoted themselves to helping the sick, aiding and teaching the poor, and helping young women in difficulties. She and her community performed invaluable work during the cholera epidemic in San Francisco in 1855, was asked by the city to take charge of the county hospital to care for the poor sick of the city, and when the arrangement was questioned two years later as violating church-state separation, she founded St. Mary's Hospital—the first Catholic hospital on the Pacific coast. In time she opened a night school for adults, the House of Mercy for unemployed women in 1855, and Magdalen Asylum in 1861 and established schools for boys and for girls and a home for the aged. In 1859 she organized the Sodality of Our Lady to finance her far-flung undertakings and adamantly refused the suggestion of the archbishop that her sisters take examinations from public school authorities and, later, dress in lay apparel to secure public funds. She died in St. Mary's Hospital, which she had directed for more than four decades, on Aug. 6.

RUSSELL, WILLIAM THOMAS B. (1863–1927), bishop. Born in Baltimore on Oct. 20, he was educated at St. Charles College, Ellicott City, Maryland, and the North American College, Rome, and was forced to return home because of illness. He continued his studies for the priesthood at St. Mary's Seminary, Baltimore, and was ordained in Baltimore in 1889. He served as pastor at St. Jerome's Church, Hyattsville, Maryland, continuing his studies at Catholic University (S.T.L.) until 1894, when he became Cardinal James Gibbons's secretary, remaining in that position until 1908, when he was named rector of St. Patrick's Church in Washington, D.C. He was made a domestic prelate in 1911 and was named fifth bishop of Charleston, South Carolina, in 1916. During his bishopric he increased the number of priests and parishes in the see, brought new religious orders into the diocese, and wrote *Maryland, the Land of Sanctuary* (1906). He was one of the four bishops on the administrative board of the National Catholic War Council and was first chairman of the National Catholic Welfare Conference when it was founded after World War I. He died in Charleston on Mar. 18.

RUTH, GEORGE HERMAN "BABE" (1895–1948), baseball player. Born in Baltimore on Feb. 6, he was raised an orphan at St. Mary's Industrial School there and early showed an aptitude for baseball. In 1914 he signed with the minor league Baltimore Orioles, where he acquired the nickname "Babe," as a left-handed pitcher. They sold him to the Boston Red Sox, who brought him up from their farm team to the major leagues in 1915. He soon established himself as one of baseball's outstanding pitchers, setting a record of 29 consecutive scoreless innings in World Series competition. But his batting prowess caused him to be converted to an outfielder and in 1919 he broke the home run record with 29 home runs. He was traded to the New York Yankees in 1920 for the then record sum of $125,000 and in the next decade and a half became one of the most colorful and most popular baseball players of all time. He broke his own home run record in 1920 with 54 home runs and again in 1921 with 59 home runs, was the American League's most valuable player in 1923, led the league in home runs in 1919–24 and 1926–31, and had a career total of 714 home runs and a lifetime batting average of .342. He established records that still exist, notably his feat of hitting 60 home runs in 1927, which was surpassed only by Roger Maris, who hit 61 in 1961 but in a 161-game season, whereas Ruth's 60 homers were in a 154-game season. He was released by the Yankees in 1935 and signed with the Boston Braves as assistant manager and player and in the last game of his career, in Pittsburgh in 1935, hit three consecutive home runs. He finished his baseball career with the Brooklyn Dodgers in 1938. He was one of the first five players elected to the Baseball Hall of Fame in 1936 and died of cancer in New York City on Aug. 16. Ruth brought baseball back into public esteem, after the Black Sox scandal of 1919, by his tremendous slugging, which completely changed the complexion of the game, and his colorful personality, which drew huge crowds wherever he appeared. He was one of the most popular figures in the history of American sports and the greatest baseball figure of all time.

RUTH, MOTHER MARY ANSELMA (1874–1957), mother general. Born in Bavaria, she was brought to Brooklyn, New York, by her parents when she was an infant. She joined the Dominicans in 1891 and took her vows the following year, studied at New Rochelle (New York) College, graduating in 1910, and later at Fordham, where she received her doctorate in 1922. She engaged in missionary work in Puerto Rico in 1910–14, was mistress of novices at her community's mother house in Amityville, New York, in 1914–38, became a subprioress, and in 1943 became its mother superior. She became president of Molloy College for Women when it was founded in Rockville Centre, New York, in 1955 and remained in that position until her death at Mary Immaculate Hospital in Jamaica, Queens, New York, on Jan. 12 after a brief illness.

RYAN, ABRAM JOSEPH (1838–86), poet. Born in Hagerstown, Maryland, on Feb. 5, he was early attracted to the religious life, studied for the priesthood at St. Mary's Seminary, Berryville, Missouri, where he joined the Congregation of the Mission, and at Our Lady of Angels Seminary, Niagara Falls, New York, and was ordained in St. Louis in 1860. He taught at several seminaries of his Congregation (the Vincentians) until 1862, when he was appointed to St. Mary's Church, Peoria, Illinois. At the outbreak of the Civil War, he unsuccessfully tried to be commissioned a military chaplain but did serve as chaplain for the Confederates several times during the war. His poetry, especially "The Conquered Banner," published in the New York *Freeman Journal* in 1865 under the pseudonym Moina, and "The Sword of Robert E. Lee," was especially popular in the South and earned him the sobriquet "Poet of the Confederacy." He engaged in pastoral work in the Nashville, Tennessee, diocese in 1864–67, transferred to Savannah, Georgia, in 1868 and became founding editor of the Augusta (Georgia) *Banner of the South,* a religious and political weekly. In 1870 he went to Mobile, Alabama, was assistant at the cathedral there until 1877, when he was appointed pastor of St. Mary's parish. He served on the staff of the New Orleans *Morning Star* from 1871 and was its editor-in-chief in 1872–75, though residing in Mobile. He retired to Biloxi, Mississippi, in 1881 and died in Louisville, Kentucky, on Apr. 22. Among his works are *Father Ryan's Poems* (1879), *Poems, Patriotic, Religious, Miscellaneous* (1880), and *A Crown for Our Queen* (1882).

RYAN, EDWARD FRANCIS (1878–1956), bishop. Born in Lynn, Massachusetts, on Mar. 10, he was educated at Boston College and the North American College, Rome, and was ordained in Rome in 1905. He engaged in pastoral work in the Boston archdiocese, became pastor of Holy Name Church, West Roxbury, Massachusetts, and in 1944 was appointed fifth bishop of Burlington, Vermont. During his episcopate, he established the *Vermont Catholic Tribune* in 1956, brought eight new religious communities into the diocese, opened new schools, reorganized the Holy Name Societies, and built twenty-three new churches in small towns and villages. He died in Burlington on Nov. 3.

RYAN, GEORGE JOSEPH (1872–1949), educator. Born in Long Island City, New York, on July 7, he was educated at St. Francis Xavier College, New York City, and entered business. He became vice president of the Long Island Savings Bank, was a delegate to the New York State Constitutional Convention in 1915, was president of the Queens Chamber of Commerce in 1917–19, and was vice president in 1920–22 and president in 1922–36 of the New York City Board of Education. He served on numerous civic, patriotic, and educational committees, served on the New York State Board of Regents from 1931 until his death, received honorary degrees from several universities, and was honored by the Vatican, France, Italy, Belgium, Spain, and Portugal. He died in Flushing, New York, on Oct. 4.

RYAN, JAMES (1848–1923), bishop. Born near Thurles, Tipperary, Ireland, on June 17, he was brought to the United States when he was seven by his parents, who settled in Louisville, Kentucky. He was educated at St. Thomas and St. Joseph colleges, Bardstown, Kentucky, and Preston Park Seminary, Louisville, and was ordained in Louisville in 1871. He taught, served as a missionary in the Peoria, Illinois, diocese, became rector of St. Columba Church, and in 1888 was consecrated third bishop of Alton (transferred to Springfield in 1923), Illinois. He convoked the first diocesan synod in 1889, drew a severe reprimand from Cardinal Ledochowski for his "irreverence" to the pope when he vehemently objected to the establishment of a permanent apostolic delegation to the United States in 1893, and saw the diocesan paper, *The Western Catholic,* established in 1896. He died in Alton on July 2.

RYAN, JAMES HUGH (1886–1947), archbishop. Born in Indianapolis, Indiana, on Dec. 15, he was educated at Holy Ghost College (later Duquesne University), Pittsburgh, Mt. St. Mary of the West Seminary, Cincinnati, Ohio, and the North American College, Rome, the Propaganda (S.T.B. 1906,

S.T.D. 1909), and the Roman Academy (Ph.D. 1908). He was ordained in Rome in 1909, taught psychology at Mt. St. Mary of the Woods College, Terre Haute, Indiana, in 1911–21, serving as president from 1920, and was executive secretary of the Department of Education of the National Catholic Welfare Conference in 1920–28. He began teaching philosophy at Catholic University in 1922, was made a domestic prelate in 1927 and a prothonotary apostolic in 1929, and was named rector of Catholic University in 1928. He was named titular bishop of Modra in 1933. He reorganized the university, brought the School of Sacred Sciences under his control, and had put the university on a sound financial basis by the time he left in 1935. He established *New Scholasticism* in 1927 and edited it the next decade and was active in civic matters. He opposed state medical services and the American Medical Association's recognition of birth control. He was appointed bishop of Omaha, Nebraska, in 1935, became that see's first archbishop when it was made an archdiocese in 1945, and died in Omaha on Nov. 23. He wrote several books, among them *A Catechism of Catholic Education* (1922), *An Introduction to Philosophy* (1924), and *On the Encyclicals of Pius XI* (1927).

RYAN, JOHN AUGUSTINE (1869–1945), sociologist. Born in Vermillion, Dakota County, Minnesota, on May 25, he was raised on the family farm and was educated at St. Thomas Seminary in 1887–92, the St. Paul (Minnesota) Seminary in 1892–98, was ordained in St. Paul in 1898 and continued his studies at Catholic University in 1898–1902 and received his S.T.D. there in 1906. He taught moral theology at St. Paul Seminary in 1902–15 and early became interested in social problems. He lectured and wrote on moral and labor problems, especially labor unions, worked for minimum wage laws for women in Wisconsin and Minnesota in 1913, and in 1915 joined the faculty of Catholic University, where he was to remain until his retirement in 1939. He was elected dean of the School of Sacred Sciences in 1919 and also taught at Trinity College, founded and was editor of *Catholic Charities Review* in 1917–20, and in 1919 was the author of the social action policy statement of the administrative committee of the National Catholic Welfare Conference (NCWC) which became known as the Bishops' Program of Social Reconstruction; of its twelve major proposals eleven were to become law under President Franklin Roosevelt's New Deal. He was appointed director of the Social Action Department of the NCWC in 1920 and became known nationally for his activities in labor, economics, and social welfare. He helped organize the Catholic Association for International Peace in 1927 and was an ardent supporter of Franklin D. Roosevelt and his New Deal. He was made a domestic prelate in 1933 and was appointed to the National Recovery Administration Industrial Appeals Board by his friend President Roosevelt in 1934. He was a tremendous force in molding Catholic socioeconomic theories and wrote profusely in periodicals and books to promulgate his ideas. Among his many books on social, economic, and labor issues were *A Living Wage* (1906), his doctoral dissertation, which was described by economist Richard Ely as "the first attempt in the English language to elaborate a Roman Catholic system of political economy," *Distributive Justice* (1916), *The Church and Socialism* (1919), *Social Reconstruction* (1920), *The Church and Labor* (1920), and, with Fr. Moorehouse Miller, *The State and the Church* (1922), a controversial text widely used in Catholic colleges which many critics believed supported the belief that once Catholics were in power they would deny religious freedom to non-Catholics; he later rewrote it with Fr. Francis J. Boland as *Catholic Principles of Politics* (1940); he also wrote *A Better Economic Order* (1935) and *A Social Doctrine in Action* (1941). He died in St. Paul on Sept. 16.

RYAN, JOHN DENIS (1864–1933), executive. Born in Hancock, Michigan, on Oct. 10, he became an oil salesman in Pennsylvania, married Nellie Gardner in 1896, and settled in Butte, Montana. In 1906 he became president of the Anaconda Copper Mining Company and also became active in the International Smelting Company and American Brass Company and several mining companies in South America. He became president of the United Metals Selling Company and the Montana Power Company. During World War I, he was on the Red Cross Council, was director of aircraft production and chairman of the Aircraft Board under President Wilson in 1918, and in Aug.–Nov. 1918 was assistant Secretary of War. After the war he left government service to return to private industry. He was known for his philanthropies, for which he was honored by the pope, and died in New York City on Feb. 11.

RYAN, PATRICK JAMES (1902–78), chaplain. Born in Litchfield, Massachusetts, on Dec. 3, he was educated at St. Thomas College and Seminary, St. Paul, Minnesota, and was ordained in 1927. He became a chaplain in the United States Army the following year and served in that capacity until his retirement in 1958. He was made a major general in 1954, was chief of chaplains in 1954–58, president of the Military Chaplains Association in 1960–61, and then became a vice president of *Catholic Digest*. He was honored by the govern-ments of the United States, England, France, Italy, and Brazil and died in Washington, D.C., on June 6.

RYAN, PATRICK JOHN (1831–1911), archbishop. Born in Cloneyharp, near Thurles, Tipperary, Ireland, on Feb. 20, he graduated from St. Patrick's College, Carlow, in 1852 but was too young to be ordained, so he went to the United States to serve under Archbishop Peter Kenrick of St. Louis. He taught at the St. Louis diocesan seminary at Carondelet, Missouri, continued his studies at St. Louis University, and was ordained in St. Louis in 1853. He served as a curate at the cathedral in St. Louis, became its rector, and was noted for his preaching. He was founding pastor of the Church of the Annunciation, St. Louis, became rector of St. John's parish there, and was one of Archbishop Kenrick's theologians at the second Plenary Council of Baltimore in 1866. While in Europe in 1868, he preached the English Lenten course in Rome for that year and while attending Vatican Council I with Archbishop Kenrick was named vicar-general and administrator of St. Louis. He was consecrated titular bishop of Tricomia and coadjutor of St. Louis in 1872; during the next twelve years he ran the archdiocese. He was appointed titular archbishop of Salamis in 1884 and later the same year he was appointed second archbishop of Philadelphia. He greatly expanded the number of religious and religious institutions in the archdiocese, tripled the number of churches and schools, was one of the incorporators of the Bureau of Catholic Indian Missions in 1894, and was appointed to the United States Indian Commission by President Theodore Roosevelt. Famed for his oratory (he was probably the outstanding pulpit orator of his day), he opened the national convention of the Republican Party in Philadelphia in 1890, lectured widely, and helped reduce anti-Catholic feeling in the United States. He was greatly interested in black and Indian missions and under his direction Mother Katharine Drexel founded the Sisters of the Blessed Sacrament devoted to helping the Indians and the blacks. He saw the Catholic population of his see grow from 300,000 to over a million, edited the *American Catholic Quarterly Review,* founded in 1876, from 1890, and died in Philadelphia on Feb. 11.

RYAN, STEPHEN MICHAEL VINCENT (1825–96), bishop. Born near Almonte, Ontario, Canada, on Jan. 1, perhaps in 1826 at Perth, he was educated at St. Charles Borromeo Seminary, Overbrook, Philadelphia, joined the Congregation of the Missions (Vincentians/Lazarists) and continued his studies at St. Mary's Seminary, The Barrens near St. Louis. He was ordained in St. Louis in 1849, taught at St. Mary's until 1851 and then taught at St. Vincent's College, Cape Girardeau, Missouri, and became its rector. He was elected visitor general of his Congregation in 1857 and served in that capacity until 1868 when he was appointed second bishop of Buffalo, New York. He backed Archbishop John Ireland's support of Fr. Sylvester Malone for regent of the University of New York in New York against Bishop McQuaid of Rochester and was also involved in disputes with the bishop of Rochester over the boundaries of their respective sees and over his position on education. He was noted for his spirited defense of the Church, concentrated, during his twenty-eight-year tenure, on establishing new parishes and schools, and founded the diocesan newspaper, the *Catholic Union* (now the *Catholic Union and Times),* in 1872. He died in Buffalo on Apr. 10.

RYAN, THOMAS FORTUNE (1851–1928), financier. Born on a farm in Lov-ington, Nelson County, Virginia, on Oct. 17, he began his business career working as an errand boy in John S. Barry's commission house and in 1872 went to New York City. He worked as a messenger boy for a Wall Street brokerage firm, married Barry's daughter in 1873, formed a firm with Barry's help, and in 1874 bought a seat on the New York Stock Exchange. With William C. Whitney, he financed streetcar and lighting projects in New York City and by 1900 he controlled practically every streetcar line in the city with the Metropolitan Street Railway Company, after running roughshod over competitors, and in 1905 he forced August Belmont to consolidate his Interborough Rapid Transit subway system with Ryan's Metropolitan Street Railway Company. He later extended these tactics to Chicago and other cities. Soon after Ryan withdrew from his transit holdings, they went bankrupt. He and Whitney organized the American Tobacco Company in the early 1890s and by 1911 it had such a monopoly on the industry it was ordered dissolved by the federal government. Ryan bought up banks, insurance companies (he bought a controlling block of shares in the Equitable Life Assurance Society in 1905), coal mines, and railroad properties in Ohio, Virginia, and West Virginia and invested in diamond mines in the Belgian Congo. In time he became a director of some thirty major corporations. Throughout his life he was constantly denounced for his unscrupulousness, ruthless business dealings, manipulation of companies, and alleged bribes, and his business dealings were the subject of several legislative investigations. He retired from active management of his many enterprises after 1910 and devoted himself and the huge fortune he had accumulated to collecting art objects and, with his wife, to philanthropic and charitable enterprises, reputedly donating some

RYAN, VINCENT JAMES

$20 million to Catholic causes, among them building and furnishing Sacred Heart Cathedral in Richmond, Virginia. When his first wife died in 1917, he married Mary Townsend (Nicoll) Lord Cuyler a few days later. He died in New York City on Nov. 23.

RYAN, VINCENT JAMES (1884–1951), bishop. Born in Arlington, Wisconsin, on July 1, he was educated at St. Francis Seminary, Milwaukee, Wisconsin, in 1902–6 and St. Paul (Minnesota) Seminary in 1906–12 and was ordained in 1912. He continued his studies at Catholic University (S.T.B.), was chancellor of the Fargo, North Dakota, diocese in 1912–36 and pastor of St. Anthony's Church in Fargo in 1918–40, administered the diocese in 1934–35, and was vicar-general in 1939–40. He was appointed second bishop of Bismarck, North Dakota, in 1940, inaugurated a period of great building activity in the diocese, was active in social work, served as president of the National Catholic Rural Life Conference in 1939–41, wrote several theological treatises, and died on Nov. 10 in Bismarck of pneumonia.

S

SADLIER, DENIS (1817–85), publisher. Born in County Tipperary, Ireland, he came to the United States with his widowed mother and his brother James (d. 1869) in 1832. Five years later he and his brother began a publishing house in New York City, D. & J. Sadlier Co., with a monthly serial edition of Butler's *Lives of the Saints* and the following year with a serial edition of the bible. In 1853 they purchased the stock and rights of publisher John Doyle and became a leading publisher of Catholic material in the United States. James opened a Montreal branch in 1840, married Mary A. Madden, who became a well-known Catholic author, and returned to New York with his family in 1860 to work with Denis. The firm acquired the *Tablet* in 1857 and became known for its editions of the bible, its line of Catholic textbooks, such as the Metropolitan Readers under the guidance of Mary Sadlier, and published some 650 titles in the nineteenth century, among them the *Catholic Directory, Almanac and Ordo* in 1864–96. Denis died in New York City on Feb. 4.

SADLIER, FRANCIS (1873–1939), publisher. Son of William H. Sadlier and Anna M. Cassidy Sadlier, he was born in New York City on Aug. 1 and was educated at St. Louis College and De La Salle Institute. He married Neva H. Hecker, grandniece of Fr. Isaac Hecker, founder of the Paulists, in 1909 and in the same year replaced his mother as head of William H. Sadlier, Inc., publisher of religious books and textbooks. He revived the business by revising the Excelsior series of U.S. history and geography and after World War I issued a series of history books for the fifth, sixth, and seventh grades and the Social Geography Series, which were very successful; the 1934 publication of *Sadlier's Baltimore Catechism with Study Lessons* was equally successful. He died in New York City on June 8.

SADLIER, JAMES (d. 1869), publisher. *See* Sadlier, Denis; Sadlier, Mary Anne.

SADLIER, MARY ANNE (1820–1903), author. Daughter of prosperous merchant Francis Madden, she was born in Cootehill, Cavan, Ireland, on Dec. 31. She early showed talent as a writer, emigrated to New York City in 1844, and, after the death of her father, moved to Montreal later that year. She married James Sadlier, who with his brother Denis had established a Catholic publishing house in New York City in 1846 and spent the next fourteen years in Montreal, where her husband was manager of Sadlier's Canadian branch. While there she published short stories and novels in several Catholic magazines and by the time they returned to New York in 1860 she was widely acclaimed for her novels and poetry and her support of the Church and Catholic charities. She became one of the most popular Catholic authors of the time and wrote some sixty books, most of them novels on Irish-American or historical themes, among them *The Blakes and the Flanagans* (1855), *Bess Conway* (1862), and *De Fromental* (1887); she also wrote on Irish history, such books as *The Red Hand of Ulster, The Old House by the Boyne, Maureen Dhu,* and *Life in Galway,* and compiled *Catechism of Sacred History and Doctrine* (1864). She remained in New York for several years after the death of her husband in 1869 and then returned to Montreal. She was awarded the Laetare Medal in 1895 and died in Montreal on Apr. 5.

SAGARD, GABRIEL (16th–17th century), missionary. Theodore Gabriel Sagard was born in France at the end of the sixteenth century, became a Recollect brother, and in 1623 was sent to Canada with Fr. Nicolas Viel and assigned to the Huron mission. He learned the Huron language and ministered to the Hurons until ordered back to France. There he published a history of Canada titled *Histoire du Canada et voyagesque les Frères Mineurs Récollets ont faits pour la conversion des infidèles.* He also compiled a 132-page Indian vocabulary and presented a memoir to the Duc de Montmorency deploring the activities of trading company agents among the Indians and suggesting a more powerful religious order for the Canadian mission—a suggestion that led to the involvement of the Jesuits in North American missions.

SAINT-COSME, JEAN FRANÇOIS BUISSON DE (1667–1707), missionary. Born in Quebec in February, he studied at the Séminaire des Missions Étrangères there and was ordained in 1690. He served as a missionary at Minas, Acadia (Nova Scotia), for a time and was then sent west to work with the Illinois Indians. He served at the Cahokia mission in Illinois until about 1698 and with the Natchez Indians at present-day Natchez, Mississippi, at the end of 1699. The missionaries were unsuccessful with the Natchez and in 1704 it was decided to abandon the mission; however, Fr. Saint-Cosme remained. Three years later, he and three French companions and a slave were murdered by the Shetimasha Indians while descending the Mississippi. The Shetimashas were almost exterminated in a war waged on them by the Natchez and other friendly tribes at the instigation of Governor Bienville of Louisiana in retaliation.

ST. JAMES, FREDDY. *See* Allen, Fred.

ST. JOHN, HECTOR. *See* Crèvecoeur, Hector St. John.

ST.-PALAIS, JACQUES MAURICE LANDES DE (1811–77), bishop. Born in La Salvetat, Hérault, France, on Nov. 15, he studied at St. Nicholas du Chartonet and St. Sulpice Seminary, Paris, and was ordained in 1836. He went to the United States, engaged in missionary work in Indiana, and in 1847 was appointed vicar-general of the diocese of Vincennes, Indiana (changed to diocese of Indianapolis in 1898), and superior of St. Charles Seminary there. He was administrator of the see in 1848 and later the same year was appointed its fourth bishop. He brought religious orders into the see, built an orphanage for boys in 1849 and for girls in 1850 in Vincennes, established new parishes and schools, and began a diocesan newspaper, the *Indiana Catholic and Record,* in 1875. While on a European trip in 1851–52, he persuaded the Benedictine Abbey of Maria Einsiedeln, Switzerland, to establish St. Meinrad's at Spencer County, Indiana, in 1854; it became an independent abbey in 1870. He refused the archbishopric of Toulouse, France, and remained as bishop of Vincennes until his death at St. Mary-of-the-Woods, Indiana, on June 28.

SALPOINTE, JOHN BAPTIST (1825–98), archbishop. Born in St. Maurice de Poinsat, Puy de Dôme, France, on Feb. 21 (or 22), he was educated at the Clermont-Ferrand seminary and was ordained in 1851. He engaged in pastoral activities for several years, taught at the Clermont-Ferrand preparatory seminary in 1855–59, and then went to the United States. He engaged in missionary activities in the Santa Fe, New Mexico, diocese and was appointed first vicar apostolic of Arizona and titular bishop of Doryla in 1868. As vicar apostolic he fought the practice of the federal government of placing Catholic Indians under Protestant missionaries, was made titular archbishop of Anazarbus and coadjutor of Santa Fe in 1884 and succeeded to the see the following year. In 1886 he attempted to curb the excesses of the Penitentes, an outgrowth of the Third Order of St. Francis probably founded by Franciscan missionaries in the seventeenth century, by ordering them to cease the practice of flagellation and carrying heavy crosses in some of their religious observations. When his order was disregarded, he ordered the Penitentes to disband and, though they continued in some sections of the archdiocese, the society was weakened. He resigned in 1894 and was appointed titular archbishop of Tomi. He retired to Banning, California, where he wrote *Soldiers of the Cross,* a source history of the pioneer Church in the Southwest. He died in Tucson, Arizona, on July 15.

SALVATIERRA, JUAN MARIA (1648–1717), missionary. Of a family of Spanish descent, he was born in Milan, Italy, on Nov. 15, studied at the Jesuit seminary in Parma, and decided to devote himself to missionary work

among the American Indians rather than marry, as his parents desired. He joined the Jesuits in Genoa in 1668, went to Mexico in 1675, continued his studies, and was ordained. He became a professor at Puebla College and then, after declining a position at the cathedral, went as a missionary to southwest Chihuahua. He worked among the Tarumari, Tubar, Guazaar, and other Indian tribes for the next decade and in 1690 was appointed *visitador* of the Jesuit missions in the northwestern district. Seven years later, after meeting Fr. Eusebio Kino, he set out to evangelize Lower California. To finance this venture he and Jean Ugarte begged and raised funds. This became the Pious Fund of California which caused trouble between the Church and the Mexican Government when California became one of the United States a century and a half later and Mexico confiscated the Fund. He founded the first of the Californian missions, Our Lady of Loreto, at Concepción Bay in Lower California late in 1697 and in the next several years established six more. He was recalled to Mexico in 1704 to serve as Jesuit provincial but returned to his missions in 1707. He died ten years later at Guadalajara on July 17 while on a journey to meet with the new viceroy of Mexico. He wrote several works on his missionary activities and explorations, among them *Cartas sobre la Conquista espiritual de California* (1698) and *Nuevas Cartas sobre lo mismo,* and was called "the apostle of California" by the noted American historian George Bancroft.

SALZMANN, JOSEPH (1819–74), missionary. Born at Munzbach, Austria, on Aug. 17, he studied there and at Linz and Vienna, where he received his doctorate in theology and was ordained in 1842. He engaged in pastoral work in his native diocese of Linz and, after a visit by John Henni, first bishop of Milwaukee, Wisconsin, in 1847, decided to go to America. He worked in a small mission in the Milwaukee diocese for a time and then became pastor of St. Mary's Church, Milwaukee. He was editor of *Der Seebote* in 1851. He decided there was a great need of a seminary in his diocese and after several years raising funds, St. Francis Seminary (which was also known as the Salesianum) was opened in Milwaukee in 1856 with Fr. Michael Heiss, later archbishop of Milwaukee, its first rector and Fr. Salzmann its procurator. Fr. Salzmann succeeded Heiss as rector in 1868, when Heiss became bishop of La Crosse, Wisconsin, and served in that position until his death. He also founded Catholic Normal School of the Holy Family, first Catholic normal school in the United States, Pio Nono College, and the American branch of the Cecilian Society devoted to the promotion of church music. He died at St. Francis, Wisconsin, on Jan. 17.

SÁNCHEZ, JOSÉ BERNARDO (1778–1833), missionary. Born in Robledillo, Old Castile, Spain, on Sept. 7, he joined the Franciscans in 1794, was sent to Mexico, and was assigned to the missionary college of San Fernando in Mexico City in 1803. He was sent to California in 1804, served at Mission San Diego in 1804–20, and in 1806 was chaplain for a military expedition against the Indians. He was stationed at Mission Purísima in 1820–21, went on an expedition with Fr. Mariano Payeras, prefect, to the interior in quest of new mission sites in 1821, and in 1827–31 was *presidente* of the missions. He adamantly opposed the secular organization plan of Governor Echeandia, which he thought would destroy the missions, and returned as a missionary to San Gabriel in 1831. He died there on Jan. 15.

SANDS, BENJAMIN FRANKLIN (1812–83), admiral. Born in Baltimore on Feb. 11, he was appointed a midshipman from Maryland in 1828 and served on coast guard survey duty in 1834–41; he was with Lieutenant Gedney when he discovered Gedney's Channel leading into New York Harbor, became a lieutenant in 1840, worked at the Naval Observatory in 1844–47, and took part in the Mexican War. He married Henrietta M. French, a Catholic, and in 1850 became a Catholic. He was advanced to commander in 1850, invented a new deep-sounding device in 1858, was chief of the Bureau of Construction in 1858–61, and was on coast survey duty on the Pacific coast when the Civil War broke out. He came east at once, applied for duty on a fighting ship, and participated in both attacks of Fort Fisher. He commanded several ships blockading the southern coast, and it was on his ship, the *Fort Jackson,* that General Kirby Smith signed articles of surrender of the last Confederate armed forces. He was made commodore in 1866, was superintendent of the Naval Observatory in Washington, D.C., in 1867–74 and during his tenure made it one of the outstanding observatories in the world. He was appointed rear admiral in 1871, retired in 1874, and served on the Catholic Indian Bureau in Washington, where he died on June 30. His autobiography, *From Reefer to Rear Admiral,* compiled by his son from notes he left, was published in 1890.

SANDS, WILLIAM FRANKLIN (1874–1946), diplomat. Son of Rear Admiral James Hoban Sands, he was born in Washington, D.C., on July 29, studied in Switzerland and Austria and Georgetown (B.A. and LL.B. 1896), and entered the diplomatic service later in 1896. He was second secretary of the American Legation in Tokyo until 1898, when he became first secretary at Seoul,

Korea, and was named chargé d'affaires the following year and was adviser to the Korean emperor. He was expelled by the Japanese when they invaded Korea in 1904, was chargé d'affaires in Panama in 1904–6, in Guatemala in 1907, and in Mexico in 1908 and married Edith Gertrude Keating in 1909, when he returned to Guatemala as envoy extraordinary. He left the diplomatic service in 1911, represented the New York banking firm of Speyer & Co. in Ecuador in 1911, the Central Aguirre Sugar Co. of Boston in Puerto Rico in 1911–12, and was manager and secretary of the Pan-American Financial Conference in 1915. During World War I, he worked for the relief of German and Austrian prisoners in Russia in 1916–18, became headmaster of the Newman School, Lakewood, New Jersey, after the war, and then set up a diplomatic training school in the State Department and held the chair of diplomacy in Georgetown's School of Foreign Service. He wrote two books on his diplomatic experiences, *Undiplomatic Memoirs* (1930) and *Our Jungle Diplomacy* (1944), was honored by France and Korea, and died in Washington, D.C., on June 17.

SANSBURY, MOTHER ANGELA (1795–1839), foundress. Marie Sansbury was born in Prince George County, Maryland, in March and was brought to Kentucky by her parents, who settled in Cartwright's Creek, Washington County. When Dominican Fr. Samuel T. Fenwick came to Kentucky in 1808, he determined to form a branch of the Dominican Sisters there, but it was not until 1822 that he secured permission to proceed; soon thereafter Marie Sansbury and eight young ladies presented themselves as candidates for the new foundation when a Fr. Wilson preached at their St. Rose's Church. He settled them in a log cabin nearby—the first Dominican convent—and Marie, with three other postulants, received the habit on Easter Sunday, Apr. 7; she took the name Angela. She was almost immediately elected Mother Prioress and made her profession early in 1823; later that year she was given a tract of land on Cartwright Creek by her father and established a new convent and school on it—the first Dominican school in the United States. When the community's spiritual adviser, Fr. Miles, was sent to Ohio at the request of Bishop Fenwick of Cincinnati, a new chaplain, Spanish Dominican Fr. Muños from nearby St. Rose Priory, was appointed. He disapproved of the lifestyle of the community (in addition to teaching, the nuns had to earn their own keep by weaving, sewing, tilling the soil, chopping wood, etc.), and to emphasize his disapproval, he ordered the community to disband when he also heard they had assumed a debt in order to build. When the sisters refused to do so, a protracted struggle ensued that was not resolved until 1830, when a new prior of St. Rose's, Fr. Stephen Montgomery, a Kentuckian, was appointed; he paid the debt and continued the community. Later in 1830 Mother Angela sent the first group of sisters from the Kentucky community, at Bishop Fenwick's request, to Ohio, where they established a branch house at Somerset. When illness beset Mother Angela late in 1830, she relinquished her superiorship, but in 1833 she was sent as prioress to St. Mary of the Springs in Columbus, Ohio, which had been founded by the Somerset house. She died at St. Mary of the Springs on Nov. 30.

SATOLLI, FRANCESCO (1839–1910), apostolic delegate to the United States. Born in Marsciano near Perugia, Italy, he was ordained in 1862, received his doctorate from the Sapienza University, Rome, taught at Perugia, and was pastor at Marsciano, becoming a Benedictine at Monte Cassion in 1872. After teaching at several Roman universities, he became rector of the Greek College in Rome in 1884, was president of the Political Academy of Noble Ecclesiastics in 1886–92, becoming titular archbishop of Lepant in 1888, and in 1889 was sent to the United States by Pope Leo XIII as papal delegate at the centennial celebration of the establishment of the American hierarchy; he also represented the pope at the World's Fair Columbian Exposition in Chicago in 1892. In 1893 he was appointed the first apostolic delegate to the United States when the permanent apostolic delegation was established, despite the opposition of many of the American bishops to its establishment. He remained in this position until 1896 (he was made a cardinal in 1895), when he was made prefect of the Congregation of Studies in Rome. He was appointed cardinal bishop of Frascati in 1903, made a final visit to the United States on the occasion of the St. Louis Exposition in 1904, and died in Rome on Jan. 8. His talks in the United States were published as *Loyalty to the Church and State* (1895).

SAVAGE, COURTENAY (1890–1946), author. Born in New York City on July 20, he was educated in private and public schools and took a course in writing at Columbia. His literary career began when he sold a story, "Rainmaker," to *Columbia* magazine. He wrote short stories, articles, and fourteen plays, was a drama critic, and became a public relations man. He became a Catholic in 1937, devoted much of his time thereafter to Catholic radio and theater work, founded the Catholic Authors Guild of Chicago, became director of public relations for the National Catholic Community Service when the United States entered World War II, and was in Europe for the National Catholic Welfare Conference when he died in Rome on Aug. 23. Among his plays were *Home Is the Hero,* a dramatization of the life of Robert Louis Stevenson, *They All Want Something,* and *The Little Dog Laughed;* he also wrote a fictional life of St. Christopher, *The Wayfarer's Friend,* and with E. B. Dewing, *Don't Bother Mother.*

SCAMMON, ELLAKIM PARKER (1816–94), educator. Born in Whitefield, Maine, on Dec. 27, he graduated from West Point in 1837, taught mathematics there, and served in the Seminole and Mexican Wars; he was one of General Winfield Scott's aids in the latter. He became a Catholic in 1846, spent 1847–54 as a member of the topographical corps surveying the Great Lakes, and resigned from the Army in 1856. He taught mathematics at St. Mary's College and Polytechnical College in Cincinnati, Ohio, and when the Civil War broke out, he rejoined the Army and became a brigadier general in 1862. He served as U.S. consul at Prince Edward Island in 1866–71, became professor of mathematics at Seton Hall College, South Orange, New Jersey, in 1875, and retired seven years later. He died in New York City on Dec. 7.

SCANLAN, LAWRENCE (1843–1915), bishop. Born in Ballytarsha, Tipperary, Ireland, on Sept. 29, he was educated at St. Patrick's College, Thurles, and All Hallows Seminary, Dublin, and was ordained in Dublin in 1868. He emigrated to San Francisco later in 1868 and engaged in missionary activities in California and Nevada. He was assistant pastor of St. Patrick's Church in 1868–70 and of St. Mary's Cathedral in 1868–70, both in San Francisco, was pastor for a brief period in Woodland, California, and served in a mining camp at Pioche, Nevada, in 1871–72 and then at Petaluma, California, earning the support of laborers on the railroad, miners, and cattlemen for his aid to down-and-outers. In 1873 he was sent to Utah, administered his 85,000-square-mile parish by himself for a time, and in 1887 was named titular bishop of Larandum and vicar apostolic of Utah when the vicariate of Utah was established. In 1891 he was appointed first bishop of Salt Lake City when the vicariate was erected into a diocese. During his bishopric he expanded the facilities of the see, built thirty churches, hospitals, and orphanages, established All Hallows College in Salt Lake City in 1895, and dedicated St. Mary Magdalene Cathedral in Salt Lake City in 1909. He died in Salt Lake City on May 10.

SCANLAN, PATRICK F. "PAT" (1894–1983), editor. Born in New York City on Oct. 8, he was educated at St. Joseph's College there (B.A.), moved to Brooklyn, and became a teacher at St. Peter's High School on Staten Island. In 1917 he joined the Brooklyn *Tablet* as managing editor on a temporary basis; he was to remain as managing editor until his retirement in 1968. He married Mae Manning in 1924 and became one of the most influential editors in the Catholic press. He wrote a weekly column, "From the Managing Editor's Desk," for fifty-one years in 2,600 consecutive issues, and wrote many of the *Tablet*'s editorials. He was a fierce opponent of Communism and the Ku Klux Klan, supported the Legion of Decency and the Catholic school system, and was active in the Catholic Press Association, serving as its president in 1924–27. He was made a Knight of St. Gregory in 1944, was honored by a dozen colleges and universities, and died in Floral Park, New York, on Mar. 27.

SCANNELL, RICHARD (1845–1916), bishop. Born in Cloyne, Cork, Ireland, on May 12, he was educated at All Hallows College, Dublin, and was ordained in Dublin in 1871. Later the same year he went to the United States, served as assistant at the cathedral in Nashville, Tennessee, became rector of St. Columba Church, East Nashville, in 1878 and the following year of the Nashville cathedral, and was administrator of the diocese in 1880–83. He was named pastor of St. Joseph's parish, West Nashville, in 1885, vicar-general of the see in 1886, and was appointed first bishop of Concordia, Kansas (transferred to Salina in 1944), in 1887. He was transferred to Omaha, Nebraska, in 1891 and held that position until his death in Omaha on Jan. 8.

SCHAAF, VALENTINE THEODORE (1883–1946), minister general. Born in Cincinnati, Ohio, on Mar. 18, he was educated at St. Francis Seraphic College in 1896–1901, joined the Order of Friars Minor in Cincinnati in 1901, and was professed in 1902. He continued his education at Franciscan monasteries at Louisville (Kentucky), Cincinnati, and Oldenburg (Indiana), where he was ordained in 1909. He taught at St. Francis Preparatory Seminary until 1918 when he resumed his studies at Catholic University (S.T.D. 1919, J.C.B. 1919, J.C.L. 1920, J.C.D. 1921) and then taught canon law at Holy Family Monastery in Oldenburg from 1921 to 1923, when he began teaching canon law at Catholic University. He was dean of the canon law faculty in 1933–36, when he was also definitor of his province, St. John Baptist, and became general definitor for English-speaking Franciscans at Rome in 1939, was named consultor of the Congregation of the Sacraments in 1940, and taught canon law at the Franciscan International House of Studies, the Atheneum Antonianum. He was designated minister general of his order by Pope Pius XII in 1945—the first American to be so honored—and died eighteen months later in Rome on Dec. 1.

SCHEERER, LOUIS ALOYSIUS C. (1909–66), bishop. Born in Philadelphia on Feb. 10, he was educated at Providence (Rhode Island) College, joined the Dominicans, and continued his education at Dominican Theological College in Washington, D.C. He was ordained in 1935 and was consecrated bishop of Multan, Pakistan, in 1960. He died in Pakistan on Jan. 27.

SCHENK, FRANCIS JOSEPH (1901–69), bishop. Born in Superior, Wisconsin, on Apr. 1, he was educated at St. Thomas Military Academy, St. Thomas College (B.A. 1922), and St. Paul (Minnesota) Seminary, and was ordained in 1926. He continued his education at Catholic University (S.T.B. 1926, J.C.D. 1928), was secretary to Archbishop Austin Dowling of St. Paul in 1928–30, and was vice-chancellor of the archdiocese in 1930–34. He taught at St. Paul Seminary in 1934–42 and was vicar-general of the archdiocese and rector of the cathedral from 1942 until 1945, when he was appointed third bishop of Crookston, Minnesota. He established a diocesan newspaper, *Our Northwest Diocese,* the Catholic Truth Organization, and the Catholic Social Service Agency. He also established some thirty churches in the diocese and set up summer boarding schools for the children of the 5,000 migrant Mexican workers who labored in the diocese each year. He was transferred to Duluth, Minnesota, as its fourth bishop in 1960, resigned in 1969, and died later in that year on Oct. 28 in Duluth.

SCHER, PHILIP GEORGE (1880–1953), bishop. Of German immigrant parents, he was born in Belleville, Illinois, on Feb. 22, was educated at the Josephinum, Columbus, Ohio, in 1893–96 and the Propaganda, Rome, in 1893–96, and was ordained in Rome in 1904. He taught at the Josephinum in 1903–4, and then went to California because of ill health and was incardinated into the diocese of Monterey-Fresno. He was curate at St. Vibiana Cathedral in 1904–5, Our Lady of Sorrows Church, Santa Barbara, in 1905–8, and was pastor of Our Lady of Mt. Carmel Church in Monticeto in 1908–11, at Hanford in 1911–18, of St. Francis Church, Bakersfield, in 1918–24, and at Capitola in 1924. He became vicar-general of the Monterey-Fresno diocese in 1930, and was administrator of the see from 1931 until 1933, when he was appointed its bishop. He paid off the debts he had inherited, developed the educational facilities of the diocese, founding ten new catechetical centers, and established eleven new parishes and churches for Mexicans, Chinese, and blacks. He suffered a stroke in 1946 from which he never recovered, and he died in Fresno on Jan. 3.

SCHERER, SISTER MARY JOSEPH (1883–1967), educator. Born in Peoria, Illinois, on Sept. 28, she joined the Sisters of Loretto at the Foot of the Cross and was educated at Creighton University, Omaha, Nebraska (B.A. 1917, M.A. 1921) and at De Paul University, Chicago (Ph.D. 1925). She taught English at Loretto academies in Kansas City, Missouri, in 1905–6, 1919–21, 1926–29, in Colorado in 1906–14, St. Mary's Academy in Denver in 1914–17, and became a professor of English at Webster College, Webster Groves, Missouri, in 1921, and served as librarian in 1929–37. She was an avid promoter of Catholic literature and authors, and in 1932 founded the Gallery of Living Catholic Authors and was its director until she resigned in 1960. She died on June 5 in St. Louis.

SCHEXNAYDER, MAURICE (1895–1981), bishop. Born in Wallace, Louisiana, on Aug. 13, he was educated at St. Joseph's Seminary, St. Benedict, Louisiana, St. Mary's Seminary, Baltimore, and the North American College, Rome, and was ordained in Rome in 1925. He was a curate at St. John's Church, Plaquamine, Louisiana, in 1925–29, chaplain at Louisiana State University in 1929–46, chaplain of the Knights of Columbus in Louisiana in 1932–44, and pastor of St. Francis de Sales Church, Houma, Louisiana, in 1946–50. In 1947 he was made a domestic prelate. He was named titular bishop of Tuscamia and auxiliary of Lafayette, Louisiana, in 1950 and became bishop of that see in 1956. He resigned in 1972 and died in Lafayette on Jan. 23.

SCHINNER, AUGUSTIN FRANCIS (1863–1937), bishop. Born in Milwaukee, Wisconsin, on May 1, he was educated at St. Francis Seminary there and was ordained in 1886. He taught at St. Francis until 1893, became secretary to Archbishop Frederick Katzer of Milwaukee and vicar-general of the diocese, and in 1905 was consecrated first bishop of Superior, Wisconsin. He resigned in 1913, but the following year he was appointed first bishop of the newly established diocese of Spokane, Washington. During his administration he greatly expanded the facilities of the see, building twenty churches, five schools, and a hospital. He also brought the Franciscans, Poor Clares, and Sisters of Charity into the diocese. He resigned in 1925 and was appointed titular bishop of Sala and died in Milwaukee on Feb. 7.

SCHLARMAN, JOSEPH HENRY (1879–1951), archbishop. Born in Breese Township, Illinois, on Feb. 23, he was educated at Francis Solanus College (now Quincy College), Illinois, and the University of Innsbruck, Austria, and was ordained in Brixen, Tyrol, in 1904 for the diocese of Belleville, Illinois. He continued his studies at the Gregorian, Rome, receiving his doctorate in philosophy and canon law in 1907, served as a curate at the Belleville cathedral in 1907–9, was chancellor of the diocese in 1909–30, and was made a domestic prelate in 1921. He was consecrated bishop of Peoria, Illinois, in 1930. He was chairman of Governor Henry Horner's Commission for the Study of Prison Problems in 1936–37, and president of the National Catholic Rural Life Conference in 1943–45 (he had prepared the constitution of the conference), and was made an Assistant at the Pontifical Throne in 1950; the following year he was given the personal title of archbishop. Interested in Mexico and Central America, he was one of the founders of Montezuma Seminary in New Mexico to train Mexican clergy. He wrote *Mexico, Land of Volcanoes* (1949), *From Quebec to New Orleans* (1930), and *Why Prisons?* (1938). He died in Peoria on Nov. 10.

SCHMIDT, AUSTIN GUILFORD (1883–1960), educator, publisher. Born in Cincinnati, Ohio, he was educated at Xavier College there, at St. Stanislaus Seminary in Florissant, Missouri, and at the University of St. Louis (B.A. 1906, M.A. 1907). He joined the Jesuits, taught at St. Ignatius High School, Cleveland, Ohio, in 1909–10 and at St. Ignatius High School, Chicago, in 1910–14, and was ordained in 1917. He continued his studies at the University of Michigan (Ph.D. 1923), was professor of education at St. Louis in 1922–25 and at Loyola University, Chicago, in 1925–52, also serving as dean of Loyola's Graduate School in 1926–32 and as director of Loyola University Press beginning in 1928. He died in West Baden, Indiana, on July 22.

SCHMIEDELER, EDGAR (1892–1963), sociologist. One of seventeen children, Louis Schmiedeler was born in Kansas City, Kansas, on Dec. 15 and was educated at St. Benedict's College, Atchison, Kansas, and St. Vincent's College, Latrobe, Pennsylvania (B.A. 1916) and St. Vincent's Seminary (M.A. 1916, S.T.L. 1917). He joined the Benedictines in 1912, taking the name Edgar, was professed in 1915, and was ordained in 1918. He taught at St. Benedict's Seminary in 1919–21 and St. Benedict's College in 1922–25 and 1927–30, and received his Ph.D. from Catholic University in 1927. He was director of the Rural Life Bureau in 1930–40 and of the Family Life Bureau of the National Catholic Welfare Conference in 1931–56. He also was founder and executive secretary of the Catholic Conference on Family Life from 1933. He taught sociology at Catholic University in 1932–35 and began lecturing at its School of Social Sciences in 1937, served as associate editor of *The Catholic Family Monthly* and *Rural Sociology,* wrote numerous articles for Catholic magazines, and was the author of several books on marriage and the family, among them *Introductory Study of the Family* (1930), *The Sacred Bond* (1940), *A Better Rural Life* (1938), and *Marriage and the Family* (1946). He died in Kansas City, Kansas, on June 8.

SCHMONDIUK, JOSEPH M. (1912–78), archbishop. Born in Wall, Pennsylvania, on Aug. 6, he was orphaned at seven and raised at St. Basil Orphanage in Philadelphia. He was educated at the Angelicum University and the Propa-

ganda, Rome (S.T.L.), and was ordained in Rome in 1936. He engaged in parish work in Aliquippa, Pennsylvania, Passaic, New Jersey, and the Ukrainian Immaculate Conception Church, Hamtramck, Michigan, in 1948–58, also serving as diocesan consultant in 1949–55, and was made a monsignor in 1953. He was a synodal judge in 1955–56, was consecrated titular bishop of Zeugma in Syria and auxiliary of the Ukrainian apostolic archeparchy of Philadelphia in 1956, and was appointed bishop of the Ukrainian Catholic diocese of Stamford, Connecticut, in 1961. In 1977 he was made archbishop of the Ukrainian Catholic archeparchy of Philadelphia. He died there the following year on Dec. 25.

SCHNELLER, JOSEPH H. (d. 1860). A priest of the New York diocese stationed in Brooklyn, he became one of a group of priests known for their fiery defense of the Church in bitter public controversies with opponents of Catholicism in the metropolitan area. A contributor to *Truth Teller,* he helped found the *Weekly Register and Catholic Diary* in 1833 to rival the *Truth Teller* when he felt the latter had become too pro-trustee in the trustee dispute racking the Church in the United States at that time; it lasted only three years. He became pastor of St. Paul's, Brooklyn's oldest Catholic church, in 1847, three years after he and Fr. Charles Constantine Pise had founded the *Catholic Expositor,* which published the first strictly Catholic poetry in the United States in English. He remained in that position until his death.

SCHREMBS, JOSEPH (1866–1945), archbishop. Born in Wuzelhofenear, Ratisbon, Bavaria, on Mar. 12, he was brought to the United States in 1877. He was educated at St. Vincent's Archabbey in Latrobe, Pennsylvania, and at Laval University in Montreal, Quebec, and was ordained at Grand Rapids, Michigan, in 1889. He served as curate at St. Mary's Church, Grand Rapids, and as curate and then pastor of St. Mary's Church, Bay City, Michigan, in 1889–1900, was pastor of St. Mary's in Grand Rapids in 1900–11, was named vicar-general of the diocese of Grand Rapids in 1902, and was made a domestic prelate in 1906. He was appointed titular bishop of Sophene and auxiliary of Grand Rapids in 1911, and later that year was appointed first bishop of the newly created diocese of Toledo, Ohio. He was made an Assistant at the Pontifical Throne in 1914, was one of the four bishops on the National Catholic War Council in 1917–19, was episcopal chairman of lay organizations of the National Catholic Welfare Conference (NCWC) in 1919–34, in which post he was one of those mainly responsible for the establishment of the National Council of Catholic Men and the National Council of Catholic Women in 1920. He also served as president of the Priests' Eucharistic League. He was appointed fifth bishop of Cleveland, Ohio, in 1921 and the following year was one of those who helped convince Pope Pius XI to allow the National Catholic Welfare Conference to be made into a permanent body. During his tenure as bishop of Cleveland, he reorganized the chancery office and the agencies of the diocese, was a firm believer in Catholic education, and opened new schools in the see. He was also a leader in church-music reform, composing several hymns and helping produce manuals of Gregorian chant and music textbooks. He was given the personal title of archbishop in 1939 and died in Cleveland on Nov. 2.

SCHRIECK, SISTER LOUISE VAN DER (1813–86), superior. The tenth of

thirteen children of a lawyer, Josephine Susanna Van Der Schrieck was born in Bergen-op-Zoom, Holland, on Nov. 14. She was educated by the Sisters of Notre Dame de Namur at Namur, Belgium, and joined them there in 1837, taking the name Louise. She was professed in 1839. In response to a plea from Bishop John Purcell of Cincinnati for nuns for his see, she and seven other nuns volunteered and in 1840 went to the United States and established in Cincinnati the first foundation of her institute outside of Belgium. She was named superior of the Cincinnati community in 1845 and superior-provincial of the country east of the Rocky Mountains in 1848, and she held that position until her death in Cincinnati on Dec. 3. While superior-provincial, she founded twenty-six convents, opened two novitiates, and increased the number of nuns in her province to some twelve hundred, most of them engaged in teaching in more than fifty schools; she also opened night schools for Catholic immigrants in the major cities in which she had schools.

SCHULER, ANTHONY JOSEPH
(1869–1944), bishop. Born at St. Mary's, Pennsylvania, on Sept. 20, he joined the Jesuits in 1886 and was educated at St. Stanislaus Seminary in Florissant, Missouri, St. Louis University, and Woodstock (Maryland) College. In 1901 he was ordained. He taught at Sacred Heart (now Regis) College, Denver, Colorado, in 1893–98 and in 1902–3 and was its president in 1903–6; he was at St. Stanislaus Seminary in 1906–7 and engaged in parish work in Texas during 1907–10 and at Denver in 1910–15. He was consecrated first bishop of the newly established diocese of El Paso, Texas, in 1915, built St. Patrick's Cathedral there, resigned in 1942, and died in El Paso on June 5.

SCHULTE, AUGUSTINE JOSEPH (1856–1937), educator. Born in Philadelphia on May 5, he was educated for the priesthood at St. Charles Borromeo Seminary, Overbrook, Philadelphia, the North American College, Rome, and the Urban College, Rome (S.T.L.) and was ordained in Rome in 1882. He was vice-rector in 1883–84 and prorector in 1884–85 of the North American College, and helped thwart the Italian Government's plan to confiscate its buildings on the grounds that the college was owned by American citizens. He returned to Philadelphia in 1885 to teach at St. Charles Borromeo, and he spent the rest of his life teaching liturgy and modern languages. He wrote articles for the *Catholic Encyclopedia* and Catholic magazines and two manuals, *Benedicenda* (1907) and *Consecranda* (1907). He died in Philadelphia on May 23.

SCHWAB, CHARLES MICHAEL (1862–1939), industrialist. Born in Williamsburg, Pennsylvania, on Feb. 18, he left school after graduating from high school in 1880, began working as a grocery clerk, and later in 1880 started at the Andrew Carnegie–owned Edgar Thompson Steel Works in Braddock, Pennsylvania, at one dollar per day. He soon became chief engineer and assistant manager, married Emma Eurana Dinkey in 1883, and was made superintendent at the Homestead (Pennsylvania) Steel Works in 1887. Two years later he returned to the Thompson Works as superintendent, was sent back to Homestead to restore peaceful labor-management relations after the bitter bloody strike of 1892 there, and did so. He became president of Carnegie Steel, Ltd., in 1897 and left in 1901 to head the newly formed United States Steel Corporation, which he had convinced J. P. Morgan to form. He resigned as president in 1903 to become head of Bethlehem Steel Company (he had bought control of it in 1901), merged with the United States Shipbuilding Company, secured control of it, and incorporated it as the Bethlehem Steel Corporation in 1904, building it into the largest independent producer in the field. He introduced executive profit-sharing and an incentive wage system for employees, and recognized the open shop. During World War I he entered the marine-engineering and armament-manufacturing field and was a major supplier of war materials to the United States and its allies. He served as director general of the Emergency Fleet Corporation in 1918 and brought the lagging ship-building program to new production highs. He was president of the American Iron and Steel Institute in 1927–32, acting as spokesman for the industry. He was renowned for his philanthropies, contributed generously to Catholic enterprises, and died in New York City on Sept. 18.

SCHWEBACH, JAMES (1847–1921), bishop. Born in Platen, Luxembourg, on Aug. 15, he was educated at Diekirch College, went to the United States in 1864, and continued his studies at St. Francis Seminary, Milwaukee, Wisconsin, and was ordained in St. Paul, Minnesota, in 1870. He was pastor of St. Mark's Church, La Crosse, Wisconsin, from 1870 to 1892 and was named vicar-general of the La Crosse diocese in 1882. He was administrator of the see in 1891, was appointed its third bishop later that year, inaugurated a program of church and school construction during his bishopric, and died in La Crosse on June 6.

SCHWERTNER, AUGUSTUS JOHN (1870–1939), bishop. Born in Canton, Ohio, on Dec. 23, he was educated at Canisius College, Buffalo, New York, and St. Mary's Seminary, Cleveland,

Ohio, and was ordained in 1897. He served as a curate at St. Columba's Church, Youngstown, Ohio, and was pastor of St. Anthony's Church, Milan, Ohio, in 1897–1903, of St. Mary's Church, Rockford, Ohio, in 1903–7, and of St. John's Church, Lima, Ohio, in 1907–13. He served as chancellor of the diocese of Toledo in 1913–21 and was made a domestic prelate in 1916. He was consecrated bishop of Wichita, Kansas, in 1921 and remained in that position until his death in Wichita on Oct. 2.

SCULLY, WILLIAM ALOYSIUS (1894–1969), bishop. Born in New York City on Aug. 6, he was educated at Cathedral College there, St. Joseph's Seminary, Dunwoodie, Yonkers, New York, and Catholic University. He was ordained in 1919, was named titular bishop of Pharsalus and coadjutor of Albany, New York, in 1945, and succeeded to the see in 1954. He retired from active administration of the diocese in 1966 but retained the title and died in Albany on Jan. 5.

SEARLE, GEORGE MARY (1839–1918), astronomer, mathematician. Son of American banker Thomas Searle and Englishwoman Anne Noble Searle, he was born in London on June 27, was orphaned soon after he was brought to the United States in 1840, and was raised by Unitarian relatives in Brookline, Massachusetts. He was educated at Harvard (B.A. 1857, M.A. 1860), where he received a prize for a paper on astronomy. On his graduation he became a mathematician on the staff of the *United States Ephemeris and Nautical Almanac* and then became an assistant at the Dudley Observatory, Albany, New York; while there he discovered the asteroid Pandora in 1858. He entered the United States Coast Survey in 1859 and taught mathematics at the

United States Naval Academy during the Civil War in 1862–64. He became a Catholic in 1862, was an assistant at the Harvard Observatory in 1866–68, and joined the Paulists in 1868. He was ordained in 1871 and taught theology at the Paulist scholasticate until 1889, and then, 1889–97, he taught science at the newly established House of Studies in Washington, D.C., and also mathematics and astronomy at Catholic University; he received a Ph.D. from Catholic University in 1896 and established his own observatory there in 1890. He was associated with the Smithsonian Astrophysical Observatory in 1900–11 and served as superior of the Paulists in 1904–09. He was then appointed Newman Club chaplain at the University of California, Berkeley, spent his last years at the Apostolic Mission House in Washington, D.C., and died in New York City on July 7. He wrote many articles for scientific and religious magazines and was the author of *Elements of Geometry* (1877), *Plain Facts for Fair Minds* (1895), *Truths About Christian Science* (1916), and several pamphlets on religious subjects.

SEELOS, FRANCIS X. (1819–67), missionary. Born in Füssen, Bavaria, on Jan. 11, he studied at Augsburg and Munich and then joined the Redemptorists. He volunteered for the American missions in 1843, made his profession at the Redemptorist novitiate in Baltimore the following year, and was ordained later in 1844 at Baltimore. He served for a time at St. James's Church there and in 1845 was sent to St. Philomena's Church in Pittsburgh, where John Neumann became his spiritual adviser. Seelos became superior of the Pittsburgh Redemptorist community in 1851 and then was sent to St. Alphonsus Church, Baltimore, where he suffered a serious illness. On his recovery he was appointed spiritual director of the Redemptorist students there, and in 1860 he refused the bishopric of Pittsburgh. He spent the rest of his life in missionary work and died of yellow fever on Oct. 4 in New Orleans, contracted while ministering to the victims of an epidemic. He was a popular confessor and was known for his sanctity. His cause for beatification was introduced by Fr. Mathias Raus, superior general of the Redemptorists in 1894–1909.

SEEP, JOSEPH (1838–1928), executive, philanthropist. Born in Voerdam, Germany, on May 7, he was brought to the United States when a boy in 1849, became a cigar maker and cotton buyer in Kentucky, and in 1859 moved to Titusville, Pennsylvania, when oil was discovered there. He became an associate with John D. Rockefeller in the oil business, established offices all over the country for the purchase of oil, and was associated with the Standard Oil and South Penn companies. He also became a director of other businesses and banking companies. He was known for his philanthropies and charities, for which he was honored by the papacy, and he died in Titusville on Apr. 1.

SEGALE, BLANDINA (1850–1941), missionary. Born in Cicagna near Genoa, Italy, on Jan. 23, she was brought to the United States when she was four by her parents, who settled in Cincinnati, Ohio. She was educated privately and in public schools, served as a nurse at the battle of Nashville in 1864, when she was fourteen, and in 1866 joined the Sisters of Mercy in Cincinnati; she was professed two years later. She taught at St. Peter's School, Steubenville, and in Dayton, Ohio, 1868–72. In 1872 she was sent to Trinidad, Colorado, and spent the next twenty years on the frontier of Colorado and New Mexico, where she met Billy the Kid,

among others. She was principal of St. Patrick's School, Pueblo, Colorado, in 1892–93 and of the Boys' Boarding School, Fayetteville, Ohio, in 1893–94. In 1897 she was assigned to work among the Italian immigrants in Cincinnati. She established centers throughout the city to aid them and helped establish the Santa Maria Italian Educational and Industrial School in 1897. She retired from public life when ninety and spent the rest of her life teaching at various schools in Ohio. She wrote several religious books and, based on diaries she had kept while doing missionary work in the Southwest, *At the End of the Santa Fe Trail* (1932); she was also editor of *Veritas Santa Maria* in 1926–31. She died at Mt. St. Joseph, Ohio, in January.

SEGHERS, CHARLES JOHN (1839–86), bishop. Born in Ghent, Belgium, on Dec. 26, he was raised by his uncle after being orphaned at an early age. He was educated at the diocesan seminary at Ghent and the American College, Louvain, and was ordained in 1863. Later that year he went as a missionary to Vancouver Island, Canada, and after a decade of missionary work among the natives and pioneer settlers, he was appointed bishop of Vancouver Island in 1873 (which diocese then had jurisdiction over Alaska) to succeed Bishop Demers, who had died in 1871. Seghers spent much time visiting settlements in Alaska, was named coadjutor to Archbishop François Blanchet of Oregon City in 1878, and succeeded to the see in 1880. He helped establish an abbey at Mt. Abbey for the Benedictines, and when no bishop could be found to succeed him at Vancouver Island, he resigned the see of Oregon City in 1884 and returned to his old see as archbishop in 1885. He was devoted to the Alaskan missions and made five trips there, founded permanent missions at

Sitka and Juneau in 1885, and on his fifth trip was murdered on Nov. 28 by a man named Francis Fuller, whose mind had become unbalanced by the hardships of the trip. Seghers is often called the "apostle of Alaska."

SEIDENBUSCH, RUPERT (1830–95), bishop. Born in Munich, Bavaria, Germany, on Oct. 13 (or Oct. 30), he emigrated to the United States, studied at St. Vincent's Seminary, Beatty, Pennsylvania, joined the Benedictines in 1850, and was ordained in 1852. He engaged in missionary work in New Jersey and Pennsylvania the next decade and in 1862 was elected prior of St. Vincent's; he was elected first abbot of St. Louis-on-the-Lake (St. John's), Collegeville, Minnesota, in 1866. He resigned his abbacy in 1875, when he was appointed titular bishop of Halia and vicar apostolic of northern Minnesota. He resigned his vicariate in 1888 and died in Richmond, Virginia, on June 2.

SEMMES, RAPHAEL (1809–77), admiral. Born in Charles County, Maryland, on Sept. 27, he was raised by an uncle when his parents died during his childhood. He was appointed to the United States Naval Academy in 1826, was given a leave of absence in 1832, studied law, was admitted to the bar, and in 1835 returned to the Navy. In 1837 he married Elizabeth Spencer. He served on various vessels and on survey duty on the southern coast and the coast of the Gulf of Mexico. He settled his family at Prospect Hill, Baldwin County, Alabama, near Pensacola, Florida, and in 1849 near Mobile, Alabama. In the Mexican War he served both afloat and ashore, was made a commander in 1855, resigned from the Navy at the outbreak of the Civil War, and became a commander in the Confederate Navy, achieving the rank of rear admiral in 1865. He was in com-

mand of the cruiser *Sumter* in 1861, which did considerable damage to Union shipping before it was bottled up in Gibraltar in January 1862. Later that year he was given command of the *Alabama*. Under his command it became the most famous naval vessel of the Civil War, and during its two-year cruise it captured or destroyed sixty-five Union vessels and sank the warship *Hatteras;* eventually, on June 19, 1864, it was sunk off the coast of France by the Union ship *Kearsage*. He escaped to England and returned to Virginia in 1865 and commanded the naval defense of Richmond until Richmond fell, when he burned his ships and surrendered. He was paroled but was arrested on his return to Mobile. By presidential order he was released after three months' imprisonment. On his return home he was driven by political pressure out of positions as probate judge of Mobile County, as professor at Louisiana State Seminary (now University), and as editor of the Memphis *Daily Bulletin*. He resumed his private law practice and wrote several books about his experiences, among them *Service Afloat and Ashore During the Mexican War* (1851), *Memoirs of Service, Afloat During the War Between the States* (1869), and the two-volume *The Cruise of the Alabama and the Sumter* (1864). He died at his home at Point Clear, Alabama, on Aug. 26.

SEMMES, THOMAS JENKINS (1824–99), jurist. Born in Washington, D.C. on Dec. 16, he graduated from Georgetown College in 1842, and after a year in the law office of Clement Cox in Georgetown he studied at Harvard Law School and received his law degree in 1845. He was admitted to the Washington bar in 1846, married Myra Eulalia Knox in 1850, settled in New Orleans, and began a law practice with Matthew C. Edwards, a partnership that was dissolved because of a speech Semmes made denouncing the anti-Catholic Know-Nothing movement; he often spoke on things Catholic and in defense of the Church. He was elected to the state legislature in 1856, was appointed U.S. District Attorney for eastern Louisiana in 1857, served as state attorney in 1859–61, and was a member of the Louisiana convention of 1861, where he helped draft the ordinance of secession. He represented Louisiana in the Confederate Assembly from 1862 until Lee's surrender and after the war returned to his law practice. He was professor of law at the University of Louisiana (Tulane) in 1873–79 and was president of the New Orleans Board of Education from 1877. He attended Louisiana's Constitutional Convention in 1879, was elected president of the American Bar Association in 1886, and died in New Orleans on Jan. 23.

SEMPLE, HENRY CHURCHILL (1853–1925), educator, author. Born in Montgomery, Alabama, on Oct. 18, he was educated at Mt. St. Mary's College, Emmitsburg, Maryland, and at the American College, Rome. In 1876 he joined the Jesuits. He was ordained in 1879, taught literature at Spring Hill College, Mobile, Alabama, and Georgetown College, was president of Immaculate Conception College, New Orleans, in 1895–99, and died in New Orleans on June 27. He was the author of *Anglican Orders* (1906), *Heaven Open to Souls* (1916), *American Liberty Enlightening the World* (1920), and several pamphlets. He also translated Hippolyte Delahaye's *St. John Berchmans* (1921).

SENAN, JOSÉ FRANCISCO DE PAULA (1760–1823), missionary. Born in Barcelona, Spain, on Mar. 3, he joined the Franciscans in 1774 and was sent to San Fernando College in Mexico City in 1784. He went to San Carlos Mission in California in 1787 and remained there until 1795, when he returned to Mexico to report on the state of the California missions. He returned to San Buenaventura Mission in 1798 and spent the rest of his life there, serving as *presidente* of the missions in 1812–15 and from 1819 until his death at Buenaventura on Aug. 24.

SENYSHYN, AMBROSE ANDREW (1903–76), archbishop. Born in Staryy Sambor, Galicia, on Feb. 23, he was educated at monastery colleges at Krechow and Lviw, Galicia and Warsaw, Poland. He was professed in the Order of St. Basil the Great in 1931 and was ordained in Krechow a few weeks later. He served as a curate at the Ukrainian Catholic College, Warsaw, in 1930–33, emigrated to the United States, and was a curate at St. Nicholas parish, Chicago, in 1933–37, and was its pastor and superior of the Ukrainian Catholic Church priests under the Order of St. Basil at Chicago in 1937–42. He was consecrated auxiliary bishop of the Ukrainian Catholic diocese of the United States in 1942, and was appointed apostolic exarch of the Byzantine rite apostolic exarchy of Stamford, Connecticut, in 1956. He became bishop of that exarchy in 1958 and in 1961 was appointed archbishop of the Philadelphia Ukrainian Catholic archeparchy in 1961. He died in Philadelphia on Sept. 11.

SERRA, JUNÍPERO (1713–84), missionary. Miguel José Serra was born at Petra on the island of Majorca, Spain, on Nov. 24. He studied under the Franciscans at Petra and Palma, joined the Franciscans at Palma in 1730, and took his vows the following year, taking the name Junípero. He was ordained in 1737, taught philosophy at St. Francis friary at Palma in 1740–43, received his doctorate in 1742, and occupied the

Duns Scotus chair of philosophy at the University of Palma in 1744–49. He was sent to San Fernando College in Mexico City in 1749, spent the first five months of 1750 at the college, and then was sent to work among the Pame Indians of Sierra Gorda. He remained with them until 1758, when he was recalled to Mexico City. He spent the next few years as an itinerant preacher throughout Mexico and teaching at San Fernando College until 1767, when he was appointed superior of a group of Franciscans appointed to replace the Jesuits, who were expelled from Spain and its territories by the king in 1767, at the Indian missions of Lower California. Two years later, when Spain began the conquest of Upper California, he accompanied Gaspar de Portolá's land expedition there and founded a mission at San Diego, the first of nine he established on the coast of California as far north as San Francisco over the next thirteen years, serving as *presidente* of them until his death. He was present at the founding of the presidio of Santa Barbara in 1782 but was prevented from establishing a mission there by Governor Philipe de Neve. He introduced agriculture and domestic animals and several European trades at the missions, raised the standard of living of the Indians, and frequently quarreled with the military over its treatment of the Indians. In 1773 he appealed to Viceroy Bucareli in Mexico City after a quarrel with the military commander, Pedro Fages, over his treatment of the Indians, and he was sustained in thirty of the thirty-two contentions he presented in his famous *Representación* to the Viceroy. He again quarreled with Neve over Serra's right to administer confirmation (he had been granted the faculty in 1778), and in 1781 Viceroy Mayorga upheld his right to do so. He is reported to have baptized some 6,000 and confirmed more than 5,300 persons, most of them Indians. He died at Mission San Carlos near Monterey, California, on Aug. 28. Serra was among the pioneer and guiding forces in the settlement of California, wrote numerous letters, and kept a *Diario* which was published more than a century after his death. He also translated a catechism into Pame. In 1931 his statue was placed in Statuary Hall in the Capitol, Washington, D.C., to represent the state of California, and in 1934 the process for his beatification was opened in Rome.

SESTINI, BENEDICT (1816–90), astronomer, editor. Born in Florence, Italy, on Mar. 20, he joined the Jesuits in Rome in 1836, studied mathematics at the Roman College, was appointed assistant to Fr. DeVico, director of the Roman Observatory, and in 1844 he was ordained. He was appointed to the chair of higher mathematics at the Roman College and made a series of sunspot drawings which were published in the 1847 Naval Observatory volume. He was forced to flee from Rome by the revolution of 1848. He went to the United States and taught at Georgetown until 1869; while there he founded the *Messenger of the Sacred Heart* in 1866, editing it until 1885. He was also the American director of the Apostleship of Prayer and the League of the Sacred Heart. He was transferred to the Jesuit scholasticate at Woodstock, Maryland, in 1969, retired to the novitiate at Frederick, Maryland, in 1885 when his health failed, and died there on Jan. 17. He published a series of textbooks on algebra, geometry, and trigonometry which never became popular and also wrote *Memoirs of the Roman College* (which included his "Catalogue of Star Colors," the first general review of the heavens for star colors), *Theoretical Mechanics* (1873), *Animal Physics* (1874), and *Principles of Cosmography* (1878).

SETON, ST. ELIZABETH ANN (1774–1821), foundress. The daughter of Dr. Richard Bayley, a prominent physician and first professor of anatomy at King's College (Columbia), New York City, and Catherine Charton Bayley, daughter of the rector of St. Andrew's Episcopal Church on Staten Island, Elizabeth Ann Bayley was born in New York City on Aug. 28. She early showed a religious bent, was educated by her father after her mother died when she was three, and became a prominent figure in New York society. In 1794 she married William Magee Seton, a successful merchant, and involved herself in social work, helping to found the Society for the Relief of Poor Widows with Children in 1797. The couple had five children, and when Seton was stricken with tuberculosis in 1803, he and Elizabeth and their oldest daughter, Anna Marie, went to Italy in the vain hope that he would be cured there. He died at Pisa, Italy, on Dec. 27, and Elizabeth returned to the United States. While in Italy she had been deeply moved by the kindness of the Italian Catholic family with whom she and her husband had stayed, the Filicchis, to her family and the appeal of the Catholicism she found around her. In 1805, despite the vigorous objections of her family and friends, she became a Catholic at St. Peter's Church in New York City. She was at once ostracized by her relatives and friends, all of whom were Protestants and were alienated by her conversion. Left almost penniless by her husband's death, she began teaching at a school in New York, but it soon closed. She then opened a boarding house for boys at a Protestant school, but when it was learned that her younger sister-in-law, Cecilia, was to become a Catholic, the boarding house was forced to close, so strong was the feeling against Elizabeth, and a movement was started to have her expelled from New York by an act of the legislature. At the suggestion of Fr. Louis DuBourg, then superior of the Baltimore Sulpicians and a professor at St. Mary's College in Baltimore, she opened a school for girls in Baltimore in 1808. She was soon joined by Cecilia and her sister Harriet, and they formed a community; Elizabeth took private vows before Archbishop John Carroll of Baltimore, who had confirmed her in New York in 1806, encouraged her to form a new community, and was her mentor. In June 1809 the community moved to a farm near Emmitsburg, Maryland, to take charge of an institution to teach poor children, the beginnings of the parochial school system in the United States. The new community applied to the Sisters of Charity of St. Vincent de Paul in France in 1810 for the rules of that order, and in 1812 Archbishop Carroll approved the rule, with some modifications. Over her objections Elizabeth was elected superior; she and thirteen others took their vows on July 19, 1813, and the Sisters of Charity were founded in the United States—the first American religious society. The order soon spread throughout the United States, and by the time of Mother Seton's death in Emmitsburg on Jan. 4, it numbered twenty communities. Her spirituality and piety caused her cause to be introduced at Rome in 1911, and she was canonized in 1975 by Pope Paul VI, with her feast day celebrated on Jan. 4—the first person born in the United States to be so honored. Her *Memoir, Letters, and Journal* were edited by her grandson Robert Seton and published in two volumes in 1869.

SETON, ROBERT (1839–1927), archbishop. The grandson of St. Elizabeth Ann Seton, he was born on Aug. 28 in Pisa, Italy, where his grandfather had died in 1803. He entered Mt. St. Mary's College, Emmitsburg, Maryland, in

1850, but in 1852 he accompanied his parents to Europe. He continued his studies in Spain and in Bonn, Germany, and in 1857 entered the Propaganda, Rome. Two years later he transferred to the American (North American) College in Rome, its first student, and in 1869 he entered the Accademia Ecclesiastici dei Nobili. He was ordained in 1865, became a papal chamberlain in 1866, and in 1867 was the first American to be made a prothonotary apostolic. He was an assistant at the cathedral in Newark, New Jersey, for a short period and then was named first chaplain of St. Elizabeth's Convent, Convent Station, New Jersey. He remained in this position until 1876, when he was named pastor of St. Joseph's Church in Jersey City, New Jersey. He was chief notary of the third Plenary Council of Baltimore in 1884, resigned his pastorate in 1901, and returned to Rome in 1902, where he acted as unofficial ambassador between the American people and the papacy and was a New York *Times* correspondent. He refused the archbishopric of Chicago when it was offered to him in 1903 but was appointed titular archbishop of Heliopolis later that year and was active in Roman ecclesiastical circles. He left Rome in 1914 because of financial reverses, spent the next several years in Europe, and returned to Convent Station in 1921. He died there on Mar. 22. He edited Mother Seton's writing, the two-volume *Memoir, Letters, and Journal* (1869) and wrote *Essays on Various Subjects Chiefly Roman* (1862), *An Old Family, or the Setons of Scotland and America* (1899), and *Memoirs of Many Years, 1839–1922* (1923).

SETON, WILLIAM (1835–1905), author. Grandson of St. Elizabeth Ann Seton and brother of Archbishop Robert Seton, he was born in New York City on Jan. 28 and was educated at St. John's (Fordham) College there, Mt. St. Mary's College, Emmitsburg, Maryland, and the University of Bonn. He traveled extensively abroad, was admitted to the New York bar, and began to practice law but left his practice to volunteer for the Union Army at the outbreak of the Civil War in 1861, becoming captain of the 4th New York Volunteers. He was wounded twice at the battle of Antietam and after his recuperation returned to the war as captain of the 16th Artillery during Grant's campaign against Richmond. After the war he devoted himself to writing, and among the books he published were *Romance of the Charter Oak* (1870), *The Pioneer* (1874), *Rachel's Fate, and Other Tales* (1882), and *Moira* (1884). After 1886 he wrote popular material on scientific subjects, especially on evolution, which his writings helped to popularize and articles on scientific themes in the *Catholic World* and the New York *Freeman's Journal* to acquaint Catholics with Darwin's theory of evolution, which he had accepted, and to encourage the study of science in Catholic institutions of higher learning. His *A Glimpse of Organic Life, Past and Present* (1897) was his attempt to reconcile Catholicism and evolution. He died in New York City on Mar. 15.

SHAHAN, THOMAS JOSEPH (1837–1932), educator. Born in Manchester, New Hampshire, on Sept. 11, he was educated at the Sulpician College, Montreal, in 1872–78, the North American College and the Roman Seminary, Rome, in 1878–82, and received his doctorate in theology and was ordained in Rome in 1882. He served as assistant at St. John's Church, New Haven, Connecticut, in 1882–83, and was chancellor of the diocese of Hartford, Connecticut, in 1883–88, and when invited to teach at Catholic University by its rector, Msgr. John J.

Keane, he first engaged in graduate studies at the University of Berlin under Adolph Harnack in 1889–91. He also studied at the Sorbonne and Institut Catholique in Paris under Louis Duchesne and finally became professor of Church history at Catholic University in 1891. He founded and was editor of the *Catholic University Bulletin* in 1895–1909 and became rector of the university in 1909, serving in that position until his retirement in 1928. He was made a domestic prelate in 1909, was appointed titular bishop of Germanicopolis in 1914, was one of the original board of editors of the Catholic Encyclopedia, serving as associate editor in 1905–13, and wrote some 200 articles for the encyclopedia. He was active in the founding of Trinity College in Washington, D.C., was president of the (later National) Catholic Educational Association in 1909–28, and in 1910 helped found the National Conference of Catholic Charities, serving as its president until 1929. He also helped found the Catholic Association for International Peace in 1927, when he was named its honorary president. During his rectorship at Catholic University, he expanded its faculty fourfold and tripled its enrollment, added new departments, enlarged its physical plant, and founded the John K. Mullen Library, began the Shrine of the Immaculate Conception, and developed the university into a center of scholarship and education of the highest order. He retired from the rectorship in 1928 to Holy Cross Academy in Washington, D.C., and died in Washington on Mar. 9. He was honored by several universities, was made an Assistant at the Pontifical Throne, and was the author of several books, among them *The Blessed Virgin in the Catacombs* (1892), *The Beginnings of Christianity* (1903), *The Middle Ages* (1904), *St. Patrick in History* (1904), and *The House of God* (1905).

SHANLEY, JOHN (1852–1909), bishop. Born in Albion, New York, on Jan. 4, he was educated at St. Vincent's College (Cape Girardeau, Missouri), St. John's College (Collegeville, Minnesota), and the Propaganda (Rome). He was ordained in Rome in 1874. He engaged in pastoral work for the next decade and a half and in 1889 was consecrated in St. Paul as first bishop of the newly established diocese of Jamestown, North Dakota (changed to the diocese of Fargo in 1897). He founded and was editor of the diocesan paper, *The Bulletin of the Diocese of Fargo,* greatly increased the number of religious, churches, and schools in the see and died in Fargo on July 16.

SHANAHAN, JEREMIAH FRANCIS (1834–86), bishop. The brother of John Walter Shanahan, who became one of his successors as bishop of Harrisburg, Pennsylvania, he was born at Silver Lake, Susquehanna County, Pennsylvania on July 13. He was educated at St. Joseph's College in Binghamton, New York, and St. Charles Borromeo Seminary in Overbrook, Philadelphia, and was ordained in 1859. He was head of the Philadelphia preparatory seminary at Glen Riddle, Pennsylvania, from 1859 until 1868, when he was consecrated first bishop of the newly created diocese of Harrisburg. He remained in that post until his death there on Sept. 24.

SHANAHAN, JOHN WALTER (1846–1916), bishop. The brother of Jeremiah Shanahan, first bishop of Harrisburg, Pennsylvania, he was born at Silver Lake, Pennsylvania, on Jan. 2, was educated at St. Joseph's College, Binghamton, New York, and St. Charles Borromeo Seminary, Overbrook, Philadelphia, and was ordained in 1869. He engaged in pastoral work in the Philadelphia archdiocese, was named superintendent of schools there in 1894, and in 1899 was appointed third bishop of Harrisburg. He held that position until his death there on Feb. 19; he was one of the founders of the Sisters of St. Casimir in 1907 devoted to teaching refugee Lithuanian children.

SHAUGHNESSY, GERALD (1887–1950), bishop. Born in Everett, Massachusetts, on May 19, he was educated at Boston College (B.A. 1909), taught in high schools in Maryland, Montana, and Utah, and in 1916 joined the Marists, taking his perpetual vows in 1918. He studied theology at the Marist College, Washington, D.C. in 1916–20 and was ordained there in 1920. He taught theology at the Marist College in Washington in 1920–23 and 1929–30, at Notre Dame Seminary, New Orleans, in 1923–24, and served on Marist Mission Bands in 1924–28. He became master of the second novitiate in Washington in 1932 and the following year was appointed bishop of Seattle, Washington. He put the finances of the diocese in order, launched a building program, convened a diocesan synod in 1938, and suffered a stroke in 1945 from which he never completely recovered. He was a contributor to the Catholic Encyclopedia, wrote *Has the Immigrant Kept the Faith?* (1925) and died in Seattle on May 18.

SHAW, JOHN WILLIAM (1863–1934), bishop. Born in Mobile, Alabama, on Dec. 12, he was educated at St. Finian's Seminary, Navan, Ireland, and the Propaganda and the North American College, Rome, and was ordained in Mobile in 1888. He became an assistant at the Mobile cathedral, engaged in pastoral work, was appointed rector of the cathedral in 1891, and served as chancellor of the diocese in 1891–1910. He was appointed titular bishop of Castabala and coadjutor of

San Antonio, Texas, in 1910 and succeeded to the see the following year. He was made an Assistant at the Pontifical Throne in 1916 and was appointed first archbishop of New Orleans in 1918 when that see was made an archdiocese. He convoked the sixth diocesan synod in 1922, the first in thirty-three years, founded Notre Dame Seminary in New Orleans in 1923, established the archdiocesan newspaper, *Catholic Action of the South* in 1932, brought new religious groups into the archdiocese, and died in New Orleans on Nov. 2.

SHEA, JOHN DAWSON GILMARY (1824–92), historian. Son of James Shea, principal of Columbia College grammar school, and Mary Ann Flannigan Shea, he worked for a Spanish merchant and learned to read Spanish fluently when a boy, studied law, and was admitted to the New York bar in 1846 but decided he wanted a religious life and joined the Jesuits in 1848, taking the name Gilmary. He decided the priesthood was not for him and left the Jesuits in 1852 and, interested in history from his boyhood, began a study of early Indian missions in the United States; with the publication of several articles on the subject in the *United States Catholic Magazine,* his career as one of the outstanding historians of the American Church began. His *Discovery and Exploration of the Mississippi Valley* (1852) was the first of almost 250 books he was to produce. He married Sophie Savage in 1854, founded and edited the *U.S. Catholic Historical Magazine* in 1859–65, was founder of the American Catholic Historical Society, and its first president, in 1887, was literary editor of Frank Leslie's secular magazines and of Sadlier's *General Catholic Directory and Almanac* in 1859–90, and in 1888 became director of the *Catholic News,* a position he held until his death. He became the outstanding authority on

American aboriginals and wrote articles on the American Indians for the Encyclopaedia Britannica and the American Encyclopedia. He wrote many pamphlets on early explorers, and 1860 saw the first issue of the *Library of American Linguistics,* a series of fifteen volumes of grammars and dictionaries of Indian languages. Among his many other books were *The Life of Pius XI* (1877), *The Catholic Churches of New York City* (1878), *The Hierarchy of the Catholic Church in the United States* (1886), *The Story of a Great Nation* (1886), and the monumental four-volume *History of the Catholic Church in the United States* (1886–92), the pioneer work in the field. Called "the father of American Catholic Church history," he was awarded the first Laetare Medal in 1883, was honored by several colleges and universities, and died in Elizabeth, New Jersey, on Feb. 22.

SHEED, FRANCIS JOSEPH "FRANK" (1897–1981), author, publisher. Always known as Frank Sheed, he was born of Irish ancestry in Sydney, Australia, on Mar. 20, was educated at Sydney University (B.A., LL.B.), and went to England in 1922 to practice law. While in London he became a member of the Catholic Evidence Guild, whose members spoke about Catholicism on street corners, and he soon became one of its most active and knowledgeable speakers. Through the Guild he met Maisie Ward, who had been one of its founders, and they were married in 1926. The couple had two children, Rosemary and Wilfrid, who later became the well-known novelist and critic. Together Frank and Maisie founded the publishing house of Sheed & Ward in London in 1926 (a branch of the firm was opened in New York City in 1933), and it soon became one of the leading publishers of Catholic books in the English-speaking world, noted for

its outstanding authors. Sheed was a sought-after lecturer and a best-selling author as well as a leading publisher and was known for his ability to present theology, history, and philosophy in a clear, understandable style. He wrote some twenty books, among them the best-selling *Theology and Sanity* (1946), a translation of St. Augustine's *Confessions* (1943), considered by many to be the best English translation of that classic work, *Society and Sanity* (1953), *Map of Life* (1933), *Communism and Man* (1938), *Theology for Beginners* (1957), *To Know Christ Jesus* (1962), and his autobiography *The Church and I* (1974). He died in Jersey City, where the family had moved in 1940, on Nov. 20.

SHEEN, FULTON J. (1895–1979), archbishop. The son of a farmer of Irish ancestry, Newton Morris Sheen, and Delia Fulton Sheen, he was born in El Paso, Illinois, on May 8. Baptized Peter, he took the name John at confirmation but later adopted his mother's maiden name and used it throughout his career. When he was a child, the family moved to Peoria, Illinois, and he was educated at St. Viator's College, Bourbannais, Illinois (B.A. 1917, M.A. 1919), where he served on the staff of its newspaper, and at St. Paul (Minnesota) Seminary. He was ordained for the Peoria diocese in 1919, continued his studies at Catholic University (J.C.B. 1920), Louvain (Ph.D. 1923), the Sorbonne, and the Collegio Angelico, Rome (S.T.D. 1924), and taught at St. Edmund's College near Ware, England, in 1925. He was also made an *Agregé en philosophie* by Louvain in 1925—the first American to receive this honor. He returned to the United States the same year and became a curate at St. Patrick's Church, Peoria, had *God and Intelligence,* the first of more than sixty books he was to write, published that year and at the end of 1926 began teaching philosophy at Catholic University, continuing until 1950. He began to attract widespread attention with his dynamic and eloquent preaching, teaching, and lecturing. In 1930 he became the first regular speaker of the "Catholic Hour" on radio (by 1950 his broadcasts were to reach 4,000,000 listeners on 118 NBC stations). He was made a papal chamberlain in 1934 and a domestic prelate in 1935, and in 1940 he conducted the first religious service to be telecast in the United States. In 1951 he began a television program entitled "Life Is Worth Living," which in time was televised on 123 ABC television and broadcast on 300 ABC radio stations, reaching an estimated 30,000,000 people each week; it received the Emmy Award in 1952. It left the air in 1957, but in 1966 he began "The Bishop Sheen Program" (he had been named titular bishop of Caesariana and an auxiliary of New York in 1951); the program was phenomenally successful. He wrote two columns, "Bishop Sheen Writes" for the secular press and "God Love You" for the Catholic press, which were syndicated throughout the country, and edited *World Mission* and *Mission*. In 1950 he was named national director of the Society for the Propagation of the Faith, and in the sixteen years of his directorship he made it the principal Catholic mission organization in the world, raising millions of dollars for the missions. He was appointed bishop of Rochester, New York, in 1966 but resigned in 1969 and was appointed titular archbishop of Newport (Wales). He spent the rest of his life teaching and writing. A fierce opponent of Communism all his life but especially in the 1930s and the 1940s, he was the most listened-to American Catholic preacher of all time and was a pioneer in the use of radio and television for religious teaching. His flamboyantly theatrical style made him internationally known for six decades as he mingled his obvious learning and scholarship with a common touch that appealed to millions. He was appointed to the Papal Commission for Non-Believers in 1969 and attended the Vatican Council II in 1969–70, where he served on the Commission on the Missions. He was also famous for his many conversions to Catholicism of prominent people, received numerous honorary degrees and awards, and was named an Assistant at the Pontifical Throne in 1976. He died in New York City on Dec. 9. Among his books, many of which appeared on national bestseller lists, were *The Life of All Living* (1929), *Old Errors and New Labels* (1931), *The Eternal Galilean* (1934), *Jesus, Son of Mary* (1947, a juvenile), *Philosophy of Religion* (1948), *Peace of Soul* (1949), *Lift Up Your Heart* (1950), *The World's First Love* (1952), *Life Is Worth Living* (five volumes, 1953–57), *Life of Christ* (1958), *This Is The Mass* (1958), *Guide to Contentment* (1967), *Those Mysterious Priests* (1974), and the autobiographical *Treasure in Clay* (posthumously published in 1980).

SHEERAN, JAMES B. (1819–81), chaplain. Born in Temple Mehill, Longford, Ireland, he emigrated to Canada in 1831 and to the United States two years later. He worked as a tailor in Monroe, Michigan, and taught at a Redemptorist school there, married about 1842, and was widowed in 1849. He joined the Redemptorists in 1855, was ordained in 1858, and was sent to the Redemptorist church in New Orleans. At the outbreak of the Civil War, he became a chaplain with the Confederate Army, was assigned to the Army of Northern Virginia, and was captured by Union forces in the Shenandoah Valley in 1864. He was imprisoned for three months and then returned to New Orleans, where he ministered to the victims of the yellow fever plague of 1867. He left the Redemptorists soon thereafter and became pastor of the Church of the Assumption in Morristown, New Jersey, where he died on Apr. 13. While serving with the Army of Northern Virginia, he kept a diary of 1861–62 which is a valuable source of information about that army and its leaders.

SHEIL, BERNARD JAMES (1888–1969), archbishop. Born in Chicago on Feb. 18, he was educated at St. Viator's College, Bourbannais, Illinois, where he was known for his athletic prowess as a baseball player (he received offers from several major league teams but refused them in order to continue his priestly vocation) and was ordained in 1910. He served as a curate at St. Mel's Church, Chicago, in 1910–17, was a chaplain at the Great Lakes Naval Training Station during World War I, 1918–19, and on his return from chaplain service served as a curate at Holy Name Cathedral in 1919–23 and was also chaplain at Cook County jail, where he began his work with young people. He was chancellor of the Chicago archdiocese in 1924–28, founded the Sheil School of Social Studies in 1925, and converted the Lewis Aeronautical College in Chicago into a four-year liberal arts college. He served as secretary to Cardinal George Mundelein and was named auxiliary bishop of Chicago in 1928, was vicar-general of the see in 1929–40, and in 1930 founded the Catholic Youth Organization, which in time became the Church's leading youth group with a membership of ten million, serving as its director until 1954. He was pastor of St. Andrew's Church in 1935–66, was administrator of the Chicago archdiocese in 1939–40 following the death of Cardinal Mundelein in 1939, and reportedly President Franklin Roosevelt, who was his friend and whose social and labor policies he warmly supported, urged his appointment as archbishop of Chicago to succeed Mundelein. He publicly denounced the anti-Semitism of Fr. Coughlin, attended many interfaith meetings when such attendance was frowned upon by Church authorities, espoused the cause of the United Nations and of Zionism, helped Saul Alinsky establish the Back of the Yards Neighborhood Council, which became a model for working-class communities, and in 1940 helped Alinsky found the Industrial Areas Foundation to organize slum communities. He established radio station WFJL in 1949 to disseminate Catholic news and developed it into the most powerful Catholic radio outlet in the United States, and in 1954 his scathing attack on Senator Joseph McCarthy attracted nationwide attention. He was made an Assistant at the Pontifical Throne in 1953, was given the personal title of archbishop by Pope John XXIII in 1959, and retired in 1966, when Archbishop John Cody removed him as pastor of St. Andrew's against his will. He retired to Tucson, Arizona, and died there on Sept. 13. Archbishop Sheil was one of the most liberal and controversial Catholic prelates of his time. He crusaded for racial justice and civil rights, championed the poor and the young, and was an active supporter of labor and labor unions, frequently appearing on picket lines with the strikers during the fierce labor battles of the 1920s and 1930s, and was often called "the apostle of Youth" and "labor's bishop."

SHERIDAN, JOHN A. LAWRENCE (1893–1964), educator. Born in Troy, New York, on Oct. 31, he was educated at Mt. St. Mary's College in Emmitsburg, Maryland, (B.A. 1917) and at St. Mary's Seminary in Baltimore (M.A. 1921), and was ordained in 1921. He taught philosophy, history, and English at Mt. St. Mary's, was acting president in 1936–37, and was elected its seventeenth president in 1937. He was made a domestic prelate in 1938 and a prothonotary apostolic in 1957. During his tenure he tripled Mt. St. Mary's enrollment and greatly expanded its facilities. He retired in 1961 because of illness and died at Mt. St. Mary's on May 18.

SHERIDAN, PHILIP HENRY (1831–88), general. He was born of Irish immigrant parents in Albany, New York, on Mar. 6 and was brought to Ohio as a boy by his parents. He entered the United States Military Academy in 1848 and graduated in 1853, after a year's suspension for attacking a cadet officer he thought had been unfair to him. He served in campaigns against the Indians in Texas and Oregon and was made a captain and chief quartermaster of army troops in southwest Missouri. He was General Halleck's quartermaster during the Corinth campaign at the outbreak of the Civil War, and in 1862 he was commissioned colonel of the 2nd Michigan Volunteer Cavalry, rising in rank within a month to brigadier general of the volunteers. He practically saved General Rosecrans' army by his fierce resistance to a Confederate advance at Stone River, and in December 1862 he was promoted to the rank of major general. During the next two years he distinguished himself for his daring and fighting ability that made him the outstanding cavalry commander of the Union armies. In 1864, when Ulysses S. Grant was promoted to lieutenant general, he gave command of all the cavalry of the Army of the Potomac to Sheridan, who reorganized his cavalry command and raided Confederate communications around Richmond in May, continuing the raids and inflicting great damage during the summer. In August he was placed in command of the Army of the Shenandoah

and was ordered by Grant to drive south and destroy all supplies of any value to the Confederacy in the Shenandoah Valley. In the next two months he methodically laid waste to the Shenandoah Valley, which had helped sustain the Confederate forces for the previous three years. He was made a brigadier general of the regular army. On Oct. 19, his ride from Winchester to Cedar Creek, turning a seemingly inevitable disaster into a victory for his forces over General Early, became legendary and caused General Grant to call him "one of the ablest of generals." In November he was commissioned a major general in the regular army for his exploits in the Shenandoah Valley. He continued his marauding raids against Lee's communications and supply lines from Winchester to Petersburg in February–March 1865, turned the Confederate flank, and forced the Confederate forces to evacuate Petersburg and retreat to Appomattox. In the final operations of the war, his command was thrown across Lee's line of retreat, and Lee's surrender to Grant followed. After the war he served as commander of the military Division of the Gulf in 1865–67; while there he encouraged the Mexican liberals and practically forced the French Government to withdraw its support of Maximilian. He was military governor of the Fifth Military District (Louisiana and Texas) in March–September 1867 and was severely criticized for the harshness of his military rule, which led President Andrew Johnson to transfer him to the Department of Missouri. He led a campaign against the Indians in 1868–69, forcing them to settle on their reservations, and he was promoted to the rank of lieutenant general in 1869. He visited Europe in 1870–71 as a military observer and witnessed several battles of the Franco-Prussian War. He married Irene Rucker at Chicago, in June 1875, and later in the year he was again sent to Louisiana. As in his previous rule as military commander of occupied states, he was heartily criticized for the severity of the military rule he imposed. When the revolt against Republican rule caused political rioting in 1878, he was placed in command of the Western and Southwestern Military Divisions, and in 1884 he succeeded General William Tecumseh Sherman as commander-in-chief of the Army. On June 1, 1888, two months before his death on Aug. 5 at Nonquitt, Massachusetts, where he had gone to restore his failing health and to finish his two-volume *Personal Memoirs* (1888), Congress bestowed on him the highest military rank in the Army at that time, general. He was one of the great military figures of the Civil War, affectionately dubbed "Little Phil" by his men, who idolized him for his just treatment and constant concern for their welfare.

SHERMAN, ELEANOR BOYLE EWING (1824–88). Daughter of Thomas E. Ewing, cabinet member and U.S. senator from Ohio, she was born in Lancaster, Ohio, on Oct. 4, was educated at the Visitation Convent, Georgetown, D.C., and in 1850 she married William Tecumseh Sherman, who had been adopted by her father in 1829 when Sherman's father died; her husband was to become one of the most famous generals of the Civil War. She was greatly interested in Catholic Indian missions through her friendship with Fr. Peter De Smet, an old family friend, and helped the missions through her brother Charles, who was appointed Indian Commissioner in 1873 and by helping to organize the Catholic Indian Missionary Association in Washington, D.C., in 1875. She also served on the U.S. Sanitary Commission in 1861–66, organized to provide spiritual and material assistance to soldiers during the Civil War, and wrote a memorial to her father, *Thomas Ewing, a Memorial* (1872). She died in New York City on Nov. 28.

SHERMAN, ELIZABETH. *See* Bentley, Elizabeth Terrill.

SHERMAN, THOMAS EWING (1856–1933), missionary. Son of William Tecumseh Sherman, famous Civil War general, and Eleanor Boyle Ewing Sherman, he was born in San Francisco on Oct. 12, was educated at Georgetown (B.A. 1874) and Yale (B.S. 1876), and studied law at Washington University, St. Louis. He joined the Jesuits in Roehampton, England, in 1878, continued his studies at Woodstock (Maryland) College in 1880–83, taught at St. Louis University in 1883–85 and the University of Detroit in 1885–87, and after further studies at Woodstock was ordained in Philadelphia in 1889. He was sent to St. Louis in 1891, attracted widespread attention with his oratorical prowess, lectured widely, and engaged in missionary work. He was a chaplain in the Spanish-American War. On his return to the United States in 1899, he devoted himself for the next decade to giving missions. He founded the Catholic Truth Society of Chicago in 1901, suffered a breakdown in 1911, and spent the next four years in a sanitarium. When he had recovered sufficiently, he traveled throughout Europe and the United States from 1915 to 1929, when he settled in Santa Barbara, California. He had another breakdown in 1931 and was confined to De Paul Sanitarium, New Orleans, where he died on Apr. 29.

SHIELDS, JAMES (1806–79), general, United States Senator. Born in Altmore, Tyrone, Ireland, on May 12, he was educated in Irish hedge schools and emigrated to the United States around 1826, after an attempt to go to Quebec ended in a shipwreck. He studied law, was admitted to the bar, and began to practice at Kaskaskia, Illinois, in 1832, fought in the Black Hawk War, and became active in Democratic politics. He was elected to the Illinois legislature in 1836, became state auditor in 1839, judge of the Illinois Supreme Court in 1843–45, and was Commissioner of the General Land Office in Washington, D.C., in 1845–47. In 1842 he was led to believe that several caustic letters in the Sagamore *Journal* ridiculing the Democrats in general and Shields in particular were written by Abraham Lincoln, and he challenged Lincoln to a duel; Lincoln accepted, but the matter was settled amicably and the duel averted. Scholars believe the letters were written by Mary Todd, later Mrs. Lincoln, and her friend Julia Jayne, though some believe Lincoln may have written at least one of the letters. When the Mexican War was declared, Shields resigned from the Land Office and was commissioned a brigadier general of Illinois volunteers. He served with distinction, was severely wounded at the battle of Cerro Gordo and of Chapultepec, and was brevetted major general in 1847. He was mustered out of the Army in 1848, was named governor of the Oregon Territory later the same year, and resigned that office when elected as a United States senator from Illinois in 1848. When his term expired in 1855, he was defeated for reelection and moved to Minnesota Territory, where he was one of the first senators from Minnesota when it was admitted to the Union in 1858. He was unsuccessful in a bid for reelection to the Senate, moved to California, where he married Mary Ann Carr in 1861, and then to Mexico, where he engaged in mining. At the outbreak of the Civil War, he returned to the Army as brigadier general of volunteers in 1861, was wounded at Winchester, where he defeated General "Stonewall" Jackson, but after decisive defeats by Jackson at Port Republic and Cross Keys in Virginia in 1862, he resigned his commission in 1863 and returned to California, resuming his law practice in San Francisco. He subsequently moved to Missouri and practiced law there. He was a railway commissioner for a time, was a member of the state legislature, serving in 1874 and 1879, was state adjutant in 1877, and in 1879 was elected to fill an unexpired term in the United States Senate, serving in January–March. He died in Ottumwa, Iowa, on June 1. In 1893 his statue was placed in the Capitol, Washington, D.C. to represent the state of Illinois.

SHIELDS, THOMAS EDWARD (1862–1921), educator. Born in Mendota, Minnesota, on May 9, he was educated at St. Francis Seminary in Milwaukee, and St. Thomas Seminary in St. Paul, Minnesota, and was ordained in 1891. He was a curate at the St. Paul cathedral in 1891–92, continued his studies at St. Mary's Seminary, Baltimore (M.A.) and Johns Hopkins University in 1895; his doctoral thesis, *The Effect of Odor Upon Blood Flow* (1895), had a great impact on psychological research. He became professor of natural science at St. Thomas Seminary in 1895 and joined the faculty of Catholic University in 1902, teaching there until his death in Washington, D.C., on Feb. 15. He began at Catholic University teaching psychology but became interested in education and in time became one of the leading Catholic educators in the United States. He founded the university's department of education in 1909 and was its first chairman, founded the first summer institute for sisters at the university in 1911, and founded Sisters College at the university in 1911 and was its first dean. He was cofounder, with Edward Pace, of the *Catholic Educational Review* in 1911, wrote a series of widely used religious textbooks, and

531

several other books, among them *Education of Our Girls* (1907), *The Making and Unmaking of a Dullard* (1909), and *Philosophy of Education* (1917).

SHIPMAN, ANDREW JACKSON (1857–1915), jurist, linguist. Born in Springvale, Fairfax County, Virginia, on Oct. 15, he was educated at Georgetown (B.A. 1878) and while a student there was converted to Catholicism. He moved to Hocking Valley, Ohio, in 1880 and became superintendent of the W. P. Rend Coal Mines; there many of the miners were Slavic rite Catholics, which led to his interest in things Catholic. He was assistant secretary to the Collector of the Port of New York in New York City in 1884–89, studied law and was admitted to the New York bar in 1886, and engaged in engineering work in New York in 1889. In 1893 he married Adair Mooney, the sister of his law partner, Edmund Mooney. He established the firm of Blandy, Mooney, and Shipman, specializing in cases involving Greek rite Catholics and ecclesiastical law, was a member of the Board of Regents of the State of New York in 1913–15, was a delegate to the New York State Constitutional Convention in 1915, and was active in the Marquette League for Indian missionaries and in several charitable institutions. He spent much time in Eastern Europe and became proficient in Russian, Polish, Greek, and Slavic languages. He became an authority on Slavic culture and on various Eastern rites performed in the United States. He worked to aid Slavic immigrants, defending them and publicizing Eastern rites, and wrote a forty-four-page pamphlet, *The Mass According to the Greek Rite* (1912), a translation of St. John Chrysostom's *Greek Mass.* He was a director of the firm that published the Catholic Encyclopedia and died in New York City on Oct. 17.

SHUSTER, GEORGE NATHAN (1894–1977), educator, author. Of German descent, he was born in Lancaster, Wisconsin, on Aug. 27, was educated at Notre Dame (B.A. 1915), and served in Army Intelligence in World War I. He continued his education at Notre Dame after the war (M.A. 1920), Poitiers, and Berlin, and in 1940 received his doctorate from Columbia. He headed the English department at Notre Dame in 1920–24, when he was also managing editor of *Ave Maria.* He taught at Brooklyn Polytechnic Institute in 1924–25 and at St. Joseph's College for Women, Brooklyn, in 1925–35, and was assistant editor of *Commonweal* in 1926–28 and managing editor in 1928–37; he left because of editorial differences with Michael Williams, editor and founder of *Commonweal,* who insisted that the magazine should support Franco after Shuster had attacked the Spanish dictator in a series of articles in the magazine. He was appointed president of Hunter College in New York City, then the largest public college for women in the world, in 1940 and served in that position for twenty years. He served on the American delegation to the United Nations Conference on International Education in 1945 and for a time was United States representative on the executive committee of UNESCO, which he had helped create at that 1945 conference. He was land commissioner for post–World War II Bavaria in 1950–52, was assistant to the president of Notre Dame and director of the Center for the Study of Man in Contemporary Society at Notre Dame in 1960–71, and became professor emeritus of English at Notre Dame on his retirement in 1971. He wrote numerous books about the Catholic influence on English literature, notably *The Catholic Spirit in Modern English Literature* (1922) and *The Catholic Church in Current Literature* (1930). He also wrote several books on the rise and menace of Nazi Germany, among them *Germans: An Inquiry and an Estimate* (1932), and on Communism, notably *Religion Behind the Iron Curtain* (1954) and his book on Cardinal Mindzenty, *In Silence I Speak* (1956). His autobiography, *The Ground I Walked On: Reflections of a College President,* was published in 1961. He was an internationally known authority on education and headed several studies of Catholic education, authoring *Catholic Education in a Changing World* in 1967. He died in South Bend, Indiana, on Jan. 25.

SIBBEL, JOSEPH (1850–1907), sculptor. Born in Dülman, Germany, on June 7, he early showed an aptitude for carving and sculpting, and was sent to Münster to study under the famous wood carver, Friedrich A. Ewertz, and clay modeling at the studio of sculptor Achterman. He emigrated to the United States in 1873 and settled in Cincinnati, Ohio, with a group of artists engaged in ecclesiastical sculpture. When this enterprise and a similar one with a secular sculptor named Rebisso failed, he came to New York City and set up a studio. He came into prominence as a sculptor when he did a series of *alto-relievos* for the cathedral at Hartford, Connecticut. He was soon commissioned to do statues for churches all over the country and became famed for his ecclesiastical sculptures; he was noted for the realism of his sculptures, the originality of his designs, and his freedom from conventionality, but his works were always in accord with history and tradition. Among his outstanding works were the statue of St. Patrick in St. Patrick's Cathedral, New York City, the series of heroic statues of four saints—Isaac Jogues, Rose of Lima, Turibius, and Kateri Takawitha—in St. Joseph's Seminary, Dunwoodie, Yonkers, New York, the statuary and decorations of St.

Paul's Cathedral in Pittsburgh, and two heroic panels, "Our Lady Comforter of the Afflicted" and "Death of St. Joseph," in the Church of St. Francis Xavier in St. Louis. He died in New York City on July 10.

SIEGMAN, EDWARD FERDINAND (1908–67), biblical scholar. Born in Cleveland, Ohio, on July 4, he joined the Society of the Precious Blood in 1922, was educated at St. Joseph's College, Indiana, St. Charles Seminary, Carthagena, Indiana, where he was ordained in 1934 and Catholic University (S.T.D. 1937). He taught Scripture at St. Charles Seminary in 1937–51 and was dean of studies in 1945–51, was an assistant professor in 1952–57 and associate professor in 1957–63 at Catholic University, received an S.S.L. at the Pontifical Biblical Institute, Rome, in 1959, and returned to St. Charles in 1963. He became professor of Sacred Scripture at Notre Dame in 1966, served on the editorial committee of the Confraternity of Christian Doctrine translation of the bible in 1951–58, was editor of the *Catholic Biblical Quarterly* in 1952–58, and died at Notre Dame on Feb. 2.

SITJAR, BUENAVENTURA (1739–1808), missionary. Born at Porrera, island of Majorca, on Dec. 9, he joined the Franciscans in 1758 and after his ordination was sent to San Fernando College in Mexico City. He was assigned to missionary work in California in 1770 and arrived at San Diego in 1771. He was present at the founding of the Mission of San Antonio, was appointed first missionary by Junípero Serra, and spent the rest of his life ministering to the Indians there. He learned the Telame language and compiled a dictionary of that language, kept a journal of an exploring expedition he accompanied in 1795, and baptized some 3,400 Indians. He died at San Antonio, California, on Sept. 3.

SIGSTEIN, JOHN JOSEPH (1875–1963), founder. Born in Chicago on Oct. 29, he was educated at St. Vincent's College (De Paul University) there. He early became interested in helping the poor, was active in the St. Vincent de Paul Society, and founded Our Lady of Victory Lodging House for Men in Chicago. In 1902 he began studying for the priesthood at Kenrick Seminary, St. Louis. He was ordained in Chicago in 1909, was a curate at St. Pius Church in Chicago for a time, and when he fell ill went to New Albin, Minnesota, as an assistant to the pastor. In 1914 he went to the Southwest, did missionary work in New Mexico, and the following year organized a group of women into the Society of Missionary Helpers of Our Lady of Victory to raise funds for missionaries. He was transferred back to Chicago in 1918, and in 1922 he founded the Society of Missionary Catechists of Our Blessed Lady of Victory to provide catechetical, social and health-care services, especially to the poor and suppressed; this society developed into Our Lady of Victory Missionary Sisters. Their first convent was established in Santa Fe, New Mexico, later in 1922, and the following year the mother house was established at Victory Noll, Huntington, Indiana. He left Victory Noll in 1938 when the society became autonomous, held its first canonical election, and elected Catherine Olberding superior general. He returned in retirement to Victory Noll in 1960 and spent the rest of his life until his death there on Mar. 13.

SINGENBERGER, JOHN BAPTIST (1848–1924), liturgical musician, composer. Born in Kirchberg, St. Gall Canton, Switzerland, on May 29, he graduated from the University of Innsbruck, Austria, in 1870. Early interested in music, he became choirmaster at the Grisons seminary, where he formed a Caecilian Society dedicated to promoting interest in church music. He was invited to become a music instructor at a normal school at St. Francis, Wisconsin, by Bishop John Henni of Milwaukee in 1873, was cofounder, with Fr. Joseph Salamann, of an American Caecilian Society, and was its first president. He was founder and first editor of its publication, *Caecilia,* the following year and soon became noted as a conductor of massed choirs. He led the movement to reform church music and to restore Gregorian chant, published a *Guide to Catholic Church Music* (1905), several choir manuals, and a collection, *Cantata* (1912); he composed fourteen Masses, six complete Vespers, twenty hymns for Benediction, and sixteen motets. He died in Milwaukee, Wisconsin, on May 29.

SKELLY, JOSEPH A. (1874–1963). Born in Germantown, Pennsylvania, on Mar. 24, he was educated at St. Vincent's Seminary there, took his vows as a Vincentian in 1895, and was ordained in 1900. He engaged in pastoral work for a time, was at St. Vincent's in 1904–14, and in 1915 was named first director of the Central Association of the Miraculous Medal, dedicated to spreading devotion to Our Lady under the title of Our Lady of the Miraculous Medal; he held this position until his death in Germantown on July 8. He began the Perpetual Novena of the Miraculous Medal in 1930, which in time spread all over the world, in some forty-five hundred churches. The Association provided funds for training priests and building several seminaries, and distributed some seventy-five million Miraculous Medals.

SKEHAN, PATRICK W. (1909–80), biblical scholar. Born in New York City on Sept. 30, he was educated at Fordham (B.A. 1929) and St. Joseph's Seminary, Dunwoodie, Yonkers, New York, in 1929–33 and was ordained in 1933. He continued his studies at Catholic University (S.T.D. 1938) and taught Semitic languages and literature there from 1951 to 1979, when he became professor emeritus. He was chairman of the Department of Semitic and Egyptian Languages in 1951–54, 1956–65, and 1967 and was made a papal chamberlain in 1954 and a domestic prelate in 1958. During these years he was also publisher-editor of the *Catholic Biblical Quarterly Review* in 1946–49, president of the Catholic Biblical Association in 1946–47, vice-chairman of the editorial board of *The New American Bible* in 1947–70, visiting professor at Johns Hopkins University in 1947–58, annual professor at the American School of Oriental Research in Jerusalem in 1954–55 and director in 1956–57, and visiting professor at the Pontifical Biblical Institute in Rome in 1969–70. He was a world-recognized authority in Semitic and scriptural studies, was a member of the international committee that translated the Dead Sea scrolls, and wrote about them. He was the author of *Studies in Israelite Poetry and Wisdom* (1971). He died in Washington, D.C., on Sept. 9.

SKINNER, RICHARD DANA (1893–1941), critic. Born in Detroit on Apr. 21, he was educated at Harvard (B.A. 1915), married Margaret Hill in 1913, was Washington correspondent for the Boston *Herald* in 1916–17, and served in the Air Force of the Army in World War I, 1917–19. After the war he joined the Guaranty Trust Co. in New York City in 1919 and left in 1921 to become president of R. D. Skinner & Co. He was vice president of Grosbeck-Hearn

Co., Inc. in 1925–29 and was on the staff of James C. Wilson & Co. in 1929–31. After serving as economic researcher at Young & Ottley, Inc., in 1931–32, he became manager of the bond department of the Emigrant Savings Bank in 1932 and became vice president of Pell, Kip & Skinner, Inc., in 1934. He was one of the founders of *Commonweal* and was its drama critic in 1924–34, was associate editor of *The North American Review* in 1935–36, and wrote *Our Changing Theatre* (1931), *Eugene O'Neill—A Poet's Quest* (1935), and *Seven Kinds of Inflation* (1937). He died in New York City on Nov. 6.

SLAVIN, ROBERT JOSEPH (1907–61), educator. Born in Dorchester, Massachusetts, on Mar. 19, he was educated at Providence (Rhode Island) College, joined the Dominicans in 1926, was professed in 1928, and continued his studies at St. Thomas Aquinas College, River Forest, Illinois (B.A. 1931), Immaculate Conception College and Catholic University, Washington, D.C., (M.A. 1934, Ph.D. 1936), and was ordained in Washington in 1934. He taught philosophy at Catholic University in 1936–47 and was appointed president of Providence College in 1947. He retained that position until his death in Providence on Apr. 24.

SLOANE, THOMAS O'CONOR (1851–1940), scientist, author. Born in New York City on Nov. 24, he was educated there at St. Francis Xavier College (B.A. 1869, M.A. 1873) and Columbia (Ph.D. 1876). He taught natural sciences at Seton Hall College, South Orange, New Jersey, in 1888–89, invented several devices, including a self-recording photometer, and served on the staff of *Scientific American, Youth's Companion,* and *Practical Electrics.* He was managing editor of *The Experimenter,* edited *Amazing Stories,* wrote books on liquid air, india rubber, chemistry, and popular science, among them *Home Experiments in Science* (1888), *Electricity Simplified* (1891), *Liquid Air and the Liquefaction of Gases* (1899), *The Electrician's Hand Book* (1905), and *Motion Picture Projection* (1921); he also translated Johannes Jörgensen's *St. Francis of Assisi* (1912). He served on the New Jersey Board of Education in 1905–11 and died in South Orange, New Jersey, on Aug. 7.

SMITH, ALFRED EMANUEL (1873–1944), governor. He was born of a poor family on New York's Lower East Side on Dec. 3 and in his youth worked as a truckman's helper, a shipping clerk, and in a Fulton Street Fish Market house (his father died when he was twelve) to help his family. He early became interested in politics, married Catherine Dunn in 1900, gained favor with Tammany Hall, and was appointed a process server in the office of the county commissioner of jurors in 1895. He was elected to the New York State Assembly in 1903, became a force in state Democratic politics in time, and served in that body until 1915, becoming majority leader in 1911 and speaker of the assembly in 1913. He gained a reputation for his progressive policies, served as vice-chairman of the State Factory Investigation Committee set up to investigate the tragic Triangle Waist Company fire in New York City that claimed the lives of 146 workers in 1911, and was largely instrumental in having a series of laws enacted regulating women's working conditions, sanitary conditions, and fire and health, and improving workmen's compensation. He distinguished himself at the state constitutional convention in 1915, was elected sheriff of New York County that fall, and was elected president of the New York City Board of Aldermen in 1917. He was elected governor of New York in 1918, despite the bitter opposition of the Republicans and William Randolph Hearst; though defeated for reelection in 1920, he was reelected in 1922, 1924, and 1926. He was a forceful and popular governor, and his administrations were noted for his administrative ability and his progressive social legislation in housing, hospitals, and state institutions; he also worked for the poor and the afflicted, workmen's compensation, and the elimination of railroad grade crossings throughout the state, the building of roads, parks, and parkways, and the passage of laws to aid the farmers of the state. In 1919 he called a special session of the legislature to ratify the woman-suffrage amendment to the United States Constitution. He opposed private development of state power facilities and resources, helped to develop the Port of New York Authority, and fought for the repeal of prohibition. He was defeated in a bid for the Democratic presidential nomination in the bitterly contested and long-drawn-out Democratic Convention in New York City in 1924 (he was nominated by Franklin D. Roosevelt), but four years later he was the Democratic Party's standard bearer—the first Catholic nominee for the presidency of the United States by a major political party. He was overwhelmingly defeated by Herbert Hoover in an election marred by bitter anti-Catholic bigotry. He retired to private business enterprises after the election, was president of the Empire State Building Corporation in 1929–44, and was active in many civic enterprises. He was defeated for the Democratic Party nomination for president in 1932 by Franklin Roosevelt, who had supported him in 1928 and whom he had urged to run for the governorship of New York in 1928, Roosevelt's springboard to the presidency. Smith broke completely with Roosevelt over the latter's New Deal policies and became his bitter political enemy, though he supported Roosevelt's administration when the United States entered World War II. He opposed Roosevelt's nomination in 1936 and 1940, and was an active member of the conservative anti-Roosevelt American Liberty League; his political power waned as Roosevelt's increased, and though he never completely abandoned politics, his later years were politically powerless. Though he had never gone to college, he received many honorary degrees and awards; he was given the Laetare Medal in 1929 and was made a papal chamberlain by Pope Pius XI in 1938. He was the author of *Progressive Democracy* (1928) and *The American Citizen and His Government* (1935); his autobiography, *Up to Now*, was published in 1929. He also wrote for the *Saturday Evening Post* in the 1930s and in 1932–34 was editor and columnist for the *New Outlook*. He died in New York City on Oct. 4.

SMITH, ALPHONSE JOHN (1883–1935), bishop. Born in Madison, Indiana, on Nov. 14, he was educated at St. Mary's College, Kansas, and the North American College, Rome, and was ordained in 1908. He served as assistant pastor of the cathedral in Indianapolis, Indiana, until 1921, when he became pastor of St. Joan of Arc Church, Indianapolis. He was consecrated bishop of Nashville, Tennessee, in 1924, encouraged native vocations and frequent communion, built fifteen churches and six schools, and died in Nashville on Dec. 16.

SMITH, AUGUSTINE. *See* Gallitzen, Demetrius Augustine.

SMITH, HENRY IGNATIUS (1886–1957), educator. Born in Newark, New Jersey, on Aug. 25, he was educated at Seton Hall College (South Orange, New Jersey), St. Joseph's College (Somerset, Ohio), the Dominican House of Studies (Washington, D.C.), and Catholic University (S.T.Lr., Ph.D., LL.D.), and was ordained a Dominican priest in 1910. He taught at the Dominican House of Studies, Washington, D.C., in 1913–16, was national director of the Holy Name Society in 1916–20 and editor of the *Holy Name Review*, and was founding editor of *Torch* in 1916–20. He was rector of St. Catherine of Siena Church, New York City, in 1916–20, began teaching philosophy at Catholic University in 1920, remaining there until his retirement in 1956, was prior of the Dominican House of Studies there in 1922–28, and in 1937 succeeded Msgr. Edward A. Pace as dean of the University's School of Philosophy. He developed it into a major center of Thomism in the United States, helped establish the Preachers' Institute (he was renowned as a preacher), became editor of *New Scholasticism* in 1937, frequently appeared on the "Catholic Hour" radio program, and wrote several religious and philosophical pamphlets. He was named dean of religious communities at Catholic University when he retired in 1956, and he died in Washington, D.C., on Mar. 8.

SMITH, JOHN TALBOT (1855–1923), author. Born in Saratoga, New York, on Sept. 22, he was educated at St. Michael's College and Seminary, Toronto, Canada, and was ordained there for the diocese of Ogdensburg, New York, in 1881. He served as a curate at Watertown, New York, became pastor at Rouses Point, New York, and in 1889 went to New York City, where he spent the next two decades writing while serving as chaplain to the Christian Brothers of De La Salle Academy and to the Sisters of Mercy of St. Catherine's Convent in 1901–4. He was editor of the *Catholic Review* in 1889–92, was one of the founders of the Catholic Summer School of America, serving as its president in 1905–9, founded the Catholic Writers Guild, and was one of the founders of the Catholic Actors Guild in 1914. In 1908 he was appointed pastor of Sacred Heart parish, Dobbs Ferry, New York, and he died there on Sept. 24. Among the books he wrote were the two-volume *History of the Catholic Church in New York* (1906), *A History of the Diocese of Ogdensburg* (1885), *Our Seminaries* (1896, reissued as *The Training of a Priest* in 1908), a devastating attack on seminary education, and a biography, *Brother Azarias* (1897).

SMITH, LEO R. (1905–63), bishop. Born in Attica, New York, on Aug. 30, he was educated at Canisius College, Buffalo, New York (B.A. 1926) and the North American College, Rome (Ph.D. 1928, S.T.D. 1930, J.C.D. 1931), and was ordained in 1929. He served as assistant chancellor of the Buffalo diocese in 1932–46 and was made a papal chamberlain in 1942 and a domestic prelate in 1946. He was named titular bishop of Marida and auxiliary bishop of Buffalo in 1952, vicar-general and episcopal moderator of the National Federation of Diocesan Youth Councils of the National Catholic Welfare Conference in 1953, and served as administrator of the diocese in 1962. He was appointed bishop of Ogdensburg, New York, in 1963 and died suddenly seven months later on Oct. 9, while attending Vatican Council II in Rome.

SMITH, MATTHEW J. W. (1891–1960), editor. Born in Altoona, Pennsylvania, on June 9, he studied journalism four years under the editors of the Altoona (Pennsylvania) *Daily Tribune* and then on the Pueblo (Colorado) *Chieftain.* He then studied for the priesthood at St. Thomas College and

Seminary, Denver, Colorado (M.A., Jour.D.), and was ordained for the Denver diocese in 1923. He became editor of the Denver *Catholic Register* in 1913 and was founding editor in 1929 of the nationally circulated *The Register* with more than thirty diocesan editions. He also founded the Register College of Journalism in 1931 and was the author of several books, among them *Letters to an Infidel* (1925), *Great Controversies* (1925), and *The Church Upon the Rock* (1941). He was made a domestic prelate in 1933 and died in Denver on June 15.

SMITH, "RED." *See* Smith, Walter Wellesley "Red."

SMITH, THOMAS KILBY (1820–57), general. Of a distinguished New England family, he was born in Boston on Sept. 23, was brought to Cincinnati as a child by his parents, and attended a military academy there. He studied law in the office of Salmon P. Chase, later Chief Justice of the United States Supreme Court, was appointed special agent for the post office in Washington, D.C., in 1853, was later named marshal for the Southern District of Ohio, and then became deputy clerk of Hamilton County, Ohio. He joined the Union Army at the outbreak of the Civil War in 1861 as a lieutenant-colonel of the 5th Regiment, Ohio Volunteers, was commander of a brigade in the 15th and 17th Army Corps of the Army of the Tennessee, serving in all its campaigns, and was on the staff of General Grant in 1863, when he was commissioned brigadier general of volunteers in command of the detached division of the 17th Army Corps. He was assigned command of the Department of Southern Alabama and Florida after the fall of Mobile in 1864 and brevetted major general. After the war he was United States consul to Panama from 1867 to 1869, when poor health caused his retirement. He settled in New York City in 1886 and engaged in newspaper work. He became a Catholic several years before his death in New York City on Dec. 14 through the influence of his wife Elizabeth Budd Smith, whom he had married in 1848.

SMITH, VINCENT EDWARD (1915–72), philosopher, author. Born in Lockland, Ohio, on Aug. 20, he was educated at Xavier University, Cincinnati, Ohio, (B.A. 1938), the University of Fribourg and Catholic University (M.A. 1942, Ph.D. 1947). He served in the United States Navy during World War II, receiving a commendation for developing a device to locate enemy radar. He married Virginia Beck in 1943, and after the war he resumed his studies at the Institutum Divi Thomas, Cincinnati, Harvard, and M.I.T. He taught philosophy at Catholic University in 1946–48, at Notre Dame in 1950–59, and at St. John's University, New York City, in 1959–66, where he was director of the Philosophy of Science Institute. He was also visiting lecturer at Sarah Lawrence College and Columbia and was editor in 1948–66 of the *New Scholasticism,* the quarterly of the American Catholic Philosophical Association, of which he was president in 1953. In 1969 he joined the faculty of Queensborough Community College, Bayside, Queens, New York. He was killed by a hit-and-run driver in New York City on May 18. He was the author of ten books, among them *Philosophical Frontiers of Physics* (1947), *Elements of Philosophy* (1957), *Philosophical Physics* (1950), and *Science and Philosophy* (1965).

SMITH, WALTER BEDELL (1895–1961), general. Born in Indianapolis, Indiana, on Oct. 5, he became interested in the military as a boy and joined the Indiana National Guard when he was fifteen. He served with the Mexican border expedition in 1916, fought in the regular army in World War I, and won a regular commission in 1920. He served in the Bureau of Military Intelligence in Washington and during the 1930s studied and taught at various military schools and graduated from the Army War College in Washington in 1937. He impressed General Omar N. Bradley and General George Marshall while at Infantry School at Fort Benning, Georgia, and in 1939 Marshall brought him to Washington to help him build up the Army. At the outbreak of World War II he was assigned to the Combined Chiefs of Staff as a lieutenant colonel, was secretary to the General Staff in 1941–42, U.S. secretary to the Combined Chiefs of Staff in 1942, and was General Dwight Eisenhower's chief of staff in 1942–45. He was with Eisenhower in the African, Sicilian, and Italian campaigns and in the invasion of France, and he conducted the negotiations that led to the surrender of the Italian Army in 1943. He drew up the plans for the invasion of Normandy and signed the document by which Germany surrendered in 1945. He was United States ambassador to Russia in 1946–49, and when he returned to the United States in 1949 became commander of the First Army as a full four-star general. He was director of the Central Intelligence Agency (CIA) in 1950–53 and reorganized and restructured it. In 1953–54 he served as undersecretary of state. He left public service in 1954 to engage in private industry as vice-chairman of the American Machine and Foundry Company, a position he held until his death in Washington, D.C., on Aug. 9. He was the author of *Eisenhower's Six Great Decisions* (1956) and *My Three Years in Moscow* (1950).

SMITH, WALTER GEORGE (1854–1924), jurist. Son of Thomas Kilby Smith, a general in the Civil War, and

Elizabeth Budd McCullough Smith, he was born in Logan County, Ohio, on Nov. 24. He was educated at the University of Pennsylvania (B.A. 1873, M.A. 1876, LL.B. 1877) and was admitted to the bar in 1877. He began his law practice in Philadelphia and in 1890 married Elizabeth Drexel, daughter of Francis Anthony Drexel, noted financier and sister of Mother Katharine Drexel; she died eight months later. He was active in Catholic affairs, was an adviser to Mother Drexel and for the Drexel Institute, and was a member of the U.S. Indian commission. He was president of the American Bar Association in 1917, contributed articles to the Catholic Encyclopedia, wrote *Life and Letters of Thomas Kilby Smith* (1898) and *Fidelis of the Cross* (1926), and received the Laetare Medal in 1923. He died in Philadelphia on Apr. 4.

SMITH, WALTER WELLESLEY "RED" (1905–82), sports writer. Son of a retail grocer, Walter Smith, and Ida Richardson Smith, he was born in Green Bay, Wisconsin, on Sept. 25, studied journalism at Notre Dame, edited the school yearbook, *The Dome,* and graduated in 1927. He began his journalism career that year with the Milwaukee *Sentinel,* moved to the St. Louis *Star* after a year, and began writing on sports. He joined the Philadelphia *Record* as a sports writer and columnist in 1936, and in 1945 became a full-time columnist for the New York *Herald-Tribune.* He was soon syndicated in 90 newspapers and by 1954 was the most widely syndicated sports columnist in the United States. His column survived in 1966 when the *Herald-Tribune* was merged with other newspapers to form the *World-Journal-Tribune,* which ceased publication in 1967. His column continued to be syndicated until four years later, when he joined the New York *Times.* The *Times* also syndi-

cated his column to 275 newspapers in the United States and some 225 newspapers in 30 foreign nations. In 1976 he was awarded the Pulitzer Prize for distinguished commentary—only the second sports columnist to be so honored (the other was Arthur Daley in 1956). In 1980 he proposed a boycott of the Olympic Games in Moscow because of Russia's invasion of Afghanistan (the column proposing the boycott was killed by the *Times),* a proposal that caused a furor but was formally endorsed by President Carter two weeks later; only 81 of 147 eligible nations participated in the games. He died in Stamford, Connecticut, on Jan. 15. Several collections of his columns appeared in book form, among them *Out of the Red, Views of Sports, The Best of Red Smith,* and *Strawberries in the Wintertime.* He always used the name Red, saying of Walter Wellesley, "I hate the name."

SMYTH, PATRICK (18th century). An unattached Irish priest from Cork, Ireland, he came to the United States in 1787 and was sent to work in Frederickstown (Frederick), Maryland, by Bishop John Carroll. He soon became dissatisfied, feeling he had been slighted by the people of Frederickstown, especially by Henry Darnell, a wealthy relative of Carroll's. Despite assurances from the bishop that this was not so, he returned to Ireland after a year in America but before doing so wrote a pamphlet entitled *The Present State of the Catholic Missions Conducted by the Ex-Jesuits in North America,* charging that former Jesuits received the best parishes, lived in luxury in mansions, and cruelly mistreated their slaves. Carroll was alarmed, since the pamphlet appeared at the same time as one by Abbé de la Poterie *(see* Bouchard, Claude Florent), and wrote at once to Archbishop Troy of Dublin, asking him to promulgate the truth about Smyth and his charges. Despite the archbishop's efforts, Smyth's preposterous accusations caused Carroll great difficulty in recruiting Irish priests for America in the next few years.

SMYTH, TIMOTHY CLEMENT (1810–65), bishop. Born in Finlea, Clare, Ireland, on Jan. 24, he was educated at Trinity College, Dublin, and at Mt. Melleray Abbey near Cappoquin, diocese of Waterford, joined the Cistercians there in 1838, and was ordained in Waterford in 1841. He was sent to the United States and in 1842 founded the Abbey of New Melleray near Dubuque, Iowa, on land donated by Bishop Jean Loras, bishop of Dubuque. He was named titular bishop of Thanasis and coadjutor of Dubuque in 1857, succeeded to the see in 1858, was administrator of the diocese of Chicago in 1858–59, and died in Dubuque on Sept. 22.

SOMERS, HERBERT GOLDSMITH (1859–1911), diplomat. He was born of American parents in Madoc, Canada, on Apr. 20, and was educated at Canandaigua Academy, New York, and the Minnesota Military Academy, Minneapolis, Minnesota, graduating and becoming a lieutenant in the United States Army in 1877. He was sent to the artillery school at Fort Monroe in 1879 and there met and married Helen Lucy Fargo in 1881 and spent 1882–85 in the cavalry. He was a military instructor at St. John's College (Fordham) in 1885–90, and after the death of his wife in 1886 he married Harriet Bard Woodcock in 1889. He was sent to South Dakota to help quell an Indian uprising and was wounded at the Battle of Wounded Knee in December 1890, resigned from the Army in 1891, and entered the diplomatic service in 1894, when he was appointed second secretary at the United States embassy in Berlin. He resigned from the diplomatic service in 1897 but returned to the diplomatic service as first secretary at the Peking embassy in 1898, in which year he and his family became Catholics there. He was chief of state in charge of the defense of Peking during the Boxer uprising in China in 1900, was minister to Cuba in 1902–5 and to Panama from 1906 until he was forced to resign in 1910 because of ill health; while he was minister to Cuba, the Platt Amendment was ratified. He died in London on Oct. 20.

SORIN, EDWARD (1814–93), educator. Born in Ahuillé, France, on Feb. 6, he studied at the diocesan seminary at Le Mans and was ordained in 1838. He joined the Congregation of Holy Cross and was professed in 1840. The following year he was sent to the United States to establish the Congregation in the diocese of Vincennes, Indiana. After a short time at St. Peter's near Vincennes, he was given a parcel of land near South Bend, Indiana, in 1842 by Bishop Célestine de la Hailandière of Vincennes to found a college. He received a state charter in 1844 and built the first building of what was to become the University of Notre Dame; he served as its president until 1865 and was also provincial superior. He brought the Sisters of Holy Cross to the United States in 1843, founded the magazine *Ave Maria* in 1865, and was appointed superior general of the Congregation of Holy Cross in 1868, holding that position until his death at Notre Dame on Oct. 31. In 1883 the prestigious Laetare Medal award was established at his suggestion, and in 1885 he founded St. Edward University in Austin, Texas.

SPAETH, OTTO LUCIEN (1897–1966), art collector. Born in Decatur, Illinois, on Jan. 7, he attended St. Francis

College, Quincy, Illinois, in 1911–14, was a lieutenant in the Army during World War I, and after the war was a bank clerk for a time and then was a salesman for Ford tractors in 1915–18. He married Eloise O'Mara in 1923 and was president of the Premier Distributing Company of St. Louis, a manufacturer of malt extract, in 1923–35. In 1935–46, he was president of the Dayton Tool and Engineering Company and of Otto L. Spaeth, Inc., of Dayton, Ohio, in 1940–46, and was a member of the War Manpower Commission in Dayton during World War II in 1940–46. An active sponsor of the arts, he introduced in 1952–54 an exhibition of American artists, among them Alexander Calder and Charles Sheeler. The exhibition was held in Cedarburg, Wisconsin, at the offices of the Metal Mold Aluminum Company, owned by the aluminum casting company of which he was board chairman. It attracted tremendous attention. He began to build what was to become an outstanding personal art collection, and in 1950 he and his wife established the Spaeth Foundation, of which he was president, to help young artists; they also sponsored the Spaeth Award for church design given annually to young artists. He was a delegate to the first Congress of the World's Catholic Artists in Rome in 1951. In 1954 he retired from business to devote himself to his collection, and in 1958 he received the Friedsam Award of the Architectural League of New York for his efforts to encourage contemporary religious architecture and art. He was president of the American Federation of Arts, a vice president of the Whitney Museum of American Art, and a founding member of Americans for Democratic Action; he also served as director and president of the Liturgical Arts Society. He died in New York City on Oct. 8.

SPALDING, MOTHEP CATHERINE (1793–1857), foundress. Born in St. Charles County, Maryland, on Dec. 23, she was orphaned when a child and was raised by her uncle, Thomas Elder. She joined the two-months-old Sisters of Charity of Nazareth, Kentucky, in 1813 when she was nineteen, and was chosen as the first mother superior; the sisters' first convent was a log cabin that they called Nazareth. In 1814 Fr. B. J. M. David, spiritual adviser of the group, opened a school staffed by the sisters— the first that the sisters were to found and operate. They made their vows in 1816 and in 1819; though urged to remain as mother superior for the rest of her life by Fr. David and the sisters, Mother Catherine refused to violate their rule limiting the term of the superior to two consecutive terms, and a new superior, Mother Agnes Higdon, was elected. Mother Catherine remained the guiding spirit of the community for the rest of her life. In 1819, the sisters opened Bethlehem Academy in Bardstown, Kentucky, the first establishment away from the mother house, and in 1824 the mother house was moved to a site near Bardstown, Kentucky. When Mother Agnes died in 1824, Mother Catherine was again elected superior, remaining as superior until 1831. She and the sisters served as nurses during the cholera epidemic in Louisville in 1832–33, and in 1834 they established St. Vincent's Orphan Asylum for the children of the epidemic's victims. She was again elected superior in 1850 and died in St. Vincent's on Mar. 20. With Fr. David she is considered the foundress of the Sisters of Charity of Nazareth.

SPALDING, JOHN LANCASTER (1840–1916), archbishop. Born in Lebanon, Kentucky, on June 2, he was educated at St. Mary's College, Kentucky,

Mt. St. Mary's College, Emmitsburg, Maryland, Mt. St. Mary's Seminary of the West, Cincinnati, Ohio (B.A. 1859), the American College in Rome and the American College at Louvain in Belgium (S.T.B. 1862, S.T.L. 1864), and was ordained at Louvain in 1865. On his return to the United States in 1865 he engaged in pastoral work in Kentucky. He became chancellor of the Louisville diocese and editor of the diocesan newspaper in 1871, was Archbishop François Blanchet's theologian at the second Plenary Council of Baltimore in 1866 and was in New York in 1872–77, writing the biography of his uncle, Archbishop Martin J. Spalding of Baltimore in 1864–72 and engaging in pastoral work. He was assistant pastor of St. Michael's Church in New York when he was consecrated first bishop of the newly established diocese of Peoria, Illinois, in 1877. He was known for his eloquent preaching, was an ardent champion and publicist of the Church, strongly supported the Catholic school system, establishing fifty-eight parochial schools during his bishopric, and with Bishop John Ireland of St. Paul he actively supported the Irish Catholic Colonization Association to encourage Irish immigrants to settle on farms in the West. He also served as president of its board of directors in 1879–91. He actively worked for the establishment of a Catholic University in the United States at the third Plenary Council of Baltimore in 1884, was on the committee that led to its foundation, and was one of those most responsible for its establishment. He opposed now-Archbishop Ireland's Faribault Plan and fought against state interference in Catholic education. He was an enthusiastic supporter of the American system and opposed the establishment of an apostolic delegation to the United States in 1893, drawing a reprimand from Rome for an article he wrote in the *North American*

Review in 1894 on it. He was a member of President Theodore Roosevelt's Anthracite Coal Strike Commission in 1902–3 and helped bring the strike to an end. He suffered a paralytic stroke in 1905 and resigned as bishop of Peoria in 1908; he was appointed titular archbishop of Scitopolis and lived in retirement until his death in Peoria on Aug. 25. During his episcopate he tripled the number of priests in the diocese to meet the needs of the Catholic populace which had increased threefold. He built 140 churches, 58 schools, numerous charitable institutions, and a new cathedral. He was one of the leading educators of his day and wrote numerous books on this and other subjects, among them *Education and the Higher Life* (1890), *Means and Ends of Education* (1895), *Thoughts and Theories of Life and Education* (1897), *Opportunity and Other Essays* (1898), *Glimpses of Truth* (1903), *Religion, Art, and Other Essays* (1905), and several volumes of poetry—notably *America and Other Poems* (1885), *God and the Soul* (1901), and *A Kentucky Pioneer* (1932).

SPALDING, MARTIN JOHN (1810–72), archbishop. Born in Rolling Fork, Kentucky, on May 23, he graduated from St. Mary's College, Lebanon, Kentucky, in 1826 and then continued his studies at St. Thomas Seminary, Bardstown, Kentucky, and the Propaganda, Rome, where he was the first American to receive his doctorate in theology. He was ordained in Rome in 1834 and on his return to the United States became pastor of the Bardstown cathedral. He was founder and editor of Kentucky's first Catholic magazine, the *St. Joseph College Minerva,* which the next year was succeeded by the *Catholic Advocate.* He was president of St. Joseph's College from 1838 until 1840, when he was appointed administrator of St. Peter's in Lexington, Kentucky. The see of Bardstown was transferred to Louisville in 1841, and in 1844 he became vicar-general of Louisville; he was appointed titular bishop of Lengone and coadjutor of Louisville in 1848 and succeeded to the see in 1850. He dedicated the cathedral in 1852, went to Europe in 1852–53 seeking religious and financial aid for his diocese, and secured the Xaverian Brothers for the diocese; on this visit he laid the foundation for an American College at Louvain, which he and Bishop Peter Lefevere of Detroit founded in 1857. He also gave encouragement and financial aid to John Henry Newman, who had just lost the suit brought against him by the ex-priest Achille. In 1855 he was the leader in the resistance to anti-Catholic Know-Nothing attacks occasioned by the visit of Archbishop Bedini, Pope Pius IX's representative, which brought on rioting and caused a massacre of German and Irish Catholic immigrants in Louisville; the day of the rioting, Aug. 5, 1855, was called "Bloody Monday." He warmly supported the establishment of the North American College in Rome and was one of the leaders in the movement to found a Catholic University in the United States, was an editor of the *Metropolitan,* and founded the Louisville *Catholic Guardian* (successor to the *Catholic Advocate)* in 1858. He sided with the Confederacy in the Civil War but fought any attempt to have the Church take a position in favor of either the North or the South. In 1864 he was appointed archbishop of Baltimore, and during his episcopate he worked to heal the wounds caused by the war and provided help for stricken Southern dioceses. He arranged, presided over, and was active at the second Plenary Council of Baltimore in 1866, to which he was the apostolic delegate; he was chiefly responsible for the Council's endorsement of the concept of the Catholic University of the United States. In 1867 he visited Rome and helped raise funds to put the North American College in Rome on a sound financial basis, was elected a member of the Commissions on Faith and Postula, which examined proposals before they were presented to the delegates to Vatican Council I in 1869–70, and at the council he warmly supported the proclamation of the dogma of papal infallibility. He was the author of a number of books, among them *Evidences of Catholicity,* a series of lectures he delivered in 1844–45 and published in 1847, *Sketches of the Life, Times, and Character of the Rt. Rev. Benedict Joseph Flaget* (1852), *Miscellanea* (1855), and *History of the Protestant Reformation* (two volumes, 1860). He died in Baltimore on Feb. 7.

SPEARMAN, FRANK HAMILTON (1859–1937), author. Born in Buffalo, New York, he was educated at Lawrence College, Appleton, Wisconsin, and in 1884 became a Catholic. He married Eugenie Lonergan the same year, entered the banking business, and became interested in politics. He began writing stories of railroad life which became very popular although he was never a railroad man. His first book, *The Nerve of Foley* (filmed as *The Runaway Express* in 1926), a collection of railroad short stories, was published in 1900, and in the next seventeen years he was to publish twenty books, short stories, essays, and novels—many of which were made into motion pictures. His most popular book was his first western railroad novel, *Whispering Smith* (1906), which was made into a film in 1915 and again in 1926. Among his other books were *The Strategy of American Railroads* (1904), a serious study of American transportation; *Held for Orders* (filmed as *The Yellow Mail); Man of Music Mountain* (1916, filmed in 1917); *Laramie Holds the Range* (1921); *The Marriage Verdict* (1923); *Spanish*

Lover (1930); and *Carmen of the Ranch,* an historical novel of California published the year he died in Hollywood on Dec. 29. He wrote many of the screen adaptations of his novels, received several honorary awards and was the recipient of the Laetare Medal in 1935.

SPELLMAN, FRANCIS (1889–1967), cardinal. Son of William Spellman, a grocer, and Ellen Conway Spellman, he was born in Whitman, Massachusetts, on May 4, was educated at Fordham (B.A. 1911), and then studied for the priesthood at the Propaganda and the North American College, Rome (S.T.D. 1916). He was ordained in Rome in 1916, returned to the United States, and served as chaplain at a home for aged women. Then he served as curate at All Saints Church, Roxbury, Massachusetts, for two years and subsequently became a member of the staff of Holy Cross Cathedral, Boston. He was circulation manager of the Boston *Pilot,* the archdiocesan newspaper, and was director of Catholic literature in 1918–22 and editor in 1924–25; he was assistant chancellor in 1922–25 and served as attaché to the Secretariat of State at the Vatican in 1925–32—the first American to serve on the Secretariat. He was made a papal chamberlain in 1926, became a domestic prelate in 1929, and was English-language announcer for the Vatican Radio when it opened in 1932. In 1931 he took a Latin copy of a papal encyclical denouncing Fascism to Paris; though trailed by Fascist agents, he reached there safely, translated the encyclical, and released it to the press. He made many friends during his Roman stay, notably Nicholas Brady, John F. Raskob, Msgr. (later Cardinal) Borgongini-Duca of the Vatican Secretariat of State, and Cardinal Eugenio Pacelli, who was to become Pope Pius XII. In 1932 he was appointed titular bishop of Sila and auxiliary of Boston, and was consecrated at St. Peter's in Rome the same year—the first American to receive episcopal consecration there. On his return to Boston, he was appointed pastor of debt-ridden Sacred Heart Church in Newton Center, Massachusetts. He proved to be an able administrator and cleared up the church's debt. In 1936 he was guide for Cardinal Pacelli on the latter's visit to the United States and arranged an interview for him with President Roosevelt; this meeting began a friendship between Roosevelt and Spellman that lasted until Roosevelt's death. He was also to be on friendly terms with succeeding American Presidents Truman, Eisenhower, Kennedy, and Johnson. In 1939 Cardinal Pacelli was elected pope, and later that year he appointed Bishop Spellman sixth archbishop of New York and military vicar for the United States Armed Forces. In the twenty-eight years of his episcopate, Spellman became one of the most influential ecclesiastical figures in the country. During his administration he wiped out an inherited $28,000,000 debt on the archdiocese and its parishes, instituted an enormous expansion of hospitals, homes for the aged, orphanages, and other charitable institutions, constructed or renovated almost four hundred schools, completely renovated St. Joseph's Seminary, and tremendously expanded the see's Catholic Charities and its services. He completely reorganized the administration of the archdiocese, raised millions for charitable causes (he became president of the Catholic Near East Welfare Association in 1939), and became involved in civic affairs on a local and national level. He helped President Roosevelt in the arrangements to send Myron C. Taylor to the Vatican as the President's personal representative in 1939—the first United States diplomatic recognition of the Vatican since 1866, was a strong advocate of greater morality in motion pictures, and caused a furor by his denunciation of *Two-Faced Woman* in 1941, of *The Miracle* ten years later, which he thought was heretical, and of *Baby Doll* in 1956, which he denounced from the pulpit of St. Patrick's Cathedral. In 1944 he pressured President Roosevelt to declare Rome a demilitarized zone when it was captured by the Americans though it conflicted with Roosevelt's policy of Germany's unconditional surrender. In 1946 he was made a cardinal by Pope Pius XII, and in 1949 he was again involved in controversy when union cemetery laborers went on strike and he ordered seminarians to bury the dead and personally led them through picket lines. Later in the same year he was involved in a headline-making dispute with Mrs. Eleanor Roosevelt: she opposed public aid for parochial schools, whereas he supported it. A letter he wrote to her, charging her with heading an "anti-Catholic campaign" and calling her "unworthy" as an "American mother," shocked many. The matter was later smoothed over when he visited her at her Hyde Park home. An implacable foe of Communism, his support of Senator Joseph McCarthy in 1953 was widely criticized. In 1966 he hosted the visit of Pope Paul VI to the United States—the first visit to this country by a reigning pontiff. In 1966 his offer to resign as archbishop of New York because he was over seventy-five was rejected by Paul. Later the same year he was again embroiled in controversy when he defended the Vietnam War in an address to American troops in South Vietnam during his Christmas visit there. He attended Vatican Council II, where he helped pass the declaration on religious liberty (its principal architect was Jesuit John Courtney Murray, whom he had brought to the Council as a peritus) and also helped pass the statement that absolved the Jews collectively of the centuries-old accusation of deicide in the crucifixion of Christ. In 1967 he was unsuccessful in an attempt to have the Blaine amendment denying state aid to parochial schools repealed. As military vicar his annual Christmas visits to American troops during World War II and the Korean and Vietnam wars, when he traveled hundreds of thousands of miles all over the world, made him one of the nation's best-known figures. He was active in advocating racial justice throughout his episcopate, fought for the rights of Catholic students, and was known for his constant concern for the welfare of the poor, the needy, the helpless, and the infirm, and for his personal kindness. His wide-ranging activities brought him a prominence in national life unmatched by any other churchman of the time and enhanced the status of the Catholic Church in the United States. He died of a stroke in New York City on Dec. 2, while preparing to visit American troops abroad as he had done every year since 1942. He was a patron of literature, sponsored the Catholic Encyclopedia for School and Home (1965) and the New Catholic Encyclopedia (1967), and was the author of a dozen books, among them *Action This Day* (1944), *Prayers and Poems* (1946), *The Foundling* (1951), *Cardinal Spellman's Prayer Book* (1952), and *What America Means to Me* (1953). He received honorary degrees from more than a score of colleges and universities, was honored by the U.S. Navy and by Belgium, and was the recipient of the Congressional Medal.

SPENCER, FRANCIS A. (1845–1913), biblical scholar. Son of an Episcopal priest, he was born in New York City on Feb. 17, became a Catholic in 1866, joined the Paulists, and was ordained in 1869. He was assigned to St. Paul the Apostle Church in New York but in

1871 left the Paulists to join the Dominicans. He became a recognized authority on liturgical music and served on a commission on church music under Cardinal James Gibbons; he was prior of St. Rose Priory in Kentucky and of St. Joseph Priory in Ohio, and was elected provincial of the Dominicans' St. Joseph's province in 1880. He translated the New Testament from the Greek, the first complete translation of the New Testament from the Greek into English under Catholic auspices, but it remained unpublished until 1937, when it was edited by Dominican Frs. Charles J. Callan and John A. McHugh. Spencer published a translation of the four gospels from the Greek in 1889. He died in Washington, D.C., on June 12.

STANG, WILLIAM (1854–1907), bishop. Born in Langenbrucken, Baden, Germany, on Aug. 21, he studied at the minor seminary in St. Nicolas, Belgium, and the American College, Louvain, and was ordained at Louvain in 1878. He went to the United States the same year, became a curate at the cathedral in Providence, Rhode Island, and was pastor of St. Ann's parish, Cranston, Rhode Island, in 1884. He then was appointed rector of the cathedral and chancellor of the diocese, and served in those positions until 1895, when he was appointed vice-rector of the American College at Louvain; three years later he became professor of moral theology there. He returned to Providence in 1899, became pastor of St. Edward Church there in 1901, and was appointed first bishop of the newly established diocese of Fall River, Massachusetts, in 1904; he remained in that position until his death in Rochester, Minnesota, on Feb. 2. He was the author of several theological and philosophical treatises, a biography of Martin Luther, a history of the Reformation, a study of the Huguenots, a study of socialism and Christianity, and a business guide for priests.

STARIHA, JOHN (1845–1915), bishop. Born in Semic, Krain (Carniola), Austria (now in Yugoslavia), on May 12, he studied there and at St. Francis Seminary, Milwaukee, Wisconsin, and was ordained in 1869. He engaged in pastoral work in the Saulte Ste. Marie and Marquette dioceses until 1871, when he joined the diocese of St. Paul, Minnesota. He became pastor of St. Francis de Sales Church there and was vicar-general of that diocese from 1897 until 1902, when he was consecrated first bishop of the newly established diocese of Lead, South Dakota (transferred to Rapid City in 1930). He resigned in 1909 because of ill health and was appointed titular bishop of Autipatris. He returned to Austria and died there in Laibach on Nov. 28.

STARR, ELIZA ALLEN (1824–1901), educator, author. Born in Deerfield, Massachusetts, on Aug. 29, she studied art in Boston, opened a studio there, moved it to Brooklyn, New York, and then to Philadelphia, and subsequently accepted a position as a tutor of a wealthy planter's family in Natchez, Mississippi. She returned to Brooklyn as a teacher in 1853 and then went back to Philadelphia, where she became a Catholic in 1854. In 1856 she moved to Chicago, where she worked with Jane Addams at Hull House. She opened an art studio and instituted an annual series of lectures on art and literature and in 1871 went to St. Mary's College, South Bend, Indiana, to establish an art department. In 1879 she left St. Mary's to study art in Italy and on her return to the United States continued her art lectures at St. Joseph's College, Chicago, which had been provided her by the archbishop and priests of the archdiocese. She wrote several books, *Pilgrims* *and Shrines* (two volumes, 1885), *Patron Saints* (two series: 1871, 1881), *Christian Art in Our Own Age* (1891), *Songs of a Lifetime* (1888), *Women's Work in Art,* and *The Literature of Christian Art,* received the Laetare Medal in 1885, the first woman recipient of that award, and in 1893 a gold medal at the World's Columbian Exposition in Chicago. She died in Durand, Illinois, on Sept. 7.

STEARNS, FOSTER (1881–1956), librarian, Congressman. Born in Hull, Massachusetts, on July 29, he was educated at Amherst College, Massachusetts, (B.A. 1903) and Harvard (M.A. 1906), graduated from General Theological Seminary, New York City, in 1909, and was ordained an Episcopal priest. He became rector of Christ Church, Sheffield, Massachusetts, and resigned when he became a Catholic in 1911. He was librarian of the Museum of Fine Arts in Boston in 1913–17 and the Massachusetts state librarian in 1917 until the United States entered World War I, when he served in the 15th Infantry of the A.E.F. and engaged in intelligence work in France. After the war he served in the American diplomatic service in Washington, Constantinople, and Paris in 1920–24. He then returned to library work as librarian at Holy Cross College, Worcester, Massachusetts, where he set up the Dinan Library in 1925–30. He entered politics in 1936, served a term in the New Hampshire legislature, was in the United States House of Representatives in 1939–45 for three terms, and was defeated in a bid for the Republican nomination for the U.S. Senate in 1944. He was the author of *Edward Everett* (1928) and *Bl. Adrian Fortescue* (1936), received awards for gallantry in action during the St. Mihiel offensive in 1918 when he was wounded, and was hon-

ored by the Vatican. He died in Exeter, New Hampshire, on June 4.

STECK, FRANCIS BORGIA (1884–1962), historian. Henry Steck was born in St. Louis on July 11, studied at St. Joseph Seminary, Teutopolis, Illinois, for five years, and in 1904 joined the Franciscans, taking the name Francis Borgia. He was ordained in 1911, taught at St. Joseph's in 1913–19, and in 1924–29 studied at Catholic University (Ph.D. 1927). He taught Spanish American history at Catholic University in 1933–47, retired to Quincy (Illinois) College in 1947 because of ill health, and died there on July 5. He wrote several books, among them *Glories of the Franciscan Order* (1920), *The Franciscans and the Protestant Revolution* (1920), *The Jolliet-Marquette Expedition, 1673* (1928), and *Marquette Legends* (1960), in which he advanced the novel thesis that Marquette was not the leader of the Jolliet expedition in 1673, that he did not write the *Narrative* of this expedition or the *Journal of the Second Voyage* (which was made in 1674–75, to the Illinois country) and that he doubted that Marquette was a priest.

STEINMEYER, FERDINAND (1720–86), missionary. Born in Swabia, Germany, on Oct. 13, he joined the Jesuits at Landsberg in 1743, and though he wished to be a missionary to China, he was sent to America instead in 1752. He engaged in pastoral work in Lancaster, Pennsylvania, until 1758, when he was transferred to St. Joseph's Church, Philadelphia, to work among the German-speaking Catholics there; he also engaged in missionary work in New Jersey and New York, though a priest entering New York at that time was subject to the death penalty, so he sometimes used the alias Farmer. He was widely known for his scholarship as a philosopher and an astronomer, and was appointed one of the first trustees of the University of Pennsylvania in 1779. He died in Philadelphia on Aug. 17.

STEVENS, MOTHER GEORGIA (1871–1946), liturgical music educator. Born in Boston on May 8, she was educated at Mrs. Gilliam's School there and the Convent of the Sacred Heart, Providence, Rhode Island, and studied music in Boston and at the Hoch Conservatorium, Frankfurt, Germany. She became a Catholic in 1895, joined the Society of the Sacred Heart (RSCJ), and took her religious studies in Roehampton, England. She was assigned to the College of the Sacred Heart (Manhattanville) in New York City, began teaching music there, and in 1916 founded the Pius X School of Liturgical Music at Manhattanville with Mrs. Justine B. Ward and became its director. She lectured on the liturgy and Gregorian chant, wrote the eight-volume *Tone and Rhythm* textbook series (1935–45) for elementary schools, and died in Boston on May 8.

STODDARD, CHARLES WARREN (1843–1909), author. Born in Rochester, New York, on Aug. 7, he was taken when a child by his parents to New York City, where they lived until they moved to California in 1855. He spent 1857–59 in New York and then returned to San Francisco, where he worked in a bookshop. He studied at a prep school of the University of California for a year but was unable to attend college because of ill health. He visited the Hawaiian Islands in 1864 to recover his health and subsequently made other trips there and to Tahiti. While in Hawaii he became a friend of Fr. Damien. On his return to the United States, he became a Catholic in 1867 and began his writing career when his *Poems,* edited by Bret Harte, were pub-

lished the same year. He became a roving reporter for the San Francisco *Chronicle* in 1873, the year he published *South-Sea Idyls,* and spent the next decade traveling in Europe (he was Mark Twain's secretary in London for a short time), the Near East, and Hawaii and writing of his travels. In 1885 he accepted a position as professor of English at Notre Dame but was soon forced to relinquish it because of illness. In 1889–1902 he was a lecturer in English literature at Catholic University—the first layman on its faculty. Illness again forced him to resign, in 1902, and he spent the next three years in Cambridge. Then, in 1905, he returned to California, where he settled in Monterey in a vain attempt to regain his health. He died there on Apr. 23. He wrote numerous books, among them *The Lepers of Molokai* (1885), *Hawaiian Life* (1894), *In the Footprints of the Padres* (1902), *Father Damien, a Sketch* (1903), *For the Pleasure of His Company* (1903, his only novel), *With Staff and Scrip* (1904), and *A Troubled Heart and How It Was Comforted At Last* (1885), the story of his conversion.

STODDARD, JOHN LAWSON (1850–1931), author. Born in Brookline, Massachusetts, on Apr. 24, he graduated from Williams College in 1871, studied for the Congregationalist ministry at Yale Divinity School, but abandoned that calling and taught the classics at Boston Latin School in 1873–74. He began a highly successful career in 1879 as a lecturer on his travels all over the world, from which he developed the ten-volume *John L. Stoddard's Lectures* (1897–98, 1901), *Glimpses of the World* (1892), and *Beautiful Scenes of America* (1902). He retired from his lecture tours in 1897, married Ida O'Donnell in 1901 (he had divorced his first wife, Mary Brown, in 1888), and moved to Europe, where he compiled his twelve-volume *The Stoddard Library: a Thousand Hours of Entertainment with the World's Great Writers* (1910). He was sympathetic to the German-Austrian coalition in World War I and wrote several pamphlets in its defense. He became a Catholic in 1922 and spent the rest of his life writing and translating books on religious subjects. Among these were the best-selling story of his conversion, *Rebuilding a Lost Faith* (1922), *Twelve Years in the Catholic Church* (1930), and his translation of Ferdinand Prat's two-volume *Theology of Saint Paul* (1926–27) and of Hilarin Felder's two-volume *Christ and the Critics* (1924). He died on his estate near Merano, Italy, on June 5.

STOKES, WALTER (1923–69), philosopher. Born in New York City on Aug. 3, he joined the Jesuits in 1942, studied at Woodstock (Maryland) College and St. Louis University (Ph.D.), and taught at St. Peter's College, Jersey City, New Jersey, spent a year studying at Cambridge, and then began teaching at Fordham. He was a pioneer in the American Thomists' reexamination of St. Thomas Aquinas' metaphysics in the light of contemporary process philosophy, with emphasis on the challenge to Thomistic metaphysics of A. N. Whitehead's process philosophy. He wrote and lectured extensively on the subject and died in New York City on Mar. 18.

STONE, JAMES KENT (1840–1921). Son of Dr. John Seeley Stone, a prominent Episcopal clergyman, and dean of the Episcopal Theological School, Cambridge, Massachusetts, and Mary Kent, daughter of the chancellor of New York, he was born in Boston on Nov. 10 and graduated from Harvard in 1861 after studying two years at Göttingen University, Germany. He fought in the Union Army during the Civil War, married Cornelia Fay in 1863, became an instructor at Kenyon College, Gambier, Ohio, and was ordained an Episcopal priest in 1866. He became president of Kenyon in 1867 and was named president of Hobart College, Geneva, New York, in 1868. After the sudden death of his wife, he became a convert to Catholicism in 1869, joined the Paulists, and was ordained in 1872. He left the Paulists in 1877 to become a Passionist, taking his vows and the name Fidelis of the Cross in 1878. He went to Buenos Aires and became superior of the Passionist community there in 1881, then worked in Argentina and Chile, and established Passionist houses in Chile, Argentina, and Brazil. He returned to the United States for a preaching tour in 1894–97 and was stationed in the United States from 1899, serving as director of Harvard's summer school from 1901 until 1908, when he was named provincial of South America. When the Carranza government barred him from Mexico in 1914, he worked for a time in Cuba and then returned to the United States. He retired in 1917, went to California the same year to recover his health, and died there in Mateo on Oct. 14. He was the author of *The Invitation Heeded* (1870) and *An Awakening and What Followed* (1920).

STORER, BELLAMY (1847–1922), diplomat. Born in Cincinnati, Ohio, on Aug. 28, he was educated at Harvard (B.A. 1867, M.A. 1870), studied law at Cincinnati University Law School (LL.B. 1869), and began practicing law in Cincinnati. He was assistant attorney for the federal Southern District of Ohio in 1869–70, married Maria Longworth Nichols in 1886, and served in the House of Representatives in 1891–95. His wife became a Catholic in 1892 and he became one in 1896. He was a warm supporter of William McKinley in the presidential election of 1900, and when elected President, Mc-

Kinley appointed him as minister to Belgium in 1897. He served until 1899, was minister to Spain in 1899–1902, and in 1902 was appointed ambassador to Austria-Hungary by President Theodore Roosevelt. Both Bellamys helped in the negotiations between the United States and the Vatican over the Friars' land problem when the United States took over the Philippine Islands after the Spanish-American War. His unsuccessful attempt to get the red hat for Archbishop John Ireland, at the instigation of President Roosevelt, caused Roosevelt to remove him as ambassador to Vienna in 1906, when the story appeared in the press and was denied officially by the President. The Storers then retired from public life, and he returned to his law practice. They both devoted themselves to philanthropic projects. He worked for Belgian relief in Cincinnati during World War I, and in 1914–15 he headed a bureau of inquiry in Rome to handle requests to Pope Benedict XV for information regarding missing soldiers; he personally paid the expenses of the bureau. He died in Paris on Nov. 12 and Maria (born Mar. 20, 1840, in Cincinnati) also died in Paris, on Apr. 30, 1932.

STRITCH, SAMUEL ALPHONSUS (1887–1958), cardinal. Born in Nashville, Tennessee, on Aug. 17, of Irish immigrant parents, he was educated at St. Gregory's Minor Seminary, Cincinnati, Ohio, and at the North American College and the Propaganda, Rome (Ph.D. 1906, S.T.D. 1910), and was ordained in Rome in 1910. He served as a curate in 1910–11 and as pastor in 1911–15 of St. Patrick's Church, Memphis, Tennessee, became secretary to the bishop of Nashville, and then chancellor of that diocese in 1915, and was superintendent of diocesan schools from 1915. He was made a domestic prelate in 1921 and later that year was consecrated bishop of Toledo,

Ohio—the youngest member of the American hierarchy. He opened the first diocesan teachers' college in the United States in 1924, began construction of a new cathedral, and built twenty-four churches while bishop of Toledo. He was appointed archbishop of Milwaukee, Wisconsin, in 1930 and despite the depression of the 1930s expanded the facilities of the see and established the *Catholic Herald Citizen* as the diocesan newspaper. He was transferred to Chicago in 1939 and during his episcopate worked to better the condition of Puerto Ricans and blacks (he insisted on racial integration in diocesan institutions and founded a branch of the Catholic International Council in Chicago in 1945). He was a leader in the movement for higher standards of morality in motion pictures and was deeply interested in the Catholic press (the diocesan newspaper, *The New World,* under his leadership increased its circulation from 10,000 in 1940 to 210,000 in 1958) and in radio and television as media of communications for the Church (he established an archdiocesan office for radio and television in 1957). He encouraged liturgical music (he appointed an archdiocesan commission on sacred music and forbade the playing of popular tunes at weddings and funerals in the see), greatly expanded the facilities of the archdiocese and Catholic Charities and its services, helped to develop the Catholic Youth Organization, instituted the Confraternity of Christian Doctrine in the see in 1941, and supported the Back of the Yards Council to improve urban living conditions. He was chairman of the board of the National Catholic Welfare Conference (NCWC) in 1939 and 1945 and chairman of the NCWC's Department of Social Action study in 1935–39, and was made a cardinal in 1946. He was active in charity and missionary work (he was chancellor of the Catholic Church Extension Society in 1939), was elected chairman of the American Board of Catholic Missions in 1931, and with Archbishop John T. McNicholas of Cincinnati, organized the Catholic Commission on Intellectual and Cultural Affairs. He served as president of the National Catholic Community Service (an agency of the USO, the United Services Organization) during World War II and in 1944 was chairman of the governing committee of War Relief Service, which he had helped to establish in 1943. He supported the United Nations and the Marshall Plan, fought Communism, secularism and materialism, anti-Semitism and persecution of the Jews, helped send assistance to Poland, and aided Italian immigrants (he helped found the American Commission on Italian Migration) and Hungarian refugees. He favored relaxing American immigration policies and opposed governmental encroachment in social assistance. A leader in the struggle for social justice, he was also known for his support of labor. He was appointed to the Roman Curia as pro-prefect of the Sacred Congregation for the Propagation of the Faith in 1958, in charge of all missionary activities of the Church—the first American to head a Curia congregation. He died less than two months later of a stroke in Rome on May 27.

STUART, HENRY LONGAN (1874–1928), author. Born in Clapham, London, he was educated at Ratcliffe College, North Kensington, London, worked as the London representative of the Shropshire Iron Works, and emigrated to the United States as a young man. He was a rancher in Colorado, became a newspaper reporter, and served in the 94th Brigade in the Royal Field Artillery during World War I. He served for a time with the Italian liaison staff and after the armistice was a staff officer in Paris in 1919; then he returned to the

United States and joined the staff of the Boston *Herald.* He began to review books and write articles for magazines, helped found and joined the staff of *Commonweal* in 1924, and wrote the novels *Weeping Cross* (1908) and *Fenelle* (1911) during temporary stays in London while also doing newspaper work and translating works of Paul Claudel and Julian Green. He died in New York City on Aug. 26.

SULLIVAN, JOSEPH VINCENT (1919–82), bishop. Born in Kansas City, Missouri, on Aug. 15, he was educated at St. John's and St. Louis seminaries and Catholic University (S.T.L. 1946), and was ordained in 1946. He continued his studies at Catholic University (S.T.D. 1949), served as a curate at Holy Name and St. Aloysius churches, Kansas City, Missouri, and was superintendent of schools of the Kansas City diocese in 1951–57. He was made a domestic prelate in 1957, was chancellor of Kansas City in 1957–67, was consecrated titular bishop of Tagamuta and auxiliary of Kansas City–St. Joseph in 1967, and also served as vicar-general of the see. In 1974 he was appointed bishop of Baton Rouge, Louisiana, and held that position until Sept. 4, when he died of a heart attack in Baton Rouge.

SULLIVAN, PETER JOHN (1821–83), general. Born in Cork, Ireland, on Mar. 15, he was brought to the United States when he was two by his parents, who settled in Philadelphia. He was educated at the University of Pennsylvania, served in the Mexican War, and was commissioned major; on his return he was made one of the official stenographers of the United States Senate. In 1848 he went to Cincinnati, was admitted to the bar, and actively opposed the Know-Nothing movement. At the outbreak of the Civil War, he rejoined the Union army, helped organize several volunteer regiments, was made colonel of the 48th Ohio Regiment, and was brevetted brigadier general of volunteers in 1865. After the war he was appointed United States minister to Colombia and served in that position until 1869, when he returned to Cincinnati and resumed his law practice. He died in Cincinnati on Mar. 2.

SUMMERS, WALTER G. (1889–1938), psychologist. Born in New York City on Mar. 23, he was educated at St. Francis Xavier College there, joined the Jesuits in 1907, studied at Woodstock (Maryland) College (B.A.) and Georgetown (Ph.D. 1919), and was ordained in Georgetown in 1921. He continued his studies at the Gregorian, Rome (Ph.D. 1923), was professor of physiology at Georgetown in 1923–30, and was professor of psychology and head of the psychology department at Fordham from 1931 until his death in New York City on Sept. 24. He was one of the Catholic pioneers in the new science of psychology in the United States, was the inventor of a lie-detecting apparatus which became widely used in police and psychiatric work, wrote numerous magazine articles, and was the author of *Textbook in Experimental Physics* (1916).

SURRATT, JOHN. *See* Surratt, Mary Eugenia.

SURRATT, MARY EUGENIA (c. 1817–65). Mary Jenkins was born of an old Maryland family in Prince Georges County, Maryland, was educated in a Catholic school in Alexandria, Virginia, and became a Catholic. She married John Harris Surratt, a plantation owner, about 1835, and when he died in 1862, leaving his family in straitened financial circumstances, she moved to Washington, D.C. and in 1864 opened a rooming house. One of the boarders was John Wilkes Booth, who, while living in the Surratt boarding house, hatched a plot to abduct President Lincoln and another plot to assassinate him. Two other members of the Booth conspiracy, George Atzerodt and Lewis Thornton Powell (alias Payne), also lodged there for a short period. Meanwhile Mary's son, John, had become a secret dispatch rider for the Confederacy and Booth interested him in the abduction plot. When the abduction attempt failed, John fled; when Lincoln was assassinated, eight alleged accomplices, including Mary, were arrested. They were tried by a military commission, and six, of whom Mary was one, were found guilty of conspiracy in the assassination on largely circumstantial evidence in 1865 and sentenced to death. Mary was hanged in Washington, D.C., on July 17. Modern historians believe the execution was a gross miscarriage of justice, that she was not involved in the assassination plot and was sentenced to death because of pressure on the military commission by Secretary of War Edwin M. Stanton and the advocate general, Joseph Holt, and the bitter anti-Confederate sentiment of the times. John was later captured and tried in a civil court in 1867. The jury voted eight to four for acquittal, but he was not released from prison until more than a year later; the government nol-prossed the indictment against him in 1868.

SWEENEY, JAMES JOSEPH (1898–1968), bishop. Born in San Francisco on June 19, he was educated at St. Patrick's Seminary, Menlo Park, California, and was ordained in 1925. He was a curate at St. Paul's Church, San Francisco, in 1925–31, was made a domestic prelate in 1939, and was director of the archdiocesan Society for the Propagation of the Faith in 1931–41. He was appointed first bishop of the newly established diocese of Honolulu, Hawaii, in 1941, and during his bishopric more than doubled the number of priests in the diocese, brought new religious orders into the see, expanded the educational and charitable institutions in the see, and organized a diocesan unit of Catholic Charities. He died in San Francisco on June 19.

SWINT, JOHN J. (1879–1962), archbishop. Born in Florence, West Virginia, on Dec. 15, he was educated at St. Charles College, Ellicott City, Maryland (B.A. 1899), St. Mary's Seminary, Baltimore (S.T.D. 1904), and was ordained in 1904. He served as assistant at Wellsburg, West Virginia, for a short time and then continued his studies at the Apostolic Mission House in Washington, D.C., in 1904–5. He was pastor at Hinton, West Virginia, in 1905–8, established the diocesan Mission Band in 1908, and spent the next fourteen years heading it while giving missions all over West Virginia and also serving as pastor of St. Patrick's Church in Weston from 1914. He was consecrated titular bishop of Sura and auxiliary of Wheeling, West Virginia, in 1922, was administrator of the see in October–December of that year, and succeeded to the see as its fourth bishop on Dec. 11. During his episcopate he greatly expanded the facilities of the diocese, building 101 churches and 43 schools and Wheeling College and several hospitals, homes for the aged, and schools of nursing. He was the author of several books, among them *The Moral Law* (1934), *Christ the Organizer of the Church* (1936), *Back to Christ* (1940), *Forgotten Truths* (1941), and *The Sweetest Story Ever Told* (1947). He was made an Assistant at the Pontifical Throne in 1929, was given the personal title of archbishop in 1954, and died in Wheeling on Nov. 13.

T

TABB, JOHN BANNISTER (1845–1909), poet. Of an old Virginia plantation family, he was born at Mattoax, Amelia County, near Richmond, Virginia, on Mar. 22 and was privately educated. An ardent supporter of the Confederacy, he was unsuccessful in an attempt to join the Confederate Army, because of poor eyesight, and became a blockade runner out of Wilmington, North Carolina, during the Civil War. He was captured in 1864 and imprisoned at Point Lookout, where he met and formed a lifelong friendship with Sidney Lanier. On his release from prison, in 1865, he studied piano, became a teacher at St. Paul's School for Boys, Baltimore, and for a few months in 1870 at Racine College, Michigan; in 1872 he became a Catholic. He then studied at St. Charles College, Ellicott City, Maryland, graduating in 1875, taught for three years at St. Peter's Boys School, Baltimore, and in 1881 entered St. Mary's Seminary, Baltimore, and was ordained in 1884. He then began teaching at St. Charles College and taught there until blindness ended his teaching career, in 1908; he died the following year in Ellicott City on Nov. 19. He was widely known for his poetry and is considered the outstanding lyrical poet of American Catholicism. Among his poetical works are *Poems* (1883), *Octave to Mary* (1893), *Poems* (1894), *Child Verse* (1899), *Two Later Lyrics* (1902), *The Rosary in Rhyme* (1904), and *Later Poems* (1910).

TAKACH, BASIL (1879–1948), bishop. Born in Vuckovar, Hungary, on Oct. 27, he was educated at the Greek Catholic Seminary at Uzhgorod and was ordained in 1902. He engaged in pastoral activities in the Mukačevo diocese, became controller of the see, and was spiritual director of the diocesan seminaries at Uzhgorod in 1919–24. He was appointed titular bishop of Zela and first bishop of the Byzantine Rite exarchate of Pittsburgh in 1924, holding the latter position until his death there on May 13. During his administration he worked to overcome friction among the various national groups in the exarchate, supported the development of Catholic fraternal groups, and enforced a 1928 ruling of the Holy See that only unmarried men could be ordained to the priesthood.

TALBOT, FRANCIS X. (1889–1953), author, editor. Born in Philadelphia, on Jan. 25, he joined the Jesuits in 1906, when he graduated from high school. He studied at St. Joseph's College (B.A. 1909) and Woodstock (Maryland) College in 1910–13, taught at Loyola School, in New York City, in 1913–16 and at Boston College in 1917–18, and finished his studies for the priesthood at Woodstock (M.A. 1913). He was ordained at Woodstock in 1921, continued his studies at the Gregorian, Rome (Ph.D.), was literary editor of the Jesuit *America* in 1923–36 and editor-in-chief in 1936–44 and was also editor of *Cath-*

olic Mind in 1936–44 and of *Thought* in 1936–40. He founded the Catholic Book Club in 1928, the Catholic Poetry Society in 1930, and the Spiritual Book Associates in 1932 and was a cofounder of Pro Parvulis Book Club, for children, in 1934; he helped organize the Catholic Theatre Conference and the Catholic Library Association and was president of Loyola College, Baltimore, in 1947–50. He was archivist at Georgetown for a short time, was parish priest at St. Aloysius Church, Washington, D.C., in 1950–52, conducted retreats at Manresa-on-the-Severn, Annapolis, Maryland, in 1952 and then became a parish priest at Holy Trinity Church, Georgetown. He contributed articles to the Encyclopaedia Britannica and wrote poetry, plays, historical works, and biographies, chief of which were *Saint Among the Savages* (1935), on Isaac Jogues, and *Saint Among the Hurons* (1949), on Jean de Brébeuf. He died in Washington, D.C. on Dec. 3.

TALON, PIERRE (1676–91), explorer. Born in Quebec, he was brought to France and soon after to Louisiana, when he was eight, by his parents, who were members of La Salle's colonization party. Soon after, he was sent to learn the language of the Cenis Indians and spent six years among them. When many of the colonists were massacred and Pierre's father died, the country was occupied by Spaniards, and Pierre and his mother and family went to Mexico City. They spent the next ten years there, becoming part of the viceroy's household, and Pierre and his brother joined the Spanish Marines; when his ship was captured by the French he became a French marine, though he wanted to return to New Spain. He then went to Brest, France, and described to the French the people and territory of southern America. While with the Cenis

Indians he may have crossed the Mississippi River. He died in France.

TANEY, ROGER BROOKE (1777–1865), jurist. Of a wealthy slave-owning family of tobacco planters, he was born in Calvert County, Maryland, on Mar. 17 and was educated at private schools and by tutors and at Dickinson College, Carlisle, Pennsylvania (B.A. 1795). He studied law in the Baltimore offices of Jeremiah Chase, one of the chief justices of the General Court of Maryland, and was admitted to the Maryland bar in 1799. He began to practice law, became involved in politics as a Federalist, served in the Maryland House of Delegates in 1799–1800, was defeated for reelection in 1800, and resumed his law practice. He was again defeated in a bid for a seat in the House of Delegates in 1802, and in 1806 married Anne Phoebe Key, sister of the author of "The Star-Spangled Banner." He was one of the defense lawyers for General James Wilkinson, who was charged with being an accomplice of Aaron Burr, and secured the general's acquittal. Defeated for election to the U.S. House of Representatives in 1812, he gained control of the Federalist Party in Maryland though he had broken with his party over the War of 1812, and was elected to the Maryland Senate for a five-year term in 1816. He moved to Baltimore in 1823, became one of that city's leading lawyers, and again broke with the Federalists, in 1824, to support Andrew Jackson for President, this time permanently though by now the party was practically dissolved. He served as attorney general of Maryland in 1827–31 and was appointed Attorney General of the United States by President Andrew Jackson in 1831 to assist the President in the struggle over the renewal of the charter of the Bank of the United States. He wrote Jackson's message vetoing the bill to recharter the bank in 1832 and was appointed Secretary of the Treasury in 1833, when, first, Louis McLane, Secretary of the Treasury, and when he was made Secretary of State, Jackson's newly appointed Secretary of the Treasury, William J. Duane, refused to withdraw government funds from the bank as Jackson had ordered; Taney did so at once. When Taney's appointment came up for confirmation in the Senate, it was rejected—the first time a presidential cabinet appointee had been rejected by the Senate—in 1834. The following year, Jackson nominated Taney for associate justice of the United States Supreme Court, but the Senate adjourned without acting on the appointment—tantamount to a rejection. In both cases the action taken by the Senate was motivated in large measure by political opposition to the President. When Chief Justice John Marshall died, later in 1835, Jackson appointed Taney fifth Chief Justice of the United States, and this time the appointment was confirmed, in 1836, though over the strong opposition of the Whigs and especially of Senators Clay and Webster. The first Catholic to hold this position, he held it until his death. During his tenure he ruled repeatedly in favor of states' rights though in sustaining fugitive-slave laws he declared free states could not refuse to surrender escaped slaves, as was required by federal law. The most notable case decided by the Supreme Court while he was Chief Justice was the *Dred Scott* case, in 1857, in which he delivered the majority opinion that slaves were not citizens but merely property and "had no rights which the white man was bound to respect" and that Congress could not exclude slavery from the territories of the United States. The ruling caused tremendous controversy throughout the entire country and especially infuriated the abolitionists and the Republicans. During the Civil War, Lincoln considered Taney his archfoe and ignored Taney's ruling against the suspension of the writ of habeas corpus. Though Taney believed whites and blacks could not satisfactorily live together in large numbers, he had as a youth manumitted the slaves he had inherited from his father and provided those too old to work with a pension for life and cooperated in projects for colonizing free blacks in Africa. He died in Washington, D.C., on Oct. 12. His decision in the *Dred Scott* case was based on his belief that as the law was written no other decision could be rendered and though at the time of his death he was scorned by the American public and feeling ran high against him and his decision in the *Dred Scott* case is considered one of the major causes of the Civil War, scholars now feel he made a significant contribution to constitutional law and was an outstanding jurist; a later Chief Justice, Charles Evans Hughes, said of him that "he was a great Chief Justice."

TANSILL, CHARLES CALLAN (1890–1964), historian. Born in Fredericksburg, Texas, on Dec. 9, he was educated at Catholic University (B.A. 1912, M.A. 1913, Ph.D. 1915) and married Helen Cecilia Parker in 1915. He taught American history at Catholic University in 1915–16, received a Ph.D. from Johns Hopkins in 1918, was acting director of the Legislative Reference Service, Library of Congress, in 1918–28, and was an adviser on diplomacy to the Senate Foreign Relations Committee in 1918–28. He taught American history at American University, Washington, D.C., in 1919–37, was Albert Shaw lecturer in diplomatic history at Johns Hopkins in 1931, and was acting dean of the graduate school at American University in 1934–35. In 1937 a radio address he made in Berlin in which he called Hitler "an inspired leader" caused a furor and on his return to the United States he was forced to resign from Catholic University. He was unable to secure an academic position until 1939, when he became professor of American history at Fordham, serving until 1944, when he went to Georgetown, where he remained until his retirement, in 1947. After World War II he became a bitter foe of Communism, was an adviser to Senator Joseph McCarthy, and accused Presidents Roosevelt and Truman of betraying the country. Best known of the several books he wrote was *America Goes to War* (1938), in which he advances his thesis that America's entry into World War I was a mistake, and *Back Door to War, 1933–1941,* which was highly critical of America's pre-World War II foreign policy, and blamed President Roosevelt for Pearl Harbor. He died in Washington, D.C., on Nov. 12.

TARPEY, MOTHER MARY CO-LUMBA (1892–1979), mother general. Elizabeth Helena Tarpey was born in Philadelphia on Jan. 4 and joined the Maryknoll Sisters in 1919, the year before the Holy See approved a group of sixty-five young women as a religious congregation, called at first the Foreign Mission Sisters of St. Dominic and later the Maryknoll Sisters of St. Dominic, and took the name Mary Columba. In 1925 she was elected first assistant to the mother general, was appointed superior of the Philippines mission in 1927, and was again elected assistant mother general in 1931. She held this position until 1947, when she was elected mother superior to succeed the foundress of the Congregation. During her generalate, two new novitiates were opened in the United States and seventy-two missions were initiated in the Orient, Latin America, and Africa and on islands in the Pacific and Indian oceans. She was reelected mother supe-

rior in 1953, and at the expiration of her second term served as superior of the midwestern region for six years. Ill the last years of her life, she died at the mother house, in Ossining, New York, on Aug. 27.

TAYLOR, VINCENT GEORGE (1877–1959), abbot. Born in Norfolk, Virginia, on Sept. 19, he studied at Belmont Abbey, North Carolina, joined the Benedictines in 1897, and was ordained in 1902. He engaged in missionary and pastoral work in North Carolina, was elected abbot ordinary of Belmont Abbey in 1924, and while serving in that post the next thirty-five years developed the Abbey and Belmont Abbey Junior College, which became a senior college in 1952; he served as its president in 1924–56. He died in Belmont Abbey on Nov. 5.

TEKAKWITHA, BL. KATERI (c. 1656–80). Daughter of a Christian Algonquin who had been raised among the French at Three Rivers, Canada, and was captured by Iroquois Indians and married to a pagan Mohawk chieftain, Kateri was born at the Indian village of Ossernenon (also called Candawaga and Caughnawaga by the Indians, now Auriesville, New York) and was orphaned as a child when her parents and her brother died during a smallpox epidemic. She, too, was a smallpox victim, which left her eyesight impaired and her face disfigured. Raised by her uncle, she was converted to Catholicism by Fr. Jacques de Lamberville, a French Jesuit missionary, in 1676. Subjected to great abuse and ostracized by her relatives and fellow Indians because of her new religion, she fled her native village in 1677 and trekked two hundred miles through the wilderness on foot to the Christian Indian village near Montreal, Canada. She made her first communion on Christmas Day, lived a life of great austerity and holiness, and in 1679 took a vow of chastity and dedicated herself to Christ. She died at Caughnawaga, Canada, on Apr. 17 and was venerated immediately for her holiness and concern for all. She was known as the Lily of the Mohawks; miracles were attributed to her, and in 1943 she was declared Venerable by Pope Pius XII; in 1980 she was beatified by Pope John Paul II.

TENNELLY, JOHN BENJAMIN (1890–1981). Born in Denver, Colorado, he was educated at St. Francis Seminary, Milwaukee, Wisconsin, St. Mary's College, Kansas, St. Mary's Seminary, Baltimore (B.A., M.A., S.T.B.) and the Collegio Angelico, Rome (S.T.D.). He joined the Sulpicians in 1913 and was ordained the same year, and taught apologetics and Scripture at St. Mary's Seminary, Baltimore, in 1917–20 and at the Sulpician Seminary, Catholic University, in 1920–35; he was president of the Sulpician Seminary in 1926–32. He became secretary of the Negro and Indian Mission Board in 1925 and was director of the Commission for Catholic Missions among Colored People and Indians from 1936 to 1976, when he retired. He died in Catonsville, Maryland, on Oct. 18.

TENNEY, SARAH BROWNSON (1839–76), author. Daughter of Orestes Brownson, Sarah Brownson was born in Chelsea, Massachusetts, on June 7. She wrote literary criticism for her father's *Brownson's Quarterly Review* and many articles and poems, which appeared mainly in Catholic magazines, three novels, *Marian Elwood* (1863), *At Anchor* (1865), and *Heremore Brandon* (1869), and a life of Prince Dmitri Gallitzen (1873). She married William J. Tenney in 1873 and died in Elizabeth, New Jersey, on Oct. 30.

TENNEY, WILLIAM JEWETT (1814–83), editor. Son of a Congregational clergyman, he was born in Newport, Rhode Island, probably in June, graduated from Yale in 1832, and began studying medicine but soon after abandoned it for law. He married Elizabeth M. Benton in 1839, was admitted to the bar, and about 1840 went to New York City, where he joined the editorial staff of the *Journal of Commerce* in 1841. He contributed editorially to the *Evening Post* in 1841–43 and 1847–48, became an editor with D. Appleton & Company in 1853, and remained with Appleton until his death. In 1861 he began editing Appleton's Annual Cyclopaedia, which he edited until his death. He lived in Brooklyn for a time and was judge of a criminal court there and was collector of the port of Elizabeth, New Jersey, during the administration of President Buchanan and held several local public offices in Elizabeth (where he had taken up residence) including president of the board of education. After the death of his first wife, he married Orestes Brownson's daughter, Sarah, in 1873. He died in Newark, New Jersey, on Sept. 20. He wrote *A Military and Naval History of the Rebellion in the United States* (1865) and *A Grammatical Analysis* (1866), edited *The Queens of England* (1852) and collaborated with Jefferson Davis on the latter's *Rise and Fall of the Confederate Government* (1881). Though the date of his conversion to Catholicism is not known, it was of tremendous importance to him and caused an estrangement with his family and friends of his earlier years.

TERESA OF THE ARCTIC. See AMADEUS OF THE HEART OF JESUS, MOTHER.

THILL, FRANK AUGUSTINE (1893–1957), bishop. Born in Dayton, Ohio, on Oct. 12, he was educated at the University of Dayton (B.A., Ph.D.) and Mt. St. Mary of the West Seminary, Cincinnati, Ohio, was ordained in Cincinnati in 1920, and continued his studies at the Angelicum, Rome, where he received his J.C.L. in 1928. He organized the Catholic Students' Mission Crusade in 1918 and was its secretary-treasurer until 1935, when he became executive counselor. He was director of the Cincinnati archdiocesan Society for the Propagation of the Faith, was made a papal chamberlain in 1928, was chancellor of the Cincinnati archdiocese in 1935–38, and became a domestic prelate in 1937. He was consecrated bishop of Concordia, Kansas (transferred to Salina in 1944), in 1938 and held that position until his death. He died in Salina on May 21.

THORMAN, DONALD (1924–77), editor. Born in Oak Park, Illinois, on Dec. 23, he entered the Servite monastery of Our Lady of Sorrows, Ladysmith, Wisconsin, in 1941 but left the following year to join the U.S. Marine Corps. He served throughout World War II in the Marines, joined the Viatorian Fathers after the war, in 1946, but left the following year and studied at De Paul University (B.A. 1949) and Loyola University (M.A. 1950), both in Chicago, and the University of Fribourg, Switzerland. After a year studying for his doctorate at Fordham he returned to help his family, taught at Loyola in 1950–55, and in 1952 became managing editor of *The Voice of St. Jude* (now *U.S. Catholic*) and married Barbara Lisowski. He was managing editor of *Ave Maria* in 1956–62, publisher of the Spiritual Life Institute of America in 1962, and the following year formed his own company, Catholic Communications Consultants. In 1965 he became publisher of the year-old *National Catholic Reporter* and remained in that position until his

death, in Kansas City, Missouri, on Nov. 30 of hepatitis contracted while visiting China with a group of reporters. He was one of the leaders in implementing the reforms of Vatican Council II, was awarded the Catholic Press Association Award posthumously in 1978, and wrote four books: *The Emerging Layman* (1962), *Christian Vision* (1967), *American Catholics Face the Future* (1968), and *Power to the People of God* (1970).

TIEF, FRANCIS JOSEPH (1881–1965), bishop. Born in Greenwich, Connecticut, on Mar. 7, he was educated at Niagara University, New York, and St. Bonaventure College, Allegany, New York (B.A. 1905) and was ordained for the Kansas City, Missouri, diocese in 1908. He was a curate at Our Lady of Lourdes Church, New York City, in 1908, pastor of Sacred Heart Church, Webb City, Missouri, in 1908–10 and of the Kansas City cathedral in 1910–16, and was vicar-general of Kansas City in 1916–20. He was consecrated bishop of Concordia, Kansas (transferred to Salina in 1944) in 1921, resigned in 1938 and was appointed titular bishop of Nisa, and died in Denville, New Jersey, on Sept. 20.

TIERNAN, FRANCES CHRISTINE (1846–1920), novelist. Daughter of Charles and Elizabeth Caldwell Fisher, she was born in Salisbury, North Carolina, and became a Catholic in her youth. She had her first novel published in 1870, and in 1887 she married James Marquis Tiernan and went to Mexico with him. She wrote some forty novels under the name of Christian Reid between 1870 and 1915, among them *Land of the Sky, Under the Southern Cross, A Daughter of the Sierra, The Picture of Las Cruces,* and *The Wargrave Trust.* She returned to Salisbury on the death of her husband, in 1898. She was the recipient of the Laetare Medal in 1909; she died in Salisbury on Mar. 24.

TIERNEY, MICHAEL (1839–1908), bishop. Born in Cahir, Tipperary, Ireland, on Sept. 29, he emigrated to the United States and spent his youth in Norwalk, Connecticut. He was educated at St. Thomas Seminary, Bardstown, Kentucky, Montreal, and St. Joseph's Seminary, Troy, New York, and was ordained in Troy in 1866. He became rector of the Hartford, Connecticut, cathedral and then in Providence, where the bishop of Hartford then lived, and became chancellor of the Hartford diocese. He was named pastor at New London, Connecticut, and then, after a year at Stamford, served there for three years and then became pastor of St. Peter's Church, Hartford. While chancellor he supervised the building of the new St. Joseph's Cathedral, Hartford, which was dedicated in 1892, and in 1894 he was consecrated sixth bishop of Hartford—the first priest of the diocese to become bishop of that see. During his episcopate, he actively promoted the temperance movement, founded St. Thomas Minor Seminary, in 1897, established a diocesan mission band, and built hospitals and charitable institutions and established sixty-nine new parishes and thirty-two new schools. He died in Hartford on Oct. 5. The present archdiocesan newspaper was established by him when he purchased the *Connecticut Catholic,* when he was chancellor, and changed its name to the *Catholic Transcript.*

TIERNEY, RICHARD HENRY (1870–1928), editor. Born in New York City on Sept. 2, he was educated at St. Francis Xavier College there (B.A. 1892), joined the Jesuits in 1892, continued his studies at Woodstock (Maryland) College (M.A.) in 1896–99, taught at Gonzaga College, Washington, D.C.,

in 1899–1901 and Holy Cross College, Worcester, Massachusetts, in 1901–03, and then continued his studies at Woodstock in 1903–7 and at Linz, Austria, in 1907–8. He taught at Woodstock in 1909–14, and in 1913 was appointed to the staff of the Jesuit weekly *America.* He was its editor in 1914–25 and also edited the *Catholic Mind,* wrote widely on education, psychology, and history, and died in New York City on Feb. 10.

TIHEN, JOHN HENRY (1861–1940), bishop. Born in Oldenburg, Indiana, on July 14, he graduated from St. Benedict's College, Atchison, Kansas, in 1881, studied at St. Francis Seminary, Milwaukee, Wisconsin, and was ordained in St. Louis in 1886. He was a curate at St. John's Church, St. Louis, in 1886–89, was rector of the Wichita, Kansas, procathedral in 1889–1911, and was named chancellor of the Wichita diocese in 1895. He was made vicar-general and a domestic prelate in 1907 and was consecrated bishop of Lincoln, Nebraska, in 1911. He was transferred to Denver, Colorado, in 1917 and resigned in 1931 because of age and declining health and was appointed titular bishop of Bosana. During his episcopacy, he added fifty-five priests to the diocese, established eighteen new schools, three hospitals and an orphanage, consecrated the cathedral (in 1921), enlarged St. Thomas Seminary, established a centralized Catholic Charities, in 1927, to handle charitable matters in the see, and saw the Sisters of Loretto establish Loretto Heights College, in 1918. He died in Wichita on Jan. 14.

TIMON, JOHN (1797–1867), bishop. Born in Conewago, Pennsylvania, on Feb. 12, he was educated at Mt. St. Mary's College, Emmitsburg, Maryland, and St. Mary-of-the-Barrens Seminary, near St. Louis, Missouri, and joined the Lazarists (Vincentians) in

1823, taking his vows in 1825. He was ordained in 1825, engaged in missionary work in Texas, Louisiana, Missouri, Arkansas, and Illinois, and became known for his conversions. He also taught at St. Mary-of-the-Barrens and in 1835 became first visitor (superior) of the American Lazarists while also serving as vicar-general of the St. Louis diocese, in 1835–47, and as prefect apostolic of Texas, in 1839–41. He declined the request of Bishop Joseph Rosati to become his coadjutor at St. Louis but was appointed first bishop of the newly established diocese of Buffalo, New York, in 1847. He ministered to the laborers on the Erie and Genesee canals and their families, fought the Know-Nothing movement, abolished trusteeism in the diocese after a long struggle, and had the legislature pass the Church Trustee Law in 1863. He founded the Brothers of the Holy Infancy in 1853 to care for destitutes and wayward boys and built St. Joseph's Cathedral and numerous other churches. He died in Buffalo on Apr. 16.

TINCKER, MARY AGNES (1833–1907), author. Born in Ellsworth, Maine, on July 18, she began teaching in public schools when thirteen, was converted to Catholicism when twenty, and was a volunteer nurse in Washington, D.C., during the Civil War until she fell ill. She moved to Boston, published short stories in the *Catholic World,* and then lived in Italy, in 1873–87. She wrote a number of very popular novels, among them *The House of Yorke* (1872), *Grapes and Thorns* (1874), *Six Sunny Months* (1878), *Signor Monaldi's Niece* (1879), *Two Coronets* (1887), and *Autumn Leaves* (1898). She died in Boston on Dec. 4.

TOBIN, AGNES (1863–1939), poet. Of a well-to-do San Francisco family, she was educated at the Convent of Notre Dame, in San Francisco, and after graduation went to Europe, where she spent most of her life; while in England she frequently stayed with the Meynell family—Alice Meynell addressed her poem "The Shepherdess" to her. She returned to the United States when her mother became ill in 1924. She wrote poetry which was praised by W. B. Yeats, Ezra Pound, Francis Thompson, and Edmund Gosse, translated Racine's *Phèdre* for Mrs. Patrick Campbell, the English actress, and much of Petrarch and the Italian sonnets of Milton. She died in San Francisco on Feb. 20.

TOBIN, DANIEL JOSEPH (c. 1875–1955), labor leader. Born in County Clare, Ireland, he emigrated to the United States in 1889 with a brother and became a sheet-metal worker and then a motorman and driver for a Boston street railway. He joined the Knights of Labor in 1896, became active in union affairs and a friend of Samuel Gompers, and in 1910 joined the Team Drivers' International; in 1907 he was elected president of the International Brotherhood of Teamsters and held that position for forty-five years, until 1952, by which time the Brotherhood had a million and a quarter members and was one of the most powerful unions in the country. He was elected treasurer of the American Federation of Labor (AFL), despite the opposition of Samuel Gompers, in 1917, was a delegate to the International Trade Union Conference, in Amsterdam, in 1918, served on President Wilson's Industrial Conference after World War I, and in 1928 resigned as treasurer of the AFL when that organization adopted a neutral attitude, rather than support the Democratic Party's nominee for the presidency, Alfred E. Smith. He was elected vice president of the AFL in 1933 and served until 1952, and continued as a member of the Federation's executive Council after he retired as president of the Teamsters, in 1952. He established the *International Teamster* in 1931 and served as its first editor and was chairman of the labor division of the National Democratic Campaign Committee in 1932, strongly supporting Franklin D. Roosevelt in the 1932 presidential campaign. He was an ardent New Dealer, strongly opposed the Taft-Hartley Act, of 1947, condemned the Congress of Industrial Organizations (CIO) when John L. Lewis founded it, and protected AFL interests in unsuccessful talks to reunite the AFL and the CIO in 1940, 1942, and 1950; he was a leader in the movement to oust Communists from the labor movement. He died in Indianapolis, Indiana, on Nov. 14.

TOBIN, JAMES EDWARD (1905–68), educator, author, editor. Born in Fall River, Massachusetts, on Jan. 17, he was educated at Boston College (B.A. 1925) and Fordham (M.A. 1928, Ph.D. 1933). He worked for the Boston *American* and the Boston *Transcript* for a time, served on the staff of the Associated Press in Boston and Baltimore in 1925–27, and married Lorraine Walsh in 1929. He taught English at Fordham in 1927–46, serving as head of the English department of the Graduate School in 1936–47, was associate editor of Fordham University Press in 1928–50, and was a member of the editorial board of *Thought* in 1939–46, serving as acting editor in 1945–46. He was editor-in-chief of Declan X. McMullen, a New York book publisher, from 1946 until 1948, when he joined the faculty of Queens College. He became a professor in 1959, was chairman of the Division of Arts in 1958–61, and was director of the School of General Studies in 1961–66, becoming its dean in 1966, a position he held until his death, of a heart attack in Tuckahoe, New York, on Oct.

31. He also taught at Molloy College for Women, Rockville Centre, New York, in 1957–60, and in 1967 Molloy named its library in his honor. He was a specialist in eighteenth-century literature, wrote poetry, and compiled bibliographies and anthologies. Among his books were *Eighteenth Century English Literature and Its Cultural Background* (1939) and *Alexander Pope* (1945); he was coauthor, with John J. Delaney, of Dictionary of Catholic Biography (1962) and edited *Joyce Kilmer's Anthology of Catholic Poetry* (1955). He served as chairman of the board of directors of the Catholic Poetry Society of America, was on the editorial board of the Catholic Book Club, and for a time was associate editor of *Spirit.*

TOBIN, MAURICE JOSEPH (1901–53), governor, cabinet member. Born in Roxbury, Massachusetts, on May 22, he was obliged to leave high school for economic reasons. He worked in the Conway Leather Factory in 1919–22 and as a telephone mechanic for New England Telephone and Telegraph Company and was district traffic manager in 1928–37. He became active in politics when he was nineteen, was elected to the Massachusetts House of Representatives in 1926 and to the Boston School Committee in 1931, became a political protégé of the powerful political leader Mayor James M. Curley of Boston, and married Helen Noonan in 1932. In 1937 and again in 1941 he defeated Curley in elections for mayor of Boston. The city was almost bankrupt when he assumed office and he put into effect an austerity budget. In 1944 he was elected governor of Massachusetts and during his term in office introduced liberal social legislation and enacted a fair employment practices law in 1946 but was defeated in a bid for reelection later in 1946. He was appointed United States Secretary of Labor by President Harry Truman in

1948 and fought against the Taft-Hartley Act, which Congress had passed the previous year, reorganized the Department in 1950, supported increased minimum-wage proposals, additional workmen's compensation benefits, and union shop negotiations with the railroads and was responsible for civilian manpower defense needs during the Korean War. He died in Scituate, Massachusetts, on July 19.

TOBIN, RICHARD MONTGOMERY (1866–1952), banker. Born in San Francisco on Apr. 9, he was educated at St. Ignatius College there, became a director of the Hibernia Bank in 1889, and was its secretary-treasurer in 1906–33. He was chairman of the Association Savings Banks of San Francisco in 1906–27, served in the United States Navy during World War I, and was assistant to the naval attaché at the American embassy in Paris and to the American commission to negotiate peace at the Versailles Peace Conference in 1918–19. He was minister to the Netherlands in 1923–29 and was the first American to be named to the Utrecht Provincial Society for Arts and Sciences. He became president of the Hibernia Bank in 1933 and remained in that position until his death, in San Francisco on Jan. 23. He served on numerous banking and civic committees and organizations, was chairman of the Federal Home Loan Bank, 12th District, in 1933, was a director of the Golden Gate International Exposition in 1940, vice president of the Catholic Association for International Peace, and was made a Knight of Malta in 1931.

TOEBBE, AUGUSTUS MARIA (1829–84), bishop. Born in Meppen, Hannover, Germany, on Jan. 15, he came to the United States and was educated at St. Mary of the West Seminary,

Cincinnati, Ohio, and was ordained in Cincinnati in 1854. He engaged in pastoral work in Cincinnati, was a theologian at the first Plenary Council of Baltimore, in 1852, was appointed bishop of Covington, Kentucky, in 1870, and held that position until his death, in Covington on May 2.

TOOLEN, THOMAS J. (1886–1976), bishop. Born in Baltimore on Feb. 28, he was educated at Loyola College and St. Mary's Seminary, Baltimore, and Catholic University (B.C.L. 1912) and was ordained in 1910. He served as a curate at St. Bernard's Church, Baltimore, in 1912–25, was appointed director of the archdiocesan Society for the Propagation of the Faith in 1925, and was consecrated bishop of Mobile (now Mobile-Birmingham), Alabama, in 1927. During his episcopacy, he established sixty-eight new parishes, organized a Bureau of Catholic Charities and a diocesan school system, was deeply concerned with the plight of blacks in the diocese and established the *Catholic Week* in 1934. He was given the personal title of archbishop in 1954, retired in 1969, and died in Mobile on Dec. 4.

TOSCANINI, ARTURO (1867–1957), conductor. Son of a tailor, Claudio Toscanini, and Paola Montani Toscanini, he was born in Parma, Italy, on Mar. 25, studied cello at the Parma conservatory for nine years, and graduated in 1885. After his graduation he was cellist in the Parma Opera and the Parma Municipal Orchestra for a year; in 1886, while playing cello in a touring orchestra in Rio de Janeiro, he was unexpectedly called on to conduct the orchestra for Verdi's *Aida*. He conducted the opera and received enthusiastic critical praise for his feat. He was named principal conductor of the touring orchestra, made his professional debut in Italy in 1886 with Alfredo Catalani's *Edmea* in Turin, and over the next few years became the outstanding conductor of his time. He conducted the world premiere of Leoncavallo's *I Pagliacci,* in Milan in 1892, the first Italian production of Wagner's *Die Götterdämmerung,* in Milan in 1895, and the world premiere of Puccini's *La Boheme* in Turin in 1897. He married Carla De Martini, a ballerina, in 1897, was named principal conductor of La Scala in Milan in 1898, and resigned in 1903 to protest the violation of his rule that there be no encores when the audience demanded one from Giovanni Zenatello; he returned to La Scala in 1906–8 but resigned again and went to New York, where he conducted the Metropolitan Opera in 1908–14. He returned to Italy in 1915, after the outbreak of World War I, and when La Scala reopened after the war, in 1920, he became its principal conductor and artistic director until 1929. He conducted the New York Philharmonic in 1926–36 and was musical director in 1933, developing it into one of the foremost orchestras in the world. He became conductor of the NBC Symphony Orchestra, which he formed in 1937, and made it world famous with its broadcast concerts and tours during the next seventeen years. An outspoken opponent of fascism, he refused to play in Fascist countries several times, was bodily attacked when he refused to play the Fascist hymn, "Giovinezza," at one of his concerts, and several years later was placed under house arrest when he continued his attacks on fascism and nazism. He was allowed to return to the United States to fulfill his obligations to NBC and vowed never to return to Italy while the Fascists were in power; he spent the rest of his life living in the United States (though he never gave up his Italian citizenship), at Villa Pauline, Riverdale, New York City. He often denounced Nazi attacks on the Jews and had his recordings destroyed by storm troopers in Germany; in 1936 he went to Palestine to conduct the Palestine Symphony Orchestra as a protest against the Nazi atrocities against the Jews. During World War II he gave benefits for the United Service Organizations (USO), for the Army and the Red Cross, and to spur the sale of war bonds. He conducted several concerts with the La Scala orchestra after the war, and when his memory, which was phenomenal and of which he was very proud, failed during an NBC Symphony concert and later during an all-Wagner concert in 1954, he never again conducted a concert. He died in Riverdale on Jan. 16.

TOUSSAINT, PIERRE (1766–1853). Born on June 27 on the island of Saint Domingue (Haiti), a slave, he was brought to New York City by his master, John Bérard du Pithon, in 1787. He was apprenticed to a hairdresser and soon became noted for his skill in creating unusual hairstyles. When his master died, in Saint Domingue, where he had gone to check on his belongings, Pierre provided for Du Pithon's penniless widow, Marie, the next twenty years and also devoted himself to aiding refugees, black and white, from Saint Domingue who had been forced to flee the island to escape the excesses of the French Revolution (Saint Domingue was a French possession). Marie freed him before she died, and he helped purchase the freedom of other slaves, including Juliette Noël, whom he married in 1811. Their home became a refuge for orphaned black children, and he devoted himself to aiding the sick and destitute, including formerly wealthy slave owners exiled from their native land, using money he earned from his trade to carry on his work. He nursed the sick victims of the numerous yellow-fever and cholera plagues that regularly ravaged New York in the early 1800s, helped raise funds for an orphanage founded in 1817 by Fr. Powers, pastor of St. Peter's Church, where Toussaint attended Mass daily for almost sixty years, and aided a servant in Baltimore named Fanny Montpensier, who helped found the Oblate Sisters of Providence, the first congregation of black sisters there. He had a wide correspondence, became the confidant of many, and at the time of his death, in New York City on June 30, was held in the highest regard and venerated by all who knew him.

TRACEY, JAMES FRANCIS (1854–1925), jurist. Born in Albany, New York, on May 30, he was educated at Georgetown (B.A. 1874) and the Albany Law School (LL.B. 1875) and practiced law in Albany from 1875; he married Lucienne Bosé in 1893. He was a lecturer at the Albany Law School from 1890 to 1905, when he was appointed associate justice of the Supreme Court of the Philippine Islands. In 1908 President Theodore Roosevelt sent his name to the Senate for confirmation as Commissioner of the Philippines and secretary of finances, but he declined the appointment. He resigned as associate justice in 1909, was active in Catholic charitable enterprises in Albany, and died at his summer home, at Altamont, New York, on Sept. 19.

TRACY, ROBERT EMMET (1909–80), bishop. Born in New Orleans on Sept. 14, he studied for the priesthood at St. Joseph Preparatory Seminary and Notre Dame Seminary, New Orleans, and was ordained in New Orleans in 1932. He was a curate at St. Leo's Church, New Orleans, in 1932–46, was archdiocesan director of the Confraternity of Christian Doctrine in 1937–46, and was Newman Club chaplain at Tulane University in 1941–66 and at Louisiana State University in 1946–59. He was made a papal chamberlain in 1947 and a domestic prelate in 1949 and was national chaplain of the Newman Club Federation in 1954–56. He was named titular bishop of Sergentza and auxiliary of Lafayette, Louisiana, in 1959 and was appointed first bishop of the newly established diocese of Baton Rouge, Louisiana, in 1961; he held this position until his death, in New Orleans on Apr. 4.

TRACY, SPENCER (1900–67), actor. Son of John Edward Tracy, a trucker, and Carrie Brown Tracy, he was born on Apr. 5 in Milwaukee, Wisconsin, where he and Pat O'Brien grew up and became lifelong friends. He enlisted in the Navy in World War I and after the war continued his high school education; he was known for his frequent truancies in elementary and early high school. He entered Ripon (Wisconsin) College in 1920 and after three years decided to go to New York City to study acting at the American Academy of Dramatic Arts. He began his acting career with a nonspeaking role in *R.U.R.* in 1922 and a one-line role in *The Man Who Came Back,* joined a stock company (where he met Louise Treadwell, whom he married a few weeks later, in 1928), and in 1930 made his first big hit in *The Last Mile,* on Broadway. When John Ford saw the play, he offered him a motion-picture contract, and he made his screen debut in *Up the River.* He made a dozen more B movies until 1933, when his role in *The Power and the Glory* evoked great critical praise. He went on to become No. 1 in Metro's Box Office Hit Parade and one of Hollywood's greatest stars, appearing in such pictures as *Captains Courageous* (1937), *Boys Town* (1938), *Northwest Passage* (1940), *Woman of the Year* (1942), with Katharine Hepburn (they were to become close friends and together a tremendous box-office draw), *Tortilla Flat* (1942), *Father of the Bride* (1950), *Bad Day at Black Rock* (1955), *The Old Man and the Sea* (1958), *Inherit the Wind* (1960), and *Guess Who's Coming to Dinner* (released posthumously in 1967). He was often called "an actor's actor" for his ability to handle practically any role and received Oscar awards for his roles as the Portuguese fisherman in *Captains Courageous* and as Father Flanagan in *Boys Town*. He died in Beverly Hills, California, on June 10.

TREACY, JOHN PATRICK (1890–1964), bishop. Born in Marlboro, Massachusetts, on July 23, he was educated at Holy Cross College, Worcester, Massachusetts, Harvard Law School, Catholic University, and St. John's Seminary, Brighton, Boston, and was ordained in 1918 for the Cleveland diocese. He became a domestic prelate and diocesan director of the Society for the Propagation of the Faith and in 1945 was named titular bishop of Metelis and coadjutor of the diocese of La Crosse, Wisconsin. He was administrator of the see in 1946 and succeeded to it in 1948. He inaugurated a $39-million building program which resulted in the construction of 196 buildings including Holy Cross Seminary and St. Joseph the Workman Cathedral, encouraged lay activities, was a promoter of the liturgical movement, and was president of the National Catholic Rural Life Conference in 1948. He died in La Crosse on Oct. 11.

TRESE, LEO (1902–70), author, columnist. Born in Port Huron, Michigan, on May 6, he was educated at Assumption College, Windsor, Ontario, Canada (B.A. 1923), and Mt. St. Mary Seminary, Detroit, was ordained in Detroit in 1927, and received his M.A. from the University of Detroit in 1929. He served as a curate in Detroit for five years and was pastor of parishes in Marysville, Melvindale, and Carlton from 1936 to 1950, when heart trouble caused him to leave pastoral work; he became chaplain at the Vista Maria girls' home, in Detroit. He wrote columns for several Catholic magazines and newspapers and was the author of *Vessel of Clay* (1950), *Many Are One* (1952), and *Tenders of the Flock* (1955); he died at Pompano Beach, Florida, on June 23.

TROBEC, JAMES (1838–1921), bishop. Born in Billichgratz, Carniola, Austria, on July 10, he emigrated to the United States and studied for the priesthood at St. Vincent's College and Seminary, Beatty, Pennsylvania, and was ordained in St. Paul, Minnesota, in 1865. He engaged in pastoral work there for the next thirty-two years and was pastor of St. Agnes Church, in St. Paul, when he was named third bishop of St. Cloud, Minnesota, in 1897. He increased the number of parishes and churches in the diocese, resigned in 1914, and was named titular bishop of Lycopolis; he died in St. Cloud on Dec. 14.

TUIGG, JOHN (1821–89), bishop. Born in Donaghmore, Cork, Ireland, on Feb. 19, he studied for the priesthood at All Hallows College, Dublin, emigrated to the United States, and continued his studies at St. Michael's Seminary, Pittsburgh; he was ordained in 1850. He became an assistant at the Pittsburgh cathedral and secretary to Bishop Michael O'Connor, founded St. Bridget's parish in Pittsburgh in 1853, and then went to Altoona, where he built a church, a convent, and a school. In 1869 he was named vicar forane of the eastern portion of the diocese, and when Pittsburgh was divided into the sees of Pittsburgh and Allegheny City, in 1876, he was appointed bishop of Pittsburgh. The division caused great bitterness, and he inherited financial problems resulting from the depression of 1873. When Bishop Michael Domenec resigned as bishop of Allegheny City, in 1872, Tuigg was appointed administrator of the see; it was suppressed in 1889 and its territory was returned to the diocese of Pittsburgh. Bishop Tuigg then reorganized the enlarged diocese. He died in Altoona, Pennsylvania, on Dec. 7.

TUMULTY, JOSEPH PATRICK (1879–1954). Born in Jersey City, New Jersey, on May 5, he was educated at St. Peter's College there (B.A. 1899), read law in several law offices, and was admitted to the bar in 1902. He practiced law in Jersey City in 1902–8, married Mary Catherine Byrne in 1903, was a member of the New Jersey Assembly in 1907–10, and at first fought the rising Woodrow Wilson's bid for governor, seeing him as a tool of the bosses and not progressive enough, but went over to Wilson's side and became one of his advisers. He fought the party bosses opposing Wilson as Wilson's progressive ideas became apparent, and when Wilson was elected governor, Tumulty served as his private secretary in 1911–13. He early supported Wilson for the presidency and continued as his secretary during Wilson's two terms as President, 1913–21—the first Catholic to be a President's secretary. He handled patronage and appointments for the President, dealt with the press, and often acted as a sounding board for the President. His objection to Wilson's second marriage, only months after the death of Wilson's first wife, Ellen Axson Wilson, as inopportune in 1915 and his suggestion it be postponed until after the 1916 presidential election annoyed the President and alienated the new Mrs. Wilson. The two men were reconciled, but a public breach took place when Tumulty conveyed a message from Wilson which was construed as an endorse-

ment of James M. Cox for the Democratic nomination for the presidency in 1920, a nomination which Wilson opposed. Tumulty returned to law practice when Wilson left the presidency. He wrote of his experiences with Wilson in *Woodrow Wilson as I Knew Him* (1921). He died in Olney, Maryland, on Apr. 8.

TURNER, THOMAS WYATT (1877–1978), educator, black Catholic leader. Born in Hughesville, Maryland, on Mar. 16, in a poor sharecropper's cabin, he was educated at Howard University, Washington, D.C. (B.A. 1901), began graduate studies at Catholic University on a scholarship but when funds ran out was forced to leave and began to teach at Tuskegee Institute. He joined the faculty of the Baltimore High and Training School in 1901, received his master's degree from Howard University in 1905, and was acting dean of its school of education in 1914–20. He became first secretary of the Baltimore branch of the National Association for the Advancement of Colored People (NAACP) in 1910 and in 1913 became a biologist at Howard University. Early a leader in the struggle for racial equality, he organized the first citywide membership drive of the NAACP in Washington, D.C., in 1915, and in 1917 organized the Committee Against the Extension of Race Prejudice in the Church to eliminate discriminatory practices against blacks, especially in Catholic institutions. In 1925 the Committee established a permanent group, Federated Colored Catholics, with Turner as its first president. A dispute arose between Turner and Fr. William Markoe, of St. Louis, over the direction the organization should take, and it split into two groups, with Turner president of an eastern group, which continued until 1952. He received his Ph.D. in botany from Cornell University in 1921 and went to Hampton Institute as its first biology department chairman, in 1924; he served in this post until his retirement, in 1945. He was the first black man to be a research cytologist for the U.S. Department of Agriculture and was a pioneer in the struggle for equal rights in the Church in the United States. He died in Washington, D.C., on Apr. 21.

TURNER, WILLIAM (1871–1936), bishop, editor. Born in Kilmallock, Limerick, Ireland, on Apr. 8, he was educated at Mungret College, Limerick, and the Royal University (B.A. 1888), the North American College (S.T.D. 1893), and Urban College, Rome, and was ordained in 1893 for the diocese of St. Augustine, Florida. He continued his studies at L'Institut Catholique, Paris, for another year and then was chairman of the philosophy department at St. Paul (Minnesota) Seminary, from 1894 until 1906, when he was appointed to the chair of philosophy at Catholic University, serving in that position in 1906–19; he was librarian in 1907–10. He was editor of the *American Ecclesiastical Review* in 1914–19 and associate editor of the *Catholic Historical Review* in 1915–18. He was appointed bishop of Buffalo, New York, in 1919, and during his episcopate he expanded the facilities of the see, was active in charitable work, established thirty new parishes, and founded the diocesan congregation the Franciscan Missionary Sisters of the Divine Child. He wrote articles for magazines and was the author of *History of Philosophy* (1903) and *Lessons in Logic* (1911). He died in Buffalo on July 10.

TWOMEY, LOUIS JOSEPH (1905–69), social-justice pioneer. Born in Tampa, Florida, on Oct. 5, he was educated at Georgetown in 1923–26 and joined the Jesuits at Grand Coteau, Louisiana, in 1926. He left the Society the following year because of his fa-

ther's illness, returned in 1929, and took his vows in 1931. He continued his studies at Loyola University, New Orleans (B.A. 1932), St. Louis University (M.A. in English 1933, in economics in 1947), taught at Spring Hill College, Mobile, Alabama, in 1933–36, resumed his studies at St. Mary's College, Kansas (S.T.L. 1940), and was ordained there in 1939. He was principal of Jesuit High School, Tampa, in 1941–45, became interested in social problems, and in 1945 went to St. Louis University's Institute of Social Order. He was founder and director of the Institute of Industrial Relations at Loyola University, New Orleans, in 1947, became regent of its law school, and helped integrate it in 1952; in 1964 he established an Inter American center at Loyola. In 1948 he began *Christ's Blueprint of the South* (now *Blueprint for the Christian Reshaping of Society),* a letter to southern Jesuits, which achieved an international circulation among the Jesuits and had a tremendous impact in the area of social justice; he also edited *Social Order* in 1962–63. He died in New Orleans on Oct. 8.

TYLER, WILLIAM (1806–49), bishop. Nephew of the noted convert Fr. Virgil Barber, S.J., he was born in Derby, Vermont, on June 5 and was converted to Catholicism with his parents when he was fifteen. He studied for the priesthood under Bishop Benedict Fenwick of Boston and at a Montreal seminary, was ordained in 1829, and engaged in missionary work in Massachusetts and Maine. He became vicar-general of the Boston diocese and in 1844 was consecrated first bishop of the newly created diocese of Hartford, Connecticut, but had his residence at Providence, Rhode Island, because there were so few Catholics (about six hundred) in Hartford (Providence had some two thousand Catholics). He was successful in getting priests from Ireland for his see and aid from the Leopold Society, Vienna, and the Lyons, France, Society for the Propagation of the Faith; he was very active in the temperance movement. He attended the seventh Provincial Council of Baltimore, in 1849, and tried to resign because of ill health but his resignation was refused. He died soon after he returned from the Council, in Providence on June 18.

U

UBEDA, BROTHER LOUIS DE (d. c. 1544). *See* Padilla, Juan de.

V

VAN BUREN, WILLIAM HOLME (1819–83), surgeon. Descended from a family of early Dutch settlers, he was born in Philadelphia on Apr. 5. He studied for a time at Yale but left before graduating to study medicine at the University of Pennsylvania, received his medical degree in 1840, and continued his studies at Paris, and on his return to the United States revolutionized the treatment of fractures in his thesis *Immovable Dressing*. He served in the Army for a time, joined the faculty of New York University in 1845, and was a professor of anatomy there in 1852–65; he resigned in 1865, when his plans to rebuild the college building which had been destroyed by fire earlier the same year were rejected. He declined the offer of President Lincoln during the Civil War to be surgeon general of the United States, became a Catholic during the war, and became a professor of surgery at Bellevue Hospital Medical College, in New York, in 1868; he remained in that position until his death on Mar. 25. He wrote notable papers on aneurysms and was considered one of the outstanding surgical teachers in the United States, was one of the founders of the United States Sanitary Commission, in 1861, served as president of the Pathological Society, and was vice president of the New York Academy of Medicine. He translated several medical treatises and was the author of *Contributions to Practical Surgery* (1865) and *Lectures on Diseases of the Rectum* (1870) and, with Dr. Edward Keyes, *Diseases of the Genito-Urinary Organs* (1874).

VAN DER VELDT, JAMES H. (1893–1977), psychologist. Herman Van der Veldt was born in Washington, D.C., on Mar. 15, joined the Order of Friars Minor in 1912, taking the name James, made his profession in 1913, and was ordained in 1919. He had been educated at Franciscan seminaries in Amsterdam and Nijmegan, the Netherlands, and Milan and continued his studies at Louvain (Ph.D. 1926, *agrégé* in philosophy 1928). He taught at the Pontifical University of the Propagation of the Faith, Rome, the next twelve years, serving as head of the psychology laboratory, and at the Pontifical Athenaeum Sancti Antonii, where he was dean of philosophy; in 1940 he returned to the United States to teach at St. Joseph's Seminary, Dunwoodie, Yonkers, New York. He left in 1945 to join the psychology and psychiatry department at Catholic University and remained there until his retirement, when he was elected professor emeritus; he then served at St. Matthew's Cathedral, Washington, D.C., until his death, in Washington on Aug. 18. He lectured widely, wrote numerous articles, and was the author of several books, among them *The City on a Hill* (1945), *Exploring the Vatican* (1947), and, with Robert P. Odenwald, *Psychiatry and Catholicism* (1952) and *Psychology for Counselors* (1952).

VAN DE VELDE, JAMES OLIVER (1795–1855), bishop. Born near Termonde, East Flanders, Belgium, on Apr. 3, he was privately educated and then studied for the priesthood at the Mechlin seminary. He taught at Puers and Mechlin for a time and then came to the United States at the behest of Charles Nerinckx in 1817 and continued his studies at Georgetown. He joined the Jesuits there, was ordained in Baltimore in 1827, and engaged in missionary work in Maryland until 1831, when he was assigned to St. Louis University. He became its vice president in 1833 and was its president in 1840–43; he was vice-provincial of the Jesuit Missouri province in 1843–48 and procurator in 1848. He was released from his Jesuit vows and appointed bishop of Chicago in 1848, had difficulties with some of the clergy who had opposed his appointment, and became embroiled in a dispute with the faculty of St. Mary of the Lake University when he ordered property, including the episcopal residence, left the university by the wills of his predecessor, Bishop William Quarter, and his brother, be returned to him as bishop, and they refused. In 1852 he attended the first Plenary Council of Baltimore, which designated him emissary to take its decrees to Rome. He resigned as bishop of Chicago later in the year, after having established seventy churches, ten schools, and the first Catholic hospital in Chicago; in 1853 he rejoined the Jesuits and was transferred to Natchez (which was transferred to Jackson in 1877), Mississippi, as its second bishop, in 1853, while still acting as administrator of Chicago in 1853–54 and of Quincy, Illinois, in 1853. He died of yellow fever in Natchez on Nov. 13.

VAN DE VEN, CORNELIUS (1865–1932), bishop. Born in Oirschot, the Netherlands, on June 16, he studied for the priesthood at the Bois-le-Duc diocesan seminary, the Netherlands, and was ordained in 1890. He went to the United States later the same year, was attached to the New Orleans diocese, and was pastor in several Louisiana parishes until 1904, when he was appointed bishop of Natchitoches, Louisiana. The see was transferred to Alexandria in 1910 at his request, and in 1929 he was made an Assistant at the Pontifical Throne. He died in Shreveport, Louisiana, on May 8.

VAN DE VYVER, AUGUSTINE (1844–1911), bishop. Born in Haesdonck, East Flanders, Belgium, on Dec. 1, he studied at the American College, Louvain, was ordained in 1870, and went to the United States. He was an assistant at St. Peter's Cathedral, Richmond, Virginia, for a time, was pastor at Harpers Ferry in 1875–81, then pastor of the cathedral and vicar-general of the Richmond diocese from 1881 to 1889, when he was appointed its sixth bishop. He greatly expanded the educational and charitable facilities of the see, founding nine parishes and building twenty-seven churches, including the new Sacred Heart Cathedral, which he consecrated in 1906 from donations made by Mr. and Mrs. Thomas Fortune Ryan. He submitted his resignation as bishop of Richmond in 1908 but withdrew it at the request of the clergy and the people of the diocese; he died in Richmond on Oct. 16.

VEHR, URBAN JOHN (1891–1973), bishop. Born in Cincinnati, Ohio, on May 30, he was educated at St. Xavier College there, Mt. St. Mary Seminary, Norwood, Ohio, and Notre Dame; he was ordained in Cincinnati, Ohio, in 1915. He was a curate at Holy Trinity Church, Middletown, Ohio, in 1915–23, chaplain at College of Mt. St. Joseph, Ohio, in 1923, and superintendent of schools of the archdiocese of Cincinnati in 1924–27. He received his M.A. from Catholic University in 1924 and his J.C.L. from Angelico College, Rome, in 1928; he was rector of St. Gregory Seminary in 1927–30 and of Mt. St. Mary Seminary in 1930–31. He was consecrated fourth bishop of Denver, Colorado, in 1931 and became Denver's first archbishop when the see was elevated to an archdiocese, in 1941; he was made an Assistant at the Pontifical Throne in 1955. During his episcopacy he unified the diocesan school system, was particularly interested in education and the press, and encouraged dialogue with non-Catholic groups. He retired in 1967; he died in Denver on Sept. 19.

VERDAGUER, PETER (1835–1911), bishop. Born in San Pedro de Torello, Catalonia, Spain, on Dec. 10, he studied at the Vich and Barcelona seminaries, emigrated to the United States, and finished his studies for the priesthood at St. Vincent's Seminary, Cape Girardeau, Missouri, and was ordained in San Francisco in 1862. He engaged in pastoral work in the Monterey–Los Angeles diocese and was pastor of Our Lady of Angels Church, Los Angeles, when he was appointed titular bishop of Aulon and vicar apostolic of Brownsville, Texas, in 1890. He was consecrated in Barcelona and installed in Brownsville in 1891; he died on Oct. 28 on his way from Santa Maria to Mercedes, Texas, while on a trip conferring the sacrament of confirmation.

VERNON, GRENVILLE (1883–1941), critic. Born in Providence, Rhode Island, on July 22, he was educated at Harvard (B.A. 1905), engaged in journalism in New York City for a time, and became editor of Dial Press. He was music critic of the New York *Times* in 1908 and of the *Herald Tribune* in 1909–21 and wrote on music for *Commonweal* in 1926–41; he became *Commonweal*'s drama critic a few weeks before his death, in New York City on Nov. 30. He wrote several plays, among them *The Dictator's Wife,* and a novel, *Image in the Path* (1917), and compiled a collection of American folk songs, *Yankee-doodle-doo* (1927).

VEROT, AUGUSTIN (1804–76), bishop. Born in Le Puy, France, on May 23, he studied for the priesthood at St. Sulpice Seminary, Paris, and was ordained in 1828. He joined the Sulpicians the next year, was sent to the United States in 1830, and taught at St. Mary's College and Seminary, Baltimore, until 1853, when he was appointed pastor at Ellicott Mills and served in several other Maryland towns. He was named titular bishop of Danaba and vicar apostolic of Florida in 1857, found only three priests and two churches in the vicariate when he took possession of it, and went to France in a successful quest for priests. He repaired old churches, established new parishes and schools, brought several religious communities into the vicariate, and encouraged immigration. He was transferred to Savannah, Georgia, as its third bishop, in 1861, while still retaining his Florida vicariate. In 1861 his sermon "A Tract for the Times: Slavery and Abolitionism," defending slavery but condemning the slave trade, was widely circulated; it was suppressed by Secretary of War Seward in Baltimore. After the Civil War he labored to repair the terrible ravages wreaked on his see during the war. When the vicariate of Florida was constituted the diocese of St. Augustine, in 1870, he became its first bishop. He attended Vatican Council I in 1870 and vigorously opposed the proclamation of the doctrine of papal infallibility and absented himself from the final vote, though he accepted it when it passed and was proclaimed by the Pope. He died in St. Augustine on June 10.

VERRAZANO, GIOVANNI DA (c. 1485–c. 1528), explorer. Born at Val di Greve, near Florence, Italy, he entered the naval service of Francis I of France and became a famous privateer, preying on Portuguese and Spanish ships (one of his prizes was the treasure ship Cortés was sending to Emperor Charles V from Mexico in 1522 with an estimated value of two million dollars. In 1524 he set out on a voyage of discovery for France to the New World, during which he explored the coast of North America probably as far south as North Carolina. He sailed into what is now New York Harbor (probably the first European to do so), up the Hudson River, and then through Long Island Sound, and along the New England coast to Maine. He returned to France later the same year. With Admiral Philippe Chabot and others he formed a partnership to finance a voyage for spice in 1526 and sailed for the Río de la Plata with five ships in 1528; what happened after is not certain. According to Spanish records he was captured under the name of Juan Florín by the Spanish off the coast of Cádiz and executed as a pirate at Puerto del Pico, Spain, by order of Charles V. Other sources claim he was killed by Indians of the island of Darién (Panama) on a trip to the West Indies. Maps his brother Hierónimo (Gerolamo) drew in 1529 based on his discoveries gave Europeans a new concept of North America.

VERTIN, JOHN (1844–99), bishop. Born in Doblice, Carniola, Austria, on July 17, he was educated at Rudolfswerth and came to the United States with his family when he was nineteen. He completed his studies for the priesthood at St. Francis Seminary, Milwaukee, Wisconsin, and was ordained in 1866. He engaged in missionary and pastoral work in northern Michigan the next thirteen years, serving as pastor at Houghton, where his family had settled, and Negaunee, and in 1879 he was appointed third bishop of Marquette, Wisconsin. He convoked the diocese's first diocesan synod, in 1899, expanded the facilities of the see, and was noted for his charities and his administrative abilities. He died in Marquette on Feb. 26.

VESPUCCI, AMERIGO (1451–1512), explorer. Son of a notary, he was born in Florence, Italy, on Mar. 9, was educated by his uncle, a Dominican friar, and was interested in astronomy, geography, and cosmography early in his life. He was attached to the Florentine embassy to King Louis XI in Paris in 1478–80, became a clerk in the Medici commercial house in Florence in 1483, was in Seville, Spain (and there met Columbus) as an agent of the Medici in 1491–92, and then embarked on the first of his voyages to the New World, in 1497, in three ships supplied by King Ferdinand of Castile. He reached the South American mainland at Guiana or Brazil, may have entered the Gulf of Mexico, and sailed along the North American coast to the Gulf of St. Lawrence; he returned to Spain on Oct. 15, 1498. He, Alonso de Ojeda, and Juan de la Cosa set out together on his second voyage on May 16, 1499, but they separated before reaching the West Indies; Vespucci went on to discover and explore the mouths of the Amazon River; he then sailed along the northern shore of South America and the West Indies and returned to Spain in September 1500 in ill health. On his recovery he entered the service of the Portuguese and set out again on May 14, 1501. He explored six thousand miles of the South American coast as far south as latitude 50° S., discovering the mouths of the Río de la Plata, and returned to Portugal on Sept. 7, 1502. He sailed again the following year on June 10 with Gonzal Coelho. They sailed along the South American coast to the Río de la Plata and returned to Portugal in 1504. He made two more voyages, with Juan de la Costa in 1503 and 1507, but left no description of either. He became a Spanish citizen in 1505 and was appointed pilot-major of Spain in 1508 and held this position until his death, in Seville on Feb. 22. It was not until the twentieth century that Vespucci's explorations were fully appreciated as scholars had long tended to belittle them though the name America was given to the new continent in Martin Waldseemüller's *Cosmographicae Introductio* (1507), which also contains a Latin translation of Vespucci's descriptions of his four journeys. Even today some scholars believe several of his explorations, notably that of 1497, were fabrications. Nevertheless he was the first to declare that South America was a new continent and not part of Asia, as was then believed. Besides his explorations, he revolutionized navigation by evolving a remarkably accurate system for computing latitude that supplanted dead reckoning, which had been used up to his time; by using it he computed the earth's circumference to within fifty miles of its actual measurement.

VEUSTER, VEN. JOSEPH DE (1840–89), missionary. Born at Tremeloo, Belgium, on Jan. 3, he was educated at the College of Braine-le-Comte, Hainaut, and in 1860 joined the Fathers of the Sacred Hearts of Jesus and Mary (the Picpus Fathers), taking the name Damien. He was sent to Hawaii as a missionary, at his request, in 1864 and was ordained that year in Honolulu. He spent the next nine years in pastoral work in the districts of Puno and Kohala, Hawaii, and in 1873, again at his request, he was sent to minister to the lepers at the leper colony on Molokai. He spent the rest of his life working among them, struggling to improve the miserable conditions he found on his arrival on the island. In 1885 he contracted the disease himself and, despite his affliction, continued working with the lepers on Molokai until his death there on Apr. 15. He was often slandered and his morals impugned during his years on the island, but a thorough investigation just before his death completely exonerated him; Robert Louis Stevenson wrote an impassioned defense of his character in 1905 in his famous *Open Letter to the Reverend Doctor Hyde of Honolulu.* His holiness and dedication were recognized by those for whom and with whom he worked, and in 1977 Pope Paul VI declared him Venerable. His statue was placed in the Capitol, in Washington, D.C., in 1931 by Hawaii as a person worthy of national commemoration.

VIADER, JOSÉ (b. 1765), missionary. Born in Gallines, Catalonia, Spain, on Aug. 27, he joined the Franciscans in Barcelona in 1788, was sent to Mexico in 1795, and joined the staff of San Fernando College, in Mexico City. He was sent to California in 1796 and worked as a missionary at Santa Clara until 1833, when he returned to Spain. While at Santa Clara, he defended the Indians against the military and the colonists; some of his correspondence is still extant.

VIEL, FRANÇOIS ÉTIENNE BERNARD ALEXANDRE (1736–1821). Son of a French physician who had emigrated to Louisiana, he was born in New Orleans on Oct. 31. He was sent to France in 1747 to study at the Oratorians' Royal Academy in Juilly, joined the Oratorians, and was ordained—the first native-born Louisianan to become a priest. He taught at Soisson and Le Mans for a time and then returned to Juilly and became rector in 1776. When the French Revolution closed the Academy, in 1792, he returned to Louisiana and was the parish priest at Attakapas the next two decades. He returned to France to help restore the Oratorians in 1812 and taught at Juilly. He died there on Dec. 16, renowned for his Latin verse; he translated several works from French to Latin.

VIEL, NICOLAS (d. 1625), missionary. A Recollect father from France, he was so persistent in petitioning his superiors to be allowed to go on the American missions that he was sent to Canada in 1623 with Théodat Sagard, a lay brother. He worked among the Hurons, learned their language, and began a dictionary. While returning to Quebec to make a retreat, he was drowned near Montreal in the rapids of Rivière des Prairies by a group of apostate Hurons —the first missionary to die in that region and the protomartyr of Canada. He was buried on June 25; the place where he was drowned is still called Sault-au-Récollet.

VOGEL, CYRIL J. (1905–79), bishop. Born in Pittsburgh on Jan. 15, he was educated at Duquesne University there and St. Vincent Seminary, Latrobe, Pennsylvania, and was ordained in 1931. He was appointed bishop of Salina, Kansas, in 1965 and served in that post until his death, in Salina on Oct. 4.

W

WADHAMS, EDGAR PHILIP (1817–91), bishop. Born in Lewis, Essex County, New York, on May 17, he was educated at Middlebury College, Vermont, where he changed his religion from Presbyterian to Episcopalian, and General Theological Seminary, New York City. After becoming a deacon in the Episcopal Church, he was converted to Catholicism in 1846, studied for the priesthood at St. Mary's Seminary, Baltimore, and was ordained in Albany, New York, in 1850. He served at the Albany cathedral for two years, when he was named its rector, became vicar-general of the Albany diocese in 1872, and was appointed first bishop of the newly established diocese of Ogdensburg, New York. He held three diocesan synods, attended the third Plenary Council of Baltimore, in 1884, enlarged St. Mary's Cathedral, doubled the number of clergy and churches in the diocese, and increased the religious from 23 to 125 and the schools from 7 to 20 as the Catholic populace of the see increased from 50,000 to 65,000. He died in Ogdensburg on Dec. 5.

WAGGAMAN, MARY TERESA Mc-KEE (1846–1931), author. Daughter of an Irish immigrant who made a fortune in the California gold rush, Mary McKee was born in Baltimore and educated at Mt. de Sales Convent, Catonsville, Maryland. She was brought to New York by her father when the Civil War broke out. In 1870, she married Dr. Samuel Waggaman and became the mother of seven children. Interested in writing from her school days, she published her first children's book in 1894, *Little Comrades, A First Communion Book,* and was launched on a writing career that made her the most prolific and popular author of religious books for children of her time. She wrote some forty books, including *The Traveling Twins,* which she wrote in her eighty-fifth year. Among her other books were *Tom's Luck-Pot* (1897), *Little Missy* (1900), *Nan Nobody* (1901), *Corinne's Vow* (1902), *Shipmates* (1914), *Grapes of Thorns* (1917), and *The Finding of Tony* (1919); she also wrote poetry and short stories. She died in Washington, D.C., on July 30.

WAGNER, ROBERT FERDINAND (1877–1953), U.S. senator. Born in Nastätten, Germany, on June 8, he was brought to the United States by his parents in 1885, when he was eight, and graduated from the College of the City of New York in 1898. He studied law at New York Law School (LL.B. 1900), early became interested in politics and attached himself to Tammany Hall, and was elected to the New York State Assembly in 1904; he was defeated in 1905 but was reelected in 1906. He married Marie McTague in 1908, served in the New York State Senate in 1910–18, and was floor leader in the Senate the last five years. He became known for his investigations of factory conditions as chairman of the New York Factory Investigating Commission (the vice-chairman was Alfred E. Smith) in 1911, which had been set up to investigate the tragic Triangle Shirt Waist Company fire, in which 147 working women died, and for the progressive social legislation he sponsored; among the measures he sponsored were bills for better working conditions, widows' pensions, and higher workmen's salaries. He worked closely with Smith in getting fifty-six of the commission's sixty recommendations enacted into law. He was elected justice of the New York Supreme Court in 1919 and protected the rights of labor while on the bench, resigned in 1926 to run for the United States Senate and was elected, and again in 1932, 1938, and 1944. In the Senate he was one of the leaders in guiding New Deal legislation in the field of social reform and labor through that body; among them the act establishing the National Recovery Administration (NRA) in 1933, the National Labor Relations Act (called "the Wagner Act") in 1935, the first social security act, the U.S. Housing Authority Act in 1937, the Railroad Retirement Act, and an antilynching bill. He opposed President Roosevelt's plan to reorganize the United States Supreme Court in 1937, helped create the Reconstruction Finance Corporation (RFC), and served on several Senate committees, among them Foreign Affairs and Banking and Currency. He supported the establishment of a Jewish state in Palestine during World War II and was chairman of the American Palestine Committee. He became a Catholic in 1946 and resigned from the Senate because of ill health in 1949; he died in New York City on May 4.

WAINSCOTT, CRICKET. *See* Blakely, Paul Lendrum.

WALDSEEMÜLLER, MARTIN (c. 1470–c. 1522), cosmographer. Born in Radolfzell, South Baden, Germany, he studied there or at the nearby University of Fribourg, Switzerland. He was a

cleric in 1514, when he became a canon at Saint-Dié, Lorraine, where he was a professor of geography at the College of Saint-Dié and lived until his death. He was early interested in geography and cartography and soon became one of the outstanding cartographers of his time. One of his most important works was his globe and map of the world in 1507, in which for the first time the name America was given to the New World; the accompanying text, *Cosmographicae Introductio,* contained in an appendix a Latin translation of the four journeys of Amerigo Vespucci and why Waldseemüller used the name America.

WALKER, FRANK COMERFORD (1886–1959), Postmaster General. Born in Plymouth, Pennsylvania, on May 30, he was taken to Montana by his parents when he was three and grew up in Butte. He was educated at Gonzaga University, Spokane, Washington, in 1903–6 and studied law at Notre Dame (LL.B. 1909) and was admitted to the Montana bar in 1909. He formed a law firm with his brother Thomas, Walker & Walker, in 1909, served as assistant district attorney of Silver Bow County, Montana, in 1909–12, and was elected to the Montana legislature in 1913. He married Hallie Victoria Boucher in 1914, served as an army lieutenant in World War I, and resumed his law practice after the war. He moved to New York in 1924, became involved in several successful business ventures, directed a chain of motion-picture theaters, and became involved in politics in New York. He supported Franklin D. Roosevelt in his gubernatorial and presidential campaigns and contributed heavily to them; he became one of Roosevelt's closest confidants and advisers. He was treasurer of the Democratic National Committee in 1932 and chairman in 1943–44; he was secretary of the President's Executive Council in 1933 and was executive secretary of the National Emergency Council from 1933 to 1935, when he returned to private business. He was an early supporter of a third term for President Roosevelt and was Postmaster General from 1940 to 1945 (he originated V-mail during World War II), when he resigned after the death of President Roosevelt. He was alternate delegate to the first United Nations General Assembly meeting, in London, in 1945 but left public life after that to return to managing his extensive business interests. He was active in Catholic charities and received the Laetare Medal in 1948; he died in New York City on Sept. 13.

WALKER, JAMES JOHN (1881–1946), mayor. Born in New York City on June 19, he studied briefly at St. Francis Xavier College there and at New York Law School in 1900–2 but did not become a member of the bar until 1912. In the meanwhile he wrote lyrics for several popular ballads, notably "Will You Love Me in December as You Do in May?" in 1905, served in the state Assembly in 1909, and attracted the attention of several Tammany Hall leaders, among them Alfred E. Smith and Tammany chief Charles E. Murphy. In 1912 he married Janet Frances Allen, a musical-comedy and vaudeville entertainer. He was elected to the state Senate in 1914 and served until 1925 and was leader of the Democrats in the Senate in 1921–25. He helped pass liberal legislation and with the support of Tammany Hall was elected mayor of New York City in 1925, overwhelming his Republican opponent, Frank D. Waterman. As mayor, he unified public hospitals, established the Sanitation Department, and supported an expanded parks and transit systems; he built the Independent subway system and constructed the Queens Midtown Tunnel and the West Side Highway. He became

immensely popular, was nationally known for his flamboyant life-style, which earned him the sobriquet Beau James, and was overwhelmingly reelected over Fiorello La Guardia in 1929. During his second term in office the exposure of several frauds led to an investigation by the legislature in 1931; the Seabury Committee was established, and its investigations revealed extensive corruption, and fifteen charges of malfeasance were leveled against him. A hearing was begun by Governor Franklin D. Roosevelt, but Walker suddenly resigned in 1932 before the hearings concluded and went into exile in Europe. While there he married Betty Compton (an actress with whom he had been conducting a well-publicized love affair) in a civil ceremony at Cannes in 1933 (his wife had divorced him earlier in the year); they were divorced in 1941, and after her death, in 1944, he returned to his Catholic faith. He returned to the United States in 1935, was assistant counsel of the New York State Transit Commission in 1937, and was appointed arbiter for the garment industry by then Mayor La Guardia in 1940. He became president of a phonograph record company and held that position until his death, in New York City on Nov. 18.

WALSH, DAVID IGNATIUS (1872–1947), U.S. senator, governor. Born in Leominster, Massachusetts, on Nov. 11, he was educated at Holy Cross College, Worcester, Massachusetts (B.A. 1893), studied law at Boston University law school (LL.B. 1897), and was admitted to the Massachusetts bar in 1897. He began a law practice with his brother Thomas, became interested in Democratic politics, served in the Massachusetts Assembly in 1899–1903, spent nine years in private law practice, and was elected lieutenant governor of Massachusetts in 1912. He was elected governor in 1913 and reelected in 1914 but was defeated in 1915. While governor, he enacted a series of reform measures, among them an improved state labor code and the establishment of state-supported university extension courses for needy students. He was a member of the state Constitutional Convention in 1917, was a delegate at large to the Democratic National Convention seven times and was elected U.S. senator from Massachusetts in 1918—the first Democratic U.S. senator from that state since 1851. He early supported President Wilson and the Versailles Treaty but broke with the President in 1919. He was defeated for reelection in 1924 but was again elected in a special election in 1926 to fill an unexpired term and remained in the Senate until 1947. While in the Senate he consistently supported the interests of minorities, generally supported the New Deal policies of President Franklin Roosevelt but did oppose his centralization policies and his attempted reorganization of the Supreme Court, in 1937. He favored tariff protection for New England industries and expansion of the Navy and the merchant marine (he was chairman of the Senate Naval Affairs committee) and a policy of strict neutrality for the United States until the United States entered the war, when he vigorously supported the war effort; after the war he voted for United States membership in the United Nations. He was defeated for reelection in 1946 and retired to private life; he died in Boston on June 11.

WALSH, EDMUND ALOYSIUS (1885–1956), educator. Born in South Boston on Oct. 10, he was educated at Boston College, joined the Society of Jesus in 1902, and continued his education at Jesuit scholasticates at Frederick and Woodstock, Maryland. He did graduate work abroad at the Universities of Dublin, London, and Innsbruck,

Austria, and was ordained at Woodstock in 1916. He taught at Georgetown and became dean of arts and sciences there in 1918 and was founder and first director of the Georgetown University School of Foreign Service in 1919. He was appointed director of the Papal Relief Mission for Russia in 1922 (while in Russia, he recovered and sent to Rome the bones of St. Andrew Bobola) and was American Catholic representative on the American Relief Administration to Russia the same year. He was named president of the Catholic Near East Welfare Association in 1927 and two years later was sent to Mexico as Vatican representative in an attempt to reconcile the Mexican Government and the Vatican. In 1931 he went to Baghdad to help establish Baghdad College, was acting president of Georgetown in 1937, and during World War II was a consultant to the War Department. He was civilian consultant to the U.S. chief of counsel during the Nuremberg war crimes trial, was in Japan in 1947–48 as Jesuit visitor general to reorganize the Jesuits there, and in 1949 he founded the Institute of Languages and Linguistics at Georgetown. He wrote several books, among them *Fall of the Russian Empire* (1928), *Ships and National Safety* (1933), *Woodcarver of Tyrol* (1935), *Total Power* (1948), and *Total Empire* (1951). He died in Washington, D.C., on Oct. 31; in 1958, Georgetown named its school of foreign service the Edmund A. Walsh School of Foreign Service.

WALSH, EMMET MICHAEL (1892–1968), bishop. Born in Beaufort, South Carolina, on Mar. 6, he studied for the priesthood at St. Bernard's Seminary, Rochester, New York, and was ordained in 1916. He served as a curate at Immaculate Conception Church, Atlanta, Georgia, in 1916 and was pastor of St. Theresa's Church, Albany, Georgia, in

1917–21, of St. Patrick's Church, Savannah, in 1921–22, and of Immaculate Conception Church, Atlanta, in 1923–27; in 1927, he was appointed sixth bishop of Charleston, South Carolina. During his episcopate there he opened new parishes, brought many new religious communities into the diocese, opened four new hospitals, was an active proponent of Catholic education, and promoted the welfare of blacks in the see. He was named titular bishop of Rhaedestus and coadjutor of Youngstown, Ohio, in 1949 and succeeded to the see in 1952. He dedicated St. Columba Cathedral in 1959 and saw Walsh College opened in 1960, held the first diocesan synod, in 1961, and expanded the facilities of the see. He died in Youngstown on Mar. 16.

WALSH, FRANCIS AUGUSTINE (1884–1938), educator. Born in Cincinnati, Ohio, on Mar. 21, he was educated at St. Francis Xavier College there (B.A. 1903), Mt. St. Mary of the West Seminary, Cincinnati, and the Gregorian, Rome (Ph.D. 1907), and was ordained in 1907. He engaged in parish work as a curate at St. Andrew's Church, Cincinnati, in 1907–8 and Sacred Heart Church, Dayton, in 1909–11, and was professor of philosophy at St. Mary's in 1911–22, except for 1918, when he was a chaplain in the Army. He was pastor of St. Andrew's Church, Cincinnati, and censor librorum of the archdiocese in 1920–23, and was also professor of philosophy at St. Joseph's College-on-the-Ohio in 1920–23 and at Summit Normal School, Cincinnati, in 1921–23, teaching summers at St. Francis Xavier University in 1920–23. He joined the Benedictines in 1923, made his novitiate at St. Bernard's Abbey, Fort Augustus, Scotland, and then went to Catholic University, where he taught philosophy until his death. He was one of the group that opened St. Anselm's

Priory in 1924, edited the *Placidian* in 1923–29, taught ethics at Trinity College from 1924, was associate editor of *Studies in Psychology and Psychiatry* in 1926–38, was regent of the seminary at Catholic University in 1931–37, and was president of the American Catholic Philosophical Association in 1933–34 and edited its review *The New Scholasticism* in 1936–38. He was active in the cause of black education and was chaplain of the Newman Club at Howard University in 1930–34, organized and was first chairman, in 1933, of the Northeastern Clergy Conference on Negro Welfare, directed the Institute of Apologetics at Catholic University, from which the Confraternity of Christian Doctrine developed, and was national director of the Confraternity in 1933–38. He was the author of several books, among them *Religion and Liturgy* (1933), *The Priest, God and the World* (1937), *Integral Philosophy* (1937), and, with Fr. Francis Xavier Lasance, *The Missal for Every Day;* he also was general editor of the Benedictine History Monograph series. He died in Washington, D.C., on Aug. 12.

WALSH, FRANCIS PATRICK (1864–1939), jurist. Born in St. Louis, Missouri, on July 20, he studied law and was admitted to the Missouri bar in 1889 and married Katherine M. O'Flaherty in 1891. He acquired a reputation as an outstanding trial lawyer, became interested in Democratic politics, and was a member of the reform group that elected Joseph W. Folk governor of Missouri in 1904. An advocate of social reform, he sponsored progressive legislation that attracted nationwide attention, was a member of the Tenement Commission in 1906–8, was an attorney for the Board of Public Welfare in 1908–14, and was president of the Board of Civil Service in 1911–13, all in Kansas City, Missouri. He supported

Woodrow Wilson for the presidency in 1912, was appointed chairman of the new Commission on Industrial Relations by President Wilson in 1913, and was cochairman, with former President Taft, of the National War Labor Board during World War I. He was chairman of the American Commission for Irish Independence after World War I and became counsel for the Irish Republic in 1920. He defended Tom Mooney in the Preparedness Day bombing in San Francisco in 1916, was active in civil liberties cases, and became recognized as one of the leading labor lawyers in the country. He was appointed a member of the New York Commission on Revision of Public Utility Laws in 1929 and chairman of the New York State Power Commission by Governor Franklin D. Roosevelt in 1931, organized the National Progressive League to support Roosevelt in the 1932 presidential campaign, and was elected first president of the National Lawyers Guild in 1936. He died in New York City on May 2.

WALSH, JAMES ANTHONY (1867–1936), founder. Of well-to-do Irish immigrant parents, he was born in Cambridge, Massachusetts, on Feb. 24, was educated at Boston College, Harvard, and St. John's Seminary, Brighton, Boston, and was ordained in Boston in 1892. He was a curate at St. Patrick's Church, Boston, in 1892–1903, became interested in missions and mission work, and in 1903–11 was director of Boston's Society for the Propagation of the Faith. He was one of the founders of the magazine *The Field Afar,* devoted to missionary activities (which later became Maryknoll's magazine) in 1907. He had met Fr. Thomas Frederick Price in 1904 at a Catholic Missionary Union meeting in Washington, D.C., in 1904, and when they met again, at the International Eucharistic Congress in Montreal in 1910, they decided to found an American society devoted to missionary work. They received the endorsement of the American hierarchy and temporary approval from Pope Pius X in 1911 to found the Catholic Foreign Mission Society (Maryknoll)—the first American mission order. They sent their first four Maryknoll fathers to South China under Fr. Thomas Price in 1918 and soon became known all over the world for their missionary work in China. Fr. Walsh was elected first superior for a ten-year term in 1929 at the first general chapter, and a permanent constitution was approved by Rome. He was appointed titular bishop of Siene in 1933, and by the time of his death, at Maryknoll, Ossining, New York, on Apr. 14, Maryknoll fathers had missions all over the Far East. He was the author of several books, among them *A Modern Martyr* (1907) and *In the Homes of the Martyrs* (1922).

WALSH, JAMES EDWARD (1891–1981), missionary, bishop. Second of nine children of William Walsh, a lawyer, and Mary Concannon Walsh, he was born in Cumberland, Maryland, on Apr. 30 and was educated at Mt. St. Mary's College, Emmitsburg, Maryland (B.A. 1910). He worked in a steel foundry the next two years and in 1912 joined the recently (1911) established Catholic Foreign Mission Society (Maryknoll). He was one of the first six students in the first class of Maryknoll Seminary, was ordained in 1915, and was one of the four men in the first departure group of Maryknoll missionaries, headed by Fr. Thomas Price, sent to China in 1918. He was named superior of the Maryknoll China Mission at Yeungkong, Kwangtung province, South China, in 1919, when Fr. Price died, and in 1924 he became prefect apostolic of the first canonically organized American mission. He founded the Little Flower Seminary in Kongmoon in

1926 and the Chinese Sisters of the Immaculate Heart of Mary there the following year. He was called Wha Lee Sou (Pillar of Truth) by the Chinese, who regarded him highly. In 1927, when he was thirty-six, he was named first bishop of the vicariate of Chiangmen (Kongmoon), in South China, and was consecrated on Sancian Island, where Francis Xavier died—the first native American to be consecrated a bishop in China. He was elected superior general of Maryknoll in 1936 and returned to Maryknoll in Ossining, New York; during his ten-year term as general he dispatched Maryknoll's first missionaries to Latin America and Africa. While on a visit to Japan in 1940 he became a secret mediator between Japan and the United States in a futile attempt to head off the threatened war between the two countries by carrying a message from Prime Minister Yosuke Matsuoka to President Roosevelt and Secretary of State Hull. He returned to China in 1948 as head of the Catholic Central Bureau in Shanghai, the agency designed to coordinate Catholic missionary activities in China. After the Communists came to power, in 1949, they closed the bureau in 1951 and arrested Walsh in 1958, charging him with being an enemy of the Chinese people, of counterrevolutionary activities, and of spying for the Vatican and for the United States, all of which he vigorously denied, and sentenced him to twenty years in prison. After he had served twelve years of his term in Ward Road Prison, in Shanghai, he was suddenly released, in 1970, with no explanation, the last of some seven thousand Catholic and Protestant missionaries expelled from China by the Communists. He returned to Maryknoll as superior general emeritus until his death, on July 29. He was the author of several books, best known of which was *The Man in*

Joss Stick Alley (1942), about a Maryknoll missionary.

WALSH, JAMES JOSEPH (1865–1942), author. Born in Archibald, Pennsylvania, on Apr. 12, he was educated at St. John's College (Fordham), New York City (B.A. 1884, M.A. 1885, Ph.D. 1889), and became a Jesuit in 1885. Ill health forced him to resign from the Jesuits after six years, and he studied medicine at the University of Pennsylvania and received his medical degree in 1895. He continued his medical studies at the Pasteur Institute and the Salpêtrière (Paris), Vienna, and Berlin, was correspondent for several American journals at the International Medical Congress in Russia, in 1897, and on his return to the United States began practicing medicine in New York City. He became an instructor and then professor at New York Polyclinic School for graduates and was professor and then dean of the Fordham University Medical School in 1905–13 and taught physiological psychology at Cathedral College. He retired from medicine in 1912 to devote himself to teaching and writing, married Julia H. Freed in 1915, wrote profusely, and was active in many Catholic organizations. He established the Fordham University Press, was on the original board of the Catholic Book Club, was twice honored by the papacy and by several Catholic universities, and was the recipient of the Laetare Medal in 1916. Besides the almost five hundred articles he wrote, he was the author of some forty books, among them *The Popes and Science* (1908), *The Thirteenth Greatest of Centuries* (1913), *Health Through Will Power* (1920), *The World's Debt to the Catholic Church* (1924), *These Splendid Priests* (1926), *Our American Cardinals* (1926), *American Jesuits* (1934), and *High Points of Medieval Culture* (1937);

he also edited *A Golden Treasury of Medieval Culture* (1937). He died in New York City on Feb. 28.

WALSH, LOUIS SEBASTIAN (1858–1924), bishop. Born in Salem, Massachusetts, on Jan. 22, he was educated at Holy Cross College, Worcester, Massachusetts, the Grand Seminary, Montreal, and St. Sulpice Seminary, Paris, and the Apollinaris and the Minerva, Rome, and was ordained in Rome in 1882. He served for a time as assistant pastor of St. Joseph's Church, Boston, and from its opening, in 1884, at St. John's Seminary, Brighton, Boston, until 1897. He was supervisor of the Catholic schools of the Boston archdiocese from 1897 until 1906, when he was consecrated bishop of Portland, Maine. He helped found the New England Catholic Historical Society and the Catholic Education Association, serving as president of the latter's school section, established new parishes, schools, and charitable institutions in the diocese, reorganized the diocesan school system, sought in vain for public aid for Catholic schools, founded the *Maine Catholic Historical Magazine,* and wrote several books. He died in Portland on May 12.

WALSH, MATTHEW J. (1882–1963), educator. Born in Chicago on May 14, he was educated at Notre Dame (Litt.B. 1903), Catholic University (Ph.D. 1907), and Johns Hopkins, and joined the Congregation of Holy Cross in 1902. He was ordained in 1907, was professor of history at Notre Dame in 1907–22, serving as vice president in 1911–22, and was a chaplain in the Army during World War I. He was president of Notre Dame in 1922–28 and president emeritus after 1928, and during his presidency inaugurated an extensive building program. He died at Notre Dame on Jan. 19.

WALSH, MICHAEL PATRICK (1912–82), educator. Born in Boston on Feb. 28, he joined the Jesuits in 1929 after graduating from high school and studied at Boston College (B.A. 1934, M.A. 1935) and Fordham (M.S. 1938, Ph.D. 1948). He was ordained in 1941 at Weston College, Massachusetts, where he received his S.T.L. in 1942, was acting principal of Fairfield University Prep School in 1942, taught biology at Boston College in 1943–45, and was chairman of the department in 1948–58. He was president of Boston College in 1958–68, expanded its staff and its physical plant, and inaugurated new programs and was president of Fordham in 1969–72, helping the university through a time of financial crisis. He returned to Boston College as chairman of the board of directors of its high school in 1972 and served in that post until 1980. He was honored by some eighteen colleges and universities for his educational contributions; he died in Boston on Apr. 23.

WALSH, PATRICK (1840–1900), journalist. Born in Ballingarry, Limerick, Ireland, on Jan. 1, he was brought to the United States in 1852 by his parents, who settled in Charleston, South Carolina. He worked as an apprentice reporter for a time, attended Georgetown in 1859–61, and when the Civil War broke out became a lieutenant in the South Carolina militia. He moved to Augusta, Georgia, in 1862 and joined the editorial staff of the Augusta *Constitutionalist* the same year, served on the *Pacificator* in 1864, *Banner of the South* in 1867, and the *Chronicle and Sentinel,* which he purchased in 1877 and combined with the *Constitutionalist.* He was general agent of the New York Associated Press in the South in 1866–92 and general manager of the Southern Associated Press, served in the Georgia legislature in 1872–76, was appointed U.S. senator from Georgia in 1894 to fill an unexpired term, and was elected U.S. senator the following year by the Georgia legislature. He died in Augusta on Mar. 19.

WALSH, ROBERT (1784–1859), author, editor. Son of a well-to-do merchant, he was born in Baltimore on Aug. 30, was educated at St. Mary's Seminary there, and was one of the first students at Georgetown, graduating in 1801. He continued his studies at St. Mary's and received his master's degree, read law under Robert Goodloe Harper, and became an ardent Federalist. He traveled in France and the British Isles in 1806–9, wrote for French and British papers, and for a time was secretary to the U.S. minister to England, William Pinkney. On his return to the United States he settled in Philadelphia, edited the *American Register* in 1809–10, and married Anna Maria Moylan in 1810, founded the *American Review of History and Politics,* the first American quarterly, which published only eight issues, in 1811–12, and founded another *American Register* in 1817, which survived only a year. With William Fry, he founded the Philadelphia *National Gazette and Literary Register,* in 1820, which he edited until 1836; he edited the *Museum of Foreign Literature and Science* in 1822–23 and founded the *American Quarterly Review* in 1827. He was a professor of English at the University of Pennsylvania in 1828–33 and a trustee of the university but retired because of ill health and moved to Paris permanently in 1837. He was American consul general in Paris from 1844 until he died there on Feb. 7. He also served as foreign correspondent of the Washington *National Intelligencer* and the New York *Journal of Commerce,* contributed articles to literary journals, edited the last twenty-

eight volumes of *The Works of the British Poets* with biographies, wrote two volumes of essays and *Didactics,* and was known for his political essays, particularly *A Letter on the Genius and Disposition of the French Government* (1810) and *An Appeal from the Judgments of Great Britain Respecting the United States of America* (1815). Edgar Allan Poe called him "one of the finest writers, one of the most accomplished scholars . . . in the country."

WALSH, THOMAS (1875–1928), author. Born in Brooklyn, New York, on Oct. 14, he was educated at St. Francis Xavier College, New York City (M.A. 1895), Georgetown (Ph.B. 1892, Ph.D. 1897), and Columbia. He became a freelance writer and developed an interest in Hispanic culture that in time made him an authority on Spanish-American matters. He served at various times on the staffs of Warner's Library of the World's Best Literature, International Encyclopedia, New York *Globe and Commercial Advertiser, The Bookman,* and the Catholic Encyclopedia, and contributed to many secular and religious magazines, including *Harper's Magazine, Scribner's, Atlantic Monthly, Ave Maria,* and *America.* He was the author of several books of poetry, among them *The Prison Ships* (1909), *The Pilgrim Kings* (1915), and *Gardens Overseas and Other Poems* (1918), and he edited *The Hispanic Anthology* (1920) and an edition of the poems of Rubén Darío (1916) and compiled *The Catholic Anthology* (1927). He was honored by several universities and foreign governments and was elected to the Royal Academy of Seville and was an associate editor of *Commonweal* at the time of his death, in Brooklyn on Oct. 29.

WALSH, THOMAS JAMES (1859–1933), U.S. senator. Born in Two Rivers, Wisconsin, on June 12, he had little formal education but received a law degree from the University of Wisconsin in 1884 and was admitted to the bar. He began to practice with his brother Henry at Redfield, South Dakota, married Elinor Cameron McClements in 1889, moved to Montana in 1890, and formed a partnership with Cornelius B. Nolan. He became a leader of the bar there and built up a profitable law practice, was defeated in a bid for Congress in 1906 and for the U.S. Senate in 1910 but was elected senator from Montana in 1912 and was reelected in each subsequent election for the rest of his life. He supported progressive legislation in the fields of woman suffrage, child labor, and antitrust legislation and helped write the eighteenth and nineteenth amendments to the U.S. Constitution. He was a firm supporter of President Wilson and his policies, including the Treaty of Versailles, the League of Nations, the World Court, and arms limitations, for which he fought vigorously. He headed the Senate investigating committee in 1922–23 that unearthed the fraudulent naval oil leases of the Harding administration and the notorious Teapot Dome and Elk Hills oil-reserve scandals. He was permanent chairman of the 1924 (at which he received 123 votes for the presidential nomination and refused the vice-presidential nomination) and 1932 national conventions of the Democratic Party. He married Nieves Perez Chaumont de Truffin (his first wife had died in 1917) and was appointed U.S. Attorney General by President Franklin D. Roosevelt in 1933 but died suddenly on a train near Wilson, North Carolina, on Mar. 2 while on his way to the presidential inauguration and to accept the appointment as Attorney General.

WALSH, THOMAS JOSEPH (1873–1952), bishop. Born in Parkers Landing, Pennsylvania, on Dec. 6, he was edu-

cated at St. Bonaventure College and Seminary, New York, and the Apollinaris, Rome, and was ordained for the Buffalo, New York, diocese in 1900. He served as a curate at St. Joseph's Cathedral, Buffalo, was secretary to Bishops Quigley and Colton there in 1900–15, was chancellor of the diocese in 1900–18, and was rector of St. Joseph's in 1915–18. He was appointed third bishop of Trenton, New Jersey, in 1918 and was made an Assistant at the Pontifical Throne in 1922. While bishop of Trenton, he established fourteen new parishes and twenty-five missions and built forty-seven elementary and eleven high schools. He was transferred to Newark, New Jersey, in 1928 as its fifth bishop and became that see's first archbishop when it was made an archdiocese, in 1937. During his episcopacy at Newark, he founded the archdiocesan paper, *The Advocate,* began a new building at the Darlington seminary and a drive to complete Sacred Heart Cathedral, and established the Mt. Carmel Guild to supervise the see's social work. He died in South Orange, New Jersey, on June 6.

WALSH, WILLIAM THOMAS (1891–1949), author. Born in Waterbury, Connecticut, on Sept. 11, he was educated at Yale (B.A. 1913) and then worked as a reporter on the Waterbury *American and Republican,* the Hartford *Times,* and the Philadelphia *Public Ledger* in 1907–18; he married Helen Gerard Sherwood in 1914. He taught English at Hartford High School in 1918, was head of the English department at Roxbury School, Cheshire, Connecticut, in 1919–33, and was professor of English at Manhattanville College of the Sacred Heart, in New York City, in 1933–47. He then retired to devote himself to writing. He wrote short stories; a novel, *Out of the Wilderness* (1935); a play, *Shekels* (1937); poetry, *Lyric Poems* (1939); essays, *Char-*

acters of the Inquisition (1940); and biographies, among them *Isabella the Crusader* (1930), *Philip II* (1937), *St. Teresa of Avila* (1943), *St. Peter the Apostle* (1948), and the posthumously published *Saints in Action* (1961); his most popular book was *Our Lady of Fatima* (1947). He was honored by the Spanish Government and received the Laetare Medal in 1941. He died in White Plains, New York, on Feb. 22.

WALWORTH, CLARENCE AUGUSTUS (1820–1900). Son of Reuben H. Walworth, last chancellor of New York State, and Mary Averill Walworth, he was born in Plattsburg on May 30, graduated from Union College, Schenectady, in 1838, and was admitted to the New York bar in 1841. He decided to give up his law practice to study for the ministry and attended General Theological Seminary, in New York City, but left after three years and in 1845 became a Catholic. In 1845, with Isaac Hecker and James McMaster, he joined the Redemptorists, studied at the Redemptorist novitiate at St. Trond, Wittenberg, and after further studies at the Redemptorist House of Studies at Witten, near Aix-la-Chapelle, he was ordained in 1848. He was sent back to the United States in 1851 as one of a mission band when the Redemptorists established an American province, and soon became known for his spellbinding oratory and preaching on the Redemptorist missions. In 1858, Frs. Isaac Hecker, Francis Baker, Augustine F. Hewitt, George Deshon, and Walworth were released from their Redemptorist vows and founded the Congregation of St. Paul (the Paulists) to give missions and especially to make converts. He disagreed with the others over the form their vows were to take before the Congregation had its constitution approved by Archbishop John Hughes of New York in 1858 and left. He was received

into the Albany diocese and stationed at St. Peter's Church, Troy, New York, but returned to the Paulists in 1861. He again resigned, in 1865, because of malaria and overwork on the missions, was appointed pastor of St. Mary's Church, Albany, in 1866, and remained in that position until his death, thirty-four years later, in Albany on Sept. 19. His verse paraphrase of the *Te Deum,* "Holy God, We Praise Thy Name" (1853), is the one commonly used in Catholic churches in the United States; he also wrote several books, among them *The Gentle Skeptic* (1863), *The Doctrine of Hell* (1873), and *Early Ritualism in America* (1893), and was a leader in the temperance movement.

WARD, ARTEMUS. *See* Browne, Charles Farrar.

WARD, JAMES HARMAN (1806–61), naval officer. Born in Hartford, Connecticut, on Sept. 25, he was graduated from the American Literary, Scientific and Military Academy (later Norwich University), Norwich, Connecticut, in 1823, studied for a time at Washington (Trinity) College, Hartford, after having been appointed midshipman, and served several years off the coast of Africa and was promoted to the rank of lieutenant in 1831. He married Sarah Whittemore in 1833, served on tours of duty in the Mediterranean and the West Indies, and in 1844–45 gave a series of lectures on ordnance at the naval school in Philadelphia which were extremely popular. He was a strong proponent of a national naval academy, and when the Naval Academy opened, in 1845, he was appointed executive officer (later designated commandant) and was head of the department of ordnance and gunnery. In 1847 he was named commander of the *Cumberland* and served along the Mexican coast during the remainder of the Mexican War; he was given command of the receiving ship *North Carolina* in the Brooklyn Navy Yard in 1857. When the Civil War broke out, he organized and was put in command of the Potomac flotilla and was killed in an attack on Mathias Point, Virginia, on June 27—the first Union naval officer to die in the war. He was the author of *Elementary Course of Instruction on Ordnance and Gunnery* (1845), *Manual of Naval Tactics* (1859), and *Steam for the Million* (1860).

WARD, JOHN CHAMBERLAIN (1873–1929), bishop. Born in West Point, Ohio, on May 25, he studied for the priesthood at St. Meinrad's Seminary, St. Meinrad, Indiana, and was ordained in 1894. He engaged in pastoral work in the Leavenworth, Kansas, diocese until 1910, when he was appointed third bishop of Leavenworth (changed to Kansas City, Kansas, in 1947), a position he held until his death there on Apr. 20.

WARD, MAISIE (1889–1975), publisher, author. Daughter of Wilfrid Ward and Josephine Mary Ward, the novelist, she was born in Shanklin, Isle of Wight, England, on Jan. 4. She early became involved in volunteer services for social causes, served as a nurse's aide in military hospitals during World War I, and in 1919 became a charter member of the Catholic Evidence Guild. Through the Guild she met Frank Sheed, and in 1926 they were married. Later the same year they founded the publishing firm of Sheed & Ward, expanded it to New York in 1933, and built it into one of the leading Catholic publishers in the world. She was the author of a series of biographies, among them *Gilbert Keith Chesterton* (1943), *Return to Chesterton* (1952), the two-volume *Robert Browning and His World* (1968), *The Tragi-Comedy of Pen Browning* (1972), and *Young Mr. Newman*

(1948). She wrote and lectured widely on Catholicism and was also involved in such activist movements as Dorothy Day's Catholic Worker, the French worker-priests, and subsidized housing in England and the United States. Though christened Mary Josephine, she was early called Maisie and used that name throughout her life. She died in New York City on Jan. 28. Her autobiography, *Unfinished Business*, was published in 1964.

WARD, WILLIAM J. (1915–81), superior. Born in Philadelphia on July 7, he joined the Oblates of St. Francis de Sales in Childs, Maryland, after graduating from Northeast Catholic High School, in Philadelphia, in 1932, and was professed in 1933. He studied at Catholic University (B.S. 1936), taught religion at Northeast Catholic High for seven years, and was ordained in Wilmington, Delaware, in 1941. He was librarian at Northeast Catholic High in 1943–45 and assistant principal in 1945–51, was superior of the De Sales House of Oblate priests in 1951–53 and of the Chestnut Hill Community of the Oblates in 1953–55 and then became principal of the new St. Francis de Sales High School, in Toledo, Ohio. After five years there he returned to Northeast Catholic High as superior of its faculty, and in 1966 became first provincial of the Toledo-Detroit province of the Oblates. He served in that position until 1970, when he was elected superior general of his order; he was reelected in 1976. He died in Philadelphia on Oct. 11.

WARDE, MARY FRANCIS XAVIER (1810–84), foundress. Mary Frances Warde was born in Mountrath, Queen's County, Ireland, and was raised by a grand-aunt, since her mother died when she was an infant. She taught children at a home for orphans operated by the newly founded Congregation of the Sisters of Mercy, and in 1830 she joined the Congregation. She received the habit in 1832, taking the name Mary Francis Xavier, was appointed superior of a convent she established at Carlow in 1837, founded convents at Naas in 1839, Wexford the following year, and Westport in 1842, and in 1843 was sent to the United States with six sisters, at the request of Bishop Michael O'Connor of Pittsburgh, to establish a foundation—the beginning of the Sisters of Mercy in the United States. She opened a hospital and a school in Pittsburgh, made a foundation in Chicago in 1846 and in Loretto, Pennsylvania, in 1848, and in 1850 opened a convent in Providence, Rhode Island, where, in 1851, with the aid of Bishop Bernard O'Reilly and a group of Catholic men, she successfully warded off an attack by a gang of Know-Nothingites intent on torching the convent. In time she opened foundations, schools, and orphanages all over the East, Midwest, and West. Blind the last months of her life, she died on Sept. 17 in Manchester, New Hampshire, where she had established a convent in 1858.

WATERS, VINCENT STANISLAUS (1904–74), bishop. Born in Roanoke, Virginia, on Aug. 15, he was educated at Belmont Abbey, Belmont, North Carolina, St. Charles College, Ellicott City, Maryland, St. Mary's Seminary, Baltimore, and the North American College, Rome. He was ordained in Rome in 1931 and served as a curate at Holy Cross Church, Lynchburg, Virginia, in 1932–36 and at Sacred Heart Cathedral, Richmond, in 1936. He was chancellor of the Richmond diocese in 1936–43, directed the diocesan Mission Fathers in 1943–45, and was appointed bishop of Raleigh, North Carolina, in 1945. He remained in that position until his death, in Raleigh on Dec. 3, and de-

spite strong opposition desegregated Catholic schools and hospitals in the diocese in 1953.

WATTERSON, JOHN AMBROSE (1840–99), bishop. Born in Bairdstown, Pennsylvania, on May 27, he was educated at Mt. St. Mary's College, Emmitsburg, Maryland, and was ordained in 1868. He taught at Mt. St. Mary's until 1877 and was its rector from 1877 until 1880, when he was appointed second bishop of Columbus, Ohio. He held that position until his death there on Apr. 17.

WATTSON, PAUL JAMES (1863–1940), founder. Lewis Thomas Wattson was born in Millington, Maryland, on Jan. 16 and was educated at St. Mary's Hall, Burlington, New Jersey, and St. Stephen (Bard) College, Annandale, New York. He studied for the Episcopal priesthood at General Theological Seminary, New York City, and was ordained in 1886. He became rector of St. John's Episcopal Church, Kingston, New York, and left in 1895 to become pastor of a church in Omaha, Nebraska. He joined the Episcopal Order of the Holy Cross in Maryland in 1898, taking the name Paul. In 1898, with Mary Lurana White, an Episcopal nun, he founded a new order called the Society of the Atonement, devoted to Anglican reunion with the Holy See, built a monastery near Garrison, New York, in 1900, and took the names Paul James. He founded *The Lamp* in 1903, launched the Church United Octave in 1908, and the following year he and seventeen members of the Society entered the Catholic Church by special dispensation of Pope Pius X, who approved the Octave in 1909. Among those in the group was Sister Mary Lurana White, who with Fr. Paul's encouragement had founded a nuns community at Graymoor in 1908. The changeover was not accomplished without some difficulty, as there were several lawsuits over the land Fr. Paul and Sister Lurana held, but they were all ended by financial settlements with the plaintiffs. Fr. Paul studied for the Catholic priesthood at St. Joseph's Seminary, Dunwoodie, Yonkers, New York, and was ordained a Catholic priest in 1910. He founded St. Christopher's Inn for homeless men and in 1916 had his octave of prayer for Christian unity extended to the universal Church by Pope Benedict XV, as the Chair of Christian Unity Octave, celebrated each year from Jan. 18 to Jan. 25. He established the Graymoor Press in 1925 and launched the "Ave Maria Hour" on radio in 1935. By the time of his death, at Graymoor on Feb. 9, the Society of the Atonement had spread to three continents.

WEBB, BENEDICT JOSEPH (1814–97), journalist, editor. Born in Bardstown, Kentucky, on Feb. 25, he was educated at St. Joseph's College there in 1821–28, became a printer and then foreman printer on the Louisville *Journal.* He published the first Catholic paper in Kentucky, the *Catholic Advocate,* in 1836–48, in Louisville, and in 1855 wrote a series of letters in the Louisville *Courier-Journal* denouncing the intolerance of the Know-Nothing movement, which had caused bloodshed and rioting in Louisville in 1854 on a day that had disgraced the city and was called "Bloody Monday"; the letters were published in book form as *Letters of a Kentucky Catholic* (1856). In 1858 Bishop Martin Spalding of Louisville, who had been one of his teachers at St. Joseph's, persuaded him to become publisher of the Louisville *Catholic Guardian,* which had been founded by the St. Vincent de Paul Society in Louisville; it was forced to suspend publication in 1862 because of the Civil War. He was a state senator in 1867–75, was editor of

the revived *Catholic Advocate* in 1869–72, wrote *The Centenary of Catholicity in Kentucky* (1884), and died in Louisville on Aug. 2. He was also known as Ben J. Webb and was sometimes erroneously called Benjamin.

WEBER, ANSELM (1862–1921), missionary. Born in New Salem, Michigan, on Nov. 10, he was educated at St. Francis College, Cincinnati, Ohio, joined the Friars Minor in 1882, and was ordained in 1889. He taught at St. Francis in 1889–98 and was then sent to minister to the Navajos at St. Michael's, Arizona. He began a school at St. Michael's, worked on behalf of the Navajos, and was successful in expanding Indian reservations. He was editor of the *Franciscan Missions of the Southwest* from 1913, wrote a two-volume English-Navaho and Navaho-English Dictionary (1912) and a catechism, and was working on a Navajo grammar when he died, in Rochester, Minnesota, on Mar. 7.

WEGNER, NICHOLAS (1898–1976), director of Boys Town. Born in Humphrey, Nebraska, he was educated at St. Joseph's Seminary, Teutopolis, Illinois, St. Paul (Minnesota) Seminary, the Gregorian, Rome (S.T.D.), and Catholic University (J.C.L.). He was ordained in Rome in 1925, was curate at St. Cecilia Cathedral, Omaha, Nebraska, was assistant chancellor in 1928–35 and chancellor in 1935–48 of the Omaha archdiocese, and in 1948 was named director of Boys Town, Nebraska, on the death of its founder, Msgr. Edward J. Flanagan. He held this post until 1973. He died in Omaha on Mar. 18.

WEHRLE, VINCENT DE PAUL (1855–1941), bishop. Born in Berg, St. Gall, Switzerland, on Dec. 19, he was educated at the diocesan seminary there and at Einsiedeln and joined the Benedictines at Einsiedeln in 1875. He was ordained there in 1882, came to the United States later the same year, and engaged in missionary and pastoral work in Arkansas and Indiana in 1882–86 and in Yankton, Dakota Territory, in 1886–88. He worked with the settlers along the route of the Great Northern Railroad in 1888–99 and founded an abbey at Richardton, North Dakota, in 1889 and St. Gall Priory near Devils Lake, North Dakota, in 1893. He was largely responsible for preserving the faith of large numbers of German-speaking immigrants in his flock, established a monastery and St. Mary's College (which became Assumption College in 1930), and was abbot in 1904–10. He was appointed first bishop of the newly created diocese of Bismarck, North Dakota, in 1910, retired in 1939, and was appointed titular bishop of Teos. He died in Bismarck on Nov. 2.

WEIGEL, GUSTAVE (1906–64), theologian. Born in Buffalo, New York, on Jan. 15, he joined the Jesuits when sixteen, entering the St. Andrew-on-Hudson, New York, novitiate in 1922, studied at Woodstock (Maryland) College (B.A. 1928, M.A. 1929) and the Gregorian, Rome, where he received doctorates in philosophy in 1929 and theology in 1931; he was ordained at Woodstock in 1933. He continued his studies in dogmatic theology at the Gregorian (S.T.D. 1937), taught theology at Catholic University in Santiago, Chile in 1937–48, and was dean of its theology faculty in 1942–48. He returned to the United States in 1948 and became professor of ecclesiology at Woodstock in 1949, a position he held until his death, in New York City on Jan. 3. He was a leader in the ecumenical movement, was the first Catholic to give a series of lectures at the Yale Divinity School, in 1960, wrote and lectured widely on

Christian unity and the need for reform in the Church, and was a member of the Vatican Secretariat for Promoting Christian Unity at the first two sessions of Vatican Council II. He was the author of *Faustus of Riez* (1938), *A Catholic Primer on the Ecumenical Movement* (1957), *Faith and Understanding in America* (1959), *The Modern God* (1963), and, with Robert McAfee Brown, coauthor of *An American Dialogue* (1959).

WELCH, THOMAS ANTHONY (1884–1959), bishop. Born in Faribault, Minnesota, on Nov. 2, he was educated at St. Paul College and Seminary, St. Paul, Minnesota, and was ordained in St. Paul in 1909. He served as Archbishop John Ireland's secretary in 1909–18 and Archbishop Austin Dowling's in 1919–22, was chancellor of the archdiocese in 1918–23 and vicar-general in 1923–25 and was made a domestic prelate in 1924. He was appointed third bishop of Duluth, Minnesota, in 1925; during his episcopate he established the Duluth *Register* in 1937 and a diocesan Confraternity of Christian Doctrine in 1938, dedicated the Cathedral of Our Lady of the Rosary in 1957, and greatly expanded the facilities of the see to meet the needs of the Catholic populace, which had grown from sixty thousand to one hundred thousand. He died in Duluth on Sept. 9.

WELDON, CHRISTOPHER JOSEPH (1905–82), bishop. Born in the Bronx, New York City, on Sept. 6, he was educated at St. Joseph's Seminary, Dunwoodie, Yonkers, New York, and Catholic University and was ordained in New York City in 1929. He served as assistant pastor at St. John's Church, White Plains, New York, was spiritual director of the Newman School for Boys, at Lakewood, New Jersey, in 1931–45, curate at St. John Chrysostom

Church, in the Bronx, in 1935–36 and at Blessed Sacrament Church, Manhattan, in 1936–42. He was a chaplain on the aircraft carrier *Guadalcanal* in 1942–46, was master of ceremonies to Cardinal Spellman in 1946–47, and was executive director of New York's Catholic Charities in 1947–50. He was made a papal chamberlain in 1947 and a domestic prelate the following year and then became president of Our Lady of the Elms College, Chicopee, Massachusetts. He was appointed bishop of Springfield, Massachusetts, in 1950, oversaw a major expansion of schools, churches, and other religious facilities in the diocese, and retired in 1977. He died in Springfield on Mar. 19.

WELSH, MARTIN STANISLAUS (1876–1961), educator. Born in Cambridge, Massachusetts, on June 4, he was educated at Boston College and St. John's Seminary, Brighton, Boston, joined the Dominicans, and was ordained in 1906. He continued his studies in Rome, taught at the Dominican House of Studies, Washington, D.C., and then became president of Aquinas College, Columbus, Ohio. He served in this position for fourteen years and was then transferred to Providence (Rhode Island) College, where he taught mathematics for thirty years, serving as vice president in 1923–31. He wrote on canon law and theology, spent the last years of his life as chaplain for the Dominican sisters in Plainville and died in Natick, Massachusetts, on June 21.

WENINGER, FRANCIS XAVIER (1805–88), missionary. Born in Wildhaus, Styria, Austria, on Oct. 31, he was educated at the University of Vienna, where he received his doctorate in divinity, and was ordained in 1830. He began teaching theology at the University of Graz but left to join the Jesuits in 1832. He taught at the University of Innsbruck, Austria, in 1834–48 and gave missions in Tyrol and Vorarlberq that were very popular. When the Jesuits were suppressed in Austria, in 1848, he emigrated to the United States, where he settled in Cincinnati, Ohio. Known for his great preaching ability, he traveled all over the United States preaching parish missions (he gave some eight hundred missions). He published a small and a large catechism in 1865 that never became popular, acquired great influence among German-speaking Catholics, and ended a long schism at St. Louis Church, in Buffalo, New York. He died in Cincinnati on June 29.

WHEELWRIGHT, ESTHER (1696–1780). Daughter of Colonel John Wheelwright and Mary Snell Wheelwright, she was born at Wells, Massachusetts (now Maine), on Apr. 10. She was captured by Abnaki Indians during a raid on Wells in 1703 and held captive until she was ransomed by Jesuit Fr. Vincent Bigot and brought to Quebec in 1708. She was taken into the household of Governor Philippe de Vaudreuil, who favored returning her to her parents but was unable to do so because of the unsettled conditions prevailing between England and France. She began studying at the Ursuline boarding school in Quebec in 1709, joined the Ursulines in 1710 but was withdrawn by the governor, who felt she should be returned to her parents. In 1712 she returned to the Ursulines as a postulant, took the habit with the name Esther-Marie-Joseph de l'Enfant Jésus in 1713, and was professed the following year. She served as a religious for more than seventy years, and was superior of the Quebec Ursulines in 1760–66 and 1769–72. She died in Quebec on Nov. 28.

WHELAN, CHARLES MAURICE (1741–1806), missionary. Born in Ballycommon, Ireland, he joined the Capuchins in 1770 at Bar-sur-Aube, France, taking the name Maurice, was professed there in 1771, and was ordained. He was vicar of the Capuchin friary at Barsur-Aube and volunteered as chaplain in the French fleet sent to aid the Americans in their struggle with England, serving on the *Jason,* which in 1781 was attached to the fleet of Admiral François de Grasse. When De Grasse was defeated by Admiral Rodney in the West Indies in 1782, Whelan was imprisoned for thirteen months in Jamaica, where he ministered to the French prisoners. After the war, he went to New York City, in 1784, began building St. Peter's Church there the next year, and became embroiled in a dispute with the trustees that was complicated by the arrival of Fr. Andrew Nugent, an Irish Capuchin. He left New York in 1786 and went to his brother's home in Johnstown, New York; the following year, he was sent as a missionary by Bishop John Carroll to Kentucky with a band of immigrants under Edward Howard. He returned to Johnstown in 1790, became rector of White Clay Creek, Pennsylvania, and ministered to the Catholics in Delaware and Maryland as well. He retired in 1805 and spent the rest of his life at Bohemia Manor, Maryland, where he died on Mar. 21.

WHELAN, JAMES (1822–78), bishop. Born in Kilkenny, Ireland, he emigrated to the United States, studied at St. Rose Convent, Springfield, Kentucky, and St. Joseph Priory, Somerset, Ohio, joined the Dominicans in 1839, and was ordained in 1846. He taught at St. Joseph's, serving as subprior in 1848–50 and as president in 1851–54, and was provincial of the Dominicans in the United States in 1854–58. He was appointed titular bishop of Marcopolis and coadjutor of Nashville, Tennessee,

in 1858 and succeeded to the see the following year as its second bishop. He resigned in 1863 because of illness brought on by the strain of the Civil War and was appointed titular bishop of Diocletianapolis. He died in Zanesville, Ohio, on Feb. 18.

WHELAN, RICHARD VINCENT (1809–74), bishop. Born in Baltimore on Jan. 28, he was educated at Mt. St. Mary's College, Emmitsburg, Maryland, and St. Sulpice Seminary, Paris, and was ordained in 1831. He engaged in pastoral work in Richmond, Virginia, in 1831–40 and was consecrated second bishop of Richmond in 1841. He founded St. Vincent's College and Seminary, near Richmond, and was its president until it closed, in 1846; in 1850, he was transferred to Wheeling, (West) Virginia as its first bishop. During his episcopacy, he built a cathedral, a diocesan seminary, and St. Vincent's College and opened new schools and hospitals. He attended the first and second plenary councils of Baltimore, in 1852 and 1866, and Vatican Council I, in 1869–70. He died in Baltimore on July 7.

WHIPPLE, AMIEL WEEKS (1816–63), general. Born in Greenwich, Hampshire County, Massachusetts, he studied at Amherst and then West Point, graduating in 1841 as second lieutenant of artillery. He transferred to the engineers and was assigned to surveying and mapping duties on the Patapsco River, the approaches to New Orleans, Portsmouth Harbor, New Hampshire, and the borders between Canada and the United States in 1844–49 and between Mexico and the United States in 1849–53. He planned a railroad route to the Pacific coast in 1853–56, was made a captain in 1855, and became a Catholic in 1857, when he was in charge of lighthouse districts from

Lake Superior to the St. Lawrence River. During the Civil War he was an engineer under Generals McDowell and McClellan, was named a brigadier general of volunteers in 1862, and was in charge of the defenses of Washington on the Virginia side in 1862. He took part in the battles of Antietam and Fredericksburg and was mortally wounded at the battle of Chancellorsville. He was brought to Washington, D.C., brevetted brigadier general on May 4, 1863, and major general of volunteers on May 6, and major general a few hours before his death, on May 7.

WHITE, ANDREW (1579–1656), missionary. Born in or near London on Dec. 27, he was educated at St. Alban's, Valladolid, and the English College, Seville, in Spain, and Douai, France, and was ordained in Douai in 1605. He was sent on the English mission the following year, was arrested and banished from England, and in 1607 joined the Jesuits at Louvain. He taught theology at Lisbon, Louvain, and then Liège, where he became prefect of studies, engaged in occasional missionary work in England in 1625–28, and in 1629 was allowed to return to England and was active in Hampshire. When George Calvert, first baron of Baltimore, decided to establish a Catholic colony in America, Fr. White joined the expedition sent to America in 1633 on the *Ark* and the *Dove* to settle in Maryland; they made land at Clement's Island on May 25, 1634, and Mass was celebrated for the first time in Maryland. He worked with the settlers and the Maryland Indians, with whom he and the settlers established good relations, and he and his companions founded numerous missions among them and the Potomac Indians in Virginia. His work was suddenly ended when civil war broke out in England and a group of Virginians (instigated by William Claiborne, of Virginia, who had been given refuge in Catholic Maryland), led by Richard Ingle, and a group of Puritans destroyed and plundered many Catholic residences and Jesuit settlements in Maryland, seized Frs. White and Thomas Copley (alias Philip Fisher), and sent them back to London in chains in 1644. Fr. White was tried for treason for his priesthood but won acquittal on his plea he had been brought to England forcibly and against his will, and was again banished from England. He went to the Netherlands, tried without success to return to Maryland, and spent the rest of his life in missionary work in England and as chaplain to a noble Hampshire family. He died probably in London on Dec. 27. Called the "apostle of Maryland," he was an important figure in early Maryland history, writing a pamphlet to attract new colonists, *Declaratio Coloniae Domini Baronis de Baltimore,* and also *Relatio itineris in Marilandiam (A Briefe Relation of the Voyage unto Maryland in English),* an account of the Indian trails in western Maryland, a grammar of the Piscataway language, and a dictionary and catechism for the Indians in their native language.

WHITE, CHARLES DANIEL (1879–1955), bishop. Born in Grand Rapids, Michigan, on Jan. 5, he was educated at St. Francis Seminary, Milwaukee, Wisconsin, and the Propaganda, Rome (Ph.D. 1907, S.T.D. 1911), and was ordained in Rome in 1910. He taught at St. Joseph's Seminary, Grand Rapids, in 1911–19, was curate at St. Andrew's Cathedral in 1911–18, and was rector of St. Joseph's Seminary in 1919–27. He was made a domestic prelate in 1925 and was consecrated bishop of Spokane, Washington, in 1927. During his twenty-eight-year episcopate, the Catholic population of the see doubled, and to meet its needs he established sixteen new parishes and thirty-one new churches, built fourteen new schools, and encouraged religious orders to open hospitals and schools in the diocese. He died in Spokane on Sept. 25.

WHITE, CHARLES IGNATIUS (1807–78), editor. Born in Baltimore on Feb. 1, he was educated at Mt. St. Mary's College, Emmitsburg, Maryland, and St. Sulpice Seminary, Paris, and was ordained in Paris in 1830. On his return to the United States he engaged in pastoral work in the Baltimore area, taught moral theology at St. Mary's Seminary, Baltimore, in 1843–45, and edited the *Annual Catholic Almanac and Directory* in 1834–57. He was a cofounder of the monthly *Religious Cabinet* in 1842, changed its name to the *United States Catholic Monthly* the next year, and edited it until its demise in 1847; he revived it as the *Metropolitan Magazine* in 1853, but it was short-lived. He helped found the diocesan weekly *Catholic Mirror* in 1849 and was its editor in 1850–55. He became rector of St. Matthew's Church, Washington, D.C., in 1857, holding this latter position until his death, in Washington on Apr. 1. He founded a school and church, an infant asylum, and a home for aged blacks, translated several French works, and published *The Life of Mrs. Eliza A. Seton* in 1853, the first full-length biography of Mother Seton.

WHITE, EDWARD DOUGLASS (1845–1921), Chief Justice of the United States. Son of Governor Edward White of Louisiana and Catherine Ringgold White, he was born in Lafourche Parish, Louisiana, on Nov. 3 and was educated at Mt. St. Mary's College, Emmitsburg, Maryland, Loyola College, New Orleans, and Georgetown. He left Georgetown when fifteen to serve with the Confederate Army during the Civil War, was captured in 1863 and paroled until the end of the war, and after the war studied law under Edward Bermudez. He was admitted to the Louisiana bar in 1868, became interested in politics, and was elected to the Louisiana state senate in 1874 and 1876. He was a state supreme court associate justice in 1879–80, retired from public life in 1881 to private practice but was active in civic affairs, helping to found Tulane University. He was elected to the United States Senate in 1891 and served until 1894 (when he married Leita Montgomery Kent). He was appointed associate justice of the U.S. Supreme Court by President Grover Cleveland. In 1910 President William Howard Taft appointed him Chief Justice—the first Southerner since Roger Taney and the second Catholic to hold that office, which he held until his death. He had a deep knowledge of civil law, was generally conservative, and wrote some seven hundred opinions while on the Court. Among his important contributions were the "rule of reason" decisions in the antitrust cases against the American Tobacco Company and the Standard Oil Company in 1911, which differentiated between legal and illegal business combinations, and the decision in 1916 upholding the constitutionality of the Adamson Act, which established the eight-hour workday for railroad workers. He was the recipient of the Laetare Medal in 1914. He died in Washington, D.C., on May 19. His statue, representing Louisiana, was enshrined in the Capitol in Washington in 1955.

WHITE, HELEN CONSTANCE (1896–1967), author. Born in New Haven, Connecticut, on Nov. 26, she was educated at Radcliffe College, Cambridge, Massachusetts (B.A. 1916, M.A. 1917), taught at Smith College, Northampton, for two years in 1917–19, and then went to the University of Wisconsin as an instructor in English. She received her doctorate in 1924 from the University of Wisconsin, became a professor there in 1926, and taught there the rest of her life. She had her first book, *The Mysticism of William Blake,* published in 1927, wrote on Anglican divines of 1600–40 and *The Metaphysical Poets* (1936), but became known chiefly for her historical novels, among them, *A Watch in the Night* (1933), *Not Built with Hands* (1935), *To the End of the World* (1939), and *Dust on the King's Highway* (1947). She was awarded the Laetare Medal in 1942, was honored by numerous colleges and universities, and was president of the American Association of University Women in 1941–47. She died in Madison, Wisconsin, on June 6.

WHITE, LINCOLN (1906–83), diplomat. Paul Lincoln White was born in Chattanooga, Tennessee, was educated at Spring Hill College, Mobile, Alabama, and began a newspaper career in 1928 with the Chattanooga *News.* He left to enter government service in 1933, joined the State Department in 1939, and by 1955 had become head of the Department's news service and its chief spokesman. He was consul general in Melbourne, Australia, in 1963–65 and retired in 1966; he had served under eight secretaries of state, from Cordell Hull, under President Franklin Roosevelt, to Dean Rusk, under President John Kennedy. He died in Searcy, Arkansas, on Apr. 25.

WHITE, STEPHEN MALLORY (1853–1901), U.S. senator. Of Irish immigrant parents who emigrated to California, he was born in San Francisco on Jan. 19, was educated at St. Ignatius College (now University of San Francisco) and Santa Clara College, graduated in 1873, began reading law, and was admitted to the bar in 1874. He became noted for his oratory, entered poli-

tics, married Hortense Sacriste in 1883, was district attorney of Los Angeles County in 1883–84, and was a member of the state senate in 1887–91. He served in the United States Senate in 1893–99, and while in the Senate he fought the railroad monopoly and corrupt practices in government, opposed imperialism (especially the annexation of Hawaii and the war with Spain), big business, and political "bossism," and favored free coinage of silver. He was an expert on international and constitutional law and was one of the lawyers representing the Church against the Mexican Government in the "Pious Funds of California" case. He died in Los Angeles on Feb. 21.

WHITFIELD, JAMES (1770–1834), archbishop. Born in Liverpool, England, on Nov. 3, he headed the family business after the death of his father, in 1787, met Ambrose Maréchal (later archbishop of Baltimore) at Lyons, France, on his return from a trip to Italy, and decided to embrace the religious life. He studied for the priesthood at St. Irenaeus (Sulpician) Seminary, in Lyons, of which Maréchal was rector, and was ordained in 1809. He joined the Jesuits in 1811 but left and engaged in pastoral work at Little Crosby, near Liverpool. In 1817 he joined Maréchal, who had become coadjutor of Baltimore, became first rector of the Baltimore cathedral, was one of the first three priests to receive a doctorate in sacred theology in the United States (from St. Mary's Seminary, Baltimore), and was appointed titular bishop of Apollonia and coadjutor of Baltimore in 1828. He succeeded Archbishop Maréchal (who died three weeks after he consecrated Whitfield) as fourth archbishop of Baltimore, later the same year. He convened the first Provincial Council of Baltimore, in 1829, a synod in 1831, and the second Plenary Council of Baltimore in 1833. He expanded the facilities of the see, expending much of his personal fortune to do so, added a tower to the cathedral, and laid the cornerstone of St. Charles College, Ellicott City, Maryland, in 1831. He died in Baltimore on Oct. 19.

WIGGER, WINAND MICHAEL (1841–1901), bishop. Of German parents, he was born in New York City on Dec. 9, was educated at St. Francis Xavier College there, and graduated in 1860 and was rejected as a seminarian by the New York archdiocese but was accepted by the Newark diocese. He studied at Seton Hall College, South Orange, New Jersey, and Collegio Brignole-Sale, Genoa, Italy, and was ordained in Genoa in 1865. He was assigned to St. Patrick's Cathedral, Newark, New Jersey, and then continued his studies at the Sapienza, Rome, receiving his doctorate in divinity in 1866. He then returned to the United States, where he engaged in pastoral work in Madison, Orange, and Summit, New Jersey, returned to Madison as pastor, and in 1881 was consecrated third bishop of Newark. He was an active supporter of the temperance movement, aided immigrants, established and was first president of the American St. Raphael Society to help German immigrants, in 1883, and helped found St. Leo house in New York City, a Catholic hostel for immigrants. He firmly believed in the Catholic parochial-school system, was unsuccessful in obtaining state aid for parochial schools in the 1892–93 state assembly, and resisted proposed legislation in 1893 that would have integrated parochial schools into New Jersey's public-school system to secure state funds for them. He attended the third Plenary Council of Baltimore, in 1884, though he had opposed convoking it, held a diocesan synod in 1886, laid the cornerstone of a new cathedral in 1899, and built new churches and schools during his episcopate. He died in Newark on Jan. 5.

WILLGING, EUGENE (1909–65), librarian. Born in Dubuque, Iowa, on Aug. 17, he was educated at Columbia College there (B.A. 1931) and the University of Michigan, where he received his B.A. in library science the following year. He was cataloguer at the Catholic University library in 1932–33 and librarian at the University of Scranton in 1933–46; he there began publication of the Index of Catholic Pamphlets in the English Language in 1937 and was editor of *Best Sellers.* He was assistant librarian at Catholic University from 1946 until 1949, when he became Director of Libraries at Catholic University, a position he held until his death, in Washington, D.C., on Sept. 20. He prepared numerous bibliographies of contemporary Catholic books, including *Weekly List of Catholic Books* and *Catholic Paperback Books,* co-authored with Herta Hatzfeld, the sixteen-part Catholic Serials of the Nineteenth Century in the United States (1959–68), and was on the original board of editors of the Image Book series of paperbooks of Catholic interest.

WILLGING, JOSEPH CLEMENT (1884–1959), bishop. Born in Dubuque, Iowa, on Sept. 6, he was educated at Loras Academy and College there (B.A. 1905), St. Mary's Seminary, Baltimore (S.T.B. 1908), and Catholic University, and was ordained in Dubuque in 1908. He was principal of St. Aloysius Institute, Helena, Montana, in 1909–10, taught at Carroll College, Helena, and was its treasurer; he was chancellor of the diocese of Helena in 1914–27. He was made a papal chamberlain in 1921, was pastor of Immaculate Conception Church, Butte, Montana, in 1927–42, was made a domestic prelate in 1939, and was vicar-general of Helena in 1939–42. He was appointed first bishop of the newly established diocese of Pueblo, Colorado, in 1941, and during his episcopate he established many new churches, increased the number of clergy, and brought new religious communities into the diocese. He was made an Assistant at the Pontifical Throne in 1958 and died in Denver on Mar. 3.

WILLIAMS, JOHN JOSEPH (1822–1907), archbishop. Of Irish immigrant parents, he was born in Boston on Apr. 27, studied at the Sulpician college at Montreal, Quebec, and St. Sulpice Seminary, Paris, and was ordained in Paris in 1845. On his return to the United States, he was made an assistant at Boston's Holy Cross Cathedral, being named rector in 1856. He was appointed pastor of St. James Church in 1857, and later that year became vicar-general of the Boston diocese. He was named titular bishop of Tripoli and coadjutor of the Boston diocese in 1866 and succeeded to the see four days after the bulls appointing him coadjutor, when Bishop John Fitzpatrick died, Feb. 13, 1866. He became Boston's first archbishop when that see was made an archdiocese, in 1875. During his episcopate, he dedicated a new Holy Cross Cathedral in 1875, established St. John's Seminary, in Brighton, in 1884, and built many schools, churches, and charitable institutions. He founded the first conference of the St. Vincent de Paul Society in New England, established the Catholic Union of Boston, was one of the founders of the North American College in Rome, and attended the second Plenary Council of Baltimore, in 1866, the first Vatican Council, in 1869–70, and the second Plenary Council of Baltimore, in 1884. He held diocesan synods in 1868, 1872, 1879, and 1886, opposed attempts to have the Vatican condemn the Knights of Labor, the Abbelen Memorial, and Archbishop Ireland's school plan (he was a close friend of Bishop Bernard McQuaid of Rochester, who condemned Ireland from his pulpit), and in 1876 became joint owner, with John Boyle O'Reilly, of the Boston *Pilot.* He died in Boston on Aug. 30.

WILLIAMS, JOSEPH JOHN (1875–1940), anthropologist. Born in Boston on Dec. 1, he joined the Jesuits in 1893, was educated at Boston College, Woodstock (Maryland) College (B.A. 1901, M.A. 1903, Ph.D. 1909), and was ordained at Woodstock in 1907. He was registrar at St. Francis Xavier College, New York City, in 1897–1900, was one of the original editors of the Jesuit magazine *America* and its managing editor in 1909–11, did mission work on the island of Jamaica, West Indies, in 1912–17, was treasurer of the Jesuit Mission of Jamaica in 1914–16 and of Woodstock College in 1917, of Holy Cross College, Worcester, Massachusetts, in 1918–22 and of the New England province of the Jesuits in 1925–28. He became a professor of anthropology at Boston College Graduate School in 1934 and became widely known for his lectures on anthropology. He wrote several books, among them the religious *Keep the Gate* (1923) and *Yearning for God* (1924) but is best known for his ethnological books, such as *Whisperings of the Caribbean* (1925), *Whence the "Black Irish" of Jamaica* (1932), *Psychic Phenomena of Jamaica* (1935), *Voodoos and Obeahs* (1932), and *Africa's God* (1937). He died in Lenox, Massachusetts, on Oct. 28.

WILLIAMS, MARY LOU (1910–81), jazz pianist. Daughter of Mose Winn (or stepdaughter) and Virginia Burley Winn, she was born in Atlanta, Georgia, on May 8 and named Mary Elfrieda Scruggs. She was a child prodigy, became a professional entertainer in her early teens, married John Williams when she was sixteen (the marriage ended in divorce a few years later), and toured the black vaudeville circuit with him. She established a name for herself with Andy Kirk's band, the Twelve Clouds of Joy, from 1929 to 1942 and then formed her own band and married its trumpeter, Harold "Shorty" Kirk in 1942 (this marriage, too, ended in divorce, six months later). In 1944 she branched out as a soloist, acquired a large following, and became known as the "Queen of Jazz." She performed all over the United States and Europe, suffered a nervous breakdown in France in 1953, and on her return to the United States gave up her career and devoted herself to helping indigent musicians. She founded and financed the Bel Canto Foundation for alcoholics. She returned to performing in 1957, when she became a Catholic. She became known for her fervent Catholicism and spent the last four years of her life as artist-in-residence at Duke University, Durham, North Carolina. She was widely recognized as an outstanding pianist, arranger, and composer, and composed for many of the big bands, among them those of Benny Goodman, Duke Ellington, Tommy and Jimmy Dorsey, Cab Calloway, Bob Crosby, and Louis Armstrong. Her career spanned six decades, and she was able to make the transition from one music style to another, from swing to bebop to progressive jazz. Among her musical contributions were her four-part "History of Jazz Piano" she performed in club appearance, the religious-inspired jazz hymn "St. Martin de Porres, or Black Christ of the Andes," and such songs as "Froggy Bottom," "Cloudy," "Pretty-Eyed Baby," and "Lonely Moments." By the time of her death she was widely acclaimed as the first woman to become a top jazz instrumentalist. She played an impor-

tant role in every jazz development from the late 1920s. She died in Durham on May 28.

WILLIAMS, MICHAEL (1877–1950), editor. Born in Halifax, Nova Scotia, on Feb. 5, he was educated at St. Joseph's College, New Brunswick, moved to Boston, and married Margaret Olmstead in 1900. He worked as a reporter for the Boston *Post* and then the New York *World* and *Evening Telegram* until 1904, when he was forced to move to Texas because of a lung condition. He then went to San Francisco and became city editor of the *Examiner* there in 1906, the day before an earthquake devastated the city. He worked for a time with Upton Sinclair in Englewood, New Jersey, coauthored with him *Good Health,* moved to California to write, returned to the Catholicism he had left in his youth while at Carmel in 1912, was special correspondent in Mexico for International News Service in 1913, continued to free-lance, and published his autobiography, *The Book of High Romance,* in 1918. He worked for the United Welfare Organizations and the National Catholic War Council during World War I, was editor of the *National Catholic War Council Bulletin* in 1919–20, and wrote *American Catholics in the War* in 1921. In 1924 he came to New York City and founded *Commonweal,* a weekly magazine, and was its editor in 1924–38 and Special Editor in 1938–45. Among the other books he wrote were *Catholicism and the Modern Mind* (1928), *The Shadow of the Pope* (1932), and *The Catholic Church in Action* (1934). He died in Hartford, Connecticut, on Oct. 12.

WILLIAMS, TENNESSEE (1911–83), playwright. Thomas Lanier Williams was born in Columbus, Mississippi, on March 26 (perhaps in 1912 or 1914), took the name Tennessee after 1939, and attended the University of Missouri in 1931–33, Washington University, St. Louis, in 1936–37, the University of Iowa (B.A. 1938), and a playwrighting summer at the New School for Social Research, New York City, in 1940. He worked at various jobs and began writing plays. He had his first play, *Cairo! Shanghai! Bombay!* produced in Memphis, Tennessee, in 1936. His depictions of lonely characters and the alienation of modern man soon attracted widespread critical attention and high praise. Among his more than a score of plays are *The Fugitive Kind* (1937), *The Battle of Angels* (1940), *The Glass Menagerie* (1945, New York Drama Critics Circle Award), *A Streetcar Named Desire* (1947, Pulitzer Prize, New York Drama Critics Circle Award), *The Rose Tattoo* (1951), *Camino Real* (1953), *Cat on a Hot Tin Roof* (1955, Pulitzer Prize, New York Drama Critics Circle Award), *Orpheus Descending* (1957), *The Night of the Iguana* (1961, New York Drama Critics Circle Award) and *Outcry* (1974). He also wrote screenplays, such as *Baby Doll* (1956), *Suddenly Last Summer* (1959), and *The Fugitive Kind* (1960), and fiction, the novel *The Roman Spring of Mrs. Stone* (1950) and short story collections, among them, *Hard Candy* (1954) and *Three Players of a Summer Game and Other Stories* (1960). His later plays were received with less enthusiasm than his earlier ones, and he became increasingly embittered at the critics in his later years. He suffered from ill health and had a mental breakdown that caused him to be confined to a mental institution for a time. He became a Catholic in 1969. His melancholia caused him to turn to drugs and alcohol, for which he was hospitalized in 1969. In New York City on the night of February 24–25 he choked to death on a plastic medicine-bottle cap. For his brilliant depictions of lonely, tortured people (who reflected his own life and anguish) he is considered one of the most important American playwrights of the twentieth century.

WILLINGER, ALOYSIUS JOSEPH (1886–1973), bishop. Born in Baltimore on Apr. 19, he was educated at St. Mary's College, North East, Pennsylvania, joined the Redemptorists, and continued his studies at Mt. Alphonsus House of Studies, Esopus, New York; he was ordained in 1911. He served in parishes in New York City, Boston, and Philadelphia, and in 1916 was sent as a missionary to Puerto Rico. He was appointed bishop of Ponce, Puerto Rico, in 1929, was named titular bishop of Bida and coadjutor of Monterey-Fresno, California, in 1946, and succeeded to the see in 1953. During his episcopate, the Catholic population of the see increased enormously, and to meet its needs he tripled the facilities of the Catholic schools in the diocese, expanded hospital services, founded a minor seminary, three retreat houses, and a Spanish weekly, and expanded ministries to blacks. He died in Fresno on July 25.

WILLOCK, EDWARD FRANCIS (1916–60), editor. Born in Boston on Apr. 22, he founded and edited, with Carol Jackson, *Integrity,* a magazine devoted to the lay apostolate, and also founded Marycrest, a community devoted to Catholic life and living, in Pearl River, New York. He engaged in free-lance writing and cartooning and was the author of *Ye Gods—* (1948) and *The Willock Book.* He died in Pearl River on Dec. 18.

WILLSON, MEREDITH (1902–84), composer, lyricist. Born in Mason City, Iowa, on May 18, he went to New York City after graduating from high school and attended the Damrosch Institute of

Musical Art (now the Julliard School). He toured for a time with John Philip Sousa's Band, became first flutist with the New York Philharmonic in 1924, and in time became a musical director with the American Broadcasting Company and the National Broadcasting Company. When he moved to Hollywood to work with NBC he composed the score for Charlie Chaplin's *The Great Dictator* (1940) and later *The Little Foxes* (1941) and in 1942 joined the Army and headed the Armed Forces Radio Service. He was a comedian on radio's "The Big Show" in the 1950s, for which he composed "May the Good Lord Bless and Keep You," and in 1957 his *The Music Man* was an immediate success, receiving the New York Drama Critics Circle and Antoinette Perry (Tony) awards for the outstanding musical of the 1957–58 season (its hit song was "76 Trombones"). He did the scores for *The Unsinkable Molly Brown* in 1960 and for *Here's Love* in 1963 and was the author of four books, *And There I Stood with My Piccolo, Eggs I have Laid, Who Did What to Fedalia?* and *But He Doesn't Know the Territory.* He died at Santa Monica, California, on June 15.

WILTBYE, JOHN *See* Blakely, Paul Lendrum.

WIMMER, BONIFACE (1809–87), archabbot. Sebastian Wimmer was born in Thalmassing, Bavaria, on Jan. 14, was educated at Ratisbon, studied law at Munich and for the priesthood at the Gregorian, Rome, and was ordained in Rome in 1831. After a year as a curate at Altötting, he joined the Benedictines at Metten Abbey, Bavaria, took his solemn vows in 1833, taking the name Boniface, and in 1846 was sent as superior of a group of Benedictines to the United States to minister to German Catholics there. He founded the first Benedictine monastery in the United States, St. Vincent's, at Latrobe, Pennsylvania, forty miles east of Pittsburgh, in 1846. It was made a priory in 1852, and when it was elevated to an abbey, in 1855, Dom Wimmer was made abbot; it was made the Cassinese Congregation of the Benedictine Order, of which he was first president, and he was confirmed in that position for life by the Holy See. During his abbacy, he provided priests for churches throughout the country, and monks from St. Vincent's established ten monasteries throughout the United States, among them St. John's Abbey and College (University in 1883), at Collegeville, Minnesota, in 1856, St. Benedict's College, Atchison, Kansas, in 1857, and Maryhelp Abbey, Belmont, North Carolina, in 1885. He died at St. Vincent Archabbey on Dec. 8.

WINKELMANN, CHRISTIAN HERMAN (1883–1946), bishop. Born in St. Louis on Sept. 12, he was educated at St. Francis Solanus College, Quincy, Illinois, and Kenrick Seminary, St. Louis, and was ordained in 1907. He served as a curate at St. Peter's Church, St. Charles, Missouri, in 1907–22, was pastor at Sacred Heart Church, Rich Fountain, Missouri, in 1922–29 and of St. Francis de Sales Church, St. Louis, in 1929–33, and was named titular bishop of Sita and auxiliary of St. Louis in 1933. He became director of the Catholic Rural Life Bureau in the see, and in 1939 he was appointed bishop of Wichita, Kansas, a position he occupied until his death there on Nov. 18.

WOLFF, GEORGE DERING (1822–94), editor. Son of a Lutheran minister, he was born in Martinsburg, (West) Virginia, on Aug. 25, was educated at Marshall College (M.A.), studied law at Easton Pennsylvania, and was admitted to the bar, though he never practiced.

He studied theology at the German Reformed Theological Seminary, Mercersburg, Pennsylvania, became a minister of the Dutch Reformed Church, was a leader of the Mercersburg movement, which had developed in the German Reformed Church, and was pastor at Tiflin, Ohio, and Norristown, Pennsylvania. He left to become principal of Norristown High School, and in 1871 he became a Catholic. He was editor of the Baltimore *Catholic Mirror* in 1871–72 and left to join the Philadelphia *Catholic Standard* as general editor; he held that position until he died, in Norristown, Pennsylvania, on Jan. 29. He was one of the founders of the *American Catholic Quarterly Review,* in 1876, and also served on its staff the rest of his life.

WOLL, MATTHEW (1880–1956), labor leader. Born in Luxembourg, Belgium, on Jan. 25, he was brought to the United States in 1891 by his parents, who settled in Chicago. He left school when fifteen to become a photoengraver's apprentice, married Irene C. Kerwin in 1899, and studied law at night at Lake Forest University, in Illinois; he graduated and was admitted to the Illinois bar in 1904. He was elected president of the International Photo Engravers Union (IPEU) in 1906, serving in that office until 1929, and edited its *American Photo Engraver* for a time, became closely associated with Samuel Gompers, and was a vice president of the Union Label Trades Department of the American Federation of Labor (AFL) in 1919–53. He became a vice president of the AFL in 1919 and served on U.S. War Labor boards in World Wars I and II. He was early interested in foreign affairs and international unions, attended the British Trades Union Congress in 1915 and 1916, was a delegate to the International Federation of Trade Unions in 1937, when the AFL affiliated with that

body, and to the Oslo conference of the International Labor Organization (ILO) in 1938; in 1943 he was elected chairman of the AFL standing committee on foreign affairs. In 1944 he became chairman of the Free Trade Committee of the AFL to promote free trade unions throughout the world. He fought Communism in the labor movement in the United States and in the occupied countries in Europe after World War II, helped organize the International Confederation of Trade Unions to offset the Communist-controlled World Federation of Trade Unions, attacked French colonial policy in Tunisia, and fought the appointment of Nazis to high posts in industry. He was a director of the National Conference of Catholic Charities in 1951–54. He wrote *Labor, Industry and Government* (1935) and, with William E. Walling, *Our Next Step—a National Economic Policy* (1934). He died in New York City on June 1.

WOOD, JAMES FREDERICK (1813–83), archbishop. Son of an English merchant, he was born in Philadelphia on Apr. 27, was a member of the Unitarian Church, and was educated in a private school in the United States and probably at an English academy. His family moved to Cincinnati, Ohio, in 1827, and he became a clerk in a bank there; in 1836 he became a Catholic. He studied for the priesthood at the Irish College and the Propaganda, Rome, and was ordained in Rome in 1844. On his return to the United States, he served as an assistant at the Cincinnati cathedral for a time, and in 1854 became pastor of St. Patrick's Church there. He was named titular bishop of Antigonia and coadjutor of Philadelphia in 1857 and succeeded to the see in 1860. During his episcopate, he finished building the cathedral, in 1864, attended the second Plenary Council of Baltimore, in 1866, built up a parochial-school system, and founded St. Charles Borromeo Seminary, at Overbrook, Philadelphia. He denounced secret societies and the Fenians and excommunicated any Catholic belonging to the Molly Maguires. He was an active proponent of the North American College in Rome, acting as treasurer of its board, was appointed Assistant at the Pontifical Throne in 1862, and attended Vatican Council I, in 1869–70, where he supported the proclamation of the dogma of papal infallibility, though forced to leave the council early because of ill health. He became Philadelphia's first archbishop, in 1875, presided over the first Provincial Council of Philadelphia, in 1880, and died in Philadelphia on June 20.

WOODLOCK, THOMAS FRANCIS (1866–1945), editor. Born in Dublin on Sept. 1, he was educated at Beaumont College, Windsor, England, London University, and St. Francis Xavier College, New York City. He joined his father and his brother in the family's brokerage business, joined *The Wall Street Journal* in 1892, and worked for the Dow-Jones News Service specializing in railroad investments. He was editor of *The Wall Street Journal* in 1902–15, was a partner in a brokerage firm on the New York Stock Exchange in 1905–18, was secretary of American International Corporation in 1918–23, and was a director of the St. Louis and Santa Fe Railroad in 1923–25 and of the Pere Marquette Railroad in 1924–25. He was appointed to the Interstate Commerce Commission by President Coolidge in 1925 and served on that body until 1930, when he resigned to return to *The Wall Street Journal.* He wrote a column for the *Journal,* titled "Thinking It Over," on contemporary problems, history, and government; a collection with that title was published in book form posthumously in 1947; he was also the author of *Anatomy of a Railroad Report*

(1894), *Ton Mile Cost* (1899), and *The Catholic Pattern* (1942) and was the recipient of the Laetare Medal in 1943. He died in New York City on Aug. 25.

WOODMAN, CLARENCE EUGENE (1852–1924), astronomer. Born in Saco, Maine, on Nov. 1, he entered Amherst College in 1869, left the following year to go to Trinity College, Hartford, Connecticut, and graduated from Trinity in 1873. He studied for the Episcopal priesthood at General Theological Seminary, New York City, in 1873–75 but instead of pursuing this career became a Catholic, in 1875. He joined the Paulists the same year, was sent to California for his health in 1878, and was ordained in San Francisco in 1879. He returned to New York City soon after and was pastor of St. Paul's Church there the next decade. He lectured on electricity at Catholic University in 1891–92, was an assistant at the Catholic University observatory in 1892–94, and served on the staff of the Smithsonian Astrophysical Observatory in 1900–1; he accompanied the Smithsonian eclipse expeditions to Wadesboro, North Carolina, in 1900 and to Hartland, Kansas, in 1918. He spent the last twelve years of his life as chaplain of the Newman Club at the University of California, Berkeley, and died at Oakland, California, on Dec. 6. He was the author of several books, among them, *Manual of Prayer* (1887) (he had been appointed to prepare the official manual of prayer for the Church in the United States by the third Plenary Council of Baltimore, in 1884), *The Bridal Wreath* (1888), *Civil and Religious Liberty* (1890), and *Poets and Poetry of Ireland* (1892).

WOZNICKI, STEPHEN STANISLAUS (1894–1968), bishop. Born in Minersville, Pennsylvania, on Aug. 17, he was educated at SS. Cyril and Methodius College and Seminary,

Orchard Lake, Michigan, and St. Paul (Minnesota) Seminary, and was ordained in 1917. He served as a curate at St. Joseph's Church, Danville, Pennsylvania, in 1918–19, was secretary to Bishop Michael Gallagher of Detroit in 1919–37, and was pastor of St. Hyacinth Church there in 1937. He was appointed titular bishop of Pelte and auxiliary bishop of Detroit in 1937, was transferred to Saginaw, Michigan, as its second bishop, in 1950, and was president of the National Catholic Rural Life Conference in 1956–57. During his episcopate in Saginaw, he established eighteen new parishes, built thirty schools and thirty-four churches, established the diocesan Council of Catholic Women in 1951 and of Catholic Men in 1953, opened St. Paul Minor Seminary, in Saginaw, in 1960, and founded the Diocesan Mission Sisters of the Holy Ghost in 1954. He was made an Assistant at the Pontifical Throne in 1967, resigned as bishop of Saginaw in 1968, and was made titular bishop of Tiava. He died six weeks after his resignation, on Dec. 10.

WRIGHT, JOHN J. (1909–79), cardinal. Born in Boston on July 18, he was educated at Boston College, Worcester, Massachusetts (B.A. 1931) while working as a librarian and for the Boston *Post,* studied for the priesthood at St. John's Seminary, Brighton, Boston, and the Gregorian, Rome, and was ordained in Rome in 1935. He worked in parishes in Scotland, England, and France, and on his return to the United States became a professor of philosophy at St. John's in 1939–43 and was secretary to Cardinals O'Connell and Cushing of Boston in 1943–47. He was made a papal chamberlain in 1946 and was named titular bishop of Aegea and auxiliary of Boston in 1947, and in 1950 was appointed first bishop of the newly established diocese of Worcester, Massachu-

setts. He was transferred to Pittsburgh in 1958, became a leader in the ecumenical movement, supported the civil rights movement, encouraged laymen to become involved in Church affairs, worked to increase the number of blacks in the parochial schools of the diocese, and denounced the Vietnam War. In 1969 he was made a cardinal and transferred to Rome as prefect of the Congregation for the Clergy—the highest-ranking American at the Vatican. Considered a liberal in secular affairs, he was regarded as a conservative in ecclesiastical matters, opposed the ordination of women, and demanded ecclesiastical obedience from the clergy and a continuation of their vow of celibacy. Known for his scholarship, he was an authority on St. Joan of Arc and accumulated a library of some six thousand volumes on her. Confined to a wheelchair from 1978 by polymyositis, which affected his legs, he died in Cambridge, Massachusetts, on Aug. 10.

WURM, JOHN (1927–84), bishop. Born in Overland, Missouri, on Dec. 8, he was educated at Kenrick Seminary, St. Louis, and St. Louis University and was ordained in 1954. He was named titular bishop of St. Louis in 1976 and was appointed bishop of Belleville, Illinois, in 1981. He died of cancer at St. John's Mercy Medical Center, St. Louis, on Apr. 27.

WYNHOVEN, PETER M. H. (1884–1944), sociologist. Born in Venray, the Netherlands, on Dec. 31, he was educated at Immaculate Conception College, Louvain, Belgium, came to the United States, and studied for the priesthood at Kenrick Seminary, St. Louis; he was ordained in 1909. He engaged in pastoral work in Louisiana, was named pastor of St. Joseph's Church, Gretna, Louisiana, in 1917, and became involved in social work, founding St. Vincent's Hotel and Free Labor Bureau in 1911, the Catholic Women's Club for Working Girls in 1918, Hope Haven Agricultural and Mechanical School in 1922, and Madonna Manor for dependent boys and girls in 1932. He was vice chancellor of the archdiocese of New Orleans in 1933–40, was made a domestic prelate in 1934, and founded the weekly *Catholic Action of the South* (1933), which he also edited. He served as chairman and director of the National Labor Relations Board of District 7 and as executive director of the Association of Catholic Charities and was president of the Catholic Press Association in 1940–43 and part of a term in 1943–44. He was pastor of Our Lady of Lourdes Church, in New Orleans, when he died, on Sept. 13 while visiting friends in Nahant, Massachusetts.

WYNNE, JOHN JOSEPH (1859–1948), editor. Born in New York City on Sept. 30, he was educated at St. Francis Xavier College there (B.A. 1876), joined the Jesuits in 1876, and studied for the priesthood at Woodstock (Maryland) College in 1879–82. He taught at St. Francis Xavier College in 1882–86 and Boston College in 1886–87 and, after theological studies at Woodstock, was ordained in 1890. He joined the staff of the *Messenger of the Sacred Heart* and was its editor in 1892–1902 and of *The Messenger* in 1902–9 and was director of the Apostleship of Prayer in 1892–97. He was in charge of the shrine of Our Lady of the Martyrs, at Auriesville, New York, in 1892–1909 and actively promoted the causes of the North American Martyrs (who were canonized in 1930) and of Kateri Tekakwitha (who was beatified in 1980), writing the material for her cause; he was appointed vice-postulator for their causes in 1923. He founded the Jesuit weekly *America* and was its first editor-in-chief, in 1909–10, was interested in the Belgian Congo missions, and helped prevent the expulsion of the Augustinian and Belgian missions from the Philippines. He formed the editorial board of The Catholic Encyclopedia in 1905 and served as one of its editors, organized the League of Daily Mass and edited its *Anno Domini* in 1914–17, and wrote several books, among them *A Shrine in the Mohawk Valley* (1905) and *The Jesuit Martyrs of North America* (1925), and edited *The Great Encyclicals of Leo XIII* (1903). He died in New York City on Nov. 30.

WYNNE, ROBERT JOHN (1851–1922), journalist, Postmaster General. Born in New York City on Nov. 18, he was educated in New York's public schools and privately, moved to Philadelphia, and became a telegrapher with the Bankers and Brokers Telegraph Company in 1870 and in a few years became chief operator of the Atlantic and Pacific Telegraph Company. He married Mary E. McCabe in 1875, entered the newspaper business, and became Washington correspondent of the Cincinnati *Gazette* in 1880 and was private secretary to Secretary of the Treasury Charles Foster in 1891–93. When Cleveland was elected President in 1892, Wynne returned to newspaper work (in 1893) and was Washington correspondent of the Cincinnati *Tribune* and the Philadelphia *Bulletin* and then of the New York *Post.* He was first assistant postmaster general in 1902–4, was appointed Postmaster General by President Theodore Roosevelt and served in 1904–5, and was consul general in London in 1905–10. He retired to private business in 1910 and was president of the First National Fire Insurance Company of the United States, in Washington, D.C., from 1915. He died in Washington on Mar. 11.

Y

YERGENS, HENRY (1870–1961), educator. Born in Philadelphia, he joined the Christian Brothers in 1889 and spent the next seventy years as teacher and administrator. He became president of St. Thomas College, Scranton, Pennsylvania, in 1932, doubled its enrollment, and secured university status for it in 1938. Two years later, he became inspector of Christian Brothers schools in the Middle Atlantic states and Ohio and held that position until he retired in 1958. He died in Ammendale, Maryland, on Jan. 8.

YON, PIETRO ALESSANDRO (1886–1943), composer. Born in Settimo Vittone, Italy, on Aug. 9, he studied music at conservatories in Milan and Turin and St. Cecilia Academy, Rome, and was substitute organist at the Vatican in 1905–7 (and again in 1919–21). He went to the United States in 1907, was organist and choirmaster at St. Vincent Ferrer Church, New York City in 1907–9 (and again in 1921–26), became an American citizen in 1923, and was in charge of music at St. Patrick's Cathedral, New York City, from 1927 until his death. He became known for his more than seventy church compositions, including thirteen masses, motets, and oratorios, and *The Triumph of St. Patrick* (1934). He was organist for the NBC Symphony Orchestra under Arturo Toscanini and was named honorary music director of St. Peter's, in Rome, in 1926. He died in Huntington, New York, on Nov. 22.

YORKE, PETER CHRISTOPHER (1864–1925), journalist. Born in Galway, Ireland, on Aug. 15, he studied at St. Patrick's College, Maynooth, emigrated to the United States, completed his studies for the priesthood at St. Mary's Seminary, Baltimore, and was ordained for the San Francisco archdiocese in 1887. He continued his studies at Catholic University (S.T.L. 1891), was editor of the San Francisco *Monitor,* the archdiocesan paper, in 1894–99, and was chancellor of the see in 1894–99. He fought the anti-Catholicism of the American Protective Association, established the Catholic Truth Society of San Francisco, and defended the teamsters in their 1901 strike. He founded the *Leader* in 1902, devoted to the cause of Irish nationalism and the rights of labor, preached the tenets of Pope Leo XIII's *Rerum novarum,* was pastor of St. Anthony's Church, Oakland, in 1903–13, served as vice president of Sinn Fein in the United States and of the National Catholic Educational Association, and was active in civic affairs. He was pastor of St. Peter's Church, San Francisco, in 1913–25 and was author of several books, among them *Lectures on Ghosts* (1897), *Text Book of Religion* (1901), *Roman Liturgy* (1903), *Altar and Priest* (1913), and *The Mass* (1921). He died in San Francisco on Apr. 5.

YOUNG, JOHN B. (1854–1928), musician. Born in Alsace, France, on Oct. 30, he joined the Jesuits in 1872 and was ordained at Woodstock, Maryland. He became organist and director of music at St. Francis Xavier Church, New York City, founded a boys' choir there which became widely recognized as one of the finest in the world, and was a leader in raising the standard of church music throughout the United States. With Pietro Yon and other organists, he worked to reform church music. He was appointed to the Papal Commission for the Revision of Church Music, compiled the Roman Hymnal, and was the author of the Justine Ward method of teaching Gregorian chant, which became widely used. Ill the last six years of his life, he died at the Jesuit house in Monroe, New York, on Sept. 26.

YOUNG, JOSUE MOODY (1808–66), bishop. Of an old Puritan family, he was born in Shapleigh, Maine, on Oct. 29 and was a Congregationalist when he converted to Catholicism, in 1828, using the name Maria instead of Moody from then on. He studied for the priesthood at Mt. St. Mary's College, Emmitsburg, Maryland, and was ordained in 1838 and engaged in pastoral work in the Cincinnati diocese until 1853, when he was appointed second bishop of Erie, Pennsylvania. The discovery of oil in his diocese in 1859 caused a great influx of Catholics, and throughout his episcopate he labored to secure priests to minister to them, doubling the number of diocesan priests. He died in Erie on Sept. 18.

Z

ZABLOCKI, CLEMENT J. (1912–83), congressman. Son of Polish immigrants, he was born in Milwaukee, Wisconsin, on Nov. 18, was educated at Marquette University there (Ph.D.), married Blanche Janic in 1937, and began teaching high school. He was elected to the state legislature in 1942 and after serving two terms was elected to the U.S. House of Representatives in 1948—the first of eighteen consecutive terms he was to serve in that body. He was strongly anti-Communist, favored a strong national defense, supported the Vietnam War and Taiwan, and was known as a conciliator who believed in legislation by consensus, rather than by confrontation. He traveled extensively, influenced Congress to exert more influence in foreign affairs, and was one of those responsible for the War Powers Act. He was elected chairman of the House Foreign Affairs Committee in 1977 and held that position until his death, at Capitol Hill Hospital, in Washington, D.C., of a heart attack on Dec. 3.

ZAHM, ALBERT FRANCIS (1862–1954), scientist, inventor. Born in New Lexington, Ohio, and brother of John, he was educated at Notre Dame (M.A. 1885), taught mathematics and mechanics there in 1885–92, and then continued his studies at Cornell (M.E. 1892) and Johns Hopkins (Ph.D. 1898). He was general secretary of the International Conference on Aerial Navigation in 1893 and 1900 and taught mechanics at Catholic University in 1895–1908. He was chief research engineer of the Curtiss Airplane Company in 1914–15 and was director of the Navy's Aerodynamics Laboratory in 1916–29, when he retired to accept the Guggenheim Chair of Aeronautics of the Library of Congress, serving in 1930–46. He did extensive pioneer research in air resistance to moving bodies, designed the Zahm shape (used by Great Britain in her rigid airships), and invented, among other things, the three-torque control for airplanes, wire tensometer, victograph protractor, and three-component anemograph, and designed and built the first wind tunnel in the United States. He wrote extensively on aerodynamics and was the author of *Treatise on Aerial Navigation* (1911). He died in Washington, D.C., on July 23.

ZAHM, JOHN AUGUST (1851–1921), scientist. Born in New Lexington, Ohio, on June 14, and brother of Albert, he was educated at Notre Dame (B.A. 1871, M.A. 1873), joined the Congregation of Holy Cross in 1871, and was ordained in 1875. He was professor of physics at Notre Dame in 1875–92, served as vice president in 1877–86, was procurator general of the Congregation in Rome in 1896–98, and was American provincial in 1898–1906. He established Holy Cross College, the Congregation's house of studies in Washington, D.C., on a permanent basis, developed the Dante and South American collections at Notre Dame, participated in expeditions to the Andes, and was a member of Theodore

Roosevelt's expedition to South America. He wrote on evolution and was the author of *Bible, Science and Faith* (1894), *Evolution and Dogma* (1896), *Scientific Dogma* (1896), *Scientific Theory and Catholic Doctrine,* the three-volume *Following the Conquistadors* (1910, 1911,1916) on his trips to South America and its history and culture, and *Women and Science* (1913). He died in Munich, Germany, on Nov. 11.

ZALESKI, ALEXANDER (1906–75), bishop. Born in Laurel, New York, on June 24, he was educated at SS. Cyril and Methodius Seminary, Michigan, the American College, Louvain, and the Biblical Institute, Rome, and was ordained in Louvain in 1931. He served as a curate at Resurrection Church in 1931–32 and St. Thomas the Apostle Church, Detroit, in 1932, and taught at SS. Cyril and Methodius in 1935–37. He was vice-chancellor of the Detroit archdiocese in 1937–49, was made a domestic prelate in 1946, and was pastor of St. Vincent de Paul Church, Pontiac, Michigan, in 1949–56. He was appointed titular bishop of Lyrbe and auxiliary of Detroit in 1950, was vicar-general in 1954–64, and pastor of St. Alphonsus Church, Dearborn, Michigan, from 1956 until 1964, when he was appointed coadjutor of Lansing, Michigan. He succeeded to the see in 1965 and was bishop of Lansing until his death there on May 16.

ZARDETTI, JOHN JOSEPH FREDERICK OTTO (1847–1902), bishop. Born in Rorschach, St. Gall, Switzerland, on Jan. 24, he was educated at the University of Innsbruck, Austria, and St. George Seminary, in St. Gall, and was ordained in 1870. He taught at St. George Seminary until 1876, when he became a cathedral canon at St. Gall, and then he went to the United States and taught at St. Francis Seminary, in

Milwaukee, Wisconsin. He was vicar-general of the Northern Minnesota vicariate in 1886–89 and was appointed second bishop of St. Cloud, Minnesota, in 1889. He remained there until 1894, when he was named archbishop of Bucharest, Romania, in 1894. He resigned in 1895 and was appointed titular archbishop of Mocissus and became a consultor of the Congregation of Ecclesiastical Affairs in 1897. He died in Rome on May 9.

ZILBOURG, GREGORY (1890–1959), psychiatrist. Born in Kiev, Russia, on Dec. 25, he studied at the Psychoneurological Institute at St. Petersburg (Leningrad), Russia, and then came to the United States and finished his studies at Columbia. He began the practice of psychiatry at Bloomingdale, New York, in 1926 and then moved to New York City, where he had a successful practice in psychiatry and psychoanalysis. He taught at New York Medical College, Butler Hospital, Catholic University, Fordham, and Woodstock (Maryland) College and wrote on the relationship of religion to psychiatry and psychoanalysis and on suicide and schizophrenia. He became a Catholic in 1954; he died in New York City on Sept. 15.

ZWIERLEIN, FREDERICK JAMES (1881–1960), author. Born in Rochester, New York, on Nov. 16, he studied at the Rochester diocesan seminary, St. Bernard's, and was ordained in Rochester in 1904. He continued his studies at Louvain, under Alfred Cauchie in 1905–6 (D.Sc., M.H. 1910) and at Campo Santo de' Tedeschi, Rome, in 1906–7 and then taught Church history and art at St. Bernard's until 1938. He wrote several historical works, among them the three-volume *Life and Letters of Bishop McQuaid* (1925–27), *Religion in New Netherland* (1910), *Reformation*

Studies (1938), and *Theodore Roosevelt and Catholics* (1956), and edited *Letters of Archbishop Corrigan to Bishop McQuaid* (1946). He died in Rochester on Oct. 5.

ZYBURA, JOHN STANISLAUS (1875–1934). Born in Subkau, Poland, on July 21, he emigrated to the United States and studied at St. Ignatius College and St. Mary's Seminary, Cleveland, Ohio, and the North American College, Rome, and was ordained in Rome for the diocese of Cleveland in 1898. He was assistant pastor of St. Anthony's parish, Toledo, Ohio, in 1902–3 and of St. Stanislaus parish, Cleveland, in 1903–4 and pastor of St. Stanislaus parish, Lorain, Ohio, in 1908–11. He then served in the Columbus, Ohio, diocese until 1915, when he was stricken with tuberculosis and retired from active duty. He died in a Colorado Springs sanitarium on Oct. 7. He translated widely from the Italian, German, and Latin during his nineteen-year illness, was the author of *Contemporary Godlessness* (1924), and edited *Present Day Thinkers and the New Scholasticism* (1927). He was elected a member of the Gallery of Living Catholic Authors in 1941—the only Polish author to be so honored up to that time.

IMPORTANT EVENTS IN THE HISTORY
OF AMERICAN CATHOLICISM

1513. Ponce de León discovers and explores the coast of Florida and lands near present-day St. Augustine.

1521. Missionaries with Ponce de León and other Spanish explorers say what are probably the first Masses within the present boundaries of the United States.

1524. Giovanni da Verrazano explores the Atlantic coast of the United States and is the first white man to enter New York Harbor.

1539. Hernando de Soto lands in Florida and reaches the Mississippi River in 1541.

1542. Francisco Coronado leads an exploring expedition into New Mexico; Fray Juan de Padilla, protomartyr of the United States, is murdered by Indians on the plains of central Kansas.

1565. St. Augustine, oldest city in the United States, is founded by Pedro Menéndez de Avilés; America's oldest mission, Nombre de Dios, is established.

1601. Mass is first said in California.

1634. Maryland is settled by Lord Calvert, the only English colony in America founded by Catholics.

1646. Isaac Jogues and John Lalande are martyred by the Iroquois at Ossernenon (now Auriesville, New York).

1649. Maryland is the first colony to offer religious freedom, with the Act of Religious Toleration, passed by the General Assembly (repealed by a Puritan regime in 1654).

1653. Mass is first said in New York.

1673. Louis Joliet and Fr. Jacques Marquette, S.J., discover the Mississippi River and explore it to the mouth of the Arkansas River.

1682. René Robert Cavelier, sieur de La Salle explores the Mississippi River to the Gulf of Mexico; Catholic Thomas Dongan appointed governor of New York.

1683. New York Assembly enacts legislation granting religious freedom to all Christians.

1688. Catholics are disenfranchised in Maryland, the only English colony founded by Catholics.

1724. Fr. Sebastian Râle, S.J., is murdered by English soldiers at Norridgewock, Maine.

1727. Ursuline Sisters from France establish what is now the oldest convent in the United States and establish the first Catholic school in New Orleans.

1769. Fr. Junípero Serra, O.F.M. founds first of California missions, at San Diego.

1773. Charles Carroll publishes his "First Citizen" letters.

1775. George Washington bans the celebration of Guy Fawkes Day in the Army.

1776. Charles Carroll, Benjamin Franklin, and Samuel Chase, accompanied by Fr. John Carroll, are sent on a mission to Canada by the Continental Congress in an unsuccessful attempt to secure Canada's cooperation in the colonists' war with England; Charles Carroll, although a Catholic, signs the Declaration of Independence as a delegate from Maryland; San Francisco de Asís mission is founded on the site of present-day San Francisco.

1779. Mass is celebrated in Alaska for the first time.

1784. Fr. John Carroll is appointed superior of the American missions by the Holy See.

1787. Two Catholics, Daniel Carroll of Maryland and Thomas FitzSimons of Pennsylvania, sign the Constitution of the United States.

1788. Mass is first publicly celebrated in Boston.

1789. Fr. John Carroll is appointed the first American bishop of the United States and ordinary of the diocese of Baltimore, the first American diocese, by Pope Pius VI's brief *Ex hac apostilicae* (the boundaries of the see were coextensive with those of the United States at that time); Georgetown, the first Catholic college, in the United States, is founded (though its first building is not ready for occupancy until 1791); Bishop John Carroll holds the first synod.

1791. St. Mary's Seminary, the first Catholic seminary in the United States, is founded by the Sulpicians in Baltimore; Pierre Charles L'Enfant designs the city of Washington as the capital of the United States.

1792. George Hoban designs the White House.

1797. The United States establishes consular relations with the Papal States.

1800. Leonard Neale is the first Catholic priest consecrated a bishop in the United States.

1808. Bishop John Carroll is appointed the first archbishop in the United States and metropolitan of the archdiocese of Baltimore; the dioceses of Boston, New York, Philadelphia, and Bardstown, Kentucky, are established as suffragan sees.

1809. Mother Elizabeth Seton founds the Sisters of Charity of St. Vincent de Paul in the United States.

1810. The first meeting of the American hierarchy is held in Baltimore.

1812. The Sisters of Loretto found the first religious community in the United States without any foreign affiliation.

IMPORTANT EVENTS

1813. New York's Court of General Sessions renders a decision favorable to Fr. Anthony Kohlmann, S.J., upholding the secrecy of the seal of confession.

1814. The first Catholic institution for children in the United States, St. Joseph's Orphanage, in Philadelphia, opens.

1821. The Cathedral of the Assumption, the mother cathedral of American Catholicism, is dedicated in Baltimore.

1822. The first strictly Catholic newspaper in the United States, *United States Catholic Miscellany,* is founded by Bishop John England of Charleston, South Carolina.

1823. Fr. Charles Richard, delegate from Michigan, is the first Catholic priest to serve in the House of Representatives.

1826. Bishop John England addresses Congress.

1828. The first hospital in the United States west of the Mississippi is opened by the Sisters of Charity at St. Louis; the New York legislature enacts a law protecting the secrecy of the seal of confession.

1829. The first Provincial Council of Baltimore is convened.

1831. Roger Brooke Taney is appointed the first Catholic in a President's Cabinet.

1834. Anti-Catholic riots led by nativists burn down an Ursuline convent in Charlestown, Massachusetts.

1836. Roger Brooke Taney is appointed the first Catholic Chief Justice of the United States.

1840. Fr. Pierre Jean De Smet, S.J., makes the first trip to the Far West to minister to the Indians.

1841. St. John's College (now Fordham) is founded.

1842. Notre Dame is founded.

1844. Anti-Catholics in Philadelphia set off riots that kill thirteen persons and wound fifty, and burn down two Catholic churches; Orestes Brownson becomes a Catholic.

1845. Isaac Hecker becomes a Catholic.

1848. Diplomatic relations are established between the United States and the Papal States; the first permanent Trappist foundation in the United States is established in Kentucky.

1852. The first Plenary Council of Baltimore is held.

1853. There are Know-Nothing demonstrations and riots all over the country protesting the visit of papal nuncio Archbishop Gaetano Bedini.

1858. The Missionary Society of St. Paul the Apostle (the Paulist Fathers) is founded, the first native religious community for men in the United States.

1859. The North American College in Rome, founded by the bishops of the United States, opens; pontifical status is granted by Pope Leo XIII in 1884.

1862. Archbishop John Hughes of New York is sent on a diplomatic mission to Europe by President Lincoln and Secretary of State William H. Seward to present the Union position and argue for the neutrality of England, France, and the Holy See in the Civil War.

1866. The second Plenary Council of Baltimore is held.

1867. Diplomatic relations between the United States and the Papal States are terminated when Congress refuses the necessary appropriation for the mission.

1875. John McCloskey, Archbishop of New York, is named the first cardinal in the United States; James A. Healy is consecrated bishop of Portland, Maine, the first man with black blood to be consecrated a bishop in the United States.

1876. Archbishop James Gibbons's *Faith of Our Fathers* is published.

1878. John P. Holland invents the first workable submarine.

1880. William R. Grace is elected the first Catholic mayor of New York.

1882. The Knights of Columbus is founded by Fr. Michael J. McGivney.

1884. The third Plenary Council of Baltimore is convened.

1886. Archbishop James Gibbons of Baltimore is named the second American cardinal.

1887. Cardinal Gibbons is instrumental in persuading the Holy See not to condemn the Knights of Labor and the works of Henry George.

1889. The Catholic University of America opens; the first Lay Catholic Congress is held.

1890. The Cahensly Memorial is presented to Pope Leo XIII.

1891. The Sisters of the Blessed Sacrament is founded by Mother Katharine Drexel; the Faribault plan is put into effect in Archbishop John Ireland's see; the Lucerne Memorial is published.

1893. The Apostolic Delegation is established in Washington, D.C., with Archbishop Francesco Satolli the first Apostolic Delegate to the United States; the Columbian Catholic Congress is held.

1896. The first Catholic women's college in the United States, Notre Dame of Maryland, opens.

1899. Pope Leo XIII's apostolic letter, *Testem benevolentiae,* concerning the errors of Americanism, is promulgated.

1904. The National Catholic Educational Association is founded.

1905. The Catholic Church Extension Society for home missions is founded.

1907. The first volume of the Catholic Encyclopedia is published (the sixteenth and final volume is published in 1914).

1908. The Church in the United States is removed from mission status under the jurisdiction of the Congregatio de Propaganda by Pope St. Pius X's apostolic constitution *Sapienti Consilio.*

1911. The Foreign Mission Society of America (Maryknoll), the first United States-established foreign mission society, is founded.

1917. The National Catholic War Council is established; the Military Ordinariate is established; Boys Town is founded by Fr. Edward Flanagan.

1919. Alfred E. Smith becomes the first elected Catholic governor of New York; the Bishops' Program of Social Reconstruction is published; the National Catholic Welfare Council (NCWC) is founded.

1925. The Supreme Court of the United States, in *Pierce* v. *Society of Sisters,* rules that Oregon law compelling all children between eight and eighteen to attend public schools only is unconstitutional.

1926. The 28th International Eucharistic Congress is held, in Chicago, the first to be held in the United States.

1928. Alfred E. Smith, the first Catholic to be nominated for the presidency of the United States by a major party, is defeated by Herbert Hoover.

1930. The Jesuit Martyrs of New York and Canada are canonized.

1939. President Franklin D. Roosevelt names Myron C. Taylor his personal representative at the Holy See.

1954. The first Image Books are published.

1960. John F. Kennedy is elected first Catholic President of the United States.

1965. The New Catholic Encyclopedia is published; Pope Paul VI visits New York, the first pope to visit the United States.

1966. The National Catholic Welfare Conference is restructured and renamed the National Conference of Catholic Bishops (NCCB); also organized, and sponsored by the NCCB, is the United States Catholic Conference (USCC).

1975. Mother Elizabeth Bayley Seton is canonized—the first U.S.-born saint.

1976. The 41st International Eucharistic Congress is held, in Philadelphia.

1977. John Nepomucene Neumann, the fourth bishop of Philadelphia, is canonized—the first male U.S. saint.

1980. Kateri Tekakwitha, the "Lily of the Mohawks," is beatified.

1984. The United States resumes diplomatic relations with the Holy See with the appointment of William A. Wilson as U.S. ambassador by President Ronald Reagan.

CATHOLIC PRESIDENT
OF THE UNITED STATES

John F. Kennedy.   1961–63

CATHOLIC JUSTICES
OF THE SUPREME COURT
OF THE UNITED STATES

Roger B. Taney.   Chief Justice 1836–64

Edward D. White.   Associate Justice 1894–1910; Chief Justice 1910–21

Joseph McKenna.   Associate Justice 1898–1925

Pierce Butler.   Associate Justice 1923–39

Frank Murphy.   Associate Justice 1940–49

William Brennan.   Associate Justice 1956–

Sherman Minton.   Associate Justice 1949–56 (became a Catholic in
    1961, five years after his retirement from the Supreme Court)

CATHOLICS WHO SERVED
IN PRESIDENTS' CABINETS

Roger B. Taney. Attorney General 1831–33; Secretary of the Treasury 1833–34

James Campbell. Postmaster General 1853–57

John B. Floyd. Secretary of War 1857–61

Joseph McKenna. Attorney General 1897–98

Robert J. Wynne. Postmaster General 1904–5

Charles Bonaparte. Secretary of the Navy 1905–6; Attorney General 1906–9

James A. Farley. Postmaster General 1933–40

Frank Murphy. Attorney General 1939–40

Frank C. Walker. Postmaster General 1940–45

Robert E. Hannegan. Postmaster General 1945–47

J. Howard McGrath. Attorney General 1940–52

Maurice J. Tobin. Secretary of Labor 1949–53

James P. McGranery. Attorney General 1952–53

Martin P. Durkin. Secretary of Labor 1953

James P. Mitchell. Secretary of Labor 1953–61

Robert F. Kennedy. Attorney General 1961–65

Anthony Celebrezze. Secretary of Health, Education, and Welfare 1962–65

John S. Gronouski. Postmaster General 1963–65

John T. O'Connor. Secretary of Commerce 1965–67

Lawrence O'Brien. Postmaster General 1965–68

Walter J. Hickel. Secretary of the Interior 1969–71

John A. Volpe. Secretary of Transportation 1969–72

Maurice H. Stans. Secretary of Commerce 1969–72

Peter J. Brennan. Secretary of Labor 1973–75

William E. Simon. Secretary of the Treasury 1974–76

Joseph A. Califano, Jr. Secretary of Health, Education, and Welfare 1977–79

Benjamin Civiletti. Attorney General 1978–81

Moon Landrieu.   Secretary of Housing and Urban Development 1978–81

Edmund S. Muskie.   Secretary of State 1980–81

Alexander M. Haig.   Secretary of State 1981–82

Raymond L. Donovan.   Secretary of Labor 1981–

Margaret M. Heckler.   Secretary of Health and Human Services 1983–

The following cabinet officers became Catholic after they left their cabinet posts:

Thomas Ewing.   Secretary of the Treasury 1841; Secretary of the Interior 1849–50. He became a Catholic in 1871, shortly before his death.

Luke E. Wright.   Secretary of War 1908

Albert B. Fall.   Secretary of the Interior 1921–23. He became a Catholic in 1935.

It is interesting to note that the first Catholic appointed to a cabinet post was Roger Taney, who was appointed Attorney General in 1831, forty-two years after George Washington was sworn in as the first President of the United States. In the first one hundred fifty years of the nation's existence, only seven Catholics served in Presidents' Cabinets; since 1939, twenty-five Catholics have been appointed cabinet members.

CATHOLICS IN NATIONAL STATUARY HALL

In 1864, the Congress designated the chamber of the House of Representatives from 1807 to 1857 as a gallery of distinguished Americans, and each state was invited to present two. In 1933, the number of statues in this National Statuary Hall was limited to one statue from each state, and the extra statues were moved to various parts of the Capitol. Among the distinguished Americans so honored are thirteen Catholics; those in National Statuary Hall are indicated in the list below by an asterisk.

Arizona: Eusebio Kino, S.J.

California: *Junípero Serra, O.F.M.

Hawaii: Damien de Veuster, SS.CC.

Illinois: General James Shields

Louisiana: Edward D. White

Maryland: *Charles Carroll

Nevada: *Patrick A. McCarran

New Mexico: Dennis Chavez

North Dakota: *John Burke

Oregon: Dr. John McLoughlin

Washington: Mother Mary Joseph Pariseau, S.P.

West Virginia: John E. McKenna

Wisconsin: Jacques Marquette, S.J.

DECEASED AMERICAN CARDINALS
(See position and year of appointment)

John McCloskey, New York. 1875

James Gibbons, Baltimore. 1886

John Farley, New York. 1911

William O'Connell, Boston. 1911

Dennis Dougherty, Philadelphia. 1921

Patrick Hayes, New York. 1924

George Mundelein, Chicago. 1924

John Glennon, St. Louis. 1946

Edward Mooney, Detroit. 1946

Francis Spellman, New York. 1946

Samuel Stritch, Chicago. 1946

James F. McIntyre, Los Angeles. 1953

John O'Hara, C.S.C., Philadelphia. 1958

Richard Cushing, Boston. 1958

Albert Meyer, Chicago. 1959

Aloysius Muench, member of the Roman Rota. 1959

Joseph Ritter, St. Louis. 1961

Francis Brennan, Prefect of the Congregation for the Discipline of the Sacraments. 1967

John P. Cody, Chicago. 1967

Terence J. Cooke, New York. 1969

John J. Wright, Prefect of Congregation for Clergy. 1969

Humberto S. Medeiros, Boston. 1973